Max-Planck-Institut für ausländisches
öffentliches Recht und Völkerrecht

Beiträge zum ausländischen öffentlichen Recht und Völkerrecht

Begründet von Viktor Bruns

Herausgegeben von
Armin von Bogdandy · Rüdiger Wolfrum

Band 210

Armin von Bogdandy · Rüdiger Wolfrum
Jochen von Bernstorff · Philipp Dann
Matthias Goldmann (eds.)

The Exercise of Public Authority by International Institutions

Advancing International Institutional Law

Springer
the language of science

ISSN 0172-4770
ISBN 978-3-642-04530-1 e-ISBN 978-3-642-04531-8
DOI 10.1007/978-3-642-04531-8
Springer Heidelberg Dordrecht London New York

Die Deutsche Nationalbibliothek verzeichnet diese Publikation in der Deutschen Nationalbibliografie; detaillierte bibliografische Daten sind im Internet über http://dnb.d-nb.de abrufbar.

Einbandentwurf: WMXDesign GmbH, Heidelberg

Gedruckt auf säurefreiem Papier

Springer ist Teil der Fachverlagsgruppe Springer Science+Business Media (www.springer.com)

Preface

The concept of global governance, which first emerged in the social sciences, has triggered different responses in the discipline of law. This volume contains our proposal. It approaches global governance from a public law perspective which is centered around the concept of international public authority and relies on international institutional law for the legal conceptualization of global governance phenomena.

This proposal results from a larger project which started in 2007. The project is a collaborative effort of the directors of the Max Planck Institute for Comparative Public Law and International Law, research fellows and friends of the Institute, as well as eminent members of the Law Faculty of the University of Heidelberg. Most of the materials contained in this volume were first published in the November 2008 issue of the German Law Journal (http://www.germanlawjournal.com). We would like to express our sincere gratitude to the journal's editors in chief, Professors Russell Miller (Washington and Lee University School of Law) and Peer Zumbansen (Osgoode Hall Law School, York University, Toronto), for the opportunity to publish our papers as a special issue of their journal. The 2008-2009 University of Idaho College of Law German Law Journal student editors deserve special recognition for their hard and diligent work during the publication process. At the Institute, Eva Richter, Michael Riegner and the editorial staff of this publication series were instrumental in bringing this publication to fruition.

The comments on some of the contributions in this volume reflect the discussions at an international workshop held at the Max Planck Institute in April 2008. We are grateful to all discussants for their valuable input. Two articles at the end of the book develop contrasting conceptualizations of the same phenomena.

This volume mirrors the authors' current views within a longer process of reflection on contemporary governance at the international level. As a matter of course, those views are not entirely homogeneous, but comprise diverging and critical voices. The discussion continues.

Heidelberg, January 2009

Armin von Bogdandy
Rüdiger Wolfrum
Jochen von Bernstorff
Philipp Dann
Matthias Goldmann

Survey

Table of Contents

I. Concept

Developing the Publicness of Public International Law: Towards a Legal Framework for Global Governance Activities

*By Armin von Bogdandy, Philipp Dann & Matthias Goldmann**

* The authors are grateful to Eyal Benvenisti, Giacinto della Cananea, Sabino Cassese, Stephan Leibfried, Erika de Wet, Jan Klabbers, Stefan Kadelbach, Nico Krisch, Ute Mager, Christoph Möllers, Christian Tietje, Christian Walter, as well as the members of the Max Planck Institute for Comparative Public Law and International Law participating in this project for comments on an earlier version, and to Lewis Enim for language review.

A. von Bogdandy et al. (eds.), *The Exercise of Public Authority by International Institutions*, Beiträge zum ausländischen öffentlichen Recht und Völkerrecht 210,
DOI 10.1007/978-3-642-04531-8_1, © Springer-Verlag Berlin Heidelberg 2010

A. Introduction: The Project in a Nutshell

The research project which this article introduces, proposes a distinctly public law approach to the deep transformation in the conduct of public affairs epitomized by the term global governance. We were intrigued to find in many policy fields an increasing number of international institutions playing an active and often crucial role in decision-making and policy implementation, sometimes even affecting individuals. Thus, a private real estate sale in Berlin is blocked by a decision of the UN Security Council Al-Qaida and Taliban Sanctions Committee;[1] the construction of a bridge in Dresden is legally challenged because the affected part of the Elbe river valley had been included on UNESCO's list of World Heritage;[2] or educational policies most relevant to our children are profoundly reformed due to the OECD Pisa rankings.[3] These examples illustrate that governance activities of international institutions may have a strong legal or factual impact on domestic issues. This calls upon scholars of public law to lay open the legal setting of such governance activities, to find out how, and by whom, they are controlled, and to develop legal standards for ensuring that they satisfy contemporary expectations for legitimacy.

This article sketches out the objective, argument and approach of our project and proceeds in three steps: a first step specifies the object of analysis (B.); a second step discusses how the phenomena thus identified should be approached in a legal perspective (C.); in a third and final step, we explain the concrete methodology of our project (D.).

In the first step, we argue that the discourse on global governance provides important new perspectives on phenomena of international cooperation (B.I.); but it is deficient from a public law perspective as the concept of global governance does not allow for the identification of what the focus of a *legal* discourse should be, i.e. those acts by which unilateral authority is exercised. Such unilateral authority is the greatest

---

1 ECJ, Case C-117/06, *Möllendorf*, 2007 ECR I-8361. On the Al-Qaida and Taliban Sanctions Committee *see* Clemens Feinäugle, in this volume.

2 Sächsisches Oberverwaltungsgericht, Case 4 BS 216/06, decision of 9 March 2007, published in 60 DIE ÖFFENTLICHE VERWALTUNG 564 (2007); *see* Diana Zacharias, in this volume.

3 Armin von Bogdandy & Matthias Goldmann, *The Exercise of International Public Authority through National Policy Assessments. The OECD's PISA Policy as a Paradigm for a New Standard Instrument*, 5 INTERNATIONAL ORGANIZATIONS LAW REVIEW 241 (2008).

challenge to the basic principle of individual freedom. Public law, at least in a liberal and democratic tradition, concerns the tension between unilateral authority and individual freedom, and is a necessary requirement for the legitimacy of public authority, which is both constituted and limited by public law (B.II.). In order to provide a basis for legal analysis and to identify phenomena that need justification, we propose focusing on *the exercise of international public authority*. We argue that any kind of governance activity by international institutions, be it administrative or intergovernmental, should be considered as an exercise of international public authority *if* it determines individuals, private associations, enterprises, states, or other public institutions. We believe that this concept enables the identification of all those governance phenomena which public lawyers should study (B.III.). Proposing this concept means complementing the concept of global governance with a concept more appropriate for legal analysis and the development of legal standards for legitimate governance. On a more general level, this concept should contribute to a deeper understanding of the historic transformation underlying the concept of global governance.[4]

In the second step, we develop a public law approach to the exercise of international public authority on the basis of international institutional law (C.). We share the aim to better understand and develop the law relating to international governance activities with recent streams of legal research such as the Global Administrative Law movement,[5] the research on an emerging international administrative law,[6] as well as the

---

4 For different interpretations of this transformation *see e.g.* JÜRGEN HABERMAS, DIE POSTNATIONALE KONSTELLATION (1998); MICHAEL HARDT & ANTONIO NEGRI, EMPIRE (2002); ANNE-MARIE SLAUGHTER, A NEW WORLD ORDER (2004). From a domestic viewpoint *see e.g.* TRANSFORMING THE GOLDEN-AGE NATION STATE (Achim Hurrelmann, *et al.* eds., 2005).

5 Benedict Kingsbury, Nico Krisch & Richard Stewart, *The Emergence of Global Administrative Law*, 68 LAW AND CONTEMPORARY PROBLEMS 15 (2005); Sabino Cassese, *Administrative Law Without the State? The Challenge of Global Regulation*, 37 NEW YORK UNIVERSITY JOURNAL OF INTERNATIONAL LAW AND POLITICS 663 (2005); Daniel C. Esty, *Good Governance at the Supranational Scale: Globalizing Administrative Law*, 115 YALE LAW JOURNAL 1490 (2006).

6 Eberhard Schmidt-Aßmann, in this volume; German original published under the title *Die Herausforderung der Verwaltungsrechtswissenschaft durch die Internationalisierung der Verwaltungsbeziehungen*, 45 DER STAAT 315 (2006).

debate surrounding the constitutionalization of international law.[7] We hold that a *synthesis* of these approaches is best suited to provide a meaningful framework for analysis and critique. The legal framework of governance activities of international institutions should be conceived of as international institutional law, and enriched by a public law perspective, i.e. with constitutional sensibility and openness for comparative insights from administrative legal thinking.

Finally, we outline how the research project was conducted, i.e. specifying the selection of thematic studies (D.I.), recapitulating the aim of and questionnaire guiding these studies (D.II.), and explaining the scope and intention of the cross-cutting analyses (D.III). We conclude by rephrasing the normative intention and underlying international ethos of this project (E.).

As was to be expected in such a new field of research, we went through an intense learning process. In this paper we lay down how we think these phenomena should now be approached. It should be stressed though that the authors of this research project do not form a monolithic block. Not every aspect of this framework is shared by all other contributions, nor do the cross-cutting studies or the thematic studies simply aim at providing evidence for the research agenda set out here. They stand on their own and display the possible diversity within the public law approach to international law. Yet, the ensuing thoughts will aid the understanding of the overall thrust of this research project. Moreover, we firmly believe that further research on the "publicness" of public international law along the lines of this paper will provide a better understanding and legal framing of global governance activities.

---

[7] Jochen A. Frowein, *Konstitutionalisierung des Völkerrechts, in* 39 BERICHTE DER DEUTSCHEN GESELLSCHAFT FÜR VÖLKERRECHT, 427 (Klaus Dicke *et al.* eds., 2000); Christian Walter, *Constitutionalizing (Inter)national Governance*, 44 GERMAN YEARBOOK OF INTERNATIONAL LAW 170 (2001); Brun-Otto Bryde, *International Democratic Constitutionalism, in* TOWARDS WORLD CONSTITUTIONALISM 103 (Ronald Macdonald *et al.* eds., 2005); Stefan Kadelbach & Thomas Kleinlein, *Überstaatliches Verfassungsrecht*, 44 ARCHIV DES VÖLKERRECHTS 235 (2006); Matthias Kumm, *The Legitimacy of International Law: A Constitutionalist Framework Analysis*, 15 EUR. J. INT'L LAW 907 (2004); Anne Peters, *Compensatory Constitutionalism: The Function and Potential of Fundamental International Norms and Structures*, 19 LEIDEN JOURNAL OF INTERNATIONAL LAW 579 (2006).

B. From Global Governance to Public Authority: A Focus for Legal Research

I. Global Governance: Strengths and Weaknesses of the Dominant Approach

This research project is motivated by our experience of strengths and weaknesses of the concept of global governance for legal research.[8] Since the mid-1990s, this concept has become a widely used analytical perspective for describing the conduct of world affairs in many disciplines.[9] Four characteristic traits of this concept are of relevance in this context. First, the global governance concept recognizes the importance of international institutions, but highlights the relevance of actors and instruments which are of a private or hybrid nature, as well as of individuals – governance is not only an affair of public actors. Second, global governance marks the emergence of an increased recourse to informality: many institutions, procedures and instruments escape the grasp of established legal concepts. Third, thinking in terms of global governance means shifting weight from actors to structures and procedures. Last but not least, as is obvious from the use of the term "global" rather than "international," global governance emphasizes the multilevel character of governance activities: it tends to overcome the division between international, supranational and national phenomena.

As becomes visible from these four characteristic traits, the concept of global governance has the merit of providing a forward looking alternative to a so-called "realist," i.e. a state-centric and power oriented world

---

[8] The origins of the term global governance can be traced back to James N. Rosenau, *Governance, Order, and Change in World Politics*, *in* GOVERNANCE WITHOUT GOVERNMENT 1 (James N. Rosenau & Ernst-Otto Czempiel eds., 1992); Jan Kooiman, *Findings, Recommendations and Speculations*, *in* MODERN GOVERNANCE: NEW GOVERNMENT-SOCIETY INTERACTIONS 249 (Jan Kooiman ed., 1993). The concept of "governance" was borrowed from economics. *See* Oliver E. Williamson, *The Economics of Governance: Framework and Implications*, 140 ZEITSCHRIFT FÜR DIE GESAMTE STAATSWISSENSCHAFT 195 (1984).

[9] Martin Hewson & Timothy Sinclair, *The Emergence of Global Governance Theory*, *in* GLOBAL GOVERNANCE THEORY 3 (Martin Hewson & Timothy J. Sinclair eds., 1999); Renate Mayntz, *Governance Theory als fortentwickelte Steuerungstheorie?*, *in* GOVERNANCE-FORSCHUNG 11 (Gunnar F. Schuppert ed., 2006); Arthur Benz, *Governance – Modebegriff oder nützliches sozialwissenschaftliches Konzept?*, *in* GOVERNANCE – REGIEREN IN KOMPLEXEN REGELSYSTEMEN 11 (Arthur Benz ed., 2004).

view, and has opened our eyes towards phenomena that this perspective, as well as traditional accounts of international law, regularly underestimate. However, there is hardly any neutral, value-free terminology for historical phenomena. Thus, global governance is strongly influenced by so-called "liberal" conceptualizations of international relations. It follows the tradition of institutionalist ideas such as regime theory in providing an alternative to the "realist" world view.[10] However, the reverse side of this origin is that global governance is impregnated with normative difficulties typical of many liberal international relation theories. Thus, global governance is mainly understood as an essentially technocratic process following a little questioned dogma of efficiency.[11]

Yet, this understanding has been challenged. For diverse reasons, stakeholders cast into doubt the legitimacy of various global governance activities, doubts which have been elaborated by numerous scholarly analyses.[12] These doubts and concerns apply centrally to international

---

[10] Michael Barnett & Raymond Duvall, *Power in Global Governance, in* POWER IN GLOBAL GOVERNANCE 1, 7 (Michael Barnett & Raymond Duvall eds., 2005); Michael Zürn, *Institutionalisierte Ungleichheit in der Weltpolitik. Jenseits der Alternative "Global Governance" versus "American Empire,"* 48 POLITISCHE VIERTELJAHRESSCHRIFT 680 (2007).

[11] *See e.g.* Robert Latham, *Politics in a Floating World, in* GLOBAL GOVERNANCE THEORY 23 (Martin Hewson & Timothy J. Sinclair eds., 2000); Martti Koskenniemi, *Global Governance and Public International Law*, 37 KRITISCHE JUSTIZ 241 (2004). On the related liberal bias of international organizations *see* Michael Barnett & Martha Finnemore, *The Power of Liberal International Organizations, in* POWER IN GLOBAL GOVERNANCE 161, 163-169 (Michael Barnett & Raymond Duvall eds., 2005). However, various critical perspectives on global governance have emerged. *See e.g.* CONTENDING PERSPECTIVES ON GLOBAL GOVERNANCE (Alice D. Ba & Matthew J. Hoffmann eds., 2005).

[12] It may suffice to cite only a few examples: Amichai Cohen, *Bureaucratic Internalization: Domestic Governmental Agencies and the Legitimization of International Law*, 30 GEORGETOWN JOURNAL OF INTERNATIONAL LAW 1079 (2005); Ruth W. Grant & Robert O. Keohane, *Accountability and Abuses of Power in World Politics*, 99 AMERICAN POLITICAL SCIENCE REVIEW 29 (2005); Robert Howse & Kalypso Nicolaidis, *Enhancing WTO Legitimacy: Constitutionalization or Global Subsidiarity?*, 16 GOVERNANCE 73 (2003); Anne-Marie Slaughter, *The Accountability of Government Networks*, 8 INDIANA JOURNAL OF GLOBAL LEGAL STUDIES 347 (2000-2001); Rainer Wahl, *Der einzelne in der Welt jenseits des Staates, in* VERFASSUNGSSTAAT, EUROPÄISIERUNG, INTERNATIONALISIERUNG 53 (Rainer Wahl ed., 2003); Joseph H. H. Weiler, *The Ge-*

institutions as important participants in, and promoters of, global governance. Generally speaking, some international institutions are seen as a risk to individual rights, collective self-determination, as well as impediments to, rather than conveyors of, global justice. With respect to individual rights, the striking absence of judicial review and procedural safeguards – even when international institutions have a deep impact upon individuals – meets with harsh critique. The listing of terrorist suspects by the UN Security Council provides the most dramatic example of governance that would be hardly permissible at the domestic level.[13] From the viewpoint of collective self-determination, international institutions are operating in considerable distance from the communities concerned, often producing outcomes that deeply impact on domestic democratic procedures. Moreover, an international institution might display features of a secretive bureaucracy (as it can also be the case with any domestic public institution)[14] or might operate more in the service of the interests of particular stakeholders or states than of global social justice. As a result, the perception of global governance in scholarship today ranges from endorsement to chastisement.[15] The policies of several institutions of global governance are questioned and, often enough, perceived as more or less illegitimate.

II. The Deficiencies of Global Governance from a Public Law Perspective

What can the response be to such claims of illegitimacy from a public law perspective? The starting point of a public law perspective is to ask whether the respective activities amount to an exercise of unilateral, i.e. public authority. Public law, at least in a liberal and democratic tradition, has a dual function: first, no public authority may be exercised

---

ology of International Law – Governance, Democracy and Legitimacy, 64 ZEITSCHRIFT FÜR AUSLÄNDISCHES ÖFFENTLICHES RECHT UND VÖLKERRECHT (ZAÖRV) 547 (2004); Michael Zürn, *Global Governance and Legitimacy Problems*, 39 GOVERNMENT AND OPPOSITION 260 (2004). For a taxonomy *see* Armin von Bogdandy, *Globalization and Europe: How to Square Democracy and Globalization*, 15 EUR. J. INT'L LAW 885 (2004).

13 *See* Clemens Feinäugle, in this volume. *See also* the contributions by Maja Smrkolj, Karen Kaiser, and Diana Zacharias, in this volume.

14 Ingo Venzke, in this volume; Ravi Pereira, in this volume.

15 For an overview *see*, BA & HOFFMANN (note 11).

that is not based on public law (constitutive function); second, public authority is controlled and limited by the substantive and procedural standards provided by public law (limiting function).[16] In particular, the second function helps to translate concerns about the legitimacy of governance activities into meaningful arguments of legality. The experience of liberal democracies teaches how important it is that legitimacy concerns can, in principle, be put forward as issues of legality.

This requires a workable concept of public authority. The concept of global governance is insufficient for this purpose. While the merits of the concept of global governance (namely the broadening of our horizons for important phenomena that influence public policy) are undisputed, it does not enable the identification of those acts which are critical because they constitute a unilateral exercise of authority. This is because global governance flattens the difference between public and private phenomena, as well as between formal and informal ones. Moreover, global governance is understood as a continuous structure or process, rather than a batch of acts of specific, identifiable actors causing specific, identifiable effects. These factors make it difficult, if not impossible, to distinguish from a global governance perspective authoritative from non-authoritative acts and to attribute the former ones to responsible actors. However, this distinction, as well as the attribution of responsibility, is crucial for the constitutive and limiting functions of public law. Only authoritative acts need to be constituted and limited by public law, and the limiting function of public law depends on identifiable actors on whom to impose limitations. Consequently, global governance cannot serve as the conceptual basis of a public law framework for authoritative acts on the international plane. We therefore suggest a new focus on the exercise of international public authority which might provide an avenue to an understanding of global governance phenomena which is more compatible with the function of public law.

---

[16] *See* EBERHARD SCHMIDT-AßMANN, DAS ALLGEMEINE VERWALTUNGSRECHT ALS ORDNUNGSIDEE 16-18 (2nd ed. 2004). *See also* Benedict Kingsbury, *International Law as Inter-Public Law*, http://www.iilj.org/courses/documents/Kingsbury,NewJusGentiumand.pdf. For a similar account *see* Jean d'Aspremont, *Contemporary International Rulemaking and the Public Character of International Law*, IILJ Working Paper 2006/12, http://www.iilj.org/publications/documents/2006-12-dAspremont-web.pdf.

III. The Exercise of International Public Authority as the New Focus

We suggest the shift towards the exercise of international public authority in order to better identify those international activities that determine other legal subjects, curtail their freedom in a way that requires legitimacy and therefore a public law framework. In other words, while the concept of global governance has a mostly functional focus, our interest is essentially a normative one: to move beyond mere functionalism. The concept of the exercise of public authority shall thus highlight issues that the concept of global governance obscures. At the same time, this shift does not mean discarding the concept of global governance entirely. The broader horizon that the notion of global governance has opened up should not be abandoned. Research on global governance has, for example, convincingly demonstrated that constraining effects do not only emanate from binding instruments or legal subjects.

Defining the exercise of international public authority requires a considerable conceptual innovation, as the concept of public authority has been coined in light of the state's monopoly of legitimate coercion and sovereign power over individuals. How exactly do we define the exercise of international public authority? For this project, we define[17] *authority* as the legal capacity to *determine* others and to reduce their freedom, i.e. to unilaterally shape their legal or factual situation.[18] An exercise is the realization of that capacity, in particular by the production of standard instruments such as decisions and regulations, but also by the dissemination of information, like rankings.[19] The determination may or may not be legally binding.[20] It is binding if an act *modifies the*

---

17 Definition is meant here as developing sufficient conceptual characterizations that cover the most important cases. We do not aim at a full definition. For details *see* HANS-JOACHIM KOCH & HELMUT RÜßMANN, JURISTISCHE BEGRÜNDUNGSLEHRE 75 (1982).

18 Our concept of authority is, thus, different from that of the New Haven School, which is defined as "the structure of expectation concerning who, with what qualifications and mode of selection, is competent to make which decision by what criteria and what procedures." *See* Myres McDougal & Harold Laswell, *The Identification and Appraisal of Diverse Systems of Public Order*, 53 AMERICAN JOURNAL OF INTERNATIONAL LAW 1, 9 (1959). In fact, this concept of authority resembles our concept of legitimacy.

19 On standard instruments *see* Matthias Goldmann, in this volume.

20 This concept of authority is similar to the concept of power developed by Barnett & Duvall (note 10). The main difference between their concept of

legal situation of a different legal subject without its consent. A modification takes place if a subsequent action which contravenes that act is illegal.[21] Yet, we hold that the concept of authority needs to be conceived in a broader way than this rather traditional definition. The capacity to determine another legal subject can also occur through a non-binding act which only *conditions* another legal subject. This is the case whenever that act builds up pressure for another legal subject to follow its impetus. Such exercise of public authority often occurs through the establishment of non-binding standards which are followed, *inter alia*, because the benefits of observing them outweighs the disadvantages of ignoring them (e.g. the OECD standards for avoiding double taxation),[22] or because they are equipped with implementing mechanisms imposing positive and negative sanctions (e.g. the FAO code of conduct for responsible fisheries).[23] Furthermore, legal subjects can also be conditioned by instruments without deontic operators (e.g. statistical data contained in PISA reports)[24] building up communicative power which the addressee can only avoid at some cost, be it reputational, economic, or other. However, such communicative power needs to reach a certain minimum threshold. This is especially the case where an instrument is equipped with specific mechanisms which ensure that the communicative power effectively has to be taken into account by the addressee. For example, in case of the OECD PISA policy, the reports are rendered effective through country rankings and repeated testing.[25]

This broad understanding of the concept of authority rests on the empirical insight that conditioning acts can constrain individual freedom and public self-determination as much as binding acts. The freedom not to obey a conditioning act is often purely fictional.[26] Accordingly, con-

---

power and our concept of authority is that authority needs a legal basis. More narrow is the definition of authority as the power to enact law unilaterally. *See* Christoph Möllers, GEWALTENGLIEDERUNG 81-93 (2005).

21 An example of such legal determination would be the refugee status determination by the UNCHR. *See* Maja Smrkolj, in this volume.

22 Ekkehart Reimer, *Transnationales Steuerrecht, in* INTERNATIONALES VERWALTUNGSRECHT 181 (Christoph Möllers, Andreas Voßkuhle & Christian Walter eds., 2007).

23 Jürgen Friedrich, in this volume.

24 von Bogdandy & Goldmann (note 3).

25 *Id.*

26 From a political science perspective *see* Barnett & Duvall (note 10); Kenneth W. Abbott & Duncan Snidal, *Hard and Soft Law in International Gov-*

siderations of principle underline this broad understanding: if public law is understood, in keeping with the liberal and democratic tradition, as a body of law to protect individual freedom and to allow for political self-determination, any act that has an impact on those values, whether it is legally binding or not, should be included if that impact is significant enough to give rise to meaningful concerns about its legitimacy. By giving governance activities which rely upon conditioning acts a legal framework, international institutions have often shown that they share this understanding; and in German domestic public law, a correspondingly broad understanding of authority has been established in recent years.[27]

However, not every exercise of authority might be qualified as *international* and *public*. This turns our attention to the second and third elements of the proposed concept: what is public and international about international public authority? We consider as international public authority any authority exercised on the basis of a competence instituted by a common international act of public authorities, mostly states, to further a goal which they define, and are authorized to define, as a public interest.[28] The "publicness" of an exercise of authority, as well as its international character, therefore depends on its *legal basis*. The institutions under consideration in this project hence exercise authority attributed to them by political collectives on the basis of binding or non-binding international acts.

Of course, this definition of publicness appears as rather formalistic and does not exhaust the meaning of publicness framed by the constitutionalist mindset of the Western tradition. Accordingly, public institutions in a liberal democracy are expected to respect and promote fundamental

---

ernance, 54 INTERNATIONAL ORGANIZATION 421 (2000); Charles Lipson, *Why Are Some International Agreements Informal?*, 45 INTERNATIONAL ORGANIZATION 495 (1991).

27 Horst Dreier, *Vorbemerkung vor Art. 1 GG, in* I GRUNDGESETZ–KOMMENTAR, margin number 125 *et seq.* (Horst Dreier ed., 2nd ed. 2004); Schmidt-Aßmann (note 16), 18 *et seq.*

28 Some put the task to discharge public duties at the heart of their approach, *see* Matthias Ruffert, *Perspektiven des Internationalen Verwaltungsrechts, in* INTERNATIONALES VERWALTUNGSRECHT 395, 402 (Christoph Möllers, Andreas Voßkuhle & Christian Walter eds., 2007). We prefer to build on the concept of public authority, but qualify it by reference to public interest.

values, such as public ethos, transparency or accessibility for citizens.[29] Our understanding of the concept of publicness is deeply imbued by and intended to carry much of this tradition, which formulates issues that need to be addressed. Nevertheless, such expectations towards public institutions should not simply be transposed to international institutions, since the differences between domestic and international institutions remain fundamental. Therefore, we believe that the legal basis of authority provides the best criterion for qualifying it as *public* and drawing the line between public and private authority that we conceive as indispensable for legal research. Accordingly, an enterprise like Volkswagen which exercises contractual authority over employees in its Brazil subsidiary cannot be considered to exercise public authority because such an enterprise is constituted under private law and is not formally charged with performing public tasks.

However, one of the main revelations of the research on global governance is that institutions based on private law or hybrid institutions which lack any relevant delegation of authority may carry out activities which are just as much of public interest as those based on delegations of authority. This is the case when such activity can be regarded as a functional equivalent to an activity on a public legal basis. To identify such functional equivalence,[30] we suggest a topical catalogue of typical instances rather than a generic definition relying on the evasive concept of the "common good." A typical instance would be, for example, any governance activity which directly affects public goods, by which global infrastructures are managed, or which unfolds in a situation where the collision of fundamental interests of different social groups has to be dealt with. Thus, an institution like ICANN, though perhaps not necessarily exercising public authority in a strict sense, should be subject to the same legal requirements which are applicable to comparable exercises of public authority, for it manages a global infrastructure (i.e. Internet domain names). Assessing such governance activities by the legal standards applicable to functionally comparable exercises of

---

[29] CARL J. FRIEDRICH, CONSTITUTIONAL GOVERNMENT AND POLITICS 247 *et seq.* (1950); KARL LOEWENSTEIN, POLITICAL POWER AND THE GOVERNMENTAL PROCESS (1957); Louis Henkin, *A New Birth of Constitutionalism, in* CONSTITUTIONALISM, IDENTITY, DIFFERENCE AND LEGITIMACY 39 (Michel Rosenfeld ed., 1994); d'Aspremont (note 16).

[30] For a similar approach relying on functional context *see* Andreas Fischer-Lescano, *Transnationales Verwaltungsrecht*, 63 JURISTENZEITUNG 373, 376 (2008).

international public authority has two main objectives. It shows that public affairs can be regulated in other, and sometimes more effective legal settings from which public institutions might even draw insights. At the same time, such reconstruction provides a framework for critique, as private forms of organization might have even more severe legitimacy deficits than public ones.[31]

As we define the object of our analysis, we should also clarify which entities we consider to be exercising international public authority. Such authority may be exercised by various formal and informal entities. In many cases public authority under international law is vested in an institution that qualifies as an international organization with international legal personality. Again, however, global governance perspectives remind and inform us that there are other institutions exercising public authority as well.[32] Some treaty regimes, for example CITES, or informal institutions, such as certain committees within the remit of the OECD, or the G8, are creatures of states which wield considerable political clout and whose acts raise concerns of legitimacy.[33] These are institutions in the sense of organizational sociology, though they might not have legal personality akin to an international organization.[34] Moreover, even in policy areas where there is a competent formal organization, public authority can be exercised through more or less informal bodies associated with it, but legally external to it, such as networks of domestic administrators.[35]

---

31 For a comparison of functionally equivalent private and public governance activities see Matthias Goldmann, *The Accountability of Private vs. Public Governance "by Information": A Comparison of the Assessment Activities of the OECD and the IEA in the Field of Education*, 58 RIVISTA TRIMESTRALE DI DIRITTO PUBBLICO 41 (2008).

32 Kingsbury (note 16).

33 On the variety of entities that are not international organizations but exercise some sort of public authority, *see* PHILIPPE SANDS & PIERRE KLEIN, BOWETT'S LAW OF INTERNATIONAL ORGANIZATION 16-7 (2001); Jan Klabbers, *The Changing Image of International Organizations, in* THE LEGITIMACY OF INTERNATIONAL ORGANIZATIONS 221, 236 (Jean-Marc Coicaud & Veijo Heiskanen eds., 2001).

34 The early European Union provides a fine example. *See* Armin von Bogdandy, *The Legal Case for Unity: The European Union as a Single Organization with a Single Legal System*, 36 COMMON MARKET LAW REVIEW 887 (1999).

35 Examples from thematic studies include: Bettina Schöndorf-Haubold, in this volume; von Bogdandy & Goldmann (note 3). *See also* Christoph Möllers,

We consider that such institutions exercise public authority if they enjoy determining capacities as defined above. The uncertainty as to which legal subject is ultimately legally responsible for the exercise of authority appears, in our opinion, to be an insufficient reason to shield such institutions from the long arm of the law. This broad concept of international institutions is based on the empirical insight that many of the informal organizations operate largely as the less legalized brethrens of formal organizations.[36] Additionally, it is supported by institutional practice: the operation and action of many informal institutions are governed by rules in a similar way to that of formal international organizations.[37]

In sum, we choose to focus on the exercise of international public authority in order to guide the attention to those activities that require normative justification. Put differently, any exercise of international public authority requires a public law framework. Our focus thus is broad and inclusive. It covers administrative as well as intergovernmental activities, even though the vast majority of activities under consideration in this project could be considered administrative in a heuristic sense.[38] We refrain from the notion of administration as the defining category since the scope and variety of activities that demand justification is broader. All public authority and not only administrative authority has to be legitimate. Moreover, using administration as the foundational concept is problematic as other concepts which usually give contour to it, such as constitution or legislative institutions and activities, are difficult to distinguish at the international level. Hence, the focus on the exercise of public authority more precisely identifies the relevant object.

Verfassungs- und völkerrechtliche Probleme transnationaler administrativer Standardsetzung, ZAÖRV 65 (2005), 351-389; Eyal Benvenisti, *Coalitions of the Willing and the Evolution of Informal International Law, in* COALITIONS OF THE WILLING – AVANTGARDE OR THREAT? 1 (Christian Calliess, Georg Nolte & Peter-Tobias Stoll, 2007).

36 *See* Anuscheh Farahat, in this volume.

37 *See id.*; Christine Fuchs, in this volume.

38 On such a concept of administration *see* Isabel Feichtner, in this volume.

C. A Public Law Approach to the Exercise of International Public Authority

The public law approach focuses on constructing a legal understanding of, and developing a legal framework for, the exercise of international public authority. This includes the question of how to identify the applicable law in order to draw a line between legal and illegal exercises of authority, as well as the question of how to develop the applicable law in light of legitimacy concerns. We understand such interests as definitional with respect to *internal* legal approaches, in contrast to *external* approaches which investigate legal phenomena with various empirical or normative interests, e.g. focusing on their societal role and effects, or their history, or on their philosophical dimensions. While external approaches are insightful for the identification and development of the law relating to the exercise of authority by international institutions (C.I.), the functions of public law cannot be achieved without an internal approach (C.II.). Based on a review of the achievements of internal approaches, we will show how this public law approach is construed as a combination of the three dominant internal approaches (C.III.).

It should be stressed that internal and external approaches are not mutually exclusive, but ideally complement each other. While external approaches ensure that internal approaches do not become detached from the role of law in societal reality and the development of new normative phenomena, internal approaches participate in construing and applying the law as an operative "social infrastructure." Moreover, internal and external arguments might intersect in the micro-structure of legal research to the point that they become difficult to distinguish. Yet, the overall outlook is fundamentally different.

I. The Contribution of External Approaches

External approaches to international law have a strong tradition within the legal discipline,[39] and the different streams within this tradition provide valuable insights when analyzing the exercise of public authority.

---

39 In particular the sociological approach, *see e.g.* MAX HUBER, DIE SOZIOLOGISCHEN GRUNDLAGEN DES VÖLKERRECHTS (1928); Anne-Marie Slaughter, *International law and international relations*, 285 RECUEIL DES COURS 13 (2000).

One important stream of research is *transnational legal process*, which follows in the footsteps of American legal realism and grew out of the New Haven School.[40] It is characterized by an emphasis on law as a continuous process of consecutive decisions instead of a stable system of rules, and by a turn away from a state-centric concept of international law.[41] This stream provides important insights as to why decisions thus produced are obeyed, whether for reasons of self-interest, identity, or as a result of repeated interaction.[42] Thus, the screen of legal analysis is extended towards new processes and actors, yet at the expenses of normative certainty, as law is considered to be a sort of amorphous process.

Transnational legal processes have much in common with so-called *managerial approaches* which focus on questions of compliance and efficiency. For them, law is one of several means for the effective and efficient regulation of society.[43] Managerial accounts, which could also be termed as functional, prevail in the study of international institutions.[44] Similarly, albeit from an observer rather than a managerial angle, is the research on legalization that investigates the conditions under which states chose harder or softer forms of legal regulation.[45] A more recent

---

[40] Harold Hongju Koh, *Transnational Legal Process*, 75 NEBRASKA LAW REVIEW 181 (1996); Michael W. Reisman, *The Democratization of Contemporary International Law-Making Processes and the Differentiation of Their Application, in* DEVELOPMENTS OF INTERNATIONAL LAW IN TREATY MAKING 15, 24-26 (Rüdiger Wolfrum & Volker Röben eds., 2005).

[41] Felix Hanschmann, *Theorie transnationaler Rechtsprozesse, in* NEUE THEORIEN DES RECHTS 347, 357 (Sonja Buckel, Ralph Christensen & Andreas Fischer-Lescano eds., 2006).

[42] Koh (note 40).

[43] Abraham Chayes & Antonia Handler Chayes, *On Compliance*, 47 INTERNATIONAL ORGANIZATION 175-205 (1993); Harold K. Jacobson & Edith Brown Weiss, *Compliance with International Environmental Accords*, 1 GLOBAL GOVERNANCE 119-48 (1995); COMMITMENT AND COMPLIANCE: THE ROLE OF NONBINDING NORMS IN THE INTERNATIONAL LEGAL SYSTEM (Dinah Shelton ed., 2000). Similar is the research on new modes of governance. *See e.g.* David M. Trubek & Louise G. Trubek, *New Governance & Legal Regulation: Complementarity, Rivalry, and Transformation*, 13 COLUMBIA JOURNAL OF EUROPEAN LAW 1-26 (2006); HARD CHOICES, SOFT LAW (John Kirton & Michael Trebilcock eds., 2004).

[44] JOSÉ E. ALVAREZ, INTERNATIONAL ORGANIZATIONS AS LAW-MAKERS 17 *et seq.* (2005).

[45] Abbott & Snidal (note 26).

variant of the tradition is the *network approach* which puts the emphasis on the outcomes produced by network structures of different actors.[46] The network approach thus goes beyond state-centrism. On a different theoretical basis, approaches based on *systems theory* arrive at similar conclusions.[47]

All these approaches shift the focus of attention from formal to informal instruments and institutions and bring powerful governance mechanisms beyond the sources of Art. 38(1) ICJ Statute as well as actors without international legal personality in the focus of the international lawyer, which should not be neglected given their political significance. Their concept of law is much more differentiated than in classical international law. Blunt contestations of the normativity of international law seldom occur, whilst stressing its limitations. This project would be unthinkable without these insights, even though some external approaches, in particular managerial ones, share the technocratic bias of global governance, which entails the aforementioned problems.

II. The Need for Internal Approaches

Nevertheless, external approaches alone do not suffice for framing international public authority.[48] Rather, the two fundamental functions of public law presuppose an internal approach to law: public law constitutes *and* limits public authority and that entails judgments that pertain to its legality.

At the moment, it is very difficult to construe a meaningful argument regarding the legality of an exercise of international public authority. Although many activities of international institutions operate on the basis of and through rules, there is often only a rudimentary legal framework constraining these activities.[49] This absence of legal stan-

---

[46] ANNE-MARIE SLAUGHTER, A NEW WORLD ORDER (2004).

[47] GUNTER TEUBNER & ANDREAS FISCHER-LESCANO, REGIME-KOLLISIONEN (2006).

[48] For a similar critique of the exclusivity of external approaches see Andreas Paulus, *Zur Zukunft der Völkerrechtswissenschaft in Deutschland: Zwischen Konstitutionalisierung und Fragmentierung des Völkerrechts*, 67 ZAÖRV 695, 708-15 (2007).

[49] An excellent example are the G8 summits, *see* MARTINA CONTICELLI, I VERTICI DEL G8 (2006).

dards leads to the difficult situation whereby international institutions exercise public authority which might be perceived as illegitimate, but nevertheless as legal – for lack of appropriate legal standards. Consequently, the discourse on legality is out of sync with the discourse on legitimacy.[50] While the legitimacy of, say, certain rules of the Codex Alimentarius may very well be cast into doubt, they are certainly not illegal, for they escape any relevant legal standard due to their non-binding character.[51] In reaction to this mismatch, some new concepts have been developed, like "accountability"[52] or "participation."[53] They reflect shared concerns about the legitimacy of the activities of international institutions. Yet, there is hardly any shared understanding about their material content. Presently, these concepts do not provide accepted standards to determine legality, but are not much more than *partes pro toto* for the concept of legitimacy.

The divergence in judgments about legality and legitimacy has several serious consequences. First and foremost, the experience of liberal democracies teaches how important it is that legitimacy concerns can, in principle, be put forward as issues of legality. As has been emphasized above, this is exactly the central role of public law. Reconstructing and furthering the legal framework of public authority is not an end in itself but enables the channeling of legitimacy concerns into legal arguments and eventually into workable rules. This channeling has a rationalizing effect. It ensures that not every single act of public authority needs to be investigated for want of legitimacy. Instead, acts that are legal are generally presumed to be legitimate.

Second, the lack of a developed legal framework is at least partly responsible for the amorphous image of international institutions. For

---

[50] Koskenniemi (note 11) suggests that the reasons for this divergence of legality and legitimacy lie in the deformalization, fragmentation, and the hegemonic traits of the current world order. On these aspects *see also* Eyal Benvenisti, *The Empire's New Clothes: Political Economy and the Fragmentation of International Law*, 60 STANFORD LAW REVIEW 595 (2007); Matthias Goldmann, *Der Widerspenstigen Zähmung, in* NETZWERKE 225 (Sigrid Boysen *et al.* eds., 2007).

[51] Ravi Pereira, in this volume.

[52] See Erika de Wet, *Holding International Institutions Accountable*, in this volume.

[53] *See* Jochen von Bernstorff, in this volume; Sabino Cassese, *Global Standards for National Administrative Procedure*, 68 LAW AND CONTEMPORARY PROBLEMS 109-26 (2005).

any understanding of international institutions by the general public, legal categories play an important role, as the domestic situation proves: the understanding of domestic public institutions rests largely on legal terminology based on doctrinal constructions. With respect to international institutions, there are hardly any legal concepts with analytical prowess to generate a general understanding. International institutions remain opaque.

Third, the lack of adequate legal concepts as well as the limited use of the legal/illegal dichotomy for judgments concerning legitimacy puts legal scholarship at the risk of being marginalized by other disciplines, in particular by economics and political science, when attempting to understand and frame world order. This would be a considerable loss, because legal scholarship has a specific, perhaps irreplaceable role in understanding and framing public authority. For these reasons, it is important to advance a legal approach to international public authority which is internal in the sense that it considers law as an autonomous discipline responsible, above all, for enabling judgments of legality.

III. The Public Law Approach as a Combination of Internal Approaches

The proposed public law approach is based on a combination of the three main existing internal approaches to global governance phenomena: constitutionalization, administrative law perspectives, and international institutional law.[54] All of them formulate important insights for a public law approach: that constitutional sensibility as well as comparative openness to administrative law concepts should inform the analysis of the material at hand, and that international institutional law should be the disciplinary basis for further inquiries. We outline the public law approach by clarifying which insights of the three internal approaches we will adopt.

First, since the early 1990s, predominantly continental scholars have developed under the label of "constitutionalization" overarching principles of a world order based on the rule of law.[55] Deductive approaches can be encountered among them as well as inductive ones. These positions constitute the intellectual basis of much of the research which

---

[54] For a reconstruction of the scholarship *see also* Ruffert (note 28).

[55] *Supra*, note 7.

goes beyond a strictly horizontal perception of the international order and consider it as (at least partly) vertical, showing traits of a public order of the international community.[56] Whereas some authors use the constitutionalist approach for a general construction of international law, others use it in order to develop a legal frame to tame governance activities of international institutions.[57] Although this stream has to battle with some serious problems, such as the reticence of the American, Chinese or Russian governments to such an understanding of international law,[58] and has stayed rather aloof from the concrete operation of international institutions, it inspires the present project. In particular, we take two elements from this approach. On the one hand, the activity of international institutions should be investigated with constitutionalist sensibility. It should be informed by the insights and concerns of constitutionalism as developed with respect to domestic institutions. This is not an argument for domestic analogies, but for comparisons that help to move beyond functionalism in the study of international institutions. Constitutionalism stresses the importance of principles such as individual freedom and collective self-determination as well as the rule of law.[59] On the other hand, we contend that the internal constitutionalization of international institutions, as proposed by the International Law Association,[60] holds much promise for responding to concerns emerging in the constitutionalist perspective: such internal

---

[56] The contrast between horizontal and vertical perceptions of world order becomes apparent by cross-reading the Separate Opinion of President Guillaume and the Joint Separate Opinion of Judges Higgins, Kooijmans and Buergenthal in the *Case Concerning the Arrest Warrant of 11 April 2000* (DR Congo v. Belgium), ICJ Reports 2002, 35 and 63.

[57] DEBORAH CASS, THE CONSTITUTIONALIZATION OF THE WORLD TRADE ORGANIZATION (2005); Ernst-Ulrich Petersmann, *Multilevel Trade Governance in the WTO Requires Multilevel Constitutionalism*, *in* CONSTITUTIONALISM, MULTILEVEL TRADE GOVERNANCE AND SOCIAL REGULATION 5 (Christian Joerges & Ernst-Ulrich Petersmann eds., 2006).

[58] In detail Armin von Bogdandy, *Constitutionalism in International Law: Comment on a Proposal from Germany*, 47 HARVARD INTERNATIONAL LAW JOURNAL 223-242 (2006).

[59] Martti Koskenniemi, *Constitutionalism as Mindset: Reflections on Kantian Themes about International Law and Globalization*, 8 THEORETICAL INQUIRIES 22 (2007).

[60] INTERNATIONAL LAW ASSOCIATION, ACCOUNTABILITY OF INTERNATIONAL ORGANISATIONS, Final Report, 2004, available at: http://www.ila-hq.org/html/layout_committee.htm.

constitutionalization, based on the founding document of an international institution, would allow for the development of legal procedures, instruments and constraints in tune with the specificities of each regime.[61]

Second, towards the end of the 1990s, other scholars started to explore the potential of administrative thinking in order to understand public law in a globalized world. Within the research on global (or international) administrative law, four directions should be distinguished: research on the administration of territories by international institutions, such as Kosovo;[62] research on normative collisions between different domestic administrative legal orders;[63] research on the effects of international law on domestic administrative law;[64] and research dealing with the law applicable to governance mechanisms beyond the domestic level.[65] Within the fourth direction, which is of most relevance to the study of international institutions, different methodologies are employed for the legal analysis of such phenomena. While some aim at the deductive development of overarching principles of public law,[66] others proceed inductively and use the normative reservoir of domestic or

---

61 Jochen von Bernstorff, in this volume; Armin von Bogdandy, *General Principles of International Public Authority: Sketching a Research Field*, in this volume.

62 On this *see* our former project, *Restructuring Iraq. Possible Models based upon experience gained under the Authority of the League of Nations and the United Nations*, 9 MAX PLANCK YEARBOOK OF UNITED NATIONS LAW (2005).

63 For this category *see* e.g. Reimer (note 22); Markus Glaser, *Internationales Sozialverwaltungsrecht*, *in* INTERNATIONALES VERWALTUNGSRECHT 73 (Andreas Voßkuhle, Christoph Möllers & Christian Walter eds., 2007); Jürgen Bast, *Internationalisierung und De-Internationalisierung der Migrationsverwaltung*, *in* INTERNATIONALES VERWALTUNGSRECHT 279 (Andreas Voßkuhle, Christoph Möllers & Christian Walter eds., 2007); Ruffert (note 28). *See also* CHRISTOPH OHLER, DIE KOLLISIONSORDNUNG DES ALLGEMEINEN VERWALTUNGSRECHTS (2005).

64 Sabino Cassese (note 53); CHRISTIAN TIETJE, INTERNATIONALISIERTES VERWALTUNGSHANDELN (2001).

65 Most of the research assembled within the Global Administrative Law movement falls into this category. *See* Kingsbury, Krisch & Stewart (note 5); Esty (note 5).

66 Benedict Kingsbury, *Omnilateralism and Partial International Communities: Contributions of the Emerging Global Administrative Law*, 104 JOURNAL OF INTERNATIONAL LAW AND DIPLOMACY 98 (2005).

European administrative law.[67] Again, others do not intend the development of overarching principles, but imagine that the actors involved in global governance will keep each other in check through mutual contestation.[68]

Even though no leading methodology for the development of global administrative standards has yet emerged, the common denominator of this strand of research, the emphasis on domestic administrative law, bears a great potential for innovation. Our approach therefore corresponds to these approaches inasmuch as we also stress the usefulness of *intradisciplinary* exchange in legal studies: the study of the law of international public institutions should be informed by the study of domestic public institutions.[69] The full development of international law as *public* international law appears hardly feasible without building on national administrative legal insights and doctrines elaborated in the past century. Public law, in order to have an impact on society, depends on bureaucracies and administrative law.

Again, this does not advocate drawing all too simple "domestic analogies": the differences between domestic institutions and international institutions are too important. Precisely for that reason, our approach differs from that of *global administrative law* as we conceive it as too "global": it risks to efface or to blur distinctions essential to the construction, evaluation and application of norms concerning public authority. Put differently, we wonder what would be the overarching legal basis of a global administrative law. Would it be general principles? Or would it have a status of its own, above positive law? The notion of *global administrative law* implies a fusion of domestic administrative and international law that does not give consideration to the fact that international legal norms and internal norms possess a categorically different "input legitimacy": state consent versus popular sovereignty, ac-

---

67 Richard Stewart, *US Administrative Law: A Model for Global Administrative Law?*, 68 LAW AND CONTEMPORARY PROBLEMS 63 (2005); Esty (note 5); Mario Savino, *EU "Procedural" Supranationalism: On Models for Global Administrative Law*, paper presented at the NYU Global Forum on 13 December 2006, on file with the authors.

68 Nico Krisch, *The Pluralism of Global Administrative Law*, 17 EUR. J. INT'L LAW 247 (2006).

69 This call for intradisciplinary comparison and inspiration has been criticized. Yet, almost all elements of international law have been developed with an eye on domestic law. Private law, in particular contracts, are an obvious example.

cording to the classical understanding. A global approach thus glosses over and threatens to obscure this fundamental difference.

Finally, the institutional law of international organizations has been used as a basis for the analysis of new global governance phenomena. *International institutional law* focuses on the externally relevant activities of international organizations as opposed to its purely internal law like staff regulations.[70] While at the outset this law was specific to each international organization, legal scholarship is in the process of extracting common principles which address the concerns and hopes that give rise to this field.[71] Developing international institutional law holds a great potential for the legal framing of international public authority, as international organizations are of enormous practical significance for the conduct of public affairs in times of global governance.[72] It is therefore no wonder that this stream of research has greatly evolved of late in order to come to terms with the changes induced by global governance. New instruments, competencies and procedures of international organizations have come into its focus.[73]

---

70 CHITTHARANJAN FELIX AMERASINGHE, I THE LAW OF INTERNATIONAL CIVIL SERVICE (2nd ed. 1994).

71 HENRY G. SCHERMERS & NIELS BLOKKER, INTERNATIONAL INSTITUTIONAL LAW (4th ed. 2003); JAN KLABBERS, AN INTRODUCTION TO INTERNATIONAL INSTITUTIONAL LAW (2002); NIGEL D. WHITE, THE LAW OF INTERNATIONAL ORGANIZATIONS (2nd ed. 2005); SANDS & KLEIN (note 33), IGNAZ SEIDL-HOHENFELDERN & GERHARD LOIBL, DAS RECHT DER INTERNATIONALEN ORGANISATIONEN EINSCHLIEßLICH DER SUPRANATIONALEN GEMEINSCHAFTEN (7th ed. 2000); PETER FISCHER & HERIBERT KÖCK, DAS RECHT DER INTERNATIONALEN ORGANISATIONEN (3rd ed. 1997); HANDBOOK ON INTERNATIONAL ORGANIZATIONS (René-Jean Dupuy ed., 1988).

72 *See* ALVAREZ (note 44).

73 *Id. See also* ALAN BOYLE & CHRISTINE CHINKIN, THE MAKING OF INTERNATIONAL LAW (2007); JURIJ D. ASTON, SEKUNDÄRGESETZGEBUNG INTERNATIONALER ORGANISATIONEN ZWISCHEN MITGLIEDSTAATLICHER SOUVERÄNITÄT UND GEMEINSCHAFTSDISZIPLIN (2005). Studies on individual instruments are too numerous to be mentioned. *See* the GAL bibliography (2006) compiled by Maurizia De Bellis, available at: http://www.iilj.org/GAL/documents/GALBibliographyMDeBellisJune2006.pdf. Many studies combine internal and external perspectives. On competencies *see* Matthias Ruffert, *Zuständigkeitsgrenzen internationaler Organisationen im institutionellen Rahmen der internationalen Gemeinschaft*, 38 ARCHIV DES VÖLKERRECHTS 129 (2000); DANESH SAROOSHI, INTERNATIONAL ORGANIZATIONS AND THEIR EXERCISE OF SOVEREIGN POWERS (2005).

In sum, constitutional, administrative and international institutional law approaches to global governance (and, thus, international institutions) share the aim of understanding, framing and taming the exercise of international public authority in the post-national constellation. None of these approaches laments the decline of the Westphalian order.[74] They rather aim at rendering the exercise of international public authority more efficient and legitimate. We therefore hold that these three internal approaches can be combined, using international institutional law as the basis for a framework of the exercise of public authority. We believe that the *law* of international institutions can place the analysis of the exercise of international public authority on a firm disciplinary basis. This assumption also rests on a degree of skepticism towards establishing an entirely new field of global or international administrative law.

In order to be commensurate to the challenge of global governance, international institutional law should encompass not only the activities of international organizations *sensu stricto* but also that of institutions with a different legal status, such as treaty regimes and informal regimes (e.g. the OSCE). A similar adaptation is necessary with respect to non-binding and non-deontic instruments. Further, international institutional law should integrate elements from the two other internal approaches. In particular, it should (1) reconstruct the exercise of international public authority by using comparative perspectives on the administrative scholarship; (2) develop a constitutionalist framework and proposing standards for critique concerning the procedures, instruments and accountability of international institutions when engaging in the exercise of public authority; and (3) reflect systematically on the interrelationships between different legal entities typical of contemporary governance, in particular the interrelations between international and domestic institutions. Since the combination contains elements of constitutionalist, administrative and institutionalist thinking focused on the phenomenon of public authority, this combination might be termed the *public law approach*.

---

[74] For a well argued book hinting in that direction *see* CHRISTIAN SEILER, DER SOUVERÄNE VERFASSUNGSSTAAT ZWISCHEN DEMOKRATISCHER RÜCKBINDUNG UND ÜBERSTAATLICHER EINBINDUNG (2005).

D. Thematic Studies and Cross-cutting Analyses: Our Research Design

On the basis of these conceptual premises, the research project of the Max Planck Institute was designed to have two layers: the conduct of thematic studies and their reflection in cross-cutting analyses. This final part shall outline the methodology and aims of these two layers.

I. Selection of Thematic Studies

Our research is based on the understanding that the analysis of the exercise of international public authority should proceed from the special to the general.[75] Even though we can build on valuable existing scholarship, there is a need to collect new material and to take into account the wide variety of forms in which public authority beyond the nation-state is exercised today. The project is therefore based on inductive research. Several thematic studies, 17 in total,[76] analyze a variety of governance mechanisms within international institutions.

The selection of these thematic studies was guided mainly by two aspects. First, cases were selected to reflect the diversity of institutions with respect to their legal status. The thematic studies therefore include traditional international organizations with legal personality (e.g. ILO, UNESCO) but also treaty regimes (e.g. CITES, Kyoto Protocol) and networks of administration (e.g. Interpol). They also include organizations that are formed under private law insofar as they fall into one of the situations catalogued above[77] (e.g. in the case of ICANN or ICHEIC).[78] For the reasons given above, we consciously go beyond the traditional scope of international institutional law scholarship.[79]

Secondly, the thematic studies were selected to represent a wide array of mechanisms and instruments, with which public authority is exercised. Looking at the instruments an institution uses, hence the way it enacts

---

[75] Ruffert (note 28), at 396.

[76] 16 of them are published in this volume.

[77] *See* Part B.III.

[78] On our understanding of international institutions, *see* part B.III.

[79] *See* SCHERMERS & BLOKKER (note 71), at § 30; SEIDL-HOHENVELDERN & LOIBL (note 71), at § 1.

its policies and influences its environment, provides a distinctive and tested public law approach. The thematic studies therefore include organizations that operate mainly through acts legally affecting individuals (e.g. UNHCR) or individual states (e.g. UNESCO), through issuing general rules or standards (e.g. CITES, FAO Code of Conduct for Fisheries), through mediation (OSCE High Commissioner) or through non-legal, real acts (e.g. the exchange of data by Interpol).

II. Questionnaire and the Aim of the Studies

Inductive research is dependent on concepts by which we grasp the world of facts. Therefore, the inductive analysis of the thematic studies was based on a conceptual framework which was originally set out in a questionnaire.[80] As explained above, the disciplinary basis of our framework is international institutional law. As our focus is on the *exercise* of authority, we rather looked at the operative side of particular exercises of authority than at the setup of the institution. More specifically, the questionnaire directed the researchers to look at the exercise of public authority from four perspectives.

First, it proposed to study the exercise of public authority from a procedure-focused understanding. We conceive such exercise primarily as a process, as *decision* and *policy-making*, and hence the role of international institutional law as structuring and channeling an ongoing process of preparing, taking and implementing decisions.[81] The analysis of

[80] The questionnaire was not designed to provide a strict question-and-answer format. Rather, it was intended as a suggestion, proposing different avenues to approach the subject as well as suggesting the testing of new notions or concepts at the subject at hand. It was meant to be less a straight-jacket and more a walking stick or road map. If a notion or a question did not apply or did not make sense, the researchers were free to leave it out. The questionnaire's intention was hence rather to unify our perspectives and concentrate the attention to similar issues.

[81] Such procedural understanding of administrative action is typical of Anglo-American administrative law. *See* Richard Stewart, *The Reformation of American Administrative Law*, 88 HARVARD LAW REVIEW 1667 (1975). For its importance in German administrative law thinking, *see* Andreas Voßkuhle, *The Reform Approach in the German Science of Administrative Law: The "Neue Verwaltungsrechtswissenschaft,"* *in* THE TRANSFORMATION OF ADMINISTRATIVE LAW IN EUROPE 89 (Matthias Ruffert ed., 2007).

the elaboration of specific actions is therefore given the same attention as the instrument which produces external effects.[82] Accordingly, the thematic studies sketch out the organizational framework of the institution, but invest equal attention to describe their processes at various stages. This includes an analysis of the procedural regime leading up to the governance activity, a deepened analysis of the adoption of the instrument or instruments by which the institution intends to cause external effects, a presentation of the means to implement the decisions and the instruments available to check the exercise of public authority by international institutions. Such procedural analysis reveals rather different forms of institutional action.

Secondly, the questionnaire framed the analysis also by paying special attention to the legal qualification of the instrument or instruments which have external effects and which therefore regularly raise the most serious legitimacy concerns.[83] It makes a difference, so the underlying assumption, whether an institution "governs" by assigning legal status,[84] by setting non-binding standards,[85] or by providing a framework for the mediation of consensual solutions.[86] In this respect the researchers rely on a specific tradition of continental legal scholarship that frames and structures the analysis of public authority according to the instruments used.[87]

---

[82] As cross-cutting analysis on this aspect, *see* Jochen von Bernstorff, in this volume.

[83] "Instrument" in this context does not mean the constituting treaty or agreement but relates to the concrete acts by which institutions intend to reach their policy objectives.

[84] For example: refugee status by the UNHCR (*see* Maja Smrkolj, in this volume); the world heritage label by the UNESCO (*see* Diana Zacharias, in this volume); or the assumption of the connection to terrorist organizations by the UN Security Council Al-Quaeda Committee (*see* Clemens Feinäugle, in this volume).

[85] For example: Codex Alimentarius Commission (*see* Ravi Pereira, in this volume).

[86] For example: OSCE High Commissioner on Minorities (*see* Anuscheh Farahat, in this volume); OECD Multinational Enterprises (*see* Gefion Schuler, in this volume).

[87] Wolfgang Hoffmann-Riem, *Rechtsformen, Handlungsformen, Bewirkungsformen, in* II GRUNDLAGEN DES VERWALTUNGSRECHTS 885 (Wolfgang Hoffmann-Riem, Eberhard Schmidt-Aßmann & Andreas Voßkuhle eds., 2007).

Thirdly, the questionnaire also inquired as to the substantive side of the institutional activity, adding yet another continental perspective.[88] It suggested analyzing the institution's specific mandate, the character of the norms that could provide material guidance and steer the institutions substantially, or pondering the question to what extent the institution is actually cut loose from (or autonomous of) the member states and the founding mission.

Finally, the exercise of international public authority requires taking into account a multi-level perspective. The exercise of international public authority mostly occurs in tandem with the exercise of domestic public authority. Moreover, international institutions not only rely on member states to gather information or implement their policies; they also cooperate in manifold ways with other organizations, be these other public international institutions or private non-governmental organizations. To grasp these increasingly dense and important mechanisms we therefore inquired into cooperation and cross-linkages with other organizations.[89]

What were the aims and expectations with regard to these thematic studies? Most importantly, they have to be seen as attempts at systematic and critical stocktaking. They intend to grasp their respective thematic field with as comprehensive a view as possible of the relevant legal rules, any accessible non-legal documents and the pertinent literature available. Their aim is thus first and foremost to carry out a diligent descriptive analysis, guided by the conceptual framework as laid down in the questionnaire. We hope to produce studies which might help other researchers to build on. In their analysis of the material, researchers were also encouraged to use comparative perspectives of domestic administrative law. Without intending any simple domestic analogies which would be naïve and mistaken, we do stress the usefulness of comparative research and intradisciplinary exchange.

Finally, researchers were encouraged to add critical perspectives to the material at hand. We regard constitutional sensibility, i.e. awareness for the demands of constitutional thinking as a central component of analyzing global governance phenomena. At the same time, the project as a

---

[88] On this difference in comparison to American scholarship, Oliver Lepsius, *Was kann die deutsche Staatsrechtslehre von der amerikanischen Rechtswissenschaft lernen?*, *in* STAATSLEHRE ALS WISSENSCHAFT (supplement to DIE VERWALTUNG) 330 (Helmut Schulze-Fielitz ed., 2007).

[89] On these aspects in a cross-cutting perspective, *see* Armin von Bogdandy & Philipp Dann, in this volume.

whole does not subscribe to one uniform normative concept. Instead, we accept (and stress) the plurality of concepts and values. Researchers were therefore free to use individually chosen concepts.

III. Cross-cutting Analyses

During the second stage of the project, cross-cutting analyses built on the thematic studies and used them to address more general themes of international institutional law under the public law approach. These analyses turned towards topics such as procedures, instruments and multilevel structure, enforcement and accountability and ultimately to "final" issues like legitimacy and principles.

Here too the intention was, first of all, one of stocktaking and comparative systematization. Given the immense heterogeneity of the institutions at hand and the lack of a common constitutional framework, readers will not find a great number of elaborate and universal doctrines in the cross-cutting studies. Instead, they rather try to develop systematizing perspectives on the material. Some of them explicitly state that general assumptions are not possible,[90] others make rather loose terminological offers and propose systematizing categories[91] and again others try to describe possible avenues or methodologies to reach more general categories.[92] Here again, the pluralism of our approach is manifest.

Going beyond our project, one could however ponder whether the construction of general doctrines would be desirable even in the long run. Different answers are possible. Some will certainly argue that such doctrines must remain overly thin or entirely useless, given that the international legal order is not on path to more integration but rather systemic fragmentation.[93] Others would doubt that at least in the foreseeable future such efforts could be fruitful and propose that energies should rather be directed to analyze particular regimes.[94]

---

90 *See* Jochen von Bernstorff, in this volume.

91 *See* Armin von Bogdandy & Philipp Dann, in this volume; Erika de Wet, *Holding International Institutions Accountable*, in this volume.

92 *See* von Bogdandy (note 61); Matthias Goldmann, in this volume.

93 TEUBNER & FISCHER-LESCANO (note 47).

94 Krisch (note 68).

Yet one can also argue that the development of common notions and concepts, able to "travel" from one regime to the next and eventually bridging them, is a fundamental function of any doctrinal work and a necessary contribution to the transparency and ultimately the legitimacy of institutional activities. This would be the approach most sympathetic to the traditions of German legal academia. In any event, these are not questions and tasks of here and now.

E. The Underlying International Ethos

This research on the public authority of international institutions has a doctrinal tendency. Yet, as with any doctrine, it is informed by more general ethical and political premises, and we hold that doctrine should make them explicit. Briefly stated, the premise of this research is a normative vision of global governance as peaceful cooperation between polities, be they states or regional federal units, a cooperation which is mediated by global institutions which are *public* in the emphatic meaning, but remain at the same time *public international* in nature. These are propelled by national governments or the corresponding organs of regional groupings (preferably democratically accountable ones), which, however, would be no longer in a position to individually block the enactment or enforcement of international law. These international institutions would in turn be conscious of their largely state-mediated (and thus limited) resources of democratic legitimacy and respectful of the diversity of their constituent polities. A democratic global federation appears to be beyond the reach of our time, just like an international community dispensing with intermediate levels of governance such as the state; but there can be a better, more peaceful and more integrated world of closely and successfully cooperating polities governed by public international institutions, and we think that elaborating the public law character of international law is an essential precondition for this.

From Public International Law to International Public Law: A Comment on the "Public Authority" of International Institutions and the "Publicness" of their Law

Comment by Stefan Kadelbach

I. Introduction

The entry onto a list of an individual or organization suspected of supporting international terrorism by a specialized sanctions committee of the UN Security Council and the effects thereon illustrate that the United Nations has the authority to take decisions which have consequences for individuals, such as travel bans and the seizing of financial assets.[1] The difficulties in reversing a sanctions listing and the reluctance

1 *See*, inter alia, UN SC Resolutions 1267 of 15 October 1999 (Taliban), 1373 of 28 September 2001 (Taliban and Al-Qaida), 1455 of 17 January 2003

A. von Bogdandy et al. (eds.), *The Exercise of Public Authority by International Institutions*, Beiträge zum ausländischen öffentlichen Recht und Völkerrecht 210,
DOI 10.1007/978-3-642-04531-8_2,

of the Court of First Instance of the European Communities to exercise jurisdiction[2] have raised questions which sound familiar within a constitutional law context. The reason is that the sanctions are implemented like public international law in general, i.e. by a model in which decisions taken at an international level have to be transformed or adopted at the state or European Union level. The result is a lacuna with respect to the protection of fundamental rights: The United Nations has the authority to act, but offers no remedy. Member State courts dispose of the capacity to grant judicial protection, but feel restrained by UN law.

This phenomenon illustrates a change in perspective. Targeted sanctions were introduced in the 1990s. They are more efficient than previous economic sanctions such as comprehensive trade embargoes which hit the population, but did not affect those responsible. The new sanctions type had been tested in sanctions against individuals from the former Yugoslavia, Haiti, Libya, Sudan, Angola and Sierra Leone before the Taliban and Al-Qaida sanctions system was set up.[3] Even though they are, as a whole, less detrimental to human rights than other sanctions, individual rights violations, from a lawyer's point of view, can be better traced back to a specific act and a responsible authority, and might thus have triggered expectations which had not been directed against the Security Council before. This perspective on the process is not exclusively one of public international law, but one of public law as well.

The current volume offers a broad spectrum of fields where international institutions in a very wide sense take decisions which used to be the sole purview of states and which, in one way or another, affect individuals. Classical examples are the international announcement of arrest

---

(reporting obligations of Member States), 1617 of 29 July 2005 (checklist of Member States actions to be taken); last update in SC Resolution 1822 of 30 June 2008.

[2] *See* CFI Cases T-306/01, *Al Barakaat v Council and Commission* [2005] ECR II-3533; T-315/01, *Kadi v Council and Commission* [2005] ECR II-3649; T-253/02, *Ayadi v Council* [2006] II-2139; and T-49/04, *Hassan v Council and Commission* [2007] ECR II-52; appeals are pending, *see* opinion of Advocate General M. Poiares Maduro of 16 January 2008 in the *Kadi* Case (C-402/05 P) and of 23 January 2008 in the *Al Barakaat* Case (C-415/05 P) who pleads for reversal.

[3] Cf. UN SC Resolutions 820 of 17 April 1993 (Yugoslavia); 841 of 16 June 1993 (Haiti); 883 of 11 November 1993 (Libya); 1054 of 26 April 1996 (Sudan); 1127 of 28 August 1997 (Angola); 1132 of 8 October 1997 (Sierra Leone).

warrants by Interpol, health standards elaborated by the joint FAO and WHO Codex Alimentarius Commission or the registration of intellectual property rights by one of the WIPO protection systems. Others of a less obvious nature are mentioned in the rich case material of this publication. Even though international institutions with administrative powers have their antecedents in 19th century administrative unions, the abundance of such organizations and agencies as well as the mass, specificity and sophistication of the output they produce mark a new quality in comparison to the past.

Scholarly reactions to this phenomenon have been diverse. In the political sciences, global governance approaches took up the institutionalist tradition and started from the assumption that international organizations replace powers the national state has lost and possess the potential to confront the negative effects of globalization.[4] Similar projections are mirrored by the debate on the constitutionalization of public international law.[5] Other approaches go a step further and ask whether international institutions are equipped with the appropriate tools to fulfill such tasks, as do different variants of good governance theories[6] and the global administrative law school.[7] Finally, there are different normative perspectives on the development of a fundamental nature. From a social philosophical perspective, the system of international institutions raises

---

[4] J.S. Rosenau, *Governance, Order and Change in the World, in* GOVERNANCE WITHOUT GOVERNMENT: ORDER AND CHANGE IN WORLD POLITICS, 1 *et seq.* (J.S. Rosenau & E.-O. Czempiel eds., 1992); M. ZÜRN, REGIEREN JENSEITS DES NATIONALSTAATS (1998).

[5] For an overview on the debate *see* S. Kadelbach & T. Kleinlein, *International Law – A Constitution of Mankind?*, 50 GERMAN YEARBOOK OF INTERNATIONAL LAW 303, 304 *et seq.* (2007).

[6] For further reference *see* J. Delbrück, *Exercising Public Authority Beyond the State: Transnational Democracy and/or Alternative Legitimation Strategies?*, 10 INDIANA JOURNAL OF GLOBAL LEGAL STUDIES 29 *et seq.* (2003).

[7] B. Kingsbury, N. Krisch & R.B. Stewart, *The Emergence of Global Administrative Law*, 68 LAW AND CONTEMPORARY PROBLEMS 15 *et seq.* (2005); N. Krisch & B. Kingsbury, *Global Governance and Global Administrative Law in the International Legal Order*, 17 EUROPEAN JOURNAL OF INTERNATIONAL LAW (EJIL) 1 *et seq.* (2006).

doubt as to whether it is "just" and "fair".[8] International lawyers analyze institutions and their decisions with respect to their legitimacy.[9]

The "public law" theory guiding the present project attempts to combine these different approaches. It follows the institutionalist supposition of global governance theory in that it stresses the importance of international organizations as actors. It takes up the constitutionalist theory of continental international law doctrine by sharing the assumption that international organizations need a rule of law basis to build on. It is related to global administrative law in its belief in the steering quality of administrative law principles; and it assumes a substantial normative stance by starting from the premise that observing principles of public law enhance the legitimacy of decisions taken beyond the state level.

In the following sections, two aspects will be explored more closely. First, an effort will be made to assess how administrative law in a broad sense fits into the legal orders of international organizations in particular and into the realm of public international law in general (below, II.). Secondly, it will be asked to what extent the public law approach adds to existing public international law thinking in terms of the legitimacy of international decision-making (III.).

II. Administrative Law beyond State Administration

1. Preceding Developments

a) International Administrative Law

Looking for precedents for the present approach, the 19th century predecessors of today's international organizations deserve attention. Some of them, such as international river commissions, the Universal Postal Union and the International Telecommunications Union, were

---

[8] R. FORST, DAS RECHT AUF RECHTFERTIGUNG 328 *et seq.* (2007).

[9] *Delbrück* (note 6); A. von Bogdandy, *Globalization and Europe: How to Square Democracy and Globalization*, 15 EJIL 885 *et seq.* (2004); R. Wolfrum, *Legitimacy in International Law, in* THE LAW OF INTERNATIONAL RELATIONS – LIBER AMICORUM HANSPETER NEUHOLD, 471 *et seq.* (A. Reinisch & U. Kriebaum eds., 2007).

initially categorized as administrative unions.[10] Consequently, the law on which they operated was referred to as international administrative law at the beginning of the 20th century, particularly in Italian and Spanish legal writings.[11] However, the term was not used in a consistent fashion. Following a tradition which goes back to *Lorenz von Stein*, a different idea of *Internationales Verwaltungsrecht* evolved which comprised international administrative law as well as domestic administrative law dealing with international aspects.[12] Although the latter, known as administrative international law, refers to administrative law rules for the resolution of conflicts of laws,[13] the approach of *von Stein* always was to comprise the reality of administration as a whole, thus encompassing different sources of law in one concept.[14] Although apparently not sharing the Hegelian connotations of *von Stein's* concept, the idea of integrating national administrative law with international institutional law is at least not ruled out by the "public authority" approach.[15]

---

10 For an overview *see* R. Wolfrum, *International Administrative Unions, in* ENCYCLOPEDIA OF PUBLIC INTERNATIONAL LAW, vol. II, 1041 *et seq*. (R. Bernhardt ed., 1995).

11 D. DONATI, I TRATTATI INTERNAZIONALI NEL DIRITTO COSTITUZIONALE, vol. I, 432, 437 *et seq*. (1906); U. Borsi, CARATTERE ED OGGETTO DEL DIRITTO AMMINISTRATIVO INTERNAZIONALE, 6 RIVISTA DI DIRITTO INTERNAZIONALE 368 *et seq*. (1912); J. Gascon y Marin, *Les transformations du droit administratif international*, 34 RECUEIL DES COURS 21 *et seq*. (1930).

12 L. VON STEIN, DIE VERWALTUNGSLEHRE, DIE LEHRE VON DER INNEREN VERWALTUNG, part II, 94 *et seq*. (1866).

13 K. NEUMEYER, INTERNATIONALES VERWALTUNGSRECHT, vol. IV, 28 *et seq*. (1936); K. VOGEL, DER RÄUMLICHE ANWENDUNGSBEREICH DER VERWALTUNGSRECHTSNORM 302 *et seq*. (1965); G. Hoffmann, *Internationales Verwaltungsrecht, in* BESONDERES VERWALTUNGSRECHT, 851, 864 *et seq*. (I. von Münch ed., 1985); cf. also C. OHLER, DIE KOLLISIONSORDNUNG DES ALLGEMEINEN VERWALTUNGSRECHTS (2005); contributions, *in* INTERNATIONALES VERWALTUNGSRECHT (A. Vosskuhle, C. Möllers & C. Walter eds., 2007).

14 For an English summary *see* K. Vogel, *Administrative Law, International Aspects, in* Bernhardt (note 10), vol. I, 2nd ed., 1992, 22 *et seq*.

15 *See also* S. Cassese, *Administrative Law without the State? The Challenge of Global Regulation*, 37 NEW YORK UNIVERSITY JOURNAL OF INTERNATIONAL LAW & POLITICS 663, 684 *et seq*. (2005).

b) European Administrative Law

A second era of international administrative law started with the emergence of European administrative law. Executive powers of the Council, the Commission and European agencies as well as the demand for rules to govern the implementation of secondary Community law entailed the need to develop a common corpus of law. Initial impulses originated from such dispersed sources as treaty law, secondary Community legislation and, above all, principles developed by the European Court of Justice. European administrative law thus came about by an abstraction from the elements thus found and by analogies to general principles of national administrative laws.[16] In a second phase, the phenomenon of "Europeanization" of national administrative law found attention.[17] German legal doctrine suggested three different consequences, depending on the stance taken with respect to the general transfer of powers to the European Union: the expectation of a complete adaptation of national administrative law to European administrative law,[18] the contrary conclusion to limit European influences to fields where this is unavoidable,[19] or the federalization of administrative law, which means the separation of two administrative law subsystems, one of which being Europeanized, the other purely national.[20] A third phase of scholarly debate concentrated on comparative administrative law, which is a prerequisite for the establishment of a solid basis for the gen-

---

16 J. SCHWARZE, EUROPÄISCHES VERWALTUNGSRECHT 1988 (2nd ed., 2005).

17 A. Hatje, DIE GEMEINSCHAFTSRECHTLICHE STEUERUNG DER WIRTSCHAFTSVERWALTUNG (1996); *contributions, in* ADMINISTRATIVE LAW UNDER EUROPEAN INFLUENCE (J. Schwarze ed., 1996); ENGLISH PUBLIC LAW AND THE COMMON LAW OF EUROPE (M. Andenas ed., 1998).

18 O. Bachof, *Die Dogmatik des Verwaltungsrechts vor den Gegenwartaufgaben der Verwaltung*, 30 VERÖFFENTLICHUNGEN DER VEREINIGUNG DEUTSCHER STAATSRECHTSLEHRER (VVDStRL) 193, 236 (1972).

19 T. VON DANWITZ, VERWALTUNGSRECHTLICHES SYSTEM UND EUROPÄISCHE INTEGRATION (1996).

20 S. KADELBACH, ALLGEMEINES VERWALTUNGSRECHT UNTER EUROPÄISCHEM EINFLUß (1999); *id.*, *European Administrative Law and the Law of a Europeanized Administration, in* GOOD GOVERNANCE IN EUROPE'S INTEGRATED MARKET, 167 *et seq.* (C. Joerges & R. Dehousse eds., 2002); cf. also TRATTATO DI DIRITTO AMMINISTRATIVO EUROPEO, vol. I, 15 *et seq.*, 399 *et seq.* (M.P. Chiti & G. Greco eds., 1997); J.H. JANS ET AL., INLEIDING TOT HET EUROPEES BESTUURSRECHT 19 *et seq.* (1999).

eration of common principles.[21] A synthesis of some of these perspectives conceives the European and national levels as a compound of administrative powers in a multi-level system where vertical and horizontal cooperation is the dominant obligation,[22] involving the need to define rules which resolve conflicts of competencies between the different actors and to find common legal principles which provide for the comparability of the systems involved, the basis for mutual recognition and the legitimacy of the decisions taken. European administrative law thus combines the abstraction method of the initial phase with conflict of law and comparative law approaches.

This new corpus of administrative law at first glance looks like an incarnation of the *Steinian* concept,[23] but there are three factors which make a difference: Firstly, this development is not a mere product of legal scholarship, but a response to the practical needs of a multilevel administration; secondly, it is guided by an overarching legal order with agreed supremacy; and thirdly, there is an international court with compulsory jurisdiction, the ECJ, which has substantially contributed to the process.

With respect to the public law approach to international institutional law, a common feature is that there are international authorities which are vested by the states with administrative powers. For a comparison with European administrative law, it seems tempting to ask whether the three above-mentioned factors are necessary for bringing about an order of legal rules, principles and institutions of a similar character. Because of the uniqueness of European integration, an answer to this question would be speculative. At any rate, to stress the differences between the European and the international planes would not falsify the public law concept. However, in order to assess the usefulness and the likelihood of an identical process within the legal orders of organizations with a global reach, it is still useful to compare the conditions at both levels.

---

21 *See*, for instance, S. CASSESE, LE BASI DEL DIRITTO AMMINISTRATIVO 53 *et seq.* (5th ed., 1998).

22 E. SCHMIDT-AßMANN, DAS ALLGEMEINE VERWALTUNGSRECHT ALS ORDNUNGSIDEE 18 *et seq.* (1998; 2nd ed. 2006); T. Groß, *Verantwortung und Effizienz in der Mehrebenenverwaltung*, 66 VVDStRL152 *et seq.* (2007).

23 As to European administrative law as a result of comparative thinking *see* L. VON STEIN, DIE VERWALTUNGSLEHRE, part I, viii *et seq.* (2nd ed., 1869).

c) Synthesis: International Public Law as Law of Multilevel Systems?

In the scholarly debate surrounding international public law, similar elements can be discerned like those contributing to European administrative law. Comparative institutional law derived common patterns of different international organizations, some of them are constitutional, others administrative in character.[24] Global administrative law concentrates on rules and principles which can be regarded as administrative law in itself. In the paper presented by *Nico Krisch* and *Benedict Kingsbury*,[25] the perspective vis-à-vis international organizations is an immanent one: the authors discern different agencies and functions which they recognize as administrative at the international level and ask by which principles their activities are guided. In a second step, the normative question is confronted as to whether the general application of principles such as accountability, participation and transparency measured against the pragmatic needs of the respective international institutions prove useful – or whether they rather entail deficiencies in effectiveness, preference for special interests or populism. The focus is on what can be found in the institutional framework; what may be external about it are the normative expectations by some observers with a similar scholarly interest. Hence, the public law approach distinguishes itself from the global administrative law theory in the strength of its normative intentions. Recent research, which investigates into the influences of international law on domestic administrative law[26] and the legitimacy of that process, opens a further dimension.[27] To integrate these trends to a single set of international public law norms appears to be a logical solution. The discursive potential of this hypothesis for the structuring of international regulating and decision-making procedures

---

24 *See* the explanation of the approach in H. SCHERMERS & N. BLOKKER, INTERNATIONAL INSTITUTIONAL LAW, §§ 22 *et seq*. (4th ed., 2003).

25 Above, note 7.

26 C. TIETJE, INTERNATIONALITÄT DES VERWALTUNGSHANDELNS (2001); F. MAYER, DIE INTERNATIONALISIERUNG DES VERWALTUNGSRECHTS (2009, forthcoming); E. Schmidt-Aßmann, *Die Herausforderung der Verwaltungsrechtswissenschaft durch die Internationalisierung der Verwaltungsbeziehungen,* 45 DER STAAT 315 *et seq*. (2006).

27 W. Kahl, *Parlamentarische Steuerung der internationalen Verwaltungsvorgänge, in* ALLGEMEINES VERWALTUNGSRECHT – ZUR TRAGFÄHIGKEIT EINES KONZEPTS, 71 *et seq*. (H.-H. Trute et al. eds., 2008).

is substantial.[28] However, the evolution of such a corpus faces conditions which are not very favorable.

First, it may be questioned whether international organizations and their member states constitute multilevel systems of a sufficiently intertwined density that they might be regarded as a compound with a multilevel administration.[29] In constitutional theory, a multilevel system presupposes structures in which law is produced autonomously at each level and public authority is exercised through shared responsibility. The concept is open enough to allow different degrees of intensity of mutual cooperation. But it is submitted that most international organizations are of a rather loose character so that they constitute different layers of authority combined with a public international law obligation of the member states to cooperate.[30] Thus, there is not much of a settled common ground for administrative law. This does not rule out that the constitutional law of the member states could demand a certain quality of legitimacy and therefore require an institutional administration which honors the rule of law and principles derived from it.

Secondly, in public international law the question of superiority is subject to a classical debate. Hence, whether the international legal order is superior to domestic law is an open question. Doubts are addressed by the theory of international constitutionalism to which the public law approach subscribes. Under the traditional monist/dualist paradigm, this is a matter of perspective. Courts in national legal orders which tend to avoid conflicts with international law obligations, as it is the case in many European states, may take a stance which privileges public international law, resolve conflicts of laws in its favor and may therefore come close to superiority. However, this may not be said of many states, and the legitimizing legal order is always at the national level.

---

28 S. Cassese, *The Globalisation of Law*, 37 NEW YORK UNIVERSITY JOURNAL OF INTERNATIONAL LAW & POLITICS 973, 992 *et seq*. (2005); E. Benvenisti, *Reclaiming Democracy: The Strategic Use of Foreign and International Law by National Courts*, 102 AMERICAN JOURNAL OF INTERNATIONAL LAW 241 *et seq*. (2008).

29 For a parallel analysis on the constitutional level *see* I. Pernice, *The Global Dimension of Multilevel Constitutionalism: A Legal Response to the Challenges of Globalisation, in* FESTSCHRIFT FÜR CHRISTIAN TOMUSCHAT, 973 *et seq*. (Pierre-Marie Dupuy et al. eds., 2006).

30 With respect to ILO and WTO *see* C. MÖLLERS, GEWALTENGLIEDERUNG 287 *et seq*. (2005).

Thirdly, whether there is an international court with jurisdiction to develop common principles, as in the European Union, again depends on the chosen organization. Although the net of international judicial bodies and tribunals has become much denser than it was ever before, their tasks rarely permit much progressive development in that field. Some organizations, like the United Nations, have their own administrative law courts, but their jurisdiction is usually limited to disputes between the organizations and their officials.[31] Others like human rights courts as well as WTO and ICSID arbitration have produced abundant case law, but do not often have the opportunity to build upon the governance of international institutions.

To sum up, conditions for the emergence of international public law are not very favorable. The desirability of an administrative law based on the rule of law is hardly to be doubted, but, for the time being, the prospects for its development remain restricted to rules that can be derived from the logic of the respective organization's powers and rules. Common administrative law as a reservoir of supplementing rules, by contrast, are problematic, not only in terms of the conditions of their formation, but also with respect to their legitimacy. The most probable consequence of this state of affairs is a plurality of international administrative law systems. Thus, the concept of international public law faces a dilemma: To restrict it to the rules found in existing institutional law would perpetuate the unsatisfactory situation which is characterized by only rudimentary standards by which activities can be reviewed. To formulate substantial standards with a view at enhancing legitimacy and acceptability of the outcome would trigger the objection to announce norms with no sufficient basis in positive law.

2. Change in Paradigm: from Private Law to Public Law as a System of Reference

The problem of how to hold the different components of international public law together is difficult to address if the outcome is expected to be not merely analytical, but also of a normative nature. The intuition of traditional international law doctrine would be to ask how the corpus of public law demanded by the present approach would fit into the categories of sources.

---

31 SCHERMERS & BLOKKER (note 24), §§ 642 *et seq*.

One of the methods suggested is an inquiry by induction into the norms on the governance of international institutions, to distillate common principles from them and to transpose the resulting rules to other institutions. This would come close to what is called general principles of international law as one variant of general principles in the sense of Article 38 (1) lit. c of the Statute of the International Court of Justice. The second approach, comparative analysis, used to be recommended as the other method of finding general principles as well. To combine both is not unusual.[32] However, there are two caveats to be made with respect to this approach, both of which are closely connected.

The first observation means to insist on the obvious: it refers to what may be called the domestic analogy objection. General principles of law are a category which was originally adopted in the statutes of international courts as a supplementary method to fill lacunae if treaties or custom did not provide appropriate rules to decide a case.[33] This method of comparative analysis is widely seen as problematic, for it involves an element of choice for which the criteria are vague; a comparative view at other legal orders thus is at risk to re-invent the own environment.[34] In order to escape this objection, the consented general principles are usually of a rather abstract character such as *pacta sunt servanda*, *bona fide* interpretation of treaties, the principle that reparation has to be made for unlawfully caused damages etc. The vast majority of (if not all) general principles have meanwhile been incorporated into treaty or customary law and thereby found an additional basis. This remark is not to say that comparative administrative law is methodologically unsound as such; but in order to counter the domestic analogy objection, it must be done in an inclusive way, making selectivity explicit and giving reasons for it. Why, for instance, the British, French or German administrative law systems are considered to be bet-

---

32 As to the difficulties of a strict distinction between general principles of law and general principles of international law *see* I. BROWNLIE, PRINCIPLES OF PUBLIC INTERNATIONAL LAW 18 *et seq.* (6th ed., 2003).

33 M. Bogdan, *General Principles of Law and the Problem of Lacunae in the Law of Nations*, 46 NORDIC JOURNAL OF INTERNATIONAL LAW 37, 39 (1977); U. FASTENRATH, LÜCKEN IM VÖLKERRECHT 100 *et seq.* (1991).

34 G. GOTTLIEB, THE LOGIC OF CHOICE. AN INVESTIGATION OF THE CONCEPTS OF RULE AND RATIONALITY 103 (1968); *see also* G. Frankenberg, *Critical Comparisons: Re-Thinking Comparative Law*, 26 HARVARD INTERNATIONAL LAW JOURNAL 411, 412 (1985).

ter sources for comparison than, for example, Chinese, Japanese or Russian law ought to be explained. The underlying assumption that systems based on the Western type constitutional state are, even for the purposes of public international law, more legitimate has to be addressed openly. The public law approach will therefore be confronted with arguments similar to constitutionalization theories of the past years.

The second remark refers to the distinction between public and private spheres. The change in paradigm involved in the public law theory deserves attention. Since *Grotius*, if not before, private law institutions have lent themselves to international law doctrine: Modern treaty law was initially developed along the lines of Roman contract law, titles to territory used to be derived from property law, the rules on state succession have roots in inheritance law, and state responsibility follows tort law thinking.[35] This is appropriate if subjects of international law are to be seen as equal. The "publicness" of classical public international law resulted from nothing more than the fact that the actors were states, but did not presuppose any legal hierarchy between them. To think in terms of public law suggests that there are superiors and entities or individuals who are their subjects. This assumption is problematic. Not only legal realists would object that whether between international organizations and their member states such a hierarchy is established depends on the distribution of powers between the organization and its member states. Regarding the UN, the permanent members of the Security Council would not look at this relationship in the same way as others. With respect to individuals as subjects of international organizations, there are very few institutions (save the European Union) with the competencies to impose obligations directly on individuals, and most of these powers are very exact.[36] Therefore, a very broad concept of "public authority" must be embraced which focuses on the impact of the decisions taken rather than on their legal effect. The criteria for drawing a line between "private" and "public" organizations still requires some refinement, however. If the disposition over public goods is the criterion, not only ICANN, but also international sports organizations such as IOC or FIFA are of interest. As with the Internet, global sporting events can be seen as public goods, and the right to or-

---

[35] Cf. H. LAUTERPACHT, PRIVATE LAW SOURCES AND ANALOGIES IN INTERNATIONAL LAW (1927).

[36] Examples are the river commissions already mentioned above (*see* note 10 and accompanying text) and the International Seabed Authority.

ganize them distributes political and economical advantages. In the end, the public law approach introduces a "public" element even for private international law institutions.[37] Apparently, even the question of what constitutes public good is guided by value choices for which criteria are yet to be found. In other words: The suggested public/private dichotomy is exposed to the criticism that it follows a predefined concept rather than being the result of the application of public law criteria.

III. Potential of International Public Law

1. Suitability of Public Law for International Organizations as a Concept of Legitimacy

The best argument for the suggested public law perspective would be if it had the potential to offer solutions other approaches cannot provide. This leads us to the question of what public law adds to other normative demands as derived from human rights, international constitutionalism and theories of legitimacy.

The present approach suggests that administrative law thinking enhances the rationality and legitimacy of international organizations. The rule of law benefit to be taken from such doctrinal methods in a continental sense is rationality and reliability,[38] and the hope is to expand that notion into the international sphere. Two methodological problems arise.

The first is the relationship between public law and its constitutional context. Public law encompasses two components, i.e. constitutional

---

[37] How this solution relates to the private law theory of "global law without a state" (*see* G. TEUBNER, GLOBAL LAW WITHOUT A STATE (1997) cannot be addressed here; but the proposal to extend the reach of fundamental rights to private organisations alone does not necessarily contradict to it. However, a latent dissent appears to occur with respect to the impact of private and public law-making on the international plane in general; *see also* C. Tomuschat, *Möglichkeiten und Grenzen der Globalisierung, in* GLOBALISIERUNG UND ENTSTAATLICHUNG DES RECHTS, 21, 28 *et seq*. (J. Schwarze ed., 2008). Under national administrative law, this would not be seen as problematic; here, the transfer of tasks to private entities usually entails a loss of legal restraints, which the functional criteria applied by the "public law" approach on the international plane would avoid.

[38] Cf. MAX WEBER, RECHTSSOZIOLOGIE 69 (2nd ed., 1967).

and administrative law. Rules and principles which make the rule of law work and help to take individual rights seriously are primarily found in administrative law. The question how far they depend on constitutional principles is of guiding interest for the whole research agenda. The answer of continental law thinking would be to take fundamental constitutional principles at face value, such as the necessity that administrative decisions have to have a legal basis and be subject to legal review if individual rights are restricted, so that a system of institutions and rules may be built upon them. Another assumption from which different institutional initiatives of good governance have started would be that administration follows an intrinsic logic and rules of "good administration" can be developed independently, with a view of the specific tasks of an organization and without having to be derived from specific constitutional traditions. The former view is not easy to defend in an institutional environment with a global reach while the latter method is likely to produce only a thin net of rules and to provoke objections from a constitutional perspective.

The second methodological difficulty is to address the objection referred to above that the corpus of law which informs public law thinking is necessarily selective in contents. This problem can be the better confronted the closer the relationship to international standards is, most of which are found in international human rights. Thus, intra-disciplinary discourse is not only promising between international institutional law and administrative law scholarship, it might also prove useful within the different branches of international law, in particular to investigate in how far the jurisprudence of international human rights' protection systems produces results suitable to be considered at the international level.

2. Reference Material – and the Targeted Sanctions Example

The work of international institutions opens a wide panorama on administrative activities in the widest sense. Seen against the background of national administrative law categories, one can recognize activities aiming at the maintenance of public order such as those of Interpol and Europol, welfare administration implemented by international development banks, and planning as designed and prepared by various OECD, UNDP or UNEP policy studies. Some of these decisions have more or less immediate external effects on individuals, others are regulatory in character. That public law thinking is useful in arriving at more reasonable and more effective results is, as a hypothesis, very plausible. The answer to the question as to how far it ultimately proves useful must be reserved to individual studies. The merit of the public law approach is to openly state this and to comprehensibly assess how far modern international institutions have taken over functions which used to be the *domaine réservé* of states. However, not all of the examples selected are equally rewarding. Thus, it is doubtful whether activities with a strong high-politics impact can be properly addressed in this way. An example is the UN targeted sanctions mechanism. Although it might have been one of the starting points for the present undertaking, it is probably not the best case to convince us that the public law approach adds much to what what already exists.

The case study devoted to that problem suggests analyzing the listing and de-listing of individuals on the sanctions list as an administrative procedure and its decisions as administrative acts. It draws the conclusion that judicial review is necessary, but, as to date, deficient.[39] This conclusion is, in effect, hard to refute. The question is whether administrative law scholarship makes it more plausible than other normative reference systems.

Following the methodology of assessing general principles, the first step in finding applicable administrative law would be to analyze whether the institutional law of the UN itself offers elements from which principles might be inferred. The Charter provides the possibility to install an independent review body which, once established, would be in a position to produce binding decisions.[40] Whether or not to set up such a subsidiary organ, however, is up to the member states, i.e. a political question.

The hypothesis for the next step is that general principles, probably found in intra-disciplinary exchange and by comparative analysis, would lead to categories which trigger the expectation of introducing a procedure closer to the rule of law. The premise is that such categories are normative in character. Historically and functionally, this assumption is correct. However, the question is which direction their normativity takes, in other words, what follows from the identification of the

---

[39] *See* C. Feinäugle, in this volume.

[40] The ICJ found that UN Charter law reflects a remote notion of checks and balances which rule out that an institution – like the General Assembly – can escape the binding consequences of a judicial body which it had entrusted with the task of legal review, *see* Opinion on the *Effect of Awards of Compensation Made by the UN Administrative Tribunal*, ICJ Reports 1954, 47 (61).

sanctions committee's listing or non-delisting decisions as administrative acts. In authoritarian systems, the categorization of an administrative act historically had the use of finding a form in law which expressed the binding character of administrative decisions. In 19th century German legal doctrine, this notion was developed in analogy to judicial decisions, thus to stress the legal authority of the executive branch in the German Empire,[41] and there are administrative law systems represented by some of the Security Council members which still rest on such a fundament.

Obviously, this is not the idea with which the "public law approach" was launched; but it shows that under this approach administrative law is not so much a reference system for analysis as it is a tool for justifying normative conclusions. The conclusion at which the case study arrives is that any administrative act encroaching upon individual rights of private individuals must be subject to judicial review. In German municipal law this conclusion was the result of constitutional development. In the Weimar Republic, *Walter Jellinek* distinguished administrative acts systematically according to whether or not an action against them could be brought.[42] It was only after the *Grundgesetz* had entered into force that the decisive reason for using the administrative act concept was to find a reference point to which the consequence of procedural rights and judicial review could to be attached.[43]

In other words, approaching institutional law with "public law" criteria involves value judgments from normative systems which are external to it and is inclined to produce an idealized version of administrative law. The interesting question is how these judgments can be justified. It is therefore still questionable whether it is less promising to plead this particular case on the basis of human rights law, all the more so since credit must be given to the new category of smart sanctions in that it is better suited than others in avoiding the suffering of innocent people. To elaborate on the system from an international perspective would have the advantage of following a path already taken.

---

41 O. MAYER, DEUTSCHES VERWALTUNGSRECHT, part I, 93 (3rd ed., 1923).

42 W. JELLINEK, VERWALTUNGSRECHT 247 *et seq*. (3rd ed., 1931).

43 H. MAURER, ALLGEMEINES VERWALTUNGSRECHT 189 *et seq.* (16th ed., 2006).

IV. Concluding Remarks

The normative implications of the public law approach open a promising field, even though they raise questions with respect to their justification, sources and methods. Objections are similar to those directed against some of the constitutionalization theories of the past years and which aim at the foundations of the implicit value judgments.

In order to avoid such criticism, it appears advisable to give more credit to the weaknesses of international law-making, i.e. its political character, its slow pace and the often very vague contents of an outcome. Thus, it appears feasible to develop principles of international public law if they can be based on, and further specify, elements already found in international institutional law, human rights law or general principles of law, all the more so those whose promotion is among the purposes of an international organization.

Intra-disciplinary exchange and comparative analysis offer a large reservoir of material which might inspire policy proposals. It is rewarding to enhance the awareness of the breadth and depth of activities with an impact on rights and prospects of individuals, to analyze them systematically and to stress the need of a more norm-oriented perspective on their activities. It therefore ought to use its potential in providing the responsible actors with material to restructure their procedural rules. The normative orientation of the concept may be criticized, but this can also be its strength in that it has the potential to open a debate on international governance with legal criteria and to put the burden of argument on the defense of some acts and procedures which are difficult to maintain.

To Tame and to Frame

*Comment by Stephan Leibfried**

I have a marked sympathy for the Heidelberg group's efforts, in recent years, to conceive and construct a more encompassing rule-bound international sphere and to unite concepts from European public law with those from political and social science. I am pleased to be able to offer my comments on their paper, "Developing the Publicness of Public International Law," though I am something of an outsider, not formally trained in international law or well-versed in the current debates and literature, and I run the risk of occasionally missing the mark. As a scholar with a general background in law, economics, sociology, social history, and political science, I have, for a number of years, been heading an interdisciplinary institute whose mission is to track the post-1970s development of OECD nation states and gauge the extent and consequences of the privatization and internationalization of responsibilities.[1] My remarks here, which focus on seven of the nine topics I

---

* I would like to thank Professor Gerd Winter from the Bremen University Law School for educating me on several key points discussed here, though he may well not be in agreement on some of my comments and should in no way be held responsible. Thanks also to Susan Gaines for helping me to clarify my thoughts and put them in intelligible English for this written commentary.

A. von Bogdandy et al. (eds.), *The Exercise of Public Authority by International Institutions*, Beiträge zum ausländischen öffentlichen Recht und Völkerrecht 210,
DOI 10.1007/978-3-642-04531-8_3,

covered at the workshop,[2] are thus concerned with the basic tenants of analytically taming and legally framing international politics, rather than with the legal nuts and bolts.

A. Moving the Hidden Agenda to Center Stage

The Heidelberg group's article is presented as a synthesis of three ways of viewing global governance phenomena – constitutionalization, global administrative law, and international institutional law[3] – but there appears to be a more ambitious hidden agenda. Their "public authority" approach comprises a new way of "understanding, framing and taming"[4] the growing jungle of international law and global governance – not a simple fusion of existing methods, but an alternative system that is firmly rooted in European public domestic law.[5] Not until late in the Heidelberg group's paper does their critique of the global administrative law approach that Benedict Kingsbury and colleagues at New York University have introduced come to the fore. And then we learn only that it is "too global," based on an impossible "fusion of domestic ad-

---

1 For an overview *see* TRANSFORMATIONS OF THE STATE? (Stephan Leibfried & Michael Zürn eds., 2005); TRANSFORMING THE GOLDEN-AGE NATION STATE (Achim Hurrelmann, Stephan Leibfried, Kerstin Martens & Peter Mayer eds., 2007). For a summary of the theoretical approach *see* Philipp Genschel & Bernhard Zangl, *Transformations of the State: From Monopolist to Manager of Political Authority*, Bremen University TranState Working Paper 2008, in print, available at: http://www.state.uni-bremen.de.

2 My original comments also include: "How is Public 'Public'", "The conclusiveness of the three delimiting characterizations of public authority (determining, conditioning and influencing)", and, as an aside, a note on the principles guiding the case selection strategy for the Heidelberg project.

3 Armin von Bogdandy, Philipp Dann & Matthias Goldmann, *Developing the Publicness of Public International Law: Towards a Legal Framework for Global Governance Activities*, in this volume, Parts A and C.II.

4 *Id.*, Part C.III.

5 Benedict Kingsbury, Nico Krisch & Richard B. Stewart, *The Emergence of Global Administrative Law*, 68 LAW AND CONTEMPORARY PROBLEMS 15 (2005); Benedict Kingsbury & Nico Krisch, *Introduction: Global Governance and Global Administrative Law in the International Legal Order*, 17 THE EUROPEAN JOURNAL OF INTERNATIONAL LAW 1 (2006).

ministrative and international law," and ignores the "categorically different 'input legitimacy'" of the different actors.[6]

I wonder if the group does not miss the mark by focusing their criticism on the global administrative law approach. The central polarizing question for all three schools of thought discussed in their paper may well be: Are all international legal phenomena generated by state entities, or is there an emergent global legal arena, a new source of law that somehow lies "beyond the state sphere" but naturally affects it? This question reaches far beyond public law into private international law and, especially at the WTO level, economic law. While I have sympathies with the state-centered approach, I would like to see this question addressed directly: What is the evidence for or against an emerging global legal arena? If it exists, what is its extent and what are its consequences? What is its relationship to state-based international law? Are the two mutually exclusive, or overlapping, or interdependent ...? Should an effort be made to block its development, and if so why? Precisely what are the advantages and disadvantages to state-generated versus global law?

B. Internal versus External

The Heidelberg group initially insisted on what they called an "internal approach" wherein the legal framework for global governance is viewed strictly according to the application and development of the law, and the analysis of the social, historical and philosophical ramifications of the law, or "external approaches," take a back seat. Here the group has shifted to a more balanced treatment, with internal approaches providing the operative infrastructure and external approaches serving as a reality check on the wider effects. But precisely how internal and external interconnect is opaque: Is it a Siamese twin relationship where neither approach can function without the other?[7] Is it a hermeneutic circle of lawyers that only overlap here and there with the normative and explanatory circles of the social scientists? Or is it a relationship of con-

---

[6] von Bogdandy, Dann & Goldmann (note 3), Part C.III.

[7] *Id.*, Parts C.I and C.II. To talk about "complements" (Part C) might suggest a twin relationship.

centric circles,[8] where black-letter law comprises a solid inner circle, surrounded by court interpretations and precedents, and then by ever wider and more distant social ramifications? A proviso maintains that internal and external arguments might intersect "to the point that they become difficult to distinguish" and implies the Siamese twin relationship, whereas the legal tradition described for the United States reflects more of a concentric circle situation.[9]

One notes an innate distrust of the social sciences,[10] however, even in this current rendition of the public authority approach: the "firm disciplinary basis"[11] for "the analysis of the exercise of international public authority" that they are seeking remains, in the view of this political scientist, elusive. Interestingly, the Heidelberg group focuses much of its energy on the legitimacy concerns that lurk behind the legal-illegal divide.[12] They point out that this emphasis on constructing legitimation via legal procedure is also a concern at the micro-level of sociology,[13] and I would add that it is also a major focus of inquiry in political science, both at the national and international levels. Perhaps, rather than internal and external, we would do better to think in terms of *integrating* social sciences and law for the purpose of interpreting the affairs of global governance, with the law maintaining sole responsibility for the "craft component" of designing and interpreting norms – the "framing". Maybe we are simply too worried about disciplinary purity and would be more productive if we just muddled through with some experimental liaisons. In this sense, at least, we might take a lesson from the American Ivy League law schools which integrate International Relations, Philosophy, Sociology etc. into their faculties whenever they see fit.

---

8 Concentric circles are also suggested by the use of "broader" versus "narrower" (*id.*, B.III).

9 *Id.*, Part C.

10 "..., the lack of adequate legal concepts as well as the limited use of the legal-illegal dimension dichotomy for judgements about legitimacy puts legal scholarship at the risk of being marginalized by other disciplines, in particular by economics and political science, on how to understand and frame the world order." (von Bogdandy, Dann & Goldmann [note 3], Part C.II).

11 *Id.*, Part C.III.

12 *Id.*, Part C.II.

13 *Id.*, Part C.II.

C. Origins of Power

We need to know a lot more about the actual origins – as opposed to the legal sources – of international public authority. State theory holds that state power, *Staatsgewalt*, is a normative construct with a factual base: in occupations, beliefs, legitimacy-chains, secularized religious traditions, and organizational might, as well as revolutions, transformations, and so forth. The Heidelberg group maintains that international public authority is presumably bestowed by state entities and thus somehow stands on this same base, but they are hard-put to identify enough specific legal empowerments to account for the observed range of international authority and must turn to miscellaneous "functional equivalents"[14] and "informal entities"[15] instead.

Their strictly legal assessment fails, however, to explain how this broad unaccounted-for international authority came into being. If it is divorced from state entities and international treaties, then it cannot claim the state's steadfast empirical base. How did it come into being? What, then, is its base in reality? Self-empowerment by transnational networks of public officials? The effective seizure of structures by multinational corporations or NGOs? Some hegemonic entity to be identified? All or some of the above? What is the best theoretical model to explain such emergent processes? Systems theory? Autopoiesis? Or?

D. International Taming by Domestic Framing

The use of domestic analogy[16] in the treatment of international politics remains embedded in the Heidelberg group's approach, despite an attempt to accommodate my workshop critique of its use. They have, to

---

14 *Id.*, Part B.III.

15 *Id.*, Part B.III.

16 *See* HEDLEY BULL, THE ANARCHICAL SOCIETY. A STUDY OF ORDER IN WORLD POLITICS 44 (3rd ed., 2002), with Forewords by Andrew Hurrell & Stanley Hoffmann, (1st ed., 1977). Specifically on the domestic analogy *see* HIDEMI SUGANAMI, THE DOMESTIC ANALOGY AND WORLD ORDER PROPOSALS (1989).

some extent, disavowed its use[17] and have removed explicit reference to the historical basis for it – that just as the emergence of the industrial state gave rise to the formation of national administrative law, globalization now gives rise to international institutional/administrative law – but they have neither excised it from their approach nor taken on the burden of proof that I challenged them with.[18]

The group admits that there are fundamental differences between domestic and international institutions,[19] but their public authority approach to international politics is not built on that distinction. Instead, defining international public authority as "legitimate international coercion" mimics the nation state's legitimate monopoly of force.[20] International public law is assigned the same functions as domestic public law.[21] Legal concepts derived from domestic administrative law comprise the sole basis for a purely *intra*disciplinary development of international administrative law.[22] I found the emphasis on instruments of domestic administrative law by all three internal methods[23] particularly surprising. There is no mention of the oft-discussed *supra*national-*inter*national learning curve. After all, EU law grew from the same domestic analogy and one would think international law could learn much from the EU experience.

---

[17] von Bogdandy, Dann & Goldmann (note 3), *inter alia*, Part B.III. In this part, they say half-heartedly they do "not advocate all too simple 'domestic analogies'".

[18] I argued that before any treatment of international politics can make unconditional use of the domestic analogy one must prove that:

1. international politics can, *in general*, be "domesticated" – and not just in some areas, say trade and environment, and for some times, say in the 1960s;
2. the "rule of law" approach is the *best fit* for such domestication;
3. the experience of taming Leviathan at the *nation state level* in the 19th and 20th century is the best model for *framing the anarchical society* in the 21st (I use anarchical society in the sense of Hedley Bull).

This would seem to be part of an international lawyer's task and should not simply be externalized to the social scientists.

[19] von Bogdandy, Dann & Goldmann (note 3), Part C.III.

[20] *Id.*, Part B.III.

[21] *Id.*, Part B.III.

[22] *Id.*, Part C.III.

[23] *Id.*, Part C.III.

From the Heidelberg group's internal perspective, legal structuring of the international sphere could, if pursued energetically, provide legitimacy in the same way that it did for the domestic sphere, through ever-more-refined rule-making – a process that, in the latter case, took several hundred years to complete. Political and social means of legitimation are not considered here.[24] This legalization strategy is presented as a crucial and hitherto unappreciated component in the emergent global governance paradigm. There is, however, little evidence that the international sphere would be consistently responsive to the sort of legalization that is applied to individual, uniform and coherent nation states. The Heidelberg group has acknowledged in very general terms that the international sphere is, despite globalization, an extremely heterogeneous cultural, political, social and geographic sphere,[25] but they do not explore or address the actual consequences of that heterogeneity and instead apply legalization generically across the entire sphere. At this stage of the public authority project, even the traditional legal delimitations of the domestic sphere, where different legal approaches involving varying degrees of legal constraint are applied to high politics, administration and the courts, are lacking – in this paper – or have yet to be formulated.

In his 1977 treatise *The Anarchical Society: A Study of Order in World Politics*,[26] Hedley Bull (1932-1985) viewed international relations as an uneasy blend[27] of anarchism (Hobbesian realism), cosmopolitanism (Kantian universalism), and a society of states (Grotian solidarist institutionalism).[28] The relative importance of these three characteristics and their respective manifestations – conflict among states, trans-national social bonds, and common rules and institutions for containing conflict

---

24 *Id.*, Part C.II: "The understanding of domestic institutions rests largely on legal terminology based on doctrinal constructions."

25 Such heterogeneity is cited as an obstacle to the evolution of "an overarching layer of common legal arguments" (*see* Armin von Bogdandy, *General Principles of International Public Authority: Sketching a Research Field*, Part D.I.2, in this volume) but is not itself analyzed in depth. It may well be that such an analysis would clarify the reasons for limiting legalization to "the development of principles in the process of internal constitutionalization of the various international institutions" (*id.*, Part E.II; emphasis mine), to a "thin", a "foot-in-the-door" mode of legalization.

26 *See* BULL (note 16).

27 BULL (note 16), 39.

28 *Id.*, 24.

– changes from epoch to epoch and issue to issue. Unlike domestic politics, international politics is a moody triple-faced beast whose character is in constant flux, shifting with every change in the weather. The Heidelberg group's definition of public authority might accommodate Grotian solidarism with a touch of Kantian zeal, but the beast's anarchic temper tantrums seem to go untended, if not unremarked. The other two internal approaches described are perhaps even more lopsided in their treatments.

The Heidelberg group does at least note that legality in international politics at present fails to confer legitimacy, and they join with Martti Koskenniemi in assigning blame to deformalization, fragmentation, and the hegemonic traits of the current world order[29] ... all institutional features of an anarchic international society. Hobbesian reality is, unfortunately, painfully apparent in international politics from Africa to the Balkans to the Mid-East, from warfare and terrorism to international financial markets. I am afraid that trying to frame it by domestic analogy is like trying to fit a large wild wolf into a small sheep's clothing – the wolf and everyone else is likely to be the worse for it.

E. Transnational Private Governance Left Out in the Cold

The Heidelberg scheme defines international public authority in narrow structural terms, as empowered by states,[30] rather than using a broader outcome-based definition that would include action in the public interest or stewardship of common goods. Private structures that perform public functions cannot meet the specified "functional equivalence" test for legitimacy,[31] and require explicit state-based empowerment.

Here, the group does not resort to domestic analogy, but they might well have attempted one from German public law – and highlighted a major weakness in their approach. Within the nation state, private par-

---

[29] von Bogdandy, Dann & Goldmann (note 3), footnote 49 and accompanying text.

[30] *Id.*, Part B.III: "We consider as *international* public authority any authority exercised on the basis of a competence instituted by a common international act of public authorities, mostly states, to further a goal which they define, and are authorized to define, as public interest."

[31] *Id.*, Part B.III.

ties ranging from rabbit breeders to large corporations form associations and assign them wide regulatory powers. Historically, such bottom-up structures comprise one of the original ways of creating public authority. In the international sphere, this would mean acknowledging institutions that are comprised of private actors as stand-alone public authorities, *if they serve a public function*, i.e., organizations like the International Standardisation Organisation (ISO) or the Forest Stewardship Council (FSC).[32] According to the Heidelberg group's use of domestic analogy, we would then require some international state-based legal anchor for those private structures, insomuch as they affect individual rights in the pursuit of public interests – basically, an international version of the German constitutional doctrine that self-administration needs a legal foundation if it is to be entrusted with certain legally binding decisions.[33] But again, we run into problems, because there is, of course, no overarching world state to delegate such power, nor does there appear to be much hope of a state treaty that would do so.

The Heidelberg group might thus be well-advised to broaden their definition of "functional equivalence" and include certain types of transnational private governance among the activities they deem worthy of normative justification. Indeed, the use of a "topical catalogue"[34] of special cases and exceptions to a very narrow definition of "publicness" may turn out to be the Achilles heel of the Heidelberg approach as presented to date. Why does the catalogue include "governance activity that directly affects public goods," the management of "global infrastructures" (like ICANN), and governance activity dealing with "col-

---

[32] One might use Lorenz von Stein's term *freie Verwaltung* to characterize these phenomena; he would have labeled public authority in the Heidelberg sense *Regierung: see* LORENZ VON STEIN, VERWALTUNGSLEHRE (1st and 2nd ed., 1866-1884), 8 parts in 10 volumes (reprinted 1962 *et seq*.). The notion of *freie Verwaltung* is developed in Part I, 7: Von Stein distinguished between (public) self government and free associations, and later folded both into one notion of "self government" (*see* JOCHEN TAUPITZ, DIE STANDESORDNUNGEN DER FREIEN BERUFE: GESCHICHTLICHE ENTWICKLUNG, FUNKTIONEN, STELLUNG IM RECHTSSYSTEM 258 (1991), note 294). Von Stein's interest was focused on conjoining "free associations" with state development through "self government".

[33] *See inter alia* the *Facharzt*–decision of the *Bundesverfassungsgericht* of 9 May 1972 (BVerfGE 33, 125, especially 156-60) that requires a legal mandate for "status-affecting" decisions.

[34] von Bogdandy, Dann & Goldmann (note 3), Part B.III.

liding fundamental interests of different social groups"? Why these particular three and only them? At the very least, we need some more explicit general criteria for admission to the catalogue, some modest theory to guide our attention to all "those activities that require normative justification."[35]

F. Global Limitations to Western Legal Thought?

This paper might leave one with the impression that the reticence of large global powers like the United States, China, and Russia to embrace the mandates of the public authority approach is the main hurdle to bringing order and legitimacy to global governance. The problem here would appear to be one of small powers versus large powers and, conceivably, resolvable.[36] But there are more fundamental disparities that may lurk behind resistance to the approach in certain regions, categorically different concepts of the common good and different traditions of statehood that could, in fact, block or limit the whole enterprise.

Hedley Bull pointed out that the historical roots of the international law enterprise are eminently Christian:[37] "That modern international society includes international law as one of its institutions is a consequence of the historical accident that it evolved out of a previous unitary system, Western Christendom, and that in this system notions of law – embodied in Roman Law, divine law, canon law, and natural law – were pre-eminent."[38] This is perhaps why it is so difficult, in today's world, to form and maintain global treaties and agreements, and some-

---

[35] *Id.*, Part B.III. The full quote is: "In sum, we choose the focus on the exercise of international public authority in order to guide the attention to those activities that require normative justification."

[36] In this paper, the group notes, without elaboration, that the constitutionalization approach is hindered by "the reticence of American, Chinese or Russian governments," leading one to suppose the same is true for the public authority project, which is purportedly inspired by constitutionalization (*id.*, Part C.III). The possibility that this reticence may actually be a deep-seated resistance on the part of these countries is not discussed here, though, in a general way, other Heidelberg sources (*see, infra,* note 42 and von Bogdandy (note 25)) do take note of such resistance.

[37] BULL (note 16), *inter alia*, 26.

[38] *Id.*, 137.

times even OECD-wide treaties: it is not just an issue of size and power, but also one of cultures and traditions that simply are not receptive to western legal doctrines. As we set our sights on the goal of global integration through law[39] – on tying "the various institutions into one legal universe"[40] – what is at the heart of the public authority approach, shouldn't we be wondering how the origins of that law might limit its globalization?[41] Can, or has, western legal doctrine finally detached from its roots enough to acquire universal applicability in a global sphere that, despite recent economic globalization, includes regions that millennia of history have set on vastly different trajectories?

G. Intra-Western Contradictions

Even in the west, we may find that differing concepts of sovereignty and the value of multilateral action may stand in the way of the public authority approach to global governance. In this paper, the Heidelberg group seems to make light of the battle between the sovereigntists, anchored in the United States, and the internationalists, anchored in western continental Europe,[42] and one might get the impression that it is

---

39 "Integration through law", after all, was first a slogan behind which European integration forces in academia did unite in the 1980s. *See* INTEGRATION THROUGH LAW: EUROPE AND THE AMERICAN FEDERAL EXPERIENCE (Mauro Cappelletti ed., 1985-1987).

40 von Bogdandy (note 25), Part A.

41 A similar argument is made in ELMAR RIEGER and STEPHAN LEIBFRIED, LIMITS TO GLOBALIZATION: WELFARE STATES AND THE WORLD ECONOMY 241 (2003), chapter 5: *The Welfare State and Social Policy in East Asia: Religion and Globalization*. This is essentially an argument about a secularized Christian legal culture being at the root of Western welfare-state building.

42 In yet another paper, they characterize these battling factions as elements of two opposing paradigms, of "particularism" and "universalism" and their view of the deep disparity between the two positions is more apparent. Here they refer to "strong resistance" to international legalization on the part of some large states, as well as to the North-South disparity in the effectiveness of international law. But they find Martti Koskenniemi's critique that their project feeds into this disparity or has, as they say a "hegemonic nature" unjustified. Perhaps if they were to address both the fundamental struggle between multilateralists and hegemonic forces within the United States and the ways in which their universal approach will affect the deep global inequalities – and vice versa – both the reasons for and the answers to such criticism would be apparent.

only a matter of time, education and experience, before the sovereigntists see the error in their ways and join the international team. I am certainly sympathetic to the goal of finding a European antidote for United States hegemony in legal thought and in international institution-building. But I do wonder if one can cure the world of what is in essence "imperialism with good manners"[43] by simply instilling more and better manners, or if it might be time to hunt down some alternative form of medicine.

In order to better understand the significance of the sovereigntist-internationalist division, we need to step back and take a look at state development in general. In the OECD world in the past thirty years, we have seen both convergence and divergence in state development. On the public-private axis there has been a net convergence since the 1950s. Nationalization and increased regulation began in the 1950s in the United States, for example, but stopped and was to some extent reversed in the late 1970s. The net result was a small shift toward the continental European position. And many European states began privatizing – with regulation – in the late 1970s, moving Europe somewhat more dramatically toward the United States position. The corridor of difference[44] between the two has thus narrowed, while its center has shifted slightly closer to the United States position.[45] Recently, in the 21st century, privatization has generally come to a halt, and now the financial crisis may actually reverse the trend with some OECD-wide nationalization, and shift the center back toward the historical European position.

On the national-international axis, on the other hand, we have seen pronounced divergence between Europe and the United States, beginning in the 1970s and picking up pace in the 1990s. Under the guise and guidance of the EU, continental European states have internationalized

---

Armin von Bogdandy and Sergio Dellavalle, *Universalism and Particularism as Paradigms of International Law*, Institute for International Law and Justice Working Papers 3 (2008), 58, available at: http://www.iilj.org/publications/2008-3Bogdandy-Dellavalle.asp. *See also, supra*, note 36.

43 BULL (note 16), 209.

44 On the concept of corridors *see* Heinz Rothgang, Stephan Leibfried & Herbert Obinger, *The State and its Welfare State: How do Welfare State Changes Affect the Make-Up of the Nation-State?* 40 SOCIAL POLICY & ADMINISTRATION 250 (2006).

45 *See* Reimut Zohlnhöfer & Herbert Obinger, *Selling-Off the Family Silver. The Politics of Privatization*, 2 WORLD POLITICAL SCIENCE REVIEW 30 (2006).

rapidly and in a systematically multilateral fashion, in both a European and a global context. Though we still occasionally decry the end of sovereignty – as demonstrated by conflicts between the German *Bundesverfassungsgericht* (Federal Constitutional Court) and the ECJ – the fact is that sovereignty for EU member states came to an end in the 1990s. The United States has also internationalized during this period, but at a much slower pace, with more caveats, and in a decidedly unilateral fashion.[46] The result is that in the realms of law, the use of force, and legitimacy, the corridor of difference between continental Europe and the United States has widened dramatically. The "great 1994 sovereignty debate" about joining the WTO[47] in the United States had no counterpart in Europe, where joining was simply a matter of politics as usual and the effect on sovereignty was hardly mentioned in parliaments or public discourse.[48]

In my field of research, welfare state studies, what was first perceived in the United States as a developmental gap or time lag is now typically viewed as a substantive difference: From the Great Depression until the 1960s, American-European differences were seen as a developmental gap, but since then they have been viewed as differing visions, as different worlds of welfare.[49] I wonder if we may be seeing a similar phenomenon when it comes to international politics, a shift in perceptions from a mere developmental gap to a substantive structural gap. Getting the United States on the public authority bandwagon is not just a matter of developing a strict dogma of international public law there. Certainly, as they point out, there are factions in the United States that are lobbying for more internationalism and multilateral engagement. But, except with respect to trade – where the economic interests of the

---

46 *See* EDWARD C. LUCK, MIXED MESSAGES: AMERICAN POLITICS AND INTERNATIONAL ORGANIZATION 1919-1999 (1999). Naturally it also helps if you are the only actor in town who can afford to act unilaterally – Europe certainly cannot, so its actions fit its potential.

47 John Howard Jackson, *The Great 1994 Sovereignty Debate. United States Acceptance and Implementation of the Uruguay Round Results*, 36 COLUMBIA JOURNAL OF TRANSNATIONAL LAW 157 (1997).

48 *See* Christoph Bellmann & Richard Gerster, *Accountability in the World Trade Organization*, 30 JOURNAL OF WORLD TRADE 31 (1996).

49 *See* Stephan Leibfried & Steffen Mau, *Introduction: Welfare States: Construction, Deconstruction, Reconstruction*, *in* WELFARE STATES: CONSTRUCTION, DECONSTRUCTION, RECONSTRUCTION, vol. 1, ANALYTICAL APPROACHES, xi, xii (*Id.* eds., 2008).

United States have led from protectionism to an open world economy that is sturdily legally protected – the United States has been entirely unreliable when it comes to multilateral international policy-making. Indeed, we should consider if what we are seeing is not just a developmental lag, or even a shift in perception, but again, a phenomenon with deeper historical roots, something that is built into the American nation-state's structure.

The American insistence on absolute sovereignty and their penchant for unilateral approaches to international relations[50] go back to the founding of the federal republic – in an anti-imperial war. They are rooted in a heritage of isolationism and a huge, sparsely populated expanse of territory. As George Washington put it in 1796: "The great rule of conduct for us in regard to foreign nations is in extending our commercial relations, to have with them as little political connection as possible... . Europe has a set of primary interests which to us have none; or a very remote relation. Hence she must be engaged in frequent controversies, the causes of which are essentially foreign to our concerns... . Our detached and distant situation invites and enables us to pursue a different course."[51] They are inherent in a politically dependent, highly partisan

---

[50] For a first overview on the causes for this development *see* Thomas Giegerich, *The Impact of the USA on Regime Formation and Implementation*, *in* MULTILEVEL GOVERNANCE OF GLOBAL ENVIRONMENTAL CHANGE, 275-304, especially section I, 275-283 (G. Winter ed., 2006); Jed Rubenfeld, *Unilateralism und Constitutionalism*, 79 NEW YORK UNIVERSITY LAW REVIEW 1971 (2004) contrasts two types of democracy in an attempt to get to the roots of this problem: the United States bottom-up "democratic constitutionalism" and the European top-down "international constitutionalism" that forms the base for post World War II international charters and institutions. *See* first his: *The Two World Orders*, 27 WILSON QUARTERLY 22-36 (2003), also presented in EUROPEAN AND US CONSTITUTIONALISM 280 (George Nolte ed., 2005).

[51] From George Washington's Farewell Address in 1796: "The great rule of conduct for us in regard to foreign nations is in extending our commercial relations, to have with them as little political connection as possible. So far as we have already formed engagements, let them be fulfilled with perfect good faith. Here let us stop. Europe has a set of primary interests which to us have none; or a very remote relation. Hence she must be engaged in frequent controversies, the causes of which are essentially foreign to our concerns. Hence, therefore, it must be unwise in us to implicate ourselves by artificial ties in the ordinary vicissitudes of her politics, or the ordinary combinations and collisions of her friendships or enmities.

Our detached and distant situation invites and enables us to pursue a different course. If we remain one people under an efficient government, the period is

legal culture,[52] and built into an extreme form of federalism that pulls the foreign-policy powers of the President into the Congressional super-majoritarian-[53] and veto system. And they are an unavoidable consequence of an inherited British[54] monist legal tradition where any international law is immediately incorporated into national "municipal" law,[55] making the American state structurally vulnerable – and, also, overly protective against ever-growing international legal influences.[56]

The United States thus has a number of effective institutional constraints on any sharp turn toward internationalization, as well as a generally ingrown system that is at odds with the everyday routines of international policy-making. It is, in essence, structurally unfit to be consistently multilateral. Add to this a democracy that was built, like most democracies, on a *de jure* disenfranchisement of the bottom half of society – while proselytizing "a democracy made in heaven" –[57] which now finds itself *de facto* disenfranchised, while the other half is substantively under-informed, and a starring role as political hegemon since World War I, and one doubts if the United States is – or ever can be – a structurally open state of the sort we would like to imagine it to be when we discuss "post-national constellations" in Germany and Europe.

---

not far off when we may defy material injury from external annoyance; when we may take such an attitude as will cause the neutrality we may at any time resolve upon to be scrupulously respected; when belligerent nations, under the impossibility of making acquisitions upon us, will not lightly hazard the giving us provocation; when we may choose peace or war, as our interest, guided by justice, shall counsel." (http://avalon.law.yale.edu/18th_century/washing.asp)

52 This legal culture can rely much less on a normative domain outside of politics. Its legal system, its "*rechtsdogmatische Durchbildung*" will always be less developed.

53 A Presidential international treaty needs a two-thirds majority in the United States Senate.

54 *See* HERSCH LAUTERPACHT, INTERNATIONAL LAW. A TREATISE, vol. 1: THE LAW OF PEACE 3 (6th ed., 1947), originally by LASSA FRANCIS LAWRENCE OPPENHEIM.

55 *Id.*, 39-40.

56 A dualist tradition would have been a better fit for the United States as it would have required a transformative act for each and every international law by Congress.

57 *See* Rubenfeld, *The Two World Orders* (note 50).

H. Staring Down the Beast

In his musings on contemporary international law, Hedley Bull calls our attention to an observation by the philosopher Martin Wright: "[Wright] has pointed out that the periods in which the claims made for international law are most extravagant ... are also the periods in which actual international practice is most marked by disorder."[58] As we make our, more or less, extravagant claims for the miracles of international law, perhaps we should be watching our backs and analyzing the growing chaos of contemporary international practice in depth – *semper apertus*! If one wants to tame a beast, after all, one must meet it head on.

---

[58] BULL (note 16), 145.

International Bureaucracies from a Political Science Perspective – Agency, Authority and International Institutional Law

*By Ingo Venzke**

A. Introduction

International bureaucracies are autonomous actors in a broader process of global governance. Their actions are oftentimes removed from the intentions and control of their creators; they affect other actors and engage in subject matters not formerly within their reach. Their factual impact remains underestimated. Little consolation can be found in the

---

* I thank the participants in this research project on the exercise of public authority by international institutions as well as Eyal Benvenisti, Dirk Hanschel, Stefan Kadelbach, Nico Krisch, Stephan Leibfried, Andrea Liese, Christoph Möllers, Christian Tietje, Christian Walter, and Michael Zürn for their insightful comments on earlier drafts.

A. von Bogdandy et al. (eds.), *The Exercise of Public Authority by International Institutions*, Beiträge zum ausländischen öffentlichen Recht und Völkerrecht 210,
DOI 10.1007/978-3-642-04531-8_4, © Springer-Verlag Berlin Heidelberg 2010

contention that international bureaucracies merely seek the effective implementation of global goals. A yawning gap unfolds between the mechanisms of control, means and ways for contesting the actions of bureaucracies and their actual exercise of public authority. These are the primary contentions motivating research on the development and conceptualization of international institutional law. This contribution sets out to corroborate these underlying contentions from a political science perspective. It subscribes to the approach that the exercise of public authority be framed in a rule-of-law context and highlights the implications of such an approach. It discards an exclusively instrumental view of international institutions that portrays them as tools in the hands of their creators or as mere instruments in pursuit of global goals. In conclusion, it emphasizes law's constitutive role in providing a space for legal and political contestation as an indispensable prerequisite for the normative desirability of autonomous international bureaucracies.

International Relations (IR) scholarship had for some time only provided a rather nebulous view of the performance of international organizations (IOs) and less formal institutions because its focus had rested on the question *why* IOs exist and persist. The question *what* IOs actually do, a conception of IOs as actors as well as an understanding and explanation of their actions, had long been largely overshadowed by the more fundamental theoretical entanglement of *whether* they matter at all. IR scholarship had been, so to speak, driving with a rearview mirror directed at those primary questions at the beginning of the road.[1] This has certainly benefited our understanding of the importance of IOs but has also come at a regrettable loss. Most importantly, this focus has left IOs as actors in a dead angle from which they have only slowly emerged to attract some attention. This contribution conceptualizes parts of IOs and less formal institutions, in particular administrative or executive organs, as bureaucracies. It thereby elucidates their sources of autonomy and authority and highlights common mechanisms to which international bureaucracies resort in the exercise of public authority. In order to grasp their autonomous actions it appears necessary to divert more attention away from the rearview mirror directed at IOs' embryonic stages under the tutelage of (dominant) constituent members. IOs have grown up. Attention should be given to the perimeters of their action, the sources of their autonomy and to *how*

---

1 *See* Alexander Wendt, *Driving with the Rearview Mirror: On the Rational Science of Institutional Design,* 55 INTERNATIONAL ORGANIZATION 1019 (2001).

they act. In short, even if it were still doubtful that IOs do matter, it is not a bad idea to at least leer at IOs as actors.[2] Otherwise they might emerge from the dead angle of research agendas to suddenly claim obedience. Jan Klabbers evocatively opens his *Introduction to International Institutional Law* with a quote from Mary Shelly's *Frankenstein*: "You are my creator, but I am your master; obey!"[3]

The aim of this contribution is to build on insights in political science in order to inform the conceptual grasp on the exercise of public authority in legal scholarship. How do international institutions exercise public authority? How can law possibly frame the exercise of such authority? While global challenges call for concerted cooperative action, public law retains and to some extend has to regain its legitimating, that is both enabling and constraining, function in framing the exercise of public authority. Public international law shares this function with domestic public law.[4] It is argued that the role of IOs, or less formal institutions, in providing the constitutive framework for the formulation and contestation of global or at least shared goals and their implementation be strengthened. This is a task for international institutional law to take.[5]

---

2 The performance of IOs and their bureaucracies has attracted a recently growing and renewed interest among political scientists. *See e.g.* AUTONOMOUS POLICY MAKING BY INTERNATIONAL ORGANIZATIONS (Bob Reinalda & Bertjan Verbeek eds., 1998); MICHAEL N. BARNETT & MARTHA FINNEMORE, RULES FOR THE WORLD. INTERNATIONAL ORGANIZATIONS IN GLOBAL POLITICS (2004); Steffen Bauer, *Does Bureaucracy Really Matter? The Authority of Intergovernmental Treaty Secretariats in Global Environmental Politics,* 6 GLOBAL ENVIRONMENTAL POLITICS 24 (2006); Andrea Liese & Silke Weinlich, *Die Rolle von Verwaltungsstäben internationaler Organisationen. Lücken, Tücken und Konturen eines (neuen) Forschungsgebiets, in* POLITIK UND VERWALTUNG 491 (Jörg Bogumil, Werner Jann & Frank Nullmeier eds., 2006); Johan P. Olsen, *Maybe it is Time to Rediscover Bureaucracies,* 16 JOURNAL OF PUBLIC ADMINISTRATION RESEARCH AND THEORY 1 (2006); JOHN MATHIASON, INVISIBLE GOVERNANCE. INTERNATIONAL SECRETARIATS IN WORLD POLITICS (2007).

3 JAN KLABBERS, AN INTRODUCTION TO INTERNATIONAL INSTITUTIONAL LAW v (2002).

4 *See* Armin von Bogdandy, Philipp Dann & Matthias Goldmann, *Developing the Publicness of Public International law: Towards a Legal Framework for Global Governance Activities*, in this volume.

5 International institutional law is a well-established field within public international law. *See e.g.* IGNAZ SEIDL-HOHENVELDERN & GERHARD LOIBL, DAS RECHT DER INTERNATIONALEN ORGANISATIONEN EINSCHLIEẞLICH DER SUPRANATIONALEN GEMEINSCHAFTEN (2000); KLABBERS (note 3); INTERNA-

Yet, such legal framing has to be mindful of the particularities of the international context, especially of persistent value conflicts and of the relatively unmediated impact that power relations might have. While legal constructions are prone to reproduce and fosterer power relations, the contribution upholds in conclusion the significance of law in approaching perennial questions of legitimate governance beyond the nation state.

The argument proceeds in three sections. The first explains the autonomy of international bureaucracies with regard to two interrelated sources: self-interested delegation by principals and bureaucracies' authority based on their characteristic traits – their strong repository of knowledge as well as expertise and their civil service. It then concentrates on the actor itself and indicates strategies and mechanisms in the exercise of public authority by which bureaucracies are likely to gain in autonomy (B.). The second section then critically revisits the argument of bureaucracies' autonomy and relates it to the possibilities and limitations of control by constituent members. It also explores whether a lack of control might be compensated by the problem solving capacity of IOs and finds that such argument faces severe factual and normative difficulties. Rather, bureaucracies' autonomy only becomes bearable in an institutional context providing ways to legally and politically contest means and ends of bureaucracies' actions (C.). The last section then draws conclusions from the analysis of the exercise of public authority by international bureaucracies for the conceptualization and construction of international institutional law. It will also locate the pitfalls of such a development in the differences between the international and national institutional contexts (D.).

B. Autonomous International Bureaucracies

Several obstacles have for some time impeded the view on autonomous international bureaucracies. The focus of IR scholarship has fallen on the primary questions of *why* IOs exist, persist, and *whether* they matter.[6] From the outset, the effect of regimes has been constantly chal-

---

TIONAL INSTITUTIONAL LAW (Henry G. Schermers & Niels M. Blocker eds., 2003). In short and in common understanding, institutional law governs international organisations' legal status, structure and functioning, *id.* at 4.

6 Bertjan Verbeek, *International Organizations. The Ugly Duckling of International Relations Theory?*, *in* AUTONOMOUS POLICY MAKING BY INTERNA-

lenged on realist premises. Regimes are arguably an academic fad that distract from the analysis of underlying power structures[7] and institutions have no independent effect on state behavior.[8] The attention given to states and structural explanations for state behavior has further impeded the conceptualization of IOs as autonomous actors.[9] However, with due regard to methodological challenges, empirical research has largely defied at least unqualified arguments on the epiphenomenality of regimes.[10] Moreover, the concepts of regime and governance have provided IOs with minor role scripts in a broader and loosely institutionalized process that again directed attention away from international bureaucracies as autonomous actors.[11] The remainder of this contribu-

---

TIONAL ORGANIZATIONS 11 (Bob Reinalda & Bertjan Verbeek eds., 1998); Lisa L. Martin & Beth Simmons, *Theories and Empirical Studies of International Institutions,* 52 INTERNATIONAL ORGANIZATION 729 (1998). For a strong argument of doubt, *see* John J. Mearsheimer, *The False Promise of International Institutions,* 19 INTERNATIONAL SECURITY 5 (1994). For an overview of contrasting positions in the earlier regime debate consult INTERNATIONAL REGIMES (Stephen D. Krasner ed., 1983) and REGIME THEORY AND INTERNATIONAL RELATIONS (Volker Rittberger ed., 1993).

7 Susan Strange, *Cave! Hic Dragones: A Critique of Regime Analysis, in* INTERNATIONAL REGIMES 37 (Stephen D. Krasner ed., 1983). *See* Jennifer Sterling-Folker, *Realist Global Governance: Revisiting Cave! Hic Dragones and Beyond, in* CONTENDING PERSPECTIVES ON GLOBAL GOVERNANCE. COHERENCE, CONTESTATION AND WORLD ORDER 17 (Alice D. Ba & Matthew J. Hoffmann eds., 2005).

8 Mearsheimer (note 6).

9 *See* ROBERT O. KEOHANE, INTERNATIONAL INSTITUTIONS AND STATE POWER: ESSAYS IN INTERNATIONAL RELATIONS THEORY 1-20 (1989); Verbeek (note 6).

10 For an overview of strategies and examples of such research *see e.g.* Robert O. Keohane & Lisa L. Martin, *The Promise of Institutionalist Theory,* 20 INTERNATIONAL SECURITY 39-51 (1995); Beth A. Simmons & Lisa L. Martin, *International Organizations and Institutions, in* HANDBOOK OF INTERNATIONAL RELATIONS 192, 199-200 (Walter Carlsnaes, Thomas Risse & Beth A. Simmons eds., 2002); HELMUT BREITMEIER, ORAN R. YOUNG & MICHAEL ZÜRN, ANALYZING INTERNATIONAL ENVIRONMENTAL REGIMES: FROM CASE STUDY TO DATABASE (2006); Bauer, (note 2).

11 *See* Friedrich V. Kratochwil & John Gerard Ruggie, *International Organization: A State of Art and an Art of the State,* 40 INTERNATIONAL ORGANIZATION 753, 759 (1986).

tion resorts to several studies that share a renewed interest in IOs and international bureaucracies as autonomous actors.

The aim of this section is to corroborate the thesis that, apart from *instruments* in the hands of one or a number of powerful actors or *arenas* for decision-making, IOs can also be autonomous *actors* exercising public authority in a broader governance process.[12] This exercise of public authority demands a legal frame as a precondition for its normative desirability. The exposition of international bureaucracies' autonomy thus serves to inform the development of international institutional law and public international law more generally.

An affirmative argument as to *whether* international bureaucracies matter compels an argument of *why* and *how* they matter. The contention shall rest on two broad and interrelated lines of reasoning. First, under rational choice premises it might simply be instrumentally rational for principals to grant IOs a certain degree of autonomy – the focus thus lies on principals' rationale for granting autonomy to agents (I.). The second line of reasoning fixates on the actor and dwells on the concept of international bureaucracies. It highlights their characteristic traits and emphasizes their strong repository of knowledge as well as expertise as a source of authority and contends that this authority is an important source of autonomy (II.). In its approach this contribution does not build on any particular paradigm in IR theory and does not follow a categorical distinction between instrumentally rationalist and constructivist approaches. It rather credits the explanatory force of each. It claims not to be negligent with regard to most thorough challenges by realists and appreciates their fundamental critique of institutions in order to maintain a beneficial critical distance to its object of analysis.

I. The Delegation of Authority

The most straightforward explanation for bureaucracies' autonomy rests on the reasons principals might have for delegating authority to agents. On the premise that actors act strategically, that is instrumentally rational in pursuit of given interests, several explanations can be offered as to why principals delegate authority. The premise translates more specifically into the claim that constituent actors (principals) delegate authority to bureaucracies (agents) and tolerate a certain degree of

---

12 CLIVE ARCHER, INTERNATIONAL ORGANIZATIONS 68-87 (2001).

autonomy of bureaucracies when they expect instrumental gains. In their rational choice analysis of delegation Hawkins *et al.* define delegation as a "conditional grant of authority from a *principal* to an *agent*"[13] and claim that "[a]ll delegation is premised upon the division of labor and gains from specialization."[14] Principals delegate authority and allow for a margin of autonomy of an agent in order to carry out a task in a way that is more efficient and/or effective compared with the principals themselves carrying out this task. Gains from specialization are likely to be greatest when the task performed by the agent is frequent, repetitive, and when it requires specific expertise or knowledge.[15]

In most plain cases of coordination problems, for instance, actors have a corresponding self-interest in achieving a particular outcome while being indifferent as to which specific action they undertake as long as the outcome is achieved. Authority might then well be delegated to an independent agent who can determine the terms of coordination.[16] An illustrative example is the drafting of the OECD Model Convention on Double Taxation, which is a highly specialized task directed at a particular outcome that is desired by all actors.[17]

In some cooperation games – typically these are variations of the Prisoner's Dilemma – principals have an incentive to cheat on their obligations. In such cases principals might first be interested in ascertaining the actions or intentions of others in order to react. To this end it would be in their respective self-interest to create agents who can provide information about norm compliance.[18] This incentive finds strong empiri-

---

13 Darren G. Hawkins, David A. Lake, Daniel L. Nielson & Michael J. Tierney, *Delegation Under Anarchy: States, International Organizations, and Principal-Agent Theory, in* DELEGATION AND AGENCY IN INTERNATIONAL ORGANIZATIONS 3, 7 (Darren G. Hawkins, David A. Lake, Daniel L. Nielson & Michael J. Tierney eds., 2006).

14 *Id.* at 13.

15 *Id.* at 13-15; Kenneth W. Abbott & Duncan Snidal, *Why States Act through Formal International Organizations,* 42 JOURNAL OF CONFLICT RESOLUTION 3, 9-16 (1998).

16 Hawkins, Lake, Nielson & Tierney (note 13), at 15-16; JACK L. GOLDSMITH & ERIC A. POSNER, THE LIMITS OF INTERNATIONAL LAW 32-35 (2005).

17 *See* Ekkehart Reimer, *Transnationales Steuerrecht, in* INTERNATIONALES VERWALTUNGSRECHT, 181 (Christoph Möllers, Andreas Voßkuhle & Christian Walter eds., 2007).

18 KEOHANE & MARTIN (note 9), at 43-44.

cal support in arms control treaties, which are frequently linked to forceful monitoring mechanisms.[19] Closely connected to this is the role of agents in enforcing agreements. Bearing in mind that principals might have an incentive to cheat on their commitments, delegating the authority to enforce the terms of an agreement to an autonomous agent increases the credibility of commitments and makes cooperation more likely.[20] This is similar to the creation of arbitrating agents.[21] Principals would grant an agent the authority to decide on future conflicts over the terms of a contract. Examples for delegation to an (compulsory) arbitrator have grown considerably over the past decade.[22] An incentive for particular political players to delegate to an agent is to create commitments that bind their successors and to thereby put their policy decision largely outside the reach of any new majority or power constellation.[23]

A most pertinent and, with regard to the development of international institutional law, most intriguing explanation for principals' delegation of authority to an international agent is that such an agent might engage

---

[19] Harald Müller, *The Evolution of Verification: Lessons from the Past for the Present*, 14 CONTEMPORARY SECURITY POLICY 333 (1993); James D. Fearon, *Bargaining, Enforcement, and International Cooperation*, 52 INTERNATIONAL ORGANIZATION 269 (1998).

[20] Hawkins, Lake, Nielson & Tierney (note 13), at 18-19; George Norman and Joel P. Trachtman, *The Customary International Law Game,* 99 AMERICAN JOURNAL OF INTERNATIONAL LAW 541 (2005); Andrew T. Guzman, *The Design of International Agreements,* 16 EUROPEAN JOURNAL OF INTERNATIONAL LAW (EJIL) 579 (2005); Barbara Koremenos, Charles Lipson & Duncan Snidal, *The Rational Design of International Institutions,* 55 INTERNATIONAL ORGANIZATION 761 (2001).

[21] Hawkins, Lake, Nielson & Tierney (note 13), at 17.

[22] *See* Bernhard Zangl & Michael Zürn, *Make Law, Not War: Internationale und transnationale Verrechtlichung als Baustein für Global Governance, in* VERRECHTLICHUNG – BAUSTEIN FÜR GLOBAL GOVERNANCE?, 12 (Bernhard Zangl & Michael Zürn eds., 2004); Bernhard Zangl, *Das Entstehen internationaler Rechtstaatlichkeit?, in* TRANSFORMATIONEN DES STAATES?, 123 (Stephan Leibfried & Michael Zürn eds., 2006); Alec Stone Sweet, *Judicialization and the Construction of Governance,* 32 COMPARATIVE POLITICAL STUDIES 147 (1999).

[23] Kenneth Abbott & Duncan Snidal, *Hard and Soft Law in International Governance*, 54 INTERNATIONAL ORGANIZATION 421, 439 (2000); Judith Goldstein, Miles Kahler, Robert O. Keohane & Anne-Marie Slaughter, *Introduction: Legalization and World Politics*, 54 INTERNATIONAL ORGANIZATION 385 (2000).

in action, which would be perceived as illegitimate if it were undertaken unilaterally by the principal itself. This is what Kenneth Abbott and Duncan Snidal call "laundering."[24] For instance, it appears more legitimate if the international financial institutions frequently link loans to the achievement of domestic reforms in the target country.[25] This channel of development assistance appears to be preferable to the imposition of conditionality by one state in relation another – in particular if the colonial past has tainted their bilateral relationship or if the more powerful state sought direct political influence.[26] Even more crucial is such action at the international level that would not only appear illegitimate in bilateral relations but would simply be illegal if it were to be undertaken by the principal itself due to domestic or international legal constraints.[27] Through the Al Qaeda and Taliban Sanctions Committee, a subsidiary organ of the UN Security Council, states can place an individual on the consolidated list of terrorist suspects with immediate consequences for this individual including the freezing of his/her financial assets. This listing is usually not subject to any discussion within the Committee, no judicial review is available and not even minimum procedural guarantees are provided.[28] A similar case in point is the refugee status determination, which states increasingly delegate to the UNHCR in order to rid themselves of "unpleasant work" not only well aware but rather embracing the procedural and normative shortcomings after this delegation.[29]

Principals might also have an interest in designing an agent as agenda setter in order to overcome a stalemate in negotiations. The agent could induce an equilibrium, which would otherwise not have been achieved. Typically the agenda setting function is delegated to an executive or governing body but also a secretariat might formally or informally take

---

24 Abbott & Snidal (note 15), at 18.

25 *Cf.* on the World Bank's legal regime Philipp Dann, *Grundfragen eines Entwicklungsverwaltungsrechts, in* INTERNATIONALES VERWALTUNGSRECHT, 7 (Christoph Möllers, Andreas Voßkuhle & Christian Walter eds., 2007).

26 Abbott & Snidal (note 15), at 18.

27 *See* Jean D'Aspremont, *Abuse of the Legal Personality of International Organizations and the Responsibility of Member States*, 4 INTERNATIONAL ORGANIZATION LAW REVIEW 91 (2007).

28 Clemens Feinäugle, in this volume; Erika de Wet, *Holding International Bureaucracies Accountable: the Complementary Role of Non-Judicial Oversight Mechanisms and Judicial Review*, in this volume.

29 Maja Smrkolj, in this volume.

up this role. For instance, the WTO is widely perceived to be a purely member-driven organization and shall only provide a common institutional framework.[30] However, the secretariat does become active on the basis of treaty provisions and beyond. The Dispute Settlement Understanding (DSU) formally provides that the Secretariat propose panelists to the parties to a dispute; should the parties not come to an agreement within 20 days, the Director General may determine the composition of the panel.[31] In so doing he/she enjoys large autonomy and is likely to further the objectives of the organization.[32] Furthermore, at times the secretariat does become active, though cautiously and in acquiescence with at least some member states, even outside any formal basis. It bears on the course of events and substantive decisions taken. In a persistent stalemate during the Uruguay Round, for example, the secretariat came to draft a text, which was in line with the prevalent objectives of the organization and which provided the reference point for discussions.[33]

In sum, a number of interrelated explanations can be offered to explain why instrumentally rational principals would delegate authority to an international agent and bear a corresponding loss of control. The extent of this delegation is then reflected in the institutional design of the organization, for instance, in the agent's formal powers in relation to the principals and in formalized decision-making procedures.[34] An agent

---

[30] Art. II(1) WTO Agreement.

[31] Art. 8(6) and (7) DSU.

[32] Armin von Bogdandy, *Law and Politics in the WTO – Strategies to Cope with a Deficient Relationship*, 5 MAX PLANCK YEARBOOK OF UNITED NATIONS LAW 609, 615-616 (2001); Joseph H. H. Weiler, *The Rule of Lawyers and the Ethos of Diplomats. Reflections on the Internal and External Legitimacy of WTO Dispute Settlement*, 35 JOURNAL OF WORLD TRADE 191, 202-206 (2001). An even stronger case could be made on the agency of judges and courts; *cf.* Karen J. Alter, *Agents or Trustees? International Courts in their Political Context*, 14 EUROPEAN JOURNAL OF INTERNATIONAL RELATIONS 33 (2008); Eyal Benvenisti, *Customary International Law as a judicial tool for promoting efficiency, in* THE IMPACT OF INTERNATIONAL LAW ON INTERNATIONAL COOPERATION. THEORETICAL PERSPECTIVES, 85 (Eyal Benvenisti and Moshe Hirsch eds., 2004). On political jurisprudence, *see* ALEC STONE SWEET & MARTIN SHAPIRO, ON LAW, POLITICS, AND JUDICIALIZATION 19-54 (2002).

[33] YI-CHONG XU & PATRICK MORAY WELLER, THE GOVERNANCE OF WORLD TRADE. INTERNATIONAL CIVIL SERVANTS AND GATT/WTO 264-265 (2004).

[34] *See* Koremenos, Lipson & Snidal (note 20); Guzman (note 20).

can, however, only then plausibly be called autonomous if its actions cannot be reduced to the interests of the principals. This means that even if the interests of the principals were known the action of the autonomous agent could not be predicated.[35] The fact that delegation is a *conditional* grant of authority does not imply that the international bureaucracy necessarily does what principals want or had expected.[36] The term "agency slack" captures actions by the agent that are undesired by the principal.[37] Agents do "implement policy decisions and pursue their own interests strategically."[38] The example of autonomous action by the WTO secretariat has already served as a case in point. In their early study of 1973, Robert Cox and Harold Jacobson pointed out that

> [R]egardless of the rigidity of their charters, ... once international organizations are established, in many instances they evolve in ways that could not have been foreseen by their founders. ... Thus, once established, organizations take on a life of their own and develop their own inner dynamics.[39]

II. The Authority of International Bureaucracies

The most straightforward case for autonomy of international institutions set out above rests on the self-interested reasons principals might have for delegating authority to agents. Drawing attention to the agents

---

[35] *See also* Yoram Z. Haftel & Alexander Thompson, *The Independence of International Organizations: Concept and Applications*, 50 JOURNAL OF CONFLICT RESOLUTION 253, 255-257 (2006) (maintaining that a difference in interest is a constitutive element of IOs' independence).

[36] Certainly there are various mechanisms for principals and other actors to improve the working of conditions and the control of international agents. That is the topic of the contribution by de Wet (note 28). For the limits of contractual or text-based delegation, *see* Jan Klabbers, *On Rationalism in Politics: Interpretation of Treaties and the World Trade Organization*, 74 NORDIC JOURNAL OF INTERNATIONAL LAW 405 (2005); Richard H. Steinberg, *Judicial Lawmaking at the WTO: Discursive, Constitutional, and Political Constraints*, 98 AMERICAN JOURNAL OF LNTERNATIONAL LAW 247 (2004).

[37] Hawkins, Lake, Nielson & Tierney (note 13), at 8.

[38] *Id.* at 5.

[39] ROBERT W. COX & HAROLD K. JACOBSON, THE ANATOMY OF INFLUENCE: DECISION MAKING IN INTERNATIONAL ORGANIZATION 7 (1973).

themselves, their characteristics and to mechanisms in the exercise of public authority, further contributes to understanding the origins of their autonomy. Conceptualizing agents as international bureaucracies brings to light the characteristic traits of bureaucracies as sources of their autonomy – their apparent rational-legal form of administration and their civil staff (1.) as well as their knowledge and expertise (2.).

1. Bureaucracies as Technical Administrators and their Civil Staff

The concept of bureaucracies has been most thoroughly developed as an analytical tool by Max Weber.[40] His conception of bureaucracies as an ideal type can plausibly guide the analysis of international institutions as actors despite the fact that reality certainly lags behind at the international level even more so than in most domestic contexts.[41] According to Weber's account, bureaucracies are a distinct organizational form. They exercise authority in a larger organizational and normative structure – an apparent rational-legal process of administration that fosters the belief in the rightness of the authority exercised.[42] Furthermore, they are staffed with civil servants who are mostly seen to be objective technocrats. Michael Barnett and Martha Finnemore adopt Weber's conceptualization of bureaucracies and concur that bureaucracies are the product of a rationalizing process and that they are prevalently perceived as part of a rational-legal exercise of power. This perception augments their authority.[43] Barnett and Finnemore define authority as "the ability of one actor to use institutional and discursive resources to induce deference from others."[44] Authority is, again following Weber,

---

40 MAX WEBER, WIRTSCHAFT UND GESELLSCHAFT 1046-1092 (2006).

41 *Id.* at 14; *cf.* Olsen (note 2). *See*, however, the cautionary remarks in ERNST B. HAAS, BEYOND THE NATION-STATE. FUNCTIONALISM AND INTERNATIONAL ORGANIZATION 96 (1964).

42 *See*, *supra*, note 39.

43 BARNETT & FINNEMORE (note 2), 17-22.

44 *Id.* at 5. *See* Bauer (note 2). Bauer refers to Claire A. Cutler, Virginia Haufler & Tony Porter, *The Contours and Significance of Private Authority in International Affairs*, *in* PRIVATE AUTHORITY AND INTERNATIONAL AFFAIRS 333, 324 (Claire A. Cutler, Virginia Haufler & Tony Porter eds., 1999) (authority "involves a surrendering of individual judgment, an acceptance of its dictates base not on the merits of any particular pronouncement but on a belief in the rightness of the authority of itself").

legitimated domination and it involves some element of consent.[45] In short, a further source of autonomy can be located, apart from deliberately delegated authority, in bureaucracies' authority and their characteristic traits.

At first glance the conceptualization of parts of institutions as bureaucracies supports the instrumental understanding of agents acting in the service of their principals. The idea of depoliticized IOs that implement the political agreements of constituent members has already figured prominently in the functionalist account of integration set out by David Mitrany. He suggests that states delegate authority to functional organs in pursuit of mutual or global goals. His work was among the first to highlight the agency and impact of institutions, in particular of autonomous bureaucracies with functionally defined tasks. Not unlike most of the explanations offered in response to why principals might delegate authority, Mitrany's functionalism rests on the belief in a separation of practical issues that are aimed at implementing uncontentious welfare goals, on the one hand, and political activities, on the other.[46] International bureaucracies would scrounge moral authority from the perceived moral significance of the goals they pursue.[47] The expansion of technical issues and the contraction of areas for politics would then lead to a true world community.[48] The submission to a technological rationality in Mitrany's functionalism is noteworthy. Functional agencies are "shaped not by any theory of political self-determination of the parties, but by the technological self-determination of each of the matters involved."[49] This distinction and premise is, however, at best only tenable in particular cases and in any event it is most contingent and vulner-

45 BARNETT & FINNEMORE (note 2), at 29.

46 DAVID MITRANY, A WORKING PEACE SYSTEM. AN ARGUMENT FOR THE FUNCTIONAL DEVELOPMENT OF INTERNATIONAL ORGANIZATION 19-24 (1943).

47 *See* BARNETT & FINNEMORE (note 2), at 21-22; Thomas Risse, *Transnational Governance and Legitimacy*, *in* GOVERNANCE AND DEMOCRACY: COMPARING NATIONAL, EUROPEAN AND INTERNATIONAL EXPERIENCES 179, 188 (Arthur Benz & Yannis Papadopoulos eds., 2006); *see also* DAVID KENNEDY, THE DARK SIDES OF VIRTUE. REASSESSING INTERNATIONAL HUMANITARIANISM 111-146 (2004).

48 DAVID MITRANY, THE FUNCTIONAL THEORY OF POLITICS 113-122 (1975); Haas (note 41), at 6.

49 MITRANY (note 48), at 250-251.

able.[50] Some technical international institutions do function smoothly without giving rise to much concern. Yet, even among some usual suspects of regulatory agencies, the pursuit of stated aims is not merely technical but is imbued with politics. In administering domain names and providing for an undisturbed functioning of the internet ICANN also takes decisions on such highly political and normative questions as to provide for domain names other than in Latin script or to provide domain names for pornographic contents, lastly, it holds the immense power to deny access to new domain names or to delete established ones.[51]

In order to understand international bureaucracies as actors in a broader governance process, it is insightful to further explore another essential part of their technocratic appearance: their staff of civil servants. Arguments relating to international bureaucracies' civil servants have a long tradition but have for some time stood in isolation to the debate on international institutions' autonomy and agency, and have only recently found renewed attention in IR scholarship.[52] The exceptions to this are functionalist accounts of regional and international integration and early studies of formal institutions. Functionalists maintain that individual loyalties are created by the functions an individual carries out. Even if civil servants are sent by national governments or selected on the basis of a national quota, the transfer of functions that comes with taking up a position in an international organization can produce a shift in loyalty.[53] This has been further supported by accounts that point to the individual socialization of bureaucrats.[54] Nu-

---

[50] HAAS (note 41), at 88. The question of what is political indeed appears to be one of subjective assessment in the eyes of the beholder rather than one of content or issue area. *See* CARL SCHMITT, DER BEGRIFF DES POLITISCHEN. TEXT VON 1932 MIT EINEM VORWORT UND 3 COROLLARIEN 26-37 (1963). On this aspect of Schmitt's concept of the political, *see* MARTTI KOSKENNIEMI, THE GENTLE CIVILIZER OF NATIONS 440-445 (2001).

[51] Jochen von Bernstorff, *The Structural Limitations of Network Governance: ICANN as a Case in Point*, *in* TRANSNATIONAL GOVERNANCE AND CONSTITUTIONALISM 257 (Christian Joerges, I. Sand & G. Teubner eds., 2004).

[52] *See* (note 2).

[53] HAAS (note 41), at 22.

[54] *See e.g.* Alastair Iain Johnston, *Treating International Institutions as Social Environments*, 45 INTERNATIONAL STUDIES QUARTERLY 487 (2001); Martha Finnemore, *Norms, Culture and World Politics: Insights from Sociology's Institutionalism*, 50 INTERNATIONAL ORGANIZATION 325 (1996).

merous studies have been offered to highlight the importance of a dedicated international staff. Yet, they have also indicated the tension between autonomy and membership influence.[55] In his early study of 1945 on administrative bodies in the international realm, Egon Ranshofen-Wertheimer reflects on his experience at the League of Nations and provides a detailed account on the work of its secretariat and the code of international officials.[56] In the same year, Arthur Sweetser pointed out that "[o]ne of the most important but least discussed elements of the general international organization on which the world's hopes are now focused will center around the kind and type of international staff which will constitute its permanent service."[57] Over the 60 years since this contention the dominant structural approaches in IR scholarship and its conceptions of unitary actors, be it states or IOs, have had their merits in their own right to the detriment, however, of an adequate theoretical reception of the impact of secretariats on the ground of their civil service.[58]

---

[55] ALEXANDER LOVEDAY, REFLECTIONS ON INTERNATIONAL ADMINISTRATION (1956); MOHAMMED BEDJAOUI, FONCTION PUBLIQUE INTERNATIONALE ET INFLUENCES NATIONALES (1958); TIEN-CHENG YOUNG, INTERNATIONAL CIVIL SERVICE. PRINCIPLES AND PROBLEMS (1958); GEORGES LANGROD, LA FONCTION PUBLIQUE INTERNATIONALE. SA GENÈSE, SON ESSENCE, SON EVOLUTION (1963); ROGER BLOCH & JACQUELINE LEFÈVRE, LA FONCTION PUBLIQUE INTERNATIONALE ET EUROPÉENNE (1963); INTERNATIONAL ADMINISTRATION. ITS EVOLUTION AND CONTEMPORARY APPLICATIONS (Robert S. Jordan ed., 1971); THOMAS G. WEISS, INTERNATIONAL BUREAUCRACY. AN ANALYSIS OF THE OPERATION OF FUNCTIONAL AND GLOBAL INTERNATIONAL SECRETARIATS (1975); YADH BEN-ACHOUR AND SABINO CASSESE, ASPEKTE DER INTERNATIONALEN VERWALTUNG (1985); YVES BEIGBEDER, THREATS TO THE INTERNATIONAL CIVIL SERVICE. PAST PRESSURES AND NEW TRENDS (1988); HANS MOURITZEN, THE INTERNATIONAL CIVIL SERVICE. A STUDY OF BUREAUCRACY; INTERNATIONAL ORGANIZATIONS (1990); JACQUES LEMOINE, THE INTERNATIONAL CIVIL SERVANT. AN ENDANGERED SPECIES (1995); ALAIN PLANTEY AND FRANÇOIS LORIOT, FONCTION PUBLIQUE INTERNATIONALE. ORGANISATIONS MONDIALES ET EUROPÉENNES (2005); JOHN MATHIASON, INVISIBLE GOVERNANCE. INTERNATIONAL SECRETARIATS IN WORLD POLITICS (2007).

[56] EGON F. RANSHOFEN-WERTHEIMER, THE INTERNATIONAL SECRETARIAT. A GREAT EXPERIMENT IN INTERNATIONAL ADMINISTRATION 239-246 (1945).

[57] Arthur Sweetser, *The World's Civil Service,* 30 IOWA LAW REVIEW 478, 478 (1945).

[58] *See* Liese & Weinlich (note 2), at 491, 500-510.

The law of many international institutions contains a provision similar to Art. 100 UNC which provides that the "Secretary-General and the staff shall not seek or receive instructions from any government or from any other authority external to the organization. They shall refrain from any action which might reflect on their position as international officials responsible only to the organization."[59] The second paragraph provides that member states should refrain from seeking influence on the Secretary-General and the staff. While practice generally contravenes the latter provision, most accounts of practitioners do point to an international staff dedicated to organizational goals, though in tension with influence of member states.[60]

While the precise impact of the civil staff hinges on the effect of national influence and control, the loyalty of civil staff and in particular the action of the head of bureaucracies is likely to have a significant influence on the autonomy of international bureaucracies.[61] In pursuing their strategies of *inter alia* interpreting their mandates, cooperating with third parties and buffering information, they must manoeuvre between competing interests among constituent members as well as third parties. This meets Ernst Haas' conception of politics as "the art of the possible."[62] However, the image of IOs' officials as "missionaries of our time"[63] must not distract from the fact that increased autonomy means less control by principals and contravenes accountability mechanisms. Democratic control cannot be sacrificed to some "heroic administrator."[64] Furthermore, picturing the staff of international civil servants as whole-heartedly dedicated to organizational goals beyond the reach of their respective national governments, might be a step too optimistic. The extent to which a dedicated civil service exists and how it relates to the balance between autonomy and the influence by other actors cannot

---

59 *See e.g.* Art. 8(2) FAO Constitution; Art. 6(4) WTO Agreement; Art. 4 Section V IBDR Articles of Agreement; Art. 11 Convention on the Organisation for Economic Co-operation and Development.

60 *See* Karl Th. Paschke, *UNO von innen – die Besonderheiten einer multinationalen Bürokratie, in* PRAXISHANDBUCH UNO. DIE VEREINTEN NATIONEN IM LICHTE GLOBALER HERAUSFORDERUNGEN 553, 565-566 (Sabine von Schorlemer ed., 2003); *see also* (note 55).

61 *See* Robert W. Cox, The Executive Head: An Essay on Leadership in International Organization, 23 INTERNATIONAL ORGANIZATION 205 (1969).

62 *See* HAAS (note 41), at 102.

63 BARNETT & FINNEMORE (note 2), at 33.

64 *See* the critique by HAAS (note 41), at 103.

be specified generally but must be examined in each particular case.[65] However, the dynamic and *esprit de corps* of bureaucracies' civil staff tends to be a further factor contributing to their autonomy.

2. *Bureaucracies' Authority Based on Knowledge and Expertise*

In addition and related to their apparent rational-legal and technocratic character, international bureaucracies oftentimes command a stronghold on knowledge and expertise, which increases their authority. Understanding *how* they exercise authority further adds to the explanation of their autonomy. The question then is not whether agents are a tool in the hands of principals for pursuing a determined goal, but the aim is rather to grasp their decisive role in defining the problems to be solved[66] and to understand how they take part in the construction of social reality. Social action is based on knowledge, views of the world as well as normative and causal convictions. To impact knowledge is to impact the social construction of reality and to thereby influence actors' behavior.[67] Weber has succinctly pointed out that "bureaucratic administration means: exercise of power by way of knowledge."[68]

An illustrative example is the rating of countries by the World Bank (WB) with regard to their eligibility for credits or loans. The WB transforms economic information into qualitative assessments of the financial credibility and economic perspective of states. This classification affects social reality – other actors receive this information and integrate it into their view forming the basis for social action.[69] The information received may be habitually, immediately and uncritically integrated. For other actors it might simply be impossible to gain similar information

---

65 Liese & Weinlich (note 2), at 514-518.

66 *See* ERNST B. HAAS, WHEN KNOWLEDGE IS POWER. THREE MODELS OF CHANGE IN INTERNATIONAL ORGANIZATIONS (1990).

67 *See* John Gerard Ruggie, *International Responses to Technology: Concepts and Trends*, 29 INTERNATIONAL ORGANIZATION 557, 569-70 (1975) (an early account). This insight stands unrelated to an actors' mode of action, be it strategic or communicative.

68 WEBER (note 40), at 226 ("Die bürokratische Verwaltung bedeutet: Herrschaft kraft *Wissen*: dies ist ihr spezifisch rationaler Grundcharakter.").

69 *See* BARNETT & FINNEMORE (note 2), at 73-120.

and resources or the will to do so might be lacking.[70] They would not have the argumentative basis for contesting doubtful claims, or there would be no basis for doubt to arise in the first place. The WB has coined particular conceptions of development, of good governance or of what constitutes a good economy.[71] In retrospect, the catastrophic effects of structural adjustment programs of the 1980s are apparent; yet, at their time they were seen as the necessary programs for achieving a well-functioning economy. Recipient states have largely lacked the resources and expertise to counter these claims.

Moreover, the demand for expert knowledge increases with the complexity and uncertainty in resolving problems or pursuing shared goals.[72] International institutions' bearing on the construction of reality and their resulting influence on actors' behavior has been demonstrated in several of the case studies. Erika de Wet observes that the International Labour Organization (ILO) has found the most effective means of promoting labor standards in promotion and persuasion. She notes that these mechanisms "rest on the assumption that increased awareness, knowledge and expertise are the critical pathways for changing government policies and behaviors."[73] More fundamentally and noteworthy, the ILO has deliberately adopted this strategy rather than aiming at the formal ratification of its conventions with the effect that less conventions are ratified but the standards set out in these conventions are largely implemented in many national labor laws.[74]

The coining of a particular concept usually unfolds in what can be described as an epistemic community, defined by Peter Haas as "a network of professionals with recognized expertise and competence in a particular domain and an authoritative claim to policy-relevant knowledge within that domain or issue area."[75] The authority of bureaucracies and their command over expertise and knowledge increase their auton-

---

70 *See* Roland Vaubel, *Principal-Agent Problems in International Organizations*, 1 REVIEW OF INTERNATIONAL ORGANIZATIONS 125 (2006).

71 Dann (note 25); BARNETT & FINNEMORE (note 2), at 165.

72 *See* Peter M. Haas, *Introduction: Epistemic Communities and International Policy Coordination*, 46 INTERNATIONAL ORGANIZATION 1, 12 (1992).

73 Erika de Wet, *Governance through Promotion and Persuasion: The 1998 ILO Declaration on Fundamental Principles and Rights at Work*, in this volume.

74 *Id.*

75 HAAS (note 66), at 3.

omy and influence.[76] Empirical studies have demonstrated the effectiveness of regimes with a focus on their impact on norm compliance by way of impacting consensual knowledge. They support the proposition that "scientific knowledge will create a consensual basis for the recognition of new cause/effect links which had not been recognized before."[77] On the basis of an international regimes database, Helmut Breitmeier finds that regimes have been responsible for a significant increase in knowledge of causes and effects with regard to environmental issues; the yardstick of this increase is the knowledge held by transnational research networks.[78]

The role that institutions play in constructing social reality by way of creating meanings, classification and norm-diffusion should be put under scrutiny and cannot comfort itself with a hint at the separation of technical from political issues.[79] Furthermore, power relations are likely to alter prevalent conceptions. These contentions shall be developed in a critical appraisal of international institutions and their exercise of public authority.

C. Critical Reflections on Autonomous International Bureaucracies

The predominant presumption appears to be that international bureaucracies implement the political directives or facilitate their realization on behalf of their constituents and pursue global or at least shared goals. Accordingly, they enjoy a combination of input and output legitimacy. A sociologically informed view of international bureaucracies

---

76 BARNETT & FINNEMORE (note 2), at 24-25.

77 Ernst B. Haas, *Is there a Hole in the Whole? Knowledge, Technology, Interdependence, and the Construction of International Regimes*, 29 INTERNATIONAL ORGANIZATION 827, 858-9 (1975).

78 BREITMEIER, YOUNG & ZÜRN (note 10); Helmut Breitmeier, *Die Output-orientierte Legitimität des globalen Regierens. Empirische Befunde aus der quantitativen Erforschung internationaler Umweltregime*, 13 ZEITSCHRIFT FÜR INTERNATIONALE BEZIEHUNGEN 39 (2006).

79 *See* BARNETT & FINNEMORE (note 2), at 31-34; HAAS (note 66), at 11.

as autonomous actors set out above casts doubt on this premise.[80] The concept of autonomy encompasses not only that international bureaucracies are actors to some degree independent from the will and intentions of their creators but also that their actions and interests do not coincide with their creators' expectations. As actors they develop a dynamic and autonomous strategy of their own. This part of the argument shall be revisited and it shall be highlighted how it turns out to be problematic. Bureaucracies' autonomous action is largely removed from control and from input legitimacy (I.). The presumption that they pursue predefined technical goals might arguably compensate for a lack of control; however, a critical reflection on bureaucracies' exercise of public authority indicates that the underlying separation of technical from political issues is at least doubtful as a categorical premise (II.). Furthermore, this critical reflection will be mindful of the possible impact and functioning of power relations.

I. Bureaucracies Unbound?

Understanding international bureaucracies as autonomous actors illustrates how they are, to some extent, removed from the intentions and control of their creators. This is also a manifest constraint on sources of input legitimacy. Input legitimacy refers to the participatory quality of the decision-making process leading to the mandate providing a conditional grant of authority to the agent.[81] The conditionality of the authority further implies that the principal has some means of control over the agent. This can be conceptualized more precisely as internal accounttability.[82] Reflections on autonomous international bureaucracies pose challenges to their input legitimacy and internal accountability. Four strategies and mechanisms in bureaucracies' exercise of public authority are particularly noteworthy.

---

[80] *See* Gayl D. Ness & Steven R. Brechin, *Bridging the Gap: International Organizations as Organizations,* 42 INTERNATIONAL ORGANIZATION 245 (1988).

[81] FRITZ WILHELM SCHARPF, REGIEREN IN EUROPA. EFFEKTIV UND DEMOKRATISCH? 17-20 (1999).

[82] *See* de Wet (note 28); Robert O. Keohane, *Global Governance and Democratic Accountability, in* TAMING GLOBALIZATION: FRONTIERS OF GOVERNANCE 130 (David Held & Mathias Koening-Archibugi eds., 2002).

First, the discussion of the WB's structural adjustment programs has already stirred the observation that principals or other affected actors frequently do not have the information, resources or knowledge to challenge decisions taken by bureaucracies.[83] The comparative advantage in information and expert knowledge in the hands of bureaucracies is a strategic resource for agents that seek to foster and expand their autonomy. To this effect they might select activities and information that are pleasant to principals and make them public while trying to conceal activities that would be viewed less favorably. Ceremonialism refers to the fact that bureaucracies seek to satisfy formal reporting requirements and allow for supervision but do so without revealing too much information.[84] Weber has pointed to the tendency of bureaucracies to increase their exclusive knowledge with the motivation to increase their power.[85] Consequently, he argues, every bureaucracy seeks to increase this comparative advantage by way of secrecy: "Bureaucratic administration tends to be administration to the exclusion of the public."[86] Furthermore, the effective functioning of an agent might call for in-transparency. The work of the OSCE High Commissioner on National Minorities (HCNM), for instance, largely depends on intransparency.[87] This is in stark contravention of principal's or a broader public's efforts to hold agents accountable. Also, the HCNM's impact stems in large from his/her authoritative articulation of standards and from determining the performance of states with regard to these standards.[88] To this end, again, he/she enjoys a superior access to information and thus making it hard if not impossible for other actors to challenge the HCNM's authority.

Second, the resort to soft- and non-binding instruments makes the control of bureaucracies more difficult because they are not (yet) subject to similar procedural requirements and would not require any national

---

83 *See* Vaubel (note 70).

84 Darren G. Hawkins & Wade Jacoby, *How Agents Matter*, *in* DELEGATION AND AGENCY IN INTERNATIONAL ORGANIZATIONS 199, 210-212 (Darren G. Hawkins, David A. Lake, Daniel L. Nielson & Michael J. Tierney eds., 2006).

85 WEBER (note 40), at 226, 1081.

86 *Id.* at 1081 ("Bürokratische Verwaltung ist ihrer Tendenz nach stets Verwaltung mit Ausschluß der Öffentlichkeit.").

87 Anuscheh Farahat, in this volume.

88 *Id.*; BARNETT & FINNEMORE (note 2), at 6.

ratification or implementation process. Nevertheless, their factual impact is oftentimes no less significant than the effect of formal and legally binding instruments.[89] Even more so, it is hardly possible to grasp international institutions' role in the construction of social reality like the World Bank's definition of development, good governance or a well-functioning economy. In addition, the working of power relations must not be neglected. The conceptions endorsed by the WB tend to be aligned with those of powerful constituent members. The exercise of public authority is then usually a mixture of coercive and productive power.[90] The latter refers to a common element of the exercise of authority and power, namely the "production, in and through social relations, of effects that shape the capacities of actors to determine their own circumstances and fate."[91] The concept of productive power gives credit to the fact that actors take decisions on the basis of a constructed social reality and it suggests that power relations persist in this construction. Bearing in mind the power of rhetoric further corroborates the critique.[92] Emanuel Adler and Steven Bernstein explain and support this suggestion *inter alia* with regard to the categorical claim that an

---

[89] *See* Eyal Benvenisti, *"Coalitions of the Willing" and the Evolution of Informal International Law, in* "COALITIONS OF THE WILLING" AVANTGARDE OR THREAT?, 1(Christian Callies, Georg Nolte & Tobias Stoll eds., 2006).

[90] Dann (note 25); Michael Barnett & Raymond Duvall, *Power in Global Governance, in* POWER IN GLOBAL GOVERNANCE, 1, 3 (Michael Barnett & Raymond Duvall eds., 2005).

[91] Barnett & Duvall (note 90), at 3.

[92] *See* SEMANTISCHE KÄMPFE. MACHT UND SPRACHE IN DEN WISSENSCHAFTEN (Ekkehard Felder ed., 2006); Eric Naim-Gesbert, *Droit, expertise et société du risque,* 123 REVUE DU DROIT PUBLIC 33, 37 (2007). Apart from a comparative advantage in knowledge, the use of rhetoric might impact the social construction to the benefit of particular actors. *See* Rodger A. Payne, *Persuasion, Frames and Norm Construction,* 7 EUROPEAN JOURNAL OF INTERNATIONAL RELATIONS 37-61 (2001); Ronald R. Krebs & Patrick T. Jackson, *Twisting Tongues and Twisting Arms: The Power of Political Rhetoric,* 13 EUROPEAN JOURNAL OF INTERNATIONAL RELATIONS 35-66 (2007). Such arguments have a long tradition. Quintilianus acknowledges his debt to Cicero and Aristotle's *Art of Rhetoric* and develops a technique of description that aligns the picture arising from the description with the interest of the speaker; *see* Quentin Skinner, *Rhetoric and Conceptual Change,* 3 FINNISH YEARBOOK OF POLITICAL THOUGHT 60-72 (1999).

open economy promotes economic growth.[93] Such a claim works to the benefit of powerful actors and has been developed and fostered by international financial institutions to the severe detriment of many recipient countries. Only under prominent expert criticism and protest has this conception started to change.[94] Power relations and the way in which international bureaucracies exercise public power – in part through the construction of social reality by way of creating meanings, classification and norm-diffusion – and their stronghold of knowledge and expertise raise further concerns about the legitimacy of their actions. Again, the argument that bureaucracies merely take executive or facilitative measures in technical issues is weak and expert knowledge might also be an expression of productive power rather than an easy cure to problems of input legitimacy.

Third, the interpretative change (so called "interpretative evolution") of constituent mandates further bears on the quality of input legitimacy.[95] Bureaucracies interpret statutory provisions to their advantage. This is in particular the case where more specific procedural norms are lacking and it is a common characteristic of constituent documents of international organizations or mandating resolutions.[96] Organs of the FAO, for example, have exploited their broad and non-specific mandates in order to produce norms in *ad hoc* procedures.[97] Cases of interpretative change rest on an informal general consent among the constituent members rather than on parliamentary ratification. Also, the standard activity of Refugee Status Determination carried out by the UNHCR or UN peacekeeping missions find no mention in the respective constituent documents. Change of this kind is a common phenomenon of

---

93 Emanuel Adler & Steven Bernstein, *Knowledge in Power: The Epistemic Construction of Global Governance*, *in* POWER IN GLOBAL GOVERNANCE 294 (Michael Barnett & Raymond Duvall eds., 2005).

94 *See* JOSEPH E. STIGLITZ, GLOBALIZATION AND ITS DISCONTENTS (2002); Michael Zürn, *Global Governance and Legitimacy Problems,* 39 GOVERNMENT AND OPPOSITION 260 (2004).

95 *See* Ian Johnstone, *The Power of Interpretive Communities*, *in* POWER IN GLOBAL GOVERNANCE 185, 186 (Michael Barnett & Raymond Duvall eds., 2005). Johnstone builds on the concept of "interpretative community" developed by Stanley Fish. *See* STANLEY FISH, DOING WHAT COMES NATURALLY. CHANGE, RHETORIC, AND THE PRACTICE OF THEORY IN LITERATURE AND LEGAL STUDIES 141-160 (1989).

96 Hawkins & Jacoby (note 84), at 206-207.

97 Jürgen Friedrich, in this volume.

growth or mission creep. Arguably, international bureaucracies expand their tasks as societies become more mindful of pressing problems.[98] Another explanation for such expansion might lie in bureaucracies struggle for survival. The CSCE/OSCE as well as NATO, for example, underwent a thorough transformation after their original *raison d'être* dismantled with the end of the Cold War. Bearing in mind power relations directs attention to the interest of powerful actors in the exchange of interpretative claims.[99]

A fourth concern with regard to input legitimacy and internal accountability lies in the fact that a bureaucracy might be captured by one or a number of members, or by third actors, and might act in contravention to the will of other members or third actors. Also, it might be part of an active strategy of bureaucracies to exploit differences between member states or to expand their permeability to third parties – that is non-principals and in particular other international organizations or international NGOs[100] – in order to increase their autonomy.[101] The development and enforcement of OECD Guidelines for Multinational Enterprises provides an example of how institutions can seek the support of NGOs in their relationship with principals. NGOs have been involved in the drafting of the Guidelines and promote them in a larger endeavor to increase corporate social responsibility.[102] However, the interaction with NGOs does not necessarily work to the institutions' advantage and institutions are not themselves immune from the influence of NGOs. The institution would lose in autonomy in relation to this capturing actor but gain in relation to others. To the extent that the bureaucracy's actions can be reduced to the will of other powerful actors, however, it could no longer plausibly be referred to as autonomous. A mixture between autonomy and capture by powerful actors can be found in the Security Council whose stated purpose is to ensure international peace and security. It's Al Qaeda and Taliban Sanctions Committee administers a consolidated list of terrorist suspects; any individ-

---

[98] HAAS (note 41), at 90-2.

[99] *See* Martti Koskenniemi, *International Law and Hegemony: A Reconfiguration,* 17 CAMBRIDGE REVIEW OF INTERNATIONAL AFFAIRS 197 (2004).

[100] For the functioning and impact of NGOs *see* in particular MARGARET E. KECK AND KATHRYN SIKKINK, ACTIVISTS BEYOND BORDERS. ADVOCACY NETWORKS IN INTERNATIONAL POLITICS (1998).

[101] Hawkins & Jocoby (note 84), at 208-210.

[102] Gefion Schuler, in this volume.

ual placed on the list faces immediate consequences in all UN Member States. Terrorism is a threat to international peace and security; yet, it stands undisputed that the vast majority of all terrorist suspects on the list are suggested by the US and included without much discussion. This evokes the thought that it serves as an instrument in the hands of the US rather than as an autonomous actor.

In sum, critical reflections from a political science perspective successfully and helpfully disturb the image of international bureaucracies as simple tools in the service of their creators. The following section will revisit the contention that international bureaucracies gain legitimacy from an effective pursuit of global or at least shared goals.

II. Bureaucracies as Technical Administrators in Pursuit of Global Goals

Output legitimacy refers to the problem solving quality of decisions.[103] It could be argued that international bureaucracies are part of the executive and do precisely what this suggests – they execute. Such an argument has already lost much of its credibility. First, the cases illustrated above show that this can also go wrong and, secondly, the claim to such output legitimacy rests on the contentious and largely untenable distinction between technical and political issues that has already been cast into doubt in the discussion of Mitrany's functionalist theory of international integration. Rather, in some cases the argument could be made that the claim to a separability of technical from political issues is itself a hegemonic move that attempts to hide political implications and power relations. It is fruitful to recall the political and normative decisions that inevitably arise even if specific goals to be pursued were given. For instance, the Security Council's prime responsibility for the stated goal of securing international peace and security can hardly inform the balance to be struck between pursuing this goal and individuals' rights to liberty. These are normative questions and reflect conflicts of interests and ideas. The submission to a "heroic administrator" following a belief in the omnipresence and exclusivity of instrumental rationality in service of a technical implementation of given policy aims is not only unwarranted but also unwelcome – it would gain the critique by Hannah Arendt who makes clear that "the self-coercive force of

103 SCHARPF (note 81), at 20-28.

logicality is mobilized lest anybody ever starts thinking – which as the freest and purest of all human activities is the very opposite of the compulsory process of deduction."[104]

Lastly, a focus on the problem solving capacity of IOs presumes that they were in fact created and function for that purpose. This might well be the case but the variety of plausible reasons that principals might have for delegating authority to an autonomous international bureaucracy have already indicated that this need not be the case. Also, institutions are mechanisms for principals to gain or maintain power.[105] A focus on the problem solving capacity would be too narrow.

In conclusion, the conceptualization of international bureaucracies as instruments of their principals or as instruments of a technical world community appears to be insufficient. Bureaucracy can and should also be seen as:

> "an institution with a raison d'être and organizational and normative principles of its own. Administration is based on the rule of law, due process, codes of appropriate behavior, and a system of rationally debatable reasons. It is part of society's long-term commitment to a *Rechtsstaat* and procedural rationality for coping with conflicts and power differentials."[106]

Recently, the call has become louder in IR scholarship to turn to the study in the domestic political context in order to learn about administrative institutions, delegation and agency.[107] A turn to the domestic

---

[104] HANNAH ARENDT, THE ORIGINS OF TOTALITARIANISM 473 (1976).

[105] Renate Mayntz, *Governance Theory als fortentwickelte Steuerungstheorie?*, *in* GOVERNANCE-FORSCHUNG 11 (Gunnar Schuppert ed., 2006).

[106] Olsen (note 2), at 3.

[107] Hawkins, Lake, Nielson & Tierney (note 13), at 4-5 ("Overall, we find the causes and consequences of delegation to IOs to be remarkably similar to delegation in domestic politics. Despite assertions that international anarchy transforms the logic of politics and renders international institutions less consequential, we find considerable overlap between the reasons why principals delegate to domestic agents and why states delegate to IOs."); Simmons & Martin (note 10), at 205 (concluding that "[a]careful look at literatures that develop theories of domestic and transnational politics, for example, should be drawn upon more systematically if we are to understand the sources and effects of international institutionalization."); Jörg Borgumil, Werner Jann & Frank Nullmeier, *Perspektiven der politikwissenschaftlichen Verwaltungsforschung*, *in* POLITIK UND VERWALTUNG 9, 18 (Jörg Borgumil, Werner Jann & Frank Nullmeier eds., 2006).

context for inspiration also draws attention to the institutional context in which autonomous bureaucracies are embedded, namely the context of a rule-of-law. A functionally equivalent context is blatantly missing at the international level. An elementary function that the national context of a rule-of-law provides is the institutional framework for contesting the actions of bureaucracies – their decisions and interpretations – both in legal and political fora.[108] This makes autonomous bureaucracies bearable. It is more fundamentally a prerequisite for their desirability and a necessary ingredient for individual and collective democratic self-determination.[109] However, some cautionary remarks will be in place with regard to the conceptualization and construction of international institutional law to this effect.

D. The Prospect of International Institutional Law in the Face of Autonomous Bureaucracies

The critical reflection on international bureaucracies' autonomy has ended with the suggestion that an institutional framework be developed as a necessary prerequisite for contesting, in legal and political fora, the means and ends of decisions taken by bureaucracies. This suggestion must first posit itself within a predominant IR scholarship that emphasizes effective governance and the role of politics in the strategic pursuit of predefined goals. Secondly, it runs the risk of unduly cloaking the exercise of power within concepts of legality.

The suggestion that institutions provide the framework for contesting the means and ends of policy choices by international bureaucracies stands in contrast to a prevalent research agenda that is focused on institutional design with an aim to increase effectiveness. Most notably, it does not inquire about the origin and constitution of ends.[110] This appears to hold as a general observation for much of the research on global governance. The concept of governance refers to the analysis of

---

[108] *See* Nico Krisch, *The Pluralism of Global Administrative Law*, 17 EJIL 247, 266-67 (2006).

[109] *See* Benedict Kingsbury, Nico Krisch & Richard B. Steward, *The Emergence of Global Administrative Law*, 68 LAW AND CONTEMPORARY PROBLEMS 15, 51 (2005).

[110] Wendt (note 1), at 1046. *See* Christian Reus-Smit, *The Strange Death of Liberal International Theory*, 12 EJIL 573, 580-585 (2001).

the relationship between the institutional design and the efficiency as well as effectiveness of the outcomes produced within and by the structures of the institution under scrutiny.[111] It is directed at the question which mechanisms are suitable to better achieve societal goals – such research does not inquire the goals to be pursued.[112] Moreover, there is a dominant corresponding trend in international law that rests on claims to universal validity of substantive convictions and loudly calls to look for effective implementation.[113] This is a plausible call and a valuable re-

---

[111] It builds on Oliver Williamson's definition of governance as "an exercise in assessing the efficacy of alternative modes (means) of organization." OLIVER E. WILLIAMSON, THE MECHANISMS OF GOVERNANCE 11 (1996). Williamson was a student of Ronald Coase who took initial and path breaking steps in exploring the relation between institutional design and efficiency of outcomes. *See* Ronald Coase, *The Nature of the Firm,* 4 ECONOMICA 386 (1937).

[112] *See* the conceptions of governance in James N. Rosenau, *Governance, Order, and Change in World Politics, in* GOVERNANCE WITHOUT GOVERNMENT: ORDER AND CHANGE IN WORLD POLITICS 1, 4 (James N. Rosenau & Ernst-Otto Czempiel eds., 1992); James N. Rosenau, *Toward an Ontology for Global Governance, in* APPROACHES TO GLOBAL GOVERNANCE THEORY 287 (Martin Hewson & Timothy J. Sinclair eds., 1999); Alice D. Ba & Matthew J. Hoffmann, *Contending Perspectives on Global Governance. Dialogue and Debate, in* CONTENDING PERSPECTIVES ON GLOBAL GOVERNANCE. COHERENCE CONTESTATION AND WORLD ORDER 249 (Alice D. Ba & Matthew J. Hoffmann eds., 2005); Sweet (note 22); Wayne Sandholtz & Alec Stone Sweet, *Law, Politics, and International Governance*, *in* THE POLITICS OF INTERNATIONAL LAW 238, 245 (Christian Reus-Smit ed., 2004); Gunnar Schuppert, *Governance im Spiegel der Wissenschaftsdisziplinen, in* GOVERNANCE FORSCHUNG. VERGEWISSERUNG ÜBER STAND UND ENTWICKLUNGSLINIEN 371 (Gunnar Schuppert ed., 2006).

[113] This appears to be the predominant drive of Anne-Marie Slaughter, *A Liberal Theory of International Law,* 94 PROCEEDINGS OF THE AMERICAN SOCIETY OF INTERNATIONAL LAW 240 (2000); ANNE-MARIE SLAUGHTER, A NEW WORLD ORDER 11 (2004); Anne-Marie Slaughter & William Burke-White, *The Future of International Law is Domestic (or, the European Way of Law),* 47 HARVARD INTERNATIONAL LAW JOURNAL 327, 335 (2006). *See* Michael Reisman, *Unilateral Action and the Transformations of the World Constitutive Process: The Special Problem of Humanitarian Intervention,* 11 EJIL 3 (2000). For a critique, *see* Andrew Hurrell, *International Law and the Changing Constitution of International Society, in* THE ROLE OF LAW IN INTERNATIONAL POLITICS: ESSAYS IN INTERNATIONAL RELATIONS AND INTERNATIONAL LAW 327, 336-46 (Michael Byers ed., 2000); Benvenisti (note 89); Martti Koskenniemi, *Constitutionalism as Mindset: Reflections on Kantian Themes About In-*

search program in response to the pressing problems of global dimensions that are beyond the reach of unilateral actions. Yet, it sometimes also comes close to what Hedley Bull has called a "premature global solidarism" that is rather oblivious to power relations and conflicting values.[114] This contribution has highlighted that the pursuit of such goals and the exercise of public authority by international bureaucracies inevitably has political and normative implications. In order to increase the legitimacy of international institutions, their conception cannot be confined to instruments for an effective implementation of agreed-upon goals but must equally encompass an arena for debating and contesting such goals and for channeling political conflict.

To the same effect Jan Klabbers has distinguished two conceptions of IOs: first as an instrument in managing common problems and second as providing a space for politics – *agorae* in the Greek ideal of political spaces.[115] The analysis of autonomous bureaucracies supports the suggestion that the latter conception be strengthened in relation to a dominant image of international organizations as managers.[116] The alternative then lies in a reappraisal of the formal – the formal basis for ethical and purposive politics.[117] One function of international institutional law then is to provide for the legal constructions constituting a space for politics. This corresponds to the conception of law as the city wall that protects the *polis*. Hanna Arendt writes on "the Greek solution":

> "In their opinion, the lawmaker was like the builder of the city wall, someone who had to do and finish his work before political activity could begin. ... Before men began to act, a definite space had to be secured and a structure built where all subsequent actions could take

---

ternational Law and Globalization, 8 THEORETICAL INQUIRIES IN LAW 9 (2007).

[114] ANDREW HURRELL, ON GLOBAL ORDER. POWER, VALUES AND THE CONSTITUTION OF INTERNATIONAL SOCIETY 55 (2007).

[115] Jan Klabbers, *Two Concepts of International Organization,* 2 INTERNATIONAL ORGANIZATIONS LAW REVIEW 277 (2005).

[116] Jan Klabbers, *The Changing Image of International Organizations, in* THE LEGITIMACY OF INTERNATIONAL ORGANIZATIONS 221 (Jean-Marc Coicaud & Veijo Heiskane eds., 2001).

[117] *Id.* at 243-45; KLABBERS (note 3), at 329-334. *See* Christian Reus-Smit, *The Politics of International Law, in* THE POLITICS OF INTERNATIONAL LAW 14, 24-31 (Christian Reus-Smit ed., 2004); Martti Koskenniemi, *Global Governance and Public International Law,* 37 KRITISCHE JUSTIZ 241 (2004); Koskenniemi (note 113); Hurrell (note 113), 312-14.

place, the space being the public realm of the *polis* and its structure the law; legislator and architect belonged in the same category."[118]

In the development of such legal structures, this project turns to the national context for inspiration. The above insights suggest that the development of international institutional law take the direction of filling in the yawning gaps in the legal structures that a comparison with the national context indicates. However, a number of remarks are in place that caution against granting unwarranted and illegitimate actions undertaken by international bureaucracies the benefit of being perceived as lawful.[119] While no uncontroversial yardstick is readily available for a normative assessment of such actions outside a framework of law and political process[120] a look at the differences between the national and international contexts indicates the limits to what a development of institutional law can achieve.

First, power relations are much more persistent and unmediated than in the national context. Institutional design is most likely the outcome of strategic bargaining reflecting power relations rather than a consideration of what is suitable to ensure legitimacy.[121] Furthermore, civil society and public scrutiny are not available to the same extent in order to perform a complementary legitimating function. Secondly, the heterogeneity of normative and factual convictions among actors is most likely higher. Third, the concept of a separation of powers can hardly be applied. Administrative and executive organs are likely to be more politicized.[122] The concept of a separation of powers is insufficiently realized in international polities that usually lack a legislative body that is functionally equivalent to democratic parliaments.[123] Fourth, when ac-

---

118 HANNAH ARENDT, THE HUMAN CONDITION 194-95 (1958).

119 *See* Carol Harlow, *Global Administrative Law: The Quest for Principles and Values*, 17 EJIL 187, 214 (2006).

120 Only the substantive yardstick of human rights might be applicable; *see* Jochen von Bernstorff, in this volume; Jürgen Habermas, *Hat die Konstitutionalisierung des Völkerrechts noch eine Chance?, in* DER GESPALTENE WESTEN 113, 142 (Jürgen Habermas ed., 2004).

121 *See* Eyal Benvenisti, *The Interplay between Actors as a Determination of the Evolution of Administrative Law in International Institutions*, 68 LAW AND CONTEMPORARY PROBLEMS 319 (2005).

122 Borgumil, Jann & Nullmeier (note 107), at 18.

123 *See* von Bernstorff, in this volume; von Bogdandy (note 32), at 625-650.

tors interpret and enforce the law and even more so when enforcement is decentralized, power relations are again reflected in interpretations.

These differences amount to the foremost obstacles in following the call for a legal framework for contesting means and ends as well as for channeling political conflict. They expose the risk of translating power relations into legal relations. Thereby they might unduly grant an imprimatur of legality and rightness.[124] While power relations and their influence on institutional design and on meanings of legal texts must not be neglected, this contribution sides with Andrew Hurrell that "power expressed through shared rules and norms is potentially more acceptable than power unmediated by rules."[125] Also, the legal form provides some armour against an easy translation of power relations into law.[126] At the international level it is thus suggested that international institutional law be developed to provide structures to make politics possible – to find institutional arrangements that bring political actors together and to provide the basis for meaningful contestation.

Yet, the argument that IOs or even more loosely regulated institutions and a development of institutional law could respond to this task faces further practical difficulties. It is precisely the stalemates and inefficiency of formal decision-making that has lead to a "flight from the plenary."[127] An administrative space for routine decision-making is indispensable for an effective response to pressing global challenges. International institutions will continue to be torn between demands for more efficiency and effectiveness and the need for an institutional framework for political contestation that can contribute to the legitimacy of decisions taken. However, an increasing resistance to or at least uneasiness concerning the legitimacy of actions undertaken by interna-

---

124 *See* Pierre Bourdieu, *The Force of Law: Toward a Sociology of the Juridical Field,* 38 HASTINGS LAW JOURNAL 814, 838 (1987) ("Law is the quintessential form of the symbolic power of naming that creates the things named ... It confers upon the reality which arises from its classificatory operations the maximum permanence."). *See also* Richard H. Steinberg and Jonathan M. Zaslof, *Power and International Law*, 100 AMERICAN JOURNAL OF INTERNATIONAL LAW 64 (2006).

125 Hurrell (note 113), at 314.

126 *See* Ingeborg Maus, Das Verhältnis der Politikwissenschaft zur Rechtswissenschaft: Bemerkungen zu den Folgen politologischer Autarkie, in POLITIK UND RECHT 76-120 (Miachel Becker & Ruth Zimmerling eds., 2006).

127 von Bernstorff, in this volume; Benvenisti (note 113).

tional bureaucracies also affects their effectiveness.[128] For example the Advocate General of the European Court of Justice has suggested that the Security Council's listing of terrorist suspects remain inapplicable and consequently ineffective as long as there are only insufficient procedural guarantees at the international level.[129] Thus, while powerful actors might well be reluctant to accept more formal institutionalized processes, such reluctance also forecloses some of the benefits.

E. Conclusion

The conceptualization of parts of international institutions as bureaucracies provides a beneficial grasp on their sources of autonomy, authority and on the way in which they exercise public authority, which might otherwise remain unseen. This is a promising emergent approach in IR scholarship. To analyze administration as a policy process further provides the basis for combining insights from domestic institutional analysis and traditional IR scholarship.[130] While bearing in mind particularities of the international context and being mindful of the pitfalls set out above, such a turn to the domestic context opens the avenue for combining political and legal scholarship on the same recurrent pivotal question: how is legitimate governance beyond the nation state possible? This contribution has attempted to provide a better view of the problems and to inform the development and conceptualization of international institutional law in response to the exercise of authority by international bureaucracies. It contends that the argument on the crucial role of law as a constitutive construction for political action is also instructive for future research in international relations.

---

[128] Zürn (note 94) (pointing to concerns about legitimacy as a significant source of non-compliance). *See also* Michael Zürn, *Introduction: Law and Compliance and Different Levels, in* LAW AND GOVERNANCE IN POSTNATIONAL EUROPE: COMPLIANCE BEYOND THE NATION-STATE 1 (Michael Zürn & Christian Joerges eds., 2005). To the same effect Thomas Frank makes the prominent argument for a compliance pull stemming from the legitimacy of international law. THOMAS M. FRANCK, THE POWER OF LEGITIMACY AMONG NATIONS 193 (1990).

[129] Opinion of Advocate General Poiares Maduro, delivered on 16 January 2008, Case C-402/05 P, *Yassin Abdullah Kadi v. Council of the European Union and Commission of the European Communities*. *See* de Wet (note 28).

[130] *See* Borgumil, Jann & Nullmeier (note 107), at 18.

II. Thematic Studies

1. The Exercise of Public Authority through Instruments Concerning Individuals

1.1 Decisions

The UN Security Council Al-Qaida and Taliban Sanctions Committee: Emerging Principles of International Institutional Law for the Protection of Individuals?

*By Clemens A. Feinäugle**

---

* The author would like to thank Prof. Dr. Armin von Bogdandy, Prof. Dr. Jan Klabbers and Matthias Goldmann for valuable comments on earlier drafts of this article, and Eric Pickett and Eva Richter for checking the language and footnotes.

A. von Bogdandy et al. (eds.), *The Exercise of Public Authority by International Institutions*, Beiträge zum ausländischen öffentlichen Recht und Völkerrecht 210,
DOI 10.1007/978-3-642-04531-8_5, © Springer-Verlag Berlin Heidelberg 2010

A. Introduction

Some time ago, one could read in the news about Mr. Abdelghani Mzoudi, the friend of the terror pilots of 9/11. He was acquitted of the accusation of aiding and abetting murder but he was not paid the owed compensation for wrongful imprisonment because his name was entered on a sanctions list of the UN. Many readers will have wondered how this could happen. Few if any will have guessed that we are in the middle of a case of international institutional law here, a process with actors on several levels (including a sanctions committee on the UN level), with different procedures and jurisdictions which can affect payments to an accused even after his acquittal. It is precisely this UN sanctions committee and its actions which form the subject of this paper.

Arguably no other subsidiary body of the UN Security Council has drawn so much attention of legal scholarship in recent years as the Al-Qaida and Taliban Sanctions Committee (in the following "the Committee"), which targets individual terrorist suspects with individual sanctions.[1]

---

[1] On the background and further development of this sanctions regime, *see* Jochen Abr. Frowein, *The UN Anti-Terrorism Administration and the Rule of Law, in* VÖLKERRECHT ALS WERTORDNUNG. COMMON VALUES IN INTERNATIONAL LAW. FESTSCHRIFT FÜR/ESSAYS IN HONOUR OF CHRISTIAN TOMU-

The Committee's activities are directed toward the fight against international terrorism. To take up this fight, the Security Council gave the Committee the task of keeping and updating a list of individuals and entities designated as being associated with Usama bin Laden, Al-Qaida and/or the Taliban, all of which are subject to the freezing of assets, travel bans and an arms embargo. "International terrorism"[2] implies by definition that this UN policy was deemed to be an international issue from the outset. It is true that in the past States have handled the issue of terrorism as a matter of domestic policy. However, with Usama bin Laden's terrorism reaching beyond Afghanistan's borders, the decentralized structure of his network, and the increasing mobility of terrorists the issue became internationalized. Therefore, the members of the UN Security Council decided to tackle this internationalized problem in the international forum of the UN, which, in the context of this sanctions regime, exercises public authority[3] through legally binding decisions. What they did not do was to provide the corresponding opportunities of review for the persons concerned by a listing. The members of the UN Security Council might thus have tried to use the international level in order to escape national standards of human rights protection and judicial review.

While the question of legal protection against the listing as a terrorist suspect is at the forefront of the legal discussion, the precise procedure of the listing and de-listing of terrorist suspects and the work of the Committee has so far taken a back seat. This paper takes a closer look at

---

SCHAT 785 *et seq.* (Pierre-Marie Dupuy, Bardo Fassbender, Malcolm N. Shaw & Karl-Peter Sommermann eds., 2006); Eric Rosand, *The Security Council's Efforts to Monitor the Implementation of Al Qaeda/Taliban Sanctions,* 98 AMERICAN JOURNAL OF INTERNATIONAL LAW (AJIL) 745 (2004); Vera Gowland-Debbas, *Sanctions Regimes Under Article 41 of the UN Charter, in* NATIONAL IMPLEMENTATION OF UNITED NATIONS SANCTIONS, 3 *et seq.* (on sanctions in general) and 15 (on the sanctions regime under Resolution 1267) (Vera Gowland-Debbas ed., 2004); Luca Radicati di Brozolo & Mauro Megliani, *Freezing the Assets of International Terrorist Organisations, in* ENFORCING INTERNATIONAL LAW NORMS AGAINST TERRORISM 377, 381 *et seq.* (Andrea Bianchi ed., 2004); ERIKA DE WET, THE CHAPTER VII POWERS OF THE UNITED NATIONS SECURITY COUNCIL 170 *et seq.* (2004).

2 SC Res. 1267 of 15 October 1999, fifth recital.

3 On the exercise of international public authority as the focus of the research project of which this contribution forms part, *see* von Bogdandy, Dann & Goldmann, *Developing the Publicness of Public International Law,* in this volume.

the Committee's tasks and procedures and tries to identify principles of international institutional law. Its principal argument is that, after repeated amendments to its guidelines, the Committee's procedures contain the germ of an administrative procedure based on the rule of law which may, to some extent, balance the lack of judicial review on the UN level. However, there is still a long way to go until a standard comparable to national judicial review has been achieved.

In the course of the legal analysis of the sanctions regime the article explains the institutional framework and the concretizing rules as well as the listing of terrorist suspects (B. I.-II.). It then focuses on the procedural regime with the listing and de-listing procedure (B. III.) before surveying the review and enforcement mechanisms (B.IV.). The concluding section extrapolates what could be emerging legal principles for the exercise of public authority by international institutions (C.).

B. Legal Analysis

I. Institutional Framework and Concretizing Rules

1. Institutional Framework

On the international level, the governance regime, *i.e.* the legal regime governing the sanctions regime, is located within the UN. The UN Charter, the founding document of the UN, forms the legal basis of this regime. It explicitly cites as one of the purposes of the UN the maintenance of international peace and security.[4]

The Security Council is the UN body entrusted with the responsibility for the maintenance of international peace and security. After the historical development in international law from the *ius ad bellum* to the prohibition of the use of force,[5] the Security Council has the singular responsibility of declaring a situation to amount to a threat to or breach of peace or an act of aggression (Art. 39 UN Charter). Apart from self-defense (Art. 51 UN Charter) this is the only case in which measures may be taken that include the use of force. In exercising this responsi-

---

4 Art. 1(1) UN Charter.

5 Albrecht Randelzhofer, *Art. 51, in* I THE CHARTER OF THE UNITED NATIONS – A COMMENTARY, paras. 1-3 (Bruno Simma ed., 2002).

bility, the Security Council has a wide discretion.[6] It adopts resolutions prescribing measures to be taken in the concrete case. Thus, the Security Council adopted resolutions 1267 (1999) of 15 October 1999 and 1333 (2000) of 19 December 2000, which established the Consolidated List of terrorist suspects and the Sanctions Committee, which was mandated to administer the sanctions regime. These resolutions of the Security Council are binding on UN Member States (Art. 25 UN Charter) and prevail over any other obligations under any other international agreement (Art. 103 UN Charter).

The Security Council has established the Sanctions Committee in accordance with Art. 29 UN Charter and delegated its responsibilities for the sanctions regime to the Committee. The Committee is thus a subsidiary organ of the Security Council, administering the Consolidated List of terrorist suspects and deciding on listings and de-listings. The Sanctions Committee is composed of all the members of the Security Council.[7] Its Chairman and the two Vice-Chairmen are appointed by the Security Council.[8] The UN Secretariat assists the work of the Committee by providing secretariat services.[9] The Committee is also supported by the Analytical Support and Sanctions Monitoring Team[10] ("the Monitoring Team") of eight experts appointed by the Secretary-General. The members of the Monitoring Team have specialized knowledge in counter-terrorism, financing of terrorism, arms embargoes, travel bans and related legal issues. The Monitoring Team operates under the direction of the Committee, but the views and recommendations expressed in its reports do not necessarily reflect the views of the Committee or the United Nations. The Monitoring Team assists the Committee, *inter alia*, by evaluating the Member States' implementation of the sanctions regime and reporting on developments that have an impact on the sanction regime's effectiveness, such as the changing nature of Al-Qaida and its continued threat.

---

6 Jochen Abr. Frowein & Nico Krisch, *Art. 39*, *in* I THE CHARTER OF THE UNITED NATIONS – A COMMENTARY, para. 4 (Bruno Simma ed., 2002).

7 Committee Guidelines in the amended version of 12 February 2007, para. 2(a).

8 *Id.* at para. 2(b) and (c).

9 *Id.* at para. 2(d).

10 This Monitoring Team was first established by SC Res. 1526 of 30 January 2004, para. 6 and was the successor of the Monitoring Group established by SC Res. 1363 of 30 July 2001, para. 4(a).

On the European Union ("EU") level, the EU Council adopts a Common Position as part of its Common Foreign and Security Policy pursuant to Arts. 11, 15 EU. The EC Council then adopts regulations based on Arts. 60, 301, 308 EC implementing this Common Position. To the extent to which the sanctions are governed by EC regulations, the sanctions are binding and directly applicable in the EC Member States.[11] As far as a sanction does not fall under EC competences, as in case of an arms embargo, that sanction must be implemented by the competent bodies on the national level. Thus, the governance of the sanction regime is carried out within a multi-level structure: the Security Council and the Sanctions Committee acting on the UN level, the EU Council acting on the European level and various national authorities acting on the national level.

2. *The Concretizing Rules: The Guidelines of the Committee*

In resolution 1390 (2002) of 16 January 2002 the Security Council mandated the Committee to promulgate such guidelines and criteria "as may be necessary" to facilitate the implementation of the sanctions measures.[12] In these "Guidelines of the Committee for the Conduct of its Work," last amended 12 February 2007, the Committee set forth, *inter alia*, the procedure of the listing and de-listing of terrorist suspects. These guidelines are the decisive legal instrument that facilitates the implementation of the measures adopted by the Security Council. The Committee decides upon the guidelines and amendments thereto by consensus.[13]

3. *The Binding Nature of Human Rights Standards for the Security Council*

Since targeted sanctions have a significant impact on individuals, the question arises whether the Sanctions Committee and the Security Council have to respect certain human rights standards such as the right of due process when implementing the sanctions regime. If the answer is in the affirmative, due to the lack of judicial review on the interna-

---

[11] Art. 249 (2) EC.

[12] *See* UN Res. 1390 of 16 January 2002, para. 5(d).

[13] Committee Guidelines in the amended version of 12 February 2007, para. 4(a).

tional level this could impose a standard of review on national and regional courts, which they must apply when deciding de-listing cases.

The question whether international human rights bind the UN Security Council in its actions has been a matter of continuous debate and is only outlined shortly here.[14] There are two main positions: one argues that the Security Council is – at least when acting under Chapter VII – not bound to respect human rights because they are overridden by the interest in maintaining international peace and security.[15] This view may be supported by UN Charter's drafters' aims and goals. The world was just emerging from the ravages of World War II and the framers intended to form a functioning Security Council with central decision-making powers; indeed, Art. 1 of the UN Charter (Purposes and Principles) mentions human rights concerns only after the maintenance of international peace and security, which is the first purpose listed. Furthermore, the wording of Chapter VII UN Charter is very broad and does not mention human rights.[16] The other position takes the view that the UN Security Council is bound by international human rights in all its actions, including under Chapter VII.[17] Although not a party to the respective human rights instruments, the UN must respect the UN Charter[18] which grants, *inter alia*, a right to due process and a right to a

---

[14] *See* August Reinisch, *Developing Human Rights and Humanitarian Law Accountability of the Security Council for the Imposition of Economic Sanctions*, 95 AJIL 851 (2001) (also citing the different positions).

[15] *See* HANS KELSEN, THE LAW OF THE UNITED NATIONS 294 (1951).

[16] *See* Anna M. Vradenburgh, *The Chapter VII Powers of the United Nations Charter: Do They "Trump" Human Rights Law?*, 14 LOYOLA OF LOS ANGELES INTERNATIONAL AND COMPARATIVE LAW JOURNAL 175, 177, 180, 183 (1991). *See also* Gabriel H. Oosthuizen, *Playing the Devil's Advocate: the United Nations Security Council is Unbound by Law*, 12 LEIDEN JOURNAL OF INTERNATIONAL LAW 549 (1999).

[17] Committee on Economic, Social and Cultural Rights, General Comment 8, The relationship between economic sanctions and respect for economic, social and cultural rights (Seventeenth session, 1997), U.N. Doc. E/C.12/1997/8 (1997); DE WET (note 1), at 199; Hans-Peter Gasser, *Collective Economic Sanctions and International Humanitarian Law*, 56 ZAÖRV 871, 880 (1996); *see International Law Association Berlin Conference (2004), Accountability of International Organisations*, 1 INTERNATIONAL ORGANIZATIONS LAW REVIEW (IOLR) 221, 250 (2004).

[18] DE WET (note 1), at 199; Bardo Fassbender, *Targeted Sanctions Imposed by the UN Security Council and Due Process Rights*, 3 IOLR 437, 446 (2006).

fair trial.[19] One systematic argument is that Art. 24 (2) UN Charter obliges the Security Council to act in accordance with the purposes of the UN and that Art. 1 UN Charter explicitly mentions the respect for human rights as one of these purposes. Another argument is that the UN, by contributing to the development of international human rights law, created the legitimate expectation that the UN itself will observe standards of due process.[20]

The former position, which denies that the Security Council is bound by international human rights, disregards the possibility that a historical perspective might be inappropriate where the Security Council targets individuals with sanctions. This development was not foreseen when the Charter was drafted. Rather, the latter position, arguing for the binding nature of international human rights, is convincing when it says that the Member States could not opt out their customary law obligations by founding the UN.[21]

II. The Listing as Terrorist Suspect

From an administrative perspective, the crucial element for the operation of the governance regime is the listing as a terrorist suspect on the Consolidated List maintained and managed by the Committee. The Committee takes the decision on whom to list as a terrorist suspect by examining whether the respective individual or entity is associated with the Taliban, Usama Bin Laden or the Al-Qaida organization.[22] The decision is taken with respect to a specific individual or entity.[23] It is followed by listing the name and other identifying data in the Consolidated List which triggers the legal consequences of the imposition of

---

[19] *See* Fassbender (note 18), 437, 446.

[20] De Wet & Nollkaemper, *Review of Security Council Decisions by National Courts*, 45 GERMAN YEARBOOK OF INTERNATIONAL LAW 166, 173 (2002).

[21] *See* Reinisch (note 14), at 858 ("... the assumption that the UN member states could have succeeded in collectively "opting out" of customary law and general principles of law by creating an international organization that would cease to be bound by those very obligations appears rather unconvincing.").

[22] SC Res. 1333 of 19 December 2000, para. 8(c); SC Res. 1617 of 29 July 2005, para. 2.

[23] *See* for details of the listing procedure, *infra*, B. III.1.

the sanctions on the listed person or entity. The Consolidated List thus has a double function: on the one hand, it reflects the decision of the Committee to subject a person to the sanctions regime. On the other hand, the Consolidated List serves as a database for the administrating levels of the EU and the UN Member States.

1. The Consolidated List of Terrorist Suspects

The Consolidated List[24] is divided into four sections: the first section contains the individuals considered as belonging to or associated with the Taliban, the second deals with the respective entities, the third section comprises the individuals considered as belonging to or associated with Al-Qaida and the fourth the respective entities. In June 2008, 380 individuals and 113 entities were listed.[25] Only eleven individuals and 24 entities were recorded as removed from the Consolidated List.[26] The names of the individuals and entities on the Consolidated List[27] are arranged in alphabetical order.

In case of individuals, the Consolidated List contains the following identification information: a permanent reference number, up to four names, title, designation, date and place of birth, aliases of good and low quality, nationality, passport number, national identification number, address, the date of entry into the Consolidated List and other data. In case of entities, the Consolidated List provides the following information: permanent reference number, name, present and former aliases, address, the date of entry into the Consolidated List and other data.

The maintenance of a list is also a typical feature of the exercise of public authority in multi-level systems: with its help, the competent authority on the national level may – on the basis of implementing national laws – act *vis-à-vis* the individual whereas at the international and regional level, the lists are necessary to ensure (or at least try to ensure) that there is legal certainty through a database explicitly identifying the

---

24 The Consolidated List was first introduced by SC Res. 1333 of 19 December 2000, para. 16(b).

25 *See* http://www.un.org/sc/committees/1267/consolist.shtml.

26 *Id.*

27 A document on the "Guidance for Searching the Consolidated List" of 18 October 2006 is available at: http://www.un.org/sc/committees/1267/pdf/sguidance.pdf.

suspects subject to the sanctions and that the lower levels implement the measures in a uniform manner.

2. The Legal Effect of the Listing

Every listed individual or entity is subject to the sanctions of a freeze of assets, a travel ban and an arms embargo by all UN members.[28] Only both elements – the listing and the sanctions – taken together generate the intended regulatory impact: the identification of the individual or entity listed and the legal consequence of the application of the sanctions.

The element of the listing may be likened – with all the prudence necessary with such comparisons – to the "*Verwaltungsakt*" that the German administrative law uses as its main instrument.[29] The difference between the sanctions regime and German administrative law, however, is that with the German "*Verwaltungsakt*" the acting authority directly addresses the citizen by prescribing a concrete behavior which directly applies to this individual.[30] In case of the listing there is *de iure* no such direct effect on the individual: *e.g.*, in the context of the travel ban, transit through the territory of UN Member States is not automatically prohibited since the individual is not the immediate addressee of the sanction. Assets are not frozen in the very moment when the UN takes the listing decision. It is still the UN Member State as the classical subject of international law that has to implement the listing by adopting a

---

[28] SC Res. 1333 of 19 December 2000, para. 2.

[29] The "*Verwaltungsakt*" requires by definition that there is a measure by an administrative body regulating a concrete, singular case with an effect on an individual outside this administration (Art. 35 of the German Administrative Procedure Act). With the "international administrative act" of the sanctions regime, the measure would be the listing and the administrative body would be the Committee. The Committee regulates because the listing triggers the legal consequence of the imposition of the sanctions. The listing concerns a concrete, singular case because the listing identifies and individualizes the targeted person. This listing has an impact on the individual outside the administration since it concerns not merely UN internal matters but imposes on UN Member States an obligation to subject – without further discretion of the UN Member States – a specific individual or entity to the sanctions. On the different instruments of international public authorities *see* Goldmann, in this volume.

[30] Directly comparable to the German "*Verwaltungsakt*" is WIPO's international registration of trademarks, *see* Kaiser, in this volume.

national law. For example, the freezing of assets still requires a transforming act providing for the asset freeze within the Member States' territory. The UN Member State remains the addressee of the UN sanctions regime. There is no direct effect on the individual. In this regard the phenomenon examined here may be referred to as a classical[31] international administrative act – compared to other international acts having *de iure* direct effect on the individual.[32]

A special feature of the UN Charter, however, generates a *de facto* effect of a listing on the listed individual: Art. 25 UN Charter says that UN Member States agree to accept and carry out the decisions of the Security Council in accordance with the UN Charter. This makes the listing decision of the Committee, which is a subsidiary body[33] of the Security Council, binding on the Member States. Furthermore, since the final addressee of the sanction is individually identifiable by the information included in the Consolidated List, the Member State does not have any discretion as to whether it implements the sanctions or not or as to whom to sanction.[34] The national level becomes the mere executing assistant of the Committee.

3. *Multi-level Aspects*

This leads to another particularity of the sanctions regime: its multilevel aspects. There are several different levels involved in the governance of the sanctions regime.

First, one must distinguish between the preconditions and the legal consequences of the sanctions regime. There are two preconditions: the decisive, formal precondition is the listing of the respective individual or entity. Prior to the listing, however, the Committee must come to the conclusion that there is a certain relationship between the individual or

---

31 Alluding to the classical period of international law with the States as the sole actors.

32 As in the case of WIPO, *see* Kaiser, in this volume.

33 *See* Committee Guidelines in the amended version of 12 February 2007, para. 1.

34 That is the difference to the general fight against terrorism that was started with SC Res. 1373 of 28 September 2001. This resolution provides for sanctions similar to the 1267 sanctions regime but does not foresee the maintenance of a Consolidated List at the UN level. That gives discretion to the States, which decide themselves whom to subject to the sanctions.

entity and the Taliban, Al-Qaida or Usama bin Laden. For the individual or entity to be put on the list, they must be "associated with" them.[35] Both preconditions were laid down in resolutions by the Security Council.[36] It is, however, the Committee that decides whether these preconditions are fulfilled. As far as the listing is concerned, the Committee even has the opportunity to influence the listing procedure by amending the respective section of its guidelines.

The legal consequences of a listing, *i.e.*, the application of the sanctions, are to be implemented by the UN Member States. There is no discretion as to the implementation. However, a similar distinction as in the German administrative law could apply here which could make a difference with regard to legal protection: German law differentiates between the discretion of the administrative body whether to act at all, and discretion regarding the means of action the administrative body chooses itself to fulfill its tasks.[37] The binding nature of the Security Council's decisions, as seen above, does not leave any discretion to the Member States as to "whether" they will act. Whether the Member States have full discretion on "how" they implement the measure remains an unanswered question. That, in turn, very much depends on the precision of the measures and the notions of asset freeze, travel ban and arms embargo. The more these measures leave room for interpretation, the wider the discretion of the national authorities implementing them. The interpretation of these terms would be a national act which could be challenged before national courts. In many national jurisdictions courts will have to take the resolutions of the Security Council into account in their findings. It might have been for this reason that the Committee has released a more precise explanation of what constitutes an "arms embargo."[38]

The fact that different levels are involved in the administration and implementation of the sanctions regime obstructs legal protection of the listed individual or entity since the competences of the different au-

---

35 *See* on this standard, *infra*, B.III.1.b.

36 SC Res. 1333 of 19 December 2000, para. 8(c).

37 HARTMUT MAURER, ALLGEMEINES VERWALTUNGSRECHT 135 (2006, 16th ed.).

38 Paper "Arms Embargo: Explanation of Terms" of 1 November 2006, available at: http://www.un.org/sc/committees/1267/pdf/ArmsEmbargo.ExplanationTermsEng.pdf. It is the only explanation of this kind so far.

thorities are not easy to perceive and the standards of review are blurred.

4. The "Sanctions Provision" as a Concise Formula for the Sanctions Regime

It would be useful to distill the results which were found above with regard to the legal effects of the listing, its multi-level aspects, and the institutional framework of the sanctions regime into one concise formula in the form of a "sanctions provision" which may read:

> Whenever an individual or entity is listed in the Consolidated List of the Committee as being associated with Usama bin Laden, Al-Qaida and/or the Taliban, all UN members are obliged to impose an asset freeze, a travel ban and an arms embargo on this individual or entity.

This "sanctions provision," on the one hand, puts the preconditions of the imposition of the sanctions (stemming from different legal documents) as well as the legal consequences of being listed into one sentence. On the other hand, it is formulated as a conditional "if – then" statement, which means that only if the preconditions are fulfilled do the legal consequences of imposing the sanctions follow.

Such a formulation of the sanctions provision enables the legal observer to recognize the preconditions required for the regime to become operative and to see the legal consequences that are triggered if these preconditions are fulfilled. Even more importantly, regarding the multi-level dimension, this sanctions provision paradigm facilitates a comprehensive understanding of the roles of the various levels involved: on the international level the Security Council as the authority prescribing the "associated with" precondition for being listed, the Sanctions Committee as the authority mandated with the listing and on the national level the UN Member States responsible for implementing the assets freeze, travel ban and arms embargo. At the same time, the subsequent question of (judicial) review of the sanctions regime can be examined more easily, since the sanctions provision allows for a clearer distinction between the named levels involved.

III. The Procedural Regime

The procedure[39] for amending the Consolidated List is laid down in the Committee Guidelines. To gain an insight into the administrative law aspects of the sanctions regime evolving from the amendments of the guidelines, it is worthwhile looking at the previous listing and de-listing procedure and to compare those standards to those now in force.

1. The Listing Procedure

a) The Previous Listing Procedure

According to the previous listing procedure the Committee was to update the Consolidated List regularly once it had agreed to include relevant information it had received from UN members or international or regional organizations.[40] Proposed additions to the Consolidated List were to include, to the extent possible, a description of the information that formed the basis for the listing.[41] They were also to include relevant and specific information to facilitate the identification by competent authorities of the persons and entities concerned, such as – in the case of individuals – the name, date of birth, place of birth, nationality etc. and in case of groups, undertakings or entities the name, acronyms, address, headquarters, subsidiaries, etc.[42] The Committee had to consider expeditiously requests to update the Consolidated List on the basis of relevant information received. It decided by consensus. If consensus could not be reached – even after further consultations – the matter had to be submitted to the Security Council.[43] The Committee had to communicate any modification to the Consolidated List immediately to the Member States and to make the updated Consolidated List available on the internet.[44]

---

[39] Generally on procedures in international institutions von Bernstorff, in this volume.

[40] Committee Guidelines in the revised version of 21 December 2005, para. 6(a).

[41] *Id.* at para. 6(b).

[42] *Id.* at para. 6(c).

[43] *Id.* at para. 4(a).

[44] *Id.* at para. 6(d) and (e).

b) The Amended Listing Procedure

According to the guidelines of 12 February 2007 the Committee is to update regularly the Consolidated List once it has agreed to include relevant information received from Member States or international or regional organizations.[45] The Member States are encouraged to establish a national mechanism or procedure to identify and assess appropriate candidates for listing.[46] They are further encouraged to seek additional information from the State(s) of residence and/or citizenship of the individual or entity concerned.[47] Member States must provide a statement of case with as much detail as possible on the basis(es) for the listing, including specific findings demonstrating the association or activities alleged, the nature of the supporting evidence (*e.g.*, intelligence, media, etc.), other supporting evidence and details of any connection with an already listed individual or entity.[48] Furthermore, Member States must use the cover sheet attached to the resolution[49] when proposing names for the Consolidated List. In addition to the information requested by the former guidelines, the information to be furnished under the amended guidelines should now include the following information for the purpose of accurate identification:

i. for individuals all available names, citizenship, gender, employment/occupation, national identification number, addresses and current location, and

ii. for entities, the tax or other identification number and other names by which it is known or was formerly known.[50]

The Committee will then consider the proposed listings on the basis of a standard which is called the "associated with" standard.[51]

The Committee takes the decision by consensus as under the previous procedure.[52] When new entries are included in the Consolidated List,

---

45 Committee Guidelines in the amended version of 12 February 2007, para. 6(a).

46 *Id.* at para. 6(b).

47 *Id.* at para. 6(c).

48 *Id.* at para. 6(d).

49 Annex I to SC Res. 1735 of 22 December 2006.

50 Committee Guidelines in the amended version of 12 February 2007, para. 6(e).

51 *See*, *infra*, in this section.

the publicly releasable portion of the statement of case must be included in the communication to the Member States.[53] It is for the State proposing a listing (the "designating" State/government) to identify those parts of the statement of case which may be released publicly.[54] The Secretariat shall, after publication but within two weeks after a name is added to the Consolidated List, notify the Permanent Mission of the country or countries where the individual or entity is believed to be located and, in the case of individuals, the country of which the person is a national. Furthermore, the Committee shall also include the publicly releasable portion of the statement of case, a description of the effects of designation, as set forth in the relevant resolutions, the Committee's procedures for considering the de-listing requests, and the provisions of resolution 1452 (2002), which governs the possible exceptions from the asset freeze.[55] After having received this notification the Member States are called upon to take reasonable steps to inform the listed individual or entity of the measures imposed on them, the Committee's guidelines, the listing and de-listing procedures, and the provisions of resolution 1452 (2002) governing exceptions.[56]

The Committee has to decide on a listing by applying the "associated with" standard, which means that a relationship between the potential terrorist suspect and Usama bin Laden, Al-Qaida and/or the Taliban must be established. The establishment of such a relationship does not, however, trigger legal consequences for the UN members, least of all for the individual concerned. It is rather by virtue of the listing on the basis of this preliminary examination that the UN members are under a duty to implement the sanctions against the named individual or entity.

Paragraph 2 of resolution 1617 (2005) sets forth that "acts or activities indicating that an individual, group, undertaking, or entity is 'associated with' Al-Qaida, Usama bin Laden or the Taliban include:

- participating in the financing, planning, facilitating, preparing, or perpetrating of acts or activities by, in conjunction with, under the name of, on behalf of, or in support of;
- supplying, selling or transferring arms and related material to;

---

52 Committee Guidelines in the amended version of 12 February 2007, para. 4(a).

53 *Id.* at para. 6(g).

54 *Id.* at para. 6(d).

55 *Id.* at para. 6(h).

56 *Id.*

- recruiting for; or
- otherwise supporting acts or activities of;

Al-Qaida, Usama bin Laden or the Taliban, or any cell, affiliate, splinter group or derivative thereof."

c) Assessment

Although the new requirements for being listed are not in a well prepared order, the different aspects form a picture of an evolving administrative procedure which can (compared with the earlier standards) at least improve the protection of the individual already in the stadium before being listed. The main elements of protection for the individual are the requirements of a statement of case,[57] the accompanying cover sheet,[58] the express introduction of the "associated with" standard, and the short time periods for notifications as well as the requirement of detailed information relating to the individual. Also, it is expressly mentioned that the Committee must agree to include someone in the Consolidated List.[59]

The statement of case imposes a duty on the designating State to provide explanations. The designating State has to justify the proposal not only by a narrative description of the respective information but also by a detailed collection of evidence that allows the Committee to assess the case objectively and to apply its "associated with" standard. The requirement of a cover sheet which is mandated by resolution[60] and annexed to the resolution as a form[61] guarantees the necessary factual background: all the information is collected by the Committee in the same way, so that nothing is forgotten and the prescribed written form ensures that nothing gets lost. The level of detail of the information reduces the risk that the wrong persons are listed or that errors concerning names occur. After the listing, the detailed data facilitates the identi-

---

57 This requirement can be seen as the principle of stating reasons as an element of the rule of law, *see* von Bernstorff, in this volume.

58 This requirement can be seen as an element of good governance, specifically transparency, *see* von Bernstorff, in this volume; International Law Association Berlin Conference (note 17), 221, 229.

59 Committee Guidelines in the amended version of 12 February 2007, para. 6(g).

60 SC Res. 1735 of 22 December 2006, para. 7.

61 Annex I to SC Res. 1735 of 22 December 2006.

fication of the individual or entity against which the competent national authorities are to take action. The application of the "associated with" standard gives the Committee's decision-making process an impetus away from a political decision and towards a decision according to written legal standards. The potential advantage for the individual is that there is at least some legal certainty as to the standards applicable to listings. The rule that the Committee must agree to any inclusion in the Consolidated List indicates that listing new individuals or entities is not merely to be thought of as being an automatic procedure after the information of the designating State is submitted to the Committee but requires a formal and informed decision. The mandate of the Secretariat to notify the Permanent Mission within two weeks after a name is added to the Consolidated List avoids putting the individual into limbo about the status of the listing and permits the person or entity to institute timely remedies against this listing. However, for the listed persons this only works in conjunction with the call upon States to inform them of the designation. This notification after a new listing is thus simultaneously the first and most important step for a de-listing. The notification should inform the individual or entity of the measures imposed on them and include the Committee's guidelines, the listing and de-listing procedures and the provisions of resolution 1452 (2002) governing exceptions. While there is no disclosure of the reasons for the listing, as is known from national administrative law,[62] the details provided in the notification, in addition to the plain information of the listing itself, make the person or entity concerned aware of the consequences of such a listing and enable them to challenge the listing by pursuing a de-listing procedure or at least by applying for an exception from the asset freeze. Thus, the protection of the individual is improved by the new amendments to the listing procedure.

2. *The De-listing Procedure*

a) The Previous De-listing Procedure

The previous de-listing procedure[63] had to be initiated by the petitioner (individual, groups, undertakings, entities) by asking the government of residence and/or citizenship to request a review of the case in the Sanc-

---

[62] Section 39 of the German Administrative Procedure Act.

[63] The latest version to be found in the Guidelines of the Committee at: http://www.un.org/sc/ committees/1267/pdf/1267_guidelines.pdf.

tions Committee.[64] At the same time, the petitioner had to provide justification for the de-listing request, offer relevant information, and request support for de-listing.[65] The petitioned government was then to approach the government originally proposing designation bilaterally to seek additional information and to hold consultations on the request.[66] Also, the designating government(s) could request additional information from the petitioned government. The governments involved could also consult with the Chairman of the Committee during their bilateral consultations.[67] If the petitioned government, after having reviewed any additional information, wished to pursue a de-listing request, it was to seek to persuade the designating government(s) to submit jointly or separately a request for de-listing to the Committee. However, the petitioned government was also able to submit a de-listing request without such an accompanying petition from the designating government.[68] The Committee decided by consensus. If consensus could not be reached, even after further consultations, the matter was to be submitted to the Security Council.[69]

b) The Amended De-listing Procedure

A recent novelty was the creation of the so-called "focal point," which can receive de-listing requests directly from individuals, entities etc.[70] It was established as part of the Security Council's endeavor to ensure fair and clear procedures for removing individuals and entities from sanctions lists.[71] The focal point is an entity which the Secretary-General was requested to establish within the Secretariat (Security Council Sub-

---

[64] Committee Guidelines in the amended version of 29 November 2006, para. 8(a).

[65] *Id.* at para. 8(a).

[66] *Id.* at para. 8(b).

[67] *Id.* at para. 8(c).

[68] *Id.* at para. 8(d).

[69] *Id.* at para. 8(e).

[70] SC Res. 1730 of 19 December 2006, para. 1.

[71] SC Res. 1730 of 19 December 2006, 5th recital; *see* also the statement of the President of the Security Council of 22 June 2006 (S/PRST/2006/28) and the respective call upon the Security Council of the Heads of State and Government in the World Summit Outcome Document of 16 September 2005 (GA Res. 60/1 of 16 September 2005, para.109).

sidiary Organs Branch).[72] It is "focal" because it works for *all* active Sanctions Committees.[73] Its main tasks are, *inter alia*, to receive de-listing requests from petitioners, *i.e.*, individual(s), groups, undertakings, and/or entities on the Sanctions Committee's list,[74] to acknowledge receipt of the request, to inform the petitioner of the general procedure for processing that request,[75] to forward the request to the designating government(s) and to the government(s) of citizenship and residence,[76] and to inform the petitioner of the Committee's decision to grant the de-listing petition or to dismiss it.[77] It is thus clear that the function of the focal point is of a purely auxiliary nature: it merely receives and forwards requests and other information.

The petitioner for a de-listing is free to choose the previous de-listing procedure via their government of residence or citizenship instead of addressing the focal point.[78] When the focal point receives the de-listing request, it forwards the request to the designating government(s) and to the governments(s) of citizenship and residence for their information and possible comments. Those governments are encouraged to consult with the designating government(s) before recommending de-listing.[79] If, after these consultations, any of these governments recommends de-listing, that government will forward its recommendation with an explanation either through the focal point or directly to the Chairman of the Sanctions Committee, who will then place the request on the Committee's agenda.[80] The Committee decides by consensus. If consensus cannot be reached, further consultations are undertaken. If consensus still cannot be reached, the matter shall be submitted to the Security Council.[81] If any of the consulted governments opposes the request, the focal point will so inform the Committee. All Committee members are

---

72 SC Res. 1730 of 19 December 2006, para. 1.

73 *See* SC Res. 1730 of 19 December 2006, para. 2.

74 Committee Guidelines in the amended version of 12 February 2007, para. 8(d)(i).

75 *Id.* at para. 8(d)(iv).

76 *Id.* at para. 8(d)(v).

77 *Id.* at para. 8(d)(viii).

78 *Id.* at para. 8(b).

79 *Id.* at para. 8(d)(v).

80 *Id.* at para. 8(d)(vi)(a).

81 *Id.* at para. 8(f).

encouraged to share information they possess in support of the de-listing request with the designating government(s) and the government(s) of residence and citizenship.[82] If, after a reasonable time (3 months), none of the consulting governments comment or indicate that they are still working on the request and require additional time, the focal point will so notify all members of the Committee and provide copies of the de-listing request.[83] Any Committee member may then, after consultation with the designating government, recommend de-listing. If, after one month, no Committee member recommends de-listing, the request shall be deemed rejected. The Chairman of the Committee shall inform the focal point accordingly.[84] The focal point will inform the petitioner of the decision once it has been taken.[85]

c) Assessment

The fact that the focal point can receive de-listing requests directly from a petitioner provides the individual with the opportunity to access directly the UN level instead of asking the State of residence or citizenship for diplomatic protection – a procedure which entails the uncertainty of the petitioned State's discretion,[86] often involves political considerations, and which usually takes some time for the decision to be taken. This is particularly detrimental when such drastic measures as an asset freeze apply, as is the case under the sanctions regime examined here. In this regard, the amendment of the de-listing procedure is no doubt an advantage for the individual.

However, this benefit of direct access to the level where the listing decision is taken which seems to promise an effective remedy is put into perspective by the fact that the focal point does not decide on the de-listing and does not even forward the de-listing request to the Sanctions Committee for decision. Instead, the designating government(s) and the government(s) of residence and citizenship have the opportunity to comment on the de-listing request first.

---

82 *Id.* at para. 8(d)(vi)(b).

83 *Id.* at para. 8(d)(vi)(c).

84 *Id.*

85 *Id.* at para. 8(d)(viii).

86 *See* Wilhelm K. Geck, *Diplomatic Protection*, *in* I ENCYCLOPEDIA OF PUBLIC INTERNATIONAL LAW 1045, 1051 (Rudolf Bernhardt ed., 1992).

Given this background, the search for principles of international institutional law in the de-listing procedure with regard to the focal point is not as fruitful as it is for the listing procedure.

IV. Review and Enforcement of the Sanctions Regime

Apart from several general obligations – mainly of the Committee – to report on the sanctions regime,[87] the determination of Usama bin Laden, Al-Qaida and the Taliban as a threat to peace, the decision to impose sanctions and the review of these decisions are measures under Chapter VII of the UN Charter and thus exclusively within the scope of the Security Council's competence. The question whether the Security Council is subject to review by other bodies, *e.g.*, by the International Court of Justice, is still a contentious issue.[88]

This must be distinguished from the review of the listing procedure and the listing itself: while amending the listing procedure is generally within the Committee's competence,[89] the review of an established listing is highly disputed.

1. Internal Review of the Listing

The established listing on the Consolidated List is in practice the most controversial issue of review with regard to the legal protection of the

---

[87] Committee Guidelines in the amended version of 12 February 2007, paras. 4(d), 5(b), 5(f), 7, 11(a), 6(i).

[88] Bernd Martenczuk, *The Security Council, the International Court and Judicial Review: What Lessons from Lockerbie?*, 10 EUROPEAN JOURNAL OF INTERNATIONAL LAW 520 (1999) (with references to further opinions on the topic in footnote 5).

[89] Committee Guidelines in the amended version of 12 February 2007, para. 5(h). The guidelines may, however, also be influenced by resolutions of the Security Council, *see* the annex to SC Res. 1730 of 19 December 2006. Before the Security Council influenced the procedure here by prescribing details of the procedure, the former de-listing procedure regulated solely by the Committee was applied for more than four years, *cf.* the adoption of the Guidelines on 7 November 2002. This internal review of the guidelines must be distinguished from judicial review which will meet the same difficulties as the judicial review of the Security Council whose subsidiary organ the Committee is.

listed individual.[90] The decision on the de-listing of a person or entity is initially an internal one taken by the Sanctions Committee on the UN level.[91] If the necessary consensus cannot be reached within the Committee, the matter may be submitted to the Security Council.[92]

There is no clear and objective standard of review to be applied in the de-listing procedure. In its latest resolution on the sanctions regime, the Security Council merely decided that the Committee "may" consider, *inter alia,* whether the individual or entity was placed on the Consolidated List due to a mistake of identity, or no longer meets the criteria of the "associated with" standard,[93] because, for example, the person is deceased or has demonstrably severed all associations with Al-Qaida and its supporters.[94] Since the Committee decides by consensus, one opposing vote can block the decision for a de-listing. There is also no duty in the Guidelines of the Committee to give reasons if the petition for de-listing is rejected. The only provision which could be said to relate to evidence within the de-listing procedure puts the petitioner at a disadvantage: it is on him to justify the de-listing request, offer relevant information and request support for de-listing.[95] This is the opposite of the presumption of innocence.

As an internal procedure conducted by the Committee itself and subject to no clear legal standard, the de-listing is a procedure that falls far short of a judicial review which would include a decision by an independent judge examining the cases on the basis of legal rules. Such legal protection is not available on the UN level.

---

90 *See e.g.* Frowein (note 1), at 793 *et seq.*; Merhdad Payandeh, *Rechtskontrolle des UN-Sicherheitsrats durch staatliche und überstaatliche Gerichte*, 66 (ZAÖRV) 41 (2006); Fassbender (note 18), at 477 (with further references in footnote 88).

91 Committee Guidelines in the amended version of 12 February 2007, para. 8(f). For the details of the de-listing procedure *see, supra,* B.III.2.

92 Committee Guidelines in the amended version of 12 February 2007, para. 8(f).

93 As described above, B.III.1.b.

94 SC Res. 1735 of 22 December 2006, para. 14.

95 Committee Guidelines in the amended version of 12 February 2007, para. 8(a).

2. *External Review of the Listing*

The question thus arises whether such legal protection could be provided by an external review of the listing by regional or national courts. Before the question is addressed as to what implications the assumed obligation of the Security Council to respect human rights[96] may have for an external review, the current practice of the European Court of First Instance (CFI) concerning cases challenging listings will be presented.

a) Practice of Regional Courts

In the sense of an *external* review within the multi-level system, the European Court of First Instance had to deal with cases brought to annul listings in the terrorist suspects list on the European level which is based on the Consolidated List entries on the UN level. The CFI has so far decided on four cases on the 1267 sanctions regime examined here, all of which are now pending before the European Court of Justice (ECJ).[97] As to the scope of review, the CFI held that the EC was bound by the obligations under the UN Charter[98] and that therefore a review of EC regulations based on Security Council resolutions was generally precluded,[99] though in case of an infringement of *ius cogens*, judicial review was possible.[100] However, with regard to the alleged infringements in the first two cases[101] of the applicants' right to property, their right to

---

96 *See* B. I. 3.

97 Case T-306/01, *Yusuf and Al Barakaat International Foundation v. Council of the European Union and Commission of the European Communities*, 2005 ECR-II 3533 (appealed to the ECJ, C-415/05); Case T-315/01, *Kadi v. Council and Commission*, 2005 ECR-II 3649 (appealed to the ECJ, C-402/05); Case T-253/02, *Chafiq Ayadi v. Council of the European Union*, 2006 ECR-II 2139 (appealed to the ECJ, C-403/06) and Case T-49/04, *Faraj Hassan v. Council of the European Union and Commission of the European Communities*, 2006 ECR-II 52 (appealed to the ECJ, C-399/06).

98 *See* Case T-306/01, *Yusuf and Al Barakaat International Foundation v. Council of the European Union and Commission of the European Communities* (note 97), at para. 243.

99 *Id.* at para. 276.

100 *Id.* at para. 277.

101 Case T-306/01, *Yusuf and Al Barakaat International Foundation v. Council of the European Union and Commission of the European Communities* (note 97); Case T-315/01, *Kadi v. Council and Commission* (note 97).

a fair hearing and their right to judicial review, the Court held that there had been no violation of *ius cogens*. In his Opinion on these two cases, the Advocate General argues that the ECJ must annul the Council regulation that lists the appellant because the regulation violates human rights guaranteed under the EC legal order.[102] In the other two cases[103] the Court held with regard to the relationship of the different jurisdictions (UN, EC, national) that it was for the national courts to grant diplomatic protection to the individual seeking to be removed from the Consolidated List on the UN level.[104] In the *Hassan* case, the CFI developed certain supranational fair trial principles that shall guide the decisions of Member States on granting diplomatic protection in cases of de-listing requests.[105]

The obligation of the Member States under EC law to allow their citizens effectively to argue their case for de-listing before the competent national authorities can be likened to the right to be heard and to defend oneself.[106] The obligation not to refuse considering a petition for de-listing too hastily based merely on the fact that the petitioner has not furnished precise and relevant information might be seen as a facilitation of defense. It should be noted, however, that this is not the same as the presumption of innocence. Thus, in multi-level terms, EU law

---

[102] Opinion of Advocate General Poiares Maduro in Case T-315/01, *Kadi v. Council and Commission* (note 97), appealed to the ECJ, C-402/05, para. 56, and Opinion of Advocate General Poiares Maduro in Case T-306/01, *Yusuf and Al Barakaat International Foundation v. Council of the European Union and Commission of the European Communities* (note 97), appealed as Case C-415/05, *Al Barakaat International Foundation v. Council of the European Union and Commission of the European Communities*, para. 56.

[103] Case T-253/02, *Chafiq Ayadi v. Council of the European Union* (note 97); Case T-49/04, *Faraj Hassan v. Council of the European Union and Commission of the European Communities* (note 97).

[104] Case T-253/02, *Chafiq Ayadi v. Council of the European Union* (note 97), at paras. 147-149.

[105] Case T-49/04, *Faraj Hassan v. Council of the European Union and Commission of the European Communities* (note 97), at paras. 115, 122.

[106] It must be kept in mind here, however, that these rights are based on European law and do not form part of an independent international administrative law, although they might inspire discussion on it. *See* Case T-49/04, *Faraj Hassan v. Council of the European Union and Commission of the European Communities* (note 97), at paras. 115, 122.

obliges the national authorities to file a de-listing request on the international (UN) level.[107]

b) What Elements Constitute a Right of Due Process?

If we assume at this point that the UN Security Council is bound[108] by international human rights, including the right of due process,[109] the question of what the elements of this right are arises.

A recent study commissioned by the UN Office of Legal Affairs argues that as a minimum standard of "fair and clear procedures" the right of due process should include *inter alia* the right of a listed person or entity to an effective remedy against an individual measure before an impartial institution or body previously established.[110] This minimum standard could be derived from a comparative analysis of the respective guarantees in international human rights treaties and national constitutional law.[111]

Specifying the single elements of the right to an effective remedy, the study clarifies that "remedy" means the establishment of any of several different options available to the Security Council, such as an international tribunal, an ombudsman office, an inspection panel, a commission of inquiry or a committee of experts.[112] "Effectiveness" includes considerations such as accessibility and speed of procedure, the fair opportunity to put forward one's case, a well reasoned decision and compliance with the decision.[113] According to a strict interpretation of the term, an effective remedy requires that the competent body has the

---

[107] The case law of the European Court of Human Rights (ECtHR), which also had to decide on a case on UN sanctions (*see* Eur. Court H. R., *Bosphorus Hava Yollari Turizm Ve Ticdaret Anonim Sirketi (Bosphorus Airways) v. Ireland*, Judgment of 30 June 2005, Reports of Judgments and Decisions 2005-VI, 107) could also be surveyed when examining external reviews of listings by regional courts.

[108] *See* B. I. 3.

[109] On the discussion of due process standards in the context of decisions on the refugee status, *see* Smrkolj, in this volume.

[110] Fassbender (note 18), at 476.

[111] *Id.*

[112] *Id.* at 479-480.

[113] *Id.* at 480.

power to take binding decisions.[114] "Impartiality" requires that matters are decided on an impartial basis, on the basis of facts and in accordance with the law, without any restrictions or improper influences.[115]

c) Application of the Due Process Standards to the Current State of Legal Protection Against UN Sanctions

If these standards are applied to the current state of legal protection of the listed individual, the suspicion that legal protection against UN sanctions is inadequate is corroborated: the "remedy" is merely the request for a de-listing addressed to the Sanctions Committee. Notwithstanding the improvement of the individual's legal situation by the option of directly petitioning the UN, rather than requesting diplomatic protection, both the State(s) of residence and/or citizenship and the designating State(s) can still prevent a de-listing request from reaching the Sanctions Committee. The newly established "focal point" thus does not improve the individual's legal protection: it is only a body that administers a request but does not have the power to decide on the de-listing. With regard to "effectiveness," accessibility is slightly improved by the establishment of the focal point. However, the Sanctions Committee is still not directly accessible for individuals or entities. Even if the de-listing request reaches the Committee, the decision is not taken "impartially," *i.e.*, in accordance with established law and procedure and without any undue influence since the Sanctions Committee, with its members being identical with those of the Security Council, remains a political body driven by the individual States' interests. It is unreasonable to assume that such a committee will objectively apply existent legal rules. Thus, legal protection with due process standards is still not available on the UN level. On the EU level, the CFI provides a remedy and is accessible and impartial within the sense of the above definition. However, as seen above, the case law of the CFI limits the legal protection against UN sanctions to violations of *ius cogens* and denies such a violation in the cases surveyed.

---

114 *See* White Paper "Strengthening Targeted Sanctions Through Fair and Clear Prcedures," prepared by the Watson Institute Targeted Sanctions Project, Brown University of 30 March 2006, 55 note 94. The paper is available at: http://watsoninstitute.org/pub/Strengthening_Targeted_Sanctions.pdf.

115 Fassbender (note 18), at 480-481.

3. *Enforcement*

The enforcement of the sanctions regime[116] is the Security Council's major interest and corresponding provisions can be traced back to the regime's initial resolution 1267 (1999). Much more than the review of the listing or the sanctions themselves, it was central to the UN's efforts from the very beginning to ensure that its Member States implement the adopted sanctions. The Committee was established at a time when there was not yet a Consolidated List to manage and was tasked with seeking information from all Member States regarding the action taken by them, monitoring violations of the regime and improving the monitoring of the implementation of the measures.[117] Soon after the Committee was formed, a committee of experts was asked to make recommendations regarding the way the sanctions could best be monitored[118] which led to the establishment of a Monitoring Group of five experts, which was to monitor implementation.[119] Later, the Monitoring Group was succeeded by the Monitoring Team of eight experts. The Monitoring Team was provided a much more detailed catalog of responsibilities, primarily dealing with monitoring and reporting to the Committee.[120] Recent mandates have also given it the responsibility of evaluating cases of non-compliance and the submission of case studies of respective States.[121] The Monitoring Team only assists the Committee and is not competent to impose any measures on States found not to be in compliance.

C. Concluding Thoughts

In summation, it may be concluded that the Al Qaida Sanctions Committee is a particularly fruitful subject-matter of study with regard to the enhancement of the law of international institutions. There are findings with respect to different categories of principles of international in-

---

[116] On the enforcement authority of international institutions *see* Röben, in this volume.

[117] SC Res. 1267 of 15 October 1999, paras. 6(a), 6(d) and 12.

[118] SC Res. 1333 of 19 December 2000, para. 15(a).

[119] SC Res. 1363 of 30 July 2001, para. 4(a).

[120] SC Res. 1526 of 30 January 2004, para. 6 and Annex to the resolution.

[121] SC Res. 1735 of 22 December 2006, para. 32 and Annex to the resolution.

stitutional law. Further, adding the ideas of the "sanctions provision" and of the listing as an international administrative act from the legal documents underlying this regime may facilitate scholarly debate.

I. Principles Enabling the Exercise of Public Authority on the International Level

The Security Council's actions are autonomous from the Member States. It decides itself whether Chapter VII is applicable and which measures are to be taken. Furthermore, its decisions are binding and the Member States do not have discretion as to whether or not to implement them. In implementing the sanctions regime the UN Member States must cooperate with the UN. This is not only true with respect to the implementation of the measures in their territory but also the provision of the necessary information to the Committee to enable it to decide about a listing.

II. Principles Restraining the Exercise of Public Authority on the International Level

There are weighty arguments in favor of the view that the Security Council, and with it the Committee, are bound by human rights.[122] This suggests that listings should be examined using human rights as a standard. The listing procedure has also experienced some interesting developments: it is now expressly provided that the Committee must first 'agree' before it includes information in the list. This procedural requirement implies the rule of law in a manner similar to two procedural obligations imposed on the Member States: the obligation to provide a statement of case with the reasons for the listing and a cover sheet for a clear identification of the individual or entity concerned.[123] The "associated with" standard is an element (even if a weak one) of legal clarity and certainty, *i.e.*, rule of law. It is reminiscent of domestic administrative law, which requires an explicit statutory basis for decisions that affect human rights. The obligations of the UN to notify the Member State of the listed person or entity of the listing and the Member State's

122 *See* B. I. 3.

123 This overlaps with the enabling principle of cooperation seen above.

obligation to inform the individual accordingly can be seen as laid down in the interest of transparency and in order to enable the listed person to challenge the listing. Nevertheless, participation and transparency are not yet sufficiently developed,[124] and reasoned decisions[125] are not available. The restraining principles must be further developed and must include the provision of reasons for the listing decision and the application of the principle of proportionality, *i.e.*, the drastic effect the listing has for the individual must be balanced and weighed against the goal of fighting terrorism.

III. The Sanctions Regime as an Example of an International Composite Administration

The sanctions regime is an example of an international composite administration.[126] Listings as well as other decisions concerning the sanctions regime are taken on the international level by the UN as centralized decisions, whereas the concomitant obligations to implement the listing decisions are decentralized, lying with the UN Member States.

IV. Principle of Accountability

The Security Council's general decision to impose sanctions on Al-Qaida, the Taliban and its supporters is a political decision and not subject to review initiated by individuals. Concerning the listing, the Security Council (and thus the Committee) can be assumed to be bound by human rights as principles restraining its actions, as seen above. These restraining principles would be meaningless if the Security Council could not be held accountable in case of human rights violations. In this regard, national or regional courts may examine listings by applying human rights as a standard of review as long as international mechanisms of judicial review are lacking. Thus, potential plans of national political actors to pursue unhindered a strict terrorism policy on the in-

---

[124] *See* de Wet, *Holding International Bureaucracies Accountable*, in this volume.

[125] As stipulated by the International Law Association (note 17), 238.

[126] *See* von Bogdandy & Dann, *International Composite Administration*, in this volume.

ternational level may boomerang on them and may be frustrated by the national or regional judiciary. Such scrutiny by national or regional courts may not disrupt effective implementation and functioning of the sanctions regime too much since such national decisions are valid only within the territory of the respective UN member or in the respective region. Rather, the UN may be motivated by this to establish judicial review on the UN level.

WIPO's International Registration of Trademarks: An International Administrative Act Subject to Examination by the Designated Contracting Parties

*By Karen Kaiser**

---

* The author would like to thank participants in the research project, especially Professor Armin von Bogdandy, Professor Rüdiger Wolfrum, Dr. Jochen von Bernstorff, Dr. Philipp Dann, Matthias Goldmann and Ingo Venzke and the participants of the International Workshop, especially Professor Giacinto della Cananea and Professor Christian Tietje for valuable comments and suggestions on the drafts, colleague Marc Jacob for reading the draft and Eva Richter for formatting.

A. von Bogdandy et al. (eds.), *The Exercise of Public Authority by International Institutions*, Beiträge zum ausländischen öffentlichen Recht und Völkerrecht 210,
DOI 10.1007/978-3-642-04531-8_6, © Springer-Verlag Berlin Heidelberg 2010

A. Introduction

Although the World Intellectual Property Organization (WIPO) is a technical intergovernmental organization with a limited mandate, it has been entrusted with a panoply of tasks. These include, *inter alia*, the international harmonization of intellectual property law, the administration of fee-based global intellectual property protection services, and the delivery of dispute resolution services to individuals. While the central role of WIPO in the continuous development of substantive intellectual property law has been questioned by developing countries,[1] the administrative activities of WIPO have remained largely unscathed by critique and, therefore, have not attracted much attention. They revolve around the international filing, registration or recognition of industrial property rights, such as patents, industrial designs and trademarks,[2] and provide an interesting perspective on the law of international institutions.

Dating back to 1891 and, thus, presenting itself as one of the earliest examples for the exercise of public authority by international institutions, the international registration of trademarks introduced the concept of an "international administrative act subject to examination by the des-

[1] Peter-Tobias Stoll, *WIPO – World Intellectual Property Organization*, in II UNITED NATIONS – LAW, POLICIES AND PRACTICE 1437 (Rüdiger Wolfrum ed., 1995).

[2] Intellectual property is traditionally divided into two branches, industrial property on the one hand and copyright and related rights on the other hand. In contrast to industrial property rights, copyright and related rights do not need to be registered.

ignated contracting parties."[3] This concept comprises administrative acts that fulfill the criteria of domestic concepts of administrative decisions, but are performed by international authorities that share their decision-making power with designated contracting parties (*i.e.* domestic authorities).[4] In comparison with modern instruments of international institutions, the "international administrative act subject to examination by the designated contracting parties" appears to be surprisingly progressive. It is, on the one hand, directly applicable in the domestic legal orders of the contracting parties, and anticipates, on the other hand, elements of modern forms of administrative cooperation between supranational and domestic authorities within the European Community (EC).

Before discussing this concept and interrelated procedural questions in more detail (C.), an introductory overview will be given of the subject area, legal regime and interests involved (B.). In the end, the international registration of trademarks will be assessed (D.) and possibilities of future developments discussed (E.).

B. The International Registration of Trademarks in Context

I. Subject Area: Trademarks

Trademarks are distinctive signs, which identify certain goods or services such as those produced or provided by a specific person or enterprise. Trademark protection helps consumers identify and purchase a product or service because its nature and quality, indicated by its unique trademark, meets their needs. The trademark holder has the exclusive right to prevent unauthorized third parties from using said trademark, or a confusingly similar trademark, so as to prevent custom-

---

3 The German translation reads "internationaler Verwaltungsakt unter Prüfungsvorbehalt" borrowing from the term "Transnationalität unter Prüfungsvorbehalt" introduced by Eberhard Schmidt-Aßmann, *Verwaltungskooperation und Verwaltungskooperationsrecht in der Europäischen Gemeinschaft*, 31 EUROPARECHT 270, 300-301 (1996).

4 Designated contracting parties are those states or intergovernmental organizations in which the international applicant wishes his trademark to be protected.

ers and the general public from being misled and the trademark itself from being exploited economically.[5] Trademarks can be protected on the basis of either use or registration. Full trademark protection, however, is properly secured only by registration.[6]

II. Legal Regime: Madrid System for the International Registration of Trademarks

The international registration of trademarks is governed by two treaties: the Madrid Agreement concerning the International Registration of Marks[7] (Madrid Agreement), concluded in 1891, and the Protocol relating to it[8] (Madrid Protocol), concluded in 1989. The Madrid Agreement and the Madrid Protocol together form the Madrid system for the international registration of trademarks (Madrid system). The aim of the Madrid Protocol was to persuade Japan, the United Kingdom and the United States of America to join the Madrid system by making some of its rules more accommodating.[9] The two treaties are parallel instruments, albeit independent from one another, and states may adhere to either one or to both. In addition, an "intergovernmental organization" which maintains its own office for the registration of trademarks may become party to the Madrid Protocol.[10] In reality, only supranational organizations fulfill this criterion, such as the EC that maintains the Of-

---

5 FREDERICK ABBOTT, THOMAS COTTIER & FRANCIS GURRY, THE INTERNATIONAL INTELLECTUAL PROPERTY SYSTEM: COMMENTARY AND MATERIALS, PART ONE 128-131 (1999); INTRODUCTION TO INTELLECTUAL PROPERTY: THEORY AND PRACTICE 183-186 (WIPO ed., 1997).

6 WIPO (note 5), 194.

7 UNTS, vol. 828, 389.

8 O.J. 2003 L 296/22.

9 The main differences are that, under the Madrid Protocol, English is introduced as the second procedural language (instead of French only), international registration can be requested on the basis of a domestic trademark application (instead of domestic trademark registrations only) and contracting parties of the Madrid Protocol can extend the period for the refusal of protection from 12 to 18 months, which is of particular importance for states and intergovernmental organizations having comprehensive official examinations. *See* 27 INTERNATIONAL REVIEW OF INTELLECTUAL PROPERTY AND COMPETITION LAW (IIC), 145, 146 (1996).

10 Madrid Protocol, Art. 14(1)(b).

fice for Harmonization in the Internal Market (Trade Marks and Designs) (OHIM).[11]

Both treaties are global protection system treaties. Global protection system treaties form one of the three groups of intellectual property treaties administered by WIPO.[12] They ensure that one international filing, registration or recognition of a given industrial property right will have effect in any of the designated contracting parties. Due to the principle of territoriality, the holder of an industrial property right registered under domestic industrial property law is only protected within the territorial boundaries inside which the domestic law is enforceable.[13] Usually, the holder interested in registering his industrial property right outside the territorial boundaries of his home country has to file additional domestic applications in the respective countries of interest. This can be costly and administratively cumbersome, as the holder has to pay different fees and submit his application in different languages, which must also be in accordance with the relevant domestic procedural rules and regulations.

Alternatively, the applicant or holder of an industrial property right may make use of the WIPO-administered global protection system treaties. These are not able to overcome the principle of territoriality, but simplify and reduce the cost of making individual applications in other countries than the home country. In the case of the Madrid system, the applicant or holder of a trademark may file a single application

---

11 Council Regulation (EC) No 40/94 of 20 December 1993 on the Community Trademark, O.J. (1994) L 11/1, Art. 2 and 111 *et seq.*; Council Regulation (EC) No 6/2002 of 12 December 2001 on Community Designs, O.J. 2002 L 3/1, Art. 2 and 62 *et seq. See also* http://oami.europa.eu/en/default.htm.

12 The other groups are intellectual property protection treaties and classification treaties. Intellectual property protection treaties, such as the Paris Convention for the Protection of Intellectual Property (Paris Convention) (UNTS, vol. 828, 305), define internationally agreed basic standards of intellectual property protection in each country. Classification treaties, such as the Strasbourg Agreement Concerning the International Patent Classification (UNTS, vol. 1160, 483), create classification systems that organize information concerning inventions, trademarks and industrial designs into indexed, manageable structures for easy retrieval.

13 On the principle of territoriality in trademark law, see Graeme B. Dinwoodie, *Trademarks and Territory: Detaching Trademark Law from the Nation-State*, 41 HOUSTON LAW JOURNAL 886-973 (2004); Friedrich-Karl Beier, *Territoriality of Trademark Law and International Trade*, 1 INTERNATIONAL REVIEW OF INDUSTRIAL PROPERTY AND COPYRIGHT LAW 48-72 (1970).

with the International Bureau of WIPO (International Bureau) through the intermediary of his home country office.[14] The application is submitted in a single language and only one set of fees is levied. A trademark so registered is equivalent to an application or a registration of the same trademark effected directly in each of the contracting parties designated by the applicant or holder of the trademark.[15] If the trademark office of a designated country does not refuse protection within a specified period, the protection of the trademark is the same as if it had been registered by that office.

III. Interests Involved: Economic Interests of Exporting Enterprises

Among the specialized agencies of the United Nations (UN), WIPO is exceptional in so far as it provides economic services to individuals.[16] Among the WIPO-administered global protection system treaties, the Patent Cooperation Treaty, concluded in 1970, is the most successful.[17] It is the global protection system treaty with the most contracting parties (137 in 2007) and the most applications filed per year (145,300 in 2006).[18] The Madrid system is the second most successful global protection system with a total of 80 contracting parties and 36,471 applica-

---

[14] According to Art. 1(3) of the Madrid Agreement, the home country is defined as (a) any country, party to the Madrid Agreement, in which the holder of a trademark has a real and effective industrial or commercial establishment, (b) if he has no establishment in such a country, the country, party to the Madrid Agreement, in which he has his domicile; or (c) if he has neither an establishment nor a domicile in such a country, the country, party to the Madrid Agreement, of which he is a national. According to Art. 2(2) of the Madrid Protocol, the applicant or holder of a trademark may freely choose his office of origin on the basis of establishment, domicile or nationality.

[15] Madrid Agreement, Art. 4(1); Madrid Protocol, Art. 4(1)(a).

[16] Edward Kwakwa, *Institutional and Procedural Reform at the World Intellectual Property Organization*, 3 INTERNATIONAL ORGANIZATIONS LAW REVIEW 143, 143 (2006). As a result, WIPO is a self-funding agency by and large, with almost 90 percent of WIPO's budget coming from fees paid by individuals, see WIPO Annual Report 2005, 26.

[17] UNTS, vol. 1160, 231.

[18] WIPO, Record Year for International Patent Filings with Significant Growth from Northeast Asia, WIPO/PR/2007/476, 8 February 2007.

tions filed in 2006.[19] This success can be attributed to the economic importance of the international registration of trademarks for enterprises wanting to acquire and maintain protection in export markets. Without international registration, unfair competitors could use similar distinctive signs to market inferior products or services. Since exporting enterprises are predominantly situated in developed countries, developed countries benefit more from the Madrid system than developing countries. In 2005, the basic fee for applications originating in least developed countries were, however, reduced to 10% of the standard amount.[20] The number of international registrations from developing countries, while not comparable to registrations from developed countries, is beginning to grow.[21]

Compared to the more successful Patent Cooperation Treaty, the Madrid system is unique in so far as it is not only the oldest global protection system, but is also the first WIPO-administered global protection system within which the EC participates.[22] The EC adhered to the Madrid Protocol in 2004. What is more, the central instrument under the Patent Cooperation Treaty is not an international registration and, thus, not an "international administrative act subject to examination by the designated contracting parties."[23]

---

19 WIPO, Germany Holds its Lead in a Year that sees Record Number of International Trademark Filings, WIPO/PR/2007/480, 15 March 2007.

20 Assembly of the Madrid Union, Fee Reduction for Applicants from Least Developed Countries, MM/A/36/2, 11 July 2005. In the period 2003/2004, only two out of 53,345 international applications originated from least developed countries.

21 *See* note 19.

22 The second WIPO-administered global protection system within which the EC participates is the Hague System for the International Registration of Industrial Designs. The EC acceded to the Hague Agreement Concerning the International Registration of Industrial Designs, Geneva Act (O.J. 2006 L 386/30), on 1 January 2008.

23 Rather, it is an international filing system that has the same effect as national filings vis-à-vis designated contracting parties. The procedure under the Patent Cooperation Treaty enhances the chances of an international applicant having his patent registered, as the international filing is published by the International Bureau together with the international search report (i.e. a listing of published document citations that might affect the patentability of the invention). However, unlike an international registration, it does not replace domestic registrations. For more details on the procedure of the Patent Cooperation Treaty see WIPO (note 5), 395-405. Its impact on international administrative

C. Analyzing the International Registration of Trademarks

The concept of an "international administrative act subject to examination by the contracting parties" introduced by the international registration of trademarks will be explored through domestic paradigms of administrative decisions (IV.). Interrelated procedural questions will be further examined by defining and delineating the parameters in which the international registration of trademarks occurs. These parameters are the institutional and normative framework (I. and II.), the procedural regime (III.) and mechanisms of control and review (V.).

I. Institutional Framework: International Administrative Union

The organizational setting of the Madrid system is an international administrative union, a special union called the Madrid Union for the International Registration of Marks (Madrid Union), which was established by the Madrid Agreement.[24] The establishment of international administrative unions dates back to the nineteenth century when the growing interdependence between states led to the realization that certain administrative matters, such as commerce, communication and transportation, could no longer be dealt with on the national level alone but needed coordination through permanent international institutions.[25] International administrative unions are understood as the historical predecessors of intergovernmental organizations. They differ insofar as they not only frequently lack international legal personality, but also the capacity to generate an autonomous will distinct from the will of their contracting parties.[26]

---

law has been discussed in SABINO CASSESE, GLOBAL ADMINISTRATIVE LAW, CASES AND MATERIALS, available at: http://www.iilj.org/GAL/documents/GalCasebook.pdf, 37 et seq.; Sabino Cassese, *Administrative Law without the State? The Challenge of Global Regulation*, 37 NEW YORK UNIVERSITY JOURNAL OF INTERNATIONAL LAW AND POLITICS 663, 682 and 685 (2006).

24 Madrid Agreement, Art. 1.

25 JOSÉ ALVAREZ, INTERNATIONAL ORGANIZATIONS AS LAW-MAKERS 28 (2005); IGNAZ SEIDL-HOHENVELDERN & GERHARD LOIBL, DAS RECHT DER INTERNATIONALEN ORGANISATIONEN EINSCHLIEßLICH DER SUPRANATIONALEN GEMEINSCHAFTEN 20 (7th ed. 2000).

26 Rüdiger Wolfrum, *International Administrative Unions*, in MAX PLANCK ENCYCLOPEDIA OF PUBLIC INTERNATIONAL LAW, http://mpepil.oup.com, para.

Today, the Madrid Union operates within the framework of WIPO and interacts with the trademark offices of the contracting parties and, in particular cases, with individuals. The trademark offices of the contracting parties can be national trademark offices, notified common trademark offices of several contracting parties,[27] such as the Benelux Office for Intellectual Property,[28] and regional trademark offices, such as the EC's OHIM. The fact that the EC and its member states are both parties to the Madrid Protocol does not lead to an additional level in the organizational setting of the Madrid system. National, common and regional trademark offices are all situated on the same level; all three forward international applications to the International Bureau. The reason is that the Madrid Protocol is – at least according to the substantive definition of mixed agreements[29] – not a mixed agreement. It was not concluded on the basis of shared, but of parallel competences. It does not fall partly within the competence of the EC and partly within the competence of its member states, but fully within the exclusive competence of both the EC and its member states.[30] This is due to the fact that Community trademarks exist independently from national trademarks and do not replace them.[31]

Like in all administrative unions operating within the framework of WIPO, the decision-making organ of the Madrid Union is an assembly of all contracting parties. As the Madrid Protocol is not a mixed agreement, the rights and obligations resulting from the membership to the

---

2 (Rüdiger Wolfrum ed., 2008); CHRISTIAN TIETJE, INTERNATIONALISIERTES VERWALTUNGSHANDELN 129 (2002); Joël Rideau, *Les institutions internationales de la protection de la propriété intellectuelle*, 72 REVUE GÉNÉRALE DE DROIT INTERNATIONAL PUBLIC (RGDIP) 730, 731 (1968).

27 Madrid Agreement, Art. 9quater; Madrid Protocol, Art. 9quater.

28 See http://www.boip.int/en/homepage.htm.

29 A mixed agreement, according to the substantive definition, is an international agreement that includes among its parties the EC, one, some or all of its member states and one or some other subjects of international law and that falls partly within the competence of the EC and partly within the competence of its member states (shared competences); see e.g. Henry G. Schermers, *A Typology of Mixed Agreements*, in MIXED AGREEMENTS 23, 25 (David O'Keeffe & Henry G. Schermers eds., 1983).

30 KAREN KAISER, GEISTIGES EIGENTUM UND GEMEINSCHAFTSRECHT: DIE VERTEILUNG DER KOMPETENZEN UND IHR EINFLUSS AUF DIE DURCHSETZBARKEIT DER VÖLKERRECHTLICHEN VERTRÄGE 160 (2004).

31 Council Regulation 40/94, Recital 5.

Madrid Protocol do not have to be shared between the EC and its member states.[32] The EC, therefore, does not have a number of votes equal to the number of their member states,[33] but may exercise its right to vote independently of its member states.[34] The Assembly is authorized not only to determine the program and adopt the budget, but also to amend the organizational provisions of the Madrid Agreement.[35] As the Madrid Union does not have any organs apart from the Assembly, it "borrows" WIPO's International Bureau for the international registration of trademarks and WIPO's Director-General for other administrative tasks.[36]

II. Normative Framework: Treaties, Regulations and Administrative Instructions

The mandate for the international registration of trademarks is contained in the Madrid Agreement and the Madrid Protocol. These treaties prescribe specific actions for all stages of the procedure and are complemented in the following ways: first by regulations implementing the international treaties (*i.e.* the Common Regulations under the Madrid Agreement and the Madrid Protocol)[37] that are adopted and modified by the Assembly; and second by instructions with details in respect of the application of the Common Regulations (*i.e.* the Administrative Instructions for the Application of the Madrid Agreement and the Ma-

---

32 Kaiser (note 30), at 199.

33 See e.g. Agreement establishing the World Trade Organization (UNTS, vol. 1867, 3), Art. IX(1).

34 Madrid Protocol, Art. 10(3)(a).

35 Madrid Agreement, Art. 10(2)(a)(v) and (ix).

36 The International Bureau is based in Geneva. WIPO's staff, drawn from more than 90 countries, includes experts in diverse areas of intellectual property law and practice, as well as specialists in public policy, economics, and administration. In 2005, WIPO's annual expenditure for its staff amounted to 189,928,000 Swiss Francs. See WIPO, Annual Report 2005, 26.

37 See http://www.wipo.int/export/sites/www/madrid/en/legal_texts/pdf/common_regulations .pdf.

drid Protocol)[38] that are established and modified by the Director-General of WIPO under Rule 41 of the Common Regulations.

III. Procedural Regime

The procedural regime governing the international registration of trademarks has a composite dimension as four actors on different levels are involved in the proceedings: first, the international applicant; second, the office of origin (*i.e.* the trademark office of his home country); third, the International Bureau; and fourth, the trademark offices of the designated contracting parties. Ergo, the proceedings leading to an international registration of trademarks are mixed insofar as both domestic (national, common and supranational) and international authorities participate.[39]

1. Three Main Procedural Stages: Application, Registration and Examination

These mixed proceedings are characterized by three main and two additional stages. The main stages are the application stage, the registration stage and the examination stage. The additional stages concern changes in the international registration of trademarks[40] and the renewal of the international registration of trademarks[41] by the International Bureau.

In the application stage, the international applicant submits his application for the international registration of his trademark through the intermediary of the office of origin.[42] A trademark may be the subject of

---

38 See http://www.wipo.int/export/sites/www/madrid/en/legal_texts/pdf/admin_instructions.pdf.

39 The filing procedure under the Patent Cooperation Treaty has also been qualified as "mixed", see CASSESE, GLOBAL ADMINISTRATIVE LAW, CASES AND MATERIALS (note 23), 37.

40 Common Regulations, Rules 25 et seq.

41 Madrid Agreement, Art. 7(1); Madrid Protocol, Art. 7(1); Common Regulations, Rules 29 et seq.; An international registration of a trademark is effective for 20 years under the Madrid Agreement (Art. 6(1)) and for 10 years under the Madrid Protocol (Art. 6(1)). It may be renewed for further periods of 20 and 10 years respectively.

42 Madrid Agreement, Art. 1(2); Madrid Protocol, Art. 2(2).

an international registration only, if it has already been domestically registered or, where the international application is governed exclusively by the Madrid Protocol, if domestic registration has been applied for in the office of origin (basic registration or application). The international application has to fulfill the formal requirements laid down in the treaties, the Common Regulations and the Administrative Instructions. As the international application must be submitted using the appropriate official form, the procedure is highly formalized and standardized.[43] The international applicant must, *inter alia*, indicate those states or intergovernmental organizations with whom he wishes the trademark to be protected. The international application is, furthermore, subject to the payment of fees.[44] These fees may be paid directly to the International Bureau or, where the office of origin accepts to collect and forward such fees, through that office.

In the succeeding registration stage, the International Bureau checks that the international application complies with the formal requirements and that the required fees have been paid. In case of irregularities, the International Bureau informs both the office of origin and the international applicant.[45] In case of compliance, the trademark is recorded in the International Register and published in the WIPO Gazette of International Marks (WIPO Gazette).[46] The International Bureau then notifies the offices of the designated contracting parties of the international registration, informs the office of origin and sends a certificate to the international applicant.[47]

The ultimate examination stage provides an opting-out mechanism for the office of a designated contracting party. Since it has the right to declare that protection cannot be granted to the trademark in its terri-

---

[43] Common Regulations, Rules 9(2)(a). There are three different official forms (MM1, MM2 and MM3) for the international application; all of them are available at: http://www.wipo.int/madrid/en/forms/.

[44] Madrid Agreement, Art. 8(2); Madrid Protocol, Art. 8(2) and (7); *see* also Schedule of Fees Prescribed by the Common Regulations under the Madrid Agreement and the Madrid Protocol and the fee calculator, both available at: http://www.wipo.int/madrid/feecalc/FirstStep.

[45] WIPO, Guide to the International Registration of Marks under the Madrid Agreement and the Madrid Protocol, para. B-22.01 (2004).

[46] Common Regulations, Rule 32(1)(a)(i). See http://www.wipo.int/madrid/en/gazette/.

[47] Common Regulations, Rules 14(1) and 24(8).

tory,[48] it may examine the international registration of the trademark, but it is not required to do so.[49] However, in case of a provisional refusal, it must notify the International Bureau within 12 or 18 months (*i.e.* the time limit specified in the treaties)[50] and indicate the grounds for refusal.[51] Any procedure following the provisional refusal, such as review, appeal or response to an objection made by a third party, is carried out directly between the holder of the internationally registered trademark and the office concerned. The holder of the internationally registered trademark has the same rights and remedies as if the trademark had been deposited directly with the office of the designated contracting party that issued the notification of provisional refusal. Once all the procedures before that office have been completed, it must send a statement to the International Bureau indicating that the provisional refusal is confirmed or is totally or partially withdrawn.[52] The provisional refusal and the statement are recorded in the International Register and published in the WIPO Gazette.[53] In addition, copies are transmitted to the holder of the internationally registered trademark.[54]

2. *Rights and Duties of Actors Involved*

The international applicant of a trademark has various rights and duties in the proceedings. Although he may not present the international application directly to the International Bureau, he may sign it, if the office of origin allows him to do so.[55] Together with the office of origin, the international applicant is entitled to be informed of irregularities

---

48 Madrid Agreement, Art. 5(1); Madrid Protocol, Art. 5(1).

49 WIPO (note 45), para. B-33.06. However, where the office of a designated contracting party finds no reason for refusing protection, it may issue a statement granting protection before the expiry of the relevant time limit. As with negative decisions on registration, this statement is recorded in the International Register, published in the WIPO Gazette.

50 Madrid Agreement, Art. 5(2); Madrid Protocol, Art. 5(2)(a) and (b); *see* also, supra, note 9.

51 Common Regulations, Rule 18(1)(a)(ii).

52 Common Regulations, Rule 17(5)(a).

53 Common Regulations, Rules 17(4) and (5)(c) and 32(1)(a)(iii).

54 Common Regulations, Rule 17(4) and (5)(b) and (c).

55 Common Regulations, Rule 9(2)(b).

with respect to his international application,[56] to receive a certificate of the international registration,[57] to be notified of facts in designated contracting parties that affect the international registration[58] and to defend his rights in case of invalidation in designated contracting parties.[59] In contrast to the original international application, the applicant or holder may present a request directly to the International Bureau for the purposes of subsequent designation, recording amendments (such as name or address) and cancellation.[60] As far as duties are concerned, the applicant or holder must fulfill the formal requirements of a request which is presented directly to the International Bureau[61] and pay the necessary fees.[62]

To a certain extent, the rights and duties of the offices (*i.e.* the International Bureau and the domestic trademark offices of the contracting parties) are mirrored in the rights and duties of the international applicant. In addition, they have rights and duties in relation to each other. Due to the mixed nature of the proceedings leading to the international registration of trademarks, their main duty is to notify one another of any decision that affects the international registration of the trademark. It is enshrined in various provisions of the Madrid Agreement and the Madrid Protocol and concretized by the Common Regulations.[63] Moreover International Bureau must publish any decision affecting the international registration of trademark in the WIPO Gazette.[64] The WIPO Gazette contains all relevant data on new international registrations, renewals, subsequent designations and changes as well as other entries affecting international registrations. It is open to the public and issued by the International Bureau on a weekly basis.[65]

---

56 Common Regulations, Rules 12 and 13.

57 Common Regulations, Rule 14(1).

58 Common Regulations, Rules 16 et seq.

59 Madrid Agreement, Art. 5(6); Madrid Protocol, Art. 5(6). See section B. V.

60 Common Regulations, Rule 25.

61 Common Regulations, Rules 24 et seq.

62 Common Regulations, Rule 10.

63 See on the principle of transparency section C. I. 2.

64 Common Regulations, Rule 32(1) and (2).

65 WIPO (note 45), para. A-07.01.

IV. Classifying the International Registration of Trademarks

The international registration of trademarks is difficult to classify, as the legal instruments of international institutional law have not yet been completely systematized.[66] Calling the international registration an "international administrative decision" would not amount to much, as this term is very vague and merely differentiates unilateral administrative decisions from bi- or multilateral administrative treaties at the international level. Therefore, this paper proposes to explore international administrative decisions through the paradigms of domestic concepts of administrative decisions.[67] By doing so, the international registration of trademarks may be qualified as an "international administrative act subject to examination by the designated contracting parties."

1. Paradigms of Domestic Concepts of Administrative Decisions

The international registration of trademarks by the International Bureau has, in contrast to the listing under the world heritage regime of the United Nations Educational, Scientific and Cultural Organization[68] and the financial sanctions regime of the UN[69], a domestic equivalent. In France, the domestic registration of industrial property rights by domestic industrial property offices is an *acte administratif individuel* (individual administrative act), taken by a public authority with regard to a definite number of individuals.[70] In Germany, it is a *Verwaltungsakt* (administrative act) in the sense of section 35 of the German Law on

---

[66] See Alvarez (note 25), at 217 et seq.; JAN KLABBERS, AN INTRODUCTION TO INTERNATIONAL INSTITUTIONAL LAW 197 et seq. (2004); Matthias Goldmann, in this volume.

[67] See on the problems of comparative administrative law Eberhard Schmidt-Aßmann and Stéphanie Dagron, *Deutsches und französisches Verwaltungsrecht im Vergleich ihrer Ordnungsideen. Zur Geschlossenheit, Offenheit und gegenseitigen Lernfähigkeit von Rechtssystemen*, 67 ZEITSCHRIFT FÜR AUSLÄNDISCHES ÖFFENTLICHES RECHT (ZaöRV) 395, 396 (2007).

[68] Diana Zacharias, in this volume.

[69] Clemens Feinäugle, in this volume.

[70] For the comparable domestic registration of patents in France, see Jean Foyer, *L'opposabilité, sur le territoire français, d'un brevet européen dont la description est rédigée en une langue étrangère*, 27 RECUEIL DALLOZ 1919, 1921 (2007).

Administrative Proceedings (*Verwaltungsverfahrensgesetz*),[71] *i.e.* "[an] order, decision or other sovereign measure taken by an authority to regulate an individual case in the sphere of public law which is intended to have direct external legal effect."[72] This seems to imply that in principle the international registration of industrial property rights, such as trademarks, also fulfills both French and German domestic criteria.

However, upon closer inspection several questions persist concerning the specific characteristics of domestic administrative acts versus international registration. For example, the assertion that international registrations are a "sovereign measure [...] in the sphere of public law" could be problematic considering that industrial property law is generally regarded as a specialized branch of private law. However, while the relationship between industrial property right holders and other individuals is indeed regulated by private law, the act of registering industrial property rights as such is a sovereign measure. It is, in other words, taken with reference to the relationship of sovereign and subject.[73]

The international registration has, moreover, a regulatory character. It bestows upon the international applicant the exclusive right to prevent unauthorized third parties from using the trademark in the territories of the designated contracting parties. From the date of the international registration, the protection of the trademark in each of the designated contracting parties is the same as if the trademark had been the subject of an application for registration filed direct with the office of the designated contracting party in question.[74] An international registration is, therefore, equivalent to a bundle of domestic registrations.

Again, the fulfillment of the "individual case" criterion raises doubt. This criterion distinguishes both the French *acte adminstratif indi-*

---

[71] BGHZ 18, 81, 92 (German Federal Supreme Court); Reimar König, *Die Rechtsnatur der Patenterteilung und ihre Bedeutung für die Auslegung von Patentansprüchen*, 10 GEWERBLICHER RECHTSSCHUTZ UND URHEBERRECHT (GRUR) 809, 810 (1999).

[72] Bundesgesetzblatt (BGBl.) (German Federal Gazette) 2003, part I, at 102. An English translation of the German Law on Administrative Proceedings is reprinted in THE RULE OF LAW IN PUBLIC ADMINISTRATION: THE GERMAN APPROACH 113-166 (HEINRICH SIEDENTOPF, KARL-PETER SOMMERMANN & CHRISTOPH HAUSCHILD eds., 2nd ed. 1993).

[73] In the fifteenth to eighteenth centuries, this was even more conspicuous. Patents were granted to individuals by the sovereign in the form of "privileges"; see WIPO (note 5), 17.

[74] Madrid Agreement, Art. 4(1); Madrid Protocol, Art. 4(1).

viduel and the German *Verwaltungsakt* from a legislative act in that it regulates a specific case and does not lay down general abstract norms applicable to an indefinite number of cases.[75] The international registration targets the international applicant, but deals indirectly with an indefinite number of individuals who might violate the exclusive right to use the trademark without authorization of the holder in the future.[76] The fact that the trademark is recorded in the International Register and published in the WIPO Gazette is reminiscent of the promulgation of a law and further underlines the general abstract effect of the internationally registered trademark.[77] This effect, however, results from the domestic trademark laws of the designated contracting parties and not from the international registration as such. The international registration merely bestows upon the international applicant the exclusive right to prevent unauthorized parties from using the trademark and places the onus upon the designated contracting parties to decide on the legal ramifications.[78]

Finally, "direct external legal effect," another criterion of the German *Verwaltungsakt*, is generally problematic in the field of international law. Even if international law and domestic law are seen as parts of one legal order, international law may not be sufficiently precise enough to be directly applicable in domestic law and might require further implementation. For example, both the inscription of properties in the World Heritage List and the inscription of individuals or groups in the UN financial sanctions list are not intended to have direct external legal consequences. They are aimed at the contracting parties or member states who are called upon to implement the obligations resulting from the listing: protection and conservation of the properties on the one hand, freezing of assets of individuals and groups associated with Usama bin Laden on the other hand.[79] The international registration, by contrast, is intended to have direct external legal consequences. The idea of simplifying the proceedings leading to multiple registrations of trademarks in other contracting parties would be thwarted if the international registration needed further domestic implementation. It is directly applied in

---

[75] MAHENDRA PAL SINGH, GERMAN ADMINISTRATIVE LAW IN COMMON LAW PERSPECTIVE 67 (2001).

[76] Foyer (note 70), 1921; König (note 71), 812.

[77] König (note 71), 812.

[78] Id.

[79] Zacharias, in this volume; Feinäugle, in this volume.

the domestic legal orders of the contracting parties[80] and, therefore, has direct external legal effect.

Borrowing from domestic concepts of administrative decisions, the international registration of industrial property rights, such as trademarks, by the International Bureau has, therefore, been labeled an "international administrative act,"[81] as it is performed by an international authority. Although the international registration is equivalent to a bundle of domestic registrations in the designated contracting parties, it is only one administrative act – *one* administrative act that has, however, direct external legal effect in the territories of *all* designated contracting parties.

2. *Reconciling Domestic Paradigms with the International Registration of Trademarks*

While the international registration of trademarks, thus far, in principle mirrors the criteria of domestic concepts of administrative decisions, in particular the German *Verwaltungsakt*, it has characteristics that cannot be fully reconciled with these aforementioned concepts. These characteristics refer especially to the mixed nature of the proceedings leading to the international registration of a trademark. The decision-making power is not concentrated in the hands of the international authority (*i.e.* the International Bureau), but shared with the relevant domestic authorities (*i.e.* the office of origin and the offices of the designated contracting parties). On the one hand, the offices of the designated contracting parties may suspend, remove or re-establish the exclusive right to prevent unauthorized third parties from using the trademark in their

---

80 *See* for the EC Art. 146 of the Council Regulation 40/94, for Germany section 112 of the Gesetz über den Schutz von Marken und sonstigen Kennzeichen (German Trademark Law; BGBl. 1994, part I, at 3082) and for France Art. R.717-1 of the Code de la propriété intellectuelle (French Intellectual Property Law; JO (3.7.1992) 8801). However, according to Art. R.717-2 of the French Intellectual Property Law, the international registration of certification trademarks (marques collectives de certification) can only be directly applied, as soon as regulations governing their use are submitted to the domestic trademark office in French; *see* also WIPO (note 45), para. B-15.04.

81 Günter Gall, D*er Rechtsschutz des Patentanmelders auf dem Euro-PCT-Weg – Erster Teil*, 7 GEWERBLICHER RECHTSSCHUTZ UND URHEBERRECHT, INTERNATIONALER TEIL (GRURInt) 417, 424 (1981); Alois Troller, *Markenrecht und Landesgrenzen*, 6 GRURInt 261, 263, footnote 8 (1967).

territories.[82] On the other hand, the internationally registered trademark remains dependent on the original trademark for a period of five years from the date of the international registration.[83] If the basic application is refused or the basic registration ceases to have effect, for example through cancellation following a decision of the office of origin or a court, the international registration will no longer be protected.

To a certain degree, this constellation resembles the "mutual recognition procedure" in the EC.[84] Within this procedure, the competent authority of one member state, the so-called *reference* member state, takes a decision that, in principle, ought to be recognized by the competent authorities of the other member states, the so-called *concerned* member states. The *concerned* member states can, however, raise objections, but only by referring to specific grounds, in the area of granting market authorizations for medicinal products, for example, by arguing that the medicinal product presents a potential serious risk to public health.[85] If the member states cannot reach an agreement on the issue, the decision-making power devolves to the European Commission.

However, the international registration procedure differs in three respects from the mutual recognition procedure. First, it is not a domestic authority of one contracting party that decides on the international registration, but an international authority (*i.e.* the International Bureau). Second, the offices of the designated contracting parties have the right to declare that a trademark cannot be granted protection in their territories, but in order to do so, they must notify the International Bureau within 12 or 18 months of their provisional refusal and indicate the grounds for refusal. Otherwise, they lose their decision-making power.

---

82 This is due to their right to declare that protection cannot be granted to the trademark in their territories, see section B. III. 1.

83 Madrid Agreement, Art. 6(3); Madrid Protocol, Art. 6(3). These provisions also apply when legal protection has later ceased as the result of an action begun before the expiration of the period of five years.

84 See for more details on the mutual recognition procedure GERNOT SYDOW, VERWALTUNGSKOOPERATION IN DER EUROPÄISCHEN UNION: ZUR HORIZONTALEN UND VERTIKALEN ZUSAMMENARBEIT DER EUROPÄISCHEN VERWALTUNGEN AM BEISPIEL DES PRODUKTZULASSUNGSRECHTS 181 et seq. (2004).

85 Report from the Commission on the experience acquired as a result of the operation of the procedures for granting marketing authorisations for medicinal products laid down in Regulation (EEC) N 2309/93, in chapter III of directive 75/319/EEC and chapter IV of directive 81/851/EEC, COM(2001) 606 final, 5.

Third, the decision of the offices or courts of the designated contracting parties to refuse protection to the trademark in their territories is definite. The International Bureau is not afforded the competencies to intervene in any way in the settlement of the substantive issues raised by a refusal of protection.[86]

3. Conclusion: A Unique Instrument of International Institutional Law

Reviewing these commonalities and differences of the international registration of a trademark with the German *Verwaltungsakt* and the mutual recognition procedure within the EC, one may call the international registration of trademarks an "international administrative act subject to examination by the designated contracting parties", as it is performed by an international authority that shares its decision-making power with the designated contracting parties. Similar to the German *Verwaltungsakt*, it may become final and conclusive such as a court decision (*Bestandskraft*).[87] The finality may either be formal or material. Formal finality means that the administrative act can no longer be challenged through remedies before the public authority or the court, because no remedies exist, the remedies have already been exhausted or the remedial time limit has expired.[88] Material finality signifies that the administrative act is binding on the public authority that has issued it as well as on the individual concerned (*res judicata*).[89]

Exactly when the international registration of a trademark reaches formal finality depends on the offices of the designated contracting parties. If they do not refuse protection within the relevant time limit, the international registration of a trademark can no longer be challenged through remedies after the expiration of five years from the date of the international registration. Up until that time, if the basic registration is refused, cancelled or withdrawn in the home country of the international applicant, the international registration will no longer be pro-

---

[86] WIPO (note 45), para. B-37.03.

[87] Singh (note 75), 80.

[88] Id., 80 et seq.; HARTMUT MAURER, ALLGEMEINES VERWALTUNGSRECHT 280 (15th ed., 2004).

[89] Singh (note 75), at 81. However, the administrative authority can abrogate the administrative act under certain conditions by withdrawal, by revocation or by reopening the administrative proceedings; *see* German Law on Administrative Proceedings, sections 48, 49 and 51.

tected. After five years, the internationally registered trademark is no longer dependent on the original trademark applied for or registered in the office of origin. However, if the offices of the designated contracting parties refuse protection within the relevant time limit, the international registration may reach formal finality at a later time, depending on the maximum time limits for seeking remedies in the designated contracting parties. In contrast to the refusal, cancellation or withdrawal of the basic registration in the home country of the applicant, the refusal of protection of the trademark in one designated contracting party does not affect the formal finality of the international registration as such or the remaining bundle of domestic registrations in other designated contracting parties.[90] The formal finality of the international administrative act subject to examination by the designated contracting parties is, thus, divisible.

As the proceedings leading to the international registration are mixed, two different relationships have to be distinguished with regard to material finality, the relationship between the international applicant and the International Bureau and the relationship between the international applicant and the offices of origin and of the designated contracting parties. While the international registration of a trademark is binding on the International Bureau as soon as it is performed, it does not have material finality in relation to the offices of origin and of the contracting parties until the formal finality is given.

V. Domestic Control and Review

Since the international registration of trademarks is equivalent to a bundle of domestic registrations, it may be reviewed by domestic institutions of the designated contracting parties (*i.e.* domestic trademark offices and courts) during the examination stage.[91] The aim of global protection system treaties is to simplify and reduce the cost of making individual applications in other countries than the home country, but not to harmonize industrial property law of the contracting parties. While the provisional refusal is communicated to the International Bu-

---

90 Compare Madrid Protocol, Art. 5(6) that does not speak of invalidation of a trademark as such, but of invalidation "of the effects [...] of an international registration" "in the territory of [a] Contracting Party".

91 See section B. III. 1.

reau in the registration phase, any following procedure (such as review, appeal or response to an objection made by a third party) is therefore carried out directly between the holder of the internationally registered trademark and the office concerned. The Madrid system contains very few legal requirements with regard to these domestic procedures. There is, however, one exception. Pursuant to articles 5(6) of the Madrid Agreement and the Madrid Protocol, invalidation may not be pronounced by the competent authorities without the holder of the internationally registered trademark "having, in good time, been afforded the opportunity of defending his rights."

In accordance with its continually increasing mandate, WIPO has established its own review mechanisms during the last decades. WIPO's Arbitration and Mediation Center and Advisory Committee on Enforcement have been mentioned in other papers.[92] One could add that WIPO is the leading domain name dispute resolution service provider accredited by the Internet Corporation for Assigned Names and Numbers (ICANN) under the Uniform Domain Name Dispute Resolution Policy (UDRP).[93] In the event that a trademark holder considers that a domain name registration infringes on his trademark, he may initiate proceedings under the UDRP. However, none of these institutions possess the power necessary to review the international registration of trademarks. WIPO's Arbitration and Mediation Center was established in 1994 to offer alternative dispute resolution options for the resolution of international commercial disputes between *private* parties.[94] Although WIPO's domain name dispute resolution service deals with trademarks, it concentrates only on *conflicts* between domain names and trademarks. Last but not least, the mandate of WIPO's Advisory Committee on Enforcement is limited to technical assistance and coordination and does not offer review.[95]

---

92 Cassese, Administrative Law without the State? (note 23), at 683 and 686.

93 *See* http://www.icann.org/udrp/udrp-policy-24oct99.htm. The UDRP was adopted by ICANN in 1999, but is based on recommendations made by WIPO in The Management of Internet Names and Addresses: Intellectual Property Issues, Final Report of the WIPO Internet Domain Process, 1999, focusing on the problems caused by the conflict between trademarks and domain names. *See* Matthias Hartwig, in this volume.

94 *See* http://arbiter.wipo.int.

95 WIPO General Assembly, Report, WO/GA/28/7, 1 October 2002, para. 114(ii) and 120.

D. Assessing the International Registration of Trademarks: Principles, Composite System and Legitimacy

The concept of an "international administrative act subject to examination by the contracting parties" has helped to shape and consolidate individual procedural principles of the law of international institutions (I.) and is an early example of composite systems[96] where the proceedings are mixed and the decision-making power is shared between the international and domestic authorities (II.). Having been established over a century ago, it does not raise the issues of legitimacy as some modern international administration instruments do (III.). However, this does not mean that there is not any leeway left for further improvement of the Madrid system.

I. Principles

Among the procedural principles that are central to the international registration of trademarks are the right to be heard and the principle of transparency. The latter allows for the effective exercise of the right to be heard and related participatory rights, such as the right to review. The foundation of these two procedural principles is strong, especially taking into account not only the Madrid system, but all WIPO-administered global protection system treaties that, in one way or another, guarantee the same principles.[97]

1. Right to be Heard

In domestic administrative law, the right to be heard prescribes that affected individuals must be given the opportunity to express their views

---

[96] On the concept and terminology of composite administrations, Armin von Bogdandy & Philipp Dann, *International Composite Administrations*, in this volume.

[97] For the right to be heard, see Hague Agreement, Geneva Act, Art. 15(1). For the principle of transparency, inter alia, see Hague Agreement, Geneva Act, Art. 10(3), 18(1).

on the facts before an administrative decision is taken.[98] It has been embodied in the above-mentioned articles 5 (6) of the Madrid Agreement and the Madrid Protocol and has been extended to international institutions. A possible point of contention could be that these provisions only concern the examination stage at the domestic level and not the procedural stages at the international level. While the right to be heard can in common law countries only be dispensed with by law, it may be denied in civil law countries, such as Germany, if the circumstances of a case do not require its observance. This would be the case, for example, if the administrative decision in question rests upon the application of an individual and does not depart from it to his disadvantage.[99] In consequence, following the German model, the right to be heard may be dispensed with at the international level, if the International Bureau registers the trademark. In this case, the administrative decision does not depart from the application to the disadvantage of the applicant. It may, however, not be denied, if the International Bureau does not register the trademark. In this case, both the international applicant and the office of origin acting as the international applicant's intermediary have to be accorded the right to be heard.

Whereas the treaties are silent on this matter, the Common Regulations state that the International Bureau has to inform both the international applicant and the office of origin of any irregularities in the international application.[100] Rules guaranteeing the right to be heard vary[101] and are dependant upon who is responsible for remedying the irregularity in question, the international applicant or the office of origin. If the office of origin is responsible, the International Bureau cannot accept proposals or suggestions directly from the applicant. It will, however, supply appropriate information to the applicant in order to give

---

98 Benedict Kingsbury, Nico Krisch & Richard B. Stewart, *The Emergence of Global Administrative Law*, 68 LAW & CONTEMPORARY PROBLEMS 15, 37 et seq. (2004-2005).

99 Singh (note 75), at 76 et seq.

100 Common Regulations, Rules 11(2), (3), (4)(a) and (6), 12(1) and 13(1). There are three kinds of irregularities: irregularities with respect to the classification of goods and services, irregularities with respect to the indication of goods and services, and other irregularities.

101 WIPO (note 45), para. B-22.02.

him the possibility of intervening with his office of origin.[102] If the office of origin does not react within the time limit, the International Bureau will, if possible, remedy the irregularity of its own accord.[103] If the responsibility for remedying the irregularity in question lies with either the office of origin together with the international applicant or the international applicant alone, they may do so within three months. If the irregularity is not remedied within this period, the international application is considered abandoned.[104]

2. *Principle of Transparency*

The principle of transparency is a fuzzy concept that lacks clarity and is difficult to evaluate.[105] Its meaning can, however, become clearer if coupled with the international institution in question. Since the international registration of trademarks concerns three different actors, the international applicant, third-parties affected by the international registration and the offices (*i.e.* the International Bureau and the domestic trademark offices of the contracting parties), the principle of transparency may be understood as an umbrella term under which the rights and duties of three different actors are interrelated.

First, under the Common Regulations, the international registration and every decision affecting the finality of the international administrative act in one of the designated contracting parties must be made known to the international applicant, as he is the intended beneficiary of the international administrative act.[106] The International Bureau is required to inform the office of origin of the international registration and to send a certificate to the then holder of an internationally registered trademark.[107] It is, likewise, requested to inform the holder of

---

[102] Id. at paras. B-23.01 and B-23.04, B-24.01 et seq. Examples for such irregularities are those with respect to the classification or indication of goods and services.

[103] Id. at paras. B-23.11 and B-24.03.

[104] Id. at paras. B-25.05 and B-25.07. An example for such irregularities would be that the international applicant has not paid any or not enough fees.

[105] Carol Harlow, *Freedom of Information and Transparency as Administrative and Constitutional Rights*, 2 CAMBRIDGE YEARBOOK OF EUROPEAN LEGAL STUDIES 285, 285 (1999).

[106] For German administrative law, *see* Singh (note 73), at 79.

[107] Common Regulations, Rule 14(1).

provisional refusals by the offices of the designated contracting parties and later confirmations or withdrawals thereof.[108]

Second, under the Common Regulations, the international registration and every decision affecting the finality of the international administrative act must also be made known to third parties. The latter might express an entitlement to use the trademark in one of the designated contracting parties, for example because of prior rights, and might object to the extension of the protection of the trademark before the office of the designated contracting party concerned. The decisions are, therefore, not merely recorded in the International Register, but also published in the WIPO Gazette.[109] In addition, anyone wishing to obtain information about the contents of the International Register has access to the following sources of information: the electronic publication on CD-ROM (ROMARIN), the electronic database, and the annual statistics.[110] The right of third parties to access general information is supplemented by their right to access specific information. Under articles 5[ter] (1) of the Madrid Agreement and the Madrid Protocol, anyone is entitled to obtain from the International Bureau copies of particular entries in the International Register.

Third, since the international registration of trademarks depends on the exchange of information because of the mixed nature of the proceedings, the offices (*i.e.* the International Bureau and the trademark offices of the contracting parties) are additionally required to notify each other of any decision that affects the finality of the international registration under both the treaties and the Common Regulations.

II. Composite System

Because the Madrid Union is an administrative union, the relationship between the two levels, (*i.e.* the International Bureau and the trademark offices of the contracting parties) is determined by heterarchy than by hierarchy. It concentrates on coordinating administrative national activities and does not exercise integrative functions.[111] The trademark offices of the contracting parties have the right to declare that protection

---

108 Common Regulations, Rule 17(4) and (5)(c).

109 Common Regulations, Rule 32(1)(a)(i) and (iii).

110 WIPO (note 45), paras. A-06.01 et seq.

111 Wolfrum (note 26), at para. 3.

cannot be granted to the internationally registered trademark in their territories and, thus, retain a substantial amount of decision-making power.

However, even though the Madrid Union does not aim at integration, it has supranational elements insofar as the International Bureau has the power to take administrative acts that are directly applicable in the territories of designated contracting parties. This power is, however, limited. For one, the international registration of a trademark is dependent on the original trademark applied for or registered in the office of origin for a period of five years. Additionally, the International Bureau is unable to extend the protection of a trademark against the will of a designated contracting party. However, if the original trademark does not cease to have effect and the office of a designated contracting party either refrains from examining the international registration of a trademark or does not notify the International Bureau of its refusal of protection within the relevant time limit, the International Bureau is the authority that ultimately decides.

III. Legitimacy

The legitimacy of the international registration of trademarks rests on four pillars: shared decision-making power of the International Bureau and domestic actors, participation of individuals in the procedure, external control and review, and effective simplification of multiple trademark registrations.

Although no democratically legitimized actors of the contracting parties are delegated to the International Bureau, the institutional link between the procedure governing the international registration of trademarks and domestic actors is strong due to the opting-out mechanism for the offices of the designated contracting parties. This opting-out mechanism leads to mixed proceedings that involve domestic actors (*i.e.* domestic trademark offices, and, in case of review, domestic courts).

Individuals have a considerable amount of influence on the procedure in two ways. First, the procedure governing the international registration of trademarks depends on their initiative (*i.e.* the international application). However, there is still potential for expanding their influence, if the Madrid system is compared to other global protection system treaties, such as the Hague Agreement and the Patent Cooperation Treaty. Under these treaties, individuals can file their international applications directly with the International Bureau and do not need an intermediary in form of an office of origin.[112] Second, individuals are guaranteed participatory rights: the right to be heard and the right to access to information on international registrations of trademarks.

Moreover, the mechanisms of external, *i.e.* domestic, control and review of the international registration of trademarks through the domestic trademark offices and courts of the contracting parties is effective, since it hardly leaves any loopholes. The only loophole is that the international applicant is denied the possibility to review a negative decision of the International Bureau. The Convention on the Grant of European Patents[113] (European Patent Convention), a regional protection system treaty, by contrast, states that decisions of different sections and divisions of the European Patent Office (EPO) can be appealed before a Board of Appeal.[114] The Boards of Appeals are integrated into the organizational structure of EPO, but reach decisions independently. In case of the Madrid system, the review of negative decisions of the International Bureau would also have to take place on the international level, as the International Bureau shares its decision-making power with the domestic trademark offices of the contracting parties only in cases where international applications receive positive decisions. The fact that a negative decision obviates the right to review need not be necessarily detrimental to the international applicant. Unlike the EPO, the International Bureau does not check substantive requirements. Failure to remedy formal irregularities on the part of the international applicant only leads to an abandonment of international applications and does not prevent the international applicant from submitting new applications. What is more, the International Bureau is called upon to help the international applicant or the office of origin, as far as possible, with remedying irregularities.

Last but not least, the Madrid Union solves the problem of simplifying and reducing the cost of making individual trademark applications in designated contracting parties effectively, and thus contributes to the output-legitimacy of the system. It has served as a model for the international registration of other industrial property rights on both the in-

[112] Hague Agreement, Geneva Act, Art. 4(1); Patent Cooperation Treaty, Art. 9(1).

[113] UNTS, vol. 1065, 199.

[114] European Patent Convention, Art. 106.

ternational and regional level and the significant number of international registrations is an indication that the system functions well.

There are negative aspects too, though. WIPO as the international organization within which the Madrid Union operates has been criticized for not sufficiently taking into account the needs of developing countries and has been perceived by developing countries as an instrument designed to buttress the economic interests of enterprises situated in developed countries.[115] This is confirmed to a certain extent by the fact that progress on the Development Agenda[116], which calls on WIPO to view intellectual property as one of many tools for development and not as an end in itself, is only slowly being achieved. Nonetheless, the impetus behind this critique does not concern the simplification of multiple registrations of industrial property rights, but the harmonization of substantive intellectual property law, which forces developing countries to adapt their domestic legal orders to a certain standard. The Madrid system can be considered neutral or, considering the fee reduction for applications originating in least developed countries, at times even friendly towards developing countries.

E. Is This as Good as It Gets or Are There Possibilities of Future Development?

Bearing in mind that international administrative unions, such as the Madrid Union, were established from the end of the nineteenth century onwards, the exercise of public authority within these unions can indeed be called progressive. The Madrid Agreement was the first global protection system treaty to introduce the concept of an "international administrative act subject to examination by the designated contracting parties," a concept that has faded into obscurity over the intervening years and, to a certain degree, had to be recreated for modern international institutions with shared decision-making power, such as for the

---

115 Ruth L. Okediji, *The International Relations of Intellectual Property: Narratives of Developing Country Participation in the Global Intellectual Property System*, 7 SINGAPORE JOURNAL OF INTERNATIONAL & COMPARATIVE LAW 315-385 (2003).

116 WIPO General Assembly, Proposal by Argentina and Brazil for the Establishment of a Development Agenda for WIPO, WO/GA/31/11, 27 August 2004.

mutual recognition procedure within the EC. The progressiveness of international administrative unions might hence raise expectations with regard to their future development. Is there a chance that the Madrid Union may expand upon its existing supranational elements?

Theoretically, this could be performed in two steps. First, the opting-out mechanism for offices of designated contracting parties could be abolished while maintaining the international registration of trademarks as a bundle of domestic registrations. The international registration would then be a "true" international administrative act, comparable to the grant of European patents under the European Patent Convention. This step would involve the Madrid Union establishing an international standard of substantive trademark law, as the International Bureau would then be obliged to verify the substantive requirements of international applications in addition to the formal ones. Substantive intellectual property law may, however, be easier to harmonize at the regional than at the international level where the different interests of developed and developing countries come into play. Although the Paris Convention and the Agreement on Trade-Related Aspects of Intellectual Property Rights[117] have harmonized substantive trademark law in many respects, it is still a fragmentary regulation.[118] Also, the Madrid Union would be required to create its own "Board of Appeals," as the domestic trademark offices and courts of the designated contracting parties would no longer be called upon to review the international registration of trademarks.

Second, the bundle of domestic registrations of trademarks could be abolished for the benefit of a unitary world or international trademark. In contrast to the first step, this step would not only entail the harmonization of international trademark law, but also endow the Madrid Union with the power to override the principle of territoriality. Hitherto, only highly integrated regional organizations, such as the Benelux Economic Union and the EC, were given such powers.[119] Consequently, they created the Benelux trademark and the Community trademark, unitary trademarks for the territories of Belgium, the Neth-

---

[117] UNTS, vol. 1869, 299.

[118] Annette Kur, *TRIPs and Trademark Law,* in: FROM GATT TO TRIPS: THE AGREEMENT ON TRADE-RELATED ASPECTS OF INTELLECTUAL PROPERTY RIGHTS, 93, 116 (Friedrich-Karl Beier & Gerhard Schricker eds., 1996).

[119] Benelux Economic Union the Uniform Benelux Law on Marks (UNTS, vol. 704, 301, 312); for the EC Art. 95 and 308 of the Treaty establishing the European Community (O.J. 2006 C 231/37) and Council Regulation 40/94.

erlands and Luxembourg and for the territories of the member states of the EC respectively.

Practically, though, it is rather unlikely that the Madrid Union will further expand on its supranational elements. The exercise of public authority within international administrative unions is still trapped within its original historical framework. Administrative matters are coordinated at the international level only when it is deemed necessary. Yet, the fact that integration is not a goal as such should not be bemoaned. It glosses over the conflict between developing and developed countries concerning the correct approach towards intellectual property and, thus, forms part of the success of the global protection system treaties. And it leaves room for less ambitious ways to develop the Madrid Union further. The Madrid Union could, for example, adapt to the progress made in other global protection system treaties. This concerns, as has been mentioned, mainly the right of individuals to file their international applications and not only their requests for subsequent designation, for recording of a change or a cancellation directly with the International Bureau. Apart from that, this is as good as it gets.

International Institutions and Individualized Decision-Making: An Example of UNHCR's Refugee Status Determination

*By Maja Smrkolj**

---

* The author would like to thank participants in the research project, especially Professor Armin von Bogdandy, Professor Rüdiger Wolfrum, Dr. Jochen von Bernstorff, Dr. Philipp Dann, Matthias Goldmann and Ingo Venzke and the participants of the International Workshop, especially Professor Giacinto della Cananea and Professor Christian Tietje for valuable comments and suggestions on the drafts, colleague Marc Jacob for reading the draft and Eva Richter for formatting.

A. von Bogdandy et al. (eds.), *The Exercise of Public Authority by International Institutions*, Beiträge zum ausländischen öffentlichen Recht und Völkerrecht 210,
DOI 10.1007/978-3-642-04531-8_7, © Springer-Verlag Berlin Heidelberg 2010

A. Introduction: The Law of International Institutions and UNHCR's Refugee Status Determination

I. International Humanitarian/Human Rights Institutions and their Perception

In autumn 2005 a group of Sudanese asylum seekers and refugees discontented with the unbearable conditions in the United Nations High Commissioner for Refuges (UNHCR) office in Cairo started a sit-in protest near the office. The protesters were, besides venting their anger at the suspension of Refugee Status Determination procedures for Sudanese refugees due to the ceasefire between the Sudanese government and Sudan's People Liberation Army, also making their frustrations heard regarding UNHCR's lengthy procedures, its failure to provide them with proper assistance, the high numbers of rejected applications, improper interviews and their general treatment by UNHCR's personnel as well as their difficult social and health conditions which had been aggravated by the lack of proper assistance. They were demanding that this situation be remedied and calling for transparent and fair procedures. Shortly thereafter they were joined by many more protesters so that in the following three months a group of between 1,800 and 2,500 people stayed around UNHCR's premises. However, meetings and negotiations with UNCHR eventually failed. The crisis ended in a tragedy. On December 30, 2005 the Egyptian security forces proceeded with the forcible removal of the protesters from the venue in an action in which 28 refugees were killed, more than half of which were children and women, with several protesters missing after the events.[1] The Cairo incident illustrates what the cited report on the events has rightly called

[1] A Tragedy of Failures and False Expectations, Report on the Events Surrounding the Three-month Sit-in and Forced Removal of Sudanese Refugees in Cairo, September-December 2005 (Azzam Fateh ed., 2006), available at: http://www.aucegypt.edu/ResearchatAUC/rc/fmrs/reports/Pages/default.aspx.

"a tragedy of failures and false expectations" regarding international humanitarian and human rights institutions.

The prevailing perception on those institutions is that of organizations responding to crises and providing support and help in all kinds of urgencies. Due to these urgencies, the legal framework for their work often seems to have a secondary meaning. At the same time the perception is also very common that there is no doubt that those institutions do follow certain rules and act according to human rights standards *per se* even if they are not explicitly bound by them. Interdependency, however, between the lack of proper legal framework and overburdening in cases where the institutions are obviously running out of capacities to perform their mandate as anticipated can lead to tragedies as the one in Cairo. As far as UNHCR's refugee status determination is concerned this study tries to add shades of grey to this black-and-white perception of international institutions while bearing in mind the questions asked by the research project presented in this volume.[2]

II. International Refugee Law and the Perspective of the Publicness of Public International Law

Although historically the recognition of persons who were forced to flee their homes as refugees was dependent on the initiative of single states,[3] today the protection of refugees is regarded as an important international issue.[4] The International Refugee Law, based in the 1951

---

2 See Armin von Bogdandy, Philipp Dann & Matthias Goldmann, *Developing the Publicness of Public International Law: Towards a Legal Framework for Global Governance Activities*, in this volume.

3 For a comprehensive historical recapitulation of the international refugee regime, *see* Laura Barnett, *Global Governance and the Evolution of the International Refugee Regime*, 14 INTERNATIONAL JOURNAL OF REFUGEE LAW (INTJREFL) 238 (2002); Guy S. Goodwin-Gil, *The Language of Protection,* 1 INTJREFL 6 (1989); WILTRUD VON GLAHN, DER KOMPETENZWANDEL INTERNATIONALER FLÜCHTLINGSORGANISATIONEN: VOM VÖLKERBUND BIS ZU DEN VEREINTEN NATIONEN (1992); Atle Grahl-Madsen, *The European Tradition of Asylum and the Development of Refugee Law, in* THE LAND BEYOND: COLLECTED ESSAYS ON REFUGEE LAW AND POLICY 34 (Peter Macalister-Smith & Gudmundur Alfredsson eds., 2001).

4 Goodwin-Gil (note 3), at 8.

Convention Relating to the Status of Refugees (CSR51)[5] and its 1967 Protocol (CSRP67),[6] provides for an interesting setting to address questions on the (new) legal framework for global governance activities.[7]

According to the UNHCR the total number of people of its concern at the end of 2006 was more then 31 million, among them 9, 7 million refugees.[8] This article focuses on an aspect of administrative activity by this very prominent international organization in the field of Refugee Law, namely the issuing of decisions on refugee status by UNHCR's field offices in the process of Refugee Status Determination (RSD). Within this so-called Mandate RSD UNHCR's staff determines whether asylum seekers fall within the criteria for international refugee protection and thus conducts an activity that is primary within the responsibility of states.[9] In 2006 in some 80 countries UNHCR received and issued decisions on 12% of all refugee status applications.[10] In this respect the NGO RSDWatch.org calls attention to the fact that each year UNHCR's offices decide on the fate of more then 80,000 individuals, which makes UNHCR the biggest RSD decision-maker in the

---

5 Convention Relating to the Status of Refugees (CSR51), Geneva, 28 July 1951, UNTS, vol. 189, 150.

6 Protocol Relating to the Status of Refugees (CSRP67), New York, 31 January 1967, UNTS, vol. 606, 267.

7 von Bogdandy, Dann & Goldmann (note 2). *See* Benedict Kingsbury, Nico Krisch & Richard Stewart, *Introduction: Global Governance and Global Administrative Law in the International Legal Order*, 17 EUROPEAN JOURNAL OF INTERNATIONAL LAW (EJIL) 1 (2006); Eberhard Schmidt-Aßmann, *Die Herausforderung der Verwaltungsrechtswissenschaft durch die Internationalisierung der Verwaltungsbeziehungen,* 45 DER STAAT 315 (2006).

8 UNHCR, Global Report 2007, 16, available at: http://www.unhcr.org/publ/PUBL/484807202.pdf. For five elements of refugee definition JAMES C. HATHAWAY, THE LAW OF REFUGEE STATUS (1991).

9 *See* UNHCR, Note on Determination of Refugee Status under International Instruments, EC/SCP/5 (24 August 1977), available at: http://www.unhcr.org/excom/EXCOM/3ae68cc04.html.

10 About 95 per cent of these adjudications were concentrated in Cameroon, Egypt, Hong Kong SAR (China), Jordan, Kenya, India, the Islamic Republic of Iran, Lebanon, Malaysia, Morocco, Pakistan, the Syrian Arab Republic, Thailand, Turkey and Yemen. UNHCR, Global Report 2006, 26-27, available at: http://www.unhcr.org/publ/PUBL/4666d25b0.pdf.

world.[11] Furthermore, while the share of UNHCR's RSD decisions continuously grows the share of government RSD decisions declines. According to a statement by Assistant High Commissioner Erika Feller, addressing the Executive Committee on the High Commissioner's Programme at its fifty-eight session in October 2007, between 2003 and 2006 the number of all refugee applications world-wide has decreased by 38% while at the same time the number of applications submitted to UNHCR has increased by 48%.[12]

III. UNHCR's Refugee Status Determination and Procedural Fairness Capacity of International Institutions

For the individual concerned the implications of an RSD decision are profound for his life and security. The issue of a Refugee Certificate, even though the Certificate as such is not formally binding, is determinative as to whether he or she is to be protected from a forcible return to his or her country of origin and is to receive special protection and assistance in rebuilding his or her life in the country other than his or her country of origin.[13] The capacity of UNHCR, its protection role and the standards it has been developing for the government-led RSD in the form of standard-setting materials, policy guidelines and training could indicate that the asylum seekers knocking on UNHCR's doors could not be better off. However, as this article tries to show, UNHCR's RSD raises significant concerns: compared to an individual national administrative act, which the decision taken within the RSD resembles, the procedural rights of the individual are everything else but satisfactory. The problems already occur in facilitating actual access to the procedure since no right exists on the part of the applicant and no legal duty on the part of UNHCR to enable him access to the procedure and to examine his application. Within the eligibility assessment procedure the applicant does not need to be provided with an interpreter or counsel, the decision can be taken on the basis of secret evi-

---

11 RSDWatch.org, UNHCR RSD continues to grow in 2006, while government RSD declines again (August 2007), available at: http://www.rsdwatch.org/index_files/Page1747.htm.

12 Statement available at: http://www.unhcr.org/doclist/admin/42a409182.html.

13 Michael Kagan, *The Beleaguered Gatekeeper: Protection Challenges Posed by UNHCR Refugee Status Determination*, 18 INTJREFL 2 (2005).

dence and the level of discretion in allowing third parties to be present and to participate in the individual procedure is very high. The field officers deciding on the cases are also not obliged to provide the applicant with reasons for the decision. And finally, there is no proper legal remedy in its classical meaning that would enable the applicant to invoke his substantial and procedural rights after the decision has been issued. Further critical points regarding this UNHCR activity highlighted in the literature and by practitioners include questions relating to the competence of UNHCR to decide individual applications, enforcement and effect of such decisions, accountability and questions of legitimacy with regard to the problem-solving potential of such decisions.[14] Doubts as to the fairness of the procedure were also confirmed by the European Court of Human Rights (ECourtHR)[15] and deficiencies have been recognized by the UNHCR itself.[16]

The other side of the coin to be considered is the role of the states, members of the United Nations, donors to the UNHCR and host states to UNHCR's field offices. Considering the growing importance of UNHCR's RSD activity, resulting in part also from the stagnation of the amount of protection afforded by the states,[17] it should not be absurd to ask oneself about the possible interests these could have in the procedure as such and in the way it has been handled.

---

[14] For explicit criticism, *see* Michael Alexander, *Refugee Status Determination Conducted by UNHCR*, 11 INTJREFL 251 (1999); Michael Kagan, *Frontier Justice: Legal Aid and UNHCR Refugee Status Determination in Egypt*, 19 JOURNAL OF REFUGEE STUDIES 45 (2006); *Id.* (note 13); Mark Pallis, *The Operation of UNHCR's Accountability Mechanisms*, 37 NEW YORK UNIVERSITY JOURNAL OF INTERNATIONAL LAW AND POLITICS 869 (2005); B.S. Chimni, *Co-Option and Resistance: Two Faces of Global Administrative Law*, 37 N.Y.U. JOURNAL OF INTERNATIONAL LAW AND POLITICS 799 (2005); RSDWatch.org, No Margin for Error: Implementation of UNHCR's Procedural Standards for Refugee Status Determination at Selected UNHCR Field Offices in 2006 (September 2006), available at: http://www.rsdwatch.org/index_files/Page397.htm.

[15] Eur. Court H.R., *D. et autres c. Turquie*, Judgment of 22 June 2006, App. no. 24245/03.

[16] UNHCR, Procedural Standards for Refugee Status Determination under UNHCR's Mandate (September 2005), 1-2, available at: http://www.unhcr.org/publ/PUBL/4316f0c02.html.

[17] This aspect is critically reflected also in the recent article by James C. Hathaway, *Why Refugee Law Still Matters*, 8 (1) MELBOURNE JOURNAL OF INTERNATIONAL LAW 89-103 (2007).

Based on the premise of the growing scope and relevance of the global governance activity by International Organizations,[18] not only with regard to national administrations but also concerning individuals,[19] it might not be that self-evident to what extent they are also capable of providing proper remedies to fairly and efficiently decide on status of individuals. Their resemblance to activities of national administrations might even lead to the assumption that no objections exist for them to not have the capacity to replace certain national administration procedures.[20] Using UNHCR as an example, the following analysis attempts to show the dangers of such an assumption.

For this purpose Part B. will proceed in 6 steps. Firstly (I.), the legal basis for UNHCR activity according to the Mandate and the level of formalization of relations towards host states will be examined. Secondly (II.), the relevance and effect of RSD decisions will be sketched out, together with the importance of fair procedure. Before addressing the procedure as such (V.), the institutional framework of the activity (III.) and substantive rules relevant for UNHCR RSD, including the question of human rights, (IV.) will be outlined. Lastly (VI.), review and oversight will be discussed. The main argument of the analysis will be the lack of procedural fairness in the conduct of RSD by UNHCR, suggesting that this failure is not coincidental but in a way backed politically by the states, since it gives them political leeway regarding the recognition of such decisions and disburdens them at the same time in preselecting persons applying for refugee protection.

---

18 Jan Klabbers, *The Changing Image of International Organizations, in* THE LEGITIMACY OF INTERNATIONAL ORGANIZATIONS 221, 222 (Jean-Marc Coicaud & Veijo Heiskanen eds., 2001); José E. Alvarez, *International Organizations: Then and Now*, 100 AMERICAN JOURNAL OF INTERNATIONAL LAW 324 (2006), B.S. Chimni, *International Institutions Today: An Imperial Global State in the Making*, 15 EUROPEAN JOURNAL OF INTERNATIONAL LAW 1 (2004).

19 *See also* Clemens Feinäugle, in this volume.

20 *See* Schmidt-Aßmann (note 7), at 322-323.

B. Legal Analysis

I. Legal Basis for Mandate RSD

The forerunner of modern RSD conducted by international institutions can be found in the era of the League of Nations' High Commissioner. At the 1928 conference convened by the Commissioner one of the concluded agreements provided for the legal basis for the representatives of the High Commissioner to determine eligibility for refugee status on behalf of governments and to participate in the national refugee offices.[21] Today, however, as this section will illustrate, the legal basis for Mandate RSD is even vaguer than in times of the League of Nations.

1. UNHCR's Mandate and Lack of Explicit Legal Basis

There is no explicit norm in the CSR51, CSRP67 or the Statute of the Office of the United Nations High Commissioner for Refugees (UNHCR Statute)[22] which would provide UNHCR with the competence to conduct individual RSD. The function is explained as part of UNHCR's international refugee protection mandate (therefore the activity is also referred to as "Mandate" RSD).

In general, CSR51 Art. 35 and CSRP67 Art. II set the legal basis for the obligation of states to accept UNHCR's role of providing international protection to asylum seekers and refugees, the obligation of states to respond to information request by UNHCR and the authoritative character of certain UNHCR statements, like standard-setting materials, policy guidelines, etc. within the exercise of its supervisory role.[23] UNHCR Statute Para. 8 further lists UNHCR's protection activities.[24]

---

[21] *See* Grahl-Madsen (note 3), at 129.

[22] UN GA Res. 428 (V) of 14 December 1950, Annex.

[23] Walter Kälin, *Supervising the 1951 Covention Relating to the Status of Refugees: Article 35 and beyond, in* REFUGEE PROTECTION IN INTERNATIONAL LAW: UNHCR'S GLOBAL CONSULTATIONS ON INTERNATIONAL LAW 619 (Erika Feller, Volker Türk & Frances Nicholson eds., 2003).

[24] These are: (a) Promoting the conclusion and ratification of international conventions for the protection of refugees, supervising their application and proposing amendments thereto; (b) Promoting through special agreements with Governments the execution of any measures calculated to improve the situation of refugees and to reduce the number requiring protection; (c) Assisting governmental and private efforts to promote voluntary repatriation or assimilation

However, the listed responsibilities are not of limiting or prescriptive nature, but are more to be regarded in the light of the main objectives. Such an all-embracing protection role of the UNHCR, also for dealing with individual cases, has also been recognized by state practice.[25] Furthermore, in difference to other human rights treaties where an international body needs approval by the state in order to intervene on behalf of an individual, CSR51 Art. 35 and CSRP67 Art. II are also interpreted in a manner that the UNHCR does not need an invitation by the state in order to exercise its protection function, including RSD.[26] Lacking any explicit legal basis, as rightly observed by Kagan, "UNHCR's Mandate allows it to choose to do RSD, but it has no specific duty to conduct RSD."[27]

2. *Deformalized Relations with Host States*

Although no formal approval of UNHCR's RSD activity is needed, conclusion of some sort of legal agreements (either in the form of stan-

---

within new national communities; (d) Promoting the admission of refugees, not excluding those in the most destitute categories, to the territories of states; (e) Endeavoring to obtain permission for refugees to transfer their assets and especially those necessary for their resettlement; (f) Obtaining from Governments information concerning the number and conditions of refugees in their territories and the laws and regulations concerning them; (g) Keeping in close touch with the Governments and inter-governmental organizations concerned; (h) Establishing contact in such manner as he may think best with private organizations dealing with refugee questions; (i) Facilitating the co-ordination of the efforts of private organizations concerned with the welfare of refugees.

25 Kälin (note 23), at 623. For questions of general competence growth of UNHCR, *see* Geoff Gilbert, *Rights, Legitimate Expectations, Needs and Responsibilities: UNHCR and the New World Order*, 10 INTJREFL 349 (1998).

26 Kälin (note 23), at 623. For the Lebanon example of opposing and disrespecting UNHCR's RSD, *see* Kagan (note 13), at 14. In 2003, however, UNHCR and the Lebanese General Security Office signed a Memorandum of Understanding providing for rights to one-year residence, freedom of movement and identity cards for registered refugees, thus affording UNHCR one year to organize resettlement possibilities for each refugee. UNCHR, Global Report 2003, at 301, available at: http://www.unhcr.org/publ/PUBL/40c6d75e0.pdf.

27 Kagan, (note 13), at 16. *See also* UNHCR, Note on Determination of Refugee Status under International Instruments (note 9).

dard UNHCR Cooperation Agreement[28] or Memorandum of Understanding) has been one of the priorities of the Office of the High Commissioner. The legal basis for such agreements can be found in the general norms of CSR51 Art. 35, CSRP67 Art. II and Art. 8 of the Statute. But, according to Zieck, as of January 2006 there should still have been some 35 countries with UNHCR's presence on their territory where no such formal agreements exist.[29] Alternatively UNHCR's presence might be guided by other agreements to which UNHCR is either a party or not (in these cases UNHCR is regarded as a third party beneficiary) or agreements to which the UN is a party, or by national legislation of respective states.[30] Some countries had, for instance, agreed to ratify both international instruments only under the condition that RSD on their territory is being conducted solely by UNHCR.[31]

The above addressed the general nature of the basic norms that provide for the legal basis for UNHCR's RSD activity and that need to be further concretized. These questions gain even more pertinence considering the reports on the standards that UNHCR's offices have (not) followed in conducting their activities,[32] read together with the practical impact and relevance of RSD decisions.

---

[28] For a Model Cooperation Agreement: MARJOLEINE ZIECK, UNHCR'S WORLDWIDE PRESENCE IN THE FIELD: A LEGAL ANALYSIS OF UNHCR'S COOPERATION AGREEMENTS 335 (2006).

[29] Among such countries are also Belgium, Greece, Netherlands, Turkey, UK, Australia, Canada and US; *id.* at 294.

[30] ZIECK (note 28), at 294. For an example of national legislation see Article 7 (Institutions with which co-operation is to be carried out) of the Regulation No. 1994/6169, Turkey, Official Gazette, 30 November 1994 (English translation available at: http://www.unhcr.org/cgi-bin/texis/vtx/refworld/rwmain. This article is the only legislative norm that refers to UNHCR although in practice it is UNHCR that conducts RSD for non-European asylum seekers.

[31] Kagan (note 14), at 46.

[32] RSDWatch.org (note 14); Pallis (note 14); Kagan (note 13); Alexander (note 14); VERDIRAME GUGLIELMO & BARBARA E HARRELL-BOND, RIGHTS IN EXILE: JANUS-FACED HUMANITARIANISM 78 (2005); Edwin Odhiambo Abuya & George Mukundi Wachira, *Assesing Asylum Claims in Africa: Missing or Meeting Standards?*, 53 NETHERLANDS INTERNATIONAL LAW REVIEW 171 (2006).

II. The Legal Effect and Actual Impact of RSD Decisions

The regulatory impact of UNHCR's RSD activity derives either from the UNHCR Refugee Certificate, if the refugee status has been confirmed or Notification of the Negative RSD Decision if UNHCR has determined that the applicant is not eligible for international refugee protection.[33] Neither of them refers to an explicit legal basis, but the latter can be derived from the refugee definition of Art. 1 CSR51 and Art. 33 CSR51, rights provided for in both treaties and the cooperation duties of the parties according to Art. 35 CSR51, Art. II CSRP67 and Art. 8 of the UNHCR Statute. These cooperation duties, however, do not oblige national administrations to recognize the Mandate Refugee Certificate as the legal basis for providing refugee protection and assistance.[34]

As observed in studies, some countries where Mandate RSD is conducted are not parties to CSR51 and CSRP67 and do not feel bound by the decisions.[35] Apart from CSR51 and CSRP67 promotion work in such cases UNHCR does not have any real enforcement mechanisms.[36] If countries are parties to both instruments the only soft enforcement mechanism would arguably be the obligation to report according to Art. 35 und 36 CSR51 and Art. II and Art. III CSRP67.

There are three groups of constellations for which the effect of RSD decisions can be observed, namely in the host country (*i.e.* the country where UNHCR has issued the decision), the country to which the refugee is to be resettled within UNHCR's resettlement program, and a third country (*i.e.* a country other than host or resettlement country), illustrating that actual impact of the decisions very often does exist, but not always to the benefit of affected individuals.

---

33 For standard Refugee Certificate and Notification of Negative RSD Decision *cf.* UNHCR, Standards (note 16), at Annex 6-1, 8-1.

34 *See* ExCom's conclusions regarding states. Here, it considered that the "very purpose of the 1951 Convention and the 1967 Protocol implies that refugee status determined by one Contracting State will be recognized also by the other Contracting States." UN GA ExCom, Extraterritorial Effect of the Determination of Refugee Status, GA Document No. 12 A (A/33/12/Add.1) (October 1978).

35 Supra, note 26.

36 Kagan (note 13), at 14-15.

In the host countries effects of RSD decisions vary significantly. For Lebanon, before signing the 2003 MOU, RSD decisions seemed to have no relevance for the national administration since they did not protect Mandate refugees from forcible return to their country of origin.[37] In Turkey the UNHCR has been conducting RSD for all non-European asylum seekers[38] because so far[39] Turkey has upheld the geographic limitation of the CSR51 and non-European refugees may only be awarded temporary residence permission. UNHCR's RSD therefore runs parallel to the national administration's procedure for obtaining temporary residence permission. During the course of the national procedure there is a separate RSD; but as practice has shown, the authorities have almost routinely been adopting UNHCR's decisions[40] and strong cooperation between the High Commissioner Office and competent authorities exists.[41] Formally UNHCR's decision has no legal value; but in practice it enables the refugee to extend his residence permit issued by the Turkish authorities and protects him from deportation or detention and thus enables the UNHCR to organize resettlement into a third country.[42] In Egypt UNHCR's decisions have had an even greater impact. Since the country does not provide for any kind of domestic asylum procedure, according to a 1954 agreement UNHCR itself assesses refugee status in Egypt. Refugees with a UNHCR identity card are allowed to stay in the country by Egyptian authorities without any further status assessment. A negative UNHCR decision, on the opposite, means that such a person is excluded from assistance and protection and has no legal status, unless he or she is able to obtain residence permits on other grounds.[43]

---

[37] *Supra*, note 26.

[38] *Supra*, note 30.

[39] In the process of EU accession the country, however, has obliged itself to lift this limitation. UNHCR, Global Report 2006 (note 10), 446.

[40] Eur. Court H.R., *D. et autres* (note 15).

[41] Elizabeth Frantz, Report on the Situation of Refugees in Turkey: Findings of a Five-week Exploratory Study, December 2002-January 2003, 16 (2003), available at: http://www.aucegypt.edu/ResearchatAUC/rc/fmrs/reports/Pages/default.aspx.

[42] *Id.* at 18.

[43] Michael Kagan, *Assessment of Refugee Status Determination Procedure at UNHCR's Cairo Office 2001-2002*, Forced Migration and Refugee Studies Working Paper No. 1, 7 (2002), available at: http://www.aucegypt.edu/ResearchatAUC/rc/fmrs/reports/Pages/default.aspx; KATARZYNA GRABSKA,

A significant number of Mandate refugees are eventually resettled into third countries, mostly to the United States, Canada, Australia and some Scandinavian countries. UNHCR referral is in these countries often necessary and the only means of accessing resettlement, meaning a positive UNHCR RSD decision is in the majority of cases the most important pre-condition for a successful resettlement.[44]

Finally, the effect of the Mandate RSD decision can be observed with regard to countries other than UNHCR RSD countries. For the United States one can conclude that again UNHCR's decision could be decisive in accessing their asylum procedure, especially if the person was declined to apply to or was rejected by the UNHCR. In practice, a negative UNHCR decision has regularly served as a basis for denying asylum. At the same time a positive decision by UNHCR does not necessary suffice for obtaining asylum in the US. The meaning of UNHCR's RSD is also not to be overlooked since according to the REAL ID Act[45] passed in 2003 an asylum officer may at any time during the procedure examine the credibility of the claim by comparing statements made by the applicant in any other context, including during the UNHCR procedure. Shortcomings of the latter can thus have direct effect on asylum procedures in the US.[46] As confirmed in several decisions of German administrative courts, Mandate refugees are not automatically granted asylum or other protection, like protection from deportation.[47]

WHO ASKED THEM ANYWAY? RIGHTS, POLICIES AND WELLBEING OF REFUGEES IN EGYPT 13, 25 (2006), available at: http://www.aucegypt.edu/ResearchatAUC/rc/fmrs/reports/Pages/default.aspx.

44 Kagan (note 43), at 7; Emily E. Arnold-Fernandez & Michael Kagan, *UN Decision-Making for Refugee Status: Implications for American Asylum Policy*, 8 ABA SECTION OF INTERNATIONAL LAW IMMIGRATION AND NATURALIZATION COMMITTEE NEWSLETTER 5 (2005).

45 P.L. 109-13.

46 Arnold-Fernandez & Kagan (note 44), at 6.

47 VG Freiburg, 07.05.2002, Decision No. 7 K 10114/00 (*cf.* also the opinion of UNHCR of 10.08.2000); OVG Lüneburg, 07.12.2005, Decision No. 11 LB 193/04; OVG Münster, 27.09.2006, Decision No. 8 A 1363/05. The cited decisions also summarize opinions issued by UNHCR on enquiries of the court. According to these opinions, Mandate refugees should enjoy international protection, however, recognition as Mandate refugee does not have any direct binding effect on German asylum procedure, but it does have strong indicative character.

In light of the preceding account, UNHCR's RSD decisions in many ways resemble an individual administrative status assessment decision. Given that their implications are of vital importance for the concerned individual, if has to be examined if the institutional framework, the procedure, including legal remedies and accountability mechanisms, correspond to those of a typical administration procedure in a rule of law state.[48]

III. The Institutional Framework

The organizational setting of the examined administrative activity is the Office of the United Nations High Commissioner for Refugees and its field offices established in 116 countries.[49] The Office was established in December 1950 as a UN agency by the United Nations General Assembly (UN GA).[50] At first it was given a limited three-year mandate. Later its mandate was extended every five years until the UN GA decided in December 2003 to remove the time limitation of UNHCR's mandate until the refugee problem is solved.[51]

Regarding the question of the legal capacity of UNHCR as such, the majority opinion considers it a "subsidiary organ" that needs authorization by the UN General Assembly in order to enter into legal relations with states, other international organizations or privates. Since UNHCR was not established by a treaty but by a Resolution of the UN GA that lacks competence to establish new international organizations as subjects of international law it enjoys international personality but is at the same time not a subject of international law.[52] This also indicates that RSD activities of UNHCR's offices should be attributed directly to the legal entity of the UN. On the other hand, however, UNHCR does enjoy a certain autonomy and distance from the UN

---

48 Schmidt-Aßmann (note 7), at 322-323.

49 UNHCR, Helping Refugees: An Introduction into UNHCR (2006 Edition), available at: http://www.unhcr.org/basics/BASICS/420cc0432.html#emergency.

50 UN GA Res. 428 (V) of 14 December 1950.

51 UN GA Res. 58/153 of 24 February 2004.

52 For assessment of the scholarly opinions, *see* VOLKER TÜRK, DER FLÜCHTLINGSHOCHKOMMISARIAT DER VEREINTEN NATIONEN (UNHCR) 115, 118 (1992); ZIECK (note 28), at 100.

GA, since according to Chapter I of the UNHCR's Statute[53] it is relatively free in providing international protection as a non-political entity that conducts its mandate under the auspices of UN GA. Apart from being obliged to consult the Advisory Committee on Refugees and to follow the policy directives given to it according to the Statute by the UN GA and the Economic and Social Council (ECOSOC), it is in no further dependence vis-à-vis the General Assembly. Furthermore there is a treaty power for co-operation with national authorities in CSR51 Art. 35 and CSRP67 Art. II.[54]

The Executive Committee of the High Commissioner's Programme (ExCom) as UNHCR's Advisory Committee, in addition to UN GA and ECOSOC, provides for the additional linkage of the mechanism to the states party to CSR51. It is a body foreseen by para 4 of the UNHCR Statute and though established at the request of the UN GA[55] by ECOSOC[56] (which also elects its members) ExCom functions as a subsidiary organ of the UN GA. It is not a substitute for the policy-making functions of the UN GA or ECOSOC but has its own executive and advisory functions. Currently it is made up of delegates from 70 Member States. It meets annually to review and approve UNHCR's programmes and budget, advise on international protection and discuss further issues with the UNHCR and its intergovernmental and non-governmental partners. ExCom's decisions are obligatory for the UNHCR but they cannot have any direct impact on RSD procedures.[57] At the same time though the potential impact of decisions regarding policy and budgeting for the RSD activity must not be overlooked. Furthermore, its Conclusions on International Protection of Refugees have as soft law an important standard setting function not only for the states but also for UNHCR.[58] Considering the fact that UNHCR has to rely almost exclusively on donations (mainly from states) since not

---

53 UN GA Res. 428 (V) of 14 December 1950, Annex.

54 TÜRK (note 52), at 118. Such treaty power can also be found in OUA Convention Governing the Specific Aspects of Refugee Problems in Africa, 10 September 1969, Art. VIII, UNTS, vol. 1001, 45.

55 UN GA Res. 1166 (XII) of 26 November 1957.

56 UN ECOSOC Res. 672 (XXV) of 30 April 1958.

57 TÜRK (note 52), at 105.

58 Erika Feller & Anja Klug, *Refugees, United Nations High Commissioner for Refugees (UNHCR)*, *in* MAX PLANCK ENCYCLOPEDIA OF PUBLIC INTERNATIONAL LAW (Rüdiger Wolfrum ed., 2008), available at: www.mpepil.com.

more than 3% come from the UN regular budget,[59] the possible impact states can have on the work of the Agency grows even further.

IV. The Sources of Substantive Rules and Standards Guiding Mandate RSD

1. The Refugee Convention and Internal Soft Law

The main body of substantive rules that binds UNHCR in assessing eligibility for refugee status comprises CSR51, CSRP67 and the Statute, most importantly the refugee definition.[60] Here, the Mandate refugee definition of the Statute (as a definition of persons to whom UNHCR's competence extends) is not completely identical with the definition of both treaties, which should consequently also mean that Mandate status is not identical with the CSR51 status. With regard to the protection territory and the addressee, the Mandate refugee enjoys *international protection* whereas CSR51/ CSRP67 refugees enjoy *protection by parties to the treaties*.[61]

Further interpretation aids to the Convention are ExCom's Conclusions on International Protection.[62] Although not formally binding and primarily addressed to parties of both treaties, arguments that they do not have a binding effect for UNHCR itself do not stand to reason.[63] The Conclusions' authority also derives from the fact that they are taken by consensus. The same should apply for further standards and manuals developed within UNHCR's Geneva Headquarters, for the purpose of additional assistance to national administrations in their

---

[59] UNHCR, UNHCR 2007 Financial Overview, available at: http://www.unhcr.org/partners/PARTNERS/45f027512.pdf.

[60] *See* Hathaway (note 11).

[61] UNHCR, Handbook on Procedures and Criteria for Determining Refugee Status under the 1951 Convention and the 1967 Protocol Relating to the Status of Refugees HCR/IP/4/Eng/REV.1, 4 (Reedited, January 1992), available at: http://www.unhcr.org/publ/PUBL/3d58e13b4.pdf. Italics added by the author.

[62] UNHCR, A Thematic Compilation of Executive Committee Conclusions (2nd Edition, June 2005), available at: http://www.unhcr.org/excom/3bb1cb676.html.

[63] Pallis (note 14), at 873; Chimni (note 14), at 820.

refugee protection activities,[64] and for the guidelines addressed to its own staff.[65] Both can be regarded as the internal law of the agency.[66]

2. *Human Rights Standards*

In his paper on the operation of UNHCR's accountability mechanisms *Pallis* further refers to human rights as the core standards for UNHCR and with respect to Mandate RSD to the due process standards of Article 14 (1) of the International Covenant on Civil and Political Rights (ICCPR).[67] He thereby alludes to a contested topic of public international law that has also been occupying the International Law Commission (ILC) under the notion of responsibility of international organizations,[68] namely human rights obligations of international organizations. According to the Commentary to the Article 8 of the draft articles, international obligations that bind an international organization may be established by "customary rule of international law, a treaty or general principles applicable within international legal order" and by rules of

64 Available at: http://www.unhcr.org/doclist/publ/3bc17bbc4.html.

65 UNHCR, Standards (note 16), further resources listed in Annex 1-1.

66 Pallis (note 14), at 874.

67 Pallis (note 14), at 872, 880, 881. On the concrete procedural standards Alexander (note 14), at 251. However, it must be noted that the authoritative ICCPR commentary does not answer the question whether asylum procedures ultimately fall under the scope of article 14 (1). But it does note that "most decisions of administrative authorities, which determine individual rights, need to be subject to full judicial review by an independent and impartial tribunal." MANFRED NOWAK, U.N. CONVENANT ON CIVIL AND POLITICAL RIGHTS: CCPR COMMENTARY 317, marg. 20 (2nd revised edition, 2005). More positive, *see* Santhosh Persaud, *Protecting refugees and asylum seekers under the International Covenant on Civil and Political Rights,* NEW ISSUES IN REFUGEE RESEARCH, RESEARCH PAPER No. 132, 15 (2006), available at: http://www.unhcr.org/doclist/research/3b8a11284.html. The recent Human Rights Committee General Comment further lists asylum seekers and refugees explicitly among the groups to which the right of access to courts and tribunals and equality before them according to article 14 CCPR must be available. Human Rights Committee, Ninetieth Session. General Comment No. 32. Article 14: Right to equality before courts and tribunals and to a fair trial, CCPR/c/GC/32, 3 (21 August 2007). On the applicability of article 14 CCPR for administrative procedures *see* Jochen von Bernstorff, in this volume.

68 The latest report: ILC, Fifty-ninth session, Fifth report on responsibility of international organizations, A/CN.4/583 (2007).

that organization.[69] If it might be possible to argue for human rights obligations such as due process as part of customary international law,[70] it is almost impossible to derive these obligations out of treaties binding UNHCR as party to the treaty or as general principles of international law. The remaining option is thus to consider if human rights could form rules of the organization or if another reasoning would be possible for UNHCR to provide for a binding effect of international human rights norms.

The application of human rights vis-à-vis UNHCR as rules of the organization might be argued by a referral to the UN-Charta. According to Art. 1, one of the purposes of the UN is to "promote and encourage respect for human rights and for fundamental freedoms" indicating that the organization and also its agencies should be bound by human rights.[71] Furthermore, the UN's own references to the universal human rights standards in various documents can serve as an indication of the commitment of the organization to adhere to human rights standards.[72] For the Mandate RSD one further argument is relevant, namely that by assessing eligibility for refugee status UNHCR is conducting an activity that is within the primary responsibility of states and should thus respectively be bound by the same human rights standards as national administrations.[73] It would exceed the scope of this article to analyze this question further.[74] However, if a legal obligation could not be derived from the Charter, one could assume a political responsibility of the UN to adhere to standards developed by the organization itself.[75]

---

69 UN GA, Official Records of the General Assembly, Sixtieth session Supplement No. 10, A/60/10, 87 (2005).

70 Pallis (note 14), at 872, 880.

71 *Id.* at 873.

72 ANDREW CLAPHAM, HUMAN RIGHTS OBLIGATIONS OF NON-STATE ACTORS 137 (2006).

73 *Id.* at 109; Ralph Wilde, *Quis Custodiet Ipso Custodes? Why and How UNHCR Governance of 'Development' Refugee Camps Should Be Subject to International Human Rights Law*, 1 YALE HUMAN RIGHTS AND DEVELOPMENT LAW JOURNAL 107 (1998).

74 For a summary of the conceptions *see* Frederic Mégret & Florian Hoffmann, *The UN as a Human Rights Violator? Some Reflections on the United Nations Changing Human Rights Responsibilities*, 25 HUMAN RIGHTS QUARTERLY 314, 316 (2003).

75 *See* ERIKA DE WET, THE CHAPTER VII POWERS OF THE UNITED NATIONS SECURITY COUNCIL 200 (2004).

V. Due Process?

1. The 2003 Procedural Standards and Their Principles

In November 2003 UNHCR for the first time released a comprehensive set of action standards addressed to the field offices for the Mandate RSD procedures. The Procedural Standards for Refugee Status Determination under UNHCR's Mandate (the Standards) were developed by the Department of International Protection and were made public in September 2005.[76] The 175 pages long Standards are not directly binding but rather provide guidelines for UNHCR's field offices on how to develop and implement RSD procedures.

The non-binding document contains several core standards to be followed by all field offices and which therefore can be regarded as common procedural principles. These are: access to UNHCR staff and RSD procedures; identification and assistance of vulnerable asylum seekers; non-discriminatory, transparent and fair procedures; timely and efficient processing of the applications; qualified and supervised staff; access to individual RSD interview; access to review procedures for rejected claims by an officer, other then the officer who decided the first instance claim; organization-wide consistency on procedures that define substantive rights in the RSD process; consistency with established policies on confidentiality, treatment of vulnerable asylum seekers and gender and age sensitivity.[77]

Standards are only a procedural tool and do, as such, neither provide guidance on the interpretation of refugee criteria nor address other substantive issues relating to RSD.[78] Therefore the Annex lists additional resources, including those on substantive questions.[79] Many of those are, however, marked as "internal" and as such bring up the question of transparency of the legal sources guiding the decision-making process.[80]

---

76 UNHCR, Standards (note 16), 1-2.

77 *Id.* at 1-2.

78 *Id.* at 1-4.

79 *Id.* at 12-1 - 12-5.

80 Chimni (note 14), at 825.

2. *Course of the Procedure*

According to the Standards, the decision on eligibility for the status of a Mandate refugee is to be carried out in three phases: reception, eligibility assessment and issuing of the decision, and appeal procedure. In addition to the standard procedure, there are further special procedures foreseen for file closure/re-opening,[81] cancellation of refugee status[82] and cessation of refugee status.[83]

During the reception phase[84] asylum seekers should receive necessary information permitting them to understand and exercise their right to apply for refugee status, including counseling. The office should also be able to identify asylum seekers with special protection or assistance needs and refer them to appropriate support or available assistance. As a general standard, every applicant and each accompanying adult family member or dependant should have an individual and confidential registration interview.[85] The applicants are then to be provided with a uniform temporary UNHCR Asylum Seeker Certificate attesting their asylum seeker status and requesting that the authorities of the host country provide them the necessary protection and assistance until UNHCR has made the final determination of the claim.[86]

The second phase[87] begins with the internal assigning of RSD files, based upon the capacity of eligibility officers as determined by their RSD supervisor. The eligibility officers do not necessarily need a degree in law. Access to RSD interview is one of the basic procedural rights of the applicants. At the interview the applicant may, upon his written consent, be accompanied by his or her legal representative.[88] As a general rule only the legal representative or designated representative of an applicant who is suffering from mental illness or disability is allowed to attend the interview, whereas participation of other third parties is limited to observation status, unless invited to participate by the eligibility officer. It should be noted that there is no explicit right for the applicant

81 UNHCR, Standards (note 16), at 9-1.

82 *Id.* at 10-1.

83 *Id.* at 11-1.

84 *Id.* at 3-1.

85 *Id.* at 3-11.

86 *Id.* at Annex 3-3.

87 *Id.* at 4-1.

88 Critically on this issue in practice Kagan (note 14), at 45.

to be provided with an interpreter. The applicants are permitted to bring witnesses to support their claim but the evidence of witnesses should not be given in the presence of the applicant. The written decision is then prepared by the eligibility officer using the standardized RSD Assessment form. The Procedural Standards recommend that offices should establish mechanisms for reviewing the quality of first instance RSD decisions before they are issued; as a minimum, at least for all negative decisions.

Generally, RSD decisions should be issued within one month after the interview. The applicants are to be notified of the decision in writing, and wherever possible in person. However, the written form, including the reasons for rejection of the application, is only strongly recommended and not compulsory.[89] Also, no obligation exists for the applicant to be informed at least orally of the reasons for rejection. On the other hand, limited disclosure of relevant information is prescribed if the disclosure could jeopardize the security of UNHCR's staff, its ability to carry out its Mandate or disclosure could endanger the source of information.

The applicants who have received a negative RSD decision[90] then have the right to appeal.[91] They are provided with the standardized Appeal Application Form[92] that they are to complete and submit to the office that decided the first instance claim. Generally, the deadline should not be less than 30 days after the notification of the decision. Appeals should be determined by a qualified protection staff member who was not involved in the adjudication or review of the RSD claim in the first instance. During the appeal procedure the appeal officer is to re-examine whether the first instance RSD decision was based on a reasonable finding of facts and correct application of the refugee criteria by reviewing the RSD file and if necessary by conducting an additional appeal interview. The latter should be the case if findings were not adequately addressed in the decision, relevant evidence was not adequately considered, if new relevant evidence is raised in the appeal, or if indications of a breach of procedural fairness exist. Reasons for the determination of the appeal are then documented in the Appeal Assessment

---

89 *Id.* at 6-2.

90 *Id.* at Annex 6-1.

91 *Id.* at 7-1 *et seq.*

92 *Id.* at Annex 7-1.

form. Applicants should then be notified of the decision in writing. Again, it is not necessary to provide reasons for the appeal decision.[93]

The actual practice[94] further adds to the ambiguity of the RSD activity notable already on the abstract level. Comparing the main principles of the Standards with the issues the 2006 RSDWatch.org report on UNHCR's field offices addressed the lack of a right to an interpreter or right to counsel as well as avoidance of accelerated rejection are among the most appalling.[95] Further, the testimonies of witnesses in the absence of the applicant and limitations regarding the disclosure of relevant information, read together with the lack of a general obligation to provide the applicant with reasons for decision, raise additional doubts as to the transparency and procedural fairness. But with regard to core elements of an effective system for determination of refugee status that UNHCR has been advocating vis-à-vis the states,[96] the Mandate RSD procedure most notably lacks the element of an independent appeal and judicial review by an independent or impartial tribunal according to ICCPR Art. 14 (1).

The latter point brings us to the key problem of the examined activity, namely the lack of proper legal remedies that would enable the applicant to invoke his rights and the prescribed and advocated standards and to achieve their obedience. The lack of such remedies obviously shows that the RSD procedure, as conducted by the UNHCR and foreseen in the Standards, does not meet the rule of law requirements for administrative procedures as they are common to liberal states. At the same time, the impact of issued decisions and the course of the procedure as such, give the impression that this is (should be) the case.

Given the above analysis, the question needs to be addressed whether the deficiencies of the procedure can partly be mitigated by the existing

---

[93] UNHCR, Standards (note 16) 7-5.

[94] *Supra*, note 14.

[95] RSDWatch.org (note 14).

[96] *See* Erika Feller, *Judicial or Administrative Protection – Legal Systems Within the Asylum Procedures*, *in* THE ASYLUM PROCESS AND THE RULE OF LAW (International Association of Refugee Law Judges) 39 (2006). *See also* UN GA ExCom, Determination of Refugee Status GA Document No. 12 A (A/32/12/Add.1) (October 1977).

review and oversight mechanisms as additional elements providing for accountability.[97]

VI. Review and Oversight

1. Internal Review of Individual Cases

Internally on the lowest level the Standards provide for some review mechanisms in procedures regarding individual cases. According to the document, its essential feature is the designation of the role of RSD Supervisor who is to be designated by the Head of Office among the staff to "oversee the RSD operation and to ensure the quality and integrity of the UNHCR RSD procedures". He is to report to the Representative or the Head of Office who is in the end accountable for the implementation of standards.[98] The RSD Supervisor is responsible for the hiring and training of the registration staff and eligibility officers, for supervising execution of the staff duties, including random monitoring of the interviews and counseling sessions. He also has to review all complaints about the procedure and should assure that at least all negative RSD decisions are reviewed by a member of protection staff other than the eligibility officer who was responsible for adjudicating the claim.[99]

A special procedure is provided for in cases where the decision is either to exclude an individual from refugee protection, to cancel or revoke refugee status, according to cancellation procedures or to terminate refugee status, pursuant to the cessation procedures.[100] Decisions in these cases have to be submitted for review and approval to the legal advisor of the appropriate bureau of the UNHCR's Headquarters. In most sensitive cases (*i.e.* exclusion of children, complex doctrinal issues on interpretative standards, and all decisions in the cancellation procedure) the Geneva Department of International Protection has to receive a copy of the submitted decision.[101] Field offices also have the possibil-

---

97 On accountability of international institutions, *see* Erika de Wet, *Holding International Institutions Accountable: The Complementary Role of Non-Judicial Oversight Mechanisms and Judicial Review*, in this volume.

98 UNHCR, Standards (note 16), at 1-7, 4-5.

99 *Id.* at 4-16.

100 *Id.* at 4-18.

101 *Id.* at 4-18.

ity to submit certain types of cases to the Headquarters if they have exhausted all possible resources but have not been able to either decide on the case or to provide information on the facts.[102]

The possibility of the recourse to the UNHCR Headquarters' experts can be regarded as a valuable help for the field officers to enhance the quality of their decisions, however, in practice difficulties might arise in the facilitation of submissions of such cases to the Geneva experts because of lack of time and resources of field offices to prepare such enquiries. Furthermore the question also arises on the implications of such submission regarding the length of the procedure.

2. *The Geneva Headquarters' Overview and Control*

On the Headquarters level three bodies conduct overview and control of the UNHCR's activity in the field with regard to effectiveness, performance, accountability to refugees and their participation: Policy Development and Evaluation Service (PDES); Inspector General's Office (IGO) and UN Office of Internal Oversight Services (OIOS).[103]

PDES was established in 2006 and has replaced the former Evaluation and Policy Analysis Unit (EPAU) established in 1999 with the task to conduct systematic analysis and assessment of UNHCR projects, programmes, practices and policies. In 2002 EPAU published UNHCR's evaluation policy, listing the evaluation principles and standards: transparency, independence of the evaluation function, consultation with UNHCR's stakeholders, including refugees, relevance and integrity.[104] The new PDES was tasked with strengthening the capacity and effectiveness of UNHCR's policy development and evaluation function and is to review the existing evaluation policy.[105] Despite reference to inclusion of refugees, work in participatory manner and a commitment to

---

102 *Id.* at 4-18.

103 For more comprehensive analysis of all three mechanisms, *see* Pallis (note 14), at 887.

104 UNHCR EPAU, UNHCR Evaluation Policy 3, 4 (September 2002), available at: http://www.unhcr.org/research/RESEARCH/3d99a0f74.pdf.

105 UNHCR, Global Appeal 2007, 308, available at: http://www.unhcr.org/static/publ/ga2007/ga2007toc.htm.

transparency,[106] the evaluation process as such cannot facilitate evaluative accountability to also suffice as participatory accountability.[107]

Since 1994 UNHCR also relies on IGO as an in-house monitoring and oversight mechanism which can also follow-up on individual complaints brought to it. Beside assessing the quality of UNHCR's management and conducting inquiries into violent attacks on staff and other incidents, it also addresses allegations of misconduct by the personnel. According to UNHCR, investigations into misconduct which directly affect its beneficiaries, including corrupt practices and other misconduct related to RSD, are the Office's priority.[108] Although IGO can be regarded as UNHCR's only participatory accountability mechanism, in practice the percentage of complaints by the refugees is astonishingly low,[109] particularly considering the 50% share of the investigations into misconduct among 100-150 investigations launched per year.[110] Most probably the reasons for this are practical difficulties in accessing the mechanism and the lack of information among refugees on its existence and on their rights.[111] ExCom's and Headquarters' documents also indicate that there has been ongoing discussion about the transparency of the inspections since reports are mostly confidential and accessible only to ExCom members through a password protected web page.[112] Also addressed was the independence of the Inspector General towards the

---

106 *Id.* at 307.

107 Pallis (note 14), at 902.

108 UNHCR, Global Appeal 2007 (note 105), at 307.

109 In the yearly reports to the ExCom IGO in the last years has not even included the statistical information on refugee complaints. In its 2004 Report it only stated: "The majority of complaints were received from UNHCR staff members. However, many of them were based on complaints made by refugees and asylum seekers." UN GA ExCom, Report on UNHCR's inspection and investigation activities A/AC.96/993, note 28, (July 2004). Pallis refers in his article to 1% (2003) - 7% (2004) of all complaints. Pallis (note 14), at 897.

110 *See* UN GA, ExCom, Report on UNHCR's inspection and investigation activities, A/AC.96/993 (July 2004), UN GA, ExCom, Report on activities of the Inspector General's Office, A/AC.96/1028 (July 2006), UN GA, ExCom, Report on activities of the Inspector General's Office, A/AC.96/1042 (July 2007).

111 Pallis (note 14), at 897.

112 Executive Office, Enhancing Independence of the Office of the Inspector General, Note for Informal Consultative Meeting, note 6, (21 July 2005), available at: http://www.unhcr.org/excom/EXCOM/42de51282.pdf.

High Commissioner.[113] However, it needs to be stressed that even by addressing these considerations IGO can only investigate on misconduct and the most egregious violations by UNHCR's staff but cannot provide for any proper legal review of RSD decisions if these have not reached the misconduct level.

A central UN-wide mechanism that can also function as UNHCR's oversight is the OIOS, established by UN GA Resolution in 1994 as an operationally independent office entrusted with the responsibilities of monitoring, internal auditing, inspection and evaluation and conducting investigations which should ensure that UN organs are operating according to their mandate.[114] As its reports to the UN GA have shown, monitoring of the proper conduct in the field represents only a small part of its activities and its focus is more on systemic problems.[115] Also access to the OIOS as a standing investigatory body is limited and no individual complaints mechanism is foreseen. Given the nature of the mechanism and restraints regarding the capacity, the potential of OIOS is in identifying grave systemic problems but it cannot function as a tool for participative accountability.

The existing mechanisms hence do not provide satisfactory review of individual cases relating to the conduct of RSD. Several suggestions and comments have been made in the literature on how to overcome this deficiency. Among them are the "establishment of an independent and impartial body to decide on the appeals, outside the branch office structure" and publication of those appeals,[116] creation of an RSD ombudsman office, and, to increase transparency, publication of reports assessing RSD procedures.[117] Regardless of which of the recommendations would seem most appropriate, there is an urgent need to improve legal review, overview, transparency and accountability of the Mandate RSD.

---

[113] *Id.* at note 3; UNHCR ExCom, Oversight: Report of the Joint Inspection Unit with Annexes, EC/54/SC/CRP.21, (23 August 2004), available at: http://www.unhcr.org/excom/EXCOM/41348eff4.pdf.

[114] UN GA Res. 48/218 B of 12 August 1994.

[115] Yearly reports available at: http://www.un.org/Depts/oios/annual_reports.htm.

[116] Alexander (note 14), at 287.

[117] Kagan (note 13), at 27. For comments, *see* B.S. Chimni, *Global Administrative Law: Winners and Loosers* 23 (2005), available at: http://www.iilj.org/GAL/documents/ChimniPaper.pdf. Pallis on the other hand also appraises the potential of IGO for individual complaints by placing its permanent representative in every office; Pallis (note 14), at 915.

C. Conclusion

I. Indispensability of UNHCR's Activity

The above remarks lead to the conclusion that Mandate RSD is a controversial activity. However, at the same time it must be acknowledged that it is basically a response by UNHCR to situations where UN Members are not willing or capable to afford protection to refugees. Its intervention therefore plays an important role in ensuring that the life and safety of many individuals are not endangered even more dramatically. As long as there are not more countries which would take on their share of international responsibility, UNHCR cannot cease to conduct RSD. On the other hand, the mere necessity of the work of UNHCR does not immunize the Office against criticism concerning the procedural shortcomings and lack of judicial review.

First and foremost, due process standards should be followed in a more thorough manner and a better legal review mechanism including more independent decision-makers should be developed. Ideally, this would mean an independent judicial-like review body. At least some improvement could already be achieved if the submission of cases to the Headquarters' experts was more formalized and was regarded as a legal remedy of the applicant and not just as a means of exercising oversight over the field officers. Secondly, review and oversight mechanisms over the conduct of the RSD in general should be improved and participation of individuals in these mechanisms should be further advocated and advanced. An ombudsman-like body which would be easily accessible to all applicants could do most in this respect. Last but not least, UNHCR should consider other means to achieve enforceability of refugee certificates vis-à-vis national administrations. An additional Protocol to the CSR51 obliging Member States to acknowledge such decisions without further substantive control admittedly sounds utopian, but there might be some room for advocating similar clauses in cooperation agreements with particular countries, especially those where currently Mandate RSD decisions are informally recognized or respected.

Altogether, the answer to the question posed at the beginning of this study, namely on the actual capacity of international institutions to decide on individual cases, seems to be ambiguous. It seems that international institutions are not able to provide for procedures like those of national administrations. At the same time in situations of humanitarian crises or human rights violations for which the international community of states has obliged itself to intervene or help but has been withdrawing itself from this obligation, not much choice has been left for these international institutions to intervene.

II. UNHCR – Handmaiden of the States

To conclude the appraisal above without asking oneself how come the lack of proper judicial review and the absence of binding force of Mandate Refugee Certificates towards national administrations have not (already) been at least partly mitigated would be very much naïve, in particular since recourse to UNHCR's RSD procedures is increasing. Overloaded field offices certainly further contribute to the deficiencies of the procedure. But, what is more important is that states are adding to this overload by disburdening themselves and are at the same time tolerating the discrepancies.

And why is this so? One answer might be that since the decisions are generally not binding they do not regard them as that relevant or that any procedural unfairness would pose a problem. However, if the positive decisions would have been taken in a more formalized procedure identical to their own they could not so easily reserve the right to further review them but would rather be expected to recognize and respect them. But at the same time, the negative decisions in particular have the practical effect of barring the applicants' access to national asylum or resettlement procedures, meaning UNHCR is in a way the agent of the states, conducting unpleasant factual pre-selection of the applicants and thereby reducing the numbers they would otherwise have to deal with. Noting the growing migration trends and inability of the international community to prevent further humanitarian crises, the motives of the states behind such attitudes are clear. It is in their interest that international institutions are doing (their) "unpleasant work" affecting rights and duties of individuals in some sort of gray area. International organizations are then characterized as not being able to provide for proper legal remedies; but in any event no appropriate solution to remedy the deficiencies could have been found so far. Despite the states being the actual stakeholders of international institutions, making use of such arguments provides them with an alibi for not being held responsible for the discrepancies of international institutions triggered by their own failure and unwillingness to fulfill international obligations.

Perhaps, in the light of such growing recourse of states to the activities of international institutions, "piercing the institutional veil"[118] should be the key metaphor for conducting future research on the legal framework for global governance activities. Although developed in a different constellation, reasoning of the European Court of Human Rights regarding Member States of the European Community[119] could pave an argument to establish responsibility of states for acts of international organizations if these had to act because of the failure of states to act, provided there was an interest of the states behind those acts, even if they did not directly approve them, or if they had not used their powers within the organizations to properly influence their activity.[120]

---

118 Metaphor used in CATHERINE BRÖLMANN, THE INSTITUTIONAL VEIL IN PUBLIC INTERNATIONAL LAW: INTERNATIONAL ORGANIZATIONS AND THE LAW OF TREATIES (2005).

119 Eur. Court H.R., *Matthews v. the United Kingdom*, Judgment of 18 February 1999, App. no. 24833/94, para 34.

120 For a similar approach, *see* Jean d'Aspremont, *Abuse of the Legal Personality of International Organisations and the Responsibility of Member States*, 4 (1) INTERNATIONAL ORGANIZATIONS LAW REVIEW 91-119 (2007).

1.2 Recommendations

Effective Governance through Decentralized Soft Implementation: The OECD Guidelines for Multinational Enterprises

*By Gefion Schuler**

* I am grateful to Prof. Dr. Armin von Bogdandy, Matthias Goldmann and fellow project participants for insightful comments and to Marc Jacob and Eva Richter for language review and copy-editing.

A. von Bogdandy et al. (eds.), *The Exercise of Public Authority by International Institutions*, Beiträge zum ausländischen öffentlichen Recht und Völkerrecht 210,
DOI 10.1007/978-3-642-04531-8_8, © Springer-Verlag Berlin Heidelberg 2010

A. Governance to Secure Corporate Social Responsibility

I. Mediation-based Governance

Botnia S.A./Metsä-Botnia Oy's construction of the Orion pulp mill in Uruguay raised concerns regarding violations of national, regional, and international law with regard to social and environmental protection.[1] On 18 April 2006, the Center for Human Rights and Environment (CEDHA), an Argentinean non-governmental organisation, submitted to Finland's National Contact Point (NCP) a "specific instance" regarding the possible non-compliance of Botnia S.A. (a Finnish enterprise) with the OECD Guidelines for Multinational Enterprises (OECD Guidelines for MNEs, Guidelines)[2] when building the envis-

---

1 OECD Watch, Quarterly Case Update, spring 2007, available at: http://www.oecdwatch.org/docs/OW_quarterlycaseupdate_english.pdf, at 4-5. For the statement of the Finnish NCP on the issue *see* Ministry of Trade and Industry, Finland's National Contact Point's Statement on the specific instance submitted by CEDHA, an Argentinean non-governmental organization, regarding Botnia S.A./Metsä-Botnia Oy's Pulp Mill project in Uruguay, 21 December 2006, available at: http://www.oecdwatch.org/docs/CEDHA_Botnia_FinnishNCP_statement.pdf.

2 OECD, Working Party on the OECD Guidelines for Multinational Enterprises, The OECD Guidelines for Multinational Enterprises: Review 2000, DAFFE/IME/WPG(2000)9, 8 September 2000 (Ministerial Booklet). This document reproduces the text of the Ministerial Booklet published at the 2000 Ministerial Council Meeting containing the Declaration on International Investment and Multinational Enterprises, the Guidelines for Multinational Enterprises (Part 1), the Decision of the OECD Council and the Procedural Guidance (Part 2), and Commentaries (Part 3).

aged pulp mill in Uruguay.[3] According to the Center for Human Rights and Environment, Botnia S.A. violated the OECD Guidelines for MNEs especially with respect to Chapter II "General Policies", Chapter III "Disclosure", Chapter V "Environment" and Chapter VI "Bribery".[4] Specific instances concerned with related issues were filed by the Center for Human Rights and Environment with the Swedish and Norwegian NCPs against Nordea, a leading financial services group of the Nordic and Baltic Sea area, for possible financing of Botnia S.A.'s pulp mill project[5] and against the Finnish state bank Finnvera for providing export guarantees to Botnia S.A.[6] Other fora that have in the meantime become involved in the issue are the International Court of Justice[7] and member institutions of the World Bank Group, the International Finance Corporation[8] and the Multilateral Investment Guarantee Agency.[9]

After the issue relating to Botnia S.A.'s alleged misbehaviour was filed, the Finnish NCP organised a hearing in cooperation with the Finnish Ministry of Trade and Industry. The meeting included representatives from both the Center for Human Rights and Environment and Botnia S.A. as well as representatives from Sweden's and Norway's NCPs. In the course of these negotiations, Finland's NCP had been in contact with the authorities in Uruguay and with representatives from Argentina's and Spain's NCPs. The Finnish NCP offered future good offices to help the parties resolve the issue.[10] On 21 December 2006 the NCP

---

3 OECD Watch, Quarterly Case Update, spring 2007, available at: http://www.oecdwatch.org/docs/OW_quarterlycaseupdate_english.pdf, at 4-5.

4 *Id.* at 4-5.

5 *Id.* at 4-5.

6 *Id.* at 4-5.

7 International Court of Justice, *Pulp Mills on the River Uruguay* (Argentina v. Uruguay), pending case, general list no 135, further information available at: http://www.icj-cij.org/docket/index.php?p1=3&p2=1&code=au&case=135&k=88.

8 International Finance Corporation, Orion Pulp Mill – Uruguay, available at: http://www.ifc.org/ifcext/lac.nsf/ content/Uruguay_Pulp_Mills.

9 Multilateral Investment Guarantee Agency, Projects, available at: http://www.miga.org/projects/index_sv.cfm?pid=690.

10 Ministry of Trade and Industry, Finland's National Contact Point's Statement on the specific instance submitted by CEDHA, an Argentinean non-governmental organization, regarding Botnia S.A./Metsä-Botnia Oy's Pulp Mill

posted a comprehensive statement on the facts and procedures of this specific instance on the internet.[11]

These procedures illustrate that responsible behaviour of MNEs in the course of investment activities is aimed to be secured through multi-level cooperation and a decentralized soft implementation mechanism. The actions taken in this specific instance exemplify that the implementation mechanism relies on mediation realized by the NCPs as well as on information collection and dissemination. The cooperation involves institutional and substantial cooperation.

The effectiveness of such governance through multi-level cooperation and decentralized soft implementation is furthermore illustrated in the following specific instance. The Czech-Moravian Confederation of Trade Unions submitted an instance to the Czech NCP alleging that a Czech subsidiary of the German company Bosch had violated the Guidelines for MNEs' chapter on employment and industrial relations (chapter IV of the Guidelines for MNEs) by denying the employees their right to organize.[12] It submitted that the Bosch subsidiary had prevented the workers from establishing a trade union and that the local management had even used physical force to prevent the workers from exercising their rights. This instance was discussed at four meetings in the Czech NCP. The Czech NCP informed the German NCP as well as the German Embassy and offered a forum for negotiations. In the course of 11 months from the filing of the instance in June 2001 until its conclusion in April 2002, the parent company changed the local management in order to enable constructive negotiations. At the fourth NCP meeting, the new management declared that there were no obstacles for the growth and development of the newly established trade union and for reaching a collective agreement.

The analyzed governance mechanism constitutes an exercise of public authority. The fact that the OECD Guidelines for MNEs and their implementation mechanism are soft law instruments does not contradict this supposition because the Guidelines' mechanisms generate consider-

---

project in Uruguay, 21 December 2006, available at: http://www.oecdwatch.org/docs/CEDHA_Botnia_FinnishNCP_statement.pdf.

11 *Id.*

12 Trade Union Advisory Committee (TUAC), TUAC Internal analysis of the treatment of cases raised with national contact points February 2001-April 2007, available at: http://www.oecdwatch.org/docs/TUAC_ListOfCases_Feb2007.pdf, at 4.

able reputational effects on actors outside the OECD. Moreover, the Guidelines regulate a subject matter of high public interest which would call for regulation in domestic or international public law in the absence of the OECD Guidelines for MNEs.

This study proposes that effective governance is achieved through multi-level cooperation and through decentralized soft mediation-based implementation. This project's perspective[13] sheds light on the governance mechanism's legal characteristics. These are in particular the necessity of a concrete mandate for the particular OECD policies, particular legal characteristics of the adherence procedure, and the *de facto* constraint to implement the Guidelines for MNEs.

II. Political Implications of Mediation-based Governance

Mediation-based governance brings about positive consequences for the effectiveness of an instrument. The NCP procedures are relatively easy to operate, they are flexible, and they do not require explicit juridical knowledge nor do they involve a financial risk. However, mediation-based governance is a political process and impartial problem-solving capacity becomes critical when a specific instance is filed on a politically sensitive issue for the government where the NCP is located. Moreover, since NCPs are mainly located in the government departments concerned with foreign investment, it is the same people who are responsible for a successful foreign investment policy who are expected to judge the behaviour of their investing enterprises. Coming back to the specific instance filed with the Finnish NCP of alleged violations of the OECD Guidelines for MNEs by Botnia S.A./Metsä-Botnia Oy in the Orion pulp mill project in Uruguay, the difficulties become explicit. Based on its decision in the comprehensive statement issued on 21 December 2006,[14] Finland's NCP stated that Botnia S.A. had complied with the

---

[13] Armin von Bogdandy, Philipp Dann, Matthias Goldmann, in this volume; Benedict Kingsbury, Nico Krisch & Richard B. Stewart, *Introduction: Global Governance and Global Administrative Law in the International Legal Order*, 17 EUROPEAN JOURNAL OF INTERNATIONAL LAW 1-13 (2006); Eberhard Schmidt-Aßmann, *Die Herausforderung der Verwaltungsrechtswissenschaft durch die Internationalisierung der Verwaltungsbeziehungen*, 45 DER STAAT 315 (2006).

[14] *See* (note 10).

OECD Guidelines for MNEs with respect to its pulp mill in Uruguay.[15] Following this statement, the Center for Human Rights and Environment filed a complaint to the Finnish Parliament Ombudsman.[16] In the complaint the Center for Human Rights and Environment cited, among other issues, concerns over the impartiality of Finland in the specific instance procedure. The Center for Human Rights and Environment claimed that the chemical supply company Kemira, the Metso Corporation, the export credit agency Finnvera and the Nordic Investment Bank were the key stakeholders in the Orion pulp mill project and that they are all enterprises with Finnish ownership. For this reason, the Center for Human Rights and Environment claimed that the Finnish NCP, located in the ministry of trade and industry, did not engage in impartial negotiations with regards to alleged violations of the OECD Guidelines for MNEs by Botnia S.A.[17]

III. The OECD's Engagement in Governance to Secure Corporate Social Responsibility

The analyzed governance aims to secure and promote responsible behaviour of MNEs during their investment activities.[18] The OECD's involvement in corporate social responsibility was part of a wider package of measures aimed at greater stability and liberalization of investment conditions between OECD states.[19] Industrialized states feared that interference by MNEs might provoke hostile reactions in developing states and possibly lead to the imposition of restrictions on the rights of foreign investors. A kind of regulatory gesture was required to help defuse mounting public concern about the lack of accountability of MNEs within the international economic system, but the majority of

---

15 The Ministry of Trade and Industry's decision on Botnia S.A./Metsä-Botnia Oy's pulp mill project: Metsä-Botnia has complied with the OECD Guidelines in Uruguay, 22 December 2006, available at: http://www.oecd.org/dataoecd/17/42/38053102.pdf.

16 Pulp Mill Conflict: Finnish Ombudsman receives complaint in Botnia S.A. Investment conflict, 31 January 2007, available at: http://www.oecdwatch.org/docs/CEDHA_vs_BOTNIA_PR_Ombudsman.pdf.

17 *Id.*

18 JENNIFER A. ZERK, MULTINATIONALS AND CORPORATE SOCIAL RESPONSIBILITY 248 (2006).

19 *Id.* at 248.

OECD member states did not want an instrument with legal sanctions against MNEs.[20] They adopted the OECD Guidelines for MNEs as a soft law code of conduct.

Concerns about the social responsibility of MNEs are not new. A need for regulation to ensure the accountability of MNEs towards workers, communities and consumers was first identified in the early 1970s.[21] It was seen with unease that, as states are the traditional addressees of international treaty and customary law, MNEs can, in contrast to their amount of power and influence, hide behind the "state veil".[22] A wide variety of international instruments addressing corporate social responsibility have since been developed to fill this regulatory gap. Sources comprise public international law instruments, NGO guidelines, individual business codes of conduct and domestic legislation.[23]

B. Analysis of the Governance

I. Governance through Multi-level Cooperation

Effective governance to promote and secure corporate social responsibility of MNEs during their investment activities is achieved through multi-level institutional and substantial cooperation. Substantial cooperation is realized by reference to other instruments relating to this area. Increased unity in the substantive prescriptions is thereby furthered. Institutional cooperation involves exchanges of views, invitation of experts from other organizations and non-member states and sharing of institutional infrastructure. This leads to a pooling of knowledge and institutions. Resulting from multi-level cooperation is rationalization and enhanced effectiveness of the particular initiatives addressing corporate social responsibility.

---

20 IOANNIS N. ANDROULAKIS, DIE GLOBALISIERUNG DER KORRUPTIONSBEKÄMPFUNG 190 (2006), ZERK (note 18), at 248.

21 ANDROULAKIS (note 20), at 128; James Salzman, *Decentralized Administrative Law in the Organisation for Economic Cooperation and Development*, 68 LAW AND CONTEMPORARY PROBLEMS 189, 212 (2004-2005); ZERK (note 18), at 22 *et seq*.

22 Ilias Bantekas, *Corporate Social Responsibility in International Law*, 22 BOSTON UNIVERSITY INTERNATIONAL LAW JOURNAL 309 (2004).

23 *Id.*

The OECD Guidelines for MNEs are a prime example of effective governance through multi-level cooperation. The OECD as the Guidelines for MNEs' institutional framework is characterized by cooperation with other organizations, non-member states and experts. The procedures that led to the revised Guidelines for MNEs in 2000 involved a variety of actors. Furthermore, the Guidelines for MNEs' implementation mechanism is characterised by multi-level institutional cooperation. With relation to substantial cooperation, the Guidelines for MNEs widely refer to substantive norms of other institutions' instruments.

1. Institutional Cooperation to Promote Corporate Social Responsibility

The multi-level cooperation to promote corporate social responsibility is realized through a network of international organisations, NGOs and experts. The principal actor of the network is the OECD.

a) The OECD as the Principal Actor

The OECD was founded in 1961 as the successor of the Organisation of European Economic Cooperation (OEEC).[24] Currently, thirty states are members of the OECD. These are the source of most of the world's direct investment flows and home to most MNEs.[25] According to Article 5 of the OECD Convention, the OECD "may (a) take decisions which, except as otherwise provided, shall be binding on all the members; (b) make recommendations to members; and (c) enter into agreements with members, non-member states and international organisations."[26] To fulfil its tasks, the OECD is provided with a budget by the member states which amounted to EUR 342.9 million in 2008.[27] The

---

[24] The OEEC was founded in 1948 to implement the European Recovery Program (Marshall Plan). *Cf.* Convention on the Organisation of Economic Co-operation and Development (Convention on the OECD), 14 December 1960, Art. 15, UNTS, vol. 888, 180.

[25] United Nations Conference on Trade and Development, World Investment Report, 2007, available at: http://www.unctad.org/en/docs/wir2007_en.pdf, at 3 and 24.

[26] Convention on the OECD (note 24), Art. 5.

[27] OECD, OECD Annual Report 2008, available at: http://www.oecd.org/dataoecd/39/19/40556222.pdf, at 11.

OECD has its Secretariat in Paris[28] which is staffed by around 2,500 employees coming from all the member states.[29] The substantive work of the OECD is conducted in about 200 Committees and Working Groups by about 40,000 senior officials from national administrations and independent experts.[30] The highest decision making organ in the OECD is the Council which convenes annually in sessions of Ministers and in between in sessions of Permanent Representatives.[31] Decisions in the Council are taken by consensus.[32] The Council is assisted by an Executive Committee[33] that meets in composition of senior officials.[34]

b) Cooperation with Other Organizations, Non-member States and Experts

The responsible body for the Guidelines for MNEs' mechanism is the Investment Committee which is attributed to the Directorate for Financial and Enterprise Affairs. The OECD member states send senior officials of national ministries and central banks to the Investment Committee. Observing states in the Investment Committee are Argentina, Brazil, Egypt and Chile, which are countries adhering to the Guidelines without being members of the OECD. International organisations, namely the International Monetary Fund, the United Nations Conference on Trade and Development, the World Bank and the World Trade Organisation send observers to the Investment Committee.[35] The

---

28 Other permanent OECD bases are in Berlin, Mexico City, Tokyo and Washington D.C.

29 *Id.* at 101.

30 *Id.* at 107.

31 Convention on the OECD (note 24), Art. 7.

32 Convention on the OECD (note 24), Art. 6.

33 Convention on the OECD (note 24), Art. 9; Council, Resolution of the Council on a new governance structure for the organisation, C(2006)78/FINAL, 24 May 2006, para. 31.

34 ROGER BLANPAIN, THE OECD GUIDELINES FOR MULTINATIONAL ENTERPRISES AND LABOUR RELATIONS, 1976-1979, 29 (1979).

35 Resolution of the Council on the Terms of Reference of the Investment Committee, C(2004)3 and CORR1, 22 April 2004; Convention on the OECD (note 24), Art. 12; Rules of Procedure of the Organisation, (C(61)21), 30 September 1962, as amended in 1962 (C(62)115(Final)) and 1970 (C(70)133(Final), rules 8(a), 9; Note by the Secretary-General, Participation of non-members in the activities of the organisation: legal aspects of the issue, C(98)211, 2 Decem-

OECD furthermore invites observers from international governmental and non-governmental organisations as well as from non-member states into the Investment Committee facilitating extensive cooperation.[36]

The Investment Committee was created by the OECD Council on 1 March 2004 by a merger of the Committee on Capital Movements and Invisible Transactions and the Committee on International Investment and MNEs (CIME).[37] The mandate of the Investment Committee among other responsibilities is to carry out the tasks assigned to it by the OECD Declaration on International Investment and MNEs and the related Council Decisions on the Guidelines for MNEs and the Procedural Guidance.[38] The Investment Committee established the Working Party of the Investment Committee that supports the Committee in its work concerning the Guidelines for MNEs.[39] A system of reporting duties from the Working Parties to the Committees to the Council enhances cooperation between the individual OECD bodies.[40]

Multi-level cooperation with the OECD as the principal institution is furthermore realized by formal relations the OECD maintains with representatives of trade unions and of businesses and industry in the

---

ber 1998, para. 3; Resolution of the Council concerning the participation of non-members in the work of subsidiary bodies of the organisation, C(2004)132/FINAL, 5 August 2004.

[36] *See* Note by the Secretary-General, Participation of non-members in the activities of the organisation: legal aspects of the issue, C(98)211, 2 December 1998; Resolution of the Council concerning the participation of non-members in the work of subsidiary bodies of the organisation, C(2004)132/FINAL, 5 August 2004.

[37] Rules of Procedure of the Organisation, (C(61)21), 30 September 1962, as amended in 1962 (C(62)115(Final)) and 1970 (C(70)133(Final), rules 22(a), 18(a)(iii); Resolution of the Council on the Terms of Reference of the Investment Committee, C(2004)3 and CORR1, 22 April 2004.

[38] Resolution of the Council on the Terms of Reference of the Investment Committee, C(2004)3 and CORR1, 22 April 2004, Art. 3; Ministerial Booklet (note 2), Council Decision, chapter II, Procedural Guidance, chapter II, Commentary on the implementation procedures of the Guidelines, chapter II.

[39] The Investment Committee: Strategy and Organisation, Mandate of the Working Party of the Investment Committee, DAF/INV(2004)1, 20 September 2004, para. 1(i).

[40] Ministerial Booklet (note 2), Procedural Guidance, chapter I D (stipulating reporting duties of NCPs to the Investment Committee) and Commentary on the Implementation Procedures, para. 3 (stipulation of reporting duties of the Investment Committee to the Council).

member countries through two organisations. These two organizations are the Business and Industry Advisory Committee (BIAC) and the Trade Union Advisory Committee (TUAC). BIAC and TUAC are officially recognized as advisory bodies to the OECD by the OECD Council.[41] A close and continuing cooperation with business and industry and trade unions through BIAC and TUAC is secured by the fact that the Guidelines for MNEs oblige the OECD Investment Committee to hold exchanges of views with the two organisations on matters covered by the Guidelines and in the experience gained from their application.[42] The exchanges of view with business representatives and trade unions enhance effectiveness and rationalisation. The early involvement of both sides of the bargaining table, business and industry through BIAC and trade unions through TUAC, makes sure that their viewpoints and objections are taken into consideration at all stages of the negotiation, adoption and implementation of the instrument. In addition to reinforcing transparency this involvement leads to higher levels of support by the people and acceptance of the instrument and thereby to increased effectiveness.[43]

---

41 BIAC was constituted in 1962 as an independent organisation with the task to represent business and industry in the work of the OECD and to express opinions on questions of common interest. TUAC is one of the oldest international trade union groupings with direct consultative status with an international organisation. It was founded in 1948 to allow European trade unions to play a full role in the administration of the Marshall Plan by the OEEC and vis-à-vis the European Recovery Program. With the creation of the OECD in 1961, TUAC was officially accredited with consultative status by the OECD, representing the organized workers of OECD member countries. TUAC maintains a permanent Secretariat in Paris. *Cf.* Labour/Management Programme (LMP) Final Reports, 2002, available at: http://www.oecd.org/document/61/0,2340,en_2649_201185_1944829_1_1_1_1,00.html; Homepages of BIAC and TUAC are available at: http://biac.org/ and http://www.tuac.org/en/public/index.phtml; BLANPAIN (note 34), 36, 40.

42 Ministerial Booklet (note 2), Council Decision, chapter II 1. The "exchanges of view" can also be requested by BIAC and TUAC. Individual MNEs also have the opportunity to express their views concerning the Guidelines, but only on issues involving their interests. *Cf.* Ministerial Booklet (note 2), Council Decision, chapter II, paras. 1-5.

43 *See* A. Laurence Dubin & Rozen Nogellou, *Public Participation in Global Administrative Organizations*, working paper, presented at the 3rd global administrative law seminar, Viterbo, 15-16 June 2007, at 26.

BIAC and TUAC are furthermore very involved in the Guidelines for MNEs' processes. TUAC in particular plays an important role since the specific instances are to a great part filed by TUAC. TUAC also takes over special training responsibilities, conducting seminars to train interested organisations (mainly representing the work force) how to initiate the implementation procedures in the NCPs.[44]

Another organisation involved in the mechanism of the Guidelines for MNEs is OECD Watch, an umbrella organisation that was established in 2003 to coordinate the work of NGOs on the OECD Guidelines for MNEs.[45]

2. Substantial Cooperation in the Field of Corporate Social Responsibility

The OECD Guidelines for MNEs form the normative nucleus of such governance.

a) The OECD Guidelines for MNEs as the Normative Nucleus

The OECD Guidelines for MNEs are part of an investment package contained in four documents. They were first adopted in 1976 and in their present form at the Ministerial Council Meeting in 2000.[46] Two of the four interrelated documents, the OECD Declaration on International Investment and MNEs and their annex, the OECD Guidelines for MNEs, stipulate substantive law. The other two documents, the Council Decision on the Guidelines for MNEs and the attached Procedural Guidance, prescribe implementation procedures for the OECD Guidelines for MNEs. The OECD's Investment Committee further prepared Commentaries on these four documents to provide information on and explanation of the Guidelines' text and the Council Decision. The commentaries are neither an integral part of the Declaration on International Investment nor of the Council Decision on the Guide-

---

44 For example, a seminar held by TUAC on the European Works Councils and the OECD Guidelines for MNEs, available at: http://old.tuac.org/statemen/communiq/TUAC%20training%20En.pdf.

45 Homepage of OECD Watch, available at: http://www.oecdwatch.org.

46 Ministerial Booklet (note 2). Previous revisions were carried out in 1979, 1982, 1984 and 1991. *See* OECD, THE OECD GUIDELINES FOR MULTINATIONAL ENTERPRISES 7 (1994); BLANPAIN (note 34), at 34.

lines.[47] While the Declaration on International Investment and MNEs and the Guidelines for MNEs are non-binding, the Council Decision on the Guidelines for MNEs and the attached Procedural Guidance are binding on adhering states.[48]

The standards stipulated in the OECD Guidelines for MNEs contain the substantive prescriptions of corporate social responsibility and are arranged in eight chapters. The prescriptions are formulated broadly and MNEs have to design specific measures in order to implement the Guidelines for MNE's standards themselves. Following a chapter on concepts and principles and one on general policies, the Guidelines address eight subject fields, namely policies of disclosure, employment and industrial relations, environment, combating bribery, consumer interests, science and technology, competition and finally taxation.[49]

The OECD Guidelines address MNEs, however they stipulate only a vague definition of an MNE. According to the OECD Guidelines, MNEs usually comprise companies or other entities established in more than one country that are linked so that they may co-ordinate their operations in various ways.[50] The Guidelines for MNEs' applicability however is not restricted to MNEs; the OECD Guidelines are also intended to direct domestic as well as small and medium-sized enterprises.[51] They are designed to influence the behaviour of those MNEs located in an adhering state, and to those MNEs located in non-adhering states that have their headquarters in one of the adhering states.[52]

b) Reference to Other Instruments

The Guidelines for MNEs are characterized by the fact that they extensively refer to substantive norms in other international treaties and soft law instruments. The OECD Guidelines explicitly state that they are

---

47 Ministerial Booklet (note 2), Commentaries.

48 Convention on the OECD (note 24), Art. 5a); Ministerial Booklet (note 2), Introduction.

49 Ministerial Booklet (note 2), OECD Guidelines on MNEs.

50 *Id.* OECD Guidelines on MNEs, chapter I, para. 3.

51 *Id.* OECD Guidelines on MNEs, chapter I, paras. 4, 5.

52 *Id.* OECD Guidelines on MNEs, Foreword.

intended to stand beside and not conflict with other instruments in the subject field of corporate social responsibility.[53]

For example, the provisions of the Guidelines' chapter on employment and industrial relations echo relevant provisions of the International Labor Organizations' (ILO) 1988 Declaration on Fundamental Principles and Rights at Work as well as the ILO's 1977 Tripartite Declaration of Principles concerning Multinational Enterprises and Social Policy.[54] Among other ILO Conventions and Recommendations, the Guidelines' chapter on employment and industrial relations furthermore refers to the ILO Conventions 182 concerning the worst forms of child labor.[55]

The text of the Guidelines' chapter on the environment reflects the principles and objectives contained in the Rio Declaration on Environment and Development in Agenda 21. It also takes into account the (Aarhus) Convention on Access to Information, Public Participation in Decision-making, and Access to Justice in Environmental Matters and reflects standards in such instruments as the ISO Standard on Environmental Management Systems.[56]

The chapter on combating bribery refers to the OECD Convention on Combating Bribery of Foreign Public Officials as well as the respective OECD Recommendations on combating bribery.[57] The Guidelines' chapter on consumer interest draws on the work of the OECD Committee on Consumer Policy, as well as that embodied in various individual and international corporate codes (such as those of the ICC), the UN Guidelines on Consumer Policy, and the OECD Guidelines for Consumer Protection in the Context of Electronic Commerce.[58]

The remaining chapters of the Guidelines for MNEs similarly refer to the relevant international norms in the respective subject matter.[59] Other organisations promote the Guidelines for MNEs, *e.g.* in the

---

53 *Id.* OECD Guidelines on MNEs, Foreword, chapters IV, V, IX.

54 *Id.* Commentary on the OECD Guidelines for MNEs, paras. 19-29.

55 *Id.* Commentary on the OECD Guidelines for MNEs, paras. 19-29.

56 *Id.* Commentary on the OECD Guidelines for MNEs, paras. 30-42.

57 *Id.* Commentary on the OECD Guidelines for MNEs, paras. 43-47.

58 *Id.* Commentary on the OECD Guidelines for MNEs, paras. 48-52.

59 *Id.* Commentary on the OECD Guidelines for MNEs, para. 52.

European Union the Guidelines for MNEs are promoted by the European Commission.[60]

II. Governance through Decentralized Soft Implementation

Effective governance to promote and secure corporate social responsibility of MNEs during their investment activities is furthermore achieved through decentralized soft implementation. This proposition is supported by the fact that the effectiveness of the Guidelines for MNEs' was significantly enhanced due to decentralization of the implementation mechanism of the Guidelines for MNEs. The enhanced decentralization was instituted as a result of the revision of the Guidelines for MNEs in 2000. Before 2000, NCPs located in the governments of adhering states only served as the initial stage of consideration for issues and conflicts arising under the Guidelines for MNEs. They regularly passed the issues to the OECD Investment Committee that was ultimately responsible for the clarification and interpretation of the Guidelines for MNEs.[61] In the revised documents NCPs were significantly strengthened. They are now the main institutions to decide on a specific instance. Today they are responsible for taking up specific in-

---

[60] Commission of the European Communities, Directorate-General for Employment and Social Affairs, Promoting a European Framework for Corporate Social Responsibility: Green Paper, COM (2001) 366 final, 18 July 2001, at 6; EC Directive on the establishment of a European Works Council on a procedure in Community-scale undertakings and Community-scale groups of undertakings for the purposes of information and consulting employees, 94/45 of 22 September 1994. This directive established European Works Councils to inform employees in the EU of their rights and to promote the OECD Guidelines for MNEs; TUAC held seminars on the European Works Councils and the OECD Guidelines for MNEs and disseminates information, available at: http://old.tuac.org/statemen/communiq/TUAC% 20training%20En.pdf.

[61] The Committee's decisions had to be taken by consensus, they had no retrospective applicability and a case was merely used to clarify the meaning of how a provision in the Guidelines should be applied in future cases. These decisions were not binding and resulted in no penalties for violation. *See* James Salzman, *Decentralized Administrative Law in the Organisation for Economic Cooperation and Development*, 68 LAW AND CONTEMPORARY PROBLEMS 189, 213 (2004-2005); Michael Klinkenberg, *Die Leitsätze der OECD für multinationale Unternehmen*, 101 ZEITSCHRIFT FÜR VERGLEICHENDE RECHTSWISSENSCHAFT 421, 421 (2002).

stances, investigating the facts, deciding whether the Guidelines for MNEs were violated and for issuing reports that name the MNE involved in the instance.[62]

Statistics on the numbers of cases filed and considered illustrate that the revised Guidelines for MNEs are more effective than before the revision in 2000. Between 1976 and 2000 just over forty specific instances were brought before an NCP. Since the 2000 revision of the Guidelines about 156 requests to consider specific instances were filed, 134 of these were actively taken up and considered and 84 of these of these have been concluded.[63]

1. Decentralized Cooperation: The Principle of Functional Equivalence

The institutional setup and the procedures for the decentralized implementation are prescribed by the Council Decision on the Guidelines and the attached Procedural Guidance.[64] According to these documents, NCPs must be instituted in each adhering state according to the principle of functional equivalence.[65] This principle effectuates the subsidiarity principle, affording discretion to the individual state with regard to the institutional arrangement of the NCP. The strengthening of the subsidiarity principle through the principle of functional equivalence provides for further evidence that decentralization is a target of OECD policies in the examined form of governance. The principle of functional equivalence merely requires states to set up their NCPs so that they meet certain basic prerequisites. These prerequisites which are binding on all adhering states include visibility, accessibility, transparency and accountability of the respective NCP.[66]

---

[62] Ministerial Booklet (note 2), Council Decision, chapter I, Procedural Guidance, chapter I C.

[63] Report by the Chair, 2007 Annual Meeting of the National Contact Points, at 14, available at: http://www.oecd.org/dataoecd/23/26/39319743.pdf.

[64] Ministerial Booklet (note 2), Council Decision, chapter I, Procedural Guidance, chapter I.

[65] *Id.* Council Decision, chapter I, Procedural Guidance, chapter I.

[66] *Id.* Procedural Guidance, chapter I; Commentaries on the Implementation Procedures, chapter I. In effect, the current NCP structure consists of: 20 NCPs single government departments; 7 NCP multiple departments; 1 bipartite NCP (involving government and business); 9 tripartite NCPs (involving governments, business, and trade unions); and 2 quadripartite NCPs (involving governments, business, trade unions and NGOs). Report by the Chair, 2007

The NCPs located in the governments of adhering states are envisaged to act according to the OECD's Procedural Guidance. The Guidelines for MNEs' implementation procedures connect national governments and the OECD. These two instruments stipulate institutional and procedural prescriptions. To this extent, NCPs are independent from national law. To the extent that the binding Procedural Guidance and the oversight procedures for the Investment Committee are effective, the national governments could be seen as an implementation organ of the international mechanism. This could be seen as constituting a form of hierarchy. However, the principle of functional equivalence prescribed in the Procedural Guidance grants discretion to the national governments. The relationship between national governments and the OECD with relation to the implementation mechanism is based on and best characterized by decentralized cooperation.

2. *Procedures for a Mediation-based Decentralized Implementation*

The procedures for implementation in specific instances are prescribed by the Council Decision on the Guidelines and the attached Procedural Guidance.[67] According to these documents, NCPs are envisioned to serve as a forum for negotiations with the aim to reach an equitable settlement between the individual MNE charged with the violation and the complainant.[68] Common functions of an NCP include the dissemination, promotion and, to the extent necessary, explanation of the Guidelines and the collection of information concerning past experience with the Guidelines for MNEs at the national level. NCPs should further provide a forum for discussion, particularly for businesses and trade unions, on problems which may arise in relation to the Guidelines and on facilities which could contribute to their solution. NCPs should stay in direct contact with other NCPs, if necessary.[69] The NCPs' main function is to provide a forum for and organize negotiations relating to the implementation of the OECD Guidelines for MNEs in specific instances.

Annual Meeting of the National Contact Points, at 20, available at: http://www.oecd.org/dataoecd/23/26/39319743.pdf.

[67] *Id.* Council Decision, chapter I, Procedural Guidance, chapter I.

[68] *Id.* Council Decision, chapter I 1, Procedural Guidelines, chapter I C.

[69] *Id.* Council Decision, chapter I, Procedural Guidance, chapter I.

The implementation procedures in a particular instance filed with an NCP have four phases. In the first phase the NCP procedures are initiated. Any interested party can file a "specific instance", a certain conduct by an MNE that is allegedly not in accordance with the OECD Guidelines for MNEs.[70] In most specific instances these interested parties are trade unions and NGOs.[71] In the second phase of the procedures, the NCP decides according to the OECD Procedural Guidance whether it has the competence to take up the specific instance.[72] One debated issue during this stage is whether specific instances must have an "investment nexus" or whether the NCP can get involved in merely trade-related instances.[73] Another debated issue relates to the consequences of existing national parallel proceedings since NCPs can neither override national rules and regulations nor override or interfere with national legal or administrative procedures.[74] If the NCP decides that it is responsible for the instance, the NCP will in the third phase of the proceedings start to facilitate negotiations between the involved

---

70 *Id.*, Procedural Guidance, chapter I C.

71 *See* Trade Union Advisory Committee (TUAC), TUAC Submission to the OECD Annual Meeting of National Contact Points (NCPs), para. 2 (2007), available at: http://www.tuac.org/en/public/e-docs/00/00/00/72/document_doc.phtml; OECD-Watch, List of OECD Guidelines cases filed by NGOs as of October 3, 2007, available at: http://www.oecdwatch.org/docs/List_OECD_Guidelines_cases_3October2007.pdf.

72 Ministerial Booklet (note 2), Procedural Guidance, chapter I C. Approximately two-thirds of the specific instances concerned MNEs' operations in non-adhering countries, but the procedural prescriptions do not determine which NCP will be responsible for an issue that took place in a non-adhering country. In practice issues arising in a non-adhering country are generally dealt with in the home country of the MNE. *See id.*, Commentary on the Implementation Procedures, para. 20.

73 *See* OECD Watch, The Guidelines for Multinational Enterprises and Supply Chain Responsibility (2004), available at: http://www.germanwatch.org/tw/kw-sup04.pdf; Trade Union Advisory Committee (TUAC), TUAC Submission to the OECD Annual Meeting of National Contact Points (NCPs), paras. 41, 44 (2007), available at: http://www.tuac.org/en/public/e-docs/00/00/00/72/document_doc.phtml.

74 Trade Union Advisory Committee (TUAC), TUAC Submission to the OECD Annual Meeting of National Contact Points (NCPs), paras. 39, 44 (2007), available at: http://www.tuac.org/en/public/e-docs/00/00/00/72/document_doc.phtml.

parties.[75] In the course of negotiations, the particular NCP might contact other NCPs or state institutions as in the case described in the introduction of this study in which the Czech NCP contacted the German NCP. Concluding the procedures with a fourth phase, NCPs are required to issue a "statement" declaring that the MNE does or does not comply with the Guidelines in the specific instance, in case the parties involved do not reach agreement.[76] In this statement, the NCP may make recommendations on the implementation of the Guidelines as appropriate.[77] The statements are envisaged to be published by NCPs in those specific instances where negotiations between the MNE and the complainant fail.[78]

3. Cooperation to Implement Effectively

Particular NCPs cooperate in the course of the specific instances as illustrated in the specific instances described above. Moreover, in order to enhance effectiveness through rationalisation of institutions the German NCP and the German Network of the UN Global Compact agreed to share their infrastructure to promote and implement their instruments in the field of corporate social responsibility. The German NCP is located in the Federal Ministry of Economics and Technology.[79] It established a working group on the OECD Guidelines (Arbeitskreis "OECD-Leitsätze") bringing together representatives of diverse government resorts, social partners, trade associations and NGOs.[80] The Ministry promotes the Guidelines on its website and composed a bro-

---

75 Ministerial Booklet (note 2), Procedural Guidance, chapter I C.

76 *Id.*, Procedural Guidance, chapter I C.

77 *Id.*, Procedural Guidance, chapter I C.

78 *Id.*, Procedural Guidance, chapter I C. This obligation is often broken by NCPs. They more often report on the proceedings when they were successful, than when they were unsuccessful. OECD-Watch, List of OECD Guidelines cases filed by NGOs as of October 3, 2007, available at: http://www.oecdwatch.org/docs/List_OECD_Guidelines_cases_3October2007.pdf.

79 Information available on the Homepage of the Federal Ministry of Economics and Technology: http://www.bmwi.de/BMWi/Navigation/aussenwirtschaft,did=177082.html.

80 Bundesministerium für Wirtschaft und Technologie, Jahresbericht für den Berichtszeitraum Juni 2006-Juni 2007, at 1, available at: http://www.bmwi.de/BMWi/Redaktion/PDF/M-O/oecd-nks-jahresbericht,property=pdf,bereich=bmwi,sprache=de,rwb=true.pdf.

chure[81] which is supplied through German embassies, the national and international chambers of commerce and via the internet. The German NCP has concluded three specific instances[82] and assisted other NCPs in seven specific instances.[83] The arrangement with the UN Global Compact foresees that the German NCP will use the procedural prescriptions of the OECD Procedural Guidance to implement the UN Global Compact when an issue comes up involving alleged violations of the standards prescribed in the UN Global Compact.[84]

III. Legal Characteristics of the Governance

The governance mechanism's legal characteristics come to light when viewed from the present project's perspective. One legal aspect that can be observed is the necessity of a concrete mandate for the particular OECD policies. Furthermore, the international adherence procedure for the Guidelines for MNEs comprises characteristics of international ratification procedures for a hard law instrument. However, national parliaments are not involved in the processes. In this context a remarkable aspect from a legal viewpoint is the *de facto* constraint to implement the Guidelines for MNEs. The *de facto* constraint is implied due to the implementation mechanism linked to the OECD Guidelines for MNEs that is binding on adhering states.

---

[81] Bundesministerium für Wirtschaft und Technologie, Verantwortliches unternehmerisches Handeln im Ausland, "Die OECD-Leitsätze für multinationale Unternehmen", (2006), available at: http://www.bmwi.de/BMWi/Navigation/aussenwirtschaft,did=26126.html.

[82] The statements of the German NCP with regard to these three cases are available for download at: http://www.bmwi.de/BMWi/Navigation/aussenwirtschaft,did=178196.html.

[83] Bundesministerium für Wirtschaft und Technologie, Verantwortliches unternehmerisches Handeln im Ausland, "Die OECD-Leitsätze für multinationale Unternehmen" (2006), available at: http://www.bmwi.de/BMWi/Navigation/aussenwirtschaft,did=26126.html.

[84] Report by the Chair, 2007 Annual Meeting of the National Contact Points, at 6, available at: http://www.oecd.org/dataoecd/23/26/39319743.pdf.

1. Necessity of a Concrete Mandate

One legal characteristic of the governance mechanism is the requirement of a concrete mandate for each policy taken. The mandate for the examined governance is attained through concretizations of the aims of the OECD set out in Article 1 OECD Convention. According to Article 1 OECD Convention the OECD aims "to promote policies designed (a) to achieve highest sustainable economic growth and employment and a rising standard of living in member countries, while maintaining financial stability, and thus to contribute to the development of the world economy; (b) to contribute to sound economic expansion in member as well as non-member countries in the process of economic development; and (c) to contribute to the expansion of world trade on a multilateral, non-discriminatory basis in accordance with international obligations".[85]

Corporate social responsibility is contained in these aims of the OECD. Corporate social responsibility is today part of economic and development policies. In that respect, a change of the meaning of the concept of economic development can be observed. An indication for corporate social responsibility as an aim of OECD policies can also be found in the aim to contribute to "sound economic expansion". However, Article 1 OECD Convention is formulated broadly. Particular OECD policies need more concrete mandates. Concretizations are formulated by the OECD Council through its permanent representatives and by experts in the Executive Committee and in the general committees.[86]

The first concretization with regard to the OECD Guidelines for MNEs is carried out in order to provide a mandate for the Investment Committee. The Investment Committee received its mandate from the OECD Council through a Council Resolution.[87] The Council resolution authorizes the Investment Committee to follow up on the work of the Committee on International Investment and MNEs (CIME). One responsibility the Investment Committee was established to carry out concerns the tasks assigned to it by virtue of the OECD Declaration on International Investment and Multinational Enterprises and related Council Decisions.[88] The specific mandate to formulate the OECD

---

85 Convention on the OECD (note 24), Art. 1.

86 BLANPAIN (note 34), at 34.

87 Rules of Procedure of the Organisation (note 37), rules 22(a), 18(a)(iii).

88 Resolution of the Council on the Terms of Reference of the Investment Committee, C(2004)3, 22 April 2004, Art. 3 no. 3.

Guidelines for MNEs was provided for by a Council resolution establishing the Committee on International Investment and MNEs (CIME) in 1975.[89]

In a second concretization the working groups are provided a mandate by the OECD Committee whose work they are established to assist.[90] With regards to the OECD Guidelines for MNEs the Investment Committee established the Working Party of the Investment Committee with the mandate among other tasks, "to assist the Investment Committee in implementing the Declaration on International Investment and Multinational Enterprises and related Decisions, including with respect to its responsibilities in relation to the 2000 Guidelines on Multinational Enterprises".[91]

2. *The Adherence Procedure*

Another legal aspect of the governance mechanism that can be traced through this project's perspective relates to the procedures for becoming an adhering state to the OECD Guidelines for MNEs. It is possible to adhere to the OECD Guidelines for MNEs without being a member state of the OECD. The Declaration on International Investment and MNEs and the related instruments have been adhered to by ten non-member states.[92] The last state to become an adhering state to the Guidelines for MNEs was Egypt in 2007. The international adherence procedures involved the signing of the OECD Declaration for International Investment and MNEs by Egypt's Minister of Investment. Internationally, the adherence procedure exhibits elements that characterise the international ratification procedure of hard law instruments. On the national level however, the soft law Guidelines are not presented to national parliaments. This is especially noteworthy in light of the follow-

---

[89] Committee on International Investment and MNEs (CIME), Experience with the OECD Guidelines for MNEs, DAFFE/IME(98)15, 3 November 1998, para. 11; BLANPAIN (note 34), 31.

[90] Rules of Procedure of the Organisation (note 37), rule 21(b).

[91] The Investment Committee: Strategy and Organisation, 'Mandate of the Working Party of the Investment Committee', DAF/INV(2004)1, 20 September 2004, para. 1(i).

[92] Argentina (1997), Brazil (1997), Chile (1997), Egypt (2007), Estonia (2001), Israel (2002), Latvia (2004), Lithuania (2001), Romania (2005) and Slovenia (2002).

ing aspect relating to the *de facto* constraint to implement the Guidelines for MNEs.

3. De facto Constraint to Implement Soft Law

A third legal feature of the governance mechanism is a *de facto* constraint to implement soft law. It was explained above that the instruments comprising the substantive investment and corporate social responsibility norms are non-binding while the instruments prescribing the institutional and procedural requirements of the implementation mechanism are binding on adhering states.[93] This qualification leads to the situation that MNEs are addressed with an instrument the implementation of which is not mandatory. However, as soon as an outside actor files a specific instance with an NCP the adhering state is required to take action with respect to the specific instance according to the OECD Guidelines for MNEs' Procedural Guidance. To the extent that the implementation mechanism is effective, the binding nature of the procedural prescriptions creates a *de facto* constraint for MNEs to implement the soft law Guidelines for MNEs.[94] It was discussed contrariwise during the negotiations of the 2000 revision whether a *de facto* constraint to implement the Guidelines was created and if so, whether this was in the parties' interest when they were setting up the implementation mechanism in a Council Decision that is binding on adhering states.[95]

IV. Accountability

Accountability of the Guidelines for MNEs is characterized by the fact that the OECD is to a large degree independent from national govern-

---

93 Convention on the OECD (note 24), Art. 5(a); *cf.* above at Part B I 2a.

94 *See* CIME, Aide-mémoire of the informal consultations between BIAC, TUAC, NGOs and the CIME Working Party on the Guidelines on the Review of the OECD Guidelines for MNEs, held on 14 April 2000, DAFFE/IME(2000)13, 15 May 2000, paras. 9-13.

95 CIME, Aide-mémoire of the informal consultations between BIAC, TUAC, NGOs and the CIME Working Party on the Guidelines on the Review of the OECD Guidelines for MNEs, held on 14 April 2000, DAFFE/IME(2000)13, 15 May 2000, paras. 9-13.

ments. All instruments examined in the Guidelines for MNEs' procedures are soft law instruments and do not need ratification in national parliaments. They are adhered to by national ministers without involvement of national governments. The Guidelines for MNEs' implementation mechanism through NCPs is to a certain degree overseen by the OECD Investment Committee. However, the oversight powers of the Investment Committee are very weak. Participation of a variety of actors from outside the OECD characterized the revision procedures of the Guidelines for MNEs in 2000. The extensive cooperation ensures participation in all stages of the Guidelines for MNEs' procedure. Accountability is therefore ensured to a certain degree through participation. Transparency is prescribed and must be given effect by adhering governments. However, *de facto* implementation of transparent procedures and disclosure of NCP documents is problematic.

1. Independence of the International Mechanism from National Governments

All four interlinked instruments of the mechanism were adopted by consensus by the OECD's highest decision making organ, the Council in composition of ministers. National parliaments are not involved in the process. OECD activities are not directly mandated by the Convention of the OECD that was officially adopted and ratified in national parliaments. Rather, the OECD's aims are concretized by the Council and the Committees, even though in the case of corporate social responsibility the general aims of the OECD provide for a starting point for concretization.

2. Internal Oversight

The responsibilities of the Investment Committee were changed in the 2000 revision and today the Investment Committee conducts a form of oversight over the mechanism.[96] An adhering state or an advisory body

---

96 Ministerial Booklet (note 2), Procedural Guidance, II 3 b): "The Committee will consider a substantiated submission by an adhering country or an advisory body on whether an NCP is responsible with regard to its handling of specific instances." Ministerial Booklet (note 2), Commentary on the Implementation Procedures, para. 4: "[The Committee] is the OECD body responsible for overseeing the functioning of the Guidelines"; *see* Report of the International Law Association, Berlin Conference (2004), Accountability of International

can make a substantiated submission on whether an NCP has correctly interpreted the Guidelines for MNEs in a specific instance. The Investment Committee was involved in the Botnia S.A. pulp mill investment described above.[97] The Center for Human Rights and Environment filed a complaint to the OECD Investment Committee for failure to correctly interpret and implement the Guidelines.[98] In case the Investment Committee decides that the NCP did not follow the procedures according to the Procedural Guidance and did not interpret the Guidelines correctly in the abstract, it can issue a clarification how the Guidelines for MNEs should correctly be interpreted.[99] The clarifications are posted on the internet.[100] This oversight function of the Investment Committee is similar to a second instance. But due to the non-binding nature of the Guidelines, the Investment Committee is precluded from acting as a judicial or quasi-judicial organ and the documents make explicit that the Investment Committee cannot reinvestigate the facts of a specific instance and review the decision of an NCP and that it cannot reach conclusions on the conduct of individual enterprises.[101] The oversight is thereby limited in the sense that the Investment Committee does not have powers to overrule the statements made by the NCPs.[102]

The Investment Committee has so far been involved in this oversight function in only a few specific instances. The benchmarks in the reports it published were not specific. In a report on a submission by the Swiss NCP on a request concerning the clarification of the procedural prescriptions, the Investment Committee did not provide for specific criteria on how to interpret the Guidelines for MNEs in the future and

---

Organisations, reprinted in: 1 INTERNATIONAL ORGANIZATIONS LAW REVIEW 221, 237 (2004).

97 Compare above at A I.

98 Pulp mill project: CEDHA appeals to OECD Investment Committee over Finnish NCP handling of Botnia S.A. specific instance, 23 January 2007, available at: http://www.oecdwatch.org/docs/CEDHA_vs_Botnia_PR_InvCom.pdf.

99 Ministerial Booklet (note 2), Procedural Guidance, chapter II 3c.

100 They are contained in the annual reports of TUAC and in the annual reports of the Investment Committee on the NCPs.

101 Ministerial Booklet (note 2), Commentary on the Implementation Procedures of the Guidelines for MNEs, para. 23.

102 *See* Report of the International Law Association, Berlin Conference (2004), *Accountability of International Organisations*, reprinted in 1 INTERNATIONAL ORGANIZATIONS LAW REVIEW 221, 237 (2004).

merely stressed that the Guidelines should be interpreted in a way to enhance their effectiveness.[103]

3. Participation and Transparency

The multi-level cooperation leads to increased participation and transparency. In addition to the cooperation displayed above,[104] the 2000 revision procedures for the Guidelines for MNEs were characterized by large-scale cooperation. In these preparation procedures for the revised Guidelines for MNEs in 2000,[105] numerous NGOs,[106] international trade union organisations, external experts and the Guidelines' addressees, MNEs, were involved and had the opportunity to state their opinions on the drafts for the revised Guidelines for MNEs on the inter-

---

[103] In July 2004, the Swiss NCP made a formal request for clarification to the Investment Committee concerning the applicability of the Guidelines and the admissibility of the case because the company was based in Switzerland and not in a foreign country. In its reply the Committee recognized that the Guidelines were applicable to both domestic and international operations of companies, but it stressed the fact that the implementation procedures involving NCPs had been created to deal with issues arising in the context of international investment and in conclusion merely encouraged the Swiss NCP to address the issue in terms of how to further the effectiveness of the Guidelines. *Cf.* Trade Union Advisory Committee (TUAC), TUAC Internal analysis of the treatment of cases raised with national contact points February 2001-April 2007, at 18, available at: http://www.oecdwatch.org/docs/TUAC_ListOfCases_Feb2007.pdf.

[104] Compare above at B I.

[105] The procedures taken to revise the Guidelines in 2000 are the result of the lessons learned from the experience the OECD made during the negotiations for a Multilateral Agreement on Investment (MAI) in 1998 when NGO opposition took the OECD and the MAI negotiators by surprise and forced the supporting governments to drop out of the negotiations. *See* GÜNTER METZGES, NGO-KAMPAGNEN UND IHR EINFLUSS AUF INTERNATIONALE VERHANDLUNGEN 69 (2006); Salzman (note 21), at 189, 196.

[106] Amnesty International, ANPED, Alliance of Northern Peoples for Environment and Development, Friends of the, Friends of the Earth, GERMANWATCH, OXFAM, Reform the World Campaign, SOMO, Centre for Research on Multinational Corporations, TOBI, NGO Task Force on Business and Industry; Tradecraft Exchange, World-Wide Fund for Nature. *See* Working Party on the Guidelines, OECD Guidelines for MNEs Proposals Submitted by BIAC TUAC and NGOs, DAFFE/IME/WPG/RD(2000)16, 9 May 2000.

net.[107] Furthermore, NGOs have a strong influence on effective implementation of the Guidelines for MNEs since the implementation mechanism relies on their participation to initiate the specific instance procedures. Participation of NGOs ensures a degree of accountability of a policy.[108] But the involvement of NGOs is ambiguous.[109] Taking NGOs as the predominant representatives of civil society, their participation is problematic since they themselves are not democratically legitimized: they are not elected, they do not necessarily involve a wide membership and they are not necessarily democratically structured.[110]

Another means to gain accountability is through transparency.[111] The Investment Committee collects information that is provided by the NCPs and publishes this information in annual reports. It thereby generates transparency regarding the institutions and procedures of the implementation mechanism.[112] The transparency during the NCPs procedures themselves is prescribed by the Procedural Guidance as a basic prerequisite that all adhering states have to further in the setup and the procedures of their respective NCPs.[113] However, there is a tension be-

---

107 Committee for Investment and Multinational Enterprises, Aide-mémoire of the informal consultations between BIAC, TUAC, NGOs and the CIME Working Party on the Guidelines on the Review of the OECD Guidelines for MNEs, DAFFE/IME(2000)13, 15 May 2000, para. 2.

108 Report of the International Law Association, Berlin Conference (2004), *Accountability of International Organisations*, reprinted in: 1 INTERNATIONAL ORGANIZATIONS LAW REVIEW 221, 230 (2004).

109 Jan Klabbers, *The Changing Image of International Organisations*, *in* THE LEGITIMACY OF INTERNATIONAL ORGANISATIONS 221, 244 (J.-C. Coicaud & V. Heiskanen eds., 2001).

110 Steve Charnovitz, *Nongovernmental Organisations and International Law,* 100 AMERICAN JOURNAL OF INTERNATIONAL LAW 348, 363 (2006); Ruth W. Grant & Robert O. Keohane, *Accountability and Abuses of Power in World Politics*, 99/1 AMERICAN POLITICAL SCIENCE REVIEW 29, 38 (2005); GÜNTER METZGES, NGO-KAMPAGNEN UND IHR EINFLUSS AUF INTERNATIONALE VERHANDLUNGEN 189 (2006).

111 Report of the International Law Association, Berlin Conference (2004), *Accountability of International Organisations*, reprinted in: 1 INTERNATIONAL ORGANIZATIONS LAW REVIEW 221, 229 (2004).

112 Report by the Chair, 2007 Annual Meeting of the National Contact Points, (2007) available at: http://www.oecd.org/dataoecd/23/26/39319743.pdf, forms part of the forthcoming Annual Report on the OECD Guidelines for Multinational Enterprises 2007.

113 Compare above at Part B IV 1.

tween the right to confidentiality of business operations and the principle of transparency and the necessity to provide information to an NCP during a specific instance procedure; and in fact, transparency is problematic. The Procedural Guidance acknowledges that while procedures in a specific instance are underway, confidentiality of the proceedings will be maintained.[114] Transparency is further aimed to be achieved for the particular specific instances. NCPs are required to issue a statement on the procedures in cases where negotiations fail and the involved parties do not reach agreement. However, statements are not posted on the internet in all required cases.

C. Assessment and Conclusion

I. Principles

From the above analysis of the mechanism two structural regularities according to which the governance is organized and effectuated become apparent. These two are multi-level cooperation and decentralization. The principle of functional equivalence is a specific expression of these two structural principles.[115]

II. Effectiveness

The implementation procedures of the OECD Guidelines for MNEs are characterized by the fact that the initiation of the mechanism is voluntary and does not take place regularly. It depends on NGOs, BIAC and TUAC and other interested actors to file a specific instance with an NCP. Implementation by NCPs is not comprehensive. Neither all substantial parts of the Guidelines are covered nor all observing MNEs in the scope of application of the Guidelines. The Guidelines for MNEs' chapters implemented through the NCPs are to a certain extent predetermined by those who file a specific instance with an NCP. Those are

---

[114] *See* Ministerial Booklet (note 2), Procedural Guidance, chapter I C 4. NCPs are advised to take appropriate steps to protect sensitive business information, *cf.* Ministerial Booklet (note 2), Commentary on the Implementation Procedure of the Guidelines for MNEs, no. 19.

[115] Compare above at Part B IV 1.

for the most part trade unions and human rights NGOs and as a consequence the chapter of the Guidelines enjoying most attention is the chapter on employment and industrial relations.[116] Other chapters are much less controlled. An analysis of the most frequently addressed NCPs – the US, Dutch and French NCPs – concluded that implementation in areas outside of labour relations was not substantial.[117] For these reasons the implementation of the OECD Guidelines for MNEs has been characterized as "piecemeal and inconsistent" in its impact.[118] However, the chapter on labour relations is a very important chapter in the context of MNEs' behaviour during investment activities. The numbers concerning utilization of NCPs set out above indicate an enormous growth in the perceived problem-solving capacity of the Guidelines for MNEs' governance mechanisms.[119]

III. Conclusion

This study proposed that effective governance is achieved through multi-level cooperation and through decentralized soft implementation based on mediation. The OECD Guidelines for MNEs were chosen as an instrument to illustrate this proposition and to prove its validity with regard to corporate social responsibility. Concerning the second proposition, it was argued that effectiveness was enhanced as a result of the 2000 revision of the Guidelines for MNEs due to further decentralization of the implementation mechanism. For future enhancement it is

---

[116] Report by the Chair, 2007 Annual Meeting of the National Contact Points 15 (2007), available at: http://www.oecd.org/dataoecd/23/26/39319743.pdf; *see* Michael Klinkenberg, *Die Leitsätze der OECD für multinationale Unternehmen*, 101 ZEITSCHRIFT FÜR VERGLEICHENDE RECHTSWISSENSCHAFT 421, 428 (2002); CORNELIA HEYDENREICH, DIE OECD-LEITSÄTZE FÜR MULTINATIONALE UNTERNEHMEN – EIN WIRKSAMES INSTRUMENT ZUR UNTERNEHMENSREGULIERUNG? 7, May 2005, available at: http://www.germanwatch.org/tw/kw05ls.pdf.

[117] For a critical assessment of the United States' implementation of the OECD Guidelines for Multinational Enterprises, *see* Christopher N. Franciose, *A Critical Assessment of the United States' Implementation of the OECD Guidelines for Multinational Enterprises*, 30 BOSTON COLLEGE INTL & COMPARATIVE LAW REVIEW 229, 232 (2007).

[118] ZERK (note 18), at 243.

[119] Compare above at B V.

necessary that the implementation of the basic prerequisites for the institutional set up prescribed by the OECD, *viz.* (namely) visibility, accessibility, transparency and accountability, is enhanced. In particular transparency needs to be implemented more vigorously. This leads to the first proposition of this study. Effective governance is achieved through cooperation. In the future, adhering governments need to enhance cooperation with the OECD and secure effective implementation of the basic prescriptions.

In view of the overall project, this study proposed that the project's perspective sheds light on legal characteristics of such governance. In particular, legal characteristics were examined as regards the necessity of a concrete mandate for the Guidelines for MNEs and the *de facto* constraint to implement the Guidelines for MNEs. Concerning the acts taken in order to become an adhering state to a soft law instrument, elements are instituted that characterise the international ratification procedures of hard law instruments without the involvement of national parliaments.

1.3 Information

The Administration of Information in International Administrative Law – The Example of Interpol

*By Bettina Schöndorf-Haubold**

* I would like to thank very much Prof. Sabino Cassese and Prof. Christian Walter for their comments and suggestions on an earlier version of this paper.

A. von Bogdandy et al. (eds.), *The Exercise of Public Authority by International Institutions*, Beiträge zum ausländischen öffentlichen Recht und Völkerrecht 210,
DOI 10.1007/978-3-642-04531-8_9, © Springer-Verlag Berlin Heidelberg 2010

A. Introduction

The photos of the presumed child abuser were published all around the world and resulted in the arrest of the wanted person in no time. Within only a few months, Interpol has twice issued public searches for wanted persons on its own initiative. The immediate success seemed to justify the measures. Does Interpol evolve into a veritable international criminal police? Since Interpol's competences for operational measures are still limited, it seems more appropriate to qualify Interpol as an agency with purely coordinative and providing functions and, accordingly, as an example for international administration.

Within the international administration, Interpol assumes a special role. This international police organization has developed only gradually from a loose association of police authorities into an intergovernmental international organization. Repressive and preventive actions against crime, thus administrative tasks at least in part, have always been central functions of this organization. At the same time, Interpol, in contrast to other administrative authorities, is limited, in principle, to acts of support. Interpol provides a platform and infrastructure for co-operation between national administrative authorities. Interpol itself does not have the competence to decide in particular cases, although such competence is a typical element of administrative work. This restriction can be explained by the wish to preserve national sovereignty. Nevertheless, the work of Interpol can be characterized as informational administrative activity[1] being a traditional area of administrative law.[2]

B. Interpol's Relevance for the International Administrative Law

I. The Subject Area: Police Activity in Danger and Crime Prevention

Interpol is the name of the International Criminal Police Organization (ICPO) with currently 186 members[3] and headquarters in Lyon (France). Regarding the number of member states, it is the second largest international organization after the United Nations. Nonetheless, Interpol has only 450 employees, one third of them delegated by the member states. With an annual budget of approximately € 45 million, the Organization is funded by the annual contributions of its member states.

According to Article 2 of the Interpol Constitution, the organization's aim is "to ensure and promote the widest possible mutual assistance between all criminal police authorities" and "to establish and develop all institutions likely to contribute effectively to the prevention and sup-

---

1 Interpol as "a modern bureaucratic police organization", *see* Mathieu Deflem & Lindsay C. Maybin, *Interpol and the Policing of International Terrorism: Developments and Dynamics Since September 11, in* TERRORISM: RESEARCH, READINGS, & REALITIES 175, 191 (Lynne L. Snowden & Bradley C. Whitsel eds., 2005).

2 EBERHARD SCHMIDT-AßMANN, DAS ALLGEMEINE VERWALTUNGSRECHT ALS ORDNUNGSIDEE, chapter 6, note 7 (2nd ed., 2004); Armin von Bogdandy, *Information und Kommunikation in der Europäischen Union, in* VERWALTUNGSRECHT IN DER INFORMATIONSGESELLSCHAFT 133, (Wolfgang Hoffmann-Riem & Eberhard Schmidt-Aßmann eds., 2000).

3 Information available on the official website of the organization, www.interpol.int. Germany became a member in 1952.

pression of ordinary law crimes."[4] Both aims describe primarily repressive police work. Notwithstanding, the prevention of crime is inseparably connected to Interpol's tasks.

At the same time, the activity of Interpol in criminal prosecution as well as in maintaining public safety is functionally limited: Interpol has no competence to conduct own investigations or to intervene on its own. This task remains with national police authorities, which can use the organization as a platform for international co-operation.

Another functional limitation is the prohibition of "any intervention or activities of a political, military, religious or racial character" (Article 3 of the Constitution). The non-interference with national political matters is an important premise for the willingness of member states to co-operate on a broad transnational level. The rule, however, gives rise to problems in the fight against international terrorism which is often motivated by political or religious reasons.[5] It is only recently that the member states of Interpol have agreed on granting the Organization a competence in the combat against international terrorism. To this end, the term "terrorism" has been depoliticized, which permits Interpol to fight against terrorism qualified as a crime.[6]

Interpol's principal task lies in the field of administration of information and of data bases. Interpol provides the infrastructure for international police co-operation, offering a global communication system, compiling databases and distributing wanted notifications. Moreover, it offers technical support or projects of continuing education to national police officers.

According to the statistics of the Commission of the European Union, Germany is one of the main users of Interpol. About 150.000 operations are guided from Germany annually, 4.800 Germans are searched for worldwide and 14.000 inquiries from Interpol concerning wanted

---

4 The Constitution of the ICPO (Interpol), 13 June 1957, last amendment at the General Assembly's 66th session (New Delhi 1997).

5 For background information on terrorism *see* ULRICH SCHNECKENER, TRANSNATIONALER TERRORISMUS (2006).

6 Deflem & Maybin (note 1), at 175. On the problems of diverging legal or political competences *see* Raymond E. Kendall, *Zentralstellen im Wandel: Interpol*, *in* KRIMINALITÄTSBEKÄMPFUNG IM ZUSAMMENWACHSENDEN EUROPA 79, 82 (Bundeskriminalamt ed., 2000).

foreigners arrive at the *Bundeskriminalamt* (Federal Criminal Police Office) in Germany.[7]

II. Interpol's Development towards an International Organization

Originally, Interpol was a mere co-operation of public authorities organized as an association of private law.[8] On the initiative of the chief of police of Vienna, an international criminal police commission was founded in 1923. Inglorious misappropriation in the time of National Socialism required a re-establishment of Interpol in 1946, initially based in Paris. In 1989, Interpol's headquarters was moved to Lyon.[9] The present statutes of the organization, called Constitution, were drafted in 1956. At the same time the organization was renamed into International Criminal Police Organization. From a loose association of police authorities, Interpol gradually evolved into an independent organization with its own tasks and competences.

Interpol's legal status remains, however, unclear.[10] The organization is not based on a treaty between states. The Constitution was adopted only by Resolution of the General Assembly. The United Nations initially granted Interpol the status of an observer as NGO. According to Article 4 of the Constitution, members of the organization are not only states but also national authorities.[11] Nevertheless, both the profile of

---

7 Commission staff working document from 21 April 2006 – Annex to the Report from the Commission on the Operation Council Common Position 2005/69/JHA (no longer published in the internet).

8 More details on the development and sociologic importance of Interpol in MATHIEU DEFLEM, POLICING WORLD SOCIETY 124 (2002); on its legal status *see* Christian Hoppe, *Internationale Kooperationsmaßnahmen*, *in* FESTSCHRIFT FÜR HORST HEROLD 209, 210 (Bundeskriminalamt ed., 1998).

9 On Interpol's history *see* MARC LEBRUN, INTERPOL (1997).

10 *See* Albrecht Randelzhofer, *Rechtsschutz gegen Maßnahmen von INTERPOL vor deutschen Gerichten?*, *in* STAATSRECHT – VÖLKERRECHT – EUROPARECHT 531, 539 (Ingo von Münch ed., 1981); Sabine Gless, *Interpol*, *in* MAX PLANCK ENCYCLOPEDIA OF PUBLIC INTERNATIONAL LAW (Rüdiger Wolfrum ed., 2008), marginal numbers 1, 5, available at: www.mpepil.com.; Michel Richardot, *Interpol, Europol,* POUVOIRS 77, 79 (2002).

11 According to Art. 45 of the Constitution, all members of the preceding organization, not necessary states, were deemed to be members of Interpol unless express objection.

the organization and its recognition by a series of states and other international organizations support the qualification as an international organization with legal personality in public international law: even if member states can have several delegates in the General Assembly,[12] each member state has only one vote. The contribution to the financing of the organization is also an indication for a membership of states. The Headquarters Agreement between Interpol and France has granted immunities and privileges. Interpol is, for these reasons, at least partly recognized as an international organization with its own legal personality in public international law.

III. The Relevance of the Interpol Legal Regime for International Administrative Law

In contrast to the notion of global administrative law, which characterizes the general part of a universally applicable administrative law,[13] international administrative law is qualified as the law of international administrative relations.[14] Apart from global principles of law, it also covers specific areas of international administrative law, which can include particular rules of administrative procedure. Thus, the purpose of the doctrine of international administrative law is to analyze the rules governing the activity of international administrative instances as well as the internationalization of national administrative law and, thirdly, to develop principles and standards for the international administrative cooperation.[15]

Several aspects of Interpol claim importance from the perspective of international administrative law: Interpol's subject area is repressive criminal prosecution and preventive danger defense. Danger prevention

---

[12] Art. 4 § 1 of the Constitution: "Any country may delegate as a Member to the Organization any official police body whose functions come within the framework of activities of the Organization."

[13] Benedict Kingsbury, Nico Krisch & Richard Stewart, *The Emergence of Global Administrative Law*, IILJ Working Paper 2004/1; for another approach to this notion concerning international administrative standard setting JOSÉ E. ALVAREZ, INTERNATIONAL ORGANIZATIONS AS LAW-MAKERS 244 (2005).

[14] Eberhard Schmidt-Aßmann, *Die Herausforderung der Verwaltungsrechtswissenschaft durch die Internationalisierung der Verwaltungsbeziehungen*, 45 DER STAAT 315, 335 (2006).

[15] *Id.* at 336.

in particular is a typical administrative activity and, thus, forms a point of reference for research on administrative law. Beyond that, both activities belong to the core of national sovereignty.

This first premise influences the institutional structure of Interpol: the decentralized allocation of competences requires the co-operation of all actors involved. Interpol represents an institutional co-operation of public authorities with a network character administered by a central General Secretariat: the organization itself does not dispose of external decision-taking powers; co-operation is characterized by the lack of hierarchy and the voluntary participation of its members.[16] The idea of a co-operation of public authorities, however, has not changed since the foundation of Interpol and does not change with its recognition as an international organization. It is the direct contact of police officers beyond the intergovernmental, diplomatic and political exchange, which pledges for expert knowledge, acceleration and efficiency in the international combat of crime.

The primary function of Interpol is the administration, the exchange and the processing of information on the international level. The rules of co-operation between Interpol and its members or between Interpol and other international organizations are deriving from contractual agreements or the organization of Interpol itself is part of an international administrative law on information (*Informationsverwaltungsrecht*).

The regulatory technique (*Steuerung*) is primarily normative:[17] the organization has created an administrative system through international resolutions and contracts, defining methods and standards of informational co-operation. The binding or non-binding character of the provisions is not always evident and has to be analyzed rule by rule.

From a perspective of administrative co-operation, Interpol acts on different levels: firstly, the General Secretariat of the organization conducts its own international administrative activity. The major part of this activity provides the basis for the international administrative co-

---

[16] On the notion of network in security law *see* Bettina Schöndorf-Haubold, *Sicherheitsnetzwerke im Europäischen Mehrebenensystem, in* NETZWERKE 149, 151 *et seq.* (Sigrid Boysen et. al. eds., 2007).

[17] On the modalities and effects of the idea of regulation by law *see* Claudio Franzius, *Modalitäten und Wirkungsfaktoren der Steuerung durch Recht, in* GRUNDLAGEN DES VERWALTUNGSRECHTS I, § 4 esp. note 42 (Wolfgang Hoffmann-Riem, Eberhard Schmidt-Aßmann & Andreas Voßkuhle eds., 2007).

operation of national police authorities connected by Interpol. These national police authorities – like the *Bundeskriminalamt* (Federal Criminal Police Office, *BKA*) in Germany – can be, on a further subordinate level, a central contact point in a network of national administrations. Finally, the international connections of Interpol through international treaties and agreements link the organization to other international organizations.

C. Administration of Information by Interpol – Legal Analysis

I. Interpol's Institutional Setting

Three different levels characterize the organizational structure of Interpol: its internal organization, the network of National Central Bureaus founded by Interpol and the organization in the context of a global security administration. Interpol connects different players on and between different levels in the combat of crime around the world.

1. Interpol's Internal Organization

The main bodies of Interpol are the *General Assembly*, the Executive Committee and the General Secretariat. In addition, Interpol runs a number of regional offices. A so-called Commission for the Control of Interpol's Files is holding a special position constantly surveying Interpol's handling of personal data.

The General Assembly – composed of the delegates appointed by member states[18] – is regarded as the highest institution of Interpol, according to article 6 of the Constitution. It is the "legislative body" of the organization deciding by simple or qualified majority voting.[19] Decisions on fundamental issues such as the budget or the exchange of information are taken in resolutions. The appendices of the General Regula-

---

[18] According to Art. 7 of the Constitution, any member state can appoint one or several delegates to represent it. Most of the delegates are not members of their governments but police officers. Thus, Interpol preserves its character as an inter-administrative agency.

[19] Every member state has one vote.

tions of the General Assembly contain the Organization's actual legal administrative regulations on information.[20]

The *Executive Committee* consists of one president elected by the General Assembly, three vice-presidents as well as nine delegates, whose appointment is based on geographical proportional representation. According to Article 22 of the Constitution, the Committee, which meets three times a year, shall supervise the execution of decisions of the General Assembly as well as the administration and work of the Secretary General.[21]

The actual administration is done by the *General Secretariat* as a permanent institution of Interpol. This office is headed by the Secretary General who is appointed by the General Assembly upon nomination by the Executive Committee. With around 450 employees, the General Secretariat is responsible for the communication and information within the organization. One third of the employees are delegated to Interpol by national police authorities. The Secretariat coordinates the exchange of information between the National Central Bureaus, maintains the databases of the organization and issues wanted notifications.

The *Commission for the Control of Interpol's Files* is not mentioned in the Interpol Constitution. It was established on the basis of the Headquarters Agreement and a concretizing *Échange de lettres* with France in 1982. Its establishment was further "legalized" by a resolution of the General Assembly.[22] The Commission consists of five persons: three data protection experts, one computing science expert and one member of the Executive Committee. For their nomination, regard is had to their expertise and independence. The experts are chosen by the General Assembly from candidates, who are named by the member states and preselected by the Executive Committee. The Control Commission

---

20 *See* infra note 37.

21 Further details in the Rules of Procedure of the Executive Committee, appendix Nr. 11.1 to the General Regulations, adopted by the General Assembly, entered into force 1 January 1995.

22 *See* the Rules on International Police Co-operation and on the Internal Control of Interpol's Archives, adopted by the General Assembly as Resolution No. AGN/51/RES/1 entered into force on 14 February 1982. These provisions will be replaced by the Rules on the Control of Information and the Access to Interpol's Data Files (infra note 37) after an amendment of the Headquarters Agreement. *See* now the revised Headquarters Agreement which was signed in April 2008.

elects its own chairman.[23] Having its own procedural rules it gets together for at least three meetings per annum. The Commission performs its tasks independently, and it is not bound by any instructions. It has to protect the official secrets. It exercises an important and – for the legal protection of individuals – indispensable administrative control over the Organization, even though it does not possess a real instrument of enforcement. In contrast, there is no jurisdictional legal protection to be found on the international level.

Furthermore, Interpol has created its own administrative sub-structures through an internal diversification of competences.[24] Interpol disposes for example of a couple of regional offices and recently established an Anticorruption Academy.[25]

2. *Network of National Central Bureaus*

The National Central Bureaus (NCB) serves as operational centers and linking platforms between the national and the international level. Each member state appoints a National Central Bureau for the international police co-operation within the framework of Interpol. In Germany, the *Bundeskriminalamt* assumes this role. The national police authorities in their function as Central Bureaus are seen as forming part of Interpol[26] without being bound by instructions of the General Secretariat.

The National Central Bureaus cooperate with other authorities of their member states, with the National Central Bureaus of other member states as well as with the General Secretariat of the Organization (Article 32 of the Constitution). Thus a three-dimensional network connecting different intra-governmental with international levels has emerged.

---

23 Art. 2 of the Rules on the Control of Information and the Access to Interpol's Data Files. With the new Resolution of the General Assembly, the complex mechanism, according to which the French government also had the right to appoint the chairman, and according to which the Permanent Court of Arbitration had to be consulted in case of a conflict, has been abolished. Yet, it remains valid until the revised Headquarters Agreement will enter into force.

24 This differentiation and diversification is a general phenomenon, *see* José Alvarez, *International Organizations: Then and Now,* 100 AMERICAN JOURNAL OF INTERNATIONAL LAW 324, 334 (2006).

25 Resolution of the General Assembly of Interpol No. AG-2006-RES-03.

26 *See* Art. 5 of the Constitution according to which Interpol comprises the General Assembly, the Executive Committee, the General Secretariat, the ad visers and the NCB.

Apart from personal contacts, the interconnection of the network takes place through the communication structure offered by Interpol. This infrastructure consists of a global communication system and several databases. The National Central Bureaus cooperate with each other through general bilateral collaboration agreements as well as upon request in particular cases. Interpol arranges the necessary contacts and provides the technical background. National Central Bureaus guarantee the transmission of information and requests in the respective state by their own information exchange systems. In this network, Interpol's role is similar to a spider in its web.[27]

3. *Interpol's Role in the Global Network of International Organizations*

On the international level, Interpol has the authority to sign agreements and thereby establish permanent relations with other inter- or non-governmental organizations (Article 41 of the Constitution). The informational network is thus extended to the international level by bilateral consensus.[28]

Interpol maintains permanent co-operation relations not only with regional organizations of police co-operation, but, above all, with other international organizations, that have a specific interest in using Interpol's information system. The co-operation is based on agreements under public international law and is furthermore reflected by provisions of the respective organization which subordinate the information flow under the Interpol legal order. Examples for such co-operation relations are the agreements with the United Nations,[29] Europol[30] or the Office

---

[27] Apart from these basic structures, there are other specific networks, established by sub-divisions of Interpol to fight terrorism, *e.g.* the Fusion Task Force.

[28] Kendall (note 6), at 86.

[29] Co-operation Agreement from 8 April 1997, adopted through Resolution of the General Assembly of Interpol No. AGN/66/RES/5. In the wake of 9 September 2001, the co-operation has been extended. In order to give a stronger support to the UN in the fight against terrorism, it has been decided to include the members of Taliban and Al-Qaida listed by the Security Council in the warrant notification system of Interpol.

[30] Joint initiative of the Secretary General of Interpol and the Director of Europol on combating the counterfeiting of currency, in particular the Euro, entered into force on 5 November 2001; *see also* Council Common Position

of the Prosecutor of the International Criminal Court[31] as well as with WIPO, the European Central Bank or with the Council of Europe.[32]

II. The Normative Regulation of the Administration of Information by Interpol

The regulation of Interpol's activities is executed normatively, *i.e.* through legal mechanisms. The legal order of Interpol is based on a cascade of rules containing provisions of different "density of regulation". Apart from these rules, the Organization has signed contractual agreements with states or other international organizations to implement and complete its legal regime. Even though Interpol's legal order cannot be considered strictly binding in terms of international law, mechanisms of "legalization" (*Verrechtlichung*) and the varying binding effect of its provisions are evidence for the strong normative impact of the Interpol regime.

1. The Cascade of Rules of Interpol's Legal Order

The basis of all Interpol regulations are the statutes – the so-called Constitution,[33] which is implemented through procedural rules with appendices issued with a two-thirds majority by the General Assembly. In addition to these primary and secondary norms of Interpol, there are further implementing rules which can be issued by the General Secretariat or the General Assembly.

The national perspective would suggest a comparison of the General Assembly to a democratic legislator and of the General Secretariat to an executive ministerial administration. In the light of its character as an organization of international co-operation of public authorities however, Interpol could also be compared to authorities of functional self-administration, which – although on an entirely administrative level – also have legislative and administrative bodies.

No. 2005/69/JI from 24 January 2005 on exchanging certain data with Interpol, ABl. EU 2005 No. L 27, 61.

[31] Entered into force on 22 March 2005.

[32] *See* list at: www.interpol.int.

[33] Entered into force on 13 June 1956.

a) "Primary and Secondary Law": Constitution and Resolutions of the General Assembly[34]

Interpol in its present form is based on a statute from 1956, which transformed the former International Criminal Police Commission into the current International Criminal Police Organization.[35] The Constitution regulates all issues of constitutional character, especially the tasks and the aims of the organization, its commitment to neutrality and its respect for human rights as well as its administrative responsibilities and its budget. Amendments to the Constitution are possible on recommendation of a member of the Executive Committee with a two-thirds majority by the General Assembly.

The Constitution is implemented through the so-called *General Regulations*[36] adopted by a two-thirds majority of the General Assembly. These rules comprehend technical provisions which first and foremost relate to the activities and sessions of the General Assembly. The actual administrative regime is laid down in its Appendices including, in particular, rules on the exchange of information and the data processing.

The *Rules on the Processing of Information for the Purposes of International Police Co-operation* (RPI)[37] contain the basic rules and definitions of the exchange of information through Interpol. This Resolution codifies a detailed administrative law of information of Interpol and, above all, sets material and procedural standards for the processing of personal data.[38] These standards apply to all bodies entering data in or using data of the system.

---

34 Apart from the Resolutions listed here, there are other Resolutions of the General Assembly which are referred to in the legal materials; the Rules Governing the Database of Selected Information and Direct Access by NCGs to that Database or the Interpol Telecommunications Regulations are examples therefore. As far as can be seen, they are not available to the public.

35 Constitution of the ICPO-Interpol, adopted by the General Assembly at its 25th session in Vienna 1956, entered into force on 13 June 1956.

36 Rules of Procedure of the ICPO-Interpol General Assembly, adopted at its 65th session in Antalya 1996, amended by Resolution No. AG-2004-RES-11.

37 Adopted as Resolution No. AG-2003-RES-04 by the General Assembly at its 72nd session in Benidorm 2003, amended by Resolution No. AG-2005-RES-15, entered into force on 1 January 2006 as amended.

38 For example retention periods for data or provisions on the amending, freezing or deleting of data.

The RPI refer to other rules which are to be issued by the bodies of Interpol. Article 25, for example, provides that the control of information and the access to personal data shall be defined in a separate set of rules. Moreover, Article 23 provides for further implementing regulations on particular aspects of information processing such as the setting up and deleting of databases as well as the regulation of their use and purpose, the determination of the level of confidentiality and the protection and control relating to the processing of particularly sensitive data.[39]

Based on Article 23(c) of the Rules on the Processing of Information for the Purposes of International Police Co-operation (RPI),[40] the General Assembly recently adopted general *Implementing Rules* dealing with principles of police co-operation and data protection.[41] Beside a series of provisions on particular facets of information processing concerning the content of databases or single information, these rules concretize the areas of responsibility between the General Secretariat, the National Central Bureaus and the data users, and specify security requirements, the access management or specific forms of co-operation.

Another example for implementing rules are the *Rules on the Control of Information and the Access to Interpol's Files*[42] which have been adopted pursuant to Article 25 of the RPI. They were also issued as an appendix to the General Regulations. These rules contain regulations on the control of Interpol data by the Control Commission, on its composition and functioning as well as on the access to data and to the Commission of individuals which are concerned by the collection of data.

As a reaction to the terrorist attacks of 9 September 2001, Interpol opened its data bases to a wider extent to other international organizations. The respective regulations can be found in the *Rules Governing Access by an Intergovernmental Organization to the Interpol Telecommunications Network and Databases.*[43] These rules form part of the ap-

---

39 *See* Art. 6.2(e), 8(f), 9(e), 10.1(e), 10.2(b) in conjunction with Art. 23 of the Rules.

40 *See* note 37.

41 Rules adopted by the General Assembly at its 76th session in Marrakesh 2007 by Resolution No. AG-2007-RES-09, entered into force on 1 January 2008.

42 Adopted by the General Assembly at its 73rd session in Cancun on 7 October 2004 by Resolution No. AG-2004-RES-08.

43 Adopted by the General Assembly at its 70th session in Budapest on 28 September 2001 by Resolution No. AG-2001-RES-08.

pendix to the RPI and can thus be seen as an appendix to the appendix to the General Regulations. The access to data by other international organizations depends on a prior permission by the General Assembly and the signing of a co-operation agreement with Interpol, in which the other organization commits itself to the rules and standards of Interpol.

The original provisions concerning the control of the information administration by Interpol were contained in the *Rules on International Police Co-operation and on the Internal Control of Interpol's Archives*[44] which were based on the Headquarters Agreement with France. Their first part (Articles 1-14) was abolished and replaced by the Rules on Processing of Information (RPI).[45] Their second part (Articles 15-18) has also been replaced by the Control Rules.[46] These provisions concerning the composition of the Control Commission on Interpol's Data Files, however, will remain valid as long as the corresponding article in the Headquarters Agreement remains unmodified.[47]

Budgetary matters are addressed in the Financial Regulations, currently redefined by the General Assembly. In addition to the matters of revenues and expenditure and the preparation of the budget, they include regulations on the tenders and public contracts by Interpol and on internal and external auditing.[48] They also belong to international administrative law. But since they form part of the internal law of international organizations they shall not be examined here.

---

44 Adopted by the General Assembly at its 51st session in Torremolinos on 14 February 1982 by Resolution No. AGN/51/RES/1, amended by the Control Rules (note 42).

45 *See* note 37.

46 *See* note 42.

47 In contrast to its future version, the present regulations still provide for a complex procedure to appoint the five members of the Commission. Under these regulations, a member of the Executive Committee and a computing expert are appointed by the president of the Commission, one member is appointed by Interpol, one by the French government and one by both of them together. If the latter fail to reach an agreement, the member is appointed by the Secretary General of the Permanent Court of Arbitration.

48 On the Financial Regulations, specified by implementing rules of the Executive Committee and by practical instructions of the Secretary General, which apparently are not published, *see* internet pages www.interpol.int.

b) Administrative Implementing Rules

These primary and secondary rules may be specified and completed through further *implementing rules*, which apparently the Organization does not always issue or at least does not publish. Article 23 of the Rules on the Processing of Information for the Purposes of International Police Co-operation (RPI) does not indicate who may be the author of such implementing rules. In its paragraph (c) however, the provision states that certain topics shall be submitted to the General Assembly.[49] This might suggest – as a conclusion in reverse – that the General Secretariat should be competent to issue the implementing rules. In fact, at least the implementing rules which concern the matters referred to in Article 23(c) are issued by the General Assembly after a statement of the Control Commission. This does not resolve the question whether there is still room for the making of general and abstract rules by the General Secretariat.

c) Administrative Setting of Standards

Interpol not only sets the rules which are of direct relevance for the entities involved in the information exchange,[50] but also indirectly coordinates the transnational operative police co-operation between individual member states through models for bilateral co-operation agreements. The Model (bilateral) Police Co-operation Agreement contains not only clauses concerning data protection but also rules on cross-border pursuit and observation[51] and is made available to the member states by Interpol in an annotated version. Since the Model Agreement explicitly refers to the legal regime of Interpol, this regime is, indirectly, applied to the relations between the member states as well. Thereby, Interpol provides a legal framework of which the member states can make use for intensifying their co-operation in police matters.

---

[49] Art. 23(c) of the Rules (note 37).

[50] On the question of legal commitment see subsequently C.II.3.

[51] Nadia Gerspacher, *The Role of International Police Cooperation Organizations*, 13 EUROPEAN JOURNAL OF CRIME, CRIMINAL LAW AND CRIMINAL JUSTICE 413, 427 (2005). Another example for an instrument for the setting of standards is the *Guide de préparation et de réponse à un attentat bioterroriste*, published by Interpol in 2007. It comprehends guidelines on administrative procedures for its member states.

For the international administrative law, the Model Agreement is of a double importance: on the one hand, it is an instrument of normative regulation without itself being legally binding. It regulates the administrative relations between states, *i.e.* legal entities distinct from itself. On the other hand, by its reference to the system of Interpol regulations, these regulations are "legalized" (*verrechtlicht*) through voluntary mutual accord.

2. *Bilateral Regulations: Treaties and Co-Operation Agreements*

The Interpol legal regime is completed by a series of treaties with constitutional and/or administrative character: firstly, the organization concluded a Headquarters Agreement with France already in 1982. This agreement addresses essential "constitutional" issues. France acknowledges Interpol's status as an international organization with legal personality, and grants immunity and privileges on French territory. Moreover, this agreement defines essential prerequisites for the administrative procedure and submits Interpol's data to an internal control, which are specified by an *Échange de lettres* between the French government and Interpol. These stipulations correspond to a large extent to the Rules on International Police Co-operation and on the Internal Control of Interpol's Archives.[52]

The co-operation agreements with other international organizations are rather of an administrative nature. They are implied by Article 41 of the Constitution and specified by implementing rules. They are concluded as treaties or memoranda of understanding by the General Secretariat, which however needs an authorization from the General Assembly. When the exchange of personal data is concerned, an opinion by the Control Commission is required in addition. The Executive Committee can object to a co-operation of this kind.

---

52 *See* note 44. The revised Headquarters Agreement, signed in April 2008, but not yet entered into force, does no longer contain provisions on administrative procedure and data control. This is probably due to the fact that the Organization has gradually elaborated a more sophisticated rule system.

3. The Question of Legal Bindingness

a) The Principles of Legal Bindingness under International Law

The majority of Interpol's rules have not been adopted through legally binding treaties under public international law. The actual diversification of the Interpol legal order is mainly taking place in the area of so-called soft law.[53]

With respect to guidelines or model provisions, this already becomes apparent from Interpol's intention to issue soft regulating mechanisms without legally binding character. However, the same must apply to the majority of resolutions adopted by the General Assembly, which do not share the legal nature of treaties under public international law. These resolutions contain compliance advices regarding its own provisions and, thereby, acknowledge not to be legally binding in a formal sense.[54] According to Article 9 of the Constitution the "members shall do all within their power, in so far as is compatible with their own obligations, to carry out the decisions of the General Assembly." These decisions are neither directly applicable, nor are they formally binding for the member states.

It is a different matter only with those agreements which Interpol concludes with individual members or other international organizations or NGOs respectively, when the legal commitment depends on the will of the parties and has to be established in individual cases.

This explains Interpol's effort to substantiate and confirm the commitment to its own positive law in every new act of law, especially on a contractual basis. Moreover, the concession of new access rights de-

---

[53] Concerning soft law *see* Alan Boyle, *Soft Law in International Law Making*, *in* INTERNATIONAL LAW 141 (Malcolm D. Evans ed., 2006); LINDA SENDEN, SOFT LAW IN EUROPEAN COMMUNITY LAW 107, 219, 235 (2004).

[54] Art. 5.1 of the RPI (note 37) illustrates the relatively weak effect of the legal commitment within the legal framework, which predominantly depends on voluntary participation: "Whenever necessary, and at least once a year, the General Secretariat shall remind the National Central Bureaus and the entities with which it has concluded a co-operation agreement of their role and responsibilities connected with the information they process through the Organization's channels, particularly with regard to the accuracy of that information and its relevance to the purpose for which it is provided."

pends on commitment to the system of rules.[55] But even the general rules set by Interpol do possess at least certain legal regulatory effects.[56]

b) Creation of Legal Regulatory Effects

A certain "hardening" or "legalization" (*Verrechtlichung*) of Interpol's rules is caused by a clear hierarchical structure of the norms and by supporting mechanisms, which create legal regulatory effects.

The texts themselves are put into a vertical relation to each other:[57] the highest position of the regulation system is the Constitution. The resolutions of the General Assembly follow in this order. They are divided into General Regulations, rules of procedure and implementing measures. To be precise, the Constitution is followed by the General Regulations with their appendices, consisting of other resolutions of the General Assembly, which in turn have appendices and implementing resolutions of their own. The implementing measures of the General Secretariat (with and without consultation of the Control Commission) are placed below the level of resolutions. Depending on the degree of participation of Interpol's other bodies; they have a higher or lower position. This ranking and differentiation between Constitution, General Regulations, appendices and implementing rules result in an internal hierarchy of the norms. This hierarchy does not give the answer to the question whether or not norms have an external binding effect. Accepting a general "rule of law," however, it binds the bodies of the organization themselves to obey the self-edicted laws and procedures. Of an even greater importance is the question of the commitment of the member states to the Interpol law regime.

Even according to the rules of international law, soft law can, to a certain extent, be legally binding:[58] some forms of full or limited self-

---

55 *See* Art. 10.1(a)(1) or Art. 20.1(a) of the RPI (note 37).

56 For general information on legal regulatory effects of administrative soft law *see* Alvarez (note 24), at 326; CHRISTOPH MÖLLERS, GEWALTENGLIEDERUNG 303 (2005); Jan Klabbers, *The Changing Image of International Organizations, in* THE LEGITIMACY OF INTERNATIONAL ORGANIZATIONS 221, 227 (Jean Marc Coicaud ed., 2001); *see also* ALVAREZ (note 13), at 257, 596, 599.

57 On this aspect, *see* HENRY G. SCHERMERS & NIELS M. BLOCKER, INTERNATIONAL INSTITUTIONAL LAW §§ 1340-1343 (2003); Sabino Cassese, *Global Standards for National Administrative Procedure*, 68 LAW AND CONTEMPORARY PROBLEMS 109, 121 (2005).

58 SCHERMERS & BLOCKER (note 57), at §§ 1196-1200.

commitment, *e.g.* through the necessity to provide reasons and justification for deviations from the provisions, create soft binding effects. This is the case with the internal law concerning the functioning of the organization, but can also be applied to the information administration "law," including the control regime, which is set to have external effects.[59]

The information exchange through Interpol is based on the voluntary participation of the respective national or international actors. Hence, the confidence in the respect for data protection standards is of special importance. All member states therefore have a great mutual interest in the protection of the legal administrative framework set by Interpol. This interest can not be equated with a true legal commitment, but the rules contain clauses which postulate their own validity and demand a certain commitment.

The mechanisms of such a limited "legalization" are, above all, provisions establishing the duty to observe the Interpol legal order as a condition for the access to, and participation in, the information exchange system of the organization. Their wording can be weaker or stronger. The use of Interpol's communication systems, for example, is explicitly bound to the respect of its rules: Article 10.1 of the Rules on the Processing of Information establishes general conditions for the processing of data and permits it only if it "complies with the Constitution and relevant provisions of the Organization's rules."[60] The creation and the assignment of the Control Commission with the duty to supervise the compliance with a part of the Interpol legal order strengthens the enforcement and, by this, the effectiveness of the rules.[61]

To some extent, legally binding effects may also result from general principles of law, especially from the human rights. Although the right to informational self-determination is partially accepted by international law, Interpol's data protection regime in its entirety cannot be considered as a specification of such generally accepted law.[62]

---

[59] In some provisions the self-commitment is explicitly laid down, *see* Art. 4.3(d) of the RPI (note 37).

[60] Other examples to illustrate this are Art. 2(c), 5.3(b), 10.1 of the RPI (note 37).

[61] Other indications of a partial "hardening" can be provisions concerning liability, sanctions, possibilities to file objections, provisos, etc.

[62] On warrants under European Law in particular *see* MARION ALBERS, INFORMATIONELLE SELBSTBESTIMMUNG 288 (2005).

Regardless of the question of legal bindingness, Interpol's rules represent a thorough codification of administrative regulations comprising material standards of information exchange, like data security or confidentiality, as well as procedural and organizational rules, like the rules on competence, supervision or control. This mirrors the concern for normative regulation on one hand and for commitment to the rule of law on the other hand, whereas the latter may anyway be required with regard to its relevance for fundamental rights.

III. The Administration of Information as the Key Function of Interpol

Interpol's core function is to support and facilitate the transnational and international police co-operation.[63] In contrast to bilateral co-operation of police authorities, this means not only operative measures like common pursuit and observation, but first and foremost the exchange of information. Competences for operative actions are neither transferred to Interpol nor to member states which act within the framework of co-operation through Interpol, because operative police actions form an important part of national sovereignty. The actual administrative measures from the perspective of national administrative law, such as extradition, determination of identity and other standard police measures of crime prevention or prosecution, remain within the responsibility of individual states.

Hence, Interpol's functions are limited to the administration of information.[64] It has, in principle, no authority to collect data through its own investigation. National competences are also preserved when it comes to the responsibility for data archives and the access to them. Interpol's actual administrative activity thus consists of providing different channels and means of information exchange (1.) within the framework of its own procedures and standards. The protection of such standards is also one of Interpol's tasks (2.). Interpol has therefore two

---

[63] The list of international agreements, which refers to Interpol's communication system, also indicates Interpol's service function, *see* at: www.interpol.int.

[64] Including its own analysis activity. Concerning this limitation *see* Paul Higdon, *Interpol's Role in International Police Cooperation*, *in* INTERNATIONAL POLICE COOPERATION, A WORLD PERSPECTIVE 29, 31, (Daniel J. Koenig & Philip K. Das eds., 2001).

functions: firstly, to provide the technical infrastructure for communication and, secondly, to secure its own formal reliability and external integrity. The latter is necessary to establish a basis of confidence which goes beyond simple bilateral relations. This twofold warranty and providing function is a major characteristic of international administration, at least in the area of public order and security (3.).

1. Providing Informational Infrastructure

Interpol offers to all police authorities involved ways and means for direct cross-border information exchange outside the intergovernmental and diplomatic channels.[65] This informational structure is based on Interpol's communication system. Several data bases and the instrument of international search warrants complement it.

a) Starting Point: Limited Competences

Outside of its providing function, Interpol has only very limited competences: according to Article 26 of the Constitution, the investigations are conducted by national authorities. The Rules on the Processing of Information[66] grant Interpol only clearly defined competences in data processing.[67] The main responsibility for information, its content and its distribution remains with its respective source, *i.e.* the National Central Bureau or an authorized national or international office.[68] The Gen-

---

[65] On Interpol's major achievement, its special information exchange structure, *see* Hoppe (note 8), at 212.

[66] *See* note 37.

[67] Although Art. 4.1(b) of the RPI (note 37) contains a general authorization ("the General Secretariat is also empowered to take any appropriate steps which may contribute effectively to combating international ordinary-law crime"), it is limited to the tasks transferred to Interpol. Art. 7(a) which refers to "information [...] obtained by the General Secretariat," has to be interpreted systematically from the regulatory context. Hence, the data obtained by Interpol, can only be secondary data resulting from primary data provided by other entities; *cf.* Art. 8 and 9 of the RPI which do not speak of Interpol as a data source. Art. 8(c) of the RPI speaks instead of the value added by the analysis work ("the value it adds to an item of information, notably when it carries out analysis work or issues a notice").

[68] Art. 5.3 of the Rules (note 37): "The National Central Bureaus, authorized national institutions and international entities shall continue to be respon-

eral Secretariat administrates the data bases and regulates the access to information with respect to possible access restrictions imposed by its respective source.

One important condition for the distribution of data via Interpol, according to Article 10.1(a) of the Rules on the Processing of Information,[69] is to respect the terms of use set by Interpol and the human rights. Furthermore, the information processing must be motivated by a specific international police interest; moreover, the aims, reputation or other interests of the organization must not be compromised; the information must be processed by the source according to the respective national law including the international duties as well as in accordance with Interpol's rules.

In cases where the compliance with these general conditions for the processing of data via Interpol is not clear, the General Secretariat together with the NCBs can take "all necessary measures" to ensure that the criteria for the processing of data are actually met. Only in urgent cases, *i.e.* in special situations of immediate physical danger, the General Secretariat is allowed to transfer relevant information to all National Central Bureaus after having informed the source of the information and on the condition that it has had no objection against the transfer of information.[70]

b) I-24/7: The Global Interpol Communication System

The infrastructure for the communication is provided by the communication system I-24/7, run by the General Secretariat. Since the beginning of the new millennium it serves as a communication basis for over 90% of Interpol's member states.

With regard to the communication network, Interpol plays a special role, which enables the member states to communicate safely. The technical requirements to access the network lie within the responsibility of the member states. However, within the framework of the technical

---

sible for the information which they provide through the police information system and which may be recorded in the Organization's files." According to Art. 5.4, the data source is also entitled to issue restrictions on the access to data.

69 *See* note 37.

70 Art. 17.1(c) with Art. 22 of the RPI (note 37).

support Interpol, if necessary, also supports states whose communication systems are below Interpol's standards.

c) Interpol Data Bases

Another element of the Interpol information system are the general and specific data bases. They have been established in accordance with Interpol's basic Rules on Processing of Information (RPI) concretized by the Implementing Rules for the RPI.[71] The Interpol regime offers several types of data bases for the Organization:[72] a general central data base for the processing of information available at the General Secretariat as well as specialized data bases, which are either connected to the central data base over an indexing system, *e.g.* analysis data bases, or which reasons are run autonomously for security.

Interpol runs data bases to search for persons and objects. Under the abbreviation ASF (automated search facility) Interpol runs a data base for stolen motor vehicles and stolen and lost travel documents. Another data base, with presently approximately 8 Mio. data sets, is used in the search for lost or forged identity cards. A data base for DNA profiles is planned for the nearest future. Moreover, a data base for missing people and unidentified bodies will also be established to be used in cases of natural catastrophes or terrorist attacks.

d) Interpol's Wanted Persons Notifications

The so-called Notices, wanted persons notifications issued in Interpol's four official languages, are the best known instrument of the organization.[73] They constitute a schematic persons search and alarm system. Interpol uses six different searching criteria and colors.

On the highest search level are the so called *Red Notices*. They are issued for persons, against who a national or international court has issued an arrest warrant. The Notice itself has not the effect of an arrest warrant. It is solely a request of the issuing entity to provisionally or fi-

---

71 *See* note 41.

72 Art. 6 of the RPI (note 37).

73 4556 Notices were issued in 2006, including 2804 Red Notices, *see* at: www.interpol.int.

nally arrest the wanted person for extradition. Red Notices can be issued either before a trial or to be able to execute a sentence.

Blue Notices are used to gain additional information on people, who are connected to a crime. Green Notices are used to issue warnings against or police information on individuals who have committed crimes and are likely to commit them again in other states. Yellow Notices are used to find missing persons or to identify people who are not capable of identifying themselves. Black Notices are used to gather information on unidentified bodies. Orange Notices are warnings against possible assaults on public security through terrorist attacks or crimes.

Implementing the resolution Nr. 1617 of the UN Security Council,[74] a new wanted notification has been established to fight terrorism: the so-called Interpol-United Nations Special Notice. With this type of Notice, the individuals listed by the Security Council of the UN can also be searched for worldwide via Interpol.[75]

The Notices consist of information about items to identify the wanted person and of legal information on the charges brought against the person, as far as they are available. An alternative to the rather formal Notice is the so-called "Diffusion". This is a message, sent from a National Central Bureau via I-24/7 to several or all other member states, with the request to find or arrest a person or to provide additional information.[76]

i) Legal Requirements

According to Article 10.5 of the RPI,[77] Notices are issued by the General Secretariat either at the request of an authorized entity or on its

---

[74] The Resolution requests the UN-Secretary General to cooperate with Interpol in order to assist the Committee 1267 of the Security Council in the best possible way at its work.

[75] Mathieu Deflem, *Global Rule of Law or Global Rule of Law Enforcement? International Police Cooperation and Counter-terrorism,* 603 THE ANNALS OF THE AMERICAN ACADEMY OF POLITICAL AND SOCIAL SCIENCE (ANNALS, AAPSS) 240, 245 (2006).

[76] 12.212 Diffusions were published in 2006. At the end of the year, 18.170 Notices and 35.385 Diffusions were in circulation; *see* at: www.interpol.int.

[77] *See* note 37.

own initiative. Usually, the National Central Bureaus are the author of a Notice. Interpol itself can issue only Green and Orange Notices.[78]

Before issuing or distributing Notices, especially to other offices than the NCBs, the General Secretariat has to evaluate, whether the issue is necessary and advisable with regard to the aims and tasks of the organization, the respect of human rights and the required security measures against possible menaces to the police co-operation, to Interpol itself or to the member states. If a Notice does not meet the formal requirements of the Constitution and other Interpol regulations, it has to be prohibited by the General Secretariat. The implementing rules, which are not accessible to the public, shall define the exact requirements and procedures for the issue. Particularly with respect to the Red Notices, the General Secretariat has been authorized by the General Assembly to forbid the issuing of a Notice, if it does not meet the requirements of a request for provisional arrest.[79]

A reference to the presumption of innocence of the wanted person is not part of the published rules and regulations. Only the corresponding pages of the internet appearance of the organization contain explicitly highlighted warnings of this kind.

ii) Legal Nature of the Notices: Are They International Administrative Acts?

The Notices issued by Interpol cannot be considered as administrative decisions on individual cases with transnational effect in the sense of an "international administrative act". They lack a character of regulation. Neither do they constitute an international arrest warrant nor are they in any other form legally binding for the individuals concerned. They, however, gain *de facto* a special relevance to the human rights through the multiplication of its recipients. Yet, this is not enough to cause a formal legal character of this measure.[80]

---

78 However, this does not result from the RPI of information. It is just stated on a fact sheet on the Notices on Interpol's websites; *see* at: www.interpol.int.

79 Information from www.interpol.int.

80 On the legal character of requests for mutual assistance, *see* FLORIAN WETTNER, DIE AMTSHILFE IM EUROPÄISCHEN VERWALTUNGSRECHT 175 (2005).

At the same time they do not entirely lack external effects. A number of states recognize the Red Notices, because of their formality and their formal supervision by the General Secretariat, as an official request for the arrest of a person. However, such a request does not legally require the action of national police authorities and can neither provide a legal basis for it. The national authorities have to decide in accordance with their national law, how they proceed with this request. Recognizing this request as a basis for an arrest, could operate an internationalization or trans-nationalization of a foreign administrative decision. The author of such a "trans-nationalized" decision, however, is not Interpol itself but the original author of this Notice. The formal admission procedure by Interpol cannot be the single cause of internalization. It is just a precondition for the recognition by the other states. The transnationalization takes place through the membership in the organization, through the supervision proviso of the General Secretariat and the recognition of the transnational effect of the information.

A successful search does not result in Interpol's further operative involvement, either. Concerned authorities or the public are supposed to contact the local police office, which then gets in touch with the issuing authority and initiates the necessary steps. Therefore, the member state usually gives the initiative for a Notice, and cooperates with one or several other member states in order to find and arrest the wanted person. Id est: existing information is just distributed through a special communication channel. Interpol's role is limited to that of a service agency.

But the Notices that are distributed by Interpol on its own initiative must have the same effect: although the General Secretariat takes a decision that is relevant for the individuals affected by the warning, it affects only the person's right to informational self-determination. It has no impact on his or her general rights and legal status, because the warning does not provide a legal basis for further police actions.

e) The Special Case of Public Searches

Coming back to the initial example of the public searches of persons suspected to have committed serious crimes: this kind of measure is not mentioned in the Interpol legal regime. Neither Interpol disposes of a special authorization to use this instrument, nor are there any procedural requirements or guaranties for legal protection. In contrast to the strict requirements for such measures in domestic law,[81] their success and effectiveness alone are not at all a sufficient basis for Interpol's activity. The public searches initiated by Interpol are not in conformity with basic requirements for criminal or administrative procedures affecting individual rights.

2. Preserving the Normative Infrastructure

Apart from this providing function, Interpol also has a normative warranty function (*Gewährleistungsfunktion*). The technical infrastructure as a basis for international administrative co-operation only works within a normative frame, which ensures a minimum level of the standards which the cooperating member states would otherwise have to maintain themselves. Of main interest are: the criteria of the information treatment concerning data security, accuracy and responsibility. From the perspective of the administrative law, Interpol has given itself an extensive system of regulations,[82] and the organization has committed itself to ensure the respect of the member states for this system.

3. Administration of Information as an (a-)typical International Administrative Activity

The core functions of Interpol are addressed to the authorities of its member states. In contrast to traditional measures under public international law, the Organization goes beyond the conventional scheme of international actors, who are neither national authorities nor individuals. The orientation on national authorities or directly on individuals is one of the main characteristics of international administration.

The direct impact on individuals is, however, not necessary. Such individual-oriented activity is in fact not Interpol's task: it has no transnational or international powers with regard to the individual. Nevertheless, its activity is directly relevant to the fundamental rights, through the multiplication of access to, and processing possibilities of personal information.

From the national perspective, this administration seems to be atypical because it is not based on "administrative decisions". In areas where na-

---

[81] *See* § 131 - § 131 c of the German *Strafprozessordnung* (Code of criminal procedure – *StPO*).

[82] *See* C. II.

tional sovereignty is strictly observed, this could, on the other hand, be a typical characteristic of international administration. If the enabling and facilitating function for other administrative activity is predominant, the administration can not be described from the decision based perspective, but has to be analyzed with regard to this particular guarantee and providing function. The fact that Interpol has created a general administrative procedural system, which does not only focus on a single procedure but takes Interpol's entire activity into account, also speaks for this.

IV. Supervision and Control

The control perspective is relevant for Interpol for two reasons: on the one hand, the question arises whether the warranty and providing function ("*Gewährleistungs- und Bereitstellungsfunktion*") of Interpol includes any control or supervision functions regarding the authorities which participate in the exchange of information. In other words, the question is whether Interpol controls the information transfer not only formally but also substantially with respect to its content. A different matter is the control of Interpol's international administration, *i.e.* the mechanisms which are used to control Interpol's own activity. Both aspects of control mechanisms are typically based on co-operation and voluntary participation. Like in the case of co-operation within a network, the control perspective rather depends on mutual confidence than on strict enforcement of positive law.

1. *Interpol as a Control Instance*

As an institution with a predominantly supporting and facilitating function, Interpol has no central, extensive control or supervision powers with regard to information exchange between authorities. In order to preserve territorial police competences, and by that in the end national sovereignties, the basic competence for the respective information and its content remains with the authorities involved.[83]

The warranty and providing function is not limited to making available the technical infrastructure, which, as such and without a normative frame, would not be sufficient to establish a confidence basis for police

---

[83] *See* Art. 5.3 and 5.4 of the RPI (note 37).

co-operation. This legal framework itself has to be protected. By administrating data bases, granting access and distributing Notices, the organization can influence the effectuation and implementation of its law. Nevertheless, the opportunities to exercise control are usually limited to an external, rather formal control.[84] Before issuing a Red Notice, the General Secretariat checks for example whether the formal application contains all information required. Nonetheless, the source remains responsible for the content; there is no control of an application's substance by Interpol.

Article 10.1(b) of the Rules on the Processing of Information (RPI)[85] underlines this by stating: "The information is considered, *a priori*, to be accurate and relevant, if it has been provided by a National Central Bureau, an authorized national institution or authorized international entity."

This fact, however, does not answer the question whether a substantive control by Interpol would be excluded entirely. Even if such a competence is not explicitly granted in the regulations, it could for once arise from the reiterated duty to respect the human rights. The presumption of correctness would also not contradict such competence. On the contrary, it can be argued that this presumption may be refuted in particular cases. Even if an obligation to control the content does not exist, such a control by the General Secretariat as well as by the Control Commission is not precluded in principle. An enforceable right of the concerned person, state or authority to control substance is, however, not adherent. Interpol's regulations are generally based less on enforcement and coercion – which the Organization could not justify anyway because of the lack of legal commitment – and more on co-operation and voluntary participation. Being part of a comprehensive network, "the General Secretariat shall remind the National Central Bureaus" "whenever necessary, and at least once a year" "of their role and responsibilities connected with the information they process through the Organization's channels, particularly with regard to the accuracy of that information and its relevance in relation to the purpose

---

84 *See* Art. 9(a) of the RPI (note 37): "The General Secretariat shall take all necessary measures to protect the security, *i.e.* the integrity, and confidentiality of information provided and processed through the police information system."

85 *See* note 37.

for which it is provided."[86] Similarly, Interpol's other control instruments are also established to provide amicable settlement of disputes.[87]

The question of Interpol's competence for control of substance arises especially in the case of the Terrorism Notices. Even if, according to Article 25 of the UN Charter, the decisions of the Security Council, *i.e.* the lists issued in Security Council resolutions, are binding only the members of the UN, it could be argued that Interpol as an international organization is bound in the same way, so that it would be precluded from a control of these lists. Such hierarchy of international administrative law could emerge, firstly, from the international obligations of the organization, or secondly, from a possible self-commitment resulting from the recognition of law regimes of other international organizations or through the commitment of Interpol's member states.

2. *Control of Interpol's International Administration*

With regard to Interpol's international administrative activity, there are several soft enforcement and supervising mechanisms. The Commission for the control of Interpol's files thereby assumes a special role. Judicial control is not envisioned.

a) Instruments of Internal Control

The Interpol legal order includes a number of report obligations of the General Secretariat vis-à-vis the General Assembly or the National Central Bureaus and other entitled entities. *E.g.* a list has to be issued annually naming all international organizations that have access to Interpol's data files; another list covers the access of national authorities. Other reporting requirements relate to the establishment and management of Interpol data bases.

---

86 Art. 5.1 of the RPI (note 37).

87 *See* Art. 4.2 of the RPI (note 37) relating to requests for information and Art. 24 concerning the dispute settlement: "Disputes that arise between National Central Bureaus, authorized national institutions, [...] or between one of these entities and the General Secretariat in connection with the application of the present Rules and the implementing rules to which they refer, should be solved by concerted consultation. If this fails, the matter may be submitted to the Executive Committee and, if necessary, to the General Assembly in conformity with the procedure to be established."

Further control mechanisms are prior consultation and approval obligations: the General Secretariat, particularly before issuing implementing measures, has to consult the Commission for the Control of Interpol's data files. In special cases, it must ask the General Assembly for permission. To establish new data bases the General Secretariat has to consult the Control Commission as well as the Executive Committee. The latter has the possibility to demand the abolishing or correcting of a data base.[88]

b) Procedures of the Commission for the Control of Interpol's Data Files

Strictly speaking, the control executed by the Commission for the Control of Interpol's data files is neither an entirely internal nor actual external surveillance. In its composition established in the original Headquarters Agreement from 1982, the Commission is appointed from experts and one member of the Executive Committee by the General Assembly and the French government. According to the future regulation, France's appointment competence is abolished, so that Interpol alone is responsible for the composition of the Commission. Consequently, it will be more difficult to preserve its independence.

According to Interpol's Control Rules,[89] the Control Commission has a threefold function: firstly, it is entrusted with the constant surveillance of the informational administration and information exchange within the framework of Interpol with a special regard to the processing of personal data and the respect for human rights. It can address advices to the General Secretariat. The advices are not binding but have to be acknowledged in so far as the Secretary General has to justify nonobservance. The Commission can, in these cases, inform the Executive Committee which then takes the necessary steps.

Secondly, the Commission exercises a consulting function and has to be consulted for example when the organization establishes new data bases or issues implementing rules relating to data protection.

Thirdly, from the perspective of individual rights the most important function of the Commission is the *processing of individual requests* and complaints which refer to accessing, correcting and deleting data. Interpol rules define this procedure as an administrative procedure of legal

---

[88] *See* Art. 6.2 or 21(b) of the RPI (note 37).

[89] *See* note 42.

remedy.[90] The individuals who are directly affected by the data processing procedure at Interpol have free access to the data. The Control Commission has to confirm and process every request as fast as possible. If the Commission finds an infringement of the data protection rules, it is, however, not allowed to take a decision on its own, for example delete data, but has to give a recommendation to the Secretary General. Nevertheless, the Commission can issue information concerning the data and inform the requester that it has exercised the controls, as requested. Regarding subjective rights, concerned persons have a right to have the request processed and examined, but there is no right to a substantial treatment or to a specific decision of the Commission that could be enforced by legal action. Subjective rights like for example to have data deleted are not granted by the legal regime. Under objective law the Commission is a soft instrument to ensure the data protection standards and thus the informational basic rights of an individual.

To fulfill its tasks, the Commission has free access to Interpol's data bases and is allowed to consult the General Secretariat as well as the National Central Bureaus. With the approval of the Executive Committee it can also address the General Assembly. The Commission is not limited to the control of Interpol's legal order, but according to Article 1(a) of the Control Rules[91] explicitly authorized to investigate fundamental breaches of the basic rights of the people concerned or the general principles of data protection. The framework of individual complaints affirms this obligation: accepted requests are examined with regard to their accordance to information processing conditions which must be respected by the Organization (Article 10 (a) of the Control Rules).[92]

From the perspective of international law of administrations, the Commission embodies a mechanism to enforce Interpol's legal order, which however like the regime itself, cannot take any legally binding decisions.

---

90 *See* especially Art. 9-11 of the Control Rules (note 42).

91 *See* note 42.

92 *See* note 42.

D. Assessment and Conclusion: Contribution to the Emergence of an General International Administrative Law

The analysis shows that Interpol exercises international administrative activity. In contrast to national administrations, its tasks do not focus on decisions in individual cases and cannot be systemized according to specific schemes of administrative procedure. Interpol rather assumes technical as well as normative functions in order to assist the international police co-operation between police authorities on different levels of the international multi-level-system. With its broadly codified legal system, it is an example for a specific field of international administrative law. The analysis of both, the legal regime and the administrative activity, reveals, that this specific international administration reverts to principles, which can be generalized for a doctrine of international administrative law. Similarly, the multi-level-dimension and the question of legitimacy are typical general issues of international administrative law.

I. Principles and Standards

There are three kinds of standards and principles which bind or at least concern Interpol's activity: the first refer to states, the second to individuals and the third to administrative procedure.

1. Standards Relating to States

Interpol's activity and the administrative co-operation within Interpol's framework are characterized by the respect for state sovereignty. Without being regulated expressly, this principle is reflected in the Interpol regime in different ways: in contrast to other information systems, *e.g.* the Schengen Information System, the co-operation via Interpol is based on *voluntary participation* of states and authorities.[93] Therefore, the Organization does not possess any externally effective decision-taking powers and relies on voluntary obedience, self-commitment and

---

[93] From a practical point of view, *see* Hoppe (note 8), at 215; on the voluntary participation as a characteristic of the co-operation of authorities in networks *see* Schöndorf-Haubold (note 16), at 152.

soft enforcement mechanisms.[94] Consequently, the responsibility is also divided between the General Secretariat and the National Central Bureaus.[95] A further consequence is the basic principle of political, military, religious and racial neutrality[96] which protects on the substantial level national and political integrity and prevents Interpol's involvement in politics.

2. *Individual Standards*

Although Interpol faces the individual only on a secondary level of the complaint procedure via the Control Commission, the administrative legal actions with respect to the processing of information are of particular importance to the human rights, for they concern the nationally and internationally accepted right to informational self-determination.[97] Hence, Interpol's legal regime considers itself bound to individual-related standards.

At the top are the basic human rights in general to which the Interpol Constitution and other rules repeatedly refer.[98]

In addition, Interpol's legal regime provides a number of informational administrative principles especially on data protection, data accuracy and confidentiality, which have direct effects only on the co-operation of authorities, but contribute indirectly to the protection of the individual.[99]

In contrast, effective legal protection is not granted within the Interpol legal system: the complaint procedure of the Control Commission, in particular, is not satisfactory with regard to the standards of rule of law. There are not granted any substantial rights for control and correction of inaccurate data nor are established any effective enforcement measures.

---

94 Evidence provides the procedure for the settlement of disputes according to Art. 24 of the RIP (note 37).

95 *See* Art. 2 and 3 of the Implementing Rules for the RPI (note 41).

96 Art. 3 of the Constitution (note 35).

97 *See* ALBERS (note 62), at 288; WETTNER (note 80), at 315.

98 *See* only Art. 2(a) of the Constitution (note 35): "in the spirit of the 'Universal Declaration of Human Rights'"; Art. 2(a), 10.1(d) and 10.3(b) of the RIP (note 37).

99 *See* only Art. 1(f), 5(a) Nr. 2 or 10.2 of the RIP (note 37).

The lack of rules which would guarantee the presumption of innocence forms another gap in Interpol's legal order. It is only information on the Organization's internet website which gives some indication that this principle is normally respected. Since the Notices and other direct decision-taking powers in individual cases do not have regulatory character, a normative fixation seems not to be obligatory. But the declaratory and clarifying effects of an explicit rule would be desirable considering the relevance to fundamental individual rights.

3. Administrative and Procedural Principles

The major part of the principles of Interpol's international administration belongs to the area of the administrative law on information. The legal regime provides an entire catalogue of standards on the processing of data. Apart from the ultimate responsibility of the data source for an information Interpol commits itself to the protection of data security, precision and to a limited extent to data accuracy.[100]

Apart from this data protection terms relating to public authorities the Interpol regulations are based on the principle of proportionality which – when the exchange of information is concerned – becomes a principle of relevance: data must not be collected, Notices issued only if "it is relevant and connected with cases of specific international interest to the police."[101] Outside the data processing standards of the Interpol regime the cooperating authorities act according to their national law. These national administrative procedures are not regulated by Interpol.

Interpol, however, provides a number of legal administrative standards for its own activity. The Control Commission in particular is submitted to the principle of good administration: it shall ensure a processing of the requests "at the earliest opportunity" is bound "by professional secrecy" and "shall take all appropriate steps to exercise its duties" (Article 5 e of the Control Rules.)[102]

---

[100] *See* Higdon (note 64), at 36.

[101] *See* Art. 10.1(a) Nr. 3 of the RIP (note 37).

[102] *See* note 42.

II. Multi-level and Network Dimension

In organization and function Interpol is multi-dimensional and has a network dimension: it is organized as a network of national and international police authorities and other entities with police tasks. Within this network Interpol itself is the central service unit. The mediating function of the NCBs, which link the different national police information networks to Interpol, gives the organization a three-dimensional orientation. An additional dimension is added through Interpol's co-operation with other international organizations. The organization therefore comprises all possible dimensions of police co-operation.[103] This network dimension is mirrored in the basic principles of the organization: the necessary non-hierarchical character results from the fact that individual contributions to the co-operation are made voluntary and from the spreading of competence and responsibility between the bodies involved.

Not only Interpol's organization but also its function is based on a multi-level structure: as an assisting institution, the organization's added value does not stem from the centralization of administrative decisions, which remain within the competence of the participating police authorities, but from the globalization and central provision of information. Without Interpol's communication system, a much bigger co-operation and organizational effort would be needed to make this information be available. Interpol provides the technical and normative infrastructure and serves as a connecting point linking the participating authorities with each other.

III. Legitimacy of International Administrative Activity

The legitimacy of Interpol's international administrative activity cannot be found in traditional administrative patterns of the legitimacy structure of the nation state.[104] Only the member states can transfer *demo-*

---

103 *See* Philip K. Das & Peter C. Kratcoski, *International Police Cooperation: A World Perspective, in* Koenig & Das (note 64), at 3, 4.

104 On the alternative legitimacy patterns of international administrations, *see* Daniel C. Esty, *Good Governance at the Supranational Scale: Globalizing Administrative Law*, 115 YALE LAW JOURNAL 1490, 1515 (2006); MICHAEL BARNETT & MARTHA FINNEMORE, RULES FOR THE WORLD: INTERNATIONAL ORGANIZATIONS IN GLOBAL POLITICS 156 (2004); Rüdiger Wolfrum, *Legiti-*

cratic legitimacy.[105] From the perspective of the German administrative law, legitimacy also seems desirable for an international administrative activity which is, although not oriented on, but with relevance to individuals. The Organization itself does not possess a democratic basis which could provide such legitimacy, even though it takes majority-based decisions in the General Assembly. The state consent as the most important source of legitimacy in international law reaches its limits when it comes to single administrative measures and individuals concerned thereof.[106]

Nevertheless, Interpol does not lack any basis of legitimacy. Given the fact, that the national actors in the organization are not the governments but the police authorities, Interpol gets one part of its legitimacy not over institutional but expert-based mediation, *i.e.* the expertise of acting persons and participating entities. The direct contact of the respectively responsible national authorities results in greater efficiency in international co-operation. This efficiency can also create a legitimating effect.[107]

Interpol's position in the world also contributes to a greater legitimacy.[108] Largely accepted as an international organization under international law, committed to political, military and religious neutrality, the Organization encounters a lot of acceptance around the globe. Appointing staff to its bodies according to geographical proportional representation system it pays attention to a well-balanced representation.

Furthermore, its legitimacy is achieved through procedures and normative standards. These standards aim at the consensus of the participating authorities, establish a certain level of data security as a precondition for communication or provide some legal protection, howsoever limited it

---

macy of International Law from a Legal Perspective, *in* LEGITIMACY IN INTERNATIONAL LAW, 1, 24 (Rüdiger Wolfrum & Volker Röben eds., 2008).

[105] On the "Tragedy of Democracy," *see* Joseph H.H. Weiler, *The Geology of International Law – Governance, Democracy and Legitimacy*, 64 ZEITSCHRIFT FÜR AUSLÄNDISCHES ÖFFENTLICHES RECHT UND VÖLKERRECHT 547, 561 (2004).

[106] *See* Allen Buchanan & Robert O. Keohane, *The Legitimacy of Global Governance Institutions*, *in* LEGITIMACY IN INTERNATIONAL LAW (note 104), at 25, 35.

[107] On the importance of efficiency and expertise for global law enforcement, *see* DEFLEM (note 75), at 248; Gerspacher (note 51), at 414.

[108] *See* Alvarez (note 13), at 332.

may be, for the individual. An essential part of Interpol's acceptance is therefore based on its legal order, in which such legitimating elements as neutrality, proportional representation, expertise, consensual procedures, material principles etc. are laid down, protected by soft enforcement mechanisms and to which the Organization commits itself. Even if Interpol's legal regime does not formally bind its addressees, the organizations legitimacy depends in a large part on the legality of its actions.[109] Legitimacy deficits appear exactly where the existing standards fall short of the standards required under the rule of law.[110]

---

[109] On the relation between legitimacy and legality, *see* Daniel Bodansky, *The Concept of Legitimacy in International Law*, *in* LEGITIMACY IN INTERNATIONAL LAW (note 104), at 309, 311.

[110] On the question of a global rule of law, *see* Sabino Cassese, *The Globalization of Law*, 37 JOURNAL OF INTERNATIONAL LAW AND POLITICS 973, 991 (2005); Sabino Cassese, *Administrative Law Without the State? The Challenge of Global Regulation*, 37 JOURNAL OF INTERNATIONAL LAW AND POLITICS 663, 689 (2005).

2. The Exercise of Public Authority through Instruments Concerning Individual States

2.1 Decisions

Flexibility and Legitimacy – The Emissions Trading System under the Kyoto Protocol

*By Petra Lea Láncos**

A. Introduction

In the field of environmental law, be it on the domestic or the international level, it is especially difficult to develop effective regulatory sys-

* I would like to thank Eric Pickett and Eva Richter for their assistance with language and editing.

A. von Bogdandy et al. (eds.), *The Exercise of Public Authority by International Institutions*, Beiträge zum ausländischen öffentlichen Recht und Völkerrecht 210,
DOI 10.1007/978-3-642-04531-8_10, © Springer-Verlag Berlin Heidelberg 2010

tems and systems for sanctions to enforce obligations.[1] The legal solutions employed under the auspices of the United Nations Framework Convention on Climate Change, as well as the Kyoto Protocol, constitute a fascinating attempt to address these problems, providing "a huge testing ground for the legal instruments of environmental policy, at the international as well as on the lower levels," mirroring "enormous creativity in the design of regulatory approaches."[2] Even though the Kyoto Protocol, "if fully implemented, will not ... avert or even slow climate change,"[3] it serves as a fine example of emerging international composite administrations,[4] where multiple actors participate in transnational institutions of a multilevel system, serving the common goal of mitigating climate change. The climate change regime's unique regard to flexibility in fulfillment is particularly prominent. This is complemented by especially stringent and complex compliance mechanisms, which have no parallel in other international forms of cooperation. A further significant characteristic of the system is the high degree of legitimacy enjoyed by its institutional organization, its procedures and procedural outcomes. Thus, the international cooperation under the framework of the Kyoto Protocol is a landmark: it achieves not only flexibility but also a high degree of legitimacy and represents a more *mature* example of the exercise of public authority by international institutions.

The present paper attempts to highlight the main features of the Kyoto Protocol and its emissions trading system, describing the distinctive institutional law solutions which lie at the heart of the climate change regime. After a brief account of climate protection in the realm of international law, the context (chapter A) and main mechanisms of the Kyoto Protocol are introduced (chapter B) followed by conclusions (chapter C). A detailed analysis from the viewpoint of international institutional law is restricted to the Kyoto mechanism of emissions trading. This serves as a basis for examining not only the institutional and composite

---

[1] Ulrich Beyerlin, *Rio Konferenz 1992: Beginn einer neuen globalen Umweltrechtsordnung?*, 54 ZEITSCHRIFT FÜR AUSLÄNDISCHES ÖFFENTLICHES RECHT UND VÖLKERRECHT (ZAÖRV) 124, 131 (1994).

[2] Michael Bothe, *The United Nations Framework Convention on Climate Change – an Unprecedented Multilevel Regulatory Challenge*, 63 ZAÖRV 239, 245 (2003).

[3] Jutta Brunnée, *The Kyoto Protocol: A Testing Ground for Compliance Theories?*, 63 ZAÖRV 255 (2003).

[4] On the concept of "composite administration," *see* Armin von Bogdandy & Philipp Dann, *International Composite Administration*, in this volume.

character, but also the hallmark of the system: its rigorous compliance regime is elaborated.

I. The Protection of the Climate System on the International Level

The world's climate system is under constant change.[5] However, scientists have shown that a byproduct of the industrialization in the last centuries has been a rapid and drastic shift in the composition of gases constituting the atmosphere, leading to the phenomenon known as global warming. Addressing the consequences of global warming through climate change management is not a regulatory field that originally belonged to international law – there have been various attempts to tackle its symptoms on the domestic level.[6] However, global warming induced by the burning of fossil fuels has proven to affect not only the domestic climate, but also the global climate system and through it the entire biosphere The consequences include desertification, floods, rise of sea levels[7] as well as the elevation of the average global temperature, thus eliminating the habitat of various species unable to adapt to changing circumstances in such a short time.[8] This way the causes of climate change boomerang on mankind by posing health risks, deteriorating the environment and disrupting traditional employment structures[9] dependent on the natural environment,[10] which in turn may lead

---

5 SEBASTIAN OBERTHÜR & HERMANN E. OTT, THE KYOTO PROTOCOL – INTERNATIONALE KLIMAPOLITIK FÜR DAS 21. JAHRHUNDERT 27 (2000).

6 Examples include the Clean Air Act (1990) of the US and its amendments, as well as the South Coast Regional Clean Air Incentives Market (RECLAIM), also foreseeing pollution trading. See Michael S. Smith, *Murky Precedent Meets Hazy Air: The Compact Clause and the Regional Greenhouse Gas Initiative*, 34 BOSTON COLLEGE ENVIRONMENTAL AFFAIRS LAW REVIEW 387-416 (2007); PASCAL BADER, EUROPÄISCHE TREIBHAUSPOLITIK MIT HANDELBAREN EMISSIONSRECHTEN 56-97 (1999).

7 Kenneth D. Frederick & David C. Major, *Climate Change and Water Resources*, 37 CLIMATIC CHANGE 7-23 (1997).

8 Bothe (note 2), at 239.

9 For an economic assessment *see* Gary Yohe & Michael Schlesinger, *The Economic Geography of the Impacts of Climate Change*, 2 JOURNAL OF ECONOMIC GEOGRAPHY 311-341 (2002).

10 OBERTHÜR & OTT (note 5), at 29; FARHANA YAMIN & JOANNA DEPLEDGE, The International Climate Change Regime 22 (2004).

to poverty, mass migration and crime constituting threats to both national and international security.[11] Gradually, members of the international community realized that, due to the transboundary nature of air pollution and its ensuing consequences as well as the high costs involved in mitigation,[12] climate change may only be effectively addressed by complementing domestic measures through institutionalized forms of transnational collaboration.[13] As a consequence, combating climate change has spilled over from the realm of domestic regulation into the field of international cooperation.

Already the 1979 Geneva Convention on Long-Range Transboundary Air Pollution as well as the 1985 Vienna Convention for the Protection of the Ozone Layer and its 1987 Montreal Protocol on Substances that Deplete the Ozone Layer constituted serious international efforts to face the problem of climate change, adopting novel solutions under international environmental law. However, these conventions targeted only specific aspects of the problem of climate change. In 1990 the Intergovernmental Panel on Climate Change published its influential First Assessment Report on the condition of the global climate system, which served as a starting point for comprehensive UN General Assembly negotiations. By way of Resolution 45/212 the General Assembly set up the Intergovernmental Negotiating Committee for a Frame-

---

[11] Victoria Dawson, *Environmental Dispute Resolution: Developing Mechanisms for Effective Transnational Enforcement of International Environmental Standards*, BERKELEY ELECTRONIC PRESS PAPER 1, 2 (2004); Stavros Dimas, *Climate Change: The Reality, the Risks and the Response*, 13 IRISH JOURNAL OF EUROPEAN LAW 5, 6-8 (2006).

[12] M. J. Mace, Chris Hendriks & Roger Coenraads, *Regulatory Challenges to the Implementation of Carbon Capture and Geological Storage Within the European Union under EU and International Law*, 1 INTERNATIONAL JOURNAL OF GREENHOUSE GAS CONTROL 253 (2007); Dennis Leaf, Hans J. H. Verolme & William F. Hunt, *Overview of Regulatory/Policy/Economic Issues Related to Carbon Dioxide*, 29 ENVIRONMENT INTERNATIONAL 303, 305 (2003).

[13] BARBARA PFLÜGLMAYER, VOM KYOTO-PROTOKOLL ZUM EMISSIONSHANDEL – ENTWICKLUNG UND AUSGEWÄHLTE RECHTSFRAGEN 5 (2004); Marta D'Auria, *Emissions Trading and Polycentric Negotiation*, 6 GLOBAL JURIST ADVANCES 1 (2006).

work Convention on Climate Change, which completed its task of drawing up the Convention by May 1992.[14]

The *United Nations Framework Convention on Climate Change* (UNFCCC, Convention) was adopted in 1992 at the so-called 'Earth Summit' held in Rio de Janeiro, "[a]cknowledging that change in the Earth's climate and its adverse effects are a common concern of humankind." With the goal of mitigating potential risks posed by climate change[15] the Convention adopted a "double track approach"[16] aimed at stabilizing greenhouse gas (GHG) concentrations in the atmosphere to prevent dangerous changes in the climate system as well as to enable ecosystems to adapt to changes already taking place. On 21 March 1994 the UNFCCC entered into force. One year later the Conference of the Parties (COP), the central body of the Convention, held its first meeting (COP 1). Already in its first session the COP 1 found that the commitments under the Convention were insufficient to meet the challenges posed by climate change. Negotiations were commenced to supplement the Convention in accordance with Article 17[17] with a protocol laying down further commitments for meeting UNFCCC goals. As a result, the Kyoto Protocol (KP) was adopted in 1997 by COP 3.[18] It entered into force on 16 February 2005 after States accounting for over 55 % of global emissions of GHGs had ratified it. The KP thereby became "the sole instrument for the implementation"[19] of the UNFCCC.

---

[14] Daniel Bodansky, *The United Nations Framework Convention on Climate Change: A Commentary*, 18 YALE JOURNAL OF INTERNATIONAL LAW 461-474 (1993).

[15] Art. 2 UNFCCC.

[16] Bothe (note 2), at 240.

[17] Art. 17 UNFCCC allows for the adoption of protocols by the Conference of the Parties by consensus; the Conference of the Parties is open only to the Parties of the Convention.

[18] By decision 1/CP.3. So far the Kyoto Protocol has received 170 ratifications (18 April 2007). For the reasons behind the resistance of one of the most substantial GHG emitter, the United States, *see* Cass R. Sunstein, *Of Montreal and Kyoto: A Tale of Two Protocols*, 31 HARVARD ENVIRONMENTAL LAW REVIEW 1-65 (2007).

[19] D'Auria (note 13), at 4; Richard L. Ottinger & Mindy Jayne, *Global Climate Change Kyoto Protocol Implementation: Legal Frameworks for Implementing Clean Energy Solutions*, 18 PACE ENVIRONMENTAL LAW REVIEW (Pace Envtl. L. Rev.) 19-86 (2000-2001).

II. The Relationship between the Convention and the Kyoto Protocol

The Kyoto Protocol reflects an attempt to 'harden' and 'widen' commitments foreseen under the UNFCCC. Together they constitute the so-called climate change treaty regime. The relationship between the KP and the Convention is marked by both differences and similarities: The KP is an international agreement that stands on its own in the sense that it constitutes a self-contained regime with its own mechanisms and compliance systems. However, emanating from the Convention it is linked to it in several ways, such as by sharing its aims, principles, certain institutions and partly even reproducing its very text. At the same time, the KP adds new and more stringent commitments to the existing ones, revamping the overall effort of mitigating climate change.

As does the Convention, the KP effectively applies the *principle of common but differentiated responsibilities*.[20] According to this principle all signatory States share the same responsibility of contributing to combating climate change, while at the same time, there is a differentiation in the allocation of commitments between developed countries (Annex I Parties) and developing countries (non-Annex I Parties). The Annex I Parties commit to binding obligations under the KP while the non-Annex I Parties are free to voluntarily bind themselves[21] to these.[22]

Furthermore, instead of simply 'dictating conduct', the KP's regulatory approach marks a move toward novel, *flexible* methods characterized by economic incentives and relying upon the self-interest of actors.[23] Although sanctions and prescriptions do play a certain role in this regulatory system, the overall approach is to enable public and private parties to identify their individual interests and to act upon them.[24] As regards further principles, the fourth recital of the Preamble of the Kyoto

---

[20] Art. 10 KP.

[21] Art. 4(2)(g) UNFCCC.

[22] This denotation stems from the country lists in Annex I and Annex II of the UNFCCC. Both Annexes list developed States (as well as those, with economies in transition, EIT). Annex II contains those Annex I countries that further undertake to financially assist developing countries in combating climate change. Thus, while all Annex II countries are Annex I countries well, the reverse is not true.

[23] D'Auria (note 13), at 6.

[24] *Id.*, at 1, 7.

Protocol affirms its adherence to the principles of the Convention as set forth in Article 3 of the Convention. The legal status of these principles (e.g., sustainable development, intergeneration equity, etc.), however, is a contentious issue: although they do not constitute precise obligations[25] but merely guide the Parties, they do go beyond being mere tools of interpretation. At the same time, the wording "being guided by" suggests that these principles are intended to be political in nature, instead of having legal force under the Kyoto Protocol.[26]

III. A System of Incremental and Differentiated Commitments

Guided by the goal of the Convention to stabilize the concentration of GHGs in the atmosphere, the KP commits the Annex I Parties to implement *inter alia* national measures which promote sustainable development through improving energy efficiency, enhancing GHG 'sinks' that trap harmful emissions and promoting scientific research on new clean technologies.[27] Most importantly, however, the Annex I Parties agree to reduce their aggregate emissions of specific GHGs[28] by five percent below 1990 levels. Therefore each Annex I Party undertakes to reduce its emissions during the first commitment period (2008 to 2012) by a certain percent.[29] Each Annex I Party is assigned a maximum amount of emission allowances,[30] which represent the amount of emissions the Party may emit during the commitment period. They may decide to fulfill their commitments either individually or jointly ('bubble'), an approach best exemplified by the European Union and its

---

25 *See* Bodansky (note 14), at 502.

26 OBERTHÜR & OTT (note 5), at 142.

27 Art. 2 KP.

28 *See* Annex A KP.

29 *See* Annex B KP.

30 The KP's base units for emission allowances are the so-called Assigned Amount Units (AAUs). Further 'emission credits' are generated privately, such as the Certified Emission Reductions (CERs), Emission Reduction Units (ERUs) and Removal Units (RMUs), depending on the nature of the mechanism under which the unit is generated or transferred; each equivalent to one metric ton of CO_2. Matthieu Wemaere & Charlotte Streck, *Legal Ownership and Nature of Kyoto Units and EU Allowances*, *in* LEGAL ASPECTS OF IMPLEMENTING THE KYOTO PROTOCOL MECHANISMS: MAKING KYOTO WORK 5, 43 (David Freestone & Charlotte Streck eds., 2005).

Member States.[31] Meeting these commitments may, however, prove burdensome from an economic perspective.[32] Therefore, to facilitate compliance with the aims laid down in Article 3, the KP also envisages three economically viable, flexible supplementary mechanisms to reduce the emission of certain harmful antropogenic gases: the emissions trading system (ETS), the clean development mechanism, (CDM) and joint implementation (JI). The ETS, applicable to certain emissions,[33] is linked with the compensatory systems of the transnational CDM and JI.[34] The ETS mechanism permits developed States to cooperate with developing countries, promoting technology transfer and at the same time providing an economically appealing common framework for collectively meeting Kyoto commitments.

As the aims and advantages of the flexible mechanisms can only be realized through securing the observance of all related provisions,[35] it is important to note the "close design link between the strength of the compliance procedure and the effective operation of the KP's market-based

---

[31] Art. 4 KP. The possibility of joint fulfilment enables Member States of the EU to construct a regional system of burden-sharing in achieving KP commitments while at the same time avoiding distortions of competition in the internal market. Ludwig Krämer, *Grundlagen aus europäischer Sicht – Rechtsfragen betreffend den Emissionshandel mit Treibhausgasen der Europäischen Gemeinschaft, in* KLIMASCHUTZ DURCH EMISSIONSHANDEL 1-45 (Hans-Werner Rengeling ed., 2001). *See* Directive 2003/87/EC of the European Parliament and of the Council of 13 October 2003, establishing a scheme for greenhouse gas emission allowance trading within the Community and amending Council Directive 96/61/EC.

[32] DAVID G. VICTOR, THE COLLAPSE OF THE KYOTO PROTOCOL AND THE STRUGGLE TO STOP GLOBAL WARMING 3 (2001).

[33] Namely: carbon dioxide (CO_2), methane (CH_4), nitrous oxide (N_2O), sulphur hexafluoride (SF_6) as well as two groups of gases: hydroflourocarbons (HFCs), and Perfluorocarbons (PFCs). In reality, not emissions, but much rather the "right to emit specified substances of a certain quantity over a defined period of time" is traded. Rutger de Witt Wijnen, *Emissions Trading under Art. 17 of the Kyoto Protocol*, in: LEGAL ASPECTS OF IMPLEMENTING THE KYOTO PROTOCOL MECHANISMS: MAKING KYOTO WORK 403 (David Freestone & Charlotte Streck eds., 2005).

[34] Art. 6 KP.

[35] OBERTHÜR & OTT (note 5), at 260.

mechanisms."[36] This design link led to the establishment of the KP's most remarkable feature: a stringent compliance regime.[37] In the analysis of the Kyoto regime the present paper shall restrict itself to the examination of the flexible mechanism of the emissions trading system. The compact, highly elaborate compliance procedures and monitoring of outcomes makes the ETS a fine example of a mature form of international composite administration.

IV. "Composite" Features and Actors' Interests

The KP establishes a composite system of governance by distributing specific competences between the international and national levels and allowing for the participation of 'regional economic integration organizations' such as the European Community.[38] Although significant regulatory power is transferred to the international plane,[39] it is characteristic of the KP's approach that it is well balanced and non-intrusive by offering flexible implementation schemes. The Parties thus retain considerable freedom in deciding exactly how they prefer to fulfill their commitments.[40] This new system of exercising public authority not only establishes relations between international institutions, regional

---

36 Jakob Werksman, *The Negotiation of a Kyoto Compliance System*, in: IMPLEMENTING THE CLIMATE CHANGE REGIME 17, 19 (Olav Schram Stokke, Jon Hovi & Geir Ulfstein eds., 2005).

37 "[W]hat emerged ... from these negotiations is a remarkable compliance system drawing on precedent from, and yet unique to, international law." *Id.*, at 17, 19.

38 Art. 20 UNFCCC and Art. 24(1) KP on the accession of regional economic integration organisations.

39 D'Auria (note 13), at 1.

40 "Emissions trading may be viewed as 'regulation lite' by critics because it frequently involves controls and allocations that are designed not to frighten the horses of the incumbents. That 'lite' quality, however, may be welcomed by many governments on the grounds that, at least on the world stage, we face global warming issues of such urgency that the best regulatory method for controlling greenhouse gases is the one that has the best chance of implementation." Robert Baldwin, *Regulation Lite: The Rise of Emissions Trading*, 3 LSE LAW, SOCIETY AND ECONOMY WORKING PAPERS 27 (2008).

economic integration organizations and national governments[41] but also builds upon the horizontal cooperation of national governments in the ambit of the various Kyoto mechanisms. Furthermore, it involves the private sector, relying on entrepreneurial interest, and actively seeks input from the scientific community and civil society,[42] which participate in the Kyoto system both vertically (observers, advisers) and horizontally (allegiances).[43] The KP thereby promotes the development of a complex, non-hierarchical, cooperative[44] network of international, regional and national institutions, and public and private actors.

Actors involved in the climate change regime pursue different interests.[45] Civil society, NGOs[46] and certain States promote environmental interests,[47] pressing for an overall reduction of harmful emissions. On the other hand, many in the private sector as well as some developing countries[48] and countries with old, inefficient industries or high fossil

---

41 An important aspect of this multilevel system of climate management is the mutually reinforcing empowerment of the international administrative entity and the national governments. Together, they gain control over the regulatory field of GHG emissions with each level acquiring a new role: international institutions gain regulatory power and national governments, though bound by international prescriptions, also gain regulatory and implementation powers over subjects potentially transcending their respective boundaries. Through this new system of administration new competences open up for all participating levels and the efficiency of each level as well as the overall project is enhanced. D'Auria (note 13), at 2.

42 "Informational cross-linkage." *See* Armin von Bogdandy & Philipp Dann, *International Composite Administration*, in this volume.

43 Joyeeta Gupta, *The Role of Non-State Actors in International Environmental Affairs*, 62 ZAÖRV 459, 467 (2003).

44 D'Auria (note 13), at 17.

45 Farhana Yamin, *The Kyoto Protocol: Origings, Assessment and Future Challenges*, 7 REVIEW OF EUROPEAN COMMUNTY AND INTERNATIONAL ENVIRONMENTAL LAW (RECIEL) 113, 114 (1998).

46 OBERTHÜR & OTT (note 5), at 58-61. Perhaps the most prominent example is the world-wide Climate Action Network International integrating over 300 NGOs concerned with climate change.

47 For example, the Alliance of Small Island States (AOSIS) face great risks of inundation induced by climate change and are therefore assiduous negotiators endorsing emissions reductions within the climate change regime.

48 Often referred to as the Group of 77; OBERTHÜR & OTT (note 5), at 55-58.

fuel production[49] follow predominantly economic pursuits.[50] They insist on the use of cheap fossil fuels, fearing that the high costs of restructuring such industries to make them more efficient and environmentally sound may be damaging to economic growth and harm their competitiveness on the global market. Developed countries are interested in preserving a high standard of living, which entails high energy consumption contributing to relatively high emission rates even in countries where environmentally friendly fuels and means of energy production exist. Finally, all States strive to retain considerable sovereignty over the field of environmental regulation; thus, stringent, unilateral international obligations excluding leeway for national divergence remain unpopular among members of the global. As will be shown below, cleavages between the interests of developed and developing countries have been internalized in the institutional organization as well as the decision-making rules foreseen for both the legislative and the enforcement bodies. The preference for consensus guarantees that interest-coalitions play a marginal role in the decision-making process. Excluding the possibility of making reservations,[51] the UNFCCC and the KP are regarded as a successful effort in accommodating the above interests, providing an attractive treaty regime[52] characterized by differentiated responsibilities of the Parties and flexible mechanisms for fulfilling international obligations in a cost-effective way.

---

49 Such as those participating in the Organization of the Petroleum Exporting Countries (OPEC) or the informal alliance JUSSCANNZ, an acronym which stands for Japan, the US, Switzerland, Canada, Australia, Norway and New Zealand. Iceland, Mexico, the Republic of Korea and other invited States, all of which are either great consumers and/or producers of fossil fuels, may also attend meetings.

50 OBERTHÜR & OTT (note 5), at 39.

51 Art. 24 UNFCCC, Art. 26 Kyoto.

52 As Baldwin puts it, emissions trading yields *political advantages*: "Trading mechanisms offer a means of introducing controls but also of avoiding major opposition from entrenched incumbents." Baldwin (note 40), at 7.

B. Legal Assessment

I. Organizational Setting

The organizational setting of the emissions trading system is the climate change treaty regime consisting of the UNFCCC and the KP. Although it has been set up under the auspices of the United Nations, except for its Secretariat,[53] the treaty regime is both institutionally as well as financially highly independent from the UN,[54] which may only participate as an 'observer' at the COP meetings.[55] The status of the treaty regime is not equivalent to that of an intergovernmental organization. However, as an entity *superiorem non recognoscentes* it is able to act effectively and independently on the international plane by way of its own bodies.[56] In this respect it shows traits similar to more traditional subjects of international law.[57] The institutional structure of the Kyoto regime is partly predetermined by the UNFCCC, from which the KP 'borrows' some of its bodies, while at the same time it also establishes its own institutions.

II. Institutional Framework

Albeit being 'own' institutions of the KP, the bodies 'shared' with the Convention do exhibit hybrid qualities, having both similarities and differences in composition and decision-making. This hybrid character is the result of the lack of identity of Contracting Parties and the inde-

---

53 Decision 6/CP.6, Institutional linkage of the Convention secretariat to the United Nations.

54 GEF, established under the auspices of the World Bank with the participation of the UNEP as well as the United Nations Development Programme (UNDP) serves as an interim financial mechanism of the Convention; Decisions 10/CP.1 and 3/CP.4.

55 Art. 13(8) KP.

56 Memorandum of Understanding on the determination of funding necessary and available for the implementation of the Convention, Decisions 1/SBI 4 and 12/CP.3.

57 Guido Acquaviva, *Subjects of International Law: A Power-Based Analysis*, 38 VANDERBILT JOURNAL OF TRANSNATIONAL LAW 345, 383 (2005); MICHAEL HEMPEL, DIE VÖLKERRECHTSSUBJEKTIVITÄT INTERNATIONALER NICHTSTAATLICHER ORGANISATIONEN 57-60 (1999).

pendence of the two international treaties.[58] All measures taken under the KP are adopted by KP bodies of the signatory States, whereas Convention bodies have no or little influence on such measures.[59] The ETS is steered by the Conference of the Parties, which in turn serves as the Meeting of the Parties (COP/MOP) to the Kyoto Protocol.[60] This COP/MOP is a KP body, and should not be confused with the COP, the supreme authority of the Convention. Although the COP/MOP creates the substantive framework of the trading system, the Secretariat, the Compliance Committee, the Expert Review Teams (ERTs) and the subsidiary bodies are principally responsible for managing the trading system and for enforcement issues.

The Meeting of the Parties is the supreme body, the highest decision-making authority of the KP. The COP/MOP's responsibility is to regularly review the implementation of the KP and to make decisions necessary for its effective implementation.[61] The COP/MOP has thus functions that could be characterized as both administrative and legislative.[62] It also has coordinating and organizational functions, since it coordinates national measures to combat climate change, but it also establishes subsidiary bodies to further the aims of the KP when necessary.[63] A link between the supreme authorities of the Convention and the KP is established by entrusting the COP/MOP with "consider[ing] any assignment resulting from a decision by the Conference of the Parties" of the Convention[64] without granting powers of decision to the COP over the COP/MOP.[65] The COP/MOP comprises the representatives of the governments of signatory States and is therefore a highly political institution. Representatives of non-party States[66] as well as the UN and its specialized agencies may participate in an observer status.[67] Finally, also

---

58 OBERTHÜR & OTT (note 5), at 305-306.

59 *Id.*, at 309.

60 Art. 13(1) KP.

61 Art. 13(4) KP.

62 OBERTHÜR & OTT (note 5), at 310.

63 Art. 13(4)(d), (h) KP.

64 Art. 13(4)(j) KP.

65 OBERTHÜR & OTT (note 5), at 312.

66 Art. 13(2) KP.

67 "Institutional cross-linkage" in the form of observational participation, *see* Armin von Bogdandy & Philipp Dann, *International Composite Administration*, in this volume.

other bodies qualified in matters covered by the KP may participate as observers, unless at least one-third of the Parties present at the COP/MOP meeting object.[68] Ordinary sessions are held annually, while extraordinary sessions are convened when necessary or upon request of the Parties.[69] Political weight and bargaining power of the individual Parties are levelled by employing consensus as the general rule in COP/MOP decision-making procedures, except in very few, albeit important cases where a 3/4 majority on a one State-one vote basis is required.[70] The relative independence of the COP/MOP from the COP of the Convention, the equal standing of Parties and the general rule of consensus in decision-making processes provides a high degree of legitimacy not only as regards the institutional design of the supreme authority of the KP but also its decisions. The COP/MOP and the Parties are further assisted in their functions by the Bonn based Secretariat.[71] The Secretariat's Methods, Inventories and Science branch secures the backbone of ETS by advancing technical methods for reporting and inventory compilation as well as by organizing the review of national inventories.

The Compliance Committee and especially its so-called Enforcement Branch play a crucial role in the operation of the emissions trading system. The Compliance Committee, a genuine Kyoto body with no Convention equivalent, was established by Decision 27/CMP.1[72] with the aim of facilitating, promoting and enforcing compliance with Kyoto commitments. Unlike the COP/MOP it is not a plenary institution, but much rather an expert body organized into different sub-divisions. It consists of a Bureau entrusted with allocating Parties' reports and questions, as well as two branches: the Facilitative and Enforcement Branch. Each branch consists of ten members who are elected by the COP/MOP from both Annex I and non-Annex I countries. The complicated decision-making procedure of the branches requires a quorum of ¾ of its members being present. If no consensus is reached, decisions

---

68 Art. 13(8) KP.

69 Art. 13(6)-(7) KP.

70 Art. 20(3) and Art. 21(4) KP (amendment of the Protocol and its Annexes as well as the adoption of Annexes).

71 Pursuant to Art. 14(1) KP "the secretariat established by ... the Convention shall serve as the secretariat of this Protocol." Note that by Decision 6/CP.6 the Secretariat has been institutionally and financially linked to the UN.

72 Decision 27/CMP.1, Procedures and mechanisms relating to compliance under the Kyoto Protocol.

are taken by a ¾ majority of members present with the additional requirement of a majority among both Annex I and non-Annex I Parties. Such a requirement of parity reflects equal consideration of the interests of both developed and developing countries, furnishing Compliance Committee decisions with further legitimacy. With regard to emissions trading, the Facilitative Branch provides advice, information and facilitation on implementation to the Parties. This reflects an approach of assisting instead of sanctioning Parties with the overall aim of successfully implementing the KP. In contrast, the Enforcement Branch is responsible for determining whether a Party in question is eligible for participation in the emissions trading system, makes corrections to the Parties' accounting of emission allowances when necessary, and applies so-called 'enforcement consequences' in cases of non-compliance.[73]

The Compliance Committee is assisted by Expert Review Teams (ERTs). The ERTs have been modelled on the Convention's so-called In-Depth Review Teams[74] and are entrusted with the "thorough and comprehensive technical assessment" of the information submitted[75] by the Parties as well as the identification of 'questions of implementation'. To this end they assess national reports, evaluate information deriving from various sources and conduct in-country visits, whereas the Parties undertake to "make every reasonable effort to respond to all questions and requests from the Expert Review Teams."[76] ERTs thus carry out the groundwork necessary for the decisions of the Compliance Committee. They are coordinated by the Secretariat, while its members are selected by the Parties and intergovernmental organizations.[77] To ensure the unbiased and efficient operation of the ERTs, members of the individual teams act in their personal capacity and must possess qualifications in the areas under review. The composition of each team must reflect a balance between Annex I and Annex II Parties; nationals of the Party under review are not eligible to be members of the team.[78] ERTs are to

[73] Werksman (note 36), at 19.

[74] Geir Ulfstein & Jakob Werksman, *The Kyoto Compliance System: Towards Hard Enforcement*, *in* IMPLEMENTING THE CLIMATE CHANGE REGIME 39, 43 (Olav Schram Stokke, Jon Hovi & Geir Ulfstein eds., 2005).

[75] UNFCCC guidelines for the technical review of greenhouse gas inventories from Parties included in Annex I to the Convention.

[76] Decision 23/CP.7, Guidelines for review under Art. 8 of the Kyoto Protocol.

[77] Art. 8(3) KP.

[78] Decision 22/CMP.1, paras. 31-35.

"refrain from making any political judgements" in their reports.[79] Instead, they are to "play an innovative and important part in the enforcement of the climate commitments"[80] by submitting technical information on the respective Party's compliance to the Compliance Committee. The information assists the Compliance Committee in determining whether there has been a violation of obligations under the KP.

Finally, the Subsidiary Body for Scientific and Technological Advice as well as the Subsidiary Body for Implementation play an important role in the design of the trading system by providing technical advice[81] that forms the basis of various COP/MOP decisions or by compiling manuals and other documents intended for assisting implementation.

III. The Emissions Trading System

1. Main Features

The emissions trading system is a flexible mechanism under the Kyoto Protocol aiming at minimizing the costs of compliance with reduction commitments and making improvements to the environment profitable in the future:[82] "Through emissions trading, a market price for emissions abatement will emerge which reflects the marginal cost of emissions abatement across all market participants. When participants have exhausted the opportunities available for domestic emission reductions ... they can elect to purchase the requisite 'assigned amounts' from other Parties (or entities). In this way, the environmental benefits are achieved, irrespective of where the reductions take place, and at a lower cost than if trading was not available."[83] The rationale of the system is

---

[79] Decision 22/CMP.1, para. 22.

[80] Ulfstein & Werksman (note 74), at 43.

[81] Also established under Arts. 9 and 10 UNFCCC.

[82] Non-Paper on Principles, Modalities, Rules and Guidelines for an International Emissions Trading Regime, 3 June 1998, available at: http://www.med.govt.nz/upload/24427/umbrellagroup.pdf. According to Pflüglmayer, the price of emission allowances will not be determined by the market, but much rather by way of political agreement. PFLÜGLMAYER (note 13), at 5.

[83] Non-Paper on Principles, Modalities, Rules and Guidelines for an International Emissions Trading Regime, 3 June 1998, available at: http://www.med.govt.nz/upload/24427/umbrellagroup.pdf.

that investing in clean technology may prove to be cheaper in the long run than purchasing emission allowances, and at the same time the surplus allowances may be sold for a high market price to Parties over-emitting and otherwise not meeting their reduction commitments.[84]

The trading system implies the creation of an emission allowances market determined by commitment periods, individual emissions caps and tradable emission allowances that constitute economic assets in the form of pollution rights. Thus, a regulatory framework had to be established to govern the main features of the flexible mechanism in terms of both its substantive and procedural aspects. The rules adopted to this end secure the functioning of the system by creating a common space in which regulation takes place at various levels, where the conditions of competition are approximated,[85] and where actors meet to interact with each other.

2. *Substantive Rules*

The emissions trading regime is based on the common rules relating to registries, transfers of allowances between these registries and the review of such transfers. The legal basis of the emissions trading system is found in Article 17 KP[86] and is also referred to in Article 3 paragraphs 10-11 KP, which set forth the basic framework of ETS without regulating details.[87] The preconditions and elements of the system are laid down in specific articles of the KP itself, legislative measures of both the COP/MOP of the KP and the COP of the Convention, which con-

---

[84] "Low cost abaters will be incentivised to reduce pollution levels and sell permits to higher cost abaters with the effect that the set level of emissions is achieved by lowest cost methods." Baldwin (note 40), at 6.

[85] Patrick Low, *Trade and the Environment: What Worries the Developing Countries?*, 23 ENVIRONMENTAL LAW (ENVTL L.) 708 (1993).

[86] Interestingly, Art. 17 KP foresees the elaboration of the rules of ETS by the COP, the institution of the Convention and not the COP/MOP: "The Conference of the Parties shall define the relevant principles, modalities, rules and guidelines, in particular for verification, reporting and accountability for emissions trading." However, Decision 18/CP.7 transferred decision-making power relating to the ETS's "modalities, rules and guidelines" to the COP/MOP. There is thus a 'mix' of Convention and Kyoto bodies in charge of defining the rules of ETS.

[87] Fanny Missfeldt, *Flexible Mechanisms: Which Path to Take after Kyoto?*, 7 RECIEL 128, 129 (1998).

cretizes the "principles, modalities, rules and guidelines" by adopting formal decisions in accordance with the general rules. Such decisions are enacted mainly on the basis of advice from the Subsidiary Body for Implementation, the Subsidiary Body for Scientific and Technological Advice as well as the Secretariat. NGOs also contribute to such decisions either indirectly by way of lobbying, or by way of direct participation in government delegations.[88] Concretizing regulatory proposals of the COP and the COP/MOP are adopted in the form of decisions under the general rules of decision-making[89] and mandate institutions or bodies of the KP to carry out specific actions. These decisions giving effect to the individual Articles of the KP and rendering mechanisms of the KP more feasible are usually very elaborate and precise and are often of highly technical nature.

3. The Procedural Regime

a) Management of the Emissions Trading System

The reduction commitments of Annex I countries span 5 year commitment periods. The Emissions Trading System, which is designed to facilitate meeting these commitments, may be analyzed here in a framework that breaks down these commitment periods into three main stages: *eligibility assessment (aa)*, *trading phase (bb)* and *commitment period compliance assessment (cc)*. In reality, the operation of the ETS reflects much rather a continuum than such clear-cut phases. However these three phases provide an adequate framework of analysis for the purposes of the present paper.

1. In the first stage, the eligibility of signatory States for participation in the ETS is assessed. This involves the allocation of allowances to the Parties according to their respective reduction commitments. The Parties in turn must meet the technical requirements for participating in flexible mechanisms. Compliance is ensured by reporting and review procedures.

2. In the next stage, provided the eligibility criteria are met, Parties can acquire and transfer allowances with a view to meeting their reduction

---

[88] Steinar Andresen & Lars H. Gulbrandsen, *The Role of Green NGOs in Promoting Climate Compliance,* in IMPLEMENTING THE CLIMATE CHANGE REGIME 169, 173 (Olav Schram Stokke, Jon Hovi & Geir Ulfstein eds., 2005).

[89] Draft Standard Electronic Format for Reporting Kyoto Units recommended for adoption by Decision 17/CP.10 para 1.

commitments. From an administrative perspective, this process requires the establishment, management and supervision of national and international registries, which track the transactions and establish uniform rules for accounting allowances between registries.

3. In the final stage, at the end of the commitment period, the Parties' compliance with their respective reduction commitments is reviewed based on the information gathered in the reporting process.

In the following, the three main stages of the emissions trading system are examined in detail to illustrate the administrative procedures under the KP.

b) Eligibility Assessment

The functioning of the ETS is premised on the sound assessment of emissions and sinks that capture GHG-s, as well as the precise allocation of the Parties' emission allowances. Therefore only those Parties to the KP which comply with specific "eligibility criteria are eligible for participation in the trading system."[90] To evaluate eligibility, a system of national reporting and review by KP bodies has been established.

According to the eligibility criteria Annex I Parties are obliged to establish and maintain national (electronic) registries for tracking holdings of emissions allowances they have been assigned, or which they have acquired or transferred.[91] They are required to compile national GHG inventories on emissions by sources and removals by sinks[92] and to supplement their respective annual reports[93] and periodic national communications under the Convention[94] with additional information related to

---

[90] The eligibility criteria are set forth in Decision 18/CP.7, para 2.

[91] Annex B of the KP itself contains the data necessary for the quantification of the emission allowances assigned to each Annex I State. Accounting takes place in compliance with Decision 13/CMP.1, (Modalities for the accounting of assigned amounts under Art. 7(4) of the Kyoto Protocol).

[92] Art. 5(1) KP; Decision 20/CMP.1, *IPCC* Good practice guidance and adjustments under Article 5, paragraph 2 of the Kyoto Protocol.

[93] In compliance with the guidelines set out in Decision 17/CP.8 and detailed in: Reporting on Climate Change – User Manual for the Guidelines on National Communications from Non-Annex I Parties.

[94] Art. 12 UNFCCC; Decision 3/CP.5, incorporating Guidelines for the preparation of national communications by Parties included in Annex I to the Convention, Part I: UNFCCC reporting guidelines on annual inventories.

the KP.[95] Together, these documents constitute the initial report first reviewed[96] by international Expert Review Teams. These compile reports for the COP on the Parties' compliance with the above obligations, identifying problems and factors related to non-compliance as "questions of implementation". ERTs may give advice or "put questions to, or request additional or clarifying information" from the Parties, while the latter are to assist the experts by supplying information and necessary facilities.[97] In their assessment ERTs are not restricted to information submitted by the Party under review, implying that they may also avail themselves of also information provided by NGOs when performing the review.[98] The draft report[99] of the respective ERT must be submitted to the Party subject to review within strict time limits. The Party then has the opportunity to comments on the report.[100] Subsequently, the ERT report is finalized in accordance with the guidelines set forth in Decision 22/CMP.1.[101] Reports are forwarded to the Enforcement Branch of the Compliance Committee, which determines whether the Party has fulfilled all requirements to be eligible for participation in the ETS.[102] After the Enforcement Branch has completed its preliminary examination, the Party is notified of the findings.[103] The Party may then provide comments in writing, and shall also be heard if it so requests. As a rule, such hearings are public. However, the Enforcement Branch may decide otherwise of its own accord or upon request of the Party concerned.[104] The Enforcement Branch "shall adopt

---

95 Decision 15/CMP.1, (Guidelines for the preparation of the information required under Art. 7 of the Kyoto Protocol), Art. 7(1)-(2) KP.

96 Art. 8(1) KP.

97 Decision 22/CMP.1, (Guidelines for review under Art. 8 of the Kyoto Protocol), paras. 5 and 6.

98 Section 153 of Decision 22/CMP.1.

99 Draft status report, draft individual inventory review report, draft review report on the national registry or draft national communication review report depending on the scope of review.

100 Decision 22/CMP.1, para. 7.

101 Decision 22/CMP.1, paras. 64, 83.

102 Decision 24/CP.7, (Procedures and mechanisms relating to compliance under the Kyoto Protocol), Section VI. paras. 1 and 3; 2/CMP.1, (Principles, nature and scope of the mechanisms pursuant to Arts. 6, 12 and 17 of the Kyoto Protocol).

103 *Id.*, at Section VII. paras. 6-7 and Section X. para. 1(a).

104 *Id.*, at Section IX. para. 2 and Section X. para. 1(b)-(c).

its preliminary finding or a decision not to proceed within six weeks of the notification or two weeks of the hearing, whichever is the shorter."[105]

Eligibility assessment also implies that the Enforcement Branch suspends Parties that no longer fulfil the eligibility criteria. Should a Party fail to continue meet the eligibility criteria, e.g., for reasons of overselling its assigned allowances[106] (in other words, not preserving the so-called commitment period reserve),[107] it shall deduct the excess emissions from the Party's next commitment period, oblige the Party to develop a compliance action plan, and suspend the Party.[108] Should the Party fail to meet other eligibility requirements under the KP, the Enforcement Branch shall suspend the Party.[109] The Party concerned may in certain cases apply to the ERT for a decision brought in an expedited procedure to review the reinstatement of eligibility[110] or may apply directly to the Enforcement Branch for reinstatement. In such cases the Enforcement Branch reviews the report of the ERT (if available) as well as the Party's action plans and subsequent annual progress reports to make a determination on the Party's reinstatement.[111]

c) Trading

After fulfilling the technical and administrative requirements of the eligibility assessment phase, Parties may commence trading their Kyoto allowances.[112] Transactions from emissions trading are tracked on both the respective national registries and the so-called International Transaction Log (ITL) administered by the Secretariat. The Log records all

---

105 *Id.*, at Section X. para. 1(d).

106 Decision 18/CP.7, para 8.

107 Amounting to 90% of the AAUs of the respective seller Party or 100% of five times its most recently reviewed inventory – whichever is lowest, Decision 18/CP.7. para. 6.

108 Decision 24/CP.7, Section XV. para. 5.

109 Namely those enshrined in Arts. 6, 12 and 17 KP, Decision 24/CP.7, Section XV. para. 4.

110 Decision 22/CMP.1, Arts. 159-160.

111 Decision 24/CP.7, (Procedures and mechanisms relating to compliance under the Kyoto Protocol), Section X. paras. 1-4; Decision 27/CMP.1.

112 Kyoto Protocol Reference Manual on Accounting of Emissions and Assigned Amounts, February 2007, at 23.

transactions[113] and includes only transactions from flexible mechanisms that have been verified, i.e., the Party is eligible for participation in the ETS, the transaction is properly accounted and the allowances of the Party have not dropped below the commitment period reserve. The ITL rejects transactions that do not meet these criteria and directs national registries to terminate such transfers (reconciliation procedure).[114] The Secretariat also manages the Compilation and Accounting Database, the official repository recording inventory estimates and corrected allowance holdings of the Parties.[115] Based on advice delivered by the Subsidiary Body for Scientific and Technological Advice, the COP/MOP decides on the standardized rules and modalities for the accounting – that is the rules regarding the addition and subtraction – of allowances.[116] All national electronic registries as well as the Log administered by the Secretariat of the Convention must conform to these accounting rules. The Secretariat cooperates with national registry administrators in developing common operational procedures and practices, promoting the compatibility and accuracy of registry systems.[117] A Standard Electronic Format for reporting and reviewing Kyoto units as well as automated checks between registries ensure unimpeded trading and review.[118] The ERT reviews the calculation and accounting of allowances as well as the capacities of the national registries in the form of annual reviews of national systems[119] and reviews of national registries.[120] Similar to review procedures under the eligibility assessment, strict time limits apply and Parties may comment on the draft report prepared by the ERT, which shall thereafter adopt the final report.[121] Subsequently, the Enforcement Branch of the Compliance Committee

---

113 *Id.,* at 15.

114 Decision 24/CP. 8, Annex, para. 25.

115 Kyoto Protocol Reference Manual on Accounting of Emissions and Assigned Amounts, February 2007, at 13.

116 Decision 13/CMP.1, (Modalities for the accounting of assigned amounts under Art. 7(4) of the Kyoto Protocol).

117 Decision 16/CP.10, (Issues relating to registry systems under Art. 7(4) of the Kyoto Protocol), paras. 4-5.

118 Decision 17/CP. 10, (Standard electronic format for reporting Kyoto Protocol units).

119 Decision 22/CMP.1, paras. 84-91.

120 *Id.*, at paras. 110-120.

121 *Id.*, at para. 94.

proceeds with the review procedure as described above in relation to eligibility assessment, and concludes by adopting a final decision.

Emission trading is not restricted to States. Indeed the Parties' governments may decide to extend trading to non-State participants as well, boosting the intensity and efficiency of the trading system.[122] However, as emissions allowances reflect international commitments of sovereign States vis-à-vis the other Parties, these may not be privately owned and the Parties remain responsible for all transfers and acquisitions on their registries.[123] For this reason, a national system for trading between private parties must put in place further rules to transform the allowances into tradable economic assets,[124] enact authorization procedures for private entities, and publicize the list of accredited traders. Finally, the Parties are to ensure the effective supervision of the market for emissions trading between such private entities.[125] Thus, the KP does not exclude domestic or regional emissions trading systems: rather, it forms an *umbrella* encompassing these markets. To avoid distortions of Kyoto commitments all transfers between such trading systems have to be accounted for[126] should they affect any transactions between the Parties.[127]

---

122 OBERTHÜR & OTT (note 5), at 254.

123 de Witt Wijnen (note 33), at 412.

124 *Id.*, at 405; the emission units allocated to the Parties may be "regarded as a mixture of a sovereign rights ... and a public property right of an Annex I Government. ... Allowances can also create property rights or quasi property rights with private entities holding allowances allocated under a domestic scheme. .... [Allowances] represent a hybrid between a purely public and a purely private right, which has been described as a 'regulatory' right. As such, they find themselves between an administrative grant and private property." Matthieu Wemaere & Charlotte Streck, *Legal Ownership and Nature of Kyoto Units and EU Allowances*, in LEGAL ASPECTS OF IMPLEMENTING THE KYOTO PROTOCOL MECHANISMS: MAKING KYOTO WORK 35, 42 (David Freestone & Charlotte Streck eds., 2005).

125 OBERTHÜR & OTT (note 5), at 254. It is important to note that transactions between private traders within the national registry are irrelevant from the point of view of the KP, as they do not lead to allowance transfers between eligible State Parties. de Witt Wijnen (note 33), at 410.

126 Kyoto Protocol Reference Manual on Accounting of Emissions and Assigned Amounts, February 2007, at 10.

127 Jürgen Lefevere, *Linking Emissions Trading Schemes: The EU ETS and the 'Linking Directive'*, in LEGAL ASPECTS OF IMPLEMENTING THE KYOTO PROTOCOL MECHANISMS: MAKING KYOTO WORK 511 (David Freestone & Charlotte Streck eds., 2005).

The cross-accounting between domestic, regional and Kyoto trading regimes thus requires 'linking' the trading systems.[128]

d) Commitment Period Compliance Assessment

At the end of the commitment period the overall compliance of the Parties with their respective reduction commitments is assessed: each Party must 'retire' a quantity of Kyoto Protocol units equal to or greater than its aggregate emissions, that is, all allowances held by the Parties at the end of the commitment period must exceed their actual emissions in the same period. The commitment period compliance assessment presupposes the conclusion of the annual review and compliance procedures for the final year. After completion, the additional period for fulfillment of commitments begins (true-up period), providing the Parties with a grace period to meet commitments and compile 'true-up reports'[129] on the Parties' transactions and holdings. The ERT compares the true-up report with the allowance units retired to a separate account on the Party's registry designated for facilitating compliance assessment. They also apply the corrections the Parties have failed to make by cancelling corresponding units, and finally, adopt a review report for the true-up period. Subsequently, the Enforcement Branch of the Compliance Committee reviews the Parties' compliance and, in cases of over-emissions, deducts "units equal to 1.3 times the quantity of the Party's excess emission from the Party's unit holdings for the subsequent commitment period"[130] (non-compliance cancellation). It is important to note that a Party may appeal to the COP/MOP against final decisions of the Enforcement Branch related to compliance assessments under Article 3 paragraph 1 KP if it "believes it has been denied *due process.*" The appeal operates to suspend the effect of the decision. By a ¾ majority vote the COP/MOP may override the decision and refer the

---

[128] See EU 'Linking Directive': Directive 2004/101/EC of the European Parliament and of the Council of 27 October 2004 amending Directive 2003/87/EC, establishing a scheme for greenhouse gas emission allowance trading within the Community, in respect of the Kyoto Protocol's project mechanisms.

[129] Decision 27/CMP. 1, Section XIII., Kyoto Protocol Reference Manual on Accounting of Emissions and Assigned Amounts, February 2007, at 26.

[130] Kyoto Protocol Reference Manual on Accounting of Emissions and Assigned Amounts, February 2007, at 63.

matter back to the Enforcement Branch.[131] This form of appeals reflects the *principle of supervision* as employed by von Bernstoff, where "parent organs ... exercise a degree of control over subsidiary organs ... including the right to overrule [their] decisions."[132] Finally, upon request and subject to review by the ERT, units in excess of emissions may be 'carried over' to the next commitment period.

e) Characteristics of Compliance Procedures

Compliance procedures under the KP are not restricted to mere reviews carried out by KP bodies but also impose obligations on national administrations, such as accounting, reporting and possibly also capacity-building obligations. With this, the climate change regime affects national administrative structures, prompting changes and amendments to these. The interaction between KP bodies and national governments is highly structured both as regards timeframes and procedures ('formalization' and 'rationalization').[133] The instruments addressed to national authorities are diverse and numerous. First, some KP Articles themselves contain specific requirements for national implementation.[134] Furthermore, COP as well as COP/MOP decisions impose detailed obligations. Finally, 'manuals'[135] and other documents compiled by KP or other bodies[136] provide assistance to Parties in fulfilling their commitments. The strict timeframes for proceedings and Parties' submissions,[137] the terminology employed by the relevant decisions as well as the possibility of hearings and the adoption of reasoned decisions resemble administrative or judicial proceedings. Together, these features

---

131 Decision 24/CP.7, Section XI. paras. 1-4.

132 Jochen von Bernstoff, in this volume.

133 *Id.*

134 Art. 3 and 7 of the KP.

135 Revised 1996 IPCC Guidelines for National Greenhouse Gas Inventories – Reference Manual, in accordance with Art. 5(2) KP, available at: http://www.ipcc-nggip.iges.or.jp/public/gl/invs6.htm. Such 'manuals', 'specifications', etc. are often incorporated into COP/MOP Decisions by reference. Jochen von Bernstorff, in this volume.

136 On such implementation support, Armin von Bogdandy & Philipp Dann, International Composite Administration, in this volume.

137 Decision 24/CP.7, Section IX. para. 11.

add up to a strict requirement of due process.[138] Since issues of legitimacy become more pressing in proportion to the "degree of formality and the autonomy of international officials,"[139] the stringent procedural rules described above are crucial for the system's formal legitimacy.

f) Features of Compliance Decisions

As noted, the aims and advantages of the complex system of emissions trading can only be achieved through securing the observance of all related rules.[140] Thus, as demonstrated above, the most characteristic feature of the Kyoto regime is its strict compliance regime. The regime of the KP thus focuses on the issues of compliance. The instruments central to the ETS are therefore the decisions adopted by the Enforcement Branch of the Compliance Committee. These come about in complex procedures of multiple stages involving various phases of periodic reporting and review as well as the cooperation of other KP bodies.

The legal basis for the binding decisions are found in the Annex of Decision 27/CMP.1 (Procedures and mechanisms relating to compliance under the Kyoto Protocol). The decisions of the Enforcement Branch are addressed to the Parties and contain findings on the compliance of the Parties with their commitments under the KP ('declaration of non-compliance'). The decision also specifies the consequences, such as suspension or reinstatement of eligibility in the Kyoto mechanisms or the deduction of allowance units from non-compliant Parties.[141] Decisions also impose obligations on non-compliant Parties to draft adequate compliance action plans and submit progress reports to the Enforcement Branch. Such decisions may be termed as 'hard law' because they contain provisions which are binding on the Parties and are reinforced by enforcement measures. The decisions are based on a variety of sources of information. These include the official reports and submissions of the Parties and the ERTs, information provided by the COP,

---

[138] Olav Schram Stokke, Jon Hovi & Geir Ulfstein, *Introduction and Main Findings*, in IMPLEMENTING THE CLIMATE CHANGE REGIME 1, 11 (Olav Schram Stokke, Jon Hovi & Geir Ulfstein eds., 2005).

[139] Daniel C. Esty, *Good Governance at the Supranational Scale: Globalizing Administrative Law*, 115 YALE LAW JOURNAL 1490, 1510 (2006).

[140] OBERTHÜR & OTT (note 5), at 260.

[141] Decision 27/CMP.1, (Procedures and mechanisms relating to compliance under the Kyoto Protocol), Section XV.

the COP/MOP and other Convention and KP bodies, and other information supplied by "competent intergovernmental and non-governmental organizations" or experts.[142] Widening the scope of such potential sources of information contributes to the decisions adopted by the Enforcement Branch being perceived as well founded. This, in turn, increases not only to the input legitimacy of the system but also to effective outputs. Final decisions "include conclusions and reasons" and are made available to the public, thus making the system more transparent.[143]

C. Conclusions

From the point of view of environmental sustainability the effective enforcement of Kyoto obligations would not necessarily result in achieving the stabilization of GHGs. From a legal point of view, despite strict, unprecedented mechanisms, ensuring effective compliance may still remain problematic. Parties may choose to over emit in subsequent commitment periods, with the consequence that deduction of emission units are merely cumulated thus "delaying the punishment forever."[144] Parties in non-compliance may also elect to simply withdraw from the KP, the procedure for which is uncomplicated.[145] Despite such weaknesses, the KP marks a new era in international cooperation by placing a greater emphasis on both the possibilities for flexible fulfilment of international obligations as well as the legitimacy of the exercise of international public authority.

Legitimacy figures as the crucial factor in the participants' overall acceptance of the KP's procedures and the outcomes of its exercise of public authority. The analysis of the Kyoto system shows that it conforms to high standards of good governance. Krisch and Kingsbury point out that examples of global governance "testify to a growing trend of building mechanisms analogous to domestic administrative law systems to the global level" with "transparency, participation, and re-

[142] *Id.*, at Section VIII. paras. 3-4.

[143] *Id.*, at Section VIII. para. 7.

[144] Stokke, Hovi & Ulfstein (note 138), at 11.

[145] *Id.*

view" being their main features.[146] The flexible mechanisms of the Kyoto Protocol seem to substantiate this observation. From an in-put legitimacy perspective it may be pointed out that the members of the COP/MOP, the supreme authority of the KP, is composed of government representatives, that is, officials democratically legitimized in their respective signatory States.[147] Members of the COP/MOP possess equal voting power in the decision-making procedure, which enhances the legitimacy of decisions taken. The general rule of consensus as well as the participation of all affected Parties forces the Parties to take the interests of all members into account in order to reach unanimity.[148] However, unanimity requirement may have deterring effects on the output of the legislative body. The 'automaticity'[149] of technically oriented procedures, the composition, professionalism and expertise of the Expert Review Teams and the Compliance Committee all contribute to the substantive legitimacy of decisions adopted on Parties' compliance, whereas strict enforcement measures ensure an efficient, predictable operation of the mechanism. The possible, indirect participation of private and non-State entities in the development and review of the trading system is weak. However, the detailed rules on decision-making, its "procedural rigor,"[150] the possibility of majority voting and the formal requirements related to decisions enhance the democratic credentials of the system. The administrative procedures are highly structured and formalized, adding to the transparency, reliability and formal legitimacy of the actions of KP bodies. The publication of documents – decisions as well as the inclusion of external experts in certain matters – provides further transparency and openness to the system, also enabling various forms of "social enforcement," such as naming and shaming or granting awards by non-State entities.[151]

Various principles contained in the KP guide the operation of the ETS. These are not only written principles contained in the Convention and

---

[146] Nico Krisch, Benedict Kingsbury & Richard B. Stewart, *The Emergence of Global Administrative Law*, 68 LAW AND CONTEMPORARY PROBLEMS 15, 19 (2005).

[147] See Jochen von Bernstorff, in this volume; Eberhard Schmidt-Aßmann, in this volume.

[148] Krisch, Kingsbury & Stewart (note 146), at 26.

[149] Stokke, Hovi & Ulfstein (note 138), at 1.

[150] Esty (note 139), at 1495.

[151] Gupta (note 43), at 467-468.

referred to by the KP, but also uncodified principles inherent in the nature of the compliance regime itself. Thus, a general principle of cooperation[152] may be abstracted from the KP and traced back to specific obligations of both the Parties to collaborate in related research, education and technological development,[153] as well as the COP/MOP to make use of information and assistance provided by other, non-Party entities.[154] The principle of constitutionality in the meaning attributed by von Bogdandy is also implied. The principle has its basis in the elaborate provisions on the specific competences of the individual KP bodies and the regulation of the Parties' obligations, signaling a highly complex division of powers. The principle of the rule of law may be deduced from the requirement that all binding acts of the Compliance Committee must include conclusions and reasons and are to be brought in the form of a formal decision.[155] Finally, the Parties may demand a hearing and lodge an appeal (although the appellate instance is political rather than legal in nature). These procedural mechanisms also mark a tendency toward the internalization of the principle of due process.[156] In sum, although the effectiveness of the ETS may be arguable, the system nevertheless constitutes a turning-point in employing novel solutions and setting the stage for the further development of multilateral environmental agreements.

---

152 See Armin von Bogdandy, *General Principles*, in this volume.

153 Art. 10(c), (d), (e) KP.

154 Art. 13(i) KP.

155 Decision 24/CP.7, Section VIII. para. 7.

156 Krisch, Kingsbury & Stewart (note 146), at 17.

The UNESCO Regime for the Protection of World Heritage as Prototype of an Autonomy-Gaining International Institution

*By Diana Zacharias**

A. Introduction

The Convention for the Protection of the World Cultural and Natural Heritage (World Heritage Convention),[1] which entered into force on

---

* The author has to thank Professor Ivan Shearer LL.M. and Matthias Goldmann for helpful comments to earlier versions of this article.

[1] UNTS, vol. 1037, 15511.

A. von Bogdandy et al. (eds.), *The Exercise of Public Authority by International Institutions*, Beiträge zum ausländischen öffentlichen Recht und Völkerrecht 210,
DOI 10.1007/978-3-642-04531-8_11, © Springer-Verlag Berlin Heidelberg 2010

17 December 1975, established a complex governance regime at the international level. The rationale behind the establishment of this regime was the international community's realization that the world contained natural and cultural sites which were so unique and outstanding that they should by no means become embroiled in the onslaught of human material progress. It was argued that these sites must be protected and conserved for posterity since they, irrespective of the territory in which they were located, belonged to all peoples and, thus, formed part of the common heritage of mankind.[2] Although the United Nations Educational, Scientific and Cultural Organization (UNESCO) regime for the protection of World Heritage is seemingly afforded with weak instruments, such as the inscription of properties on the World Heritage List or on the List of World Heritage in Danger, its activities increasingly play a role, not least in national administrative procedures. The cases of Yellowstone National Park in the United States,[3] Cologne Cathedral[4]

---

[2] *See* World Heritage Convention, Preamble, recitals 2, 5 and 6; in literature *e.g.* Germana Canino, *Il ruolo svolto dall'UNESCO nella tutela del patrimonio mondiale culturale e naturale, in* LA PROTEZIONE DEL PATRIMONIO MONDIALE CULTURALE E NATURALE A VENTICINQUE ANNI DALLA CONVENZIONE DELL' UNESCO DEL 1972, 1, 45-46 (Maria C. Ciciriello ed., 1997); MARIA E. E. CASTELLI, PROTECCIÓN JURÍDICA DEL PATRIMONIO CULTURAL DE LA HUMANIDAD 17-21 (1987); MANLIO FRIGO, LA PROTEZIONE DEI BENI CULTURALI NEL DIRITTO INTERNAZIONALE 281-310 (1986); Rudolf Dolzer, *Die Deklaration des Kulturguts zum "common heritage of mankind", in* RECHTSFRAGEN DES INTERNATIONALEN KULTURGÜTERSCHUTZES 13, 17-20 (Rudolf Dolzer, Erik Jayme & Reinhard Mußgnug eds., 1994); Frank Fechner, *Prinzipien des Kulturgüterschutzes, in* PRINZIPIEN DES KULTURGÜTERSCHUTZES 11, 33-34 (Frank Fechner, Thomas Oppermann & Lyndel V. Prott eds., 1996); Markus Müller, *Kulturgüterschutz: Mittel nationaler Repräsentation oder Wahrung des Gemeinsamen Erbes der Menschheit?, in* PRINZIPIEN DES KULTURGÜTERSCHUTZES 257, 268-271 (Frank Fechner, Thomas Oppermann & Lyndel V. Prott eds., 1996); Sabine von Schorlemer, *Der internationale Schutz von Kulturgütern gegen Umwelteinflüsse, in* PRINZIPIEN DES KULTURGÜTERSCHUTZES 225, 246-47 (Frank Fechner, Thomas Oppermann & Lyndel V. Prott eds., 1996).

[3] *See* JEREMY RABKIN, WHY SOVEREIGNTY MATTERS 46-48 (1998).

[4] *See* Kerstin Odendahl, *Protecția bunurilor culturale în dreptul internațional – literă moartă sau protecție eficientă?*, 4 II CAIETE DE DREPT INTERNATIONAL 11-17 (2006); Diana Zacharias, *Cologne Cathedral versus Skyscrapers – World Heritage Protection as Archetype of a Multilevel System*, 10 MAX PLANCK YEARBOOK OF UNITED NATIONS LAW (MAX PLANCK UNYB) 273-366 (2006).

and Dresden Elbe Valley in Germany,[5] and Kakadu National Park in Australia[6] are only a few examples in this regard.

In the following explanations, the regime for the protection of world heritage will be examined more closely. The examination will reveal a prototype scenario whereby an international institution has attained a wide range of autonomy. It has its own organizational structure, though not legally independent; self-contained decision-making structures that have, to a large extent, been emancipated from the multilateral processes due to a deviation from the principle of consensus; consultation powers extensively involving experts in its proceedings, who are democratically unaccountable to the citizens of the States Parties to the underlying international agreement; instruments capable of having binding effect towards the States Parties; and it maintains a dialogue with local authorities, without utilizing the central government as mediator. Naturally the tendency become more and more autonomous raises questions of legitimacy since autonomy is tantamount to less input-legitimacy. However, the case of the world heritage regime demonstrates that autonomy can at the same time also lead to a gain of efficiency and effectiveness, which contributes to a higher level of output-legitimacy. Thus, the world heritage regime provides for a fine example of the advantages and disadvantages of international bureaucracies.

I. Background, Objectives and Legal Foundations of the Convention

The idea of international cooperation and support concerning the protection of world cultural heritage was already established in the nine-

---

5 *See* German Federal Constitutional Court, 17 LANDES- UND KOMMUNALVERWALTUNG (LKV) 509-513 (2007); Higher Administrative Court of Saxony, 60 DIE ÖFFENTLICHE VERWALTUNG (DÖV) 564-568 (2007); Armin von Bogdandy & Diana Zacharias, *Zum Schutz der Weltkulturerbekonvention im deutschen Rechtsraum*, 26 NEUE ZEITSCHRIFT FÜR VERWALTUNGSRECHT (NVwZ) 527-532 (2007); Ulrich Fastenrath, *Der Schutz des Weltkulturerbes in Deutschland*, 59 DÖV 1017-1027 (2006); Michael Kilian, *Die Brücke über die Elbe: völkerrechtliche Wirkungen des Welterbe-Übereinkommens der UNESCO*, 18 LKV 248-254 (2008).

6 *See* S. Javed Maswood, *Kakadu and the Politics of World Heritage Listing*, 54 AUSTRALIAN JOURNAL OF INTERNATIONAL AFFAIRS 357-372 (2000); BEN BOER & GRAEME WIFFEN, HERITAGE LAW IN AUSTRALIA 87 (2006).

teenth and early twentieth century.[7] It gained momentum in 1946 after the Egyptian government decided to build the Aswan High Dam, which would have flooded the valley containing the Abu Simbel and Philae temples, which are treasures of ancient Egyptian civilization. In 1959, UNESCO, following a request for assistance by Egypt and Sudan, launched an international protection campaign. That campaign facilitated the dismantling of the temples, relocation to dry ground and their subsequent reassembly. This logistical effort cost approximately US$ 80 million, half of which was donated by some 50 countries, illustrating the importance of shared responsibility in the conservation of outstanding cultural sites. Its success led to other protection campaigns, such as saving Venice and its lagoon in Italy and the archaeological ruins at Moenjodaro in Pakistan, as well as the restoration of the Borobodur Temple compounds in Indonesia.[8]

Against this background, voices were raised calling for the institutionalization of international support. Hence, UNESCO initiated, with the help of the International Council on Monuments and Sites (ICOMOS), which is an international non-governmental organization of professionals dedicated to the conservation of historic monuments and sites,[9] the preparation of a draft convention on the protection of world heritage. The impetus for the convention's content came not least from the United States. At a White House Conference in Washington D. C. in 1965 Russell Train, an American conservationist and legal advisor to the then US President Richard Nixon, recommended the establishment of an international trust "to identify, establish, develop and manage the world's superb natural and scenic areas and historic sites for the present and future benefit of the entire world citizenry". Train, who is regarded

---

[7] *See* UNESCO World Heritage Centre, WORLD HERITAGE: CHALLENGES FOR THE MILLENIUM 26-28 (2007). The brochure can be downloaded under: http://whc.unesco.org/documents/publi_millennium_en.pdf.

[8] *See* UNESCO World Heritage Centre, Brief History, available at: http://whc.unesco.org/en/169/.

[9] Maria C. Ciciriello, *L'ICCROM, l'ICOMOS e l'IUCN e la salvaguardia del patrimonio mondiale culturale e naturale*, *in* LA PROTEZIONE DEL PATRIMONIO MONDIALE (note 2), at 110, 119 and 122; Gilbert H. Gornig, *Der internationale Kulturgüterschutz*, *in* KULTURGÜTERSCHUTZ – INTERNATIONALE UND NATIONALE ASPEKTE 17, 45-46 (Gilbert H. Gornig, Hans-Detlef Horns & Dietrich Murswiek eds., 2007).

as one of the spiritual fathers of the world heritage concept[10] (a concept which was later for the first time enshrined in para. 1 of the 1970 Declaration of Principles Governing the Sea Bed and Ocean Floor[11]), also stressed the importance of the international community's acceptance that "throughout the world there exist natural and cultural areas of such unique values that they are truly a part of the heritage not only of the individual nations but of all mankind".[12] In 1968, the International Union for Conservation of Nature and Natural Resources (IUCN, now called World Conservation Union), which is, like ICOMOS, a non-governmental organization, developed similar proposals for its members, which are States and government agencies, political and economic integration organizations, international and national non-governmental organizations and affiliates.[13] These proposals were approved by the Stockholm Conference on the Human Environment, the first global intergovernmental meeting on the environment.[14] Eventually, the World Heritage Convention was adopted by the General Conference of UNESCO on 16 November 1972 in Paris. Currently, the Convention has some 184 countries as States Parties.[15]

---

10 *See* David J. Haigh, *World Heritage – Principle and Practice: a Case for Change*, 17 ENVIRONMENTAL AND PLANNING LAW JOURNAL 199 (2000).

11 *See* ROBIN R. CHURCHILL & ALAN V. LOWE, THE LAW OF THE SEA 227 (3rd edition, 1999).

12 Quoted by Harold K. Eidsvik, *The World Heritage Convention Yesterday, Today and Tomorrow*, *in* PROCEEDINGS OF A WORKSHOP SESSION ON CRITICAL ISSUES FOR PROTECTED AREAS HELD DURING THE 18TH SESSION OF THE GENERAL ASSEMBLY OF IUCN 15 (1990).

13 IUCN Statutes, Part III, s. 4; the Statutes are available at: http://www.iucn.org/members/Documents/Statutes.pdf.

14 *See* Action Plan for the Human Environment, Recommendation No. 99, Report on the United Nations Conference on the Human Environment 1972, available at: http://www.unep.org/Documents.multilingual/Default.asp?DocumentID=97&ArticleID=1511&l=en.

15 UNESCO World Heritage Centre, *World Heritage: States Parties*, available at: http://whc.unesco.org/en/statesparties/. About the history of the Convention in more detail, *see* Thomas Fitschen, *Internationaler Schutz des kulturellen Erbes in der Welt*, *in* INTERNATIONALER KULTURGÜTERSCHUTZ UND DEUTSCHE FRAGE 183, 185-189 (Wilfried Fiedler ed., 1991); Francesco Francioni, *Thirty Years On: Is the World Heritage Convention Ready for the 21st Century?*, 12 ITALIAN YEARBOOK OF INTERNATIONAL LAW 13, 15-16 (2002); BARBARA GENIUS-DEVIME, BEDEUTUNG UND GRENZEN DES ERBES DER MENSCHHEIT IM VÖLKERRECHTLICHEN KULTURGÜTERSCHUTZ 140-143 (1996);

The World Heritage Convention seeks to protect immovable[16] and tangible cultural heritage (monuments, groups of buildings, and sites) and natural heritage (natural features, geological and physiographical formations, and natural sites) that exemplify "outstanding universal value" (see recitals 7 and 8 of the Preamble and arts. 1 and 2 of the Convention). Hence, it can be framed within the broader context of international environmental law.[17] Moreover, the Convention views the protection of world heritage as primarily a domestic matter;[18] States Parties are requested to take responsibility for world heritage listings that are located within their territories. This is noted, for instance, in art. 4 sentence 1 of the Convention. The provision reads that each State Party recognizes that the duty of ensuring the identification, protection, conservation, presentation and transmission to future generations of the cultural and natural heritage situated on its territory belongs primarily to that State.

However, the World Heritage Convention is not least a reaction to the observation that the protection of world cultural and natural heritage at the national level is often a piecemeal process due to the scale of financial investment it requires coupled with insufficient economic, scientific and technical resources of the country where the property is located (*cf.* recitals 3 and 7 of the Preamble). Hence, the idea of solidarity comes into play, and the Convention facilitates the international community's participation in the protection of world heritage by granting collective assistance which, although not absolving the State concerned of its responsibility, serves as an effective complement thereto (*cf.* recital 8 of the Preamble). The provision for said collective assistance is art. 6 para. 1 of the Convention. It states that the States Parties, whilst fully respecting the sovereignty of the States on whose territory the cultural

---

Robert L. Meyer, *Travaux Préparatoires for the UNESCO World Heritage Convention*, 2 EARTH LAW JOURNAL 45-81 (1976); MARTIN P. WYSS, KULTUR ALS EINE DIMENSION DER VÖLKERRECHTSORDNUNG 125-131 (1992); Russell Train, *The World Heritage Convention – The First Twenty Years and Beyond*, speech held at the 16th session of the World Heritage Committee on 7 December 1992, available as Doc. WHC-92/CONF.002/12 of 14 December 1992 at: http://whc.unesco.org/archive/repcom92.htm#inf1.

16 *See* KERSTIN ODENDAHL, KULTURGÜTERSCHUTZ 136 (2005).

17 *See* Maswood (note 6), at 357.

18 *See* Ljudmila Galenskaya, *International Co-operation in Cultural Affairs*, 198 III RECUEIL DES COURS 265, 277 (1986); GENIUS-DEVIME (note 15), at 288-289; WYSS (note 15), at 130-131.

and natural heritage of outstanding universal value is situated, recognize that such heritage constitutes a world heritage for whose protection it is the duty of the international community as a whole to cooperate. This recognition manifests itself in the States Parties undertaking, in accordance with the provisions of the Convention, to assist in the identification, protection, conservation and preservation of such heritage; this assistance must take place, if necessary, in a financial, artistic, scientific or technical manner (*cf.* arts. 4 sentence 2 and 6 para. 2 of the Convention).[19]

Moreover, governance under the World Heritage Convention is defined in art. 7 as a system of international cooperation and assistance designed to support States Parties in their efforts to conserve and identify the world heritage. As such, the Convention has often been qualified in academic discourse as a cooperation agreement providing measures which are secondary to those present in individual States.[20] This qualification, however, is a simplification because it neglects both the institutional setting and the existing compliance mechanisms.[21] It seems to be more adequate to speak of an agreement establishing an international regime which deals with the protection of world cultural and natural heritage as a typically non-transboundary problem[22] and is characterized by an emphasis on cooperative aspects. First and foremost the cooperative aspects do not affect the relationship between the States Parties to the Convention but rather the relationship between the international institution and the individual State Party, which implies a multilevel dimension.

II. Governance of World Heritage Protection in Action: A Survey

The activities of the international institution established under the World Heritage Convention are molded by decisions in individual cases and are, thus, typical executive decisions from a national point of view. In this respect, one can distinguish between two types of decisions:

---

19 SABINE VON SCHORLEMER, INTERNATIONALER KULTURGÜTERSCHUTZ 134 (1993).

20 *See* Fitschen (note 15), at 183, 196; Müller (note 2), at 257, 269 with further references.

21 *See* Zacharias (note 4), at 273, 318-322.

22 *See* Maswood (note 6), at 357, 358.

The first type is the inscription of a property on the World Heritage List (art. 11 para. 2 of the Convention) and, as the case may be, additionally on the List of World Heritage in Danger (art. 11 para. 4 of the Convention). The *actus contrarius* of listing is the deletion of a property from the World Heritage List or its removal from the List of World Heritage in Danger. Currently, 851 properties have been inscribed on the World Heritage List, 660 of which are cultural, 166 natural and 25 mixed properties.[23] From 1977 to 2006, 58 sites were inscribed on the List of World Heritage in Danger, 16 of which have eventually been removed; two were removed and later re-inscribed.[24] A deletion of a property from the World Heritage List has been exercised on a single occasion, in the case of the Arabian Oryx Sanctuary in Oman.[25] However, on several occasions the States Parties concerned were cautioned that non-compliance with their duties under the Convention would result in delisting.[26]

The second type is the allotment of international assistance, financed by the World Heritage Fund (art. 13 paras. 1, 3 and 6 of the Convention). International assistance may include, *inter alia*, emergency assistance for sites that have suffered or are in imminent danger of severe damage due to sudden and unexpected natural or man-made phenomena; preparatory assistance for the drafting of nominations for the World Heritage List; technical cooperation covering the provision of experts and/or equipment for the conservation or management of world heritage sites; assistance for either the training of specialized staff at all levels in the fields of identification, protection, conservation, presentation and rehabilitation of world heritage or for education, information and awareness-raising (see arts. 22 and 23 of the World Heritage Convention as well as paras. 235 and 241 of the Operational Guidelines 2005[27]).

---

23 UNESCO World Heritage Centre, World Heritage List, available at: http://whc.unesco.org/en/list; *see also* UNESCO World Heritage Centre (note 7), at 36-37.

24 UNESCO World Heritage Centre (note 7), at 45.

25 UNESCO World Heritage Centre, Twenty-two sites inscribed on the UNESCO's World Heritage List, and one deleted during the Committee meeting in Christchurch, available at: http://whc.unesco.org/en/news/365; *see* for the situation before the 2007 meeting Peter Strasser, *"Putting Reform into Action" – Thirty Years of the World Heritage Convention*, 11 INTERNATIONAL JOURNAL OF CULTURAL PROPERTY 215, 219 and 254 (2002).

26 *See* Zacharias (note 4), at 273, 276 with references.

27 Available at: http://whc.unesco.org/archive/opguide05-en.pdf.

In 2005 the total annual amount allocated for international assistance was approximately US$ 1 million. This figure has been steadily declining since 2002. From 1998 to 2005 787 grants were approved, amounting to nearly US$ 20 million. Non-State actors, mainly the International Centre for the Study of the Preservation and Restoration of Cultural Property in Rome (ICCROM), a scientific organization with currently 119 Member States,[28] and IUCN, were allocated approximately a seventh of the total funds. These funds were primarily used for training programs at the regional level.[29]

The procedures for the inscription of a property on the World Heritage List and for the allotting of international assistance commences with a nomination for listing or a request for assistance by the State Party in which the property constituting the cultural or natural heritage is situated.[30] The nomination or request is evaluated by the so-called Advisory Bodies (*i.e.* ICOMOS, IUCN and, in cases concerning a request for assistance, also ICCROM.[31] The Intergovernmental Committee for the Protection of the Cultural and Natural Heritage of Outstanding Universal Value, which is also known as the World Heritage Committee and is established under art. 8 of the Convention, bases its decisions on the Advisory Bodies' evaluations and recommendations.[32] Once a property has been inscribed on the aforementioned lists or international assistance has been allotted, a process of monitoring ensues.[33]

On the basis of a synopsis of the historical foundations, the declarations in the Preamble and the wording of the majority of provisions of the World Heritage Convention, one could draw the conclusion that international assistance is the defining characteristic governing the protection of world heritage. The entire Convention exudes the idea that the international community must, as a bearer of guarantee to balance defi-

---

28 *See* ICCROM, *ICCROM Member States*, available at: http://www.iccrom.org/eng/00about_en/00_01govern_en/memstates_en.shtml; Ciciriello (note 9), 110, 111-112.

29 *See* UNESCO World Heritage Centre (note 7), 50.

30 *See* arts. 11(1), 13(1) and 19 of the World Heritage Convention and para. 120 of the Operational Guidelines 2005.

31 *See* art. 13(7) of the Convention; paras. 35, 37, 143 to 146 and 248 to 250 of the Operational Guidelines 2005.

32 *See* arts. 11(2), 13(3) and 21(3) of the Convention; paras. 153 to 160 and 247 to 254 of the Operational Guidelines 2005.

33 *See* UNESCO World Heritage Centre (note 7), 20.

ciencies, offer assistance to those States Parties which, although willing, cannot sufficiently cope with the task of protecting and conserving the world heritage sites in their territories. Therefore, the international institution is concerned with exercising a quintessential State-esque function. Since the protection of world heritage is governed primarily through the distribution of funds, an administration of public services would appear to be an apt categorization.

Social reality, however, appears to suggest otherwise since the inscription of properties on the World Heritage List has, over time, become an important yardstick for adjudging the reputation of States – not least in the developed countries where the prospect of receiving financial support from the international community rarely plays a decisive role in nominations. The listing is not a classical means of regulatory administration. Nor is it a unilateral infringement of the rights of the State Party concerned, whereby the State Party occupies a subordinate position to that of the international institution. Furthermore, the World Heritage Committee has rightly pointed out that it is not allowed to use the instruments laid down in the World Heritage Convention as a means of punishing or sanctioning a State Party.[34] Reconciliation of this definitional ambiguity requires a compromise categorization. For instance that the governance mechanism is a special type of cooperative regulatory administration because it unilaterally determines the duties of the State Party (although a request is regularly necessary) or that it is an accreditation or certification administration. Either way, it is a multifaceted administration, responsible for delivering services as well as determining, or even giving rise to, duties incumbent upon States Parties.

B. Legal Analysis

I. Institutional Framework

The World Heritage Convention was adopted by the General Conference of UNESCO on the basis of art. 1 para. 2 lit. c of the UNESCO Constitution.[35] The international bureaucracy for the protection of world cultural and natural heritage operates under the umbrella of

---

[34] *See* e.g. UNESCO World Heritage, *World Heritage in Danger*, available at: http://whc.unesco.org/pg.cfm?cid=158.

[35] UNTS, Vol. 4, No. 1580.

UNESCO. However, the World Heritage Convention does not constitute a monolithic administrative authority consisting of only one actor but entrusts a series of actors with collective administration, in particular the General Assembly of States Parties, the World Heritage Committee and its Secretariat (World Heritage Centre), the Advisory Bodies (ICOMOS, IUCN and ICCROM), the Director-General and the General Conference of UNESCO. The role and competencies of these bodies at the international level as well as their relationship and responsibilities towards each other are not precisely defined in the Convention and leave room for discussion.

The General Assembly of States Parties, the meetings of which take place biannually during the ordinary sessions of the General Conference of UNESCO,[36] has two tasks: it elects the members of the World Heritage Committee and determines the size of the World Heritage Fund (arts. 8 para. 1 and 16 para. 1 of the Convention). During its infancy, the General Assembly dealt in principle only with these aforementioned matters.[37] Issues of "other business" were rarely raised. One can find, for instance, calls to reflect upon problems related to world heritage threatened by various causes, including war,[38] or an appeal for assistance of a world heritage site that had been damaged during an earthquake.[39] Following the adoption of a resolution that sought to ensure an equitable representation of different regions and cultures in the Committee at its 7th session in 1989,[40] the General Assembly extended its field of deliberation. At its 9th session in 1993, the General Assembly "recommended that its future sessions devote more time to debates of substance aimed at defining general policy directives for the implementation of the Convention" and adopted on that occasion a declaration concerning the increasing threats to world cultural and natural heritage sites.[41] This decision, which had the potential to start a mission creep

---

36 *See* in this context the Rules of Procedure of the General Assembly of States Parties to the World Heritage Convention, available at: http://whc.unesco.org/en/garules/.

37 *See* Strasser (note 25), at 215, 228.

38 6th General Assembly Report, para. 22, available as Doc. CC-87/CONF.013/6 of 31 October 1987 at: http://whc.unesco.org/archive/ga87.pdf.

39 7th General Assembly Report, para. 20, available as Doc. CC-89/CONF.013/6 of 13 November 1989 at: http://whc.unesco.org/archive/ga89.pdf.

40 *Id.* at para. 12.

41 9th General Assembly Report, paras. 30 and 32, available as Doc. CC-93/CONF.003/6 of 2 November 1993 at: http://whc.unesco.org/archive/ga93.pdf.

via institutional practice, can be regarded as an attempt to gain more influence on, and more power to control, the World Heritage Committee.

Accordingly, at the next session in 1995 the General Assembly paid great attention to the controversial issue of new monitoring activities related to the way in which world heritage sites were conserved. It decided to defer the discussion until the 11th session in 1997 and requested that the Committee prepares a report and a proposed resolution.[42] This instigated a debate questioning whether the General Assembly had the right to initiate such an action, in particular whether it could give instructions to the Committee.[43] Hence, the Bureau of the World Heritage Committee during its 24th session in June/July 2000 asked the Legal Advisor of UNESCO for clarification regarding the division of competencies between Assembly and Committee. In his reply, the Advisor argued that there was a "general legal principle of deferring to the plenary body which can deal with any question related to the Convention". Following this view, the Bureau noted that "the World Heritage Convention is different from many other international conventions in that all the substantive powers are assigned to the Committee and not to the General Assembly. The Committee can transfer powers to the General Assembly."[44] Thus, the General Assembly with its aforementioned decisions found at the 9th and 10th session acted *ultra vires*; it does not have extensive reserve competencies which facilitate the substantial governance of the World Heritage Committee, particularly with regard to the prescription of general policy. Rather, the General Assembly merely functions as electing body and as guardian over the budget; additionally, it fulfils tasks that are delegated to it by the Committee.

The World Heritage Committee forms the core of the international institution for the protection of world heritage. According to art. 8 sentence 1 of the Convention, it is established within UNESCO. The institutional bond to UNESCO manifests itself in the Director-General of UNESCO appointing, as part of the UNESCO Secretariat, the secretariat which shall assist the Committee (art. 14 para. 1 of the Conven-

---

[42] 10th General Assembly Report, paras. 15 to 31, available as Doc. WHC-95/CONF.204/8 of 22 November 1995 at: http://whc.unesco.org/archive/genass95.htm.

[43] *See* Strasser (note 25), at 215, 229.

[44] Report of the Bureau of the World Heritage Committee, 24th session, VI para. 7, quoted by World Heritage Committee Report, 26th session, para. 37, available as Doc. WHC-02/CONF.202/12 of 4 June 2002 at: http://whc.unesco.org/archive/2002/whc-02-conf202-12e.pdf.

tion), preparing the Committee's documentation and the agenda of its meetings, and having the responsibility for the implementation of its decisions (art. 14 para. 2 of the Convention). Thus, the Committee is at first merely a Conventional organ, but through its secretariat it is affiliated with UNESCO and it, thus, operates effectively as a sub-organ of UNESCO. The reason for this parallel structure may be that the organs and sub-organs of UNESCO cannot be used, not least because of budgetary reasons, for regimes which do not include all Members of the organization.

The Committee consists, and this is a further institutional multi-level aspect, of representatives of 21 States Parties to the World Heritage Convention that are elected for a term of six years by the General Assembly (arts. 8 para. 1 sentences 2 and 3 and 9 para. 1 of the Convention).[45] Furthermore, art. 8 para. 2 of the Convention stipulates that the composition of the Committee shall ensure an equitable representation of the different regions and cultures of the world. This requirement, which can be categorized as an element fostering legitimacy, indicates that the Committee is not a mere rubber stamp for the elected States Parties. Rather, it is desirable that the representatives of the States, who must be "persons qualified in the field of the cultural or natural heritage" (art. 9 para. 3 of the Convention), do not originate from the State that appoints them.[46] This desideratum is in practice, however, rarely observed. The Committee meets at least once a year and manages its meetings according to Rules of Procedure,[47] which it has adopted pursuant to art. 10 para. 1 of the Convention. It establishes its Bureau (consisting of the chairperson, five vice-chairpersons and a recording secretary)[48] which meets during the sessions of the Committee as frequently as deemed necessary and is responsible for the daily affairs of the Committee.[49]

The main functions of the Committee are (in cooperation with States Parties), *inter alia*, to identify cultural and natural properties of outstanding universal value which are to be protected under the World Heritage Convention and to inscribe those properties on the World

---

[45] *See also* Fitschen (note 15), at 183, 198.

[46] Haigh (note 10), at 199, 201.

[47] Available at: http://whc.unesco.org/pg.cfm?cid=223.

[48] *See* about the actual members UNESCO, Bureau of the World Heritage Committee, available at: http://whc.unesco.org/en/bureau/.

[49] Maswood (note 6), at 357, 361.

Heritage List (art. 11 para. 2 of the Convention); to examine the state of conservation of properties inscribed on the World Heritage List through a process of reactive monitoring and periodic reporting (arts. 11 para. 7 and 29 of the Convention); to decide which properties inscribed on the World Heritage List are to be inscribed on, or removed from, the List of World Heritage in Danger (art. 11 paras. 4 and 5 of the Convention); to decide whether a property should be deleted from the World Heritage List (*cf.* art. 11 para. 2 of the Convention; para. 192 of the Operational Guidelines 2005); to define the procedure by which the requests for international assistance are to be considered and to carry out studies and consultations, if necessary, before reaching a decision (art. 13 paras. 1 and 3 of the Convention); to periodically review and evaluate the implementation of the Convention (*cf.* arts. 11 para. 7 and 29 of the Convention); and to adopt and revise the Operational Guidelines (*cf.* art. 11 para. 5 of the Convention; para. 24 of the Operational Guidelines 2005). Moreover, the Committee develops strategic objectives in order to facilitate the implementation of the World Heritage Convention which are periodically reviewed and revised to ensure that new threats towards world heritage are addressed effectively (para. 25 of the Operational Guidelines 2005).[50] Thus, the World Heritage Committee has a very wide range of competencies, covering nearly all administrative activities under the World Heritage Convention. It is the central decision-making body in an operative sense.

Additionally, the Committee is free to determine its own procedures. It can, within the framework of the Convention, implement its objectives and prioritize the order of its actions and has complete autonomy with respect to its final decisions. This is already indicated by the fact that, on the one hand, it determines the criteria that govern whether a property belonging to the cultural or natural heritage may be inscribed on the World Heritage List and in the List of World Heritage in Danger (art. 11 paras. 2 sentence 1 and 5 of the Convention) and that, on the other hand, the contractual arrangements concerning international assistance are concluded on its behalf and not on behalf of UNESCO (art. 13 para. 3 of the Convention). Thus, the Committee is afforded with a measure of legal personality and forms insofar a sub-organization of

---

[50] The first "Strategic Orientations" adopted by the Committee in 1992 are contained in annex II of Doc. WHC-92/CONF.002/12 (note 15). In 2002, the World Heritage Committee revised its strategic objectives; the Budapest Declaration on World Heritage is available as Doc. WHC-02/CONF.202/5 at: http://whc.unesco.org/archive/2002/whc-02-conf202-25e.pdf#decision.9.

UNESCO. The legal personality is, however, limited to the tasks laid down in the World Heritage Convention. More precisely, it can be described as the sum of external competencies and powers of the Committee to fulfill effectively its functions under the Convention towards (other) subjects of international law.[51]

The World Heritage Centre, which operates under its full name "UNESCO World Heritage Centre", was established in 1992 to serve as the Committee's secretariat.[52] It is assigned with primarily organizational and promotional tasks (*cf.* art. 14 para. 2 of the Convention; Budapest Resolution on World Heritage 2002;[53] para. 28 of the Operational Guidelines 2005). It generally supports the administrative activities of the Committee and its Bureau; in particular it communicates and collaborates with the States Parties and the Advisory Bodies (*cf.* rule 43 of the Rules of Procedure of the World Heritage Committee 2003). Furthermore, it works in close cooperation with other sectors and field offices of UNESCO (para. 27 of the Operational Guidelines 2005); it functions insofar as a liaison office between World Heritage Committee and UNESCO.

ICOMOS and IUCN, which had been quite active in the process of drafting the World Heritage Convention, and ICCROM are explicitly named as Advisory Bodies to the World Heritage Committee in arts. 13 para. 7 and 14 para. 2 of the Convention. The roles of the Advisory Bodies are, *inter alia*, to advise on the implementation of the Convention in the field of their expertise (art. 13 para. 7 of the Convention); to monitor the way in which world heritage properties are conserved and review requests for international assistance submitted by States Parties; to evaluate properties nominated for inscription on the World Heritage List and to present evaluation reports to the Committee; and to attend meetings of the Committee and its Bureau in an advisory capacity (art. 8 para. 3 of the Convention; paras. 31, 33, 35 and 37 of the Operational Guidelines 2005). Moreover, the Committee can call on other international and non-governmental organizations with appropriate competence and expertise to assist in the implementation of its programs and

---

[51] *See* about legal personality in international law, *e.g.*, ICJ, *Reparations Case*, ICJ Reports 1949, 174; Bardo Faßbender, *Die Völkerrechtssubjektivität internationaler Organisationen*, 37 ÖSTERREICHISCHE ZEITSCHRIFT FÜR ÖFFENTLICHES RECHT UND VÖLKERRECHT 17-49 (1986).

[52] *See* Circular Letter No. 16 of the General-Director of UNESCO of 21 October 2003, available at: http://whc.unesco.org/circs/circ03-16e.pdf.

[53] *See* note 50.

projects (para. 38 of the Operational Guidelines 2005), since the enumeration in art. 13 para. 7 of the Convention is non-conclusive. The Advisory Bodies do not form part of the institutional structure of UNESCO in the narrow sense of the word; they remain on the periphery as external experts. However, they play an important role in the international institution's activities. Through evaluation and recommendation, they regularly predetermine the later decision of the World Heritage Committee.

Finally, the General Conference of UNESCO receives the reports of States Parties concerning their legislative and administrative measures *vis-à-vis* the World Heritage Convention and of the World Heritage Committee (art. 29 paras. 1 and 3 of the Convention). It is not itself a part of the governance mechanism for the protection of world heritage.

In summary, the international institution consists of various bodies within the structures of UNESCO as well as of non-governmental and intergovernmental organizations. The World Heritage Committee, which would be better described as "intergovernmental", is the executive core of the institution, whereas the General Assembly of States Parties, the World Heritage Centre and the Advisory Bodies revolve around it, the latter not least by providing practical assistance. The Committee's integration into UNESCO is achieved not least by the activities of the World Heritage Centre and by the Committee's duty to report to the General Conference of UNESCO. Moreover, the Committee has decision-making autonomy; in particular the General Assembly of States Parties is not entitled to give binding orders to it.

II. Substantial Steering by Means of Operational Guidelines

The general task of the international institution for the protection of world heritage, and therefore the World Heritage Committee, is to take measures "for the protection of the cultural and natural heritage of outstanding universal value". This is expressed in recital 8 of the Preamble to the World Heritage Convention which reads that the Convention shall establish an effective system of collective protection of the cultural and natural heritage of outstanding universal value as well as through the Committee's full name, laid down in art. 8 para. 1 sentence 1 of the Convention.

This vague prescription of objectives notwithstanding, the World Heritage Convention also contains definitions for world cultural and natural heritage in arts. 1 and 2. These definitions determine and refine the objects pertaining to the type of protection which the Convention strives for. Furthermore, the Convention states with greater precision the instruments the Committee can utilize of in order to fulfill its objective. Thereby, the Convention focuses, as already mentioned, on listing and granting assistance. Accordingly, art. 11 para. 2 of the Convention stipulates that the World Heritage Committee shall establish, keep up to date and publish, under the title "World Heritage List", a list of properties forming part of the cultural heritage and natural heritage, which it considers as having outstanding universal value in terms of such criteria as it shall have established. Furthermore, the Committee shall establish, keep up to date and publish, whenever circumstances shall so require, under the title "List of World Heritage in Danger", a list of the property appearing in the World Heritage List for the conservation of which major operations are necessary and for which, in principle, assistance has been requested by the State Party concerned (art. 11 para. 4 sentence 1 of the Convention). Again, art. 11 para. 5 of the Convention stipulates that the Committee should define the criteria on the basis of which a property belonging to the cultural or natural heritage may be included in the World Heritage List or in the List of World Heritage in Danger. Thus, the Convention itself endows the Committee with the competence to formulate the requirements which a property must meet in order to qualify for inscription on one of the two lists.

Art. 13 of the World Heritage Convention reads that the World Heritage Committee shall receive and study requests for international assistance formulated by States Parties with respect to property forming part of the cultural or natural heritage, situated in their territories, and included or potentially included in the lists referred to in art. 11 of the Convention (para. 1 sentence 1). The Committee shall decide on the action to be taken with regard to these requests and determine, where appropriate, the nature and extent of its assistance (para. 3). Furthermore, it shall determine in that context the order of priorities for its operations, thereby bearing in mind, *inter alia*, the respective importance for the world cultural and natural heritage of the property requiring protection, the need to give international assistance to the property most representative of a natural environment or of the genius and the history of the peoples of the world (para. 4). These prescriptions of actions remain vague and allow to the Committee a broad margin for evaluation and appreciation. In particular, the notions "respective importance for the world heritage" and "most representative of a natural environment or of the genius and the history of the peoples" invites considerable interpretation. The Convention does not explicitly stipulate that the Committee is obliged to make general and abstract inferences based upon said notions nor does it exclude it from doing so; instead, the Committee's duty to make inferences concerning certain points also suggests a need to clarify additional aspects in the Convention.

After all, the World Heritage Convention comprises fundamental notions that need to be delineated. In particular this applies to the crucial notion "outstanding universal value" as a prerequisite for the enshrining of a property on the World Heritage List. This notion was left deliberately[54] undefined in the Convention.[55] The term was introduced to limit the Convention's application to the protection of the most important places of cultural and natural heritage in the world.[56] That is the reason why the Convention provides that the Committee decides on the criteria for the inscription of properties on the lists.

The Committee fulfilled this task during its first session by issuing the "Operational Guidelines for the Implementation of the World Heritage Convention".[57] The original version of the Operational Guidelines was based on a "Main Working Paper" prepared by the Committee's Secretariat in cooperation with the Advisory Bodies,[58] since the World Heritage Convention does not comment on the procedure or form in which the necessary delineation shall take place. Over the past thirty years, the Operational Guidelines have been revised twelve times,[59] and their content has been extended from 27 paragraphs in 1977 to 290 paragraphs, including 9 annexes, in February 2005.[60]

The reform procedure which brought about the Operational Guidelines 2005 commenced with a decision by the World Heritage Committee in

---

54 *See* Strasser (note 25), at 215, 217.

55 *See* Mark M. Boguslavsky, *Der Begriff des Kulturguts und seine rechtliche Relevanz*, *in* RECHTSFRAGEN DES INTERNATIONALEN KULTURGÜTERSCHUTZES (note 2), at 3, 7.

56 Sarah M. Titchen, *On the Construction of "Outstanding Universal Value,"* 1 CONSERVATION AND MANAGEMENT OF ARCHAEOLOGICAL SITES 235, 236 (1996); Fitschen (note 15), at 183, 191.

57 *See* note 27.

58 *See* World Heritage Committee Final Report, first session, para. 56, available as Doc. CC-77/CONF.001/9 of 17 October 1977 at: http://whc.unesco.org/archive/repcom77.htm.

59 UNESCO World Heritage Centre (note 7), at 32.

60 *See also* Strasser (note 25), at 215, 247; Zacharias (note 4), at 273, 307.

1999 to organize an international meeting of experts.[61] As a consequence, in the following year the "International Expert Meeting on the Revision of the Operational Guidelines for the Implementation of the World Heritage Convention" took place, where experts of cultural and natural heritage from all regions of the world and representatives of the Advisory Bodies analyzed the existing provisions and recommended a number of changes.[62] On the basis of these recommendations the World Heritage Centre, through a collaborative process involving its own personnel as well as representatives of States Parties and of the Advisory Bodies,[63] prepared a first draft of the revised Operational Guidelines.[64] In the course of discussions, this draft was modified several times. Thereby, the World Heritage Committee invited the States Parties to the Convention to provide comments on the then prevailing draft with annotated revisions.[65] Furthermore, it gave the Centre and the Advisory Bodies the task of reviewing these comments, verifying that they complied with its decisions and subsequently integrated them into the Operational Guidelines.[66] Thus, the Operational Guidelines which, according to a decision of the Committee, entered into force on 2 February 2005[67] can draw legitimacy from the participation of experts and of

---

[61] *See* World Heritage Committee Report, 23rd session, chapter XIII para. 12, available as Doc. WHC-99/CONF.209/22 of 2 March 2000 at: http://whc.unesco.org/archive/repcom99.htm.

[62] International Expert Meeting on the Revision of the Operational Guidelines for the Implementation of the World Heritage Convention, Final Report, available as annex to Doc. WHC-2000/CONF.202/17 of 30 May 2000 at: http://whc.unesco.org/canterbury/final-eng.pdf.

[63] World Heritage Committee Report, 24th session, chapter VI para. 4, available as Doc. WHC-2000/CONF.204/21 of 16 February 2001 at: http://whc.unesco.org/archive/repcom00.htm.

[64] *See* World Heritage Committee Report, 26th session, annex II, available as Doc. WHC-02/CONF.202/14A of 23 May 2002 at: http://whc.unesco.org/archive/2002/whc-02-conf202-14ae.pdf; Strasser (note 25), at 215, 248-250.

[65] World Heritage Committee Report, 25th session, chapter VI, available as Doc. WHC-01/CONF.208/24 of 8 February 2002 at: http://whc.unesco.org/archive/repcom01.htm#sec6.

[66] World Heritage Committee, Decisions adopted at the 27th session, para. 10, available as Doc. WHC-03/27.COM/24 of 10 December 2003 at: http://whc.unesco.org/archive/decrec03.htm#sec10.

[67] World Heritage Committee, Decisions adopted by the World Heritage Committee at its 7th extraordinary session, chapter 4A para. V, available as

States Parties, which is the typical dual legitimacy structure used for the international institution and its activities under the World Heritage Convention. In fact, a number of States Parties tabled comments and proposals for alternative formulations to the drafts of the revised Operational Guidelines,[68] so that the Bureau could rightly note that there was "teamwork" on the part of the Secretariat, the Advisory Bodies and the representatives of States Parties.[69]

The Operational Guidelines play an essential role in the implementation of the Convention. A note in the original version stated that "these guidelines, which will need adjusting or expanding to reflect later decisions of the World Heritage Committee, are of crucial importance, in that they provide a clear and comprehensive statement of the principles which are to guide the Committee in its future work".[70] In fact, the Committee in its work treats the Operational Guidelines as if they were not merely a nonbinding commentary to the Conventional provisions but binding secondary law. As far as one can discern, there are no deviations from or violations against the Guidelines in practice. The Committee acts within the procedural rules and observes the substantial stipulations, which underpins the Convention.

Notwithstanding, the legal quality of the Operational Guidelines is not clear.[71] The Committee describes them as "flexible working documents",[72] not least since they can be amended much more easily than the Convention. Primarily, the Operational Guidelines, which are general and abstract rules, are akin to the internal law of an international organization. The Committee has bound itself by abstract norms with

---

Doc. WHC-04/7EXT.COM/17 of 13 January 2005 at: http://whc.unesco.org/archive/2004/whc04-7extcom-17e.pdf.

[68] *See* World Heritage Committee (note 65), chapter VI para. 1 (3rd prong).

[69] Bureau of the World Heritage Committee Report, special session, chapter III para. 22, available as Doc. WHC.2000/CONF.202/4 Rev. 1 (SPE) of 16 January 2001 at: http://whc.unesco.org/archive/repbur00ss.htm#sec3.

[70] Note 1 sentence 2 under para. 3 of the Operational Guidelines 1977, Doc. CC-77/CONF.001/9 of 19 October 1977, 56, available at: http://whc.unesco.org/archive/repcom77.htm.

[71] *See* with regard to the dispute about the legal significance of the Operational Guidelines during the 1996 session World Heritage Committee Report, 20th session, chapter XVII para. 7 and annexes 1-4 to IX, available as Doc. WHC-96/CONF.201/21 of 10 March 1997 at: http://whc.unesco.org/archive/repcom96.htm; Strasser (note 25), 215, 246.

[72] *See* UNESCO World Heritage Centre (note 7), at 32.

regard to, for instance, making use of margins of appreciation when deciding whether a property belongs to the cultural or natural world heritage or not, and exercising discretion when deciding whether, and what kind of, international assistance is to be granted. Thus, the Operational Guidelines do not only serve the standardization and simplification of the administrative procedures but also guarantees more transparent, foreseeable and calculable decisions at the international level. As a consequence, the States Parties can prepare their national heritage or rather environmental and historic monument protection policies for international deliberation and know with certainty, *inter alia*, whether construction planning or investments will be granted.[73]

Moreover, the Guidelines function as external governance instruments. They have the character of an administrative regulation in the sense of the notion used in German law. Although they are not directed to subordinate authorities, they foster a uniform administrative practice of the States Parties, especially regarding nominations of properties for inscription on the World Heritage List. Accordingly, the Operational Guidelines 2005 identify as their key users not only the Committee and the Advisory Bodies but also the States Parties, which are mentioned from the outset (para. 3) and are, furthermore, directly addressed by a series of provisions. For instance, the Guidelines encourage the States Parties to ensure the participation of stakeholders in the identification, nomination and protection of world heritage properties (para. 12), to bring together their cultural and natural heritage experts in regular intervals to discuss the implementation of the World Heritage Convention (para. 14) or to participate in the implementation of the Global Strategy for a Representative, Balanced and Credible World Heritage List[74] (para. 56). With these provisions, the Guidelines aim at educating the States Parties how to improve their national administrative procedures; they function as State-directed codes of conduct. Furthermore, the Guidelines, by containing the criteria for a property to be inscribed on or deleted from the World Heritage List as well as the priority prin-

---

[73] *See e.g.* World Heritage Newsletter No. 27 of May to August 2000, available at: http://whc.unesco.org/news/27newsen.pdf, which mentions that one important function of the Operational Guidelines is to ensure that States Parties to the Convention are "well informed about the principles which guide the work of the World Heritage Committee".

[74] *See* World Heritage Committee Report, 25th session, available as Doc. WHC-01/CONF.208/14 of 31 October 2001 at: http://unesdoc.unesco.org/images/0012/001264/126443e.pdf.

ciples for the granting of assistance, help the States Parties recognize which properties situated in their territories are of such a value that they should be conserved for future generations. Thus, they create an international standard for determining the historic monuments and natural sites which in any case deserve domestic protection, irrespective whether they are listed or not (*cf.* also art. 12 of the Convention).

III. Procedural Regime

The administrative procedure is loosely stipulated in the World Heritage Convention. The relevant provisions are specified and completed by the Operational Guidelines and by the Rules of Procedure[75] which guide the internal decision-making process of the World Heritage Committee.

1. Three-Part Structure of the Procedure of Decision-Making

a) Procedure of Listing

Before being able to initiate the procedure of listing by the nomination of a property, the States Parties have to prepare and submit to the World Heritage Committee a Tentative List.[76] The Tentative Lists,[77] include, with documentation about the location and significance, the heritage sites that the States Parties plan to nominate in the next five to ten years.[78] Thus, they are planning tools, since they allow the Committee and the Advisory Bodies to compare nominated sites with similar ones that might be nominated in future so that they can select only those of outstanding universal value.[79] As previously mentioned, States Parties are encouraged to prepare their Tentative Lists with the participation of a wide variety of stakeholders, including site managers, local and regional governments, local communities, NGOs and other interested parties and partners (para. 64 of the Operational Guidelines 2005).

---

[75] *See* note 47.

[76] *See* art. 11(1) sentence 1 of the Convention.

[77] Available at: http://whc.unesco.org/en/tentativelists.

[78] *See* art. 11(1) sentence 2 of the Convention, para. 62 of the Operational Guidelines 2005.

[79] *See* para. 70 of the Operational Guidelines 2005.

However, in practice at least half of the European countries do not involve local stakeholders in the preparation of their Tentative Lists and at least two thirds draft their Lists without any public consultation.[80]

The States Parties formally nominate properties, on the basis of the Tentative Lists, for inclusion on the World Heritage List. They can only nominate sites located within their boundaries.[81] In the case of sites that extend beyond national borders a joint transboundary or transnational nomination can be made;[82] then, a horizontal cooperation between States Parties takes place. Para. 123 of the Operational Guidelines 2005 indicates that the participation of local people in the nomination process is essential to foster shared responsibility with the State Party in the maintenance of the property. Thus, the States Parties are encouraged to prepare nominations in conjunction with site managers, local and regional governments, local communities, NGOs and other interested parties (*cf.* also para. 12 of the Operational Guidelines 2005). Again, neither the Convention nor the Guidelines stipulate an obligation of the States Parties to involve local stakeholders or to carry out a public consultation. Even governments of territorial entities below the level of the State Party need not be given the possibility to participate, which can prove problematic particularly in federal states. The World Heritage Convention contains a federal clause in the form of art. 34, but it only clarifies that federal or central governments have exactly the same obligations for the implementation of the Convention as those States whose governments take a unitary form and places the responsibility on the national government to persuade the lower levels to carry out the provisions of the Convention notwithstanding the lack of direct federal or central government power.[83]

The States Parties' nomination dossiers – which must contain details about the property, the justification for inscription, the state of conservation, the actual operating protection system and the management plan (*cf.* para. 132 of the Operational Guidelines 2005) – are evaluated by the Advisory Bodies, that is by ICOMOS for cultural heritage and IUCN

---

[80] *See* UNESCO World Heritage Centre (note 7), at 35.

[81] *See* Fitschen (note 15), at 183, 192-193.

[82] *See* paras. 134, 135 and 139 of the Operational Guidelines 2005.

[83] *See* Australian High Court, *Commonwealth v. Tasmania* (Franklin Dam Case) [1983] 158 CLR 1; Ben Boer, *Article 34*, *in* THE 1972 WORLD HERITAGE CONVENTION, 355, 356 (Francesco Francioni ed., 2008); von Bogdandy & Zacharias (note 5), at 527, 530; Zacharias (note 4), at 273, 330-331.

for natural heritage sites. A joint evaluation by both of them takes place in the case of mixed sites and some cultural landscapes (*cf.* paras. 144 to 146 of the Operational Guidelines 2005). The Advisory Bodies examine whether or not the properties nominated by the States Parties have outstanding universal value, meet the additional conditions of integrity and/or authenticity and the requirements of protection and management (para. 143 of the Operational Guidelines 2005). Thereafter, they forward their recommendations to the World Heritage Committee. The concerned States Parties may send, at least two working days before the opening of the new session of the Committee, a letter to the Chairperson if they think they have identified factual errors in the evaluation of their nomination made to the Advisory Bodies. Thereafter, this letter will be distributed to the members of the Committee and may be read by the Chairperson following the presentation of the evaluation (para. 150 of the Operational Guidelines 2005). Thus, the States Parties have the possibility to make a counter-statement to the Advisory Bodies' evaluation.

The participation of the Advisory Bodies at evaluation stage is not explicitly stipulated in the World Heritage Convention. According to art. 11 para. 7 of the Convention, the Committee shall, with the agreement of the States concerned, coordinate and encourage the studies and research needed for the drawing up of the World Heritage List and of the List of World Heritage in Danger. This indicates that the Committee is allowed to enlist the support of experts for the purposes of assessment whether a property forms part of the world heritage. Moreover, art. 13 para. 7 of the Convention, with regard to the granting of international assistance, reads that the Committee shall cooperate with international and national governmental and non-governmental organizations that have similar objectives to those of the Convention; thereby, ICCROM, ICOMOS and IUCN are named as examples. Hence, it seems reasonable that the Committee uses the expertise of these organizations also for the evaluation of nominated properties.

The World Heritage Committee decides whether a property should be inscribed on the World Heritage List, or whether the nomination should be referred back to the State Party for additional information or deferred for more in depth assessment, or a substantial revision by the State Party (*cf.* art. 11 para. 2 of the Convention; paras. 153, 159 and 160 of the Operational Guidelines 2005). The Committee is not bound by the Advisory Bodies' evaluations and recommendations,[84] although in

84 *See* World Heritage Committee (note 71), chapter XVII para. 8.

practice it regularly avoids making use of its capacity to deviate. In order to include a property in the World Heritage List the consent of the State concerned is necessary (art. 11 para. 3 sentence 1 of the Convention), which is usually seen to have been given with the submission of the nomination. Furthermore, art. 11 para. 6 of the Convention states that the Committee, before refusing a request for inclusion in the World Heritage List or the List of World Heritage in Danger, shall consult the State Party in whose territory the property in question is situated. Thus, the procedure is framed by strong consensual elements.

The World Heritage Committee's decisions need not be based on unanimity; rather, art. 13 para. 8 of the Convention reads that decisions of the Committee shall be taken by a majority of two-thirds of its members present and voting. This means a further weakening of the already remote representation of the States Parties through the Committee but strengthens the autonomy of the Committee at the national level.

b) Procedure for Granting Assistance

Like the procedure of listing, the procedure of granting international assistance starts with an initiative of the State Party concerned.[85] The States Parties must submit a formal request for assistance according to arts. 13 para. 1 and 19 sentence 1 of the World Heritage Convention, which they are, in principle, only entitled to do when they have paid their contribution to the World Heritage Fund (*cf.* para. 237 of the Operational Guidelines 2005).[86] The requests should contain any information and documentation necessary to enable the Committee to arrive at a decision (art. 19 sentence 2 of the Convention); and must even be supported by experts' reports whenever possible (art. 21 para. 1 sentence 2 of the Convention).

The Advisory Bodies, which means ICOMOS and ICCROM in the case of cultural sites, ICOMOS, ICCROM and IUCN in the case of mixed sites, and IUCN in the case of natural sites,[87] evaluate the requests and make recommendations. This support of the World Heritage Committee can be based on art. 13 para. 7 in conjunction with art. 21 para. 3 of the World Heritage Convention reading that the Committee, before coming to a decision, shall carry out such studies and consulta-

---

85 *See* GENIUS-DEVIME (note 15), at 316-317.

86 UNESCO World Heritage Centre (note 7), at 47.

87 *See* paras. 248 to 250 of the Operational Guidelines 2005.

tions as it deems necessary. Additionally, art. 24 of the Convention stipulates that international assistance on a large scale shall be preceded by detailed scientific, economic and technical studies. Thus, an evaluation by experts is recognized by the Convention as an important procedural stage in certain cases. Moreover, one can argue that the constant consultation of experts over a period of more than thirty years has led to a duty to consult them, at least if the nomination is not going to be refused already because of formal reasons. Thus, the mere possibility of consultation has become an obligation *via* "institutional practice".[88]

Thereafter, the Committee decides on the action to be taken with regard to the request, determines, where appropriate, the nature and extent of its assistance and authorizes the conclusion, on its behalf, of the necessary contractual arrangements with the government concerned (*cf.* arts. 13 para. 3 and 26 of the Convention). After all, one can also discern a three-part structure of the administrative procedure, consisting of application, evaluation and formal decision.[89]

2. *Reporting and Monitoring*

The implementation of the World Heritage Convention in general and of the obligations arising from listing or granting assistance in particular by the States Parties is mainly supervised by the World Heritage Committee and by the General Conference through periodic reporting and reactive monitoring. Periodic reporting means a six-year cyclical review of States Parties' policies and legislation, as well as the organization, management and conservation of the world heritage sites situated in the prevailing territories.[90] It shall provide an assessment of the application to the Convention by the State Party and also an analysis whether the outstanding universal value of the properties inscribed on the World Heritage List is being maintained over time. Reactive monitoring takes place in reference to properties that are under threat, which means that they are inscribed, or plan to be inscribed, on the List of World Heritage in Danger, and in the procedures for the eventual deletion of prop-

---

[88] *See* JOSÉ E. ALVAREZ, INTERNATIONAL ORGANIZATIONS AS LAW-MAKERS 87 (2005).

[89] *See* Strasser (note 25), at 215, 218; LÉON PRESSOUYRE, THE WORLD HERITAGE CONVENTION – TWENTY YEARS LATER 46 (1996).

[90] *See* arts. 11(7) and 29 of the Convention; para. 199 of the Operational Guidelines 2005.

erties from the World Heritage List.[91] It is primarily a policy guidance tool, aimed at providing benchmarks, orientations and deadlines to the actions of the States Parties.[92] Finally, there must be monitoring of the implementation of international assistance within one year of the completion of the activities for which the assistance had been granted (para. 256 of the Operational Guidelines 2005).

When the reporting or monitoring reveals a breach of Convention duties and obligations on behalf of the States Parties, the international institution only has a limited arsenal of instruments at hand to ensure compliance, since there is no legal penalty, sanction, or remedy provided for under the World Heritage Convention.[93] If a property is included in the World Heritage List, the Committee can, as a measure of compliance,[94] either inscribe it on the List of World Heritage in Danger or threaten to delete it completely from the World Heritage List.[95] These measures have the potential to stimulate the motivation of the State Party to take the necessary steps to avert the threat to the property or to encounter its negative results not least because they are means of naming and shaming.[96] They announce publicly that the present steps taken by the State Party in order to protect the property forming part of the world heritage are insufficient. Thus, they can be interpreted as measures of "reputation enforcement".[97] The effectiveness of these measures has been well demonstrated in the case of Cologne Cathedral, where the Mayor of the City of Cologne was eventually prepared to make concessions with regard to the construction planning concerning the surroundings of the Cathedral.[98]

---

91 Para. 169 of the Operational Guidelines 2005.

92 UNESCO World Heritage Centre (note 7), at 20.

93 BOER & WIFFEN (note 6), at 70.

94 *See* Zacharias (note 4), at 273, 310-322.

95 BOER & WIFFEN (note 6), at 70.

96 *See* CHRISTINA HOTZ, DEUTSCHE STÄDTE UND UNESCO-WELTERBE. PROBLEME UND ERFAHRUNGEN MIT DER UMSETZUNG EINES GLOBALISIERTEN DENKMALSCHUTZKONZEPTES 42 (2004).

97 *See* Giandomenico Majone, *Delegation of Regulatory Powers in a Mixed Polity*, 8 EUROPEAN LAW JOURNAL 319, 337 (2002); Peter T. Leeson, *Contracts without Government*, 18 JOURNAL OF PRIVATE ENTERPRISE 35-36 (2003).

98 *See* Zacharias (note 4), 273, 366.

IV. Legal Effects of Listing

The legal classification of listing is disputed. According to some scholars, the inscription of a property on the World Heritage List does not constitute obligations of the State Party in whose territory the property is situated; decisive for the existence of world heritage and for the State Party's obligations resulting from that status are only the substantial criteria mentioned in arts. 1 and 2 of the Convention. The listing is at best a formal confirmation of a status that is already given, and has the function of a clarification;[99] it has, thus, merely a declaratory character. To corroborate this opinion one could argue on the basis of art. 3 of the Convention. This provision reads that it is for each State Party to identify and delineate the different properties situated on its territory mentioned in arts. 1 and 2. Thus, the State Party concerned would appear to be capable in conclusively assessing the quality of a property that is to be nominated. Moreover, art. 11 para. 1 sentence 1 of the Convention stipulates that every State Party shall submit to the Committee an inventory of property forming part of the cultural and natural heritage, situated in its territory and suitable for inclusion in the World Heritage List. One could read this passage in the sense that the qualification as world cultural or natural heritage is fixed before the inscription on the World Heritage List takes place.

However, this view overlooks the complex assessment procedure at the international level that includes an evaluation of the Advisory Bodies. This procedure would be entirely superfluous if the listing had no effects under international law; the World Heritage Committee could restrict its activities to automatically including the national lists in the World Heritage List. Notwithstanding, the inscription on the List is not a necessary constituent factor for further measures; in particular it is not a compelling prerequisite for the eligibility of the affected property for international assistance. Instead, assistance can already be granted if a property is potentially suitable for inclusion in the List (*cf.* arts. 13 para. 1 sentence 1 and 20 of the Convention).

Hence, the effects of listing must be linked directly with the world heritage status of the property or must be related to the property's protection. Since the World Heritage Committee examines whether a property forms part of the world heritage, its final positive decision ascertains this quality in a legally binding way so that the State Party cannot arrive at a deviating assessment. Thus, the decisions can be described as

---

[99] *See* Fastenrath (note 5), at 1017, 1019 and 1026-1027.

accreditation, which means a formal positive determination of the qualitative status with which various rights or duties are directly linked; with regard to the latter they have constitutive effect. This qualification of listing was rightly recognized by the High Court of Australia which stated in *Queensland v Commonwealth* that "[f]rom the viewpoint of the international community, the submission by a State Party of a property for inclusion in the World Heritage List and [the later] inclusion of the property in the List by the Committee are the means by which the status of a property is ascertained and the duties attaching to that status are established. The State Party's submission of a property is some evidence of its status but the Committee's listing of a property is conclusive. [...] As the procedures for evaluation adopted by the Committee are extensive, the Committee's decision [...] assures the international community that the property has outstanding universal value as part of the cultural heritage or natural heritage." These procedures placed the State Party "under an international duty to protect and conserve" the property in question.[100]

The aspect that the accreditation gives rise to duties incumbent upon States Parties is also emphasized by a body of literature which argues that the listing carries with it a "heavy international responsibility [for the State Party] to protect and enhance the World Heritage values over the years"; hence, the State Party, when nominating a property, "must be fully aware of the long term obligations" connected with the positive decision of the World Heritage Committee which it strives for.[101] The rationale behind these duties is that the inscription of a property on the World Heritage List consolidates and, thus, activates the State Party's primary obligations under the Convention with regard to the objective of protection and conservation. These obligations are formulated vaguely and openly in arts. 4 and 5 of the World Heritage Convention but the accreditation of a property concentrates these abstract rules into sufficiently concrete stipulations which bind the State Party, since all questions of interpretation and evaluation are decided.[102] As a conse-

---

100 *Queensland v. Commonwealth* [1989] 167 CLR 232, 240-242.

101 Jane A. Vernhes, *Implementation of the World Heritage Convention in South East Asia and the Pacific*, *in* PROCEEDINGS OF A WORKSHOP SESSION ON CRITICAL ISSUES FOR PROTECTED AREAS, held during the 18th session of the General Assembly of IUCN on 1 December 1990, at 26; *see* Haigh (note 10), at 199, 205-206; VON SCHORLEMER (note 19), at 132-133.

102 von Bogdandy & Zacharias (note 5), at 527-528; Zacharias (note 4), at 273, 308.

quence, the State Party shall endeavor, *inter alia*, to integrate the protection of that item of world heritage into comprehensive planning program (art. 5 lit. a of the Convention) and to take the appropriate legal, scientific, technical, administrative and financial measures necessary for the protection, conservation, presentation and rehabilitation of this heritage (art. 5 lit. d of the Convention). The last point could, for example, mean that the State Party has to pass a historic monument act or to take efficient supervisory measures in the field of construction planning to ensure that regional or local governments which are not addressees of the Convention for their part protect the properties which have the status of world heritage.[103]

V. Oversight

The oversight of the international institution is restricted to the General Conference of UNESCO receiving and, should the need arise, reacting to the World Heritage Committee's biannual reports on its activities according to art. 29 para. 3 of the Convention. This weak instrument might be regarded as being sufficient in the light of the consensual administrative procedure which requires an intensive consultation between the Committee and the States Parties and is, to a large extent, able to guarantee that faults are avoided or at least revised. Thus, the reports have the function of enabling the General Conference to control whether the general policy of the Committee is in line with the targets of the World Heritage Convention. Consequently, this oversight appears to be more a political than a strict, legal one.

C. Assessment and Conclusion

I. Principles

There are a series of principles that determine the shape and the activities of the international institution for the protection of world heritage. These principles can be divided into four groups.

---

[103] *See* with regard to the measures of the federal, state and municipal level in Germany Zacharias (note 4), 273, 331-360.

The first group consists of principles which constitute, not least as Conventional objectives, the coordination of the world heritage protection system, laid down in the Preamble of the World Heritage Convention. These are the principle of ecologically sustainable development,[104] which is consolidated by the precautionary principle and the intergenerational principle,[105] the principle of cooperation, and the principle of subsidiarity.

The principle of ecologically sustainable development, which is a leading substantial principle, is prominent in all recitals of the Preamble of the Convention, since they suggest the increasing threats to the stock of world cultural and natural heritage by both the traditional causes of decay, changing social and economic conditions and to the need to preserve this heritage as part of the common heritage of mankind. Moreover, art. 5 lit. a of the Convention states that the world heritage must be given a "function in the life of the community", and art. 5 lit. d of the Convention stipulates that it must be identified, protected, conserved, presented and rehabilitated. Thus, the maintenance of the world heritage has priority even over achieving a balance with the economic development.

The precautionary principle is mentioned in art. 5 lit. c of the Convention stipulating that the State Party shall endeavor to develop "scientific and technical studies and research" and to work out the necessary operating methods as well as making it "capable of counteracting the dangers" that threaten its cultural or natural heritage. This means that the State Party is not allowed to take deliberate action that might damage the world heritage site. A detailed assessment of the likely environmental impacts on the site must be conducted.[106] The inter-generational principle is contained within art. 4 sentence 1 of the Convention. The provision reads that each State Party recognizes a duty to ensure the "transmission to future generations" of the world heritage. This duty requires that the degree of present damage must be kept to a minimum so that it does not erode the world heritage and destine it to a "death of a thousand cuts".[107]

The principle of cooperation, which is a formal, structural principle, can be deduced from the sum of provisions in the Convention providing

---

104 *See* Haigh (note 10), at 199, 208 and 211-212.

105 *See* FRIGO (note 2), at 189.

106 Haigh (note 10), at 199, 211.

107 *See id.* at 199, 208.

that the World Heritage Committee can only act on an initiative of the State Party concerned or with the consent of the State Party or must, at least, consult the State Party (*cf.*, *e.g.*, arts. 11 paras. 1, 3 and 6, 13 paras. 1 to 3 and 19 of the Convention). In the context of the World Heritage Convention, the principle is meant to apply vertically and not horizontally, although art. 7 of the Convention appears to indicate a different conclusion. The principle of subsidiarity which is closely connected with the principle of cooperation and can be understood both formally, with regard to competencies, and substantially, with regard to the manner and extent of the measures to be chosen, states that international assistance only takes effect when the State Party is not able to adequately fulfill the task of world heritage protection within its own resources. It is laid down in particular in recitals 3 and 5 of the Preamble and in arts. 4, 7, 21 para. 1 and 25 of the Convention.

The second group concerns the representation of the States Parties in the governing bodies of the international institution or, more generally, the formal relation or connection between the national and the international level. It is, thus, a structural principle. The appointment of World Heritage Committee members follows the principle of an equitable representation of the different regions of the world (*cf.* art. 8 para. 2 of the Convention). The first and the second group of principles belong to the substantive and institutional framework of the international institution or describe the international institution in its entirety as a governance regime.

The third and the fourth group of principles contain legal principles governing decision-making. The third group is related to the administrative procedure, and the fourth group consists of material prescriptions for the final decision. Regarding procedure, one can discern the principle that no action shall be made without the initiative or at least consent of the State Party concerned (*cf.* arts. 11 paras. 1, 3 and 6, 13 paras. 1 to 3 and 19 of the Convention), apart from measures to enhance compliance for which the majority vote in the Committee has special importance. One could in this context also mention voluntary subjection to the decision-making power of the international level with regard to specific properties. Furthermore, one can identify the principle that decisions must be preceded by evaluations made by external experts, which means by the Advisory Bodies (*cf.* arts. 13 para. 7 and 21 para. 3 of the Convention; paras. 143 to 151 of the Operational Guidelines 2005). A third procedural principle is the principle of transparency. Any final decision of the World Heritage Committee must be made public; and even the application (nomination or request) of the State Party and the reports of the Advisory Bodies are published (*cf.* para. 187 of the Operational Guidelines 2005). Regarding material provisions, one might investigate a principle of burden-sharing, since art. 25 of the Convention provides that, as a general rule, only part of the cost of work necessary shall be borne by the international community; the contribution of the State benefiting from international assistance shall constitute a substantial share of the resources devoted to each program or project, unless its resources do not permit this.

II. Multilevel Dimension

The relationship between the international and the national level is hierarchical. The World Heritage Committee is the central decision-making body at the international level. It makes decisions that legally bind the States Parties who have subjected themselves to its power. However, the State Party's general duties under the Convention that are consolidated by the Committee's decision to inscribe a property on the World Heritage List are formulated in such a way that affords the State Party with a broad scope for action. In particular, it can, to a large extent, decide which measures it may take to protect, conserve and rehabilitate the listed property (*cf.* arts. 4 sentence 2 and 5 of the Convention). However, the situation is somewhat dissimilar when the State Party avails itself of the granted international assistance. In which case, it must comply with the conditions set out in the agreement with the Committee (*cf.* art. 26 of the Convention).

III. Legitimacy: Experts versus Representation?

The legitimacy of the governance of world heritage protection is based on four pillars: the representation of the States Parties in the World Heritage Committee, albeit flawed; the substantive formulation of the Committee's activities within the broad scope already set out in the Convention ratified by the States Parties; the intensive participation of the State Party concerned in the procedures of listing and granting assistance which guarantees that the rights and interests of the State Party are considered; and, finally, the inclusion of and reference to external expertise. The deficits that characterize the representation of States Parties could be counterbalanced by efficiency gains and increased acceptance of the entire governance mechanism through reliance on independent expertise.

On the one hand, the governance of world heritage protection is articulated in the body of literature as highly efficient.[108] In fact, the consensual and cooperative approach results in a high acceptance of the Committee's decisions by the States Parties. Moreover, the often intensive consultations with public authorities "at the grass roots level" like regional governments and municipalities which are regarded as "partners in the protection and conservation of World Heritage" (para. 40 of the Operational Guidelines 2005) in the processes of consultation and evaluation are suited to give the World Heritage Committee and the Advisory Bodies a factual, though not legal, standing in administrative procedures on the national, regional or local level. The Committee and Advisory Bodies are known by the domestic authorities and there seems to be, thus, no psychological obstacle to involve them as experts bringing in the global perspective.

On the other hand, the efficiency and acceptance of the UNESCO world heritage regime suffer from three weaknesses. Firstly, the Committee can, in principle, only become active upon an explicit request of a State Party. The absence of said request negates the inscription of a property on the World Heritage List as well as the protection of the international community,[109] even if the State Party deliberately (be it for political, economic or religious reasons) neglects the cultural or natural heritage.[110] In order to remedy this situation the Convention itself would need to be amended. Similarly the rules concerning the members of the Committee requires amendment in order to guarantee the full representation of all States Parties, since the current democratic deficits in the appointment of the Committee's members are compensated by the States Parties' strong participatory rights in the administrative procedure.

Furthermore, there are no adjudicative mechanisms present in the Convention to afford the States Parties with the possibility to review Committee decisions, in particular the referral or deferral of a nomination and, thus, the refusal to enshrine a nominated property in the World

---

[108] ODENDAHL (note 16), at 137.

[109] FRANK FECHNER, RECHTLICHER SCHUTZ ARCHÄOLOGISCHEN KULTURGUTS 98-99 (1991); GENIUS-DEVIME (note 15), at 316; ODENDAHL (note 16), at 137.

[110] Fitschen (note 15), at 183, 200; *see* Francioni (note 15), at 13, 30-32.

Heritage List at present or the inscription of a property on the List of World Heritage in Danger. Since the States Parties are also not able to take action in any external tribunal such as the International Court of Justice or the Permanent Court of Arbitration[111] (exemplified in the cases of Cologne Cathedral and Dresden Elbe Valley where a system of dispute settlement or management could have been helpful), perhaps a kind of appellate body should be established within the framework of the UNESCO world heritage regime for cases of conflict.[112]

Ultimately, the compliance mechanisms at hand are problematic insofar as they cannot efficiently guarantee that the States Parties act in accordance with the Convention, since the ultimate threat for a State Party which does not comply with its Conventional duties is delisting and, thus, withdrawing the international protection from a property that has outstanding universal value.[113] Hence, the Committee, for example, abandoned its plan to inscribe Kakadu National Park on the List of World Heritage in Danger in view of a proposed uranium mine in an enclave within the Park because of the resistance mounted by Australian Government. This decision reflected a "rational choice to prevent defection and non-compliance that could potentially be more damaging to the heritage regime".[114] The national authorities must carefully weigh such a decision. Moreover, they may consider the delisting simply as one kind of cost among others of, for instance, a measure of planning.[115] As the German Federal Constitutional Court held in its preliminary decision of 29 May 2007 concerning the Dresden Elbe Valley where it stated that the City of Dresden, if necessary, would accept the loss of the title of world heritage when the wish of the people to construct a bridge over the Valley, as articulated in a local referendum, was to be respected;[116] here a decision which was found on the local level by a means of direct democracy was regarded as having more weight than a

---

[111] *See* BOER & WIFFEN (note 6), at 70.

[112] *See* Francioni (note 15), at 13, 36.

[113] *See* Zacharias (note 4), at 273, 320-322.

[114] Maswood (note 6), at 357, 358.

[115] *See* Markus Scheffer, *Der Volkswille als Leerformel*, FAZ No. 123 of 30 May 2007, 37.

[116] Federal Constitutional Court (note 5), at 513. *See* Dieter Bartetzko, *Pilatus lebt*, FAZ No. 130 of 8 June 2007, 33; Reinhard Müller, *Bürgerwille und Völkerrecht*, FAZ No. 136 of 15 June 2007, 12.

decision of the autonomous, expertocratic international institution.[117] A solution to such cases would be, again, an amendment to the Convention which allows sanctions. But this would mean a change to the Convention's character.

After all, the international institution for the protection of world heritage is an example of a widely autonomous regime. The autonomy guarantees to a certain degree independence from the States Parties and their ideas, which is expressed at best by the restricted competences of the General Assembly of States Parties towards the World Heritage Committee. Consequently, the institution can focus more precisely on its core task, without having the obligation and need to extensively consider national polities. However, it is just this point which undermines its acceptance by administrative authorities of the States Parties, which must implement the World Heritage Convention into their national legal systems. The institutional distance strengthens the impression of national bureaucracies that the international level does not sufficiently acknowledge regional and local interests, that it is too technocratic and, to say it in one word, remote.

---

[117] *See* Daniel Hildebrand, *Waldschlößchen ohne Brücke: über Aussetzung und Selbstausschaltung von Demokratie*, 40 KRITISCHE JUSTIZ 184-192 (2007). Regarding supposed democratic deficits of the world heritage regime and possible reforms, *see* Natasha Affolder, *Democratising or Demonising the World Heritage Convention?*, 38 VICTORIA UNIVERSITY OF WELLINGTON LAW REVIEW 341-361 (2007).

The UNESCO Regime for the Protection of World Heritage

*Comment by Ute Mager**

The elaborate description and legal analysis of the UNESCO regime documents a rather developed international administration and cooperation in the field of the protection of cultural and natural sites of outstanding value. Therefore it serves very well as an example for proving the value of the international composite administration model.

First of all, the UNESCO regime is a good and convincing example for the existence and exercise of international public authority. The heart of the regime, governed by the World Heritage Convention, concerns the relations between an organ of an international organisation, the World Heritage Committee, and the State Parties. In substance, the protection of cultural and natural sites is a concern which the States themselves regard as their responsibility. The World Heritage Committee offers its assistance under the condition that, first, the site is of sufficient importance for mankind and second, the State requests such assistance.

The instruments used to reach the goal of the convention are:

- substantive and procedural norms in the convention itself as well as regulations or guidelines,
- binding decisions,
- financial or technical assistance,
- reporting duties, and
- the involvement of expert committees.

* I would like to thank Eric Pickett for his very helpful comments on a previous draft of this article.

A. von Bogdandy et al. (eds.), *The Exercise of Public Authority by International Institutions*, Beiträge zum ausländischen öffentlichen Recht und Völkerrecht 210,
DOI 10.1007/978-3-642-04531-8_12, © Springer-Verlag Berlin Heidelberg 2010

The modes of action are formed by cooperation between the World Heritage Committee, States and expert committees. This is true for the development of guidelines as well as for the decision-making process. A site is only included on the World Heritage list and financial or technical assistance are only granted at the request of the State and after evaluation of experts. Only the decision of delisting is a unilateral decision, though it should be noted that this decision is taken with the participation of experts.

I agree with the author's view that the modes of action are similar to public services (*Leistungsverwaltung*) provided on the domestic level. In particular, there is no contradiction between the decision to list a site being coupled with the imposition of obligations and conditions; benefits granted by national public authorities are also never granted unconditionally.

Guidelines are a very interesting phenomenon, bearing similarities to instruments in national administrative law. Their function is to ensure the uniform application of the convention. This objective implies that they are a mixture of administrative regulation with purely internal effects (*Verwaltungsvorschriften* in German law) binding only the international organization, as well as executive order law with external effects (*Rechtsverordnungen* in German law), which have external effects. Perhaps it does not make sense to differentiate too strictly between internal and external effects because, even more than in the domestic situation, it is difficult to maintain a sharp distinction between an international organization's mode of action having purely internal effects and it having "external effects" on the members.

However, I disagree with the author's view that the relationship between the international and the national level is hierarchical. The existence of legally binding decisions is not enough for the use of the term of hierarchy. Even the fact of subordination would not be sufficient. There is subordination if one person or organisation has to accept the unilaterally taken decision of another person or organisation. There is hierarchy if the competences of one person or organisation are of overriding importance and encompass the competences of another person or organisation. In the case of the UNESCO regime the powers of the World Heritage Committee and the State Party involved are not the same. The State has no power to list a cultural or natural site on its territory on the World Heritage list. It has no competence to grant itself international assistance for the protection. On the other hand, the World Heritage Committee has no power to protect the site in the territory of a State. Taking into account the fact that the World Heritage

Committee can only act on the request of the State, I doubt very much that there is any subordination in the relation between the World Heritage Committee and a State Party; in any event, there is surely no hierarchy. Furthermore, the author speaks only of hierarchy under the subtitle of Multilevel Dimensions, whereas in the rest of the very convincing legal analysis the aspect of cooperation in the relations between the World Heritage Committee and the State Parties is stressed. This fact can be regarded as evidence for the misleading effects of the concept of "multilevel-administration", as is pointed out in the contribution of Armin von Bogdandy and Philipp Dann.[1] In any event, in my opinion, it is of eminent relevance for the establishment of the concept of international composite administration that the notions taken from the language of national administrative law are used in their specific sense.

The weaknesses of the UNESCO Regime enumerated by the author seem to be the typical weaknesses in international composite administration: action only on request, no adjudicatory powers, no sanctions beyond delisting. A comparison with the instruments of national protection of cultural and natural sites and especially with the European Flora-Fauna-Habitat-Regime could deepen the understanding of the differences between national, European and international administration and perhaps enhance some ideas for further development of the international regime.

Finally the UNESCO-Regime shows an amazing variety of sources of legitimacy and therefore enjoys a high level of legitimacy for its actions. In this sense it is a good model for other areas of international composite administration.

To conclude: The UNESCO-Regime is a very well chosen example for the value of the concept behind the term international composite administration. Whereas the concept of multilevel-relations is misleading and the term network is not helpful in understanding the relation between the World Heritage Committee and State Parties, the concept of international composite administration opens the way for enlightening and innovative legal analysis.

---

1 *See* Armin von Bogdandy & Philipp Dann, *International Composite Administration*, in this volume.

2.2 Recommendations

Regulating Minority Issues through Standard-Setting and Mediation: The Case of the High Commissioner on National Minorities

*By Anuscheh Farahat**

* I would like to thank Jürgen Bast, Jochen von Bernstorff and Lewis Enim for their helpful discussions and comments on earlier drafts.

A. von Bogdandy et al. (eds.), *The Exercise of Public Authority by International Institutions*, Beiträge zum ausländischen öffentlichen Recht und Völkerrecht 210, DOI 10.1007/978-3-642-04531-8_13, © Springer-Verlag Berlin Heidelberg 2010

A. Introduction

On 17 February 2000 the OSCE High Commissioner on National Minorities (HCNM) submitted a recommendation to the Senate of the Babes-Bolyai University (BBU) in Romania. In this recommendation he formulated inter alia: "It is important for the staff of a University to reflect the University's multi-cultural character [...] Therefore, an Equal Opportunity Commission should be established within the university to encourage the hiring of minority and female staff – on the basis of academic credentials – regulate guidelines on the recruitment and promotion of staff in this context and monitor performance against clear and transparent success/failure criteria."[1]

The following article describes the work of the HCNM as peace-building through standard-setting and mediation. We will see that the HCNM exercises public authority during the procedures, which govern his shaping activities as well as his monitoring activities.

1 Recommendation on Expanding the Concept of Multi-culturalism at the Babes-Bolyai University, Cluj-Napoca, Romania, 17 February 2000, available at: http://www.osce.org /documents/hcnm/2000/03/2745_en.pdf.

The first chapter of this article will therefore outline the benefit of a perspective emphasizing the exercise of public authority with regard to the idiosyncrasies of the activities of the HCNM, explaining the political background, the aims and tools of the HCNM (B.). The second chapter of the article concerns the legal analysis of the activities of the HCNM. This includes a short introduction of the institutional framework in which the HCNM is embedded, a typology of the central instruments of the HCNM, and an exploration of the monitoring and enforcement mechanisms (C.). Against the background of this analysis, the last chapter will extrapolate principles of the HCNM's tasks and provide a criticism of the HCNM's work and procedures (D.).

B. Minority Protection as an Instrument for Security – An Introduction

I. Historical Background – Minority Protection after the Cold War

The HCNM was established in 1992 primarily against the background of the fall of the Iron Curtain and a myriad of evolving conflicts in the former Soviet Block. The rising tensions in the former Republic of Yugoslavia, Georgia and South Ossetia as well as in Abkhazia caused well-founded fear of ethnic tensions and violent conflicts within and between the new states in Central and Eastern Europe.[2] Therefore, the logic in 1992 during the Helsinki Conference was to prevent minority related tensions within a participating state from escalating into an inter-state conflict through the intervention of the HCNM at the "earliest possible stage".[3]

The general idea behind the establishment of the HCNM was that tensions between national minorities within one state could pose a threat to peace and stability between neighboring states if they developed into a more violent conflict. The term "High Commissioner *on* National Minorities" is used instead of "High Commissioner *of* National Minorities". This reflects that the focus is on minority protection as a tool

---

2 CHRISTIANE HÖHN, ZWISCHEN MENSCHENRECHTEN UND KONFLIKTPRÄVENTION 292 (2005); WALTER A. KEMP, QUIET DIMPLOMACY IN ACTION 4 (2005).

3 Para. 3 of the Mandate.

for guaranteeing peace and political stability within the OSCE area and not primarily as an independent value.[4]

II. Characteristics of the HCNM's Work – Peace-Building and Stability Through the Standard-Setting and Mediation in a Tense Political Area

The first characteristic of the HCNM's work is that he acts in the context of an international body, the OSCE, whose legal nature is still highly debatable. Even the legal nature of all OSCE-documents, on which the work of the HCNM is based, is still controversial. The categorizations vary between international treaties without the classical state responsibility and jurisdiction,[5] soft law with binding political effect,[6] and strictly non-binding political commitments.[7] The only thing which can be said with some certainty is that the OSCE-documents do not constitute international treaties in the classical and formal sense. Nevertheless, they are aimed at producing, at the very least, strong commitments and are in fact very effective.[8]

---

[4] KEMP (note 2), at 54-55; Rob Zaagman, *The CSCE High Commissioner on National Minorities: An analysis of the Mandate and the Institutional Context*, in THE CHALLENGE OF CHANGE: THE HELSINKI SUMMIT OF THE CSCE AND ITS AFTERMATH 113, 127, 140 (Arie Bloed ed., 1994).

[5] JULIA MARQUIER, SOFT LAW: DAS BEISPIEL DES OSZE-PROZESSES 212, 219 (2004); JAN KLABBERS, THE CONCEPT OF TREATY IN INTERNATIONAL LAW 126 (1996).

[6] Ulrich Fastenrath, *The Legal Significance of CSCE/OSCE Documents*, OSCE-YEARBOOK 1995/1996 411, 418; Theodor Schweisfurth, *Die juristische Mutation der KSZE, in* RECHT ZWISCHEN BEWAHRUNG UND UMBRUCH 213, 224 (Ulrich Beyerlin ed., 1995); Theodor Schweisfurth, *Zur Frage der Rechtsnatur, Verbindlichkeit und völkerrechtlichen Relevanz der KSZE-Schlussakte*, 36 ZEITSCHRIFT FÜR AUSLÄNDISCHES ÖFFENTLICHES RECHT UND VÖLKERRECHT (ZAÖRV) 681, 695 (1976); MARCUS WENIG, MÖGLICHKEITEN UND GRENZEN DER STREITBEILEGUNG ETHNISCHER KONFLIKTE DURCH DIE OSZE 59-64, 72 (1996); Rob Zaagman, *Focus on the Future*, 6 HELSINKI MONITOR 40, 42 (1995).

[7] KNUT IPSEN & VOLKER EPPING, VÖLKERRECHT 529-530 (5th ed., 2004).

[8] For a detailed analysis of the effectiveness *see* Comparative Case Studies on the Effectiveness of the OSCE High Commissioner on National Minorities, CORE WORKING PAPERS 6, 7, 8 and 10 (Wolfgang Zellner, Randolf Oberschmidt & Claus Neukirch eds., 2002), available at: http://www.core-hamburg.de/CORE/pub_workingpapers.htm.

Against this background, the first High Commissioner has developed two instruments, which are central for the fulfillment of his tasks: general recommendations and country-specific recommendations. Both were not foreseen by his Mandate.

The general recommendations fulfill the function of developing general strategies and standards for the protection and political integration of national minorities in all participating states. They serve as standards – usually particularizing existing international obligations – for his expectations vis-à-vis the OSCE-states concerning a specific aspect of minority protection. The term standard in this context is understood as including all commitments and responsibilities below the level of formally binding rights and obligations.

The country-specific recommendations create concrete requirements for each state and each situation. These requirements are generated on the basis of the general recommendations developed by the HCNM, which form thematic compilations of international minority-related standards and rights.

In this respect the HCNM exercises public authority in two ways also present in domestic administrative law:[9] firstly he acts as a *standard-setter* by particularizing international rights and standards, and secondly as a *monitoring-body* by supervising the compliance of the participating states with these standards.

The focus on the exercise of public authority through the HCNM's work allows a structuring of the institutional arrangement and the activities of the HCNM[10] and provides legal criteria to assess the principles governing the work of the HCNM.[11]

Of special interest is the exercise of public authority for tackling traditional international issues, such as conflict prevention in this specific case. This might inform us about the general effectiveness of this kind of the exercise of public authority for conflict prevention.[12]

---

9 RICHARD J. PIERCE, SIDNEY A. SHAPIRO & PAUL R. VERKUIL, ADMINISTRATIVE LAW AND PROCESS 285-308 (4th ed., 2004); HARTMUT MAURER, ALLGEMEINES VERWALTUNGSRECHT 6-9 (16th ed., 2006); Karsten Herzmann, *Monitoring als Verwaltungsaufgabe*, DEUTSCHES VERWALTUNGSBLATT (DVBl) 670-674 (2007); PAUL CRAIG, ADMINISTRATIVE LAW 398-405 (5th ed., 2003).

10 Chapter C.

11 Chapter D.

12 Chapter D.

C. Independent Standard-Setting and Mediative Monitoring Within the OSCE-Framework

The following chapter analyzes the legal framework of the HCNM's work. In the first section of this chapter, few comments as to the role of the HCNM in the OSCE-framework will be made. The second section will deal with the question in how far the HCNM's work is directed by his Mandate. The third section will illustrate a typology of the instruments of the HCNM: general recommendations and country-specific recommendations. The examination of the implementation and the monitoring-procedures will finally reveal several interesting multi-level aspects of the HCNM's work.

I. The Institutional Framework – An Independent Office within a Broader Context

The HCNM is an "instrument" of the OSCE,[13] possessing legal personality under Dutch law according to Section 2 para. 1 of the Dutch HCNM Act.[14] The HCNM is on the one hand a bureaucracy comprising 25 staff members in The Hague (HCNM) and, on the other hand a person (the High Commissioner), which is consensually appointed by the Permanent Council[15] for a period of three years.[16] Beside this appointment the role of the HCNM within the OSCE framework is characterized by his independence from the other institutions of the OSCE. This is emphasized by the fact that the High Commissioner has full discretion concerning the decision to intervene[17] and a formal consultation or request is rarely required by the Mandate.[18]

---

13 Para. 2 of the Mandate.

14 HCNM Wet, 31 October 2002, Staatsblad 2002, at 580.

15 The Mandate originally conferred this power to the Committee of Senior Officials (CSO), which was followed by the Senior Council (SC). Meanwhile this task shifted to the Permanent Council (PC).

16 Para. 9 of the Mandate.

17 Paras. 3, 13 of the Mandate.

18 Paras. 7, 17 of the Mandate.

II. Programming an International Public Authority – Clear Objectives and Vague Competences

The main legal basis for the work of the HCNM is the Mandate as it was concluded in 1992 in Copenhagen by a consensus of the then participating states. The legality of OSCE-documents aside, the Mandate fulfills in fact the same function as any other founding document establishing an institution within an international organization. It is intended to be the legal basis of the HCNM's work, to define the aims and competences as well as the procedures he has to follow. Otherwise it would be of no value to establish rules regulating his work at all.

The provisions of the Mandate contain objectives as well as competences. The general objective of the HCNM is, according to said Mandate, to "provide 'early warning' and – if appropriate – 'early action' [...] in regard to tensions involving national minority issues which [...] have the potential to develop into a conflict within the OSCE area, affecting peace, stability or relations between participating States [...]."[19] Hence, the objective to provide an early warning mechanism is quite clear.

The field of application is defined negatively by exclusion of three specific situations: national minority issues in situations "involving organized acts of terrorism",[20] purely inner-state conflicts[21] and violations of the Conference on Security and Co-operation in Europe (CSCE) commitments "with regard to an individual person belonging to a national minority".[22]

Conversely, concrete actions are described vaguely and at a very abstract level as the Mandate neither includes any concrete means which can or should be taken nor any procedural rules.[23] Therefore, it is the High Commissioner himself who developed concrete mechanisms and measures to reach his objectives, among those the two types of recommendations mentioned above. These recommendations have been de-

19 Para. 3 of the Mandate.

20 Para. 5 b of the Mandate.

21 Para. 2 of the Mandate.

22 Para. 5c of the Mandate.

23 Para. 12 of the Mandate: The HCNM "*may* during a visit [...] discuss the questions with the parties, and *where appropriate* promote dialogue [...]" (emphasis added); Para 13: "*If* [...] [the HCNM] concludes that that there is a prima facie risk [...], he/she *may* issue an early warning." (emphasis added).

veloped in a uniform structure and with certain reoccurring elements, which lead to a kind of standardization of the work of the HCNM not foreseen by the Mandate. In the next section this will be demonstrated with regard to the procedural and substantial regime of these two instruments.

III. Standard-Setting and the Emergence of a Pyramid of Norms – A Typology of the Instruments of HCNM Public Authority

This section aims at displaying a typology of the instruments of the HCNM in order to highlight their use as an exercise of public authority. The first and second section demonstrates that the work of the HCNM has generated a high level of standardization through unitary forms (1.) and procedures (2.). In the third section the substantive aspects regarding the regulatory instruments will be illuminated (3.). Pursuant to the special focus on the exercise of public authority it is of particular interest that the typology of instruments reveals a pyramid of norms, as to be disclosed in the fourth section (4.). Finally it will become clear that this is not just a political accident, but required for normative reasons (5.).

1. Standardization of the Form and the Development of the Central Instruments

The general recommendations and the country-specific recommendations can be qualified as the central instruments of the HCNM because they are the most effective instruments used for the implementation of minority protection standards in the participating states.[24] The country-specific recommendations were created by the first High Commissioner to address the states involved in certain situations concerning the protection of minority rights. Their idea is to loosely replicate in written and more formalized form, what the High Commissioner had tried to convey to the parties during his visit. They suggest concrete steps for a solution.[25] At the same time they fulfill an informative function for

---

24 *See* Zellner, Oberschmidt & Neukirch (note 8).

25 Kemp (note 2), at 56.

other OSCE-organs, especially the Chairman-in-Office, to whom the High Commissioner submits the recommendations regularly.[26]

While the country-specific recommendations aim essentially at the solution of a concrete conflict, the general recommendations serve as guidelines for the requirements of the HCNM vis-à-vis the participating countries. They are directed at the participating states as they set standards for their behavior towards minorities within their territory. Their aim is to try to provide coherent political and legal concepts in specific fields of minority protection. As the general recommendations are elaborated by expert groups,[27] it is clear that they do not impose any obligations on the member states,[28] but can create standards in the sense defined above.[29]

In order to underline the suggestion that the HCNM's work is an exercise of public authority the two types of recommendations will be analyzed first with special regard to the standardization of the form, before then examining the standardization of the procedure through which these instruments are decided upon. Standardization of the form is one of the main characteristics of administrative procedures. However, the Mandate itself does not prescribe any specific form for the general or for the country-specific recommendations.

a) The Form of the General Recommendations

To be a useful tool in the hands of the HCNM and to inform the OSCE-states about the minority related requirements concerning specific themes, general recommendations have a written form and are made public on the website of the HCNM.

---

26 *Id.* at 58. The OSCE Chairmanship is held by one participating State for one calendar year and is supposed to co-ordinate the decision-making process and to set priorities for the activities during that year. The Chairmanship is headed by the Chairman-in-Office (CiO), which is usually the Foreign Minister of the State concerned. His tasks are defined as the co-ordination of and consultation on current OSCE business and he presides over Summits and the Ministerial Council, the two central decision-taking organs of the OSCE. For further information *see* OSCE HANDBOOK (2007), available at http://www.osce.org.

27 The detailed procedural aspects will be explained under point III.2.

28 Para. 34, sentence 2 of the Mandate.

29 *See* B. II.

Another interesting aspect is the repeated and almost formalized reference to the normative framework of international minority protection out of which the content of the general recommendations is formed. In the first four of his five general recommendations the HCNM has always referred to the international law provision on which he based his recommendations. In the last of his guidelines[30] he did not mention any standard or right with reference to minority issues any more. Instead he elaborated his standards more or less independently. This was criticized in the literature.[31] Apparently the lack of citation of concrete norms of international law is seen as a formal deficit affecting the recommendations' success and usefulness.

This illustrates that through the development of the first four general recommendations the High Commissioner had already established formal standards for the elaboration of this instrument which were not only accepted but also expected by the different actors involved in minority issues. The self-binding effect with regard to this new formal requirement reveals a first standard-setting function of this procedure.

b) The Form of the Country-Specific Recommendations

The country-specific recommendations usually take the form of a follow-up letter addressed to the foreign minister of the country concerned after a visit of the High Commissioner and after a process of dialog between him and the parties involved.[32] As the country-specific recommendations are not foreseen by the Mandate, there exist no requirements as to their form.

2. *Standardization of the Procedure Regarding the Central Instruments*

Not only the standardized form of the instruments of public authority take, but as well of the procedure through which they are decided upon, is characteristic for any legal administrative regulation. Therefore it is telling to examine elements of standardization in the procedures regard-

---

[30] Recommendation on Policing in Multi-Ethnic Societies, available at: http://www.osce.org/ documents/hcnm/2006/02/17982_en.pdf.

[31] Arie Bloed, *Comments on the new set of Recommendations on Policing in Multi-Ethnic Societies*, 17 HELSINKI MONITOR 184, 187 (2006).

[32] *Id.*

ing the two central instruments, through which the HCNM exercises public authority.

a) Procedure for the General Recommendations

The strong institutionalized influence of experts is of special interest regarding the procedure for making general recommendations. The Mandate prescribes in considerable detail the possible involvement of experts in the work of the HCNM. According to para. 31 of the Mandate the High Commissioner "may decide to request assistance from [...] experts with relevant expertise in specific matters". For that purpose he will set "a clearly defined Mandate and time-frame for the activities of the experts".[33] Finally the High Commissioner "will be responsible for the activities and for the reports of the experts and will decide whether and in what form the advice and recommendations will be communicated to the states concerned".[34] In addition, the procedure concerning the elaboration of the general recommendations is regulated by para. 35 of the Mandate, which prescribes that the experts "will be selected by the High Commissioner with assistance of the Office for Democratic Institutions and Human Rights (ODIHR) from a resource list established at the ODIHR as laid down in the Document of the Moscow Meeting".

Despite the detailed procedural prescription, the reality of the HCNM's work is quite different. Until 1999 it was the Foundation on Inter-Ethnic Relations (FIER) that organized an international expert consultation on different themes. In spite of its formally independent character, the FIER worked hand in hand with the High Commissioner and his office, which were located in the same building as the FIER in The Hague.[35] The first expert consultations on request of the High Commissioner lead to the elaboration of The Hague Recommendations Regarding Education Rights of National Minorities. After the dissolution of the FIER in 1999 and its incorporation in the office of the HCNM, it is now the High Commissioner himself who invites the expert group

---

33 Para. 32 of the Mandate.

34 Para. 34 of the Mandate.

35 KEMP (note 2), at 100; Kemp formulates that "its very *raison d'être* was to serve the High Commissioner", due to the fact that the FIER was founded on the initiative of the first HCNM, Max van der Stoel, who was also adviser to the Board of Directors of the FIER.

and who publishes the general recommendations. The draft recommendation of the expert group is edited by the High Commissioner and then "endorsed" through publication.

Regardless of these differences between the wording of the Mandate and the *de facto* procedure, the reality of the elaboration of the general recommendations is characterized by a surprisingly high standardization. All general recommendations have been elaborated by expert groups on a formal request of the High Commissioner who finally endorsed the general recommendations, after he had edited them.

b) Procedure for the County-Specific Recommendation

The procedure followed for the country-specific recommendations developed by the High Commissioner also reveals differences in comparison to the formal procedure described in the Mandate. The High Commissioner has full discretion as to whether a situation might become a conflict situation and therefore needs his involvement. The procedure in para. 7 of the Mandate, prescribing the requirement of a formal request of the Senior Council in cases "when a particular national minority issue has been brought to the attention of the Council of Senior Officials (CSO)",[36] was never followed. The only two statements of the Senior Council – during a crisis in Estonia in 1993[37] and concerning the issue of Crimea in 1994[38] – were formulated as invitations for the involvement of the HCNM or as support for his activities. A formal mandate by the Senior Council or Permanent Council has never been a prerequisite to the involvement of the HCNM.[39]

In order to consider whether a situation requires his involvement or not, the HCNM receives "information regarding the situation of national minorities and the role of the parties involved from any source",[40] including media and non-governmental organizations. He also receives specific reports from parties directly involved regarding developments

---

[36] Now Senior Counsel.

[37] 22nd CSO Journal no. 2, annex 2, 30 June 1993.

[38] 27th CSO Journal no. 3, annex 2, 23 September 1993, the CSO expressed his support for "the continued activities of the High Commissioner on National Minorities in the Ukraine".

[39] Zaagman (note 4), at 170.

[40] Para. 23a of the Mandate.

concerning national minorities.[41] The latter can be governments, regional and local authorities as well as representatives of associations, non-governmental organizations, religious and other groups of national minorities directly concerned, which are authorized by the persons belonging to those national minorities to represent them.[42] Apart from the representatives of a concrete minority the most important non-governmental organizations involved in the work of the HCNM are the European Centre for Minority Issues (ECMI) in Flensburg (Germany) and the Minority Rights Group (MRG) in London (UK). The latter are frequently consulted and provide information and data for the HCNM.[43]

Since the beginning of his work the HCNM has clearly avoided the need to reach the formal stage of early warning as it is foreseen in the Mandate by paras. 13, 14 and 15 as well as the "early action"-procedure of para. 16. The first High Commissioner Max van der Stoel thought that bringing a conflict into the stage of early warning would probably aggravate the tensions, as the topic would then be discussed publicly in the Permanent Council. He preferred to enlarge his spectrum of activities in the first stage before coming to the warning.[44] Conflict identification and fact finding therefore constitute the most important area of activities of the HCNM nowadays.

Here the visits in a country of concern, according to paras. 23, 24 of the Mandate, are of special importance in order to ascertain concrete problems and interests involved, to monitor the tensions and to analyze the structure of a specific conflict. The Mandate does not explicitly require any consent of the countries concerned, but requires a previous consultation of the Chairman-in-Office.[45] Practically the High Commissioner has often informed the Chairman-in-Office prior to his departure and sometimes even asked his opinion as to whether the HCNM should become involved in a situation. However, the main objective of this provision of the Mandate, namely that the Chairman would consult the involved parties on the basis of the information provided by the HCNM,

---

41 Para. 23b of the Mandate.

42 Para. 26 of the Mandate.

43 Interview with Krzysztof Drzewicki, Senior Legal Adviser of the HCNM, 29 May 2007 in The Hague.

44 KEMP (note 2), at 83-84.

45 Paras. 27-30 of the Mandate.

has never been followed in this strict sense.[46] To gather more information about a conflict the High Commissioner sometimes uses the existing ODIHR missions in a country as his "eyes and ears".[47]

During the first visit the High Commissioner usually tries to uncover the root causes of a conflict and to establish a permanent dialog between the parties concerned as well as to foster an atmosphere of understanding between the parties. Round tables and discussion groups are the main tools in this arena. This stage of fact finding and visits functions as a facilitator of dialog and participation. Here the High Commissioner tries to come to an acceptable solution for all parties involved, he tries to understand their interests as well as the technical and political obstacles to a solution of the conflict. Against this background his aim is to mediate a possible solution between the parties. These solutions are then laid down in the concrete recommendations.

After the visit, the High Commissioner – in accordance with para. 18 of the Mandate – submits strictly confidential reports to the Chairman-in-Office. He provides information about his visit and his assessment of the situation as well as an overview of the positions of the different actors and parties involved. In this report he also provides the results of his confidential discussions with different actor as well as background information. In contrast to the diplomatic formulation of the recommendations, these reports are more open and combined with an honest political assessment of the situation concerned.[48]

Unlike these reports, the country-specific-recommendations are more carefully formulated and describe specific suggestions, which in his opinion might solve the conflict. These recommendations are exclusively addressed to the participating states involved. They are usually not sent to the minority group in question, but there have been occasions when the High Commissioner has asked the government to forward his recommendations to the minority representatives.[49] Due to the fact that the country-specific-recommendations are usually not sent to the minority party this mechanism is frequently described as "quiet diplomacy".[50]

---

46 KEMP (note 2), at 91.

47 *Id.* at 96; Margit Sarv, *Integration by Reframing Legislation*, *in* CORE WORKING PAPER 7 (note 8).

48 KEMP (note 2), at 91.

49 KEMP (note 2), at 56.

50 *Id.*

The term "quiet diplomacy" also describes the fact that the recommendations are usually withheld from the public from the outset to ensure a time without public scrutiny and in which the parties can act in good-faith.[51] During this period of confidentiality quiet diplomacy activities can be pursued and the state has time to consider, react and already implement recommendations. The foreign minister of the country concerned always has the possibility to respond to the recommendation before they are made public.[52] Finally most letters until 2001 were made public in order to inform all interested parties about the opinions and recommendations of the High Commissioner and the government concerned.[53] This was originally rendered possible through a formal decision by the Permanent Council by which the letters became an official OSCE document. Later they were simply released into the public domain some time after the High Commissioner reported their contents to the Permanent Council.[54] Contrary to this practice the country-specific recommendations were withheld from the public under the second High Commissioner, Rolf Ekéus.

After the dialog in form of the country-specific recommendation and the follow-up letters of the foreign minister the High Commissioner decides, whether a successful solution has been found. Otherwise he can decide to continue the monitoring of the situation. In the worst case he deems that his scope for action is exhausted without success. In this case he has to inform the Permanent Council about this assessment.[55]

Here an even stronger standardization of the procedure takes place despite several deviations from the Mandate. The general idea of the vague provisions of the Mandate has been transformed into an effective detailed procedure by the High Commissioner. This procedure contains the unifying elements of fact finding, dialog and a suggestion for the solution of a tension.

---

51 JONATHAN COHEN, CONFLICT PREVENTION INSTRUMENTS IN THE OSCE: AN ASSESSMENT OF CAPACITIES 64 (1998); KEMP (note 2), at 59.

52 This procedure follows the right to comment recommendations elaborated by experts as it is foreseen by para. 34 of the Mandate.

53 Para. 34 of the Mandate.

54 *Id.*

55 Para. 20 of the Mandate.

c) Particularizing General Standards through a Mediative Approach

The elaboration-procedure of the country-specific recommendations is characterized by a cooperative and dialog-oriented process, which includes the parties directly involved. The idea is to adjust the international standard of minority protection to the country-specific situation by searching for a solution together with the parties involved. This includes tension-reducing projects such as workshops and round-tables.[56] The aim of this procedure is not primarily to end up with a shaming of the state acting contrary to international standards. Rather the focus of the procedure established by the High Commissioner is to find a solution for a specific conflict which respects the interests of both parties involved as far as possible – the state's as well as the minority's. The described procedure involves the conflicting parties from the beginning and the High Commissioner himself takes more the role of a mediator of a conflict who finally articulates his recommendations. To particularize international norms regarding minority protection is indeed a kind of mediative process by the High Commissioner in the sense that it aims at brokering two diverging positions with the help of a third actor, without the need for coercive measures. The process includes elements of communication, formulation and manipulation as they are characteristic of mediative procedures.[57] Nevertheless his activity differs from traditional mediation-theories as he simultaneously acts as a monitoring-body for the compliance with international standards and obligations.[58] The mediative character of specifying more general norms and standards seems to be an appropriate approach to reach at the same time compliance with standards and the solution of a conflict.

d) Conclusion

The forms of the two central instruments as well as their procedures reveal standardization, which is a characteristic effect of administrative procedures. Nevertheless this is only a first formal indicator. To further

---

[56] KEMP (note 2), at 74-75.

[57] Saadia Touval & Ira William Zartman, *Introduction: Mediation in Theory*, *in* INTERNATIONAL MEDIATION IN THEORY AND PRACTICE (Saadia Touval & Ira William Zartman eds., 1995).

[58] Ratner qualifies the HCNM as a "normative intermediary". Steven Ratner, *Does International Law Matter in Ethnic Conflicts?*, 32 NYU JOURNAL OF INTERNATIONAL LAW AND POLITICS 591, 668-684 (2000).

corroborate the thesis of the recommendations as an exercise of public authority we take a closer look at the substantive law governing these instruments.

3. *"Translation" of International Law – the Substantive Framework*

As described above, general recommendations usually refer to all the relevant norms and standards on an international or regional level. Out of these norms and standards the requirements, aims, and policy guidelines concerning a specific topic of minority protection are developed. The general recommendations "translate"[59] different responsibilities and legal obligations out of a myriad of international and regional treaties and agreements as well as "best practices" on the national level in relation to minority issues into a concrete set of requirements concerning a specific topic.[60] It is crucial to bear in mind that even national arrangements or international norms which may not be directed to all OSCE-states – as they are for example not party to a cited treaty or agreement – are transformed through this mechanism into standards addressed to all OSCE participating states.[61]

For the country-specific recommendations the High Commissioner can in principle freely decide on which provision he will base his recommendations or warnings in a concrete case. He chooses the particular standards or rights, which he considers being the most accepted by the involved parties.[62] This discretion is a key factor for the success of the High Commissioner's work as it allows him to be sensitive to the needs of each actor involved. Furthermore it strengthens his credibility by avoiding a "one size fits all"-solution in the sensitive area of minority protection.

Two other aspects of the substantive standards governing the work of the High Commissioner contribute to an adequate method of dealing with crucial minority protection related issues: firstly he refers to the general recommendations while formulating concrete suggestions in the country-specific recommendation; secondly he refers to international obligations, *e.g.* to higher norms, while elaborating his thematic standards in the general recommendations.

---

59 HÖHN (note 2), at 324; Ratner (note 58), at 624.

60 HÖHN (note 2), at 322-327.

61 *Id.* at 349-352.

62 *Id.*

In the practice of the HCNM one can hence observe a substantive standardization as the counterpart to the above described formal standardization. The standardization in these two aspects allows for a further classification of the exercise of public authority through the HCNM's activities as we will see in the next section.

4. The Pyramid of Norms in the Activities of the HCNM

If we consider on the one hand that there exists a certain flexibility in the applicable substantive law and that on the other hand the HCNM acts in a mere political framework, one might ask why these instruments should represent anything more than mere politics. How can we conclude that the two types of recommendations can be conceived of as an exercise of public authority at all?

A first argument can be drawn from the fact that the described typology and substantive standardization reveals a pyramid of norms, which is quite similar to the pyramids of norms governing the exercise of public authority at a domestic level.

Both types of recommendations refer to international obligations concerning minority protection. This includes all relevant OSCE Documents, the Framework Convention on National Minorities, Art. 27 International Covenant on Civil and Political Rights, the European Convention on Human Rights, documents of the United Nations (UN) concerning minorities etc. The notion "international standard" in the documents of the HCNM characterizes the *aquis* of the minority protection rights and standards existing on a regional and international level.[63] Therefore, we can state that the international obligations on minority protection constitute a first layer of substantive law.

The general recommendations translate these various international standards and norms into concrete standards concerning one specific aspect of minority protection. The general recommendations form a quasi-secondary level law set by the HCNM.

The country-specific recommendation in turn particularizes the general recommendations, as it formulates concrete suggestions for the solution of a situation of tension. It differs from the exercise of public authority in the national context insofar as it is aimed rather at advising and enabling the parties to find a solution between them and forms in this respect part of a mediation process. Nevertheless the country-specific

---

63 Ratner (note 58), at 591, 659.

recommendation is the last step in the procedure particularizing a general norm, though which the latter is applied to a concrete situation.

Recalling the high level of formal standardization, we see that the instruments of the HCNM constitute a formalized specification, as they transform general standards into concrete ones through a formally standardized procedure. They therefore fulfill an administrative function.[64] It is precisely the difference between politics and law that the latter allows for particularizing abstract requirements within a formalized procedure. Through the pyramid of norms and the standardization of form and procedure, we can qualify the two recommendations as the exercise of public authority.

5. *Just Practice or Normative Points of Reference?*

Hitherto it has only been outlined that a pyramid of norms exists in the practice of the HCNM. However, the idea of the exercise of public authority through the tools used by the HCNM is still fragile as it does not answer the question whether this pyramid evolved accidentally due to the strategic ideas of the current High Commissioner. In other words, is there any normative reason why the High Commissioner is cannot ignore the general recommendations while elaborating a specific one?

This is critical especially because of their explicit non-binding character as recommendations of experts, according to para. 34, sentence 2 of the Mandate. It is a core element of modern legal systems that standards are always modifiable through democratic procedures unless there is a hierarchy of standards, through which the higher standard determines the lower one.[65] Even if the specific recommendations are more detailed than the general ones, they normatively form part of the same rank of norms as they are both enacted by the High Commissioner on the basis of the Mandate. The Mandate does not prescribe any hierarchical rela-

---

64 Max Weber, *Bürokratismus, in* IV WIRTSCHAFT UND GESELLSCHAFT 159, 186-189 (Edith Hanke ed., 2005); MAX WEBER, RECHTSSOZIOLOGIE 123-126 (Heinz Maus & Friedrich Fürstenberg eds., 1967); NIKLAS LUHMANN, LEGITIMATION DURCH VERFAHREN 204-207 (Heinz Maus & Friedrich Fürstenberg eds., 1969).

65 HANS KELSEN, REINE RECHTSLEHRE 228-230 (1960); ALF ROSS, THEORIE DER RECHTSQUELLEN 359-369 (1929); Adolf Merkl, *Prolegomena einer Theorie des rechtlichen Stufenbaus, in* GESELLSCHAFT, STAAT UND RECHT 252, 272-285 (Alfred Verdross ed., 1931).

tion between these two instruments nor include the general recommendations any instruction to elaborate specific ones. Consequently the *lex posterior*-rule, which applies in all cases of absence of a hierarchy,[66] would have to be applicable in this context.

Therefore, to assume a binding effect of the general recommendations, it is necessary to identify a normative argument for the primacy of the general over the specific recommendations.[67]

The recourse to the principle of sovereign equality as it is laid down in Art 2, no. 1 of the Charter of the United Nations and the principle of impartiality laid down in paras. 4 and 8 of the Mandate allow arguing for a binding effect of a standard for the elaboration of others at the same rank. The principle of impartiality in the Mandate can be interpreted as a translation of the general principle of equality within the context of the HCNM. The ratio behind the principle of impartiality is not only that a neutral behavior of the High Commissioner is useful for his credibility vis-à-vis the participating states. In fact it is the idea that the participating states have agreed upon the OSCE-commitments as equal parties on the basis of sovereign equality. This premise for the agreement would be destroyed if unequal requirements were born out of these commitments through their application by the HCNM.

The general recommendations particularize the regulations in a variety of international treaties and the OSCE-commitments concerned with minority protection. They therefore constitute a tool for reviewing the compliance with international treaties and commitments. If the High Commissioner decides against this background to base a country-specific recommendation concerning one participating state on the requirements defined within the general recommendation, it is not possible for him to apply a different standard vis-à-vis another state. The general recommendations compile international standards of minority protection concerning a specific thematic aspect. As a compilation of the *aquis* in international minority protection they are addressed to all OSCE participating states. They serve as a guideline for the minority protection in each member state and set out the expectations of the HCNM. To apply a standard set out in the general recommendations in one case and a different and even contradictory standard in another case would constitute an unequal treatment of two states which would ex-

---

[66] JÜRGEN BAST, GRUNDBEGRIFFE DER HANDLUNGSFORMEN DER EU 222 (2006).

[67] *Id.*

pect that the benchmark for their activities in the field of minority protection would be these general recommendations.

There is no doubt that it is also possible to interpret the general recommendations as mere informative compilations for the protection of minorities, *i.e.* as pure policy guidelines. This interpretation nevertheless has to be abandoned as soon as the High Commissioner himself explicitly applies the standard set out by the general recommendations in order to review a state's behavior. In this case the principle of impartiality in the Mandate and the general principle of sovereign equality transform the general recommendations from mere informative instruments into self-binding ones. As long as the general recommendations are not formally amended by the High Commissioner he is then bound to apply the same benchmark in every case.

Due to these principles the High Commissioner is normatively bound by the general recommendations while elaborating a specific one. From this perspective the general recommendations are comparable to the communications of the European Commission.[68] They fulfill the function of a secondary level law, advancing a hierarchy of different levels of provisions within the framework of the HCNM as they create a new layer of law not provided by the Mandate but nevertheless applied by the HCNM.

IV. Effective Soft Law through a Manifold Monitoring System

After charting the main instruments of the HCNM with all their procedural and substantial aspects, it is now necessary to ascertain how useful these instruments are in legal practice and how a minimum of effectiveness is guaranteed. The recommendations – the specific as well as the general ones – are all non-binding instruments.[69] Their implementation is entirely dependent upon the discretion of the recipient state.[70] The transformation depends on the national legal system and subjects concerned. Despite this explicit characterization as non-binding a remarkable debate nonetheless ensued surrounding the recommendations questioning the difference between hard law and soft law within the

68 LINDA SENDEN, SOFT LAW IN EUROPEAN COMMUNITY LAW 140, 143-145 (2004).

69 Para. 34 of the Mandate.

70 KEMP (note 2), at 59.

context of the OSCE, due to the enormous effectiveness of the recommendations.[71]

There already exists a wealth of scholarly literature testifying that the standards set by the HCNM are in fact at least as effective as hard law even if they remain in the sphere of standards, as provisions under the level of formal international law.[72] There is no need for reiteration here. Instead, it suffices to make a note of the effectiveness of the recommendations of the HCNM and to stress three aspects of specific interest for the focus on the exercise of public authority through the HCNM's work.

1. Enforcement of International Law

The first interesting aspect with regard to enforcement mechanisms of international bureaucracies is that the HCNM serves as a monitoring body for several international treaties containing provisions with regard to minority protection. The HCNM bases the general recommendations explicitly not only on the OSCE commitments but also on formal international law. By doing so he fulfills monitoring functions for international treaties external to his own international organization.

2. Implementation through Capacity Building

Already the elaboration of the country-specific recommendation illustrates that the High Commissioner is focused on the elimination of all practical and political obstacles to the effective enforcement of minority rights. During the fact-finding and mediation process the High Commissioner already tries to initiate round-tables and work-shops concerning the respect of minority protection rights. These activities sometimes also include policy training.[73] The HCNM furthermore tries to

---

[71] John Packer, *Making International Law Matter in Preventing Ethnic Conflicts*, 32 NYU JOURNAL OF INTERNATIONAL LAW & POLITICS 715-724 (2000); Ratner (note 58), at 659-668; HÖHN (note 2), at 205-231.

[72] Packer (note 71); Ratner (note 58); COHEN (note 51); Sarv (note 47); Volodymyr Kulyk, *Revisting A Success Story, in* CORE WORKING PAPER 7 (note 8), at 1-146; David Galbreath, *The Politics of European Integration and Minority Rights in Estonia and Latvia,* 4 PERSPECTIVES ON EUROPEAN POLITICS AND SOCIETY 36, 45 (2003).

[73] KEMP (note 2), at 74-75.

secure financial support for the establishment of infrastructure necessary for a continued institutional dialog and the guarantee of equal treatment of minorities in the social, political and economic spheres.[74] It is a characteristic of the HCNM's monitoring mechanism that it is based on capacity building taking into account the specific needs of each conflict situation.

3. Implementation though Multi-Level Cooperation

Finally, one of the motors for the effective implementation of the standards set by the HCNM is an alliance with other actors in the field of minority protection. In this sense the fruitful relations between the HCNM and the European Union (EU) is of particular importance. During the accession procedure for aspiring new EU members the country-specific recommendations of the HCNM have found their way into the monitoring reports prepared annually by the European Commission for each of the candidate states.[75] They were also explicitly referred to in the strategy paper concerning the accession of 2000.[76] In this respect the HCNM plays a key role in the policy development of the EU's foreign and enlargement policies,[77] whereby the EU plays at the same time a major role for the effective enforcement of the HCNM's recommendations. Through this avenue he increasingly influences the emerging inner-EU-standards of the protection of national minorities through his guidelines and state recommendations.[78] The cooperation between the EU and the HCNM can be described as an in-

---

[74] Kemp describes the vivid example of the Crimean Conflict in the Ukraine, during which the HCNM organized for example a donor conference in 1996; Kemp (note 2), at 222-229.

[75] For the example of Estonia *see* Sarv (note 47), at 79-83, 108-110.

[76] COM (2000) 704 final, Regular Report from the Commission on Estonia's Progress towards Accession, at 18-20, COM (2000) 706 final, Regular Report from the Commission on Latvia's Progress towards Accession, at 23.

[77] Galbreath (note 72), at 36-53, 45. For the latest development *see* Krzysztof Drzewicki, *National Minority Issues and the EU Reform Treaty. A Perspective of the OSCE High Commissioner on National Minorities,* 2 SECURITY AND HUMAN RIGHTS (SHR) 137-146 (2008).

[78] For the influence of external minority protection on the internal EU-standard of minority protection: EU Network of independent experts on fundamental rights, Thematic comment no. 3, available at: http://www.ec.europa.eu/justice_home/cfr_cdf/doc/thematic_comments_2005_en.pdf.

strumental cross-linkage, as the EU also uses the instruments developed by the HCNM.

Another example of a fruitful, though not unambiguous, cooperation is the relation between the HCNM and the Council of Europe (CoE) and his work in the field of minority protection. The two organizations mutually refer to their documents when assessing minority related conflicts. They also increased the practice of "enhanced cooperation",[79] a mechanism aimed a establishing a permanent dialog between the CoE organs and the HCNM through a coordination group and a regular consultation between the so called "focal points" of the OSCE and the CoE.[80] One striking example of this mutual influence is the development of minority protection in Estonia, where the desire to ease the country's entrance into the CoE enforced the implementation of the HCNM's requirements.[81] The fragmentation because of overlapping activities of the HCNM and the CoE with diverging interpretations of minority protections standards can be at least reduced by these mechanisms. The cooperation in this case is not only instrumental, but at the same time institutional as the HCNM and the CoE established an own coordination group guaranteeing a regular dialog and exchange.

In this light the monitoring mechanisms used by the HCNM's work can be characterized by cooperation, mediation and recourse to international norms.

D. Confidentiality and Mediation as Two Sides of One Coin – Principles and Perspectives

This last chapter will outline principles which can be identified in the law of the HCNM as described above. The function and consequences of these principles are to be assessed. Thereby their ambivalent character regarding efficiency on the one and legitimacy and transparency on the other hand is demonstrated. Finally suggestions for lessons to be drawn out of the use of these tools in a political context concerning effective conflict prevention will be presented.

---

79 Krzysztof Drzewicki & Vincent de Graaf, *The Activities of the OSCE High Commissioner on National Minorities: July 2004-June 2005*, 4 EUROPEAN YEARBOOK OF MINORITY ISSUES (EYMI) 595-613, 600, 601 (2004/2005).

80 For the OSCE this is the High Commissioner.

81 Sarv (note 47), at 33.

I. Structuring Axes of Conflict Prevention through Minority Protection – Four Principles

The law of the HCNM is governed by four principles which are derived from the Mandate and the function of the HCNM as prescribed by it. These principles are not all named explicitly in the Mandate, but are widely accepted in the literature. These principles should be understood as structural principles, constituting scholarly abstractions which define legal structures in the positive law governing the activities of an international public authority, in this case of the HCNM.[82]

1. Principle of Impartiality

The first principle is the principle of impartiality which is indispensable for the High Commissioner to act as a credible mediator. Para. 4 of the Mandate explicitly states that the High Commissioner "will act independently of all parties directly involved in the tensions" and para. 8 of the Mandate declares that the he will be a personality "from whom an impartial performance of the function may be expected".

2. Principle of Independence

The second principle is related to the first and can be described as the principle of independence or of discretion. While the principle of impartiality concerns the distance from the parties of a conflict, the principle of independence stresses the independence of the High Commissioner to all other OSCE-institutions and -organs. Despite the fact that the HCNM acts "under the aegis of the Senior Council" according to para. 2 of the Mandate, and despite the obligations to report and to cooperate, which have been described above with regard to the recommendations-mechanism, the HCNM is in general independent from the political influence of all other OSCE-institutions and the participating OSCE-states.

---

82 *See* for a detailed explication of this term and the distinction between structural, guiding and legal principles, Armin von Bogdandy, *General Principles of International Public Authority*, in this volume.

3. Principle of Confidentiality

The third principle is the principle of confidentiality, which is aimed at avoiding a loss of face by one of the parties during the mediation process. This principle becomes evident in the requirement of a strictly confidential report of the High Commissioner to the Chairman-in-Office in para. 18 of the Mandate. It is reflected in the confidential character of the consultation of the participating states concerned by the Chairman-in-Office in para. 19 of the Mandate. Finally the explicit requirement and recognition of confidentiality in para. 22 of the Mandate, with regard to information provided to the implementation meetings on human dimension issues, illustrates the principle of confidentiality.

4. Principle of Participation and Dialog

The fourth and final principle is the principle of participation and dialog. It is based on numerous provisions of the Mandate according to which the High Commissioner is bound to take into account the views, assessments and positions of different actors. The most important aspect is that he has to receive information form non-governmental organizations, especially form minority representatives as well as from the governments of the states involved and from local authorities.[83]

II. The Ambivalence of the Principles – Effectiveness through Intransparency

All of the above mentioned principles bare an ambivalent character. The ambivalence is caused by the fact that the HCNM acts as a political advisor and a legal monitoring body at the same time.

1. Principle of Impartiality

Public authorities as well as all instances destined to solve conflicts are obliged to act unbiased. The credibility of the instances executing or applying law in specific situations depends to a great extent on the im-

---

83 Paras. 11a, 23, 26 of the Mandate.

partiality of their actions.[84] At least if impartiality is not required for a decision-making body, an impartial review process is often required.[85] Furthermore, impartiality of decision-making is always required, if a public authority acts in the field of adjudication,[86] as the HCNM does through his country-specific recommendations. As there is no judicial review of the HCNM's activities, the HCNM as a decision-making body has to act impartial.

Despite this principle the political context of his activities reveals some inconsistencies concerning this principle. Until 2001 the activities of the HCNM were in practice limited to fourteen eastern participating states of the OSCE.[87] It was only recently that the HCNM became involved in the conflict concerning the Kurds in Turkey. On the contrary nearly all minority related problems in the eastern participating states have been addressed by the HCNM regardless of the violent quality of the tensions. The vagueness of the term of "terrorism" in para. 5, b) of the Mandate allows for a very vague demarcation between conflicts in and outside the scope of the HCNM. This raises the risk of a "double standard" applied by the HCNM.[88] Be it only imagined or real, the double standard poses a serious threat to the credibility of the HCNM and as a result also to the efficiency of his work.

2. *Principle of Independence*

The autonomy of public authorities is a principle known not least in the context of the administrative law in the USA concerning the Independent Agencies as well as in the UK with respect to the Non-Depart-

---

84 ADMINISTRATIVE LAW 292, 327, 328 (Mark Elliot, Jack Beatson & Martin H. Metthews eds., 3rd ed., 2005); Zhiyong Lan, *A Conflict Resolution Approach to Public Administration, in* PUBLIC ADMINISTRATION LAW 189, 197-198 (Julia Beckett & Heidi O. Koenig eds., 2005); JEAN-FRANCOIS LACHAUME, DROIT ADMINISTRATIF 604-605 (13th ed., 2002); RENÉ CHAPUS, DROIT ADMINISTRATIF GÉNÉRAL 98, 1111 (15th ed., 2001); Peter Badura, *Das Verwaltungsverfahren, in* ALLGEMEINES VERWALTUNGSRECHT 511-512 (Hans-Uwe Erichsen ed., 13th ed., 2006).

85 CRAIG (note 9), at 469; LACHAUME (note 84), at 122.

86 PIERCE, SHAPIRO & VERKUIL (note 9), at 474-783; CRAIG (note 9), at 98-103.

87 *See* country recommendations at: http://www.osce.org/hcnm.

88 Ratner (note 58), at 684.

mental Public Bodies.[89] These administrative bodies are usually afforded with certain autonomy from other organs and the involved parties in its decision-making and enforcement-procedures. Independent agencies are characterized by the appointment of their members by a higher authority and by the deliberative character of their decision-making process.[90] Against this background it is consistent that the High Commissioner acts in an independent manner, while exercising public authority. He acts independently from other organs and elaborates his general recommendations together with expert groups in a deliberative process. Besides, the political character of his work and the lack of judicial enforcement results in a strong political dependence on other OSCE-organs as well as on other international actors like the EU and the CoE.

3. *Principle of Confidentiality*

Contrary to the principle of confidentiality, which governs the work of the HCNM, the exercise of public authority on the domestic level – especially through administrative procedures – is often characterized by the principle of transparency and access to documents.[91] The general idea behind free access to such documents is that persons concerned by the activity of a particular authority should be able to follow the procedure and the reasoning of a decision in detail in order to be able to initiate a well-founded review of the decision.[92] The principle of transpar-

---

89 Pierce, Shapiro & Verkuil (note 9), at 95-97.

90 *Id.*

91 Art. 255 TEC; Sweden: Chapter 1, § 3 Constitution of Sweden (1.1.1975); USA: Freedom of Information Act (FOIA), 5 U.S.C.A. § 552, Pub. L. 89-554, 6 September 1966, 80 Stat. 383; Canada: Access to Information Act, Bill C-43, R.S. 1985 Chapter A-1, 1 July 1983; Australia: Freedom of Information Act, A 1989-46, Gazette 1989 No S 164, 10 May 1989; for a more detailed overview: PUBLIC ACCESS TO GOVERNMENT-HELD INFORMATION: A COMPARATIVE SYMPOSIUM (Norman S. Marsh ed., 1987); ÖFFENTLICHKEIT VON UMWELTINFORMATIONEN. EUROPÄISCHE UND NORDAMERIKANISCHE RECHTE UND ERFAHRUNGEN (Gerd Winter ed., 1990).

92 Rolf Gröschner, *Transparente Verwaltung: Konturen eines Informationsverwaltungsrechts*, 63 VERÖFFENTLICHUNGEN DER VEREINIGUNG DEUTSCHER STAATSRECHTSLEHRER (VVDStRL) 346, 355 (2004); Johannes Masing, *Transparente Verwaltung: Konturen eines Informationsverwaltungsrechts*, 63 VERÖFFENTLICHUNGEN DER VEREINIGUNG DEUTSCHER STAATSRECHTSLEHRER (VVDStRL) 379-441 (2004).

ency is necessary to guarantee the rule of law, in particular the binding effect of statues on public authorities. It is also useful to guarantee an effective participation of the persons concerned in the administrative procedure.[93]

There is no equivalent for the general principle of transparency in domestic administrative procedures even if we take into account possible restrictions[94] to this principle in a national context. The principle of confidentiality in the context of the HCNM has the rationale to increase compliance with the standards of minority protection set or compiled by the HCNM and there is no regulation at all requesting a transparent procedure by the HCNM. The need for confidentiality in order to foster compliance is caused by the specific political field in which the activities of the HCNM take place. The public access to documents, namely the country-specific recommendations, would constitute an instrument of "naming and shaming". While this might be an efficient instrument to enforce the compliance with concrete legal standards in the monitoring mechanisms of human rights treaties, it is doubtful in a context where the aim is the prevention or solution of a concrete conflict. Here the parties involved have to find solutions which not only comply with the standards referred to by the HCNM, but which are indeed acceptable to both sides in order to find a sustainable solution.[95] The aim of the activities of the HCNM is to find a solution together with the parties involved and therefore the door for remarkable commitments and compromises has to remain open, which is achieved through strict confidentiality.

However, even if this specific context explains the need for confidentiality in the context of the HCNM, it is possible to improve the balance between confidentiality and transparency. With regard to the functions of the principle of transparency it would at least be important to inform the minority party concerned about the content of the recommendations and not to leave the decision about information of the latter to the

---

93 Regulation (EC) No 1049/2001 of the European Parliament and of the Council of 30 May 2001, regarding public access to European Parliament, Council and Commission documents, recital (2).

94 Art. 4(3) Regulation (EC) No 1049/2001; Masing (note 92), 385; Matthias Jestaedt, *Das Geheimnis im Staat der Öffentlichkeit*, 126 ARCHIV DES ÖFFENTLICHEN RECHTS 204, 225 (2001).

95 Rob Zaagman, Conflict Prevention in the Baltic States: the High Commissioner on National Minorities in Estonia, Latvia and Lithuania 10 (1999).

discretion of the state authorities. This would also produce a stronger compliance with the principle of impartiality as mentioned above.

4. Principle of Participation and Dialog

Participation of the persons concerned in the decision-making process occurs in domestic administrative procedures, thus in procedures regulating the exercise of public authority.[96] Participation is an instrument to legitimate the decision from an in-put perspective.[97] The principle of participation and dialog in the context of the HCNM fulfills a similar function as it takes into account the views and requirements of the specific minority concerned and hence legitimates the solution to be found in the recommendations. Nevertheless, there are two major differences to be identified. Firstly, the participation in the context of the activities of the HCNM is by no means justiciable by the minority whereas this is usually the case with regard to domestic exercise of public authority. Secondly, the principle of dialog and participation in the context of the HCNM fulfills more a mediating function than a simple participatory function as national procedures do. This mediating function has only recently been sparsely introduced into national procedures regulating the exercise of public authority.[98] Here the domestic administrative law can benefit from the experiences of the HCNM in the use of mediation as part of the exercise of public authority.

Despite the success of this cooperative and mediative approach of the HCNM it remains problematic that there is no formal procedural provision enabling the parties concerned to voice their interests in the process of conflict solution. Furthermore the fact that the formal procedures for the selection of experts in the Mandate has never been followed and the lack of any judicial review makes it hard to prove the impartiality of the experts involved and poses a threat to the credibility of the HCNM in the eyes of the parties.

---

96 CRAIG (note 9), at 101; GEORGES DUPUIS, MARIE-JOSÉ GUÉDON & PATRICE CHRÉTIEN, DROIT ADMINISTRATIF 469-472 (10th ed., 2007); FRANZ-JOSEPH PEINE, ALLGEMEINES VERWALTUNGSRECHT 192 (6th ed., 2002).

97 *Id.*

98 Sophie Boyron, *Mediation in Administrative Law*, 13 EUROPEAN PUBLIC LAW 263, 266 (2007); CHRISTOPH A. STUMPF, ALTERNATIVE STREITBEILEGUNG IM VERWALTUNGSRECHT 289-290 (2006).

E. Conclusion

The comparative analysis of the principles characterizing the work of the HCNM with procedures regulating the exercise of public authority at the domestic level – namely administrative procedures – indicates a tension between efficiency of the used instruments with regard to the aim of stable conflict prevention on the one hand and a lack of certainty and control on the other hand. It is doubtful whether the tension can be solved and whether it would be even wishful to adjust the HCNM's procedure to domestic administrative principles in all respects.

Nevertheless two suggestions should be made to make use of these results in the future.

The HCNM's work provides a vivid example for the use of mediation processes in cases were the exercise of public authority has to take into account multiple interests. This encourages and informs the introduction of mediative elements in international administrative procedures.

At the same time the work of the HCNM illustrates the usefulness of tools known in the domestic regulation of the exercise of public authority for the purpose of a right based approach to conflict prevention. The monitoring of international obligations is enforced through international jurisdiction. The example of the HCNM illustrates a combination of monitoring on the one hand and specific mediative solutions on the other. It is for this combination that the standardized specification of norms can be used very effectual in the field of conflict prevention. It allows a comprehensive approach, taking into account the idiosyncrasies of every specific situation in order to generate more sustainable solutions to conflicts.

2.3 Information

Governance through Promotion and Persuasion: The 1998 ILO Declaration on Fundamental Principles and Rights at Work

*By Erika de Wet**

---

* The research was conducted during a sojourn at the Max Planck Institute for Comparative Public Law and International Law, Heidelberg (Germany), with the financial support of the Alexander von Humboldt Foundation. This contribution also forms part of a so-called VICI Project of the Netherlands Organisation for Scientific Research (NWO) titled: *The emerging international constitutional order: the implications of hierarchy in international law for the coherence and legitimacy of international decision-making*. The author would like to thank Mr. Lee Swepston and Ms. Anne Trebilcock for critical comments to earlier drafts.

A. von Bogdandy et al. (eds.), *The Exercise of Public Authority by International Institutions*, Beiträge zum ausländischen öffentlichen Recht und Völkerrecht 210,
DOI 10.1007/978-3-642-04531-8_14,

A. Introduction

I. Promotion, Persuasion and the Mandate of the International Labour Organization

The current contribution will elaborate on the manner in which the Declaration of the International Labour Organization (ILO) on Fundamental Principles and Rights at Work[1] (hereinafter the 1998 Declaration) functions as an instrument of governance for the purpose of promotion and persuasion. The purpose of this activity is to improve the observance by States of certain principles contained in the 1998 Declaration. At the outset one should stress that this governance technique is a trade mark of the ILO as a whole and not only of the 1998 Declaration. The basic premise of the ILO is to rely on cooperation and dialogue rather than sanctions in its efforts to realize its goals.

Public promotion and moral persuasion involve mobilizing peer pressure and shaming through the threat, or act, of exposing breaches of international labour standards to the international community. Technical assistance, which constitutes a particular concretisation of promotion and persuasion, ranges from advising on legislative reform and training of government officials to strengthening the capacity of governments, workers organisations and employers organisations for realizing international labour standards.[2] The ILO does not have the means or the mandate to engage in governance techniques such as black-listing or the imposition of financial sanctions, as may be the case with, for example, the United Nations Security Council. Instead, its governance techniques are more comparable to those of many human rights supervisory bodies within the United Nations system. All of these systems rely on reporting, dialogue and technical assistance as a mechanism for enforc-

---

1 Adopted by the International Labour Conference, 86th Session, 18 June 1998. See International Labour Conference, Record of Proceedings, Nos. 20 and 22 (86th Session Geneva 1998).

2 Austina Reed and Charlotte Yates, *The ILO Declaration on Fundamental Principles and Rights at Work: The Limitations to Global Labour Standards*, *in* THE AUTO PACT: INVEST, LABOUR AND THE WTO 249 (Maureen Irish ed., 2004). Within the national context the social partners are also mobilized around the 1998 Declaration through technical assistance projects. This, in turn, can lead to institutional and legislative reform in areas pertaining to the eight fundamental Conventions. Available at: http://www.ilo.org/dyn/declaris/DECLARATIONWEB.INDEXPAGE. See also, *infra*, note 44.

ing certain international obligations and none of them possess any coercive powers.

In the case of the ILO the 1998 Declaration attempted to intensify the impact of these techniques by placing certain fundamental principles at the centre of its activities and thereby sharpening the focus of its governance techniques. This implies that the public authority exercised by the 1998 Declaration takes the form of "determination through influence."[3] The promotional activities encourage the ILO's tripartite constituents (see section A.2. below) to adopt legislation and practices that further a particular public interest in the form of decent working conditions. In this manner the tripartite constituents are pressured to conform to a certain behaviour, which implies a de facto (albeit sometimes modest) limitation of their freedom to determine labour conditions without external constraints. The influence exercised in this manner can be avoided, but this would result at the cost of loosing face or reputation. The promotional activities are "public" in as far as they take place within the framework provided for and in accordance with the principles articulated by the ILO Member States in the ILO Constitution.

1. The Origin and Purpose of the ILO

Before engaging in an analysis of the technique of promotion and persuasion as embodied in the 1998 ILO Declaration, one should explain the institutional setting in which this instrument functions, including the origin and purpose of the ILO. The ILO is the United Nations specialized agency, which seeks the promotion of social justice and human rights since the end of the First World War through the creation of decent working-conditions. Its standard-setting activities are directed principally at the workforce in the formal as well as informal economy.[4] The ILO was founded in 1919 and is the only surviving significant crea-

---

[3] For a definition of "public authority," *see* von Bogdandy, Dann and Goldmann, in this issue.

[4] The formal economy pertains to income-generating activities that take place within a formal regulatory framework. The informal economy concerns those income generating activities which take place outside the formal regulatory framework. *See* Reed and Yates (note 2), at 248. For the extent to which international labour standards address people in the informal economy, *see* Anne Trebilcock, *International Labour Standards and the Informal Economy, in* LES NORMES INTERNATIONALES DU TRAVAIL: UN PATRIMOINE POUR L'AVENIR. MÉLANGES EN L'HONNEUR DE NICOLAS VALTICOS 588 *et seq.* (ILO ed., 2004).

tion of the Treaty of Versailles, which also brought the League of Nations into being.

Attempts to internationalize labour regulation date back to the nineteenth century when, in the wake of the industrial revolution, labour activists such as Robert Owen (1771-1853) and Daniel Legrand (1783-1859) advocated the need for an international labour organisation. In 1901, these efforts resulted in the foundation of the forerunner to the ILO, the International Association for Labour Legislation, based in Basel. Before the outbreak of the First World War, the Association engaged in the translation and publication of European labour laws and initiated the first two labour Conventions, which banned the use of white phosphorous and regulated night work in industry by women and young persons.[5]

The creation of the ILO at the end of the First World War was underpinned by four motivations. First, improving working conditions was considered a humanitarian issue. Second, there was a broad consensus that industrial peace and international peace were closely related and there was considerable fear for social disorder due to deteriorating labour conditions. Thirdly, there was economic concern about the consequences of the cost of production of social reform and the unequal playing field that would result, if such reforms were undertaken only by some. Finally, the parties at the table in Versailles were convinced that if social protection was not increased, world peace would be severely threatened by countries that undermined labour standards and promoted social dumping.[6] The adoption of the ILO Constitution in Part XIII of the Treaty of Versailles created an institutional framework for the setting and implementation of international labour standards. This framework was subsequently complemented by the Declaration of Philadelphia of 1944, which in 1946 became an integral part of the Constitution and reaffirmed the fundamental principles on which the ILO is based.[7] In 1946, the ILO became the first specialized agency of the

---

[5] International Labour Office, Women and Work: Selected ILO policy documents, 3 (1994); HÉCTOR G. BARTOLEMEI DE LA CRUZ *ET AL.*, THE INTERNATIONAL LABOUR ORGANIZATION 4 *et seq.* (1996).

[6] CHRISTINE KAUFMANN, GLOBALISATION AND LABOUR RIGHTS: THE CONFLICT BETWEEN CORE LABOUR RIGHTS AND INTERNATIONAL ECONOMIC LAW 49 (2007); Nicolas Valticos and Geraldo Von Potobsky, *International Labour Law, in* I INTERNATIONAL ENCYCLOPEDIA OF LABOUR LAW AND INDUSTRIAL RELATIONS 34 *et seq.* (ILO ed., 1994).

[7] KAUFMANN (note 6), at 51.

United Nations (UN), in accordance with Article 57 of the UN Charter.[8]

2. *Organs and Standard Setting*

A unique feature of the ILO is its tripartite structure, in accordance with which representatives of governments, employers and workers are represented in all of its executive bodies.[9] The inclusion of representatives of workers and unions alongside those of governments in the norm-setting activities of the ILO was aimed at strengthening the acceptance and enforcement of the international labour standards by those most affected by these standards. The ILO executive bodies concern in particular the International Labour Conference and the Governing body. The International Labour Conference meets annually in Geneva and each Member State is represented by two government delegates, an employer delegate and a worker delegate. The International Labour Conference establishes and adopts international labour standards, sets a discussion forum for important labour issues, as well as supervises the application of international labour standards at the national level.[10]

The Governing Body constitutes the executive council of the ILO and is composed of 28 government members, 14 employer members and 14 worker members. During its three annual meetings in Geneva it sets the policy of the ILO, including the setting of the agenda of the International Labour Conference and bi-annual budget, which are then submitted to the International Labour Conference for adoption, as well as the election of the Director-General of the ILO.[11] The International Labour Office is the permanent secretariat of the ILO and constitutes the focal point for the overall activities of the organization. It is ac-

---

[8] The agreement also specifically committed the ILO to operating consistently with the purposes of the UN Charter and, in particular, Art. 55. *See* Janelle Diller, *UN Sanctions – The ILO Experience, in* UNITED NATIONS SANCTIONS AND INTERNATIONAL LAW 197 (Vera Gowlland-Debbas ed., 2001).

[9] KAUFMANN (note 6), at 50.

[10] Valticos and Von Potobsky (note 6), at 40 *et seq.*

[11] Ten of the government seats are permanently held by States of chief industrial importance. Representatives of other member States are elected in the Conference every three years, taking into account geographical distribution. The employers and workers elect their own representatives respectively. *See also* Valticos and Von Potobsky (note 6), at 42 *et seq.*

countable to the Governing Body and functions under the leadership of a Director General, who is elected for a five-year renewable term.[12] The International Labour Office currently employs almost 2000 officials at the Geneva headquarters and 40 field offices around the world.[13]

The standard setting activity of the ILO has traditionally been achieved through Conventions and Recommendations.[14] Conventions are international treaties that are open to ratification by Member States. Recommendations are intended to guide national action, but are not open to ratification and are not legally binding. Member States are obliged to bring all Conventions and Recommendations to the attention of their Parliaments or other authorities that are competent to ratify international treaties and enact implementing legislation, within 18 months after the adoption of the respective instrument by the International Labour Conference.[15]

The ratification rate of most of the Conventions has remained low throughout the years.[16] On the one hand, it would not be accurate to measure the impact of the ILO Conventions exclusively on the basis of their formal ratification. The ongoing dialogue between the International Labour Office and States means that many labour laws that are adopted are influenced by the standards reflected in these Conventions, regardless of whether they are ratified. On the other hand, the formal

---

12 Valticos and Von Potobsky (note 6), at 43; *see also*: https://www.ilo.org (last visited 3 June 2008).

13 The ILO has international legal personality and currently consists of 181 member States. *See* Art. 39 ILO Constitution, text available at: https://www.ilo.org (last visited 3 June 2008).

14 In light of the tripartite nature of the ILO, no reservations against ILO Conventions are possible. Valticos and Von Potobsky (note 6), at 40; KAUFMANN (note 6), at 50.

15 Art. 19(5)(b) ILO Constitution, text available at: https://www.ilo.org (last visited 3 June 2008).

16 For example, of the 17 Conventions adopted by the Conference during the 1980s, the highest number of ratifications registered for any of these instruments were 73. Of the 14 Conventions adopted during 1990, only the Prohibition of the Worst Forms of Child Labour Convention, 1999 (No 182) attracted a high number of ratifications. Of the remaining conventions, the highest ratification rate was 20. *See* William R. Simpson, *Standard-Setting and Supervision: A System in Difficulty*, *in* LES NORMES INTERNATIONALES DU TRAVAIL: UN PATRIMOINE POUR L'AVENIR. MÉLANGES EN L'HONNEUR DE NICOLAS VALTICOS 52 (ILO ed., 2004).

ratification rate and impact of the Conventions do suffer as a result of several factors pertaining to their substance and manner of adoption. These factors include the increasingly detailed and sectoralized (specialized) nature of the Conventions; the tendency of the workers' group to secure maximum protection that remains out of reach for many developing countries[17]; the lack of involvement of the ILO regional field offices during the standard-setting process; as well as insufficient appreciation of the social realities by the technical units of the International Labour Office and certain interests groups within the Governing Body, where many of the standards initiate.[18] In addition, the intensification of globalization during the 1990s resulted in a discussion of the utility of international labour standards in the post Cold War era. Many governments argued that they deprive countries of their competitive advantage.[19]

By the mid 1990s, it was clear that the ILO standard-setting mechanism was facing severe challenges. The organization had to redefine its role and priorities in order to survive in the post Cold War era. The ILO commenced with a renewal process which inter alia resulted in the withdrawal of several older standards, following a Governing Body review of all pre-1985 standards between 1995 and 2002.[20] At the time it also designated 73 Conventions as fully up to date.[21] In addition, The ILO decided to sharpen its profile by concentrating its promotional ac-

---

17 European Union Member States in particular tend to force standards to their level of achievement, without considering the needs of developing countries. For their part, many developing countries do not sufficiently take part in the negotiation process.

18 Simpson (note 16), at 50 *et seq.*

19 KAUFMANN (note 6), at 50.

20 Of the prior 185 conventions, Nos 4, 15, 20, 21, 28, 31, 34-40, 43, 46, 48-51, 60, 61, 64-67, 86, 91 and 104 have been withdrawn. Of the 195 Recommendations, Nos. 1, 5, 11, 15, 37-39, 42, 45, 50, 51, 54, 56, 59, 63-66, 72 and 73 have been withdrawn. *See* KAUFMANN (note 6), at 51; Brian A. Langille, *Core Labour Rights – The True Story (Reply to Alston)*, 16 EUROPEAN JOURNAL OF INTERNATIONAL LAW 425 (2005).

21 In 1997 the International Labour Conference adopted an amendment to the ILO Constitution, which would allow for the abrogation of a convention in force but recognized as obsolete if two-thirds of delegates voted for such a measure. This amendment has been ratified by more than 80 states but still falls short of the requirements for entering into force. Available at: http://www.ilo.org.

tivities on so-called fundamental rights and principles at work. This decision ultimately resulted in the adoption of the 1998 Declaration which, as will be explained below, was identified as a feasible vehicle for the promotion of these rights and principles.

3. The Adoption of the 1998 Declaration: Streamlining and Focusing Promotional Activities

The text of the 1998 Declaration and its follow-up mechanism, which was adopted unanimously by the International Labour Conference on 18 June 1998, had been negotiated over a period of two years and in close collaboration with all ILO tripartite constituents (governments, employer organizations and workers organizations).[22] Input was also received from United Nations specialized agencies and non-governmental organizations (NGOs) with ILO observer status. However, unlike the tripartite constituents of the ILO, these entities do not have voting rights within the organization and their influence was therefore indirect.

The timing of the 1998 Declaration was the result of the concerns during the 1990s both within and outside the ILO over the processes of globalization and the possible social consequences of trade deregulation.[23] On the one hand, there was a quest for more flexibility in labour standards, whilst on the other hand there were concerns that the lowering of international labour standards would result in social dumping practices, where cheaply manufactured goods were sold below the cost of production. Within the ILO the conviction grew that in order to promote international labour standards effectively in these circumstances it needed to adopt a more flexible approach. Its promotional activities should focus in particular on standards which enjoy universal acceptance, as the universality claim would strengthen the moral and political case for their implementation.[24] In addition, the promotion should focus on the principles embodied in the standards, rather than the detailed standards themselves.

---

22 ILO Press Release, 98/23, 29 May 1998.

23 ILO Press Release, 98/23, 29 May 1998.

24 International Labour Conference, Report VII, *Consideration of a possible Declaration of principles of the International Labour Organization concerning fundamental rights and its appropriate follow-up mechanism*, 5 (86th Session, Geneva 1998).

At the United Nations World Summit for Social Development,[25] which took place in Copenhagen on 12 March 1995,[26] a consensus emerged in relation to four categories of ILO standards which should be respected in employment relations, namely freedom of association and the effective recognition of the right to collective bargaining; the elimination of forced or compulsory labour; the abolition of child labour and the elimination of discrimination in respect of employment and occupation.[27] The 117 Heads of State and Government in Copenhagen encouraged governments to enhance the quality of work and employment by fully implementing ILO Conventions on fundamental rights in States that have ratified them and to take into account the principles embodied in those Conventions in States that have not.[28] Subsequently, the Council of Ministers of the World Trade Organisation (WTO) expressed its renewed commitment to internationally recognized core labour standards in the Final Declaration of the World Trade Organisation (WTO) meeting at Singapore in 1996,[29] as did the OECD in its study of core labour rights and international trade, also published in 1996.[30]

Following the Singapore WTO Ministerial Conference, the ILO Governing Body decided to place the issue of a "Declaration on Fundamen-

---

[25] Final Copenhagen Declaration and the Program of Action, Report of the World Summit for Social Development, Copenhagen, 6-12 March 1995, UN Doc. A./CONF./166/9, para. 54(b).

[26] The ILO participated in the negotiations leading up to the adoption of the Programme of Action on workers' fundamental rights at the Copenhagen summit. See International Labour Conference, Report VII, *Consideration of a possible Declaration of principles of the International Labour Organization concerning fundamental rights and its appropriate follow-up mechanism,* 1 (86th Session, Geneva 1998).

[27] International Labour Conference, Report VII, *Consideration of a possible Declaration of principles of the International Labour Organization concerning fundamental rights and its appropriate follow-up mechanism,* 5 (86th Session, Geneva 1998). See also Art. 2(a)-(d) of the 1998 Declaration, text available at: http://www.ilo.org (last visited 3 June 2008).

[28] ILO Press Release, 98/23, 29 May 1998.

[29] WTO Singapore Ministerial Declaration, 13 December 1996, WTO Doc. WT/MIN(96)/DEC, 18 December 1996, para. 4, available at: http://www.wto.org (last visited 3 June 2008).

[30] *See also* OECD, TRADE EMPLOYMENT AND LABOUR STANDARDS: A STUDY OF CORE WORKERS' RIGHTS AND INTERNATIONAL TRADE (OECD Publishing, Paris 1996); OECD, INTERNATIONAL TRADE AND CORE LABOUR STANDARDS (OECD Publishing, Paris 2000).

tals Principles and Rights at Work" on the agenda of the 86th Session of the International Labour Conference. The initiative came from within the employers group and was eventually supported by a number of governments and the workers' group.[31] As far as the scope of the Declaration was concerned, the ILO constituents ultimately agreed to limit it to the same four categories of rights and principles mentioned in the Copenhagen Declaration.[32]

As far as the choice of a declaration as format for the promotion of fundamental labour standards is concerned, one should keep in mind that by the time the Singapore Ministerial meeting took place in 1996, it was clear that the promotion of labour standards through the inclusion of social clauses in free trade agreements had very little chance of success.[33] A non-binding declaration, which in the United Nations system constitutes a "formal and solemn instrument suitable for rare occasions when principles of lasting importance are being enunciated,"[34] was a feasible substitute. From the perspective of promotion and persuasion, the format of a declaration was supposed to add special weight to the moral and political standing of its contents, since it resembles a special moment in the history of the ILO.[35] In essence therefore, the substance and form of the 1998 Declaration attempts to enhance its promotional impact by focusing on universally accepted principles (which underlines their moral authority) and by choosing a format (declaration) with a particular pedigree within the United Nations system.

---

[31] International Labour Conference, Report VII, *Consideration of a possible Declaration of principles of the International Labour Organization concerning fundamental rights and its appropriate follow-up mechanism*, 4 (86th Session, Geneva 1998).

[32] GB 270/3/1, 270th Session, November 1997, para. 19.

[33] International Labour Conference, Report VII, *Consideration of a possible Declaration of principles of the International Labour Organization concerning fundamental rights and its appropriate follow-up mechanism*, 5 (86th Session, Geneva 1998).

[34] International Labour Conference, Report VII, *Consideration of a possible Declaration of principles of the International Labour Organization concerning fundamental rights and its appropriate follow-up mechanism*, 7 (86th Session, Geneva 1998); Memorandum of the United Nations Office of Legal Affairs, E/CN.4/L.610/, 2 April 1962.

[35] The Declaration of Philadelphia, which constitutes an integral part of the ILO Constitution, is the only binding Declaration ever adopted by the International Labour Conference.

B. Legal Analysis

I. The Nature and Scope of the Fundamental Principles in the 1998 Declaration

1. The Relationship with the ILO Constitution and ILO Conventions

The 1998 Declaration departs from the premise that the obligation to respect the principles of freedom of association and the effective recognition of the right to collective bargaining; the elimination of forced or compulsory labour; the abolition of child labour and the elimination of discrimination in respect of employment and occupation, arise from the ILO Constitution itself.[36] The obligation to respect, promote and realize these four categories of principles thus arises from the very fact of membership in the ILO and the 1998 Declaration does not establish new legal obligations for Member States.[37] By linking a non-binding vehicle for promotion to binding legal obligations in this manner, the persuasive character of the vehicle is strengthened. The underlying message is that although the "packaging" of the obligations may be non-binding, States cannot distance them from the substance contained therein.

As far as the right to freedom of association is concerned, it is well established that the obligation to respect this principles stems directly from the Constitution, given that Article I(b) of the Declaration of Philadelphia (which forms an integral part of the ILO Constitution) describes this principle as essential for sustained progress.[38] The remaining categories of fundamental principles are also mentioned in the Constitution, but in less strong language.[39] In fact, the references to these prin-

[36] Art. 2(a)-(d) of the 1998 Declaration, text available at: http://www.ilo.org (last visited 3 June 2008).

[37] GB. 270/3/1, 270th Session, November 1997, para. 18.

[38] *See* Max Rood, *New Developments within the ILO Supervisory System*, *in* LABOUR LAW, HUMAN RIGHTS AND SOCIAL JUSTICE 90 (Roger Blanpain ed., 2001); KAUFMANN (note 6), at 59.

[39] The principle of forced labour is not explicitly mentioned in the Preamble or the Declaration of Philadelphia, but is derived from the values proclaimed in these texts (in particular dignity and equal opportunity). *See* Francis Maupain, *Revitalization Not Retreat: The Real Potential of the 1998 ILO Declaration for the Universal Protection of Workers' Rights*, 16 EUROPEAN JOURNAL OF INTERNATIONAL LAW 444 (2005); GB.270/3/1, 270th Session, November 1997, para. 18.

ciples in the Preamble to the ILO Constitution are no stronger than references to other principles such as health and safety and social security, which were not included in the 1998 Declaration. This does raise the question why only these four categories of fundamental principles were included in the 1998 Declaration as opposed to all principles, which enjoy constitutional reference.

Support for their inclusion can be found in the fact that the ILO has for many years in practice acknowledged these four categories as representing fundamental standards, which have to be distinguished from those standards which represent essential infrastructure for the protection of workers and social progress; as well as standards aimed at ensuring specific levels of protection for (certain categories of) workers.[40] Their inclusion was also motivated with the argument that the four categories of fundamental principles constituted process-oriented standards which create the legal framework necessary for negotiating other labour standards of a substantive nature. The core principles would therefore form a prerequisite for the realisation of any substantive rights.[41] However, it is questionable whether any of the principles embodied by the categories of fundamental rights are indeed only process-oriented. The mere fact that they are formulated in a flexible manner and do not prescribe any concrete outcome does not detract from the fact that they are essentially directed towards the achievement of a substantive goal. Seen in this light, it is difficult to see why these principles would necessarily be less substance oriented (or necessarily more process oriented) than those aimed at health and safety at the workplace, for example, or why they would necessarily be more fundamental.

During the drafting process Member States insisted that the principles contained in the 1998 Declaration only encompass the essence of the obligations, as opposed to any detailed legal obligations that come with

---

[40] CLARENCE WILFRED JENKS, LAW, FREEDOM AND WELFARE 103 (1963); Mouloud Boumghar, *La Déclaration de l'organisation international du travail du 18 Juin 1998 relative aux principes et droit fondamentaux au travail: une technique juridique singulière de relance des conventions fondamentales*, 10 AFRICAN YEARBOOK OF INTERNATIONAL LAW 369-370 (2002).

[41] GB.270/3/1, 270th Session, November 1997, paras. 16, 19; International Labour Conference, Report VII, *Consideration of a possible Declaration of principles of the International Labour Organization concerning fundamental rights and its appropriate follow-up mechanism*, 430-431 (86th Session, Geneva 1998); Langille (note 20).

ratification of the relevant Conventions.[42] This raises the question of the exact scope of the "essence of the obligations."[43] In particular, it was unclear at the time of the adoption of the 1998 Declaration if and to what extent they would overlap with the obligations in the eight fundamental Conventions[44] that cover the same categories as the 1998 Declaration.[45] Stated differently, the question arose whether the difference in scope between the principles and Conventional obligations would lead to a fragmentation of ILO Standards within the ILO itself. However, in practice this risk seems less relevant, as the ratification rate of the fundamental Conventions has – since the adoption of the 1998 Dec-

---

42 KAUFMANN (note 6), at 76.

43 *See* Philip Alston, *Core Labour Standards and the Transformation of the International Labour Regime*, 15 EUROPEAN JOURNAL OF INTERNATIONAL LAW 494 (2004) (claiming that the 1998 Declaration detaches the core rights themselves from the details of the relevant conventions and the work done by the supervisory bodies in applying those standards over the years).

44 The ILO classified those Conventions which contain the core ILO standards as fundamental Conventions. It concerns standards which the ILO has for many years in practice acknowledged as being of a fundamental nature. They include the Freedom of Association and Protection of the Right to Organize Convention, 1948 (No. 87) (148 ratifications); Right to Organize and Collective Bargaining Convention, 1949 (No. 98) (158 ratifications); Forced Labour Convention, 1930 (No. 29) (172 ratifications); Abolition of Forced Labour Convention, 1957 (No. 105) (167 ratifications); Minimum Age Convention, 1973 (No. 138) (150 ratifications); Worst Forms of Child Labour, 1999 (No. 182) (165 ratifications); Equal Remuneration Convention, 1951 (No. 100) (164 ratifications); Discrimination (Employment and Occupation) Convention, 1958 (No. 111) (166 ratifications). Status of ratifications available at: http://www.ilo.org (last visited 3 June 2008). For the reporting obligations entailed by these Conventions, see section B.II.1.

45 *See* Art. 1(b) of the 1998 Declaration, text available at: http://www.ilo.org (last visited 3 June 2008). The ILO's Governing Body has also designated another four conventions as priority instruments, thereby encouraging member states to ratify them because of their importance for the functioning of the international labour standards system. These include Labour Inspection Convention, 1947 (No. 81) (137 ratifications); Labour Inspection (Agriculture) Convention, 1969 (No. 129) (46 ratifications); Tripartite Consultation (International Labour Standards) Convention, 1976 (No. 144) (122 ratifications); Employment Policy Convention, 1964 (No. 122) (97 ratifications). Status of ratifications available at: http://www.ilo.org (last visited 3 June 2008).

laration – improved to the point where the vast majority of States are now also bound by the Conventional obligations.[46]

On a formal level the promotional impact of the 1998 Declaration has therefore been successful, as it has lead to a higher number of Conventional ratifications.[47] At the same time, however, many States that have ratified the fundamental Conventions have not yet brought their laws and practices in line with their Conventional obligations. Cynics would therefore argue that their ratification had more to do with escaping the reporting burden that the 1998 Declaration imposes, than genuine progress in implementing fundamental ILO standards.[48] Even though such cynicism would not be justified in all cases, one should indeed be cautious not to equate the successful promotion of the principles in the 1998 Declaration with the formal ratification of the eight fundamental Conventions, but also to give due consideration to the extent to which they have been implemented.

2. *Relationship with Other International Regulatory Regimes*

As far as the risk of fragmentation in the application of standards is concerned, one should keep in mind that standards similar to the ILO core labour standards have also been included in other international (human rights) instruments, to which ILO Member States may be a party. These include the International Covenant on Civil and Political Rights (ICCPR); the International Covenant on Economic, Social and Cultural Rights (ICESCR); the United Nations Convention on the Rights of the Child (CRC); the European Convention of Human Rights (ECHR); the European Social Charter (ESC); and the European

---

[46] The supervisory machinery which is based on reports compiled by States and the ILO respectively (see B.II below) also focuses on the standards as defined in the respective fundamental Conventions. For example, the Director General's 2005 Global Report, *A Global Alliance against Forced Labour* (2007), 5 *et seq.*, stated that the ILO's definition of forced labour comprises two basic elements. These include work or service that is exacted under the menace of a penalty and is undertaken involuntarily. It then draws on the work of the ILO's supervisory bodies when supervising ratified Conventions to elaborate on the contents of these elements.

[47] Maupain (note 39), at 455; Simpson (note 16), at 63.

[48] Simpson (note 16), at 63.

Union Charter of Fundamental Rights (EU Charter).[49] References to labour standards also increasingly feature in the programs of the Bretton Woods institutions such as the World Bank and the International Monetary Fund (IMF), regional Development Banks and the United Nations Global Compact for the advancement of ten universal principles in the areas of human rights, labour, the environment and anti-corruption.[50]

This overlap in mandates implies that fragmentation of standards can result from the manner in which these other instruments are interpreted and applied in practice. These supervisory bodies are in no way bound by the ILO Constitution, ILO Conventions or Recommendations, or the 1998 Declaration. There is no guarantee that they will interpret the core rights and principles contained in the 1998 Declaration (or any other ILO instrument) – to the extent that it overlaps with its own mandate – in a manner that corresponds to the ILO's own vision in this regard.[51] It would, of course, not be accurate to attribute such potential fragmentation exclusively to the existence of the 1998 Declaration. The risk of inconsistent interpretation of standards initially adopted in ILO Conventions and Recommendations and subsequently also guaranteed in international or regional human rights instruments would also exist in the absence of the 1998 Declaration. However, it is fair to argue that the adding of any additional international instruments (such as the 1998 Declaration) to the existing body of international standards complicates the interpretation process with which international supervisory bodies is confronted with and in this manner increases the risk of fragmentation.

---

49 For example the right to freedom of association in Art. 22 ICCPR; the prohibition of forced labour in Art. 8(3) ICCPR; the prohibition of exploitative child labour in Art.32 Convention on the Rights of the Child and Art. 10(3) ICESCR; the prohibition of discrimination in employment and occupation in Art. 2(2) and Art. 6 ICESCR.

50 For the 10 principles of the Global Compact, which became operational on 26 July 2000, See: http://www.unglobalcompact.org/AboutTheGC/TheTen Principles/index.html. The wording on labor standards were taken from the 1998 Declaration.

51 Alston (note 43), at 477. *See also* Information Note on Corporate Social Responsibility and International Labour Standards, para. 6, ILO Doc. GB.286/WP/SDG/4(Rev.), 2003, text available at: https://ww.ilo.org (last visited 3 June 2008).

A few selected examples will illustrate that the relationship between the 1998 Declaration and other (human rights) instruments can be one of cooperation or one of competition, depending on the case at hand. Cooperation would imply an affirmation by other international monitoring bodies of the ILO's own interpretation of the scope of the rights and principles contained in the 1998 Declaration. This, in turn, would reinforce the promotional impact of the 1998 Declaration. Competition, on the other hand, would imply a different interpretation of the scope of such rights and principles. The resulting fragmentary effect would weaken the promotional impact of the 1998 Declaration.

An example of cooperation can be found in the fact that an ILO representative is present during the reviewing procedures foreseen under the ICCPR, ICESCR and ESC. In addition, the supervisory mechanisms for the ILO, ICCPER, ICESR and ESC allows for the coordination of state reports in relation to overlapping areas.[52] The human rights supervisory bodies do also in practice often refer to ILO practice when interpreting rights and obligations that overlap with ILO core labour standards.[53]

The risk of competing mandates and resulting fragmentation in the application of standards seems more prominent in relation to the programs of the Bretton Woods institutions. Whilst the IMF structural adjustment programs have thus far not included any requirements on compliance with the principles contained in the 1998 Declaration, the World Bank nowadays regularly imposes conditions regarding harmful child labour on its financial assistance.[54] However, the conditions imposed by the Bank require domestic regulation of child labour, without referring to the 1998 ILO Declaration. The definition of the standards at stake is therefore left to the States with the risk of fragmenting or

---

52 See Arts. 66 *et seq.* ICESCR; Art. 40 ICCPR; and Arts. 21 *et seq.* ESC, texts available at: https://www.unhchr.ch (last visited 3 June 2008).

53 For example, when defining forced labour, the Committee on Economic, Social and Cultural rights (the supervisory body to the ICESCR) referred to the Forced Labour Convention of 1930 (No. 29) and the Abolition of Forced Labour Convention of 1957 (No. 105), as well as Art. 8(3) ICCPR. *See* Committee on Economic, Social and Cultural Rights, General Comment No. 18 (Right to Work), 6 February 2006, E/C.12/GC/18, para. 9, text available at: https://www.unhchr.ch (last visited 3 June 2008).

54 *See* KAUFMANN (note 6), at 108 *et seq.*

even undermining the rights and principles in the 1998 Declaration.[55] Similarly, the World Bank has commenced with the mainstreaming of gender equality into its programs, but without referring to the 1998 ILO Declaration.[56] A recent move towards cooperation can be found in the Performance Standards on Social and Environmental Sustainability, adopted by the International Finance Corporation of the World Bank Group on 30 April 2006. These standards, which are aimed at private sector projects in emerging markets, explicitly refer to observance of core ILO labour standards.[57]

This reference to private sector projects also touches on the issue of the growing number of private corporate social responsibility initiatives and their potential fragmentary impact on the 1998 Declaration.[58] Although the 1998 Declaration primarily (some would even say only)[59] addresses States, the reality is that non-State actors have an increasing impact.[60] Towards the end of the first reporting cycle under the 1998 Declaration follow-up procedure (see section B.II.1. below), the ILO had surveyed 300 corporate initiatives on labour standards. However, only a handful attempted to define their mandate with reference to core international labour standards.[61] It is therefore fair to question whether, when implemented at the enterprise level, these private corporate initia-

---

55 In addition, the notion of harmful child labour is narrower than the ILO approach which is aimed at the elimination of child labour.

56 WORLD BANK, ENGENDERING DEVELOPMENT THROUGH GENDER EQUALITY IN RIGHTS, RESOURCES AND VOICE, SUMMARY (World Bank, Washington 2000); KAUFMANN (note 6), at 38.

57 Principle 2, available at: http://www.ifc.org/ifcext/enviro.nsf/Content/SustainabilityPolicy (last visited 3 June 2008); Sec. IV of the OECD Guidelines for Multinational Enterprises, which resembles the core ILO standards, available at: http://www.oecd.org/. *See* Schuler, in this issue.

58 *See* KAUFMANN (note 6), at 108 *et seq.*

59 Maupain (note 39), at 452.

60 A fact recognized during the drafting process. *See* ILO, Report of the Director General, *The ILO, Standard Setting and Globalization,* International Labour Conference, 85th Session, 1997, 14. *See also* Alston (note 43), at 470; KAUFMANN (note 6), at 76.

61 Alston (note 43), at 477. Information Note on Corporate Social Responsibility and International Labour Standards, Para. 6, ILO Doc. GB.286/WP/SDG/4(Rev.), 2003, available at: www.ilo.org (last visited 3 June 2008).

tives correspond in substance to the core ILO labour rights and principles.

In summary therefore, the promotional impact of the 1998 Declaration in relation to other regulatory regimes is mixed. Whereas there are indications of cooperation between the ILO and a number of international institutions, this cooperation is still underdeveloped. The same applies to cooperation with the private sector, whose social initiatives often take no (visible) account of the 1998 Declaration.

II. Overseeing the Implementation of the 1998 Declaration

1. Reporting Under the Follow-up Mechanism to the 1998 Declaration

The oversight mechanism in place for the 1998 Declaration is based on the premise that the ILO's role is first and foremost to create awareness for the fact that progress and social justice can be a sound investment for stability and the long-term competitiveness of the economy.[62] The 1998 Declaration attempts to create such awareness through reporting and technical assistance.[63] It provides for two types of reporting, namely State reporting that involves governments and workers' and employers' organisations in the respective Member States, and a thematic Global Report, prepared by the International Labour Office. These reports serve as an empirical basis for a dialogue with States, which is aimed at identifying problem areas and promoting solutions. In addition, it provides a basis for identifying areas where the ILO can assist States in overcoming problems in implementation through technical assistance, as well as assist the ILO itself in orienting its work.[64]

---

62 ILO, Report of the Director General, *The ILO, Standard Setting and Globalization, International Labour Conference*, 85th Session, 1997, 11.

63 Para. IV.2, Annex to 1998 ILO Declaration, available at: http://www.ilo.org (last visited 3 June 2008) (providing for a review of the entire follow up process, which has been scheduled to take place in 2008).

64 An example is the creation of the Special Action Programme on Forced Labour, which grew out of the discussion of the first Global Report on that topic. It filled an operational void in the ILO's work in support of Member States' efforts to eliminate modern as well as traditional forms of forced labour. See: http://www.ilo.org/sapfl/lang--en/index.htm. *See also* International Labour Conference, Report VII, *Consideration of a possible Declaration of principles of the International Labour Organization concerning fundamental rights and its appropriate follow-up mechanism*, 12 (86th Session, Geneva 1998). See also Hi-

The State reporting obligation in the follow-up mechanism is directed at Member States who have not yet ratified (all of) the fundamental Conventions. It requires annual reporting by States and the information provided in this manner is subsequently compiled by the International Labour Office in an Annual Review, which is then reviewed by a group of five Expert Advisers.[65] This group is appointed by and reports to the Governing Body. It adds its own introduction to the Annual Review received from the International Labour Office, draws attention to aspects that seem to call for more in-depth discussion, and may propose to the Governing Body any adjustment that they think desirable to the reporting procedure.[66]

One should point out that the reporting obligation described in the follow-up obligation does not introduce a new obligation, but rather clarifies the modalities for an obligation that has its roots in Article 19(5)(e) and Article 19(6)(b) and (d) of the ILO Constitution. These articles oblige each Member State to report to the Director General of the ILO, at appropriate intervals as requested by the Governing Body, on the position of its laws and practice in respect of specific, *non-ratified* Conventions and Recommendations.[67] In this manner, Member States have the opportunity to explain their laws and practice on issues covered by the instruments in question, as well as the reasons preventing ratification.[68] Generally speaking (in as far as all ILO Conventions are concerned), this reporting obligation is only triggered when requested by the Governing Body. States are also not obliged to come up with additional information (as can be the case when reporting on *ratified* Conventions).[69]

---

lary Kellerson, *La Déclaration de 1998 de l'OIT sur les principes et droits fondamentaux: Un défi pour l'avenir*, 137 REVUE INTERNATIONALE DU TRAVAIL 245 *et seq.* (1998).

65 ILO Governing Body, Minutes of the 274th Session, 6th Sitting (1999); See also para. II.B.3 of the Annex to the 1998 ILO Declaration, available at: https://www.ilo.org (last visited 3 June 2008).

66 Momar N'Diaye, *The Annual Review and the Promotion of the 1998 Declaration on Fundamental Principles and Rights at Work: Developments and Initial Impact Assessment, in* LES NORMES INTERNATIONALES DU TRAVAIL: UN PATRIMOINE POUR L'AVENIR. MÉLANGES EN L'HONNEUR DE NICOLAS VALTICOS 421 (ILO ed., 2004); Simpson (note 16), at 63; Rood (note 38), at 88.

67 N'Diaye (note 66), at 420; Rood (note 38), at 88.

68 Rood (note 38), at 89.

69 *Id.*

The follow-up mechanism under the 1998 Declaration fine-tunes this obligation in relation to the non-ratified fundamental Conventions, both in terms of the emphasis of the reports and their frequency. In relation to the emphasis, the questions articulated in the report forms focus on identifying the type of technical cooperation required for overcoming difficulties in giving effect to the rights and principles in the 1998 Declaration. This differs from the reporting forms approved by the Governing Body under Articles 19 of ILO Constitution, which mainly focus on the legal provision in place in relation to the relevant Conventions and Recommendations.

The reporting procedure under the follow-up mechanism is also more arduous in terms of frequency than that under article 19 of the ILO Constitution, as it requires *annual* reporting in relation to the legal situation concerning all non-ratified fundamental Conventions.[70] In fact, the annual reporting cycle is even more frequent than in the case of ratified Conventions in accordance with Article 22 of the ILO Constitution. The State reporting cycle for ratified fundamental Conventions and priority Conventions[71] is currently two years, while for all other ratified Conventions (with the exception of those conventions that are shelved), reports must be submitted every five years, or more often if requested. The state reporting under the 1998 Declaration commenced in 2000 with a governmental reporting rate of 56%. By the end of the first cycle the reporting averaged at 62%, while since 2006 it has been close to 100%.[72]

In accordance with the tripartite nature of the ILO, the reporting procedure under the 1998 Declaration must also involve the social partners in the form of workers and employers organisations. This obligation also stems from the ILO Constitution, notably Article 23(2), according to which a copy of government reports under Article 19 of the ILO Constitution must be communicated to the most representative employers' and workers' organizations within the respective member State. Although the rate of formal comments by the social partners re-

---

[70] Para. A.1. and Para. B.1, Annex to 1998 ILO Declaration, available at: https://www.ilo.org (last visited 3 June 2008); see also Simpson (note 16), 63; Rood (note 38), 92; Kaufmann (note 6), 73.

[71] *See* (note 45).

[72] Although the reporting rate has increased significantly since 2006, the number of countries subject to the follow-up mechanism has shrunk, as the fundamental Conventions become increasingly ratified. *See* N'Diaye (note 66), at 419.

mains low, at an average of 37% of reports received,[73] the actual input of the social partners in the annual reports is higher. In States which have ratified the Tripartite Consultation (International Labour Standards) Convention 1976 (No. 144), the annual reports are drawn up in consultation with the social partners, who then do not submit additional, separate comments. However, in 2004 the Expert Advisors drew attention to the low reporting rate and suggested expanded participation of civil society groups during the reporting process. This suggestion was, however, not met with much enthusiasm by workers and employers organizations.[74] This reluctance seems to be related, at least in part, to a fear on the part of these social partners of a (further) dilution of their influence in the ILO if additional civil society groups were involved in the reporting process.

The State reporting is complemented by the annual Global Report, drafted by the International Labour Office under the auspices of the Director-General and submitted to the International Labour Conference for examination. It is thematic in nature and covers the four fundamental rights in cycles of four years. In this manner it attempts to give a regular global overview of the situation regarding a particular fundamental principal. The first Global Report was issued in 2000 and addressed freedom of association. The subsequent reports respectively focused on forced labour, child labour, and discrimination respectively. The second cycle commenced in 2004 with a report on Organizing for Social Justice, followed by the 2005 study on a Global Alliance against Forced Labour; the 2006 Report on the End of Child Labour within Reach and the 2007 Global Report on Discrimination at Work.[75]

When drafting the Global Report, the International Labour Office draws on the annual reports provided by member States under follow-up mechanism to the 1998 Declaration (and Article 19 ILO Constitution) where it concerns non-ratified fundamental Conventions, as well as Article 22 of the ILO Constitution, where it concerns ratified fun-

---

73 Comments are mainly received from the International Confederation of Free Trade Unions, which concentrate on the principle of freedom of association and the right to collective bargaining. At the same time, the input by the workers' and employers' organizations increased in 2005 to more than for the whole period between 2000 and 2004. *See* N'Diaye (note 66), at 417, 419; Alston (note 43), at 474.

74 ILO Doc. GB.289/4; N'Diaye (note 66), at 424.

75 Texts available at: http://www.ilo.org (last visited 3 June 2008).

damental Conventions.[76] The Global Report serves to highlight those aspects of the right in question that require greater attention and serves as a basis for determining priorities for technical cooperation.[77]

One could therefore conclude that whilst the promotional impact of the 1998's supervisory mechanism evidences success on the formal level (higher ratification rate of ILO fundamental Conventions), it remains debatable whether it has succeeded in mobilizing the social partners to participate in the promotional procedures, and whether the formal ratifications were also accompanied by extensive implementation of the relevant obligations in practice. During the first cycle of reporting, substantive success was also hampered by the fact that the ILO had difficulty in absorbing the resources which were made available (notably by the United States government) for the purpose of technical assistance. This was due to a lack of sufficiently trained and experienced staff who could respond to the high number of governmental requests for assistance.[78]

2. The Complaints Procedure for the Violation of Freedom of Association

Additional supervisory mechanisms to the ones provided for in the follow-up mechanism to the 1998 declaration are, in principle, only available to the extent that Member States have ratified the respective fundamental Conventions. Where this has happened, Member States are bound by the reporting and complaints ("naming and shaming") procedures provided for in and Articles 22, 24 and 26 of the ILO Constitu-

[76] Para. II.B.1, Annex to 1998 ILO Declaration, available at: http://www.ilo.org (last visited 3 June 2008).

[77] For example, since the launch of the follow-up plan, the ILO has attempted to shed light on old and new manifestations of forced labour and to address them through technical cooperation. *See* Maupain (note 39), at 446, 456.

[78] The problem of absorption of extra budgetary resources affects the ILO as a whole and is not exclusively related to funds provided under stimulus of the Declaration. The reasons (such as slow recruitment) are largely systemic. For instances where resources have been effectively applied in relation to requests for technical assistance under the follow-up mechanism, see: http://www.ilo.org/dyn/declaris/DECLARATIONWEB.PROJECTSLIST?var_language=EN. See also N'Diaye (note 66), 419.

tion.[79] There is, however, one instance in which an additional supervisory procedure exists within the ILO – regardless of whether the Member States have ratified the relevant fundamental Conventions. Already in 1951, the ILO Governing Body created the Committee on Freedom of Association (CFA) with the purpose of examining complaints pertaining to the violation of freedom of association in ILO member States. The CFA is a tripartite body, to which governments of ILO member States, as well as organisations of workers or employers, whether national or international, can file complaints. Complaints are directed at the government of an ILO Member State of the ILO, irrespective of whether the State concerned has ratified the Freedom of Association and Protection of the Right to Organise Convention of 1948 (No. 87) or the Right to Organize and Collective Bargaining Convention of 1949 (No. 98).[80]

Since its establishment in 1951, the CFA has dealt with more than 2300 alleged violations of trade union rights. Despite being non-biding, its conclusions carry considerable weight and its problem-solving, non-legalistic approach to trade union issues has often been praised.[81] On the one hand, the procedure represents moral persuasion through "naming and shaming," as it is directed at exposing specific violations of trade union rights by a particular country. On the other hand, it is also promotional as it is engaged in finding solutions for specific problems which can also serve as an example to other ILO member States.[82]

It is important to highlight that this procedure was introduced long before the adoption of the 1998 Declaration and functions independent from it. A similar procedure does not exist for any of the other core

---

79 *See* Rood (note 38), at 88 *et seq.* and Simpson (note 16), at 66 *et seq.* (generally on reporting and complaints procedures).

80 This committee should be distinguished from the tripartite Fact-finding and Conciliation Commission on Freedom of Association (FCCA), which was created in 1950 through agreement between the United Nations Economic and Social Council (ECOSOC) and the ILO Governing Body (enclosed under B in *ILO, Law on Freedom of Association, Standards and Procedures*, Geneva 1995). This body also deals with alleged violations of trade union rights in countries that have not ratified the relevant fundamental Conventions. However the FCCA mechanism can only be triggered if the countries concerned have consented to the authority of the FCCA and is not used frequently. *See* Simpson (note 16), at 68; Rood (note 38), at 59, 89 *et seq.*

81 Simpson (note 16), at 68.

82 See Simpson (note 16), at 68 *et seq.*; Alston (note 43), at 445.

principles enshrined in the 1998 Declaration and is unlikely to be introduced in the near or intermediate future, due to insufficient support from ILO member States.[83] The extra dimension of promotion and persuasion represented by this procedure will therefore remain limited to the principle of freedom of association.

C. Assessment and Conclusion

The 1998 Declaration attempts to revitalize the role of the ILO in the globalized economy by singling out certain core labour standards and devising a special reporting procedure, accompanied by technical assistance, in order to promote their observance within Member States. The promotional technique has been successful on the formal level as it has lead to a significant increase in ratification of the eight fundamental ILO Conventions that concretize the principles contained in the 1998 Declaration. Stated differently, the concentration of the promotional activities on "core business" strengthened the fundamental standards of the ILO amongst its different stakeholders on the formal level. However, formal ratification does not in and of itself constitute effective substantive implementation of the obligations in question and it remains debatable whether the technique of promotion and persuasion is itself (in the absence of coercive powers) sufficient to ensure such implementation. This factor, as well as criticism pertaining to the substance and addressees of the 1998 Declaration, raises questions about its legitimacy.

For the purpose of this contribution, legitimacy involves both substantive and procedural legitimacy.[84] Substantive legitimacy implies that there is agreement by those affected on the content of the norms in question and therefore also an implicit acceptance that all affected will abide by such norms.[85] Procedural or institutional legitimacy rests on accepting the make-up of the decision-making process and institutions and entities involved in making the decisions. Procedural legitimacy is more likely conferred on those decision-making processes which qual-

---

83 International Labour Conference, Report VII, *Consideration of a possible Declaration of principles of the International Labour Organization concerning fundamental rights and its appropriate follow-up mechanism*, 3 (86th Session, Geneva 1998); Maupain (note 39), at 444.

84 Reed and Yates (note 2), at 246.

85 *Id.*

ify as representative of those affected by them and which are characterized by transparency and accountability.[86]

As far as the substance of the 1998 Declaration is concerned, authors have criticized it for being highly selective and not based on the consistent application of any compelling economic, philosophical or legal criteria.[87] This criticism is not so much directed at the fact that the four categories of core labour standards were included in the 1998 Declaration, but rather at the fact that only these categories were included whereas other standards – which can also be traced back to the ILO Constitution – were not and in this manner "demoted" to a lower status. Moreover, since their adoption, the principles in the 1998 Declaration have benefited from additional promotional activities and resources made available for technical assistance. Even though the resources in question were specifically made available by States for this purpose and did not imply a diversion of existing resources away from other standards, such differential treatment enhanced the perception that those categories of labour standards not included in the 1998 Declaration were relegated to second class standards.[88]

Criticism is further directed at the procedural legitimacy of the 1998 Declaration's follow-up mechanism, both in terms of its (lack of) representativeness and its weak accountability mechanisms. Due to the ILO's unique tripartite structure, non-state actors in the form of employers' and workers' organizations have always had a formalized role in any decision-making processes, including those pertaining to the 1998 Declaration and its follow-up mechanism. This singles out the ILO from most other international organizations where such a formalized role does not exist. However, given the challenges that unions and labour movements face within many domestic jurisdictions, it is questionable whether those participating are indeed representative of those affected by the impact of the 1998 Declaration.

Unions and labour movements in many countries have lost legitimacy within their own national borders, as more and more workers find themselves outside labour relation frameworks which might once have protected them.[89] Moreover, whereas private capital and States have de-

---

86 *Id.*

87 KAUFMANN (note 6), at 71.

88 Alston (note 43), at 458, 488. For a denial of the existence of any hierarchy in relation to ILO standards, see Maupain (note 39), at 447.

89 Reed and Yates (note 2), at 252; Alston (note 43), at 475.

veloped the capacity for international coordination and action, unions have remained nationally bound institutions with weak international coordinative institutions and capacity. As a result, labour movements tend to be far-removed from where the decision-making takes place, which further weakens their credibility within their respective domestic jurisdictions. In essence, the legitimacy of the tripartite system itself is at stake and this constitutes one of the most fundamental challenges confronting the efficacy of the 1998 Declaration and that of the ILO as a whole.[90] When raising this point one has to acknowledge that it is not easy to identify other actors outside of the organised labour movement, that would be more representative of those affected by the impact of the 1998 Declaration (or ILO standards in general). However, this fact would arguably not suffice to dispel the ILO's own legitimacy concerns. In relation to the 1998 Declaration, the social partners should therefore reconsider the advice of the Expert Advisors in 2004, according to which the participation of civil society groups during the reporting process should be expanded.[91]

Noticeably absent from all ILO accountability mechanisms – including those pertaining to the 1998 Declaration – is any form of coercion such as (financial) sanctions or exclusion from ILO membership. Instead, it relies on public promotion, moral persuasion and the provision of technical assistance, which simultaneously function as mechanisms of supervision ("enforcement") and accountability. These methods are similar to those applied by most United Nations supervisory bodies in the field of human rights and rest on the assumption that increased awareness, knowledge and expertise are the critical pathways for changing government policies and behaviours.[92] Thus, the assumption embedded in ILO practices is that once countries agree to take action to improve labour rights and working conditions, the greatest obstacle to their correction of poor labour standards lies in lack of knowledge and expertise (which can be overcome by technical assistance).

However, it is questionable whether these mechanisms are sufficient in an era where the 1998 Declaration's moral authority is facing strong competition from financially powerful institutions such as the World Bank and the IMF and other actors who propagate a model in which the market, as opposed to defined minimum standards, is paramount in

---

90 *Id.*

91 ILO Doc. GB.289/4; N'Diaye (note 66), 424.

92 Reed and Yates (note 2), at 250.

determining the allocation of resources and rights.[93] It is therefore likely that a certain disparity between the formal success of the promotional technique represented by the 1998 Declaration (i.e. high ratification rate of fundamental ILO Conventions) and substantive success (effective implementation of the relevant obligations and participation of all affected parties in the implementation process) will remain a reality in future.

93 Reed and Yates (note 2), at 251; Alston (note 43), at 474.

The WTO Committee on Trade in Financial Services: The Exercise of Public Authority within an Informational Forum

*By Joseph Windsor**

---

* The author is grateful to Armin von Bogdandy for collaboration on related articles, the staff at the Max Planck Institute for Comparative Public Law and International Law and fellow project participants for insightful comments, the GLJ staff and Eva Richter for painstaking editing, and Salát Orsolya and Sandra Yue for stalwart friendship.

A. von Bogdandy et al. (eds.), *The Exercise of Public Authority by International Institutions*, Beiträge zum ausländischen öffentlichen Recht und Völkerrecht 210,
DOI 10.1007/978-3-642-04531-8_15, © Springer-Verlag Berlin Heidelberg 2010

A. Introduction

The Committee on Trade in Financial Services (hereinafter, Committee or CTFS)[1] is a committee subsidiary to the Council for Trade in Services (CTS), which itself reports to the General Council of the WTO. Shortly after the WTO Agreement entered into force, the CTS established the Committee in its Decision on Institutional Arrangements for the General Agreement on Trade in Services (Institutional Decision).[2] The Committee acts primarily as a forum for dissemination of regulatory information specific to the often opaque financial services sector. This permits a meeting of national finance ministers and experts, as opposed to (mere) trade negotiators and representatives, who may not be in a position to understand the unique nature of national financial regulation. Fundamentally, a state's finance sector underlies all other sectors of international trade, since any transaction for goods or services requires compensation, usually monetary, thereby making the financial sector function as a sort of central nervous system for global trade.[3] The financial services sector, therefore, is peculiar among WTO trade sectors. Indeed, the regulatory constellation for financial services within WTO law is unique: it includes two annexes to the General Agreement on Trade in Services (GATS) and two Protocols to GATS, negotiations extended well beyond the Uruguay Round and the Marrakesh Agree-

---

[1] Sometimes referred to as the Financial Services Committee, it should not be confused with the Financial Services Committees of either NAFTA or the U.S. House of Representatives.

[2] S/L/1, 4 April 1995, para. 3.

[3] *See* Juliane Hernekamp, *Ausgewählte Dienstleistungssektoren, in* WTO-RECHT 418 (Meinhard Hilf & Stefan Oeter eds., 2005); Peter Morrison, *The Liberalisation of Trade in Financial Services and the General Agreement on Trade in Services*, 5 SINGAPORE JOURNAL OF INTERNATIONAL & COMPARATIVE LAW 593, 593 (2001); J. Steven Jarreau, *Interpreting the General Agreement on Trade in Services and the WTO Instruments Relevant to the International Trade of Financial Services*, 25 NORTH CAROLINA JOURNAL OF INTERNATIONAL LAW & COMMERCIAL REGULATION 1, 8 (1999).

ment's entry into force, and there is a *sui generis* set of heightened commitments called the Understanding on Commitments in Financial Services.[4] The Committee also acts as a monitoring body, overseeing both the implementation of legal commitments under the relevant Protocols and the specific progress of China under the Protocol on the Accession of the People's Republic of China.[5]

Following a brief introduction to the sector of financial services and the Committee as a body exercising public authority, part B analyzes the Committee in the context of international institutional law, considering its institutional setting, mandate, meeting procedure, decision-making, and review. Part C then surveys this legal landscape, giving attention to legal principles and questions of legitimacy.

I. Trade in Financial Services: The Legal Regime

The CTFS administers the application of GATS in the trade sector of financial services, a field that, by its interstate nature, is necessarily a concern of international law.[6] Specifically, the institutional context of the WTO/GATS sets the framework for regulatory activity. Article I:2 GATS defines trade in services in four modes: (a) the cross-border supply of a service between WTO Members, (b) the consumption of a service abroad in another Member's territory, (c) the supply of a service through a commercial presence in another Member's territory, and (d) the supply of a service through the presence of natural persons in another Member's territory. GATS's Annex on Financial Services, in turn, more specifically regulates financial services, in particular defining "financial services" extensively in paragraph 5(a). Its three subsectors are insurance, banking, and securities services (although the GATS definition uses only two categories). By way of illustration, financial services include, *inter alia*, direct insurance, reinsurance, actuarial services, claim settlement services, acceptance of deposits, all types of lending, issuance of credit and securities, asset and portfolio management, and transfer of

---

4 LT/UR/U/1, 15 April 1994.

5 WT/L/432, 23 November 2001, Section 18.

6 For the author and a co-author's full analysis of financial services under GATS, *see* Armin von Bogdandy & Joseph Windsor, *Annex on Financial Services*, *in* VI MAX PLANCK COMMENTARIES ON WORLD TRADE LAW 640-666 (Rüdiger Wolfrum, Peter-Tobias Stoll & Clemens Feinäugle eds., 2008).

financial information. Subject to certain exceptions, "services supplied in the exercise of governmental authority" and services supplied by a "public entity" are not covered by GATS disciplines.[7] GATS itself contains general obligations of most-favored-nation (MFN) treatment and transparency (Articles II-III). Beyond this, Members can inscribe further-going obligations to trade liberalization in their so-called schedules of specific commitments, which are then legally an integral part of GATS (Articles XIX-XXI). Clarifying the regulatory implications of the somewhat complicated schedules of specific commitments is one of the activities undertaken by the Committee.[8]

The Committee therefore operates at the overlap of international trade law, international financial regulation, and national financial regulation. A perusal of the preambles to the WTO Agreement and GATS illustratively includes a broad range of interests and objectives, including social welfare, environmental protection, sustainable development, economic growth, and aid to developing countries. The implications for national policy can be significant not only for state legislative, executive, and administrative regulators, but also ultimately for private suppliers and consumers of financial services.

II. The Committee as a Forum for Monitoring and Discussion

The CTFS engages in various forms of regulation. In the years following the adoption of the Second Protocol[9] to GATS, sometimes referred to as the Interim Agreement, the CTFS monitored its acceptance and ratification by Members who had undertaken commitments in accordance with it. Similarly, since the adoption of the Fifth Protocol,[10] often called the Financial Services Agreement, the Chair of the Committee

---

[7] Art. I:3(b) GATS in conjunction with paras. 1(b)-(d), 5(b)-(c) of the Annex on Financial Services.

[8] A useful (albeit partially outdated) list of schedules is: FINANCIAL SERVICES COMMITMENTS AND MFN EXEMPTIONS, available at: http://www.wto.org/english/tratop_e/serv_e/finance_e/finance_commitments_e.htm. *See also* SCHEDULES OF COMMITMENTS AND LISTS OF ARTICLE II EXEMPTIONS, available at: http://www.wto.org/english/tratop_e/serv_e/serv_commitments_e.htm#commit_exempt.

[9] S/L/11, 24 July 1995.

[10] S/L/45, 3 December 1997.

has at every meeting "invited" the Members that have yet to accept it to provide information on the status of their domestic processes. Since 2003, only Brazil, Jamaica, and the Philippines have continued to lag behind in their national legislative processes of acceptance.

The Committee also acts as a forum for discussion. In its meetings, Members are able to voice complaints, raise political defenses, give reasons and explanations, make proposals, and identify issues in need of clarification. In particular, the CTFS is mandated to provide technical assistance to developing and least-developed countries.[11] As a practical matter, the CTFS receives communications from various Members or groups of Members, assigns them a WTO document symbol, and circulates them among the other WTO Members in advance of Committee meetings.

III. An Outlier in the Law of International Institutions

One question should be addressed at the threshold of the present analysis: does the Committee really belong in a discussion of the emerging law of international institutions? To put it another way, how much public authority is actually being exercised here? The CTFS has been selected for various reasons. Firstly, the WTO is one of the most influential international organizations, having even been called an "embryo world government".[12] In administering its trade agreements, the WTO exerts a tremendous influence on national public policy-making and national administrative agencies. Instead of generalizing and surveying the entirety of the organization – a feat which would fail simply for reasons of space – the present contribution undertakes a microcosmic view of one of the almost forty councils, committees, and working groups operating under the auspices of the WTO's general assembly, whether it is meeting as the General Council, the Ministerial Conference, the Dispute Settlement Body, or the Trade Policy Review Body.[13] While the activities of these bodies vary greatly, the CTFS has been selected not only for the underlying importance of the financial sector for interna-

---

11 *See* S/FIN/W/29/Rev.1, 17 September 2003.

12 *Trade: At Daggers Drawn*, THE ECONOMIST 17, 22, 8-14 May 1999.

13 For an overview of WTO structure and subsidiary bodies, *see* WTO ORGANIZATION CHART, available at: http://www.wto.org/english/thewto_e/whatis_e/tif_e/org2_e.htm.

tional trade, but also because its diplomatic, soft-law mode of operation may, to a large extent, characterize the orientation of the WTO as a whole (even the compulsory jurisdiction of the dispute settlement system foresees consultations and good offices, conciliation, and mediation before the establishment of a Panel).[14] In this sense, a closer analysis of one of the WTO bodies may provide insights which might be cautiously extrapolated onto the organization generally.

Secondly, the network of international financial regulators and standard-setting bodies represents one of the most highly regulated sectors in global governance.[15] The organizational mandates vary widely in terms of purpose, geography, addressees, etc., so the necessity for horizontal cooperation, coordination, and deference in this sector is all the more acute. When the Organization for Economic Cooperation and Development (OECD), for example, makes a presentation at a CTFS meeting, this makes a subtle contribution to the setting of financial industry standards, because a common frame of reference is promoted among the more than 150 WTO Members. The Committee is, of course, not among the most prominent of the international financial regulatory institutions, but the present analysis is meant to shed light on the significance of a single inconspicuous component in the vast governance network.[16]

Finally, the CTFS has been chosen intentionally as a borderline case study – as a sort of outlier among international institutions. One of the defining characteristics of the law of international institutions is its departure from the traditional sources of public international law enshrined in Article 38 of the ICJ Statute. Informal, soft-law instruments and nonbinding governance methods become objects worthy of legal

---

[14] Arts. 4-5 of the Understanding on Rules and Procedures Governing the Settlement of Disputes (DSU).

[15] *See generally* Sydney J. Key, *Trade Liberalization and Prudential Regulation*, 75 INTERNATIONAL AFFAIRS 61, 69-70 (1999); David Zaring, *Informal Procedure, Hard and Soft, in International Administration*, 5 CHICAGO JOURNAL OF INTERNATIONAL LAW 547, 585-592 (2004-2005).

[16] Important international financial regulatory organizations include the OECD, the Bank for International Settlement (BIS) and the Basel Committee on Banking Supervision, the International Accounting Standards Committee (IASC), the International Organization of Securities Commissioners (IOSCO), the International Association of Insurance Supervisors (IAIS), the Financial Stability Forum (FSF), as well as the World Bank and the International Monetary Fund (IMF).

analysis.[17] Thus, the Committee's informality, collegiality, and political consensus-building should not be considered insurmountable obstacles to its analysis from the perspective of international institutional law. The Committee engages in varied activities that can be considered exercises of public authority: the administration of regulatory information, including naming-and-shaming and giving international notice of non-compliance and regulatory peculiarities; oversight and review of acceptance and implementation of international obligations in national financial systems; constructive rulemaking in the form of clarification and negotiation of Members' schedules of specific commitments, thereby contributing to the setting of state regulatory practice; a sort of notice-and-comment forum for proposed amendments to GATS and the Annex on Financial Services; and a forum for formal communications which trigger open discussion and thereby act as an informal complaint procedure between Members. The Committee's exercise of public authority may be more political bark than legal bite, but its watchdog role over the financial services sector under GATS gives teeth to its influence on national financial regulation. In this sense at least, it certainly exercises public authority.

B. Legal Analysis

I. The WTO as Institutional Framework

As stated above, the Committee operates as one of numerous subsidiary bodies in the WTO. While an institutional analysis of the WTO is, of course, beyond the scope of the present chapter, some contextualization should be of assistance. Established on 1 January 1995 by the WTO Agreement,[18] the WTO meets, with representation of all Members, either at a Ministerial Conference or as the General Council, which in turn can also convene as the Dispute Settlement Body or the Trade Policy Review Body, depending on which function is to be performed.[19]

---

17 *See* Zaring (note 15), at 594-595 ("the regulatory cooperation studied here transcends the concept [of 'soft law' in international relations] ... Even if it is nonbinding, how does that matter if it is obeyed? ... In this sense, regulatory cooperation, both hard and soft, amounts to administration by agreement in a way just as substantial as agreement by treaty.").

18 33 ILM 1144 (1994).

19 Art. IV WTO Agreement.

The General Council is the WTO's highest decision-making body and meets regularly in Geneva. Three Councils operate under the General Council's general guidance: the Council for Trade in Goods, the Council for Trade-Related Aspects of Intellectual Property Rights, and the CTS.[20] The CTS, in turn, has established four of its own subsidiary bodies, namely, the Committees on Trade in Financial Services and Specific Commitments and the Working Parties on Domestic Regulation and GATS Rules. By way of comparison, the WTO's structure includes around two dozen committees and working parties on this lowest organizational level, each reporting to one of the three main Councils or to the General Council itself.[21]

According to Article XXIV:2 GATS, delegates from all WTO Members may participate in all of the CTS's subsidiary bodies and, thus, also in the Committee. The CTS established the CTFS in 1995 in paragraph 3 of the Institutional Decision, on the basis of its power, under Article XXIV:1 GATS and Article IV:6 WTO Agreement, to establish such bodies. According to paragraph 2 of this decision, the Committee is subordinate to the CTS and is to "carry out responsibilities as assigned to it by the Council"; however, paragraph 1 empowers the Committee to "establish its own rules of procedure". The Committee regularly submits to the CTS an Annual Report of the Committee on Trade in Financial Services.[22]

The CTFS elects its own Chair under the procedures outlined in the Guidelines for Appointment of Officers to WTO Bodies.[23] The various committees, councils, and working groups in the WTO, however, have developed a practice of informal consultations to ensure a proper distri-

---

[20] Art. IV:5 WTO Agreement.

[21] *See* WHOSE WTO IS IT ANYWAY?, available at: http://www.wto.org/english/thewto_e/whatis_e/tif_e/org1_e.htm. This excludes other sub-committees, negotiating groups, and working parties on the accession of specific candidates. *See* WTO BODIES & OTHER ENTITIES, CHAIRPERSONS AND ASSOCIATED DOCUMENT SERIES, available at: http://www.members.wto.org/bodiesandseries/Public/main.asp.

[22] The most recent is S/FIN/18, 13 November 2007. The minutes of the meeting on 12 November 2007 are contained in S/FIN/M/55, 16 November 2007. As of May 2008, this was the most recent meeting, with a meeting scheduled for 3 June 2008.

[23] WT/L/31, 7 February 1995.

bution of the heads of these bodies.[24] Such consultations work out consensus on a slate of chairpersons for the four bodies reporting to the CTS, which then takes note thereof, before the CTFS elects its Chair by consensus. Those elected generally chair the Committee for one year. The composition of the CTFS blends two levels in the multilevel international legal order. That is, its meetings bring together national representatives of WTO Member governments without specific requirements as to whom a government may send. The Committee may thus comprise a mixture of trade officials, financial regulators, diplomats, and ministers of finance or their aides, and this mixture of national representatives meets, at the international level, as one subsidiary body within a larger international organization. The Committee's immediate legal foundation is a decision internal to the international organization, but of course this ultimately derives its validity from the international treaty on which the organization itself is based. The Committee enjoys legal autonomy only as far as its procedure is concerned; its substantive mandate is limited by both the decision on which it is founded and any assignments from the superior body to which it reports.

II. Substantive Mandate

1. General Mandate

The CTS adopted the Institutional Decision pursuant to Article XXIV GATS. Paragraphs 1 and 2 are formulated generally, setting up a framework for "[a]ny subsidiary bodies that the Council may establish". Paragraph 3 goes on to create the CTFS, stating that it has the mandate laid down in paragraph 2, which contains a catalogue of responsibilities in addition to any other tasks that the CTS may assign.

Thus, the six subparagraphs of paragraph 2 make up part of the Committee's mandate; in the context of financial services, they include:

a) To review and survey continually the application of GATS and the Annex on Financial Services to the financial services sector;

b) To formulate proposals or recommendations on any matter relevant to financial services;

---

[24] *See* CURRENT WTO CHAIRPERSONS, available at: http://www.192.91.247.23/english/thewto_e/secre_e/current_chairs_e.htm.

c) To consider proposals for amendment of the Annex on Financial Services and to make recommendations, where appropriate, to the CTS in this respect;

d) To provide a forum for technical discussions and to conduct studies and examinations of national measures and of the financial services sections of Members' schedules of specific commitments and lists of MFN exemptions;

e) To provide technical assistance to developing countries, whether already Members or seeking membership, regarding GATS obligations in the financial services sector; and

f) To cooperate with other subsidiary bodies under GATS or any international organizations active in the financial services sector.

Because paragraph 2 of the Institutional Decision was drafted as a general template for any sectoral committee, it is necessarily abstract and general. The Institutional Decision explicitly leaves the Committee's mandate open for any future "responsibilities assigned to it by the Council [for Trade in Services]". Three main tasks have indeed been subsequently assigned to the CTFS: it has been instructed to monitor Members' acceptance of, respectively, the Second and Fifth Protocols to GATS on financial services and, notably, to carry out transitional review of the financial services sector under Section 18 of Chinese Accession Protocol.

2. *Monitoring of GATS Protocols*

Since GATS entered into force along with the WTO Agreement, negotiations have continued with respect to Members' schedules of specific commitments. An individual Member can unilaterally improve the commitments in its schedule, or, occasionally, certain groups of Members have negotiated a set of commitments, all of which enter into force simultaneously, effectively as a new agreement. Several such agreements have been reached in the form of Protocols to GATS, and the Second and Fifth Protocols deal with schedules of commitments in the financial services sector. Although the Second Protocol no longer has legal relevance, the commitments annexed to the Fifth Protocol account for much of the current state of the law in the international financial services sector.

The CTFS has had the task of monitoring the status of acceptance of each Protocol by those Members that annexed new financial services commitments.[25] Since its entry into force, all Members concerned have accepted the commitments they annexed to the Fifth Protocol except Brazil, Jamaica, and the Philippines, so that the Committee's monitoring task continues with respect to this Protocol.[26]

3. *Transitional Review Mechanism*

The Chinese Accession Protocol[27] was drafted and adopted in 2001 in response to many Members' concerns about the Chinese legal order's compatibility with WTO law, given China's "socialist market economy", the relatively high number of state-owned enterprises, and the one-party system.[28] Section 18 of the Accession Protocol tasks the CTFS, alongside fifteen other subsidiary bodies, with the Transitional Review Mechanism. Section 18, paragraph 1, requires the Committee to "review, as appropriate to [its] mandate, the implementation by China of the WTO Agreement"; for its part, China is required to "provide relevant information" to the Committee ahead of meetings. The regulatory, administrative, and legal content covered by this mandate is not only quite technical, but also very broad; however, it should be kept in mind that the review mechanism has a merely monitoring function and is not equipped to enforce the law.[29] Paragraph 1 does, however, require (and empower) the Committee to issue reports to the CTS, which then is to report to the General Council.

---

25 Regarding the Second Protocol, *see* S/L/13, 24 July 1995, para. 3; regarding the Fifth Protocol, *see* S/L/44, 3 December 1997, para. 3.

26 *See* STATUS OF ACCEPTANCES OF THE FIFTH PROTOCOL TO THE GENERAL AGREEMENT ON TRADE IN SERVICES, available at: http://www.wto.org/english/tratop_e/serv_e/finance_e/finance_status_5prot_e.htm; S/FIN/M/53, 30 November 2006, paras. 3-7.

27 WT/L/432, 23 November 2001. *See also* Xin Zhang, *Implementation of the WTO Agreements*, 23 NORTHWESTERN JOURNAL OF INTERNATIONAL LAW & BUSINESS 383, 408-410 (2003).

28 *See* Julia Ya Qin, *WTO Regulation of Subsidies to State-owned Enterprises (SOEs) – A Critical Appraisal of the China Accession Protocol*, 7 JOURNAL OF INTERNATIONAL ECONOMIC LAW 863 (2004); Zhang (note 27), at 409-410.

29 *See* William Steinberg, *Monitor with No Teeth*, 6 UNIVERSITY OF CALIFORNIA DAVIS BUSINESS LAW JOURNAL 2, section IV (2005).

4. *Forum for Discussion*

Much of the CTFS's mandate revolves around the dissemination of information and the clarification of GATS rules for and in the sector. The importance of this informational function in the exercise of public authority should not be understated.[30] The Institutional Decision's listing of responsibilities leaves the Committee's area of competence wide open. The Committee, then, is programmed as a forum for technical discussion, particularly for the benefit of developing country Members, as a forum for clarification of GATS disciplines as applied to financial services and Members' schedules of specific commitments, and, to some degree, as a forum for standard-setting and notice-and-comment rulemaking.[31] Regarding the latter, the CTFS does not engage in standard-setting or rulemaking *per se*; nonetheless, it is not inaccurate to say that the forum provided by the Committee serves as one (possible) phase in such informal rulemaking in the highly regulated financial sector.

III. Flexible Practice Instead of Fixed Rules of Procedure

1. *General Practice and Decision-making*

Paragraph 1 of the Institutional Decision states that the Committee "shall establish its own rules of procedure, and may set up its own subsidiary bodies as appropriate". Thus far, the Committee appears to have avoided laying down any definite rules of procedure, instead relying on an adaptable, diplomatic approach to its meetings; it has not established any subsidiary bodies. As far as can be determined from publicly accessible documentation, the procedure involves the distribution by airgram of an agenda before each meeting. This pre-distributed agenda is listed

---

[30] *See* Schmidt-Aßmann, in this volume ("Here, even more than in national administrative law, it holds true: administrative law is first and foremost law on the administration of information!"); Daniel C. Esty, *Good Governance at the Supranational Scale*, 115 YALE LAW JOURNAL 1490, 1533 (2006).

[31] In BLACK'S LAW DICTIONARY 1358 (Bryan A. Garner, Editor in Chief, 8th ed., 2004) *informal rulemaking* is defined as: Agency rulemaking in which the agency publishes a proposed regulation and receives public comments on the regulation, after which the regulation can take effect without the necessity of a formal hearing on the record. Informal rulemaking is the most common procedure followed by an agency in issuing its substantive rules. Also termed *notice-and-comment rulemaking*.

at the beginning of the minutes of each meeting (with the document symbol WTO/AIR/...), but the airgrams are not available on the WTO's website. Typical agenda items include the acceptance status of the Fifth Protocol, technical issues (for example, e-commerce or sectoral classifications), recent developments, and presentations by other bodies active in the field (for example, the World Bank or the OECD). More recently, the agenda has included the abovementioned transitional review under the Chinese Accession Protocol. At meetings, the Chair presides, and representatives, as desired or as necessary, make statements, put questions, and respond to communications.

The Committee apparently makes decisions by consensus, as no annual report has yet recorded formal dissent to the decisions made. This has the effect that – at least from an external point of view – disagreement in the CTFS is minimized, appearing only occasionally in the minutes as disagreement expressed during meetings but not as formal nays. Indeed, nothing like voting is apparent from the Committee's documents. Members are thus able to record objections and express concerns in the Committee's documents – even apparently anonymously. One example can be seen in the minutes of an early meeting in 1995. Negotiations in the financial services sector had been extended beyond GATS's entry into force. The months leading up to the Second Protocol on financial services were contentious.[32] This may have led certain Members to wish to remain anonymous: although the minutes ordinarily do name the countries taking action or making statements, the minutes of this meeting record several instances of simply "one delegation" or "another delegation" making statements, criticizing developments, or responding.[33]

2. *Monitoring of the Fifth Protocol*

During meetings, the Chair regularly "invites" delegates from certain Members to provide information on the continuing processes of domestic implementation of the Fifth Protocol. This involuntary, if not necessarily particularly invasive, means of disseminating information is usually the first agenda item at Committee meetings. Members that have yet to accept the Fifth Protocol (currently, only Brazil, Jamaica,

---

32 For an account of financial services negotiations, *see* von Bogdandy & Windsor (note 6), at margin nos. 4-12.

33 S/FIN/M/3, 29 May 1995, paras. 6-7; S/FIN/M/7, 26 July 1995, paras. 19-20.

and the Philippines) are called on to provide information on the status of acceptance in their national legislatures and the reasons why it remains outstanding. The inquiry, by now, is not particularly rigorous, and delegations sometimes simply respond that no new developments have occurred since the last report.[34] Considering that the negotiated Agreement entered into force for many Members a decade ago, the value of this information may now lie more in naming-and-shaming than in updating foreign regulators, despite occasional expressions of concern by other Members.[35] This also has the effect of providing other Members with notice that the given Member's schedule of specific commitments, as annexed to the Fifth Protocol, has not yet been implemented in the national regime.

3. *Transitional Review Mechanism*

Transitional review under Section 18 of the Chinese Accession Protocol similarly displays the Committee's high level of informality. Usually a handful of other Members submit communications in advance of the review, and these are circulated among all Members. During meetings, then, the Chinese representative responds at length to the submissions, after which the delegations engage in an extended question-and-answer session.[36] Thematically, transitional review covers the full range of banking, securities, and insurance services in the Chinese system, for example, minimum capital requirements for foreign direct investment, the operation of grandfather clauses in insurance law, or regulations on priority of debt repayment for domestic and overseas depositors. The sixth review took place on 12 November 2007, and Section 18, paragraph 4, of the Chinese Accession Protocol calls for eight annual reviews with a final review in the tenth year after accession. The CTFS delivers a for-

---

[34] *See* S/FIN/M/52, 4 May 2006, para. 4; S/FIN/M/53, 30 November 2006, paras. 4-5.

[35] The United States, Japan, Switzerland, and the European Communities have recently expressed concern over the delays. S/FIN/M/52, 4 May 2006, para. 5; S/FIN/16, 28 November 2006, para. 2.

[36] Transitional review sessions have apparently been extensive, judging from the number of paragraphs covered in the minutes of meetings: S/FIN/M/37, 24 October 2002, paras. 11-71; S/FIN/M/43, 4 December 2003, paras. 21-74; S/FIN/M/47, 26 November 2004, paras. 14-77; S/FIN/M/50, 23 September 2005, paras. 6-55; S/FIN/M/53, 30 November 2006, paras. 12-73; S/FIN/19, 14 November 2007, paras. 30-106.

mal, succinct report to the CTS, listing the date of review, the communications received in advance of review, and a reference to the minutes of the meeting.[37]

Committee documents are adopted by consensus, and the informality of the review mechanism allows for some level of evasiveness. Thus, transitional review has not only been praised for its contribution to transparency and dialogue, but also sharply criticized for its lack of effectiveness and sanctions.[38] The merits of Section 18 review depend on the criteria used to evaluate it. As a forum for clarifying uncertainty regarding opaque regulations and as a means of creating political pressure via on-the-record criticism, the mechanism has been quite successful. As an effective means of securing speedy compliance and implementation, it has been rather poor.

4. Poorly Defined Powers: The Adoption of the Second Protocol

One open question regards the legal basis of the Committee's decision-making powers and whether it could, without consensus, make binding or even nonbinding decisions. This has not become an issue because, even in critical, quarrelsome periods, the Committee has maintained its modest profile and not attempted to appropriate greater significance, neither within the WTO nor in the international financial sector. Yet its decision-making powers remain poorly defined. While nothing currently suggests that the issue will become a problem in the foreseeable future, at least the potential exists that a dispute could arise. Two meetings on 26 July 1995 illustrate the lack of clarity. Dissatisfied with the counteroffers of certain Members and concerned about a "free rider" threat, the United States withdrew its broad MFN offer from Committee negotiations, leaving the EC scrambling to salvage some part of the progress made theretofore. The EC led the way to the conclusion of the stopgap Second Protocol[39] – a negotiated set of financial services commitment that entered into force together on an MFN basis, although

---

[37] The six reports thus far have been formulaic: S/FIN/7, 25 October 2002; S/FIN/11, 4 December 2003; S/FIN/13, 26 November 2004; S/FIN/15, 23 September 2005; S/FIN/17, 30 November 2006; S/FIN/19, 14 November 2007.

[38] For positive comments, *see* S/FIN/M/47, 26 November 2004, paras. 37, 51; S/FIN/M/50, 23 September 2005, paras. 39, 46; Zhang (note 27), 408-410. For negative remarks, *see* S/FIN/M/50, 23 September 2005, para. 47; S/FIN/M/53, 30 November 2006, paras. 48, 71; Steinberg (note 29), sections IV-V.

[39] S/L/1, 24 July 1995.

not all WTO Members (notably, the United States) attached commitments. At the meetings, the Committee discussed, *inter alia*, the "procedural issues" involved in adopting the Second Protocol and three related implementing decisions. The description of the Secretariat's explanation is worth quoting at length:

> On the question of the legal basis for the [adoption of the Second Protocol and related decisions], the Secretariat explained that there was no doubt that these Decisions could be taken by the Committee and the Council for Trade in Services by consensus, and that the Council for Trade in Services rather than the General Council was empowered to take the Decisions being discussed; there were many precedents to such decisions being taken by consensus which had had more far-reaching consequences ... Their legal validity had never been challenged, and they had been accepted by Panels as "relevant GATT provisions" ... It was also clear that the Second Decision being considered did not introduce any fundamental changes in the rights and obligations of Members ... Therefore, a Decision to extend the term of the rights and obligations that the Annex provided seemed to be absolutely within the capacity of the Services Council to establish necessary procedures ... Delegations expressed satisfaction with this explanation.[40]

Admittedly, the nature of the Second Protocol played a significant role here: it was essentially a plurilateral agreement, binding only for the "Members concerned" and not for each and every WTO Member, although it applied on an MFN basis. The text proper did not include any new commitments to financial services liberalization. Instead, the set of negotiated schedules of commitments were annexed to the Protocol, and they would only enter into force if all annexing Members accepted it in their national processes by the date specified or if otherwise decided despite any lagging Members. In terms of legal substance, then, the decision to adopt the Second Protocol was based on an already negotiated, reciprocal compromise. Who, then, was going to object? Nonetheless, legally speaking, the maneuver appears to have been, at least, the rubber-stamping of a *questionable*, albeit *unquestioned*, legal basis for action or, at most, a procedural assertion of uncertain institutional powers in the protective shadow of current consensus. Again, neither the actual nor the theoretical significance of the Committee's decision in this case should be overstated; the Japanese delegation even made a point of stressing that, in its understanding, the decisions were

---

40 S/FIN/M/7, 26 July 1995, para. 17.

"purely procedural" and "did not prejudge in any way [its] final position".[41]

Other formulations in the Secretariat's statement appear similarly presumptuous. Lack of previous challenge to legal validity is not necessarily tantamount to legal validity, and lesser significance does not *ipso facto* heal any lack of empowerment that might exist. That the "[d]elegations expressed satisfaction with this explanation", of course, also would not sanction any procedural or substantive overstepping of institutional bounds. The benignity of the decision-making thus far belies the fact that delegated decision-making can raise serious issues of legitimacy.[42]

Perhaps more problematic is the legal basis for the Committee's decisions adopting the Second and Fifth Protocols. Assuming that the legal power to adopt such texts actually does reside with the CTS, and not with the General Council,[43] it remains unclear from public documents whether the CTS can and did delegate the relevant decision-making power to the CTFS. The respective decisions adopting the Protocols were made by the Committee itself; the parallel third paragraphs read, "The Committee on Trade in Financial Services shall monitor the acceptance of the Protocol by Members concerned and shall, at the request of a Member, examine any concerns raised regarding the application of paragraph 2 above."[44] Here, too, expedience and a lack of any dissent apparently sufficed to sidestep formal procedural delegation: it is not entirely clear under what powers deriving from the Institutional Decision (absent any subsequent empowerment by the CTS) the CTFS either could adopt the two Protocols or could assign itself(!) the compulsory task of monitoring their acceptance by Members. While the content of the Protocols is well within the Committee's sectoral mandate, it is not clear why the agreements, which are akin to the four plurilateral trade agreements in Annex 4 to the WTO Agreement,

---

41 S/FIN/M/8, 26 July 1995, para. 4.

42 Esty (note 30), at 1503-1504. However, unchallenged institutional practice can itself clarify powers. *See* JOSÉ E. ALVAREZ, INTERNATIONAL ORGANIZATIONS AS LAW-MAKERS 87 *et seq*. (2005).

43 In the Secretariat's explanation quoted above, this is indeed assumed. It seems indisputable that the CTS's mandate to "oversee the functioning of [GATS]" (Art. IV:5 WTO Agreement) includes adoption of agreements such as the Second and Fifth Protocols.

44 S/L/13, 24 July 1995, para. 3; S/L/44, 3 December 1997, para. 3 (omits "on Trade in Financial Services").

needed to be separately adopted by a WTO-wide body at all (as opposed to simply the subset of Members concerned); thus, there is at least the appearance that the Committee decided to adopt the Protocols as a means of appropriating not only the task of monitoring but even the decision-making power regarding the task. Here, again, the lack of objection by WTO Members and the CTS does not supply a proper legal basis.

5. Participation of Other International Organizations

While the WTO has a primarily intergovernmental nature and is Member-driven, consultation and cooperation with other international organizations is foreseen in several relevant provisions.[45] As the meetings bring together high-level finance officials and their aides, widening the circle of participants and attendees would complicate the proceedings of the Committee and disrupt the heretofore collegial atmosphere and practice. Although the meetings are not open to the public, six international organizations currently enjoy observer status: the African, Caribbean and Pacific Group of States (ACP), the IMF, the OECD, the UN, the United Nations Conference on Trade and Development (UNCTAD), and the World Bank.[46] The CTFS, for its own meetings, has the power to grant or revoke observer status and ad hoc observer status.[47]

Beyond such observer status, several briefing sessions held for CTFS delegations display the thoroughly networked nature of the sector. On 10 October 2001, the Basel Committee on Banking Supervision, the IAIS, and the IOSCO held a joint briefing session in Geneva for delegations ahead of a Committee meeting the next day. During the session, the standard-setting financial organizations reported on their respective areas of competence, and the session was mostly well-received.[48] On the

---

[45] Institutional Decision, para. 2(f); Arts. VII:5, XXVI GATS; Art. V WTO Agreement.

[46] *See* International intergovernmental organizations granted observer status to WTO bodies, available at: http://www.wto.org/english/thewto_e/igo_obs_e.htm.

[47] WT/L/161, 25 July 1996, Annex 3; S/FIN/M/13, 29 April 1997, para. 5; S/FIN/M/26, 29 June 2000, para. 44; S/FIN/M/28, 20 November 2000, para. 31.

[48] S/FIN/M/31, 1 June 2001, para. 16; S/FIN/M/32, 9 November 2001, paras. 43-44.

morning of 22 July 2002, ahead of a Committee meeting that afternoon, the IMF and the World Bank jointly held a similar briefing session on their Financial Sector Assessment Programme and its relation to financial services trade.[49] On 26 February 2003, the World Bank also held a briefing session entitled "Finance for Growth: Policy Choices in a Volatile World" on the morning of a Committee meeting.[50] Additionally, during the afternoon meeting the IMF representative commented extensively on an IMF paper entitled "Financial Sector Stability, Reform Sequencing and Capital Flows" discussing the relationship between specific commitments in financial services and capital movements.[51] On 23 March 2004 the OECD held a briefing and information session during a meeting, presenting a document entitled "Managing Request-offer Negotiations under the GATS: The Case of Insurance Services" as part of a joint OECD/UNCTAD project; the presentation was followed by an extensive question-and-answer period.[52] And on 12 November 2007 UNCTAD reviewed its recent Expert Meeting on Trade and Development Implications of Financial Services at a CTFS meeting.[53] Such cooperation is regulated by the Rules of Procedure set up by the WTO's General Council, such that the Committee has broad discretion over the form and degree of interaction.[54] However, concern has been expressed over the level of discontinuity resulting from such inter-institutional exchange and policy-overlap.[55] Fragmentation, in part, may even have induced the negotiators of GATS to include the so-called prudential carve-out in paragraph 2(a) of the Annex on Financial Services[56] – a catchall exception which permits a WTO Member to take measures for prudential reasons (such as to protect investors or policy holders or to ensure the integrity or stability of the financial system), any provision in GATS notwithstanding.

---

49 S/FIN/M/34, 26 April 2002, paras. 27-32; S/FIN/M/35, 8 July 2002, paras. 36-37.

50 S/FIN/M/39, 7 April 2003, paras. 56-57.

51 S/FIN/M/39, 7 April 2003, paras. 12-18.

52 S/FIN/M/44, 21 April 2004, paras. 25-62.

53 S/FIN/M/55, 16 November 2007, paras. 12-29.

54 WT/L/161, 25 July 1996, Annex 3; Institutional Decision, para. 2(f).

55 S/FIN/M/32, 9 November 2001, para. 44; S/FIN/M/54, 2 July 2007, paras. 15-22.

56 Apostolos Gkoutzinis, *International Trade in Banking Services and the Role of the WTO*, 39 INTERNATIONAL LAWYER 877, 902 (2005).

The intergovernmental WTO affords limited opportunity for private actors to participate directly, whether as individuals or collectively as NGOs, lobbies, or multinational corporations, and the same holds true for the Committee's proceedings. In theory, such actors can instead lobby national governments, including especially, but not only, their own government.[57] Because the governmental delegations to the Committee call for a high level of expertise, meetings evince a high level of technocracy, especially by and among the representatives from developed countries, which not only have greater resources and know-how, but also have more capital invested in the financial services sector. The exclusion of NGOs and the public may be seen as an affirmation of the Committee's collegial practice, its technical regulatory area, and its tendency toward technocracy: beyond the necessary financial delegations from Member governments and a few select international financial organizations, opening the participant circle to the uninitiated might compromise the definite, albeit limited, functional niche that the Committee has carved out for itself.

6. *Multilevel Aspects*

As the CTFS is a forum for the dissemination of information, financial information regularly flows from the national level to the international level. This takes place both voluntarily and on demand with varying levels of legal and political pressure. Information is frequently supplied voluntarily at meetings as recent developments in financial services, allowing Members to discuss the functioning of their specific commitments under GATS and the regulatory peculiarities of their financial services markets. The Committee's monitoring of the acceptance of the Fifth Protocol also represents the flow of information from the national to the international level. More pressure, if not quite compulsion, to provide information is exerted on China under Section 18 of the Chinese Accession Protocol. As discussed above, Section 18 requires China to provide information to the CTFS, although the vague parameters of the duty leave enough slack for China *legally* to avoid providing any information it desires to withhold, whatever the *political* consequences of such evasiveness might be.[58]

---

[57] Steve Charnovitz, *Opening the WTO to Nongovernmental Interests*, 24 FORDHAM INTERNATIONAL LAW JOURNAL 173, 199-200 (2000).

[58] Steinberg (note 29), at sections III-IV; Zhang (note 27), at 408-409.

The Committee's annual reports, decisions, and the minutes of meetings represent information transferred in the opposite direction, that is, from the international to the national level. (This transfer is not identical with a transfer of the information to the public at large, because CTFS documents, in particular the minutes of meetings, are initially circulated as "restricted" among Members before eventually being derestricted and made generally accessible).[59] Again, the CTFS apparently adopts decisions and reports by consensus, meaning that dissent is handled during drafting, so that the Committee speaks in its documents with a relatively singular voice with disharmonious voices usually "noted" by the Chair in the minutes of meetings. As stated above, the consensus procedure effectively affords each delegation a veto, which in the CTFS has occasionally led to the compromise of dissent voiced under anonymity (with respect to the general public, though probably not within the Committee).

Some horizontal cooperation between the Committee and other international organizations has taken place, although it may be more properly characterized as consultation at the Committee's discretion. Several international organizations have held briefing and information sessions at or in conjunction with meetings.

IV. Reporting and Decisional Activity

1. Central Regulatory Instruments

The combination of the Committee's informality with the recommendatory, soft-law nature of its decision-making means that it exercises a diffuse kind of public authority, spread across its decisions, reports of minutes, and annual reports to the CTS. Since its inception in 1995, two significant tasks have been added to the Committee's governance activities. Firstly, its consecutive tasks to monitor Members' acceptance of the Protocols is a standard agenda item reported in the minutes of meetings and annual reports. Secondly, since 2001, the CTFS has carried out annual transitional review of China's implementation of WTO law in the financial services sector. Formulated generally: within a dense network of domestic and international financial institutions, the Committee engages in soft-law, multilateral decision-making and the dissemina-

---

[59] WT/L/452, 16 May 2002.

tion of sectoral information as a means of regulating national legal regimes for trade in financial services.

In adopting the Institutional Decision as the legal basis and framework for the CTFS's regulatory activity, the CTS availed itself of Article XXIV GATS. Paragraphs 1 and 3 of the Institutional Decision mandate and empower the Committee to report at least annually to the CTS. As discussed above, the legal basis for Committee decisions is somewhat equivocal; however, the Committee's modest powers, consensus procedure, and prudent self-restraint have thus far meant that its decisions and their bases have been uncontested. Questions as to the scope of its decision-making power thus remain purely theoretical – for the time being. At any rate, the nonbinding legal nature of Committee decisions may deflate any disputes that do arise.

The Institutional Decision generally formulates the CTFS's mandate in the financial services sector. From this basis and including subsequent tasks assigned by the CTS, the Committee has developed, in its decisional and reporting practice, a small set of agenda items that circumscribe the range of subject matter typically covered. These include monitoring the acceptance of the Fifth Protocol, recent developments in financial services trade, and the clarification of technical issues in the sector. Instead of legally obligating the given addressees, the CTFS usually phrases its reports and decisions in admonitory or recommendatory language. Because the Committee's purpose is largely to disseminate information *among its own participants*, which constitute "a discrete regulatory community,"[60] the legal and political intensity of the language chosen tends to be indirectly proportional to the prominence of the legal act. In other words, the mildest language appears in the prominent annual reports to the CTS; whereas the reports of the minutes of meetings use somewhat stronger language to identify culprits, call on Members to undertake specified activity or reform, and make decisions by consensus. Presumably, the most disputatious (and, thus, most productive) work among CTFS delegations is carried out off the record in "informal consultations in small group configurations."[61]

The addressees of the Committee's legal instruments are WTO Members generally, via the CTS as overseeing body. Here, it is worth reiterating that these addressees reflexively include the Members' delegations

---

[60] S/FIN/M/35, 8 July 2002, para. 19; S/FIN/M/37, 24 October 2002, para. 83.

[61] *See* S/FIN/M/54, 2 July 2007, para. 20.

to the Committee itself; indeed, they might even be seen as the *primary* addressees, since the flow of information regarding the functioning of WTO law and financial services law in other jurisdictions pertains particularly to the financial regulators typically sent as delegates to Geneva. Indirectly, then, the Committee's work also implicates national lawmakers, who have the dual task of implementing GATS schedules of commitments and structuring the national trade regime in compliance with GATS disciplines. Furthermore, the Committee's regulatory and administrative activity affect national financial service suppliers[62] whose commercial activity is the ultimate regulatory object of GATS in the sector. Committee documents are available initially to Members and later made accessible to the public at large, depending on restriction status, most easily accessible on the WTO's website.

2. *Multilevel Aspects*

At first glance, the decisional and reporting activity at the CTFS appears to be directed top-down, in terms of multilevel governance: an international organization acts through a subsidiary body to disseminate technical information to member states and to monitor their compliance with public international law in a highly regulated sector. On closer inspection, the levels become less clearly distinct. Expertise from the national level flows directly into the Committee via the national delegations. And the international level's superiority in the hierarchy is mitigated by the CTFS's consensus procedure, although significant political pressure can be exerted on national regulators both by the naming-and-shaming of non-complying Members and by the red-flagging of national regulatory peculiarities. In this sense, even without requiring compulsory action, the Committee is one administrative actor in the larger network of standard-setting bodies and international administrative agencies active in the financial sector.

A state's financial sector underlies every other trade sector, and compliance with international financial standards, such as the banking and capital adequacy standards referred to as Basel II, remains voluntary

---

[62] Para. 5(b) of the Annex on Financial Services defines "financial service supplier" as "any natural or juridical person of a Member wishing to supply or supplying financial services but the term 'financial service supplier' does not include a public entity." *See* von Bogdandy & Windsor (note 6), margin nos. 20-21.

but extremely beneficial.[63] Therefore, within the "discrete regulatory community" of this network, the myriad bodies necessarily rely heavily on horizontal, informal cooperation. Perhaps expectedly, this (over) abundance of standard-setters and international institutions has raised issues of overlap and fragmentation in public international law in the sector.[64] However, the principle of consensus has, here more than elsewhere, remained relatively strong because the economically strongest states form an exclusive club that other states are all too eager to join. Regulation in the financial services sector is thus *de jure* largely voluntary, diminishing misgivings about fragmentation. But the *de facto* inequality between major players and developing countries raises issues of legitimacy.

V. Review by the CTS

The Institutional Decision requires the Committee to report no less than annually to the CTS. An assessment of the CTS's opportunity to review the activity of the CTFS can only be called unremarkable. Since 1998, the CTS's annual reports to the WTO General Council have simply included under "Work of the Subsidiary Bodies" a reference, without further comment, to the annexed copy of the Committee's annual report.[65] Prior to this, CTS reports included brief descriptions of the Committee's negotiations toward the Fifth Protocol and a recommendation that Ministers abide by the prescribed timeframe.[66] Recently,

---

63 *See* BIS, BASEL II: REVISED INTERNATIONAL CAPITAL FRAMEWORK, available at: http://www.bis.org/publ/bcbsca.htm; Michael S. Barr & Geoffrey P. Miller, *Global Administrative Law*, 17 EUROPEAN JOURNAL OF INTERNATIONAL LAW 15 (2006).

64 This abundance of "multilateral international institutions and standard-setting bodies with a mandate to discuss the international financial regulatory and supervisory framework" contributed to the adoption of the prudential carve-out in para. 2(a) of the GATS Annex on Financial Services as a means of limiting WTO law's (and thus, by extension, the Committee's) impact on domestic regulatory autonomy. Gkoutzinis (note 56), 902-904. Due to the potential fragmentation, "soft regulatory convergence on the basis of international standards and codes" has been suggested in place of attempts to harden regulations. *Id.*, 913-914.

65 *See, e.g.*, S/C/26, 1 December 2006, para. 8, Annex I.

66 S/C/3, 6 November 1996, paras. XXXIV-XL, XLIII.

CTS reports have also incorporated, by reference, the Committee's Section 18 review of Chinese implementation into its own Section 18 review.[67] Thus far the CTS has simply rubber-stamped the Committee's activity.

Institutionally, this (potential) review is external to the Committee but internal to the WTO. Were the Committee ever to test the limits of its mandate or undertake controversial action, the standard of review would presumably be the Institutional Decision, which, however, not only leaves the Committee's mandate open to further assignments by the CTS, but also fails to provide much power independent of the CTS.[68] It is difficult to imagine the Committee's attempting to make any formal decision without the consent, tacit or explicit, of the CTS. The Committee's modest practice has avoided the necessity of testing the limits of its accountability. It seems reasonable to assume that the CTS and the General Council – but *only* these two superior WTO bodies – have the power to initiate review of Committee action and would have broad discretion to craft sanctions, as necessary. Again, unless practice changes drastically, such a situation is highly unlikely.

This lack of significant review also stems, in large part, from the nature of the financial services sector. Because it is highly complex and highly regulated, the trade representatives throughout the rest of the WTO may, as a general rule, defer to the financial technocrats in the CTFS. As long as the Committee remains collegial in practice and uncontroversial in content, this sectoral deference and absence of demand for clear lines of accountability will likely remain common practice at the CTFS.[69]

C. Assessment

I. Principles

As a subsidiary committee within the GATS institutional framework, the CTFS is immediately involved in promoting the general obligations of MFN treatment and transparency (Articles II-III GATS) as well as

---

67 *See* S/C/26, 1 December 2006, para. 2; S/C/M/85, 12 December 2006, paras. 20-21.

68 *See* the chapeau and para. 2(b)-(c).

69 But *see* Lori M. Wallach, *Accountable Governance in the Era of Globalization*, 50 UNIVERSITY OF KANSAS LAW REVIEW 823, 826-841, 862-864 (2002).

specific commitments in market access and national treatment (Articles XVI-XVII).[70] At least theoretically, these disciplines are in line with the economic principle of non-discrimination. Furthermore, GATS and the WTO itself are based largely on the economic principle of comparative advantage.[71] The WTO also places significant emphasis on promoting equality among its Members, specifically for developing and least developed countries.[72] Of course, whether developing countries have sufficient resources to take meaningful advantage of this normative equality, and whether the WTO's trade system would even benefit them, if they *could* take advantage of it, are open questions.[73] More specifically to GATS and financial services, the Committee's work toward defining the contours of the prudential carve-out – the catchall exception for "prudential reasons" in financial services[74] – promotes what has been called the principle of derogation in global administrative law.[75] The law governing international institutions, by its multilevel nature, requires "flexibility mechanisms to accommodate intense national political pres-

---

[70] For the WTO's own assertion of principles, *see* PRINCIPLES OF THE TRADING SYSTEM, available at: http://www.wto.org/english/thewto_e/whatis_e/tif_e/fact2_e.htm.

[71] *See* THE CASE FOR OPEN TRADE, available at: http://www.wto.org/english/thewto_e/whatis_e/tif_e/fact3_e.htm; Alan O. Sykes, *Comparative Advantage and the Normative Economics of International Trade Policy*, 1 JOURNAL OF INTERNATIONAL ECONOMIC LAW 49 (1998).

[72] *See* preambular paras. 2, 4-6, Arts. III:4, IV, V:3, XV:1, XIX:2, XXV:2 GATS. The Institutional Decision, para. 2(e), also mandates the CTFS "to provide technical assistance to developing country Members and developing countries negotiating accession to the [WTO]."

[73] *See* Victor Murinde & Cillian Ryan, *Globalization, the WTO and GATS*, *in* HANDBOOK OF INTERNATIONAL BANKING 751-763 (Andrew W. Mullineux & Victor Murinde eds., 2003); ISABEL LIPKE & MYRIAM VANDER STICHELE, FINANZDIENSTLEISTUNGEN IN DER WTO: LIZENZ ZUM KASSIEREN? 37-38 (World Economy, Ecology & Development ed., 2003).

[74] Para. 2(a) Annex on Financial Services. *See* von Bogdandy & Windsor (note 6), at margin nos. 22-24. The Committee debated on the prudential carveout during seven meetings in 2000-2001 (S/FIN/M/25-31).

[75] Esty (note 30), at 1536-1537. The principle can be seen as a specific instance of the principle of subsidiarity, applicable in politically charged situations to maintain or increase accountability, and divorced from geographical considerations.

sures ... [and] promote good governance by transferring politically sensitive decisions to national officials with greater accountability".[76]

Beyond international trade law, the Committee's role in the international regulatory network also has implications for general principles of public international law. Its openness to all Members, collegial practice, and consensus decision-making reflect the principle of the sovereign equality of states and the related principle of consensus as basis for international legal obligation. While both of these principles may be diminishing in international law, the continued, cooperative regulatory work of bodies like the CTFS flows from traditional notions of sovereignty. Perhaps most directly, however, the Committee's activity promotes the principle of transparency. In particular, its regular discussion of recent developments in financial services trade fosters regulatory transparency. As the U.S. trade representative put it, Members' presentations "emphasiz[e] transparency in their regulatory frameworks for financial services ... [T]ransparency regarding consultations with the public was beneficial and helped avoid unintended consequences of regulation. The Committee would benefit from other countries relating their practices in the future. She agreed ... that this issue was particularly relevant in the financial sector, which was highly regulated and where lack of transparency could therefore effectively mean lack of access to markets."[77]

Other principles may also be developing in the law of international institutions. Highly technical regulatory areas – such as the international financial sector, but also space law or any number of international environmental and health law sectors – may require a principle of sectoral deference among international actors. The subject matter of international institutional law is too varied, too technically complex, for any single institution to be comprehensive. This can be seen, too, in the complex adjudication of WTO panels. Article 8(4) DSU contemplates the Secretariat's maintaining indicative lists of potential panelists, indicating their "specific areas of experience or expertise". Moreover, paragraph 4 of the Annex on Financial Services requires panelists in disputes over financial matters or prudential regulatory issues to have "the necessary expertise relevant to the specific financial service".[78] While the WTO Appellate Body, in contrast, *is* a standing court, its jurisdiction is

---

76 *Id.* at 1536.

77 S/FIN/M/37, 24 October 2002, para. 83.

78 *See also* von Bogdandy & Windsor (note 6), at margin nos. 29-30.

limited to questions of law, so the potential lack of sector-specific expertise is far less significant.[79] The exclusivity of the club of financial representatives, whether in the CTFS or in any of the international financial regulatory organizations, exemplifies the administrative necessity for sector-specific expertise.

The other side of this sectoral deference *between* sectors is the cooperative networking *within* sectors. As one forum in a network of financial regulatory institutions, the Committee has some role in the setting of standards[80] such as Basel II or the Core Principles of the Joint Forum of the Basel Committee, the IOSCO, and the IAIS.[81] Because such standards are "mere" soft law, toward which aspiring financial regulators can orient reforms, one author has called such standard-setting a case study of the "proselytization imperative".[82] When the CTFS meets, and especially when it provides a forum for such direct standard-setters to present information, it engages in such "proselytization of minimum standards from developed countries to less developed countries".[83] Soft-law proselytization, then, becomes an alternative to hard-law compulsion. Common standards in complicated regulatory areas such as the financial services sector provide an efficient form of rulemaking: they craft nonbinding standards that states nonetheless frequently seek to implement on the national level.[84] In the Committee's case, it facilitates not simply the generalized setting of such standards, but also the implementation of its Members' schedules of specific commitments.

---

79 Eric H. Leroux, *Trade in Financial Services under the World Trade Organization*, 36 JOURNAL OF WORLD TRADE 413, 432 (2002).

80 For a Committee debate about what role the Committee and the WTO have in standard-setting, *see* S/FIN/M/42, 12 November 2003, paras. 49-69.

81 THE JOINT FORUM, CORE PRINCIPLES: CROSS-SECTORAL COMPARISON (BIS ed., 2001), available at: http://www.bis.org/publ/joint03.pdf.

82 Zaring (note 15), at 580-585.

83 *Id.* at 583.

84 *Id.* at 592 ("Whatever standard is chosen has a good chance of developing an adoptive momentum by virtue of the advantages regulators see in being a part of the 'network' of regulators applying the same schema to their regulated industry"); Michael P. Malloy, *Emerging International Regime of Financial Services Regulation*, 18 TRANSNATIONAL LAWYER 329, 347-349 (2005) ("[Basel II] seems to represent the emergence of a new kind of source of law: an international administrative practice involving rule proposal for public comment, revision in light of public comments, and adoption, implementation, and enforcement at the national level.").

Within the WTO, the CTFS provides a forum for informational exchange, provides technical assistance to developing countries, and provides guidance on the implementation of GATS generally and by specific Members, thereby promoting legal certainty by coordinating the national execution of WTO law.

II. Legitimacy

The Committee's exercise of public authority raises fewer questions than many international institutions, owing to its peripheral role in the international financial network, its collegiality and informality, its non-binding decision-making and reporting, and especially its focus on consensus-building. Instead, questions shift toward the cleft between industrialized and developing countries; the availability of the resources, capacity, and expertise necessary to take meaningful part in meetings and negotiations; and the lack of both openness to the public and participation of NGOs. In terms of legitimacy, the Committee fares moderately, open to both criticism and praise.

Some scholars bifurcate legitimacy into process (or input) legitimacy and results (or output) legitimacy; the former can further be assessed *ex ante* or *ex post*.[85] In the CTFS, then, process legitimacy *ex ante* appears to be too opaque. The CTFS consists of delegations of ministers or other high-level trade representatives, but the compositions of delegations are neither set nor readily apparent from publicly accessible WTO documents. One might also object that, in the CTFS, all delegations are equal, but some are more equal than others: "from the perspective of smaller developing countries, global regulatory institutions including the WTO ... might already appear to be 'administering' them at the bidding of the industrialized countries."[86] Moreover, only a handful of international organizations have observer status, excluding NGOs, watchdog groups, and the public at large. However, "while many reports and minutes of meetings are published online, actual participation in meetings at all levels [of the WTO] is crucial in order to understand the nature and depth of political negotiations and compromises which

---

85 *See* Venzke, in this volume.

86 Benedict Kingsbury, Nico Krisch & Richard B. Stewart, *The Emergence of Global Administrative Law*, 68 LAW & CONTEMPORARY PROBLEMS 15, 27 (2004-2005).

lie behind formal pronouncements."[87] Process legitimacy *ex post* may be even more problematic due to the almost complete lack, in practice, of meaningful review by the CTS, combined with the exclusion of NGOs. While the low profile of Committee activity has arguably made such oversight superfluous, the increasing significance of the WTO and GATS and the continued debate over the lack of transparency may eventually demand openness at all levels.

The assessment of results legitimacy is more positive. The CTFS may not be in high demand as a topic for debate in legal journals or newspaper editorials, but it has certainly found its highly specific, highly complex niche of influence in the network of international financial regulators. No other forum has the expertise and institutional positioning to speak with the Committee's level of credibility regarding the modest but significant area where international trade law, GATS schedules of specific commitments, and national banking, securities, and insurance regulation converge.

III. Conclusion

The foregoing discussion has been intended to help to illustrate the multifaceted nature of the law of international institutions. One actor among the myriad international financial regulators plays its seemingly minor role in the tremendously intricate choreography of one of most complex sectors of global governance. Other players certainly have more prominent roles and greater influence. The Basel Committee's effects, for example, can hardly be understated, but at the same time it lacks the institutional framework and compulsory dispute-settlement jurisdiction that the CTFS enjoys in the WTO. The IMF and the World Bank enjoy an enormous budget but have a limited mandate related specifically to developmental aid. The OECD has a wide mandate but lacks the credibility that flows from a broad representation of the international community. Due in large part to this versatility and diversity, this network of international financial administrators exerts an ever-increasing influence on the world economy, public international law, and national administrative law.

---

[87] Ngaire Woods & Amrita Narlikar, *Governance and the limits of accountability*, 53 INTERNATIONAL SOCIAL SCIENCE JOURNAL 569, 577 (2001).

International institutional law will only grow in significance in the foreseeable future. Already, the received sources of international law in Article 38 of the ICJ Statute no longer circumscribe the sphere of the law's influence on the international stage.[88] The Committee can be seen as an outlier, a borderline case, among international regulatory institutions – one that begins to show the definitional boundaries of the still uncertainly defined area. It may well be that the observer will scrutinize the motley gestalt of international institutions – each with a limited mandate, limited membership, and limited powers – and will come to the conclusion that the whole of international institutional law is greater than the sum of its parts.

88 *See* Kingsbury, Krisch & Stewart (note 86), at 29-31.

3. The Exercise of Public Authority through General Instruments

3.1 Secondary Law

The Administration of the Vocabulary of International Trade: The Adaptation of WTO Schedules to Changes in the Harmonized System

*By Isabel Feichtner**

* I would like to thank Professor Armin von Bogdandy, Jürgen Friedrich, Marc Jacob and Eva Richter for their help. This project has been supported by the European Social Fund.

A. von Bogdandy et al. (eds.), *The Exercise of Public Authority by International Institutions*, Beiträge zum ausländischen öffentlichen Recht und Völkerrecht 210, DOI 10.1007/978-3-642-04531-8_16, © Springer-Verlag Berlin Heidelberg 2010

A. The Object and Objectives of the Case Study

A common language is indispensible for reaching and maintaining understanding in all inter-subject relations, including international relations. One element of today's common language in the field of international trade in goods is the Harmonized Commodity Description and Coding System (the Harmonized System/HS) which is maintained by the World Customs Organization (WCO). The HS provides for a common vocabulary by classifying all traded goods according to a nomenclature. This common vocabulary facilitates, and avoids misunderstandings in communications about products. It thus reduces transaction costs and consequently is of eminent economic importance for today's globalized trade relations. Take for example WTO tariff negotiations with respect to chocolate: While one party might assume that the product commonly referred to as white chocolate is included in the negotiations on chocolate, the other trading partner might assume that it is excluded for the reason that it does not contain cocoa and thus does not qualify as chocolate. Reference during the negotiations to specific positions of the HS nomenclature reduces the probability of such misunderstandings. If during the exemplary tariff negotiations parties would refer to the HS heading Chocolate no party could later claim that the negotiated tariff should also apply to white chocolate since the HS classifies the product which is commonly referred to as white chocolate under the heading Sugar Confectionary (and there under a specific sub-position) whereas chocolate containing cocoa is classified under the heading Chocolate.[1] The vocabulary of the Harmonized System is a point of reference for many legal norms which relate to international trade in goods – in my example the legal obligation to comply with the negotiated tariff concession (Art. II GATT) and not to discriminate against like products (Art. I, III GATT). While the HS provides the vocabulary, these norms provide the grammar of a common language of international trade.[2]

The object of this study is the adaptation of World Trade Organization (WTO) schedules of concessions – in which Members' tariff commitments with respect to certain goods are laid down and which are negotiated and structured on the basis of the HS – to changes of the Harmonized System.[3] Two characteristics of the adaptation of WTO goods schedules to HS changes motivate this study. First, the administration of the HS in the WCO and its reception in the WTO is an instance of intensive cross-linkage between the WTO and another international institution, the WCO; and second, the adaptation of schedules in the WTO is a rare occasion of effective administration within the WTO.

While the Harmonized System is administered within the WCO, i.e. regularly adapted to changes in trade and needs of its users, interpreted and explained, the adaptation of WTO schedules to HS changes, which can also be characterized as administration, takes place within the WTO. This paper attempts to clarify the subject-matter linkage which exists due to this division of labor, where the WCO administers the vocabulary to which the rules of the WTO relate, as well as the (limited)

---

1 To be sure, even when the HS is used, classification of products will frequently be contentious. *See, e.g.* the dispute between the European Communities on one side and Brazil and Thailand on the other concerning the classification of salted frozen boneless chicken cuts, *EC – Chicken Classification*, WT/DS269, 286/R (panel report), WT/DS269, 286/AB/R (Appellate Body Report).

2 The metaphor of the HS as a vocabulary therefore seems more fitting than that of the HS as the language of international trade which is often used. *See, e.g.* the WCO referring to the HS as a universal economic language, http://www.wcoomd.org/home_wco_topics_hsoverviewboxes_overview_hsharmonizedsystem.htm; PETROS C. MAVROIDIS, TRADE IN GOODS. THE GATT AND THE OTHER AGREEMENTS REGULATING TRADE IN GOODS 73 (2007) (depicting the HS as supplying the common language to describe goods).

3 In the following when I speak of schedules of concessions I mean schedules of concessions with respect to goods which are annexed to the General Agreement on Tariffs and Trade (GATT) and according to Art. II:7 GATT form an integral part of the GATT.

institutional linkages. Such clarification provides a starting point for a legal conceptualization of inter-institutional linkages. Inter-institutional linkages are often neglected in legal research on international institutions which frequently focuses on one institution, its organs and external "vertical" relations with its Members.[4] However, functional differentiation and sectoral fragmentation of international law heighten the importance of inter-institutional relations and consequently the need to conceptualize them.[5] With respect to the linkages between the WTO and the WCO such conceptualization should address, *i.a.*, the relationship between the settlement of classification disputes within the WCO and the WTO.[6]

The focus of the study is on the schedule adaptation process within the WTO organs. It provides insights into an area in which the WTO engages in effective administration. With effective administration I mean activities (mainly) within the lower specialized bodies of the WTO with a strong involvement of the organization's bureaucracy – the secretariat – which are conducted in pursuit of the organization's tasks and produce external effects.[7] While administration in the WTO frequently re-

---

[4] For a study that aims at a conceptualization of horizontal cross-linkages, *see* Kal Raustiala & David G. Victor, *The Regime Complex for Plant Genetic Resources*, 58 INTERNATIONAL ORGANIZATION 277-309 (2004). Cross-linkages between international dispute settlement organs are relatively well-studied and there have been several attempts to conceptualize them in legal terms. *See e.g.* JASPER FINKE, DIE PARALLELITÄT INTERNATIONALER STREITBEILEGUNGSMECHANISMEN. UNTERSUCHUNG DER AUS DER STÄRKUNG DER INTERNATIONALEN GERICHTSBARKEIT RESULTIERENDEN KONFLIKTE (2004); HEIKO SAUER, JURISDIKTIONSKONFLIKTE IN MEHREBENENSYSTEMEN (2008).

[5] Moreover institutional linkage seems to be a more plausible and also a more desirable solution to the perceived dangers of fragmentation than, for example, a hierarchy of norms which does not leave room for politics. For an approach that stresses inter-institutional cooperation, *see* Gunther Teubner & Andreas Fischer-Lescano, *Regime Collisions: The Vain Search for Legal Unity in the Fragmentation of Global Law*, 25 MICHIGAN JOURNAL OF INTERNATIONAL LAW 999-1046 (2004).

[6] This could provide a principled answer to the question whether in the *EC – Chicken Classification* the WTO panel or rather the HS Committee of the WCO should have decided the classification question. *See* (note 1).

[7] This could also be characterized as the exercise of public authority. *See* Armin von Bogdandy, Philipp Dann and Matthias Goldmann, *Developing the Publicness of Public International Law: Towards a Legal Framework for Global Governance Activities*, in this issue (employing a wide definition). Administra-

sults in non-binding instruments[8] or consists of assistance and support to Members,[9] the adaptation of schedules is an exception in that it results in a relatively large amount of binding secondary law, namely decisions on procedures and waiver decisions, and eventually the certification of adapted schedules. The adaptation of schedules is characterized on the one hand by a widely informal managerial approach – albeit based on formal procedures – which aims at the efficient transposition of HS changes into WTO Members' schedules and on the other hand the objective to maintain formal legality in the external relations between WTO Members – an objective which is achieved by the granting of waivers. A further feature is the key part which the secretariat and chairpersons play in the adaptation process. These findings contradict the generalizing depictions of the WTO as a purely member-driven organization with a weak secretariat and contribute to a more differentiated picture of the activities taking place routinely within the organization and outside the multilateral negotiation rounds.[10]

My aim is to present the institutional law and practice relating to the adaptation of schedules so as to contribute to a more differentiated picture of the law-making and administrative processes within the WTO. The criteria according to which I have chosen to structure this study are, firstly, the legal framework constituted by the primary law of the WTO Agreement, including the General Agreement on Tariffs and Trade (GATT) 1994, secondary procedural law laid down in formal legal decisions, as well as other guidelines or generally applied rules even

---

tion as used and defined here, however, is a narrower term since it does not encompass acts taken by the highest political organs that are preceded by processes of inter-state diplomatic bargaining.

8 For example the recent draft guidelines to further the practical implementation of Art. 6 of the SPS which explicitly provide that they shall "not add to nor detract from the existing rights and obligations of Members under [...] any [...] WTO Agreement" G/SPS/W/218, para. 2 (25 February 2008); on the activities of the FTSC see Joseph Windsor, in this issue.

9 For example in the form of workshops organized by the secretariat for national administrators.

10 For other works which stress the role of secretariat or chairpersons, *see* Joseph H.H. Weiler, *The Rule of Lawyers and the Ethos of Diplomats*, 35 JOURNAL OF WORLD TRADE 191 (2001) (on the secretariat's role in dispute settlement); Gregory Shaffer, *The Role of the Director-General and Secretariat: Chapter IX of the Sutherland Report*, 4 WORLD TRADE REVIEW 429 (2005); John S. Odell, *Chairing a WTO Negotiation*, 8 JOURNAL OF INTERNATIONAL ECONOMIC LAW 425 (2005).

though not formally adopted, and institutional practices of a general nature. I opt for such a broad framework of analysis because a legal analysis restricted to positive legal requirements derived from treaty law and formal sources of secondary law loses sight of important practices and processes which impact on the shape and application of the procedures in question.[11] Secondly, the role of bodies and organs of the WTO as well as the WCO in the process of schedule adaptation is observed and in particular the impact of the WTO Secretariat and committee chairpersons on the process. Thirdly, attention is paid to compliance with the procedures and the effectiveness of the process in achieving the objective of schedule adaptation, as well as, where possible, the underlying interest structures – the politics of the process. Attention to actors and interest structures is important in order to understand the process and to identify potential legitimacy deficits and seems more meaningful than the otherwise often-adopted distinction between political and technical matters and related differentiations with respect to legitimacy requirements. This study thus constitutes a doctrinal as well as a hermeneutical exercise. As a caveat it has to be noted that my observations on processes, practices, effects and motivations are predominately based on the publicly available minutes of the formal meetings of the relevant WTO bodies and thus limited by the information contained therein and the conclusions and interpretations this information permits.

B. The Harmonized System

I. The Harmonized System, Its Objectives and Uses

The Harmonized System consists of a Nomenclature, Section, Chapter and Subheading Notes as well as General Rules for the interpretation of the Harmonized System.[12] The nomenclature is divided into 21 sections, 99 chapters, 1241 headings, and more than 5000 sub-positions, re-

---

[11] On the different ways of modification and development of law under the GATT 1947 and the important role of institutional practices in this respect, *see* WOLFGANG BENEDEK, DIE RECHTSORDNUNG DES GATT AUS VÖLKERRECHTLICHER SICHT 115-130 (1990).

[12] Art. 1(a) International Convention on the Harmonized Commodity Description and Coding System (HS Convention). The convention and nomenclature can be found on the WCO's website, at: http://www.wcoomd.org/home_wco_topics_hsoverviewboxes.htm.

sulting in a 6 digit classification system. Each traded product can be subsumed under one six-digit position; it cannot, however, come under more than one position. Take again white chocolate: this product falls under Section IV: Prepared Foodstuffs; Beverage, Spirits and Vinegar; Tobacco and manufactured Tobacco Substitutes, Chapter 17: Sugars and sugar confectionary, Heading 17.04: Sugar confectionary (including white chocolate), not containing cocoa and sub-position 1704.90: Other.[13]

The Harmonized System is annexed to and forms an integral part of the International Convention on the Harmonized Commodity Description and Coding System (HS Convention) which was established under the auspices of the Customs Cooperation Council – which is now the World Customs Organization (WCO) – and replaces the Brussels Convention on Nomenclature for the Classification of Goods in Customs Tariffs of 1950.[14] The HS Convention entered into force on January 1, 1988. As of March 2008, 133 countries and customs/economic unions were parties to the convention. These are obliged to use the HS nomenclature for their customs tariff and statistical nomenclatures. They are allowed to introduce further subdivisions beyond the 6 digit level of the HS (Art. 3:3 HS Convention) and most industrialized countries do so.[15] E.g. the Combined Nomenclature of the European Community extends the 6 digit HS code by two further digits thus creating a further level of sub-positions.[16] All in all more than 200 countries and economies use the HS nomenclature as the basis for their customs tariffs and trade statistics.[17]

---

[13] The classification under the residual position "Other" results from the fact that the only other sub-position is titled "Chewing gum, whether or not sugar-coated."

[14] The Brussels Convention had replaced the so-called Geneva Nomenclature of 1937.

[15] If a country wants to impose a specific customs duty on white chocolate, which according to the HS falls under the residual position "Other," it needs to create a further (seventh) level of differentiation in order to separate white chocolate from the other products falling under this residual position.

[16] The Combined Nomenclature (a tariff and statistics nomenclature) of the European Community is established by Regulation 2658/87.

[17] *See* http://www.wcoomd.org/home_wco_topics_hsoverviewboxes_hsharmonizedsystem.htm. WCO Members are not obliged to become parties to the HS Convention and at the same time parties to the HS Convention do not necessarily have to be Members of the WCO (Art. 11(c) HS Convention).

The HS is a multipurpose tool which is used not only by the contracting parties to the HS Convention and other states, but also private entities and international institutions. The main objective of the HS Convention is designated in its preamble as the facilitation of international trade;[18] it is also used for purposes unrelated to trade such as the imposition of internal taxes, economic research and analysis,[19] or the monitoring of controlled goods, such as e.g. endangered species, hazardous waste or ozone-depleting substances.[20]

While the HS is relevant for various international institutions,[21] not only in the economic sector, its relevance is greatest within the WTO which shares with the WCO the objective of facilitation of international trade.[22] Several WTO agreements, such as the Agricultural Agreement and the Information Technology Agreement refer for their product coverage to the Harmonized System, the draft rules of non-preferential origin have been based on the HS,[23] and most importantly WTO schedules of concessions for goods are based on the HS nomenclature. Today practically all WTO Members base their national tariffs, i.e. their structured lists of product descriptions[24] according to which customs duties are imposed and administered, on the HS nomenclature and have schedules which are based on the HS even though not all WTO Mem-

---

[18] HS Convention preamble, first recital.

[19] *See* http://www.wcoomd.org/home_wco_topics_hsoverviewboxes_hsharmonizedsystem.htm.

[20] Monitoring is facilitated when the controlled items can be identified by reference to a HS position.

[21] Examples are the Convention on International Trade in Endangered Species of Wild Fauna and Flora (CITES), the Basel Convention, The United Nations Food and Agricultural Organization, or the Montreal Protocol. The trade statistical systems of the UN (*e.g.* the Standard International Trade Classification (SITC) and Central Product Classification (CPC)) are also based on the HS nomenclature.

[22] According to the WTO Agreement's preamble expansion of trade in goods is one of the objectives of the WTO.

[23] With respect to rules of origin it is interesting to note that the Technical Committee on Rules of Origin which carries out the main technical work of harmonizing non-preferential rules of origin was established by the WTO and is a WTO body, but operates under the auspices of the WCO with the WCO Council exercising supervision over it (Art. 4:2 Agreement on Rules of Origin).

[24] Peter Van den Bossche, The Law and Policy of the World Trade Organization 379 (2005).

bers are parties to the HS Convention.[25] The tariff data available on the WTO website now is also presented in a standardized form by using the HS nomenclature.[26]

As has already been illustrated, the Harmonized System facilitates the negotiation of tariff concessions. It reduces transaction costs by enabling negotiators to refer to a HS position for a specific product line under negotiation with a common meaning ascribed to it by the HS. During the Uruguay Round tariff negotiations were based on the Harmonized System nomenclature,[27] and on August 1, 2004 WTO Members agreed to finalize the results of the currently on-going non-agricultural market access negotiations of the Doha Round in the HS 2002 nomenclature.[28]

After agreement has been reached on concessions, the HS, including the notes and general rules of interpretation, as well as explanatory notes and WCO classification decisions of the HS Committee help WTO Members to interpret and determine the content of concessions and to monitor compliance with the obligation in Art. II GATT to grant the negotiated concessions.[29] The HS is also relevant for the interpretation of other WTO obligations relating to goods; most importantly the HS classification of a product can be one factor in the determination of the "likeness" of products, a prerequisite for obligations of non-discrimination in the form of most-favored nation treatment (Art. I GATT) or national treatment (Art. III GATT).[30]

---

25 As of 31 March 2006, 78 WTO Members (counting the EC-25 as one) were contracting parties to the HS Convention, http://www.wto.org/English/thewto_e/coher_e/wto_wco_e.htm.

26 *See* http://www.wto.org/english/news_e/news07_e/tariff_sept07_e.htm.

27 VAN DEN BOSSCHE (note 24), at 401, 419.

28 WT/L/579, Annex B, paragraph 5. That tariff negotiations are conducted on the basis of the HS does not mean that WTO Members are limited by the product differentiations which the HS provides. They may further differentiate and negotiate tariff cuts with respect to only a subgroup of a product group subsumed under a subposition of the HS.

29 The relevance of the HS for the interpretation of concessions has been confirmed by the Appellate Body in *EC—Computer Equipment*, WT/DS62, 67, 68/AB/R, para. 89 and *EC –Chicken Classification* (note 1), para. 199.

30 Appellate Body Report in *Japan – Alcoholic Beverages* WT/DS 8, 10, 11/AB/R, at 21, 22.

II. Administration of the Harmonized System of Commodity Coding and Description in the WCO

For it to remain viable as a common vocabulary the HS has to be regularly adapted to changes in reality, such as the development of new products and changing trade patterns, as well as to changes in the needs of its users.[31] To ensure its commonality the HS should be uniformly interpreted. These two demands – for continuous adaptation as well as uniform interpretation – explain certain institutional features of the HS Convention, in particular the entrustment of specialized committees with the development and interpretation of the Harmonized System, as well as the facilitated amendment procedure.

Amendments to the HS Convention are prepared by the HS Committee, which is established under the HS Convention and which is composed of one representative of each contracting party (Art. 6:1 HS Convention), and the Review Sub-Committee and the HS Working Party which have been established by the HS Committee according to Art. 6:8 HS Convention. The HS is revised – and the HS Convention amended accordingly – every 4-6 years.[32] Apart from changes in technology or patterns of international trade (Art. 7:1 (a) HS Convention), societal and environmental concerns with respect to certain goods are also reasons for HS changes.[33] Proposals from contracting parties to the

[31] The HS Convention recognizes in its preamble the "importance of ensuring that the Harmonized System is kept up to date in the light of changes in technology or in patterns of international trade," recital 11.

[32] In 1988 the WCO Council endorsed a conclusion by the HS Committee to review the HS at regular intervals of 3 to 4 years. So far revisions to the HS have entered into force in 1992, 1996, 2002 and 2007, they are referred to as the HS1992, HS1996, HS2002 and HS 2007 changes.

[33] The 2007 HS amendments include changes due to technological progress, changes in trade patterns and amendments for social and environmental reasons. The latter entailed *i.a.* the inclusion of new subheadings to facilitate the monitoring and control of certain species of fish (FAO), pesticides (Rotterdam Convention) or ozone-depleting substances (Montreal Protocol). The HS 2007 changes further take into account the structure of other international agreements, *e.g.* the WTO's Information Technology Agreement. *See* for a summary of the HS 2007 amendments the report of the representative of the WCO to the Committee on Market Access at its meeting on 30 March 2005, G/MA/M/39, paras. 4.9-4.19.

convention as well as international institutions[34] are first considered by the Review Sub-Committee. Proposals which have been approved by the Review Sub-Committee are submitted to the HS Committee[35] which aggregates these proposals and at the end of the review period makes a proposal for an amendment (Art. 7 HS Convention).[36] Decisions on amendment proposals by the HS Committee have to be taken by a two-thirds majority.[37] An amendment proposal which is made by the HS Committee is examined by the WCO Council[38] (Art. 8:1 HS Convention). If no Council member who is a contracting party to the HS Convention requests that a proposal be referred back to the HS Committee for re-consideration, the Council recommends the amendment to the contracting parties. An amendment is deemed to be accepted 6 months after its notification by the Secretary General unless a contracting party has objected to a proposed change (Art. 16:3 HS Convention). In case of an objection the respective HS change does not enter into force for any contracting party. An amendment to the HS Convention enters into force on January 1 of the second or third year after notification depending on whether the amendment has been notified before or after April 1 (Art. 16:4 HS Convention).

The interpretation of the HS is also entrusted to the HS Committee. After acceptance and before entry into force of HS changes the HS Committee establishes and amends explanatory notes to the HS, aided by the HS Working Party, and approves correlation tables (between the former and the amended HS nomenclature) established by the WCO

---

[34] Proposals by national governments are often prompted by private sector initiatives that are addressed to the customs or trade ministry and are considered by all agencies which have an interest in the matter; as an example of an international institution proposing a HS change, *see* Decision 13.37 of the Conference of the Parties of CITES according to which the secretariat shall "liaise with the World Customs Organization to promote the establishment and use of specific headings within the standard classifications of the Harmonized System for tortoises and freshwater turtles and for products thereof".

[35] Rule 2(b) Rules of Procedure of the Review Sub-Committee.

[36] The amendment proposals are drafted by the HS Working Party.

[37] Art. 6 HS Convention and Rule 19 of the Rules of Procedure of the HS Committee.

[38] Members of the Council are the contracting parties to the Convention establishing a Customs Cooperation Council. These are not necessarily also all parties to the HS Convention.

Secretariat.[39] These documents are not legally binding but important aids for the exercise of implementing HS changes.[40] To further ensure the uniform interpretation of the HS nomenclature, the HS Convention provides for the settlement of classification disputes by the HS Committee (Art. 10 HS Convention). To settle disputes, the HS Committee is entitled to make recommendations which the parties to a dispute may in advance agree to accept as binding (Art. 10:4 HS Convention). These recommendations can be adopted by a simple majority.[41]

The entrustment of specialized committees with the negotiation of amendments and the interpretation of the HS, the possibility of majority voting in these committees, the facilitated amendment procedure through presumption of acceptance of HS changes if no objection is voiced and the lack of a ratification requirement are meant to provide for expertise and efficacy and justify the characterization of the maintenance of the HS as an administrative activity within the WCO.

III. The Politics of HS Administration

Even though the maintenance of the HS at first sight appears as a highly technical matter, and even though the HS constitutes a public good[42] and its administration lies in the common interest of the contracting parties to the HS Convention, it may give rise to conflicts of interests between its users. Such conflicts concern first the question of which terms shall constitute the vocabulary of international trade and second the denomination of goods according to the established terms.

---

39 Up to the HS96 changes correlation tables were prepared by the CCC Secretariat without involvement of the HS Committee.

40 Explanatory notes, classification opinions and other advice on interpretation is presumed to be accepted by the WCO Council unless a contracting party to the HS Convention requests referral of the matter to the Council within a specified time period (Art. 8:2 HS Convention). Some contracting parties have put the explanatory notes into law, see statement of the representative of the WCO to the Committee on Market Access at its meeting on 30 March 2005 (note 33), para. 4.36.

41 Art. 6:4 HS Convention and Rule 19 of the Rules of Procedure of the HS Committee.

42 The HS nomenclature constitutes a public good in the economic meaning of the term since it is non-excludable and its consumption is non-rivalrous.

Important economic, but also social or environmental interests may be attached to the creation or deletion of a subheading of the Harmonized System nomenclature which might not be shared by all users or even opposed by some. E.g. certain users might have an interest in the creation of a sub-heading for a certain product because they want to differentiate their domestic tax system[43] with respect to this product, e.g. impose an environmental tax on it, or because they wish to restrict trade with respect to it or impose a customs duty. To be sure, if no specific sub-heading is created this does not necessarily frustrate the realization of these interests, since the HS nomenclature allows for further individual differentiation beyond its 6 digit-level; however, such differentiation is costly.

While the aforesaid conflicts of interest relate to the abstract decision as to which product groups receive their own heading, i.e. which terms make up the Harmonized System vocabulary, further conflicts of interests relate to the concrete question of how to classify a certain commodity, i.e. what that product is called according to the agreed-upon vocabulary of the HS. This question arose e.g. in the WTO dispute between the European Communities on the one side and Brazil and Thailand on the other with respect to salted frozen boneless chicken cuts which the EC subsumed under one heading of the HS nomenclature, Brazil and Thailand under another. The involved interests were economic in nature. A higher tariff applied to the heading favored by the EC than to the heading favored by the opponents. This dispute shows that, while uniform interpretation and classification is essential and for this reason should fall within the competence of the WCO, it should not be treated as a merely technical enterprise.[44]

---

[43] In some countries tax laws make reference to HS classification of products.

[44] In *EC—Chicken Classification* (note 1) the AB upheld the panel's finding that the products in question are covered by the EC's tariff commitment of heading 02.10 of its schedule which corresponds to heading 02.10 of the HS nomenclature. The WCO had taken the position that the dispute settlement procedures provided for in the HS Convention should have been followed by the parties to the dispute before the panel took a decision on a violation of WTO law, in this case Art. II GATT (*see* panel report para. 7.53). Subsequent to the adoption of the AB report, the HS Committee adopted a classification decision with the same result (classification decision No 1, 40th Session, October 2007, available at: http://www.wcoomd.org/files/1.%20Public%20files/PDFandDocuments/Harmonized%20System/HS_COMM_Classifications_Decisions/CLHS40Eng.pdf. On this dispute and the question where it should have been

C. The Adaptation of WTO Schedules to the Harmonized System

I. The Interrelationship of Legal Obligations Under the HS Convention, the GATT and Municipal Constitutions

First it should be noted that the HS Convention and the GATT are legally unrelated. The HS Convention clarifies that it does not impose any obligations on the contracting parties in relation to the rates of custom duties they impose (Art. 9 HS Convention) and the GATT does not impose on WTO Members an obligation to use a certain tariff nomenclature.[45]

However, the obligations under the HS Convention and the GATT are factually interrelated. The contracting parties to the HS Convention are obliged to implement amendments to the Convention by the time these amendments enter into force.[46] Most contracting parties, mandated by municipal constitutional law, do so by adopting implementing legislation.[47] The transposition of HS changes into national tariffs in turn affects WTO Members' obligations under WTO law. The implementation of a HS change may – as will be seen – affect the value of a tariff concession. In any case however the disparity between the national tariff and the schedule, which results from the domestic implementation of HS changes, affects the possibility to monitor whether a WTO Member is in compliance with its obligation not to impose higher tariff rates on imported products than those laid down in its respective schedule (Art. II GATT).

Thus in order to comply with their international obligations under the HS Convention, with WTO law and municipal constitutional law, states and customs unions, including the EC, ideally first adapt their WTO schedules to HS changes and subsequently, until these changes

---

adjudicated, *see* Hendrik Horn & Robert L. Howse, *European Communities – Customs Classification of Frozen Boneless Chicken Cuts*, 7 World Trade Review 9, 32 *et seq.* (2008).

45 GATT panel report in *Spain – Unroasted Coffee*, BISD 28S/102, para 4.4.

46 A Developing Country contracting party may, according to Art. 4(1) HS convention, delay the application of all or some subheadings.

47 According to Art. 12 regulation 2658/87 the EU Commission publishes annually the complete version of the combined tariff together with the duty rates in form of a regulation.

become binding through the entry into force of the respective amendments to the HS Convention, incorporate them into their national tariffs in compliance with municipal constitutional law. As will be seen in the following, this sequence is mostly not achieved in practice and WTO schedules are not adapted before HS changes are implemented domestically. This necessitates the suspension of Art. II GATT through waivers to maintain legality.

II. The Impact of HS Changes on WTO Schedules

The incorporation of HS changes into WTO schedules in all cases results in formal changes to the schedules, but may also result in substantive changes which affect the value of concessions.[48] The value of tariff concessions may be substantially affected by HS changes when two HS positions are merged into one. This is the case when a WTO Member had adopted different bound rates with respect to the two formerly distinct product groups, or a bound rate with respect to one, but not the other.[49] A change of the scope of the tariff concession in such a case can be avoided when a sub-heading is created beyond the six-digit level of the Harmonized System. However, the creation of further subheadings is sometimes not feasible since it would result in undue complexity. In such a case different methods have been identified how the affected concessions could nonetheless be maintained or at least their value not materially undermined. Thus, Members could apply the lowest rate of any previous tariff line to the merged new tariff line, they could apply the tariff rate which was previously applied to the tariff line with the majority of trade, the trade weighted average rate for the new line or the

48 Concessions which are included in the schedules and which may be affected by adaptation to HS changes are not only tariff concessions. However the impact of HS changes is greatest with respect to tariff concessions which shall be the focus of the following observations.

49 For a more detailed analysis of how the adoption or changes of the HS nomenclature can affect tariff concessions, *see* Dayong Yu, the Harmonized System – Amendments and their Impact on WTO Members' Schedules, WTO Staff Working Paper ERSD-2008-02, at 12, 13, available at: http://www.wto.org/english/res_e/reser_e/ersd200802_e.htm; *see also* WTO Procedures for Introduction of HS2002 Changes to Schedules of Concessions, WT/L/405, Attachment A, at 3, 4.

arithmetic average of the previous rates in case the trade weighted average cannot be calculated due to insufficient trade data.[50]

III. The Adaptation of WTO Schedules to HS Changes

1. The Need for Procedures for the Adaptation of WTO Schedules to HS Changes

With respect to the adaptation of schedules to Harmonized System changes, legal procedures serve three purposes. First, they formally legalize the resulting modifications of the treaty, second, they are intended to increase the efficiency of the adaptation exercise, and third, procedures serve Members to safeguard their benefits from other Members' concessions.

Schedules – according to Art. II:7 GATT – constitute an integral part of the GATT and as such, via Art. II:2 WTO Agreement, an integral part of the WTO Agreement. Consequently, each change to a Member's schedule – be it formal or substantive – is a change to the WTO Agreement and may not be made unilaterally by a WTO Member. Since the treaty amendment procedure foreseen in the GATT 1947 was deemed to be too complicated and time-consuming for mere formal changes to schedules which did not affect the value of concessions, the CONTRACTING PARTIES adopted a decision which foresees that such changes are formally adopted and enter into force through certification by the Director General.[51] This is the so-called rectification procedure. Another procedure – set out in Art. XXVIII and a decision of the GATT Council[52] – allows Members to withdraw and modify the value of concessions. In order to safeguard other Members' rights in these concessions it requires renegotiation between the Member that wishes to modify concessions and Members which have a right or special interest with respect to the concessions in question.[53] It further

---

50 L/5470/Rev. 1, Annex 1, para 4.2.

51 Procedures for Modification and Rectification of Schedules of Tariff Concessions, Decision of 26 March 1980, L/4962, BISD 27S/25.

52 Decision of 10 November 1980, C/113 and Corr. 1, BISD 27S/26.

53 Members which may participate in Art. XXVIII GATT renegotiations are Members which have an initial negotiation right or a principal supplying interest. On principal supplying interest see also the Understanding on the Interpretation of Art. XXVIII of the General Agreement on Tariffs and Trade 1994.

foresees that formal effect will be given to the negotiated changes of concessions in accordance with the rectification procedure through certification mentioned above.[54]

These procedures enable Members to modify schedules outside the treaty amendment procedure and at the same time provide for safeguards against the impairment of benefits deriving from concessions. However, they are insufficient for the timely adaptation of a great number of schedules to the HS which partly results in mere formal changes to schedules, but also necessitates large-scale and complex renegotiations of concessions. Further procedures are required which enable a timely and effective adaptation of schedules and ensure that Members have the opportunity to maintain their benefits from concessions.

2. *The Procedures Concerning the Introduction of the HS and the Incorporation of HS Changes into WTO Schedules*

a) Aims and Content of the HS Procedures

The first procedures for the adaptation of schedules of concessions to the Harmonized System (HS procedures) were adopted under the GATT 1947[55] and subsequently replaced by procedures for the adaptation of schedules to the HS changes of 1992, 1996, 2002 and 2007.[56] The HS procedures supplement the existing procedures on the rectification of schedules and modification of concessions. In the following I will mainly refer to the HS2007 procedures.

The HS procedures lay out the documentation which a WTO Member has to provide when it is introducing HS changes to its schedule and sets out procedures for review of this documentation. On the basis of this documentation and its review the other WTO Members can determine whether the HS changes affect the value of concessions in which they have a special interest and thus whether to enter into bilateral renegotiations of concessions on the basis of Art. XXVIII GATT. If renegotiation is not deemed necessary the rectification procedures will be

---

54 BISD 27S/26.

55 L/5470/ Rev. 1.

56 L/6905 (aimed at the incorporation of HS1992 changes into GATT schedules as well as any future changes and used for the incorporation of HS1992 and HS1996 changes); WT/L/407 and WT/L/605 (for HS2002 changes); WT/L/673 (for HS2007 changes).

followed.[57] The required documentation consists mainly of that part of the schedule which is affected by HS changes and which is transposed into the newest version of the HS nomenclature and the indication of any changes in the scope of concessions.[58] Three main principles can be identified which underlie the HS procedures. These are the guiding substantive principle of the maintenance of concessions, the principle of efficiency and the principle of transparency. In addition, the procedures are characterized by substantial technical assistance provided by the secretariat.

i) Maintenance of Concessions

If possible existing tariff bindings are to remain unchanged by the adaptation of schedules to the HS.[59] In order to achieve this aim, Members should – where necessary – create new sub-headings.[60] Only where this would result in undue complexity of national tariffs, concessions may be changed.[61] If the value of concessions is negatively affected by the adaptation exercise and consequently bilateral renegotiations take place, then these shall aim at maintaining a general level of reciprocal and mutually advantageous concessions.[62]

ii) Efficiency

The stated aim of the first HS procedures was the simplification and acceleration of the existing GATT procedures for modification of concessions.[63] Simplification and facilitation were also the main impetus of the revisions and amendments of the initial HS procedures over the course of the different amendments to the HS Convention and in the light of the experiences made with the transposition of HS changes.[64]

---

57 WT/L/673, para. 17.

58 WT/L/673, para. 4 and Annex 1.

59 WT/L/673, para. 4.

60 WT/L/673, Annex 2, para. 4.

61 Preferably according to the methods set out above to avoid a negative impact on the value of concessions, *see* WT/L/673, Annex 2, para. 5.

62 L/5470 Rev. 1 Annex 1, para 1.

63 L/5470 Rev. 1 Annex 1, para 1.4.

64 *See* WT/L/673, preamble, recital 6.

Elements which shall improve efficiency are – apart from the clear documentation of changes made to the schedules – timelines for the submission of the required documentation and the review of draft files,[65] cooperation with the WCO,[66] assistance by the secretariat, and multilateral review.[67] The multilateral review of draft files with the adapted parts of schedules by the Committee on Market Access gives the committee members the opportunity to verify the changes made to schedules and to determine whether the value of concessions is affected and bilateral renegotiations under Art. XXVIIII have to take place.[68]

When there are no objections remaining at a multilateral review session regarding a schedule, the schedule can be considered approved by the committee and can subsequently be certified according to the rectification procedures.[69]

iii) Transparency

Various requirements of the procedures are intended to ensure the transparency of the process of schedule transposition. These are first of all the distribution of the submitted documentation by the secretariat to all Members. Secondly, if Members opt for changing concessions instead of introducing new subheadings, they have to explain their reasons for doing so.[70] Thirdly, transparency has been enhanced by moving to multilateral review of the submitted documentation and draft files prepared by the secretariat. These reviews take place during informal sessions. However, the secretariat notifies Members of any modifica-

---

65 Draft files are the electronic files with the transposed parts of the schedule (WT/L/673, Annex 1). For the timelines in the HS2007 procedure, *see* WT/L/673, paras. 2, 11, 12.

66 This cooperation is implicit in the procedures which foresee that schedule transposition and preparation of concordance tables by the WTO Secretariat shall be based on information provided by the WCO, WT/L/673, para. 7.

67 An attempt to increase efficiency through electronic verification of schedule changes by the secretariat foreseen in the HS 2002 procedures (WT/L/407) failed due to unforeseen difficulties the secretariat encountered with this exercise.

68 WT/L/673, paras. 13-15.

69 *Id.* at para. 16.

70 L/6905, para. 1; WT/L/673, Annex 2, para. 5.

tions to the draft files.[71] Members that are engaged in bilateral discussions and consultations, including renegotiations of concessions under Art. XXVIII GATT, should report on the status of these consultations at the multilateral sessions.[72] The secretariat shall submit periodic reports on the status of its work on the transposition of developing country schedules (see below), the status of multilateral review, approval and certification.[73] The transparency requirements laid out in the HS procedures serve two purposes – on the one hand to increase the efficiency of the transposition exercise and on the other hand to enable Members to secure their rights in concessions granted by other Members.

iv) Technical Assistance

While the first HS procedures merely stated that the secretariat would be available to assist governments in negotiations and consultations and that special account would be taken of the needs of developing countries consistent with Part IV of the GATT,[74] this assistance has increasingly been specified and substantiated. The first HS2002 procedures foresaw that developing countries could request technical assistance from the secretariat for the preparation of the relevant documentation[75] and the amended HS2002 procedures as well as the HS2007 procedures, which are based on the former, now entrust the secretariat with the preparation of the entire documentation for developing country Members.[76] Developing Country Members are expected to examine the draft files prepared by the secretariat and to either approve them or submit specific comments. When a developing country Member remains passive the draft file can nonetheless be submitted for multilateral review.

---

[71] WT/L/673, paras. 13, 14.

[72] WT/L/673, para. 15.

[73] WT/L/673, para. 17.

[74] L/5470, Rev. 1, Annex 1, para. 4.5.

[75] WT/L/407, Attachment B, para. 8.

[76] WT/L/605, para. 1; WT/L/673, para. 2 (these HS 2007 procedures foresee that developing country Members may opt for preparing their draft files themselves). The secretariat prepares this documentation by incorporating HS changes into the schedules in the Consolidated Tariff Schedules Database, an electronic database which is not legally binding (WT/L/673, preamble, recital 5). Regarding the transposition the secretariat has to follow a methodology laid out in an annex to the procedures, WT/L/673, para. 5 and Annex 2.

It can, however, only be certified once the developing country in question has approved it.[77]

This move to substantial technical assistance has been motivated – not by considerations of justice – but the objective of efficiency. The secretariat provides expertise as well as the necessary resources to prepare developing countries' documentation. Previously, developing countries had often either not submitted any documentation at all or incomplete documentation so that the transposition exercise could not be completed.

b) The Legal Instrument

With the establishment of the WTO the HS procedures are adopted by the General Council as legally binding decisions; under the GATT 1947 they were adopted by the GATT Council. These decisions can thus be classified as acts of secondary law. Many of the requirements they lay down are mandatory.[78] As they concern the modification of treaty law, namely of the schedules, which determines the legal relationship between the individual Members, the procedures can further be characterized as external law of the organization.[79] With the entry into force of the WTO Agreement the legal decisions which adopted procedures under the GATT 1947 have become an integral part of the GATT 1994 and thus have been elevated to the status of primary law.[80]

c) The Legal Framework for the Adoption of HS Procedures

The legal basis for the adoption of binding HS procedures within the WTO is unclear. While it is a noteworthy aspect of the increased legalization and formalization in the WTO as opposed to the GATT 1947 that the documents containing the WTO HS procedures are titled "de-

---

77 WT/L/673, paras. 8-12, 16.

78 For the distinction between the form of a legally binding decision and the mandatory nature of its content, *see* BENEDEK (note 11), at 118.

79 Benedek therefore seems to be mistaken when he groups the procedures for negotiations under Art. XXVIII (note 52) with rules of procedures of the GATT organs and collectively qualifies them as internal rules; BENEDEK (note 11), at 122.

80 *See* introductory note to the GATT 1994, para. 1 (the so-called incorporation clause).

cision" and explicitly refer to Articles IV:2 and IX:1 WTO Agreement,[81] neither Art. IV:2 which establishes the General Council as a plenary organ of the WTO nor Art. IX:1 WTO Agreement which concerns decision-making by the WTO and codifies the consensus practice of the GATT provide for such a legal basis. It is doubtful whether a decision-making competence exists in the WTO which is similarly broad as the decision-making competence of the GATT CONTRACTING PARTIES under Art. XXV:1 GATT.[82] Commonly it is assumed that the only general powers of the Ministerial Conference to take decisions which are legally binding for the Members in their external relations – apart from decisions on accession and amendment proposals – are those concerning the adoption of authoritative interpretations in Art. IX:2 (which is also a genuine competence of the General Council) and the granting of waivers in Art. IX:3 WTO Agreement.

The WTO HS procedures have – as the HS procedures under the GATT 1947 – been negotiated and drafted by a committee, namely the Committee on Market Access.[83] The Committee on Market Access was established by the General Council – acting on behalf of the Ministerial Conference – on the basis of Art. IV:7 WTO Agreement.[84] It is a sub-

---

[81] WT/L/407; WT/L/605; WT/L/673. The legal documents of the GATT 1947 to which the HS procedures are annexed neither refer to a legal basis in the GATT nor are they entitled "decision", L/5470/Rev.1, L/6905.

[82] It is sometimes discussed whether Art. IV:1, cl. 2 WTO Agreement entails a general competence to take legally binding decisions. Pieter J. Kuijper, *Some Institutional Issues Presently Before the WTO, in* THE POLITICAL ECONOMY OF INTERNATIONAL TRADE LAW 81, 82 (D. L. M. Kennedy & J. D. Southwick eds., 2002). On the broad decision-making power under Art. XXV:1 GATT, *see* Frieder Roessler, *The Competence of GATT*, 21 JOURNAL OF WORLD TRADE LAW 73 (1987).

[83] Under the GATT 1947 the HS procedures were established by the Committee on Tariff Concessions which had been created in 1980 by the GATT Council; Minutes of the Council meeting on 29 January 1980, C/M/138, at 10.

[84] WT/GC/M/1, 11, 12. The terms of reference of the committee are contained in document WT/L/47; the rules of procedure which the committee according to Art. IV:6 WTO Agreement may establish for itself, subject of approval of the Council for Trade in Goods, are based on the rules of procedure for meetings of the General Council and contained in G/L/148. It is interesting to note that it was stated by the chairman at the first committee meeting that until the committee had adopted its rules of procedure, it "would conduct its business on the basis of common sense and GATT practice" (G/MA/M/1, para. 1.1).

sidiary organ of the Council for Trade in Goods which is established by the WTO Agreement and operates under the general guidance of the General Council (Art. IV para. 5 WTO Agreement). Membership in the Council for Trade in Goods as well as the Committee on Market Access is open to representatives of all Members. According to its terms of reference laid down by the Council for Trade in Goods it is within the mandate of the Committee on Market Access "to ensure that GATT Schedules are kept up-to-date, and that modifications, including those resulting from changes in tariff nomenclature, are reflected".[85] The rules of procedure of the Committee on Market Access and the Council for Trade in Goods foresee that matters on which no consensus can be reached are to be referred to the higher body – from the Committee on Market Access to the Council for Trade in Goods,[86] and from the Council for Trade in Goods to the General Council.[87]

Further opportunities for oversight of the higher bodies with respect to the working of the lower bodies are created by the rules on reporting. According to these, the Committee on Market Access annually reports to the Council on Trade in Goods and the Council on Trade in Goods reports once a year to the General Council.[88] The reports shall be factual in nature.[89] It can however be observed that in general these reports are not discussed by the body to which the reporting obligation is owed.[90]

d) The Process of Establishing the Procedures

While the process leading to the adoption of HS procedures is only to a limited extent framed by positive law, there are regularities and practices that are followed which can also be detected in other areas of work

---

85 WT/L/47, para. C.

86 Rule 33 of the Rules of Procedure of the Committee on Market Access, G/L/148.

87 Rule 33 of the Rules of Procedure of the Council for Trade in Goods, WT/L/79.

88 Procedures for an Annual Overview of WTO Activities and for Reporting Under the WTO, adopted by the General Council on 15 November 1995, WT/L/105, para. 1.

89 *Id.* at para. 1.

90 According to the procedures the Council for Trade in Goods and the General Council "take note of reports". *Id.* at para. 4.

of the WTO – some of which merit a characterization as institutional practice or even customary law of the organization.[91]

In the WTO it is – as it was under the GATT 1947 – common practice that consultations are taken outside formal meetings and are conducted in informal meetings of interested delegations. The HS procedures were established during informal consultations of delegations to the Committee on Market Access and the committee only returned to formal mode when the procedures were ready for approval.[92] Before the procedures are approved by the committee, delegations submit the procedures for approval to the competent government agency in their capitals.[93] While there are public minutes of the formal committee meetings, there is no publicly accessible record of informal meetings. To ensure greater transparency a practice has developed in recent years that the chairperson of the committee gives a short summary of the outcomes of informal discussions at the next formal committee meeting.[94]

The committee approves the draft procedures by consensus.[95] Subsequently they are referred to the Council for Trade in Goods[96] and from there to the General Council for adoption.[97] So far there has been no further discussion of the procedures within the Council for Trade in

---

[91] On customary law under the GATT 1947 and its importance for the evolution of the GATT, *see* BENEDEK (note 11), at 126-130.

[92] *See e.g.* the proposal by the Chairman of the Committee on Market Access with respect to the HS2007 procedures, G/MA/M42, para. 4.4.

[93] *See e.g.* G/MA/M/26, para. 3.1.

[94] *See e.g.* G/MA/M/38, Add. 1, para. 1.2.

[95] While the first HS2002 procedures and the HS2007 procedures were approved in formal meetings, the second procedures on the transposition of HS 2002 changes were only agreed upon by the committee during an informal meeting, *see* statement of the chairperson in the minutes of the meeting of 30 March 2005, G/MA/M/38, Add.1, para. 1.2. The first procedures for the introduction of HS2002 changes were approved by the committee *ad referendum*, G/MA/M/29, para. 2.18.

[96] The second HS2002 procedures were directly submitted by the committee to the General Council, G/MA/M/38, Add.1, para. 1.2.

[97] With respect to the first GATT HS procedures concerning the adoption by contracting parties of the HS nomenclature, there was some discussion in the Committee on Tariff Concessions on the procedure for adopting the procedures. It was finally proposed by the chairman that the committee adopt the procedures and that they would be transmitted to the Council for approval (TAR/M/10 paras. 3.1 *et seq.*).

Goods or in the General Council which usually refer to the consensus in the lower body as the basis for their own consensus.

The secretariat – more precisely the Market Access Division of the secretariat – is strongly involved during this process. At a preliminary stage it provides the committee members with information on the HS revisions drafted in the HS Committee as well as their implications for schedules.[98] The secretariat is further substantially involved before and during the consultation stage, makes suggestions for procedures, drafts the final decisions and gives legal opinions.[99]

Leadership by the chairperson of the committee[100] often plays a crucial role in achieving compromise. In one instance the chairman has taken the initiative and proposed changes to the HS2002 procedures when it turned out that the difficulties encountered with these procedures would not allow for a timely conclusion of the transposition of schedules. [101]

Cooperation between the WTO and the World Customs Organization regarding schedules, which is regulated only to a very limited extent by positive law – the WCO has been granted observer status in the Council for Trade in Goods and the Committee on Market Access[102] – is a further important element in the process of establishing HS procedures. The secretariat maintains close contacts with the WCO by attending the meetings of the HS Committee. Representatives of the WCO regularly attend formal committee meetings and report on and explain impending HS changes to facilitate the development of new HS procedures.[103]

The informality of the process, its locus within a specialized committee and the engagement of the expertise of WTO Secretariat and WCO officials can be explained by the aims to achieve efficacy in the decision-making process and adequacy of the resulting procedures. Several safeguards have been established with a view to address the intransparency

---

98 *See e.g.* the information notes of the GATT Secretariat, TAR/W/22, TAR/W/81, TAR/W/89.

99 *See e.g.* G/MA/M/37, paras. 3.2-3.6 and G/MA/M/45, para. 6.4.

100 The chairperson of the committee is appointed for one year after informal consultations among Members on the distribution of chairperson posts for the different WTO organs; on the practice of chairperson appointments *see:* http://www.wto.org/english/thewto_e/secre_e/current_chairs_e.htm.

101 G/MA/M/37, para. 3.2.

102 *See* http://www.wto.org/english/thewto_e/igo_obs_e.htm.

103 *See e.g.* G/MA/M/39, paras. 4.9-4.19.

resulting from informality and to avoid that the procedures are only attributable to a small number of trade representatives actually participating in the informal negotiations and experts from the secretariat. All Members are notified when the issue of HS procedures is put on the agenda for a formal meeting and thus can – if interested – consult with their capitals and attend the formal meeting to raise any objections they may have. Due to the consensus requirement each Member has a veto power. The institutional links to the higher organs by the need for approval or through reporting often seem like mere formalities since the higher organ mostly relies on the consensus formed within the lower organ. However, they are more than that. Most importantly the referral chain from Committee on Market Access to Council for Trade in Goods and then General Council ensures that a Member has the opportunity to contest an alleged consensus within a lower body.

Lastly, it should be noted that the objective of efficacy and timely establishment of procedures has not always been achieved. The process has often been lengthy and the procedures have consequently been adopted so late that there was not sufficient time for schedule adaptation between their adoption and the entry into force of HS changes.[104] It seems, however, that with the HS2007 procedures a procedure has been set up which works well in practice and therefore might become the template for a procedure which will be generally applicable to future HS changes.

3. *The Implementation of the Procedures and Their Informal Modification*

The process of schedule adaptation is characterized by a great degree of flexibility in the application and modification of the formal HS procedures. With respect to compliance with the requirements set out in the procedures it is noteworthy that the committee – instead of sanctioning non-compliance – has opted for an approach that aims at assisting WTO Members in meeting the requirements.

Just as with the process of establishing the HS procedures, secretariat and chairpersons are strongly involved in the implementation pro-

---

[104] *E.g.* the HS2007 procedures have only been adopted by the General Council on 15 December 2006.

cess.[105] Beyond rendering technical assistance to developing countries as foreseen in the procedures, the secretariat serves as a distributor of information – e.g. it provides necessary information on the submission of documentation, the status of the transposition exercise and renegotiations[106] – and a repository of expertise with which it assists Members, e.g. by holding workshops on the technicalities of the transposition exercise.[107]

In the following sections the informality of the implementation process, as well as the managerial approach to compliance shall be illustrated by way of examples.

a) Informal Change of Rules – The Issue of General Reservations

The procedures on withdrawal and modification of concessions foresee that a Member which believes it has a principal supplying interest in a concession granted by another Member should submit a claim of interest within 90 days following the submission of documentation by that Member. It has to do so in order to secure its rights to participate in Art. XXVIII GATT renegotiations.[108] This time period was deemed to be too short for the submission of specific claims due to the amount of documentation to be reviewed by the contracting parties in the transposition exercise. Upon a proposal by the United States in 1986[109] the Committee on Tariff Concessions of the GATT 1947 accepted that it should suffice to make general reservations to the change of concessions within the 90 day period. No formal decision was taken on this matter[110] – it was later stated that there had been "tacit agreement" in the

---

105 One example of the crucial role of the chairpersons in the implementation process has been the engagement of one chairman in getting Members to approve their HS2002 schedules after multilateral review. To induce Members to give their approval – which is a prerequisite for the certification of schedules – this chairman wrote letters to and successfully initiated bilateral meetings with the respective delegations, G/MA/M/44, para. 3.1.; G/MA/M/45, paras. 6.5., 6.6.

106 *See e.g.* G/MA//TAR/2/Rev. 40 on the submission of HS96 documentation and G/MA/W/23/Rev. 4 on the situation of schedules.

107 *E.g.* G/MA/M/38 Add. 1, para. 1.1.

108 Procedures for Negotiations under Art. XXVIII, BISD 27S/26, 27, para. 4.

109 TAR/W/61.

110 TAR/M/21, para. 2.9.

committee[111] – and thus the formal procedures for renegotiation were informally amended.[112]

In the following years, and especially with respect to the 1996 HS changes, the practice of submitting general reservations created a problem. Because the general reservations often were not specified afterwards, neither bilateral re-negotiations of concessions nor the certification of the adapted schedules could take place. For lack of consensus on a solution in the Market Access Committee, the issue was taken by two delegations, namely Switzerland and Norway, outside the committee and to the Council for Trade in Goods. The solution found after a series of informal consultations once again was not a formal and legally binding decision, but a statement by the chairman of the Council for Trade in Goods to the effect that all general reservations not specified within a certain time limit would be considered removed and that such reservations in future should as far as possible be specified.[113] Upon request the chairman indicated that his statement, to which no objection was raised, was not a formal decision by the Council for Trade in Goods, but a statement of the chairman which would be entered into the minutes of the meeting.[114] Nonetheless it was effective and in the following most of the general reservations were specified and the remaining ones considered as having been withdrawn.[115]

b) Complementary Practices and Compliance Management – The Issue of Missing or Incomplete Documentation

Another problem encountered in particular during the HS96 transposition exercise was deficient submission of the required documentation.

---

111 C/M/205, P. 13 (*see* statements by the US and EC delegates).

112 An initiative by a group of developing countries for a formal amendment extending the 90 days time limit did not achieve consensus. Since there was no consensus in the committee the matter was taken to the Council and the CONTRACTING PARTIES where consensus could also not be reached due to objections by some contracting parties that such an amendment might delay the transposition process too much. The CONTRACTING PARTIES consequently referred the matter back to the Committee on Tariff Concessions for an appropriate solution (SR.42/5, at 5).

113 G/C/M/23, para. 2.5.

114 G/C/M/23, para. 2.9.

115 G/MA/M/14, para. 3.2.

As a consequence the committee in an informal meeting in the year 2000 – *i.e.* already four years after the HS96 changes entered into force for parties to the HS Convention – agreed that the secretariat should prepare an informal list on the status of the pending submissions of HS96 documentation to enhance transparency.[116] It was further agreed that the secretariat would continually update this list and that individual Members would have to explain themselves in informal meetings. In the following the secretariat regularly updated the list, informal review sessions were frequently held and this practice was generally welcomed as a successful acceleration of the adaptation of schedules to HS96 changes.[117]

IV. HS Waivers

1. The Function of Waivers in the Administration of Schedule Adaptation

Deficient compliance with the requirements of the HS procedures and the issue of general reservations discussed above, but also late adoption of procedures and capacity restraints of the secretariat have obstructed the timely adaptation of schedules to HS changes and their subsequent certification. While the committee attempts to address these challenges in a pragmatic and often informal way, there is at the same time a strong desire to maintain formal legality in the external relations between WTO Members. This is evidenced by the extensive practice of the General Council to grant so-called HS waivers to WTO Members who implement HS changes domestically without having adapted and certified schedules.[118]

The HS waiver suspends the application of the provisions of Art. II "to the extent necessary for the purpose of enabling [...] Members to implement domestically the recommended amendments to the Harmo-

---

[116] G/M/MA/23, para. 2.5.

[117] *See e.g.* G/M//MA/26, para. 23. Due to capacity problems of the secretariat the informal meetings could not take place as often as intended, *see e.g.* G/M/MA/34, para. 3.2; G/M/MA/35, para. 2.2.

[118] *See e.g.* TAR/M/28, para. 2.1 referring to the function of HS waivers under the GATT; on WTO Members' need for a waiver when they are implementing HS2002 changes domestically, but have not yet completed the procedures to introduce these changes into their schedules, *see* G/MA/M/31, para. 4.1.

nized System nomenclature pending incorporation of such changes into their schedules of concessions."[119]

2. *The Legal Framework for the Adoption of Waivers*

The legal basis for the adoption of HS waiver decisions is Art. IX:3 WTO Agreement which authorizes the Ministerial Conference to waive an obligation imposed on a Member by the WTO Agreement or any of the Multilateral Trade Agreements. Between the meetings of the Ministerial Conference, the General Council exercises the waiver competence (Art. IV:2 WTO Agreement). According to Art. IX:3 WTO Agreement a waiver decision can be adopted by three-fourths of the Members.[120] While under the GATT 1947 waiver decisions and decisions on accessions were routinely taken by vote, this practice has been abandoned with the establishment of the WTO and waivers are now exclusively taken by consensus.[121] Requests for waivers concerning the GATT – according to Art. IX:3 (b) WTO Agreement – shall be submitted to the Council for Trade in Goods which shall consider such a request within a time period that shall not exceed 90 days.

The only substantive requirement for waivers set out in Art. IX:3 WTO Agreement and the Understanding in Respect of Waivers of Obligations under the General Agreement on Tariffs and Trade 1994 ("the Understanding") is the existence of exceptional circumstances. This requirement has however never been specified and in the past has not provided for a substantive limitation of the waiver power. According to Art. IX:4 WTO Agreement waiver decisions have to have a termination

---

[119] *See e.g.* WT/L/675.

[120] According to footnote 4 to Art. IX:3 WTO Agreement, consensus is required for a decision to waive obligations subject to a transition period or a period for staged implementation.

[121] On 15 November 1995 the General Council agreed that decisions concerning waivers and accessions would also be taken in accordance with Art. IX:1 WTO by consensus and that only when consensus could not be arrived at, should voting take place in accordance with the relevant provisions; Decision-Making Procedures under Arts. IX and XII of the WTO Agreement, Statement by the Chairman, as agreed by the General Council on 15 November 1995, WT/L/93. The statement also specifies that a Member may request a vote at the time the decision is taken.

date, shall be reviewed annually by the Ministerial Conference and can be subject to conditions.[122]

3. Qualification of the Waiver Decision

Since a waiver decision changes the pre-existing legal situation by freeing the addressee from having to comply with the waived obligation it has to be characterized as a legally binding decision.[123] Waiver decisions bind all Members of the organization in that no Member can successfully claim that the obligation which has been waived has been violated by the addressee of the waiver.[124] For the duration of the waiver, the decision thus modifies the primary treaty law. The obligation which is being waived cannot serve as a standard against which the legality of the waiver decision can be measured.[125]

4. The Practice of Granting HS Waivers

The amount of HS waiver decisions is extensive and far outnumbers the waivers granted of other WTO obligations in different contexts.[126]

HS waiver requests are submitted to the Committee on Market Access. There the requests are discussed in formal and informal meetings and after approval referred to the Council for Trade in Goods together with

---

[122] The legal requirements that waivers may only be of a limited duration and have to be reviewed annually did not exist under the GATT 1947 and were negotiated during the Uruguay Round.

[123] H. G. SCHERMERS & N. M. BLOKKER, INTERNATIONAL INSTITUTIONAL LAW § 811 (3rd revised ed., 1995).

[124] A Member may however bring a non-violation complaint against a Member which received a waiver. This possibility is acknowledged in the Understanding.

[125] This ability to change legal obligations established by primary law distinguishes waiver decisions from other acts of secondary law which usually establish a level of law beneath primary law and thus a hierarchy of norms. Due to these characteristics Benedek characterized the granting of waivers under GATT 1947 as a special form of lawmaking by secondary law ("sekundärrechtliche Rechtsfortbildung") note 11, 141.

[126] Of the 35 waiver decisions (including extension decisions) taken in 2001, 23 were HS waiver decisions; for the waivers granted in 2001 see Note by the WTO Secretariat, Paragraph 6 of the Doha Declaration on the TRIPS Agreement and Public Health: Information on Waivers, IP/C/W/387, at 13.

a draft decision. The Council for Trade in Goods approves a request usually on the basis of approval in the committee and without discussion and transmits it to the General Council for adoption. Under the GATT 1947 and later under the WTO HS waivers were granted for 6 months only. Later this practice was changed and starting in 2000 HS waivers were granted for 12 months.

Two main themes can be identified with respect to the practice of granting HS waivers. On the one hand waivers are perceived as a necessary element to ensure the formal legality of trade relations during the process of schedule adaptation to the HS and on the other hand the need is expressed to counter the danger that waivers perpetuate a state of exceptions and thus obstruct the effectiveness of the process of schedule adaptation.

a) Waiver Decisions as a Necessary Element of the Process of Schedule Adaptation

As has been noted above certain general deficits of the adaptation process led to a general need for waivers to maintain legality in the external relations between WTO Members. This general and systemic need for waivers resulted in certain specific characteristics of the HS waiver process. Starting with the HS1996 transposition, waivers were granted on a collective basis.[127] This means that one waiver decision was drafted and Members could submit requests to be included in the decisions. Even though it was from time to time stressed by Members that a so-called collective waiver decision in fact constituted individual decisions grouped together in one,[128] the granting of collective waivers nonetheless signified that these waivers were deemed a necessary element of the adaptation process in the common interest of the organization.

Further aspects of this "institutionalization" of the HS waiver are that the secretariat often drafts the waiver decision[129] and that the committee chairpersons regularly remind committee members to request necessary

---

127 For the collective waivers granted by the General Council for the HS1996, HS2002 and HS2007 transposition exercises *see* G/MA/W/23/Rev. 4.

128 G/MA/M/6, para 2.1.9 (statement by the Swiss representative).

129 The first collective HS waiver concerning the transposition of HS2007 changes was drafted together with the HS2007 procedures by the Market Access Division with the help of the Legal Affairs Division, the draft waiver is contained in G/MA/W/82.

extensions of waivers in time so that the requests can be considered at the meetings of the Council for Trade in Goods and the General Council before expiry of the waivers.[130] Even though the positive law does not foresee this, in practice waivers have been granted from time to time with retroactive effect.[131]

However not all waivers are granted for general systemic reasons common to many Members. Frequently waivers are granted because Members need more time for the submission of documentation or conclusion of renegotiations of concessions. The impression that waivers were often granted and extended quasi-automatically and could lead to permanent situations endangering legal security and predictability of tariff concessions has led to the imposition of procedural safeguards beyond those set out in the primary law.

b) Limitations on Waivers

There are several mechanisms which aim at restricting and controlling waivers. One important bilateral control mechanism, intended to safeguard the reciprocity of benefits from concessions, is foreseen in the waiver decisions themselves. They provide that Members – pending the entry into force of the results of negotiations and/or consultations under Art. XXVIII GATT – will be free to suspend concessions initially negotiated with the Member under the waiver to the extent that they consider that adequate compensation is not offered by the Member concerned.[132]

Further, multilateral, control is enabled by regular (twice-yearly) reports by the committee to the Council for Trade in Goods which are prepared by the secretariat. With respect to HS96 waivers, they contain factual information in an annex on the number of waivers granted, which Members they are granted to and for which HS changes.[133] This reporting practice goes back to the GATT 1947. It was a compromise between the delegations from developed and developing contracting parties. While some delegations, led by a proposal from the Swedish

---

130 *See e.g.* G/MA/M/42, para. 3.11.

131 *See e.g.* the decision of 15 June 1999 which extended the HS96 collective waiver and was granted with retroactive effect to 30 April 1999, WT/L/303, footnote 1.

132 *See e.g.* WT/L/675, para. b(iii).

133 The latest report of 6 May 2008 is contained in G/MA/198.

delegation, had wanted to restrict the waiver practice by requiring that contracting parties requesting a waiver should submit a full and detailed report to the committee on how they intended to finalize the HS implementation during the period covered by the waiver,[134] this proposal was met by opposition of developing countries, the main beneficiaries of waivers. Compromise was reached after informal consultations and on the basis of a proposal by the chairman,[135] which foresees the just mentioned reporting.

A further compromise was reached with respect to the practice to grant collective waivers. In 2000 after the issue of general reservations with respect to HS96 documentation was solved, discussion ensued in the committee about ending the practice of extending the collective waiver with respect to the transposition of HS96 changes. There was strong opposition to this proposal in the committee by developing country delegations. The compromise finally agreed upon foresaw that the collective waiver would be extended one last time for the duration of one year under the condition that all of the required documentation be provided. This solution was accompanied by the agreement to hold informal meetings on the status of HS96 documentation (see section III.3.b above). The HS2002 and 2007 collective waivers were also granted on the condition of the submission of documentation.

V. The Politics of Schedule Adaptation in the WTO

All WTO Members have an interest that schedules conform to the Harmonized System for the reasons stated earlier in this paper. As long as the adaptation does not affect the value of concessions Members' interests do not conflict. Where however concessions are substantially affected, economic interests of the granting and the benefitting Member may collide. WTO law foresees that the resolution of these conflicts does not take place within WTO bodies, but that they are resolved outside the institutional structure in bilateral negotiations.

What is addressed within the WTO, is the uncertainty that arises as to how economic interests might be affected by schedule adaptation. Since all Members are in the same position of uncertainty there is again a

---

134 Proposal by Sweden, TAR/W/88 (23 September 1993).

135 This proposal was based on proposals submitted by delegations; for the chairman's proposal *see* TAR/M/36, Annex, at 3.

common and shared interest to devise and implement procedures in a manner that all Members are able to detect when their economic interests are affected. Once safeguards are instituted that enable Members to distinguish between schedule adaptation which affects their economic interests and schedule adaptation which does not, and thus between mere technical changes and others, there is little reluctance to entrust the organization, i.e. the secretariat, with wide-ranging tasks with respect to the technicalities of schedule adaptation.

It should be noted however that the capacity of developing Members to benefit from these safeguards is much more limited than that of developed countries since they often will not have the resources available to review all documentation and attend all informal meetings. While technical assistance is rendered by the secretariat to developing Members, this assistance in effect mainly benefits the other Members since it ensures that the respective developing Member's schedule is properly transposed and thus its concessions to other Members are safeguarded.[136]

As a device to maintain formal legality during the adaptation process, the adoption of HS waiver decision frequently lies within the common interest of the organization. This explains why mostly HS waivers are granted easily and mostly without much discussion as compared to other waivers which frequently result from the need to reconcile conflicting interests.[137]

D. Conclusions

Overall, the process of schedule adaptation to the Harmonized System is characterized by a problem-oriented and managerial approach aiming

---

[136] Developing country Members are further disadvantaged with respect to the renegotiation of concessions due to the transaction costs incurred in such renegotiations and their limited bargaining power.

[137] *See e.g.* the so-called TRIPS waiver (WT/L/540) , granted to facilitate the importation by Members of generic drugs in case of public health crises, or the Kimberley waiver (WT/L/518) which was granted to legalize trade restrictions implementing the Kimberley Process Certification Scheme to combat trade in so-called blood diamonds. On both waiver decisions, Isabel Feichtner, *The Waiver Power of the WTO: Opening the WTO for Political Debate on the Reconciliation of Competing Interests*, 20 EUROPEAN JOURNAL OF INTERNATIONAL LAW (2009), forthcoming in issue 3.

at efficiency which is accompanied by a relatively large number of formal and binding legal decisions. Both characteristics – effective pragmatism with strong involvement of the secretariat on the one hand and formal legal decisions by the WTO organs on the other – are relatively unusual at least according to common depictions of the work of the political organs and secretariat within the WTO.

The first characteristic can be explained by the common interest of the organization as well as its Members in the HS and its effective transposition into schedules and the eminent importance this has for international trade in goods. The formal legal procedures enable this process and support its efficiency by codifying successful practices; they ensure transparency and thus enable Members to safeguard their benefits from concessions. The waiver decisions maintain formal legality where the process of schedule adaptation would otherwise lead to a violation of Art. II GATT. The maintenance of formal legality in the external relations of WTO Members through waivers is important in regard of the high degree of legalization and judicialization in the WTO.

Finally it is interesting to note that with respect to the administration of the HS one can detect a reversal of roles between the WTO and the WCO. While the WTO is often depicted as the locus for political negotiations on trade matters and the WCO as the organization taking care of the technicalities of trade, another picture is presented here. As has been indicated above, agreement on HS changes which is to be achieved within the WCO, will frequently require the balancing of different interests and thus might for its legitimacy necessitate an open political process characterized by reason-giving. At the WTO the incorporation of the adopted HS changes into the schedules is then a mainly technical matter requiring technical expertise and assistance, as provided by the WTO Secretariat.

Convention on International Trade in Endangered Species of Wild Fauna and Flora (CITES) – Conservation Efforts Undermine the Legality Principle

*By Christine Fuchs**

---

* The author is grateful to Angela Dunker, Philipp Dann, Rüdiger Wolfrum, Armin von Bogdandy, Geranne Lautenbach, Matthias Goldmann and fellow project participants for valuable and constructive comments and to Lewis Enim and Eva Richter for language check and editing.

A. von Bogdandy et al. (eds.), *The Exercise of Public Authority by International Institutions*, Beiträge zum ausländischen öffentlichen Recht und Völkerrecht 210,
DOI 10.1007/978-3-642-04531-8_17, © Springer-Verlag Berlin Heidelberg 2010

A. Introduction

CITES is acknowledged as one of the most successful international environmental treaties in the world.[1] CITES is not just a conservation treaty, it is also a trade instrument that attempts to strike a balance between these often competing values.[2]

The purpose of CITES, as stated in the first paragraph of its preamble, is to protect wild fauna and flora for current and future generations. Wild fauna and flora are described as an irreplaceable part of the natural systems of the earth and as being valuable from aesthetic, scientific, cultural, recreational and economic points of view.[3] CITES establishes international co-operation for the protection of certain species from over-exploitation through international trade.[4] The purpose of adopting the Convention was not only to avoid aggravation of an ecological prob-

---

[1] Elisabeth M. McOmber, *Problems in Enforcement of the Convention on International Trade in Endangered Species*, 2 BROOK. J. INT'L L. 673, 674 (2002).

[2] ROSALIND REEVE, POLICING INTERNATIONAL TRADE IN ENDANGERED SPECIES. THE CITES TREATY AND COMPLIANCE 28 (2002).

[3] Convention on International Trade in Endangered Species of Wild Fauna and Flora (CITES), 3 March 1973, Preamble (1), (2), available at: http://www.cites.org/eng/disc/text.shtml.

[4] CITES, Preamble (4).

lem, but also to prevent a penalization of countries, in particular the US, with stricter ecological legislation.[5]

The trade in species that the Convention is intending to regulate is mainly a South-to-North phenomenon that is driven by consumer demand for fashion and food products, as well as rare animals and plants for medical/pharmaceutical research, exhibition or collection purposes.[6] The market is worth between $5 billion and $17 billion every year.

In order to ascertain reasons for the success of CITES this paper examines how public authority is exercised under the Convention. At the same time it raises the question of how efforts to establish and reinforce an effective mechanism for the protection of species has made CITES lose sight of an aspect of the rule of law: the legality principle. The obligation on member states to penalize trade in protected species provokes the question whether the intention to safeguard our wealth in species contemporaneously encroaches upon this fundamental principle of justice.

This paper tackles these questions in three steps. Part A analyses the two main interests CITES aims to balance, namely species preservation and economic development (I.). This is followed by a brief introduction to CITES' activities (II.).

To render an analysis possible as to whether or not CITES' methods threaten or infringe the legality principle, Part B provides an insight into CITES' institutional structure and mode of work. It first explores CITES' institutional characteristics as a treaty regime (I. 1.), the functions and the composition of CITES' organs (I. 2.), and CITES' cooperation with other organizations (I. 3.).

The subsequent paragraph focuses on CITES' substantive activities which comprise, most significantly, the listing of species on its three appendices (II. 1.) and the development of concrete rules for this listing procedure (II. 2.). The amendment procedure is described (III) as well as the result of CITES' listing activities: the three appendices (IV.). Furthermore, the obligations for member states that are linked to the appendices (IV. 1.) as well as the implementation of these obligations (IV. 2.) are set forth in detail. Finally, the way in which CITES reviews its own effectiveness (V. 1.), the monitoring procedures (V. 2.) and the enforcement mechanisms of CITES (V. 3.) are considered in turn.

---

5 Peter H. Sand, *Whither CITES? The Evolution of a Treaty Regime in the Borderland of Trade and Environment*, 1 EUROPEAN J. INT'L L. 29, 31 (1997).

6 *Id.* at 30.

The article concludes with Part C which deals with CITES' legitimacy, whereby particular attention is given to the aforementioned questions regarding the legality principle (II. 2.).

I. Two Contrasting Interests: Preservation and Sustainable Development

CITES' members and involved NGOs represent various attitudes towards wildlife which reflect their political, ethical, religious and cultural differences that range from the view that wildlife should be economically exploited, to the belief that individual animals have the right to continued life and freedom from pain.[7] NGOs usually represent the more extreme views of the spectrum while Government positions tend to be in the middle.[8]

CITES' primary concern is the conservation of species. Its preamble lists the economic value among species' values, and the Convention does not generally prohibit but merely strives to coordinate trade in species that may become endangered. This underlines the fact that the Convention does not one-sidedly favor an unlimited conservation approach, nor does it neglect trade interests outright. The Convention text does not however refer to the need to balance environmental and development interests in the way envisaged by the sustainability principle. The Brundtland Report and Agenda 21 both stress the concept of "sustainable development", that is the need to strike a balance between development and environmental protection.[9]

CITES' member states that seek to resume trade in species (the so called "consumptive use block"), in particular the African elephant, are of the opinion that the use of species provides both incentives to local people to conserve, as well as funds to improve enforcement and customs ser-

---

[7] DAVID S. FAVRE, INTERNATIONAL TRADE IN ENDANGERED SPECIES: A GUIDE TO CITES 878 (1989); Saskia Young, *Contemporary Issues of the Convention on International Trade in Endangered Species of Wild Fauna and Flora (CITES) and the Debate Over Sustainable Use*, 1 COLO. J. INT'L ENVTL. L.& POL'Y 167, 173 (2003).

[8] FAVRE (note 7), at 882.

[9] Brundtland Report of the World Commission on Environment and Development: Our Common Future; United Nations Conference on Environment & Development, Agenda 21, UN Doc. A/42/427.

vices.[10] The economic value of species is even considered to be the only value that will help conserve wildlife. It is argued that a preservationist approach, that is an approach which opposes any commercialization of endangered species, places a disproportionate share of the costs on poorer range states while sustainable use provides a source of revenue for conservation measures.[11] Furthermore, social and economic issues, such as the destruction inflicted on the humans living alongside protected wildlife, must also be taken into account.[12]

These arguments are rejected by preservationists as being unproven. Proponents of trade resumption are accused of placing relatively too little importance on the survival of species compared to the importance placed on the exploiters. Any trading in a threatened species is said to encourage poachers because it establishes a market where income is generated from the killing of the species, thereby thwarting the Convention's objectives.[13] Global trade is seen as the second most crucial reason for the decline of species after habitat loss.[14] Preservationists emphasize the need to base decisions on whether or not to permit trade in a species exclusively on scientific advice rather than on the needs of the exploiters who, in any event, frequently exceeded quotas. In cases of scientific uncertainty, preservationists insist that the burden of proving that trade is not detrimental lies on the traders, independent of economic and social pressures.[15] Placing an emphasis on economic value leaves species without any apparent use unprotected.[16]

While the text of the Convention does not elaborate on the linkages between trade and sustainable development, the 13th Conference of the Parties (CoP) meeting urged the parties to utilize the Principles and Guidelines for the Sustainable Use of Biodiversity.[17]

---

[10] Patricia Birnie, *The Case of the Convention on Trade in Endangered Species*, *in* ENFORCING ENVIRONMENTAL STANDARDS: ECONOMIC MECHANISMS AS VIABLE MEANS? 233, 241, (Rüdiger Wolfrum ed., 1996).

[11] Young (note 7), at 183; Catharine L. Krieps, *Sustainable Use of Endangered Species under CITES: Is It a Sustainable Alternative?*, 17 U. PA. J. INT'L ECON. L. 476, 477 (1996).

[12] Young (note 7), at 184.

[13] Birnie (note 10), at 241.

[14] McOmber (note 1), at 674.

[15] Birnie (note 10), at 241.

[16] Young (note 7), at 185.

[17] Conf. 13.2(a).

The CITES' Strategic Vision adopted by CoP-14 confirms that sustainable trade in wild fauna and flora can make a major contribution to achieving the broader objectives of sustainable development and biodiversity conservation.[18] The Strategic Vision provides a framework for the future development of Resolutions and Decisions. It takes into account issues such as:

1. Meeting the UN Millennium Development Goals;
2. Significantly reducing the rate of biodiversity loss by 2010;
3. Achieving deeper understanding of the cultural, social, and economic issues at play in producer and consumer countries; and
4. Promoting wider involvement of civil society in the development of conservation policies and practices.

These developments indicate a shifting of CITES towards a more comprehensive approach, increasingly taking into account the various interests and actors concerned. Yet, while the draft of the Strategic Plan 2008-2013 stated as one of its four goals to adopt balanced wildlife trade policies compatible with human well-being, livelihoods, and cultural integrity, the final version of the Strategic Vision omitted this goal.[19]

II. Introduction to CITES' Activities

CITES uses a three-tiered system of appendices to classify species that are already threatened with extinction, those that may become threatened unless trade in them is regulated, as well as those protected within any member state which needs the cooperation of other states to ensure the effectiveness of the protection.[20] There are approximately 5,000 fauna species and 28,000 flora species listed on the three CITES appendices. In certain cases they include entire groups, such as primates, cetaceans (whales, dolphins and porpoises), sea turtles, parrots, corals, cacti and orchids. While some creatures, such as bears, elephants, tigers and whales, are the most widely known species listed by CITES, the majority of species included are less popularized species, such as aloes, corals, mussels and frogs.[21]

---

18 Conf. 14.2 Annex Goal 3; Objective 3.4; SC54 Doc. 6.1, Annex 2.

19 SC54 Doc. 6.1.

20 Art. II.

21 *See* http://www.cites.org/eng/disc/species.shtml, last visited: April 2007.

CITES' main activities include the amendment of its appendices, the monitoring of implementation of the Convention by member states, and enforcement measures. The implementation itself is a task entrusted to the member states. CITES' activities in this latter context are limited to supporting and assisting its members.

B. The Exercise of Public Authority by CITES: A Legal Analysis

I. The Institutional Framework

1. CITES' Characteristics as Treaty Regime

CITES is a treaty regime. It has not been established as an international organization, yet its structure and functioning, in many respects, resembles those of international organizations. CITES satisfies the conditions required of international organizations. It is an association of states established by and based upon a treaty that pursues common aims, and which has organs that fulfill functions.[22] Typically, international organizations are founded with a generally and vaguely termed framework treaty which is then dynamically concretized by treaty bodies. Executive tasks are carried out by a Secretariat.[23] Both aspects are also true of CITES.

2. Function and Composition of CITES' Organs

At the international level, CITES operates through CoPs which take place every two and a half years, a Secretariat, the executive Standing Committee[24] and two functional, subsidiary or technical committees: the Animals and the Plants Committee.[25] While the CoP and the Secre-

---

[22] Rudolf L. Bindschedler, *International Organisations, General Aspects, in* EPIL, vol. 2, 1289 (Rudolph Bernhardt ed.,1995)

[23] EBERHARD SCHMIDT-AßMANN, DAS ALLGEMEINE VERWALTUNGSRECHT ALS ORDNUNGSIDEE 321 (2006).

[24] Conf. 11.1 (Rev. CoP14) (a).

[25] Conf. 11.1 (Rev. CoP14) (b).

tariat are provided for by the Convention, the other committees have been established by resolution of the CoP.[26]

The essential actors at the national level are Management Authorities, designated to issue export and import permits as well as certificates for species, and Scientific Authorities which advise on all scientific matters.[27]

The Convention thus relies on national as well as international bodies to perform its central tasks. The examination of the composition and the functions of CITES' institutions will further underline this composite administrative dimension of the treaty.

a) Conference of the Parties (CoP)

CITES' main decision-making body, the CoP, is composed of government representatives. Fourteen CoPs have been held to date.[28]

The role of CoPs is viewed quite divergently. Sometimes they are described as issue-specific global legislatures. At the other end of the spectrum they are envisaged as nothing more than a forum in which lawmaking is undertaken by states. They are compared to a diplomatic conference, with the additional advantage that they permit continuous processes and cooperative engagements of technical experts, policymakers, and lawyers. The truth may well lie between those two extremes.[29]

b) Secretariat

The CITES Secretariat is entrusted with executive functions in a way typical for international organizations and treaty regimes.[30] The Secre-

---

[26] Conf. 11.1 (Rev. CoP14).

[27] Art. IX(1), (2).

[28] *See* http://www.cites.org/eng/CoP/index.shtml.

[29] Jutta Brunnée, *Reweaving the Fabric of International Law? Patterns of Consent in Environmental Framework Agreements, in* 177 DEVELOPMENTS OF INTERNATIONAL LAW IN TREATY MAKING 101, 106 (Rüdiger Wolfrum &Volker Röben eds., 2005).

[30] Rüdiger Wolfrum, *Means of Ensuring Compliance with and Enforcement of International Environmental Law*, 272 RECUEIL DES COURS. COLLECTED COURSES OF THE HAGUE ACADEMY OF INTERNATIONAL LAW 9, 48 (1998).

tariat is provided by the Executive Director of UNEP with the assistance of intergovernmental and non-governmental agencies and bodies and located in Geneva.[31] CITES was one of the first multilateral environmental agreements (MEAs) with a professional full-time Secretariat.[32]

c) Standing Committee

In 1979, following a recommendation of the Secretariat, the then existing advisory Steering Committee was re-established by resolution as a permanent executive Standing Committee. The Standing Committee's functions are "general policy and general operational direction" and overseeing the operation of the Convention between meetings of the CoP.[33] This includes providing guidance and advice to the Secretariat,[34] overseeing the Secretariat's budget and all financial activities,[35] providing coordination and advice to other committees and working groups,[36] drafting potential CoP resolutions,[37] and performing any other functions that are entrusted to it by the CoP.[38]

Members of the Standing Committee are elected by the CoP.[39] The Committee comprises 14 regional party representatives, plus Switzerland, the depositary government,[40] and the previous and the next host country.[41] Between one and four members represent each of the six geographic regions.[42] Africa, the region with the most parties, has four

---

31 Art. XII(1); Birnie (note 10), at 238.

32 REEVE (note 2), at 43.

33 Conf. 11.1, (Rev. CoP14) Annex 1, (a).

34 Conf. 11.1, (Rev. CoP14) Annex 1, (b).

35 Conf. 11.1, (Rev. CoP14) Annex 1, (c).

36 Conf. 11.1, (Rev. CoP14) Annex 1, (d).

37 Conf. 11.1, (Rev. CoP14) Annex 1, (f).

38 Conf. 11.1, (Rev. CoP14) Annex 1, (i).

39 Conf. 11.1, (Rev. CoP14) Annex 1, (a)(III).

40 Conf. 11.1, (Rev. CoP14) Annex 1, (a)(i)(B).

41 Conf. 11.1, (Rev. CoP14) Annex 1, (a)(i)(C).

42 Conf. 11.1, (Rev. CoP14) Annex 1, (a)(i)(A).

representatives. Each regional representative has an alternate member authorized to act in case of his absence.[43]

Elected members serve an approximate five-year term that ends with the second CoP meeting following their election.[44] Only the regional members or alternate regional members have the right to vote, with the Depositary Government voting only to break a tie.[45] Decisions are, in practice, made by consensus.

d) The Technical Committees

The Animals and Plants Committees are the technical committees. Their members are chosen by the regions. North America and Oceania each elect one person, while the other four regions elect two. Additionally, there is a specialist on zoological nomenclature (Animals Committee) and a specialist on botanical nomenclature (Plants Committee) who are appointed by the CoP, bringing the total number of members to twelve.[46] Even though not expressly required, members tend to be from Scientific Authorities. Their terms in office last about five years, ending with the second CoP after their election.[47]

The Committees' main functions are to provide advice and guidance to all other bodies, including proposals to amend the appendices;[48] cooperate with the Secretariat to assist Scientific Authorities;[49] review and assess species that are significantly affected by trade;[50] review species included in the appendices;[51] advise range states on management techniques and procedures if requested;[52] draft potential CoP resolutions;[53]

---

43 REEVE (note 2), at 47; Conf. 11.1, (Rev. CoP14) Annex 1, (a)(ii).

44 REEVE (note 2), at 48; Conf. 11.1, (Rev. CoP13) Annex 1, (a)(iii).

45 Conf. 11.1, (Rev. CoP14) Annex 1, (b)(i).

46 Conf. 11.1, (Rev. CoP14) Annex 2, (a).

47 REEVE (note 2), at 51; Conf. 11.1, (Rev. CoP14) Annex 2, (c).

48 Conf. 11.1, (Rev. CoP14) Annex 2, (a).

49 Conf. 11.1, (Rev. CoP14) Annex 2, (d).

50 Conf. 11.1, (Rev. CoP14) Annex 2, (f), (g).

51 Conf. 11.1, (Rev. CoP14) Annex 2, (h).

52 Conf. 11.1, (Rev. CoP13) Annex 2, (i).

53 Conf. 11.1, (Rev. CoP13) Annex 2, (j).

and perform any other functions assigned to them by the CoP or the Standing Committee.[54]

3. CITES Co-Operation with Other Organizations

A characteristic feature of CITES lies in its cooperation with other organizations. The Secretariat contracts several organizations to carry out specific tasks, such as the specialist groups of the IUCN (World Conservation Union) Species Survival Commission, which is a "knowledge network" of roughly 7,000 volunteers, the IUCN Environmental Law Centre, the UNEP World Conservation Monitoring Centre and TRAFFIC (Trade Records Analysis of Fauna and Flora in Commerce). TRAFFIC has 22 offices which monitor wildlife trade and provide data to the Secretariat and national authorities. Occasionally, other NGOs are contracted by the Secretariat for specific tasks.[55]

On the whole, the composition of CITES' organs and its cooperation with other organizations indicate that CITES follows the typical form of a composite administration, notably in international organizations and treaty regimes. CITES' work is based on linkages between different international bodies as well as those at the national and international level.

II. CITES' Substantive Programming

The following paragraphs will serve to draw a more distinctive picture of CITES' foremost function: the listing of species on its appendices as well as the development of the regulatory framework for listing decisions.

1. The Mandate of CITES to Amend its Appendices

CITES is mandated to list species in one of three appendices.[56] Appendix I includes all species that are threatened with extinction, and that are or may be affected by trade. Trade in specimens of these species under-

---

54 Conf. 11.1, (Rev. CoP13) Annex 2, (k).

55 Reeve (note 2), at 46.

56 Art. II.

lies the most stringent provisions and is only authorized in exceptional circumstances.[57]

Appendix II includes species which may become threatened with extinction unless trade in them is strictly regulated, as well as species which are not at risk themselves but resemble threatened species (so-called "look alike" species)[58] that are included in order to protect their threatened counterparts.[59]

Appendix III includes all species which are protected within any member states that need the co-operation of other parties in trade control.[60]

2. *Concretization of the Mandate Through CoP Resolutions*

The mandate of CITES to conserve wild fauna and flora through the listing of species in its three appendices is rather vague and abstract. This made further concretization through resolutions of CoPs necessary. These resolutions have brought about a considerable reform of the Convention's mode of work.[61]

For treaty regimes it is a common phenomenon that decision making power gradually shifts from the states parties to the CoP.[62] Typically, environmental problems need to be addressed in a flexible manner, which keeps pace with evolving knowledge, or readiness to act. Thus, initial agreements only comprise general commitments of the parties, while the success of the treaty regime largely depends on its adaptation capacities. This shifting of the decision-making power to the CoP thus helps to strike a balance between the interests of state sovereignty, which is safeguarded by consent requirements, and efficiency, that is, the capacity to respond to new circumstances.[63]

---

57 Art. II(1).

58 Birnie (note 10), at 235.

59 Art. II(2).

60 Art. II(3).

61 Birnie (note 10), at 237.

62 Brunnée (note 29), at 102.

63 *Id.* at 104.

a) Form of and Procedure for CoP Resolutions

The Convention provides the CoP with the opportunity to make recommendations but does not specify the form of those recommendations.[64] Since 1994 they have taken the form of "resolutions", "revised resolutions", and "decisions". Resolutions are designed to take long-term effect, while decisions are generally only valid from one meeting of the CoP to the next.[65] In practice, however, decisions with long-term effect are being increasingly approved.[66] In 1994 the CoP decided to compile all its decisions not recorded in resolutions into a document that was to be updated after each meeting of the CoP.[67] Recommendations have grown into a body of rules which, although not considered legally binding, transformed the regime in an unforeseeable way.[68]

CoP resolutions contain language that is typical for legally binding provisions ("shall") and, arguably, they affect the rights and obligations of the parties under the agreement. Non-compliance with them triggers reactions under the compliance regime. This entails their classification as *de facto* lawmaking, that is, they have a *de facto* effect on parties as if they were binding.[69]

Until 1985, resolutions were adopted by a simple majority of the parties present and voting. The argument that wider support would improve implementation, led to the introduction of the requirement of a two-thirds majority of votes cast. In practice, parties try to achieve a consensus.

The recommendations become effective on the date when they are notified to the parties, unless otherwise provided.

The recommendations have made the CITES regime more dynamic and flexible than it would be if changes in its procedures were only brought about by treaty amendments. Amendments have to be adopted by a two-thirds majority of the votes cast.[70] They enter into force for the parties which were in favor of them 60 days after two-thirds of the par-

---

[64] Art. XI(3)(e).

[65] REEVE (note 2), at 40.

[66] *Id.* at 41.

[67] REEVE (note 2), at 40.

[68] Sand (note 5), at 35.

[69] Brunnée (note 29), at 111, 115.

[70] Art. XVII(1).

ties have deposited an instrument of acceptance.[71] The Gaborone amendment which is intended to permit the accession to the EU shows the delay treaty amendments may cause. It was approved at CoP-4 in 1983, and still has not entered into force.[72]

Until 1994, voting at CoP meetings on proposals to amend the appendices and on CoP resolutions was public. At CoP-9 an option for a secret ballot was introduced, in spite of expressed concerns about a loss of transparency. A vote can be by secret ballot if so requested by ten parties.[73] Although this is meant to be only an exception, in practice the secret ballot is being used more and more often for strongly contested proposals.[74]

b) Content of Concretizing Resolutions

CoP resolutions significantly revised the grounds upon which decisions concerning the categorization of species are based. At the First Meeting of the CoP, the "Berne criteria" were adopted which specified the method used to list species and to transfer them from one Appendix to the other.[75] Decisions were to be based on data on population, habitat, trade and similar factors. This method was preferred to a strict application of precise biological data because it helped to ensure the protection of species whose survival status was unknown due to scientific or financial reasons. These criteria were rejected, mostly by African states, as being too vague and unscientific.[76]

In 1981, CoP-3 adopted a resolution which permitted the ranching of Appendix I species that were no longer considered endangered, if the ranching was "primarily beneficial to the conservation of the local population".[77]

---

71 Art. XVII(3).

72 REEVE (note 2), at 41.

73 *Id.* at 42.

74 *Id.* at 43.

75 WILLEM WIJNSTEKERS, THE EVOLUTION OF CITES 51 (2003).

76 McOmber (note 1) at 683; Johan L. Garrison, *The Convention on International Trade in Endangered Species of Wild Fauna and Flora (CITES) and the Debate Over Sustainable Use*, 12 PACE ENVTL. L. REV. 301, 312 (1994).

77 McOmber (note 1), at 683; Sand (note 5), at 45.

In 1992, the CoP-8 decided to revise the criteria and the 1994 Conference finally agreed on more specific criteria for amendments.[78]

Dissatisfaction about the listing criteria was wide-spread. Industrialized states' efforts to assign charismatic mega fauna such as elephants, rhinoceroses, and tigers to Appendix I were considered as a form of cultural imperialism.[79] At the same time environmentalists argued that the failure to list species such as the Atlantic bluefin tuna and the Brazilian mahogany resulted from powerful economic interests overruling sound science. The Berne Criteria were also criticized for making it virtually impossible for certain species to be down listed from Appendix I to Appendix II. The members regarded science as a means to both serve procedural "rule of law" values, and help to achieve a substantively correct listing result.

The Ford Lauderdale Criteria changed in particular four aspects. First, they introduced quantitative guidelines for the assignment of species to an appendix. Second, the criteria gave biology a priority over trade status. Third, the criteria recommended parties to down-list Appendix I species which failed to meet the new quantitative criteria. Finally, the criteria authorized "split-listing".

This much contested question, whether or not to permit the split-listing of a species (that is the listing of different populations of a species in different appendices), had particular relevance with respect to elephants. South African countries rejected the 1989 listing of all elephant populations in Appendix I. In 1997, the parties reached a compromise and agreed to leave the highly threatened East African populations on Appendix I, while downgrading the Southern African elephants to Appendix II.[80]

Further changes included the request for input from intergovernmental organizations for all species.[81] A precautionary principle was established for cases of uncertainty about the status of a species or impact of trade on a species, as well as a proportionality principle.[82]

After the adoption of the criteria, listing decisions have continued to be political decisions since the parties are not under an obligation to vote

---

78 McOmber (note 1), at 684; Sand (note 5), at 46.

79 FAVRE (note 7), at 876.

80 McOmber (note 1), at 695.

81 *Id.* at 685.

82 *Id.* at 686; Conf. 9.24 (Rev. CoP13).

for the listing of a species even when it meets the quantitative guidelines. Instead they act in accordance with their own conservation priorities given the unfeasibility of a comprehensive protection of all species.

III. Procedure to Amend Appendices

1. General Amendment Procedure

CITES' appendices are amended in several steps. Amendments to Appendix I or II can be proposed for consideration at the next CoP meeting by any party.[83] Additionally, there is a postal procedure for urgent cases.[84] The proposal is communicated to the Secretariat. The Secretariat consults the other parties and interested bodies and communicates the response to all parties.[85]

Amendments are adopted by a two-thirds majority of parties present and voting. Abstaining parties are not counted.[86] Amendments enter into force 90 days after the meeting for all parties except those which make a reservation.[87] Any party may, by notification in writing to the Depositary Government, make a reservation with respect to the amendment.[88] Parties who enter reservations with respect to Appendix I species are recommended to treat the species as if it were listed in Appendix II, and to report trade in their annual reports.[89] Current editions of appendices are published periodically and distributed to the parties by the Secretariat.[90]

Hence, the Convention does not provide for formal state consent to the modification of appendices. Pursuant to Article 11 of the Vienna Convention of the Law of Treaties, states can express their consent by "any other means if so agreed". Typically, when dealing with the amendment of annexes, formal consent requirements are discarded. Those tend to

---

83 Art. XV(1)(a).

84 Art. XV(2).

85 Art. XV(1)(a).

86 Art. XV(1)(b).

87 Art. XV(1)(c).

88 Art. XV(3).

89 REEVE (note 2), at 36.

90 Art. XII(2)(f).

be adopted at sessions of the CoP and do not require the deposit of instruments of acceptance by parties to become effective. Rather, it is common to presume acceptance unless a party explicitly opts out.

Those annexes usually contain only technical detail rather than substantive commitments. Yet, in the case of CITES the decisions about amendments to appendices are among the most controversial issues in the ambit of the Convention and impact directly on obligations of parties and individuals.[91] In this aspect CITES differs from most other treaty regimes. This fact underlines the high level of power CITES exerts on its members.

2. *Co-operation With Other Actors in the Preparation of Amendments*

It is not exclusively CITES which works to amend Appendices. The IUCN Species Survival Commission and TRAFFIC International are authorized to review the proposals for amendments.[92]

IUCN's Species Survival Commission collects information on the status and biology of species from its Specialist Group network and the scientific community as a whole, while TRAFFIC collects data on the trade and use of species from its own sources as well as the CITES trade database. They both publish their analyses of proposals to amend the appendices online. A summary booklet is produced and widely distributed before and during the CoPs, with a view to enabling participants to base their decisions on accurate and up-to-date scientific data.

Before CoP-14 in 2007 they engaged in intensive consultations involving hundreds of experts around the world for three months. Thirty-six proposals have been analyzed covering a wide range of species from mammals, such as the African elephant and leopard, to commercially important timber species, including three species of Central American rosewood, and commercially valuable marine species of sharks, eels and coral. One third of the animal species proposed this time were marine species.[93]

The indicated NGOs thus play a significant role with regard to amendment proposals.

---

91 Brunnée (note 29), at 108.

92 Reeve (note 2), at 32.

93 Available at: http://www.iucn.org/themes/ssc/news/2007_articles/cities.htm.

3. Observers at CoP Meetings

One aspect of particular significance during the procedure leading to an amendment of the appendices is the participation of observers at CoP meetings. Governmental or non-governmental bodies or agencies qualified within the field of action of CITES may attend CoP meetings without a right to vote unless at least one-third of the parties present object.[94] The United Nations, its specialized agencies, and the International Atomic Energy Agency, as well as any state that is not a party to the Convention, may be represented at meetings of the Conference by observers who do not vote.[95]

At its thirteenth meeting the CoP specified requirements under Article XI(7)(a) such that a registration by the Secretariat would require a prior demonstration that the organization is qualified in protection, conservation or management of wild fauna and flora; and is an organization in its own right, with a legal persona and an international character, remit and program of activities.[96] Rule 3, paragraph 5, of the Rules of the Procedure for CoP meetings established a one-month deadline to inform about observers.

The CoP further recommended that the parties make every effort to ensure that chosen venues for meetings have space for observers and that the Secretariat and the host country make every effort to ensure that each approved observer is provided with at least one seat in the meeting rooms, unless one-third of the party representatives object. Finally, it instructed the Presiding Officers to make every effort to allow observers to make interventions.

The Secretariat is further asked to ensure that informative documents prepared by observers are distributed to the participants in the meeting, and not to provide sponsorship through the Sponsored Delegates Project to any representative who is also an observer for an NGO.[97]

In practice, NGOs participate actively in CoP meetings. They make verbal interventions, suggest amendments to CoP recommendations, and participate in working groups at the discretion of the chairs of the sessional committees.[98]

---

94 Art. XI(7).

95 Art. XI(6).

96 Conf. 13.8.

97 Conf. 13.8.

98 REEVE (note 2), at 38.

IV. The Central Instruments

1. Obligations for Its Members Set Forth by CITES

The central regulatory impact of CITES is intended to derive from the appendices in connection with the obligation of member states to coordinate international trade in accordance with the Convention and to prohibit and penalize trade in contravention of it.[99]

The export of Appendix I species requires an export permit, which is only granted when authorities of the state of export have advised that the export will not be detrimental to the survival of that species. Further conditions of a permit are that the authorities are satisfied that the specimen was not obtained in contravention of the laws of that state for the protection of fauna and flora, that any living specimen will be so prepared and shipped as to minimize risks of injury, damage to health or cruel treatment, and that an import permit has been issued for the specimen.[100]

The import requires an import permit and either an export permit or a re-export certificate. An import permit requires that the authorities of the state of import have advised that the import will be for purposes which are not detrimental to the survival of the species concerned, are satisfied that the recipient of a living specimen will care for it adequately, and that the specimen is not to be used for primarily commercial purposes.[101] This limits trade to specimens used primarily for scientific and educational purposes, and, in some instances, to hunting trophies.[102]

The re-export or introduction from the sea of any specimen underlies similarly strict regulations.[103]

The export of Appendix II species requires an export permit which is granted under the same conditions applicable to Appendix I species.[104] A Scientific Authority in each party monitors exports and advises to limit the granting of permits if necessary.[105]

---

99 Art. II(4), VIII(1)(a).

100 Art. III(2).

101 Art. III(3).

102 Birnie (note 10), at 237.

103 Art. III(4), (5).

104 Art. IV(2).

105 Art. IV(3).

The import merely requires the prior presentation of either an export permit or a re-export certificate. Other requirements necessary with respect to Appendix I species need not to be fulfilled here.[106]

The export of specimens of species listed in Appendix III from any state where it is listed in Appendix III requires an export permit.[107] The import requires the prior presentation of a certificate of origin and, where the import is from a state which has included that species in Appendix III, an export permit.[108]

There are exemptions from the requirements of Articles III, IV, and V. For example, for the benefit of scientists[109] and, at the discretion of the states' authorities, traveling exhibitions.[110]

CITES thus obliges its members to make concrete actions concerning the control of international trade through the issuing of export and import permits. Groups of individuals actually affected by the prescriptions are exporters and importers of wildlife and wildlife products.

2. *Implementation of CITES*

The implementation of the Convention is a responsibility of the member states. States have a duty to prohibit trade in contravention of CITES.[111] They are under an obligation to take appropriate measures to enforce the provisions of CITES, including penalties for trade in, or possession of, such specimens and the confiscation or return to the state of export of such specimens.[112] Even Articles III, IV, and V are formulated in broad general terms and require national legislation to make them effective.[113]

---

106 Art. IV(4).

107 Art. V(2).

108 Art. V(3).

109 Art. VII(6).

110 Art. VII(7).

111 Art. II(4).

112 Art. VIII(1).

113 Birnie (note 10), at 243.

a) CITES' Support for Implementation

CITES assists its members in the implementation of their obligations under the Convention in several different ways. CoPs helped to interpret some of the vague treaty provisions, for example the phrase "any readily recognizable part or derivative"[114] of specimens to lead to more conformity and effective implementation.

Where the non-detriment finding is concerned, in many cases CITES does not support its members. The parameters for non-detriment finding are not specified in the Convention or in any resolutions.[115]

The setting of export quotas has evolved into a standard practice to fulfill the non-detriment condition. Quotas establish the maximum number of specimens of a species that may be exported over the course of a year without causing a detrimental impact on its survival. The CoP usually sets quotas only for species of special concern while most quotas are set voluntarily by parties.[116]

To support the implementation, the Secretariat also undertakes scientific and technical studies in accordance with programs authorized by the CoP.[117] Another important strategy to facilitate implementation is the organization of capacity-building training seminars for officials from CITES Management Authorities and enforcement services, since institutional and financial constraints, especially in developing countries, are often the cause for failure of implementation.[118]

b) Implementation by the EU

The European Community enacted binding regulations to implement CITES in 1982. These were subsequently amended and enforced by a landmark judgment of the European Court of Justice in 1990 which held an unsubstantiated French CITES import permit to infringe Community law.[119]

---

114 Art. 1(b)(II), (III).

115 Conf. 10.3 (h); James B. Murphy, *Alternative Approaches to the CITES "Non-detriment" Finding for Appendix II Species*, 2 ENVTL. L. 531, 540 (2006).

116 Conf. 10.14 (Rev. CoP13); Conf. 10.15 (Rev. CoP12); Conf. 12.3 (Rev. CoP13); available at: http://www.cites.org/eng/resources/quotas/index.shtml.

117 Art. XII(2)(c).

118 Sand (note 5), at 51.

119 Sand (note 5), at 55.

At present, CITES is implemented by the EU through regulation No. 338/97 9th December, 1996. The regulation includes four annexes, which contain, *inter alia*, all the species from CITES appendices.[120]

c) Implementation by Non-Members

Non-members may also be required to comply with treaty provisions when they intend to trade with member states. Trade with non-member states is regulated in Article X and elaborated through resolutions of the CoP. Parties can only accept permits and certificates from non-party states whose competent authorities and scientific institutions are included in the most recent list compiled by the Secretariat, or after consulting with the Secretariat. Parties importing Appendix I and II species must also require certificates stating that the competent scientific institution in the non-party state has made a non-detriment finding, and that the specimens were not illegally obtained. Before allowing trade in Appendix I species with non-party states, parties are further required to consult with the Secretariat, and to only allow the trade of wild specimens in special cases for conservation or welfare purposes.

V. Review, Monitoring and Compliance Enforcement

1. Review of CITES

CITES' organs themselves review CITES' effectiveness. The CoP, as well as the Secretariat, may make recommendations to improve CITES' effectiveness.[121]

Member states also have a certain degree of control over CITES' activities. Parties can object if they feel that the Secretariat is being too intrusive in its reports on infractions.[122]

2. Monitoring

To make the monitoring of the implementation possible, parties are required to transmit an annual report to the Secretariat listing the number

120 Art. 3.

121 Arts. XI(3)(d), (e); XIII(3); Art. XII(2)(h).

122 Sand (note 5), at 49.

and type of permits granted, exporters and importers and the states with whom they are trading and the numbers or quantities and types of specimens.[123] Furthermore, they have to furnish a biennial report on legislative, regulatory, and administrative measures taken to enforce the provisions of the Convention.[124] These reports are made public if the law of the party so permits.[125]

The collection, analysis, and dissemination of information on compliance is essential for a compliance system. These tasks are undertaken by the Secretariat. CITES relies mainly on party reports, but also on information from NGOs and International Organizations, from organizations such as Interpol and the World Customs Organization (WCO). CITES disperses one of the best information sources available to any environmental treaty, with independent case studies and reports on seizures and prosecutions being publicized in the TRAFFIC Bulletins.[126] NGOs, such as IUCN, WWF (World Wide Fund for Nature), and TRAFFIC, provide data on the status of species, the threat to them posed by trade, and the strictness of observance of the Convention which enables the Secretariat to identify problems and to engage in counter measures.[127]

The Secretariat may also be asked to make an *ad hoc* visit to any party to verify information, or in cases of serious non-compliance.[128]

When the Secretariat is convinced that any species included in Appendix I or II is adversely affected by trade or that the Convention is not implemented effectively, it communicates such information to the Management Authority of the parties concerned.[129] The concerned states inform the Secretariat of any relevant facts and, propose remedial action.[130]

The Secretariat draws the attention of the parties to any matter which pertains to the aims of CITES[131] and it prepares annual reports on the

---

123 Art. VIII(6), (7).

124 Art. VIII(7).

125 Art. VIII(8).

126 Sand (note 5), at 50.

127 Birnie (note 10), at 239; Sand (note 5), at 49.

128 Reeve (note 2), at 62.

129 Art. XIII(1).

130 Art. XIII(2).

131 Art. XII(2)(e).

implementation of the Convention.[132] Within the monitoring mechanism the Secretariat has thus further reaching competences than secretariats under the majority of treaty regimes.[133]

3. Compliance Enforcement

Compliance with CITES is promoted through two mechanisms, trade suspension and Significant Trade Review. In addition to those measures certified, non-compliance leads to negative publicity and politically harmful media coverage.[134] Thus, public pressure can help to improve compliance.

Countries that continue to violate CITES can face a recommendation of trade sanctions issued by the Standing Committee or the parties.[135] Trade sanctions were not explicitly provided for in CoP Resolution 11.3 (Rev. CoP14) which deals with non-compliance response. They are, however, used in practice.[136]

The Standing Committee initiates collective action against non-compliance from member states as well as third states. It recommends parties to take stricter domestic measures than those provided by the treaty, including suspension of trade, as envisaged in article XIV(1).[137] In the case of non-member states, these measures are used when the state concerned persistently refuses to provide comparable documents pursuant to article X.[138]

At the time of writing, 31 countries are subject to a recommendation to suspend trade. In the case of Djibouti, Guinea-Bissau, Liberia, Mauritania, Rwanda, and Somalia, a suspension of all trade has been recommended due to a lack of adequate national legislation. Mauritania and Somalia are additionally subject to a recommendation of a comprehensive trade suspension due to a failure to provide annual reports. Niger is

---

132 Art. XII(2)(g).

133 Wolfrum (note 30), at 49.

134 Sand (note 5), at 49.

135 Murphy (note 115), at 537.

136 REEVE (note 2), at 91.

137 Sand (note 5), at 38.

138 *Id.* at 39.

subject to a recommendation to suspend all trade because of enforcement matters.[139]

The procedure for Significant Trade Review for Appendix II species may lead, as a last resort, to a suspension of trade in the affected species with the state concerned issued by the Standing Committee.[140]

CITES thus disposes of two rather sophisticated and complex enforcement mechanisms.

C. Legitimacy

I. Input Legitimacy

This final section of the paper will address the question of whether or not CITES represents a legitimate regime. To shed light on this problem, the input legitimacy will first be considered.

Government members form the main decision-making body of CITES and have, therefore, a quite central position. On the other hand, the Secretariat and the Committees' strong position, founded upon expertise procured from external experts, is notable. CITES is comparatively open to NGO participation which means that it leaves room for influence by affected individuals. The central position of states, the reliance on science, and the involvement of NGOs indicate existing efforts to ensure CITES' input legitimacy.

II. Output Legitimacy

1. Effectiveness

CITES' output legitimacy is hotly debated where CITES' effectiveness is concerned. The status of a species depends on a multitude of factors, such as the state of their habitat and impacts by alien invasive species that the Convention has no influence on. The effectiveness of the Con-

---

139 *See* http://www.cites.org/eng/news/sundry/trade_suspension.shtml.

140 Conf. 12.8 (Rev. CoP13) (s).

vention can therefore not be correlated directly with the conservation status of a species.[141]

CITES' effectiveness in regulating global trade seems doubtful considering that the global illegal trade in wildlife is estimated to be worth $5 to $10 billion every year. Only drugs and arms generate more illegal income.[142]

The Species Survival Network's review of international trade in birds found nine species of birds and thirteen countries for which quotas established under the significant trade process had been exceeded between 1994 and 1999.[143] The study further detected an omission of range states in fifteen reviews of significantly traded birds, quota-setting without biological data, lack of peer review of field studies, lack of uniform standards for non-detriment findings, lack of follow-up recommendations, and a failure of importing states to comply with trade suspensions. A further problem is that reviews consider only a limited number of species while the majority of species remains unheeded.[144]

The quota system is criticized for being uncontrolled, unscientific, and open to abuse. Parties often exceed quotas. In 1999, sixty-seven quotas for fauna and two for flora were reportedly exceeded. Half of these were exceeded by at least 150% and two were exceeded by over 1000%.[145]

The Significant Trade Review process is also criticized by some as being complex, difficult to understand, and ineffective.[146] The Significant Trade Review process was however successful in some cases. The committees reviewed more than 200 animal taxa, succeeded in limiting trade to a sustainable level and in increasing cooperation among range states, for example, with Caspian Sea range states regarding sturgeon and paddlefish. High cost of scientific studies and lack of a scientific consensus to determine when a species is endangered pose additional problems.

There is a notably sharp decline of some Appendix I species, such as the Kenyan rhinoceros population which dropped from 18,000 rhinos in 1968 to only 400 rhinos in 1992. A similar decline is notable with re-

---

141 Sand (note 5), at 54.

142 McOmber (note 1), at 674.

143 Murphy (note 115), at 541.

144 *Id.* at 542.

145 *Id.* at 540.

146 *Id.* at 534, 541.

spect to tigers.[147] When affluent states such as the United States lack adequately trained personnel, it is not surprising that poorer range states' record of controls is not any better.[148]

The implementation of provisions relating to Appendix II species are hampered by the lack of accurate information on the health of a species and levels of trade which prevents parties from assessing whether trade will be detrimental to the survival of the species. The overwhelming percentage of all CITES species are listed in Appendix II which makes the significance of precise non-detriment findings all the more obvious.[149] Decisions taken in the absence of reliable scientific data need to be avoided.

And still, some positive outcomes of CITES are undeniable. In spite of its limited budget of approximately US $5 million annually, the Secretariat of CITES has a strong position.[150] Its Infraction Reports are now perceived as reliable and impartial documents that help to reinforce national implementation and accountability.[151]

Some changes in consumer demands are attributed to CITES. The food and fashion industries shifted away from products from Appendix I listed species, such as turtle soup, or leopard fur coats. Medical/pharmaceutical research, and partly the pet trade, substituted captive-bred for wild-caught animals. Crocodile leather is increasingly obtained from CITES controlled ranching operations and plants such as orchids and cacti are artificially propagated. In many cases CITES listed species have been replaced by other species.[152]

2. *The Legality Principle*

One further legitimacy question is commonly neglected by CITES' organs as well as researchers. The obligation of member states to penalize the trade in and possession of protected species[153] entails the question of whether the criminal norms that are consequently adopted at the na-

---

147 Krieps (note 11), at 462.

148 *Id.* at 473.

149 Murphy (note 115), at 533.

150 REEVE (note 2), at 45.

151 Sand (note 5), at 50.

152 *Id.* at 54.

153 Art. VIII(1)(a).

tional level are legitimate. The decision about form and content of criminal provisions remains exclusively within the purview of each member state. And yet the references to CITES contained in the legislation may present a legitimacy problem shared by criminal norms that are adopted in order to implement the Convention. The EC regulation for the protection of species,[154] for example, automatically incorporates all species on CITES' appendices. The regulation is then implemented through national criminal norms containing dynamic cross-references to the EC regulation. The Austrian,[155] German,[156] Hungarian,[157] and Dutch[158] criminal legislation refer to the lists of protected species contained within EC Regulation No. 338/97.[159] Denmark,[160] France,[161] Italy,[162] Luxembourg,[163] Poland,[164] Slovenia,[165] and Belgium[166] criminalize

---

[154] EC Regulation No. 338/97 of 9 December 1996, OJ L 61, 3.3.1997.

[155] Bundesgesetz über die Überwachung des Handels mit Exemplaren wildlebender Tier- und Pflanzenarten Artenhandelsgesetz – ArtHG) – Trade in Species Act from 30 January 1998, BGBl. I No. 33/1998, last changed by BGBl. I No. 29/2006.

[156] Section 66, Federal Nature Conservation Act from 3 April 2002, BGBl. I No. 22/2002; Section 330 (1)(3), Criminal Code from 13 November 1998, BGBl. I 3322, last changed by BGBl. I 1690.

[157] Government Decree No. 271/2002 (XII.20) on the Implementation and Enforcements of CITES (2002), amended by Government Decree No. 283/2004.

[158] Flora and Fauna Act from 1 April 2002, Stb. 1998, 402, last changed by Stb. 2002, 236; Act on Economic Offences from 22 June 1950, Stb. 1950, K258, last changed by Stb. 2002, 542.

[159] Tobias Garstecki, *Implementation of Article 16, Council Regulation (EC) No. 338/97, in the 25 Member States of the European Union.* A Traffic Europe Report for the European Commission, 7 (2006), available at: http://www.traffic.org/general-topics/.

[160] Ministry of Environment and Energy Statutory Order No. 84 of 23 January 2002.

[161] Art. 215 and Art. 414, Customs Code of 8 July 1963, Décret No. 63-673, Journal Officiel from 12 July 1963.

[162] Law 150/92, Gazz. Uff. No. 44 from 22 February 1992.

[163] Art. 12 Law of 21 April 1989, Journal Officiel No. 33 from 26 May 1989.

[164] Arts. 127-131 Nature Conservation Act of 16 April 2004, Journal of Laws 04.92.88.

[165] Art. 40 Decree on the Course of Conduct and Protection Measures in the Trade in Animal and Plant Species, OG of the RS 52/04.

violations of this EC Regulation. Portuguese law,[167] on the other hand, does not provide for any criminal but only administrative sanctions in order to implement CITES.[168]

It is not merely the commercial conduct which is criminalized. Small-scale wildlife trade offences are also criminalized.[169] In Denmark, for instance, the importation in good faith for non-commercial use (for example tourist souvenirs) of specimens in Appendix II, usually result in confiscation[170] whereas such importation of Appendix I specimens usually results in fines.[171]

Hence, a modification to the appendices of CITES automatically alters domestic criminal law without any control by the legislature. Moreover, the criminal proscriptions do not specify the trade in which species is criminalized. To ascertain the species concerned, it is necessary to peruse a current edition of CITES' appendices. Consequently the involvement of CITES' appendices causes a loss of power of the national legislature which goes hand in hand with a loss of clarity for addressees of the statutes.

Primarily, the question arises whether such criminal proscriptions conform to the legality principle – provided that this principle is a relevant concept for measuring legitimacy. What status does the legality principle enjoy in existing national legal systems? What elements are encompassed by it? And what is its status and content within international law?

---

166 Art. 127 Loi-Programme of 27 December 2004, Service Public Federal Chancellerie du Premier Ministre from 31 December 2004, available at: http://www.ejustice.just.fgov.be/doc/rech_f.htm.

167 Art. 32/1 Decreto-Lei No. 114/90, from 5 April 1990, Diário da República I No. 80, p.1669.

168 ROB PARRY JONES AND AMELIE KNAPP, ENFORCEMENT OF WILDLIFE TRADE CONTROLS IN EU MEMBER STATES: COUNTRY PROFILES, 108 (2006), available at: http://www.traffic.org/enforcement.

169 Garstecki (note 159), at 7.

170 Monika Anton, *A Preliminary Overview of Court Cases and Challenges in the Prosecution of Crime related to Wildlife Trade in the EU, in* PROCEEDING OF THE INTERNATIONAL EXPERT WORKSHOP OF THE ENFORCEMENT OF WILDLIFE TRADE CONTROLS IN THE EU, 43 (Monika Anton, Nicholas Dragffy, Stephanie Pendry & Tomme Rozanne Young eds., 2001), available at: www.traffic.org/enforcement.

171 PARRY-JONES AND KNAPP (note 168), at 29.

Since the French Revolution, this principle has been hailed as a fundamental guaranty. That being said, not all national legal systems base their criminal law on the principle of legality. Rather, there are examples for legal orders founded on the doctrine of substantive justice. Under the latter doctrine, any conduct that is harmful or threatening to society is punished independently of any legal criminalization at the time of action.[172] Society is thus favored over the individual. The Soviet Union and the Nazi criminal law are examples for the application of the doctrine.[173]

Nowadays, most democratic civil law states recognize the principle of strict legality as fundamental. The principle sets out four conditions for proscriptions that criminalize and penalize certain actions: (i) they are enacted by parliament, rather than by customary rules or secondary legislation enacted by the ministers; (ii) they may not be retroactive; (iii) they may not be applied analogously; and (iv) they must be as specific and clear as possible.[174] The requirement of a written law passed by a central authority which has the sole responsibility for the adoption of criminal law is seen as a logical condition for the effectiveness of legal certainty.[175] These principles prevent the risk of judicial abuse and arbitrary application of the law and are considered a part of fundamental justice.

By contrast, common law countries have both common law offences, resulting from judgments, as well as statutory offences. Hence, proscriptions are not necessarily enacted by parliament, nor do they fulfill the principle of non-retroactivity in the way it is applied under civil law systems. It follows that the principle has a different content within common law systems.[176]

One aspect of the legality principle as it is recognized in civil law countries, which makes the influence of CITES on criminal law problematic, is its requirement of solely legislative responsibility for criminal proscriptions as the CoP changes the content of the statute with its decision to add species to the appendices. States do not even have to declare

---

[172] ANTONIO CASSESE, INTERNATIONAL CRIMINAL LAW 139 (2003).

[173] *Id.* at 140.

[174] *Id.* at 141.

[175] Mauro Catenacci, *Nullum Crimen Sine Lege, in* The INTERNATIONAL CRIMINAL COURT, COMMENTS ON THE DRAFT STATUTE, 159, 162 (Flavia Lattanzi ed., 1998).

[176] CASSESE (note 172), at 142.

their willingness to be bound by those changes. Rather they have to actively opt-out. The second aspect which poses problems with respect to CITES' influence is the condition for statutes to be as specific and clear as possible. This too is problematic since norms with dynamic references do not contain all relevant information.

Does international law contain similar requirements for criminal provisions which make CITES' effect on criminal statues problematic also from an international law perspective?

Historically, international law has applied the doctrine of substantive justice, since states used to be unwilling to enter into treaties establishing criminal liabilities. Additionally, customary rules had only evolved in a rudimentary manner and only with respect to prohibiting and punishing war crimes. The international community thus had no choice but to rely upon the doctrine of substantive justice when crimes against peace and crimes against humanity had to be addressed by the Nuremberg Tribunal.[177]

After World War II, international law witnessed a gradual shift towards the principle of legality. Various newly adopted human rights treaties laid down the principle for national courts.[178] Additionally, the Universal Declaration of Human Rights[179] and the Third and Fourth Geneva Conventions of 1949 contributed to the principle being accepted as a fundamental human right.[180]

Today, international criminal proscriptions, irrespective of whether they flow from conventions, custom, or general principles of law, must satisfy the principle of legality. The statutes of the ICTY, ICTR, and the ICC[181] formulate a legality requirement.[182] The principles of legality are

---

177 *Id.* at 143.

178 Art. 15 UN Covenant on Civil and Political Rights; Art. 7 European Convention on Human Rights; Art. 9 American Convention on Human Rights; Art. 7(2) African Charter on Human and People's Rights; Susan Lamb, *Nullum Crimen, Nulla Poena sine Lege in International Criminal Law*, *in* I THE ROME STATUTE OF THE INTERNATIONAL CRIMINAL COURT. A COMMENTARY 733 (Antonio Cassesse ed., 2002).

179 Art. 11(2) Universal Declaration of Human Rights.

180 CASSESE (note 172), at 144; Art. 99(1) Third Convention; Art. 67 Fourth Convention; Additional Protocol I, Art. 2(c); Additional Protocol II, Art.6(c).

181 Arts. 22-24 ICC-Statute; Per Saland, *International Criminal Law Principles*, *in* THE INTERNATIONAL CRIMINAL COURT, THE MAKING OF THE ROME STATUTE – ISSUES, NEGOTIATIONS, RESULTS 189, 190 (Roy S. Lee ed., 1992).

a general principle of international law and have become part of customary law.[183] Hence, this principle is not merely a concept in domestic legal systems, it is also recognized at the international level.

At the international level this principle requires that: (i) there be no crime without a law (*nullum crimen sine lege*), nor a punishment without a law (*nulla poena sine lege*); (ii) no retroactive application of laws; (iii) no analogies as bases for punishment, and (iv) crimes have to be defined in a clear and unambiguous way to ensure that people are aware which acts constitute a crime.[184] The level of specificity required remains debated since existing criminal justice systems do not agree on the issue. Arguably, the crime must be defined as clearly as possible, which is interpreted less strictly than in continental European law.[185]

The second significant difference between the international and national continental European level concerning the scope of the legality principle, relates to the requirement of a law enacted by parliament. In contrast to civil law systems, international law permits customary law as a source of criminal provisions where international as well as national crimes are concerned. However, the legality question is particularly controversial where customary international criminal proscriptions are concerned.[186] In some instances, customary international law fails to comply with the requirement of legality, and codification is thus advocated to address this weakness. General principles of law may also be a source of criminal law as stated in Article 15(2) ICCPR. They are, however, the source of criminal law that is most likely to fall short of the principle of legality.[187] The decisive question remains, whether a proscription is known or could have been known to any ordinary reasonable person anywhere in the world.[188]

---

182 M. CHERIF BASSIOUNI, INTRODUCTION TO INTERNATIONAL CRIMINAL LAW 219 (2003).

183 GERHARD WERLE, PRINCIPLES OF INTERNATIONAL CRIMINAL LAW 32 (2005); BASSIOUNI (note 182), at 221.

184 BASSIOUNI (note 182), at 218; WERLE (note 183), at 33; Lamb (note 178), at 733; WARD N. FERDINANDUSSE, DIRECT APPLICATION OF INTERNATIONAL CRIMINAL LAW IN NATIONAL COURTS 223 (2006).

185 WERLE (note 183), at 33.

186 BASSIOUNI (note 182), at 221.

187 *Id.* at 224.

188 *Id.* at 225.

Legislation containing dynamic references to CITES is less transparent than legislation containing all relevant details. References to appendices are also less transparent than those of conventions, since the former can be changed more easily and become binding upon states unless they enter reservations. The mandate of the CoP to decide on the inclusion of species, which is hailed as an important step towards safeguarding endangered species causes, is at the same time, a loss of clarity of criminal provisions. Moreover, the utilization of tacit consent makes the problem even more acute, since there is no need for parliamentary consent.

On the other hand, customary law and general principles of law are recognized as source of criminal law yet these sources are even more likely to be unknown to reasonable persons and they lack parliamentary control. Are CITES' appendices, as a consequence, unproblematic with respect to the legality principle in international law?

The existence of un-codified international crimes is opposed. The fact that customary law and general principles of law are even less transparent does not absolve the international community from accomplishing CITES' mandate in a way that takes account of international and national legality principle standards. Efforts to make species protection more effective may not detract from the fundamental value of the legality principle. CITES should not leave this principle unheeded. Instead it should work to ensure that references to its appendices are as transparent as possible. It should promote participation of legislatures to legitimate them.

There are those who argue that the principle makes the criminal system inflexible and unable to comply immediately with the constant changes of public opinion.[189] Indeed, the mandate of the CoP to change CITES' appendices arguably makes CITES better able to quickly respond to conservation needs. Nevertheless, it must be noted that criminal sanctions can only be effective if they are clear enough. The appendices are difficult enough for customs officers. So how accessible are they for importers and exporters?

The Convention does not include concrete guidelines for the listing of species. These have instead been drafted by the CoP. Modifications are adopted with a two-thirds majority of votes cast and by secret ballot. Decisions depend on conservation priorities of the states. All this makes the listing procedure even less amenable to parliamentary control and less clear for addressees.

---

189 Catenacci (note 175), at 160.

States that fail to abide by the obligation to penalize contraventions may face enforcement measures under the compliance regime which makes it essential that CITES itself respects and safeguards the principle of legality in its work. It does not suffice to place all responsibility on member states to safeguard this principle.

D. Conclusion

CITES represents a fascinating example of the exercise of public authority by an international institution. Since its inception in 1973 it evolved into one of the most effective multilateral environmental agreements, balancing conservation and economic interests. Its institutional features, including its strong Secretariat and close cooperation with expert NGOs, as well as its main activities, the listing of species, compliance monitoring and decisions on enforcement measures, are factors which render this success possible. At the same time, the influence of CITES on national criminal provisions poses several problems to the legality principle as it exists at the international level, as well as within national legal systems. This problem has not yet been discussed. CITES and its members should take account of it to ensure that responsive strategies can be developed.

3.2 International Public Standards

Legal Challenges of Non-binding Instruments: The Case of the FAO Code of Conduct for Responsible Fisheries

*By Jürgen Friedrich**

---

* I gratefully acknowledge the helpful comments received from Armin von Bogdandy, Philipp Dann, Isabel Feichtner, Matthias Goldmann, Jan Klabbers and of the participants of the project on "The Law of International Administration" in 2007 and the international workshop on "The Exercise of Public Authority by International Institutions" in 2008, both at the Max Planck Institute for Comparative Public Law and International Law, as well as the German-Israeli Minerva School 2008 at the Minerva Centre for Human Rights in Tel Aviv, Israel. A PhD thesis on the role, limits and legitimacy of nonbinding instruments in environmental governance and law by this author is forthcoming.

A. von Bogdandy et al. (eds.), *The Exercise of Public Authority by International Institutions*, Beiträge zum ausländischen öffentlichen Recht und Völkerrecht 210,
DOI 10.1007/978-3-642-04531-8_18, © Springer-Verlag Berlin Heidelberg 2010

A. Introduction

Faced with the reluctance of states to transfer sovereign powers to the international level, traditional international organizations often resort to voluntary instruments when attempting to respond to pressing issues of public concern such as sustainable development. One salient example is the attempt of the United Nations Food and Agriculture Organization (FAO) to improve the dire state of global fisheries resources by means of the non-binding Code of Conduct for Responsible Fisheries (CCRF).[1] After years of extensive and dynamic development of fishing capacities in response to an increasing demand from a growing world population, the worldwide production of fisheries seems to have now reached its ceiling. The FAO estimates that three quarters of fish stocks are either fully exploited (50 percent) or overexploited and depleted (25 percent).[2] Any solution to this state of affairs faces complex regulatory challenges. The regulation of collective goods, in this case including the global common space of the high seas, goes beyond mere coor-

---

[1] Food and Agriculture Organization of the United Nations (FAO), Code of Conduct for Responsible Fisheries (CCRF), Report of the Conference of FAO, Twenty-Eighth Session, 20-31 October 1995, Annex 1 to the CCRF (Background to the Origin and Elaboration of the Code), also available at: ftp://ftp.fao.org/docrep/fao/005/v9878e/v9878e00.pdf. General literature on the CCRF includes: William Edeson, *Closing the Gap: The Role of 'Soft' International Instruments to Control Fishing*, 20 AUSTRALIAN YEARBOOK OF INTERNATIONAL LAW 83 (1999); Gerald Moore, *The Code of Conduct for Responsible Fisheries, in* DEVELOPMENTS IN INTERNATIONAL FISHERIES LAW 85 (Ellen Hey ed., 1999).

[2] FAO, The State of World Fisheries and Aquaculture 2006 (2007), Part I, available at: http://www.fao.org/docrep/009/A0699e/A0699e00.htm.

dination problems as analyzed by other case studies in this volume.[3] It requires cooperation across jurisdictional zones by a multitude of different actors with various economic and social interests in a subject area marked by fierce economic competition. Free riding must be prevented through monitoring and enforcement at sea. Further, it is now understood that long-term sustainable use largely depends on the protection of the living and non-living environment of the resource, from which derives the need for an ecosystem approach. Uncertainty over reproduction levels and impact of environmental degradation makes a precautionary approach to fisheries management indispensable for successful regulation. The complexity and high level of uncertainty additionally calls for a highly flexible and adaptable regulation.

Aware of these complex regulatory exigencies, one is left to wonder whether a voluntary instrument of an organization without any enforcement capabilities could actually be of any use. Clearly, the capacity of the CCRF is indeed limited. It is not an instrument which regulates access to resources or establishes substantive management measures such as quotas. These difficult decisions and their enforcement, which often harbor the greatest potential for conflicts of interests, are left to states and regional fisheries organizations. However, even if management and enforcement is or will have to be conducted in this decentralized way, the FAO by means of the CCRF fulfils other important functions which accommodate some of the regulatory necessities indicated. In addition to setting global principles and standards for fisheries governance, the CCRF and further related bodies of norms constitute a collection of concrete measures that illustrate how these modern principles and concepts could be implemented. The institutional machinery of the FAO further resorts to numerous subtle ways through which states are drawn into flexible and discursive learning processes that often trigger important paradigm shifts of domestic law and policies towards more sustainable practices. These processes are further enhanced through various other actors at various levels of governance which also respond to the activities of the FAO.

If the CCRF and related activities fulfill such significant functions, the question of legitimacy arises. However, a meaningful legitimacy assessment must be based on a differentiated and regime-specific assessment of the governance potential and the limitations of a particular instrument in exercising public authority. And in identifying the legitimacy and accountability challenges it is paramount to overcome generalizing

---

3 *See* Karen Kaiser, in this volume.

assumptions. On the one hand, it is not sufficient to simply point to the consensual intergovernmental nature of the adoption of an instrument and the formal control of an international organization by states. As this case will illustrate, a number of institutional activities are conducted in relative autonomy from governmental instruction, and oversight mechanisms are often weakly developed. On the other hand, is it not sufficiently differentiated to question the legitimacy of these activities without taking into account existing intra-institutional procedures as well as the possible legitimacy safeguards provided in particular at the domestic level.

With a view to pursue the necessary two-pronged assessment of effectiveness and legitimacy in the case of the CCRF, the study first takes an intra-institutional perspective in order to assess how, and to what extent, the FAO acts as an autonomous actor that is not only the agent of states (sections B.I–B.III.). In order to achieve this objective, this study will scrutinize the institutional structures and possible dynamics in light of two variables: autonomy and routine. Autonomy indicates the distance from purely intergovernmental processes and control. Routine points to the potential for reiterated interaction through which networks of specialized government officials, international civil servants and private actors establish common norms and identities – a process which may lead to even greater dissociation of the respective institutional bodies from the will and interests of state governments. As indicated, this perspective helps to clear the sight for a number of activities occurring in the context of the CCRF besides the unanimous adoption by governments of the main instrument. The first one is the continuous subsequent norm production by subsidiary bodies under the normative framework of the CCRF (B.II.). Secondly, the decentralized implementation of the norms is centrally administered by the FAO by means of various activities, including promotional activities, capacity building and the monitoring of implementation (B.III).

Following this intra-institutional analysis, the case study broadens the perspective to assess the particular functions and limitations of the CCRF in governing the issue area of global fisheries. Thus, it takes a look at the horizontal and vertical linkages to other public and private actors as well as institutions other than the FAO. It hereby accentuates the important integrative and coordinative functions of the CCRF and related instruments in a complex and decentralized multi-level system of norm implementation (B.IV.).

On the basis of the analysis of the institutional structure and the functions of the instrument, the concluding remarks will then point to specific legitimacy challenges and possible remedies (Part C.). As will be seen, such legitimacy issues arise from the way in which bureaucrats and largely uncontrolled specialist bodies take over important tasks of norm development and distribution of resources at a level which is largely detached from public discourse. In addressing these concerns with legal means, legal scholarship cannot simply suggest a return to hard law at the expense of flexibility and effectiveness. It must develop proposals which allow maintaining the effectiveness of the institution while formalizing it to the extent that appears necessary to meet any legitimacy gaps. The final considerations will hint at the potential of procedural law and a rights-based approach to participation as possible responses.

B. The Code of Conduct as the Basis of a Complex Governance Mechanism

I. Institutional Framework

The institutional framework of the governance mechanism is crucial for determining the degree of autonomy and routine of the different activities of the FAO.

The CCRF has been unanimously adopted by the Conference of the Food and Agriculture Organization, and thus by all 189 FAO Member States and the European Union.[4] The main body responsible for FAO fisheries policy is the Committee on Fisheries (COFI), a subsidiary body of the executive organ of the FAO, the FAO Council.[5] COFI was instrumental in the drafting of the CCRF and oversees the implementation process. It meets every two years and is open to any Member State and Member Organization (EU).[6] In the last meeting period between 2005 and 2007, 131 Member States of the FAO were members of the Committee. The government representatives attending the meetings of COFI are not diplomats, but government officials from specialized

4 On the FAO in general Jean-Pierre Dobbert, *Food and Agriculture Organization of the United Nations, in* ENCYCLOPEDIA OF PUBLIC INTERNATIONAL LAW, 413 (Rudolf Bernhardt ed., 1995).

5 Art. V(6) FAO Constitution.

6 Rule III of the Rules of Procedure of the Committee on Fisheries (COFI), available at: http://www.fao.org/Legal/index_en.htm.

state ministries, usually those responsible for agriculture and fisheries.[7] In addition, approximately 30 environmental, social and industry NGOs and a great number of the most important international organizations, including the World Bank (WB), the World Trade Organization (WTO), the International Maritime Organization (IMO) and numerous regional fisheries organizations participate in the meetings as observers.[8] This makes COFI the main international policy and discussion forum for fisheries issues.

Important substantive work, including the drafting of technical guidelines for the implementation of the CCRF, is conducted by two sub-committees established by COFI, namely the Sub-Committee on Fish Trade and the Sub-Committee on Aquaculture.[9] Also open to all members, the meetings have a smaller number of participants (usually between 40 to 60 government representatives). The meetings usually take place in the gap year between COFI meetings. Taken together, the meetings at COFI and the sub-committees thus establish a meeting routine of three meetings in two years by the main policy makers. These meetings, although a far cry from the daily routine of a bureaucracy, undoubtedly raise the possibility for the emergence of transgovernmental networks comprising sub-units of governments that interact on the basis of particular (and perhaps newly constructed) shared understandings and identities. The substantive outcome of this interaction may be different from that of negotiations through diplomatic channels.[10] This relative independence from diplomacy at the highest political level is further increased by the possibility of decision making by majority vote in the aforementioned bodies.[11]

The only body exclusively composed of civil servants, formally independent of governments[12] and working on a daily routine is the FAO

---

[7] In the case of Germany, this is the Ministry of Food, Agriculture and Consumer Protection.

[8] Rule III of the Rules of Procedure of the COFI.

[9] The power to establish sub-committees derives from Rule XXX para. 10 of the General Rules of the Organization, available at: http://www.fao.org/Legal/index_en.htm.

[10] Similarly, albeit in a more general context, JOSÉ ALVAREZ, INTERNATIONAL ORGANIZATIONS AS LAW-MAKERS, 2005, 247; ANNE-MARIE SLAUGHTER, A NEW WORLD ORDER, 2004.

[11] Art. V(5) FAO Constitution and Rule V of the Rules of Procedure of the COFI.

[12] Art. VIII(2) FAO Constitution.

Secretariat. Its Fisheries and Aquaculture Department is responsible for all CCRF-related activities, and its work is guided by the CCRF. Composed of 74 professional staff at the headquarters alone, the Department disposes of considerable human resources. It does not only indirectly influence the meetings of COFI by preparing drafts and participation in discussion, but carries out important functions in the follow-up procedures and the coordination with other international organizations. Overall, it can be seen that in particular the Secretariat carries out its activities in relative autonomy from governments. Oversight, which could seriously restrain its discretion, is weak. The only relevant mechanisms in this regard are budget decisions of the higher level bodies and an internal reporting mechanism; no formal external review mechanism exists. The same applies to COFI and its sub-committees. The weak oversight and the already mentioned voting procedures as well as the composition of these bodies distance them from intergovernmental diplomatic processes. In this sense, one may also speak of autonomy in their case, even though it is of a different kind and exists only to a much lesser degree than that of the Secretariat.

II. Development of Global Norms for Responsible Fisheries

The following legal and institutional analysis will illustrate how the different organs of the FAO engage in norm production on the basis of broad mandates without substantial procedural or substantive guidance. The different instruments form a cascade of norms which gain in specificity the further these activities are removed from the highest political level.

Three categories of norms produced in the context of the CCRF can be distinguished:

1. The main instrument of the CCRF adopted by the FAO Conference;
2. The International Plans of Action (IPOAs) and a Strategy for Improved Information usually adopted by COFI; and
3. The Technical Guidelines and related supplements as elaborated under the auspices of the FAO Secretariat.

1. Mandate for Norm Development

The FAO Constitution does not specifically mandate the FAO Conference to adopt a code of conduct. It only endows the Conference with the power to issue recommendations to members, associate members and organizations.[13] In addressing individuals, non-state actors, fishing entities and non-Member States besides Member States, the CCRF deviates from the nomenclature provided for in the Constitution. The institutional practice of the FAO thus transcends these formal requirements, a fact that indicates a mission creep with regard to the instruments used. A substantive mandate for these normative activities can be deduced from the very general objectives outlined in the FAO Constitution, namely the promotion of the conservation of natural resources and improvement of processing, marketing and distribution of food and agricultural products.[14] While the adoption of the CCRF and the IPOAs by governing bodies can be directly based on these broadly phrased constitutional provisions, the FAO Secretariat is given a similarly wide mandate for the elaboration of Technical Guidelines in Resolution 4/95 of the FAO Conference.[15]

2. Procedural Regime

Inasmuch as the mandates of the Constitution and the Resolution for all norm-producing activities remain broad and general, specific procedural requirements for the development and adoption of the CCRF and the implementing instruments are largely wanting. In the absence of any pre-existing procedural rules, the organs and sub-entities of the FAO have used their broad unspecific mandates to develop the norms in ad hoc procedures. Particularly in the case of lower level bodies and the Secretariat, the lack of procedural guidance reinforces their relative autonomy from the highest political level. It also facilitates the access and influence of independent experts and NGOs. The lack of specific procedural law thus further reduces the intergovernmental character of norm development.

---

13 Art. IV(3) and (4) FAO Constitution.

14 Art. I(2)(c) and (d) FAO Constitution.

15 FAO Conference Res. 4/95 of 31 October 1995, para. 5, empowers the FAO "... to elaborate, as appropriate, technical guidelines in support of implementation of the Code". Compare the Report of the Conference of FAO, Twenty-Eighth Session, 20-31 October 1995.

This is less the case for the main instrument of the CCRF. Even if the drafting was heavily influenced by experts and the FAO Secretariat as well as NGOs, all important decisions in the elaboration processes of the main instrument were taken by higher political bodies. This indicates – as confirmed by participants – that the technical specialist input remained secondary, leaving the political objectives as the dominant influence.[16] Political control is less pronounced in the development of the International Plans of Action and the Strategy for Improving Information. Here, the experts' drafts underwent an elaboration process involving few political decisions. Finally, the procedures of elaboration and adoption of the so-called "Technical Guidelines for Responsible Fisheries"[17] under the auspices of the FAO Secretariat display clear signs of autonomous bureaucratic activity. Acting on the basis of a broad mandate lacking specific procedural rules, the FAO Fisheries Department is almost constantly engaged in the development of guidelines and supplements. It does so with considerable autonomy from any interference of the governing bodies through expert consultations, sometimes with the help of other international or non-governmental organizations.[18] Individual governments most often function as sponsors, but the Fisheries Department mainly relies on its own expertise.[19]

Occasionally, following a direct request by COFI, the Secretariat develops a specific set of guidelines. In a recent example, COFI initiated the development of technical guidelines regarding marine protected areas even against the expressly stated will of a Member State.[20] This not only suggests that states take this activity seriously even though the matter "only" concerns the elaboration of voluntary technical guidelines supplementing a non-binding instrument. The incident also illus-

---

16 William Edeson, *The Role of Technical Bodies, in* DEVELOPMENTS OF INTERNATIONAL LAW IN TREATY MAKING 63, 82 and 90 (Rüdiger Wolfrum & Volker Röben eds., 2005).

17 As of June 2007, 15 Technical Guidelines had been developed by or under the auspices of the Fisheries Department.

18 The Technical Guidelines on Marine Protected Areas are being developed by the FAO with the World Bank and the NGO International Union for the Conservation of Nature (IUCN).

19 This was the case for the development of the Technical Guidelines on Aquaculture.

20 FAO, Report of the Twenty-Sixth Session of the Committee on Fisheries, 7-11 March 2005, para. 103, available at: ftp://ftp.fao.org/docrep/fao/008/a0008e/a0008e00.pdf.

trates the readiness of COFI to act by majority decisions at this lower level of normative activity, thereby underscoring its autonomy from consensual intergovernmental processes.

3. Characteristics and Content of the CCRF and Implementing Instruments

This section takes a closer look at the characteristics and the content of the norms produced by the FAO. It thereby aims to illustrate why the development of these norms is significant for fisheries law and governance. Since various treaty law instruments already deal with fisheries issues, one must question what the added value of such an instrument could be. And considering the variety of different instruments produced at different levels of the FAO, the respective role of each body of norms – and therefore of the different institutional bodies of the FAO – will be addressed with the intent of further exploring the interplay of governmental and expert input.

The expressly voluntary CCRF and its implementing instruments[21] fill some of the gaps left by the limited scope of other fisheries instruments.[22] The framework of the United Nations Convention on the Law of the Sea (UNCLOS)[23] establishes generally worded duties to cooperate,[24] but UNCLOS hardly comprises elements of sustainable development or modern ecosystem and precautionary approaches. The UN Fish Stocks Agreement of 1995 (FSA)[25] incorporates precautionary and ecosystem considerations and transcends the zonal approach of UNCLOS,

---

[21] Art. 1(1) CCRF; *e.g.* International Plan of Action to Prevent, Deter and Eliminate Illegal, Unreported and Unregulated Fishing (IPOA-IUU), para. 4; Technical Guidelines usually include a preliminary phrase that they have "no formal legal status", *e.g.* FAO Technical Guidelines on Aquaculture Development, 2007.

[22] The potential of the CCRF to complement more limited fisheries instruments is emphasized by Edeson (note 1), 90.

[23] United Nations Convention on the Law of the Sea (UNCLOS), 10 December 1982, UNTS, vol. 3, 1833.

[24] Arts. 64, 118 and 197 UNCLOS.

[25] Agreement for the Implementation of the Provisions of the United Nations Convention on the Law of the Sea, 10 December 1982, Relating to the Conservation and Management of Straddling Fish Stocks and Highly Migratory Fish Stocks (Fish Stocks Agreement, FSA), 4 December 1995, UNTS, vol. 88, 2167.

but is limited in its scope *ratione materiae*. Neither the FSA nor the FAO Compliance Agreement[26] have achieved the ratification numbers necessary for their mechanisms to function effectively.[27] In contrast thereto, the norms of the CCRF and implementing instruments are addressed to FAO Member States, but also to non-members as well as fishing entities,[28] governmental and non-governmental organizations at all levels of government and – contrasting with other soft and hard law instruments – to all persons involved in some way or another with conservation, management or development of fisheries.[29] Facilitated by its non-binding nature, the CCRF thus generalizes the requirements of the Compliance Agreement and important parts of the FSA for all states, and concretizes the general duties of UNCLOS with regard to all fisheries and for all states. Similarly wide and comprehensive is the scope of territorial application and the scope *ratione materiae*. The territorial scope of the CCRF is defined as "global",[30] and the CCRF comprises all activities related to fisheries ranging from conservation and management to trade of fish products and aquaculture.[31] With this extensive scope, the CCRF is applicable across the jurisdictional zones of UNCLOS and the regional boundaries of regional fisheries organizations.

The role of the CCRF is not only supplementary. As can be seen, it establishes the only framework for fisheries governance that integrates all actors involved in such activities worldwide. Being non-binding, the norms of the CCRF can easily link the activities of a large variety of state and non-state actors even across sectoral boundaries. The significance hereby goes beyond mere coordination, but constitutes a step forward in the progressive development towards modern fisheries gov-

---

26 Agreement to Promote Compliance with International Conservation and Management Measures by Fishing Vessels on the High Seas (Compliance Agreement), 24 November 1993, UNTS, vol. 148, 1860.

27 The FSA had been ratified by 65 States as of 1 March 2007. Important fishing nations such as China and Taiwan, Peru, Chile, Indonesia, Thailand, Republic of Korea, the Philippines, Malaysia, Mexico, Vietnam and Argentina are still missing. As of April 2007, only 35 States had ratified the Compliance Agreement.

28 This term can be understood as a reference to Taiwan, province of China, which is not recognised as a Member State.

29 Art. 1(2) CCRF.

30 Art. 1(2) CCRF.

31 Art. 1(3) CCRF.

ernance. The main instrument of the CCRF represents a remarkably innovative and complete statement of principles for fisheries and is as such unequalled in international governance and law.[32] Two of the central elements of the concept of sustainable development, namely the principle of sustainable use and the principle of integration of environmental considerations and development needs,[33] are specified for the context of fisheries.[34] A related principle that is manifest throughout the CCRF and implementing instruments is the precautionary principle.[35] What is of importance is finally its clear ecosystem orientation.[36]

The main achievement of the CCRF and implementing instruments lies in the translation and concretization of the general principles and concepts into fisheries-specific rules and proposals for action.[37] If all instruments are seen together, the addressees are confronted with a rather complete system of norms that can be directly implemented without necessitating much further consideration or concretization. The thematic sections in the code constitute a first concretization. They cover a range from fisheries management and operations to aquaculture development, research, coastal management and trade.[38] In mostly general-abstract terms, the provisions in these articles outline what actions should be taken by states and private actors in order to implement the principles in the different substantive areas. For example, the thematic section on fisheries management translates the general principle to apply the precautionary approach[39] into factors that states need to take into account in fisheries management to implement this approach. These include environmental and social conditions and non-target fisheries as well as natural phenomena.[40] The CCRF is thus an instrument which combines principles marked by general and abstract language and norms generally circumscribing desirable measures.

---

32 Moore (note 1), at 96.

33 PHILIPPE SANDS, PRINCIPLES OF INTERNATIONAL ENVIRONMENTAL LAW 253 (2nd ed. 2003).

34 Arts. 2(a) and 6(1) CCRF.

35 Art. 6(5) CCRF.

36 The ecosystem approach is manifest in Arts. 6(1), (2), (3) and (8) CCRF.

37 Moore (note 1), at 98.

38 Arts. 7-12 CCRF.

39 Art. 6(5) CCRF.

40 Arts. 7(5.2) and (5.5) CCRF.

While the CCRF nevertheless remains quite general and abstract, a higher degree of specificity is achieved by the International Plans of Action.[41] Their normative-worded rules address specific problems such as the decline of sharks or illegal fishing. IPOAs can contain norms prescribing in detail the requirements for national law and policy. For example, the IPOA on Illegal, Unreported and Unregulated Fishing specifies in detail the kind of information that vessel monitoring systems or authorizations to fish should contain.[42] Sometimes timetables for the adoption of national plans of action are included.[43] The recent Strategy for Improving Information on Status and Trends of Capture Fisheries[44] aims to concretize and implement the CCRF chapter on research[45] by calling on states to establish data collection systems at the national and global level.

A further concretization of both CCRF and IPOAs is achieved by the Technical Guidelines and supplementary documents developed by the FAO Secretariat, sometimes in cooperation with other international organizations and NGOs. The Technical Guidelines are texts usually containing general explanations of the provisions of the CCRF that are relevant for the issue.[46] Most importantly, they additionally include general or specific suggestions and recommendations on how these objectives can be achieved and enhanced. Annexes to the Technical Guidelines include guidance on specific technical subjects.[47] Recently, the FAO Secretariat has even started to develop supplements to Technical Guidelines – so-called "companion documents" – which reach an even

---

41 So far, four IPOAs have been developed. These are the IPOA for Reducing Incidental Catch of Seabirds in Longline Fisheries (IPOA-Seabirds), the IPOA for Conservation and Management Sharks (IPOA-Sharks) and the IPOA for the Management of Fishing Capacity (IPOA-Capacity), all adopted in 1999, and the IPOA-IUU, adopted in 2001. All IPOAs are available at: www.fao.org/fi.

42 IPOA-IUU, paras. 42-49.

43 IPOA-IUU, para. 25.

44 FAO, Strategy for Improving Information on Status and Trends of Capture Fisheries, available at: www.fao.org.

45 Art. 12 CCRF.

46 All Technical Guidelines and Accompanying Supplements are available at: www.fao.org.

47 *See* FAO Technical Guidelines for Responsible Fisheries on Fishing Operations contain an Annex III which outlines a "Proposed System for the Marking of Fishing Gear".

higher degree of specificity.[48] Finally, the Guidelines often include references to or include as annexes very specific guiding non-binding instruments of other international organizations. Examples are the Guidelines of the International Council for the Exploration of the Sea or the Ballast Water Control Forms of the IMO.[49]

The emerging picture points to a division of labor between the CCRF and treaty law on the one hand, and between the various bodies of norms produced at the FAO on the other. As the different sets of norms stem from different institutional levels of the FAO with differing governmental input, their interplay illustrates the various contributions from the political level and the expert-driven bodies of the FAO. The different sets of norms amount to a cascade of soft law norms ranging from the more general and rarely altered norms developed at the highest political level and the more specific action plans adopted by COFI to specific and highly flexible norms developed and administered by the experts of the FAO Secretariat.

It is in particular the norm production of the FAO Secretariat which could be described in terms of autonomous bureaucratic activity. The norms at the most specific and normatively lowest end of the cascade of norms, the Technical Guidelines and supplementary norms, must not be formally adopted by a political body. Rather, a very general mandate and the almost complete lack of substantive or procedurally constraining rules allow the FAO Fisheries and Aquaculture Department of the FAO Secretariat to engage in comparatively autonomous norm production on a routine basis. Sometimes, the Secretariat even develops Technical Guidelines on issues that are not explicitly mentioned in the CCRF, but which should, according to the Secretariat and experts, be dealt with in order to implement its objectives.[50] This underscores its independent input. Autonomy from the political level enables it to swiftly act upon new developments and to adapt the norms of the CCRF to

---

48 *See* "Compliance to FAO Technical Guidelines for Responsible Fisheries: Health Management for Responsible Movement of Live Aquatic Animals" as announced in FAO Technical Guidelines for Responsible Fisheries No. 5 Aquaculture Development, Suppl. 2.

49 FAO Technical Guidelines for Responsible Fisheries No 2: Precautionary Approach to Capture Fisheries and Species Introductions, FAO 1996.

50 For example, the CCRF does not address movement of live aquatic animals, but the FAO Secretariat has developed the FAO Technical Guidelines on Aquaculture Development, Suppl. 2 on "Health Management for Responsible Movement of Live Aquatic Animals," FAO 2007.

technological or scientific developments, adding flexibility to the overall mechanism.[51] Generally speaking, this division of labor in which the highest political level decides on the main objectives, but delegates the concretization to lower level bodies and bureaucracies, balances political and bureaucratic expert-driven input which is necessary for a functioning mechanism. However, the need for such discretion does not render superfluous the elaboration of specific pre-determined procedural law and improved access of the public to these processes as discussed further below.

Finally, the norms of the CCRF carry the potential to provide the first common framework for the discourse on international fisheries issues of all relevant actors, with the effect that their respective governance is coordinated and altered towards more effective resource protection. The extent to which this potential materializes will be assessed in Part IV.

III. Central Management of Compliance and Implementation

Developing norms in the manner described above is only one part of the institutional activities undertaken by the FAO. Another part that is less visible but nevertheless influential is compliance management. Its main elements are a reporting mechanism as well as implementation assistance. Both are important features of a non-confrontational managerial strategy known from compliance mechanisms in multilateral environmental agreements and highlighted by scholars for their compliance-inducing effects.[52]

1. Mandate and Procedural Regime

The FAO Conference has mandated the FAO to give advice to developing countries and establish an Interregional Assistance Program.[53] The

---

51 Edeson (note 16), at 85.

52 Rüdiger Wolfrum, *Means of Ensuring Compliance with and Enforcement of International Environmental Law*, 272 RECUEIL DES COURS 25, 110 (1998); ABRAHAM CHAYES & ANTONIA HANDLER CHAYES, THE NEW SOVEREIGNTY: COMPLIANCE WITH INTERNATIONAL REGULATORY AGREEMENTS 154 and 197 (1995).

53 FAO Conference Res. 4/95 (note 15), at para. 4.

Secretariat is also charged with the monitoring of implementation, and must report accordingly to the COFI.[54] Similar to the norm production activities, these broad and general mandates are hardly qualified or constrained by further substantive or procedural specifications. While the FAO Secretariat remains under the oversight of the COFI for much of the reporting activities, the assistance and advisory functions of the Secretariat take place in relative autonomy from direct political influence. On the basis of the general mandate, the FAO Secretariat enjoys wide discretion in the organization and running of the financial, technical and legal assistance to developing countries and in the collection of information on implementation.

2. *Monitoring of Implementation by Means of Voluntary Reporting Mechanisms*

The reporting mechanism is based on voluntary questionnaires. They are sent out to states as well as organizations, including regional fisheries organizations and NGOs. The results provide the input for the progress report on implementation presented by the Secretariat to COFI biennially.[55] The five progress reports between 1999 and 2007 show that a significant number of countries responded to the questionnaires sent to them by the Secretariat.[56] Certainly as a consequence of the non-binding nature of the norms in question, the Secretariat has treated the reports from states and organizations in such a manner that it is impossible from outside the Secretariat to individualize the information, *i.e.* to link information to a specific state. The monitoring mechanism in this respect deviates from most compliance control procedures under international environmental or human rights law. Without the possibility to individually assess a country's compliance, the possibility of naming and shaming largely fails. Instead of assessing individual compliance, the mechanism serves to identify problems and maintain a dia-

---

[54] Art. 4(2) CCRF; FAO Conference Res. 4/95 (note 15), para. 6; references to reporting to and of FAO are equally included in all of the IPOAs, *see* IPOA Seabirds, para. 24, IPOA-Sharks, para. 31, IPOA-Capacity, para. 44, IPOA-IUU, para. 87.

[55] FAO, Committee on Fisheries, Report of the Twenty-Second Session, 17-20 March 1997, para. 29.

[56] Numbers of reporting countries: 69 in 1999, 103 in 2001, 105 in 2003, 49 in 2005, 70 in 2007. All reports are available at: http://www.fao.org/fi/body/cofi/cofi.asp.

logue on implementation. Thus, notwithstanding its limitations, it fulfils other important functions as a reporting mechanism. One is the generation of information on the general behavior of most actors. This increase in transparency is essential for reassurance, and thus for achieving cooperation in collective action constellations. In addition, the monitoring by the Secretariat has the effect that states are continuously confronted with the rules of the CCRF, since it generally keeps the issue of implementation on both the national and the international agendas. Since discussions of fisheries issues at both levels are accordingly based on the CCRF, the reporting exercise structures the national and international discourse. Finally, the implementation review provided by the reporting mechanism enables national and international actors to receive feedback on effectiveness which is a prerequisite for learning processes.

Although conducted by the Secretariat, the political bodies and in particular the COFI largely guide the reporting process. In concretizing the mandate in the Resolution, the FAO Council in 1997 followed a proposition from COFI on the reporting format. The main content of the questionnaires has also been decided upon and approved by COFI.[57] The questionnaires are continuously revised by the Secretariat, but it is in this regard acting on the basis of specific suggestions from COFI.[58] In other words, the functions of the Secretariat in the monitoring process are more or less confined to traditional secretarial functions.

3. *Implementation Assistance*

The CCRF and the implementing instruments serve as a basis for the formulation and design of capacity building projects and for mechanisms of legal, financial and technical assistance. More concretely, the FAO provides the institutional platform, executive know-how and funding to help local communities and developing states with implementation. For example, the advisory service of the Fisheries Department assists governments in the formulation and revision of fisheries

---

57 FAO Council, Report of its Hundred and Twelfth Session, 1997, CL 112/REP, para. 29; Report of the Twenty-Second Session of the Committee on Fisheries, 1997, FIPL/R562 (En), para. 29.

58 The 2001 revision was based on an improved format suggested by COFI at its 23rd session in 1999.

legislation[59] and multilateral fisheries agreements such as the Convention on the Sustainable Management of Lack Tanganyika.[60] By means of the Global Partnership for Responsible Fisheries ("FishCode") and a corresponding financing institution ("FishCode trust fund") which draws on external donations as well as regular program resources of the FAO, the FAO further funds and manages capacity building projects designed to help states, but also communities, fishermen and fish workers to shift to responsible fisheries.

Again, the analysis of these compliance-inducing activities reveals a considerable degree of autonomy for the Secretariat of the FAO, but it does not act without a mandate. Besides, this relative autonomy for the civil servants of the Secretariat seems warranted, because a political body could hardly conduct these activities effectively. Any improvement of these processes would have to pay tribute to these necessities. The need for improved legitimation of these autonomous activities becomes apparent when they are viewed within the context of the significance of the CCRF in fisheries governance worldwide.

IV. Significance of the Institutional Activities for Fisheries Governance and Law

The significance of the CCRF and the related bureaucratic activities can only be fully appreciated by taking into account the implementation activities of the instrument's addressees and other institutions. Broadening the perspective lets the CCRF emerge as the framework and point of reference for actors at the international, supranational, national, regional and private levels. The pathways of influence may be structured for the sake of clarity by conceiving of horizontal and vertical linkages, even if communication structures mainly build on non-hierarchical persuasive processes. Within both of these dimensions, instrument-based mechanisms linking different instruments can be distinguished from institutional ones deriving from the way institutions engage with each other as actors.

---

59 FAO Secretariat has recently assisted in the revision of pertinent legislation of a number of developing countries, including Angola, Namibia, Malaysia, The Maldives, Vietnam, Barbados, and Antigua and Barbuda.

60 The Convention text is available at: www.faolex.fao.org.

1. Horizontal Dimension: Integration of Actors and Instruments across Regime Boundaries

a) Instrument-based Linkages

Linkages between the CCRF and other fisheries instruments are mainly achieved by rules of reference.

As mentioned already, the CCRF and the implementing instruments frequently refer to treaty law (UNCLOS, Compliance Agreement, WTO)[61] and other non-binding instruments (*e.g.* IMO Codes).[62] The effect is the incorporation of the rules of these instruments into the CCRF. The rules of the CCRF are thereby harmonized through these treaties, but more importantly, these norms then provide the common framework for all actors that adhere to the CCRF.

Second, other non-binding and binding instruments entail references to the CCRF. The need for the implementation of the CCRF is explicitly called for in the non-binding Johannesburg Plan of Implementation which was endorsed by the UN General Assembly.[63] It is interesting to observe that this document explicitly mentions the IPOAs and the FAO Technical Guidelines alongside the CCRF – a fact which underscores the significance of the norm production of the FAO Secretariat.

Treaty instruments either explicitly (*e.g.* Lake Tanganyika Convention[64]) or implicitly incorporate the norms of the CCRF, and thus effectively "harden" them. An implicit reference is the way in which the CCRF supplements the Fish Stocks Agreement (FSA) and UNCLOS through rules of references to international standards in these treaties. The Fish Stocks Agreement contains an obligation to apply "generally recommended international minimum standards for the responsible conduct of fishing operations" through cooperation in regional fisheries management organizations.[65] As the wording and negotiating history suggests, this can be understood as a clear reference to norms outlined

---

61 Arts. 6(14) and 11(2) CCRF (WTO), Arts. 1(1), 3(1) and (2) CCRF (UNCLOS); Art. 1(1) CCRF (Compliance Agreement).

62 Arts. 8(4.1) and (10.1) CCRF.

63 World Summit on Sustainable Development, Johannesburg Plan of Implementation, para. 31 (c), endorsed by GA Res. 57/253 of 20 December 2002.

64 Article 7 section 2(b) Lake Tanganyika Convention, available at: http://faolex.fao.org.

65 Art. 10(c) FSA.

in the CCRF and implementing instruments.[66] As a consequence, the norms of the CCRF then partake in the enforcement mechanism of the FSA through which non-cooperative states can be excluded from access to the resources.[67] A similar example of references to "generally recommended international minimum standards"[68] can be found with respect to the duty of states to maintain the maximum sustainable yield which is included in the FSA and UNCLOS. If understood as a reference to the CCRF, its norms would effectively qualify the kind of management and conservation measures states have to take under both treaties.[69] The function of the references to rules and standards in UNCLOS is to make international practices and norms obligatory for all Member States regardless of whether particular states are party to a treaty entailing these norms or not, *i.e.* regardless of whether they are binding upon these states.[70] Given this dissociation of the obligations in UNCLOS and the membership to a third treaty, it can be logically concluded that practice but not consent is the decisive criterion, *i.e.* that even rules and standards of non-binding instruments such as the CCRF qualify as references if they are widely accepted.[71] By importing precau-

---

[66] The FSA was elaborated in parallel to the CCRF, often by the same delegates, so that from a historical perspective, a reference to "responsible fishing" is likely to be a reference to the FAO CCRF.

[67] Art. 8(4) FSA.

[68] Art. 5(b) FSA and Arts. 61(3) and 119(1)(a) UNCLOS. For the duty to take measures and the duty to cooperate with a view to take such measures compare Art. 64 UNCLOS in conjunction with Art. 5 FSA; Arts. 61(2) and 117 UNCLOS.

[69] These are the duties that derive from Art. 64 UNCLOS in conjunction with Art. 5 FSA; Arts. 61(2) and 117 UNCLOS.

[70] Rüdiger Wolfrum, *IMO Interface with the Law of the Sea Convention, in* CURRENT MARITIME ISSUES AND THE INTERNATIONAL MARITIME ORGANIZATION 223, 231 (Myron Nordquist & John Norton Moore eds., 1999); David Vignes, *La valeur juridique de certaines règles, normes ou pratiques mentionnées au TNCO comme 'généralement acceptées'*, 25 ANNUAIRE FRANÇAIS DE DROIT INTERNATIONAL 712, 716 (1979); Louis B. Sohn, *Generally Accepted International Rules*, 61 WASHINGTON LAW REVIEW 1073, 1075 (1986); ROBIN CHURCHILL AND VAUGHAN LOWE, THE LAW OF THE SEA 107-108 (3rd ed. 1999).

[71] Rüdiger Wolfrum, Volker Röben and Fred Morrison, *Preservation of the Marine Environment, in* INTERNATIONAL, REGIONAL AND NATIONAL ENVIRONMENTAL LAW 225, 233 (Fred Morrison & Rüdiger Wolfrum eds., 2000); International Law Association, Final Report of the Committee on Coastal State Jurisdiction Relating to Marine Pollution 38 (2000); Bernhard Oxman, *The*

tionary and ecosystem considerations into the law of the sea, the norms of the CCRF in this way contribute to modernization and flexibilization of UNCLOS.

b) Inter-institutional Linkages

The CCRF and implementing instruments play a role in inter-institutional cooperation. An outstanding example is the Global Program on Sustainable Fisheries ("ProFish") established by the World Bank in association with a number of states, organizations and institutions, including the FAO. Financed by the World Bank Development Grant Facility, one of three main activities of the partnership is to build national and regional consensus with a view to implement the CCRF.[72] An indirect role is played by the CCRF in horizontal cooperation between the FAO Fisheries Department of the FAO and the Secretariat of the Convention on International Trade in Endangered Species of Wild Flora and Fauna (CITES). Both cooperate closely in the attempt that only responsibly managed fisheries are allowed to be traded under CITES. The cooperation is formalized by a Memorandum of Understanding between the FAO and CITES.[73]

2. Vertical Dimension: Coordination of Implementation Efforts in a Multi-level System

The CCRF also serves to influence and coordinate the policies and fisheries management of various actors at various levels of governance, including the domestic one. Some examples should suffice to highlight this function of the CCRF.

Duty to Respect Generally Accepted International Standards, 24 NEW YORK UNIVERSITY JOURNAL OF INTERNATIONAL LAW AND POLICY 109, 110 (1991-1992).

72 World Bank website, www.worldbank.org/fish; David Freestone, The Role of the World Bank and the Global Environment Facility in the Implementation of the Regime of the Convention on the Law of the Sea, in THE LAW OF THE SEA: PROGRESS AND PROSPECTS 307, 322 *et seq.* (David Freestone, Richard Barnes & David Ong eds., 2006).

73 Memorandum of Understanding between FAO and CITES, available at: http://www.cites.org/eng/disc/sec/index.shtml.

a) Regional Level

Cooperation in regional fisheries organizations is emerging as a key strategy for sustainable fisheries, especially where regional organizations have the mandate to issue binding management measures. The CCRF and implementing instruments have proven to be of relevance for these regional administrations. Parts of the CCRF have gradually been transformed into binding measures of regional fisheries bodies.[74] A particularly salient example for the influence of norms is the implementation of the IPOA-IUU by the Commission for the Conservation of Southern Bluefin Tuna through a binding Resolution on Illegal, Unregulated and Unreported Fishing. The Resolution essentially establishes a system of authorized fishing based on a public record of authorized vessels.[75] In particular regional fisheries bodies of the FAO have adapted their founding documents to correspond with the objectives of the CCRF. The case of the newly created South West Indian Ocean Fisheries Commission illustrates that newly created regional fisheries organizations even include express references to the CCRF instead of enumerating guiding principles.[76]

It is possible to further chart the influence of the principles of the CCRF and related instruments at the European Union's policy-making level. In particular, the EU Commission draws upon the FAO norms for policy suggestions. For example, the Green Paper adopted by the EU Commission on the future of the Common Fisheries Policies expressly draws on the CCRF as an expression of the "large worldwide consensus on the overall objective of fisheries policy" when suggesting the basic principles of the new policy.[77] In the context of the reform of the Common Fisheries Policy, the EU Commission has also developed a

---

[74] FAO, Independent External Evaluation of the Food and Agriculture Organization, *FAO: The Challenge of Renewal,* Working Draft, para. 630 (July 2007), available at: http://www.fao.org/unfao/bodies/IEE-Working-Draft-Report/K0489E.pdf.

[75] Commission on the Conservation of Southern Bluefin Tuna (CCSBT), Res. on Illegal, Unregulated and Unreported Fishing (IUU) and Establishment of a CCSBT Record of Vessel over 24 meters, 7-10 October 2003, amended by a resolution adopted at the Eleventh Annual Meeting of 19-22 October 2004, available at: www.ccsbt.org.

[76] Statute of the South West Indian Ocean Fisheries Commission, para. 5, available at: http://www.intfish.net/orgs/fisheries/swiofc.htm.

[77] European Commission, Green Paper on the Future of the Common Fisheries Policy, COM (2001) 135 final, 20 March 2001.

voluntary "European Code of Sustainable and Responsible Fisheries Practices" directed at its fishing sector which is based on the framework of the CCRF.[78] Furthermore, the International Action Plans are implemented by Community Action Plans.[79]

b) Domestic Level

Overall, states are increasingly acting in compliance with or working towards achieving compliance with the CCRF. According to the most recent progress report on the results of the self-reporting exercise, 95 percent of the responding FAO Members reported to have legislation and policies in place which are partially or totally in conformity with the CCRF, and 9 out of 10 states reported to be either in conformity or were working towards conformity in both policy and legal domains.[80] This is confirmed by a recent independent expert evaluation. According to this study, the CCRF and the implementing instruments have had "a very considerable impact" on worldwide fisheries management by both developing and developed states.[81]

As non-binding norms, the CCRF and implementing instruments can be implemented at the national level without specific legislation. They are thus often directly implemented by national administrations, for example by means of national plans of action.[82] Proper implementation of the code, however, often requires enacting or reforming fisheries legislation. The new fisheries law of Tanzania can serve as an example for a

---

[78] European Commission, European Code of Sustainable and Responsible Fisheries Practices (2004).

[79] European Commission, Communication from the Commission to the Council and the European Parliament laying down a Community Action Plan for the conservation and sustainable exploitation of fisheries resources in the Mediterranean Sea under the Common Fisheries Policy, COM (2002) 535 final, 9 October 2002, para. 3.4.3.

[80] FAO, Committee on Fisheries, Twenty-Seventh Session, 5-9 March 2007, COFI/2007/2, Progress in the implementation of the 1995 Code of Conduct for Responsible Fisheries, related International Plans of Action and Strategy, para. 6.

[81] *FAO, The Challenge of Renewal* (note 74), at para. 425.

[82] Compare *e.g.* the Mexican Plan of Action to implement the IPOA-Sharks, 'Plan de Acción Nacional para el Manejo y Conservación de Tiburones, Rayas y Especies Afines en México', available at: ftp://ftp.fao.org/FI/DOCUMENT/IPOAS/national/mexico/PANMCT_VERSIONFINAL.pdf.

far-reaching legislative implementation of the CCRF. The Tanzanian Fisheries Act of 2003[83] incorporates the concept of responsible fishing as well as the principles, objectives and several of the specific tools suggested in the CCRF, such as vessel monitoring systems and fishing authorizations.[84]

c) Private Level

The norms of the CCRF and IPOAs provide an ideal and welcome basis for market-based enforcement activities of NGOs. An outstanding example is the eco-labeling initiative of the Marine Stewardship Council. Its "principles and criteria for sustainable fishing" represent the leading standard against which fisheries are assessed before being certified. It is based on the CCRF.[85] About six percent of the world's total wild capture fisheries are now engaged in this program, including 42 percent of the global wild salmon catch.

In contrast to binding norms, codes of conduct are generally well suited for marketing purposes, because compliance indicates ethical business behavior beyond legal requirements. Whether or not this is the main motivation, the CCRF and implementing instruments form the basis for self-regulation of fishermen or industry associations. Illustrative examples in this regard are the Code of Conduct for a Responsible Seafood Industry of the Australian Seafood Industry Council,[86] the Canadian Code of Conduct for Responsible Fishing Operations designed by local fishermen[87] or the code of conduct of the Federation of European Aquaculture Producers.[88]

---

[83] The Fisheries Act, 2003, available at http://faolex.fao.org/docs/pdf/tan53024.pdf.

[84] The numerous references to responsible fisheries can be understood as dynamic implicit references to the CCRF.

[85] MSC website, available at: http://eng.msc.org/.

[86] The Code of Conduct is available at: http://www.seafoodsite.com.au/sustainable/code.php.

[87] The Code of Conduct is available at: http://www.fisheriescouncil.ca/pdf/FCCFishingOperations6.pdf.

[88] The Code of Conduct is available at: www.feap.info.

3. Implementation Difficulties

Despite the numerous implementation efforts, the problems "on the ground" are far from being solved. Fish stocks continue to deteriorate in most parts of the world. Part of the reason may be that significant implementation gaps remain in many areas and parts of the world. Indeed, the progress reports to COFI indicate that progress has not been rapid. The largest implementation problems persist with regards to the implementation of the ecosystem and precautionary approach as well as the overexploitation of stocks.[89] Predominant constraints for more rapid progress are insufficient resources and institutional incapacity as well as awareness deficits in developing countries.[90] Regarding shrimp aquaculture, for instance, studies suggest that only a few countries have so far implemented the strategies of the CCRF.[91] A case study of Bangladesh – an important shrimp producing country – published in 2005 serves as a case in point. Little effort had been made in this signatory state to understand or implement the CCRF.[92]

4. The Division of Labor between Non-binding and Binding Instruments

The continuously dire state of fisheries and aquaculture highlights the immense task of achieving cooperation and sustainable resource management under conditions of fierce economic competition and strong market forces. If used as mere alternatives to binding law, voluntary codes of conduct seem to be inadequate to solve these kinds of regulatory problems.[93] In fact, the CCRF and implementing instruments were

---

89 FAO, Committee on Fisheries, Twenty-Sixth Session, 7-11 March 2005, COFI/2005/2 Progress in the implementation of the 1995 Code of Conduct for Responsible Fisheries, related International Plans of Action, paras. 33-36.

90 FAO, *The State of World Fisheries and Aquaculture 2006* (2007), Part II, available at: http://www.fao.org/docrep/009/A0699e/A0699e00.htm.

91 David Barnhizer, *Waking from Sustainability's "Impossible Dream": The Decisionmaking Realities of Business and Government*, 18 THE GEORGETOWN INTERNATIONAL ENVIRONMENTAL LAW REVIEW 595, 677 (2006).

92 Nazmul Alam, Kwei Lin, Amararatne Yakupitiyage, Harvey Demaine and Michael Phillips, *Compliance of Bangladesh Shrimp Culture with the FAO Code of Conduct for Responsible Fisheries: A Development Challenge*, 48 OCEAN AND COASTAL MANAGEMENT 177, 186 (2005).

93 Barnhizer (note 91), at 674.

not intended as and could not be the sole solution. Binding international, regional and national laws have not become superfluous for effectively dealing with complex collective action problems such as the one at hand. The ratification procedures ensure that national or regional measures, such as the quotas and strict monitoring and enforcement of illegal fishing, confront the contravening economic interests of the fishing industry.

The analysis in this last section, however, also highlights that the CCRF is not without significance. Supported by the institutional machinery of the FAO, it serves as a flexible framework and point of reference for a truly global and progressive discourse on fisheries issues. By means of this instrument, the FAO coordinates, integrates and ultimately influences the main public and some private actors across sectoral boundaries. What first appears to be a rather toothless non-binding instrument develops force and impact through horizontal and vertical connections. The soft form facilitates linkages across institutions and regimes in a way that hard law hardly ever could in practice. It further contributes to the emergence of a dialogue between all interested actors which – as it is structured along the lines of these norms – may ultimately contribute to a (re)construction of the values and the interests of these actors.[94] Non-binding instruments such as the CCRF therefore perform important tasks in a division of labor between non-binding and binding instruments.

C. Conclusion

The CCRF proves to be much more than yet another non-binding intergovernmental declaration of a mere hortatory character. Although implementation is still unsatisfactory, the FAO has managed to establish a modern and influential normative framework and collection of best practices which provides the basis for functional cooperation and management efforts of many important actors in fisheries governance at various levels of governance and across functional divides. By making use of its extensive institutional machinery and institutional relations, it uses a flexible non-binding instrument to initiate and structure a learn-

---

[94] *See* on constructivism in the context of international institutions and bureaucracies Ingo Venzke, in this volume.

ing and socialization process that integrates actors which could not necessarily be reached through binding law.

A closer inspection of the intra-institutional processes and structures reveals that much of the normative development and implementation management central to this mechanism is not occurring at the highest political level of the FAO, but on lower political levels or at the FAO Secretariat. The instrument appears to derive much of its potential from institutional activities marked by significant autonomy from intergovernmental processes and routine. An important amount of externally relevant decisions are taken either by the Secretariat or by lower level organs and experts which are only to a limited extent controlled by the higher political decision-making bodies. In particular the Secretary-General and the Secretariat are insufficiently accountable to the governing bodies.[95]

Now, executive discretion is nothing unusual in legal systems.[96] The autonomy of bureaucracies is well known from domestic legal systems. The example of the FAO indeed shows that autonomy and related informality are beneficial for a mechanism which strives to instigate flexible learning processes on the basis of progressive norms. Autonomy from intergovernmental processes facilitates the translation of principles into progressive and concrete actionable measures and best practices as well as their continuous revision as learning processes advance. Capacity building efforts that flexibly adapt to the particularities of different regions and local conditions can hardly be pursued at the highest political level.

Inasmuch as the need for flexible instruments and autonomous decision-making leads to the emergence of such structures in international organizations, there is a corresponding need for public law and procedure to provide a legal framework for this exercise of public authority.[97] It is thus proposed to resolve the underlying tension between flexibility and legitimate exercise of authority through legal formalization not of the instrument itself, but of the intra-institutional processes.

This presumes that first, there is a legitimacy issue at all and second, that procedural law could be an adequate response.

---

95 *FAO: The Challenge of Renewal* (note 74), Box 4.3.

96 Eyal Benvenisti, *Public Choice and Global Administrative Law: Who's Afraid of Executive Discretion?*, IILJ Working Paper 2004/3 (GLOBAL ADMINISTRATIVE LAW SERIES), available at: www.iilj.org.

97 *See* Jochen von Bernstorff, in this volume.

Regarding the first question, it can be generally said that any exercise of public authority with impact on behavior must be legitimate, whether it is exercised through binding or non-binding instruments.[98] More concretely, the legitimacy issue in this case arises in connection with two basic considerations.

One is the necessity for intra-institutional control by states in times where states remain the main actors and the state level the main source of legitimacy. Although the main instrument itself is supported by the approval of state representatives, a legitimacy model which only takes this sole decision into account proves to be insufficient in light of various autonomous institutional activities. Formalization through predetermined procedural law indicating lines of responsibility and specific decision-making procedures could strengthen the delegational link and thus legitimize these activities without necessarily abrogating flexibility.[99]

The second consideration concerns the linkage between the institution as a whole and the state level. Given the non-binding nature of the instrument which depends to a large extent on implementation by states, legitimacy seems at first sight to be secured at the national level. While it is beyond the scope of this contribution to comprehensively consider these difficult questions,[100] one aspect should be stressed here. Whether the code is indirectly implemented by acts of the national or supranational executive or a national parliamentary act, the entire exercise only makes sense if the instrument can be implemented without calling into question its content, process of elaboration etc. It is in the interest of all actors that implementation is comprehensive and the package not reopened so as not to upset the balance of different economic, environmental and social aspects. In particular developing countries, due to limited resources, often need to rely on the international standards as a reliable and legitimate source of norms. In other words, in the name of effective cooperation it is in the interest of all participants in the international processes that the instrument is sufficiently legitimated already at the international level. Inasmuch as environmental decision-making shifts from national parliaments to the international level, and given

---

[98] Armin von Bogdandy, *Lawmaking by International Organizations: Some Thoughts on Non-Binding Instruments and Democratic Legitimacy*, *in* DEVELOPMENTS OF INTERNATIONAL LAW IN TREATY-MAKING 171, 173 (Rüdiger Wolfrum & Volker Röben eds., 2005).

[99] *See also* Jochen von Bernstorff, in this volume.

[100] *See* Rüdiger Wolfrum, in this volume.

that a global public sphere is at best in a weak stage of its development, international institutions must even for non-binding instruments establish pre-determined procedures which ensure that national publics and the political opposition are linked to these processes. This is necessary to uphold the legitimating function of the national public discourse which is essential for the legitimation of both international norm production and national implementation.

Provided that they indeed strive to link international processes to national level debates, regional and local groups as well as NGOs have a role to play in this respect.[101] So far, at the FAO, neither associations of affected stakeholders nor individuals or the public play a significant role. Nor have notice-and-comment procedures that include the general public as emerging in particular in the OECD been undertaken. This lack of openness to potentially affected individuals or groups and the general public is a lacuna in particular in environmental law where access to information and participation of the public in environmental policy-making and administration is increasingly seen to be essential.[102]

To be sure, this is not an argument for direct voting rights of NGOs, but rather for more transparency through improved rights-based access to information about these processes, as well as formalized participation of the public in policy-making in international fora, for example through notice-and-comment procedures. A recommendation to this effect has been adopted by the Meeting of the Parties of the Aarhus Convention in the detailed Almaty Guidelines in 2005.[103] These Guidelines call for the application of the principles of the Aarhus Convention not only at the state or EU level, but also at the level of international institutions. Even if only perceivable as a long-term objective, the exten-

---

101 Jochen von Bernstorff, *Zivilgesellschaftliche Partizipation in Internationalen Organisationen: Form globaler Demokratie oder Baustein westlicher Expertenherrschaft?*, *in* DEMOKRATIE IN DER WELTGESELLSCHAFT, SONDERBAND SOZIALE WELT (Hauke Brunkhorst ed., 2009).

102 Convention on Access to Information, Public Participation in Decision-Making and Access to Justice in Environmental Matters, 28 June 1998, Arts. 6 and 7, UNTS, vol. 447, 2161.

103 United Nations Economic Commission for Europe, Report of the Second Meeting of the Parties to the Convention on Access to Information, Public Participation in Decision-Making and Access to Justice in Environmental Matters held in Almaty, Kazakhstan, 25-27 May 2005, Decision II/4 entitled "Promoting the Application of the Principles of the Aarhus Convention in International Forums", ECE/MP.PP/2005/2/Add.5, 20 June 2005.

sion of Aarhus Principles to the international arena could be a promising step forward, especially if access to information and public participation are secured by means of an institutionalized review. Again, the precondition for such a review is formalization. Legal procedures that formalize decision-making and allow for access to information and public participation thus emerge as a realistic strategy through which the apparent need for flexible instruments and executive discretion could be satisfied while safeguarding the long-term legitimacy of the overall mechanism.

Why Would International Administrative Activity Be Any Less Legitimate? – A Study of the Codex Alimentarius Commission

*By Ravi Afonso Pereira**

---

* I am grateful to António Manuel Hespanha, Armin von Bogdandy, Dario Bevilacqua, Gonçalo de Almeida Ribeiro, Jochen von Bernstorff, Matthias Goldmann, Miguel Poiares Maduro, Philipp Dann and Vera Eiró for comments. An earlier draft of this article was presented at a workshop on *The Exercise of Public Authority by International Institutions: A Proposal for the Development of International Institutional Law*, convened by the Max Planck Institute for Comparative Public Law and International Law. I thank the commentator, Eyal Benvenisti, and the participants, for their valuable comments.

A. von Bogdandy et al. (eds.), *The Exercise of Public Authority by International Institutions*, Beiträge zum ausländischen öffentlichen Recht und Völkerrecht 210,
DOI 10.1007/978-3-642-04531-8_19, © Springer-Verlag Berlin Heidelberg 2010

A. Introduction

This article examines the regulatory activity performed by the Codex Alimentarius Commission (Commission), which is the international body responsible for setting food standards and which has been the object of growing attention by lawyers. The main problem is that Codex standards, although they are not binding, strip national regulators of their discretion. This occurs because the Agreement on the Application of Sanitary and Phytosanitary Measures (SPS Agreement) and the Agreement on Technical Barriers to Trade (TBT Agreement)[1] refer to them as relevant international standards. Furthermore, the World Trade Organization (WTO) Appellate Body has been construing its provisions in a way that makes it virtually impossible for national regulators to set higher levels of protection. From this it follows that, unless national constituencies are afforded the possibility to participate in the

---

[1] Both the SPS Agreement and the TBT Agreement are multilateral agreements on trade in goods under the World Trade Organization.

regulation of food safety at the outset before the Commission, when it comes down to setting national food standards national regulators are unable to fully respond to their concerns. This is all the more so if one considers that, while being undisputed that science plays a major role in the preparation of Codex standards, many issues the Commission has to address cannot be settled in strictly scientific terms. Instead, the latter enjoys a wide degree of discretion in striking a balance between fair trade and consumers' health. The political dimension surrounding the issues the Commission has to address coupled with the legal effect of Codex standards raises questions about its legitimacy. Yet any assessment of the legitimacy of the Commission is necessarily incomplete unless it takes into account the comparative performance of national regulatory authorities.

B. The Institutional Framework of the Commission

I. The Establishment of the Commission

The Commission was established through resolutions adopted at the eleventh session of the Food and Agriculture Organization Conference in 1961 and at the sixteenth World Health Assembly in 1963[2] as a critical component of the Joint Food and Agriculture Organization (FAO) / World Health Organization (WHO) World Food Program. Thus, it was created under a joint program of two international organizations.[3] Its statutes are contained in the World Health Assembly resolution of 1963.[4] Its objectives are broadly formulated, which means that the Commission's mandate is characterized by a wide degree of discretion.[5]

---

2 FAO and WHO, Understanding the Codex Alimentarius Commission, 7, available at: ftp://ftp.fao.org/docrep/fao/008/y7867e/y7867e00.pdf.

3 Today's international organizations are increasingly being established by other international organizations rather than by governments. *See* Eric Stein, *International Integration and Democracy: No Love at First Sight*, 95 AMERICAN JOURNAL OF INTERNATIONAL LAW (AJIL) 489, note 2 (2001).

4 WHO, Resolution WHA16.42, para. 1.

5 An evaluation report proposes the development of a comprehensive and clear mandate for Codex. *See* W. Bruce Trail *et al.*, *Report of the Evaluation of the Codex Alimentarius and Other FAO and WHO Food Standards Work*, para. 76-77, available at: http://www.who.int/entity/foodsafety/codex/en/codex_eval_report_en.pdf.

It could hardly be otherwise since lack of knowledge to discharge full-blown food safety regulations was the reason the Commission was established in the first place. The substantive program of the Commission and its work priorities are laid down in advance in a strategic plan stating goals, listing program areas and planned activities with a clearly defined timetable.[6] Apart from that, there is no substantive legal instrument narrowing down the scope of its mandate, which seems to be a common feature in international institutional law.[7] However, the Commission adopts principles, guidelines and definitions some of which are of a substantive character such as its four statements of principle concerning the role of science[8] or the ones relating to risk analysis,[9] all of which are self-binding.

II. The Organizational Structure of the Commission

1. Main Bodies

The Commission elects a chairperson and three vice-chairs from its membership to serve for one ordinary session of the Commission eligible for re-election up to three consecutive years. The work of the Commission and its subsidiary bodies is assisted by a secretariat of six professional and seven support staff housed at FAO Headquarters in Rome within the Food and Nutrition Division[10] and funded jointly by FAO and WHO. The Executive Committee (composed of a chairperson, three vice-chairs and seven representatives from geographical groups[11]) acts on behalf of the Commission as its executive organ between its sessions, which for a long period of time were held every two

---

6 CAC, ALINORM 07/30/REP, para. 138 and Appendix IV.

7 Jochen von Bernstorff, in this volume.

8 CAC, ALINORM 95/37, para. 25 and Appendix 2.

9 CAC, ALINORM 97/37, para. 28 and Appendix II.

10 Prior to January 2002, the Codex secretariat was not a clear separate unit within FAO and the Codex secretary was an FAO staff member with responsibilities also for FAO's other food standards work.

11 Members elected on a geographical basis are expected to act within the Executive Committee in the interest of the Commission as a whole.

years.[12] It is incumbent upon each committee session to consider the timing of the following one.[13]

2. *Subsidiary Bodies*

Solely focusing on the sessions of the Commission might be misleading. In fact, by the time the Commission is scheduled to adopt a standard very little remains to discuss, since all controversial issues have already been addressed at the committee level. One finds committees addressing horizontal issues such as the Codex Committee on Food Labeling, committees that are focused on a single commodity such as the Codex Committee on Milk and Milk Products and one also finds coordinating committees for specific regions or group of countries. Instead of committees, the Commission may decide to establish *ad hoc* intergovernmental task forces that may later give rise to the establishment of a committee.

3. *Membership*

Membership is open to all member states and associate members of FAO and WHO interested in international food standards. Committee membership is open to members of the Commission who have notified the Director-General of FAO or WHO of their desire to be considered as members thereof or to selected members designated by the Commission. Membership of regional coordinating committees is only open to members of the Commission belonging to the region or group of countries concerned.

4. *Observer Status*

Any other Commission member or any member or associate member of FAO or WHO which has not become a member of the Commission may participate as an observer at any committee if it has notified the Director-General of FAO or WHO of its wish to do so. For instance,

---

[12] The Commission began holding annual sessions from 1963 to 1972. Thereafter, it adopted a biennial meeting pattern until 2003 when it decided to start meeting annually again.

[13] CAC, ALINORM 03/41, para. 150.

before becoming a Commission member in 2003,[14] following an amendment of the Commission's rules of procedure allowing regional economic integration organizations to become members,[15] the European Community had been participating in the work of the Commission and its subsidiary bodies as an observer.[16] These countries may participate fully in the discussions of the committee and shall be provided with the same opportunities as other members to voice their opinions including the submission of memoranda, which excludes the right to vote or to move motions (whether substantive or procedural). International organizations which have formal relations with either FAO or WHO should also be invited to attend sessions of those committees which are of interest to them, albeit in an observatory capacity.[17] Intergovernmental organizations and international non-governmental organizations may attend, upon invitation by the Directors-General of FAO or WHO, all committee sessions as observers.[18] There are at present 46 international organizations, 157 international non-governmental organizations[19] and 16 UN organizations enjoying observer status within the Commission.

5. National Codex Contact Points

Finally, reference should be made to the national codex contact points which act as a link between the Codex Secretariat and member countries, coordinating all relevant Codex activities at the national level by giving notice of draft standards to be adopted by the Commission and by providing opportunity for comments from national food industry, consumers and traders, thereby ensuring that national governments are provided with an appropriate balance between policy and technical ad-

---

[14] EC Council Decision 2003/822 of 17 November 2003, O.J. 2003 L 309.

[15] CAC, ALINORM 03/41, paras. 19-24 and Appendix II.

[16] In 1991, the European Community became a member of FAO alongside EC Member States.

[17] CAC, ALINORM 04/27/41, para. 14 and Appendix II.

[18] CAC, Rules of Procedure, Rule IX-1 and ALINORM 99/37, para. 71 and Appendix IV. However, they may not attend the sessions of the Executive Committee.

[19] International Non-governmental Organizations in Observer Status with the Codex Alimentarius Commission, Report by the Secretariat (CAC/30 INF/2), available at: ftp://ftp.fao.org/Codex/CAC/CAC30/if30_02e.pdf.

vice.[20] It also makes it easier for the members of the Commission to exchange information and coordinate activities.

III. The Legal Nature of the Commission

Scholars disagree on the legal nature of the Commission. Some think of it as a hybrid intergovernmental-private administration[21] while others look at it as an intergovernmental structure.[22] In my view, it does not strictly fit either category.[23] The fact that private parties may participate as observers at the standard-setting procedure is not enough to warrant the organization a hybrid legal nature, since only government representatives are allowed to vote as full members. On the other hand, private parties do play an important role reducing member countries' bargaining power and the truth is that standards are frequently adopted by consensus.[24] Yet the adoption of Codex standards does not require unanimity. I should further note that the Commission is not entirely independent from its mother organizations. The Directors-General of FAO and WHO are key players in the agenda setting of the Commission.[25] It comes as no surprise that an independent evaluation of the Commis-

---

20 CAC, ALINORM 99/37, para. 72 and Appendix IV. *See* List of Codex Contact Points, Report by the Secretariat (CAC/30 INF/1), available at: ftp://ftp.fao.org/Codex/CAC/CAC30/if30_01e.pdf.

21 Benedict Kingsbury, Nico Krisch & Richard B. Stewart, *The Emergence of Global Administrative Law*, 68 LAW AND CONTEMPORARY PROBLEMS (LAW & CONTEMP. PROBS.) 15, 22 (2005).

22 Alexia Herwig, *Transnational Governance Regimes for Foods Derived from Bio-Technology and their Legitimacy, in* TRANSNATIONAL GOVERNANCE AND CONSTITUTIONALISM 199, 204 (Christian Joerges, Inger-Johanne Sand & Gunther Teubner eds., 2004).

23 Which points less to the singularity of the Commission than to recent developments in the law of international organizations. *See* José E. Alvarez, *International Organizations: Then and Now*, 100 AJIL 324, 333 (2006) (stating that "[international organizations] [...] are for all practical purposes a new kind of lawmaking actor, to some degree autonomous from the states that establish them").

24 CAC, ALINORM 03/41, para. 30 and Appendix III and ALINORM 04/27/41, para. 14 and Appendix II.

25 CAC, Rules of Procedure, Rule VII-1, Rule V-3 and Rule XI-6.

sion's activity recommended greater autonomy by way of proposing and executing its work program.[26]

C. The Standard-Setting Procedure

I. Sequence

The Commission has adopted its own Rules of Procedure as well as other internal procedures necessary to achieve its objectives that together with other materials such as general principles, guidelines and definitions form the Commission's Procedural Manual[27] intended to help its members and organizations with observer status participate effectively in the work of the Joint FAO/WHO Food Standards Program. This section examines the procedural regime of food standards on a sequential basis. Since the sessions of the Commission are only convened for a short period once a year, it is the Executive Committee that, assisted by the Secretariat, handles the standard-setting process.

1. Eight-step Uniform Procedure

The regular uniform procedure encompasses eight steps. It is up to the Commission to decide whether to establish a standard and initiate the procedure. However, decisions to elaborate standards may also be taken by subsidiary bodies subject to subsequent approval by the Commission (step one). The Secretariat consults the Joint FAO/WHO expert bodies[28] or, in the case of milk and milk products the International Dairy Federation and collects all relevant available scientific data (step two). This provides the members of the Commission and interested international organizations with the necessary information on which to base their comments including possible implications of the proposed draft standard for their economic interests (step three). The Secretariat

---

[26] Trail *et al.* (note 5), at para. 87.

[27] CAC, Procedural Manual of the Codex Alimentarius Commission, 15th ed., Rome, available at: ftp://ftp.fao.org/codex/Publications/ProcManuals/Manual_15e.pdf.

[28] Joint FAO/WHO Expert Committee on Food Additives (JECFCA); Joint FAO/WHO Meeting on Pesticides Residues (JMPR); Joint FAO/WHO Expert Meetings on Pesticide Specifications (JMPS).

then receives the comments and forwards them onto the subsidiary body or other body concerned which has the power to consider such comments and to amend the proposed draft standard (step four). The proposed draft standard is then submitted through the Secretariat to the Executive Committee for critical review and to the Commission with a view to its adoption as a draft standard (step five). In doing so, the Commission should give due consideration to the outcome of the critical review and to any comments that may be submitted by any of its members regarding the implications which the proposed draft standard may have for their economic interests. Upon adoption, the draft standard is then submitted by the Secretariat to all members and interested international organizations for comment on all aspects, including possible implications of the draft standard for their economic interests (step six). The Secretariat receives said comments and conveys them to the subsidiary body or other bodies concerned, which has the power to consider such comments and amend the draft standard (step seven). Finally, the draft standard is submitted through the Secretariat to the Executive Committee for critical review and to the Commission, together with any written proposal received from members and international organizations for amendments at this stage (step eight).[29]

2. Step 5/8 Procedure (With Omission of Steps 6 and 7)

The Commission may authorize, on the basis of a two-thirds majority of the total votes cast, the omission of steps 6 and 7. Recommendations to omit steps shall be notified to members and interested international organizations as soon as possible after the session of the Codex committee concerned. When formulating recommendations to omit steps 6 and 7, Codex committees shall take all appropriate matters into consideration, including the need for urgency, and the likelihood of new scientific information becoming available in the immediate future. The Commission may at any stage in the elaboration of a standard entrust any of the remaining steps to a Codex committee or other body different from that to which it was previously entrusted.[30]

---

[29] At its Thirty-first Session the Commission adopted eighteen standards following the Uniform Procedure (ALINORM 08/31/REP, Appendix VII, Part 1).

[30] ALINORM 04/27/41, Appendix II. At its Thirty-first Session the Commission adopted nineteen standards with omission of steps 6 and 7 (ALINORM 08/31/REP, Appendix VII, Part 2).

3. Five-step Accelerated Procedure

An accelerated procedure can be employed, essentially consisting of steps 1 to 5 at the end of which a text is adopted as a Codex standard. This is generally employed when an immediate need for a standard is identified and/or there is already broad consensus on the issue under consideration. The Commission, the Executive Committee or the subsidiary body concerned (subject to subsequent confirmation by the Commission or the Executive Committee) can invoke the accelerated procedure on the basis of a two-thirds majority of the total votes cast.[31]

4. Decision-making by Consensus

Decisions are normally reached by consensus. Only in noticeable politically sensitive subjects can one expect government representatives to push for a voting, as they might otherwise incur in political costs at national level.

5. Publicity

Meetings of the Commission should be held in public, unless the latter decides otherwise.[32] Public voting is utilized where no consensus is reached, unless the Commission determines that a sensitive issue should be decided by secret ballot.[33] The Codex standard is published and issued to all member states and associate members of FAO and/or WHO and to the international organizations concerned.[34] It is also made available to the general public in the Commission's website as a portion of the Codex Alimentarius.[35]

---

[31] CAC, Procedural Manual (note 27), 25. At its Thirty-first Session the Commission did not adopt any standard under the Accelerated Procedure (ALINORM 08/31/REP, Appendix VII).

[32] CAC, Rules of Procedure, Rule VI-6, 11.

[33] CAC, Rules of Procedure, Rule VIII-5, 12. That was the case concerning the Standard on Beef Hormones.

[34] CAC, Procedural Manual (note 27), 26.

[35] Available at: http://www.codexalimentarius.net.

II. Functional Separation Between Risk Assessment and Risk Management

I have briefly described the standard-setting procedure on a sequential basis. I will now examine it against the background of the science-politics divide. I should start by noting that the procedure is embedded in the idea of an analytical distinction between risk assessment and risk management when conducting risk analysis.[36] Risk assessment lies primarily with the Joint FAO/WHO expert bodies and consultations at step two of the standard setting procedure, whereas risk management lies with the Commission and its subsidiary bodies.[37] Such functional separation[38] aims at ensuring the scientific integrity of the risk assessment, avoiding confusion over the functions to be performed by risk assessors and risk managers and to reduce any conflict of interests.[39] Risk assessment should be based on all available scientific data and use quantitative information to the greatest extent possible. The report of the risk assessment should indicate any constraints, uncertainties, assumptions and their impact on the risk assessment. It should also record minority opinions. In turn, risk managers should base their decisions on risk assessment taking into account other factors that might be relevant for the protection of consumers' health and for the promotion of fair practices in food trade. When making a choice among different risk management options, which are equally effective in protecting the health of the consumer, the Commission and its subsidiary bodies should seek and take into consideration the potential impact of such measures on trade among its member countries and select measures that are no more trade-restrictive than necessary.

The functional separation between risk assessment and risk management informs us that it is up to scientific bodies to calculate risk and up to accountable decision-makers to determine what level of risk is acceptable. Whenever risk is not quantifiable, that is in situations of scientific uncertainty,[40] science runs out and it is up to decision-makers to

---

[36] Thorsten Hüller & Matthias Leonhard Maier, *Fixing the Codex? Global Food Safety Governance Under Review*, *in* CONSTITUTIONALISM, MULTILEVEL TRADE GOVERNANCE AND SOCIAL REGULATION 267, 281-286 (Christian Joerges & Ernst-Ulrich Petersmann eds., 2006).

[37] CAC, ALINORM 03/41, para. 146 and Appendix IV.

[38] CAC, ALINORM 97/37, para. 28 and Appendix II.

[39] CAC (note 37), para. 9.

[40] FRANK H. KNIGHT, RISK, UNCERTAINTY AND PROFIT (1921).

regulate on the basis of what they believe are their constituents' desires. The critical moment of the risk analysis and of the Codex standard-setting procedure generally is the activity performed by the Joint FAO/WHO expert bodies, where science is the official language and member countries are not at all represented. Thus, whatever happens following the scientific report is heavily influenced by the latter, which means that relevant input coming from member countries and organizations enjoying observer status at later stages of the procedure is somewhat neglected. The normative implication of that separation is that whenever one is dealing with risk assessment one only needs to make sure that experts are unbiased and that scientific information is not manipulated whereas risk management and decisions made under uncertainty raise quite different concerns. In the absence of objective scientific support, the members of the Commission will most likely disagree on the level of acceptable risk let alone the very necessity of adopting a Codex standard. Disagreement is perfectly justified given the fact that national delegations respond to the concerns of their respective constituencies, which may favor different levels of acceptable risk or prefer more or less precautionary approaches under uncertainty. There should be no problem with that but for the fact that national regulators are striped of their discretion in determining what they consider adequate levels of health protection through the Appellate Body's interpretation of the SPS Agreement.[41] Yet I argue that it would be wrong to assume that leaving it up to national regulators[42] settles the issue. I will come back to this in the last section of the article.

---

41 Robert Howse, *Democracy, Science and Free Trade: Risk Regulation on Trial at the World Trade Organization*, 98 MICHIGAN LAW REVIEW 2329 (2000) (arguing that, quite to the contrary, the Appellate Body has been interpreting the SPS Agreement in a way that enhances the quality of rational democratic deliberation about risk and its control).

42 Dario Bevilacqua, *The "EC-Biotech Case": Global v. Domestic Procedural Rules in Risk Regulation: The Precautionary Principle*, 6 EUROPEAN FOOD AND FEED LAW REVIEW 331 (2006).

D. Codex Standards

I. Classification of Standards

Two basic distinctions should be made in providing a classification of standards. First, one should look at the subject matter addressed by a standard. Second, one should consider its object.

1. Subject Matter

One should distinguish between food safety standards and all other standards. The former contain provisions for maximum levels of pesticide residues, contaminants and food additives. The other category encompasses commodity/product standards that define what a commodity is (*e.g.* species of sardines) or how it is made and what it may contain (*e.g.* cheddar cheese, corned beef), quality descriptors as part of commodity standards which are often grading characteristics (*e.g.* color of different types of asparagus) and non-health related standards. While food safety standards strike a balance between consumers' health and fair practices in trade, all other standards are specifically targeted at fair trade and informed consumer choice. The distinction is important because the SPS Agreement only covers food safety standards. Technical standards fall under the TBT Agreement. On the other hand, the distinction may be misleading suggesting that only food safety standards are controversial.

2. Object

One should also distinguish between standards containing substantive requirements and standards containing merely procedural requirements. The latter are adopted in the form of guidelines on processes and procedures (*e.g.* codes of practice) which are intended to augment the application of core standards rather than act as principal standards themselves and which may be adopted whenever an agreement is not possible on a commodity or residue standard.[43]

---

[43] David G. Victor, *The Sanitary and Phytosanitary Agreement of the WTO: An Assessment After Five Years*, 32 NEW YORK UNIVERSITY JOURNAL OF INTERNATIONAL LAW AND POLITICS 865, 886 (2000).

II. Legal Effect

The most controversial issue is the legal effect of Codex standards. Under the founding instrument of the Commission one can find no requirement for member countries to adopt national regulatory measures conforming to Codex standards, which means that they were initially conceived of as a non-binding instrument. Member countries are free to decide whether to adopt them or not. At present, following the abolition of the Acceptance Procedure,[44] member countries are no longer required to notify the Commission of the implementation of standards and since the notification procedure provided for in the SPS Agreement only applies to SPS measures not covered by international standards,[45] monitoring of member countries' compliance seems to depend largely on trade disputes. But there is more to it than that. In fact, as one scholar puts it, "[Codex standards] now potentially have binding application through the SPS Agreement".[46]

1. SPS Agreement

The SPS Agreement covers national sanitary and phytosanitary measures which may, directly or indirectly, affect international trade.[47] When adopting SPS measures WTO members are required either (i) to base them on international standards, guidelines or recommendations where they exist, (ii) to conform them with such instruments or (iii) to provide scientific evidence demonstrating that stricter measures are required for an adequate level of protection.[48] If national measures fall short of meeting at least one of these requirements they may be challenged before the WTO dispute settlement bodies. If one considers that the Appellate Body has been interpreting the relevant provisions of the

---

44 CAC, ALINORM 05/28/41, para. 34 and Appendix IV.

45 SPS, Annex B, 5. The SPS Committee has recently adopted revised recommended procedures on implementing the transparency obligations of the SPS Agreement. One significant change in the revised recommendations encouraged WTO members to notify new or changed measures which conform to international standards.

46 Victor (note 43), 892.

47 SPS, Art 1.1.

48 *Id.* at Art 3.1-3.3. Annex A 3(a) expressly recognizes the Commission as the relevant standard-setting organization for food safety.

SPS Agreement in a way that strips national regulators' discretion to deviate from international standards and that members may eventually face sanctions if non-compliance persists, Codex standards might be undergoing a hardening process.[49] In *EC – Hormones*, while rejecting the idea that international standards, guidelines and recommendations are binding norms[50] and stating that "[...] a Member may decide to set for itself a level of protection different from that implicit in the international standard",[51] the Appellate Body makes clear that the right of a member to define its appropriate level of protection is not, however, an absolute or unqualified right.[52] In fact, while being at first sight friendly to an interpretation of Art 5.1 SPS, which refers to the scientific risk assessment on the basis of which states may determine higher levels of protection, which allows for other than quantifiable evidence to be included,[53] by requiring "a rational relationship between the measure and the risk assessment",[54] even if mitigated by disagreements within the scientific community,[55] the Appellate Body makes it virtually impossible for a member to set a higher level of protection.[56] This is all the more so if one considers that Art 5.5 SPS requires each member to "avoid arbitrary or unjustifiable distinctions in the levels it considers to be appropriate in different situations" and providing a justification of different levels of protection across the range of comparable risks may

---

49 Christine Chinkin, *Normative Development in the International Legal System, in* COMMITMENT AND COMPLIANCE: THE ROLE OF NON-BINDING NORMS IN THE INTERNATIONAL LEGAL SYSTEM 21, 31-34 (Dinah Shelton ed., 2000).

50 AB Report, *EC – Measures Concerning Meat and Meat Products (Hormones)*, WT/DS26/AB/R and WT/DS48/R, para. 165. On this critical issue the Appellate Body reversed both panel reports finding international standards to be binding via Art 3.1 SPS. US Panel Report, WT/DS26/R/USA, para. 8.44 and Canada Panel Report, WT/DS48/R/CAN, para. 9.47.

51 *Id.* at para. 172.

52 *Id.* at paras. 173-177.

53 *Id.* at paras. 186-187.

54 *Id.* at para. 193.

55 *Id.* at para. 194.

56 *See* Howse (note 41), at 2349 (stating that "sufficiency" of scientific evidence does not refer to some threshold of scientific proof or certainty [...] but rather to the extent of the obligation of a Member to engage in scientific investigation *within* the process of rational democratic deliberation").

be too costly.[57] Therefore students of the Commission seem to agree on characterizing its standards as *de facto* binding norms.[58]

2. *TBT Agreement*

The TBT Agreement does not expressly refer to the Commission but the Appellate Body has decided that Codex standards are "relevant international standards" under Art 2.4 and Annex 1.2.[59] Even if it is up to the complaining party to demonstrate that the Codex standard is not ineffective or inappropriate to achieve the objectives pursued by the TBT measure,[60] deference to a Codex standard is most likely to occur. It would be wrong to assume that standards falling under the TBT Agreement do not raise concerns when compared to standards falling under the SPS Agreement. Notwithstanding important differences,[61] standards falling under the TBT may also incorporate a delicate balance between efficiency and distribution to the extent that they may relate not only to product characteristics but also to related process and production methods.[62]

3. *European Law*

The multi-level dimension of Codex standards is impressive. Aside from their legal effect in the international legal order, they penetrate into European law not only through their implementation by EC food-

---

57 *Id.* at 2352 (arguing that by failing to justify different levels of protection national regulators impede their citizens' ability to engage in informed rational democratic deliberation about regulatory choice).

58 Dario Bevilacqua, *Il principio di trasparenza come strumento di* accountability *nella* Codex Alimentarius Commission, 57 RIVISTA TRIMESTRALE DI DIRITTO PUBBLICO 651, 657 (2007).

59 AB Report, *EC – Trade Description of Sardines*, WT/DS231/AB/R, para. 227.

60 *Id.* at para. 275.

61 Joost Pauwelyn, *Non-Traditional Patterns of Global Regulation: Is the WTO 'Missing the Boat'?, in* CONSTITUTIONALISM, MULTILEVEL TRADE GOVERNANCE AND SOCIAL REGULATION (note 36), at 199, 208-215.

62 TBT Agreement, Annex 1(2). Yet the presumption of conformity of Art 2.5 seems to cover only technical regulations.

stuffs legislation[63] but much more interestingly when referred to by the European Court of Justice (ECJ) and the Court of First Instance in clarifying the meaning of provisions contained therein.[64] Thus far Codex standards have only been referred to in support of administrative decisions – made either by the EU Administration[65] or by national administrative authorities[66] – implementing EU legislation. It remains to be seen how the European Courts will decide in those much more interesting cases where a private party invokes a Codex standard against EU legislation containing stricter requirements.[67] Another interesting question is whether, in the absence of EC legislation, compliance with Codex standards may be invoked by Member States to justify – under Article 30 EC – national legislation otherwise in breach of the free movement of goods. Confronted with the issue, the ECJ decided that a Member State may not impose additional requirements – even if conforming to Codex standards – on products of the same type imported from another Member State when those products have been lawfully manufactured and marketed in that Member State and consumers are provided with proper information.[68] However, in a later case,[69] the EU Commission seems to signal that it will consider national administrative practices conforming to Codex standards to be justified under Article 30 EC. That position alone is meaningful since it informs us that the EU Commission will not initiate proceedings against a Member State under Article 226 EC. Nonetheless, because a case may also be brought before the ECJ for a preliminary ruling, whether the ECJ will endorse the EU Commission's deference to Codex standards or stick to its decision in *Deserbais*[70] is not yet clear.

---

63 EC Regulation 852/2004 of 29 April 2004, O.J. 2004 L 139.

64 Sara Poli, *The European Community and the Adoption of Food Standards within the Codex Alimentarius Commission*, 10 EUROPEAN LAW JOURNAL 613, 616-617 (2004).

65 Case C-236/01, *Monsanto Agricoltura Italy and others*, 2003 ECR I-8105, para. 79.

66 Case C-196/05, *Sachsenmilch*, 2006 ECR I-5161, paras. 29 and 34.

67 I am grateful to Dario Bevilacqua for pointing out this important difference.

68 Case 286/86, *Ministère public v. Deserbais*, 1988 ECR 4907, para. 15.

69 Case 192/01, *Commission v. Denmark*, 2003 ECR I-9693, para. 27.

70 Case 286/86 (note 68).

E. Accountability

This section discusses the extent to which the activity performed by the Commission is held accountable. One should start by noting that, when compared to other international standard-setting organizations, the Commission is at first sight fairly accountable. Most countries are represented and NGOs may participate as observers. In addition, meetings are held in public, fully documented and made public in the Commission's website.[71] Its activity is guided by strict procedural rules and relies heavily on scientific assessments. It has to report to FAO and WHO. One also needs to consider that it would be a mistake to require from global governance institutions to exhibit the same kind of accountability that one finds at the state level.[72] Global power-wielders have no corresponding public they might be accountable to, which means that an electoral system would prove inadequate. Furthermore, one should bear in mind that there is no "single problem of global accountability"[73] and that what might constitute an abuse of power relies heavily on the subject area, institutional framework and legal instrument at stake.[74] However, following the public awareness of food-related trade disputes and the reference made by the SPS Agreement to Codex standards, at some point it became clear that the standard-setting activity performed by the Commission was not subject to law to a satisfactory degree. An independent expert evaluation was fixed to carry out a comprehensive study on necessary adjustments of the Commission to the changed circumstances since its establishment in 1963.[75] I will proceed by reviewing the most important proposals made by students of the Commission, beginning with non-judicial accountability mechanisms and then turning to judicial review.

---

71 Available at: http://www.codexalimentarius.net.

72 Ruth W. Grant & Robert O. Keohane, *Accountability and Abuses of Power in World Politics*, 99 AMERICAN POLITICAL SCIENCE REVIEW 29, 34 (2005).

73 *Id.* at 41.

74 Daniel C. Esty, *Global Governance at the Supranational Scale: Globalizing Administrative Law*, 115 YALE LAW JOURNAL 1490 (2006); Stein (note 3).

75 Trail *et al.* (note 5).

I. Non-judicial Accountability Mechanisms

1. Notice-and-Comment

One author has suggested that right at the outset, when the Executive Committee is reviewing a proposal draft coming from a subsidiary body or from a member country, it is necessary to introduce a notice-and-comment requirement.[76] At present there is no requirement to give notice and private parties are only eventually offered the possibility to participate and comment on the draft proposal depending on their awareness. Another problem concerns the way in which national industries and consumers are consulted by the time each member country is notified for comment at step 3 of the standard-setting procedure. First of all, members should, according to domestic administrative procedures, keep national publics informed of draft standards proposed for discussion when they have yet to be discussed at Codex committees and not only after already scheduled for adoption by the Commission. Second, while it is virtually impossible to ensure that national contact points reach out to all potentially affected interests, governments should at least provide information to national constituencies of which interests are being consulted. One way of accomplishing this is to require a public docket on each draft standard to be kept within the secretariat of national contact points and also made available online for consultation. The docket would also mention the names of the persons comprising the national delegation attending Codex meetings. Such a mechanism would raise public awareness of what is being negotiated and pressure governments to better respond to national constituencies' desires. In turn, that would strengthen national delegations' bargaining power within the Commission. Since the political costs of disregarding national interests would be higher, member countries might use that argument to oppose other countries' regulatory strategies and pressure for their own solutions.[77] On the other hand, that might polarize what would otherwise be more consensual positions on any particular subject and eventually impair the adoption of important standards. The truth is that, since Codex committees, together with the scientific report

---

[76] Bevilacqua (note 58), at 663.

[77] Robert D. Putnam, *Diplomacy and Domestic Politics: The Logic of Two-Level Games*, 42 INTERNATIONAL ORGANIZATIONS 427, 440 (1988) (showing how the domestic constraints under which a negotiator operates amount to a bargaining advantage that can be exploited at the international level). *See also* THOMAS C. SCHELLING, THE STRATEGY OF CONFLICT 19-28 (1960).

and other political factors, are required to take into account the economic interests of the states, the information gathered by national delegations regarding national economic interests should be fully disclosed.[78] This is all the more so given the fact that national delegations are easy targets for industry capture. National delegations attending Codex meetings are composed not only of government officials but also of industry representatives. While understandable to some degree, given regulators lack of knowledge on technical issues, the line might be crossed at some point and national economic interests might be taken for national industry's interests. In order to avoid that, national delegations should include consumer representatives. While there are considerable costs involved, it is the only way of bringing into the standard-setting procedure a democratic legitimating ground.

2. *Observer Status*

Widening the debate implies a much more cautious selection of organizations as observers. The expert report pointed out that the eligibility criteria for NGOs to obtain observer status falls short of ensuring that they really speak on behalf of an international community.[79] It only requires NGOs to have membership in three or more countries and these can be from the same geographic region[80] whereas they should consist of general representation, impartiality and protection of common interests.[81] When applying, candidates should be required to document their activity, membership and purposes in order to avoid conflict of interests.[82] By allowing the Commission to better identify which public candidates really represent, the application materials could also be used as a source of information to make sure that there is a genuine balanced representation among observers not only geographically but also regarding economic interests. If one has a look at official data one realizes that NGOs representing the industry largely outnumber consumer NGOs.[83]

---

78 Bevilacqua (note 58), at 669.

79 Trail *et al.* (note 5), at para. 147.

80 CAC, ALINORM 99/37, para. 71 and Appendix IV.

81 Bevilacqua (note 58), at 663-664.

82 *Id.*

83 CAC (note 19). Only 9 out of 157 are consumer representatives.

3. Participation of Developing Countries

Due to the fact that developing countries face severe financial constraints, a Codex Trust Fund was launched in 2003 to enable low-income and lower-middle-income countries to both prepare for and participate effectively in the Commission and its subsidiary bodies' meetings.[84] A small portion of funds is also made available to enable developing countries to prepare and present technical/scientific positions and data related to Codex work. Applications are channeled through the national contact points. Another strategy is to make arrangements for Codex committees to be hosted by developing countries. While generous, the Trust Fund gives rise to the awkward situation of allowing the international community to determine developing countries regulators' incentives thereby disempowering national governments. Whether to fight malaria first or negotiate the labeling of foods containing GMOs will be decided by funds made available by the international community and not by national constituencies. In fact, one might perceive the willingness of rich countries to fund developing countries participation not as a generous act but rather aiming at smuggling more industry representatives into their delegations. Furthermore, the Trust Fund may turn out to be ineffective. The importance given to science in the standard-setting procedure eventually diminishes the contribution of developing countries because even with unlimited funding developing countries lack the knowledge and skill to provide sufficient scientific evidence on any given level of protection. Funds would be better allocated in capacity building programs[85] rather than on participation. In fact, developing countries may prefer, based upon reasons other than trade-related, lower but effective standards of protection to higher but unenforceable ones. Efforts are underway for the Joint FAO/WHO expert committees to include experts from developing countries.[86]

---

84 It is hoped that approximately USD 4 million per year will be made available.

85 FAO, WHO, OIE, the World Bank and the WTO have established a global program in capacity building and technical assistance called the Standards and Trade Development Facility, available at: http://www.standardsfacili ty.org/.

86 FAO and WHO, Enhancing developing country participation in FAO/WHO scientific advice activities, available at: ftp://ftp.fao.org/docrep/fao /010/a0873e/a08 73e.pdf.

4. Transparency

Considering the role risk assessment plays in the standard-setting procedure, ensuring transparency in the selection of experts becomes critical. Thus, all experts are required to declare any interests that could constitute a real, potential or apparent conflict of interests.[87] While it is very difficult to find experts without any industry contact whatsoever, information on each case should be disclosed. It is also important to make sure that FAO and WHO pay honoraria and not only cover the attendance costs of meetings in order to avoid capture by the food industry.[88] Documenting scientific conflicts through the publication of minority reports and making summary reports available online for public comment and peer review[89] provide valuable material for Codex committees to base their decisions on. While time-consuming it should not take as long as a "second opinion" expert consultation procedure would. While transparency in the selection of experts leads to impartial performance in risk assessment, which is meaningful given their crucial role in the standard-setting procedure, it does not solve the problem of how to bring into account decisions made by risk managers regarding the establishment of levels of acceptable risk and judgments made under uncertainty. Furthermore, even if unbiased professionals, experts, just like any other individual, cannot avoid bringing value-laden choices into their judgments. Transparency alone provides no solution for that concern.

II. Judicial Review

1. Constraints of the International Legal System

The mechanisms put forward thus far, such as "notice and comment", "statements on conflicts of interests", "public docket" and "public interest funding", bear a resemblance to the legal regime underpinning administrative activity in many different national legal systems.[90] Yet at

---

[87] FAO and WHO, FAO/WHO Framework for the Provision of Scientific Advice on Food Safety and Nutrition, available at: http://www.fao.org/ag/AGN/agns/files/Final_Draft_EnglishFramework.pdf, 18-19.

[88] Herwig (note 22), at 220.

[89] FAO and WHO (note 87), 22.

[90] Kingsbury, Krisch & Stewart (note 21); Esty (note 74).

the domestic level individuals are entitled to challenge administrative decisions before courts, whereas at the international level judicial review is generally unavailable. In most cases, because international norms are not ripe and still need to be implemented by national regulatory authorities it makes perfect sense not to have them immediately reviewed. Individuals may later challenge the national implementing measures before domestic courts. Furthermore, it is difficult to determine exactly which interests are affected by international norms, which makes it a long shot for individuals to meet standing requirements. Yet, while falling short of corresponding to judicial review witnessed in domestic legal systems, proposals have been made which credit for forging a doctrinal consistent solution for independent review of Codex standards under the constraints of the international legal system.

2. *Institutional Differentiation*

Scholars have suggested that the WTO dispute settlement bodies and mainly the Appellate Body might provide an adequate legal framework under which the standard setting performed by the Commission might be scrutinized.[91] The most interesting idea behind the gatekeeper function of the Appellate Body is the expansion of the object of disputes brought before WTO tribunals. In fact, the WTO Dispute Settlement Understanding (DSU) is conceived of to challenge trade-restricting *domestic* measures and not *international* norms. On the other hand, its interpretation of the scope of the SPS/TBT Agreements as well as of Codex standards themselves determine the extent to which the latter become *de facto* binding which means that, if WTO tribunals start making requirements concerning Codex's standard-setting procedures for standards to gain the legal effect that raises the cost of enacting non-conform domestic regulation, the Commission will be under pressure to start meeting those requirements. It is argued that such form of institutional differentiation would enhance the legitimacy of the activity performed by the Commission. While the interplay between standard-setting international organizations and the WTO has been acknowl-

---

91 Joanne Scott, *International Trade and Environmental Governance: Relating Rules (and Standards) in the EU and the WTO*, 15 EUROPEAN JOURNAL OF INTERNATIONAL LAW (EJIL) 307, 311-312, 330-333 (2004); Michael Livermore, *Authority and Legitimacy in Global Governance: Deliberation, Institutional Differentiation and the Codex Alimentarius*, 81 NEW YORK UNIVERSITY LAW REVIEW 766, 789 (2006).

edged,[92] I find it difficult to expect from the DSU, the interpretation of which keeps avoiding weighing public values against international trade, to compensate for the internal deficiencies of representation and equality one can find at the Commission. Even if one could find within the DSU a fair balance between competing public values,[93] one would still run up against what Koskenniemi calls "structural bias"[94] let alone the admissibility of using non-WTO law in the WTO dispute settlement mechanism.[95] [96]

---

[92] Armin von Bogdandy, *Law and Politics in the WTO – Strategies to Cope with a Deficient Relationship*, 5 MAX PLANCK YEARBOOK OF UNITED NATIONS LAW 609, 633-641 (2001) (arguing that the incorporation of non-binding standards set up by international organizations might be a way to meet WTO's mismatch between politics and law).

[93] Robert Howse, *From Politics to Technocracy-And Back Again: The Fate of the Multilateral Trading Regime*, 96 AJIL 94, 109-112 (2002) (arguing that recent decisions of the Appellate Body, instead of a trade bias, "do justice to the delicate interrelationship of values and interests").

[94] Martii Koskenniemi, *Fragmentation of International Law: Difficulties Arising from the Diversification and Expansion of International Law*, Report of the Study Group of the International Law Commission, available at: http://daccess-ods.un.org/TMP/3983809.html, 143.

[95] Markus Böckenförde, *Zwischen Sein und Wollen – Über den Einfluss umweltvölkerrechtlicher Verträge im Rahmen eines WTO-Streitbeilegungsverfahrens*, 63 ZEITSCHRIFT FÜR AUSLÄNDISCHES ÖFFENTLICHES RECHT UND VÖLKERRECHT 971 (2003) (arguing against the direct applicability of non-WTO law while making room for the possibility of having the latter be referred to when clarifying provisions of the covered agreements). *See* Joost Pauwelyn, *The Role of Public International Law in the WTO: How Far Can We Go?*, 95 AJIL 535, 561-562 (2001) (arguing that the wording of the DSU does not exclude the application of non-WTO law); Lorand Bartels, *Applicable Law in WTO Dispute Settlement Proceedings*, 35 JOURNAL OF WORLD TRADE 499 (2001) (claiming – on the basis of a distinction between jurisdiction and applicable law – for prima facie applicability of a variety of sources of international law subject to the rule that the dispute settlement body may not add to or diminish the rights and obligations provided in the covered agreements). *See also* Koskenniemi (note 94), at 65-101 (claiming that the rationale of special regimes such as the WTO is the same as that of *lex specialis* and arguing against the possibility of there being any self-contained regime "[...] completely cocooned outside international law").

[96] In *EC – Approval and Marketing of Biotech Products*, US Panel Report, WT/DS291/R; Canada Panel Report, WT/DS292/R and Argentina Panel Report WT/DS293/R, the panel admits the use of non-WTO law for interpretative

F. The Legitimacy of International Administrative Activity

I. Models of Administrative Law

This section starts by discussing three different conceptions of administrative law.[97] This digression is important in order to demonstrate that the problems raised by the activity performed by the Commission perfectly match the ones addressed by administrative lawyers in domestic legal systems.

1. The Formalist Model

According to established wisdom administrative law evolved from the liberal project of subjecting public power to law. Yet what lies behind nineteenth century European public law scholarship is its own agenda of being accepted as science by mainstream positivist legal thought.[98] One was led to believe that administrative activity could be traced back to legislative intent expressing people's will and the growth of bureaucracies was accepted as a means to rationalize subjectivity.[99] Administrative law was therefore designed under a transmission belt to ensure that the administration actually effectuated constituents' desires.[100] Ingenious versions of non-delegation doctrines were invented. Yet while apparently placing limits on what legislatures might pass on to the ad-

---

purposes whenever the relevant rules of international law are applicable in the relations between all WTO Members (para. 7.68), yet leaving open the question whether admissibility extends to those cases where the relevant rules of international law are applicable in the relations between all parties to the dispute but not between all WTO Members (para. 7.72).

97 JERRY L. MASHAW, DUE PROCESS IN THE ADMINISTRATIVE STATE 16-24 (1985).

98 Michael Stolleis, *Verwaltungsrechtswissenschaft und Verwaltungslehre 1866-1914*, 15 DIE VERWALTUNG (DV) 45, 49-50 (1982).

99 MAX WEBER, WIRTSCHAFT UND GESELLSCHAFT 565 (1921). *See* Gerald E. Frug, *The Ideology of Bureaucracy in American Law*, 97 HARVARD LAW REVIEW (HARV. L. REV.) 1276 (1984) (arguing that the stories of bureaucratic legitimation are based on failed attempts to combine-yet-separate objectivity and subjectivity, whereas, since each is a "dangerous supplement" of the other, no line between the two can ever be drawn).

100 Richard B. Stewart, *The Reformation of American Administrative Law*, 88 HARV. L. REV. 1669, 1675 (1975).

ministration to rule on, such doctrines were in fact a powerful legitimating source of administrative activity within the authorized range of delegation, the confines of which were in turn far from being precise and easily manipulable.[101] Administrative lawyers are aware of the fact that lawmaking is not a province of parliament both because national governments and regulatory authorities with broad mandates are also engaged in rulemaking activity and the parliament itself is limited by constitutional principles.[102] While German public law scholarship, being heavily influenced by the classic article by Böckenförde,[103] for the most part, works under the formalist model – also known as the classic model[104] – at the same time there is a widespread understanding that the latter is falling apart.[105]

One could try to analyze the activity performed by the Commission under this model simply by conceiving it as an extension of national regulatory activity. On the other hand, given its broad mandate one cannot escape recognizing the Commission's virtually unfettered discretion and consequently the need to abandon a formalist model of administrative law. Yet that tells us less about the specificity of the Commission than of the inability of the formalist model to adequately capture administrative activity. In fact, even at the domestic level one can find broad delegation of rulemaking powers to administrative bodies,

---

[101] Frug (note 99), at 1303-1305.

[102] ARMIN VON BOGDANDY, GUBERNATIVE RECHTSETZUNG (1999).

[103] Ernst-Wolfgang Böckenförde, *Demokratie als Verfassungsprinzip, in* I HANDBUCH DES STAATSRECHTS 887 (Josef Isensee & Paul Kirchhof eds., 1987) (the author made some minor changes to the original version of the article in: II HANDBUCH DES STAATSRECHTS 429 (Josef Isensee & Paul Kirchhof eds., 2004)).

[104] EBERHARD SCHMIDT-AßMANN, DAS ALLGEMEINE VERWALTUNGSRECHT ALS ORDNUNGSIDEE 89 (2006) and *Verwaltungslegitimation als Rechtsbegriff*, 116 ARCHIV DES ÖFFENTLICHEN RECHTS (AöR) 329 (1991) and Hans-Heinrich Trute, *Die demokratische Legitimation der Verwaltung, in* I GRUNDLAGEN DES VERWALTUNGSRECHTS 307, 311-317 (Wolfgang Hoffmann-Riem, Eberhard Schmidt-Aßmann & Andreas Voßkuhle eds., 2006).

[105] Ulrich R. Haltern, Franz C. Mayer & Christoph R. Möllers, *Wesentlichkeitstheorie und Gerichtsbarkeit. Zur institutionellen Kritik des Gesetzesvorbehalts*, 30 DV 51 (1997). *See also* Wolfgang Hoffmann-Riem, *Gesetz und Gesetzesvorbehalt im Umbruch – Zur Qualitäts-Gewährleistung durch Normen*, 120 AöR 5 (2005); Karl-Heinz Ladeur & Tobias Gostomzyk, *Der Gesetzesvorbehalt im Gewährleistungsstaat*, 36 DV 141 (2003).

which equally raises the question of the extent to which the latter respond to constituents' desires.

2. *The "Expertise" Model*

Alternatively, one might try to analyze the Commission under an "expertise model" of administrative law, which essentially relies on the special knowledge of experts rather than lay politicians to legitimate administrative activity.[106] Under this model administrative law lays down strict rules of eligibility for the appointment of experts making sure that they are in fact high-qualified professionals and establishes accountability mechanisms aiming at ensuring unbiased professionalism such as statements on conflicts of interests and peer review. It also sets procedural requirements by imposing a duty on the administration not only to hear all interested parties but, more importantly, to effectively address all relevant issues by undertaking a study of possible alternatives before reaching its decision ("hard look" doctrine[107]). A duty to give reasons is also to be understood as an important legal tool developed by the expertise model.

There are no real proponents of the "expertise model" anymore at least in its original form, but it would be wrong to assume that it has been altogether abandoned.[108] Deliberative conceptions of democracy[109] – much in vogue concerning the debate on the legitimacy of the European Union[110] but also easily adjustable to the economic rationale of international trade law[111] – simply reproduce the technocratic narrative of the

---

106 JAMES M. LANDIS, THE ADMINISTRATIVE PROCESS (1938).

107 STEPHEN G. BREYER AND OTHERS, ADMINISTRATIVE LAW AND REGULATORY POLICY 347-357 and 383-384 (2006).

108 STEPHEN G. BREYER, BREAKING THE VICIOUS CIRCLE: TOWARD EFFECTIVE RISK REGULATION (1993).

109 What follows would not apply to strictly procedural versions of deliberative democracy. The problem with those versions is that democratic deliberation cannot be legitimate by itself, that is without reference to any procedure-independent standard. David Estlund, *Beyond Fairness and Deliberation: The Epistemic Dimension of Democratic Authority, in* DELIBERATIVE DEMOCRACY, 173, 181 (James Bohman & William Rehg eds., 1997).

110 Christian Joerges & Jurgen Neyer, *Transforming Strategic Interaction into Deliberative Problem-Solving*, 4 JOURNAL OF EUROPEAN PUBLIC POLICY 609 (1997).

111 Howse (note 41).

"expertise model."[112] They do so by arguing that individual preferences need to be liberated from institutional constraints within the market on the basis of which they were shaped through a truly autonomous process of preference formation.[113] That process relies heavily on technical expertise.

As I pointed out, when analyzing the standard-setting procedure, scientific assessments are a critical component when setting the appropriate level of risk for a food product. Furthermore, when discussing the accountability mechanisms of the Commission, one could find several rules and procedures representative of an expertise model of administrative law. However, no matter how important it is to ensure that food experts are not captured by the industry, the main problem with analyzing the Commission under the expertise model is, once again, the model itself. Even if unbiased professionals, experts, just like any other individual, cannot avoid bringing value-laden choices into their judgments.[114]

3. The "Interest-representation" Model

Pluralist theorists[115] sought to bring back to the administrative process a democratic legitimating ground. The "interest-representation" model of administrative law consists in neutralizing agency bias towards regulated industries by making it bestow adequate consideration to all relevant interests differently affected by possible policy alternatives.[116] Instead of shielding administrative activity against organized interests as the expertise model did, administrative law now supports interest-group participation in administrative decision-making. In fact it desperately needs it as the legitimating source of its activity now understood

---

112 Martin Shapiro, *"Deliberative," "Independent" Technocracy v. Democratic Politics: Will the Globe Echo the E.U.?*, 68 LAW & CONTEMP. PROBS. 341, 351 (2005).

113 CASS R. SUNSTEIN, AFTER THE RIGHTS REVOLUTION. RECONCEIVING THE REGULATORY STATE 40-41 (1990).

114 MASHAW (note 97), at 18; Andreas Voßkuhle, *Sachverständige Beratung des Staates*, *in* III HANDBUCH DES STAATSRECHTS 425, 437-438 (Josef Isensee & Paul Kirchhof eds., 2005).

115 DAVID B. TRUMAN, THE GOVERNMENTAL PROCESS (1951).

116 Stewart (note 100), at 1760-1813.

as a surrogate political process through legal procedures rather than through electoral mechanisms.

The standard-setting activity carried out by the Commission could be presented in light of this model. Member countries – in coalition with national industries – pressure for a food standard that resembles national regulatory practices. Administrative law is not about pursuing the common good and invalidating standards based on national or industrial biases but about making sure that there is a balanced representation of interests in the standard-setting procedure and keeping a record of all activity so that at the end of the day everyone knows which interests are reflected in the food standard. Yet the "vital cockpit" in administering this conception of administrative law is the judiciary, which is precisely lacking to a satisfactory degree at the international level.[117] Once again, I argue that that tells us less about the specificity of international administration than about some imperfections within the "interest-representation" model.[118]

II. Why Would International Administrative Activity Be Any Less Legitimate?

It follows from our discussion of different models of administrative law that when extending each conception of administrative law to international administrative activity one is struck by the fact that there always seems to be something lacking. Something that, at the domestic level, one holds dear, be it electoral mechanisms under the formalist model, mechanisms that guarantee impartial and objective scientific findings under the expertise model or judicial review under the "interest-representation" model. However it also follows that the actual role those elements play in domestic administrative law needs qualifications.

One easy reaction to the deconstruction of each model of administrative law would be to argue that by doing so one misses the aggregate value of the different mechanisms, which, if combined, might legitimate administrative activity. A different strategy that goes in the same direction comes from the scholarship on Global Administrative Law and

---

[117] Richard B. Stewart, *U.S. Administrative Law: A Model for Global Administrative Law?*, 68 L. & CONTEMP. PROBS. 63, 75 (2005).

[118] MARTIN SHAPIRO, WHO GUARDS THE GUARDIANS? – JUDICIAL CONTROL OF ADMINISTRATION 74-75 (1988); Stewart (note 100), at 1770-1781.

consists in regarding the fact that, at the global level, no single constituency can claim for itself absolute legitimacy for controlling regulation as something positive and normatively defensible.[119] The institutional disorder of global regulation, the argument goes, by leaving open the question of ultimate authority and balancing accountability to the different constituencies gives rise to the mutual accommodation of the concerns of each while allowing for smooth functioning of the global system. The problem is that behind fragmentation lies a calculated effort on the part of powerful states to protect their dominance and discretion.[120] There is nothing legitimate about that.

Which institution should one trust regulatory activity depends on the relative strengths and weaknesses of all potential institutional alternatives.[121] Hence any assessment of the legitimacy of the Commission is necessarily incomplete unless it takes into account the comparative performance of national regulatory authorities. Accomplishing this requires further research. In the remaining part of the article I put down some thoughts that I hope might serve as inspiration to students of the Commission. The point is that if one considers that the national regulatory process is severely imperfect and likely subject to capture by the national food industry, the case for a stronger democratic legitimacy chain loses some of its appeal. In fact, the stakes of national food industry are high enough for it to do all it can to pressure national regulators to set food standards at any given level that most benefits its interests. One can expect the adoption of national regulatory measures that harm

---

[119] Nico Krisch, *The Pluralism of Global Administrative Law*, 17 EJIL 247, 262-274 (2006).

[120] Eyal Benvenisti & George W. Downs, *The Empire's New Clothes: Political Economy and the Fragmentation of International Law*, 60 STANFORD LAW REVIEW 595 (2007) (arguing that fragmentation makes it difficult for weaker states to create coalitions through cross-issue logrolling and increases the transaction costs that international bureaucrats and judges face in trying to rationalize the international system or to engage in bottom-up constitution building).

[121] What follows draws heavily on the scholarship of Miguel Poiares Maduro on European constitutionalism. *See* MIGUEL POIARES MADURO, WE THE COURT – THE EUROPEAN COURT OF JUSTICE AND THE EUROPEAN ECONOMIC CONSTITUTION 103-149 (1998); Miguel Poiares Maduro, *Europe and the constitution – What if this is as Good as it Gets?*, *in* EUROPEAN CONSTITUTIONALISM BEYOND THE STATE 74 (Joseph H. H. Weiler & Marlene Wind eds., 2003). *See also* NEIL K. KOMESAR, IMPERFECT ALTERNATIVES. CHOOSING INSTITUTIONS IN LAW, ECONOMICS AND PUBLIC POLICY (1994) (developing the framework for comparative institutional analysis).

consumers both by limiting the variety in food products and by increasing prices. Domestic courts may, on occasion, depending on the pedigree of the national administrative system, invalidate some measures but they are more likely to defer to administrative discretion backed-up by scientific findings. Those negative effects on consumers can only be prevented by the WTO regime, which closely examines national regulatory measures containing higher levels of health protection than the ones set in Codex standards. Yet, as previously noted, the adjudicative process of the WTO also suffers from biases which render it unlikely for a fair balance between free trade and consumers' health to take place. While insufficiently responsive to consumers' concerns, the standard-setting activity of the Commission removes most costs of national regulation. It also channels consumers' preferences in a much more effective way than what one otherwise achieves through the adjudicative process before the WTO. At the same time, it maximizes resources by pooling the expertise and regulatory instruments of all member states. Furthermore, being an organized institutional setting pursuing long-term goals, the Commission reduces the transaction costs of cooperation between states thereby avoiding the costs of litigation before the WTO. The Commission may be highly imperfect and yet still superior to any other alternative in the regulation of food safety. As Komesar puts it "[i]nstitutional superiority is not always obvious, and superiority is often a choice of bad over worse."[122]

---

[122] KOMESAR (note 121), at 255.

4. Public Authority through Private Law Instruments?

ICANN – Governance by Technical Necessity

*By Matthias Hartwig**

1. Introduction

One of the most curious instances of international administrative governance is the Internet Corporation for Assigned Names and Numbers (ICANN). On the one hand, ICANN is neither an international or-

* I would like to thank Matthias Goldmann for fruitful discussions and Lewis Enim and Eva Richter for their corrections of the text.

A. von Bogdandy et al. (eds.), *The Exercise of Public Authority by International Institutions*, Beiträge zum ausländischen öffentlichen Recht und Völkerrecht 210,
DOI 10.1007/978-3-642-04531-8_20, © Springer-Verlag Berlin Heidelberg 2010

ganization, nor even an entity under international law, but a non-profit corporation under Californian law. On the other hand, it administers access to the Internet and sets the standards around the world. The principal participants in setting the standards and organizing the Internet are private corporations. Although national governments are involved, they are formally reduced to an advisory role *vis-à-vis* the organization. The roles are generally reversed in international law, private persons function as consultants only and it is up to the governments as representatives of states to make binding decisions.[1] Under the standard model of international law an international organization or an international authority may set rules only after having been empowered to this end by states. ICANN, however, has never been vested with such powers by any international treaty. Further, international actors are usually bound by the rules established by an international organization or authority only by accepting such an obligation through international treaties and agreements. The rules set by ICANN, however, are accepted and implemented without any such international legal instrument having been concluded. Nevertheless, ICANN establishes rules which are of greater importance than most acts of international organizations and they are more widely and more strictly accepted and respected than binding decisions of most international organizations. One could make the argument that ICANN decisions are more authoritative than those of the UN Security Council in the sense that ICANN decisions are less frequently violated. The reason why ICANN's decisions enjoy such broad acceptance and are followed so strictly is practical in nature: ICANN's rules are necessary for the operation of the Internet, without which the Internet would not run, and without the Internet today's world would not run.

2. History of ICANN

None of the aspects of ICANN mentioned above can be understood without taking into consideration the development of the Internet. The Internet started out in the 1960s as a U.S. military research project.[2] At

---

1 *See* Art. 71 UN Charter on the cooperation between the Economic and Social Council of the United Nations and non-governmental organizations.

2 As a matter of fact the research into the possibility of establishing an Internet was undertaken by the Defense Advanced Research Projects Agency, which had been founded in 1958 in response to the sputnik shock in the USA.

a later stage educational and research institutions, government contractors, scientists and technology specialists were incorporated into the program.[3] The object of the whole project was to connect computers for the purposes of exchanging information. The ultimate goal was to link different networks, which meant developing a network of networks.

The first rules and standards of this network were proposed by students who formed informal working groups. They cautiously called their ideas "Requests for Comments", indicating that they intended the development of standards to be the result of an open discussion of the Internet community, a characteristic which continues today. The organization of this network was somewhat anarchic; whoever was interested could participate in the formulation of the rules which should govern the Internet. In 2000 ICANN even held elections in which all registered users should elect the members of the Board of Governors. However, owing to the deficient structure of the elections, the result did not really reflect the composition of the Internet users' community.[4] The attempt to involve the Internet users in the decision-making process through elections at a world level was accordingly ended by an ICANN decision in 2002.

Besides these bottom-up approaches to Internet governance the U.S. government was not disengaged from the development. The early responsibilities of the military were later transferred to the National Science Foundation, which entered into a cooperative agreement with the Network Solutions Incorporation.[5] With the creation of ICANN in 1998 the U.S. government intended to guarantee a management of the Internet which was not government controlled and followed the bottom-up principle in the field of policy making. The stakeholders of the Internet had to be represented in its structures of the Internet. The main principles of the United States policy were laid down in the Memoran-

---

See Jonathan Weinberg, *ICANN and the Problem of Legitimacy*, 50 DUKE LAW JOURNAL 187, 192 (2000/2001).

3 Peter K. Yu, *The Origins of CCTLD Policymaking*, 12 CARDOZO JOURNAL OF INTERNATIONAL AND COMPARATIVE LAW 387 (2004).

4 Thus, the director of the Board who should represent Africa was elected by 67 of 130 votes, Africa having almost 800 million inhabitants, *see* Jochen von Bernstorff, *Democratic Global Internet Regulation? Governance Networks, International Law and the Shadow of Hegemony*, 9 EUROPEAN LAW JOURNAL 511, 521 (2003).

5 Weinberg (note 2), at 198.

dum of Understanding in November 1998, which now forms the basic document by which the Department of Commerce delegates certain powers to corporations, and in the Bylaws of ICANN.[6] It has to be stressed that by delegating powers to ICANN the U.S. government, although excluding governmental influences on ICANN, maintained an important supervisory function as it was able revoke the delegated powers any time.

3. The Impact of the Assignment of Names and Numbers on the Internet[7]

One might wonder why the assignment of Internet numbers matters in politics. The Internet only functions if different computers can enter into contact with each other. In order to make this possible, number groups comparable to phone numbers (so-called Internet protocols) are assigned to each computer. Without such a number a computer cannot be contacted from an external location. As numbers are generally more difficult to remember it has become common practice to give names to the addresses, each number corresponding to one or several names. These names must have a specific structure, which is due to the complexity of the Internet. Therefore a Domain Name System was developed, the DNS. It turned out that it would not be feasible just to have names on the same level; it became evident that they had to be organized in a certain way. This organization was accomplished by the hierarchization of certain parts of the name, comparable to the area code of the telephone system. To this end so-called top level domains (TLDs) were introduced which either had a generic code such as ".com", ".org", or ".net", covering specific areas of activities respectively

---

6 The Memorandum of Understanding can be found under http://icann.org. The Memorandum has been several times amended, *see* http://www.ntia.doc.gov; it was supplemented by a Joint Project Agreement between ICANN and the Department of Commerce, last amendment of 29 September 2006, http://www.ntia.doc.gov/ntiahome/domainname/icann.htm. The Bylaws are the "charter" of ICANN which has been adopted by ICANN, last amendment of 29 May 2008, http://www.icann.org/en/general/bylaws.htm. Amendments to the Bylaws require a majority of two thirds of the Board of Governors.

7 For the following *see* Daniel Karrenberg, *The Domain Name System Explained for Non-Experts, in* INTERNET GOVERNANCE: A GRAND COLLABORATION, UNITED NATIONS, 22 (Don MacLean ed., 2004).

(".com" for commercial, ".org" for non-profit organizations, ".net" for network providers) or a country code, such as ".de" for Germany, ".us" for the United States, or ".uk" for the United Kingdom. The abbreviations of country names as a rule follow the standards set up by the International Organization for Standardization.[8] On a lower level, one always finds the domain name, to the left of the TLD names. The TLD names are saved in specific servers; the location of servers is listed in the so-called root servers which are at the top of the hierarchy. The vast majority of these root servers are located in the USA, among them the Master of the root servers, which has the main steering function. These root servers contain all information about the location of TLDs. Therefore, as a rule, if a computer does not know where to send an email, the so-called cache server will address the root servers. When starting up, a cache server will address all root servers in order to get the current list of the root servers. This will enable it to know where to send the query for the location of the TLD. If the name of a top-level domain is not included in the list, the root servers will not indicate it. Everything there depends on the inclusion of the name insertion, *quod non est in actis non est in mundo*. If a TLD name is eliminated from the root servers, it will be impossible to contact any address containing this TLD name. All these addresses will be excluded from the normal Internet communication – death by silence, if you will. Therefore, the power to manage the list of the top-level domain names in the root servers comes close to the power to decide on life or death in the Internet.[9]

Although the administration of the Internet seems to concentrate on technical issues, a political impact cannot be excluded. It starts with the definition of a state. For example, does Palestine have a right to a top level domain name, such as ".ps",[10] or the European Union to the top level domain ".eu",[11] although both of them are not in the list of states of the International Organization for Standardization? What is the situation of Catalonia, being only a *comunidad autonoma* of Spain, has

---

[8] http://www.ccnso.icann.org/workinggroups/draft-issues-paper-idn-cctlds.pdf. However, there are exceptions: the abbreviation of the United Kingdom by the ISO is GB, not UK.

[9] Stefan Bechtold, *Governance in Namespaces*, 36 LOYOLA OF LOS ANGELES LAW REVIEW 1256 *et seq.* (2003).

[10] The question has been answered affirmatively.

[11] In 2005 the top level domain name ".eu" has been introduced by a resolution of ICANN, *see* http://www.icann.org/en/announcements/announcement-23mar05.htm.

it a right to an own country code?[12] When should the use of ".su" for Soviet Union – actually phased out – end, or that of ".zr" for Zaire? Does Taiwan have a right to the top level domain name ".tw"? The Peoples' Republic of China contested it in 2003, without, however, insisting in the withdrawal of this name.[13] Furthermore, what is the character of country codes? Do they form part of the national heritage and are they therefore not subject to free disposal by a private corporation, as South Africa, for instance, claims? To what extent can states dispose of their country code? Lucky Tuvalu, one of the smallest states in the world, with the very appealing country code ".tv", has already increased its state income by more than $ 20 million by leasing its country code to television companies.

A further not purely technical problem linked to the administration of the Internet is which generic top-level domains should be established. Recently, a conflict broke out over a new top level domain name ".xxx" which was supposed to be reserved exclusively for pornographic material. As pornographic sites are among those most frequented in the Internet – 25% of all Internet researches are directed to pornographic sites[14] – one could come to the conclusion that it would make sense to supplement the top level domains by an ".xxx", from a standpoint focusing exclusively on demand. However, political concerns, especially of the United States, prevailed, and in the end the proposal was not adopted.[15]

It has long been disputed whether domain names will only be available in ASCII characters[16] or whether internationalized domain names will be admissible in other additional scripts, such as Cyrillic,[17] Chinese,

---

12 In 2005, ".cat" for Catalonian speaking persons or organizations has been introduced, though not as a country code top level domain name, but rather as a generic top level domain name, *see* http://www.icann.org/en/minutes/resolutions-15sep05.htm.

13 It should be mentioned that Hong Kong possesses its own country code top level domain, namely ".hk".

14 http://Internet-filter-review.toptenreviews.com/Internet-pornography-statistics.html.

15 The proposal was rejected by ICANN in 2006 and again in 2007.

16 ASCII means American Standard Code for Information Interchange and is based on the English alphabet.

17 The President of the Russian Federation demanded that the Cyrillic alphabet be introduced into the Internet, http://technology.timesonline.co.uk/tol/news/tech_and_web/article4119960.ece.

Arabic or Hebrew.[18] This is not only a technical question, but concerns the representation of different cultures in the Internet. Further problems may arise out of trademark concerns. Who may use which name? Will it be sufficient to follow the principle of first come first served or will it be necessary to grant minimum protection for trade marks against so-called DNS squatters who try to get domain names which they can sell? Finally, it falls within the administration of the Internet to decide who should register and administer the domain names below the top level. The policy in this context will decide on the structure of the administration – monopolistic, oligarchic or free market oriented.

4. Structure, Functions and Competences of ICANN

4.1. Structure of ICANN

Although ICANN is a private organization (as explained above), it is not a creation of private persons. Rather, its activities are governed by a Memorandum of Understanding of 25 November 1998 (MoU) between the U.S. government, represented by the Department of Commerce (DoC) and ICANN. The MoU's objective was to implement a DoC policy statement, in which the intention was expressed to privatize the technical management of the Internet names and addresses in order to allow for the development of robust competition. ICANN's effectiveness depends on its recognition by the DoC, which can withdraw the recognition at anytime and transfer the functions of ICANN to another organization.[19] To a certain extent it fulfills the tasks of a U.S. government state agency. Consequently, the traditional models of (national)

---

[18] ICANN issued guidelines for the use of internationalized domain names in 2003, http://www.icann.org/general/idn-guidelines-20jun03.htm. In March 2008, the ICANN board voted to develop final fast-track implementation proposals for a limited number of International Domain Names with respect to the country code top level domain names. In the future, the ccTLD names can be written not only in ASCII, but likewise in other characters than ASCII, such as Cyrillic, Hebrew, Chinese or Arabic.

[19] *See* para. 5 of the Amendment to the Memorandum of Understanding between the Department of Commerce (DoC) and the Internet Corporation for Assigned Names and Numbers (ICANN), 4 November 1999, http://www.icann.org/en/nsi/amend1-jpamou-04nov99.htm.

administration would qualify ICANN as a state actor[20] or a public private partnership.[21]

The main body of ICANN is the Governing Board, which has the exclusive power to decide on the corporation's policy and which finalizes the contracts with the registries through the CEO, who is a member of the Governing Board. Six members of the Board are elected by so-called support organizations, which represent different interest groups maintaining business contacts with ICANN, such as the Country Code Names Supporting Organization, the Generic Name Supporting Organization, and the Address Supporting Organization. Pursuant to Art. VII of the Bylaws, a further eight members are elected by a nominating committee. According to a complex formula, the principal interests should be represented, for example the Intellectual Property Constituency of the Generic Names Supporting Organization, an entity which was designed to reflect academic interests. Consumer and other public interest groups are also represented on the Board. These groups are selected by the Noncommercial Users Constituency of the Generic Names Supporting Organization, which represents the interests of users having no commercial interest in the Internet. This constituency forms the largest group of persons in this system. In addition, representatives of the so-called advisory committees are non-voting members in the nominating committee. There are four advisory committees: the Governmental Advisory Committee (GAC), the At-Large Advisory Committee, the Security and Stability Advisory Committee, the Root

---

[20] Jennifer Arnette-Mitchell, *State Action Debate Reborn Again: Why the Constitution Should Act as a Checking Mechanism for ICANN's Uniform Dispute Resolution Policy*, 27 HAMLINE JOURNAL OF PUBLIC LAW AND POLICY 307, 310 (2006); this view is not shared by Volker Röben, *International Internet Governance*, 32 GERMAN YEARBOOK OF INTERNATIONAL LAW 416 (2000). Röben focuses on the fact that the effectiveness of the administration relies on the acceptance by the Internet Service Providers, but he overlooks the fact that the powers of this corporation derive from a delegation of power by the U.S. Department of Commerce.

[21] ICANN President's Report: ICANN – The Case for Reform, 24 February 2002, www.icann.org/general/lynn-reform-proposal-24feb02.htm; Nico Krisch & Benedict Kingsbury, *Introduction: Global Governance and Global Administration in the International Legal Order*, 17 EUROPEAN JOURNAL OF INTERNATIONAL LAW 3 (2006); Robert Uerpmann-Wittzack, *Multilevel Internet Governance, Involving the European Union, Nation States and NGO's, in* MULTILEVEL REGULATION AND THE EU, 163 (Andreas Follesdal, Ramses A. Wessel & Jan Wouters eds., 2008).

Server System Advisory Committee and the Technical Liaison Group. Among these advisory committees, the At-Large Advisory Committee is of a specific interest.[22] It was created in 2002 in order to give Internet users the possibility of participating in the formulation of ICANN's Internet policies. The Committee is composed of 15 members from the five regions as defined by ICANN. In each of these regions a Regional At-Large Conference deals with questions pertaining to the Internet. In certain cases, the At-Large Advisory Committee may have a non-voting representative in the Subdivisions of the ICANN, *i.e.* the Generic Names Supporting Organization and the Country Code Names Supporting Organization. Similarly, it may have liaisons in the working groups of ICANN, including the Board of Governors. It also appoints 5 members – one from each region – to the Nominating Committee. Its impact on the ICANN's activities is mainly advisory in nature.

The Governmental Advisory Committee (GAC) has been given a specific role which reflects the development of the Internet governance. The GAC is composed of representatives of state governments, public authorities and representatives of international organizations such as the International Telecommunication Union. According to its founding principles, ICANN should be free from government influences – with the exception of the U.S. government. At the very beginning the Bylaws of ICANN excluded all government representatives from being members of ICANN organs.[23] The GAC was conceived as a type of independent governmental conference which cooperated with ICANN; it did not qualify as an organ of ICANN in a strict sense.[24] The situation changed with the reform of the ICANN Bylaws in 2002 when, due to the pressure from governments outside the United States and as a consequence of the terror attacks of 2001, it became evident that public interests, among them security interests, were concerned by the management of the Internet. Since 2002 the GAC may send non-voting liaison to all ICANN bodies, the Board of Governors included. In this way the governments are integrated in the structure of ICANN and they gain influence although they do not have voting rights.[25] The private structure of ICANN was upheld in the reform of 2002, however, a pro-

---

22 Art. XI(2(4)) of the Bylaws.

23 Art. V, sec. 5 of the Bylaws of 1998.

24 Wolfgang Kleinwaechter, *From Self-governance to Public-Private Partnership: The Changing Role of Governments in the Management of the Internet's Core Resources*, 36 LOYOLA OF LOS ANGELES LAW REVIEW 1104 (2003).

25 Art. VI, sec. 1, 9.1.a of the Bylaws of 2002.

vision was included in the Bylaws according to which ICANN recognizes that governments and public authorities are responsible for public policy and duly takes into account governments' or public authorities' recommendations.[26] This has been implemented by the obligation of the Board of Governors to grant a special treatment to proposals made by the GAC. The GAC can put issues to the Board of Governors and its advice on public policy matters must be duly taken into account. If the Board of Governors does not want to follow the advice, it must therefore provide reasons whereupon the GAC and the Board will then seek a mutually acceptable solution; if they do not reach such a solution, the Board of Governors has to explain why it cannot follow the advice of the GAC, and the statement will be without prejudice to the rights or obligations of GAC members with respect to public policy issues falling within their responsibilities.[27] The GAC cannot force ICANN to follow its proposals.[28] Nevertheless some authors assume that it is factually impossible for ICANN to take decisions against the will of the GAC, as states preserve their competences for public policy issues which include the competence to take the administration of the Internet under control by means of a national frame.[29]

4.2. Functions and Powers of ICANN

In order to fulfill its mission to coordinate the Internet's systems of unique identifiers, and in particular to ensure the stable and secure operation of the Internet's unique identifier systems, ICANN assigns, through its Board of Governors, the principal identifiers for the Internet, especially the domain names and the Internet protocols.[30] In order to implement its decisions, ICANN enters into agreements with the

---

26 Art. I, sec. 2.11 of the Bylaws of 2002.

27 Art. XI sec. 2 (21)(k) of the Bylaws of 2002.

28 Principle 2 of the Operating Principles of GAC reads: "The GAC shall provide advice and communicate issues and views to the ICANN Board. The GAC is not a decision making body. Such advice given by the GAC shall be without prejudice to the responsibilities of any public authority with regard to the bodies and activities of ICANN, including the Supporting Organisations and Councils." *See*: http://gac.icann.org/web/home/GAC_Operating_Principles.pdf.

29 Uerpmann-Wittzack (note 21), at 156 *et seq*.

30 Art. I sec. 1 of the Bylaws.

registries of domain names. It is not within ICANN's powers to administer the registries where Internet users have to subscribe in order to have access to the Internet as set up by ICANN. Instead, the domain names are administered by registries which might be private corporations, state entities or public private partnerships managing a TLD name, be it a generic TLD (gTLD) or a country code TLD (ccTLD). The registries conclude contracts with the registrars. As a rule, the latter are private corporations which assign Internet addresses to users. If a new ccTLD name is introduced the respective state has to determine the registry which should manage the top level domain and which has to be accredited by ICANN, for example DENIC for ".de", AFNIC for ".fr",[31] Nominet for ".uk", or EURid for ".eu".[32] As far as generic top-level domains are concerned, ICANN may choose the company which should administer the respective domain, for example VeriSign for the gTLD ".com". Despite its monopoly position, ICANN is generally free to decide whether or not to enter into any such agreement with a specific registry.

The registry agreements between ICANN and the registries of gTDL establish commitments of these registries to respect the policies of ICANN and to oblige the registrars to follow them.[33] This obligation includes even policies which come into force after the conclusion of the registry agreement.[34] The policies of ICANN to be respected embrace for example the principle of allocating registered names on a first come first served basis, prohibitions in warehousing or speculation of domain names, maintenance of and access to accurate and up-to-date informa-

---

31 Association à but non lucrative, *see*: www.afnic.fr.

32 Uerpmann-Wittzack (note 21), at 146 *et seq*.

33 Evelyn Lagrange, *L'Internet Corporation for Assigned Names and Numbers: un essai d'identification*, 108 REVUE GÉNÉRALE DU DROIT INTERNATIONAL PUBLIC 295, 333 (2004).

34 *See e.g.* Art. III sec. 3.1(b) of the Registry Agreement between ICANN and VeriSign of 1 March 2006: "At all times during the term of this Agreement and subject to the terms hereof, Registry Operator will fully comply with and implement all Consensus Policies found at: http://www.icann.org/general/consensus-policies.htm, as of the Effective Date and as may in the future be developed and adopted in accordance with ICANN's Bylaws and as set forth below." The agreement is available at http://www.icann.org/en/tlds/agreements/verisign/registry-agmt-com-01mar06.htm.

tion concerning domain name registrations, and so on.[35] In this way ICANN can enforce its policies throughout the Internet. In case of repeated violations of the policies, punitive, exemplary or other damages might be awarded by arbitrators. If the registry fails to cure a fundamental and material breach and if such a breach and failure has been finally determined by an arbitrator or court, ICANN may terminate a registry agreement.[36] Beyond these sanctions it can refuse the renewal of an agreement if the registry violated its obligations. ICANN's monetary liability under these registry agreements is limited to the amount of the registry fees.

The economic impact of the agreements between ICANN and the registries should not be underestimated. For example, the contract with VeriSign, a U.S. corporation, on the management of the generic domain name ".com", is of a high economic value.[37] VeriSign at one time controlled 85% of the market of generic registrations.[38]

ICANN does not conclude registry agreements with ccTLD registries as with the gTLD registries. However, the national registries authorized by each state for the assignment of names under its ccTDL have to be accredited by ICANN.[39] For this purpose, the national registries exchange letters with ICANN in which they commit themselves to securing and enhancing the stability and interoperability of the Internet's Domain Name System.[40] Starting with the German TLD registry DENIC in 2006 the national registries somehow unilaterally undertake the commitments vis-à-vis ICANN. As a rule there is no general obligation to follow all policies of ICANN, and no sanctions are foreseen in the event that a national registry violates ICANN policies. The

---

[35] ".com" Registry Agreement between ICANN and VeriSign of 1 March 2006 (note 34).

[36] *See e.g.* Art. VI sec. 6.1. of the Registry Agreement between ICANN and VeriSign of 1 March 2006 (note 34).

[37] Guillaume Le Floche, *Le sommet mondial de Tunis sur la Société de l'information*, 51 ANNUAIRE FRANÇAIS DE DROIT INTERNACIONAL 470 (2005).

[38] Milton Mueller, John Mathiason & Lee W. McKnights, *Making Sense of "Internet Governance": Defining Principles and Norms in a Policy Context, in* MacLean (note 7), 118.

[39] Lagrange (note 33), 295, 336.

[40] *See e.g.* exchange of letters between the Egyptian University Network as registry of ".eg" and ICANN, http://www.icann.org/en/cctlds/eg/eg-icann-letters-02nov08-en.pdf; further exchange of letters between national registries and ICANN can be found under the same link.

ccTLD registries are considered to form part of the public interest. The Principles and Guidelines for the Delegation and Administration of Country Code Top Level Domains, which have been adopted by the GAC in 2005 enshrined in section 4.1.1.: "Ultimate public policy authority over the relevant ccTLD rests with the relevant government or public authority; how this authority is exercised is determined by applicable law."[41] Thereby, any supervisory function exercised by ICANN is excluded.

The powers of a registry are delegated by the respective government, and only the government may re-delegate these powers.[42] ICANN's role is reduced to coordinating the Internet's system of top-level unique identifiers, and to ensure their stable and secure operation.[43] In the past, however, ICANN exercised the power to suspend or to end the use of a top level domain name. It froze the ".iq" (Iraq's country code), because the Chef Executive Officer of the registry managing this country code – the InfoCom – was accused of being a terrorist.[44] The Iraqis were forced to use generic domain names to continue their Internet presence. It is also not quite clear if ICANN has such a power after the ccTLD registries were qualified as part of public interest not subject to any supervision by ICANN. As a matter of fact, ICANN has the technical capacity to disconnect a registry of a specific ccTLD from the Internet.

The above described structure of the administration of domain names in the Internet on the one hand guarantees certain competitiveness, as ICANN concludes agreements with various registries; the registries contract with different registrars, so that registrants, that are users, ultimately have a certain choice where to register. On the other hand, ICANN can enforce its policies, at least vis-à-vis the gTLD registries, by stipulating in the registry agreements an obligation to respect these policies, and as ICANN (as the chief administrator of the Internet domain names) has a monopolistic position; the registries have to accept these commitments.

Apart from establishing contacts with the registries, ICANN's most important task is to develop the policies which are to govern the Inter-

---

41 http://gac.icann.org/web/home/ccTLD_Principles.pdf; Wittzack (note 21), at 158.

42 Sec. 7.1 of the The Principles and Guidelines for the Delegation and Administration of Country Code Top Level Domains.

43 Sec. 6.1.

44 Le Floche (note 37), at 464, 473.

net. These include, for example, the Inter-Registrar Transfer Policy which allows registrants to transfer their domain from one accredited registrar to another.[45] This possibility is designed to promote competition in the domain name space. Another policy develops principles for the allocation of Autonomous System Numbers to Regional Registries.[46]

Another – and perhaps one of the most important – policy of ICANN concerns the settlement of disputes surrounding domain names. ICANN developed a rapid, cheap and reasonable procedure for the resolution of conflicts over domain name ownership. It did so in close cooperation with WIPO, which led to the establishment of the Uniform Dispute Resolution Policy, which entered into force on 1 November 1999.[47] Pursuant to this policy, disputes are to be decided by an arbitration tribunal composed of three judges. According to paragraph 15 (a) of the Rules for a Uniform Domain Name Dispute Settlement the arbitration panel shall decide a dispute "on the basis of the statements and documents submitted in accordance with the Policy, these Rules and any rules and principles of law that it deems applicable". The panel may transfer or cancel a domain name,[48] it may not grant any form of compensation. At the time of writing, almost 6,000 cases have been settled. The decisions of these tribunals do not prevent the parties to the dispute from submitting the dispute to a competent municipal court.[49] These courts are not limited in their decisions to the legal rules which have been applied by the arbitration tribunal under the Uniform Domain Name Dispute Settlement Policy, but may come to different con-

---

45 *See* for the Inter-Registrar Transfer Policy: http://www.icann.org/en/transfers/.

46 *See* for the Allocation Policy of Autonomous System Numbers to Regional Registries: http://www.icann.org/en/general/global-policy-asn-blocks-31jul08-en.htm.

47 http://www.icann.org/udrp/udrp-policy-24oct99.htm.

48 Sec. 3(b) of the Uniform Domain Name Dispute Settlement Policy, http://www.icann.org/dndr/udrp/policy.htm.

49 *See* Section 4(k) of the Uniform Domain Name Dispute Resolutions Policy, http://www.domainregistry.de/disputeresolution.html; Karen Webb, *The "Appeal" of the Internet – Looking at the Uniform Domain Name Dispute Resolution Policy and How it is Newly Influenced by the Anticybersquatting Consumer Protection Act,* 43 SANTA CLARA LAW REVIEW 1431 (2003).

clusions.[50] While a case is pending before a municipal court and after the decision of such a court the decision of the arbitration tribunal will not be executed; the competent registry will neither cancel nor transfer the domain name under dispute.

5. Governance

Governance of the Internet has two facets: first, who is governing ICANN, and second, how is ICANN governing the Internet.

5.1. Who Is Governing ICANN?

This question is implicitly answered by ICANN's structure as described above. To sum up the main characteristics: following the philosophy of the bottom-up approach, governments formally play an advisory role within ICANN. ICANN's policies are formulated after input from various stakeholders, such as the registries and commercial and noncommercial users. As a rule, they participate in two ways in ICANN's decision-making procedures: first, they exercise advisory and consulting functions, the Board of Governors being the competent organ making the final decisions. The Board of Governors was conceived as a coordinator of the network and a translator of community consensus into decisions.[51] This structure contrasts with the classical model of international organizations, which are normally governed by the member states through their representatives in the decision-making organs. In ICANN the national governments are somehow bypassed. Instead, private individuals, be they physical or legal persons, are directly acting at an international level and are responsible for maintaining and foster-

---

50 *See* the case between the Spanish city of Barcelona and a private enterprise which used "barcelona.com" as an internet address. The Administration Panel under the Uniform Domain Name Dispute Resolution Policy of 5 May 2000 decided that domain name had to be transferred to the city of Barcelona, *see* http://www.wipo.int/amc/en/domains/decisions/html/2000/d2000-0505.html; the United States Court of Appeals for the Fourth Circuit decided that the Spanish trademark law was not applicable by U.S. courts, and that under U.S. law the private enterprise was the legitimate owner of the domain name, *see* http://www.icannwatch.org/article.pl?sid=03/06/03/0056220&mode=thread.

51 von Bernstorff (note 4), at 519.

ing international interest and goodwill, namely transnational communication. The second way in which stakeholders participate in the governance of ICANN are the elections as described below (9.2).

The only, albeit important, exception to the exclusion of direct governmental participation in the activities of ICANN is the role assumed by the U.S. government through the Department of Commerce. It gave the concession to ICANN to manage the domain name system and the Internet, and it can revoke this concession at any time, as described above. Even if the United States has yet to exercise direct influence on how ICANN fulfills its task, its position is strong because ICANN derives its power from the U.S. government.

5.2. How Is ICANN Governing the Internet?

As a counterpart to ICANN's horizontal structure – and its character as a private corporation – it does not govern through unilateral binding decrees or resolutions. Rather, ICANN enforces its policies through the conclusion of contracts with the registries which have to respect these. If ICANN decides that a certain TLD name should not be admitted, this decision is not binding in the sense that states or the Internet users have to respect it. ICANN just does not include such a name in its offer. This is true for all gTLD names, and to a certain degree also with regard to ccTLD names; for even if they form part of the public interest of the respective state, at least in doubtful cases – *e.g.* Palestine or Taiwan – ICANN has to decide whether it assigns a TLD name to such an entity or not.

Although ICANN policies do not have a directly binding effect on registries, registrars and Internet users, the registry agreements concluded between ICANN and the registries refer to these policies and oblige the registries to respect the policies. Of course, no registry is forced to conclude such an agreement with ICANN. Any relation with ICANN seems to presuppose voluntariness. However, as ICANN is the only organization which can give access to the Internet as it is structured today, that is through the assignment of TLDs, everybody who wants to be connected to the Internet, be it directly, as a registry, or indirectly, as registrar or user, has to enter into a contractual relationship and thereby to bow down to the conditions of ICANN. The monopoly position of ICANN in its crucial role for the Internet domain name system leaves no choice. As previously mentioned, the situation of ccTLD registries is somehow different, since ICANN has to accredit those which are empowered by the respective state organ without any freedom of choice. But even the ccTLD registries accept the policies of ICANN through the above mentioned letters of exchange for fear of a disintegration of the Internet if they do not respect the rules established by ICANN. The nature of the Internet, or in other words, the need for uniformity of the basic rules which govern the Internet is the most forceful argument for the recognition of these rules.

Therefore, the powerful position of ICANN is derived from its monopoly over Internet administration which is due to the structure of the Internet. The basic principle of the Internet is the interconnectivity of different computers and networks. This interconnectivity can be guaranteed only if there are rules which make it possible for different computers to contact each other. It seems evident that the question of addresses is of utmost importance: whoever wants to take part in Internet communication has to comply with the rules concerning the assignment of Internet addresses. It seems quite logical that the uniformity of the rules is best guaranteed by a single "legislator". The logic of the Internet favors monopolistic structures. Of course, everybody is free to establish an alternative Internet.[52] However, this would run counter to the Internet's objective of having a universal scope, that is, everybody being able to communicate with everybody else. If there were an alternative Internet, the question of compatibility and interconnectivity would arise again on a higher level, and again institutions would have to be created in order to establish the necessary links and the rules which govern them. In other words, the Internet does not "run itself", but requires management, which in turn means that someone must set the rules. At present, this task is incumbent upon ICANN. The structure of the Internet facilitates the need to respect ICANN's policies: the lack

---

52 There are other options, such as the Open Root Server Network, which, however, is considered to be just a supplement to ICANN. It shall guarantee that, in case a certain root zone is eliminated from the root server – for example, all addresses which end .de – the addresses can be reached. The idea behind the establishment of such an Open Root Server Network is to reduce the power of the U.S. agencies, *see* Wissenschaftliche Dienste des Deutschen Bundestages, Die Regulierung des Internets – Strukturen, Aufgaben und Arbeitsweisen von ICANN, DENIC, CENTR, CORE und ORSN, 28 November 2005, 29, http://www.bundestag.de/wissen/analysen/2005/2005_11_281.pdf.

of an alternative and the fear of Internet disintegration provide the strongest incentives for complying with ICANN's rules.[53]

6. Legal Principles Governing the Activities of ICANN

ICANN is not acting in a space without legal rules. The first layer of legal principles is established by ICANN itself, *i.e.* in the Bylaws, especially in Art. 1 sec. 2. They include the enhancement of the operational stability, reliability, security, and global interoperability of the Internet, the self-limitation to matters which require global coordination, participation of groups affected by the Internet governance, competition in the registration of domain names, transparency in the decision-making, neutrality – that is nobody should be privileged or discriminated for reasons not pertaining to the operability of the Internet –, and accountability – that is ICANN should be controlled in a due procedure. The only principle comparable to a fundamental right is the commitment to fairness[54] and the principle of non-discrimination.[55]

The Bylaws themselves stipulate in Art. 1 sec. 2: "These core values are deliberately expressed in very general terms, so that they may provide useful and relevant guidance in the broadest possible range of circumstances. Because they are not narrowly prescriptive, the specific way in which they apply, individually and collectively, to each new situation will necessarily depend on many factors that cannot be fully anticipated or enumerated. Moreover, because they are statements of principle rather than practice, situations will inevitably arise in which perfect fidelity to all core values simultaneously is not possible. Any ICANN body making a recommendation or decision shall exercise its judgment to determine which core values are most relevant and how they apply to the specific circumstances of the case at hand, and to determine, if necessary, an appropriate and defensible balance among competing values."

Principles which have a specific impact on ICANN's activities are transparency, accountability and participation. These principles are

---

53 Tamar Frankel, *Governing by Negotiation: The Internet Naming System*, 12 Cardozo Journal of International and Comparative Law 449, 453 (2004).

54 Art. I sec. 2 item 8 of the Bylaws.

55 Art. II sec. 3 of the Bylaws.

elaborated in greater detail in a document of January 2008 entitled "ICANN Accountability and Transparency Frameworks and Principles" (the "Frameworks and Principles Paper"), which synthesizes the philosophy of ICANN in this regard.[56] It states that there are three dimensions of accountability:

a. towards the stakeholders as represented in the various organs and bodies of ICANN;

b. corporate and legal accountability, which covers the obligations that ICANN has under through the U.S. legal system and under its Bylaws; and

c. participating community accountability, which is designed to ensure that the Board performs its tasks in keeping with the wishes and expectations of the ICANN community.

The only express reference in the Frameworks and Principles Paper to legal norms is the section on corporate and legal accountability. The legal obligations are derived from Californian and U.S. American law, albeit in a very generic way. Given that ICANN is constituted under Californian law, this is hardly surprising. Apart from this reference to legal norms, the Frameworks and Principles Paper does not specify the notion of accountability. Accountability is differentiated only with respect to various groups involved in ICANN's work. The quintessence of accountability is that ICANN has to pay due attention to the interests of these groups. The wishes and expectations which are submitted by them should be duly considered. In this sense the content of the accountability is not substantive but procedural by nature; exaggerating somewhat, one could say that the supreme law of the corporation is the will of its stakeholders and of the Internet community. This very generic way of identifying accountability criteria makes it quite difficult to implement the principle. By making the wishes of the stakeholders and the Internet community the focus, it becomes difficult to prove a violation of the accountability principle. The various stakeholders and Internet users do not share an identical interest. ICANN always has to strike a balance between conflicting interests. Therefore, it will be difficult to prove that in a given decision ICANN did not duly take into consideration the wishes of an affected group.

The principle of accountability is related to the principle of transparency. Transparency involves *inter alia* informing the Internet commu-

---

[56] http://www.icann.org/en/transparency/acct-trans-frameworks-principles-10jan08.pdf.

nity of proposals, plans and policies of ICANN. This enables the various interest groups to articulate their interests and participate in the elaboration of ICANN's policies. The principle of transparency is implemented by means of an Information Disclosure Policy,[57] a statement on Financial Accountability, and an external audit process.

The principle of participation is closely linked to the principles of accountability and transparency. The principle of participation mandates the participation of the Internet community and the various stakeholders in ICANN's decision-making process. It is an expression of the above-described bottom-up approach, which endows ICANN with a democratic character. The basic principle of ICANN does not consist of values such as human dignity or freedom of expression, or the protection of property (none of which are mentioned in the Bylaws) but in implementing the will of the diverse interest groups.

Since there are no international agreements which steer ICANN's policies, no guiding principles for this organization are established at an international level by treaty. A more difficult question is whether ICANN is bound by customary international law. Not being a classical international organization, and for that reason not a subject under international law, ICANN is not a direct addressee of any obligations under international law. But the question is whether ICANN has to respect certain rules of international law which could be relevant to its activities due to the fact that it is exercising functions of an international public interest. A private corporation exercising public functions for the international community is – with very few exceptions[58] – such a new phenomenon in international law that to date conventions on this subject matter have not been concluded and customary law has not yet developed any applicable principles. However, one could imagine that, in the future, should it become common practice for governance in the international field to be exercised by private corporations, certain rules and limitations under international law would be developed with regard to the form and the manner in which these functions are fulfilled. These rules would have to be respected irrespectively of the character of the actor who is exercising this function.

---

57 http://www.icann.org/en/transparency/acct-trans-frameworks-principles-10jan08.pdf.

58 *See e.g.* the International Committee of the Red Cross which was established as an association under Swiss law.

All in all, one can say that the scarcity of substantive rules which could guide the policy of ICANN reflects the basic character of this institution as a private corporation. Private corporations do not establish a bill of rights, but very concrete policies which are closely related to their activities. ICANN is aware of its importance for the Internet community. Therefore it formulates rules, which in a way will provide a procedural means which tempers its enormous power over the Internet by involving the Internet community in its decision-making procedures and by establishing accountability towards the Internet community.

7. Judicial Control

As described above ICANN is not beyond the law. The obligations deriving from its own Bylaws as well as and Californian and United States law can be enforced through a combination of quasi-judicial and judicial procedures. ICANN's Bylaws provide for an internal reconsideration of a decision at the request of an individual affected by the decision; this procedure provides for an internal review of decisions made by the Board of Directors in case a person feels unfairly treated or believes that a decision of the Board of Directors violates procedural requirements.[59] The so-called Reconsideration Committee is a subsidiary organ of ICANN's Board of Directors. It can issue recommendations, amend or overturn a decision which has not been taken by the Board of Directors as a whole. Second, the Bylaws provide for an Independent Review Panel, which is operated by an international arbitration provider, the International Centre for Dispute Resolution, a body which provides mediation and alternative dispute resolution services.[60] This Review Panel can be addressed by any person materially affected by a decision of ICANN. The International Review Panel can declare an action of ICANN incompatible with the Articles of Incorporation or the Bylaws and may make recommendations to the Board of Directors. Fi-

59 Art. IV sec. 2 of the Bylaws. In 2008 no such request was lodged, *see* Board Reconsideration, Annual Report 2008, https://cai.icann.org/files/meetings/cairo2008/reconsideration-report-06nov08.pdf; in the years before not many requests were filed, *see* list of requests at http://www.icann.org/en/committees/reconsideration/.

60 Art. IV sec. 3 of the Bylaws.

nally, an ombudsman is appointed who can investigate, publish his findings and give recommendations to the Board of Directors.[61]

The specific internal review procedure shows that ICANN does not conceive itself as a "normal" corporation under civil and corporate private law. By granting additional internal legal protection ICANN recognizes that specific interests of its users are at stake which go beyond the interests involved in a normal private contractual relationship. This type of dispute settlement is much more common with public administrations, where the parties are quite often involved (especially the individuals) try to find a solution to the conflict before internal organs of the respective entity or authority. This may help to avoid long lasting proceedings before courts. The reason why this internal dispute settlement is more likely to be found within public administrations derives the fact that, in contrast to private corporations, public administrations are not supposed to defend their own interest, but take into consideration the common interest, including the interests of individuals. ICANN by providing such dispute settlements just proves its proximity in character to organs of public administration.

The dispute settlement procedures established in the Bylaws can be considered to be effective and swift. However, a closer scrutiny shows that they correspond to the requirements of a judicial control only to a limited extent: the Reconsideration Committee is not an independent body and, therefore, can only offer "administrative" self-regulation. The ombudsman is independent, but as all classical ombudsmen he has no real judicial powers. While the ombudsman may investigate conflicts between affected persons and ICANN, he cannot deliver binding decisions. The Independent Review Panel may hand down such decisions as it is an independent body, but it has no power to quash a decision of the Board of Directors or to grant compensation. It is limited to a declaration of incompatibility with an act found in the ICANN Bylaws. The Uniform Domain Name Dispute Resolution Policy may only restitute a cybersquatted domain name, it cannot decide on damage claims. Those have to be brought before U.S. courts.[62]

If a dispute should arise between ICANN and a Registry, the registry agreements provide for a settlement of the dispute by arbitration pursuant to the rules of the International Court of Arbitration of the International Chamber of Commerce; the arbitration procedure should take

[61] Art. V of the Bylaws.

[62] http://cybersquatting.com/index.php?page=legal-actions.

place in the Los Angeles County in English.[63] As described above, ICANN cannot impose sanctions, such as the termination of a registry agreement, on a registry without an anterior decision by an arbitration court which determines a breach of the registry agreement. ICANN has no right to unilateral sanctions against registries. In this context the judicial control has an enormous importance for the limitation of ICANN's power.

An individual affected by the decision of ICANN can lodge a law suite against ICANN before a U.S. court, which will apply Californian or U.S. law respectively.[64] In this regard, ICANN is treated as a normal private corporation, and as long as it has this legal form it will be subject to U.S. jurisdiction. As the case may be a lawsuit between ICANN and another private person could also arise before a municipal court of another state.[65]

8. Legitimacy

8.1. The Problem of Legitimacy

The question of ICANN's legitimacy is of specific interest. Although the corporation manages an international public good, that is the access to the Internet, it is not formed by or subject to an international agreement, but rather is the creation of the U.S. government and has been delegated its authority by this government.[66] Therefore, the classical form of legitimacy of an international organization, that is the principle of consent which is achieved by the accession of the member states to the treaty establishing the international organization, as well as their participation in the bodies of the international organization, does not apply to ICANN.

---

63 Art. 5 sec. 5.2 b of the .biz Registry Agreement; Art. 5 sec. 5.1 b .com Registry Agreement of 1 March 2006, http://www.icann.org/en/tlds/-agreements/verisign/registry-agmt-com-01mar06.htm.

64 *See* list of law-suites in which ICANN has been involved, available at: http://www.icann.org/en/general/litigation-moore.htm.

65 *See pool.com v. ICANN*, before the Superior Court of Justice, Ontario, Canada, http://www.icann.org/en/general/litigation-pool.htm.

66 Lagrange (note 33), at 295, 337 *et seq.*

The question of legitimacy is likewise not solved by the fact that ICANN is established as a private corporation and that it concludes contracts with its partners who "voluntarily" enter into the agreements. As a rule, the question of legitimacy does not arise in contractual relations with the same intensity as it does in public law relations, which are mostly vertical. The consent which the partners give to the contract justifies all obligations resulting therefrom. *Volenti non fit iniuria.* However, as it has been described above, the partners of ICANN do not enjoy a free choice when dealing with ICANN. Contracting with ICANN is not the result of their free will. Rather, they are forced to do so for lack of an alternative if they want to participate in the Internet. Due to its monopoly, ICANN's position in the administration of a public good, that is access to the Internet more closely resembles that of a state agency. The legitimacy of state agencies, which as a rule are not established through direct elections, is in great part derived from the legal framework and the substantive principles which give direction to the decisions of these organs. As has been shown above, the principles which ICANN has to respect are quite vague, so that it would be difficult to enforce them.

8.2. Input Legitimacy

The lack of legitimacy conveyed by governments is compensated by two forms of input legitimacy. First, the groups and persons affected by the ICANN decisions participate in the decision-making process by exercising an advisory function. Their comments and proposals are to be duly taken into consideration by the Board of Directors. In a way, it is the weakest form of input legitimacy as there is no real obligation to follow the proposals. However, in practice interest groups' proposals play an important role in the development of ICANN policies. A defect in this type of legitimacy lies in the difference between the power of the interest groups affected by ICANN. As it turned out, the commercial interests are much better represented before ICANN than the interests of the common users.[67]

The second form of input legitimacy derives from the participation in the election of the members of the executive and advisory and electoral bodies by the respective interest groups which have a seat in specific

---

[67] von Bernstorff (note 4), at 522 *et seq*.

ICANN organs. In some of these bodies the "transmission belt" of democratic legitimacy is continued in the sense that its members are elected by the respective groups. For example, the At-large Constituency, which is elected at a regional level by Internet users, participates in the election of the Board of Governors through the nomination of five members to the nomination committee.

8.3. Output Legitimacy

For ICANN, output legitimacy is much more important than input legitimacy. Whether an institution has output legitimacy depends on how it fulfills its functions. Legitimacy does not require that the institution has the highest performance in an absolute sense. An institution already enjoys legitimacy if without its activities the situation were worse. If an institution cannot be replaced in the fulfillment of its functions because there is no alternative, its legitimacy also derives from its position.

In the case of ICANN output legitimacy flows from the efficient management of the Internet, which is mostly undisputed, and from the fact that ICANN actually, as a matter of fact, cannot be substituted by another organization as it holds the monopoly in the distribution of the top level domain names. Everybody who wants to use the connectivity of the Internet has to defer to the rules set up by ICANN. The rules of ICANN are accepted if for no other reason than the fact that there is no alternative. It does not mean that all decisions of ICANN are undisputed, but it does mean that, once they have been taken, they have to be complied with. This situation was concisely phrased as "Code is Law".[68]

9. Criticism of ICANN

The administration of the Internet by ICANN is not free from criticism. It is considered inappropriate that a national corporation under Californian law and under the supervision by the U.S. Department of Commerce manages the Internet which is considered to be a common good. Therefore, the World Summit of the Internet Society, which took

---

68 Wolfgang Kleinwächter, *Beyond ICANN vs. ITU, in* MacLean (note 7), 33.

place in Geneva in 2003 and in Tunis in 2005, discussed the topic extensively. The Tunis Agenda for the Information Society emphasized in para. 29 the full involvement of governments in the management of the Internet, and it places the governments even before the private sector.[69] In para. 35 lit. a the Tunis Agenda underlines that "policy authority for Internet-related public issues is the sovereign right of states. They have rights and responsibilities for international Internet-related public policy issues." It does not exclude the private sector when stating: "The private sector has had, and should continue to have an important role in the development of the Internet, both in the technical and economic field." The governments should have "an equal role and responsibility for international Internet governance and for ensuring the stability, security and continuity of the Internet".[70] Besides, questions concerning the interests of only one state should not be decided by other states. In this sense the Tunis Agenda declares in para. 63: "Countries should not be involved in decisions regarding another country's country code Top-Level Domain (ccTLD)."

A Working Group on Internet Governance, established by the Secretary General of the United Nations, identified as one problem of the Internet governance that "a vacuum within the context of existing structures, since there is no global multi-stakeholder forum to address Internet-related public policy issues. It came to the conclusion that there would be merit in creating such a space for dialogue among all stakeholders. This space could address these issues, as well as emerging issues, that are cross-cutting and multidimensional and that either affect more than one institution, are not dealt with by any institution or are not addressed in a coordinated manner."[71] The Working Group proposed four models. One of them aims at strengthening the participation of the governments and at the replacement of the U.S. government in the supervision of ICANN. A more radical proposal envisages the transfer of the most important competences of ICANN to a World Internet Corporation for Assigned Names and Numbers. A third one declares that a specific oversight organization is not required, but like-

---

[69] Available at: http://www.itu.int/wsis; the same ranking between the governments and the private sector can be found in para. 24 dealing with Internet governance.

[70] Para. 68 of the Tunis Agenda for the Information Society.

[71] Para. 40 of the report of the Working Group on Internet Governance to the Tunis World Summit of the Information Society, http://www.wgig.org/docs/WGIGREPORT.pdf.

wise favors more government participation. The fourth model proposes the establishment of an International Internet Council which should defend the interests of the public vis-à-vis ICANN. All the proposals share the common position of national governments in that the administration of the Internet should be strengthened. This should be an answer to the critique that in the management of the Internet public interests are at stake on which not only a private corporation under the supervision of one government should take decisions.

The U.S. government, while recognizing that public interests are concerned by the Internet administration and accepting the responsibility of each country for its ccTLD, strictly rejects the idea of giving up its supervisory function. In 2008 the government declared that it does not intend to transfer the authoritative control over the Internet administration to ICANN,[72] and the European Union did not insist in such a transfer fearing that the Internet governance could become too bureaucratic and open to abuse by governments which want to obstruct the freedom of information. Therefore, the basic structures of the Internet administration were maintained, including the competences of ICANN. To date, the World Summit of the Information Society has not had an impact on a substantial readjustment of the structure of ICANN to meet the requirement of an adequate consideration of the interests at stake. As a result of the World Summit of the Information Society, an Internet Governance Forum has been established by the UN Secretary General.[73] The Internet Government Forum is to offer a multi-stakeholder policy forum for discussion on the further development of the Internet outside ICANN. Thus far, three meetings have been held.[74]

---

[72] Letter of the National Telecommunications and Information Administration to the Chairman of ICANN of 30 July 2008, http://www.ntia.doc.gov/comments/2008/ICANN_080730.html; this letter refers to a former declaration of 2005 by the Government on the U.S. Principles on the Internet's Domain Name and Addressing System, Kieren McCarthy, *Bush Administration Annexes Internet*, THE REGISTER, 1 July 2005, http://www.theregister.co.uk/2005/07/01/bush_net_policy/.

[73] *See* para. 72 of the Tunis Agenda for the Information Society.

[74] *See* http://www.intgovforum.org/cms/index.php/aboutigf.

10. ICANN: Private Corporation or Public Authority?

The analysis of ICANN raises the question whether this organization can be ranked among international institutions which exercise international public authority as understood in the frame of this project.[75] In the case of ICANN, each of the three terms contained in the concept of "international public authority" involves difficulties that require detailed consideration.

10.1. The Public Character of ICANN

Prima facie, the private law character of ICANN and the contracts it concludes seem to exclude any assumption that it exercises *public* authority. However, upon closer inspection, ICANN loses its purely private law character. This has to do, first, with the existence of some principal-actor relationships linking ICANN to the will of public entities. The competences of ICANN are delegated by the U.S. government, and the U.S. government can re-delegate these competences if it wishes to do so. The U.S. government further exercises supervisory functions in the public interest. Further, even if government representatives do not participate in the voting by the organs of ICANN they factually play an important role by influencing how ICANN exercises its functions. They have liaison persons in various organs of ICANN, among them the Board of Directors. A special provision obliges ICANN to take into consideration the proposals of governments. ICANN further recognizes the public interests of each state in the management of its ccTLD. By accepting the policies and administration of the states in this field ICANN integrates decisions of public actors into its

Second, the functions which ICANN carries out are of a public character. ICANN administers a scarce common good, which is the access to the Internet, and decides on its assignment. Scarce technical facilities which serve basic needs of society normally are managed by the state, other public entities, or under their supervision. A prominent example is the International Telecommunication Union, being among other

[75] *See* Armin von Bogdandy, Philipp Dann & Matthias Goldmann, *Developing the Publicness of Public International Law: Towards a Legal Framework for Global Governance Activities*, in this volume.

things in charge of the administration of radio frequencies.[76] It is shaped as a classical international organization based on an international treaty and composed of and controlled by the member states. Even if the purely technical administration of the Internet can be fulfilled by a private corporation it is beyond doubt that issues of public interest are at stake. ICANN's Bylaws recognize public law interests linked to the administration of the Internet. The management of the ccTLDs is qualified as forming part of public interests. It fits into this line of argumentation that the World Summit of the Information Society tried to enlarge the state control over the Internet, because it identified in the Internet governance public policy issues.

It follows from this that ICANN can be qualified as exercising *public* authority. This conclusion is in line with the views of other scholars who qualify ICANN's activities without hesitation as an element of global administration.[77] Even though their concept of global administration might differ from the concept of international public authority which lies at the core of this project, there seems to be a shared conviction that the mentioned public elements in the organizational setup of ICANN justify this qualification.

10.2. The International Character of ICANN

The *international* character of the functions carried out by ICANN could be cast into doubt because of the stronghold of the U.S. government on the basic infrastructure and its unwillingness to share its power with other states. However, in order to get an idea of the true character of ICANN, one has to take into consideration two important aspects: first, international stakeholders, especially of the governments of almost all states participate in the administration of the internet access. Second,

---

[76] Art. 1 para. 2(a) of the ITU Constitution.

[77] Bruno Carotti & Lorenzo Casini, *Complex Governance Forms: Hybrid, Multilevel, Informal, in* GLOBAL ADMINISTRATIVE LAW, 29 *et seq*. (Sabino Cassese et. al., eds., 2008). Available at: http://iilj.org/GAL/documents/GAL Casebook2008.pdf. In the preface to this book the editors emphasize with respect to private organizations exercising global governance: "Moreover, there are other significant examples of innovative governance methods, mechanisms and principles, of which any fully-rounded theory of global administration would have to take account."; Krisch & Kingsbury (note 21), at 3; Kleinwaechter (note 24), at 1104; von Bernstorff (note 4), at 511.

ICANN's activities do not only have an factual impact on the internet management in all countries, but it is the objective of this corporation to influence and form a communication system on an international level. For both reasons one has to qualify ICANN as an international institution.

10.3. Does ICANN Exercise Public Authority?

A third question is whether ICANN exercises public *authority* by the unilateral legal determination of others. If the question is put directly in this manner it has to be answered negatively. The policies of ICANN are not directly binding; ICANN does not unilaterally issue acts which establish obligations for individuals or states. ICANN enters into contact with private parties only through contracts which establish obligations for the other party. Nevertheless, ICANN could be considered exercising authority by factually determining others in a unilateral way. One has to take into account the monopoly which ICANN exercises in the administration of Internet access by the assignment of Internet addresses. ICANN decides with which registry of gTLD names it concludes a registry agreement. Even if ICANN has to respect the principle of non-discrimination, it is free to choose among corporations which want to function as registry. As ICANN is the only organization offering access to the Internet via assignment of Internet addresses, there will normally be more than one competitor. In such a constellation the choice of ICANN with whom it concludes the contract is a unilateral act. The corporations which want to become a registry of a gTLD have no choice but to conclude the agreement with ICANN for lack of an alternative.[78] They have to accept the conditions under which ICANN concludes the agreement, among them all the policies which ICANN has elaborated. The registry agreements, as a rule, do not only refer to current policies concerning the conclusion of an agreement, as has been shown above, but also to policies adopted at a later stage. So, a corporation has no choice with whom to conclude the registry agreement, it has no real influence on the content of these agreements and it has even to accept a subsequent unilateral change of the content of the

---

[78] As has been shown above, the situation with the ccTLD is different, as ICANN's power is somehow counterbalanced by the obligation to accredit the proposed registries of the ccTLD names. In this sense a balance is struck between the public authority of ICANN and the public interest of the States.

agreement. Therefore, the agreement cannot be conceived as being based on the free consent but is somehow unilaterally dictated by ICANN. In spite of the form of an agreement through which ICANN enforces its policies, in essence ICANN unilaterally exercises public authority through the administration of a public good.

With regard to the ccTLD registries, ICANN is not exercising unilateral authority in the same way as with regard to gTLD registries because, as explained above, states consider the management of the ccTLD as part of their public interest. There is no contract regulating the division of authority between the states and ICANN in the management of the ccTLD. ICANN unilaterally recognizes the public interests of states in its Bylaws, and the ccTLD registries which derive their powers from the respective states somehow unilaterally declare their compliance with the policies of ICANN. They do so because they recognize the crucial role of ICANN in the management of the Internet and for lack of an alternative. ICANN can enforce its policies because of its unique position.

The case of ICANN is of special interest for the legal conceptualization of global governance for it shows that private law elements may be introduced into the administration of international public goods. This parallels the development in municipal administrative law, where an ongoing privatization of the legal forms of administration can be observed. The case of ICANN exemplifies that the main criteria for what is international public authority is not the form in which it is exercised. More important is the objective of the administration. If it is a public good, there is a public interest. Wherever the public interest is at stake, organs or organizations are established which should take care of the public interest, and at the last instance they exercise unilateral power to fulfill their task.

International Administration of Holocaust Compensation: The International Commission on Holocaust Era Insurance Claims (ICHEIC)

*By Steven Less**

---

* In the interest of transparency, one of the features of international institutional law with which my case study is concerned, I would like to mention that I have encouraged and assisted relatives in submitting claims to ICHEIC, but stand in no other relationship to the organization than that of a critical observer. In memory of the drowned and in honor of the saved, I dedicate this article to Miriam (Maier) Less, John H. Less, and Carol (Less) Shachtman.

A. von Bogdandy et al. (eds.), *The Exercise of Public Authority by International Institutions*, Beiträge zum ausländischen öffentlichen Recht und Völkerrecht 210, DOI 10.1007/978-3-642-04531-8_21, © Springer-Verlag Berlin Heidelberg 2010

A. Background

I. Contextual Considerations

The most important change in public international law over the past century has been a re-direction of its focus exclusively on states to a broadened scope of subjects including, most importantly, individual human beings. This shift in the status of individuals may be directly traced to the widely acknowledged need, in the aftermath of the Second World War, for a more adequate response to the Holocaust and other large-scale atrocities than that offered by traditional international law. Substantive concerns led to the development of human rights law.[1] Victims' demands for compensation or restitution for the material injuries caused by genocidal Nazi persecution spurred a parallel procedural revolution. The innovation lay in national and international recognition of individuals' rights to assert such claims on their own behalf against their own governments, foreign states and foreign private entities.[2]

---

[1] *See, e.g.*, Daniel Levy & Natan Sznaider, *The Institutionalization of Cosmopolitan Morality: The Holocaust and Human Rights*, 3 JOURNAL OF HUMAN RIGHTS 143, 143-144 (2004).

[2] *See, e.g.*, Richard M. Buxbaum, *A Legal History of International Reparations*, 23 BERKELEY JOURNAL OF INTERNATIONAL LAW 314, 314-317 (2005); Thomas Buergenthal, *International Law and the Holocaust*, *in* HOLOCAUST

In relation to other procedural-institutional changes in international law which have likewise found their impetus in awareness of the horrors perpetrated by Nazi Germany during World War II, the International Commission on Holocaust Era Insurance Claims (ICHEIC) represents a unique development. This institution is distinguishable from both a traditional claims commission and an arbitral tribunal.

Classically, claims commissions have been established under bilateral, lump-sum, postwar reparations settlements to resolve demands for compensation by individuals. An example of such a commission may be found in the context of the Nazi Persecution (*Princz*) Agreement[3] between the United States and Germany, which facilitated compensation of a small group of American citizens who survived Nazi concentration camps.[4] The settlement in the *Princz* case,[5] including its claims processing arrangement, corresponded to the traditional practice under customary international law. Pursuant to that practice, claims of individuals against a foreign state may only be espoused by the state of which they are citizens.[6]

RESTITUTION: PERSPECTIVES ON THE LITIGATION AND ITS LEGACY, 17 (Michael J. Bazyler & Roger P. Alford eds., 2006).

3 Agreement Between the Government of the Federal Republic of Germany and the Government of the United States of America Concerning Final Benefits to Certain United States Nationals Who Were Victims of National Socialist Measures of Persecution, 19 Sept. 1995, 35 ILM 195 (1996). For the implementing legislation, see Holocaust Survivors Claims Act, Section 119, incorporated by reference in Pub. L. No. 104-99, Section 211, 109 Stat. 26, 37-38 (1996).

4 Following a lump-sum payment of $2.1 million by Germany to the US in 1995 for distribution to Hugo Princz and 10 other survivors, US implementing legislation entitled similarly situated persons to have their claims adjudicated by the Foreign Claims Settlement Commission, an agency within the US Dept. of Justice. Claims found by the Commission to satisfy eligibility requirements were awarded with distributions from an additional German lump-sum payment to the US in 1999 of $18 million. *See* www.usdoj.gov/fcsc/holocaustclaims.htm. This Internet citation and all which follow were last accessed on 13 July 2008.

5 Princz v. Federal Republic of Germany, 26 F.3d 1166 (D.C. Cir. 1994) (settled following dismissal for lack of subject matter jurisdiction by reason of the defendant's sovereign immunity).

6 *See* Ronald J. Bettauer, *Holocaust Claims: The Role of the United States Government in Recent Holocaust Claims Resolution*, 95 ASIL PROCEEDINGS 37-38 (2001).

The United Nations Compensation Commission (UNCC), which processed claims resulting from the Iraqi invasion and occupation of Kuwait in 1990, represented a similar compensation approach. However, the UNCC's establishment within a multilateral framework rendered it an atypical example of a postwar claims commission. The UNCC, moreover, constituted a subsidiary organ of the UN Security Council, was multinational in composition and processed an unprecedented number of individual damage claims.[7] Nevertheless, the UNCC still relied on the state espousal doctrine.[8]

As indicated, ICHEIC also differs from an arbitral tribunal such as the Claims Resolution Tribunal (CRT), which made awards under the US court-supervised settlement in the *Swiss Banks Litigation*.[9] Finally, ICHEIC was not set up – at least formally – as a public foundation, or an agency of such a foundation, to administer an out-of-court settlement under national law.[10] It stood, however, in close proximity to the German Foundation "Remembrance, Responsibility and the Future," a domestic nongovernmental institution charged with distributing a fund

---

[7] *See* John J. Chung, *The United Nations Compensation Commission and the Balancing of Rights Between Individual Claimants and the Government of Iraq*, 10 UCLA JOURNAL OF INTERNATIONAL LAW AND FOREIGN AFFAIRS 141, 147-148 (2005); Norbert Wühler, *Institutional and Procedural Aspects of Mass Claims Settlement Systems: The United Nations Compensation Commission, in* INSTITUTIONAL AND PROCEDURAL ASPECTS OF MASS CLAIMS SETTLEMENT SYSTEMS 17-22 (The International Bureau of the Permanent Court of Arbitration ed., 2000).

[8] *See* Wühler (note 7), at 17.

[9] *See In re* Holocaust Victim Assets Litigation, 105 F. Supp. 2d 139 (E.D.N.Y. 2000), aff'd, 413 F.3d 183 (2d Cir. 2001) (hereinafter *Swiss Banks Litigation*). The settlement covered claims not only related to the dormant accounts of Holocaust victims in Swiss banks, but also looted assets, denials of asylum, slave labor and insurance policies. In exchange for payment of $1.25 billion by the Swiss banks, the plaintiffs dropped all claims against the banks and the Swiss government for damages related to the Holocaust and the war. Decisions over individual claims were left to the Claims Resolution Tribunal (CRT), which operated essentially as an arm of the District Court. *See* Burt Neuborne, *Preliminary Reflections on Aspects of Holocaust-Era Litigation in American Courts*, 80 WASHINGTON U. LAW QUARTERLY 795, 801 (20002).

[10] The plaintiffs' lead counsel in the Swiss banks case, who also served as a principle lawyer in the forced and slave labor suits against German companies and as a trustee of the German Foundation saw the German Foundation (*see, infra*, note 11) as such an entity. *See* Neuborne (note 9), at 821.

stocked with equal contributions by German industry and the German government. The German Foundation was meant to implement a bilateral executive agreement between the United States and Germany resolving compensation claims primarily relating to the use of slave and forced labor by German companies.[11]

ICHEIC can be seen as a largely private or hybrid private-public and national-international form of regulatory authority. From its inception, ICHEIC advertised itself as a global mechanism for processing insurance claims against non-state-owned insurance companies and responding to related humanitarian concerns that continued to beg a response more than half a century after Germany's military defeat and the removal of its Nazi regime. The following examination of ICHEIC – which completed its claims and appeals processing in March 2007 and officially closed shop in June 2007,[12] but whose humanitarian programs have ongoing significance – offers a case study of an administrative manifestation of the above-noted "epochal break"[13] in international law's history.

---

11 Agreement Concerning the Foundation "Remembrance, Responsibility and the Future" of 17 July 2000, 39 ILM 1298 (2000). The German Foundation, which provided the framework for a $5.2 billion out-of-court settlement, was established under German domestic law by the *Gesetz zur Errichtung einer Stiftung "Erinnerung, Verantwortung und Zukunft"* (EVZStiftG) (Law on the Creation of a Foundation "Remembrance, Responsibility and the Future"), 2 Aug. 2000, BGBl. I-1263, last amended by Art. 1 of the *Gesetz vom 21. Dez. 2006* (Law of 21 Dec. 2006), BGBl. I-3343. *See* Bettauer (note 6), 39. The executive agreement was intended to facilitate the dismissal of multiple class action lawsuits in the US through the creation of the German Foundation, on the one hand, and the provision of a "statement of interest" by the State Department to seized courts, on the other. This mix of domestic and international aspects warrants reference to the German Foundation as a "hybrid settlement." *See* Neuborne (note 9), at 820.

12 *See* Press Release, ICHEIC Announces Successful Completion of Holocaust Era Insurance Claims Process, 20 March 2007, and the Chairman's Cover Letter (accompanying an ICHEIC "legacy document," cited, *infra*, note 44, 18 June 2007, both available at www.icheic.org.

13 Levy & Sznaider (note 1), at 143.

II. Moral Qualms

Does assessing ICHEIC as an administrative process bureaucratize Holocaust compensation and obscure or devalue the moral significance of the issues with which the Commission has dealt? Those with misgivings may join the numerous critics who have questioned the legitimacy of the litigation which began in the 1990s on behalf of Holocaust victims to resolve claims involving dormant bank accounts, forced labor, stolen artwork and insurance policies, as well as the path taken under the bilateral executive agreement to reach "closure" of outstanding issues through the German Foundation. The controversy is not new. A commonplace of Holocaust compensation discourse – voiced by those asserting claims as well as those confronted with them – has been that no pecuniary redress can ever restore the victims to the position in which they found themselves prior to the crime against humanity perpetrated against them. Justice is said to be unattainable in this context. Moral responsibility, it is argued, can never find closure. Thus, some have labeled Holocaust-related litigation as inappropriate and pecuniary resolution of Holocaust-era claims as degrading.[14]

Material disputes concerning the Holocaust undeniably also contain "extra-legal components."[15] Morals and memory are no less at stake where Holocaust victims have asserted claims for material loss.[16] Con-

---

14 For references to the original postwar debate over the propriety of Holocaust compensation and its more recent manifestation, *see* Libby Adler & Peer Zumbansen, *The Forgetfulness of Noblesse: A Critique of the German Foundation Law Compensating Slave and Forced Laborers of the Third Reich*, 39 HARVARD JOURNAL ON LEGISLATION 1, 54-57 (2002); MICHAEL J. BAZYLER, HOLOCAUST JUSTICE: THE BATTLE FOR RESTITUTION IN AMERICA'S COURTS 286-293 (2003).

15 Vivian G. Curran, *Competing Frameworks for Assessing Contemporary Holocaust-Era Claims* 25 FORDHAM INTERNATIONAL LAW JOURNAL 107 (2001) (Symposium issue).

16 *See id.*, 111-113; Adler & Zumbansen (note 14); Roman Kent, *It's Not About the Money: A Survivor's Perspective on the German Foundation Initiative, in* HOLOCAUST RESTITUTION: PERSPECTIVES ON THE LITIGATION AND ITS LEGACY, 205, 213-214 (Michael J. Bazyler & Roger P. Alford eds., 2006); Edward B. O'Donnell, Ambassador, Special Envoy for Holocaust Issues, Compensation and Restitution for Victims of the Holocaust, Remarks at the Claims Conference Board of Directors, New York City, 11 July 2006, available at www.state.gov/p/eur/rls/rm/69488.htm; Pierre A. Karrer, *Mass Claims Proceedings in Practice: A Few Lessons Learned*, 23 BERKELEY JOURNAL OF

sequently, emphasis may instead be better placed on revealing details of the genocide which occurred and its individual impact, thereby responding to the victims' unassuaged need for "re-individualization."[17] Notwithstanding this forceful argument, consideration of the property rights of those who – as victims of an unparalleled industrialized mass murder – were simultaneously robbed in what has been called "thefticide,"[18] the greatest mass theft in history, seems natural and necessary.[19] Their compensation, whether resulting from litigation or within the framework of an administrative process, involves recognition of "a simple, straightforward and virtually universally acknowledged basic legal right that civilized societies afford their citizens."[20]

III. Introduction to the Subject-Matter, Regime and Interests Involved in the ICHEIC Process

1. Addressing an Ignored Dimension of the Holocaust

Under traditional international law, individuals who suffered damage during wartime have had to look to their governments to represent their interests once hostilities ended and the victorious states entered

INTERNATIONAL LAW 463 (2005). For Nobel laureate and Holocaust survivor Elie Wiesel, remembrance of the *Shoah* and its victims was a "sacred" task and "had to do with something other than financial evaluation... [I]t had to do more with morality and even theology." STUART E. EIZENSTAT, IMPERFECT JUSTICE. LOOTED ASSETS, SLAVE LABOR, AND THE UNFINISHED BUSINESS OF WORLD WAR II ix (foreword by Elie Wiesel, 2003).

17 *See* Curran (note 15), at 116-117.

18 *Id.*, at 120 (quoting Deputy Treasury Secretary Stuart Eizenstat, the principal representative of the US government on Holocaust issues during the Clinton Administration).

19 For the view that claiming individual as well collective monetary compensation for Jewish victims of Nazi persecution is an understandable, natural and legitimate notion, *see* Siegfried Moses, *Die jüdischen Nachkriegsforderungen* (Tel Aviv 1944), reprinted in: IUS VIVENS: QUELLENTEXTE ZUR RECHTSGESCHICHTE (Wolf-Dieter Barz, Andreas Roth & Stefan C. Saar eds., 1998). The expectation that Germany would restore property it had taken or provide material reparation for the loss it caused reflects nothing less an "elementary principle of justice and human decency." NANA SAGI, GERMAN REPARATIONS, A HISTORY OF THE NEGOTIATIONS 76 (1980).

20 Curran (note 15), at 120.

into agreements for reparations with those they defeated. This model was largely applied after World War II as well despite its inadequacy in view of the enormity of Germany's crimes. Millions of people were stateless or unwilling to return to their original countries after fleeing Nazi persecution and surviving the atrocities committed by Nazi Germany. Their interests could only be represented by the states to which they fled. In the case of Jewish survivors, that was for many the new State of Israel. Jewish non-governmental organizations, represented by the Claims Conference, [21] also articulated the claims of Jews outside Israel as well as the Jewish people as a whole with regard to the loss of private assets belonging to individuals who were exterminated during the Holocaust leaving no heirs. Ultimately, postwar Germany agreed to provide reparations to Israel as well as some individual compensation and humanitarian assistance to certain categories of persons who had been damaged.[22] Bilateral and multilateral agreements for reparations were also entered into with Western countries and, after the reestablishment of diplomatic relations following German reunification and the end of the Cold War, with former Communist-bloc countries as well.[23] However, efforts to achieve justice for Holocaust survivors were stymied by the omission of significant classes from among those who received remedial payments.

One class widely neglected in both the international reparations agreements and domestic German restitution and compensation legislation comprised holders and beneficiaries of insurance policies purchased before the war. As in the case of dormant Swiss bank accounts from the Holocaust-era, litigation over which resulted in a settlement for $1.25 billion in 2000,[24] insurance policies also involved substantial amounts of assets. Estimates of the value of life insurance policies alone extended up to $15 billion.[25] Figures such as this rested on compelling evidence

---

[21] The Conference on Jewish Material Claims Against Germany (Claims Conference). *See* http://www.claimscon.org.

[22] *See* Agreement between the State of Israel and the Federal Republic of Germany (Luxembourg Agreement), 10 Sept. 1952, 162 UNTS 206 and German *Wiedergutmachung* legislation (*see*, *infra*, note 27).

[23] For details regarding postwar Germany's financial response to Nazi persecution, *see* German Federal Ministry of Finance, Compensation for National Socialist Injustice: Indemnification Provisions (2006 edition).

[24] *See* note 9.

[25] *See* Sidney Zabludoff, ICHEIC: *Excellent Concept but Inept Implementation, in* HOLOCAUST RESTITUTION: PERSPECTIVES ON THE LITIGATION AND

that insurance policies, particularly for the large Jewish population in Eastern Europe, were "the poor man's Swiss bank account."[26]

2. *Legal Interests: Material Redress vs. Immunity from Unjustified Claims*

Surviving policyholders and beneficiaries who demanded that the insurance companies fulfill their contractual obligations or compensate for damages encountered an overwhelmingly negative and often demeaning response. In addition to requiring death certificates and documented proof of ownership of a policy or entitlement to benefits, insurers also often declared that the policies had meanwhile been closed or that the claimants' injuries were only nominal in view of postwar currency devaluations. Faced with potential legal liability, insurers raised substantive arguments which ignored the special circumstances surrounding the claims. Thus, payments were frequently denied on the grounds that policies had lapsed due to nonpayment of premiums. Insurers often insisted, moreover, that policies had previously been satisfied by payments made under government directive into blocked and later confiscated bank accounts, or that the claims were extinguished by prior payments under Germany's compensation or restitution laws[27] or under its postwar international reparations agreements.[28] In many cases,

---

ITS LEGACY 260, 267 (Michael J. Bazyler & Roger P. Alford eds., 2006). Total sums ranging up to $29 billion for life, property, dowry and education insurance were mentioned in the class action cases on insurance. *See* Sven F. Kellerhof, *Versicherer zahlen Millionen-Entschädigung*, WELT-ONLINE, 20 March 2007, http://www.welt.de/wirtschaft/article770075/Versicherer_zahlen_Millionen-Entschaedigung.html.

[26] Bazyler (note 14), at 110. See also Press Release, $16 Million Paid to Holocaust-Era Insurance Claimants from ICHEIC Humanitarian Fund, 30 March 2004, available at http://www.icheic.org/newsroom.html. *But see* The International Commission on Holocaust Era Insurance Claims (ICHEIC), Lessons Learned: A Report on Best Practices, June 2007, 7-8 (hereinafter ICHEIC, Lessons Learned), available at http://www.icheic.org/pdf/ICHEIC%20Best%20Practices%20Paper.pdf (maintaining that the analogy, which raised claimants' expectations, was relativized by ICHEIC's own research).

[27] *See Bundesentschädigungsgesetz* (BEG) (Federal Compensation Law), 29 June 1956, BGBl. I-559, and the *Bundesrückerstattungsgesetz* (BRüG) (Federal Restitution Law), 19 July 1957, BGBl. I-734. *See* BAZYLER (note 14), at 144.

[28] *See* Detlev Vagts & Peter Murray, *Litigating the Nazi Labor Claims: The Path Not Taken*, 43 HARVARD INTERNATIONAL LAW JOURNAL 503, 510-528

insurers maintained that the policy-issuing company had ceased conducting business or was nationalized by a postwar communist regime, or that relevant records no longer existed.[29]

When litigation began, the insurance companies also raised significant procedural defences. Insurers questioned the jurisdiction of the courts or the appropriateness of adjudicating Holocaust era insurance claims under the political question doctrine as well as the notions of *forum non-conveniens* and comity. Further, defendants argued that such claims were barred under prevailing statutes of limitations and treaties, in particular, the London External Debt Agreement[30] and the Two-Plus-Four Treaty.[31] The insurers additionally denied the standing of the claimants to represent the designated class where collective suits were lodged.

In the class actions brought before American courts against the insurance companies which issued the original policies or their successors – many of which had meanwhile become multinational conglomerates doing billions of dollars of business in the United States, plaintiffs nevertheless sought judicial review and financial redress. They asserted that the companies had breached their contractual obligations and were unjustly enriched by appropriating assets to which they lacked any entitlement.[32] These arguments were bolstered legally and morally by the

---

(2002) (for analysis of what the authors consider powerful legal defences of German industry which the plaintiffs would have had to overcome for the forced labor cases dismissed in connection with the German Foundation agreement to proceed). *But see* Adler & Zumbansen (note 14) (identifying significant weaknesses in these traditional defences).

[29] See BAZYLER (note 14), at xvi, 117, 138; Derek Brown, *Litigating the Holocaust: A Consistent Theory in Tort for the Private Enforcement of Human Rights Violations*, 27 PEPPERDINE LAW REVIEW 553, 560 (2000).

[30] Agreement on German External Debts (London Debt Agreement), 27 Feb. 1953, 333 UNTS 3.

[31] Treaty on the Final Settlement with Respect to Germany (with Agreed Minute) (Two-Plus-Four Treaty), 12 Sept. 1990, 1696 UNTS 124. In effect, the London Debt Agreement of 1953 (note 30) postponed consideration of the liability of German companies until the conclusion of a peace treaty with Germany, something which the Two-Plus-Four Treaty of 1990 functionally represents. *See* Adler & Zumbansen (note 14), at 30-37; Neuborne (note 9), at 813-816.

[32] For an overview of the litigation, *see* Michael J. Bazyler, *Nuremberg in America: Litigating the Holocaust in United States Courts*, 34 U. OF RICHMOND LAW REVIEW 1 (2000-2001).

assertion of collusion. Evidence indicated that companies had in many cases willingly and profitably worked together with the Nazi regime. When indemnifying claims by making payments into blocked accounts, for example, companies had been allowed to keep a transaction fee and paid less than the policies' face value. Some companies insured facilities in concentration camps, including Auschwitz. The head of Germany's largest insurer, Allianz, for instance, was the second Minister of Economy under the Nazi regime and belonged to the inner circle of supporters of SS chief Heinrich Himmler.[33]

3. Regime: Globalized Compensation of Holocaust-Era Insurance Claims

With the establishment of ICHEIC as an alternative to litigation, its founders imagined that the need for adjudicating the parties' conflicting legal positions on an issue which had previously eluded a satisfactory response could be avoided by means of a central, unified or standardized regime for compensation. ICHEIC was, thus, envisaged as a way of providing expedited redress to deserving individuals who had lacked a remedy under national and international law for many decades. As a non-judicial, regulatory mechanism,[34] ICHEIC represented for its advocates a pragmatic solution meant to provide already elderly Holocaust victims, and in some cases their families, with a small measure of justice rather than the recognition of legal rights.[35] It ultimately resulted in compensatory payments for about half of those who submitted claims, either on the basis of named or identified policies or on humanitarian grounds. Direct humanitarian payments to individuals resulted where evidence showed that policies had existed although an issuing company could not be further specified, the company no longer existed or had been nationalized, or the policy had been confiscated. Significant humanitarian distributions to social programs were also made from separate funds contributed by member insurance companies in recognition of "heirless" claims.

---

33 *See id.*, 114-116.

34 *See* Holocaust Era Insurance Restitution after AIA v. Garamendi: Where Do We Go From Here? Hearings Before the House Committee on Government Reform, 108th Cong., 1st Sess., 54, 62 (16 Sept. 2003) (hereinafter Hearings 2003) (Statement of Lawrence S. Eagleburger, Chairman, ICHEIC).

35 *See, e.g.*, O'Donnell (note 16).

IV. Overview of the Activity of ICHEIC

1. Purpose and Legal Basis

Indisputably, Germany's postwar international reparations agreements as well as national compensation programs developed in the 1950s and 1960s were deficient and incomplete with respect to lost or stolen assets of Holocaust victims, including those relating to insurance policies. After the Cold War and following German unification in 1990, the major obstacles to seeking compensation for claims previously relegated to the back-burner appeared to have disappeared.[36] Class action lawsuits filed in American courts against European insurance companies focused renewed attention on the matter during the 1990s.[37] Because of the claimants' advanced age, time was of the essence, if survivors were personally to receive any redress for wrongs they had suffered.[38] This bolstered the demands of survivors' groups as well as the US government for an expedited process to resolve the insurance issue. Ultimately, however, the financial threat posed by the lawsuits, the negative publicity they gave the defendant companies, as well as potential federal regulatory sanctions[39] provided the prime impetus for an agreement which offered the companies an alternative to costly litigation.[40]

ICHEIC was intended by its founders as a mechanism for pursuing individual claims against European insurance companies which would al-

---

36 *See* note 31.

37 By the end of 1998, 25 insurers had been sued. *See* BAZYLER (note 14), at 132. The National Association of Insurance Commissioners (NAIC), in which all state insurance regulators participate, formed a working group to examine the matter; insurance commissioners in several states held hearings at which the companies were questioned on their non-payment histories. *Id.*, 69.

38 Holocaust survivors were dying at a rate of 10% per year. *See* Stuart E. Eizenstat, *The Unfinished Business of World War II*, *in* HOLOCAUST RESTITUTION: PERSPECTIVES ON THE LITIGATION AND ITS LEGACY 297 (Michael J. Bazyler & Roger P. Alford eds., 2006).

39 *See* H.R. 1210, Holocaust Victims Insurance Relief Act of 2003, 108th Cong., 1st Sess. (11 Mar. 2003). *See*, moreover, H.R. 1905, Comprehensive Holocaust Accountability in Insurance Measure, 108th Cong., 1st Sess. (1 May 2003), recognizing the authority of states to pass laws requiring insurance companies to disclose policyholder names and the current status of Holocaust era insurance policies, and creating a federal cause of action permitting claimants to sue insurers for payment of such policies in federal court.

40 *See* EIZENSTAT (note 16), at 339.

low both claimants and the companies to avoid protracted litigation in US courts and shield the companies from threatened governmental restrictions on their business in the United States. As such, and in view of "the national interest in maintaining amicable relationships with current European allies," it also represented the preferred policy choice of the US government and received its clear endorsement.[41]

A Memorandum of Understanding (MOU) signed on August 25, 1998 by several major European insurance companies, American state insurance regulators, several international non-governmental Jewish and survivor organizations, and the State of Israel constituted ICHEIC's legal basis.[42] Under the MOU, the new entity was delegated a sizeable bundle of competences relating to development of a just process for collecting and facilitating the signatory companies' processing and settling of insurance claims from the Holocaust period. ICHEIC's authority encompassed: the formulation and implementation of procedures for filing, investigating, valuating, and resolving such claims; negotiation with European insurers to provide information about and settlement of unpaid insurance policies; promulgation of an audit program and monitoring to assure company compliance with the MOU and ICHEIC decisions; and establishment and administration of a related humanitarian fund.

2. *Scope*

The MOU committed member insurance companies to providing access to policyholder data, making contributions to the humanitarian fund to

---

41 *See* American Insurance Association v. Garamendi, 539 U.S. 396, 396-397, 421-423 (2003) (striking down California's attempt to force insurance companies licensed in the state, including the subsidiaries of European companies, to reveal the names of their Holocaust-era policyholders). The Court's holding rested primarily on its determination that the US government, through the executive agreement which led to the German Foundation and its provision for the Foundation to work with ICHEIC, had clearly formulated national foreign policy on the issue of Holocaust-era insurance claims and that the state law directly conflicted with this legitimate exercise of executive authority and was accordingly preempted. *See also In re* Assicurazioni Generali S.p.A. Holocaust Insurance Litigation, 340 F.Supp. 2d 494, 500, 503-505 (SDNY 2004) (hereinafter *Generali II*) (dismissing multiple suits against Generali on the basis of unambiguous executive branch policy favoring resolution of claims by ICHEIC).

42 The MOU is available at http://www.icheic.org/pdf/ICHEIC_MOU.PDF.

be administered by ICHEIC and covering the costs of ICHEIC's investigation of claims, as well as oversight and auditing of the insurers' compliance with the agreed claims process.[43] Roughly $500 million was ultimately received by ICHEIC for compensatory payments of eligible claims and humanitarian purposes from ICHEIC member companies and from funds made available through the conclusion of side-agreements relating to parallel processes.

To identify and expeditiously resolve unpaid insurance Holocaust-era insurance claims, ICHEIC issued rules and guidelines which the participating companies were obligated to apply. ICHEIC, moreover, negotiated and concluded agreements with partner entities, seeking to ensure analogous application of its prescriptive efforts, particularly with regard to relaxed standards of proof and policy valuation.

ICHEIC also developed criteria for making humanitarian awards where claimants had only anecdotal information about the existence of a policy and could not name a specific company, and where no additional documentation could be found. Such awards were paid by ICHEIC out of a separately maintained section of the humanitarian fund.

B. Legal Analysis

I. Institutional Framework

1. Is ICHEIC "Public" and "International"?

ICHEIC was chartered as a *Verein* (private association) under Swiss law. Its principle US address was in Washington, D.C., but claims were processed at an office established in London.[44] ICHEIC thus appears to be a private, nonprofit institution representing the signatories of the

---

[43] *See* Megan Hoey, *Holocaust Era Insurance Claims: Compensating the Unimaginable*, 30 AUSTRALIAN ALTERNATIVE LAW JOURNAL 134, 140 (2005).

[44] Initially outsourced, claims processing in-house came at a later stage. *See* ICHEIC's "legacy document": LAWRENCE S. EAGLEBURGER & M. DIANE KOKEN, WITH CATHERINE LILLIE, FINDING CLAIMANTS AND PAYING THEM: THE CREATION AND WORKINGS OF THE INTERNATIONAL COMMISSION ON HOLOCAUST ERA INSURANCE CLAIMS 42 (2007), available at http://www.icheic.org/pdf/ICHEIC%20Legacy%20Document.pdf. ICHEIC also established a call-center in New York, whose operations were outsourced to the Claims Conference. *See id.*, 21, 42.

MOU and subject primarily to Swiss and British law. If ICHEIC was not legally constituted as an international organization, with a headquarters in the United States, that lay in the shared intention of the signatories to impede litigation before American courts.[45] A glance behind ICHEIC's formal veil, however, reveals the inadequacy of defining the legal personality of ICHEIC as that of a purely private, nongovernmental, domestic-law entity. ICHEIC may instead be better conceived as a hybrid public-private and national-international body with regulatory functions regarding a subject of transborder public concern.

The MOU which established ICHEIC represents a private associational agreement with a public and international dimension.[46] It was signed by and reflected the interests of national and sub-national authorities as well as nongovernmental organizations and private parties. However, ICHEIC's qualification as a hybrid private-public institution not only derives from the partially "public" source of the competences it was delegated by the MOU. ICHEIC's public component may also be seen in its socio-political purpose of expediting the non-adjudicative processing of Holocaust era insurance claims where the resolution of conflicting private interests through litigation threatened a delay offensive to basic conceptions of human rights.

In setting out the public-private, national-international institutional framework of ICHEIC, the MOU envisaged an entity whose membership would equally balance the competing interests at stake. Half of the 12 members of ICHEIC were to be designated by American state insurance regulators from the National Association of Insurance Commissioners[47] as well as the World Jewish Restitution Organization (WJRO),[48] the Conference of Jewish Material Claims Against Germany

---

45 *See id.*, 42; BAZYLER (note 14), at 136; EAGLEBURGER, KOKEN & LILLIE (note 44), at 42.

46 *See* Hearings 2003 (note 34), at 11, 12 (Statement of Rep. Henry A. Waxman, Ranking Minority Member of Committee on Government Reform).

47 *See* note 37.

48 Major Jewish organizations established the WJRO in 1992 to pursue restitution of Jewish communal property and redress for material damage to individual Jews in Eastern Europe during the Holocaust. *See* http://www.jafi.org.il/education/worldwide/synagogues/part2e.html.

(Claims Conference), and the State of Israel. The other half were to be designated by the signatory European insurance companies.[49]

Appointment of an independent Chairperson unaffiliated with any of the persons or entities otherwise represented in ICHEIC was left to the 12 regular Commission members. ICHEIC formally began with the appointment of former US Secretary of State Lawrence S. Eagleburger as its Chairman in October 1998. ICHEIC's Chairman was supported by two senior staff, consisting of a Chief Operational Officer and a Chief Financial Advisor, and a combined staff of about 20 persons in the Washington and London offices.[50] While the MOU appears to establish a relatively compact institution, the ICHEIC articles of association allowed for the formation of committees,[51] which consisted of delegates of Commission members, to address particular tasks. As a result, ICHEIC meetings sometimes involved almost 100 people.[52]

In its provision for observers, the MOU reflects the unusual "mix of negotiating partners"[53] which lent a multi-dimensional or hybrid character to the entity it created. Each of the two above-mentioned interest groups was to designate two alternate representatives with observer status. Five additional observers were foreseen. Of these, three were to be designated by the WJRO together with the Claims Conference and the State of Israel, one by the "European Economic Commission" and one by the US Department of State.[54] This grant of observer-status to delegates of supranational as well as national and subnational governmental authorities further manifests the semi-public and international personality of ICHEIC.

---

49 The signatory insurance companies were Allianz, AXA, Basler Leben, Generali, Zurich Financial Services, and Winterthur Leben. Basler Leben resigned shortly after signing the MOU.

50 *See* ICHEIC Holocaust Era Insurance Claims Processing Guide 8 (1st Edition, 22 June 2003), available at http://www.icheic.org/pdf/ICHEIC_CPG.pdf (hereinafter ICHEIC Claims Processing Guide);

51 *See* EAGLEBURGER, KOKEN & LILLIE (note 44), at 20. Despite the legacy document's reference to the articles of association, they are absent from the ICHEIC website.

52 *See id.*, 19.

53 Bettauer (note 6), at 39.

54 Presumably, the "European Economic Commission" referred to the Commission of the European Communities. For indications of the more active role than that of a mere passive observer played by the US government in ICHEIC, *see* note 41.

2. *ICHEIC and the Trilateral Agreement*

Another unusual feature of ICHEIC relates to its side-agreements or "partnerships." Separate operating agreements were concluded on claims processing with what ICHEIC termed "partner entities."[55] ICHEIC's attempt to establish a global or integrated process for resolving all outstanding insurance claims and pursuing related humanitarian purposes involved agreements with MOU signatory companies,[56] agreements with governmental restitution/ compensation organizations and/or insurance industry associations,[57] and an agreement with a Jewish restitution/ compensation organization.[58]

The most important and elaborate of ICHEIC's side-agreements was that with the German Foundation and the German Insurance Association (GVD) (hereinafter Trilateral Agreement),[59] This instrument places

---

55 *See* ICHEIC Claims Processing Guide (note 50), 9; EAGLEBURGER, KOKEN & LILLIE (note 44), at 31-32.

56 Agreement was entered into by ICHEIC and the WJRO with Assicurazioni Generali S.p.A. (Generali) in 2000. In 2001, the Generali Fund in Memory of the Generali Insured in East and Central Europe Who Perished in the Holocaust (Generali Trust Fund/ GTF), established in Israel, was recognized in a further agreement as the implementing organization. *See* ICHEIC Claims Processing Guide (note 50), 9. This arrangement ended in Nov. 2004, when the Generali Policy Information Center in Trieste, Italy, assumed claims-processing functions. *See* EAGLEBURGER, KOKEN & LILLIE (note 44), at 29. Agreement was concluded in 2003 with AXA, Winterthur and Zurich on the terms of claims processing and additional funds for ICHEIC. *See id.*, 30.

57 ICHEIC, the German Foundation and the German Insurance Association (*Gesamtverband der deutschen Versicherungswirtschaft*) (GDV); ICHEIC and the General Settlement Fund (Austria); ICHEIC and the Buysse Commission (Belgium); ICHEIC and the *Sjoa* Foundation (the Netherlands); ICHEIC and the Drai Commission (France). *See* ICHEIC Claims Processing Guide (note 50), 10-14.

58 While an official text is unavailable, the Humanitarian Claims Processing Agreement between ICHEIC and the Conference on Jewish Material Claims Against Germany is referred to in INTERNATIONAL MASS CLAIMS PROCESSES: LEGAL AND PRACTICAL PERSPECTIVES 36 (Howard M. Holtzmann & Edda Kristjansdottir eds., 2007).

59 Agreement Concerning Holocaust Era Insurance Claims among ICHEIC, the German Foundation and the German Insurance Association, 16 Oct. 2002, available at http://www.icheic.org/pdf/agreement-GFA.pdf. The 111-page document, consisting of a main agreement and eleven annexes, served

ICHEIC in a peculiar light for the following reasons: it finally got the claims process off the ground after an ineffective start; it resulted in the publication of about 360,000 potential policyholder names, thereby alerting many potential claimants to their possible eligibility for receiving an award; it provided ICHEIC with the bulk of its funding;[60] and it effectively shielded the European insurers from the jurisdiction of American courts. Although the German Foundation came about through separate negotiations and entailed formal recognition of ICHEIC as an autonomous entity,[61] the Trilateral Agreement for practical purposes transformed ICHEIC into a *de facto* implementing organ of the German Foundation.[62] Accordingly, ICHEIC may be said to represent an example of hybrid public-private as well as national-international administration also when seen from this perspective.[63]

---

as a model for similar agreements sought with Austria and France. *See* ICHEIC Claims Processing Guide (note 50), at 11-12.

[60] Most of the funds available for payment of claims under the ICHEIC process came from the German Foundation's DM 10 billion (€ 5.1 million) fund, to which German insurance companies had contributed about 10%. In total, DM 550 million resulted for ICHEIC from the side-agreement among the German Foundation, the German Insurers Association and ICHEIC, of which DM 200 million was for named or matched policies, with the remaining DM 350 million for humanitarian purposes, including claims resolved under the humanitarian claims process. *See id.*, 10-11.

[61] *See Satzung der Stiftung "Erinnerung, Verantwortung und Zukunft"* (Statutes for the "Remembrance, Responsibility and the Future" Foundation), available at http://www.stiftung-evz.de/eng/foundation_remembrance_responsi bility_and_future/statutes/, which lists ICHEIC among the institutional partners operating in the subject-area of the Foundation that "will assume functions assigned to them by the Foundation Act and relevant contracts. They are not organs of the Foundation, which will work together with them to fulfill the purpose of the Foundation ...," as envisaged under Section 7 of the EVZStiftG (note 11), amended 11 June 2007, Section 9.

[62] For the German insurers, ICHEIC could indeed be considered an administrative sub-organ of the German Foundation. *See* Eizenstat (note 38), at 300; Kai Hennig, *The Road to Compensation of Life Insurance Policies: The Foundation Law and ICHEIC, in* HOLOCAUST RESTITUTION: PERSPECTIVES ON THE LITIGATION AND ITS LEGACY 251, 254 (Michael J. Bazyler & Roger P. Alford eds., 2006).

[63] Evidence of ICHEIC's hybrid quality may be seen in the fact that, under the executive agreement signed on 17 July 2000 (note 11), the US and Germany agreed that insurance claims against German companies that fell within the handling procedures of ICHEIC would be processed by the companies and the

II. Substantive Aspects

1. Mandate

Under the MOU's normative framework, ICHEIC was charged with establishing a just process to collect insurance claims from the Holocaust period[64] and to facilitate their processing by signatory companies. Signatory companies agreed to determine the claims' current status following ICHEIC guidelines, which were to be negotiated and established by consensus among the ICHEIC membership. The scope and structure of the ICHEIC claims process was extended through ICHEIC's partnerships agreements. *Inter alia*, they contributed to ICHEIC's operating funds and the funds from which claimants were paid. As part of the agreements, the partner organizations stipulated that they would process claims in a manner broadly consistent with ICHEIC rules and guidelines, and that ICHEIC would be provided with copies of all offers and denials.[65]

The following six primary normative prescriptions, addressed to both ICHEIC and the member companies, constitute the claims mechanism established by the MOU or what may be considered ICHEIC's "substantive programming:"

First, ICHEIC is to "initiate and conduct an investigatory process" to assess the current status of claims filed (MOU, Section 4). For purposes of the investigatory process, ICHEIC is given authority for obtaining information about victims of the Holocaust from relevant archives such as *Yad Vashem* in Jerusalem. Beyond this, it is delegated two related functions: first, promulgating an "audit mandate" which shall outline the work of the auditing firms engaged by ICHEIC or the member companies to insure that there is reasonable review of the insurers' files; and second, establishing a review mechanism to assess the acceptability of previous investigatory work by the companies (MOU, Section 4 (a)).

Under the same subsection, participating insurers or insurance regulators are committed to ensuring "complete and unfettered access" to the

---

GDV on the basis of these procedures and additional processing rules to be accepted by ICHEIC, the German Foundation and the GDV.

64 Holocaust-era insurance claims were defined as those relating to policies issued to Holocaust victims between 1920 and 1945. *See* MOU (note 42), Section 4.

65 For a general description, *see* EAGLEBURGER, KOKEN & LILLIE (note 44), at 31.

relevant data by the auditing firms to the extent necessary for their work. This duty is further qualified by the stipulation that "[s]uch access shall be in accordance with local insurance authorities and laws." And, as if this had not sufficed to cause paralysis, dispute seems to have been pre-programmed into the ICHEIC process under Section 4 (b) of the MOU. Here, ICHEIC appears charged with assuring potential claimants' adequate notification of the possibility to submit claims. The provision reads: "[ICHEIC] will address the issue of a full accounting by the insurance companies and publication of the names of Holocaust victims who held unpaid insurance policies."

Second, ICHEIC is to "establish a claims and valuation process" to resolve and pay individual claims at no cost to the claimants (MOU, Section 5). This entails promulgation of claims processing guidelines and "establishment of relaxed standards of proof that acknowledge the passage of time and the practical difficulties of the survivors, their beneficiaries and heirs in locating relevant documents, while providing protection to the insurance companies against unfounded claims."

Third, the MOU requires that each participating company "establish its own dedicated account" for immediate payment of claims found valid and attributable to that insurer by virtue of named or matched claims (MOU, Section 7).

Fourth, the insurance companies are obligated under the MOU, Section 8, to contribute to a Special (Humanitarian) Fund which consists of two sections and respective, separately maintained accounts. These accounts allow for compensation under the "Specific Humanitarian Section" in cases where claimants are unable to attribute their policies to a particular and currently existing insurance company (Section 8 (A)(1)), or where policies were nationalized or confiscated (Section 8 (A)(2)). Under the "General Humanitarian Section" (Section 8 (B)), for which the insurers' contributions are understood to "give due consideration to the category of 'heirless claims,'" funds "shall be used for the benefit of needy victims of the Holocaust and for other Holocaust-related humanitarian purposes."

Fifth, member companies are required to cover the expenses of ICHEIC and each insurer individually will bear the costs of auditing its records "and any expenses relating to the processing or investigation of claims" against itself (MOU, Section 9).

Sixth, the MOU (Section 10) requires the signatories to "work to achieve exemptions from related pending and future legislation… for those insurers that become signatories to the MOU and which fully co-operate with the process and funding of ...[ICHEIC]."

2. *Secondary Rules*

ICHEIC announced initiation of the claims process in February 2000. Despite ICHEIC's so-called "outreach program," which consisted of a global campaign advertising the possibility of claiming previously unpaid Holocaust-era insurance policies, very few potential policyholder names were initially revealed.[66] Yet, this was very often precisely the basis upon which individuals could decide whether to file claims when they could not name a specific company or knew nothing of a policy's existence. Critics saw the slow process and limited release of policyholder names as evidence of the insurance companies' bad faith in view of the advanced age of the claimants. A result was negative media attention, litigation, regulatory sanctions under US state legislation and repeated Congressional hearings.

Clearly, the program outlined in the MOU required further specification with regard to ICHEIC's investigatory process, the auditing of insurers' processing work and the processing of humanitarian claims, valuation of policies and standards of proof. The development of the relevant secondary rules, which became essential elements of the ICHEIC normative framework, took place only gradually and without direct public input. At least initially, ICHEIC's committees[67] served as a forum for negotiations and facilitated the relevant compromises required for the Commission to reach the consensus necessary for adop-

---

[66] By mid-Nov. 2000, ICHEIC's website listed only 39,000 of the more than 519,009 names that were eventually published by the end of 2003. *See* Press Release, International Commission on Holocaust Era Insurance Claims announces publication of additional 20,000 Holocaust-era insurance policies, 16 Nov. 2000, available at http://www.icheic.org/pdf/2000-1116.pdf; EAGLEBURGER, KOKEN & LILLIE (note 44), 37. For a response to critics, echoing insurers' argument that full disclosure would drive up the cost of claims processing without offsetting the need for further investigation, *see* Letter from Lawrence S. Eagleburger, ICHEIC Chairman, to Tom Davis, Chairman, Committee on Government Reform 1, 9, 10 (23 Oct. 2003); available at http://www.icheic.org/pdf/2003-1023.pdf.

[67] *See* note 51 and accompanying text.

tion of such rules.[68] After negotiating impasses, however, the consensus requirement was abandoned and the insurers agreed to abide by the Chairman's directives.[69]

Valuation guidelines enabling companies to calculate offers were finalized in 2002, distributed to MOU-members and posted on the ICHEIC website.[70] Guidelines for policies issued in Germany, which varied somewhat from those otherwise applicable, were included in ICHEIC's side-agreement with the German Foundation and the GDV in October 2002.[71]

Relaxed standards of proof[72] were adopted by ICHEIC to ensure thorough investigation by the companies of every claim regardless of the kind of evidence submitted and serious assessment of "the strength and plausibility of non-documentary or unofficial documentary evidence."[73] Where the claimant could prove the existence of a policy, the burden shifted to the company to demonstrate the policy's status. It was up to insurer to show an adjustment of the policy's value or its previous payment. To substantiate an assertion that the company had already fulfilled its contractual obligations, it had to produce proof from its own records or other external documentary evidence. The rules take account of the difficulties companies faced in satisfying their burden of proof because of the destruction of documents during the war or in the normal course of business. Thus, any documentary evidence that payment was made to the insured or a beneficiary, whether from the company's own records or external sources, was acceptable. However, where the

---

68 *See In re* Assicurazioni Generali S.p.A. Holocaust Insurance Litigation, 228 F. Supp.2d 348, 357 (2002) (hereinafter *Generali I*) (citing evidence of the understanding of Chairman Eagleburger and Generali regarding consensus).

69 BAZYLER (note 14), at 158. For a critical assessment, tracing many of ICHEIC's problems to the "inept governance" which resulted from abandonment of the committee approach to consensus-building in favor of decision-making by the Chairman based on solely on consultation with the head of the London office and selected ICHEIC members , *see* Zabludoff (note 25), 262-263.

70 ICHEIC Guide to Valuation Procedures (edition 22 Oct. 2002), available at http://www.icheic.org/pdf/ICHEIC_VG.pdf.

71 *See* Trilateral Agreement (note 59), Annex D.

72 *See* ICHEIC, Standards of Proof (15 July 1999), available at http://www.icheic.org/pdf/ICHEIC_SP.pdf; *see also* Trilateral Agreement (note 59), Annex B.

73 ICHEIC Claims Processing Guide (note 50), at 20.

company could not show that the policy was paid or its value should otherwise have been adjusted, it was called upon to offer full payment of the sum insured using the valuation guidelines.[74]

Succession guidelines also formed an important component of the ICHEIC process. They determined the ability of claimants to inherit benefits of a policy from the person originally entitled to payment upon the death of the insured or maturity. In contrast to the secondary norms already described, the succession guidelines were not separately posted on the ICHEIC website. They were, however, also part of the Trilateral Agreement and published in that context.[75]

3. *Rules Specifically Concerning ICHEIC'S Humanitarian Funds*

The MOU delegates to ICHEIC administrative functions concerning the distribution of humanitarian funds. Those functions have noteworthy multilevel features.

Criteria for evaluating claims which could not be matched to a particular or existing company or policy under the ICHEIC process, but which nevertheless demonstrated plausibility, were developed under the supervision of the Senior Counselor to ICHEIC. Chairman Eagleburger appointed former US National Security Advisor Samuel R. Berger to this post. Berger also acquired responsibility for overseeing the process for handling the respective humanitarian awards provided for under MOU, Section 8 (A). The actual task of evaluating Section 8 (A)(1) claims was contracted out to the Claims Conference.[76]

ICHEIC also decided on allocations from the general humanitarian fund reserved for the benefit of needy Holocaust victims worldwide.[77] Acting on behalf of ICHEIC, the Claims Conference distributed the

---

74 *Id.*, 22-23.

75 *See* Trilateral Agreement (note 59), Annex C.

76 *See* Hearings 2003 (note 34), at 75-76 (Statement of Chairman Eagleburger). For detailed treatment of the humanitarian claims aspect of the ICHEIC process in the context of a comparative survey, *see* Holtzmann & Kristjansdottir (note 58).

77 The ICHEIC's competence to make such allocations is recognized under the law establishing the German Foundation in Section 9 (4) nos. 3 and 5 as well as Section 9 (5), EVZStiftG (note 11).

bulk of this money to various social welfare programs.[78] Additionally, ICHEIC earmarked a portion of the fund for strengthening Jewish culture and heritage, to counteract the Nazis' efforts to achieve their obliteration, and to memorialize those who did not survive.

Decisions regarding the appropriate programs and the best approach toward allotting payments for social welfare as opposed to Holocaust-related education were made by ICHEIC *ad hoc* and drew criticism for their lack of transparency. According to Eagleburger, however, prior consultation with the "humanitarian community" as well as with US insurance regulators overcame this objection.[79] He referred in this respect to the ICHEIC Service Corps, which was run by Hillel Foundation and the University of Miami under the fiscal oversight of the Claims Conference.[80] Further humanitarian distributions have gone to programs administrated by other private institutions or governmental agencies.[81]

III. Procedural Aspects

1. ICHEIC's Procedural Functions

Claims processing was regulated under guidelines promulgated by ICHEIC. A copy of these guidelines, dated 22 June, 2003 and designated as a "first edition," was posted on the ICHEIC website.[82] As de-

---

78 The Claims Conference (*see* note 21) was asked by ICHEIC to implement the distribution of the fund, which began in 2003 with allocations originally earmarked through 2011. *See* http://www.claimscon.org/index.asp?url=news/icheic_new_grants.

79 ICHEIC's proportional allocation of funds for social welfare (80%) and educational purposes (20%) was also defended as being "[i]n keeping with general practice for funds reclaimed from Holocaust-related assets..." EAGLEBURGER, KOKEN & LILLIE (note 44), at 61.

80 *See* Hearings 2003 (note 34), at 76 (Statement of Chairman Eagleburger). The ICHEIC Service Corps Program encouraged voluntary social assistance to Nazi victims by students. *See* ICHEIC, Humanitarian Fund, http://www.icheic.org/fund.html.

81 Initiative to Bring Jewish Cultural Literacy to Youth in the Former Soviet Union (developed and run by the Jewish Agency for Israel) and the ICHEIC Program for Holocaust Education in Europe (established and administered by the *Yad Vashem* International School for Holocaust Studies).

82 ICHEIC Claims Processing Guide (note 50).

scribed in the guidelines, ICHEIC assumed responsibility for sending claims it received to the appropriate companies/entities for further processing. ICHEIC did not seek, in the first instance, to evaluate such policies. In contrast to the process established under the CRT regime for resolving insurance claims related to the Swiss banks settlement, ICHEIC was not an arbitral tribunal. It was, however, committed to ensuring that: (1) claims that named an insurance company were sent to and reviewed by that company; (2) claims that did not name a company were checked by those MOU-member companies (or companies associated with programs covered by ICHEIC side-agreements) which sold policies in the country where the claimant lived; and (3) offers or denials on claims were determined in accordance with ICHEIC guidelines.[83]

In other words, in addition to determining the framework of claims processing by developing the secondary norms previously discussed, ICHEIC played a direct three-fold administrative role in the overall claims process: it facilitated the transfer of claims to the companies for their evaluation and decisionmaking, tracked the progress of the companies' handling of claims, and verified resulting decisions against ICHEIC guidelines. The process itself fell into the three following stages in cases where claimants managed to identify a particular company: 1) filing and assignment to appropriate company or companies/partner organization or entity (under the relevant ICHEIC side-agreements); 2) company evaluation and determination; and 3) appeals.[84]

2. *Role of the Companies in Claims Processing*

In the second stage of the process, the company/ partner entity was required to search its records to determine the existence of claimed policies. Evidence of prior compensation or restitution was also sought at this stage. Under the Trilateral Agreement, a significant multilevel aspect of the ICHEIC claims process may be seen in this connection: the GDV together with the *Bundeszentralkartei* (BZK) (Federal Filing Agency) were namely charged with making an initial check for previous governmental compensation or restitution covering claims before the named company was required to proceed with its own search. Accord-

---

83 *See id.*, 14.

84 Appeals are considered in greater detail, along with monitoring, in the context of oversight in Part B V.

ing to the ICHEIC guidelines, policies that had previously been subject to decisions under the German Federal Compensation Law[85] were ineligible for compensation under the ICHEIC claims process.[86] For companies covered by the Trilateral Agreement, a positive result on this check therefore generally meant no further obligation by the company to investigate or evaluate a claim.

Following the BZK check, the companies evaluated claims for which there had been no previous compensation. They were bound to do so taking into account all information provided by the claimant, data discovered by the insurer during investigation of its records, and any supporting data submitted by ICHEIC as a result of its own search of additional archives. Final assessments by the insurers required application of the relaxed standards of proof and the valuation guidelines previously mentioned. Copies of the companies' determination to offer an award or deny a claim were sent simultaneously to the claimant and ICHEIC.

3. Claims Matching by ICHEIC

ICHEIC played a unique role during the second stage of claims processing by independently attempting to match claims with policyholder names. The massive investigatory work which this necessitated was the result of a fundamental compromise. Rather than release all policyholder names for the relevant period, companies agreed to make their archives available to ICHEIC or auditors operating within the ICHEIC process. To ensure payment where justified despite many claimants' inability to name a particular company, ICHEIC did the following two kinds of archival searches: 1) it compared names of policyholders submitted to ICHEIC by claimants with those provided by the insurance companies; and 2) it compared claimants names with a further database containing the companies' lists of names plus names obtained from public or governmental archives.[87] Resulting matches were communicated to the claimants and the appropriate companies.

---

[85] *See* note 27.

[86] *See* ICHEIC Claims Processing Guide (note 50), 19; Trilateral Agreement (note 59), Section 2 (1)(C).

[87] *See* Hearings 2003 (note 34), at 73-75. In the relevant cases, claims were matched under the Trilateral Agreement against the list of Holocaust-era insurance policies compiled by the *Bundesanstalt für Finanzdienstleistungsaufsicht*

An unpublished manual entitled "ICHEIC Protocols and Procedures for Matched Claims" provided secondary rules formalizing the procedural standards to be applied in these cases.[88] The primary normative basis for ICHEIC's research, Section 4 of the MOU, broadly provides that ICHEIC "shall initiate and conduct an investigatory process to determine the current status of ... insurance policies issued to Holocaust victims... [and] assess the remaining unpaid ... policies" of this nature. Section 4 continues with a delegation of competence relevant to archival work: "[R]easonable review will be made of the participating companies' files, in conjunction with information concerning Holocaust victims from Yad Vashem and the United States Holocaust Memorial Museum and other relevant sources of data."

Cases of "unnamed claims," where claimants were unable to identify an insurance company, were handled somewhat differently. These claims were transferred by ICHEIC (or the GDV in the case of the Trilateral Agreement) to all relevant companies.[89] The result of the companies' search for evidence of a policy was communicated to ICHEIC,[90] whereupon it in turn notified the claimants. When matches were found, the companies processed the claims following the rules for named claims. In the event companies' investigations failed to locate a policy, the claimants were informed of their possible eligibility for a humanitarian payment under MOU, Section 8 (A)(1), the processing of which has already been mentioned.[91]

IV. Central Regulatory Instrument: Claims Decision and Award Letters

While award or denial decisions contractually affected the financial relations of private actors, this is only one of the competing frameworks

---

(BAFin) (German Federal Agency for the Supervision of Financial Services). *See* ICHEIC Claims Processing Guide (note 50), at 37.

88 *See id.*

89 *See id.*, 35.

90 Under the Trilateral Agreement (note 59), Annex A, Section 24, companies reported their findings to the GDV, which in turn communicated this information to ICHEIC.

91 *See* Part B II 3.

for understanding their significance.[92] From a legal perspective, final decision letters from the insurance company in cases of named or matched claims may be seen as a central regulatory instrument in the ICHEIC claims process. Doing so recognizes their particularly public regulatory significance for both the company and the external addressee, *i.e.* the individual claimant.

Decision letters provided an assessment of claims based on ICHEIC procedural guidelines, relaxed standards of proof, succession rules and valuation guidelines. They were thus directly based on secondary norms related to the MOU or to ICHEIC's side-agreements. The decision letters included reference to this legal basis, for example where particular valuation rules were mentioned on the enclosed valuation sheet. However, no particular form was prescribed for this instrument.

A positive decision letter did not directly confer on the claimants any legal rights. Rather, it communicated a private contractual offer of payment to its addressees, who could accept or ignore this as they saw fit. While the decision letter included reasons for the company's determination and documents relevant to the claim, this had no binding effect. This instrument did not represent an acknowledgement of legal liability by the deciding company. Contractual rights arose only upon acceptance of the award, which required consent to its conditions,[93] including the waiver of any and all rights and benefits which the claimant might then have "or ever had, up to the date of ... [the] release, relating to, or in any way connected with ... the policy or any claims related to it...."[94]

The multilevel reporting requirements surrounding decision letters indicate public regulatory dimensions of the claims process. Seen as the functional equivalent of a lower level of public regulatory authority, the companies bore certain reporting duties vis-à-vis claimants and the "higher levels" represented by ICHEIC, the German Foundation and the GDV. Specifically, companies had to include the following items together with their determination regarding a claimant's entitlement to a claimed policy: all documents relevant to the claim and the company's decision; notice of the possibility of appeal within a specified time-

---

[92] *See* Curran (note 15).

[93] These included, *e.g.*, the claimant's agreement to share the payment with other entitled persons who make a claim or seek compensation with regard to the policy in question. *See* Trilateral Agreement (note 59), Annex F, Consent and Waiver, Section (e).

[94] *Id.*, Section (a).

frame; an appeal form; and a copy of the Appeals Guidelines.[95] At the same time, ICHEIC's claims processing procedure called for companies to communicate the outcome of their claims assessments to the higher administrative levels in the form of a copy of the decision letter and accompanying documentation.[96]

The ICHEIC's award offer under the humanitarian process with respect to plausible but unmatched claims, or claims against companies no longer in existence,[97] was of course no less central to ICHEIC's mandate than the companies' decision letters. Most of what has been said about decision letters also applies to the award letters. However, the latter reveal even more distinct international public regulatory contours, since they issued directly from ICHEIC, as did the respective humanitarian payments, rather than from a particular insurer.

Evidence of the public regulatory character of ICHEIC decision and award letters can be further derived from the fact that they may eventually be susceptible to public scrutiny and thereby also serve a memorializing function. Section 10 of the Trilateral Agreement provides for archiving data relating to ICHEIC claims. It obliges ICHEIC to retain or offer to the German Foundation "records generated during the processing of the claims and the appeals process" after the conclusion of the claims process.[98]

---

95 ICHEIC Claims Processing Guide (note 50), at 33-34.

96 These "higher levels" were the ICHEIC and, in the case of German companies covered by the Trilateral Agreement, the German Foundation. *See id.*

97 *See* MOU (note 42), Section 8 (A)(1).

98 *See* Trilateral Agreement (note 59); *see also* ICHEIC, Concluding Meeting of the International Commission on Holocaust Era Insurance Claims, Washington D.C., March 20, 2007, 21, available at http://www.icheic.org/pdf/Meeting%20Presentation%203-20-07.pdf (hereinafter ICHEIC, Concluding Meeting) (indicating that the US Holocaust Memorial Museum would continue to store key documents, research data and claims files following ICHEIC's closure).

V. Oversight of the Claims Process

1. Monitoring

a) Audits

The ICHEIC regime provided for audits of claims processing and decision-making by both its own member companies and other organizations in Section 4 (a) of the MOU. Subsequently developed "Audit Standards" set the template for evaluation of the insurers' performance.

Under the standards, the companies were audited in a first stage with respect to their efforts to find, collect, safeguard and make accessible the records necessary for establishing claims. Auditing in this regard was carried out by internationally recognized accounting firms appointed by the insurers themselves. A second stage of auditing focused on evaluation of the companies' process for receiving claims and searching records for matches, as well as for issuing decision letters with the proper notifications and relevant supporting documents. Peer review of the actual handling of claims and use of ICHEIC standards and procedures subject to the initial audit was carried out at this second stage largely on the basis of selective sampling by a firm appointed by ICHEIC. Auditing reports were submitted to a special ICHEIC committee: the Audit Mandate Support Group.

Because of ICHEIC's fractured regime, the auditing process varied depending on the company or partner organization and the audit-category concerned. Thus, in the case of the Generali Trust Fund, ICHEIC commissioned an auditing firm to examine claims handling procedures and processing. On the other hand, audits of German non-MOU insurers, ten of which were selected by mutual consent, were carried out by the *Bundesanstalt für Finanzdienstleistungsaufsicht* (Federal Financial Supervisory Authority/ BaFin) with the participation of ICHEIC observers.[99] The BaFin audits covered the companies' compliance with the terms of the Trilateral Agreement, which incorporated claims handling requirements similar – but not identical – to ICHEIC's Audit Standards. To audit the processing by the Claims Conference of humanitarian claims under Section 8 (A) of the MOU, ICHEIC commissioned yet another international auditing firm.

The role played by audits in the ICHEIC process may be overstated. Audit reports only became publicly available on the ICHEIC website

---

[99] Trilateral Agreement (note 59), Annex I.

after ICHEIC claims processing was substantially completed. For audits carried out by BaFin in connection with the Trilateral Agreement, a possibility existed for appeal by dissatisfied ICHEIC observers to the Appeals Panel.[100] The Panel, in turn, had authority to direct a company to make payments where necessary,[101] but its decision was confidential and not appealable in a court of law.[102]

b) Decision Verification System

Oversight was augmented by an internal system developed to check whether companies were making decisions in keeping with the relevant guidelines. The Decision Verification System aimed in particular at ensuring the companies' consideration of all pertinent evidence and their comprehensive responses to the claimants. For this purpose, the ICHEIC Claims Team in London was charged with reviewing all named-company claims concerning the MOU-companies, the GTF and the companies covered by the Trilateral Agreement.[103] The verification system extended on a "rolling basis" to all decisions made since the beginning of the ICHEIC claims process. Moreover, the Claims Team also conducted verification focusing specifically on denials of well-documented claims.[104]

The ICHEIC Claims Team could raise questions with companies, track their responses and make follow-up inquiries. But the Decision Verification System threatened recalcitrant companies only with the application of "pressure" to "ensur[e] the continued effectiveness of the claims team as a means of receiving prompt responses on the issues about which they inquire."[105] Results of ICHEIC's verification efforts were never published. During a substantial portion of ICHEIC's existence, critics have accordingly questioned whether the London office served

---

[100] *Id.*, Annex I, Sections 11-23.

[101] *Id.*, Section 21.

[102] *Id.*, Section 22.

[103] *See* ICHEIC Decision Verification System, available at http://www.icheic.org/pdf/ICHEIC_VP.pdf.

[104] *See id.*

[105] *See id.*

as anything more than a "post-office" for transmittal of claims to the companies.[106]

c) ICHEIC Monitoring Group

Annex K of the Trilateral Agreement provided for an *ad hoc* monitoring group. Originally convened in 2002, the Monitoring Group consisted of a chairman and representatives appointed by the MOU companies, the US regulators and the Jewish groups/ the State of Israel. According to paragraph 4 of Annex K, the Monitoring Group would, "from time to time," be charged at the behest of Chairman Eagleburger or its own chairman, "with reviewing and verifying that all members of ICHEIC are complying with ICHEIC rules, procedures and decisions, including decisions of the Chairman, and are doing so as effectively and efficiently as possible." Otherwise, the Monitoring Group could commence review, as set out in paragraph 5, based on "information of a pattern of noncompliance by a company or companies" or "a concern relating to the consistency or effectiveness of claims processing," as identified by members of ICHEIC, the Appeals Panel or the audit process.[107] In 2003, the Monitoring Group was asked to evaluate the claims verification process. Any assessment it may have made remained unpublished.[108]

d) External Monitoring

More meaningful monitoring took place outside ICHEIC itself. Formal oversight by means of periodic governmental reporting occurred at the national level in Germany and the United States. In addition, informal oversight in the United States resulted from congressional hearings and,

---

106 *See* Zabludoff (note 25), at 262. For a more scathing critique, indicting ICHEI as "a storefront enabling a consortium of companies to effectively deny thousands of claims as they see fit under the guise of a US-sanctioned settlement," *cf.* Hearings 2003 (note 34), at 140, 143 (Statement of Daniel Kadden). *See also Generali I* (note 68), 356-357 (describing ICHEIC as "entirely a creature of the six founding insurance companies" and "the company store"). With respect to ICHEIC's outsourcing of core functions, *see*, *supra*, note 44 and, implicitly self-critical, ICHEIC, Lessons Learned (note 26), at 14.

107 Trilateral Agreement (note 59), Annex K, Section 5.

108 The Monitoring Group's ineffectiveness was also criticized in congressional testimony by Daniel Kadden. *See* Hearings 2003 (note 34), at 140, 143.

at the state level, in the form of reports published by state regulatory authorities.

The German federal government was statutorily required to report semi-annually to the Bundestag on the status of distributions and cooperation with partner organizations of the German Foundation.[109] American federal law similarly obligated the Secretary of State to report to appropriate congressional committees on the status of the German Foundation Agreement, including those aspects of it involving ICHEIC.[110] In both cases, however, the dependency on information provided by ICHEIC limited the efficacy of governmental reporting.[111]

Reports by the New York Banking Department provide one example of monitoring at the state level in the United States. The Banking Department was statutorily required to explain the status of work done by its Holocaust Claims Processing Office (HCPO) *inter alia* with regard to

---

109 *See Beschluss des Deutschen Bundestages vom 28. Juni 2001* (Decision of the German Bundestag of 28 June 2001) (*Bundestagsdrucksache* 14/6465); with regard to ICHEIC, *see, e.g., Fünfter Bericht der Bundesregierung über den Stand der Auszahlungen und die Zusammenarbeit der Stiftung "Erinnerung, Verantwortung und Zukunft" mit den Partnerorganisationen, Bundestagsdrucksache* 15/5936 (21 July 2005) (Fifth Report of the German Government on the Status of Distributions and the Cooperation of the Foundation "Remembrance, Responsibility and Future" with Partner Organizations).

110 *See* Pub. L. 107-288, Section 704, Foreign Relations Authorization Act of 2003.

111 The limitations for effective oversight are manifest in the State Department's open acknowledgment that it "was unable to obtain such information on the ICHEIC claims process as required by Section 704 (a)(3)-(7)" and its referral in this connection to publicly available statistics on the ICHEIC website. *See* US Dept. of State, Bureau of European and Eurasian Affairs, Report to Congress: German Foundation "Remembrance, Responsibility, and the Future," March 2006, available at www.state.gov/p/eur/rls/rpt/64401.htm. *But see* Review of the Repatriation of Holocaust Art Assets in the United States, Hearing before the Subcommittee on Domestic and International Monetary Policy, Trade and Technology, 109th Cong., 16, Appendix 1, Best Practices in Holocaust Era Claims Restitution, NY State Banking Dept. Research Paper (27 July 2006) (Testimony of Catherine A. Lillie, Director, Holocaust Claims Processing Office, NY State Banking Dept.), available at http://www.claims.state.ny.us/sp060727.pdf, qualifying as a "best practice" ICHEIC's provision to US insurance regulators of a monthly report on the status of claims filed by US residents or by a US regulatory agency on their behalf.

insurance claims.[112] In this case, the connection between the entities was particularly close, since the director of the HCPO represented US regulators on the ICHEIC Monitoring Group after September 2003.[113]

Perhaps the most effective oversight of ICHEIC came in the form of the congressional hearings which took place before the Committee on Government Reform of the US House of Representatives.[114] Notwithstanding federal legislators' lack of formal authority over ICHEIC, the House Committee drew national public attention to problems of accountability in the ICHEIC process. An example of the impact of the hearings may be seen in connection with that held on September 24, 2002, concerning proposed legislation to induce European insurance companies to release policyholder information and otherwise cooperate with ICHEIC.[115] It seems to be no coincidence that the Trilateral Agreement, which brought the non-MOU German companies into the ICHEIC system, was signed shortly thereafter, on October 16, 2002.

To be sure, the Supreme Court's 2003 decision in *Garamendi*,[116] striking down similar state disclosure legislation, removed enormous pressure on the insurers. Undeterred, however, the Committee on Government Reform held further hearings that year to discuss future congressional strategy with respect to federal legislation which would allow ICHEIC to achieve its purpose.[117] Renewed calls for congressional action con-

---

112 *See* NY Consolidated Laws Service, Banking Law, Art. II, Section 37-a (2007).

113 Holocaust Claims Processing Report, Report to the Governor and the Legislature, 15 January 2007, 10 (New York State Banking Dept. ed., 2007).

114 For comprehensive links to the testimony presented, see the website of Rep. Henry A. Waxman, www.henrywaxman.house.gov, as well as that of the Committee on Oversight and Government Reform, http://oversight.house.gov/.

115 *See* Hearing on H.R. 2693, The Holocaust Victims Insurance Relief Act of 2001, Before the Subcommittee on Governmental Efficiency, Financial Management and Intergovernmental Relations, Committee on Government Reform, 107th Cong., 2nd Sess. (24 Sept. 2002).

116 American Insurance Association v. Garamendi, 539 U.S. 396 (2003).

117 *See* H.R. 1210 (note 39), and H.R. 1905, Comprehensive Holocaust Accountability in Insurance Measure, 108th Cong., 1st Sess. (1 May 2003) (introduced in the House), recognizing the power of the states to place conditions on insurance companies operating within their territory.

spicuously preceded a court-approved settlement of the last major class action involving Holocaust-era insurance claims in February 2007.[118]

2. Appeals

ICHEIC provided claimants a cost-free means of contesting decisions on named company claims or matched, unnamed company claims in the case of negative claim assessments.[119] However, ICHEIC's composite features complicated oversight of the claims process with respect to appeals. Two independent review-bodies heard appeals during the third stage of the ICHEIC claims process. The ICHEIC Appeals Tribunal considered appeals on decisions from all member companies and on German MOU-company decisions dated before October 16, 2002. The Tribunal operated in accordance with specially provided Rules of Procedure[120] and Expert Determination Rules.[121] The Tribunal was comprised of a President, a Vice President and independent Arbitrators. It was deemed to have its seat in London.

Under ICHEIC's side-agreement with the German Foundation and the GDV, another body – the Appeals Panel – considered appeals on decisions from German insurance companies, including MOU-member companies, dated on or after October 16, 2002. The Appeals Panel was deemed to be located in Geneva, Switzerland. This adjudicative body consisted of three members, one of whom was appointed as Chairman. Its determinations on appeals petitions were governed by the Appeals Guidelines found in Annex E to the Trilateral Agreement.

---

118 *See* Joseph B. Treaster, Settlement Approved in Holocaust Victims' Suit Against Italian Insurer, N.Y.TIMES, 28 Feb. 2007, Section C, 3; *In re* Assicurazioni Generali S.p.A. Holocaust Ins., Slip Copy, 2007 WL 601846, S.D.N.Y., 27 Feb. 2007 (hereinafter *Generali Settlement*).

119 There was no right to appeal concerning unnamed and unmatched claims or the humanitarian awards of ICHEIC. *See* ICHEIC Claims Processing Guide (note 50), at 35.

120 ICHEIC Appeals Tribunal Rules of Procedure, available at http://www.icheic.org/pdf/ICHEIC_Appeals.pdf. The ICHEIC Appeals Process is detailed in the ICHEIC Claims Processing Guide (note 50), at 38-45.

121 *See id.*, at 43.

Various ICHEIC claims were ineligible for consideration under ICHEIC's own appeals processes and fell instead within the divergent parallel processes of ICHEIC's partners.[122]

C. Assessment

I. Principles

Substantive principles central to the ICHEIC process included the application to claims processing of relaxed standards of proof taking account of genocide, wartime conditions and the passage of time, as well as valuation guidelines making allowance for currency changes, interest and prior compensation/ restitution assessments. Salient procedural principles included the provision to claimants, without charge, of assistance with claims filing and evaluation, including research in appropriate archives, the application of processing guidelines that required insurers to communicate all essential facts and documents, and possibility for appeal.

Analogous core principles have been applied in other mass claims processes.[123] The truly significant and distinctive feature of ICHEIC, however, was its attempt to administrate a universal nonadversarial process to resolve Holocaust-related claims by private parties against private entities. This development represents a departure from the traditional approach of international law, under which damage claims by individuals following an armed conflict fell within the general scope of war damages and were subsumed in and dependent on reparations agreements between States.[124] For those who insist that this tradition main-

---

[122] *See id.*, at 44-45 (with regard to the Sjoa Foundation, the GTF and the Buysse Commission, which offered a second review rather than the possibility of petition to an appellate body).

[123] With respect to the UNCC, for example, *see* Chung (note 7).

[124] For unwaivering support by prominent German academics for this traditional approach, *see*, *e.g.*, Karl Doehring, *Reparationen für Kriegsschäden*, *in* JAHRHUNDERTSCHULD – JAHRHUNDERTSÜHNE: REPARATIONEN, WIEDERGUTMACHUNG, ENTSCHÄDIGUNG FÜR NATIONALSOZIALISTISCHES KRIEGS- UND VERFOLGUNGSUNRECHT, 41 (Karl Doehring, Bernd J. Fehn & Hans G. Hockerts eds., 2001); Christian Tomuschat, *Ein umfassendes Wiedergutmachungsprogramm für Opfer schwerer Menschenrechtsverletzungen*, 80 DIE FRIEDENS-WARTE/ JOURNAL OF INTERNATIONAL PEACE AND ORGANIZATION 160-167

tains its currency, additional payments made in response to private claims relating to World War II were the result of moral pressure and constitute charitable distributions rather than legal or quasi-legal redress.[125] A powerful argument insists, however, that there is an evolving consensus favoring the principle that victims of gross violations of human rights are entitled to reparations. The remedies provided by monitoring bodies under human rights treaties, as well as a recent UN General Assembly resolution which adopted rules on reparations for gross violations of human rights law and serious violations of international humanitarian law,[126] indeed point to an "emerging right of victims to

---

(2005) (with an English summary, 12). See also Rainer Hofmann, *Victims of Violations of International Humanitarian Law: Do They Have an Individual Right to Reparation against States under International Law, in* VÖLKERRECHT ALS WERTORDNUNG. COMMON VALUES IN INTERNATIONAL LAW. FESTSCHRIFT FÜR CHRISTIAN TOMUSCHAT/ ESSAYS IN HONOUR OF CHRISTIAN TOMUSCHAT, 341, 349 (Pierre-Marie Dupuy *et al.* ed., 2006), for an indication that this view has been reflected in the consistent practice of all post-war governments of the Federal Republic of Germany.

125 See Doehring (note 124), at 41; Rudolf Dolzer, *The Settlement of War-Related Claims: Does International Law Recognize a Victim's Private Right of Action? Lessons after 1945*, 20 BERKELEY JOURNAL OF INTERNATIONAL LAW 296-341, 335 (2002) (characterizing the German Foundation as an "arrangement [...] intended both to continue Germany's moral atonement for the suffering inflicted at its hands, and to assuage perceived social forces [sic] positioned to potentially cause economic losses by, for example, boycotts and similar activities."). This depiction comes disconcertingly close to that which refers to representatives of the "Jewish-American establishment" and class action lawyers as being engaged in an enterprise to "shakedown" or "extort" payments in the name of Holocaust victims for their own personal, political and financial motives. See NORMAN FINKELSTEIN, THE HOLOCAUST INDUSTRY: REFLECTIONS ON THE EXPLOITATION OF JEWISH SUFFERING (2001). The failure of such critics to appreciate "the essential moral value that formed the heart of these processes" or the legitimacy of the American approach to mass injury cases is noted, e.g., by Melvyn I. Weiss, *A Litigator's Postscript to the Swiss Banks and Holocaust Litigation Settlements: How Justice Was Served, in* HOLOCAUST RESTITUTION: PERSPECTIVES ON THE LITIGATION AND ITS LEGACY 103, 109-111 (Michael J. Bazyler & Roger P. Alford eds., 2006) and EIZENSTAT (note 16), at 345.

126 UN GA Res. 60/147 of 16 Dec. 2005. *See* DINAH SHELTON, REMEDIES IN INTERNATIONAL HUMAN RIGHTS LAW (2nd ed., 2005) 143-152 (surveying the 15 years of work of the UN Sub-Commission on Promotion and Protection of Human Rights and the UN Commission on Human Rights to identify basic principles and guidelines on reparations which culminated in this resolution.

reparation."[127] With its focus on easing formal requirements in order to allow for compensation of individuals who were victims of Nazi genocide, the ICHEIC process reflects and contributes to this growing trend.[128]

As a regulatory alternative to litigation meant to avoid the adjudication of legal rights, the ICHEIC process paradoxically provided "compensation" to those who could establish a plausible claim and who had not previously received redress even where a company could not be identified, the company no longer existed, the company was nationalized, or the policy was confiscated or paid into a blocked and subsequently plundered account. Under Section 6 of the MOU, claims awards are expressly labeled "compensatory." In the above-mentioned situations where the formalities of a legal claim may have been absent, claims were thus redressed as if legal rights were at stake.

II. Multilevel or Composite Aspects

To speak of "upper" and "lower" levels of regulatory authority in the ICHEIC process may sound artificial. The insurance company members of ICHEIC independently assessed claims, despite their commit-

---

127 Manfred Nowak, *The Right of Victims of Gross Human Rights Violations to Reparations, in* RENDERING JUSTICE TO THE VULNERABLE. LIBER AMICORUM IN HONOUR OF THEO VAN BOVEN 203, 223 (Fons Coomans *et al.* ed., 2000) (referring to Special Rapporteur van Boven's first draft of Principles and Guidelines on a Right to Reparation for Victims of (Gross) Violations of Human Rights and International Humanitarian Law, UN Doc. E/CN.4/1997/104). *But see* Christian Tomuschat, *Dafur – Compensation for the Victims*, 3 JOURNAL OF INTERNATIONAL CRIMINAL JUSTICE 579, 587 (2005) (denying the existence of individual compensation claims under customary international law); Albrecht Randelzhofer, *The Legal Position of the Individual under Present International Law, in* STATE RESPONSIBILITY AND THE INDIVIDUAL: REPARATION IN INSTANCES OF GRAVE VIOLATIONS OF HUMAN RIGHTS 231, 242 (Albrecht Randelzhofer & Christian Tomuschat eds., 1999), (denying that any fundamental change has occurred with respect to the reparation of individuals under international law).

128 *See* EIZENSTAT (note 16), at 353 (offering cautious recognition of such a trend: "Although I would like to think my teams and I helped write a new page in creating civil liability for the violation of human rights, we provided scant legal precedent" which, however, "does not diminish the legal and diplomatic implications of what we accomplished.").

ment to follow certain standards and procedures. The MOU recognizes as much. Section 5 states: "The initial responsibility for resolving claims rests with the individual insurance companies...." Hierarchical regulatory features might be seen where the member companies implemented the Chairman's "memoranda," if these instruments are understood rather as directives.[129] However, the companies were never formally integrated into a hierarchical regime. The ICHEIC process has been seen as significantly flawed as a consequence. Its member companies fought bitterly for and were largely able to maintain their autonomy. The primary example of this was their successful prevention of a more wide-scale publication of potential policyholder names than the approximately 519,000 which ultimately appeared on the ICHEIC website. How many names were supplied to ICHEIC on condition that they remain confidential is unknown, but some 8 million policyholder names from the Holocaust period were said to exist in company records.[130] This flew in the face of the MOU mandate, under Section 4 (b), for ICHEIC to "address the issue of a full accounting by the insurance companies and publication of the names of Holocaust victims who held insurance policies."

The ICHEIC process also reveals a horizontal dimension in ICHEIC's side-agreements. Attention has previously been directed toward the most important of these – the Trilateral Agreement – but related parallel processes also handled insurance claims in Austria,[131] Belgium,[132]

---

[129] *See, e.g.*, ICHEIC Memorandum: Laws of General Application, 4 Feb. 2004 (detailing – in a noticeably directive-like communication – laws relating to currency conversion which are to be taken into account in the processing of ICHEIC claims). The legal nature of the Chairman's memoranda apparently evolved during ICHEIC's existence. *See* note 69 and accompanying text; ICHEIC, Lessons Learned (note 26), at 4.

[130] *See* Hearings 2003 (note 34), at 33, 36 (Statement of Ambassador Randolph M. Bell, Special Envoy for Holocaust Issues, US Dept. of State) (referring to the total number of names registered in the companies' files from 1920 through 1945). *See* Hennig (note 62), at 255 (indicating that the German insurance companies themselves had compiled a database – monitored by the German Federal Financial Supervisory Authority – which contained 8.5 million names.

[131] *See* Agreement Between the International Commission on Holocaust Era Insurance Claims and the General Settlement Fund of the Republic of Austria, 8 Dec. 2003, available at http://www.icheic.org/pdf/agreement-RAGSF%20(eng).pdf.

France,[133] and the Netherlands,[134] as well as with respect to Generali.[135] Moreover, a group of three MOU-companies signed their own separate agreement with ICHEIC.[136] The communication of claims information between the parties was agreed to in ICHEIC's side-agreements and processing by ICHEIC's partners took place according to rules similar to ICHEIC's. But there were significant variations. Thus, the level of funding, valuation standards and filing deadlines differed, as did the regulation of appeals, auditing and publication of potential policyholder names. The resulting lack of consistency, *i.e.*, fragmentation, in Holocaust-era claims processing provoked critics to call the ICHEIC system "Balkanized."[137]

Fragmentation on the horizontal plane also resulted from decisions of the arbitral mechanism established under the court-approved settlement in the *Swiss Banks Litigation*. While predominantly concerned with claims to dormant Swiss bank accounts, the Claims Resolution Tribunal (CRT) also assessed Holocaust-era insurance claims against a number of Swiss companies and some of their affiliates. Filing deadlines and other rules applicable to the CRT system differed from those of ICHEIC.[138]

---

[132] *See* Operating Agreement between ICHEIC and *La Commission Pour le Dédommagement des Membres de la Communauté Juive de Belgique* (Buysse Commission), 14 July 2003, available at http://www.icheic.org/pdf/agreement-buysse.pdf.

[133] With respect to the *Commission pour l'indemnisation des victimes de spoliations intervenues du fait des législations antisémites en vigueur pendant l'Occupation* (CIVS) (Commission for the Compensation of Victims of Spoliation under the anti-Semitic Legislation in force during the Occupation), *see* http://www.civs.gouv.fr/. Formal signed agreements did not result, however, in the cases of France and the Netherlands, although member companies of the Dutch Insurance Association joined the ICHEIC.

[134] With respect to the *Sjoa* Foundation, *see* http://www.stichting-sjoa.nl/.

[135] *See* the Generali Implementation Agreement, 16 Nov. 2000, and the Generali Implementing Organization Agreement, 30 April 2001, respectively available at http://www.icheic.org/pdf/agreement-generali.pdf and http://www.icheic.org/pdf/agreement-gtf.pdf.

[136] *See* AWZ-Settlement Agreement, 11 July 2003, available at http://www.icheic.org/pdf/agreement-awz.pdf (concluded among AXA, Winterthur Life Insurance Company, Zurich Life Insurance Company, the WJRO and ICHEIC).

[137] Hearings 2003 (note 34), at 140, 144 (Statement of Daniel Kadden).

[138] CRT also provided for relaxed standards of proof in its Rules Governing the Claims Resolution Process (as Amended), available at http://www.crt-

Whether the CRT was able to do a better job resolving Holocaust-era property claims is open to question. In contrast to ICHEIC, however, it handled only a relatively small number of insurance claims.[139] Certainly, a more limited disclosure of the names of potential claimants occurred in the context of the *Swiss Banks Litigation*. Notwithstanding the four million bank accounts opened between 1933 and 1945, and the recommendation of Paul Volcker, chairman of the Independent Committee of Eminent Persons which supervised a $200 million audit to identify dormant accounts, to publish 36,000 names, the banks ultimately revealed the names of only 23,700 account owners and 400 holders of a power-of-attorney.[140]

III. Legitimacy

Whether the ICHEIC process can be judged as having adequately addressed the interests of those affected is questionable at best. This assessment rests on consideration of the following factors: representation of the claimants, their ability to affect the outcome, the transparency of the process, the alternative of having the issue judicially resolved, the duration of the process, its costs, the amount of funding made available for distribution to claimants, and disclosure of policyholders' names.

The fact that government officials as well as representatives of important Jewish nongovernmental organizations and the State of Israel belonged to or participated in ICHEIC does not necessarily offset an important objection raised by survivors. Some insisted that they gave no authorization for negotiation in their name and would have preferred to

---

ii.org/_pdf/governing_rules_en.pdf. Its rules on valuation referred to ICHEIC's valuation guidelines, *see* Section 4.2, Amendment to No. 2 Settlement Agreement, 9 Aug. 2000, available at http://www.swissbankclaims.com/pdfs_Eng/Amendment2.pdf.

[139] *See* Swiss Banks Settlement Fund Distribution Statistics as of November 15, 2007, *Holocaust Victim Assets Litigation*, CV 96-4849, available at http://www.swissbankclaims.com/Documents_New/11_15_st.pdf (indicating 88 approved and 391 "no match" decisions) (hereinafter Distribution Statistics).

[140] *See* Eizenstat (note 38), at 302; Deposited Assets Class, *Holocaust Victim Assets Litigation*, CV-96-4849, http://www.swissbankclaims.com/DepositedAssets.aspx .

have had their day in court.[141] Arguably, class action lawyers, such as those who played a vital role in negotiations leading to the Swiss bank settlement and the German Foundation Agreement, more effectively represented the insurance claimants than the ICHEIC members who unilaterally assumed this function.[142] A persistent criticism has been that ICHEIC members were, in any event, not representative enough, inasmuch as "[t]he interests of the victims were represented by 'non-survivor organizations.'"[143] Furthermore, no possibility existed for survivors to help shape the ICHEIC process by commenting on the various secondary rules or side-agreements adopted.[144] Provision for such input was, by way of contrast, an important feature of the Swiss banks settlement. Judicial approval of this settlement in fact rested to a significant degree on the opportunity of the class-action plaintiffs and interested parties to have the court consider their views on the allocation plan proposed by a court-appointed Special Master.

With respect to the information required for meaningful input, the litigation approach offered a model of transparency. Summaries of the

---

141 *See, e.g.*, Si Frumkin, *Why Won't Those SOBs Give Me My Money? A Survivor's Perspective, in* HOLOCAUST RESTITUTION: PERSPECTIVES ON THE LITIGATION AND ITS LEGACY 92, 95 (Michael J. Bazyler & Roger P. Alford eds., 2006).

142 Positive assessment of the role of the class action lawyers, not unexpectedly, comes from those who acted as such. *See, e.g.*, Robert A. Swift, *Holocaust Litigation and Human Rights Jurisprudence, in* HOLOCAUST RESTITUTION: PERSPECTIVES ON THE LITIGATION AND ITS LEGACY 50, 53 (Michael J. Bazyler & Roger P. Alford eds., 2006); Weiss (note 125), at 103.

143 *See* Jolie Bell, *Maybe Not the Best Solution, But a Solution: The German Foundation Agreement,* 6 CARDOZO JOURNAL OF CONFLICT RESOLUTION 107, 151 (2004). A result may have been a disproportionate allocation of humanitarian funds for educational and remembrance purposes rather than for health care and social services for elderly and financially needy survivors (20% and 80%, respectively), a problem meanwhile acknowledged, for example, by Stuart Eizenstat. *See* Eizenstat (note 38), at 303; *see also* David A. Lash & Mitchell A. Kamin, *Poor Justice: Holocaust Restitution and Forgotten, Indigent Survivors, in* HOLOCAUST RESTITUTION: PERSPECTIVES ON THE LITIGATION AND ITS LEGACY 315 (Michael J. Bazyler & Roger P. Alford eds., 2006); Thane Rosenbaum, Losing Count, N.Y. TIMES, 14 June 2007, Section A, 31.

144 *See* Bell (note 143), at 151-152 (criticizing also this aspect of the Trilateral Agreement). *See also* Zabludoff (note 25), at 265 (noting that even a proposal to appoint an ombudsman to receive complaints from claimants on the handling of claims bore no fruit).

proposed plan for allocation and distribution of settlement funds were mailed to the almost 600,000 persons who returned "Initial Questionnaires" concerning a draft settlement. Moreover, copies of the Special Master's two-volume, 900-page report were available cost-free upon request as well as posted in the Internet prior to the public hearing held by the District Court in November 2000.[145]

This kind of transparency was largely absent from the ICHEIC process. Not surprisingly, critics explained the discord within ICHEIC and its lack of public support, most pronounced in ICHEIC's early stages,[146] by pointing to Chairman Eagleburger's "secret diplomacy" and purported reliance on advice from selectively consulted ICHEIC members and staff.[147]

Assessment of the ICHEIC's output legitimacy calls for comparison with its alternatives. It is unclear whether the ICHEIC process was superior to what might have resulted from litigation.[148] A judicial deter-

---

145 *See* Chronology: *In re Holocaust Victim Assets Litigation*, http://www.swissbankclaims.com/Chronology.aspx (June 11, 1999: Initial Questionnaire; September 11, 2000: Statement From Burt Neuborne, Lead Settlement Class Counsel).

146 *See* EIZENSTAT (note 16), at 267 (mentioning among ICHEIC's early "administrative failings" an episode in which its chairman resigned for twenty-four hours).

147 *See* Zabludoff (note 25), at 263. With regard to ICHEIC's secrecy, *see also* BAZYLER (note 14), at 155-156; Hearings 2003 (note 34), at 140, 144 (Statement of Daniel Kadden); *id.*, 11, 12 (Statement of Rep. Henry A. Waxman).

148 For observers more favorably disposed toward the litigation approach, *see* Adler & Zumbansen (note 14); Bell (note 143), at 154; Burt Neuborne, *A Tale of Two Cities: Administering the Holocaust Settlements in Brooklyn and Berlin, in* HOLOCAUST RESTITUTION: PERSPECTIVES ON THE LITIGATION AND ITS LEGACY 60, 77 (Michael J. Bazyler & Roger P. Alford eds., 2006); Graham O'Donoghue, *Precatory Executive Statements and Permissible Judicial Responses in the Context of Holocaust-Claims Litigation*, 106 COLUMBIA LAW REVIEW 1119 (2006) (arguing that the federal courts' dismissals of Holocaust litigation rested on mistaken application of the doctrines of judicial abstention and federal preemption of state law, as well as the notion of international comity). *See also* EIZENSTAT (note 16), at 342 (acknowledging the essential role of the lawsuits for the diplomacy which led to the settlements); Dinah Shelton, *Reparations for Historical Injustices*, 50 NETHERLANDS INTERNATIONAL LAW REVIEW 289, 303 (2003) (underscoring the value of lawsuits, even where they do not lead to favorable court judgments, in focusing attention on the legitimacy of the asserted claims). For Swiss and German criticism of the Holocaust litigation in American courts, *see, e.g.*, Samuel P. Baumgartner, *Human Rights and Civil*

mination would necessarily have had to rest on complex procedural and substantive legal doctrines often difficult to square with the singular situation in which Holocaust survivors found themselves. This posed serious risks for the claimants, as demonstrated by the refusal of the District Court in the Generali litigation to retain jurisdiction following the Supreme Court's articulation of separation of powers and federalism concerns in *Garamendi*.[149] However, the persistence of class action lawyers and legislators induced Generali to settle even after the District Court's dismissal.[150]

Under the Swiss banks settlement, payment of the claimants does not appear to have taken longer than the nine-year ICHEIC process. More than six years after the banks settled, over $500 million of the $1.35 billion settlement fund was still unpaid.[151] Insurance awards continued to be ordered by the CRT through October 2006 – seven years into the settlement.[152] Despite his unwavering support for ICHEIC, Eizenstat acknowledged, its "slow and costly start."[153] The time-lag between conclusion of the settlement and initial distributions in the Swiss banks case was 2 ½ years.[154] In the case of ICHEIC, only $7 million worth of

---

Litigation in United States Courts: The Holocaust-Era Cases, 80 WASHINGTON UNIVERSITY LAW QUARTERLY 853 (2002). According to their detractors, such lawsuits are "less about questions of law, than ... about power." *Id.*, 845, quoting (in translation) Burkhard Heß, *Entschädigung für NS-Zwangsarbeit vor US-amerikanischen und deutschen Zivilgerichten*, 44 AKTIENGESELLSCHAFT 145, 154 (1999).

149 *See Generali II* (note 41), 357 (dismissing multiple claims against Generali in light of *American Insurance Association v. Garamendi*, 539 U.S. 396 (2003)). For a résumé of the *Generali* litigation and negative assessment of ICHEIC in this regard, *see* Lawrence Kill & Linda Gerstel, *Holocaust-Era Insurance Claims: Legislative, Judicial and Executive Remedies, in* HOLOCAUST RESTITUTION: PERSPECTIVES ON THE LITIGATION AND ITS LEGACY 239, 248 (Michael J. Bazyler & Roger P. Alford eds., 2006)

150 *See* Treaster (note 118) (reporting that Generali agreed to add $35 million more to what it already paid to resolve claims on Holocaust-era policies). *See also Generali Settlement* (note 118), at 2.

151 *See* EIZENSTAT (note 38), at 301.

152 *See* Distribution Statistics (note 139). Under the Swiss banks settlement, $50 million was allocated for payment of Holocaust-era Swiss insurance claims. By Nov. 2007, eighty-eight claimants had been awarded a total of $1,023,480 by the CRT. See *id.*

153 EIZENSTAT (note 38), at 300.

154 *See* Neuborne (note 148), at 68.

claims had been paid, while administrative expenditures had run up to $90 million, by July 2002, four years after its inception.[155] After six years, 61% of all the eligible 80,000 claims still awaited processing and only 5.5% (approximately 4500) had received offers.[156]

As intended, the ICHEIC process spared claimants legal costs which would have arisen in connection with class actions. But a comparison of approaches hardly disfavors litigation in this respect. For the many dozens of lawyers who participated, it was estimated that legal fees would come to just over 1% of the roughly $8 billion recovered as a result of all the negotiations to resolve outstanding Holocaust-era claims.[157] ICHEIC, in contrast, ran up administrative costs amounting to almost 20% of the $550 million placed at its disposal.[158]

Serious questions remain regarding the adequacy of ICHEIC's funding. According to a prominent expert on economic issues pertaining to Holocaust-era claims, the amount which ICHEIC was expected to distribute by way of redress of recognized claims and for humanitarian purposes represented only 3% of the value (in 2003) of Holocaust-era insurance policies which were unpaid at the time ICHEIC was founded in 1998.[159] Moreover, the estimated total value of these policies – some $15 billion – excluded claims relating to non-life insurance policies, *e.g.*

---

155 *See* EIZENSTAT (note 38), at 300.

156 *See* Kill & Gerstel (note 149), at 242. *See also* Zabludoff (note 25), at 260 (criticizing ICHEIC's nine-year duration as a failure to meet its mandate). Further comparison may be made with the German Foundation regime under which payments ended in June 2007. This was more than 8 years after announcement by the German government and German companies of their intention to create the Foundation. *See* http://www.stiftung-evz.de/eng/foundation_remembrance_responsibility_and_future/press_contact_newsletters/press_archive/year_2007/press_release_04_2007_2007_06_11/.

157 *See* EIZENSTAT (note 16), at 345 (indicating that this is "a pittance" compared to contingency fees commonly awarded in successful mass injury tort litigation, which can range from 15% to 30% of the total award); *see also* Neuborne (note 9), at 804. Litigation, however, continued over this issue. *See In re Holocaust Victim Assets Litigation*, Slip Copy, 2007 WL 805768 (E.D.N.Y. 2007) (containing a report to the District Court on Neuborne's fee as the Lead Settlement Counsel involved in the allocation of German Foundation funds and recommending an amount significantly below that proposed by Neuborne).

158 *See* EIZENSTAT (note 38), at 300; ICHEIC, Concluding Meeting (note 98).

159 *See* Zabludoff (note 25), at 260, 267.

casualty insurance.[160] Under the ICHEIC process, attention focused exclusively on life insurance.[161] Valuation of policies under this process also failed to consider several relevant factors bearing on the true value of the claims at issue, thereby further throwing the adequacy of offers made by the insurance companies into question. Arguably, policyholders were entitled to stock issued or dividends paid out by their insurance companies over a sixty-year period.[162] In agreeing to relinquish their claims for contractual damages under the ICHEIC process, claimants also gave up potential common law and statutory remedies which allow recovery of extra-contractual damages as well as punitive damages.[163]

In comparison with the disclosure of account-holders which occurred under the court-supervised Swiss banks settlement,[164] a more significant number of policyholder names were published within the framework of the ICHEIC process – something due in no small measure to ICHEIC's own extensive archival research.[165] Notably, the names posted on ICHEIC's website overwhelmingly belonged to possible holders of policies purchased from German insurers – a result of the Trilateral Agreement. Only a small portion of these, however, were revealed by the companies themselves.[166] In the end, both German and

---

160 *Id.*, 260. *See* Joseph B. Treaster, *Deal Struck on Claims of Nazi Era*, N.Y. TIMES, 31 Jan. 2007, Section C, 1 (referring to an estimate by Sidney Zabludoff of $18 billion at 2007 rates). While many owners held casualty insurance, they received no indemnities from their insurers following the devastation of Jewish property during the "*Kristallnacht*" pogrom of Nov. 1938, which entailed total losses of $270 million (estimated at 2003 rates). *See* BAZYLER (note 14), at 114.

161 *See* Zabludoff (note 25), at 260, 267.

162 *See* Bell (note 143), at 147-148.

163 *See id.*, 149.

164 *See* note 140 and accompanying text.

165 The CRT, however, did publish a list of 37 names of Holocaust-era insurance policyholders in 2005. *See* http://www.crt-ii.org/_insurance/faqs_in.phtm.

166 *See* Kill & Gerstel (note 149), at 242; *see also* BAZYLER (note 14), at 146-153 (identifying as motives for the insurers' stonewalling the desire to avoid potential costs and, more importantly, to "demonstrate that the entire [disclosure] movement was bogus from the outset, that in fact no significant claims for unpaid policies from [the] Holocaust era ever existed." *Id.*, 152.

other insurers, whether MOU-members or not, successfully avoided full disclosure regardless of which approach they faced.[167]

IV. Concluding Critique

Did ICHEIC exercise too much international regulatory authority concerning Holocaust-era compensation issues or too little? Could the underlying insurance claims have been better resolved through an international apparatus for processing mass claims similar to the UNCC?[168] Transnational compensation claims are often dealt with by regulatory mechanisms whose institutional role has long been recognized under public international law. At its core, the UNCC was such a mechanism.[169] If the mass of individual claims arising from the Iraqi invasion of Kuwait in 1991 could be resolved on this basis,[170] was a different

---

167 For criticism that the disclosure of some 350,000 policyholder names under the Trilateral Agreement was "not even close to a disgorgement," *see* Bell (note 143), at 150.

168 *See* Roland Bank, *New Programs for Payments to Victims of National Socialist Injustice*, 44 GERMAN YEARBOOK OF INTERNATIONAL LAW 307, 352 (2001) (submitting, with regard to the Swiss banks settlement, the German Foundation and the Austrian funds for reconciliation and compensation, that "a multinational solution would have been preferable"). Without specifically naming the UNCC as a precedent, Bank, mentions the possibility that the UN could create an international compensation mechanism for "situations involving responsibilities of States and/or companies from different States" for massive violations of human rights. *Id.*, 352.

169 *See* notes 7 and 8.

170 According to the UNCC, more than 2.6 million claims of individuals, corporations, and governments, were submitted by nearly 100 governments, as well as international organizations, where individuals were unable to have claims submitted by governments. Approximately $368 billion in compensation was sought. *See* http://www2.unog.ch/uncc/theclaims.htm. Determinations on the merits of some 2.5 million eligible claims of individuals which were deemed more urgent were made from 1991 to 1996, with payment of awards for these categories of claims completed in 2000. *See* David D. Caron & Brian Morris, *The UN Compensation Commission: Practical Justice, Not Retribution*, 13 EUROPEAN JOURNAL OF INTERNATIONAL LAW 183, 187-188 (2002) (asserting that "[this] first phase of the UNCC's work is one of the most significant and underreported success stories of the United Nations"). In comparison, the German Foundation paid out about € 4.37 billion to 1.66 million former forced and slave laborers between 2000 and 2007. *See* http://www.stiftung-evz.de/eng/

regulatory approach appropriate to deal with those consequences of the Holocaust at issue in the ICHEIC context?

Intended essentially as an administrative process under the direction of the Security Council,[171] the UNCC might be more specifically described as an international administrative dispute-settlement mechanism with some judicial functions.[172] However, the UNCC's authority did not cover claims concerning Iraq's own citizens. The various categories of claims which it had authority to resolve, including those of individuals, could only be submitted by governments.[173] Claims were considered to be directed against Iraq, and the funds for awards came from economic sanctions imposed on Iraq by the Security Council.[174] These features alone indicate that the UNCC regime rested upon a recognition of State responsibility for injuries to foreigners under the traditional international law doctrine of diplomatic protection.[175] Ultimately, therefore, the legal framework of the UNCC mirrored that of traditional inter-State adjudication.[176]

---

foundation_remembrance_responsibility_and_future/press_contact_newsletters /press_archive/year_2007/press_release_04_2007_2007_06_11/. Under the ICHEIC process, 48,000 claimants were awarded $306.24 million by the time it ended in March 2007.

171 *See* Danio Campanelli, *The United Nations Compensation Commission (UNCC): Reflections on Its Judicial Character*, 4 THE LAW AND PRACTICE OF INTERNATIONAL COURTS AND TRIBUNALS 107, 112 (2005).

172 *See id.*, 139.

173 For an overview and analysis of the claims categories, processing modalities and institutional aspects of the UNCC, *see* Norbert Wühler, *United Nations Compensation Commission, in* ENCYCLOPEDIA OF PUBLIC INTERNATIONAL LAW, VOL. IV, 1068 (R. Bernhardt ed., 2000); *See* SHELTON (note 127), at 404-412.

174 *See* Caron & Morris (note 170), at 196-197 (denying that, because of the diversion of oil revenues for funding of awards made by the UNCC and the relation between the UNCC and the oil-for-food program imposed on Iraq by the Security Council, the UNCC constituted a disguised sanctions device).

175 For an exposition of the classical regime concerning reparations, *see* SHELTON (note 127), at 50-103.

176 *See* Heidy Rombouts, Pietro Sardaro & Stef Vandeginste, *The Right to Reparation for Victims of Gross and Systematic Violations of Human Rights, in* OUT OF THE ASHES: REPARATION FOR VICTIMS OF GROSS AND SYSTEMATIC VIOLATIONS OF HUMAN RIGHTS VIOLATIONS 418 (K. De Feyter, S. Parmentier, M. Bossuyt & P. Lemmens eds., 2005) (erroneously placing ICHEIC in the same category); Norbert Wühler, *The United Nations Compensation Commis-*

A major factor contributing to the relatively successful UNCC approach was its simple factual context.[177] Iraq could be and was held liable for its invasion of Kuwait and the resulting damage. Moreover, control of Iraq's oil exports by the Security Council facilitated the creation of a compensation fund of unprecedented proportions. ICHEIC was different. No opportunity existed for establishing a postwar reparations claims commission under traditional principles of international law in the case of Holocaust-era insurance claims. These claims involved private contractual rights and the obligations of private business entities. Compensation depended upon contributions to a settlement fund by such entities. For the most part, funding for ICHEIC came from the German Foundation. The alternative which Germany and the companies belonging to the German Foundation initiative would have preferred, namely a treaty or executive agreement with the United States explicitly extinguishing private claims in favor of a lump-sum arrangement to be implemented by the German Foundation,[178] never materialized. The United States steadfastly rejected such an approach,[179] which led the parties to adopt an unusual alternative: an agreement by the US government to support defendants in Holocaust claims litigation before American courts by submitting a "Statement of Interest" referring to the German Foundation (including its provisions on

---

sion, *in* STATE RESPONSIBILITY AND THE INDIVIDUAL: REPARATION IN INSTANCES OF GRAVE VIOLATIONS OF HUMAN RIGHTS 228 (Albrecht Randelzhofer & Christian Tomuschat eds., 1999).

177 *See* Tomuschat (note 127), at 589.

178 *See* EIZENSTAT (note 16), at 269. Some on the German side, however, also disfavored this approach, fearing it would serve as a general invitation to renegotiate Germany's post-war international reparations agreements. *See* Otto Graf Lambsdorff, *The Negotiations on Compensation for Nazi Forced Laborers*, *in* HOLOCAUST RESTITUTION: PERSPECTIVES ON THE LITIGATION AND ITS LEGACY 170, 176 (Michael J. Bazyler & Roger P. Alford eds., 2006).

179 The US government "would not [agree to] take a formal legal position barring U.S. citizens from their own courts." *Id.* While separation of powers concerns might have had some bearing on the American government's position, precedent exists for claims settlement agreements which include such a ban. *See* *Dames & Moore v. Reagan*, 453 U.S. 654 (1981). However, where claims were asserted by Nazi victims against private parties rather than a foreign state and the US could find itself aligned with companies implicated in the Holocaust, this was legally more precarious and politically unthinkable. *See* O'Donoghue (note 148), at 1136-1137.

ICHEIC) as the appropriate mechanism for resolving Holocaust-era claims.

As a regulatory remedy with a mixed national and international structure providing "rough justice" rather than the more individualized redress normally available through a judicial process,[180] ICHEIC had serious flaws, as enumerated above particularly in Part C, II and III. It clearly reveals numerous discrepancies with the basic requirements for any legitimate modality of reparation in the case of gross and systematic violations of human rights.[181] Consequently, litigation continued.[182]

ICHEIC's central conceptual problem was its overly faithful adherence to the axiom that "collective cataclysms must be handled through collective mechanisms."[183] Advocates of "collectivization" or globalized claims mechanisms which employ general categories as opposed to individual assessments for resolving mass compensation claims posit the destabilizing impact of individualized consideration or its ineffectiveness.[184] In reality, however, a different calculus may apply: the higher a claims process' regard for individual situations, the greater the likelihood of its effectiveness and broad acceptance, with social stability reinforced as a result. Individualization, particularly in the context of claims mechanisms allowing recovery of damages related to the Holocaust-era and a crime that aimed at the physical and spiritual extermination of Jews as a group, is essential for achieving the "climate of internal

---

[180] *See* EIZENSTAT (note 16), at 353.

[181] *See* Rombouts *et al.* (note 176), at 487 (formulating prerequisites in light of which the legal adequacy of a reparations mechanism may be assessed, *i.e.*, timeliness, representation/participation, adequacy of amount, acceptance, effectivity, equality, causality).

[182] See Joseph B. Treaster, *Appeals Court Extends Time for Suit on Holocaust Insurance Payments*, N.Y. TIMES, 3 Oct. 2007, Section C, 4 (referring to the *Generali Settlement*). *See also*, Treaster (notes 118 and 150); *In re Assicurazioni Generali S.p.A. Holocaust Ins.*, Slip Copy, 2007 WL 3129894 (S.D.N.Y., 26 Oct. 2007).

[183] *See* Tomuschat (note 133), at 586.

[184] *See id.*; Roland Bank, *Processing of Claims for Slave and Forced Labor: Expediency versus Accuracy?*, *in* HOLOCAUST RESTITUTION: PERSPECTIVES ON THE LITIGATION AND ITS LEGACY 190, 195-196 (Michael J. Bazyler & Roger P. Alford eds., 2006) (describing the German Foundation approach as a trade-off between "individual justice and a contribution to general justice for the large majority of victims" by means of expedited processing, which avoided the delay and costs of litigation, using simplified criteria in favor of the latter).

understanding"[185] and "reconciliation"[186] supported by proponents of claims collectivization. Under the ICHEIC process, notwithstanding the compensatory payments that many thousands of claimants received, challenges were understandably raised concerning the large proportion of claims rejected and the adequacy of funding provided by the insurers. Moreover, the question of the insurance companies' complicity with the Nazi regime remained unresolved and unsettling.[187]

A deeper explanation for the continuing legal challenge may be found in a widespread dissatisfaction with ICHEIC on a moral level. Was the ICHEIC process anything more than a fig-leaf which permitted the insurance companies to continue business as usual and the governments of the United States and Germany to dispose of an uncomfortable diplomatic problem, as some critics suggest?[188] In essence, ICHEIC was an administrative arm of the German Foundation.[189] By acceding to the Trilateral Agreement, the ICHEIC in effect allowed Allianz, the largest German insurance company[190] and one of ICHEIC's key founding members, to play by another set of rules.[191] Among other things, Allianz could thereby contribute exclusively to the German Foundation and ignore its prior commitment to provide separate funding to

---

[185] Tomuschat (note 133), at 587.

[186] Bank (note 184), at 196.

[187] *See* Bell (note 143), at 112 (referring to this continuing "source of contention").

[188] *See id.*, at 144 (noting that the German Foundation Agreement has been seen as providing a neat diplomatic way of removing an irritant to US-German relations). The objection that the *Generali Settlement* (note 118) initially approved by a lower Federal court in Feb. 2007 amounted to a "cover up" by failing to require full disclosure of policyholders' names, *see* Rosenbaum, Losing Count (note 143), could be lodged with respect to ICHEIC as well. Rosenbaum notes elsewhere the absence of "a true and complete accounting" in the Holocaust compensation cases, and that the "pillaging enterprises, in most cases, purchased the silence of history for a few pennies on the dollar, thereby exploiting the unfortunate conspiracy of time." *See* THANE ROSENBAUM, THE MYTH OF MORAL JUSTICE: WHY OUR LEGAL SYSTEM FAILS TO DO WHAT'S RIGHT 76 (2006).

[189] *See* note 62 and accompanying text.

[190] Allianz AG of Germany, the second largest insurance company in the world and owner of over 30 American subsidiaries, was said to have collected $6.2 billion in premiums in the US in 1996. *See* BAZYLER (note 14), at 112.

[191] *See* note 63.

ICHEIC specifically to compensate insurance claims.[192] To this extent, ICHEIC might be termed an elaborate shell game.[193]

Viewed more positively, the ICHEIC process may have achieved a measure of re-individualization and, perhaps, satisfaction at least for those who did receive some compensation. Payments, at least symbolically, represented acknowledgment of the claimants' injury and slightly dented the insurers' pocketbooks. Irrespective of the pecuniary outcome, moreover, the ICHEIC process established a record which testifies to the economic dimensions of the Holocaust. The documentation relating to claims, thus, contributes toward establishing historical truth and memorializing the victims. ICHEIC's archival research and publication of policyholder names had a similar effect, as did the portion of the ICHEIC humanitarian fund earmarked for educational and remembrance purposes.[194]

Unsurprisingly, debate over ICHEIC's achievement eludes simple resolution. ICHEIC abounds in paradoxes: it sought compensation for the non-compensable and individualized redress for a collective injury; it was a private entity and a form of international administration, and it was an autonomous regime and an appendage of a domestic administrative program. Where questions prevail over answers, as in so many matters concerning the Holocaust, additional consideration appears justified.

---

[192] *See* EIZENSTAT (note 16), at 268; Kent (note 16), at 211.

[193] As in a shell game, observers are likely to be distracted by appearances, losing track of the primary object of their interest. Understanding the true nature of ICHEIC requires one to "follow the money." Most of ICHEIC's funding came from the German Foundation. Half of the $5 billion fund administrated by the German Foundation was contributed by the German government, while the other half came from German industry. German industry received an approximate 40% tax deduction on its contribution. In other words, German taxpayers rather than German corporations footed about two-thirds of the bill – an additional reason for describing ICHEIC as a semi-public entity. *See* BAZYLER (note 14), at 88, 100; Deborah Sturman, *Germany's Reexamination of Its Past through the Lens of the Holocaust Litigation, in* HOLOCAUST RESTITUTION: PERSPECTIVES ON THE LITIGATION AND ITS LEGACY 215, 223 (Michael J. Bazyler & Roger P. Alford eds., 2006).

[194] *But see* ROSENBAUM (note 182), at 77 (identifying the central flaw in the various Holocaust compensation arrangements as a failure to provide the "moral remedy of having the story of atrocity [and pillaging] told and the historical truth revealed").

III. Cross-Cutting Analyses

Inside Relative Normativity: From Sources to Standard Instruments for the Exercise of International Public Authority

*By Matthias Goldmann**

* For comments on earlier drafts I am grateful to Armin von Bogdandy, Eyal Benvenisti, Giacinto della Cananea, Jan Klabbers, Russell Miller, Christian Walter, as well as the fellow participants in this project and in the German-Israeli Minerva School on Global Public Policy and the Law of International Administration, Tel Aviv, March 2008. I am further indebted to Lewis Enim and Eva Richter for their diligence with language and editing. All errors are mine.

A. von Bogdandy et al. (eds.), *The Exercise of Public Authority by International Institutions*, Beiträge zum ausländischen öffentlichen Recht und Völkerrecht 210,
DOI 10.1007/978-3-642-04531-8_22, © Springer-Verlag Berlin Heidelberg 2010

A. Introduction

This article suggests a tentative model for the legal conceptualization of the great variety of instruments by which international institutions exercise public authority, brought to light by the thematic studies of this project. If one were to display this variety of instruments on a scale that ranges from binding international law to non-legal instruments, hardly any thinkable step on this scale would remain empty. Situated at the top end of the scale one would find binding instruments[1] such as interna-

[1] I use the term "binding" instrument as a heuristic category, defined as those instruments which can be ascribed to one of the traditional sources of international law stipulated in Article 38(1) of the Statute of the ICJ. On the difficulties related to the distinction between binding and non-binding norms, *see* Part E.

tional treaties,[2] periodic treaty amendments,[3] decisions on individual cases with binding effect[4] or decisions having the potential to become binding by way of domestic recognition.[5] While these instruments clearly have external legal effects, other instruments seem to be purely internal rules of procedure, although they have in fact considerable repercussions for national administrations.[6] Next come various types of soft, *i.e.* non-binding legal instruments.[7] Some of these instruments operate in the shadow of binding instruments.[8] Others are kept in purely

---

2 World Bank loan or financing agreements, *see* Philipp Dann, *Accountability in Development Aid Law: The World Bank, UNDP and Emerging Structures of Transnational Oversight*, 44 ARCHIV DES VÖLKERRECHTS 381 (2006).

3 Amendments to CITES Annexes, *see* Christine Fuchs, in this volume; and to the WCO Harmonized Commodity Description and Coding System, *see* Isabel Feichtner, in this volume.

4 Listings of terror suspects by the UN Security Council Taliban and Al-Qaida Sanctions Committee, *see* Clemens Feinäugle, in this volume; conferral of world heritage status by the UNESCO World Heritage Committee, *see* Diana Zacharias, in this volume; waivers for WTO members for implementing changes in the Harmonized System, *see* Isabel Feichtner, in this volume; decisions by the Enforcement Branch of the Compliance Committee for the Emission Trading System on, *e.g.*, the reduction of emission rights due to past non-compliance, *see* Petra Láncos, in this volume.

5 International trademark registrations, *see* Karen Kaiser, in this volume.

6 The "HS Procedure" for adapting WTO scales of concessions to changes in the WCO Harmonized Commodity Description and Coding System, *see* Isabel Feichtner, in this volume; the accounting rules for the administration of ETS allowances, *see* Petra Láncos, in this volume; and the Operational Guidelines of the World Heritage Committee, *see* Diana Zacharias, in this volume.

7 The term "non-binding legal instrument", which I use in a strictly heuristic sense, is not an oxymoron. Rather, it is based on a relative concept of law which comprises both *binding law* and *non-binding law*, *see* Part B.I. On the problems related to a conceptual distinction between binding and non-binding law *see* Part E.

8 Refugee Status Determination by UNHCR, *see* Maja Smrkolj, in this volume; ILO Declaration on Fundamental Principles and Rights at Work, *see* Erika de Wet, *Governance Through Promotion and Persuasion*, in this volume; general and country-specific recommendations of the OSCE High Commissioner on National Minorities, *see* Anuscheh Farahat, in this volume.

soft form, like product standards or codes of conduct,[9] but also decisions concerning individuals.[10] In the lower part of the scale one would find instruments containing non-binding rules that are foremost aimed at facilitating consultation,[11] or soft private law instruments.[12] At the bottom end one would discover non-legal instruments that are devoid of any deontic elements,[13] but nevertheless have a high legal or political impact on the affected policy area. Examples of this class of instruments include factual assessment reports,[14] indicators,[15] reports on implementation and compliance,[16] and databases.[17]

---

9 Codex Alimentarius, *see* Ravi Pereira, in this volume; FAO Codes of Conduct for Responsible Fisheries, *see* Jürgen Friedrich, in this volume; OECD Guidelines for Multinational Enterprises, *see* Gefion Schuler, in this volume.

10 Interpol notices, *see* Bettina Schöndorf-Haubold, in this volume.

11 Proceedings before National Contact Points in case of complaints for violations of the OECD Guidelines for MNEs, *see* Gefion Schuler, in this volume; country visits and confidential follow-up reports by the OSCE High Commissioner on National Minorities, *see* Anuscheh Farahat, in this volume; as well as the HS Procedure, *see* Isabel Feichtner, in this volume.

12 Decision letters concerning ICHEIC insurance claims, *see* Steven Less, in this volume.

13 Only instruments with a significant prevalence of deontic vocabulary expressing commands, requests, and recommendations may be termed legal. As it is sometimes difficult to make a precise distinction between facts and norms at a theoretical level, my distinction between "legal" and "non-legal" instruments is rather heuristic than systematic. In most cases, though, it will not cause any practical difficulty. On the differences between facts, norms and normative facts, *see* ROBERT BRANDOM, MAKING IT EXPLICIT 623-6 (1994). For a critical assessment, *see* Jürgen Habermas, *From Kant to Hegel. On Robert Brandom's Pragmatic Philosophy of Language*, 8 EUROPEAN JOURNAL OF PHILOSOPHY 322 (2000).

14 Risk assessment reports containing scientific information for risk management within the Codex Alimentarius Commission, *see* Ravi Pereira, in this volume; reports assessing eligibility for the Emission Trading System, *see* Petra Láncos, in this volume.

15 Armin von Bogdandy & Matthias Goldmann, *The Exercise of International Public Authority through National Policy Assessment. The OECD's PISA Policy as a Paradigm for a New International Standard Instrument*, 5 INTERNATIONAL ORGANIZATIONS LAW REVIEW 241 (2009).

16 Many examples are mentioned in the thematic studies. *See*, for example, the review mechanism in the Committee on Trade in Financial Services installed

The position of an instrument on this scale should not be taken as indication of its effectiveness. Rather, as the thematic studies reveal, each of the instruments surveyed in this project has its way of effectively contributing to the exercise of public authority[18] in the policy area concerned. This is no coincidence as one criterion for the compilation of the instruments surveyed was that they have a perceptible impact on public policy. The driving interest behind this project is not so much the questions whether, why and to what extent international instruments are effective,[19] nor why policymakers opt for a particular type of instrument in a particular situation,[20] but first and foremost to provide a legal account of effective international public authority, and to further develop the legal framework within which such authority is situated. The purpose of such a legal account is to foster both the effectiveness and the legitimacy of international public authority. Legal concepts serve as analytical tools, provide a medium for critique, and have the capacity of transposing imponderable discourses about legitimacy into more precise, sustainable, manageable and reliable concepts of legality.[21] This is due to the law's capacity to rationalize fundamental conflicts about questions of justice through the use of formalistic arguments about rights and obligations.[22] Certainly legal arguments are not free of

---

on the basis of China's Accession Protocol to the WTO, *see* Joseph Windsor, in this volume.

17 In the context of Interpol, *see* Bettina Schöndorf-Haubold, in this volume.

18 On the concept of public authority, *see* Armin von Bogdandy, Philipp Dann & Matthias Goldmann, in this volume.

19 This is what distinguishes this project from research on compliance. *See* ANDREW GUZMAN, HOW INTERNATIONAL LAW WORKS (2008); COMMITMENT AND COMPLIANCE (Dinah Shelton ed., 2000); INTERNATIONAL COMPLIANCE WITH NONBINDING ACCORDS (Edith Brown Weiss ed., 1997). For a critical viewpoint, *see* JACK L. GOLDSMITH & ERIC A. POSNER, THE LIMITS OF INTERNATIONAL LAW (2005).

20 *See* Kenneth W. Abbott & Duncan Snidal, *Hard and Soft Law in International Governance*, 54 INTERNATIONAL ORGANIZATION 421 (2000); Charles Lipson, *Why are Some International Agreements Informal?*, 45 INTERNATIONAL ORGANIZATION 495 (1991).

21 On this agenda, *see* Armin von Bogdandy, Philipp Dann & Matthias Goldmann, in this volume, Part B.II.

22 This is the common denominator of otherwise very different legal theories within the communicative paradigm, *see* FRIEDRICH KRATOCHWIL, RULES,

contingency. Nevertheless, I consider the formalism of legal discourse as preferable to "pure" moral reasoning because it "enable[s] the legal profession to continue to carry out its legal job without having to transform itself into a legislative agency ("realise policy") or a priesthood of right and wrong".[23]

It is submitted that this legal account of international public authority requires a legal conceptualization of the *instruments* by which public authority is exercised. This follows from our approach[24] for at least three reasons. Two reasons are rather practical. First, our approach focuses on the *exercise* of international public authority. Accordingly the authoritativeness of an international institution's policies depends primarily on the kinds of instruments involved. Consequently an account of typical instruments would facilitate the identification of policies by which public authority is exercised. Second, the legal standards to be developed for ensuring the legitimacy of each exercise of international public authority, *i.e.* the concrete rules addressing competence, procedures, participation, transparency, accountability, judicial review, etc., cannot possibly be the same for all instruments. Obviously an international treaty that receives domestic ratification and has no immediate repercussions for individuals poses a legitimacy challenge that is different from that of a technical code adopted by a secretive round of government experts or an instrument affecting the financial interests of named individuals. The response of international institutional law to international public authority, therefore, needs to be specific to the type of instrument in question. The development of instrument-specific standards accentuates the administrative law bequest of our approach, as it entails a concretization and specification of constitutional princi-

---

NORMS, AND DECISIONS 200 (1989); MARTTI KOSKENNIEMI, FROM APOLOGY TO UTOPIA 563 *et seq.* (2nd ed., 2005); JÜRGEN HABERMAS, FAKTIZITÄT UND GELTUNG 272 *et seq.* (1992).

[23] Martti Koskenniemi, *Introduction, in* SOURCES OF INTERNATIONAL LAW xi, xiii (Martti Koskenniemi ed., 2001). This idea is also a driving factor for constitutionalist approaches, *see* Anne Peters, *Compensatory Constitutionalism: The Function and Potential of Fundamental International Norms and Structures*, 19 LEIDEN JOURNAL OF INTERNATIONAL LAW 579, 610 (2006). Comprehensive on the role of the rule of law for channeling disagreement on questions of justice, *see* SAMANTHA BESSON, THE MORALITY OF CONFLICT 205 *et seq.* (2005).

[24] By "our approach", I mean the concept set out in Armin von Bogdandy, Philipp Dann & Matthias Goldmann, in this volume. It goes with out saying that not all aspects of this approach are shared by all participants in the project.

ples. The third reason is epistemological and depends on the first two reasons. There is no direct access to reality, but only through the intermediation of concepts.[25] If there are good practical reasons for conceptualizing typical instruments in law, the concepts need to be *legal* ones. As each scholarly discipline has a specific interest in reality, it needs to define its own concepts for approaching reality. Thus, the aesthetics of the color blue are meaningless for the spectral analysis of a blue-colored pigment. Therefore, as instruments are to play a major role in the development of the law of international institutions, they need to be *legally* conceptualized.

This conceptualization of instruments should have the potential to cover diverse forms of public authority and include binding and non-binding legal as well as non-legal instruments. Presently the legal status of many of these instruments is all but clear.[26] The revealed plurality of instruments stands in marked contrast to the narrow limits of the classical doctrine of the sources of international law as stipulated in Article 38(1) of the ICJ Statute (hereinafter "sources doctrine"). Article 38 only provides for customary law, general principles of law, and treaties. Looking at the instruments under analysis in the thematic studies, only a few of them could be considered as "secondary"[27] treaty law,[28] and again fewer could be taken as representations of customary international law.[29] A large portion of the instruments of public authority, for which I will use the shorthand term "alternative instruments", simply escape the sources doctrine because of their lack of binding force (non-binding law), or of legal rules (non-law). The term "soft law", though commonly used, assembles a very heterogeneous array of non-binding

---

[25] "Gedanken ohne Inhalt sind leer, Anschauungen ohne Begriffe blind." (Thoughts without content are empty, intuitions without concepts are blind): IMMANUEL KANT, CRITIK DER REINEN VERNUNFT 75 (2nd ed., 1787).

[26] For a detailed analysis, *see* Part B.

[27] The term "secondary" does not allude to HERBERT L.A. HART, THE CONCEPT OF LAW 79 (1st ed. 1961), but to the concept of secondary, or delegated, legislation as used in the context of EU law. *See also* JURIJ ASTON, SEKUNDÄR-GESETZGEBUNG INTERNATIONALER ORGANISATIONEN ZWISCHEN MITGLIEDSTAATLICHER SOUVERÄNITÄT UND GEMEINSCHAFTSDISZIPLIN (2005).

[28] Changes to CITES appendixes, *see* Christine Fuchs, in this volume; modifications of the Harmonized System, *see* Isabel Feichtner, in this volume.

[29] *See* de Wet (note 8).

instruments.[30] Because it does not provide any meaningful conceptualization, the term "soft law" is not much more than a slightly more elegant way of saying "underconceptualized law". Thus, a large part of the instruments by which international institutions exercise authority remains beyond the reach of meaningful legal concepts.

The lack of a legal account of alternative instruments is all the more disconcerting as their legitimacy raises at least as many questions as that of binding international law.[31] For example, alternative instruments might affect *democratic procedures* by facilitating two-level games in which national executives bypass their parliaments and other national stakeholders by agreeing on effective international instruments that do not require domestic ratification.[32] Democratic decision-making might also be compromised by uncertainty about the competencies and procedures required for adopting alternative instruments. Who is authorized to adopt what kind of alternative instrument? While statutes of international organizations, professional associations, etc., usually stipulate whether an organ of the organization may adopt binding rules, alternative instruments are frequently adopted in the absence of a comparable statutory rule of competence and sophisticated rules of procedure ensuring participation, accountability, etc. Further, alternative instruments may affect *legal certainty* because they might modify the meaning of a binding rule without modifying the text of that rule.[33] Finally, alternative instruments might infringe *individual rights*. Interpol notices, for example, might have serious consequences for those named in them.[34]

---

[30] In this article, "soft law" is used in reference to the bindingness, and not to the degree of textual precision of an instrument.

[31] This is the reason for Jan Klabbers' philippic against soft law, *see* Jan Klabbers, *The Undesirability of Soft Law*, 67 NORDIC JOURNAL OF INTERNATIONAL LAW 381 (1998). *See also* Martti Koskenniemi, *Global Governance and Public International Law*, 37 KRITISCHE JUSTIZ 241, 243 (2004); Eyal Benvenisti, *"Coalitions of the Willing" and the Evolution of Informal International Law, in* COALITIONS OF THE WILLING: AVANTGARDE OR THREAT? 1 (Christian Callies, Georg Nolte & Peter-Tobias Stoll eds., 2006).

[32] Kerstin Martens & Klaus D. Wolf, *Paradoxien der Neuen Staatsräson. Die Internationalisierung der Bildungspolitik in der EU und der OECD*, 13 ZEITSCHRIFT FÜR INTERNATIONALE BEZIEHUNGEN 145 (2006); Eyal Benvenisti, *Exit and Voice in the Age of Globalization*, 98 MICHIGAN LAW REVIEW 167 (1999-2000).

[33] Illustrative is the ECJ Case 322/88, *Grimaldi v. Fonds des Maladies Professionnelles*, 1989 E.C.R. 4407.

[34] Bettina Schöndorf-Haubold, in this volume.

As a result one could say that alternative instruments face many of the well-known legitimacy problems of global governance.[35]

This article attempts to sketch an approach that has the potential to cover a diverse range of instruments of international public authority and thereby to shed some conceptual light onto the "opacity" of instrumental pluralism in the postnational constellation.[36] This approach rests on the conviction that lawyers should not deplore relative normativity[37] but seek to get it under control. The envisaged account combines internal and external perspectives. It aims at building bridges between the instrumental plurality of global governance revealed by external, or material, perspectives, and the internal, or formal, viewpoint of law that follows the binary logic of the difference between legal and illegal.[38] This requires the formulation of multiple rules of identification for multiple types of instruments of public authority. Each of these rules of identification will identify one type of instrument, called standard instruments, of international institutions according to formal parameters. Standard instruments constitute the backbone of international institutional law: they enable the identification of instruments that are comparable to a degree that justifies the development and application of one identical legal regime that sets up rules regarding competence, procedure, judicial review, etc.

Part B provides the theoretical groundwork for the envisaged legal account. Reviewing various scholarly strategies that aim at coming to terms with alternative instruments, it argues that a successful account requires a relativist and internal viewpoint. On this basis, Part C introduces the concept of standard instruments, elaborates the parameters that serve as a toolbox for the definition of rules of identification, and suggests tentative rules of identification for a number of standard instruments that emerge from the project. Part D explores some elements

---

35 For many others, *see* Joseph H. H. Weiler, *The Geology of International Law – Governance, Democracy and Legitimacy*, 64 ZEITSCHRIFT FÜR AUSLÄNDISCHES ÖFFENTLICHES RECHT UND VÖLKERRECHT (ZAÖRV) 547 (2004).

36 JÜRGEN HABERMAS, DIE POSTNATIONALE KONSTELLATION (2003).

37 *See* Prosper Weil, *Towards Relative Normativity in International Law?*, 77 AMERICAN JOURNAL OF INTERNATIONAL LAW (AJIL) 413 (1983).

38 On the difficulty to distinguish external from internal views, *see* Klaus Günther, *Legal Pluralism or Uniform Concept of Law?* 5 NO FOUNDATIONS. JOURNAL OF EXTREME LEGAL POSITIVISM 5 (2008). On the internal perspective of this project, *see* Armin von Bogdandy, Philipp Dann & Matthias Goldmann, in this volume.

of their respective legal regimes. Part E concludes with some observations, drawn from the present approach, on what it means in terms of legal theory to consider an instrument "binding".

B. Approaching Alternative Instruments: Theoretical Vantage Points

This section makes the case for a conceptualization based on a relative concept of international legal normativity and assuming an internal perspective. It claims that this standpoint is best suited for a legal account that aims at covering a wide spectrum of alternative instruments and at facilitating discourse about their legality. In making this point this section also reviews the ways in which different streams in international legal scholarship presently conceptualize alternative instruments. It thereby corroborates the initial assumption that alternative instruments are underconceptualized at present, and shows how the envisaged account relates to contemporary research. Because non-legal instruments rarely have been conceptualized in international law,[39] this section largely focuses on the literature on binding and non-binding legal instruments, without any claim to completeness.

---

[39] Gauthier de Beco, *Human Rights Indicators for Assessing State Compliance with International Human Rights*, 77 NORDIC JOURNAL OF INTERNATIONAL LAW 23 (2008). National law perspectives are similarly rare, *see* Bradley C. Karkkainen, *Information as Environmental Regulation: TRI and Performance Benchmarking, Precursor to a New Paradigm?*, 89 GEORGETOWN LAW JOURNAL 257 (2000-2001); Christian Bumke, *Publikumsinformation. Erscheinungsformen, Funktionen und verfassungsrechtlicher Rahmen einer Handlungsform des Gewährleistungsstaates*, 37 DIE VERWALTUNG 3 (2004). Remarkably more research has been carried out on the Open Method of Coordination, which also comprises non-legal instruments, *see* David M. Trubek & Louise G. Trubek, *Hard and Soft law in the Construction of Social Europe: The Role of the Open Method of Co-ordination*, 11 EUROPEAN LAW JOURNAL 343 (2005); Christian Engel, *Integration durch Koordination und Benchmarking*, *in* EUROPÄISCHES VERWALTUNGSVERFAHRENSRECHT 408 (Hermann Hill & Rainer Pitschas eds., 2004). On research from other disciplines, *see* Dirk Lehmkuhl, *Governance by Rating and Ranking*, Paper presented at the 2005 Annual Meeting of the International Studies Association, on file with the author.

I. Absolute vs. Relative Concepts of Law

One fundamental distinction in the debate about alternative instruments is that between absolute, or binary, and relative, or gradual, concepts of law.[40] Absolute positions make a categorical distinction between (binding) law and (non-binding) non-law. A rule is either part of (binding) law or it remains in the penumbra of politics or morals. Relative positions, however, assume that different grades of legal normativity are conceivable.[41] In the case of international law, some relativists suggest a continuum ranging from non-law to *ius cogens*.[42]

Contemporary accounts of international law that pursue an absolute concept of law claim that only the sources enumerated in Article 38(1) of the ICJ statute may give rise to *legal* obligations. All rights and obligations entail basically the same legal effects while non-binding instruments are considered mere "legal facts"[43] or "political" instruments.[44]

---

[40] On this distinction, *see* Dinah Shelton, *International Law and 'Relative Normativity', in* INTERNATIONAL LAW 145, 167-8 (Malcolm Evans ed., 2003); Anne Peters & Isabella Pagotto, *Soft Law as a New Mode of Governance: A Legal Perspective*, New Modes of Governance Project, Paper No. 04/D11, 6 (2006).

[41] For reasons of conceptual clarity, it should be added that absolute and relative positions can be combined both with uniform accounts of law, which assume that there is only one overarching international legal order, and with pluralist accounts, which embrace the view that there is a heterarchy of different legal orders. On uniform and pluralist accounts, *see* Günther (note 38), at 6. On the relationship between legal pluralism and the monism vs. dualism debate, *see* Armin von Bogdandy, *Pluralism, Direct Effect, and the Ultimate Say: On the Relationship Between International and Domestic Constitutional Law*, 6 INTERNATIONAL JOURNAL OF CONSTITUTIONAL LAW 397 (2008).

[42] Pierre Eisemann, *Le Gentlemen's agreement comme source du droit international*, 106 JOURNAL DU DROIT INTERNATIONAL 326 (1979); Richard Baxter, *International Law in Her Infinite Variety*, 29 INTERNATIONAL AND COMPARATIVE LAW QUARTERLY 549, 563 (1980); Alan E. Boyle, *Some Reflections on the Relationship of Treaties and Soft Law*, 48 INTERNATIONAL AND COMPARATIVE LAW QUARTERLY 901, 913 (1999); Christine M. Chinkin, *The Challenge of Soft Law: Development and Change in International Law*, 38 INTERNATIONAL AND COMPARATIVE LAW QUARTERLY 850, 866 (1989). Willem Riphagen proposes a circular, rather than a linear relationship, *see* Willem Riphagen, *From Soft Law to Ius Cogens and Back*, 17 VICTORIA UNIVERSITY OF WELLINGTON LAW REVIEW 81 (1987).

[43] Jean d'Aspremont, *Softness in International Law: A Self-Serving Quest for New Legal Materials*, 19 EJIL 1075 (2008).

The term "soft law" is therefore considered a misnomer.[45] Certainly, scholars entertaining an absolute concept of law do not simply pass over alternative instruments. Rather, the effects of non-binding instruments on the traditional sources of international law are acknowledged. Accordingly, non-binding instruments are seen as important evidence of the existence of *opinio iuris*; as rules of interpretation for the concretization of general clauses like "good faith" or indeterminate treaty provisions; as means for facilitating implementation of indeterminate treaty provisions; and as limitations to the scope of domestic jurisdiction.[46]

Absolute concepts of law find their origin in positivist legal theories, which are primarily focused on the national level.[47] Two central arguments are presented in favor of an absolute concept of international law. The first is the idea of state sovereignty and of a predominantly horizontal international order. These principles dictate strict adherence to voluntarism and make anathema the idea that legal obligations might arise against or without the will of states.[48] The second is the general positivist concern of ensuring a "pure" concept law that is uncontaminated by values, morals and political considerations.[49]

---

44 Anthony Aust, *The Theory and Practice of Informal International Instruments*, 35 INTERNATIONAL AND COMPARATIVE LAW QUARTERLY 787 (1986); Michael Bothe, *Legal and Non-legal Norms – A Meaningful Distinction in International Relations?*, 11 NETHERLANDS YEARBOOK OF INTERNATIONAL LAW 65, 95 (1980); WOLFGANG HEUSEL, "WEICHES" VÖLKERRECHT. EINE VERGLEICHENDE UNTERSUCHUNG TYPISCHER ERSCHEINUNGSFORMEN 47 (1991).

45 Bothe (note 44), at 95.

46 Daniel Thürer, *Soft Law*, *in* IV ENCYCLOPEDIA OF PUBLIC INTERNATIONAL LAW 452 (Rudolf Bernhardt ed., 2000); *see also* the statements in *A Hard Look at Soft Law*, *in* PROCEEDINGS OF THE 82ND ANNUAL MEETING 371 (American Society of International Law ed., 1988). The list could be continued. This account is shared by scholars arguing from very different theoretical standpoints, including traditional positivist as well as constructivist approaches. *See* KRATOCHWIL (note 22).

47 Theorists like Austin, Kelsen, Hart, and Luhmann generally follow an absolute approach.

48 See the strictly horizontal view of the international legal order in Weil (note 37), at 417-9. Further, the distinction between legal acts and legal facts is based on a voluntaristic concept of law, *see* d'Aspremont (note 43), at 4.

49 Weil (note 37), at 421.

The first argument presents more an empirical than a theoretical challenge.[50] On a theoretical level relative normativity can be reconciled with a strictly voluntaristic approach to international law if one considers that states might simply choose to create instruments of varying legal normativity.[51] Empirically the contemporary state of the international order brings the sovereignty argument considerably under stress because it looks more and more vertical. International institutions exercise considerable public authority that is only remotely related to state consent.[52] As the thematic studies of this project amply demonstrate, majority votes, bodies with limited composition and expert committees are now part of daily international affairs. Consensual acts might affect states that never consented to them.[53] But even if all these developments were seen as exceptions that prove the rule of a still largely horizontal international order characterized by state sovereignty, empirical proof would still militate against the exclusion of non-binding legal instruments from the concept of law. The thematic studies in this issue show that such instruments function as independent sources of public authority.[54] Some of them look like law and function like law, *i.e.* they govern public affairs by enabling a distinction between legal and illegal behavior. They are used in situations where practical reasons impede the adoption of law under the sources doctrine[55] or where an existing treaty framework proves insufficient.[56] Non-binding legal instruments, therefore, put limits to state sovereignty just as much as instruments falling under the sources doctrine because states chose them to do so. As a result, for empirical reasons, sovereignty and state consent cannot be invoked as arguments for limiting non-binding legal instruments to the role of mere auxiliaries to the traditional sources of international law

---

50 Insofar I agree with Oscar Schachter, *The Twilight Existence of Nonbinding International Agreements*, 71 AJIL 296, 301 (1977).

51 Ulrich Fastenrath, *Relative Normativity in International Law*, 4 EJIL 305, 325 (1993).

52 *See* Ingo Venzke, in this volume.

53 This is particularly the case of financial regulations which are usually made by developed states.

54 *See* Part A. For further examples of effective governance through alternative instruments, *see* JOSÉ E. ALVAREZ, INTERNATIONAL ORGANIZATIONS AS LAW-MAKERS 217 *et seq.* (2005). For the literature about compliance with alternative instruments, *see* note 20.

55 Ravi Pereira, in this volume; Gefion Schuler, in this volume.

56 Jürgen Friedrich, in this volume.

and leaving them essentially before the doors of the concept of law.[57] Such an absolute concept of law is unconvincing if one sees the role of public international law in providing a comprehensive framework for the international order.[58] Consequently absolute concepts of law either need to be modified so as to take full account of alternative instruments or should be abandoned for the purposes of this article.

In recognition of this problem three intriguing strategies extend the *absolute* concept of law into the field of alternative instruments by proposing rules of recognition that reach farther than the sources doctrine and would cover a significant number of non-binding legal instruments. The first strategy, proposed by van Hoof, proceeds on the basis of H.L.A. Hart's concept of law and suggests five "points of recognition" for determining all relevant manifestations of consent or agreement that he considers to be rules of international law.[59] Those points of recognition allow treating certain non-binding legal instruments and instruments falling under Article 38(1) of the ICJ Statute all the same. The second approach is Andrew Guzman's rational choice model of international law. Guzman observes that reputation has a far greater, and retaliation a far lesser role for state compliance with international rules than traditional theories of international law suggest. Consequently he defines international law comprehensively as "those promises and obligations that make it materially more likely that a state will behave in a manner consistent with those promises and obligations than would otherwise be the case". This definition clearly includes non-binding law.[60] The third strategy is proposed by both Brunnée and Klabbers. They

---

[57] In addition, it is difficult to conceptualize the agreement or promise contained in such instruments in other normative orders like politics or morals, *see* JAN KLABBERS, THE CONCEPT OF TREATY IN INTERNATIONAL LAW 121 (1996).

[58] On this purpose of public law, *see* Armin von Bogdandy, Philipp Dann & Matthias Goldmann, in this volume.

[59] GODEFRIDUS VAN HOOF, RETHINKING THE SOURCES OF INTERNATIONAL LAW (1983). Those points of recognition comprise abstract statements (declarations etc. which indicate a state's conviction to be bound), travaux préparatoires, characteristics of the text of an instrument (*e.g.* language employed, name and preamble of a document), follow-up mechanisms and subsequent practice. *Id.* at 215-279.

[60] Andrew T. Guzman, *A Compliance-Based Theory of International Law*, 90 CALIFORNIA LAW REVIEW 1823, 1878 *et seq.* (2002).

rely on Lon Fuller's eight criteria for the morality of law[61] in order to draw the distinction between law and non-law.[62] This is a promising way of accommodating any non-binding legal instrument within an absolute concept of law because state consent does not play a role in Fuller's model. As Klabbers concedes, Fuller's criteria are not designed to determine the validity of laws, a factor that Fuller presupposes, but rather to ensure their legitimacy.[63] Klabbers suggests giving up the categorical distinction between validity and legitimacy that is so fundamental for modern legal positivist thinking.[64] This distinction also lies at the heart of the second argument listed above. While I fully share and endorse the positivist view that the strength of law lies in its enabling a formalized, rational discourse that produces relatively clear, timely, and enforceable decisions, I do not think that the concept suggested by Brunnée and Klabbers raises concerns in this respect. Most of Fuller's criteria are quite formal and can be applied easily and without too much contingency.

My reservations about absolute concepts of law, including those that react on contemporary instrumental diversity, lie elsewhere, on a more pragmatic level. If the objective of the envisaged conceptualization is to enable the law to provide a comprehensive framework for the international order and the exercise of public authority within this order, *i.e.* to ensure its effectiveness, legitimacy, and conformance with human rights norms,[65] absolute concepts of law do not seem to be very helpful. If the

---

61 According to LON FULLER, THE MORALITY OF LAW 33-91 (1964), legal norms (as opposed to moral norms) require generality; promulgation; limited retroactivity; clarity; absence of contradictions; not requiring the impossible; constancy through time; and congruence between official action and declared rule.

62 Jutta Brunnée, *Reweaving the Fabric of International Law? Patterns of Consent in Environmental Framework Agreements, in* DEVELOPMENTS OF INTERNATIONAL LAW IN TREATY MAKING 101 (Rüdiger Wolfrum & Volker Röben eds., 2005); Jan Klabbers, *Constitutionalism and the Making of International Law. Fuller's Procedural Natural Law,* 5 NO FOUNDATIONS. JOURNAL OF EXTREME LEGAL POSITIVISM 84, 91 (2008).

63 Klabbers (note 62), at 106. *See also* Jan Klabbers, *Reflections on Soft International Law in a Privatized World,* 16 FINNISH YEARBOOK OF INTERNATIONAL LAW 313, 322 (2005 (2008) (pleading for the use of purely formal criteria for the identification of legal rules).

64 Klabbers (note 62), at 108.

65 On these aims *see* Armin von Bogdandy, Philipp Dann & Matthias Goldmann, in this volume.

scope of the rule of recognition is extended in order to include non-binding legal instruments, instruments that are not equal are put on an equal footing. For example, nobody doubts that instruments outside the scope of the sources doctrine are not susceptible to giving rise to damages or claims before international courts. The envisaged conceptualization should mirror such differences. One-size-fits-all solutions run the risk of downplaying important differences and preclude the formation and application of adequate legal standards that are specific to each type of instrument. As valuable as the proposal by Brunnée and Klabbers is for other purposes,[66] it does not provide a basis for developing the envisaged conceptualization of instruments of public authority that would allow treating different instruments differently and like instruments alike. This objective seems to require a relative concept of law that includes additional categories besides "law" and "non-law" and allows determining not only *whether* an instrument is valid but also *how* it is valid.[67]

Two important caveats should be added. First, discarding absolute concepts of law for the purposes of this project does not amount to assuming that such concepts are "wrong". The choice between absolute and relative positions is a matter of definition and definitions cannot be right or wrong. They can only be more or less convenient for understanding reality.[68] Relative concepts might simply provide more convenient solutions measured by the aims of this article.[69] Second, the preceding argument only supports the view that a relative concept of law is necessary for *defining different categories of instruments* and describing

---

66 In fact, the concept suggested by Klabbers and Brunnée is of great value insofar as it approximates our concept of international public authority, *see* Armin von Bogdandy, Philipp Dann & Matthias Goldmann, in this volume. The concept of international public authority seems to be more inclusive insofar as it also encompasses non-legal instruments, and less inclusive insofar as it approaches purely private self-regulation with more caution.

67 Similar Peters & Pagotto (note 40), at 9; Christian Tietje, *Recht ohne Rechtsquellen?*, 24 ZEITSCHRIFT FÜR RECHTSSOZIOLOGIE 27 (2003).

68 KARL POPPER, DIE BEIDEN GRUNDPROBLEME DER ERKENNTNISTHEORIE 368 (2nd ed., Troels Eggers Hansen ed., 1994); HANS ALBERT, TRAKTAT ÜBER KRITISCHE VERNUNFT 35-44 (5th ed., 1991).

69 My main point of contention with proponents of absolute concepts like d'Aspremont (note 43) therefore seems to be a different idea of the purpose of the concept of law, which I see not only as a means of coordination, but as constitutive of an international public order.

their legal effects. It does not include the claim that *the legal regime* that will be applicable to each category of instruments necessarily needs to be based on a relative concept of law. Rather, each category of instrument resembles a self-contained regime that is subject to judgments that follow the binary code of legality versus illegality.[70] The maintenance of a binary structure does not cause relative theories to lose their *raison d'être*.[71] Their *raison d'être* is to extend legal discourse to those instruments of public authority that have hitherto remained largely below the radar of legal discourse. Even if the legality of an alternative instrument is an on/off matter a relative understanding still allows a more precise assessment of the legal effects of the instrument and does not have to refer instruments that are constitutive of public authority to substantially different spheres like morality or politics. This is the main point of a public law approach.

II. External vs. Internal Standpoints

The preceding section deals with the theoretical concept of law that this article should endorse. Legal theory assumes the external standpoint of an outside observer of legal operations.[72] Ultimately, however, the present project, and this includes this article, does not aim at fostering legal theory. Its objective is the development of international institutional law and doctrine so as to facilitate discourse about the validity and legality of instruments. This is essentially an internal perspective. This section argues that an internal perspective requires basing the envisaged conceptualization on purely formal criteria.

At this point it must be noted that a large share of scholarly analysis of alternative instruments is written from a functionalist perspective and assumes an exclusively external standpoint. Thematically as well as personally this stream of legal research overlaps with other disciplines, in

---

70 On soft law as a self-contained regime, *see* Hartmut Hillgenberg, *A Fresh Look at Soft Law*, 10 EJIL 499 (1999). The concept of self-contained regime should be used *mutatis mutandi*, as it usually refers to regimes falling under the sources doctrine.

71 *But see* KLABBERS (note 57), at 157 *et seq*.

72 For the distinction between external and internal approaches, *see* HART (note 27), at 88-90.

particular with social sciences.[73] Although the need for internal conceptualizations finds recognition in this research[74] it pursues different interests. For example, it describes the use of alternative instruments, their advantages and disadvantages, the reasons why states comply with them, the challenges they imply for democracy, etc. As a consequence of these research interests instruments are judged and classified not according to formal criteria only but also according to material criteria such as their actual effects, the peculiarities of the issue area concerned, the likelihood of states' compliance, etc.

Likewise, legal theory that endorses a relative concept of law maintains an external, observing perspective and frequently uses other than explicitly formal criteria for classifying instruments. For example, according to the theory proposed by Gunther Teubner and Andreas Fischer-Lescano, law, as opposed to other communicative systems, presupposes institutionalized processes of secondary norm-formation,[75] which is a material criterion referring to social reality. Other theories like the New Haven School and Transnational Legal Process even gloss over the difference between law and other normative discourses like politics and morals, proposing neither formal nor material criteria for distinguishing different kinds of instruments.[76]

What is the problem with the recourse to material criteria? Why do internal approaches need to be based on purely formal criteria? Internal perspectives, *i.e.* the perspectives of those who need to make decisions about the validity and legality of certain instruments, etc., require *ex ante* judgments. Only formal criteria allow such judgments. The operator with an internal perspective cannot wait until the instrument causes

---

73 Abbott & Snidal (note 20); HARD CHOICES, SOFT LAW (John J. Kirton & Michael J. Trebilcock eds., 2004); Lipson (note 20); Kal Raustiala, *Form and Substance in International Agreements*, 99 AJIL 581 (2005); SHELTON (note 19); Christine M. Chinkin, *Normative Development in the International Legal System, in* COMMITMENT AND COMPLIANCE 21, 30 (Dinah Shelton ed., 2000); Pierre-Marie Dupuy, *Soft Law and the International Law of the Environment*, 12 MICHIGAN JOURNAL OF INTERNATIONAL LAW 420, 431 (1990-1991).

74 ALVAREZ (note 54), at 258.

75 GUNTHER TEUBNER & ANDREAS FISCHER-LESCANO, REGIME-KOLLISIONEN 43 (2006).

76 Myres S. McDougal, *International Law, Power and Policy: A Contemporary Conception, in* 82 RECUEIL DES COURS 137, 162 *et seq.* (1953); Harold Hongju Koh, *Transnational Legal Process,* 75 NEBRASKA LAW REVIEW 181 (1996).

certain effects, is being complied with or not, before he or she makes a judgment about its legal quality that will allow him or her to determine the conditions for its validity and legality. Rather, the insider needs to be able to legally qualify an instrument in the moment he or she chooses to make use of it. Only by way of formal criteria the operator within a legal system may anticipate the legal quality of the instrument he or she intends to adopt and apply the legal regime provided by international institutional law for instruments of this kind. Formal criteria would enable the identification and classification of an instrument before its "normative ripples"[77] appear. For this reason the ensuing internal conceptualization hinges on the exclusive use of formal criteria.

C. From Sources to Standard Instruments

I. The Concept of Standard Instruments

This section proposes the concept of standard instruments as a category for the legal conceptualization of instruments of international public authority from an internal, doctrinal perspective. This concept is not entirely new or revolutionary, neither in domestic nor in international law. In addition, it harmonizes with the established sources doctrine.

A standard instrument is a combination of a rule of identification for authoritative instruments of a specific type and a specific legal regime that is applicable to all instruments coming under the rule of identification. The two elements of standard instruments need to be carefully distinguished. The *rule of identification* identifies specific instruments that belong to a certain category of authoritative acts to which the same legal regime applies.[78] It is based on a relative concept of law and assumes an internal perspective by reliance on formal criteria. The *legal regime* is the second element of standard instruments. It determines conditions for the validity and legality of the instruments that fall under the rule of identification (hereinafter: standardized instruments) that relate to issues such as competence, procedure, or review. From our public law

---

[77] Klabbers, *Reflections* (note 63), at 322.

[78] The rule of identification is constituted by formal criteria only and designed for an internal standpoint. I therefore refrain from using the term rule of recognition, which Hart uses for the analysis of the law from an external perspective.

perspective the legal regime is at the highest level guided by principles of public law that are of constitutional significance for the institution within whose penumbra the instruments have been created.[79]

The proposal to think in standard instruments instead of sources has a long tradition in European legal orders. The definition of standard instruments played a crucial role in the development of an administrative law in some continental legal orders.[80] Developed as doctrinal concepts with the purpose of rendering administrative activity more effective and legitimate, they later were instrumental in the assertion of judicial review against administrative action. The law of the European Union comprises written and unwritten standard instruments that are crucial for the allocation of competence among its organs.[81]

In international law, the idea of standard forms is all but new. International lawyers have conceptualized certain types of international instruments, often alternative instruments, in a more or less abstract manner.[82] For example, René Jean Dupuy suggested declaratory and programmatory law as instrumental categories in the penumbra of customary and treaty law.[83] Further examples include conceptualizations of generally accepted standards[84] and codes of conduct.[85] A large amount

---

79 On the concept of a pluriverse of internal constitutional principles *see* Armin von Bogdandy, *General Principles*, in this volume.

80 On Germany and Italy, *see* von Bogdandy & Goldmann (note 15).

81 Jürgen Bast, *Legal Instruments, in* PRINCIPLES OF EUROPEAN CONSTITUTIONAL LAW 373 (Armin von Bogdandy & Jürgen Bast eds., 2006).

82 Comprehensively HENRY SCHERMERS & NIELS BLOKKER, INTERNATIONAL INSTITUTIONAL LAW, sec. 1196 *et seq.* (4th ed., 2003).

83 René Jean Dupuy, *Declaratory Law and Programmatory Law: From Revolutionary Custom to "Soft Law", in* DECLARATIONS ON PRINCIPLES 247 (Robert Akkerman, Peter van Krieken und Charles Pannenborg eds., 1977). Similarly, *see* Hiram E. Chodosh, *Neither Treaty Nor Custom: The Emergence of Declarative International Law*, 26 TEXAS INTERNATIONAL LAW JOURNAL 87 (1991). However, both authors include external and internal parameters in the proposed rules of identification.

84 Bernard Oxman, *The Duty to Respect Generally Accepted International Standards*, 24 NEW YORK UNIVERSITY JOURNAL OF INTERNATIONAL LAW AND POLITICS 109 (1991-1992). This concept of standards needs to be distinguished from the concept of standards proposed by EIBE RIEDEL, THEORIE DER MENSCHENRECHTSSTANDARDS (1986), who understands as standards normative rules of different legal quality emerging from an array of sources, ranging from practices of interpretation to principles in a Dworkinian sense.

of writing relates to resolutions of international organizations with a particular focus on those of the UN General Assembly.[86] The conceptualization suggested in the following builds on these proposals. It goes beyond them in two ways. First, in keeping with the adoption of an internal viewpoint, my conceptualization is based on a single set of purely formal parameters. Second, in keeping with the chosen relative concept of law, my conceputalizaiton takes full account of the public authority exercised by such instruments and not only their significance for the classical sources of international law. The proposal is, thus, based on the hope that an approach that looks closer at the specific authority of an instrument will foster the normative project of advancing international institutional law in a fragmented legal order.

The concept of standard instruments is in harmony with general international law. Like self-contained regimes, standard instruments do not exist in isolation from general international law.[87] Thus, whenever their legal regime provides no specific rules, standard instruments are subject to general international law, including international institutional law, treaty law or customary law. Moreover, even international treaties could be conceptualized as a particular standard instrument. The main difference between thinking in terms of standard instruments and a refurbished theory of sources of law is that the notion of a standard instrument is not limited to legal instruments but equally encompasses non-legal instruments.

The realization of this proposal requires two moments of "doctrinal constructivism".[88] First, the definition of rules of identification; second,

---

[85] Hellen Keller, *Codes of Conduct and their Implementation: The Question of Legitimacy, in* LEGITIMACY IN INTERNATIONAL LAW 219 (Rüdiger Wolfrum & Volker Röben eds., 2008).

[86] Krzyzstof Skubiszewski, *A New Source of the Law of Nations: Resolutions of International Organisations, in* RECUEIL D'ÉTUDES DE DROIT INTERNATIONAL EN HOMMAGE À PAUL GUGGENHEIM 508 (1968); Jochen A. Frowein, *The Internal and External Effects of Resolutions by International Organizations*, 49 ZAÖRV 778 (1989); BLAINE SLOAN, UNITED NATIONS GENERAL ASSEMBLY RESOLUTIONS IN OUR CHANGING WORLD (1991); on binding resolutions, *see* ASTON (note 27).

[87] Martti Koskenniemi, *Fragmentation of International Law: Difficulties Arising from the Diversification and Expansion of International Law*. Report of the Study Group of the International Law Commission, UN Document A/CN.4/L.682, 13 April 2006, 100.

[88] *See* von Bogdandy & Goldmann (note 15), at part IV.A.3.

the definition of the applicable legal framework. The first moment will be the subject of the remaining part of this section while the second will be thematized in section D.

II. Defining Standard Instruments: Theoretical Basis

The following sections develop the parameters of which the rules of identification of standard instruments are composed. These parameters could thus be called the meta-rule of identification, or a toolbox for doctrinal construction, which establishes a common framework of reference. Each standard instrument will be defined as a specific constellation of these parameters. The parameters themselves rest on both empirical and normative considerations.

Regarding the empirical facet, I elaborated earlier in this article that this meta-rule of identification needs to be limited to strictly formal parameters as opposed to substantive ones. However, the conceptualization of instruments somehow needs to be linked to the world of the factual, as the concept of public authority on which this project is based also rests upon factual considerations, in particular on the empirical insight that there are instruments beyond the sources doctrine that put effective constraints on the will of their addressees. Therefore, a link has to be established between the pure formality of the parameters, which is owed to the needs of an internal perspective, and the world of the factual. In other words, the selection of formal parameters for inclusion into the meta-rule of identification must be made on the basis of generalized factual considerations, *i.e.* considerations about the abstract ability of each parameter to indicate the authoritativeness of an instrument. As in H.L.A. Hart's concept of law, in which the rule of recognition pertains to acceptance as a social fact, but buffers the realm of law against the factual due to its formal nature, in this internal conceptualization, it is the meta-rule of identification that provides the link between the factual and the normative and that autonomizes legal concepts from concepts stemming from other discourses. This link to the world of the factual is achieved by reference to theories surrounding compliance with hard and soft international instruments.

For this purpose I rely on a broad specter of compliance theories in order to extricate a set of parameters that have some significance for the authority of an instrument.[89] This cumulative application of different and sometimes contradictory, theoretical strands could be shunned as eclectic and inconsequential. However, my aim is to identify the widest possible range of parameters for the identification of instruments of public authority. As each theory stems from a different theory about law and society, it would be insufficient to limit oneself to one theory and thereby construe the meta-rule of identification on a too narrow concept of society. To the contrary, it is more probable that each theory reveals a particular aspect of the truth. Furthermore, the requirement to achieve theoretical coherence should not be overstretched. The concrete rules of identification that are the ultimate aim of this article relate to legal doctrine, not to legal theory in the narrower sense. There is hardly a doctrinal concept in international law that rests on one single contradiction-free theoretical basis. The doctrine of the sources of international law is probably the best example in this respect, as neither positivist nor naturalist theories have thus far provided a conclusive explanation of all its features.

Admittedly, even this eclectic approach would require a detailed, critical assessment of each compliance theory. I limit myself to identifying four main factors that are deemed to have an impact on compliance by various theoretical strands because this article cannot provide the necessary, detailed assessment. The first factor is *enforcement*. Based on a rationalist model it encompasses all types of incentives or disincentives that make compliance more favorable for the addressees of a rule. Enforcement mechanisms can have harder or softer forms, ranging from military intervention[90] to the threat of reputational damage.[91] The second factor is *management techniques* that the rationalist model of the mana-

---

[89] Although compliance is normally understood as the mere conformity of behavior with a rule irrespective of the impact of the rule on this result, while the impact of a rule on behavior is termed its effectiveness, most of the literature – theoretical and empirical – is about compliance as effectiveness can hardly be measured. On the difference between compliance and effectiveness, *see* Raustiala (note 73), at 610.

[90] This is the position of positivist mainstream in an Austinian or Kelsenian tradition, but also that of non-constructivist rational choice accounts such as GOLDSMITH & POSNER (note 19).

[91] This is the main argument in rationalist-constructivist accounts, *see* GUZMAN (note 19); George Norman & Joel P. Trachtman, *The Customary International Law Game*, 99 AJIL 541 (2005); George Downs, David Rocke & Peter Barsoom, *Is the Good News About Compliance Good News About Cooperation?*, 50 INTERNATIONAL ORGANIZATION 379 (1996).

gerial school considers decisive for compliance, such as sufficient and precise information concerning the content of rules and policies, monitoring, dispute settlement and capacity building.[92] Third, quite different schools identify a number of reasons contributing to the *acceptance* of an instrument, such as the influence of its author or its symbolic validation, as factors fostering compliance.[93] Finally, a decidedly constructivist strand of the literature singles out elements of *persuasion*, such as justificatory discourse that shapes not only the instrument, but also the identity and interests of its authors.[94]

Apart from providing the link to the factual, the carving out of the parameters needs to take into account certain normative considerations that follow from the overall thrust of this project to ensure the legitimacy of public authority. Thus, it plays a decisive role for the qualification of an instrument whether individuals are directly affected by it or whether the interface of another governance level has the potential for providing relief. Moreover, accounting must be made for the existence and length of a "transmission belt" of delegated authority.

III. Parameters for the Definition of Standard Instruments

The factors for compliance as well as the normative premises listed above will now be extrapolated to a set of formal parameters, the metarule of identification. This is a toolbox for the ensuing formulation of

---

92 ABRAM CHAYES & ANTONIA CHAYES, THE NEW SOVEREIGNTY (1995). On the different impacts of normative vs. hortatory, general vs. specific instruments, *see* Dinah Shelton, *Law, Non-Law and the Problem of "Soft Law", in* COMMITMENT AND COMPLIANCE 1, 3 (Dinah Shelton ed., 2000); Peter Haas, *Choosing to Comply: Theorizing from International Relations and Comparative Politics, in* COMMITMENT AND COMPLIANCE 43, 52 *et seq.* (Dinah Shelton ed., 2000).

93 This includes the New Haven School, *see* McDougal (note 76); and Transnational Legal Process, *see* Harold Koh, *Why Do Nations Obey International Law?*, 106 YALE LAW JOURNAL 2599 (1997); THOMAS FRANCK, THE POWER OF LEGITIMACY AMONG NATIONS (1990).

94 Jutta Brunnée & Stephen Toope, *Persuasion and Enforcement: Explaining Compliance with International Law*, 13 FINNISH YEARBOOK OF INTERNATIONAL LAW 273, 292 (2002 (2004)); Michael Barnett & Raymond Duvall, *Power in Global Governance, in* POWER IN GLOBAL GOVERNANCE 1 (Michael Barnett & Raymond Duvall eds., 2005).

concrete rules of identification. Three main groups of parameters can be distinguished: genetic, textual, and follow-up related parameters. There is no "sacred" rule as to which parameters should be part of a concrete rule of identification.[95] The decision must be made according to practical considerations: those parameters that most adequately capture the specificity of the public authority exercised through a certain type of instrument should be chosen as defining parameters. Consequently not all of the following parameters will always be part of a specific rule of identification. Some parameters will be of relevance for a larger number of rules of identification than others.

1. Genetic Parameters

Genetic parameters refer to various circumstances in the process leading up to the adoption of a particular instrument.

a) Author

The legal personality of the institution adopting an instrument (*e.g.* states, international organizations, private associations) as well as the legal framework and composition of the decision-making body within the institution have an impact on the legitimacy of an instrument. Authorship is a crucial category for input legitimacy and for effectiveness because an instrument's author's authority might induce compliance. In practical terms it might be decisive for the effectiveness of an instrument that it has received the blessing of the hegemon of the time. But such aspects cannot be formulated as a formal parameter. Only the abstract legal personality of the author is to be considered.

b) Procedure

A large part of the procedural parameters will usually not be decisive for the classification of an instrument. Rather, procedure is one of the primary fields to which the legal regime of a standard form is supposed to apply, because the adoption procedure is a crucial factor for ensuring

---

[95] *See* JÜRGEN BAST, GRUNDBEGRIFFE DER HANDLUNGSFORMEN DER EU 20, 101 *et seq.* (2006).

the legitimacy and also the effectiveness of an instrument.[96] However, it might matter for the qualification of an instrument that it is part of a larger process leading to the adoption of another instrument or that it concludes the process. Presumably only few preparatory instruments will require specific conceptualization because the conceptualization of the concluding instrument will normally suffice. Only if the preparatory instrument frames the concluding instrument in a decisive way or if said instrument has specific significance for the legitimacy or effectiveness of the concluding instrument, do normative reasons require a legal conceptualization of the preparatory instrument.

c) Promulgation

The role of the promulgation of an instrument is acknowledged in a number of theories about compliance, in particular managerial theories of compliance. It seems evident that it matters for the authority of an instrument whether it is adopted by solemn declaration[97] or official publication, whether it is disclosed or not,[98] or copyrighted.[99] All these aspects are formal and can therefore be determined *ex ante*. This justifies the elevation of aspects concerning the promulgation of an instrument to the rank of potential parameters.

2. *Textual Parameters*

Textual parameters refer to the text of the instrument. It is not necessary for an instrument to dispose of a written text, but most in fact do.

---

[96] Note that in the law of the European Union, the applicable procedure largely depends on the competence, not on the instrument used, *id.* at 351.

[97] The OECD Guidelines for Multinational Enterprises, *see* Gefion Schuler, in this volume.

[98] The Export Credits Arrangement, which used to be confidential. Also, the Basel group developed confidential rules. Likewise, the Security Council's reasoning behind putting someone on or removing him from the list of terrorists remains secretive, *see* Clemens Feinäugle, in this volume.

[99] Official Commentary on the OECD Model Convention on Double Taxation, *see* Ekkehart Reimer, *Transnationales Steuerrecht, in* INTERNATIONALES VERWALTUNGSRECHT 181 (Christoph Möllers, Andreas Voßkuhle & Christian Walter eds., 2007).

a) Designation

In EU law, due to consistent practice, the abstract designation given to an instrument, like "regulation" or "decision", is a safe indicator for the type of standard instrument chosen.[100] But the terminological practice of international institutions seems to be too heterogeneous, both within and across institutions, to give much significance to the designation of an instrument. This will therefore regularly not be a meaningful parameter.

b) First Level Addressees

This parameter concerns the direct addressee of an instrument, *i.e.* the individual or group to which the instrument is explicitly addressed. It matters mostly from a normative perspective because this is the counterpoint to authorship for determining whether there has been a delegation of authority and how many links the chain of delegation has.[101]

c) Second Level Addressees

The term "second level addressee" refers to the person or group that, according to the instrument, is affected. Sometimes the first and second level addressees are identical, as in the case of an instrument addressed to states that only affects their situation.[102] However, a number of activities by international institutions are addressed to states, while they explicitly concern individuals and affect them indirectly,[103] for example by requiring states to impose obligations, grant rights, or change the legal situation of individuals.[104] This parameter is to be taken into account

---

[100] BAST (note 95), at 146; FLORIAN VON ALEMANN, DIE HANDLUNGSFORM DER INTERINSTITUTIONELLEN VEREINBARUNG 44 (2006).

[101] In most of the thematic studies of this project, instruments are addressed to states. However, some instruments are addressed directly to individuals. *See* Steven Less, in this volume; Karen Kaiser, in this volume; Maja Smrkolj, in this volume; Gefion Schuler, in this volume.

[102] Maja Smrkolj, in this volume; Karen Kaiser, in this volume (on individuals); Petra Láncos, in this volume (on states).

[103] On indirect legal effects, *see* PETER KRAUSE, RECHTSFORMEN DES VERWALTUNGSHANDELNS 25 (1974). This largely corresponds to the distinction between *acte juridique* and *fait juridique*, *see* d'Aspremont (note 43).

[104] Anuscheh Farahat, in this volume; Clemens Feinäugle, in this volume.

for the same reasons as the first level addressee. However, it may only be taken into account if the second level addressee is explicitly mentioned. Not every indirect, remote effect may count.

d) Deontic vs. Non-Deontic Instruments

Mostly for normative reasons a distinction between whether an instrument contains deontic language or not must be made. In the terminology used here this corresponds to the question whether the instrument may be considered as law.[105] While deontic language reduces the choice of action of the addressees irrespective of whether it defines goals or means, the dissemination of mere information, though it might have a normative impact, leaves the addressees with greater leeway. Thus, while instruments of "governance by information"[106] might very well be seen as exercising public authority, the authority is less focused than in cases of legal rules. Moreover, a distinction may be drawn based on whether an instrument contains more hortatory or obligatory language. However, this parameter is not particularly clear-cut and should therefore be used with care.

e) General vs. Specific Instruments

It is easier to distinguish whether the instrument is addressed to specific individuals or whether it sets up a general rule. Normally international institutions set up general rules that have to be implemented at the domestic level. A notable exception is WIPO.[107] This division of work is about to change. Indeed, the recent awareness for the activities of international organizations is not least due to their increasing adoption of specific instruments concerning (but not necessarily directly addressing) individuals.[108] This puts individuals more in the focus of interna-

---

105 *Supra,* note 13.

106 *See* Matthias Goldmann, *The Accountability of Private vs. Public Governance "by Information". A Comparison of the Assessment Activities of the OECD and the IEA in the Field of Education*, 58 RIVISTA TRIMESTRALE DI DIRITTO PUBBLICO 41 (2008).

107 Karen Kaiser, in this volume.

108 The most prominent example are certainly the Security Council antiterrorism lists, *see* Clemens Feinäugle, in this volume.

tional institutions because it removes the "armor" of national implementation and perhaps even national judicial review.

f) Superior vs. Subordinate Instruments

Another formal parameter relates to the position of an instrument within a cascade of norms ranging from abstract to concrete that affect the relevant issue area. From the viewpoint of democratic legitimacy and individual rights it makes a significant difference that an instrument is backed by another instrument and merely concretizes it in respect of some details.

3. Parameters Concerning Follow-up

The third group concerns parameters that provide for incentives for compliance, or disincentives for non-compliance, and that play the predominant role in the enforcement approach to compliance.

a) Hard Enforcement: Sanctions, Damages or Direct Implementation

Hard enforcement mechanisms like sanctions, reprisals or damages may be used only in case of a violation of binding international law, *i.e.* acts under the sources doctrine as well as secondary acts endowed with the same legal effects.[109] In a rationalist interpretation hard enforcement gives these instruments particular bite. Therefore, it needs to be determined carefully that the instrument is supposed to trigger such sanctions. This is relatively easy if an instrument is subject to a special self-contained regime that qualifies the use of these sanctions. Otherwise, it must be determined in accordance with the rules of interpretation stipulated in Articles 31-33 of the Vienna Convention on the Law of Treaties. Besides sanctions, direct implementation is another form of hard enforcement. It takes place in the event that the institution adopting an act has the means to implement the decision directly, *e.g.* by withdrawing benefits or allocating a grant.

---

109 ASTON (note 27).

b) Proceedings before International Courts or Other *Fora*

This is, strictly speaking, another element of hard enforcement. But due to its high significance from a legal perspective it deserves specific consideration. The determination that an instrument may serve as the basis of a claim before an international court or other forum for judicial dispute settlement is not significantly different from that concerning means of hard enforcement.

An important sub-parameter relates to the question as to who might have recourse to judicial recourse. This might not only be decisive for the legitimacy of the instrument, particularly if individuals are directly affected.[110] Also, incentive structures for judicial recourse might be significantly different if, for example, class actions are possible.[111] Furthermore, normative reasons compel a further distinction between independent judicial recourse and quasi-judicial, administrative complaint procedures.

c) Soft Enforcement: Monitoring, Reporting and Reputation

Monitoring and reporting mechanisms are a probate means of inducing compliance, both because they reduce managerial difficulties such as lack of transparency and information, and because they are a means of exerting pressure on non-compliant rule addressees. However, significantly different results in compliance are to be expected depending on whether the addressee, the international institution, or independent actors collect the data. Monitoring might be particularly effective if it is carried out in a horizontal direction[112] or if intermediate levels are involved.[113] Also, the publicity of the data and reports multiplies their reputational repercussions. Furthermore, reporting obligations not in-

---

[110] *See*, most notably, Clemens Feinäugle, in this volume; Maja Smrkolj, in this volume.

[111] Anne van Aaken, *Making International Human Rights Protection More Effective: A Rational Choice Approach to the Effectiveness of Provisions of Ius Standi*, 23 CONFERENCES ON NEW POLITICAL ECONOMY 29 (2006).

[112] *See* Haas (note 92).

[113] For example, the FAO Code of Conduct for Responsible Fisheries owes much of its effectiveness to monitoring and implementation by regional fisheries organizations, *see* Jürgen Friedrich, in this volume.

volving specific negotiation and mediation elements are not always effective.[114]

Apart from international courts and tribunals there are other *fora* for dispute settlement that might impose soft sanctions.[115] The proceedings before National Contact Points established under the OECD Guidelines for Multinational Enterprises are a fine example of such quasi-judicial settlements. The sanction consists in the issuance and publication of a statement by a National Contact Point. For enterprises with a reputation to lose this outlook might amount to a substantial threat. Again, who may trigger the procedure becomes a matter of great significance.

The parameters thus defined should be sufficient for the definition of most standard instruments. Nevertheless, I do not claim that the list could not be continued. In particular, non-textual instruments like physical acts might require additional parameters that could be defined analogously.

IV. Identification of Some Preliminary Standard Instruments

Having established the parameters, this section proposes a preliminary set of standard instruments developed on the basis of the instruments analyzed in the thematic studies covered in this issue, and defines their rules of identification by means of the parameters. While the parameters have been developed deductively, the following part is more inductive, making the construction of rules of identification an overall dialectical exercise.

The thematic studies reveal that basically all governance mechanisms comprise a host of instruments all of which contribute in different ways to the exercise of public authority, be it that they are part of a cascade of instruments that step-by-step concretizes a broad statutory provision,[116] establish the results of discussions,[117] ensure uniform interpreta-

---

[114] For negative examples, *see* de Wet (note 8); for positive examples, *see* Anuscheh Farahat, in this volume.

[115] *See* Aust (note 44), at 791.

[116] Jürgen Friedrich, in this volume; Bettina Schöndorf-Haubold, in this volume.

[117] Minutes or official reports of meetings and conferences, *see* Bogdandy & Goldmann (note 15).

tion,[118] foster the implementation of another instrument,[119] or otherwise. Which of these instruments are to be framed as standard instruments? On the one hand, every instrument could qualify provided that a substantive argument were made that it reaches a minimum threshold of authority. On the other hand, a careful balance must be struck between the need to formalize international public authority and the practice requirement of leaving enough leeway for the spontaneous development of new modes of decision-making as well as substantive decisions. Without spontaneity as a resource of innovation and critique,[120] one would run the risk of suffocating progress and reform by too tight a formalist straightjacket. Likewise, over-simplifications will be normatively questionable while exaggerated specificty will be impractical.[121]

How to strike this balance? Creating hierarchies like the identification of a "central instrument" might serve heuristic purposes but are highly contingent and not always easy to achieve.[122] A normatively sound way of making this choice is to focus on those instruments that are addressed to another legal subject whether they stand in a horizontal or a vertical relationship; these instruments are most likely to raise issues of self-determination and legitimacy. The following focuses mostly on these instruments. For reasons of clarity the standard instruments suggested in the following are grouped according to their second level addressee.

1. Instruments Concerning Individuals

a) International Administrative Decisions

A number of instruments retrieved in the thematic studies affect the legal situation of individuals, namely listings by the UN Taliban and Al Qaida Sanctions Committee, UNHCR Refugee Status Determination

---

118 Isabel Feichtner, in this volume.

119 *See* de Wet (note 8): Technically, the 1998 ILO Declaration on Fundamental Principles only corroborates preexisting conventional obligations, although it exceeds their significance; Gefion Schuler, in this volume.

120 Gunther Teubner, *Neo-Spontanes Recht und duale Sozialverfassung in der Weltgesellschaft?*, *in* ZUR AUTONOMIE DES INDIVIDUUMS 437, 446 *et seq.* (Dieter Simon & Manfred Weiss eds., 2000).

121 Peters & Pagotto (note 40), at 7.

122 Anuscheh Farahat, in this volume (referring to "central instruments").

and International Trademark Registrations by WIPO.[123] All of these instruments contain an element of decision-making concerning individuals whose legal situations are indirectly affected. This also applies to the determination of refugee status: although the UNHCR holds that this status follows directly from the Refugee Convention, the determination of this status by the competent international organization has an authoritative status that cannot, and is not, ignored at the domestic level. The Madrid System is slightly different in that it allows national authorities to opt out of a specific trademark registration. Although this mechanism affects individuals more directly than a decision imposing a duty to adopt an act affecting the individual, there is still an intermediate level of governance that filters the legal relationship between the international level and the individual. This justifies applying the same standards to it.

Applying the parameters in a systematic manner, the rule of identification for international administrative decisions could be defined as a deontic, not merely a hortatory act by, or delegated by, a public international institution, addressed to another level of governance, and having individuals as second level addressees, subject to hard enforcement. The strong – though indirect – legal repercussions of such instruments on individuals justify calling it an "administrative" decision, a term that illustrates well the main thrust of this kind of instrument.

b) International Administrative Recommendations

Some decisions affecting individuals are merely hortatory in character. This is the case, for example, with the statements rendered by National Contact Points in case of a specific instance under the Procedural Guidance relating to the OECD Guidelines for Multinational Enterprises.[124] These statements are not subject to hard enforcement and therefore cannot be considered binding law. Nevertheless, they are rendered within an elaborate non-binding legal framework and use legal discourse to resolve a dispute. One could have doubts about the international character of these statements because they are rendered by national administrations. However, in doing so, the National Contact Points act purely on the basis of binding and non-binding international

---

[123] *See* Clemens Feinäugle, in this volume; Maja Smrkolj, in this volume; Karen Kaiser, in this volume.

[124] Gefion Schuler, in this volume.

law. The system of National Contact Points, thus, features the peculiarity of a decentralized implementation in which regular meetings and information exchange provide for uniformity.

Applying the parameters it is possible to define international administrative recommendations as deontic, hortatory and specific instruments rendered by public institutions on the basis of international law, directly addressed to individuals and not subject to hard enforcement. The quasi-judicial process in which the statements of National Contact Points are produced is deliberately not included in this rule of identification. As this procedure appears crucial for the legitimacy and effectiveness of the instrument it should rather be subject to the legal regime of international administrative recommendations.

c) International Administrative Information Acts

Interpol Notices are a case in point for international acts of non-deontic content. Interpol Notices are not to be equated with requests for judicial assistance. Even though some states in practice treat them like requests they are mere announcements by Interpol that a member has issued, or will issue, a respective request for assistance. By issuing a Notice Interpol does not attribute rights or duties to an individual, like in the case of international administrative decisions, but merely forwards information. Nor does it impose any hard or soft obligation on its members to obey the corresponding request by the member entity.[125] There is no deontic element in the pure and simple dissemination of information. Nevertheless, as the issuance of a Notice has a grave factual impact on the individual concerned, human rights concerns militate for the definition of a standard instrument. By means of the parameters, international administrative information can be described as non-deontic instruments by international institutions addressed to public entities revealing information about specific individuals.

Having said that, a difference exists between the non-deontic dissemination of a Notice and the decision by Interpol underlying this dissemination. The latter is addressed to the applicant state and will be considered in the following section.[126]

---

[125] Bettina Schöndorf-Haubold, in this volume.

[126] Certainly, these distinctions are difficult to draw. Similar problems can be observed in German police law, where it is controversial whether the issuance of a search request according to section 30 Federal Police Act (Bundespolizeige-

2. *Instruments Concerning States*

a) International Public Decisions

Decisions on requests for issuance of a Notice by Interpol are subject to examination by the Interpol General Secretariat to test their formal accuracy and necessity, including respect for human rights. Such decisions therefore entail a considerable margin of appreciation on the part of the international institution. They are addressed to a state or another public entity, even though its second level addressee might be an individual. In this sense this instrument resembles other state-directed decisions by international institutions, such as decisions of the UNESCO World Heritage Committee to include a monument or natural site in the list of world heritage or to award a grant to an enlisted site,[127] or decisions on eligibility for the Emission Trading System or on non-compliance by the Enforcement Branch of the Compliance Committee of the Kyoto regime.[128] Another example would be the approval of loans by the World Bank Executive Board.[129]

All these decisions do not contain abstract rules but attribute rights and obligations to public entities,[130] mostly states. As they are implemented directly by the adopting international institution they are subject to hard enforcement and, therefore, can be considered binding. They are equivalent of international administrative decisions although both their first and second level addressees are states. Interestingly, it seems that in none of the mentioned cases a plenary body decides on the measure but only limited bodies or secretariats. This is an issue for the legal regime, not for the rule of identification of international public decisions, because this greatly affects the legitimacy of the instrument. By means of the parameters they could be defined as deontic, specific instruments by international institutions, addressed to other public entities as first and second level addressee and subject to direct implementation.

---

setz of 19 October 1994, Bundesgesetzblatt (1994) I-2978), and the request of the individual affected to withdraw the pending search, are to be qualified as administrative decisions (Verwaltungsakte). *See* Michael Drewes, *Section 30*, *in* BUNDESPOLIZEIGESETZ, margin number 4 (Karl-Heinz Blümel et al. eds., 3rd ed. 2006).

[127] Diana Zacharias, in this volume.

[128] Petra Láncos, in this volume.

[129] *See* Dann (note 2).

[130] Jochen von Bernstorff, in this volume (calling them "operational decisions").

b) International Public Recommendations

A number of instruments that are directed to states or other public entities are not subject to hard enforcement. For example, the OSCE High Commissioner on National Minorities issues specific recommendations concerning the situation of minorities in an individual state.[131] Similarly, the Committee on Freedom of Association of the ILO issues non-binding conclusions on alleged violations of the freedom of association,[132] and the Committee to the Harmonized Commodity Description and Coding System (Harmonized System) within the World Customs Organization (WCO) issues recommendations in order to settle classification disputes among member states.[133] Within the OSCE there seems to be no consistent practice as to the public accessibility of such recommendations. The public accessibility of such recommendations is a form of soft enforcement that gives these instruments considerably more weight. But it seems to be too sensitive an issue to be included in the rule of identification of this standard instrument. Instead, it seems more advisable to develop legal principles pertaining to public accessibility.

International public recommendations can be defined as deontic, hortatory instruments concerning an individual case issued by international institutions and addressed to states or other public entities that are not necessarily subject to soft enforcement mechanisms.

c) International Secondary Law

A few international institutions have the power to adopt abstract rules that have the same legal effects for their members as international treaties. Among the thematic studies in this issue this is the case with amendments to the appendices of CITES.[134] CITES amendments technically become constituent parts of the international treaty and are subject to the sanctions regime, which includes trade sanctions. Similarly, amendments to the Harmonized System within the WCO modify the underlying treaty. If no state party objects within six months the Harmonized System, an integral part of an international convention, is

---

131 Anuscheh Farahat, in this volume.

132 de Wet (note 8).

133 Isabel Feichtner, in this volume.

134 Christine Fuchs, in this volume.

amended. Slightly different are waivers of obligations arising from agreements within the frame of the WTO, which change the content of treaty obligations only with respect to specific members.[135] Other instruments do not formally affect the obligations arising under an international treaty but create new ones. The COP/MOP of the Kyoto Protocol adopts accounting rules for the Emission Trading System that need to be implemented by member states and that are subject to enforcement measures by the compliance committee.[136]

At an abstract level one could define such secondary law as deontic, general instruments by international institutions addressed to states or other public entities that are subject to hard enforcement. Admittedly, this definition might be too broad to account for the considerable differences between the many variants of international secondary law such as waivers, opting-out[137] or contracting-in[138] procedures.[139] These instruments seem to require more refined subcategories. But this would go beyond the scope of instruments covered by this project.

d) Internal Operational Rules

The legal quality of certain types of rules that are situated at a medium level of norm concretization seems to provide some difficulty in the thematic studies in this issue.[140] For example, the Operational Guidelines by the UNESCO World Heritage Committee are subordinate to the provisions of the Convention but need to be meticulously observed by states if they want to succeed with their applications. The Kyoto COP has adopted functionally similar principles, modalities, rules and guidelines. Another example is the Common Regulations under the Madrid Agreement and Madrid Protocol adopted by the assembly of

---

[135] Isabel Feichtner, in this volume.

[136] Petra Láncos, in this volume.

[137] Decisions by the Council of the International Civil Aviation Organization.

[138] ILO Conventions, *see* de Wet (note 8).

[139] For a comprehensive analysis, *see* ASTON (note 27).

[140] *See* Christine Fuchs, in this volume ("*de facto* lawmaking"); Maja Smrkolj, in this volume ("internal soft law"); Diana Zacharias, in this volume ("binding secondary law").

member states.[141] The Interpol General Assembly has adopted a variety of resolutions setting out operational procedures for the submission of requests for notices. Each of these resolutions is annexed to a comprehensive internal document called General Regulations.[142] Similarly, the mandate of the UN Taliban and Al Qaida Sanctions Committee is specified in Committee guidelines, and Refugee Status Determination by UNHCR receives normative guidance from the Executive Committee's Conclusions on International Protection of Refugees.[143] The decisions and resolutions of the CITES COP specify the provisions of the convention by determining, among others, the criteria for the listing of specific animals, *i.e.* for the adoption of secondary law.[144] Another case of operational rules for the adoption of secondary law are the HS procedures adopted by the WTO General Council for the adaptation of WTO schedules of concessions to changes in the Harmonized System of the WCO, yet with the difference that they do not merely concretize previous commitments, but provide for their flexibilization and amendment by establishing a new procedural framework on a questionable legal basis.[145]

Those rules thus concretize the provisions of an international treaty whenever specific decisions are being taken.[146] Formally they are only of internal significance for the respective international institutions and add nothing to the obligations arising under the treaty. Nevertheless, they have a crucial impact on the outcomes of the procedures and decisions for which they provide the set-out. Also, the establishment of such operational guidelines involves a considerable degree of discretion. As the international institution has the possibility of implementing them directly they are subject to hard enforcement. Therefore, this type of subordinate instrument should be conceptualized as a standard instrument. By reference to the parameters it could, thus, be defined as a deontic and not only a hortatory instrument dependent on superior standards that is authored by actors within international institutions

141 Diana Zacharias, in this volume; Petra Láncos, in this volume; Karen Kaiser, in this volume.

142 Bettina Schöndorf-Haubold, in this volume.

143 Clemens Feinäugle, in this volume; Maja Smrkolj, in this volume.

144 Christine Fuchs, in this volume.

145 Isabel Feichtner, in this volume.

146 CITES is an exception. However, the secondary law that the resolutions prepare is specific with regard to the animal concerned.

and addressed to actors within international institutions who adopt instruments having individuals or states and other public entities as their first or second level addressees, subject to direct implementation.

e) International Public Standards

Another large group of instruments is constituted by multilateral agreements drafted within an international institution that are not subject to hard enforcement. Some of these instruments have received considerable public attention. The list includes the OECD Guidelines on Multinational Enterprises, the Codex Alimentarius, the ILO Declaration on Fundamental Principles and Rights at Work, and the FAO Code of Conduct for Responsible Fisheries.[147]

These instruments, although their names vary, have a significant number of common parameters. They are deontic, specific instruments at a low level of concretization, authored by international institutions and addressed to states, private or other public entities, sometimes cumulatively. The public promulgation of these instruments should be taken as another defining element as it is key to their effectiveness. A further sub-division of this standard instrument could be considered for international public standards that are enforced by soft mechanisms going beyond monitoring and reporting.[148] Some international public standards are implemented by other international or regional organizations through reference in their hard law. The classical case is the relationship between the WTO SPS Agreement and the Codex Alimentarius.[149] Such linkages boost compliance with these standards considerably. It could also be framed as a formal criterion. The drafters of the international public standard are very well aware of this "hardening" of their instrument, so that an *ex ante* application of specific legal standards should be possible.

---

[147] *See* Gefion Schuler, in this volume; Ravi Pereira, in this volume; de Wet (note 8); Jürgen Friedrich, in this volume.

[148] The OECD Guidelines on Multinational Enterprises. *See* Gefion Schuler, in this volume.

[149] Ravi Pereira, in this volume.

f) International Implementing Standards

Implementing instruments are usually subordinate to international secondary law or international public standards. A case in point is the rules concretizing the Code of Conduct for Responsible Fisheries such as International Plans of Action and Technical Guidelines for Responsible Fisheries that are developed by the FAO Secretariat.[150] Another example is the explanatory notes to the Harmonized System drafted by the HS Committee.[151] Implementing standards could thus be defined as instruments of international institutions addressed to states and subordinate to treaty law, international secondary law or international public standards. Usually they are not enforced by hard means but only by reporting.

The classification of general recommendations issued by the OSCE High Commissioner on National Minorities is no clean slate. While previous general recommendations that advise states on minority related policies on specific issues indicated the international rights or standards on which they were based, this practice ceased in 2006.[152] This instrument oscillates between the form of an implementing standard and an international public standard. Should the practice continue it might raise questions of competence.

g) Preparatory Expert Assessments

Most preparatory instruments remain below the radar of conceptualization as a standard instrument. Only some of them deserve closer consideration. The Codex Alimentarius Commission adopts standards on the basis of risk assessment reports prepared by the Joint FAO/WHO expert bodies. These reports summarize available scientific information about the risks to consumers' health related to a certain food standard including minority opinions and enduring uncertainties. Considering that these reports need to interpret scientific data and make choices between sometimes diverging opinions they are certainly not free from normativity. However, the reports as such do not contain deontic operators and refrain from risk assessment, which is the sole task of the Codex Alimentarius Commission. Nevertheless, the division of work between the Commission and the expert bodies in the standard-setting

---

150 Jürgen Friedrich, in this volume.

151 Isabel Feichtner, in this volume.

152 Anuscheh Farahat, in this volume.

procedure justifies considering them as an independent standard instrument for the exercise of public authority and not only as a preparatory instrument that does not call for specific conceptualization. Accordingly, International Expert Assessments could be defined as non-deontic instruments of international institutions requested by a body of the same or another international institution as part of a law-making or standard-setting procedure that limits the discretion of the requesting institution or body.

A deontic variant of the same standard instrument can also be observed. The operational guidelines of the World Heritage Committee provide for the consultation of Advisory Bodies composed of independent expert organizations on every application for inclusion in the list of world heritage or for financial support. Granted, there is no division of work as in the case of the Codex Alimentarius Commission. Rather, the discretion of the World Heritage Committee is not limited, even though in practice it regularly follows the Advisory Bodies.[153] However, the practice of preparatory expert recommendations seems to have acquired customary status within the World Heritage Committee. Their conceptualization as a standard instrument is therefore justified because of their role as accessory instruments to the international public decisions rendered by the World Heritage Committee. Similar considerations apply to recommendations by Expert Review Teams within the framework of the Kyoto protocol.[154]

h) National Policy Assessments

Finally, some policies rely on the gathering and dissemination of information. For example, the OECD PISA policy consists in large-scale empirical assessments of educational achievements of students in the participating states. The periodic and public nature of the assessment reports, coupled with country rankings, make this an effective instrument for influencing national educational policy. This policy is not subject to any predefined standards, as opposed to, *e.g.* the Transitional Review Mechanism by which the WTO Committee on Trade in Financial Services supervises China's implementation of GATS obligations, or compliance monitoring as carried out by the ILO. Some policies, however, like the OECD Environmental Policy Review, constitute interme-

153 Diana Zacharias, in this volume.

154 Petra Láncos, in this volume.

diate forms that only partly monitor the implementation of predefined international standards. And even monitoring instruments may concretize, or even change, the meaning of the standards to which they refer. In addition, some of these instruments draw more or less specific recommendations from the material, while others do not. National Policy Assessments should, therefore, be broadly defined as predominantly non-deontic instruments by international institutions addressed to another entity that are subject to soft means of enforcement.[155]

V. A Continuing Task

The preceding taxonomy of standard instruments is rather preliminary. Its relatively small empirical basis makes any claim to completeness impossible. Further standard instruments could be envisaged, in particular in relation to monitoring and reporting activities, while some of the proposed standard instruments could benefit from more fine-tuning. A particular challenge yet to be considered is that of purely private instruments that are not linked in any way to public entities or international institutions by any chain of delegation. In this respect, the only examples within the scope of the thematic studies in this issue are the instruments adopted by ICHEIC, in particular claim decision letters.[156] As a general rule, in case such instruments assume functions that can be qualified as equivalents to those of instruments of public authority, they should be measured by the same standards as instruments of public authority.[157] Whether this applies to ICHEIC claim decision letters is questionable. In spite of the undisputed socio-political significance of ICHEIC, at the end of the day, those instruments amount to means for the facilitation of private dispute settlement that are sufficiently explained and framed by the terms of private law.

It is to be expected that the elaboration of standard instruments is a continuous task. Once the legal requirements for specific standard instruments have been spelled out it is to be expected that some decision-makers will look into ways to strip them off by taking recourse to hitherto unknown and not yet legally framed instruments. The entirety of

---

155 For an earlier definition, *see* von Bogdandy & Goldmann (note 15).

156 Steven Less, in this volume.

157 Armin von Bogdandy, Philipp Dann & Matthias Goldmann, in this volume.

standard instruments will never correspond exactly to the full range of instruments of public authority. All that can be achieved is an approximation. There is thus the concrete prospect of an endless cat-and-mouse game. But this game is preferable to an uncontrolled plague of mice. And with the parameters as tools for the development of rules of identification it can be ensured that each new mouse will soon be followed by the cat.

D. Construing the Legal Regime of Standard Forms

I. Methodological Observations

Once standard instruments have been defined their legal regimes, *i.e.* the legal standards determining their validity and legality, need to be elaborated. This is still a very distant goal. Methodically the elaboration of a standardized legal regime for each standard instrument is a task that cannot, and should not, be carried out by scholarship alone. It requires multiple rounds of exchange between theory and practice, until a legal regime emerges. What scholarly discourse can achieve, however, is the abstraction of structural principles, *i.e.* significant regularities in the legal regimes of instruments of the same type.[158] The extrapolation of structural principles should be followed by a profound normative critique based on the overarching idea of ensuring legitimate and effective public authority. This would be the main contribution of legal scholarship for initiating a communicative process in which domestic and international policy-makers, civil society, as well as domestic and international judges elaborate the legal regime. Concerns about the role attributed to international law scholarship in this method might be mitigated by the fact that it is not unusual for concepts of international law, even for prominent ones like *mare liberum* or *ius cogens*, to be formulated in the first instance by scholars as a claim that later finds recognition in international legal practice. Nevertheless, each scholarly proposal needs to strike a careful balance between apology and utopia, and requires awareness of the risk that it might strengthen, rather than diminish, power imbalances.

---

[158] On structural principles, *see* Armin von Bogdandy, *General Principles*, in this volume.

Whether and how the elements of the legal regime thus elaborated acquire legal normativity is a difficult question. In particular, the legal regime needs to rank above the standardized instruments that it regulates. Within one international institution it is relatively easy to conceptualize higher ranking rules that could take the form of internal constitutional principles or customary legal commitments emerging from consistent institutional practice.[159] Elements of legal regimes that transcend institutional borders might only emerge in the long run. Customary law, international constitutional principles[160] or certain human rights[161] might lend themselves as levers of normativity and hierarchical superiority to an emerging overarching international institutional law. Theses problems are familiar from the discourses about the constitutionalization of international law and global administrative law. It goes without saying that any definitive solutions cannot be proposed in the frame of this article.

II. Elements of Legal Regimes

An exhaustive consideration of structural similarities or dissimilarities in the legal regimes of the standardized instruments described above would be beyond the scope of this article, in particular because the other cross-cutting analyses of this project reveal these aspects extensively.[162] Nevertheless, a few selected observations should be made as to how the above conceptualization might translate into specific legal regimes for each standard instrument that goes beyond general principles of international institutional law. These observations will be based on comparisons of the different regimes.

---

[159] Armin von Bogdandy, *General Principles*, in this volume; von Bogdandy & Goldmann (note 15).

[160] Stefan Kadelbach & Thomas Kleinlein, *International Law – A Constitution for Mankind? An Attempt at a Re-appraisal with an Analysis of Constitutional Principles*, 50 GERMAN YEARBOOK OF INTERNATIONAL LAW 303 (2007).

[161] von Bogdandy & Goldmann (note 15).

[162] Jochen von Bernstorff, in this volume; Armin von Bogdandy & Philipp Dann, in this volume; Erika de Wet, *Holding International Institutions Accountable*, in this volume; Volker Röben, in this volume.

1. *Rules of Conflict*

Normative conflicts between instruments belonging to categories are all but impossible. Two different dimensions of normative conflicts are conceivable. First, conflicts might emerge within one policy of the same international institution, *e.g.* among different bodies involved. In this case the taxonomy of instruments might provide for some hierarchy that serves as a default rule of conflict and excludes the application of, *e.g.*, the principle of *lex posterior.*[163] Second, conflicts might emerge between instruments belonging to entirely different regimes, such as trade and human rights. This recalls the familiar discussion about the fragmentation of international law. Some instruments, like waivers of concessions under WTO law, are means for the proceduralization of such conflicts. However, most instruments do not contain such mechanisms. There might, therefore, be some need to develop principles for collision management in a fragmented normative environment. The principle of mutual recognition might be a candidate for this.[164]

2. *Competence: The Principle of Adequate Concretization*

Competence is at present a doctrinal category that hardly constrains the activities of international institutions. This is due to the tension between the principles of attributed and implied powers.[165] The tendency of international institutions to increase their autonomy[166] makes the latter principle likely to prevail, and international institutions arrogate competencies not explicitly provided for in the founding instrument.[167] This development has serious repercussions for national power balances.[168] But, although greater clarity in relation to competencies is desirable, one should not cherish hopes that are likely to be disappointed.

---

163 *See*, however, Anuscheh Farahat, in this volume.

164 Kalypso Nicolaidis & Gregory Shaffer, *Transnational Mutual Recognition Regimes: Governance without Global Government*, 68 LAW & CONTEMPORARY PROBLEMS 263 (2005).

165 Jan Klabbers, *The Changing Image of International Organizations, in* THE LEGITIMACY OF INTERNATIONAL ORGANIZATIONS 221 (Jean-Marc Coicaud & Veijo Heiskanen eds., 2001).

166 Jochen von Bernstorff, in this volume; Ingo Venzke, in this volume.

167 *See* the examples in Anuscheh Farahat, in this volume; Isabel Feichtner, in this volume; Joseph Windsor, in this volume.

168 For the example of PISA, *see* von Bogdandy & Goldmann (note 15).

Even in developed multilevel legal orders, such as Germany or the European Union, formal rules on the vertical division of competencies have not necessarily been an effective device for limiting "mission creep" at the "upper" level, and this is the case in spite of powerful courts with jurisdiction to enforce rules of competence.[169] Compensation might be afforded through an increase in the complexity of the procedural regimes. Thus, the WTO General Council adopted the HS procedures on a doubtful legal basis but at least pursuant to an inclusive process that mitigates concerns regarding legitimacy.[170] Further, internal constitutional principles could be elaborated that relate to the question which standard instruments a particular body of the institution might use. This might prevent issues like the questionable adoption of secondary law by the WTO Committee on Trade in Financial Services.[171]

One further observation can be made. Whenever international institutions dispose of relatively broadly formulated competencies in their statutes, these rules are further and further concretized through mandates, operational rules, etc. Remarkably, operational rules can be regularly observed in case of administrative instruments as well as international public decisions and recommendations, *i.e.* whenever an international instrument is adopted that concerns individuals, states or other entities as first or second level addressees.[172] This resembles the essentiality principle (*Wesentlichkeitsgrundsatz*) in German constitutional law, according to which the essential features of a measure that affects fundamental rights need to be determined by acts of parliament. This principle is thought to limit the discretion of the administration in order to secure the impact of parliament on such decisions.[173] As of now, there is no equivalent principle in international institutional law that would require the plenary body that bears overall political responsibility for a certain policy to set out the essential features of that policy in a general manner instead of delegating this task to a subsidiary body, plenary or non-plenary, or to the secretariat. So far all that can be observed

---

[169] Some exceptions confirm the rule; *see* ECJ, Case C-376/98, *Germany v. Parliament and Council* (Tobacco Advertising), 2000 E.C.R. I-8419; Bundesverfassungsgericht, Case 2 BvF 1/01 (Altenpflegegesetz), 106 BVerfGE 62.

[170] Isabel Feichtner, in this volume.

[171] Joseph Windsor, in this volume.

[172] *See also* Jochen von Bernstorff, in this volume.

[173] Helmuth Schulze-Fielitz, *Art. 20 (Rechtsstaat), in* GRUNDGESETZ-KOMMENTAR, margin number 113 (Horst Dreier ed., 2nd ed., 2006).

in this respect are certain structural similarities in international institutional practice: international operational rules are usually adopted by plenary organs[174] while non-plenary, expert bodies or secretariats often take the concrete decision on the basis of these operational rules.[175] Switching from a descriptive to a normative perspective, one could postulate a principle of adequate concretization by politically responsible bodies for reasons of individual rights protection and democratic legitimacy. The example of the UN Taliban and Al Qaida Sanctions Committee demonstrates the detrimental effects on individual rights of international administrative decisions based on insufficiently specific operational rules.[176] A lack of democratic legitimacy could be diagnosed for the operational rules of the World Heritage Committee, which are adopted by the Committee itself.[177] As with most international organizations the competencies of UNESCO are formulated in fairly broad terms. Non-plenary bodies and secretariats could be considered to lack the necessary competence to set out international operational rules that guide the adoption of administrative decisions, recommendations and information acts.

3. Procedure

Procedure is probably the issue that raises the most debate. A comparison of the current procedural regimes of some instruments belonging to the same type of standard instrument reveals interesting structural similarities.

In case of international public decisions and recommendations, decisions are usually not taken by plenary organs but instead by limited bodies like expert committees or secretariats.[178] It seems that the idea of state consent, fundamental as it is for international law, is unhinged by the idea that no state should be its own judge. It logically follows from the reduced role attributed to state consent that such instruments are

---

174 CITES recommendations; rules within the Emission Trading System of the Kyoto Protocol; the HS procedures of the WTO.

175 The Enforcement Branch of the Kyoto Compliance Committee.

176 Clemens Feinäugle, in this volume.

177 The World Heritage Committee Operational Guidelines.

178 Petra Láncos, in this volume; Diana Zacharias, in this volume; Anuscheh Farahat, in this volume; Christine Fuchs, in this volume; Jochen von Bernstorff, in this volume.

often adopted by majority votes,[179] which smoothes decision-making in the bodies in charge. The same involvement of experts through specialized, non-plenary bodies can be observed in the case of preparatory expert assessments. In addition to the reason just mentioned, state consent might also be considered inappropriate in this case because it would destroy the aura of objectivity surrounding these instruments. While this reasoning would be questionable, it is normatively acceptable as preparatory expert reports are followed by political decisions of responsible committees.

Besides these specific instruments there are some general instruments that involve a high degree of expertise, namely international implementing standards within the FAO Fisheries regime and the OSCE regime on national minorities. Again, this seems to imply the belief that implementation is primarily a technical matter. This approach, although questionable, is consistent as long as the implementing standard explicitly refers to some superior standards that at least formally serve as the source of the obligations arising under the implementing standard. However, when this link to a superior standard is cut off, like in the case of general recommendations of the OSCE High Commissioner on National Minorities, this form of expert-driven standard-setting becomes questionable. In this case, it would be better to opt for an international public standard. Those instruments are usually adopted by high-level political bodies that seem to foster both the legitimacy and the effectiveness of the ensuing standards. This should apply *a fortiori* if issues like human rights or environmental matters are concerned where reciprocity is not a pertinent reason for states to comply.

Further elements of legal regimes could certainly be considered. However, the above list might suffice as a first impression of this instrument-specific approach. Of course, at the moment the elements of legal regimes that were mentioned are not much more than proposals based on structural similarities or dissimilarities. For the time being it appears that the common ground among the legal regimes of instruments that fall into the same category, but belong to entirely different institutional frameworks, is limited. This is partly due to the fact that some legal regimes are not very consolidated, in particular if they relate to instruments produced by secretariats instead of plenary bodies.[180] Further, at this stage, international institutional law seems hardly developed

---

[179] Petra Láncos, in this volume; Diana Zacharias, in this volume.

[180] Anuscheh Farahat, in this volume; Steven Less, in this volume.

enough to make a meaningful distinction between elements of legal regimes that are a precondition for the validity of the instrument and such elements that make the instrument illegal and voidable but not invalid.[181] Nevertheless, the above observations might provide the starting point for normative claims that eventually become a legal rule. Admittedly, this goal is still a long way ahead.

E. Inside Relative Normativity: The Elusive Quest for Bindingness

What are the larger doctrinal repercussions of this excursion into relative normativity? Four insights come to mind. First, alternative instruments do not only play a role at the margins of public authority. Second, the preceding section revealed several similarities in the legal regimes of instruments belonging to the same type, but also a few discrepancies. Legal conceptualization is therefore worth its price and helps understanding, but also criticizing, the exercise of authority by international institutions. Third, individuals are probably more affected by the activities of international institutions than is commonly believed. Even though international institutions often do not have direct access to individuals, but only through the interface of states and other entities, this intermediate level hardly has a negative effect on the efficiency of the instruments. The fourth and probably main insight is that the authority and legal regimes of instruments which classical doctrine considers binding, and those that it holds to be non-binding, do not vary that much. Internal operational rules are a case in point. Are these instruments "binding"? There seems to be no unequivocal answer to this. On the one hand, they are subject to one of the most effective enforcement mechanisms, which direct implementation by the international institution which has adopted them. On the other hand, they do not necessarily stand on a firm legal basis as they might be adopted by a body which has no competence for the adoption of binding rules. This raises the question whether the concept of bindingness, which has been hitherto used in a heuristic sense as previously defined,[182] is theoretically tenable.

---

181 BAST (note 95), at 329.

182 *Supra*, notes 1 and 7.

In classical accounts of international law the decisive criterion for determining the binding nature of an instrument is the "intent" of its drafter. This is not a formal criterion, a fact that makes it difficult to grasp in a practical sense. Besides, it is doubtful what the "intent" of the "parties" is – is it the intention of the persons involved in the negotiations, of the minister or heads of government who bear the political responsibility? But even if one were Hercules and knew exactly and in all details the mental state and intentions of the parties, the problem of drawing the line precisely would not be solved. What is the intent to be "bound" supposed to refer to? Is it the explicit or implicit assumption that an infringement of the act will entail damages or will give rise to a claim that can be enforced before a competent court?[183] The concept of intent, therefore, appears to be inconclusive.[184]

But even if it were agreed that the possibility of triggering any form of hard enforcement or court proceedings was a conclusive, unequivocal sign of an instrument's binding nature, this concept would be out of sync with the sources doctrine. Some international treaties that might even have received ratification by the parliaments of their respective parties contain soft, indeterminate language so that no possible violation could ever be determined and that damages or court proceedings would never take place.[185] Reputational damage also is not a conclusive criterion because it might occur irrespective of whether the violated norm was "binding" or "non-binding". At most, violating binding obligations might entail higher reputational costs,[186] which only amounts to a gradual, not a categorical difference. Likewise, in a constructivist reading, non-binding norms may as well have an impact upon the preferences and identity of their authors and addressees. Therefore, any attempts to find a sort of "higher morality" in binding law beyond the

---

[183] In this sense, *see* Baxter (note 42), at 549; Hanspeter Neuhold, *The Inadequacy of Law-Making by International Treaties: "Soft Law" as an Alternative?*, *in* DEVELOPMENTS OF INTERNATIONAL LAW IN TREATY MAKING 39, 48 *et seq.* (Rüdiger Wolfrum & Volker Röben eds., 2005); Roger Alford, *Federal Courts, International Tribunals, and the Continuum of Deference*, 43 VIRGINIA JOURNAL OF INTERNATIONAL LAW 675 (2003). On the elusiveness of referrals to the intention to be bound, *see* KLABBERS (note 57), at 65 *et seq.*

[184] For an impressive deconstruction of intent *see* KLABBERS (note 57), at 65 *et seq.*

[185] d'Aspremont (note 43), at 10 (accepting reference to these instruments as "soft law").

[186] Jürgen Friedrich, in this volume.

mentioned sanctions or an increased reputational risk are speculative and on the edge of metaphysics.

With binding instruments adopted by international organizations the situation is not much better. Neither the designation of international instruments as "binding" nor the competencies of the adopting body are conclusive indicia of binding effect. Operational rules by bodies without the competence to make "binding" decisions might nevertheless be binding due to direct implementation. Middle-of-the-road concepts like "*de facto* bindingness" are helpless attempts to preserve a distinction of whose failure they are the best evidence. Jan Klabbers, therefore, takes the view that any international agreement could be considered binding.[187] In my view, the concept of an instruments binding nature, though it has an undeniable heuristic value, is theoretically elusive and is not a meaningful criterion for a theoretically sound distinction between different kinds of instruments expressing different kinds of commitments.

This journey to the heart of relative normativity, thus, brought us beyond the concept of bindingness. The same methodology could be extended to the realm of the traditional sources and be used for the reconceptualization of various sub-forms of these instruments that practice has developed. End-of-the-world scenarios in the face of relative normativity are exaggerated. A theoretically sound approach to legal doctrine will always find pragmatic ways for the inclusion of new forms of public authority into the international legal order.

---

187 KLABBERS (note 57), at 164.

Goldmann Variations

Comment by Jan Klabbers[1]

I

It has long been a source of discomfort among international lawyers that sources doctrine never quite lived up to its promise. For one thing, the very term 'source' seems misplaced – it suggests that law somehow originates organically, in much the same way that rivers have their source, springing naturally from mountain streams and eternal snow. Therewith, the very term source immediately wrong-foots aspiring international lawyers, by suggesting the absence of human agency. And when human agency is (as it has to be) re-introduced, it is typically re-introduced in terms of power; terms which, at first sight, seemingly have little to do with the notion of law.

However, upon closer inspection, sources doctrine has never failed to disappoint. At least in its standard version (the one to be found in article 38, paragraph 1, of the ICJ Statute), it appears to be both over-inclusive and under-inclusive. It is over-inclusive in its listing of the writings of the most highly qualified jurists as one of the things the ICJ may apply – few authors nowadays can meaningfully be said to have patented the truth. Even though the caveat is made that such writings are but subsidiary means for the determination of rules of international law, it nonetheless seems perfectly clear that the ICJ will not be caught relying too much on the writings of a single author, and probably never did – occasional claims by individual authors to the contrary notwith-

1 The present text is written as a comment on Matthias Goldmann, *Inside Relative Normativity: Public Authority and International Institutions*, in this volume. All references to Goldmann will be to this source.

A. von Bogdandy et al. (eds.), *The Exercise of Public Authority by International Institutions*, Beiträge zum ausländischen öffentlichen Recht und Völkerrecht 210,
DOI 10.1007/978-3-642-04531-8_23,

standing.[2] By the same token, the Court may, perhaps, be willing to find inspiration in domestic judicial decisions and international precedent, but is unlikely to decide cases on this basis without there being a more convincing argument available: a treaty provision, a firmly established rule of customary international law. Indeed, if the 2007 *Genocide* decision is anything to go by, the ICJ is unlikely to rely too much on the findings of international courts other than the ICJ itself – least of all perhaps on the ICTY.[3] Likewise, the Court has been markedly reluctant, in its almost 90 years of existence, to speak in terms of general principles of law.

But more interesting for present purposes is the under-inclusiveness of present-day sources doctrine, a circumstance that has been lamented by many since at least the 1960s, when the effects of decolonization made clear that international institutions could adopt all sorts of instruments which would not find recognition in terms of traditional sources doctrines. Hence, many have been attempts to somehow come to terms with manifestations of a global opinion which would somehow not be cast in recognizable terms of sources doctrine. In Utrecht, Bos,[4] followed by his pupil Van Hoof,[5] developed ideas about 'recognized manifestations of consent'. While this would help consider some resolutions of the General Assembly of the United Nations (GA, hereafter) as being law-making in nature, it hinged too much on equating the activity of voting in favor of resolutions with expressing consent to be bound. Since all resolutions depend in one way or another on counting heads and thus on voting (consensus decision-making too can only be conceptualized in such terms), but not all become law, this failed to do the trick.

---

[2] Perhaps most audacious is Seyersted's claim that *Certain Expenses* was really decided in accordance with an, at the time, unpublished article of his in which he set out a theory of inherent powers of international organizations, and which he had sent to the ICJ. *See* FINN SEYERSTED, COMMON LAW OF INTERNATIONAL ORGANIZATIONS (2008).

[3] *See* Application of the Convention on the Prevention and Punishment of the Crime of Genocide (Bosnia and Herzegovina v. Serbia and Montenegro), judgment of 26 February 2007, paras. 403-407.

[4] Bos devoted a few articles to setting out his approach, and provided a synthetic version in MAARTEN BOS, A METHODOLOGY OF INTERNATIONAL LAW (1984).

[5] *See* GODEFRIDUS F.H. VAN HOOF, RETHINKING THE SOURCES OF INTERNATIONAL LAW (1983).

Others spoke in terms of equating the GA with a world parliament, and then took the next step of equating GA emanations with parliamentary emanations, followed by the (again logical) next step that since (as in domestic situations) parliaments may often have law-making powers, so too could the GA be established as a law-making body.[6] Apart from containing a few too many shortcuts and a rather selective domestic analogy,[7] this too stumbled on the same problem as the Bos and Van Hoof theory: how to tell the GA's legislative acts (if one accepts the theory to begin with) from its non-legislative acts? For surely, not all resolutions aspire to lay down the law. Some are, at face value, obviously hortatory, and some are even clearly misguided (the 'Zionism is racism' resolution comes to mind), but the distinction between law-making and hortatory cannot be captured by simply equating the GA to a law-making body.

More recently, attempts to theorize sources have focused on social science approaches, in two distinct ways (or maybe three). One is manifested in Boyle and Chinkin's recent monograph on the making of international law.[8] They start from the (more or less) sociological premise that non-governmental organizations are an important site of social legitimacy, and therefore NGOs ought to be included more in the making of international law. And to some extent, they also demonstrate that increasingly, NGOs find a place at the negotiating table. Still, they stop short of rising beyond traditional sources doctrine; they cannot integrate NGOs into a more subtle, nuanced, and appropriate theory of international law-making.

Goldsmith and Posner, in their much lamented (and, truth be told, highly lamentable) *The Limits of International Law*,[9] start from the other end, so to speak. Employing game theory and rational choice theory, they end up suggesting the continued relevance of state consent: states only accept things that are to their benefit. Rather amazingly, their universe does not contain international organizations, or any

---

6 This is most easily associated with Taslim O. Elias, *Modern Sources of International Law, in* TRANSNATIONAL LAW IN A CHANGING SOCIETY: ESSAYS IN HONOR OF PHILIP C. JESSUP, 34-69 (Wolfgang Friedmann *et al.* eds., 1972).

7 While many parliaments may have law-making powers, they rarely get to exercise them in isolation from the executive.

8 *See* ALAN BOYLE & CHRISTINE CHINKIN, THE MAKING OF INTERNATIONAAL LAW (2007).

9 *See* JACK L. GOLDSMITH & ERIC A. POSNER, THE LIMITS OF INTERNATIONAL LAW (2005).

other actors for that matter, other than states. In such a setting, obviously, the traditional sources problem can hardly exist: when there are only two states and no international organizations, at the very least sources doctrine is unlikely to be upset by the output of organizations. But even that is a wisdom they aim to undermine, expecting the impossible from customary international law, then concluding that custom fails to meet these (unrealistic) expectations, and subsequently suggesting that much that is often called customary law does not deserve the label law because it is, well, ineffective.[10] And while Andrew Guzman's rational choice approach is far more subtle than the one employed by Goldsmith and Posner,[11] it too stumbles in the end over the circumstance that the chosen method simply is not very appropriate for coming to terms with law-making in a complicated setting. While rational choice may play a useful role in settings where individual positions can easily be aggregated, and while game theory can be very useful in explaining behavior where a limited number of actors are involved, their use is limited when it comes to explaining where international law comes from, how it is made, and most of all, how it can be recognized and distinguished from non-law.

Most of these pitfalls are avoided in what may well be the most ambitious recent attempt to rework sources doctrine in recent years: José Alvarez' monumental study on law-making by international organizations.[12] Still, he shares with Goldsmith & Posner an insistence on a social science approach, testing the legal nature of instruments by looking for their 'normative ripples', their effects on the behavior of actors. And this is bound to remain insufficient, because, as Goldmann so ably puts it, this way *ex ante* judgments can never be made: one would need to await any normative ripples prior to being able to claim that law exists. This, needless to say, undermines some of the more relevant functions of law, such as allowing the subjects of the law to engage in planning their future actions by informing them beforehand what behavior they may engage in, and what behavior they will not be allowed to engage in.

---

10 *See* in more detail my review of the work in 16 FINNISH YEARBOOK OF INTERNATIONAL LAW 401-407 (2005).

11 *See* ANDREW T. GUZMAN, HOW INTERNATIONAL LAW WORKS: A RATIONAL CHOICE THEORY (2008).

12 *See* JOSÉ E. ALVAREZ, INTERNATIONAL ORGANIZATIONS AS LAW-MAKERS (2005).

II

It is the great merit of Goldmann's piece that he manages to take the discussion on sources doctrine to another level. He realizes all too well that any relevant sources doctrine (whether one employs the term or not) will have to reckon with what Hart referred to as the internal perspective of those endowed with the task of somehow applying the law, be they judges, police officers, or administrators.[13] This, in turn, makes Goldmann opt for a purely formal approach, for it is only a formal approach which allows for judgments to be made on the legal nature of instruments *ex ante*. Looking merely for the effects of instruments on human behavior may result in excellent sociology, but that is what it will remain: sociology. And the sociologist, typically, observing the behavior of people with respect to traffic lights, cannot justify normative conclusions on this basis. It does not follow from the circumstance that a majority of pedestrians stops in front of a red light that, in law, they ought to do so. More tellingly still, those who have participated in traffic in busy cities will realize that there may well be a serious disjuncture between what traffic rules say and what people do: the sociologist observing Amsterdam traffic might even reach the conclusion that the color red signifies the right to proceed rather than the obligation to stop.

Instead of borrowing from the social sciences, Goldmann borrows from administrative law, and that seems a sensible thing to do, as of course domestic lawyers have been confronted with exercises of public authority for many years. In so doing, he presents what he refers to as standard instruments, providing a lengthy taxonomy ranging from international public decisions to international administrative recommendations, and from internal operational rules to even national policy assessments. All of these aspire in one way or another to exercise public authority, or exercise such authority in fact, and therewith engender legal effects, to such an extent that they can and should be studied by international lawyers. In turn, the taxonomy takes into account a number of different factors, such as authorship, addressees, procedure, designation, deontic content, and measures of enforcement.

This alone, however impressive, is not yet sufficient, for it may well be the case that an international public decision is taken which on its contents would seem to be binding and effective, but happens to be taken

---

[13] *See* HERBERT L.A. HART, THE CONCEPT OF LAW (1961).

by an institution lacking the competence to take it, or is taken by the proper authority but following a shortcut procedure. Thus, Goldmann adds a few other things to the taxonomy in order to determine validity of the standard instruments: powers (i.e. competences), procedure, and conflict rules.

In doing so, Goldmann renders a great service to international institutional law and, indeed, global governance generally. The framework as developed makes the exercise of public authority by international actors a bit more transparent and traceable, and therewith controllable. Those familiar with my own work will not be surprised that I have great sympathy for the exercise, and am duly impressed by the quality of the ensuing work. And yet, a few thorny issues remain unresolved or, at least, under-illuminated.

III

On some of these Goldmann himself is frank and open. Thus, he explicitly notes that his work (indeed, the entire project of which it forms a part) is limited to coming to terms with the exercises of public authority, leaving private authority untouched. This is fine as far as things go, and clearly understandable, but it does mean that there are two huge categories of instruments that remain out of sight. The first of these, obviously, is when power is exercised by private authority. This is not much of a problem perhaps (perhaps…) when private authority works under color of public authority – perhaps the prison wardens at Abu Ghraib might fall into his category.

But it becomes more problematic when private authority acts without reference to public authority. Then again, it may be countered that this traditionally has been a problem for law: surely, one cannot assign legal blame to a company that refuses to make certain products because making other products is more profitable. Thus, pharmaceutical companies exercise great power in that they can threaten to make Viagra instead of cancer drugs or aids medication unless their inventions meet with generous protection under intellectual property law.[14] Soft drink manufacturers invade education by providing badly needed resources in return for rights to install vending machines, thus potentially steering the con-

---

[14] *See* the excellent study by SUSAN K. SELL, PRIVATE POWER, PUBLIC LAW: THE GLOBALIZATION OF INTELLECTUAL PROPERTY RIGHTS (2003).

tents of education and, in the process, making parental control over soft drink consumption well-nigh impossible.[15] And personally, I still blame Microsoft for forcing me to quit using the word-processing program WordPerfect, and having to start using Microsoft's Word: the former was simply no longer compatible with the generally available operating system, despite being more closely attuned to my word-processing needs. Still, as noted, these are emanations of power that law traditionally has had a hard time addressing: it is difficult legally to argue with market decisions without questioning the very basis of a market-based economy – and the accompanying legal system.

Goldmann is also open in suggesting that his taxonomy does not accommodate non-intentional law-making, however difficult to operationalize that very category is. But important it is: no legal system can completely exclude the normative effects of customs and usages, generating expectations among participants and actors which, over time, may well demand to be honored. Even within international institutional law such mechanisms have been able to play a role, the most prominent example perhaps being the way in which the decision-making procedure within the Security Council has come to depart from the text of article 27, paragraph 3, of the UN Charter.[16]

In short, Goldmann presents a model of great value for the study of international public authority, and in particular the inclusion of non-deontic acts (including national policy assessments) is original and politically highly relevant. But his model does not amount to a new sources doctrine; at best, it nuances accepted doctrine. This owes much, of course, to the circumstance that the international legal order is not a full-fledged public order. Sir Gerald Fitzmaurice may well have had a point when arguing that treaties are best considered sources of obligations rather than sources of law,[17] but in the international legal order, that particular distinction is still difficult to make. While not one would

---

15 Very insightful (and very disturbing) is the study by ERIC SCHLOSSER, FAST FOOD NATION: WHAT THE ALL-AMERICAN MEAL IS DOING TO THE WORLD (2002).

16 And approved by the ICJ in 1971, in Legal Consequences for States of the Continued Presence of South Africa in Namibia (South West Africa) notwithstanding Security Council Resolution 276 (1970), advisory opinion, ICJ Reports 1971, 16.

17 *See* Sir Gerald Fitzmaurice, *Some Problems regarding the Formal Sources of International Law, in* SYMBOLAE VERZIJL, 153-176 (Frederik M. van Asbeck *et al.* eds., 1958).

mistake a private law contract for 'law', its closest analogy in international law (a treaty between two states) is generally considered as law. And that can be so precisely because the international legal order is not a fully-fledged public order.

IV

As noted, Goldmann does quite a service to international institutional law: this piece, and the project it is a part of, may well come to be regarded by future international institutional lawyers as seminal, in line with Tammes' contribution on law-making by international organizations[18] or Virally's exposition of the theory underlying functionalism.[19] Still, on the level of detail there are a few points worth considering.

On some points, the explanatory and the normative uncomfortably run into each other. One such point is Goldmann's suggestion that lawyers "should not deplore relative normativity but seek to get it under control."[20] This creates some discomfort, in two ways. First, it fails to recognize that relative normativity, in the sense used here, is not just something to deplore or not to deplore like, say, the roundness of the earth, or the laws of gravity. Relative normativity is not a fact of life, but rather a political phenomenon; it is eminently arguable that what Prosper Weil aimed to do in his classic piece was precisely to get it under control.[21] This then leads to the second discomfort: normative relativity (i.e. the sentiment that some norms are more important than others) need not necessarily be expressed in the formal status of instruments, but may also be manifested in the wording used. Indeed, Weil on this point is still highly relevant, claiming that law is at its best, and most useful, when it maintains a 'simplifying rigor': allowing law to come in various shades of grey makes law indistinguishable from morality or, worse, politics. Therewith it loses its unique selling point, and might as

---

[18] *See* Arnold J.P. Tammes, *Decisions of International Organs as a Source of International Law*, 94 RECUEIL DES COURS 265-363 (1958).

[19] Michel Virally, *La notion de fonction dans la théorie de l'organisation internationale, in* MÉLANGES OFFERTS À CHARLES ROUSSEAU: LA COMMUNAUTÉ INTERNATIONALE, 277-300 (Suzanne Bastid *et al.* eds., 1974).

[20] Goldmann (note 1), Part A.

[21] *See* Prosper Weil, *Towards Relative Normativity in International Law?*, 77 AMERICAN JOURNAL OF INTERNATIONAL LAW 413-442 (1983).

well stop existing. Indeed, one could even go a step further and suggest that by giving up law's simplifying rigor, the commodification of international law is facilitated.[22]

On another point too, the academic and the normative intersect uncomfortably when Goldmann aims to combine the need for formalization with what he calls the "practice requirement of leaving enough leeway for the spontaneous development of new modes of decision-making as well as substantive decisions."[23] The difficulty here is that not only may a proper balance be elusive (and will depend on one's political preferences anyway), but it would seem that policy-makers tend to be very creative in circumventing prescribed procedures and recognized categories, to such an extent that one hardly needs to worry on their behalf. As noted above, no legal system can fully exclude spontaneous law-making; but all legal systems will have to worry seriously about creating loopholes for those to whom the ends justify the means. It seems here that Goldmann, while endorsing control of public power, at the same time opens the door for public power to leak away and become uncontrollable.

Focusing yet more closely, one question-mark concerns the distinction between international administrative decisions, and international administrative recommendations (and likewise the distinction between international public decisions and international public recommendations). The recommendations are said not to be subject to hard enforcement, and therewith only be recommendations. But that, surely, misses an important point: it misses the point that even when designated as recommendations (and thus perhaps unsupported by hard enforcement), such recommendations nonetheless aim to change – or at least to affect – the existing legal situation. If not hortatory as to their linguistic contents, these have little to distinguish them from decisions other than their very designation, and that would seem to suggest that Goldmann risks falling into the very trap he aims to avoid: by focusing on enforcement and designation, he loses sight of the normative ambitions of instruments, and therewith of the way in which they exercise public authority.

---

[22] *See* Jan Klabbers, *The Commodification of International Law*, 1 SELECT PROCEEDINGS OF THE EUROPEAN SOCIETY OF INTERNATIONAL LAW 341-358 (2006).

[23] Goldmann (note 1), Part C.IV.

Mildly puzzling is the inclusion of conflict rules among the elements of legal regimes. While Goldmann is no doubt correct in suggesting that some mechanisms may need to be developed to solve normative conflicts in a pluralist world, such conflict rules will not normally affect the validity or legality of the emanations of public authority.[24] Therefore, they operate on a different footing than do rules on competence or procedure. Whereas *détournement de pouvoir* may, in some scenarios, result in invalidity, mere conflict with an existing rule will not do so, and most assuredly cannot if the conflicting rule forms part of a different subsystem. Put differently, possible conflict with the precautionary principle will not invalidate a WTO rule which demands free trade in genetically modified organisms, and neither does the WTO rule invalidate the precautionary principle. It is highly arguable that not even conflict with obligations under the UN Charter results in invalidity or illegality;[25] it is only with respect to *jus cogens* that such could possibly be claimed, and in that case it is doubtful whether the designation of 'conflict rule' does justice to the *jus cogens* phenomenon.

Finally, there is a fairly surprising, and most likely untenable, claim towards the end of the paper: the concept of bindingness, so Goldmann suggests, is "theoretically elusive" (which indeed can happily be acknowledged) and, so he continues, is not meaningful when it comes to making a distinction "between different kinds of instruments expressing different kinds of commitments."[26] Therewith, in the end, he does away with the distinction between law and non-law altogether.

But doing so is problematic. Not only does Goldmann shoot himself in the foot, for if bindingness is no longer meaningful, then there is no point in insisting between valid and invalid, legally or illegally produced norms. Part of the point of bindingness, if you will, is that it functions as shorthand for saying that the norm at issue has met an x-amount of tests and passed all of them. Such a norm, when emanating from an institution, is adopted in accordance with prescribed procedure; it is adopted by the proper organ; it does not run counter to any substantive limits, and its wording suggests that its addressees, both direct and indirect ones, ought to do something or refrain from doing something. Such

---

24 For general discussion and specific application to the EU, *see* JAN KLABBERS, TREATY CONFLICT AND THE EUROPEAN UNION (2009).

25 *See* Jan Klabbers, *Straddling Law and Politics: Judicial Review in International Law, in* TOWARDS WORLD CONSTITUTIONALISM, 809-835 (Ronald St.J. MacDonald & Douglas M. Johnston eds., 2005).

26 Goldmann (note 1), Part E.

a norm is called binding so as to distinguish it from norms which are invalid (not to be recognized by the law, and thus eventually not binding) or illegal (and thus arguably not binding) or hortatory (and thus not binding). It also distinguishes norms which are in force from those that have yet to acquire legal force, or those that have been terminated. Shorthand it may be, but it is the sort of shorthand inextricably tied up with legal thought. In much the same way that one cannot think of Romeo without thinking of Juliet, or Tristan without Isolde, or Jack without Jill if you will, one cannot think of law without also thinking of it in terms of instruments being binding or non-binding.

Now perhaps the problem here has an identifiable origin. In the sentence just before the one dispensing with bindingness, he suggests that it is my view that "any international agreement could be considered binding."[27] If that were indeed the case, it is understandable that he feels the need to distance himself from that position. Curiously though, my position is not quite what Goldmann claims it to be; as a result, his distancing act may not have been all that necessary to begin with.

In the work of mine Goldmann refers to, I make two points which are relevant for present purposes. The first is not that I see any agreement as binding by definition, but rather as giving rise to a presumption as to legally binding force. If and when two states (or more, obviously) reach an agreement, such agreement must be presumed to be binding as a matter of international law, simply because there are no other positions available as meaningful presumptions: morality and politics are not normative orders which can be employed at will,[28] and a presumption of non-bindingness would be utterly unworkable. Still, the presumption of bindingness is only that: a presumption, and true to its presumptive nature, it can be rebutted. One circumstance possibly allowing for rebuttal is when the context suggests that the agreement should not be taken as binding. Thus, agreement reached within the plenary body of an international organization, and expressed in an instrument labeled recommendation, may well rebut the presumption of bindingness, unless, on surrebuttal, it can be established (by way of example) that somehow the states adopting it had the intention to be governed by

---

27 *Id.* He does so under reference to JAN KLABBERS, THE CONCEPT OF TREATY IN INTERNATIONAL LAW (1996).

28 Politics can actually, but only in the sense that every legally binding agreement springs from political agreement. Politics is not available as a distinct normative order; in fact, its normative order is law, as centuries (nay, millennia) of political and legal thought will testify.

the terms of the instrument. In the latter case, it may well be regarded as binding after all.

The second relevant point made in that work is that the fine nuances of politics and morality can be expressed, if necessary, in the precise language of an instrument. Thus, an absolute prohibition to stop using chemical weapons may not require a superbinding instrument, or the form of *jus cogens*, but can simply be phrased as an absolute prohibition which, if words mean anything at all, is stronger than a command to try and endeavor to refrain from using chemical weapons.[29] While accepting that there are limits to what language can express, international lawmakers, nonetheless, have decidedly some room left to push the envelope: whereas legal instruments are devised with great creativity, the language used in those instruments is often remarkably similar – to the point of being bland. Perhaps then creative talent ought to be utilized in the language of instruments, rather than in finding new forms – most of them having the purpose, moreover, to escape from public scrutiny.

V

Still, all this takes nothing away from Matthias Goldmann's remarkable achievement – and from the remarkable project at large, for it is also clear that much of the thoughts going into the article owe something to the larger surroundings in which they were conceived and developed. Goldmann has written a highly relevant piece on a highly relevant topic. The challenge now lies with the rest of us to pick up the ball and run with it.

This running with the ball could take place in several directions. Some of these have been, however implicitly perhaps, suggested above: expansion into a veritable sources doctrine, ironing out some of the uncertainties surrounding differences between decisions and recommendations, that sort of thing. But surely, there are other avenues to explore as well. One topic of gigantic proportions hitherto left largely undiscussed by international lawyers is privatization: what are the effects of privatization on the international legal order? How will it come to affect global governance, and in particular the legitimacy thereof?

---

[29] The example is not entirely random: under Article 1 of the Chemical Weapons Convention, states agree "never under any circumstances" to purchase chemical weapons, use them *et cetera*.

Another is the very notion of legal powers of international institutions. While this has recently met with some conceptualization,[30] the larger question still is whether it is actually appropriate to think of international organizations and organs in terms of their powers, for in practice it often seems that such powers are unlimited. Moreover, the EC experience suggests that even when exercising one's own proper competence, one can nonetheless still interfere with someone else's.[31] And if that is so, then analyzing the work of organizations in terms of their powers may not be the most appropriate way of doing things – and this would then have to influence the legal regimes applicable to standard instruments for the exercise of international public authority.

---

30 *See* DAN SAROOSHI, INTERNATIONAL ORGANIZATIONS AND THEIR EXERCISE OF SOVEREIGN POWERS (2005).

31 For brief discussion in a limited setting, *see* Jan Klabbers, *Restraints on the Treaty-making Powers of Member States Deriving from EU Law, in* THE EUROPEAN UNION AS AN ACTOR IN INTERNATIONAL RELATIONS, 151-175 (Enzo Cannizzaro ed., 2002).

General Principles of International Public Authority: Sketching a Research Field

*By Armin von Bogdandy**

* I am grateful to Sabino Cassese and Christian Walter as well as Eyal Benvenisti, Giacinto della Cananea, and Stefan Kadelbach for comments on an earlier version of this paper, to Marc Jacob for language review and Eva Richter for editorial assistance.

A. von Bogdandy et al. (eds.), *The Exercise of Public Authority by International Institutions*, Beiträge zum ausländischen öffentlichen Recht und Völkerrecht 210,
DOI 10.1007/978-3-642-04531-8_24, © Springer-Verlag Berlin Heidelberg 2010

A. Introduction

The term *principle* is ubiquitous in the thematic studies and the cross-cutting studies of this research project on the exercise of public authority by international institutions. Apparently its legal analysis and normative framing is difficult to achieve without principles. This is no specificity of this undertaking: Legal research on the public authority of international institutions regularly deals with the issue of principles.[1] *General* principles for all international institutions are of specific interest as they might tie the various institutions into one legal universe. Yet, precisely their variety, even heterogeneity raises the question if such principles can be anything but "stars which give little light because they are so high." This quotation from Francis Bacon's "On the Advancement of Learning" precedes Edward Carr's classical study on the problems of a sweeping, *principled* and idealistic approach to international phenomena.[2]

The aim of this contribution is therefore not so much a discussion of individual principles, which is done in other studies of this research project. A first aim is to study more closely how principles are used in legal discourses (B.). I will distinguish between structural principles, guiding principles and legal principles. This makes it easier to grasp the various meanings and scholarly agendas pursued under the term *principle*. In section C. I discuss the impact of emerging principles of international authority on the general evolution of public international law and its scholarship in times of global governance. Thereby I hope to add further support to our general approach and to prepare the ground for the most difficult part of this contribution, the one on the development of general principles (D.). In section D., I will first review possible legal

---

1 Benedict Kingsbury, Nico Krisch & Richard Stewart, *The Emergence of Global Administrative Law*, Institute for International Law and Justice (New York University School of Law) Working Paper 2004/1, available at: http://www.iilj.org/papers/2004/2004.1.htm, later published in 68 LAW AND CONTEMPORARY PROBLEMS 2 (2005); Eberhard Schmidt-Aßmann, *Die Herausforderung der Verwaltungsrechtswissenschaft durch die Internationalisierung der Verwaltungsbeziehungen*, 45 DER STAAT 315 (2006); Eberhard Schmidt-Aßmann, in this volume; Giacinto della Cananea, *Dai vecchi ai nuovi principi generali del diritto*, *in* I PRINCIPI DALL'AZIONE AMMINISTRATIVA NELLO SPAZIO GIURIDICO GLOBALE 11 (Giacinto della Cananea ed., 2007).

2 Francis Bacon, *On the Advancement of Learning*, cited according to EDWARD HALLET CARR, THE TWENTY YEARS' CRISIS. AN INTRODUCTION TO THE STUDY OF INTERNATIONAL RELATIONS 302-307 (1940), vii.

bases of general principles (D.I.), suggesting *internal* constitutionalization as the best path in light of the heterogeneity and fragmentation of international law. Second (D.II.), I will discuss the roles of international and domestic judges in that process, stressing their common, but differentiated responsibility. Eventually, some individual principles of international institutions will be outlined in light of the principles of the European Union (E.).

B. Objects and Interests

The word *principle* defines only vaguely an object and a scholarly interest. Legal theory is not very helpful here, since it offers a plenitude of diverging and even contrasting conceptualizations.[3] This can be no different for such a basic legal term like "principle." This study employs an inductive approach focussing on the actual usages of the term within this research project. Here three main usages of the term and three corresponding concepts can be distinguished: principles in the sense of structural principles, in the sense of guiding principles and in the sense of legal principles. These categories are not mutually exclusive, and normatively it appears desirable that those principles which convey the fundamental ideas of liberal democracies are at the same time structural, guiding and legal principles. Sadly, this is not always the case on the international level.

I. Structural Principles for Doctrinal Constructions

A scholarly, doctrinal interest aims, above all, at principles in the sense of structural principles (*Ordnungsprinzipien*). Structural principles are scholarly abstractions which define legal structures within the positive law in the sense of significant regularities. The primary aim is to order

---

[3] On such theories, *see* RICCARDO GUASTINI, DISTINGUENDO. STUDI DI TEORIA E METATEORIA DEL DIRITTO 115 *et seqq*. (1997); András Jakab, *Prinzipien*, 37 RECHTSTHEORIE 49 (2006). In international law, *see* Martti Koskenniemi, *General Principles: Reflexions on Constructivist Thinking in International Law*, *in* SOURCES OF INTERNATIONAL LAW 359, 361 *et seq*. (Martti Koskenniemi ed., 2000).

the legal material *via* a system based on principles.[4] Examples include recurrent important norms concerning the relationship between international institutions and states, such as the principle of attributed competence, their internal organization or recurrent patterns of procedure or decision-making, such as the principle of consensus.

There is, at least in continental Europe, a general understanding that the identification and elaboration of such principles by means of abstraction, labelling, extrapolation, and arrangement of material belongs to the core areas of legal research. Many texts that aim at presenting an entire field of law often already exhibit the term "principle" in their title.[5] Many believe that the functional legitimacy of legal scholarship depends on this activity. Legal material needs to be arranged and thereby rationalized according to principles, and this scholarly arrangement is understood as essential for the law to fulfil its function of social ordering. Such abstractions appear particularly important in a field as heterogeneous and fragmented as the one of this study. Contrary to an occasionally voiced suspicion, such a systematic approach implies neither positivistic restrictions nor innovation-adverse conservatism. Rather such doctrinal constructions may help to apply principles established in one international legal regime on other regimes thereby furthering their progressive development.

II. Guiding Principles and the Framing of Discourses

In the international discourse, and correspondingly in the studies of this research, objectives pursued *via* an international legal regime are often

---

4 Koskenniemi (note 3), at 381 *et seq.*; EBERHARD SCHMIDT-AßMANN, ALLGEMEINES VERWALTUNGSRECHT ALS ORDNUNGSIDEE, margin number 3, 5 (2nd ed., 2004). Sometimes the term *principle* only indicates something like *general features. See* RICCARDO MONACO, SCRITTI DI DIRITTO DELLE ORGANIZAZZIONI INTERNAZIONALI 279 *et seqq.*, 459 *et seq.* (1981).

5 The book that founds the discipline in Germany carries the title FRIEDRICH FRANZ VON MAYER, GRUNDSÄTZE DES VERWALTUNGSRECHTS 46 *et seq.* (1862). For today, *see* CHITTHARANJAN FELIX AMERASINGHE, PRINCIPLES OF THE INSTITUTIONAL LAW OF INTERNATIONAL ORGANIZATIONS (2nd rev. ed., 2005); ALVIN LEROY BENNETT & JAMES K. OLIVER, INTERNATIONAL ORGANIZATIONS – ISSUES AND PRINCIPLES (7th ed., 2002).

called principles; they can be labelled *guiding principles.*[6] Such objectives can be found in the constituent treaties, in secondary legislation, but often also in legal instruments devoid of a binding character; in all cases these objectives are legally established, and hence part of the law. Thus, Article 3 of the United Nations Framework Convention on Climate Change lays down *principles* which are to guide the Parties, and the World Bank commits to the principles on development aid of the *Paris Declaration.*[7] The *International Law Association* also uses the term in this sense.[8] Such principles seek to line up a specific activity without providing for possible sanctions in case of non-observance. As regards domestic law, including for present purposes the law of the European Union, it appears preferable to distinguish doctrinally between objectives and principles. However, this is not the case on the international level, which is less differentiated.

Guiding principles, even if they do not aim to determine the line between legal and illegal behaviour, are important, since they structure and focus the discourse in an international institution.[9] In order to better understand this point, the metaphor of international law as a "universal language" is helpful.[10] Communication is a process ridden with prerequisites, in particular at the international level, and principles constitute a form of "vocabulary" by means of which the diverse political, economic, or ethical concerns can be introduced into the international process and treated in a common mode of communication. This is par-

---

6 On this type, *see* Riccardo Monaco, *Sources of International Law*, *in* IV ENCYCLOPEDIA OF PUBLIC INTERNATIONAL LAW (EPIL) 467, 473 (Rudolf Bernhardt ed., 2000).

7 For instance, in the case of the UNESCO World Heritage Convention the Preamble sets out the principle of ecologically sustainable development, which is consolidated by the precautionary principle and the inter-generational principle, the principle of cooperation, and the principle of subsidiarity. *See* Diana Zacharias, in this volume.

8 International Law Association, *Accountability of International Organisations*, Final Report, 2004, available at: http://www.ila-hq.org/html/layout_committee.htm.

9 Erwin Grochla, *Organisationstheorie*, *in* HANDWÖRTERBUCH DER ORGANISATION 1797 (Erwin Grochla ed., 2nd ed. 1980).

10 On the understandings of international law based on communication theory, *see* Friedrich Kratochwil, *How do Norms Matter?*, *in* THE ROLE OF LAW IN INTERNATIONAL POLITICS: ESSAYS IN INTERNATIONAL RELATIONS AND INTERNATIONAL LAW, 35 (Michael Byers ed., 2000).

ticularly important as international institutions do not aim at the application of largely predetermined law, but at political design.

III. Legal Principles and the Dual Function of Public Law

The third group consists of legal principles. Legal principles are general and important norms whose main function is the attribution of the binary qualification of legal/illegal in light of overarching values.[11] For sure, principles do not determine any such attribution in a mechanical or deductive sense, but they are often crucial in arguing about such attribution. They operate therefore at the core of the legal system. To many they appear as the most promising tool to frame the action of international institutions in a way that makes them efficient as well as respectful of liberal and democratic values. By developing such principles which transcend the legal practice of individual international institutions, legal scholarship performs its critical function *vis-à-vis* legal practice and stimulates its further development. However, unlike political claims or philosophical constructions, the concrete potential within the legal realm needs to be kept in sight: to postulate utopian ideas as legal principles usually harms the normativity of law.

Legal principles of international public authority have engendered interest in the past primarily out of a hope of supporting within international law a realm of administrative rationality in the tradition of functionalist conceptions of peace.[12] Accordingly, principles of international public authority aim to further their effective operation; the principle of implied powers and that of cooperation might serve as examples. This supportive attitude has determined the scholarly interest in the principles of international institutions for a long time.

More recent is the concern that the operation of these institutions might conflict with the values of the rule of law or democracy.[13] The activities

---

[11] Koskenniemi (note 3), at 368 *et seq.*

[12] EDWARD HALLET CARR, THE TWENTY YEARS' CRISIS. AN INTRODUCTION TO THE STUDY OF INTERNATIONAL RELATIONS 302-307 (1940). For a path breaking work, *see* DAVID MITRANY, A WORKING PEACE SYSTEM, AN ARGUMENT FOR THE FUNCTIONAL DEVELOPMENT OF INTERNATIONAL ORGANIZATION (4th ed., 1946).

[13] Matthias Ruffert, *Perspektiven des Internationalen Verwaltungsrechts*, *in* INTERNATIONALES VERWALTUNGSRECHT 395, 404 (Christoph Möllers, Andreas Voßkuhle & Christian Walter eds., 2007). See on the rule of law also the Focus

of the sanctions' committee of the UN Security Council or the Codex Alimentarius Commission are important examples.[14] Some even suspect that the operation of some international institutions might be potentially authoritarian.[15] For that reason legal principles now have the additional function of helping to meet a potential bureaucratic unlashing on the international level. This is particularly true for politics which eventually concern the individual citizen. Since many international institutions are only rudimentarily constrained by their founding treaties a taming *via* general principles appears as a possible alternative. Legal principles have been crucial in taming national bureaucracies as well as the institutions of the European Union. It appears apposite to develop such principles also with respect to the authority of international institutions. Yet, the specificities of international institutions need to be addressed, such as their heterogeneity or the lack of a common legal basis.

There is certainly a tension between the two objectives of an efficient and at the same time liberal operation of an international institution. This tension is not to be understood as a paradox. Rather, one here finds a general feature of public law thinking as this tension represents a basic characteristic of public (and particularly administrative) law.[16] Yet, even if there is consonance between international and domestic public law on this point, one needs to see that at the international level not only the protection of individuals is at stake, but also the protection of democratic self-determination of political collectives. In light of this the present contribution investigates general principles, i.e. principles which can apply to all forms of international public authority. Specific principles of individual fields of international law are not considered, such as

---

in MAX PLANCK YEARBOOK OF UNITED NATIONS LAW (MAX PLANCK UNYB) 12 (Armin von Bogdandy & Rüdiger Wolfrum eds., 2008).

14 *See* the contributions by Clemens Feinäugle, Ravi Afonso Pereira, Jochen von Bernstorff, Erika de Wet, Ingo Venzke, Rüdiger Wolfrum, in this volume.

15 MICHAEL HARDT & ANTONIO NEGRI, EMPIRE (2001); Anthony D'Amato, *On the Legitimacy of International Institutions*, *in* LEGITIMACY IN INTERNATIONAL LAW 83, 92 (Rüdiger Wolfrum & Volker Röben eds., 2008).

16 SCHMIDT-AßMANN (note 4), at 16 *et seq*.

the principle of sustainable development[17] or the principle of common but differentiated responsibility.[18]

C. Public Law Principles and the Evolution of the Field

I. Developing the Publicness of Public International Law

As argued in the contribution that sets out our general research agenda, we believe that a public law approach to the law of international institutions is a way to further legal understanding of the phenomena of global governance.[19] A reflection on principles supports this approach. The development of general principles of international public authority, such as the principle of attributed competence, or of human rights protection, aims at the strengthening of the publicness of public international law.[20] So far the general principles of international law correspond mainly to private law principles or principles of litigation between equal subjects, i.e. private law litigation.[21] The emergence of the public law component together with principles of international public authority is not just a sectoral phenomenon since international institutions are of considerable importance in many fields of international law.[22] Therefore this development heralds an overall strengthening of the publicness of public international law and evolves the general principles of international law.

We propose as the disciplinary point of departure for studying global governance phenomena the discipline of international institutions. This

---

17 Jürgen Friedrich, Christine Fuchs, in this volume. For principles in international environmental law, *see* Ulrich Beyerlin, *Principles, in* THE OXFORD HANDBOOK OF INTERNATIONAL ENVIRONMENTAL LAW (Jutta Brunnée, Daniel Bodansky & Ellen Hey eds., 2007).

18 Petra Láncos, in this volume.

19 *See* Armin von Bogdandy, Philipp Dann & Matthias Goldmann, in this volume.

20 On the concept of publicness, see *id.* at Part A III.

21 Hermann Mosler, *General Principles of Law, in* II EPIL 511, 518 *et seq.* (Rudolf Bernhardt ed., 1995).

22 José Alvarez, *International Organizations: Then and Now*, 100 AMERICAN JOURNAL OF INTERNATIONAL LAW (AJIL) 324 (2006); JOSÉ ALVAREZ, INTERNATIONAL ORGANIZATIONS AS LAW-MAKERS 184 *et seq.* (2005).

approach is confirmed when studying the relevant principles since that discipline presents studies on the principles of cooperation, of attributed competence, or of accountability. At the same time the new interest in international institutions in light of the phenomenon of global governance should result in a development of these principles.[23] Therefore one should not only study principles of such international institutions which are subjects of international law but also of other institutions such as treaty organs or informal institutions which exercise public authority.[24] Above all, the demands resulting from these principles should be framed in more stringent ways.

This approach seeks principles which guide and tame the public authority of international institutions. Yet, its objective is not a general rollback of such institutions. In this respect it is different to, for example, Anne-Marie Slaughter's approach, which locates public authority above all in networks of domestic administrations emasculating international institutions.[25] Our approach, by contrast, does not question the public authority of international institutions as such.

II. Principles of Domestic Authority: The Role of Comparative Thinking

The development of principles of international authority raises the question of comparison: what is the role of domestic public law principles in this process? Not considering such principles would be adverse to the "nature" of legal thinking since comparison is one of its most important features. Not taking into account the domestic context would furthermore miss the point that international institutions have been modeled on domestic experiences.[26] That is why a comparative method is promising. At the same time it is a truism that the principles of international public authority cannot be simple copies of domestic principles because international institutions are different: the domestic analogy, based on the assumption that an exercise of international authority parallels an exercise of domestic authority in all essential ele-

---

23 As example, *see* UGO DRAETTA, PRINCIPI DI DIRITTO DELLE ORGANIZZAZIONI INTERNAZIONALI (2nd ed., 2006).

24 *See* Anuscheh Farahat, in this volume.

25 ANNE-MARIE SLAUGHTER, A NEW WORLD ORDER (2004).

26 *See* Jochen von Bernstorff, in this volume.

ments, cannot convince in most cases. This leads to the question of a framework for comparison between international institutions and those of nation states or the European Union.

So far the most important application of public law principles beyond the nation state has happened with respect to the European Union. Therefore the relevant discussion might provide guidance for our topic. Within the framework of the public law of the European Union the development of public law principles is mainly due to the phenomenon of the Union's public power over private legal subjects. Such authority is the keystone of the dominant understandings of public law. European as well as national authorities can affect citizens or private enterprises without their consent. This unilateral power conflicts with the fundamental idea of modern constitutionalism: the freedom of the individual. This issue defines the core problem of public law. The corresponding *leitmotiv* of principles of public law is how to constitute, organize and channel this troublesome unilateral power. In fact, much of the current interest in international institutions is based on the concern that these institutions might evade the legal framing of public authority.

The acts of international institutions only very rarely bind individuals directly. One of the exceptions is the law of international public service. Thanks to well-established international administrative tribunals a satisfactory set of principles exists.[27] Far more critical is international public authority exercising administrative functions over individuals in cases of failed states or similar situations.[28] Both cases remain sidelined in this study, which is mainly concerned with the "routine" situation of functioning statehood. In this "routine" situation direct exercise of authority by international institutions over individuals is extremely rare. Examples include the determination of the refugee's status by the UNHCR in states which have delegated this task to this institution.[29] For the rest, not even the sanction lists of the UN Security Council bind individuals directly.[30] The WIPO trade mark unfolds legal conse-

---

27 *See* CHITTHARANJAN FELIX AMERASINGHE, I THE LAW OF INTERNATIONAL CIVIL SERVICE (2nd ed. 1994); ROBERTO MALKASSIAN, EL FUNCIONARIO INTERNACIONAL 63 (1980) (assuming the emergence of common general principles for all international organizations).

28 On this, *see Restructuring Iraq. Possible Models Based Upon Experience Gained Under the Authority of the League of Nations and the United Nations*, Max Planck UNYB 9 (Armin von Bogdandy & Rüdiger Wolfrum eds., 2005).

29 Maja Smrkolj, in this volume.

30 Clemens Feinäugle, in this volume.

quences directly for individuals, but national institutions can suspend the effect.[31] Therefore the principles of international institutions concern actions for which the implementing states or the implementing European Union have at least some political and legal responsibility, precisely because there is no direct effect and supremacy. This lack of direct authority of international institutions needs to be reflected in the relevant principles.

If comparability between domestic public authorities and international institutions were to exist only in case of a legal determination of individual legal positions, an international public law would remain a very limited phenomenon, at least with respect to most countries of the world. However, it appears outdated to consider only acts directly binding individuals as the exclusive focal point of public law. In fact recent research on domestic public law is expanding beyond this focus. Hence the research on international or global administrative law rests on the plausible assumption that the exclusive focus on legal determination of individuals is too restrictive in light of liberal democratic principles: as developed in the contribution on the research agenda (A.II.), an exercise of public authority can also occur through a non-binding act which only *conditions* another legal subject.[32] In this *authority of public institutions to determine others* by binding, but also by non-binding acts whenever put in a constraining framework, we see the level of comparison between domestic authorities and international institutions.

Yet, in most cases arguments against strictly analogical reasoning abound. Any comparison must take into account that acts of international institutions come neither with direct effect nor with supremacy and that the legal situation of the individual is mostly framed by the domestic implementing measure. The construction of analogies is further complicated by the fact that – as comparative administrative law tells us – there are few generally recognized principles for such types of administrative activities which are not directly binding on individuals. As a consequence, any transposition of domestic legal doctrine needs to be carefully construed.

Summing up, I submit that any domestic principle applicable to domestic public authority provides for a perspective to juridically examine international public authority. This can be seen as quintessential to the public law approach to international law with its constitutionalist dis-

31 Karen Kaiser, in this volume.

32 Similarly, *see* della Cananea (note 1); Ruffert (note 13), at 407, 414.

position. There is a presumption that an established principle of domestic public authority raises an issue to which the law of an international institution should provide a principled answer, which, however, in most cases will differ from that given in domestic legal orders. At the same time, the more an international authority impacts an individual, the stronger the assumption is that international principles require legal arrangements which are functionally equivalent to what is to be expected in the domestic realm. But a strict analogy can almost never apply for reasons which also militate against a broad category of principles of global administrative law, to which I turn now.

III. Principles of an International or Global Administrative Law?

A much further reaching and bolder approach is presented by the proposal of an international administrative law, and even more so the idea of a global administrative law as a new field of research or even a new discipline.[33] In discussing these approaches further aspects of the principles of international institutions come to light. Here, the public authority of international institutions is conceived as a mere aspect of a much broader phenomenon. In contrast to the traditional separation of domestic (national or unional) law and international law, a field emerges which embraces international and domestic administrative activity. Such a novel field implies a claim of overarching principles: the establishment of a specific field of legal research goes hand in hand with the formulation of principles which shape the entire field.

Eberhard Schmidt-Aßmann's approach conceives an international administrative law as "administrative law originating under/in *international law*" and divides it into three "functional circles," following the logic of his doctrine on European administrative law: a body of law governing international administrative institutions, a body of law *determinative* of national administrative legal orders, and a body of law on *cooperative* handling of common problems.[34] On the horizon appears a new jurisprudential sub-discipline focussing on – *inter alia* –

---

33 This topic was one of the main themes of the German public law association in 2007. *See* Giovanni Biaggini & Claus Dieter Classen, *Die Entwicklung eines Internationalen Verwaltungsrechts als Aufgabe der Rechtswissenschaft*, 67 VERÖFFENTLICHUNGEN DER VEREINIGUNG DEUTSCHER STAATSRECHTSLEHRER (2008).

34 Schmidt-Aßmann (note 1), at 336.

overarching principles of international and national administration. The international development would thus *in principle* reproduce the European one, a widespread aspiration not only in Europe.[35]

This understanding leans, however, towards a proto-federal conception of global order which I do not think tenable. This becomes particularly evident with respect to general principles. The development of overarching principles has been a pillar of a common administrative law in a federal state[36] as well as in the European Union.[37] In particular the development of a supranational composite administration rests – from a legal perspective – on the function and competences of the ECJ and common principles of an integrated legal order, as enshrined in Article 6 EU. The idea of a fundamental consonance of European and national administration under the EC Treaty has been established for some time and is promoted by the constitutionalization of the respective legal positions.[38] This is an important element furthering the federal unity within the process of European integration.

Should there be similar overarching principles on the international level that would be a considerable step towards a world federation. Yet there is very little evidence for such an evolution. The proto-federal global administrative law rests on assumptions which appear to me even more problematic than the constitutional understanding of international law which is not, by necessity, federal.[39] Similarly, the proponents of a global administrative law assert the advent of a "single, if multifaceted global administrative space distinct from the domains of international law and domestic law," built by overarching principles.[40] The term

---

35 Anne-Marie Slaughter & William Burke-White, *The Future of International Law is Domestic (or, The European Way of Law)*, 47 HARVARD INTERNATIONAL LAW JOURNAL 327 (2006). Similarly the report of the International Law Association (note 8).

36 ERNST FORSTHOFF, I LEHRBUCH DES VERWALTUNGSRECHT 40 *et seq.* (10th ed. 1973).

37 Schmidt-Aßmann (note 1), at 393 *et seq.*

38 *See*, e.g., Case C-28/05, Dokter, 2006 E.C.R. I-5431, paras. 71-75. The administrations of the Member States are bound by the principles developed for the EU's own administration: a federal constellation through and through.

39 See Armin von Bogdandy, *Constitutionalism in International Law: Comment on a Proposal from Germany*, 47 HARVARD INTERNATIONAL LAW JOURNAL 223, 232 et seq. (2006).

40 Kingsbury, Krisch & Stewart (note 1), at 2, 13, 16, 24 *et seq.*; SABINO CASSESE, OLTRE LO STATO 38 *et seq.*, 55 (2006). Later Krisch appears to have

"space" is revealing: *space* or *area* have become the proxy for *federal* in *Eurospeak*: the EU is an *area* of freedom, security and justice, a research *area*, not least an *area* of free movement, each with its administrative dimension.[41]

In my understanding, there is little ground for a global doctrine of principles encompassing international and domestic public authorities. The respective general legal and institutional context appears to be too diverse: European administrative law is based upon the principles of direct effect and supremacy, on the principle of vertical and horizontal constitutional compatibility (Article 6 TEU), on the essentially uniform political system of the EU, which is rooted in its territory and citizens, on a judiciary endowed with strong competences, and on a largely parliamentary legislature. All this, in short: a federal unity, cannot be traced beyond the Union.[42]

If global administrative law is in some respects too broad, it appears too narrow in others. It appears of little use only to investigate principles which deal exclusively with administrative activity. Given the underdeveloped differentiation of public authorities on the international level, general principles remain crucial, for example human rights. At stake are general principles of public authority, i.e. principles of public law.

This argument does not deny that many international norms, and in particular international principles, are important, even determinative for domestic administrative procedures. For example, the law of the WTO[43] or the human rights instruments establish some principles;[44]

---

noticed the problem. *See* Nico Kirsch, *The Pluralism of Global Administrative Law*, 17 EUROPEAN JOURNAL OF INTERNATIONAL LAW (EJIL) 247 (2006).

41 For the close link between global administrative law and international constitutionalism, *see* CASSESE (note 40), at 185 *et seq.*

42 And its assumption is not prevalent among international law scholars, *see* only the contributions by Eyal Benvenisti, Stefan Kadelbach, Helen Keller, Thilo Marauhn, Georg Nolte, Stefan Oeter, Andreas Paulus, Anne Peters, Erika de Wet & Andreas Zimmermann, 67 ZEITSCHRIFT FÜR AUSLÄNDISCHES ÖFFENTLICHES RECHT UND VÖLKERRECHT (ZAÖRV) 585-824 (2007).

43 *See e.g.*, WT/DS2/AB/R *US – Standards for Reformulated and Conventional Gasoline*, Report of the Appellate Body adopted on 29 April 1996; WT/DS58/AB/R *United States – Import Prohibition of Certain Shrimp and Shrimp Products, Recourse to Article 21.5 DSU.*

44 Such as procedural guarantees binding upon national administrations emanating from Art. 6 ECHR. On this aspect, *see* Christoph Grabenwarter &

moreover, some international treaties lay down specific requirements for domestic administrations.[45] Yet these norms explicitly address only domestic administration.

Is it possible to assert a principle of parallelism so that international law addressed to domestic administrations applies also to international institutions? That might be a possible political or moral maxim. In the legal context, however, as set out in B.II., the legal basis as well as the legal and factual context of domestic principles on the one side and international principles on the other side appear to be so diverse that it is more promising to conceive different, although interlinked phenomena. As a consequence one should not strive for overarching principles, even if there is some overarching consolidated law in particular in human rights guarantees.[46]

I agree with the proponents of a global administrative law that there should be a theoretical and doctrinal framework for international, supranational and national public law which conceptualizes their linkages and which guides the transfer of insights as well as the construction of analogies. Yet, I find neither the theory nor the doctrine of administrative law convincing at this point in time in this respect. Moreover, this approach blurs categories which are indispensible for attributing political and legal responsibility: the lack of an elaborate doctrine of sources as well as the lack of a doctrine of direct effect is no coincidence.

IV. Public Law Theory as the General Framework

The framework should be developed as an overarching theory and doctrine of public law. The phenomenon of interest is less that of *admini-*

Katharina Pabel, *Art. 6*, *in* EMRK/GG, KONKORDANZKOMMENTAR 653 (Rainer Grote & Thilo Marauhn eds., 2006).

45 *See Aarhus-Convention on Access to Information, Public Participation in Decision-Making and Access to Justice in Environmental Matters*, 38 INTERNATIONAL LEGAL MATERIALS 517 (1999). *See also* Christian Walter, *Internationalisierung des deutschen und europäischen Verwaltungsverfahrens- und Verwaltungsprozessrechts – am Beispiel der Aarhus-Konvention*, 40 EUROPARECHT 302 (2005); Rüdiger Wolfrum, *Ansätze eines allgemeinen Verwaltungsrechts im internationalen Umweltrecht*, *in* ALLGEMEINES VERWALTUNGSRECHT – ZUR TRAGFÄHIGKEIT EINES KONZEPTS (Thomas Groß, Christoph Möllers, Christian Röhl & Hans-Heinrich Trute eds., 2008).

46 Ruffert (note 13), at 415.

stration but rather the more general phenomenon of public authority. Public authority, i.e. the competence to unilaterally determine the conduct of others, is the fundamental problem of public law as it collides with the fundamental idea of constitutionalism: freedom. The phenomenon of public authority corresponds to the phenomenon and the discipline of public law. This understanding flows from the tradition of the *Ius Publicum*[47] which aims at establishing a legal framework for any exercise of public power. This approach opens broad interfaces both within and outside legal scholarship. Moreover it avoids the problems of delimitation which the concept of *administration* and the corresponding concept of *constitution* give rise to. The debate on a European Constitution revealed how problematic it is to use the concept of a constitution even within a supranational context.[48] This problem grows worse with respect to a field of law which – due to its sources – belongs to international law. This problem cannot be avoided by simply using the complementary concept of *administration*. Hence the principles of international institutions should be understood as concretizations of general principles of public law formulated in the tradition of liberal constitutionalism and adapted to the structures and requirements of multilevel systems and global institutions.

In the formulation of international principles for the exercise of public authority one can distinguish between three basic constellations. The first is the one pursued in this contribution: principles to guide and frame the activities of international institutions which need to be implemented by domestic institutions to have legal effects with respect to the individual.

The second constellation concerns international principles for international institutions whose acts directly affect private subjects in particular the international administration of territories.[49] The third constellation consists of international legal principles for domestic administrative activity.[50] In this third constellation again three situations might be

---

47 *See* MICHAEL STOLLEIS, NATIONALITÄT UND INTERNATIONALITÄT. RECHTSVERGLEICHUNG IM ÖFFENTLICHEN RECHT DES 19. JAHRHUNDERTS 20 *et seq*. (1998).

48 Christoph Möllers, *Pouvoir Constituant – Constitution – Constitutionalisation, in* PRINCIPLES OF EUROPEAN CONSTITUTIONAL LAW 183 (Armin von Bogdandy & Jürgen Bast eds., 2006).

49 Von Bogdandy & Wolfrum (note 28); Smrkolj (note 29).

50 CASSESE (note 40), at 67 *et seq*.

distinguished: a) principles for a basic rule of law standard (e. g. Article X GATT, Article 14 ICCPR, b) principles that force domestic administrations to consider extra-territorial interests as a response to global interdependence,[51] and c) principles regarding the cooperation of domestic administrations within composite administration.[52]

D. On the Development of General Principles

I. On the Legal Bases

Structural principles can be generated through scientific abstraction. By contrast, for guiding principles and particularly for legal principles scientific efforts do not suffice. The problem is related to the issue of how to deal with gaps in international law, i.e. situations in which decision according to the letter of the positive legal texts appears unsatisfactory.[53] I will argue that, given the lack of an overarching international constitution, of a general international judiciary as well as in light of the heterogeneity of international institutions, their *internal* constitutionalization appears to be the most promising avenue for developing general principles to constrain their exercise of public authority. This is best explained in the context of other approaches.

1. Traditional Approaches

One of these other approaches is the "mortgage theory" (or "theory of technical-legal delegation").[54] It comes in two versions: in a first, radical version, the competences of international administrative institutions are understood as domestic competences delegated by the states as if the in-

---

51 On this problem in the context of the WTO, *see* L. Bartels, *Art. XX of GATT and the Problem of Extraterritorial Jurisdiction. The Case of Trade Measures for the Protection of Human Rights*, 36 JOURNAL OF WORLD TRADE 353-403 (2002).

52 For duties to cooperation, *see* Armin von Bogdandy & Philipp Dann, in this volume.

53 ULRICH FASTENRATH, LÜCKEN IM VÖLKERRECHT 125 *et seq.* (1991); Koskenniemi (note 3), at 372.

54 KATHRIN OSTENECK, DIE UMSETZUNG VON UN-WIRTSCHAFTSSANKTIONEN DURCH DIE EUROPÄISCHE GEMEINSCHAFT 222 *et seq.* (2004).

ternational institution were a domestic agency;[55] the international institution would then have to comply with all the legal obligations that are incumbent upon its Member States under domestic law.[56] This understanding is rarely championed today, confirming an important principle: the principle of the autonomy of international institutional activity *vis-à-vis* internal law. The second version of the "mortgage theory" contends that international institutions are subject to the international law obligations of the states supporting them. The legal basis of this is in itself a general principle, i.e. the principle that a legal subject cannot free itself from a legal obligation towards a third subject by creating a new subject of law. Henry Schermers and Niels Blokker hold that "[s]tates which have founded an international organization are bound by general principles of law. These principles will also be applicable in the legal order of the organization."[57] This approach certainly lies within the limits of what is legally tenable; however, because of the vagueness of the statement "general principles of law," it only provides a platform for further reasoning in the context of Article 38 § I lit. c ICJ-Statute. In this sense the ICJ states in a classical obiter dictum "international organisations are subjects of international law and, as such, are bound by any obligation incumbent upon them under general rules of international law (...)."[58]

One line of concretizing thought is based on qualitative comparative methodology, comparing domestic principles of public law of different domestic orders. *Global* or *international administrative law*, to take a recent example, is the desire to transpose established principles of domestic administrative law to international institutions. Another school operates in the framework of natural law theory. Important authors include Alfred Verdross or Hersch Lauterpacht;[59] this approach remains

---

55 This was in fact the dominant understanding in the 19th and early 20th century. *See* Part D.I.1.

56 There are tendencies in this direction in DAN SAROOSHI, INTERNATIONAL ORGANIZATIONS AND THEIR EXERCISE OF SOVEREIGN POWERS 33 *et seq.* (2005).

57 HENRY SCHERMERS & NIELS BLOKKER, INTERNATIONAL INSTITUTIONAL LAW § 1575 (3rd ed., 1995).

58 Interpretation of the Agreement of 25 March 1951 between the WHO and Egypt, Advisory Opinion of 20 December 1980, ICJ Reports 1980, 73, 89-90.

59 For a reconstruction of the positions, *see* Béla Vitanyi, *Les positions doctrinales concernant le sens de la notion de principes généraux de droit reconnus*

important.[60] The best case in this respect can be made for principles of human rights applying to international institutions, by now often considered independent from domestic law.[61] A similar argument is developed within the framework of international customary law in the sense of Article 38 § I lit b ICJ-Statute. Human rights laid down in international treaties are interpreted as customary law principles and – by way of progressive development – enriched with requirements for international administrative action.[62]

These lines of thinking can be attacked on good grounds. In the methodical canon of a positivism focused on legal texts or state will, it is usually possible to negate the legal relevance of general principles, if their validity has not been ordered explicitly.[63] Conceptions which see international law as being largely fragmented tend to a similar position.[64] But problems also abound under different methodological premises. Natural law arguments are beset with well known difficulties. In a similar line, the comparison of administrative legal systems can easily conclude that there are hardly principles in the sense of Article 38 § I lit. c ICJ-Statute.[65] Comparative research is largely limited to a few legal systems and its findings mostly regard administrative action directly af-

---

par les nations civilisées, 86 REVUE GÉNÉRALE DE DROIT INTERNATIONAL PUBLIC 48 et seq. (1982).

60 *See* OSCAR SCHACHTER, INTERNATIONAL LAW IN THEORY AND PRACTICE 50 *et seq.* (1991).

61 For a path breaking treatment, *see* Bruno Simma & Philip Alston, *The Sources of Human Rights Law: Custom, Jus Cogens and General Principles*, 12 AUSTRALIAN YEARBOOK OF INTERNATIONAL LAW 82 (1992); Niels Petersen, *Customary Law Without Custom?*, 23 AMERICAN UNIVERSITY INTERNATIONAL LAW REVIEW 275 (2008).

62 Alexander Orakhelashvili, *The Acts of the Security Council: Meaning and Standards of Review*, 11 MAX PLANCK UNYB 143, 177 (2007).

63 HANS KELSEN, PRINCIPLES OF INTERNATIONAL LAW 438 *et seq.* (1966); Gabriel H. Oosthuizen, *Playing the Devil's Advocate: the United Nations Security Council is Unbound by Law*, 12 LEIDEN JOURNAL OF INTERNATIONAL LAW 549 (1999).

64 HEINRICH TRIEPEL, VÖLKERRECHT UND LANDESRECHT 83 *et seq.* (1899); MYRES MCDOUGAL, STUDIES IN WORLD PUBLIC ORDER 987 (1960); IBRAHIM SHIHATA, THE WORLD BANK LEGAL PAPERS 265 *et seq.* (2000).

65 Carol Harlow, *Global Administrative Law: the Quest for Principles and Values,* 17 EJIL 168 (2006). *See also* the contributions in the Symposium Issue of the EJIL, 2006, Number 1.

fecting the legal positions of individuals, which is rarely the case with international institutions. Similarly the proof of international customary law is beset with chronic difficulty,[66] and the expansive interpretation of human rights is met with vehement critique from important states.

This is maybe why the European Court of First Instance, in its judgment of 21 September 2005,[67] has chosen the approach of examining the compatibility of decisions by UN bodies with *jus cogens*. The result of this judgment is unsatisfactory from a human rights perspective, but it reflects the vagueness and the problems of this legal construction[68] as well as the hegemonic structure on which important parts of international law rest. There seems to be a hardly resolvable tension between the suitability of *jus cogens* to tame the actions of international institutions and its universal credibility, a tension which should be resolved, in case of doubt, in favor of universal credibility.

2. *The Promise of Internal Constitutionalization*

A more promising approach aims at the internal constitutionalization of international institutions; it features prominently in a report of the International Law Association.[69] This constitutionalization is usually based on the institution's constituent instrument, and enriches its often rudimentary requirements through progressive interpretation in light of other important international norms, but also in light of requirements formulated by domestic legal orders for the acceptance of the institution's acts. Internal constitutionalization seeks to develop the operation of an international institution in light of the values of constitutionalism.

This approach needs to be distinguished from a constitutionalization of an international treaty with respect to a domestic legal order, in particu-

---

66 Koskenniemi (note 3), at 359, 387; Holger Hestermeyer, *Access to Medication as a Human Right*, 8 MAX PLANCK UNYB 101, 158 (2004).

67 Case T-306/01, Yusuf, 2005 E.C.R II-3533, paras. 304 *et seq.*

68 Stefan Kadelbach, *Jus Cogens, Obligations Erga Omnes and Other Rules – The Identification of Fundamental Norms, in* THE FUNDAMENTAL RULES OF THE INTERNATIONAL LEGAL ORDER 21 (Christian Tomuschat & Jean Marc Thouvenin eds., 2006).

69 *See* International Law Association (note 8). For the UN, *see* ERIKA DE WET, THE CHAPTER VII POWERS OF THE UNITED NATIONS SECURITY COUNCIL 191 *et seq.* (2004).

lar *via* direct effect and supremacy. Heralded by European Union law, this has been proposed as a possible route for other international institutions, in particular the UN and the WTO. I am doubtful whether such constitutionalization of international treaties is legally and politically convincing for institutions such as those investigated in this research.[70]

In contrast to constitutionalization as a general approach, internal constitutionalization is far more circumscribed since it does not affect the position of international law in the domestic systems. With respect to the development of general principles framing the exercise of international authority, this approach has three main advantages. First, it is based on the constituent treaty and therefore provides for a firm legal basis, not beset with the problems of the sources under Article 38 § I lit. b and c ICJ-Statute. Second, it is highly flexible. It leaves room for the specific logic and settings of the various institutions. In most constituent instruments, one will find a basis to argue the applicability of general normative considerations, but these bases vary, as well as the institutional practice on which any argument should build upon. Third, this approach fits with the largely fragmented state of international law without giving up the project of a public law framework. Granted, this pluralist approach will not yield a universe of general principles in a strict sense as they are known under domestic constitutions. Yet, striving for general principles which apply equally for all the exercises of any international authority might be a fruitless project given the diversity within the international legal order.[71] This pluralist understanding does not assert a uniform set of international principles for the exercise of international authority, but rather a pluriverse of general principles of different international institutions, which are, however, interlinked, thereby forming an overarching layer of common legal arguments.

Under this pluralist approach, I see much potential for a framing and taming of international institutions based on general principles. I do not know of an international institution today that would simply repudiate the demand for an embedding of its activity in the *rule of law* or in *good*

---

70 *See* Armin von Bogdandy, *Law and Politics in the WTO. Strategies to Cope with a Deficient Relationship*, 5 MAX PLANCK UNYB 609 (2001); Armin von Bogdandy, *Pluralism, Direct Effect, and the Ultimate Say*, 6 INTERNATIONAL JOURNAL OF CONSTITUTIONAL LAW 397-413 (2008).

71 *Report of the Study Group of the International Law Commission*, U.N. GAOR, 58th Sess., U.N. Doc. A/CN.4/L.682 (13 April 2006); Nico Kirsch, *The Pluralism of Global Administrative Law*, 17 EJIL 247 (2006).

governance; this can be interpreted as an acknowledgement of principles. It is obvious that otherwise the institution would lose legitimacy and endanger its existence. Notwithstanding a range of theoretical questions as to the formulation of principles, there seem to be, from a practical point of view, sufficient legal bases for a principle-oriented embedding of the exercise of international authority.[72] A historic perspective shows that development of principles has mostly started with the scholarly assertion of a principle.[73] But much more important than the scholar has been the judge in that process, to whom I now turn.

II. Who Should Do What: The Role of International and Domestic Judges

A structuring and framing of the activities of international institutions by principles is possible and meaningful. At the same time, limits and problems have come to light. Legal principles require institutions which impose them on the acting public authorities. Erika de Wet's contribution on accountability shows that this can be done by various institutions. Yet, a principle-oriented embedding of international administrative activity is hardly feasible without a strong judiciary.[74]

A uniform set of general principles has in the past always required a powerful overarching court capable of exercising judicial review. The lack of such an institution on the international level is a further reason why general principles of international public authority will be different to those in domestic settings. But the problem is even more serious: as only a few international institutions are subject of direct judicial review, indirect control is of utmost importance. This control can be exercised by international courts, in particular the International Court of Justice or the European Court of Human Rights. Given, however, that

---

[72] Numerous legal starting points can be found in the report of the International Law Association (note 8).

[73] Cananea (note 1), at 42.

[74] Erika de Wet & André Nollenkaemper, *Review of Security Council Decisions by National Courts*, 45 GERMAN YEARBOOK OF INTERNATIONAL LAW 166 (2002); Christian Walter, *Grundrechtsschutz gegen Hoheitsakte internationaler Organisationen*, 129 ARCHIV DES ÖFFENTLICHEN RECHTS 39 (2004); Sienho Yee, *The Responsibility of States Members of an International Organization for Its Conduct*, *in* INTERNATIONAL RESPONSIBILITY TODAY 435 (Maurizio Ragazzi & Oscar Schachter eds., 2005).

international acts require in most instances domestic implementation, the task of indirect control mostly lies with the domestic judiciary, the ECJ included.

At this point the question is how and to what extent the domestic judiciary should compensate the lack of an international judiciary and under which principles it should examine international acts. The domestic courts could use international legal principles. The European Court of First Instance has followed this approach albeit limiting itself to principles of *jus cogens*.[75] The advantage of this approach is that it contributes to a more rapid development of such principles as there will be more decisions. Its disadvantage is that it might disrupt the development of international institutions. Moreover it could appear paternalistic with respect to other domestic legal orders since stating illegality on the basis of international law entails a universal claim. Less disruptive and less paternalistic might be the definition of requirements of application within the domestic legal order. This is the approach of the German Federal Constitutional Court, and it is shared by Advocate General Maduro in his opinion on Kadi.[76] Under this approach domestic judicial decisions contribute indirectly to the development of international principles by defining domestic requirements for acceptance to which the interpretation of the constituent treaty can respond, and which eventually might even become relevant via the legal source of Article 38 § I lit. c ICJ-Statute. This approach appears better in tune with the limited competences of most courts.

On this path, it will take more time to develop international legal principles. At the same time, this winding path might prove more successful since it responds better to the complexities of the formation of international legal principles in a heterogeneous world. The drawback of this approach might be a further fragmentation of the law and a reversion to traditional dualism that might damage the linkages between domestic and international law. This danger can be met if the domestic courts interpret the pertinent domestic principles in light of international law, contributing thereby to the global, but pluralistic debate. Thus domestic courts could participate together with legal scholarship in a development of international principles which guide and frame international institutions without endangering them.

---

[75] *Supra*, note 67.

[76] AG Poires Maduro, in Case C-402/05 P, Yassin Abdullah Kadi v Council of the European Union and Commission of the European Union, 16 January 2008.

E. Some General Principles — A Sketch

The following text presents some general principles for the exercise of international authority as an overarching layer of common legal arguments for different international institutions. At the same time, it is based on the insights of research on the principles of the European Union.[77] There are many texts which conceive the European Union as a simple species of the genus *international institution*.[78] Although I do not share this understanding for the reasons to be developed, a comparative presentation appears promising. The aim is to indicate parallels, but also differences in order to grasp the specific quality of international public authority. Due to reasons of space these issues can only be sketched out briefly.

Research on the principles of the public authority of the European Union has revealed that the relationship between the Union and its Member States deeply affects all principles of the Union's public authority. Therefore a comparative inquiry with respect to international institutions should start with this issue.

I. The Relationship Between International Institution – Member State

1. Autonomy and Sovereignty

The principle of the autonomy of community law is fundamental to the European legal order. It is a structural principle which explains many features of that legal order, and it is a legal principle which the ECJ defends emphatically. While international institutions were for a long time considered common institutions of the Member States,[79] their autonomy has become a legal principle within the law of international institutions. First of all there is a principle of legal autonomy of legal acts of international institutions with respect to domestic law. Due to their le-

---

[77] For that field of research, *see* Armin von Bogdandy, *Constitutional Principles*, *in* von Bogdandy & Bast (note 48), at 3.

[78] *See* MANUEL DIEZ DE VELASCO VALLEJO, LAS ORGANIZACIONES INTERNACIONALES 137 *et seq.* (12th ed. 2006); SCHERMERS & BLOKKER (note 57), at § 58.

[79] David Kennedy, *The Move To Institutions*, 8 CARDOZO LAW REVIEW 841, 962-964 (1987).

gal basis in an international source of law the validity of such acts is independent from domestic sources. This independence is an important functional prerequisite of international institutions as the alternative clearly demonstrates. If the action of international institutions occurred on the basis of delegated domestic competences, i.e. in sense of the strict mortgage theory, efficient action on the international level would hardly be possible given the differences between the various domestic legal orders. The example of European integration also shows that this legal autonomy is one of the reasons why national governments pursue political projects on the international level. The legal scope for action is far broader, and it is usually more difficult for affected domestic groups to organise resistance on the international level. The importance of this autonomy is well evidenced by the UN sanctions lists.[80] In most domestic legal orders a similar act would be unlawful for many reasons.

The autonomy of the legal validity of international legal acts based on an international source is a general structural principle and a general legal principle; it is at the basis of Article 27 of the Vienna Convention on the Law of Treaties. Many decisions of international and domestic courts ascertain this autonomy. To my knowledge, no domestic court has ever examined the validity of an act of an international institution on the basis of its domestic law. Either the court examines its legality under international law; here the court examines whether the act conforms to superior international law.[81] Or the international act is examined on the basis of domestic law; the domestic court then does not discuss legality or validity, but rather the applicability within the domestic legal order.[82] Another part of this autonomy is that international institutions enjoy broad immunities before domestic courts.[83]

The principle of autonomy can also be observed in the organizational structure of international institutions. The capacity to form an independent will is constitutive for an international organization; this entails

---

80 *See* Clemens Feinäugle, in this volume.

81 *Supra,* note 67.

82 AG Poires Maduro, in Case C-402/05 P, Yassin Abdullah Kadi v. Council of the European Union and Commission of the European Union, 16 January 2008, paras. 24, 38 *et seq.*

83 *See* August Reinisch, International Organizations Before National Courts (2000); Kirsten Schmalenbach, Die Haftung internationaler Organisationen 69 *et seq.* (2004).

by necessity some autonomy with respect to the Member States.[84] Every institution discussed in this research project has some autonomy with respect to its Member States. There is always a secretariat with some autonomous range of action. CITES is important in this respect as it is one of the first treaty regimes with a professional full-time secretariat.[85] Moreover in many international organizations some majority decisions are possible. This latter form of autonomy can, however, only be formulated as a structural principle. A legal principle that forces states to provide some autonomy to international institutions does not exist. Yet if there is a complete lack of autonomy, international law does not permit to conceive an institution as an international organization with the consequence that any decision is directly attributable to the Member States.

Whereas the principle of the autonomy of international law is well established, a principle of the autonomy of internal law appears doubtful. Granted, hardly anybody will argue that an act by an international institution determines the validity of national law. In that respect autonomy exists. However, a principle of the autonomy of domestic law has been argued as a principle under the law of the European Union with the aim to protect certain topics against supranational interference. So far the proponents of such a principle have not succeeded in demonstrating such a principle beyond the principle of subsidiarity.

Different to European Union law, the acts of international institutions do not have direct effect and supremacy within the domestic legal order. This autonomy of domestic law is important for international law as the lack of direct effect and supremacy provides for relief regarding pressures of legitimacy. The lack of direct effect and supremacy can be seen as a structural principle which distinguishes international institutions from supranational ones. The Court of First Instance misses this point in its decision in the Yussuf case. Its decision is trapped in an antiquated monism irreconcilable with the autonomy of community law. This should not be interpreted as singing the praises of dualism; I rather advocate a conception of the interaction along the lines of a legal pluralism

---

84 SCHERMERS & BLOKKER (note 57), at § 44. On autonomy, *see* Ingo Venzke in this volume.

85 *See* Christine Fuchs, in this volume.

that acknowledges the many linkages between the different legal orders.[86]

With respect to the protection of the autonomy of states against interference from international institutions, there is certainly the principle of sovereignty. Yet, all expressions of that principle in the context of the law of international organizations, such as the principle of domestic jurisdiction (*domaine réservé*) have proven to be an ineffective protection.[87] The same holds true for the emerging principle of subsidiarity in international law; it does not limit the intensity by which international actions might impact on domestic politics.[88]

2. *Loyal Cooperation and Procedural Principles*

International institutions, similar to the European Union, hardly ever act alone and directly with respect to private legal subjects. They operate in most cases together with domestic institutions, be it in the shaping of politics, be it their implementation. This requires coordination, and correspondingly the thematic studies reveal detailed duties of cooperation. The various forms of interaction can be summarized by the concept of composite administration.[89] The concept rests on the insight that global governance needs the autonomy of the component institutions as well as their capacity for common action. Whereas the element of independence finds expression in the principle of autonomy, the interaction of the different authorities can be brought together under the principle of cooperation. The fundamental idea of such composite authorities is that public duties can be better discharged in cooperation between domestic and international institutions rather than by an isolated domestic administration. This also justifies the ensuing drawbacks of national self-determination.

These duties can be interpreted as an expression of a general principle of cooperation.[90] In fact, many years ago the ICJ declared that "the very

---

[86] In detail Armin von Bogdandy, *Pluralism, Direct Effect, and the Ultimate Say*, 6 INTERNATIONAL JOURNAL OF CONSTITUTIONAL LAW 397-413 (2008).

[87] Jochen von Bernstorff, in this volume.

[88] Isabel Feichtner, *Subsidiarity*, *in* EPIL (Rüdiger Wolfrum ed., 2009).

[89] Bogdandy & Dann (note 52).

[90] Konrad Ginther, *Mitgliedschaft in Internationalen Organisationen, Grundfragen*, 17 BERICHTE DER DEUTSCHEN GESELLSCHAFT FÜR VÖLKER-

fact of Egypt's membership of the Organization entails certain mutual obligations of co-operation and good faith incumbent upon the Organization."[91] There are remarkable attempts to establish the principle of cooperation as a general principle of international law even beyond the law of international institutions. According to Wolfgang Friedmann's famous categorization of international law, the cooperation between states is the defining principle of an era which has overcome the more traditional international law focused on mere coexistence or coordination.[92] The principle of cooperation has the character of a structural, guiding, and legal principle. The latter entails a common responsibility of all participating authorities for the realization of the objectives of the international regime in question.

If there exists a principle of cooperation its importance should, however, not be exaggerated, as the limits of such a principle's functional capacity are evident. The principle of federal loyalty alone cannot organize administrative cooperation within a federal state,[93] and the principle of loyal cooperation alone does not provide the basis for an effective supranational polity.[94] Only in very few cases can such an abstract principle have a direct regulatory function or even determine a certain behavior as illegal; far more detailed and precise rules are required for day-to-day business. This is especially so for forms of cooperation beyond national borders, which can not rely on either a basic trust or an intuitive reciprocal acquaintance on the part of the various authorities; rather a good measure of ignorance and mistrust often dominates the relationships.

Nevertheless it is possible to deduce from the abstract principle of cooperation in extreme situations some specific duties as the ECJ has shown on the basis of Article 10 EC.[95] With respect to international compound administration one can deduce from the principle of coop-

---

RECHT (REPORTS OF THE GERMAN SOCIETY OF INTERNATIONAL LAW) 13, 21 (1975).

91 ICJ (note 58), at 93.

92 WOLFGANG FRIEDMANN, THE CHANGING STRUCTURE (1964).

93 BERNHARD SCHLINK, DIE AMTSHILFE 145 *et seq.* (1982).

94 Gert Meier, *Europäische Amtshilfe – Ein Stützpfeiler des Europäischen Binnenmarktes*, 24 EUR 237, 245 *et seq.* (1989).

95 Armin von Bogdandy, *Links between National and Supra-national Institutions*, *in* LINKING EU AND NATIONAL GOVERNANCE, 24 (Beate Kohler-Koch ed., 2003).

eration in particular procedural rights of states.[96] Of special importance appear to be rights to information, a right to be heard and a right to contest, if the action of an international institution affects an individual state.

The principle of cooperation has – similar to the principle of autonomy – an institutional expression. In all institutions one finds organs, staffed with officials from the members. Most thematic studies show that these organs play a leading role in the shaping of politics. The preeminence of states in the organs of an international institution is only a structural principle, not a legal principle.

3. The Principle of Attributed Competence

Competence is the legal cipher for power. Accordingly any insight into the public authority of international institutions must lead to a legal interest in their competences. Well established and undisputed is the principle that international institutions are not original subjects of power. Neither are their actions protected by human rights guarantees. Hence the legal principle that an international institution only acts legally if there is a legal base: the principle of attributed competence.[97] The thematic studies show a consistent practice that this applies not only to international organizations, but also to the actions of treaty organs or non-formalized organizations.[98] Furthermore, the studies show that non-binding acts also require some legal basis, i.e. acts commonly qualified as soft law.[99] This confirms the premise of the study to use a broad concept of public authority.

Unfortunately, many features of this principle are vague. The vagueness of the principle of attributed competence is no coincidence but rather the expression of a fundamental tension within the law of international

---

[96] *See* Jochen von Bernstorff, in this volume; CASSESE (note 40), at 108 *et seq*.

[97] Reparation for Injuries Suffered in the Service of the United Nations, Advisory Opinion of 11 April 1949, ICJ Reports 1949, 174, 185; Eckart Klein, *Reparation for Injuries Suffered in Service of the UN (Advisory Opinion)*, *in* IV EPIL 174-176 (Rudolf Bernhardt ed., 2000); DE VELASCO VALLEJO (note 78), at 137.

[98] Petra Láncos, Christine Fuchs, Anuscheh Farahat, in this volume.

[99] For the legal basis for the guidelines of the OECD, *see* Gefion Schuler, in this volume; Farahat (note 24).

organizations between its functional autonomy and its guidance through its founding treaty which conveys democratic legitimacy.[100] In that respect the principle of attribution is undermined by the principle of implicit competence which allows the deduction of powers to act from the general aims of an international institution. Many activities described in the studies of this research find their legal basis only in such an implicit competence.

At this point a fundamental difference with respect to the law of the European Union comes to the fore. European constitutional law knows *the principle of constitutional legality*. This principle has two aspects: negative and positive legality.[101] According to the *principle of negative legality*, every act that can be attributed to the Union must be consistent with higher ranking law, i.e. the totality of the current treaty norms as well as those general principles of law to be found at the same level as the treaty norms. This creates a strict internal hierarchy within Union law. The tremendous success of the constitutionalization of the EC Treaty is revealed by the fact that today the principle of negative legality appears trivial in the EU context. Yet, obvious as the validity of this institute may appear today, it was anything but evident to the early Community.[102] Such hierarchization is due to the ECJ's rigorous "hierarchization" case law. Starting from the premise of an autonomous legal order, the ECJ consistently concluded that the procedures for amending the treaties are exclusively those foreseen and provided for by the treaties (now Article 48 EU Treaty). This jurisprudence prevents any extralegal influence on the part of the Member States. The treaties' strict normativity does not permit the temporary suspension of the treaties' provisions by informal agreements,[103] nor can a persistent practice by the institutions derogate primary law.[104] Even acts enacted unanimously by the Council are completely subject to primary law. This leads to a striking dichotomy, well-known in constitutional theory, between the

---

[100] *See* JAN KLABBERS, AN INTRODUCTION TO INTERNATIONAL INSTITUTIONAL LAW 60 *et seq.* (2002).

[101] *See* Armin von Bogdandy & Jürgen Bast, *The European Union's Vertical Order of Competences: The Current Law and Proposals for its Reform*, 39 COMMON MARKET LAW REVIEW 227 (2002).

[102] Karl Carstens, *Die kleine Revision des Vertrags über die Europäische Gemeinschaft für Kohle und Stahl*, 21 ZAÖRV 1, 14, 37 (1961).

[103] Joined Cases 90 and 91/63, Commission v. Belgium and Luxembourg, 1964 E.C.R. 1329, 1345.

[104] Case 68/86, United Kingdom v. Council, 1988 E.C.R. 855, para. 24.

Member States' status and their capacities to act. As treaty-creating and -amending actors they remain largely outside the scope of the Union's jurisdiction, yet they can only exercise this capacity according to the difficult procedure foreseen in Article 48 EU Treaty; in substance this means that the Union's constitutional order is largely protected. At the same time, the Member States' representation through the Council means that they are at the focal point of the public power constituted by the treaties. In this capacity, however, they are fully subject to the Union's primary law. This simultaneous exclusion and inclusion of the "masters of the Treaties" bears a remarkable resemblance to the foundation of constitutional legality in the Member States: the parliaments represent the sovereign, yet are strictly bound by their respective constitution and its legislative procedures.[105]

Only on the basis of this strict normativity does the *principle of positive legality* flourish. This principle implies that an enabling provision is a necessary proviso. Any act at the level of secondary Union law must possess a legal basis which can be traced back to the treaties. The legal basis can either be contained in the treaties themselves or in an act of secondary law, which in turn is based on the treaties.[106] Whereas negative legality is (only) concerned with delimiting an assumed public power, the requirement of an enabling norm is situated one step before and asks about the act's legal basis.

That the founding treaty of an international institution operates in this way as the standard for the law produced by that institution is a rather new phenomenon. A hierarchization of the sources of law is essentially alien to traditional international law (with the exception of *jus cogens,* in itself a new development).[107] In international institutions it is generally recognized that the founding treaty can be implicitly changed by a later deviating practice, and some understand the principle of implied powers in a way that international organizations can move into new areas of competence unless it is specifically denied by Member States.[108] Fur-

---

105 Niklas Luhmann, *Verfassung als evolutionäre Errungenschaft*, 9 RECHTSHISTORISCHES JOURNAL 176 *et seq*. (1990).

106 The question whether State actions must also have a basis in the national constitutions in the same way is very controversial. *See* CHRISTOPH MÖLLERS, STAAT ALS ARGUMENT 256 *et seq*. (2000).

107 Kadelbach (note 68).

108 Advisory Opinion 12 August 1922, PCIJ 1922, Series B, No. 2, 23-25, 39; Corfu Channel Case/Preliminary Objection (United Kingdom of Great Britain and Northern Ireland v. Albania), ICJ Reports 1948, 15 *et seqq*.; Corfu Channel

thermore the doctrine of *ultra vires*, an essential element of the principle of attributed competence, only applies according to the main understandings if the field of activity of an international institution is clearly overstepped.[109]

In light of a broad concept of public authority, this loose understanding hardly convinces;[110] *implied powers* should only be understood as a specific teleological interpretation of a positive competence, but not a further legal basis. There is an urgent need to formulate standard instruments by which international institutions exercise public authority and stricter requirements to uphold negative and positive legality; the International Law Association provides sensible proposals under its principle of constitutionality.[111]

Case/Merits (United Kingdom of Great Britain and Northern Ireland v. Albania), ICJ Reports 1949, 4 *et seqq.*, 25; M. Barnett & M. Finnemore, *The Power of Liberal International Organizations, in* POWER IN GLOBAL GOVERNANCE 161, 182 (M. Barnett & R. Duvall eds., 2006); DE VELASCO VALLEJO (note 78), at 138; Georg Nolte, *Lawmaking through the Security Council, in* DEVELOPMENTS OF INTERNATIONAL LAW IN TREATY MAKING 237, 239 *et seq.* (Rüdiger Wolfrum & Volker Röben eds., 2005). For a critique *see* Andreas Zimmermann, *"Acting under Chapter VII (...)" – Resolution 1422 and Possible Limits of the Powers of the Security Council, in* VERHANDELN FÜR DEN FRIEDEN, LIBER AMICORUM TONO EITEL 253 (Jochen A. Frowein, Klaus Scharioth, Ingo Winkelmann & Rüdiger Wolfrum eds., 2003); Rüdiger Wolfrum, *Der Kampf gegen die Verbreitung von Massenvernichtungswaffen: Eine neue Rolle für den Sicherheitsrat, in* WELTINNENRECHT, LIBER AMICORUM JOST DELBRÜCK 865 (Klaus Dicke, Stephan Hobe, Karl-Ulrich Meyn, Anne Peters, Eibe Riedel, Hans-Joachim Schütz & Christian Tietje eds., 2005).

109 On *ultra vires* acts and their disputed effects, *see* Rudolf Bernhardt, *International Organisations, Internal Law and Rules, in* II EPIL 1316-1317 (Rudolf Bernhardt ed., 1995); Eckart Klein, *Die Internationalen und Supranationalen Organisationen, in* VÖLKERRECHT 352-354 (Wolfgang Graf Vitzthum ed., 2004); IGNAZ SEIDL-HOHENVELDERN & GERHARD LOIBL, DAS RECHT DER INTERNATIONALEN ORGANISATIONEN EINSCHLIEßLICH DER SUPRANATIONALEN GEMEINSCHAFTEN 221 (2000); HERIBERT FRANZ KÖCK & PETER FISCHER, DAS RECHT DER INTERNATIONALEN ORGANISATIONEN 561 (1997); Hersch Lauterpacht, *The Legal Effects of Illegal Acts of International Organizations*, CAMBRIDGE ESSAYS IN INTERNATIONAL LAW 88 (1965); Ebere Osieke, *The Legal Validity of Ultra Vires Decisions of International Organizations*, 77 AJIL 239-256 (1983).

110 On this point, *see* Jochen von Bernstorff in this volume.

111 International Law Association (note 8), at 12 *et seqq.*

There are also uncertainties with respect to which institutions have the competence to determine an infringement of the principle of attributed competence. Traditionally this competence lies with the acting institution. This is certainly unsatisfactory. The German Federal Constitutional Court has established the yardstick of the so-called "Integrationsprogramm" (integration program);[112] the potential of this doctrine needs to be proven.[113] One might consider differentiated requirements of a legal basis corresponding to various effects of decisions of international institutions: this corresponds with the overall approach of this research.[114]

II. The Relationship between International Institutions and Private Subjects

There is space only for a few lines on principles regarding the relationship between international institutions and private subjects, in particular individuals. The EU-Treaty puts the principle of freedom of the individual in Article 6 para. 1 right at the beginning. Although the importance of international human rights has steadily grown, there is little ground to consider the freedom of the individual as the foremost principle of international law.

Within the law of the European Union the principles of the rule of law and of the protection of private legal subjects are of increasing importance. The public authority of the European Union is bound by human rights, in particular by the European Convention on Human Rights, as interpreted by the European Court of Human Rights. Furthermore a seamless web of legal protection against public authority is required. Granted, the legal order of the European Union does not fully live up to these principles. Some acts are difficult, even impossible to challenge. Nevertheless, the difference between the European Union and international institutions is evident, given that what is the rule with respect to international institutions is a rare exception in European Union law.

---

112 *See* Bundesverfassungsgericht (BVerfG, Federal Constitutional Court), 2 BvE 2/07, paras. *42 et seq.* with further references.

113 Mehrdad Payandeh, *Rechtskontrolle des UN-Sicherheitsrates durch staatliche und überstaatliche Gerichte*, 66 ZAÖRV 41 (2006).

114 *See* Bogdandy, Dann & Goldmann, in this volume.

However, it seems that this unsatisfactory situation is about to change. In particular the response to the UN sanctions list might have triggered the impetus to develop and uphold legal principles protecting the individual against acts of international institutions;[115] it can be built by coherently developing established doctrine.[116] These principles and the mechanisms of review need to be respectful of the specificities of international institutions, which is assured by their development in the process of internal constitutionalization. Accordingly, the doctrinal construction might vary from institution to institution. At the same time, the development of such principles protecting the individual against international institutions can draw on the EU experiences.[117]

On this note this article ends. Its aim was to discuss possible functions, impacts, bases and elements of general principles of international public authority. While the article remains rather skeptical about the prospects of a general doctrine of general principles similar to those in domestic legal orders, it sees and advocates the development of principles in the process of internal constitutionalization of the various international institutions. On this basis, a comparative doctrinal discourse can distill legal arguments that are of general use when construing the authority of international institutions. Such arguments are useful irrespective of whether the principle amounts to a classic source of general principles. Accordingly, I see a future for general principles of international public authority, less as a source of law, but as condensed comparative legal arguments.

---

[115] Clemens Feinäugle, in this volume.

[116] ICJ Opinion, Effect of Awards of Compensation made by the United Nations Administrative Tribunal, ICJ Reports 1954, 57.

[117] August Reinisch, *Securing the Accountability of International Organizations*, *in* INTERNATIONAL ORGANIZATIONS 535, 538 *et seq.* (Jan Klabbers ed., 2005).

Is There a Global Administrative Law?

*Comment by Sabino Cassese**

1. An Important Intellectual Exercise

We are currently engaged in a very important intellectual exercise – no less important, indeed, than that undertaken by the 19th century "founding fathers" of public law, such as Laferrière in France, Gerber, Laband and Mayer in Germany, and Orlando and Romano in Italy. Scholars in New York, Rome, Heidelberg and elsewhere are working on a new area of legal theory and practice: that of global law.[1]

---

* This paper offers some reflections on Armin von Bogdandy's piece entitled "General Principles of International Public Authority: Sketching a Research Field", in this volume. Thanks are due to Euan MacDonald, Mariangela Benedetti, Lorenzo Casini, Elisabetta Morlino, and Gianluca Sgueo for their comments.

1 *See* the Global Administrative Project launched by New York University in 2005 (http://www.iilj.org/GAL/default.asp), the research on Global Administrative Law led by the Institute for Research on Public Administration (IRPA) in Rome (http://www.irpa.eu/index.asp?idA=161), and the Project on The Exercise of Public Authority by International Institutions at the Max-Planck-Institut für ausländisches öffentliches Recht und Völkerrecht at Heidelberg (http://www.mpil.de).

A. von Bogdandy et al. (eds.), *The Exercise of Public Authority by International Institutions*, Beiträge zum ausländischen öffentlichen Recht und Völkerrecht 210,
DOI 10.1007/978-3-642-04531-8_25, © Springer-Verlag Berlin Heidelberg 2010

This scholarly work has three main features. It is, firstly, a truly global effort. Jurists from all over the world are engaged in such research, some providing in-depth analyses of individual global regimes, while others seek to deduce from the many and varied governance experiences a body of common principles and rules.

It is worth noting that a scholarly endeavor of this sort has not been undertaken since the 17th century. Indeed, ever since the attack from legal positivism led to the collapse of natural law approaches to the discipline, law has been conceived of as exclusively the product of nation-states, with international law conceptualized mainly on the basis of "contractual" relations between them. As a consequence, the study of each national system of law has become for the most part limited to national "schools" of lawyers, with occasional raids into foreign legal systems permitted to scholars of a more comparative bent.

Secondly, this endeavor deals with an entirely new subject-matter; one that has developed only relatively recently, chiefly in the last twenty years. It encompasses a vast array of different treaties, rules, standards, institutions, and procedural arrangements established beyond national frontiers either by states themselves, or by other global institutions, in order to deliver services, establish further standards, monitor compliance, or act as "clearing houses" more generally.

This body of law is confusing, at least when viewed through the lens of traditional conceptual criteria. It is law, but in most cases non-binding. It does boast established institutions, but these can most often proceed only tentatively at best, because their authority is not yet widely recognized.

Thirdly, in the study of this field one cannot rely upon the usual paradigms of public law. These have been developed in national contexts as a set of values, principles, and rules necessary to the proper functioning of domestic institutions. For example, regular elections at the national and local levels serve the purpose of democracy; and the due process of law is instrumental to the protection of fundamental rights. But can they be transposed mechanically to an entirely new environment, beyond the state? Can new wine be poured into old bottles?

2. Bogdandy on the Legal Nature and Principles of the Global Arena

Armin von Bogdandy's paper on "Principles of International Public Authority" is a very rich and complex contribution to this new field. It examines not only the principles of international public authority, but also the legal nature of the global arena more generally.

Von Bogdandy's argument rests upon the following five basic assumptions:

1. to exercise public authority means to unilaterally govern the conduct of third parties, even without their consent;
2. there exists no one single and unitary body of law, nor a proto-federal legal order, nor a legal space, that can be called "global";
3. the direct exercise of authority by international institutions over individuals is extremely rare, and in the global arena there is thus, for the most part, neither direct effect nor supremacy of global norms; as a rule, the decisions of international institutions do not unilaterally affect private parties, but are addressed to national administrations;
4. the relationship between international institutions and national legal systems can be understood as based on two principles: the principle of autonomy (or independence) and the principle of delegation;
5. international institutions are subject to the principle of attributed competence: they cannot acquire powers on their own initiative; rather, their competences are attributed to them by national governments.

Von Bogdandy ends with five main conclusions:

1. while there is little evidence of the development of overarching principles at the international level, some principles regulating international public authority are emerging;
2. a hierarchization of sources of law is establishing itself in the operation of international institutions; in each regulatory regime, the founding treaty of each institution operates as the framework for the law that it produces;
3. international institutions are subject to the principle of cooperation in their relations both with national governments and with other global bodies, and to specific procedural duties (the duty to inform affected parties, their right to be heard, etc.);

4. the protection afforded to individuals against action taken in violation of their rights by international institutions is at present unsatisfactory, although this is beginning to change;

5. the relevant global legal principles remain under-developed, due to the fact that only a few international institutions are subject to direct judicial review.

3. What Is Law in the Global Arena?

The first point that I want to discuss here concerns the very concept of law in the global arena, and the related concepts of binding force and authority.

In domestic legal orders there is a clear-cut dichotomy between legal and non-legal prescriptions; and this is because there is a higher authority that establishes the dividing line between what is and what is not law. This picture, however, changes as we move into the global arena. There, we are confronted by a world that is highly formalized, but not in strictly legal terms. For example, many World Bank "legal" instruments are simply referred to as "policy" documents; yet in many cases these can scarcely be considered less important than statutes passed by national parliaments. They regulate important aspects of the Bank's activity, such as the duty to perform an environmental impact assessment and all of the procedural requirements related to this.[2] Private parties in

---

[2] Elsewhere, I have defined the World Bank's operative policies as "*ad hoc* international administrative norms": *see* S. Cassese, *Global Standards for National Administrative Procedures*, 68 LAW & CONTEMPORARY PROBLEMS (LAW & CONTEMP. PROBS.) 109 (2005). Moreover, NGOs and local communities have increasingly been addressing the World Bank's policies within the context of global compliance mechanisms; *see*, for instance, M. Circi, *The World Bank Inspection Panel: The Indian Mumbai Urban Transport Project Case*, *in* GLOBAL ADMINISTRATIVE LAW: CASES, MATERIALS, ISSUES, 55 *et seq*. (S. Cassese, B. Carotti, L. Casini, M. Macchia, E. MacDonald & M. Savino eds., 2nd ed., 2008); A broader analysis of the World Bank social policies can be found in A. Vetterlein, *Economic Growth, Poverty Reduction, and the Role of Social Policies: The Evolution of the World Bank's Social Development Approach*, 13 GLOBAL GOVERNANCE 513 (2007). *See also* K. Tomasevski, *The Influence of the World Bank and IMF on Economic and Social Rights*, 64 NORDIC JOURNAL OF INTERNATIONAL LAW 385 (1995), M. Nesbitt, *The World Bank and de facto Governments: A Call for Transparency in the Bank's Operational Policy*, 32 QUEENS LAW JOURNAL 641 (2006-2007), K.W. Simon, *World Bank Wants a New Ap-*

India or South Africa can appeal to these standards, and ask that global and national governance bodies comply with them. Must we concede that anything that is not binding is, *ipso facto*, not law? If there is an area of law in which the Latin motto "*ubi societas, ibi ius*" holds true, then surely it must be the global arena.

At this point, a second dichotomy emerges, related to the first: that between binding ("hard") and non-binding ("soft") law. The basic question that we might pose in this regard is as follows: is a formally binding commitment to obey a rule the only means of producing rule-conforming behavior?

Even in domestic legal orders, not all rules are binding or compulsory. National legislation also establishes incentives and issues guidelines; it seeks not only to compel, but also to promote, to correct, to educate, and so on.

An example from the global arena is provided by the standards generated by the Codex Alimentarius Commission. These are not, in and of themselves, compulsory; they are, however, in effect given binding force by the World Trade Organization.[3] One authority produces rules;

---

proach to Consultations with Civil Society, 1 INTERNATIONAL JOURNAL OF CIVIL SOCIETY LAW 41 (2003).

[3] *See,* for a general overview of the Codex Alimentarius Commission within the World Trade Organization, J. Vapnek, *Legislative Implementation of the Food Chain Approach*, 40 VANDERBILT JOURNAL OF TRANSNATIONAL LAW (VAND. J. TRANSNAT'L. L.) 987 (2007); J. Kurtz, *A Look behind the Mirror: Standardisation, Institutions and the WTO SPS and TBT Agreements*, 30 UNIVERSITY OF NEW SOUTH WALES LAW JOURNAL 504 (2007); T.P. Stewart & D.S. Johanson, *The SPS Agreement of the World Trade Organization and International Organizations. The Roles of the Codex Alimentarius Commission, the International Plant Protection Convention, and the International Office of Epizootics*, 26 SYRACUSE JOURNAL OF INTERNATIONAL LAW & COMMERCE 27 (1998-1999). An analysis of the complex relationship between the global standards of the Codex Alimentarius Commission and domestic states is provided by D. Livshiz, *Updating American Administrative Law: WTO, International Standards, Domestic Implementation and Public Participation*, 24 WISCONSIN INTERNATIONAL LAW JOURNAL 961 (2006-2007). A more general overview is provided by K. Claire, *Power, Linkage and Accommodation: The WTO as an International Actor and Its Influence on Other Actors and Regimes*, 24 BERKELEY JOURNAL OF INTERNATIONAL LAW 79 (2006). A further analysis of the Codex Alimentarius standards and their connection to the FAO and WTO is given by M.D. MASSON-MATTHEE, THE CODEX ALIMENTARIUS COMMISSION AND ITS STANDARDS (2007). It is worth noting that the standards can also diverge. *See*, for instance, E. D'Alterio, *Relations between Global Law and EU Law*, *in*

another endows them with binding force. The rule is not binding from its inception, only becoming so because another authority imposes conformity upon those under its jurisdiction. Therefore, in this case the rule is binding in the field of global trade, but not in other areas, creating a "dédoublement".

A third point, again related, concerns the concept of authority. Power, not authority, is central in the global arena. Power can be exercised through authoritative means (such as the "command and control" models familiar from domestic administrative systems), but also through agreements, contracts, incentives, standards and guidelines.

4. The Global Legal Space

The area beyond the state is not only "global" from an economic point of view; rather, there also exists a global legal space, encompassing a vast number of different regulatory bodies, a mass of rules, a great quantity of procedures, and a complex array of links both to national bureaucracies and civil society.

What is missing is one general and unitary body of global law. Instead, there are numerous (at least two thousand) global regimes. However, both the administrative actors and the judicial bodies (where these exist) within each individual regime establish links to, and rules of engagement with, other regimes. Cooperation, division of labor and dialogue are common among global regimes and their constituent institutions. This law is generated through a process of accretion and accumulation, and the cooperative dialogue between regimes means that the principles of each should not be interpreted and applied in a vacuum. It is in this process that some have recognized the emergence of a general body of law at the global level.[4]

GLOBAL ADMINISTRATIVE LAW: CASES, MATERIALS, ISSUES (note 2), 105; H.S. Shapiro, *The Rules That Swallowed Exceptions: The WTO SPS Agreement and Its Relationship to GATT Articles XX and XXI – The Threat of the EU-GMO Dispute*, 24 ARIZONA JOURNAL OF INTERNATIONAL & COMPARATIVE LAW 199 (2007).

[4] "The current range of international legal obligations benefits from a process of accretion and cumulation" (Arbitral Tribunal, *Southern Bluefin Tuna* case, n. 52, 14 August 2000). "[...] the principles underlying the Convention [on Human Rights] cannot be interpreted and applied in a vacuum" (European Court of Human Rights, *Bankovic v. Belgium and others*, 12 December 2001).

Moreover, each national legal order has developed a certain number of common rules, and these now provide core standards that can be shared and even codified at a supranational level (take, for example, the Council of Europe's codification of rules on administrative procedure[5]).

Given that the global legal order is fragmented (or, perhaps more accurately, that there is not one unitary legal order at the global level, but rather many different and self-contained legal regimes), there are no general legal principles common to all. But some common understandings are developing: the duty to respect human rights and the rule of law; the obligation to inform and to hear interested parties before a decision is taken (as held, for example, in the *Juno Trader* case before the International Tribunal of the Law of the Sea[6]); a number of due process of obligations; and substantive duties relating to principles of fairness and reasonableness, amongst others.

5. The Global Legal Space as a "Marble Cake": Shared Powers

The widely-used expression "multilevel governance" is misleading, insofar as there is no clear-cut separation of competences between national governments and global institutions, structured within a definite hierarchy, of the type that this expression seems to suggest. Rather, the global arena is characterized by the spread of powers between the global and the national levels of government. For instance, environmental protection is at once a global and a national task, and competen-

---

"The scope of special laws is by definition narrower than that of general laws. It will thus frequently be the case that a matter not regulated by special law will arise in the institutions charged to administer it. In such cases, the relevant general law will apply." (UN Study Group on the Fragmentation of International Law, *Conclusions*, 2006).

5 COUNCIL OF EUROPE, THE ADMINISTRATION AND YOU. PRINCIPLES OF ADMINISTRATIVE LAW CONCERNING THE RELATIONS BETWEEN ADMINISTRATIVE AUTHORITIES AND PRIVATE PERSONS, Strasbourg 1996.

6 International Tribunal of the Law of the Sea, The "*Juno Trader*" Case (*Saint Vincent and the Grenadines v. Guinea-Bissau*), case no. 13, December 18, 2004 (www.itlos.org/cgi-bin/cases/case_detail.pl?id=13&lang=en); *see* D. Agus & M. Conticelli, *The International Tribunal for the Law of the Sea (ITLOS): The Juno Trader Case, in* GLOBAL ADMINISTRATIVE LAW: CASES, MATERIALS, ISSUES (note 2).

cies in this field are not merely shared by global and national bodies; rather, areas of jurisdiction overlap and compete with each other. The line between the national and the international is becoming increasingly blurred (see, for example, the Cybersquatting cases before the dispute resolution panels of the World Intellectual Property Organization).[7] In the case of shared powers of this sort, the rule is not strict separation and rigid hierarchy, but rather permeability, intermingling, interpenetration.

Global institutions derive their jurisdiction and their powers from national governments. It does not necessarily follow, however, that of all their powers originate in a direct delegation by states. For example, there are international institutions that were not established by national governments, but by other international bodies (for example, the Codex Alimentarius Commission).[8]

Moreover, cooperation in the global arena does not occur only between international institutions and national governments, but also among international institutions themselves. The global order can be illustrated by the well-known metaphor of the marble cake, as there are no clear dividing lines between layers (national and global) and (global) sectoral regimes; rather, the two worlds are linked both vertically and horizontally through a complex array of relations and networks.

---

7 *See*, for example, World Intellectual Property Organization, Arbitration and Mediation Center, Administrative Panel Decision, decision of 22 July 2003 *Keisanki Kabushki Kaisha, dba Casio Computer Co., Ltd v. Fulviu Mihai Fodoreanu*, Case No. DRO2003-0002 ("Casio"); decision of 4 August 2000; *Excelentisimo Ayuntamiento de Barcelona v. Barcelona.com Inc.*, Case No. D2000-0505. Decisions are available at: http://arbiter.wipo.int/domains/decisions/index-cctld.html.

8 *See* MASSON-MATTHEE (note 3). Further information is available in J.A. Bobo, *The Role of International Agreements in Achieving Food Security: How Many Lawyers Does It Take to Feed a Village?*, 40 VAND. J. TRANSNAT'L. L. 937 (2007).

6. Legitimacy through the Law

There exists no cosmopolitan democracy, no planetary constitution, no global parliament. Is this cause for concern?

Here again it is necessary to return to certain basic questions. Why do we want national governments to be legitimate? Simply put, the answer might run something as follows. National governments exercise their power through authority: they oblige and impose. Therefore, they must be run on the basis of the consent of the governed. Through recurrent elections, politicians are chosen and kept under control by the people.

A number of differences emerge, however, when we move from the national to the global context. Firstly, global bodies do not normally exercise power through authority: they do not seek to simply impose their will, but rather to influence the behavior of national bureaucracies and private parties through a variety of different mechanisms.

Secondly, global bodies are usually established in order to keep national governments under control, or to provide services or pursue goals that governments alone are unable to. Therefore, they put limits on the activities of national executives. In this regard, we might suggest, they are on the same "side" as the people, formally speaking at least.

Thirdly, periodic elections are not the only means of legitimizing public power. Global institutions seek to forge their legitimacy through ensuring openness, dialogue and the participation of private parties ("Legitimation durch Verfahren")[9] in the decision-making process. Examples of this abound within global regimes: consider, for instance, the International Preliminary Examination procedure for the protection of inventions, established by the Patent Cooperation Treaty; or the complaints procedure before the World Bank Inspection Panel.

Judicial protection is not guaranteed by every global regulatory regime. However, many do establish mechanisms that can act as a surrogate for formal judicial protection, for example granting "*ex ante*" participation rights to affected private parties or national governments, establishing quasi-judicial procedures and ensuring some degree of independence from decision-making bodies.

---

9 N. LUHMANN, LEGITIMATION DURCH VERFAHREN (1969).

Finally, there are now around 110 extra-national courts around the world (most of them with jurisdiction in criminal matters).[10] Technical and scientific expertise often play an important role in the controversies brought before these courts (see, for example, the *Apples and Fire Blight* case before the World Trade Organization Dispute Settlement Body[11] and the *Southern Bluefin Tuna* case before the Arbitral Tribunal of the United Nations Convention on the Law of the Sea[12]). There also exist some internationalized forms of administrative review of domestic agencies (for example, the NAFTA Chapter 19 Panels[13]); and there are

---

[10] *See* the Project on International Courts and Tribunal International (PICT) and the synoptic chart, available at: http://www.pict-pcti.org/publications/synoptic_chart/Synop_C4.pdf.

[11] The relevant decisions in this case are Panel Report, *Japan – Measures Affecting the Importation of Apples*, WT/DS245/R, 15 July 2003 and Report of Appellate Body, *Japan – Measures Affecting the Importation of Apples*, WT/DS245/AB/R, AB-2003-4, 26 November 2003: *see* A. Albanesi, *The WTO 'Science-Fest': Japan Measures Affecting the Importation of Apples, in* GLOBAL ADMINISTRATIVE LAW: CASES, MATERIALS, ISSUES (note 2), at 178 *et seq.*

[12] Arbitral Tribunal established under Annex VII of the United Nations Convention on the Law of the Sea, *Australia and New Zealand v. Japan*, Award on Jurisdiction and Admissibility, 4 August 2000. *See also* B. Carotti & M. Conticelli, *Settling Global Disputes: The Southern Bluefin Tuna Case, in* GLOBAL ADMINISTRATIVE LAW: CASES, MATERIALS, ISSUES (note 2), at 145 *et seq.*

[13] NAFTA Article 1904 establishes a mechanism that provides an alternative to judicial review by domestic courts of final determinations in antidumping and countervailing duty cases: the Binational Panel system. This system uses panels consisting of US and Canadian or Mexican panelists to review antidumping and countervailing duty decisions taken by national administrative authorities. The Panel may uphold or remand the national administrative action, and its decisions are binding. The Binational Panel system represents an internationalized form of administrative judicial review of domestic agencies: it reviews decisions of domestic agencies; its decisions are based on domestic law, not international trade rules; and the private parties involved (e.g. firms) have a right to initiate panel review. For an overview on this topic, *see* G.R. Winham & A. Heather, *Antidumping and Countervailing Duties in Regional Trade Agreements: Canada-U.S. FTA, NAFTA and beyond*, 3 MINNESOTA JOURNAL OF GLOBAL TRADE 1 (1994); G.R. Winham & G.C. Vega, *The Role of NAFTA Dispute Settlement in the Management of Canadian, Mexican and U.S. Trade and Investment Relations*, 28 OHIO NORTHERN UNIVERSITY LAW REVIEW 651 (2001-2002); E.J. Pan, *Assessing the NAFTA Chapter 19 Binational Panel System: An Experiment in International Adjudication*, 40 HARVARD INTERNATIONAL LAW JOURNAL 379 (1999). *See also* M. Macchia, *Reasonableness and Proportionality: The NAFTA Binational Panel and the Extension of Administra-*

many more bodies that provide some sort of judicial review by acting as quasi-independent courts, open to the petitions of the affected citizens, and following adversarial or quasi-adversarial procedures. These are often referred to as, for example, "compliance committees"[14] or "inspection panels"[15]. In many regards, these latter bodies resemble the French

---

tive Justice to International Relations, in GLOBAL ADMINISTRATIVE LAW: CASES, MATERIALS, ISSUES (note 2), at 86 *et seq*.

14 The term "compliance committee" is used in multilateral environmental agreements (MEAs). *See* Convention on Biological Diversity, COP-MOP 1 Decision BS-I/7, *Establishment of Procedures and Mechanisms on Compliance under the Cartagena Protocol on Biosafety*, Kuala Lumpur, 23-27 February 2004; Meeting of the Parties to the Convention on Access to Information, Public Participation in Decision-making and Access to Justice in Environmental Matters, Report of the First Meeting of the Parties, Addendum, *Decision I/7 Review of Compliance* adopted at the first meeting of the Parties held in Lucca, Italy, on 21-23 October 2002, ECE/MP.PP/2/Add.8, 2 April, 2004; Commission for environmental cooperation, *Adoption of the Revised Guidelines for Submissions on Enforcement Matters Under Articles 14 and 15 of the North American Agreement on Environmental Cooperation*, 28 June 1999, Council resolution 99-06.

15 The term "inspection panel" is used by the Multilateral Development Banks (MDBs, consisting of the World Bank Group and the four Regional Development Banks: The African Development Bank, The Asian Development Bank, The European Bank for Reconstruction and Development, The Inter-American Development Bank Group). *See* International Bank of Reconstruction and Development, I.B.R.D. Res. 93-10 (Sept. 22, 1993); International Development Association, IDA Res. 93-6, Sept. 22, 1993 (the two Resolutions are identical and are reprinted in World Bank, *World Bank Operational Manual: Bank Procedures*, 17.55, annex A, 1997); Asian Development Bank, *Establishment of an Inspection Function*, ADB Doc. R225-95 (Nov. 10, 1995); IFC/MIGA's Office of the Compliance Advisor/Ombudsman, (*see also* Compliance Advisor/Ombudsman – CAO, *Operational Guidelines,* April 2004); European Bank for Reconstruction and Development – EBRD, *Independent Recourse Mechanism: As Approved by the Board of Directors on 29 April 2003* (2003), (*see also Independent Recourse Mechanism Rules of Procedure: As Approved by the Board on 6 April 2004*); Inter-American Development Bank (IDB), *IDB's Independent Investigation Mechanism (IIM)*, (*see also* the rules and procedures of IDB's IIM); African Development Bank, Board of Director, *Enabling Resolution* B/BD/2004/9-F/BD/2004/7-B/BD/2004/10, June 30, 2004. Asian Development Bank, *Review of the Inspection Function: Establishment of a New ADB Accountability Mechanism*, May 2003. For an overview, *see* E. Suzuki & S. Nanwani, *Responsibility of International Organizations: The Accountability Mechanisms of Multilateral Development Banks,* 27 MICHIGAN JOURNAL OF INTER-

Conseil d'État in the period between 1800 and 1872, when the Council was not legally recognized as a judicial body despite the fact that it was exercising *de facto* judicial review.

7. Is There a Global Administrative Law?

Finally, let me return to the question contained in the title of this contribution: is there a global administrative law?

This question must, in my view, be answered in the affirmative. This law has the following features.

1. Notwithstanding some areas of overlap, global administrative law should be distinguished from traditional international law. "*Ius gentium*", "*Ius inter gentes*" and the law of the nations refer to the law established between the governments of states to regulate relations between states as legal entities. Despite displaying some features to the contrary, this law is still largely non-hierarchical, voluntaristic and contractual in nature. Global law, on the other hand, consists in large part of the rules produced by international organizations of various different kinds.

2. International law is mainly based on transactions, while global law has developed a more robust hierarchy of norms. This hierarchy has developed within each individual regulatory regime; it is now emerging among the different regulatory regimes as well (for example, the European Court of Justice, in the *Kadi* case,[16] has recognized the primacy of United Nations law over European law).

NATIONAL LAW 177 (2006); W. Namita, *Human Rights Accountability of the IMF and the World Bank: A Critique of Existing Mechanisms and Articulation of a Theory of Horizontal Accountability*, 12 UNIVERSITY OF CALIFORNIA DAVIS JOURNAL OF INTERNATIONAL LAW & POLICY 331 (2005-2006).

[16] Judgment of the Court (Grand Chamber) 3 September 2008, joined cases C-402/05 P and C-415/05 P. See also A. Sandulli, *Caso Kadi: tre percorsi a confronto*; S. Cassese, *Ordine comunitario e ordine globale*; E. Chiti, *I diritti di difesa e di proprietà nell'ordinamento europeo*; M. Savino, *Libertà e sicurezza nella lotta al terrorismo: quale bilanciamento?*; G. Vesperini, *Il principio del contraddittorio e le fasi comunitarie di procedimenti globali*; and G. della Cananea, *Un nuovo nomos per l'ordine globale, in* GIORNALE DI DIRITTO AMMINISTRATIVO 1088-1104 (2008).

3. As already noted, there currently exist around two thousand international organizations,[17] which are often capable of reproducing other such organizations (in fact, many of them were themselves established by other global bodies). They conclude treaties and make rules, and can no longer be considered as the mere agents of states. Indeed, they can even create standards that are aimed at transforming the internal structure of national governments.

4. Perhaps the most important global bodies are those that carry out a standard-setting function. These standards are generally addressed to national governments; but this does not mean that private parties are not affected by them. For example, the food that we eat is subject worldwide to the standards of the Codex Alimentarius Commission.[18] The standards established by the Forced Labor Convention (1930) are addressed to national governments, but affect private individuals (see, for example, the case of *Myanmar and the International Labor Organization*[19]).

5. Such bodies are at the top of many sectoral regimes. These regimes do not, however, exist entirely independent of each other, but rather are linked in myriad different ways – either in relatively structured "regime complexes",[20] or simply through the significant

---

[17] Union of International Associations, YEARBOOK OF INTERNATIONAL ORGANIZATIONS, München, Saur, 2005.

[18] *See* Kurtz (note 3); Livshiz (note 3). *See*, with particular reference to the interactions with the US system, D.M. Strauss, *International Regulation of Genetically Modified Organisms: Importing Caution into the U.S. Food Supply*, 61 FOOD & DRUG LAW JOURNAL 167 (2006), or, also, S. Keane, *Can a Consumer's Right to Know Survive the WTO: The Case of Food Labeling*, 16 TRANSNATIONAL LAW & CONTEMPORARY PROBLEMS 291 (2006-2007).

[19] Commission of Inquiry, ILO, *Forced Labor in Myanmar (Burma), Report of the Commission of Inquiry Appointed under Article 26 of the Constitution of the International Labor Organization to Examine the Observance by Myanmar of the Forced Labor Convention, 1930* (No. 29), Geneva, 2 July 1998. *See also* E. Morlino, *Labor Standards: Forced Labor in Myanmar*, *in* GLOBAL ADMINISTRATIVE LAW: CASES, MATERIALS, ISSUES (note 2), 1 *et seq*.

[20] A regime complex can be defined as "an array of partially overlapping and non hierarchical institutions governing a particular issue-area ... [R]egime complexes are marked by the existence of several legal agreements that are created and maintained in distinct fora with participation of different sets of actors. The rules in these elemental regimes functionally overlap, yet there is no agreed upon hierarchy for resolving conflicts between rules. Disaggregated decision-making in the international legal system means that agreements reached in one

areas of overlap in their respective fields of jurisdiction (e.g., trade and labor; trade and human rights; environmental protection and human rights; etc.)[21].

6. The global and the national levels interact in a number of different ways: for example, national governments act as law-makers at the global level, but are also the addressees of global substantive and procedural standards.

7. A global administrative law has thus developed, in terms of which global regimes are encouraged, and sometimes compelled, to ensure and promote the rule of law and procedural fairness, transparency, participation, and the duty to give reasons throughout all areas of their activity.

8. Dispute settlement by mandatory adjudication remains, as yet, the exception rather than the rule within the global legal order. Traditional diplomatic relationships and negotiations survive and operate side by side with compulsory and binding adjudication by su-

---

forum do not automatically extend to, or clearly trump, agreements developed in other forums."; *see* K. Raustiala & V. David, *The Regime Complex for Plan Genetic Resources*, 2 INTERNATIONAL ORGANIZATION 279 (2004).

[21] The many linkages between protection of human rights and protection of the environment have long been recognized. Principle 1 of the 1972 United Nations Conference on the Human Environment (Stockholm Declaration) declared that man has a fundamental right to freedom, equality and adequate conditions of life, in an environment of a quality that permits a life of dignity and well-being. It also recognized the responsibility of each person to protect and improve the environment for present and future generations. Almost twenty years later, in Resolution 45/94, the UN General Assembly recalled the language of Stockholm, stating that all individuals are entitled to live in an environment adequate for their health and well-being. The resolution called for enhanced efforts towards ensuring a better and healthier environment. In contrast to the earlier documents, the 1992 Rio de Janeiro Conference on Environment and Development formulated the link between human rights and environmental protection largely in procedural terms (*see* Principle 10). This angle was further developed in 1998, with the conclusion of the Convention on Access to Information, Public Participation in Decision-making and Access to Justice in Environmental Matters (Aarhus Convention). The Convention focused on the same issues as Principle 10 of the Rio Declaration and Principle 1 of the Stockholm Declaration, but in a more concrete manner, which strengthens the areas of overlap between human rights and environmental issues. For a comment on the Aarhus Convention, *see* M. Macchia, *Legality: The Aarhus Convention and the Compliance Committee, in* GLOBAL ADMINISTRATIVE LAW: CASES, MATERIALS, ISSUES (note 2), 71 *et seq*.

pranational courts and the non-binding decisions of different quasi-judicial bodies.

9. Global regulatory regimes become effective through various means. For example, within the WTO, a number of different mechanisms are used to ensure that the rules of the regime are enforced: mutual support, dumping/antidumping, subsidies/countervailing measures, non-implementation of WTO judicial decisions/retaliation, etc.[22]

10. As there are no periodic elections at the global level, procedural accountability plays a dominant role in making global bodies responsible to global society.

11. Membership in multilateral institutions can also enhance democracy at the national level: "as international bodies come into interaction with national centers of power, they can check abuses by those national centers [...] and force them into a better level of democratic performance."[23] Perhaps the clearest example of this phe-

---

[22] On the retaliation principle and on countervailing measures, *see* K. Anderson, *Peculiarities of Retaliation in WTO Dispute Settlement*, 2 WORLD TRADE REVIEW 123 (2002); T. Giannakopoulos, *Safeguarding Companies' Rights in Competition and Antidumping/Antisubsidies Proceedings*, 43 COMMON MARKET LAW REVIEW 268 (2006); T. Jurgensen, *Crime and Punishment: Retaliation under the World Trade Organization Dispute Settlement System*, 39 JOURNAL OF WORLD TRADE 327 (2005); Y.H. Ngangjoh & R.R. Herran, *WTO Dispute Settlement System and the Issue of Compliance: Multilateralizing the Enforcement Mechanism*, 1 MANCHESTER JOURNAL OF INTERNATIONAL ECONOMIC LAW 15 (2004); J. Pauwelyn, *Enforcement and Countermeasures in the WTO: Rules Are Rules – Toward a More Collective Approach*, 94 THE AMERICAN JOURNAL OF INTERNATIONAL LAW 335 (2000). In this regard, an important case arose before the WTO Appellate Body with reference to the reactions of WTO Member States against the Continued Dumping and Subsidy Offset Act of 2000 (also known as the "Byrd Amendment") approved by the US Senate. *See* WTO Appellate Body Report, *United States – Continued Dumping and Subsidy Offset Act of 2000 ("Byrd amendment")*, WT/DS217, 234/AB/R, 27 January 2003 and Panel Report, *United States – Continued Dumping and Subsidy Offset Act of 2000*, WT/217/R, WT/DS234/R, 16 September 2002. For an analysis of the case, *see* M. Benedetti, *EU Countermeasures against the US Byrd Amendment, in* GLOBAL ADMINISTRATIVE LAW: CASES, MATERIALS, ISSUES (note 2), 185 *et seq*.

[23] R.O. Keohane, S. Macedo & A. Moravcsik, *Democracy-Enhancing Multilateralism*, IILJ Working Papers, Global Administrative Law Series, 2007/4, available at: http://iilj.org/publications/documents/2007-4.GAL.KMM.web.pdf.

nomenon in practice is provided by the European Convention on Human Rights, which provides for individual complaints to be brought before the European Court of Human Rights, which in turn has compulsory jurisdiction over its Member States.[24] These two features "give rise to a potentially expansive process of transnational dispute resolution".[25]

[24] Council of Europe, Convention for the Protection of Human Rights and Fundamental Freedoms, as amended by Protocol No. 11, Art. 34.

[25] Keohane et al. (note 23), at 27.

Procedures of Decision-Making and the Role of Law in International Organizations

*By Jochen von Bernstorff**

---

* I thank the participants in the MPI research project on the exercise of public authority by international institutions as well as Eyal Benvenisti, Giacinto della Cananea, Christian Tietje and Christoph Möllers for their insightful comments and critique on earlier drafts. Many thanks also to Eva Richter, Lewis Enim and Eric Pickett for proof-reading and formatting.

A. von Bogdandy et al. (eds.), *The Exercise of Public Authority by International Institutions*, Beiträge zum ausländischen öffentlichen Recht und Völkerrecht 210,
DOI 10.1007/978-3-642-04531-8_26,

A. Introduction

There is no general body of procedural law for decision-making in international organizations. At the same time, many of the more than 230 existing international organizations (IOs) exercise public power through legislative and regulatory activities involving a myriad of decisions taken within these institutions every day. These decisions shape societal perceptions of a wide range of pressing humanitarian-, ecological, technical- and scientific issues and direct actions taken in these fields. From a rule of law perspective any exercise of public power outside a limiting framework of public law is reason for concern. According to the domestic rule of law traditions, public law is supposed to prescribe the form in which public power is exercised. It regulates the process of decision-making by establishing binding procedures, including procedural rights of participants and affected individuals. In case of unlawful exercise of power by public officials affected persons and entities have legal recourse to an independent court or tribunal. If formalized procedural constraints for the exercise of public authority are important at the national level they are all the more so at the international level since conflicts over substantive legal standards and disagreement over community values are usually more acute.

Despite the lack of a general body of administrative law guiding the work of international bureaucracies, there is of course some law to turn to. It is the law which forms the basis of the functioning of each individual international institution, such as the treaty constituting a particular IO, the rules of procedure of individual organs and internal rules such as financial- or staff regulations. Some of these rules may be set forth in the IO's founding treaty or constitution. However, constitutions are generally phrased in broad terms and notoriously unclear about the powers different bodies possess; rules of procedures usually only refer to individual organs and voting-procedures, rather than prescribing the entire process of decision-making which will often be scattered over a number of organs.[1] Financial and staff regulations as well as internal guidelines and rules of operational decision-making tend to be IO-specific and therefore appear to solely reflect particular institutional practices. There are of course a number of decisions and opinions of the ICJ and its predecessor on the scope of explicit and implied powers of IOs, but they are of a limited and rather ambiguous nature. Remarka-

1 HENRY G. SCHERMERS & NIELS M. BLOKKER, INTERNATIONAL INSTITUTIONAL LAW 1 § 707 (1995).

bly, Felice Morgenstern's classic conclusion regarding the state of legality in international organizations by and large still holds true today: "As a system of law all this does not amount to very much."[2]

The absence of a general body of procedural law for IOs would not be problematic if it could be assumed that international institutionalization is an inherently beneficial undertaking. The question of legal limits and judicial control would then not become relevant in the first place. There is, however, a growing uneasiness about the way public power is exercised beyond the national realm. Scholars have noted a change of perception regarding international organizations.[3] The growing number and increased effectiveness of IOs has indeed brought new questions to the fore. Can the UN Security Council legislate in the field of nuclear non-proliferation and terrorism on behalf of the world community and arguably violate human rights and due-process standards by setting up lists of terror-suspects?[4] How complicitous is the international patent-protection regime in denying access to live-saving drugs for millions of H.I.V. victims in Africa? Who takes the responsibility for World Bank structural adjustment-programs with socially disastrous repercussions for the affected populations and why are some persons granted a potentially life-saving international refugee-status by UNHCR and others not?

In more general terms, there is an increased interest in how decisions are taken in IOs, in whether they can be deemed legal, and in the question who actually bears responsibility for the distributional effects of such decisions towards which constituencies.[5] The aim of this paper is

---

2 F. Morgenstern, *Legality in International Organizations*, 48 BRITISH YEARBOOK OF INTERNATIONAL LAW 241 (1976-77). The standard-reference in the field, Schermer's and Blokker's INTERNATIONAL INSTITUTIONAL LAW (note 1) likewise describes decision-making processes within various IOs without reference to a general procedural law.

3 J. Klabbers, *The Changing Image of International Organizations*, *in* THE LEGITIMACY OF INTERNATIONAL ORGANIZATIONS 221-255 (V. Heiskanen ed., 2001); J.E. Alvarez, *International Organizations: Then and Now*, 100 THE AMERICAN JOURNAL OF INTERNATIONAL LAW (AJIL) 324-347 (2006); D. Kennedy, *The Move to Institutions*, 8 CARDOZO LAW REVIEW 841 *et seq*. (1987) (on early perceptions of IOs, in particular regarding the League of Nations).

4 Feinäugle, in this volume; de Wet, in this volume.

5 On the changing role of public actors in times of globalization, *see* S. Leibfried & M. Zürn, *Von der nationalen zur postnationalen Konstellation*, *in* TRANSFORMATIONEN DES STAATES? 19-64 (S. Leibfried ed., 2006). On accountability *vis à vis* various constituencies, *see* N. Krisch, *The Pluralism of Global*

to more closely examine how decisions are taken in IOs and what role general international law plays in this regard. The paper is divided into four parts. In the subsequent part I attempt to explain why procedural controls of decision-making in IOs can be deemed necessary in the first place (B.). In the second part, I will briefly describe the role of various procedural principles in the domestic rule of law tradition (C.). In the third part, I will undertake an actor-oriented analysis of procedures of decision-making in IOs hereby drawing on the case studies presented in this project (D.). The main focus in this part will be put on the question of whether or not IOs in fact already rely on general procedural principles imported from the domestic rule of law tradition. The last part will discuss two strategies of international lawyers to construct general procedural constraints for the activities of IOs (E.).

B. IOs as Autonomous Actors and the Need for Enhanced Procedural Controls

Are enhanced procedural controls really needed in IOs? The underlying thesis of this paper is that IOs act with a high degree of autonomy in decision-making and that this fact has been concealed by the assumption that sovereign members always remain in full political control of the organization.

I. The Organizational Setting

Already the first half of the 19th century-IOs were modeled on the idea of the separation between political legislation on the one hand and technical administration by administrative bodies on the other hand. According to this concept, sovereign member states establish and direct the organization by designing and controlling its main organs. The foundation of an international organization is based on sovereign consent expressed by the adoption of an international instrument. The convention usually establishes a principal plenary organ, in which political decision-making in form of resolutions and standard-setting can take place. The political organs usually decide on the basis of the one state

---

Administrative Law, 17 EUROPEAN JOURNAL OF INTERNATIONAL LAW 247-278 (2006).

one vote principle hereby respecting the principle of sovereign equality. National representatives take responsibility for their participation in such organs under national criteria and are legitimized by national procedures, which remain outside the realm of general international law. The constitution generally also establishes an executive board or council as an executive supervisory organ usually consisting of a limited number of national representatives, representing the membership.[6]

Political organs (plenary and council) on the one hand and the secretariat on the other fulfill different functions. The plenary proceduralizes the "political" on the basis of the principle of sovereign consent, whereas the "technical" is based on the ideal of efficient administrative implementation and supposed to be handled by the secretariat and subordinated bodies.[7] To date most international institutions officially maintain an organizational hierarchy by delegating tasks to the secretariat or subordinated bodies and by creating mandates. According to the organizational blue-print political decisions are taken by member states in the plenary organs or a council or board, consisting of a smaller number of member states. Their promotion and implementation is then delegated to technical committees or the management of the organization. Plenary organs can also create new mandates in order to institutionalize certain policies by appointing special representatives, rapporteurs or ad hoc committees for specific tasks. Plenary organs are supposed to be responsible for rule making and for guiding the secretariat in the implementation of standards and strategic goals politically.

II. Conceptual Legacies and the Assumption of Sovereign Control

If responsibility was merely delegated, a control problem could – at least in theory – not occur. Sovereign member states theoretically could always direct the organization politically by taking respective decisions regarding mandated activities and delegated tasks in plenary (congress/assembly) or the council (board). From a historical perspective, the idea of controlling the work of IOs through general procedural standards or even through external judicial bodies would have conflicted with a number of general assumptions regarding the nature of in-

---

6 SCHERMERS & BLOKKER (note 1), at § 409.

7 I. SEIDL-HOHENVELDERN & G. LOIBL, DAS RECHT DER INTERNATIONALEN ORGANISATIONEN 124 (7th ed., 2000).

ternational organization. First, external control would have meant that the decisions taken by sovereign member states in the plenary could be controlled by a higher form of political or legal institution. In the minds of 19th century international lawyers such an institution would have presupposed the foundation of a World-State with a World-Court, which in itself was considered a utopian and politically undesirable aspiration.[8] The creation of IOs in the 19th and twentieth century could only be brought about, if the overall institutional set-up did not convey the impression that its future operations would fundamentally conflict with the doctrine of national sovereignty. Second, international organizations were supposed to serve functions of the general welfare, which was in itself considered "a good thing."[9] They were conceptualized as entities rendering assistance and advice to member states in the fulfillment of certain administrative functions, rather than fulfilling such functions themselves. Decisions taken on the international level were generally regarded as having no effects on individuals outside the organization. Such effects were supposed to occur only through an act of national implementation, called transformation.

This assumption of sovereign control not only rendered midwife-services in the historical process of creating the first IOs, it remains a conceptual legacy of the law of international organization. It therefore does not come as a surprise that 20th century academic literature on IOs dealt primarily with the question of strengthening IO-performance and its legal personality *vis à vis* its sovereign and allegedly much more powerful member states. With their focus on high politics, questions of war and peace and hegemonic powers, authors considered autonomous decision-making of international bodies more of an unachieved or utopian goal than a problem.[10] Scholarly attempts in the interwar period to decouple the foundations of the international legal order from the sovereign will of states were aimed precisely at enhancing the legal autonomy of new international institutions like the League of Nations.[11]

---

[8] For an influential German 19th century critique of "civitas maxima" conceptions in international law, *see* C. KALTENBORN VON STACHAU, KRITIK DES VÖLKERRECHTS 73 (1847).

[9] On this general assumption, *see* Klabbers (note 3), at 221-255.

[10] E.H. CARR, THE TWENTY YEARS' CRISIS 1919 – 1939. AN INTRODUCTION TO THE STUDY OF INTERNATIONAL RELATIONS 186 (1940).

[11] J. V. BERNSTORFF, DER GLAUBE AN DAS UNIVERSALE RECHT. ZUR VÖLKERRECHTSTHEORIE HANS KELSENS UND SEINER SCHÜLER 59-61, 107-110 (2001).

IOs themselves also had no interest in portraying themselves as autonomous actors and instead ritually complained about the lack of commitment or disruptive power politics of individual member states, blocking important projects the IO could otherwise pursue.[12] The ambiguous or indeed paradoxical nature of international organizations, which is characterized by the need to create a new political actor, without openly infringing the sovereignty of its member states, was concealed by the organizational hierarchy, according to which sovereign states seemingly remained in full political control of the organization.[13] As a consequence a number of developments and pathologies in the work of international bureaucracies remained theoretically invisible for a long time. Not only international legal scholarship but also predominant strands in International Relations (IR) theory seem to have underrated the degree of autonomy such actors can assume.[14] In particular, the need for specific legal controls of international bureaucracies was not perceived.

III. The Creation of Autonomous Actors Exercising Public Authority

As Inis Claude argued in his "Swords into Plowshares," the 19th century administrative unions already enjoyed a high degree of autonomy which did not sit comfortably with the prevailing assumptions of sovereign political control. The invention of the "secretariat" as a permanent genuinely international machinery of administration was the crucial step in the creation of autonomous political actors on the international level. The Bureau of the International Telegraphic Union became the prototype of a secretariat staffed by international civil servants tasked to carry out functions of research, correspondence and publication as well as the preparation of decisions for future conferences. This first phase of international organization was already marked by the emergence of a diverse group of new participants in the business of international affairs, including scientific experts, private interest groups and humanitarian organizations, which exerted considerable influence

12 M.N. Barnett & M. Finnemore, Rules for the world. International organizations in global politics 20-30 (2004).

13 I.L. Claude, Swords into plowshares. The problems and progress of international organization 39 (1956).

14 On IO-autonomy in IR-theory, *see* Venzke, in this volume.

on decisions taken by the secretariat, without necessarily involving the political organs of the IO. This phenomenon destabilizes the conceptual hierarchy between decision-making in state dominated political organs and the seemingly technical implementation of such decisions by the secretariat.[15] Due to their unrivalled technical expertise in specific regulatory fields the bureaus of the first administrative unions quickly got involved not only in the implementation but also in the preparation and drafting of decisions to be adopted in plenary by member states.[16]

With the proliferation of IOs in the second half of the 20th century and the impact of their policies, which today can be felt at every corner of the world, the trend toward administrative autonomy and influence has become more visible. IOs also had an increasing impact on the structures of domestic administrative law in their member states.[17] The following observations regarding structures of decision-making in international organizations stand in contrast to the original assumption that IOs have a hierarchical internal structure based on law that allows for significant political and legal control of the work of the organization.

1. Mission-Creep

Firstly, many IOs have started to engage in activities beyond their original mandate, as set out in their constitution, operating in these fields on a doubtful legal basis. Many of the activities of international bureaucracies described in the case studies are not mentioned in the constitution of the respective IOs.[18] Can such actions still be considered legal? Two potentially limiting principles of the law of international organization are relevant in this context: The principle of domestic jurisdiction and the *ultra vires* doctrine. The principle of domestic jurisdiction had been enshrined in the League of Nations Covenant (Art. 15, para. 8) and was given expression in Art. 2 para. 7 of the UN Charter.[19]

---

15 CLAUDE (note 13), at 39-40.

16 SEIDL-HOHENVELDERN & LOIBL (note 7), at 124.

17 As a comprehensive analysis of this phenomenon C. TIETJE, INTERNATIONALISIERTES VERWALTUNGSHANDELN (2001).

18 On the terror lists of the UN Security Council, *see* Feinäugle, in this volume.

19 On Art. 2(7) UN-Charter, *see* J.A. Frowein, *Are There Limits to the Amendment Procedures in Treaties Constituting International Organizations, in*

The original idea behind the domestic jurisdiction doctrine was that there were issues which were *per definitionem* within the exclusive realm of sovereign national discretion. This restrictive approach to international jurisdiction was confirmed in various judgments and opinions of the Permanent Court of International Justice.[20] Its applicability suffered from the fact that it was theoretically and politically impossible to come up with a concrete list of issues, which by their nature could not be regulated by international law.

On the issue of the *ultra vires* doctrine, the ICJ opined in the *Certain Expenses* case that "when the Organization takes action which warrants the assertion that it was appropriate for the fulfillment of one of the stated purposes of the United Nations, the assumption is that such an action is not *ultra vires* the Organisation."[21] Given that the purposes of an IO are usually not phrased in narrow language and are open to interpretation, the liberal approach towards implied powers taken by the ICJ in this case did not help to make the *ultra vires* doctrine an effective and constraining legal principle. In fact, by deducing implied powers from the purposes of the IO, the ICJ reduced the scope of application of the *ultra vires* doctrine to an extent, which made it virtually meaningless. In the *Nuclear Weapons* advisory opinion[22] the ICJ took a more restrictive approach returning to a narrowly interpreted principle of attribution of powers as originally applied by the Permanent Court of Justice in its opinion on the *Jurisdiction of the European Commission of the Danube* case.[23] A more restrictive approach indeed seems necessary to turn these principles into meaningful limitations on the proliferation of new competencies in some IOs.

LIBER AMICORUM FOR I. SEIDL-HOHENVELDERN 201-218 (Gerhard Hafner *et. al.* eds., 1998).

[20] On the critique of this principle by interwar-scholarship, *see* V. BERNSTORFF (note 11), 88-91.

[21] *Certain Expenses of the United Nations*, Advisory Opinion of 20 July 1962, ICJ-Reports 1962, 168.

[22] *Legality of the Use by a State of Nuclear Weapons in Armed Conflict*, Advisory Opinion of 8 July 1996, ICJ-Reports 1996, at 80-81.

[23] *Jurisdiction of the European Commission of the Danube between Galatz and Braila*, advisory opinion, 1926 Publ. PCIJ, Series B, No. 14, at 64. *See* J. KLABBERS, AN INTRODUCTION TO INTERNATIONAL INSTITUTIONAL LAW 80 (2002). For a critique of the "revisionist" nuclear weapons advisory opinion, *see* N.D. WHITE, THE LAW OF INTERNATIONAL ORGANISATIONS 99-102 (2005).

2. The Flight from the Plenary

Secondly, plenary organs have often ceased to function as an effective political control mechanism. Formal decision-making in plenary bodies is often considered unproductive, since controversial political debates "block" decision-making in these fora.[24] Political struggles between rich donors and the biggest contributors on the one hand and developing countries on the other hand often lead to a stalemate situation, since the poor have the votes and the rich have the money. In addition, delegation and mandating as classic instruments of plenary organs for steering an international organization inevitably entails a loss of control. Once a task has been delegated to an institutional structure it inevitably takes on a life of its own. This effect is concealed by the hierarchical structure involved in delegation or mandating. Usually the creation of a new mandate involves reporting obligations of the new mandate holder *vis à vis* its creator.[25] However, the degree of institutional autonomy established by an act of delegation or mandating will not be severely limited by such reporting obligations. Strong states oftentimes have an interest in autonomous decision-making in expert bodies because they have more influence in these informal processes through higher scientific and bureaucratic resources.

IOs also increasingly engage in horizontal delegation to other IOs and private institutions, hereby incorporating and enforcing external decisions taken in other institutions without having procedures in place to politically assess and control them. The WTO, for instance, relies upon and "hardens" decisions taken in the WHO/FAO Codex Alimentarius Commission by a dynamic reference in the SPS Agreement.[26] The effect of such forms of delegation to external technical expertise can be the disempowerment of other political bodies on the international and national level. Delegation to technical committees is often justified by higher scientific expertise of these bodies. However, most regulatory decisions involve normative assumptions and trigger redistributive outcomes that cannot be reduced to seemingly objective scientific inquiries;

---

24 On this problem within the FAO, *see* *FAO: The Challenge of Renewal. An Independent External Review of the Food and Agriculture Organisation*, 2007, FAO-document on file with author.

25 On delegation, *see* Venzke, in this volume.

26 Pereira, in this volume.

each time someone wins and someone loses.[27] Another example is the intense co-operation between Interpol and the UN Security Council Counter Terrorism Committee.[28] By connecting the committee with a global data platform for police enforcement activities, the implementation of individualized sanctions becomes possible in practice. This increase in efficiency by dynamic incorporation of standards and decisions between IOs comes with a price. It separates the political organs of the organizations from the relevant decision-making procedures. Decision-making and responsibility fall apart.

3. The Reign of Expert Bodies and Decision-Making Affecting External Entities

While initially the framework of regulatory decisions was clearly delineated by national representatives taking political decisions being implemented later by technical bodies, in practice there is often an inversion of these roles. More and more regulatory decisions are framed and prepared by technical committees and only formally adopted by national representatives, who are left with a rubber-stamping role. Internal hierarchies are replaced by technical subordination. Moreover, even large states often neglect their supervisory-functions in executive boards or councils unless they take a particular interest in a specific project. Due to the complexity of technical, economic and social issues at hand, decisions regarding programs, projects and policies prepared by the secretariat or management of the organization are not always scrutinized in a thorough fashion by governmental supervisory bodies before being adopted lock, stock and barrel as proposed by the secretariat. Secretariats often either have specific knowledge of the relevant issues or are in a position to incorporate such knowledge through the involvement of external experts and consultants. Such knowledge puts secretariats and expert-committees in a position to shape the general (global) understanding of the issues at hand. Such understandings and interpretations of social phenomena and international standards are disseminated by autonomous promotional and capacity-building activities of the secretariat.[29] Given that expert committees are often composed of

---

27 I have made this argument elsewhere. J.v. Bernstorff, *Democratic Global Internet Regulation? Governance Networks, International Law and the Shadow of Hegemony*, 9 EUROPEAN LAW JOURNAL 511-526 (2003).

28 Schöndorf-Haubold, in this volume.

29 On this aspect in the FAO-context, *see* Friedrich, in this volume.

specialists from governmental departments that deal with a particular issue area, they often share a common worldview.[30] Barnett and Finnemore refer to the "social construction power" of IOs because they use their knowledge to help to create social reality.[31]

Furthermore, decision-making by technical committees and secretariats increasingly entails at least indirect effects on individuals and other entities outside the organizational setting. In the case studies presented in this research project a number of such decisions are dealt with in detail. The attribution of a certain status or right, such as the recognition of refugee status by UNHCR[32] or the recognition of a trade mark by WIPO[33] would fall into this category. In addition, decisions to put a specific case, person or site on a formalized list, such as the listing of endangered species under CITES[34], or a listing as a world cultural heritage sites by UNESCO[35] need mentioning in this context.[36] Listing-procedures frequently trigger legal or political consequences for the listed entity and indirectly also for third parties, be they individuals, member-states or non-member states. As a result, questions regarding a

---

[30] So called "epistemic communities," consisting of scientists, representatives of specific professions and national experts, provide institutions with shared perceptions of various issues ranging from technical standards to bioethical considerations, which serve as a basis for decision-making within the institution. These contributions help to reduce societal complexity for the actors within the organization and have a considerable impact on the development of global standards. Such activities take place in technical committees or through informal contacts with staff members of the secretariat of the organization. Once the epistemic community has succeeded to transform their world-view into a global standard within one institution it tries to convince other organizations to adhere to these standards in related areas. And once recognized globally, such standards can effectively be used at home to pressure national legislators to reform national regulations portrayed as being out of step with global standards. It goes without saying that such lobbying activities proliferate where commercial interests are affected by global decision-making. *See* P.M. Haas, *Introduction: Epistemic Communities and International Policy Coordination*, 46 INTERNATIONAL ORGANIZATION 1-35 (1992).

[31] BARNETT & FINNEMORE (note 12), at chapter 1 (2004).

[32] Smrkolj, in this volume.

[33] Kaiser, in this volume.

[34] Fuchs, in this volume.

[35] Zacharias, in this volume.

[36] Feinäugle, in this volume.

fair hearing, access to justice and legal remedies have become more acute.

In summary, the conceptually cemented assumption regarding the nature of international organization according to which sovereign member states control and direct the organization politically through internal hierarchies seems to be contradicted by the inherent tendencies of autonomous decision-making in IOs and other global governance-institutions. The creation of such institutions should, however, not be portrayed as a one sided process, which inevitably leads to a loss of influence on the part of state actors. Oftentimes states only gain influence on other actors and regulatory issues through the creation of international institutions. State representatives themselves can increase their freedom of action *vis à vis* domestic constituencies by creating and using international institutions.[37] It is often in the interest of some member states that technical committees initiate new standards. At the same time states have created a new actor, which cannot be fully controlled even by the strongest member states, let alone by less powerful actors. In the following, I will describe how procedures are used to gain control of the exercise of public authority on the national level.

C. Controlling the Exercise of Public Authority through Procedures

Procedures are the magic formula of the enlightened political mind. They promise to transform the reign of arbitrary power into the legitimate exercise of public functions in the interest of the citizens.[38] They domesticate the political "machine" and bring progress, reason and truth or in the words of Francois Guizot, the French nineteenth-century historian and statesman: "Toutes les combinaisons de la machine politique doivent donc tendre, d'une part, à extraire de la société tout ce qu'elle possède de raison, de justice, de vérité, pour les appliquer a son gouvernement; de l'autre, à provoquer les progrès de la société

---

37 M. ZÜRN, REGIEREN JENSEITS DES NATIONALSTAATES. GLOBALISIERUNG UND DENATIONALISIERUNG ALS CHANCE 245 (1998).

38 N. LUHMANN, LEGITIMATION DURCH VERFAHREN 11-26 (1969).

dans la raison, la vérité, et à faire incessamment passer ces progrès de la société dans son gouvernement".[39]

The insistence on "truth" as the end of political procedures reveals the archaic roots of the enlightened belief in proceduralization. Public procedures, applied originally in post medieval court proceedings had replaced archaic rituals with an outcome allegedly predetermined by supernatural forces. Societies invented procedures in order to decide under conditions of uncertainty in a manner that allowed a reduction of societal complexity.[40] Proceduralized decision-making had become the "truth-machine" of modern society.

According to Max Weber's sociological account of national bureaucracies, administrative procedures fulfill two main functions: formalization and rationalization of the exercise of public power.[41] Both functions are closely related to the concept of "Rechtsstaat", coined 1848 by the German liberal lawyer Robert von Mohl.[42] Legal systems make use of administrative procedures in order to formalize processes of public decision-making and enforcement.[43] The law prescribes in detail in which form public power shall be exercised. It regulates the process of decision-making by establishing binding procedures.[44] In fact, the concept of the rule of law in the Western tradition is based on the assumption that public power is exercised in and through administrative procedures on the basis of legislation. If power is exercised unlawfully, the individual has recourse to legal remedies in an independent tribunal. Procedures based on legal rules formalize public decision-making processes and facilitate their judicial review. To date a number of procedural principles have emerged in domestic legal systems, which aim to enhance the control of administrative power. An official assessment of the Swedish government of procedural principles recognized within all EU-

---

[39] M. Guizot, *Histoire des origines du gouvernement représentatif en Europe*, vol. 1, 78 (1851), quoted in Id.

[40] LUHMANN (note 38), at 11-26.

[41] M. WEBER, WIRTSCHAFT UND GESELLSCHAFT 125-130 (2006).

[42] M. STOLLEIS, PUBLIC LAW IN GERMANY, 1800 - 1914, 229-235 (2001).

[43] For the national realm, *see* E. SCHMIDT-AßMANN, DAS ALLGEMEINE VERWALTUNGSRECHT ALS ORDNUNGSIDEE. GRUNDLAGEN UND AUFGABEN DER VERWALTUNGSRECHTLICHEN SYSTEMBILDUNG 305-310 (1998).

[44] On the German and Italian domestic tradition, *see* G.d. Cananea, *Beyond the State: The Europeanization and Globalization of Procedural Administrative Law*, 9 EUROPEAN PUBLIC LAW 563, 565-566 (2003).

states *inter alia* lists the following legal principles: the principle of legality and proportionality and impartiality, the right to a fair hearing, the right to have access to information, the obligation to give reasons for a particular decision in written form and the obligation to give instruction on a right to appeal.[45]

In terms of rationalization procedures enable civil servants to structure the process of decision-making. The imposed structure allows the planning and co-ordination of the contributions to this process by the participants. The procedure also clarifies on a general basis who can become a participant in the decision-making process, and when and in which form his or her voice will be taken into account by those who will make the final decision. It permits the selecting of information which is relevant to the process by excluding other information as irrelevant or belated. It excludes alternatives, reduces complexity and thus facilitates the gradual convergence of perspectives among participants regarding the matter at hand. This process according to Niklas Luhmann enables the system to construct the outside world in a way that enables the participants to reach a decision.[46] Needless to say they hereby enormously impact the substance of the decisions taken at the end of the procedure.

The reign of expertise and new informal ways of decision-making, which include private actors, also confront domestic administrative law with new procedural arrangements, which cannot easily be integrated in the various administrative law traditions.[47] The control problem can not only be observed at the international level.[48] Due to the increasing linkages between domestic and international bureaucracies described in the case studies a clear separation between these levels of decision-making can no longer be upheld. The main difference is that on the national level courts can potentially exercise meaningful judicial control whereas

---

[45] Quoted in E. Schmidt-Aßmann, *Verwaltungsverfahren und Verwaltungskultur*, NEUE ZEITSCHRIFT FÜR VERWALTUNGSRECHT (NVwZ) 40, 43 (2007).

[46] LUHMANN (note 38), at 11-26.

[47] On expertise in German administrative law, *see* A. Voßkuhle, *Sachverständige Beratung des Staates, in* III HANDBUCH DES STAATSRECHTS DER BUNDESREPUBLIK DEUTSCHLAND 45 *et seq.* (J. Isensee & P. Kirchhof eds., 2005).

[48] For Pereira there is no difference between the domestic and the international level regarding the legitimacy problems involved in administrative decision-making. *See* Pereira, in this volume.

decisions produced on the international level often escape such judicial controls.

D. Procedures of Decision-Making in IOs

In the following two types of decisions of IOs shall be differentiated: rule-making decisions and operational decisions.[49]

I. Rule-Making Decisions

The political process of rule-making and standard-setting consists of a number of decisions often scattered over various organs of the IO. Procedures vary from IO to IO. Two general stages of such processes can be identified: the initiative- and drafting-stage and the adoption-stage. According to the original concept of international organization, governments are the main initiators of decision-making processes within the organization. In fact they have a right of initiative through the plenary organs or the council in most IOs.[50] The preparation of an initiative and the creation of a first draft are often coordinated between particular groups of states before being tabled in the political organs.[51] Governments are frequently lobbied by private interest groups to run rule-making initiatives on the international level. This holds true for

---

[49] For a more complex analytical matrix of decision making in IOs, *see* R.W. COX & H.K. JACOBSON, THE ANATOMY OF INFLUENCE. DECISION MAKING IN INTERNATIONAL ORGANIZATION (1973).

[50] SCHERMERS & BLOKKER (note 1), § 711. On the complex relationship between the Council and the Assembly of the International Seabed Authority, *see* Wolfrum, in this volume.

[51] In organizations with a universal membership cross-regional political groupings such as the Organisation of Islamic States (OIC), the Non-Aligned Movement (NAM) and the European Union (EU) have a political filtering function regarding individual initiatives. In particular the European Union coordinates common EU-initiatives as well as EU-member states-initiatives within such institutions in a substantive fashion. Likewise over the last years an astonishing revival of the Non-Aligned Movement (NAM) could be observed, leading to an improved coordination of NAM-countries in universal institutions. Often such groupings run their own initiatives, which will formally be tabled by one member country representing the grouping in plenary.

humanitarian- and economic issues alike. They offer to provide interested governments with background research and a first draft of a new standard or multilateral agreement and to assist them in lobbying other delegations regarding specific initiatives. As the case study for the OECD-export credit arrangement in this research project shows, private interest groups in co-operation with national bureaucrats play a major role in drafting new standards in this field.[52]

Some IOs foresee a formal right of initiative of the secretariat of the organization, the most prominent example being the European Commission. Secretariats also usually involve external expertise into the drafting process of such initiatives. Often, and in particular in the EC-context, drafts produced by interested private institutions are made into an official initiative without substantive changes. Within the UN the Secretary General has the right to propose items for the agendas of the main organs.[53] Even in the absence of a formal right of initiative secretariats claim powers of initiative from the nature of delegated functions and instructions. In particular the international financial institutions as well as development agencies, such as UNDP and UNICEF seem to be driven by a series of program and project initiatives generated predominantly by the management of these organizations.[54] Furthermore, secretariats usually have no problem in finding governments that are willing to table their initiatives, which usually benefit from the secretariat's high level of technical expertise.[55]

The adoption of decisions of a rule-making nature usually takes place in plenary organs in a formalized fashion governed by the respective organ's rules of procedure. Most organizations rely on the one state one vote principle. However, mechanisms of weighted voting are a well established exception to that rule. Voting under the unanimity-rule, originally upheld by the Permanent Court of International Justice in its *Treaty of Lausanne* advisory opinion (1925)[56], has been replaced by

---

52 Goldmann, in this volume.

53 Security Council, Provisional Rule 6; General Assembly, Rule 13; ECOSOC, Rule 10.

54 P. Dann, *Grundfragen eines Entwicklungsverwaltungsrechts, in* INTERNATIONALES VERWALTUNGSRECHT 21-25 (C. Möllers, A. Voßkuhle, C. Walter eds., 2007).

55 SCHERMERS & BLOKKER (note 1), at § 714.

56 PCIJ, Series B, no. 12, 29. On this problem, *see* C. Tomuschat, *Obligations Arising for States Without or Against their Will,* 241 RECUEIL DES COURS /

(qualified) majority-voting in many international organizations. For instance, the adoption of a new convention by the General Assembly does not require a unanimous vote. Given that the binding effect on individual member states in any event depends on subsequent ratification majority voting does not seem to contradict with the principle of sovereign consent. More problematic in this regard are non-binding instruments, which are frequently adopted in plenary organs allowing for majority voting. Such non-binding standards are often taken as a basis for the secretariat and other committees within the organizations in order to engage in a wide range of implementation activities.[57] Their adoption against the will of a number of member states increases the aforementioned political autonomy of IOs *vis à vis* their member states. Majority voting is therefore sometimes modified by so called opting out procedures, according to which states can lodge an objection against the decision of the majority and thus avoid being bound by the act.[58] In many organizational settings decisions are not taken by voting but by consensus (acclamation).[59] This means in practice that debates are continued until no one present in the room further raises objections against a specific proposal and therefore a minimum-level of acceptance of the decision among all participants has been reached.

An increasing number of universal IOs allow for NGO participation in the process of negotiating and adopting new standards. The UN for instance, grants consultative status to international and national NGOs on the basis of Art. 71 of the UN Charter. Such a status can provide NGOs with access to ECOSOC deliberations and other negotiations in various UN-fora. Each main organ and agency within the UN has its own internal rules of procedure regarding the rights of participation of affected NGOs.[60] Despite increased openness towards NGOs and public participation, governments still play a dominant role in general rule-making in IOs. Procedures tend to be formalized and based on the principle of sovereign equality.

ACADÉMIE DE DROIT INTERNATIONAL DE LA HAYE 199-374 (1993); KLABBERS (note 23), 228-229.

57 CITES is a good example. *See* Fuchs, in this volume.

58 On opting out, *see* M. Fitzmaurice, *Expression of Consent to be Bound by a Treaty as Developed in Certain Environmental Agreements*, *in* ESSAYS ON THE LAW OF TREATIES, 59, 66 (J. Klabbers ed., 1997).

59 SCHERMERS & BLOKKER (note 1), at § 771.

60 G. DAHM & R. WOLFRUM, VÖLKERRECHT 240 *et seq.* (2002).

II. Operational Decisions

By far the greatest number of IO-decisions, many of which with direct effects on external entities, are taken outside plenary organs. They are usually considered as operational decisions taken in order to implement rules adopted in plenary or in the framework of explicitly or implicitly delegated tasks and mandates. Most of the case studies of this issue deal with decisions taken in secretariats and subordinated intergovernmental bodies and expert-commissions or committees of IOs.

Two rationales behind the delegation of decision-making to such bodies can be discerned. The first rationale concerns the quest for objective and expertise-driven decisions. For some tasks government-representatives are considered lacking the necessary impartiality and expertise. For instance, the UNESCO world heritage committee consists of independent experts who are supposed to decide impartially on the granting of the desired world heritage status. Another example from the case studies is the FAO/WHO Codex Alimentarius Commission, consisting of governmental experts and private interest-groups tasked with regulating global food-safety standards. Governmental delegations to the Commission often include industry-representatives. However, despite its "technical" mandate, the Commission deals with highly politicized issues such as the assessment of GMO-products.[61] The findings of the Commission, even though being of a non-binding nature, determine whether or not specific food-products can be banned by national governments. The reason for this is that the decisions of the Commission can effectively be "hardened" and enforced by WTO-mechanisms.

The second reason for the delegation of decisions to smaller bodies is the attempt to increase the effectiveness of decision-making.[62] A smaller body is usually more likely to make decisions in a reasonable time frame. In terms of facilities and translation deliberations in smaller sized bodies are less costly than those in the plenary organs. Executive boards, councils and governing bodies, composed of a smaller number of government representatives were established out of this functional necessity. Most of these boards officially function under the authority of the plenary, some however have their own independent executive

---

61 Pereira, in this volume.

62 With a critique of the call for effective implementation and the corresponding mindset, *see* M. Koskenniemi, *Constitutionalism as Mindset: Reflections on Kantian Themes About International Law and Globalization*, 8 THEORETICAL INQUIRIES IN LAW 9 (2007).

powers.[63] A prime example is the UN Security Council, which has developed a system of subcommittees consisting of national diplomats from the permanent missions of the members of the Security Council in New York.[64] The division of labor between the council and the plenary regarding policy decisions depends on the constitution of the respective IO and is not always clear cut.[65]

Operational decisions can be regarded as complex processes of decision-making often involving the secretariat, the governing board, technical committees and external experts. In the case of the World Bank a decision to finance a country project is prepared by the civil servants and taken by the World Bank board of directors.[66] Similarly, UNICEF country programs are prepared by the management of the organization, adopted by the UNICEF executive board lock, stock and barrel to be subsequently implemented through individual projects based on decisions taken by the staff members of the organization.[67]

Implementation of such projects on the ground frequently involves the use of external expertise provided by scientists and NGOs. The promotion of standards through secretariats might also involve activities of norm-concretization through manuals, guidelines and commentaries. Such autonomous acts of norm-concretization, however, involve an element of norm-creation.[68] On the international level this is particularly relevant because norm-concretization through the secretariat or a functional committee may have direct influence on how domestic legislators eventually regulate the issues at hand. This indirect form of global rule-making through model-legislation can have an enormous regulatory impact even though it is based on non-binding standards and

---

63 SCHERMERS & BLOKKER (note 1), at § 409-421.

64 On the powers of the Security Council, *see* G. Nolte, *The Limits of the Security Council's Powers and its Functions in the International Legal System: Some Reflections, in* THE ROLE OF LAW IN INTERNATIONAL POLITICS – ESSAYS IN INTERNATIONAL RELATIONS AND INTERNATIONAL LAW 315-326 (Michael Byers ed., 2000).

65 R. Wolfrum, in this volume.

66 Dann (note 54), at 21-25.

67 On program-management in IOs, *see* D.T.G. Dijkzeul, *Programs and the Problems of Participation, in* RETHINKING INTERNATIONAL ORGANIZATIONS PATHOLOGY AND PROMISE 197-233 (D.T.G. Dijkzeul ed., 2003).

68 H. KELSEN, REINE RECHTSLEHRE. EINLEITUNG IN DIE RECHTSWISSENSCHAFTLICHE PROBLEMATIK 98 (1934).

autonomous promotional activities by often not more than a handful of international civil servants, experts and private interest-representatives. This is illustrated in the case studies in this issue on the Code of Conduct for Responsible Fisheries and on the OECD-activities in the field of taxation.[69]

In terms of the state of formalization and rationalization of operational decision-making the first observation is that subordinated technical committees and secretariats of IOs in general enjoy a high degree of discretion regarding the implementation of their mandate. However, there is an obvious need to fill the substantive legal void left by the constitution of the IO with internal organizational structures aiming at the rationalization of decision-making-processes. Such structures are usually adopted by the bodies themselves in order to allow for a certain degree of internal managerial control and efficiency. As the case studies presented in this research project prove, all international bureaucracies take recourse to internal guidelines, rules of procedures and regulations, which set out internal procedures of decision-making. The level of formalization of such internal rules depends on the organization. Such rules are usually developed autonomously by the secretariat, management or the respective committees.

These internal rules intend to structure the process of decision-making and regulate which entities within and outside of the organization must be involved at which stage of the process. They may involve arrangements for incorporating external expertise from NGOs, scientists and other private interest groups through the secretariat and committees, either in the preparation phase (background studies for standard setting and programs) or in the implementation phase (project partners operating on the ground).[70] Both the World Bank and UNICEF for instance have a highly complex internal program cycle based on internal guidelines which governs internal decision-making by sequencing meetings and the submission of documents for country programs. In terms of the types of procedures used in different substantive fields of governance striking similarities with national bureaucracies can be observed. For example programs and project-cycles are also being used in the field of the administration of subsidies in the national realm.[71] As can be seen in

---

69 Friedrich, in this volume.

70 L. Dubin & R. Nogellou, *Public Participation in Global Administrative Organizations*, 3RD GLOBAL ADMINISTRATIVE LAW SEMINAR (June 15-16, 2007) (on file with author).

71 Dann (note 54), at 21-25.

the case studies in this issue some IOs have even shaped procedures according to domestic legal principles replicating procedures of a fair hearing, public access to information, the right to reasoned decisions and access to judicial relief on the international level.

1. Fair Hearing and Reasoned Decision-Making

In terms of the right to fair hearing, the UNHCR-case study in this issue demonstrates that the determination of a refugee-status has striking commonalities with the procedure of recognition of such a status under national immigration law.[72] The affected individual is generally heard by the UNHCR-staff before the decision is taken and there is an internal appeal-mechanism open to the respective individuals. Decisions in the appeal-procedure will then be taken by another UNHCR-staff member. The internal UNHCR-standards for determining refugee status "simulate" due-process procedures, which can be found in national administrative settings. The main difference is the lack of access of the affected individual to independent review by an administrative court or tribunal.

Another example for "simulated" due process are the revised guidelines of the UN-Security Council Counter Terrorism Committee regarding the listing of individual terror suspects falling under the Council's asset-freeze sanction regime. As described in the case study, the revised guidelines have introduced the duty to state the reasons why a particular person should be listed in more detail.[73] According to the guidelines states are now also supposed to inform the listed individual of the fact that he or she was listed. They also foresee the establishment of a focal point mandated to receive individual complaints and requests for instituting the de-listing procedure. In particular the Security-Council example shows, however, how far IOs still are from taking domestically established procedural legal principles seriously.

---

[72] Smrkolj, in this volume. On the due process principle from a comparative perspective, *see* G.d. Cananea, *Equivalent Standards under Domestic Administrative Law: A Comparative Perspective, in* II INVESTMENT TREATY LAW – CURRENT ISSUES 116-125 (F. Ortino, L. Liberti, A. Sheppard, H. Warner ed., 2007).

[73] Feinäugle, in this volume.

2. *Public Participation and Access to Information*

In line with domestic developments in administrative culture a number of IOs have adopted policies in order to enhance public participation and public access to information. The OECD for instance tries to enhance public participation by so called notice- and comment-procedures and by open processes of consultation with NGOs on certain issue-areas.[74] However, the results of public participation-processes are never binding for the bureaucracy. Final decisions are taken by governmental bodies or the secretariat of the IO.

The most progressive developments regarding these principles can be found in organizational settings in the field of environmental law. The Aarhus convention sets out specific rights of participation for the public and interested individuals. In the Almaty-Guidelines of 2005[75] the member states of the UN-Economic Commission for Europe foresee the application of these principles not only at the state or EU-level, but also at the level of IOs. The Aarhus principles include the active dissemination of information on all environmental policy-making processes through the internet as well as access to relevant drafts and meetings within the respective IOs.[76] Remarkably, states are obliged to actually take into account comments and proposals of NGOs and other individuals participating in these fora.[77] As Jürgen Friedrich suggests in his case study on the rather untransparent FAO policy-making procedures in fisheries-issues, the extension of Aarhus principles to the international arena could function as an additional accountability mechanism, especially if access to information and public participation are secured by means of an institutionalized review. [78]

On this issue the ILA-report entitled on "Accountability of IOs" also recommends that IOs implement the "*principle of transparency*" and the "*principle of access to information*" by adopting all normative deci-

---

74 Goldmann, in this volume; Dubin & Nogellou (note 70).

75 United Nations Economic Commission for Europe, Report of the Second Meeting of the Parties to the Convention on Access to Information, Public Participation in Decision-making and Access to Justice in Environmental Matters held in Almaty, Kazakhstan, 25-27 May 2005, Decision II/4 entitled *Promoting the Application of the Principles of the Aarhus Convention in International Forums,* ECE/MP.PP/2005/2/Add.5, 20 June 2005.

76 Almaty Guidelines (IV), UN-Doc. Nr. ECE/MP.PP/2005/2/Add.5.

77 Almaty Guidelines (V/ 37), UN-Doc. Nr. ECE/MP.PP/2005/2/Add.5.

78 Friedrich, in this volume.

sions in a public vote and opening meetings of non-plenary organs to the public.[79] According to the ILA-recommendations non-plenary organs should also grant an appropriate status to members and third states particularly affected by decisions of these organs.[80] Furthermore non-plenary organs should increase public access to information and provide information regarding their activities to all member states including the texts of draft decisions under consideration.[81] It should not be overlooked in this context that many IOs or organs within them are still reluctant to grant open access to files and negotiations at an early stage of decision-making. The UN-Security Council[82] and the WTO are infamous examples for secret negotiations behind closed doors.[83]

3. Access to Independent Review

Some IOs have reacted to widespread criticism of their policies by introducing quasi-judicial complaint mechanisms on the international level. As referred to in the case studies in this volume, the World Bank inspection panel, Interpol's control commission and the OECD-guidelines on corporate social responsibility[84] for instance foresee the submission of individual complaints by external actors. Notably, such review mechanisms tend to confine the applicable standards to the ones the IO has given itself in the form of internal rules and guidelines.[85] As a result, such mechanisms add to the fragmentation of standards in the law of international institutional law. They do not explicitly allow for the application of general international law and usually do not provide for an appeal. Hence, the main difference compared to national bureaucracies rooted in the rule of law tradition remains the absence of general public law-structures, in which these types of procedures are embedded. The introduction of effective judicial control, however, could potentially help to remedy illegal effects on third parties and re-

---

79 F. Berman, *et al., ILA-Berlin Conference (2004) on Accountability of International Organizations,* 1 INTERNATIONAL ORGANIZATIONS LAW REVIEW 221, 229 (2004).

80 *Id.*, at 230.

81 *Id.*, at 231.

82 Feinäugle, in this volume.

83 Dubin & Nogellou (note 70).

84 Schöndorf-Haubold, in this volume.

85 *Id.*

orient the activities of the international institution in general international law. At the same time and somewhat paradoxically, effective judicial review itself is greatly facilitated by the existence of a general law of administrative procedures.[86]

Generally speaking operational decisions in IOs are of course not taken at random. They usually follow certain internal procedures of decision-making based on particular rationalities. However, only in exceptional cases are such internal structures shaped according to general legal principles regulating the effects such decisions might have on third parties. Procedural rules usually aim at the internal rationalization of decision-making rather than trying to make decisions more transparent, let alone attempting to institute an external judicial or transparent political review.

E. Strategies to Bring General International Law Back in

International lawyers have reacted to the control-problem in different ways. A growing number of authors attempt to bring the constraining force of law to bear in decision-making of international bureaucracies. This is also one of the main motives behind this research project, which analyzes how the exercise of public authority through international institutions could be framed from a public law perspective.[87] Two other and somewhat related strategies should be mentioned in this context: First, the claim for internal constitutionalization of IOs through the progressive development of existing principles of the law of international organizations or through comparative analysis of various domes-

---

[86] Schmidt-Aßmann, *Verwaltungsverfahren und Verwaltungskultur*, NVwZ 40, 43 (2007).

[87] von Bogdandy, *et al.*, in this volume; *see* on the "Global Administrative Law"-approach B. Kingsbury, N. Krisch & R. Stewart, *The Emergence of Global Administrative Law*, 68 LAW AND CONTEMPORARY PROBLEMS 15 (2005); S. Cassese, *Administrative Law Without the State? The Challenge of Global Regulation*, 37 NEW YORK UNIVERSITY JOURNAL OF INTERNATIONAL LAW AND POLITICS 663 (2005); D. C. Esty, *Good Governance at the Supranational Scale: Globalizing Administrative Law*, 115 YALE LAW JOURNAL 1490 (2006).

tic administrative law traditions.[88] Second, the demand that IOs adhere to human rights standards.

I. Internal Constitutionalization

In its 2004 report on the accountability of international organizations the International Law Association recommended a number of general procedural principles for decision-making in IOs. The report's aim was to contribute to the "progressive development" of international law in that area and left open the question of the respective sources of the postulated procedural principles. Some clearly stemmed from national administrative law traditions.[89] A number of recommendations attempt to strengthen hierarchical mechanisms of political supervision. Under the "*principle of supervision*" parent organs should have a duty to exercise a degree of control over subsidiary organs which corresponds to the functional autonomy granted, including the right to overrule decision of subsidiary organs.[90] Questions related to *ultra-vires* and implied powers are subsumed under the "*principle of constitutionality*",[91] obliging the organs of the IO to carry out their functions in accordance with the rules of the organization. Constitutionalization in this context is understood as strengthening internal reformalization without addressing the question of conformity with substantive rules of international law.

The International Law Association was reluctant to set out recommendations for specific types of procedures, instead formulating a general "*principle of procedural regularity*"[92] according to which IOs should prevent abuse of discretionary powers, avoid errors of fact and law and ensure respect for due process and fair treatment. Another principle recommended which stems from national administrative traditions is

---

[88] On this approach, *see* Cananea (note 72). On the evolution of administrative norms, *see* E. Benvenisti, *The Interplay between Actors as a Determinant of the Evolution of Administrative law in International Institutions*, 68 LAW AND CONTEMPORARY PROBLEMS 319-340 (2005).

[89] For due process from a comparative perspective, *see* Cananea (note 72).

[90] F. Berman, *et al.* (note 79), at 221, 237.

[91] *Id.*, at 236.

[92] *Id.*, at 239.

the "*principle of objectivity and impartiality*"[93]. The principles recommended by ILA try to transfer procedural principles from various national rule of law-traditions to the global level. The report also takes up the classic claim of amending Art. 34 para. 1 of the ICJ-Statute in order to give IOs locus standing before the court.[94] Through such a mechanism of direct judicial action the recommended principles could then be confirmed by universal adjudication.

The procedural principles set forth in the report are an attempt to re-constitutionalize decision-making in international bureaucracies. Their aim is to strengthen internal hierarchies and to introduce elements of the rule of law-tradition for decision-making on the global level. Law is supposed to preside over efficiency or as Jan Klabbers has put it: "a constitutional approach would radically reject the proposition that the end justifies the means"[95]. A constitutional sensibility certainly must be welcomed and can be seen as a driving element behind this volume. The question, however, is whether the strategy to re-entrench internal organizational hierarchies alone could solve the control problem in practice. After all, many national bureaucracies, particularly those from Western states, do not seem to have severe problems with the general loss of control over expert bodies and functional committees. They have contributed to this development in the past. Other countries often do not have the resources to contribute to more effective supervision. Many national actors therefore are likely to resist the proposed strategy of internal constitutionalization or will not be able to live up to the expectations raised by it.

II. Human Rights

A further strategy of imposing legal limits on IO decision-making to be dealt with in this context is the insistence on strict adherence of international bureaucracies to human rights standards. Such demands were triggered by the dramatic social consequences of particular economic policies of international financial and trade institutions, by the death of thousands of Iraqi children as a result of the UN-Security Council's

---

93 *Id.*, at 239.

94 *Id.*, at 291.

95 J. Klabbers, *Constitutionalism Lite*, 1 INTERNATIONAL ORGANIZATIONS LAW REVIEW 31, 58 (2004); M. Koskenniemi (note 62).

sanctions program, the disputed listing of terror suspects by its Anti-Terrorism Committee, UNHCR's involvement in forced repatriation of refugees and by many other human rights-sensitive issues administered and enforced by international bureaucracies. The argument that human rights should apply to IOs has been advanced from both a procedural and a substantive angle.[96] Criticism has been based on a number of rights, ranging from the right to a fair hearing (Art. 14 ICCPR) to the right to food and water (Art. 11 ICESCR).

Legally the question of whether or not IOs are bound by international human rights norms without having ratified the two principal human rights covenants or other human rights conventions is far from being clarified.[97] According to a frequently used argument in the UN-context, the promotion of human rights is one of the principle goals of the organization, as set out in the UN-Charter. Human rights violations committed by the organization itself therefore cannot be justified.[98] One could also argue that some human rights norms are part of international customary law and as such are binding also upon IOs.[99] If that is the case the question needs to be asked which norms have acquired the status of customary law and to what extent such necessarily vague customary norms can actually set limits to concrete activities of international bureaucracies. In the absence of compulsory judicial review on the global level these uncertainties are not likely to disappear in the near future. Instead, decentralized judicial controls by national and regional courts might potentially have an impact on the development of universal standards in this area. [100]

---

[96] F. Mégret & F. Hoffmann, *The UN as a Human Rights Violator? Some Reflections on the United Nations Changing Human Rights Responsibilities*, 25 HUMAN RIGHTS QUARTERLY 314-342 (2003).

[97] von Bogdandy, in this volume; de Wet, in this volume.

[98] B. Fassbender, *Targeted Sanctions Imposed by the UN-Security Council and Due Process Rights*, 3 INTERNATIONAL ORGANIZATIONS LAW REVIEW 437-485, 468-469 (2006). On this problem, *see* A. Reinisch, *Developing Human Rights and Humanitarian Law Accountability of the Security Council for the Imposition of Economic Sanctions*, 95 AJIL 851-872 (2001).

[99] Most commentators accept that IOs are in principle bound by international customary law, *see* J.E. Alvarez, *International Organizations: Then and Now*, 100 AJIL 324-347 (2006).

[100] See de Wet, *Holding International Institutions Accountable: The Complementary Role of Non-Judicial Oversight Mechanisms and Judicial Review*, in this volume; G.d. Cananea, R*eturn to the Due Process of Law: The European*

Despite – or perhaps precisely because of the vagueness of human rights entitlements the power of human rights-discourse to politically constrain international bureaucracies seems unmatched by any other strategy of re-legalization. The discursive scandalization of certain IO-policies by international NGOs based on human rights language has proven to have a political effect on IOs. Social mobilization through media-driven campaigns has put a number of IOs on the defensive. As a reaction, many IOs have paid lip-service to human rights protection by officially declaring their commitment to these principles. "Human Rights Mainstreaming" has become a big issue in most IOs these days. Whether these initiatives are just a strategy of accommodation in the face of public resistance or the beginning of the acceptance of general legal constraints imposed by international law, remains to be seen. One thing, however, seems clear: scandalization alone might divert public attention from problematic IO-routines which are less suitable for globalised media-coverage but nonetheless have a strong impact on the daily lives of individuals.[101]

F. Conclusion

Wolfgang Friedmann at the height of the Cold War in his famous "The changing structure of international law" considered international co-operation through international organizations as the most important future project for international law. Organized co-operation was supposed to rescue mankind from "ruinous and destructive competition and exploitation of the resources of the earth short of war"[102]. Since then international law has indeed helped to bring about and stabilize many new organizational entities dealing with the most important economic, social and security-related issues of the planet. It seems, how-

---

Union and the Fight Against Terrorism, Comment on Court of First Instance judgment of December 16, 2006, Case T-228/02, Organisation de Modjahedins de l'Iran v Council, 32 E.L. Rev. 2007, 895-906 (on file with author). On the role of national courts see E. Benvenisti, *Reclaiming Democracy: The Strategic Uses of Foreign and International Law by National Courts*, 102 AJIL 241 (2008).

101 For a general critique of human rights discourse along these lines, see D. KENNEDY, THE DARK SIDES OF VIRTUE 3-35 (2004).

102 W.G. FRIEDMANN, THE CHANGING STRUCTURE OF INTERNATIONAL LAW 94 (1964).

ever, as if the role of international law remained confined to the creation of these new entities as powerful new actors without helping to embed them in procedural and substantive legal structures of a general nature. As a result, these actors have relied on flexible internal structures of decision-making, hereby increasing their individual autonomy in the process of developing and implementing global rules. They produce a myriad of political decisions every day, often taken in the absence of a specific and binding legal basis. The resulting fragmentation of institutional practice not only impedes effective legal controls but also makes it more difficult for the public sphere to effectively address and contest political outcomes and redistributive effects of global governance.[103] In the meantime Friedmann's dystopia, consisting of destructive competition, exploitation of resources short of war and an increasing global "apartheid" created by extreme poverty continues to unfold.

---

[103] Insisting on a space for politics, *see* J. Klabbers, *Two Concepts of International Organization*, 2 INTERNATIONAL ORGANIZATIONS LAW REVIEW 277, 292 (2005).

The Contributions by Jochen von Bernstorff and by Maja Smrkolj*

Comment by Christian Tietje

I. Introduction

In order to analyse the exercise of public authority by international institutions, it is necessary not only to take a look at the power and authority granted to international institutions by their respective founding treaties – constitutions – but also to focus on how international institutions actually apply their respective powers on a daily basis. In this regard, the law in action[1] is of course always substantive law (whether

* Jochen von Bernstorff, *Procedures of Decision-Making and the Role of Law in International Organizations*, in this volume; Maja Smrkolj, *International Institutions and Individualized Decision-Making: An Example of UNHCR's Refugee Status Determination*, in this volume.

A. von Bogdandy et al. (eds.), *The Exercise of Public Authority by International Institutions*, Beiträge zum ausländischen öffentlichen Recht und Völkerrecht 210, DOI 10.1007/978-3-642-04531-8_27,

hard or soft law) based on certain procedures determining the way in which the substantive law is made or applied. According to Hans Kelsen, the validity of law depends, *inter alia*, on adherence to existing procedural requirements.[2] This, however, is not only true with regard to law-making in a legislative sense, but also concerning administration. Procedure – and decision-making as a central element of procedure – is thus crucial for the legitimacy of law as such.[3] These very general thoughts highlight the importance of the topic addressed by Maja Smrkolj and Jochen von Bernstorff.

This comment is structured as follows: first, the content of the two papers will briefly be outlined. Second, some general remarks on the topic of the two papers shall be made, thus not focusing on the individual papers separately. In this regard, the following issues will be discussed: (1) some general aspects of the decision-making powers of international organizations (IOs) with regard to the concept of international organizations as such; (2) whether a more precise distinction between different types of IOs is necessary; (3) the necessity of differentiating between decision-making with "internal" and "external" effects in order to highlight the dualistic character of administrative law of international organizations.

II. Content of the Two Papers

1. General Perspectives on Decision-Making in International Organizations

The paper by Jochen von Bernstorff addresses in general the question of procedures relating to decision-making in international organizations. In doing so, the author starts his analysis from the classical per-

---

1 "Law in action" in this regard is not strictly meant to refer to the respective school of legal theory, but certain associations with legal realism are intended.

2 For details *see, e.g.*, Eugenio Bulygin, *Das Problem der Geltung bei Kelsen, in* Hans KELSEN – STAATSRECHTSLEHRER UND RECHTSTHEORETIKER DES 20. JAHRHUNDERTS, 80, 82 *et seq.* (Stanley L. Paulson & Michael Stolleis eds., 2005).

3 On details namely with regard to the law-making procedure *see* NIKLAS LUHMANN, LEGITIMATION DURCH VERFAHREN 174 *et seq.* (3rd ed., 1993).

spective that IOs are not only increasingly important in the international system, but that they also increasingly exercise functions of public authority, which have been in the past exclusively in the domain of the nation state. In the author's opinion, this phenomenon contrasts with a lack of sufficiently clear and precise legal rules concerning the procedure of decision-making in international organizations. The author clearly underlines his concern about the "exercise of public power outside a limiting framework of public law".

In order to make the main point of the paper more clear, in part one of his analysis, the author discusses "IOs as autonomous actors and the need for enhanced procedural controls". He does this by first providing an outline of the idea of international organizations, specifically by contrasting political decision-making dependent on the will of member states and the increasing independence of the administrative organs of international organizations. In this regard, von Bernstorff also outlines the general institutional structure of international organizations.

The specific aspect of an increasing autonomy in the exercise of public authority is analysed in more detail in the next part of the paper. In this regard, the author gives examples of (1) "mission-creep", *i.e.* the way IOs increasingly engage "in activities beyond their original mandate", (2) "the flight from the plenary", *i.e.* the phenomenon that "plenary organs often ceased to function as an effective political control mechanism", and (3) the fact that "more and more regulatory decisions are framed and prepared by technical committees" and that member states in this regard are "left with a rubber-stamping role" and that all this has an increasingly direct or indirect effect "on individuals and other entities outside the organizational setting".

The second part of Jochen von Bernstorff's paper discusses the rationale and importance of the exercise of public authority through procedures in general. In this regard, the author draws on legal history and the sociology of law in order to stress the importance of procedural law. This part is followed by a detailed section on different procedures of decision-making in IOs, namely with regard to rule-making decisions and operational decisions. Concerning operational decisions, von Bernstorff identifies certain procedural principles which are applied in the process of decision-making in a number of IOs. He specifically focuses on the principles of a fair hearing and reasoned decision-making, public participation and access to information, and finally access to independent review mechanisms.

The papers ends with a discussion of two main strategies of how "to bring general international law back in", namely through internal constitutionalization and human rights.

2. The Example of UNHCR's Refugee Status Determination

The paper by Maja Smrkolj is a case study on decision-making. It addresses refugee status determination by the UNHCR, specifically with regard to the procedure applied in this regard.

The paper starts with an introduction to the Refugee Convention and its protocol and the factual relevance of refugee status determination. In the second part of the paper, the author provides a legal analysis of refugee status determination. As a starting point for her entire analysis, she clearly demonstrates that there is no explicit legal basis for UNHCR's refugee status determination, but that this is only part of the general mandate of the organization. In contrast to this absent (or at least very vague) legal basis, an individual refugee status determination by UNHCR has far reaching consequences for the respective person within the national legal orders of the parties to the Refugee Convention.

As to the applicable law for the determination of refugee status, the author emphasises that almost no hard law exists. Aside from of the Refugee Convention and its protocol, which contain only very general provisions, details on the procedure are only laid down in documents of the Executive Committee of the High Commissioner's Programme and UNHCR itself. Even though one may argue that these documents have a legally binding effect, they are at least *prima facie* only of an internal character. Moreover, it is highly controversial whether general human rights law is applicable to any international organization.

In the next part of the paper, the author provides a detailed assessment of whether due process standards apply to refugee status determination. The bases for this analysis are UNHCR's 2003 procedural standards and their principles. Maja Smrkolj demonstrates that there are severe procedural deficiencies, specifically the lack of a right to an interpreter or right to counsel, the lack of a general obligation to provide reasons for a decision, and – most importantly – the lack of an independent appeal and judicial review by an independent and impartial tribunal, even though there are certain mechanisms for an internal monitoring and oversight procedure within UNHCR.

In the concluding section of the paper, the author, after pointing out how important the work of UNHCR is, tries to provide some answers to the question of why there is such a lack of due process guarantees. One possible explanation in this regard could be, according to the author, that UNHCR's refugee status determination has no legally binding effect in a strict sense, but that the final legal effect concerning individual persons only comes about within national legal orders. As states do rely to a large extent on UNHCR's determination, it could be that they use UNHCR as an "alibi" as long as it suits them. This leads to the situation that the states have no desire and thus make no attempt to provide more concrete legislation disciplining UNHCR's work.

III. Comments

1. General Aspects of the Decision-Making Powers of International Organizations with Regard to the Concept of International Organizations as Such

A first aspect that shall be addressed in terms of comments on both papers concerns the general conception of international organizations and its implication for the topic of decision-making.

As indicated in the paper by Jochen von Bernstorff, the development of the legal concept of international organizations is important with regard to decision-making. This is due to the fact that any possibility of decision-making having external effects beyond the internal structure of the respective organization is legally and political possible only by recognizing the independent legal status of international organizations. However, it is important to note that the recognition of the independent legal status of international organizations[4] only became accepted in academic writing in the 1920s and in state practice only with the advisory opinion of the ICJ in the Reparation for Injuries case[5] in 1949.[6]

---

[4] On the origin of the term "international organization" *see* Pitman B. Potter, *Origin of the Term International Organization*, 39 AMERICAN JOURNAL OF INTERNATIONAL LAW (AJIL) 803 *et seq.* (1945).

[5] ICJ, Reparation for Injuries Suffered in the Service of the United Nations, Advisory Opinion of 11 April 1949, ICJ Reports 1949, 174 *et seq.*

[6] *See* comprehensively on the historical development of the concept of legal personality of international organizations Bardo Fassbender, *Die Völkerrechts-*

Until then, international organizations were mostly qualified as mere administrative unions without any legal personality in public international law. However, as it was obvious already in the 19th century that the administrative unions of that time in fact did carry out somehow autonomous functions and practiced decision-making,[7] complicated legal constructions were developed in order to explain their status. The predominant view of that time was that the administrative unions did not have any legal relevance as such, but that only their organs were of interest. The organs of the administrative unions, however, were not considered as being something independent, but exclusively as being organs of the member states. Thus, from a strictly legal standpoint, there were always as many organs of a respective administrative union as there were member states. The problem of this approach is of course obvious: it is necessary to argue that, with regard to any decision-making or other expression of a will of the administrative union, a pre-existing decision concerning the respective matter by all member states individually was necessary.[8]

It was only with the establishment of the League of Nations that a new conception evolved. The League was considered by the majority of scholars to be a confederation and as such, by prevailing legal definition of that time, a subject of law. The other possible option of recognizing the League as an independent legal personality without the need to classify it as a confederation was only put forward by a few scholars. This legal opinion was only recognized with the advisory opinion of the ICJ in the Reparation for Injury case of 11 April 1949.[9]

Why this history? Only the historical development may explain why we still have so many problems with decision-making by international organizations today. The core problem in this regard is that – because of the historical development of the concept of international organizations as such – public international law recognizes their independent legal existence as subjects of international law on the one hand, but of course

---

subjektivität internationaler Organisationen, 37 ÖSTERREICHISCHE ZEITSCHRIFT FÜR ÖFFENTLICHES RECHT UND VÖLKERRECHT 17 *et seq.* (1986).

7 For details *see, e.g.*, Paul S. Reinsch, *International Unions and Their Administration*, 1 AJIL 579 *et seq.* (1907); for a detailed empirical assessment on all international organizations established between 1815 and 1964 *see* Michael Wallace & David J. Singer, *Intergovernmental Organizations in the Global System*, 1815-1964, 24 INTERNATIONAL ORGANIZATION 239 *et seq.* (1970).

8 For details *see* Fassbender (note 6), 19 *et seq.*

9 Fassender (note 6), 19 *et seq.*

still makes the existence of the organization dependent upon the will of the member states on the other.[10]

The at least *prima facie* paradox of recognizing international organizations as subjects of international law on the one hand and insisting on the dominant role of member states on the other is also the underlying reason for the legal distinction between international and supranational organizations. As is widely known, the traditional legal perspective is that only supranational organizations – most prominently of course the EC – have the competence of decision-making with direct effect in member states' national legal orders.[11] Moreover, most national constitutions only provide for the possibility of recognizing a direct legal effect of decisions by an international organization within the national legal order with regard to supranational organizations.[12] With regard to other international organizations, the predominant view is still that their decisions need to be transformed into domestic law by some legislative act or other legal act of the state, depending on the respective constitutional order.[13] This concept is also rooted in the theory that international organizations do not have decision-making power independent of the will of the member states.[14] Decision-making by international organizations is thus – as secondary public international law – considered to be public international law and, just as any other source of interna-

---

[10] *See* already Jurisdiction of the Europ. Com. of the Danube, Advisory Opinion, PCIJ Ser. B., No. 14, 64 (1927): "As the European Commission [for the Danube] is not a state but an international institution with a special purpose, it only has the functions bestowed upon it by the Definitive Statute with a view to the fulfilment of that purpose, but it has the power to exercise those functions to their full extent, in so far as the Statute does not impose restrictions on it."

[11] *See, e.g.*, PAUL J. G. KAPTEYN & PIETER VERLOREN VAN THEMAAT, INTRODUCTION TO THE LAW OF THE EUROPEAN COMMUNITIES 82 *et seq.* (3rd ed., 1998); HENRY G. SCHERMERS & NIELS M. BLOKKER, INTERNATIONAL INSTITUTIONAL LAW § 61 (4th ed., 2003).

[12] *See* Article 24 para.1 and Article 23 para. 1 German Basic Law (Grundgesetz).

[13] KAPTEYN & VERLOREN VAN THEMAAT (note 11), 82 *et seq.*

[14] SCHERMERS & BLOKKER (note 11), § 209: "A rule of thumb is that, while states are free to act as long as this is in accordance with international law ... , international organizations are competent to act only as far as powers have been attributed to them by the member states."

tional law, it is dependent on the will of states.[15] Any autonomous character of decisions by international organizations is not visible.[16]

The question, however, is whether the traditional legal conception is still convincing; can it explain the factual importance of decision-making by international organizations? As can be seen in the case study by Maja Smrkolj and with regard to numerous further examples, the distinction between supranational and international organizations is diminishing. One may thus ask whether the conventional conception of international organizations as such is still adequate and valid.

Moreover, it is worth noticing that there is at least one international organization which still works on the basis of a strict dependence of any activity on the will of the members and which, because of this, is close to failure: the WTO. The insistence of WTO members that the WTO is a "member driven" organization is the principal reason for many of the problems we see in the development of world trade law. The institutional system of the WTO and its entire culture do not fit into an international economic system shaped by globalization. It is obvious that a system built on ideas of the GATT 1947 era is not able to cope with the challenges of today – but this is exactly the situation with regard to the WTO.[17]

2. Necessary Differentiation between Different Types of IOs

As a second point, one may ask whether it is adequate to analyse decision-making in international organizations as such. This comment suggests that, with regard to decision-making, there is no such thing as "the" international organization. Rather, it seems to be necessary to develop a typology of different international organizations and different mechanisms of decision-making. The most important distinction in this regard is of course the one between technical (or special) and political

---

[15] For this predominant view *see, e.g.*, IAN BROWNLIE, PRINCIPLES OF PUBLIC INTERNATIONAL LAW 3 *et seq.* (7th ed., 2008).

[16] Jurisdiction of the Europ. Com. of the Danube, Advisory Opinion, PCIJ Ser. B., No. 14, 64 (1927) (note 10).

[17] For details *see* Debra P. Steger, *The Culture of the WTO: Why it Needs to Change*, 10 JOURNAL OF INTERNATIONAL ECONOMIC LAW 483 *et seq.* (2007); *The Atlantic Council of the United States, Transatlantic Leadership for a New Global Economy*, Policy Paper 2007.

(or general) international organizations.[18] This distinction is not only important because of the different mechanisms of decision-making that are applied within different international organizations, but also concerning questions of legitimacy. It seems to be clear that legitimacy of decision-making in international organizations may not be based exclusively on the concept that it derives from the will of the member states. Instead, it seems necessary to apply more of a functional approach. This does not mean to exclusively apply an output-oriented perspective in order to assess legitimacy. Instead, a pluralistic conception of legitimacy seems to be adequate.[19] However, in order to apply such a pluralistic conception of legitimacy, one needs to closely look at a specific international organization and not to international organizations as such. This is due to the fact that the tasks assigned and fulfilled differ significantly with regard to the various international organizations.

Moreover, in order to adequately analyse decision-making in international organizations it seems to be necessary to take a closer look at the different mechanisms of decision-making that exist. In this regard, one may just mention the consensus principle as opposed to decision by consent, majority voting with or without opting-out procedures and weighted voting.[20] There are always different rationales behind these different mechanisms and thus again different conceptions of legitimacy.

Finally, with regard to the increasing importance of the administration of international organizations – the executive branch – and its role in decision-making, it is also necessary to differentiate between different types of international organizations. This is already indicated by the well-known differentiation between "secretary general" and "director general". There is a long-standing and well-analysed substantial difference with regard to the competences of the secretariat depending on whether the respective chief officer is called "secretary general" or "di-

---

[18] SCHERMERS & BLOKKER (note 11), §§ 63 *et seq.*

[19] For details on the pluralistic concept of legitimacy in general *see, e.g.*, Wolfgang Hoffmann-Riem, *Gesetz und Gesetzesvorbehalt im Umbruch*, 130 ARCHIV DES ÖFFENTLICHEN RECHTS 5, 66 *et seq.* (2005); UTZ SCHLIESKY, SOUVERÄNITÄT UND LEGITIMATION VON HERRSCHAFTSGEWALT – DIE WEITERENTWICKLUNG VON BEGRIFFEN DER STAATSLEHRE UND DES STAATSRECHTS IM EUROPÄISCHEN MEHREBENENSYSTEM 588 *et seq.* (2004).

[20] For the different mechanisms of decision-making *see, e.g.*, SCHERMERS & BLOKKER (note 11), §§ 771 *et seq.*

rector general".[21] Moreover, there are even international organizations that do not list the secretariat as a main organ, *e.g.* the WTO. This of course has important repercussions on the power and the legitimacy of decision-making by the secretariat.

3. The Dualistic Character of Administrative Law of International Organizations

As a further point of comment, some specific aspects concerning decision-making in international organizations as an important element of international administration as such shall be addressed.

As a starting point, it is submitted that in order to assess decision-making in international organizations it is necessary to be precise about the constitutional role we assign to the different organs and sub-organs of international organizations. This of course directly leads to the well-known question whether there is something like a separation of powers doctrine within international institutional law. Without giving a conclusive answer to this hotly contested question,[22] it is submitted that there are quite a few similarities between concepts of national constitutional law concerning the role of the administration and the problems of decision-making in international organizations as highlighted in the two papers. The two most important issues in the regard are, first, the autonomy of the administration, and, second, the differentiation between decision-making with internal and with external effects. Both aspects are important with regard to the so-called dualistic character of administrative law.[23]

As to the first point – the autonomy of administration – it is worth recalling that, from the perspective of domestic constitutional law, administration is more than the branch of government exclusively responsible for the execution of legislative orders. Instead, it is one of the basic ideas of separation of powers to grant every branch of government cer-

---

21 SCHERMERS & BLOKKER (note 11), § 435.

22 Some thoughts on a separation of powers within international organizations are, *e.g.*, formulated by Eckart Klein, *Das Recht der Internationalen Organisationen, in* VÖLKERRECHT, 349 (Graf Vitzthum ed., 2007); *see also* CHRISTOPH MÖLLERS, GEWALTENGLIEDERUNG 253 *et seq.* (2005).

23 On this concept *see* EBERHARD SCHMIDT-AßMANN, DAS ALLGEMEINE VERWALTUNGSRECHT ALS ORDNUNGSIDEE 16 *et seq.* (2nd ed., 2006).

tain autonomy as such. In public international law, this of course directly goes back to the aforementioned concept of international organizations as subjects of international law and the role of the secretariat as the legal representative of an international organization. If one thus recognizes the autonomy of international administration, it is necessary to not only focus on the remaining or diminishing influence of member states in decision-making processes in international organizations, but to ask for truly governance-oriented functions of the international administration. An important element from this perspective – just as in domestic law – could be the legal discussion on public goods, specifically with regard to international organizations and the provision of global public goods.[24]

The second similarity between national and international administrative law concerns the distinction between decision-making with internal and external legal effects. For a long time both national and international law followed the concept of a strict and clear differentiation between law with internal and external effects. Thus, the internal law and decision-making with exclusively internal effects in international organizations was not regarded as being part of public international law as such for a considerable period.[25] Even though this approach is not accepted anymore, some aspects of the distinction remain valid, namely with regard to procedural issues. In this regard it is important to note that the administration not only has responsibilities with regard to individual rights of persons being affected by their decisions and activities, but also concerning the effectiveness and efficiency of its own functioning.[26] These two rationales of administration are usually referred to as the dualistic character of administration. With regard to the internal/external distinction, the dualistic character of administration calls for different standards of procedure of decision-making. In cases where decision-making has external effects on individual rights positions, due process aspects of procedure gain relevance. If the decision-making at issue is only of an internal character, standards of effectiveness and efficiency are of predominant importance. However, whereas it is hard to argue

---

[24] On global public goods *see* comprehensively GLOBAL PUBLIC GOODS – INTERNATIONAL COOPERATION IN THE 21ST CENTURY (Inge Kaul, Isabelle Grundberg & Marc A. Stern eds., 1999); PROVIDING GLOBAL PUBLIC GOODS: MANAGING GLOBALIZATION (Inge Kaul ed., 2003).

[25] For this discussion *see*, *e.g.*, GEORG DAHM, JOST DELBRÜCK & RÜDIGER WOLFRUM, VÖLKERRECHT, vol. I/1, 29 *et seq.* (2nd ed., 1989).

[26] SCHMIDT-AßMANN (note 23), 17 *et seq.*

that individual due process standards apply in a decision-making situation that does not affect individual rights, the principles of effectiveness and efficiency always apply.

The implications of this concept become evident if one takes a look at the analysis of UNHCR's Refugee Status Determination. Maja Smrkolj makes a strong argument on problems of individual due process rights in this regard. However, from a strictly legal point of view, the paper does not identify the individual rights at issue that call for individual due process guarantees. In fact, this could actually be difficult. There are hardly any specific (*i.e.* with the exception of general human rights) individual rights guarantees in public international law for refugees, with the exception of the Refugee Convention.[27] The main question is thus whether UNHCR is bound by the Convention. If this is not the case, it is hard to see how individual rights are affected by UNHCR's Refugee Status Determination. Moreover, even if one is of the opinion that individual rights are affected, it would be necessary to focus not only on due process guarantees, but also to take considerations of effectiveness and efficiency into account.

In sum, it is submitted that a critical analysis of the procedure of decision-making in international organizations has to take into account both sides of the dualistic character of administrative law: its function in disciplining the exercise of public authority, namely with regard to individual rights, but also the importance of an effective and efficient administration.

---

[27] DAHM, DELBRÜCK & WOLFRUM, VÖLKERRECHT, vol. I/2, 191 *et seq.* (2nd ed., 2002).

The Enforcement Authority of International Institutions

By Volker Röben

A. von Bogdandy et al. (eds.), *The Exercise of Public Authority by International Institutions*, Beiträge zum ausländischen öffentlichen Recht und Völkerrecht 210,
DOI 10.1007/978-3-642-04531-8_28,

A. Introduction

I. Implementation and Enforcement

One of the most striking features of international institutional law that emerges from the several case studies collected in this issue is that enforcement authority is now vested in international institutions alongside the more familiar types of public authority almost as a matter of course. Enforcement of international law by international institutions needs to be distinguished from other closely related concepts of public authority that are in turn the subject of closer studies collected in this issue. As discussed by von Bogdandy, Dann and Goldmann,[1] international institutions often dispose of an implementation authority which in turn is subject to a branch of international institutional law. The responsibilities and indeed the authority of international institutions do not stop at the mere implementation of their legal base. However, enforcement involves a categorically different exercise of public authority. It concerns the interaction with another subject of law. Insofar as enforcement essentially empowers an international institution to confront States it deeply interferes with the sovereign's conduct, and its very existence may seem counterintuitive.

II. The Concept of Enforcement by International Institutions

Enforcement aims to ensure effectiveness of the law, primarily involving the exercise of public power. A law-internal perspective of enforcement is possible nevertheless. For enforcement will be subject to legal regulation. Such regulation will constitute the power that may be exercised to react to the possible reaction to the norm violation, and shape the procedure for determining whether there has been a norm violation in the first place, the principles guiding the use of the available enforcement powers. As such, thinking about enforcement is emphatically within the remit of (international) law scholarship.

Enforcement may be defined as public action with the objective of preventing or responding to the violation of a norm. While this definition is inspired by (national) administrative law, it is just as much applicable to public international law. For the definition relates to the concept of

---

1 *See* von Bogdandy, Dann & Goldmann, in this issue.

the rule of law and the normativity of any legal order, including public international law, not to the background of a domestic constitutional system.

However, a number of caveats are in order for the purposes of this paper. Only international institutions are of relevance, not the State, and its inherent enforcement authority over individuals. Quite differently, the prime interest here lies in enforcement action by international institutions against States.

Furthermore, public action needs to be understood not just as legally binding action but in the broad sense of public authority amicable to this project. All action that merely conditions the addressee to comply with the norm in question instead of violating it is also covered.

The objective of enforcement finally needs to be understood specifically. Enforcement closely relates to compliance, which remains the objective of all enforcement in the international realm where punishment has no role. Contra-factual compliance, *i.e.* compliance that would otherwise not occur, will be the result of both the prevention and the repression of norm violation by an act of public authority.

Enforcement as such may be distinguished from compliance control and related terms. The focus of this paper remains on international public authority so that its working definition of enforcement cannot focus on all coordinated, negotiated, assisting or otherwise managerial action, aiming at furthering or controlling compliance with the norms of a given treaty or institutional regime. Such managerial concerns for ensuring compliance are well catered for in the vast and impressive literature on the managerial analysis of international institutions.[2] But, for the reasons set forth in the introductory paper, this project's law-internal concern is primarily with analysing such international public authority the exercise of which triggers specific public law concerns.

III. Objective and Plan of Paper

The case studies of this research project show, however, that the domain of enforcement authority of international institutional law has by now matured to the point that a doctrinal reconstruction along the lines set

---

2 *See* ABRAM CHAYES & ANTONIA HANDLER CHAYES, THE NEW SOVEREIGNTY: COMPLIANCE WITH INTERNATIONAL REGULATORY AGREEMENTS 311 (1995).

forth in the introductory paper[3] appears worthwhile. Our objective is thus modest. First of all it is to provide a stocktaking and systematisation of the bewildering variety of enforcement authority that international institutions wield. It will be argued that a proper systematisation of the enforcement authority of international institutions should encompass at least five elements. The plan of the paper in support of this objective is the following: I will propose to identify several mechanisms of enforcement that each embodies a specific strategy across the several sectors of substantive law and which are put at the disposition of international institutions (B.). I will then examine the addressees of these enforcement mechanisms (C.), the procedures that regulate the application of these mechanisms (D.) as well as institutional issues (E.), and, finally, any principles guiding the allocation and exercise of enforcement authority that can be identified (F.).

Parts B. to F. of the paper are essentially concerned with a doctrinal reconstruction of the legal data at hand. This will not exhaust the subject though. For enforcement authority is a public resource to be spent wisely. Part G. will therefore adopt a governance perspective and undertake to identify criteria that may guide the international legislator in deciding on how to shape the authority to enforce of a given international institution.

In its concluding Part H. the paper will then inquire about the wider ramifications for public international law brought about by the emergence of an institutionalised – a vertical – enforcement dimension that complements traditional horizontal enforcement.

B. Mechanisms of Enforcement

There are several ways doctrinally to reconstruct the data assembled in the various case studies. This paper suggests that the reconstruction be oriented by a typology of enforcement mechanisms. For the purposes of this typology, an enforcement mechanism is characterised by the strategy brought to bear to react to the norm violation and the type of public authority that goes with it. Essentially four mechanisms of enforcement can be distinguished: persuasion (I), incentives and disincentives (II), force (III), sanctions (IV), and quasi-judicial dispute settle-

3 *See* von Bogdandy, Dann & Goldmann, in this issue.

ment (V).[4] The specifically legal quality of the public authority employed to administer these mechanisms matures correspondingly: The persuasion mechanism exclusively relies on the international institution conditioning the addressee, incentives and disincentives additionally change the addressee's legal situation, and both force and sanctions provide for the imposition of new legal obligations on the addressee.

I. Persuasion

International institutions may rely on persuasion to enforce legal obligations. The core strategy here is to persuade the norm addressee to comply with its international legal obligations even though it may not be inclined to do so. Persuasion in this sense will seek to achieve transparency about both treaty demands and the ways to achieve compliance, and it will incidentally determine the question of whether the norm addressee – mostly States – is currently in compliance or not. The assumption is that such transparency is not self-evident, but needs to be constituted by way of a dialogue between the international institution and the norm addressee. The norm addressee will then be asked to submit reports on its national implementing measures to the international institutions in regular intervals, which will be discussed with a view to securing that treaty obligations are complied with. If applicable, the international institution may issue recommendations for any steps needed to be taken to bring the State into compliance, and it may follow up on these recommendations through various means. The public authority that the competent international institution may use in a persuasion context is "soft"; it resides in the loss of prestige for the States that the international institution can bring about by making its findings public.

Persuasion in this sense is probably one of the oldest and, quantitatively speaking, still the most prevalent if not pervasive means of enforcement by international institutions. It can be found across the spectrum of international institutional, as a brief survey touching on the areas of human rights, international peace and security, international environmental law and international economic law will show:

---

[4] Obviously, the terminological designation given to the several mechanisms is not of primary importance and may be subject to debate.

1. Human Rights

Institutionalised human rights treaties extensively provide for enforcement by persuasion. The 1998 ILO Declaration on Fundamental Principles and Rights at Work,[5] the OSCE's High Commissioner on National Minorities,[6] and possibly the OECD's PISA Policy[7] understood as the international assessment of national policy in a human rights sensitive area give a good illustration of this.

2. International Peace and Security

While developed and honed to maturity in the human rights context, persuasion has now become a standard means of enforcement in all areas where States are under an international obligation to take complex implementing action in their national legal system. A powerful example is provided by the numerous resolutions on anti-terrorism of the UN Security Council adopted under Chapter VII UN Charter. These resolutions set forth complex schemes for economic legislation that Member States need to enact in order to cut the funding stream for terrorist activities. To ensure the effectiveness of these substantive resolutions the Security Council has accompanied them with an extensive reporting scheme. States are to report on the implementation of the resolutions' requirements to committees of the Security Council specifically created for that purpose, which will discuss them with State representatives. The committees will be assisted in their task by groups of experts, monitoring developments in the Member States.[8] All of this serves to persuade Member States, in the sense identified above, effectively to comply with the resolutions.

3. International Environmental Law

Other examples for the use of the reporting technique and thus persuasion as an enforcement means are provided by the extensive fabric of in-

---

5 de Wet, in this issue.

6 Farahat, in this issue.

7 von Bogdandy & Goldmann, in this issue.

8 *See* most recently, S/RES/1822 (2008).

ternational environmental law. The FAO Code of Responsible Fisheries is a case in point.[9]

4. *International Economic Law*

Also, as The WTO Committee on Trade in Financial Services illustrates, international economic law employs the mechanisms of persuasion. This Committee provides a forum for Parties to discuss relevant issues of the Agreement on Trade in Services.[10] Such discussion will provide the transparency inducing a State to comply with its obligations under the WTO Agreement. Arguably, the OECD's disciplines for national export credits institutions also belong to the category of persuasion. This flexible non-binding regulatory framework contains procedures of notification and consultation with the OECD in case a State does not want to comply with the regime's substantive provisions.[11] The transparency brought about by these procedures will work not just directly on the State concerned, but it will also work indirectly. For the non-complying State now has to countenance reciprocal non-compliance of other States, triggering a subsidies race which is in no one's interest.

II. Incentives and Disincentives

As several case studies of this project show, international institutional law has moved beyond traditional persuasion-based enforcement. Enforcement may also consist of conditioning the decision-making process of the norm addressee through incentives for norm-compliance and/or disincentives against norm-violation. Such incentives and disincentives will be administered by international institutions unilaterally.

International institutional law has given shape to at least two groups of incentive-based enforcement mechanisms. A first group is composed of treaty based compliance control regimes, which primarily employ positive incentives (1). A second group is composed of liability regimes (2).

---

9 *See* Friedrich, in this issue.

10 *See* Windsor, in this issue.

11 Andrew Moravcsik, *Disciplining Trade Finance: The OECD Export Credit Arrangement*, 43 INTERNATIONAL ORGANIZATION 173 (1989).

1. Compliance Control Regimes

Major multilateral treaties increasingly provide not just for substantive regulation of the matter at hand but also for the enforcement of these provisions through elaborate compliance regimes. These compliance regimes essentially set forth incentives for compliance, removing the causes for non-compliance with the treaty's provisions. These incentives may comprise technical, economic and other assistance, which is administered by an international institution.[12]

Such non-compliance procedures have become a standard of international environmental law in particular,[13] but other treaties designed to protect an international public good – such as non-proliferation etc. – will now also comprise such a compliance regime. A hugely influential model for such a compliance control regime remains the Non-Compliance Procedure under the Montreal Protocol to the Vienna Convention on the Protection of the Ozone Layer.[14] This procedure allows Parties to apply to the Implementation Committee for technical and economic support in the fulfilment of their treaty obligations to phase out ozone depleting substances.[15] It is characteristic that a potentially non-complying Party itself but also the Protocol's Secretariat may seize the Implementation Committee. The Kyoto-Protocol on Climate Change essentially copies this procedure. The Facilitative Branch of the KP's Compliance Committee is competent for handling cases where a Party requires and requests international compliance assistance of a technical or financial nature.[16]

---

[12] *See* Jutta Brunnée, *Enforcement Mechanisms in International Law and International Environmental Law*, 3 ENVIRONMENTAL LAW NETWORK INTERNATIONAL REVIEW 3, 11 (2005) ("non-complying parties are most likely to be states with genuine capacity limitations").

[13] *See* Jan Klabbers, *Compliance Procedures*, *in* INTERNATIONAL ENVIRONMENTAL LAW 995, 990 (2007) (giving examples). *See also* Friedrich, in this issue (considering Implementation Assistance provided by FAO to States under the Code of Conduct for Responsible Fisheries).

[14] *See* Jan Klabbers, *Compliance Procedures*, *in* INTERNATIONAL ENVIRONMENTAL LAW 995 (Daniel Bodansky, Jutta Brunnée & Ellen Hey eds., 2007).

[15] However, the threat of sanctions such as export restrictions is not excluded should the Party fail to meet the commitments indicated by the MOP, *see* Klabbers (note 14), at 997.

[16] Láncos, in this isssue.

2. Liability Regimes

Any liability regime allows to react to a norm violation and to make good any consequences of such a violation through compensation of the victim. Beyond this remedial action effect the availability of a liability regime will also have the effect of preventing norm violations in the first place. The certain expectation that damages will have to be paid will act as a disincentive to violating the norm in the first place.

General international law provides for damages through, *i.e.*, the law of State responsibility. The law of State responsibility applies to all types of obligations under international law. It provides that the violation of any primary obligation incumbent on a State will trigger a set of secondary obligations including damages for that State. The right to claim damages lies with the State to which the primary obligation was owed. The law of State responsibility is of a general nature. The fact that it applies across all international law entails a lack of specificity leaving room for more specialized regimes adapted to the circumstances of a given area of law.

Any specialized regime will require an international institution administering it.[17] The UN Claims Commission was essentially set up to deal with Iraq's liability arising from its internationally unlawful invasion of Iraq.[18] The International Commission on Holocaust Era Insurance Claims (ICHEIC) may also be seen as a case in point as this institution took it upon itself to seek to enforce secondary (monetary) claims of individuals for primary human rights atrocities committed during the Holocaust.[19] Other international institutions such as the World Bank are empowered to insert provisions for damages into their contracts with States.

---

[17] In the recent past, several more such regimes have come into existence. A recent example from 2005 is the so-called Liability Annex (VI) to the 1991 Protocol on Environmental Protection in Antarctica, which, *e.g.*, puts the Antarctic Treaty Secretariat in charge of the contingency funds. *See* D. J. Bederman & S. P. Keskar, *Antarctic Environmental Liability: The Stockholm Annex and Beyond*, 19 EMORY INTERNATIONAL LAW REVIEW 1383 (2005).

[18] *See* Less, in this issue.

[19] This is, of course, a somewhat idiosyncratic way of looking at the mandate of the ICHEI. For a detailed analysis, *see* Less, in this issue.

III. Legal Sanctions

The incentive-based mechanisms discussed are qualitatively improved upon in terms of effective legal enforcement whenever genuine sanctions lie against a State in violation of its treaty obligations. There may be different definitions and understandings of sanctions. But, in the context of this paper, sanction should be understood to involve the detrimental change in the addressee's legal situation brought about in response to the latter's prior action. The case studies bear out that international institutions apply two forms of sanctions. One is that the Party concerned is put under additional substantive obligations. The other type of sanction involves removal of certain of the concerned Party's rights and privileges. International institutions may find the legal base for their sanctioning decisions either in the constitutive treaty (1) or in a contractual arrangement (2).

1. Constitutive Treaties: The Case of the Kyoto Protocol with Marrakech Accords

This novel concept of enforcement through legal sanctions is now being realised as part of the international climate change regime, which is based on the UN Framework Convention and the Kyoto Protocol (KP). In 2007 the KP's Meeting of Parties (MOP) adopted a set of rules implementing the KP's provisions. These so-called Marrakech Accords[20] not only flesh out the emission trading provisions of the Protocol but more importantly, they also stipulate an innovative enforcement mechanism including sanctions of both types identified above. The Accords provide for an autonomous administrative-law style procedure conducted by a newly created Enforcement Branch leading to binding decisions:[21]

Under the Marrakech Accords, questions of non-compliance can be raised by a Party with respect to itself, or by any Party with respect to another, provided the question is supported by corroborating information. The newly created Enforcement Branch of the KP's Compliance Committee will conduct a preliminary investigation within three weeks

---

[20] Available at: http://www.unfccc.de/cop7/documents/accords_draft.pdf. The legal status of the Marrakech Accords is a decision of the COP/MOP, not a separate international treaty. This does not, however, affect its bite since the Accords will be treated as having the same legal quality as the KP itself.

[21] For discussion, *see* Láncos, in this issue.

of the submission to determine whether the question is supported by sufficient information, is not *de minimis* or ill-founded, and is based on the requirements of the Protocol. Institutionally, the Enforcement Branch is a sub-organ of the Compliance Committee, which is itself an organ of the Meeting of Parties, but with limited membership. If it decides to proceed, the Branch may consider information from expert review teams staffed by experts serving in a personal capacity (ERTs), the Party that submitted the reference, reports from treaty bodies including the Facilitative Branch of the Compliance Committee, as well as from the Party concerned. After finding a case of non-compliance, the Enforcement Branch may decide on the consequences of that breach of treaty law, and also follow through on that decision (*vollziehen*). The powers of the Enforcement Branch comprise both forms of legal sanctions identified above. In case that a Party does not meet its substantive GHG emissions reduction obligations, the Committee may decide to increase the concerned Party's GHG emission reduction obligations by up to a third for the subsequent reduction period. The Committee's decision changes the concerned Party's substantive obligations under the treaty. It does not constitute physical force nor any other extra-legal means of pressure. But it is automatic, not subject to agreement by the concerned Party. This is a case of sanctioning by imposition of additional obligations. In case a Party does not fulfil its procedural obligations under the emissions trading scheme of the KP, the Committee may decide to exclude that Party from further participating in the scheme. This is sanctioning by removal of a privilege or right. The Party concerned has the right to be heard by the Enforcement Branch, and it may challenge any decision by the Enforcement Branch before the KP-MOP. However, the review is for procedural errors of the Branch only.

The KP Compliance Committee's enforcement mechanism is the most advanced and complex realisation of the "sanctions" type enforcement mechanism to-date. Similar albeit less advanced systems have been inserted in other environmental treaties.[22] A somewhat less complex mechanism was realised under the CITES regime. The power of the CITES' Standing Committee to curtail a Party's right to trade in certain species is nevertheless an instance of a legal sanction for non-comp-

---

22 The procedure established under the Cartagena Protocol on Biosafety includes rules on the admissibility of submissions, admissible information, and on the measures that can be taken against the Party concerned. *See* Doc. UNEP/CBD/BS/COP-MOP/1/15 (14 April 2004), Annex.

liance.[23] And UNESCO, an institution charged with the protection of the global cultural heritage, may remove a site from the coveted World Heritage List that it maintains if the requirements for such designation are no longer met.[24]

2. *Contractual: The World Bank*

Sanctions in the above sense may also be employed by international institutions on the basis of a contract. The World Bank may enforce the contractual duties of the recipient State through sanctions in the shape of the suspension or even termination of the financing of projects. Unilateral and bilateral rules regulate in detail, under which circumstances the Bank can suspend or cancel its financial support for a project.[25] But the Bank can also declare the acceleration of its payment of dues or even demand a refund of already paid sums. These sanctions will be used to enforce the standards on corrupt, fraudulent or collusive behaviour on the side of the recipient or the performance requirements that the recipient is under. While based on a contract, such sanctions can be considered to form part of public authority for the World Bank may impose them unilaterally.

IV. Force

Ultimately, international institutions may be empowered to use force to enforce certain international law. Force here is physical power. In a world of sovereign States such a stark mechanism must be the exception, but the UN Charter does provide for it. Chapter VII UN Charter authorizes the Security Council to take action including force to ensure that a Member State respects its obligation under the Charter, and in particular Art. 2(4) UN Charter. Doctrinally, the public authority of the Council legally to decide on the use of force is to be distinguished from the actual exercise of this force, which may be carried out be the Council itself (Art. 43 UN Charter) or by States acting pursuant to its authorization.

---

23 *See* Fuchs, in this issue.

24 *See* Zacharias, in this issue.

25 General Conditions IBRD, Art. VII; also OP 13.50.

The Security Council may make use of its powers only pursuant to a well-defined procedure with important voting rules, namely the veto of one of the permanent five members. While often considered an obstructive element to the effective functioning of the Charter system it can also be seen as an important constraint on the very broad power of an international institution. Additionally, certain principles underlie and harness the use of the force-enforcement mechanism by the Security Council. The use of force by the Council is to be proceeded by non-forcible economic and other sanctions and the use of positive incentives for the State to comply with its obligations under the Charter.[26] The Security Council also emphasizes the need for a negotiated solution to any crisis, involving the groupings of the most interested States and any regional organisations in the efforts to resolve the crisis peacefully. However, the background of such negotiations is formed by the fact that the Security Council can resort to the use of force if it considers doing so necessary.

V. (Quasi-)Judicial Dispute Settlement

Judicial dispute settlement is an enforcement mechanism in its own right. The central enforcement effect lies in the finding of a breach of international law by a court, resulting in a considerable loss of prestige as well as the obligation to correct the illegal behaviour. Factors determining the effectiveness of this mechanism are a court with mandatory jurisdiction and the power of an international institution unilaterally to seize the court. Examples are far and few between. The example of European integration demonstrates this amply with the European Court of Justice's enjoying mandatory jurisdiction over cases involving EU law and the European Commission being empowered to seize the Court in any instance of a Member State violating its obligations under the EC treaty. The International Tribunal for the Law of the Sea has mandatory jurisdiction over disputes involving the Deep Seabed Authority under UNCLOS Part XI on Deep Seabed Mining.[27] Otherwise, the WTO through its Dispute Settlement Body and also ITLOS rely on decentralized enforcement, however, in that a Party to the treaty needs to seize the court.

---

[26] *See* Volker Röben, *Managing Risks to Global Stability*, *in* INTERNATIONAL LAW TODAY: NEW CHALLENGES AND THE NEED FOR REFORM? 51 (Doris König, Peter-Tobias Stoll, Volker Röben & Nele Matz-Lück eds., 2008).

[27] *See* Wolfrum, in this issue.

It is probably not too much of an exaggeration to say that the effectiveness of international judicial enforcement takes a quantum leap whenever private actors have access to an international court or tribunal. Such access may be of a direct or indirect variety as is the case with the referral procedure (Art. 234 EC). Private parties' access rights are very rare, again with the exception of the EC and the deep seabed mining regime of UNCLOS.

C. Addressees of Enforcement Action by International Institutions

The several case studies collected in this volume demonstrate that the panoply of addressees of enforcement action by international institutions reaches from States (I) to individuals (II).

I. States

The multi-level governance model is based on the interaction between international institutions and sovereign States. International institutions rapidly emerge as policy-makers, rule-makers, and rule-implementers. Their prime interlocutors remain the sovereign States, which are to domestically further implement and enforce the measures adopted by international institutions. Consistently with this model, international institutions need to address their enforcement action to States.

But, international institutions may also reach through the sovereign shell in certain instances and address a range of sub-state actors and institutions as well. For instance, under the OCED's export credits discipline, those sub-state institutions that manage "official support" for export credits and credit guarantees as well as so-called tied aid are addressees.

II. Individuals and Other Entities

Several case studies of this project demonstrate that the decisions of international institutions increasingly reach through to individuals. International institutions may attribute to them a certain status or right, such as the recognition of a refugee status by UNHCR[28] or the allocation of a trade mark by WIPO.[29] So-called listing-procedures trigger legal consequences for the listed entities and individuals. The UN Security Council's Al-Qaida and Taliban Sanctions Committee is the striking case in point.[30] Multinational enterprises are the object of certain OECD-Guidelines[31] and non-governmental organisations engaged in fishing of the FAO Code of Conduct for Responsible Fisheries.[32]

These are, however, decisions of a primary nature, *i.e.* they determine rights and obligations of individuals and other entities. Enforcement of this primary law is left to the States, which are placed under an international law obligation to take any requisite enforcement action towards their nationals.[33] The framework for international enforcement is complemented by state-internal enforcement, the machinery of which may have to be set up in the first place by each Party. Obviously, Parties will at some point direct their attention to the internal rule of law institutions in place in each State Party. The role of the international institution is restricted to providing technical assistance and coordination concerning the domestic enforcement. Such is the role of the WIPO Enforcement Committee.[34] Under traditional international institutional law this was considered a bright line rule stipulating a limit to the potential reach of international institutions.

However, on closer inspection this may well be an overly formalistic view of things. Clearly, individuals will at least be indirectly affected whenever the relevant international institution in turn enforces the domestic enforcement obligations incumbent on the State. As a result,

---

28 *See* Smrkolj, in this issue.

29 *See* Kaiser, in this issue.

30 *See* Feinäugle, in this issue.

31 *See* Schuler, in this issue.

32 *See* Friedrich, in this issue.

33 For instance, international registration by WIPO bestows upon the applicant the exclusive right to prevent unauthorized third parties from using the trademark in the territories of the designated contracting parties; the enforcement of which right, however, would have to take place in the national courts.

34 *See* Kaiser, in this issue.

questions regarding fair hearing and legal protection for individuals become pertinent from the enforcement angle as well. The received (continental) doctrine of administrative law holds lessons as to how to tackle these questions short of, in particular judicial remedy, which may not always be an option.[35]

D. Procedure

All of the above enforcement mechanisms require that the international institution completes a certain procedure before being allowed to apply. The institution will follow a procedure that has at covers at least the following five elements: clarification of the applicable law, implicit or explicit determination of non-compliance,[36] the decision on the consequences of that finding, the application of this decision, and follow-up.

Additionally, a review procedure may be provided for. Conceptually speaking, the international institution's decision on the enforcement action may be subject to an administrative or even judicial review, which may be internal or external to the institution. The several case studies of this project demonstrate that enforcement mechanisms are indeed increasingly subject to review of one type or another. The World Bank inspection panel, Interpol's control commission,[37] and the OECD-guidelines on corporate social responsibility[38] for instance foresee the submission of individual complaints by external actors. In most instances the institution's general review mechanisms will also cover the institution's enforcement action to the extent that internal rules and guidelines provide so. Any such review serves to limit the enforcement power of international institutional and therefore is functionally quite distinct from the use of (quasi-)judicial review as an enforcement mechanism.

But the KP system envisages a specialised procedure for the review of any enforcement measures taken. Under this system, Parties who feel they have been denied due process will have the right to appeal a non-

---

[35] *See* Feinäugle, in this issue.

[36] It is obvious that the mere fact that an international institution finds a State to be in violation of its international obligations will in itself often enforce that obligation.

[37] *See* Schöndorf-Haubold, in this issue.

[38] *See* Schuler, in this issue.

compliance determination to the MOP.[39] The enforcement branch's decision will stand pending an appeal, and it may be overturned only by a three-fourths majority vote of the MOP. If a Party's eligibility to participate in the Protocol's three flexibility mechanisms has been suspended, there are expedited procedures for reinstatement.

While varying in degree across the several areas of law referenced in this project, it can safely be stated that States increasingly bind enforcement by international institutions to judicial or administrative control and review. This is not the classic inter-state dispute settlement machinery epitomized by the International Court of Justice. Rather it is a matter of devising specialized procedures and organisational structures. The procedures will be the more formal the more effective the enforcement authority to be controlled is to the point of including (quasi)judicial elements. The increase in effective and justiciable enforcement authority vested in international institutions, by the same token, changes the overall gestalt of the international institutions concerned.

E. Organisation

Effective enforcement of international law and the rise of international institutionalism are two concepts that are inexorably intertwined. Effective enforcement requires independent actors – an international institution – which can handle the complex legal and factual issues arising in an independent and neutral manner. The increasingly complex enforcement mechanisms presuppose the existence of institutions with a concomitant level of organisational complexity. Thus, legal sanctions cannot be operated by States acting either individually or in ad-hoc cooperation with other States. Rather they can only be applied by an organisationally differentiated body such as the Enforcement Branch of the Kyoto Protocol.

Effective enforcement mechanisms presuppose an organisationally differentiated international institution for their functioning, but they do not necessarily require an international organisation. While it is true that force can be exercised only by the UN – the archetype of an international organisation – it is equally true that the Meeting of Parties of the KP can take legal sanctions against Parties. Importantly, this latter institution had both the ability and flexibility to *develop* an organisa-

[39] Decision 24/CP.7 Annex, Art. XV.

tional set-up commensurate to sanctions as a new enforcement mechanism not provided for under the treaty.[40]

In this respect, a number of models emerge from the State practice as evidenced by the case studies of this project. At the one end, a fully centralised set up marked by institutional autonomy can be conceived. It would comprise a specialised limited membership body which can examine cases of non-compliance of its own motion and take relevant action, as required. The body would have the right of initiating the enforcement procedures, or such right of initiative would be vested in another body or organ of the international institution. Finally, review of the enforcement action taken, if any, would again be conducted within the institution. The Kyoto/Marrakech system comes closest to this model. The other end of conceivable organisational set ups is marked by decentralisation where most of these functions are entrusted to States, acting individually or jointly.

Several intermediate stages between these two extremes are conceivable and realised in practice. In particular, there can be lateral linkage between centralised and decentralised organisational elements. One example of such a solution is FAO and its voluntary Code of Responsible Fisheries (CCFR). The norms of the CCRF partake in the decentralised enforcement mechanism foreseen, *e.g.*, in the UN Fish Stocks Agreement (FSA).[41] Since FSA contains an obligation to apply "generally recommended international minimum standards for the responsible conduct of fishing operations" through cooperation in regional fisheries management organisations, this can be understood as a reference or linkage to norms outlined in the CCRF. Another instance of such lateral enforcement by another institution is the European Union's basing its admission of new Member States on the recommendations of the OSCE High Commissioner on Minorities.[42] Fitting enforcement powers and organisational structure of the international administration is a matter of institutional choice.

---

40 Decision 25/CP.7 plus annex, adopted at the eighth plenary meeting of the Conference of the Parties to the UNFCCC (Doc. FCCC/CP/2001/13/Add.3 [21 January 2002], at 64-77). Similarly, the Montreal Protocol's non-compliance procedure was adopted by that Protocol's MOP (Doc. UNEP/OzL.Pro.10/9 [3 December 1998], Annex II).

41 *See* Friedrich, in this issue.

42 *See* Farahat, in this issue.

F. Principles

Enforcement by international institutions against States is in need of legitimacy. Issues of legitimacy become more pressing in proportion to the "degree of formality and the autonomy of international officials."[43] Effective enforcement arguably involves the highest degree of formality and autonomy of international officials on all categories of international institutional decision-making. Consistently, regardless of the classic State-consent reasoning, the legitimacy of effective enforcement authority including sanctions wielded by international institutions vis-à-vis States is now perceived to require the respect of certain principles. Among these principles are adequate procedural safeguards and defence rights for States in the original proceeding as well as a quasi-judicial review of the institution's decisions.

The case studies collected here bear out this point. This is clearly demonstrated by the deep seabed mining provisions of UNCLOS,[44] and also by the KP system for enforcing States Parties' GHG emission reduction obligations.[45] And the enforcement of international law against States as per KP is circumscribed by strict procedures both of an administrative and a quasi-judicial type that will tie the discretion of the international officials put in charge of the enforcement machinery.[46] This applies both to the enforcement action directed against States and against individuals. The enforcement of international law against individuals per UN Security Council resolutions calls for ever improving protection for the targeted individual and other entities against abuse.

G. Criteria for the Design of Enforcement Mechanisms

While persuasion used to be the only enforcement mechanism for a long time, modern treaties increasingly provide for incentives, disincentives, force, and legally binding sanctions. Such a development might

---

[43] Daniel C. Esty, *Good Governance at the Supranational Scale: Globalizing Administrative Law*, 115 YALE LAW JOURNAL 1490, 1510 (2006).

[44] *See* Wolfrum, in this issue.

[45] *See* Láncos, in this issue.

[46] Olav Schram Stokke, Jon Hovi & Geir Ulfstein, *Introduction and Main Findings*, *in* IMPLEMENTING THE CLIMATE CHANGE REGIME 1, 11 (Olav Schram Stokke & Geir Ulfstein eds., 2005); Láncos, in this issue.

seem counterintuitive to the received notions of legal sovereignty, for, clearly, providing an international institution with the power to enforce international law through sanctions reaches deep into national sovereignty of States subject to it. The provision of effective enforcement is a matter inherently in need of a justifying rationale; put differently, enforcement raises governance issues. First of these issues, enforcement makes sense only if compliance by States with their international obligations is not assumed, which was a central tenet of international law scholarship for a long time.[47] The more realistic worldview reflected in the burgeoning literature on compliance control/enforcement implicitly acknowledges the increasing depth of international law and the fact that international norms will not always stipulate the course of conduct that States would wish to adopt anyway. A further consideration is that all the models that can be chosen from are clearly identified. It is a noble task of legal scholarship to order the mass of legal provisions at hand at any time.[48] At best, this effort of reconstruction will yield a consistent structure storing innovative as well as time-tested concepts and model solutions that are potentially "horizontally" relevant for many if not all areas of law. Parts B. to F. of the paper were devoted to constructing such a contemporary model of the enforcement authority vested in international institutions. Finally, one will need to look for criteria for evaluating the several models and the respective advantages and disadvantages that they present in deciding on the best fit between abstract model solution and the matter at hand.[49]

---

[47] This may still explain much of the workings of some of the most effective international institutions such as Interpol (*see* Bettina Schöndorf-Haubold, in this issue). Given the strong preference of competent national authorities for cooperating with each other through Interpol, the chance of being factually barred from further cooperation arguably makes any formal enforcement of the cooperative requirements superfluous.

[48] EBERHARD SCHMIDT-AßMANN, DAS ALLGEMEINE VERWALTUNGSRECHT ALS ORDNUNGSIDEE (2nd ed., 2004); *see also* Eberhard Schmidt-Aßmann, *Die Herausforderung der Verwaltungsrechtswissenschaft durch die Internationalisierung der Verwaltungsbeziehungen*, 45 DER STAAT 315 (2006). The present paper owes much to this publication, which is itself firmly rooted in the German administrative law tradition. This assumes a primarily inductive, reality-driven reasoning, while complementarily inductive, constitutional-law driven reasoning is not excluded *per se*.

[49] On the methodology applied here, *see* ADRIAN VERMEULE, MECHANISMS OF DEMOCRACY: INSTITUTIONAL DESIGN WRIT SMALL (2007).

Parts B. to F. having laid the ground, Part G. will now undertake to identify criteria for the design of the enforcement mechanism proper for the substantive law regime at hand. Essentially two such criteria may be conceived of. One criterion is the legal qualification of the standards (I). A second, explanatorily more powerful criterion is the complexity of the cooperation intended (II).

I. Legal Qualification of Substantive Standards?

Intuitively, one would assume that the legal qualification of the substantive standards controls the choice of the enforcement mechanism. However, no strong correlation between the two can be observed in practice, as the examples of the non-binding Codex Alimentarius being enforced by binding decisions of the WTO DSB[50] and of non-binding FAO Code of Fisheries being enforced laterally[51] amply illustrate.

II. The Complexity of the Cooperation Intended

Mere legal analysis will not do the job. Rather, one needs to venture into adjacent disciplines such as economic theory. The economic literature on enforcement of international law redirects attention to the fact that the design of international institutions ultimately is best explained as a result of the cooperation of States. Or, in other words, institutions serve the cooperative needs of the principals, *i.e.* States.[52] Economic theory informs us that if States truly want to make their cooperation work, they need effective enforcement, containing at least these three elements: verifiable information, credibility and potency.[53] An effective en-

---

50 *See* Pereira, in this issue.

51 *See* Friedrich, in this issue.

52 *See, e.g.*, Duncan Snidal, Barbara Koremenos & Charles Lipson, *The Rational Design of International Institutions*, 55 INTERNATIONAL ORGANIZATION 761 (2001). I shall follow these assumptions for the purpose of this paper making abstraction from the rich literature on the identity and aspirations of institutions.

53 *See, e.g.*, Scott Barrett, *An Economic Theory of International Environmental Law*, *in* INTERNATIONAL ENVIRONMENTAL LAW 231, 249-52 (Daniel Bodansky, Jutta Brunnée & Ellen Hey eds., 2007).

forcement regime also has to meet certain requirements of legitimacy and acceptability. They relate particularly to institutionalised processes of decision-making including the dispute settlement subject to procedural guarantees and certain organisational standards.

Economic theory of law would furthermore point out that effective enforcement will deter States from norm violation in the first place.[54] Or, put differently, effective enforcement being in place will make it more likely that norms are complied with in the first place, making use of the enforcement mechanism superfluous. States would want to ensure compliance in this way with norms that legally protect areas of cooperation to which they attach particular importance and which require significant change in behaviour. In other words, the greater the value of a specific cooperation the greater the likelihood that States will install effective enforcement mechanisms "to make the deal stick".[55] Occasional enforcement would then have a normative effect of its own, stabilizing the primary norm by ensuring that it is internalised by the addressee(s).

It is thus the type, intensity, and complexity of the cooperation reflected in the primary standards that matters most. Climate change serves as an illustration. Any effort to protect the climate requires that each State needs to make considerable investments. Such cooperation will need to be protected by enforceable law.

Of course, there are also limits to the usefulness of this push for effective enforcement. These limits result from the need to strive for universality of international law-backed cooperation. Achieving such universality or at least the participation of the greatest number of States possibly requires more than simply effective enforcement through sanctions. It requires most often enforcement through positive incentives. For the reasons set out above, such incentives are the instrument of choice whenever lack of capabilities is the primary reason why States or a group of States cannot meet their international obligations.[56] Consis-

---

[54] *See* Scott Barrett, *An Economic Theory of International Environmental Law, in* INTERNATIONAL ENVIRONMENTAL LAW 231, 252 (Daniel Bodansky, Jutta Brunnée & Ellen Hey eds., 2007).

[55] *See* Joseph Weiler, *The European Court of Justice in the Arena of Political Integration*, 31 JOURNAL OF COMMON MARKET STUDIES 417 (1993).

[56] This implies a matter of public choice. The involvement of many particularly many developing countries in the treaty regime may have to be traded off with the set up of an effective system of sanctions approved by a smaller group of states. Of course, the trade off may change over time as the system matures.

tently, the most recent enforcement systems to be operated by international institutions contain both sanctions and incentives.

H. What Enforcement Tells Us about International Law

On the basis of the legal data assembled in this issue, the domain of enforcement can be considered a viable part of international institutional law across its several substantive areas. This legal data on enforcement can be fitted into a general doctrinal reconstruction resting on three elements: the several mechanisms of enforcement, each mechanism embodying a specific strategy of reacting to a norm violation and bringing about compliance (persuasion, incentives and disincentives, force, and sanctions), the procedures and the organisation of the international institution applying the enforcement mechanism(s), and the potential addressees of this public authority.

This identification of the legal structure of enforcement vested in international institutions serves the rationale of any "*Allgemeines Verwaltungsrecht*" and more specifically the idea of a consistent system, *Ordnungsidee*, which is to systematize the several specific solutions, serve as "storage" for solutions implemented, and allow for the comparison between them so as to guide the search for the best solution in future instances. Given the twin concerns of effectiveness and respect for sovereign sensibilities, the design of the enforcement powers of a given international institution will have be tailor-made. The search for such a design may be aided and inspired by the models that have been implemented in practice. Of particular relevance in this respect may in the future be the models of the KP and the WTO DSB that serve institutionalised treaty regimes through which the international community administers global public goods.

But the chapter "enforcement" of international institutional law also goes a long way towards strengthening the publicness of public international law of which it is part and parcel. For, the publicness of public international law and the very quality of public international law as a legal order can be considered to hinge on its at least occasional enforceability. While it is true that law (including public international law) is motivational in its own right, lack of at least occasional contra-factual enforcement of the law will undermine the belief in the law as binding prescript and thus the very underpinning of any legal order,[57] weakening the contribution that international law can make to global governance.

As an essentially horizontal legal order, international law traditionally provides for enforcement mechanisms adapted to its horizontal structure. The law of State responsibility serves as an example. International institutional law now adds vertical enforcement to the traditional horizontally operating mechanisms. In small albeit growing segments, international law can now be vertically enforced by international institutions vis-à-vis States. International environmental law and international economic law may be considered the most innovative references ("*Referenzsysteme*") in this respect.

57 NIKLAS LUHMANN, DAS RECHT DER GESELLSCHAFT (2004).

The Enforcement Authority of International Institutions – Some Remarks and Suggestions for Further Analysis

Comment by Dirk Hanschel

A. Overview

The article by Volker Röben gives a good account of the enforcement authority in various institutional contexts, drawing from examples in the fields of human rights, international peace and security, and, in particular, international economic and environmental law which display the most innovative cases. The use of enforcement mechanisms is explained as an exercise of public authority and thus an expression of the publicness of international law, which is illustrated by various case studies from this volume. Hence, the analysis is rooted within the research agenda of this book and adds an important dimension to it. This comment follows the course of Röben's argument and deals with the various sections of his article (B – H).

A. von Bogdandy et al. (eds.), *The Exercise of Public Authority by International Institutions*, Beiträge zum ausländischen öffentlichen Recht und Völkerrecht 210, DOI 10.1007/978-3-642-04531-8_29, © Springer-Verlag Berlin Heidelberg 2010

B. Mechanisms of Enforcement

In looking at the various mechanisms of enforcement, the article convincingly differentiates between persuasion, incentives and disincentives, legal sanctions, force and (quasi-)judicial dispute settlement. The concept of enforcement is explained in the context of the related notions of compliance control and implementation. Röben claims that enforcement "involves a categorically different exercise of public authority" as compared to implementation, because it "concerns the interaction with another subject of law". He stresses that his analysis cannot "focus on all coordinated, negotiated, assisting or otherwise managerial action, aiming at furthering or controlling compliance with the norms of a given treaty or institutional regime". Notwithstanding this fact, the wide array of enforcement mechanisms covered in the article may suggest that enforcement as an expression of public authority is the central means of establishing compliance, be it legal compliance (*i.e.* the existence of domestic rules corresponding to an international obligation) or factual compliance (*i.e.* the correspondence of a factual domestic situation with an international obligation).[1] The direct nexus to compliance is also reflected by the fact that in the section on incentives and disincentives the author deals with compliance control regimes. One might add that compliance does not usually occur by coincidence, but is achieved through active measures of domestic implementation and, if necessary, international enforcement.[2] However, compliance may also exist by

---

[1] I have made this argument elsewhere, *see* Dirk Hanschel, VERHANDLUNGSLÖSUNGEN IM UMWELTVÖLKERRECHT 61 *et seq.* (2003). For the distinction of different forms of compliance *see*, for example, Kal Raustiala & David G. Victor, *Conclusions, in* THE IMPLEMENTATION AND EFFECTIVENESS OF INTERNATIONAL ENVIRONMENTAL COMMITMENTS: THEORY AND PRACTICE, 661 (David G. Victor, Kal Raustiala & Eugene B. Skolnikoff eds., 1998). A further distinction can be made between procedural and substantive compliance, *see* Edith Brown Weiss, *Compliance with International Standards: Environmental Case Studies – Remarks,* THE AMERICAN SOCIETY OF INTERNATIONAL LAW – PROCEEDINGS of the 89th Annual Meeting 212 (1995).

[2] Building on the definition of enforcement used in this article, one might understand implementation as an autonomous process of ensuring compliance by enacting rules and policies, whereas enforcement tries to ensure compliance vis-à-vis another subject of law. However, implementing rules and policies are usually addressed to or at least affect other legal subjects within the national legal order, as well (in particular individuals), so that the distinction between the two terms becomes more difficult.

mere coincidence, be it because the appropriate rule or factual situation within a state precedes the corresponding international obligation, or be it because the rule or situation was prompted by other factors (*e.g.* domestic policy considerations, private activities or changes of the economic situation within a country). In this context, Röben aptly points to the tools of counterfactual analysis which may help to filter out such cases of non-causal compliance.[3]

The analysis suggests that enforcement may be defined as "public action with the objective of preventing or responding to the violation of a norm". One might add that, while enforcement usually constitutes a reaction to non-compliance, it does not always presuppose a violation. In areas such as international environmental law or human rights law, the term "violation" is sometimes carefully avoided, since it is not deemed useful to put states in the pillory where non-compliance happens due to inadvertence or lack of capacity.[4] The notion of non-compliance entails the advantage that it can capture a variety of reasons for non-observance as well as various degrees of non-compliance.[5] It may also provide an indicator for the appropriateness and legitimacy of the resulting type of enforcement action. Still, a violation will be the most common cause of enforcement.

The different forms of enforcement are well illustrated by pertinent examples from the various case studies in this volume. Hence, the analysis provides an important cross-cutting function. The aspect of persuasion which the author aptly describes as "probably one of the oldest and, quantitatively speaking, still the most prevalent if not pervasive means of enforcement by international institutions" could be further elaborated by looking at negotiation analysis.[6] This might generate additional insight on how to distinguish between modes of arguing and bargaining, the former referring to persuasion, the latter to strategic behavior,

---

[3] Peter M. Haas, Robert O. Keohane & Marc A. Levy, INSTITUTIONS FOR THE EARTH. SOURCES OF EFFECTIVE INTERNATIONAL ENVIRONMENTAL PROTECTION 18 *et seq.* (1993).

[4] *See*, for example, Rüdiger Wolfrum, MEANS OF ENSURING COMPLIANCE WITH AND ENFORCEMENT OF INTERNATIONAL ENVIRONMENTAL LAW 31 *et seq.* (1999).

[5] On the adequate reaction to different degrees of non-compliance *see* Abram Chayes & Antonia Handler Chayes, *On Compliance,* 47 INTERNATIONAL ORGANIZATION 198 (1993).

[6] *See*, for example, Howard Raiffa, NEGOTIATION ANALYSIS. THE SCIENCE AND ART OF COLLABORATIVE DECISION MAKING (2003).

and how this distinction correlates with social science concepts regarding the interaction between institutional design and negotiation processes (such as constructivist versus rational choice theories).[7] Looking at these concepts would require venturing into neighboring disciplines, but might provide interesting lessons for legal scholarship.

Röben goes on to distinguish between incentives and disincentives on the one hand and sanctions on the other. One might also consider classifying disincentives (*e.g.* by way of removal of advantages or privileges) as negative sanctions. This is illustrated by the fact that the notion of sanctions is, according to the author, "understood to involve the detrimental change in the addressee's legal situation brought about in response to the latter's prior action", either by imposing additional substantive obligations onto the party or by removing certain rights and privileges. In the latter case the distinction between sanctions and disincentives becomes blurred. While positive sanctions are potentially at odds with sovereignty, negative sanctions or disincentives are usually less intrusive when they merely take away privileges or rights having been conferred upon a party through an international agreement.

As far as incentives are concerned, it should be interesting to look in greater detail at their effectiveness in the light of "carrots-and-sticks", sunshine or management approaches developed in the literature.[8] With regard to sanctions, the article distinguishes between unilateral and contractual approaches, raising important questions of public authority and legitimacy. The Kyoto Protocol indeed constitutes a highly advanced case reflecting the former approach, including the imposition of additional mitigation burdens and the exclusion from the emission-trading scheme. Here the question arises whether the separation of facilitation and enforcement as envisaged by the two branches of the compliance committee is convincing, or whether facilitation is tantamount to set-

---

7 *See*, for example, Elinor Ostrom, *A Behavorial Approach to the Rational-Choice Theory of Collective Action,* 92 AMERICAN POLITICAL SCIENCE REVIEW 1 (1998); James G. March & Johan P. Olsen, REDISCOVERING INSTITUTIONS: THE ORGANIZATIONAL BASIS OF POLITICS (1989); Arild Underdal, *Explaining Compliance and Defection: Three Models,* 4 EUROPEAN JOURNAL OF INTERNATIONAL RELATIONS 5 (1998).

8 *See* Thomas Bernauer, *The Effect of International Environmental Institutions: How We Might Learn More*, 49 INTERNATIONAL ORGANIZATION 351 (1995); Abram Chayes & Antonia Handler Chayes, THE NEW SOVEREIGNTY: COMPLIANCE WITH INTERNATIONAL REGULATORY AGREEMENTS 3, 22 *et seq.* (1995); Hanschel (note 1), 234 *et seq.*

ting incentives and thus falls within the scope of a wider notion of enforcement as employed in this article. In the further course of his analysis, the author gives a hint by claiming that "incentives are the instrument of choice whenever lack of capabilities is the primary reason why States or a group of States cannot meet their international obligations". Finally, when looking at the contractual approach of the World Bank, the question arises how such a seemingly horizontal approach could be conceptualized as a use of public authority, as examined within the research agenda of this volume. The convincing answer given in this article is that while the obligation and enforcement options are agreed upon by contract and thus horizontally, the actual use of enforcement measures follows a vertical track justifying the domestic public law analogy.

The article further distinguishes between force and (quasi-)judicial dispute settlement. As opposed to legal sanctions, force is understood as "physical power", *e.g.* as mandated by the UN Charter under strict preconditions. Here, questions of legitimacy become particularly pressing, and one may wonder whether the constraining elements of the pertinent procedures of the Security Council, including the granting of veto power, the priority of non-forcible sanctions and the prerogative of a negotiated settlement provide adequate safeguards. The section on judicial and quasi-judicial enforcement mentions the European Court of Justice, the WTO Dispute Settlement Body and the International Tribunal for the Law of the Sea. This relevant list might be further expanded so as to include, for example, the quasi-judicial role of human rights committees under the Covenants or dispute settlement and implementation/compliance bodies under international environmental agreements, especially with regard to state complaint procedures.[9]

C. Addressees of Enforcement Action by International Institutions

When characterizing enforcement by the interaction between an international institution and "another subject of law", it is crucial to determine the addressees of enforcement action by international institutions. Here, the author differentiates between states and individuals as well as

[9] *See* Eibe Riedel, *The Examination of State Reports, in* THE MONITORING SYSTEM OF HUMAN RIGHTS TREATY OBLIGATIONS, 95 (Eckart Klein ed., 1998); Wolfrum (note 4).

other entities. Since they are the main actors of international law which enter into multiple obligations, states naturally constitute the key addressees of enforcement action. Interestingly, the article also mentions sub-state actors and institutions as potential addressees. More research might be desirable in order to elaborate which actors and institutions are relevant in this context, *e.g.* to what extent sub-national entities in federal states are addressed. The article stresses that individuals will "at least be indirectly affected whenever the relevant international institution [...] enforces the domestic enforcement obligations incumbent on the State". This, indeed, raises particularly pressing questions "regarding fair hearing and legal protection for individuals". Hence, enforcement authority vis-à-vis states poses minor problems of legitimacy when compared to such authority with regard to individuals who are not usually in a position to influence international rule-making. Examples such as the UN Security Council's Sanctions Committee are therefore most striking, raising concerns as to the legitimacy of the exercise of public authority. Here, the enforcement by international institutions is complemented by regional and by "state-internal enforcement". In the absence of effective judicial remedies at the global level, continental administrative law may hold some lessons that can be used in order to deal with these concerns. In this context, one may refer to the European Union as an international institution that does provide rather effective judicial remedies, particularly in the light of the recent ruling of the European Court of Justice in the cases of *Yassin Abdullah Kadi* and *Al Barakaat International Foundation*.[10] The decision shows that courts can fulfill an important review function limiting the international enforcement authority. Another lesson is that enforcement may constitute a complex multi-level game involving global, regional and national institutions.[11]

---

[10] Here the Court annulled a Council regulation to the extent that it froze Mr. Kadi´s and Al Barakaat´s funds, after the appellants had been listed by the UN Sanctions Committee, *see* Judgment of the Court (Grand Chamber) 3 September 2008, Joint Cases C-402/05 P and C-415/05 P.

[11] *See* Armin von Bogdandy, *Links between National and Supranational Institutions: A Legal View of a New Communicative Universe, in* LINKING EU AND NATIONAL GOVERNANCE, 24 (Beate Kohler-Koch ed., 2003).

D. Procedure

The section on procedure precisely describes the various elements of compliance regimes such as the system existing under the Kyoto Protocol. The analysis makes a basic distinction between the determination of non-compliance (*e.g.* through monitoring and reporting) and reactions to non-compliance. Here the author avoids the term "violation" and uses the more flexible non-compliance terminology. Reactions depend on the degree of non-compliance, on the underlying reasons and on the question of whether non-compliance concerns substantial or procedural obligations.[12] Drawing on the various case studies in this volume, the author reaches the conclusion that "enforcement mechanisms are indeed increasingly subject to review of one type or another", be it "judicial or administrative control and review". The latter mechanisms serve to limit enforcement power and thus constitute the opposite of enforcement through (quasi-)judicial bodies. One might add that complaint procedures as a means of establishing quasi-judicial control may also be used for enforcement purposes, as the individual complaint procedures of the human rights covenants show.[13] They thus fulfill the opposite function of, for example, the right to appeal against a decision of the compliance committee of the Kyoto Protocol. Moreover, while there may be a development towards stricter control and review, some cases still reveal a clear absence of effective review mechanisms, especially where institutions at a regional and national level merely execute decisions of international institutions which are hardly remediable. This stresses the importance of the research agenda of this volume as an attempt to strengthen legitimacy by doctrinal efforts drawing on the domestic public law analogy.

---

[12] *See* THE OXFORD HANDBOOK OF INTERNATIONAL ENVIRONMENTAL LAW, vol. IV (Daniel Bodansky, Jutta Brunnée & Ellen Hey eds., 2007), in particular the chapters by Ronald B. Mitchell, *Compliance Theory: Compliance, Effectiveness and Behaviour Change in International Environmental Law,* 893 and by Jan Klabbers, *Compliance Procedures,* 995.

[13] *See*, for example, Hilary Charlesworth, *Individual Complaints: An Overview and Admissibility Requirements, in* INDIGENOUS PEOPLE, THE UNITED NATIONS AND HUMAN RIGHTS, 74 (Sarah Pritchard ed., 1999).

E. Organization

In this section the author convincingly outlines the interconnections between effective "enforcement of international law and the rise of international institutionalism", stressing the fact that effective enforcement mechanisms require an international institution in order to function. To some extent, this argument can also be made in a reverse fashion, since international institutions will usually operate more effectively when they provide functioning enforcement mechanisms. One should emphasize that enforcement may consist of elements at the international and at the national level; different models are conceivable and exist in practice. As far as the international level is concerned, it might be worthwhile to elaborate the significance of the usual "tit for tat game" when negotiating international institutions: In order to achieve consensus, compromises can be made with regard to various aspects of the deal, such as the institutional design, the decision-making procedures, the substance of the resulting obligations, their binding or non-binding character, the range of Member States and finally the quality of the enforcement mechanisms. The result may be, counter-intuitively, that an institution provides weak enforcement mechanisms, because this allows for greater membership or for the agreement on more substantial obligations. While the more progressive parties may hope that effective enforcement will follow later so that the institutions develop "teeth", others may only have signed up for the initial deal because they know that the obligations can hardly be enforced.[14]

F. Principles

The author aptly points out that "the legitimacy of effective enforcement authority including sanctions wielded by international institutions vis-à-vis States is now perceived to require the respect of certain principles", such as "adequate procedural safeguards and defense rights for States in the original proceeding as well as a quasi-judicial review of the institution's decisions". Examples are the seabed mining provisions of UNCLOS as well as the enforcement system under the Kyoto Protocol. The question would be to what extent these examples provide the

---

[14] I have made this argument elsewhere, *see* Dirk Hanschel, *Environment & Human Rights – Cooperative Means of Regime Implementation,* 3 YEARBOOK OF HUMAN RIGHTS & ENVIRONMENT 189 (2000).

necessary principles or rather procedural devices that need to be driven by principles yet to be developed. As Röben stresses, the enforcement of UN Security Council resolutions vis-à-vis individuals requires adequate safeguards against abuse, and other cases from this volume display similar deficiencies. The European Court of Justice has shown that such principles may not only be developed at the global, but also at the regional level if regional institutions are involved in the enforcement/implementation process. Evidently, domestic courts can provide protection, as well, although their remedies may not always be effective when the actual decisions affecting the individual are made at the global level.

G. Criteria for the Design of Enforcement Mechanisms

The notion that states will generally comply with their obligations may, indeed, be challenged by empirical evidence. As the author points out, "international norms will not always stipulate the course of conduct that States would wish to adopt anyway". International institutions will usually be more ambitious in assuming that states will change their behavior due to an international obligation, regardless of their domestic policy aims and intentions. It is this ambitious assumption that has been challenged by empirical evidence, so that *Henkin's* view that "almost all nations observe almost all principles of international law and almost all their obligations almost all of the time" may be contested.[15] This is why effective enforcement measures are so important.

At the same time the analysis suggests that enforcement by international institutions causes frictions with national sovereignty and thus requires a "justifying rationale". Starting from this premise, Röben undertakes to "identify criteria for the design of the enforcement mechanism proper for the substantive law regime at hand", distinguishing between "the legal qualification of standards" and "the complexity of the cooperation intended". The often weak relation between that legal qualification and the design of the enforcement mechanism may sound less counter-intuitive when one considers the fact that the institutional design is part of the overall "tit for tat" in the negotiations, as elaborated above. Thus, strong enforcement may well be a compensation for weak or non-binding rules and thus part and parcel of the overall deal

---

15 Louis Henkin, HOW NATIONS BEHAVE 47 (1979). For a more cautious assessment *see* Abram Chayes & Antonia Handler Chayes (note 5), 178.

or compromise. The author points to this fact when mentioning the "complexity of the cooperation intended". One may claim that effective enforcement mechanisms become more likely when the value of an intended cooperation increases, although – depending on the case – a high value may also be attributed to the success of less complex cooperation. In practice, the perceived value of cooperation often varies between the actors, which is why compromises need to be struck that can result in seemingly hybrid constructions potentially displaying strong enforcement of weak obligations.

Economic theory as referred to by the author helps to analyze the value of international institutions in securing a deal.[16] Thus, effective enforcement may "make it more likely that norms are complied with in the first place, making use of the enforcement mechanism superfluous". This can help to stabilize expectations. Hence, the "type, intensity, and complexity of the cooperation reflected in the primary standards" influence the design of the enforcement mechanism. The climate change regime, which imposes substantial costs on at least some of the Member States, is an example of an international institution that requires effective enforcement. However, the effectiveness of the current compliance system is still limited (in spite of its elaborated design) so that the overall deal is weakened, which may appeal to the interest of some of its parties. This shows that divergent interests play an important role, especially in multi-party negotiations, so that a determination of an institution's value becomes more challenging.

H. What Enforcement Tells Us about International Law

A doctrinal reconstruction of general enforcement elements appears very useful, even though the idiosyncrasies of the various cases studies in this volume render this a rather difficult task. Due to concerns of sovereignty on the one hand and effectiveness on the other, the design of each enforcement system is indeed "tailor-made". Again one might add that the bargaining situation leading to the creation of the respective institution, including the nature of the issue and the consensus between

---

[16] Further economic theories, such as contract theory and various kinds of cost-benefit analysis, might also be helpful to look at, *see* for example Ian Ayres & Robert Gertner, *Strategic Contractual Inefficiency and the Optimal Choice of Legal Rules*, 101 THE YALE LAW JOURNAL 730 (1992).

the actors as to the aim of cooperation, as well as membership, substantive rules and finally the enforcement system of that institution, play an important role. The constraints and requirements of a particular bargaining situation expand the number of categories that need to be taken into account when diagnosing a given enforcement system, including remedies based on principles which limit the exercise of public authority. International institutions are built through the "art of the possible", and a weakening of enforcement authority through effective legal remedies may or may not be in the interest of their makers. This merely underlines the importance of the research agenda of this volume, namely to convince decision-makers from a doctrinal point of view that such remedies are what intrinsically *should be* a part of every international institution, especially if the institution can take decisions with direct or indirect effect on individuals. The domestic public law analogy referred to by the author (including the rationale of administrative law or of a consistent system – "Ordnungsidee") may help to make such a point more convincing.[17] To some extent, the design of remedies and other limitations to enforcement authority may follow existing models, such as the compliance procedure used under the Kyoto Protocol or the WTO Dispute Settlement Body which may hence provide a tool-kit for future use.

The case studies analyzed in this volume justify the author's conclusion that enforcement is "a viable part of international institutional law across its several substantive areas". Enforcement indeed constitutes "part and parcel" of the exercise of public authority. Without at least occasional enforceability the "publicness of public international law and the very quality of public international law as a legal order" may be challenged. Depending on the underlying theoretical assumptions, the existence of international law may or may not hinge on enforcement. But without enforcement its "contribution [...] to global governance" would at least be weakened. International institutional law adds a new perspective, because it increasingly allows for vertical enforcement of an otherwise horizontal legal order. This aspect is crucial, since it triggers the analogy with the exercise of domestic public authority which in turn makes claims for limitations of international public authority very convincing.

---

[17] *See* Eberhard Schmidt-Aßmann, DAS ALLGEMEINE VERWALTUNGSRECHT ALS ORDNUNGSIDEE: GRUNDLAGEN UND AUFGABEN DER VERWALTUNGSRECHTLICHEN SYSTEMBILDUNG (2nd ed., 2006).

Holding International Institutions Accountable: The Complementary Role of Non-Judicial Oversight Mechanisms and Judicial Review

*By Erika de Wet**

A. Mapping the Territory

The current contribution focuses on the oversight over international institutions, which is used as a synonym for the accountability of such entities. It departs from the principle that all entities exercising public authority have to account for the exercise thereof.[1] The growing power

---

* The research was conducted during a sojourn at the Max Planck Institute for Comparative Public Law and International Law, Heidelberg, Germany with the financial support of the Alexander von Humboldt Foundation. This contribution also forms part of a so-called VICI Project of the Netherlands Organisation for Scientific Research (NWO) titled: *The emerging international constitutional order: the implications of hierarchy in international law for the coherence and legitimacy of international decision-making*.

[1] Report of the International Law Association, Berlin Conference (2004), Accountability of International Organizations, reprinted in: 1 INTERNATIONAL

A. von Bogdandy et al. (eds.), *The Exercise of Public Authority by International Institutions*, Beiträge zum ausländischen öffentlichen Recht und Völkerrecht 210,
DOI 10.1007/978-3-642-04531-8_30, © Springer-Verlag Berlin Heidelberg 2010

of international institutions in areas that were formerly regulated domestically, along with the growing impact of their conduct on (the rights of) States and non-State actors alike, has thus far not been matched by a shift in accountability relationships beyond those applicable within the confines of the territorial State.[2] Understandably therefore the calls for the accountability of international institutions have increased in recent years, as it is seen as essential for ensuring their credibility and for securing control over public power.[3]

For the purpose of the current contribution, accountability refers to the obligation of international institutions to give a reasoned account of the manner in which they exercise public authority. Of particular importance in this context are normative acts such as standard-setting or rule-making, or the determining of a particular course of conduct.[4] Decisive is not whether the normative act is legally binding in the formal sense, but rather whether it has a *de facto* impact on the rights and interests of States and/or non-State actors.[5] The exercise of public authority in the form of a normative act further implies a relationship between an actor and a forum (constituency), a particular conduct which has to be accounted for, as well as forms of or mechanisms for accountability.[6] Whereas the relationship between the actor and the forum should contain an element of distance, (as opposed to self-control) the accountability mechanisms may be judicial as well as non-judicial, (*i.e.* political, administrative or financial) or any combination of these.[7] The account-

---

ORGANIZATIONS LAW REVIEW 225 (2004). Hereinafter referred to as ILA Report.

2 Deirdre Curtin & André Nollkaemper, *Conceptualizing Accountability in International and European Law*, 36 NETHERLANDS YEARBOOK OF INTERNATIONAL LAW 6, 9 (2005).

3 Nico Krisch, *The Pluralism of Global Administrative Law*, 17 EUROPEAN JOURNAL OF INTERNATIONAL LAW 277 (2006); Bimal N. Patel, *The Accountability of International Organisations: A Case Study of the Organisation for the Prohibition of Chemical Weapons*, 13 LEIDEN JOURNAL OF INTERNATIONAL LAW (LJIL) 572-573 (2000). *See also* von Bogdandy, Dann & Goldmann, in this issue.

4 *See* ILA Report (note 1), at 230.

5 *See* von Bogdandy, Dann & Goldmann, in this issue, at part C.II.

6 Mark Bovens, *Analysing and Assessing Accountability: A Conceptual Framework*, 13 EUROPEAN LAW JOURNAL 450 (2007); Curtin & Nollkaemper (note 2), at 10.

7 ILA Report (note 1), at 226.

ability mechanisms further imply some standard for assessing the conduct of the actor, as well as the possibility of sanctions which can vary from legally enforceable measures to naming-and-shaming.[8]

The actors concern (a specific organ or sub-entity of) an international institution. The international institutions range from organizations created under international law by an international agreement among States, possessing a constitution and organs separate from its Member States,[9] to the more amorphous ones that have non-State actors as members and/or do not constitute subjects of international law. It is the *de facto* impact of an international institution on the rights of States and/or non-State actors which triggers the accountability requirement, rather than the question whether the international institution constitutes a subject of international law in the formal sense.

I. The Constituencies

Some authors argue that the forum (constituency) under which accountability arises is one of the most controversial issues pertaining to international accountability, as it touches on the issue of who should control public authority.[10] For example, if one views the matter from the perspective of the sovereign equality of States, the Member States of an international institution are the primary constituency with a vital interest in policing the public authority exercised within the international institution.[11] From the liberal democratic perspective, this position is open to criticism, given the great disparity in power and population between States.[12] This reality would not be reflected in a "one State one vote" model of accountability. In addition, such a formalistic notion of the sovereign equality of States would not necessarily be representative

---

8 Philip Dann, *Accountability in Development Aid Law: The World Bank, UNDP and Emerging Structures of Transnational Oversight*, 44 ARCHIV DES VÖLKERRECHTS, 384-385 (2006). *See also* Curtin & Nollkaemper (note 2), at 4.

9 *See* definition in ILA Report (note 1), at 222.

10 Krisch (note 3), at 252.

11 Benedict Kingsbury, Nico Krisch & Richard Stewart, *The Emergence of Global Administrative Law*, 68 LAW AND CONTEMPORARY PROBLEMS 45 (2005).

12 Nigel D. White, *Accountability and Democracy within the United Nations: A Legal Perspective*, 13 INTERNATIONAL RELATIONS 6 (1997).

of the electorate in any particular State.[13] From the perspective of liberal democracy, the national constituency in the form of the national electorate is the primary one. The domestic electoral process thus has to ensure accountability for the exercise of public authority also on the international level.[14]

However, for internationalists the international community (of States) as a whole constitutes the main constituency. This relates to the fact that many international institutions produce effects which reach well beyond national boundaries and cannot be left exclusively to national constituencies. In addition, certain subject matters such as environmental protection or human rights protection by their very nature concern all States.[15] The cosmopolitan view, on the other hand, attributes less importance to the role of States as part of the constituency and emphasizes the role of civil society in the international legal order. According to the cosmopolitan view, the global community of citizens, as for example represented by NGOs, constitutes the primary constituency.[16]

This contribution departs from the premise that there is not necessarily one primary constituency for the purposes of accountability or oversight within any particular international institution.[17] Instead, the constituency entitled to claim accountability from an international institution can consist of a variety of international actors (with or without international legal personality), provided their interests or rights are affected by the conduct of the international institution in question.[18] On the one hand, multiple constituencies can lead to a conflict between different constituencies within the same international institution, especially if the constitutive instrument does not provide for a clear hierarchy between them. However, it is also possible that the day-to-day relationship between the constituencies is characterized by mutual accommodation, as a result of which they fulfill a complementing role for the purpose of accountability of a specific act of public authority.[19]

---

13 *Id.* at 8.

14 Krisch (note 3), at 254, 277.

15 *Id.* at 254.

16 *Id.* at 255; Bovens (note 6), at 457; Patel (note 3), at 575.

17 Krisch (note 3), at 260; Curtin & Nolkaemper (note 2), at 10.

18 ILA Report (note 1), at 226.

19 Krisch (note 3), at 266-267.

II. Retrospective versus Prospective Accountability

Since the concept of accountability has not acquired a clearly defined legal meaning in international law,[20] there is a tendency to define it very broadly. For example, the International Law Association (ILA) endorsed a three-layered model. The first level of the ILA model concerns the extent, to which an international institution, in the fulfillment of its functions as established in its constituent instruments, is subjected to forms of scrutiny and monitoring, irrespective of potential and subsequent liability in a legal sense.[21] The second level concerns tortuous liability for injurious consequences arising out of acts or omissions not involving a breach of any rule of international and/or institutional law (*e.g.* environmental damage as a result of lawful nuclear or space activities). The third level of responsibility arises out of acts or omissions which constitute a breach of international (institutional) law (*e.g.* violations of human rights or humanitarian law, breach of contract, gross negligence, or as far as institutional laws concerned, acts of organs which are *ultra vires* or violate the law of employment relations).[22]

Whereas the second and third levels correspond to classic legal notions of State responsibility (*Staatshaftung*), as well as responsibility of international organizations,[23] the first level of accountability is broader. It encompasses a range of procedures for scrutinizing the behavior of international institutions which can be of a non-judicial nature. Moreover, it is sometimes interpreted as including retroactive as well as prospective elements of accountability. The retrospective elements mainly concern oversight through which international institutions give account

---

[20] Curtin & Nollkaemper (note 2), at 5. *See generally* Ruth Grant & Robert Keohane, *Accountability and Abuses of Power in World Politics*, 99 AMERICAN POLITICAL SCIENCE REVIEW 29 (2005).

[21] ILA Report (note 1), at 226.

[22] *Id.* at 226.

[23] *See* Giorgio Gaja (Special Rapporteur of the International Law Commission), First Report on Responsibility of International Organizations, UN Doc. A/CN.4/532, 26 March 2003; *Id.*, Second Report on the Responsibility of International Organizations, UN Doc. A/CN.4/541, 2 April 2004; *Id.*, Third Report on Responsibility of International Organizations, UN Doc. A/CN.4/553, 13 May 2005; *Id.*, Fourth Report on Responsibility of International Organizations, UN Doc. A/CN.4/564, 28 February 2006; *Id.*, Fifth Report on Responsibility of International Organizations, UN Doc. A/CN.4/583, 2 May 2007, all available at: http://www.un.org/law/ilc/.

of prior conduct, such as reporting requirements or non-judicial complaints procedures. The prospective elements entail notions of participation in and transparency of decision-making, as well as reasoned decision-making.[24] Participation as a tool for accountability implies the inclusion of the various constituencies whose interests are affected by the decision-making process.[25] Transparency for its part requires access of affected constituents to information regarding the manner in which normative decisions are taken.[26] Closely related to the principles of participation and transparency is reasoned decision-making, which adds visibility to the different interests at stake and the role of the various stake-holders in the decision-making process.[27]

Proponents of the inclusion of prospective elements in the first level of accountability argue that the distinction between prospective and retrospective elements is artificial, as these concepts are inter-dependent. For example, reasoned decision-making can provide benchmarks for oversight, while broad participation assists in informing constituents who may subsequently be involved in oversight functions. A purely retrospective definition of accountability would not sufficiently take account of this reality.[28] However, such a broad definition of "first level accountability" risks becoming too diffuse to have any added value.[29] If one is striving for the development of a workable "first level accountability" concept, conceptual clarity is of the essence. For this reason the current contribution limits the notion of "first level accountability" to retroactive mechanisms of oversight.[30] It regards notions such as participation, transparency and reasoned decision-making as separate and distinct concepts which complement accountability in a complex process of responsible international governance.[31]

---

24 Curtin & Nollkaemper (note 2), at 8.

25 *See* ILA Report (note 1), at 230.

26 *Id.* at 229.

27 Kingsbury, Krisch & Stewart (note 11), at 39; ILA Report (note 1), at 238. *See* von Bernstorff, in this issue.

28 ILA Report (note 1), at 238; Curtin & Nollkaemper (note 2), at 8.

29 Dann (note 8), at 384.

30 *Id.* at 384-385. *Compare* Curtin & Nollkaemper (note 2), at 11.

31 One could even argue that participation and transparency are prerequisites for efficient oversight mechanisms. For example, the quality of the oversight mechanisms themselves would be significantly enhanced if they were well-reasoned and transparent.

The subsequent passages first analyze the extent to which first level accountability mechanisms are present in the case studies covered by this project. More specifically, this part of the analysis focuses on the non-judicial procedures present for retroactive oversight within the respective international institutions themselves. Thereafter the analysis focuses on oversight procedures provided outside of the international institutions, notably judicial review by regional and domestic courts.

When dealing with judicial review during which the behavior of an international institution is measured against binding norms of international law, one is moving away from first level accountability to second and third level accountability. One is then dealing with a situation where the violation of a primary obligation under international law can trigger the responsibility of an international institution and/or that of its Member States. The subsequent analysis focuses on the procedural dimensions of judicial review, *i.e.* its utility as a procedural technique for ensuring oversight. The contribution does not examine in any depth the substantive standards for measuring the conduct of international organizations, such as proportionality or substantive human rights norms.[32]

By contrasting non-judicial oversight procedures with judicial review, the author attempts to illustrate the complementary function of the different levels of accountability (first versus second and third level of accountability). Since the non-judicial mechanisms are mostly centralized (existing within the respective international institution itself) while the judicial mechanisms are decentralized (existing within in the respective Member States), the author also attempts to illustrate the layered nature of the complementing oversight mechanisms.

The non-judicial as well as judicial procedures under discussion reflect a formal, command and control approach to accountability. From the perspective of legal certainty, these procedures constitute an obvious starting point, as their formalized (institutionalized) nature makes it possible to define and analyze them in legal terms. This is not intended to deny that informal and less visible accountability mechanisms such as behind-the-scenes political pressure could also be very effective under certain circumstances. However, exactly because of their informal and invisible nature, such political mechanisms are difficult to define in legal

---

32 *See generally* ERIKA DE WET, THE CHAPTER VII POWERS OF THE UNITED NATIONS SECURITY COUNCIL (2004).

terms and could only be of secondary importance in a legal order adhering to the principle of legal certainty.

B. Oversight

The sub-sections on oversight divide the different mechanisms into two loosely defined categories. The first concerns general oversight mechanisms, which include all procedures which are not characterized by an individual(ized) complaints procedure and are not of a judicial nature. In addition, these procedures all generate from within the international institution itself and are therefore of a centralized nature. Most of them amount to accountability towards Member States in accordance with the sovereign equality of States model outlined above. This is particular the case with the vertical and intermediate oversight mechanisms as defined below, as Member States feature prominently in these oversight mechanisms. Where the States constituting the oversight body are perceived as acting on behalf of the large majority of States as a whole, the oversight mechanism is also representative of the internationalist accountability model. Certain centralized non-judicial oversight procedures further resemble the cosmopolitan accountability model, which is directed to civil society (the global community of citizens). This applies notably to the horizontal oversight mechanisms and to some extent also to the intermediate mechanisms.

The second category focuses on individual(ized) complaints procedures, which can either be of a centralized or decentralized nature. Only the decentralized complaints procedures in the form of judicial review before regional or domestic courts amount to full-fledged judicial proceedings. The centralized complaints procedures resemble the cosmopolitan accountability model, to the extent that it guards over the interests of specific individuals or groups within the global community of citizens. However, these procedures also reveal a tension between the cosmopolitan accountability model on the one hand and the sovereign equality of States and internationalist models of accountability, on the other hand. The individual protection guaranteed by the complaints procedures are sometimes diluted by influence of Member States or the interests of the international community (of States) as a whole on the complaints procedures.

Decentralized complaints procedures in the form of judicial review are also a manifestation of the cosmopolitan accountability model. In addition, judicial review can be representative of the liberal democratic accountability model, as it is sometimes directed at strengthening parliamentary control over the manner in which the executive exercises public authority on the international level.

I. General Oversight

General oversight can take several potentially complementing forms, which can broadly be divided into vertical, horizontal and intermediary oversight. Where parent organs exercise formal supervision over a subsidiary organ, this would constitute vertical oversight as there is a relationship of hierarchy between the respective organs.[33] In such a relationship the supervisory and controlling power implies the right of the parent organ to question the way in which the subsidiary organ has exercised its competencies. It can also impose sanctions, which can vary from the right to overrule the decision of the lower body to milder sanctions such as public or confidential criticism.

For example, in the case of INTERPOL, the Executive Committee can overrule decisions of the Secretariat on the basis of information provided by the independent expert Commission for the Control of INTERPOL's Files.[34] However, in the case of the OECD Guidelines for Multinational Enterprises, OECD's Investment Committee can merely issue abstract clarifications on the Guidelines in instances where it is of the view that the National Contact Points did not interpret the Guidelines correctly. It cannot make determinations pertaining to specific enterprises, nor can it overrule a decision of the National Contacting Points.[35]

In the case of the UNESCO Regime for the Protection of World Heritage, the vertical oversight which the General Conference exercises over the World Heritage Committee is limited to its election of the Committee's members and the determination of its budget.[36] The General Conference is not entitled to give any binding orders to the World Heritage Committee which remains an autonomous body within the interna-

---

33 Bovens (note 6), at 460; Dann (note 8), at 392.

34 *See* Schöndorf-Haubold, in this issue.

35 *See* Schuler, in this issue.

36 *See* Zacharias, in this issue.

tional institution.[37] Similarly, in the case of the FAO's Code of Conduct for Responsible Fisheries, budgeting and internal reporting seem to be the main mechanism of the FAO Council and FAO Conference over the Committee of Fisheries (COFI) and the secretariat.[38] Much of the norm-creating activity of these bodies takes place in a relative autonomy from political influence of higher bodies.[39] The same applies to the conduct of the High Commissioner on National Minorities of the OSCE, whose country missions are organized independently from other OSCE bodies. Disapproval within the OSCE of the manner in which the High Commissioner exercises his functions can nonetheless prevent his re-election, seen as he is appointed by the Permanent Council (a plenary body) by consensus for a period of three years.[40] The OSCE example reflects that superior organs can strengthen their control over subsidiary organs by attaching time-limits to the mandates of lower bodies. Discontent with the manner in which the lower body exercises its mandate can result in its non-extension by the higher body.

The level of independence exercised by the higher body during the oversight procedure is likely to be more profound in instances where the composition of the higher body significantly differs from that of the lower bodies. Stated differently, such independence is not likely to be present where the Member States composing the higher body corresponds to a large extent to that of the lower body. This is particularly noticeable in relation to reporting, which seems to have become a prominent procedure for vertical supervision within all the international institutions under discussion. For example, within the WTO regime, the Committee on Trade and Financial Services is subsidiary to the Council for Trade in Services of the WTO and reports to the WTO Council on an annual basis.[41] The fact that the Council for Trade in Services is also a plenary body means that the membership of the subsidiary organ and the reviewing organ overlaps. This overlap does not extend to the specific individuals representing the States on the different bodies, as different expertise is required within the different bodies. Notably in the case of the Committee on Trade and Financial Services, the work is of a highly technical nature. These factors (overlapping

[37] *Id.*

[38] *See* Friedrich, in this issue.

[39] *Id.*

[40] *See* Farahat, in this issue.

[41] *See* Windsor, in this issue.

membership and technical nature of the work of the Committee) make it unlikely that the WTO Council will exercise review in any strict manner or reach a different conclusion than the Committee. In fact, the Council's reports to the WTO General Council merely refer to the report of the Committee, which constitutes an annex to its own report, without any further comment.[42]

Particularly problematic in terms of overlap of membership between the higher and the lower bodies is the Al-Qaeda/Taliban Sanctions Committee. The regular reporting to the Security Council as required by the Committee Guidelines amounts to nothing more than self-reporting, given that the composition of the Sanctions Committee is the mirror image of the composition of the Security Council.[43] Moreover, the veto right of the five permanent members implies that any attempt within the Security Council to overrule a decision pertaining to listing or de-listing by the Al-Qaeda/ Taliban Sanctions Committee, is highly unlikely.

In all of the case studies covered, the supervisory organ is compiled of Member States of the international institution, which reflects that vertical oversight is first and foremost directed towards States in accordance with the sovereign equality model. To the extent that one accepts these supervisory bodies as being representative of the international community (of States) as a whole, the vertical oversight would also be representative of the internationalist model. In contrast, the horizontal oversight exercised over some international institutions resembles the cosmopolitan accountability model, as it involves scrutiny of normative activity by NGOs or other members of civil society.[44] The horizontal oversight can have its root in the constitutive document of the international institution or another formal decision, but frequently also occurs on a voluntary basis. Typical for this type of oversight is the absence of the involvement or intervention of a hierarchically superior body (composed of Member States) in the oversight procedure itself. The sanction is typically limited to social (peer) pressure or public naming-and-shaming. For example, the publication by the OECD's Investment Committee of information compiled by the National Contact Points in relation to the OECD Guidelines for Multinational Enterprises gener-

---

42 *Id.*

43 *See* Feinäugle, in this issue.

44 Bovens (note 6), at 460.

ates the possibility for review by the general public.[45] Similarly, the disclosure policies of the World Bank that provide rules for access to World Bank documents have introduced a measure of public scrutiny.[46]

In between horizontal and vertical oversight one encounters various forms of intermediate supervision. In such instances the oversight would have a formal basis in, for example, the constitutive document of the international institution or resolutions adopted in accordance with the constitutive document.[47] The supervision as such is exercised by an independent body which does not have a direct hierarchical relationship with the body that is being supervised. It nonetheless takes place in the shadow of hierarchy, as the supervising body acts on the authority of a higher body and also reports to it. Sanctions – which can either be imposed by the higher body itself or by the independent body on the authority of the higher body – vary in intensity. The accountability generated by intermediate oversight seems to be directed primarily at the Member States composing the hierarchically superior organ in whose shadow the oversight is executed. However, the case studies reveal that intermediate oversight is also linked to the cosmopolitan accountability model when accompanied by horizontal oversight.

In relation to the case studies covered, the World Bank in particular has introduced several mechanisms of intermediate oversight, some of which are also connected with horizontal oversight. One such mechanism is the Department of Institutional Integrity, which investigates allegations of fraud and corruption in the World Bank projects and of misconduct of the Bank's staff. This Department, which has unrestricted access to Bank records, documents and properties, is institutionally separate from the regular staff and reports directly to the President.[48] Sanctions in case of substantiated allegations can result in various disciplinary measures including the termination of a contract with the World Bank and a debarment from re-hiring.[49] One can draw a parallel between this procedure and that of the Inspector General of UNHCR, who investigates severe misconduct affecting UNCHR bene-

---

[45] Although the peer review first and foremost has a bearing on the behavior of Member States, it also reflects on the OECD's ability to regulate the behavior of multinationals. *See* in this issue the contribution by Gefion Schuler.

[46] Dann (note 8), at 388.

[47] Bovens (note 6), at 467.

[48] Dann (note 8), at 390.

[49] *Id.* at 391.

ficiaries, including corrupt practices and other misconduct related to Refugee Status Determination.[50] The inspection reports are submitted to the Executive Committee of the High Commissioner's Program, which functions as a subsidiary organ of the General Assembly.[51]

A second, intermediate mechanism of the World Banks is the fiscal control proscribed by its Articles of Agreement.[52] It consists of the auditing of the Bank's financial Statements by an external private company who is chosen by and reports back to the Audit Committee of the Board of Executive Directors. The sanctions attached to the auditing are mild, as they are limited to the publishing of the audit reports. This also adds an element of horizontal oversight, as the audit reports are accessible to a potentially vigilant public.[53]

The World Bank's third mechanism for intermediate reporting is constituted by the Independent Evaluation Group. This group is organized independently from the Bank's other departments, but reports directly to the Board of Executive Directors and in this manner functions in the shadow of a hierarchically superior organ. It rates the efficacy of the World Bank's operation programs in accordance with four standards which were derived from the Bank's own objectives, namely outcome sustainability, institutional impact, and Bank and borrower performance.[54] As the Group's findings are made public to the Member States and the broader public, it simultaneously enhances horizontal accountability.[55] Also in this instance one can draw a parallel with UNHCR's oversight mechanisms. The Policy Development and Evaluation Service (previously known as the Evaluation and Policy Analysis Unit), conducts independent systematic assessments of a wide range of UNCHR projects, programs, practices and policies. The evaluations are presented

---

50 *See* Smrkolj, in this issue.

51 *Id.*

52 Dann (note 8), at 390.

53 *Id.*

54 *Id.* at 392.

55 *Id.* at 393.

to the Senior Management Committee of UNCHR and are also available to the general public.[56]

Finally, one can mention the State reporting procedure under the 1998 ILO Declaration. These reports are analyzed by five independent Experts Advisers with whom the States do not have a direct hierarchical relationship. However, since they are appointed by and responsible to the Governing Body, the Expert Advisers function in the shadow of the tripartite executive organ of the ILO. Although (mild) sanctions in the form of public criticism is a possibility, the process is more geared towards identifying problems in the implementation of ILO fundamental Conventions, than exposing bad behavior by States.

This brief overview reveals that the measures for general oversight are mainly representative of the sovereign equality of State model of accountability. Member States play a central role in relation to both vertical and intermediate oversight mechanisms. This model sometimes overlaps with the internationalist accountability model, for example where the Member States participating in the supervisory organ is representative of the large majority of States in the world. The cosmopolitan accountability is present (although in nascent form) through horizontal oversight. The liberal democratic model was not visibly present in the case studies under discussion. In addition, the oversight mechanisms under discussion remain rather weak for the most part, regardless of whether one is dealing with vertical, horizontal or intermediate oversight or any combination thereof. Stated differently, although the sovereign equality of States model of accountability is the dominant one, this does not necessarily mean that this is a strong form of accountability or necessarily stronger than the other accountability models identified here.

II. Individual(ized) Oversight

1. Centralized (Non-Judicial) Complaints Procedures

In relation to the individualized complaints procedures present in the case studies, one can distinguish between centralized complaints procedures within the institution itself and decentralized complaints procedures taking place within the Member States of the international institution. The centralized individual complaints procedures provided for in

---

[56] *See* Smrkolj, in this issue.

the respective case studies do not amount to judicial proceedings in the sense of binding (enforceable) decisions characterized by impartiality, independence and even-handedness.[57]

The most extreme example is that of the Al-Qaeda/Taliban Sanctions Committee's proceedings. Although the affected individuals can submit a request for delisting through the United Nations Focal Point, they have no right to consideration of their request. In addition, they have no right to be heard before the Sanctions Committee and are not provided with reasons for the Sanctions Committee's decisions which are taken by political consensus.[58] This procedure reflects the tension between the cosmopolitan accountability model and the sovereign equality of States model, with the scale tipping clearly in the direction of the latter. Moreover, if one were prepared to accept that the Security Council and its Sanctions Committee represented the international community of States as a whole, the oversight procedure would also reflect a tension between the cosmopolitan accountability model and the internationalist accountability model.

In contrast, the individual complaints procedure before the Inspection Panel of the World Bank seems to be slightly more protective of the interests of (members of) civil society, as it is composed of external experts who function independently from the Bank's management. However, the procedure does not result in binding decision against the Bank, neither does it provide for compensation for affected individuals.[59] Similarly, individuals who are affected by INTERPOL's inclusion of certain data in its files have the right to file a complaint with the independent Commission for the Control of INTERPOL's Files. However, they do not have a right to the removal of such data in case the Commission finds in their favor. Such removal remains within the discretion of the Secretary General.[60] Also in case of the UNHCR's Refugee Status Determination procedure one is not dealing with a judicial procedure in the true sense. Although the applicants have the right to be heard and the right to appeal, there is no obligation to provide them with reasons or to interview witnesses in their presence. In addition, a

---

57 *See* Erika de Wet & André Nollkaemper, *Review of the Security Council Decisions by National Courts*, 45 GERMAN YEARBOOK OF INTERNATIONAL LAW 171 (2002).

58 *See* Feinäugle, in this issue.

59 Dann (note 8), at 389.

60 *See* Schöndorf-Haubold, in this issue.

positive decision is not binding on the domestic authorities that have parallel proceedings for determining the residence status of refugees.[61] In essence, these individualized complaints procedures reveal that the impact of cosmopolitan accountability models within international institutions is still significantly diluted by accountability models directed at the Member States or in some instances the international community of States.

2. *Decentralized Judicial Review by Regional and Domestic Courts*

The question arises whether the cosmopolitan accountability model can be strengthened through decentralized oversight mechanisms that are available to individuals whose rights are affected by the decisions of international institutions. More specifically, the question arises whether decentralized judicial review before regional or domestic courts can fulfill this role.

In this context one should note that decentralized judicial review is sometimes explicitly provided for and regulated on the international level, as in the case of the WIPO's regime for the international registration of trademarks. Third parties who are affected by the decision of the International Bureau of the WIPO to register an international trademark can file a complaint against this decision with their respective domestic courts. These courts can overrule the International Bureau's decision by refusing to recognize a trademark in the respective Member State's territory.[62] The clear legal framework within which this review takes place, combined with the fact that one is dealing with a binding judgment in the legal sense, strengthens the quality of the oversight that is being exercised. In this instance judicial review thus constitutes a useful avenue for strengthening the cosmopolitan accountability model.

The matter is more complicated where the decentralized review procedures are not explicitly provided for. In these instances the review of a normative decision of an international institution takes place incidentally, in instances where individuals challenge measures that implement decisions of an international institution before their domestic or regional courts. In the process, the courts may also be confronted with reviewing indirectly the scope and/or legality of decisions of an interna-

---

61 *See* Smrkolj, in this issue.

62 *See* Kaiser, in this issue.

tional institution.[63] The first challenge facing the court during incidental review is determining whether it has the implicit competence to engage in incidental review, given that such competence was not explicitly provided for. If it answers this question in the affirmative, it will then be confronted with interpreting the substance of the respective international normative measure.

At this point it is worth distinguishing between three situations with which courts can be confronted, by referring to pertinent examples of the European Court of Justice (ECJ) and the Court of First Instance (CFI) – all of which concern binding decisions of the Security Council. In the first situation, the ECJ had to interpret the scope of the EU's implementing measures and incidentally that of the relevant Security Council resolutions. However, in this situation neither the legality of the implementing measures, nor that of the Security Council resolutions themselves were at issue. In the second scenario, the ECJ was confronted with challenges to the legality of the implementing measures, but could avoid an incidental review of the legality of the respective Security Council measures. In this instance the Security Council measures were formulated in broad terms, as a result of which those responsible for their implementation had discretion as to how to achieve the desired result. The third scenario concerned disputes about the legality of measures of implementation which incidentally also touched on the legality of the respective Security Council resolution. In this instance the relevant Security Council resolutions were formulated in arrow terms which did not (seem to) allow the Member States (or the EU) any discretion in relation to their implementation.

As far as the first two scenarios are concerned, the ECJ has in the past not hesitated to exercise its competence of review. The first example (pertaining to the first scenario mentioned above) concerns the *Bosphorus* decision.[64] In that instance, the ECJ had to determine the scope of EC Regulation 1990/993[65] and in particular, whether it authorized the impoundment by the Irish authorities of two aircrafts leased to the applicant by the former Yugoslav airline JAT. As the respective EC Regu-

---

[63] The possibility to take action against international institutions directly before domestic courts remains very limited, as those with separate international legal personality such as the United Nations and the World Bank enjoy immunity before domestic courts. *See* Dann (note 8), at 389.

[64] Case C-84/85, *Bosphorus Hava Yollari Turzim ve Ticaret AS v. Minister for Transport, Energy and Communications and Others*, 1996 ECR I-3953.

[65] EC Regulation 1990/93 O.J. 1993 L 102, 14.

lation implemented a Security Council sanctions regime against the former Federal Republic of Yugoslavia, the ECJ also had to determine the scope of Security Council Resolution 820 of 17 April 1993.[66] The ECJ took into account the purpose of the sanctions regime in concluding that the limitation of the international right to property of the applicant (who effectively lost three years of a four year lease) was proportionate under the circumstances.[67] However, neither the legality of EC Regulation 1990/1993 nor the sanctions regime from which it resulted was at issue.

The second example (concerning the second scenario) is that of the *Segi* case.[68] In this case, the ECJ reviewed the EU measures implementing Security Council Resolution 1373 of 28 September 2001, which *inter alia* requested United Nations Member States to freeze all funds and other financial assets or economic resources to those involved in terrorist activity.[69] In order to ensure consistent implementation of this resolution in its Member States, the EU implemented this resolution through a series of measures which *inter alia* resulted in the blacklisting of the Basque organization *Segi*.[70] The applicants filed an action for damages in relation to the relevant EU measures, on the basis that it violated their right to judicial protection in accordance with Article 6(2) of the EU Treaty. According to their line of argument, the violation resulted from the fact that they had no means of challenging Segi's inclu-

---

[66] *Bosphorus* decision (note 64), at para. 15.

[67] *Id.* at para. 26.

[68] Case C-355/04 P, *Segi, Araitz Zubimendi Izaga, Aritza Galarraga v. Council of the European Union* 2007 ECR I-01657, para. 57.

[69] *See* Mielle Bulterman, *Fundamental Rights and the United Nations Financial Sanctions Regime: The Kadi and Yusuf Judgments of the Court of First Instance of the European Communities*, 19 LJIL 757 (2006).

[70] *See* Common Position 2001/931/CFSP on the application of specific measures to combat terrorism O.J. 2001 L 344, 90; Regulation (EC) No. 2580/2001 on specific restrictive measures directed against certain persons and entities with a view to combating terrorism O.J. 2001 L 344, 70; Decision 2001/927/EC establishing the list provided for in Article 2(3) of Council Regulation (EC) No. 2580/2001 on specific restrictive measures directed against certain persons and entities with a view to combating terrorism O.J. 2001 L 344, 83; Common Position 2002/340/CFSP updating Common Position 2001/931/CFSP on the application of specific measures to combat terrorism O.J. 2002 L 116, 75 and Common Position 2002/462/CFSP updating Common Position 2001/931/CFSP on the application of specific measures to combat terrorism and repealing Common Position 2002/340/CFSP O.J. 2002 L 160, 32.

sion in the blacklist, due to the nature of the Common Positions that were adopted under the so-called third Pillar of the EU Treaty. This claim effectively also constituted an indirect challenge to the validity of the relevant Common Position.[71]

In reviewing the matter and concluding that EU law indeed provided for an avenue of judicial protection in this case, the ECJ emphasized the applicants' right to a remedy and access to a court of law.[72] However, it is important to note that Security Council Resolution 1373 (2001) clearly left States the discretion to implement the obligations contained therein in accordance with (international) human rights obligations. For example, it did not identify the persons to be blacklisted in a manner that appeared to suspend any avenue of (domestic) judicial protection for such individuals.[73] As a result, the question whether the respective implementing measures were in accordance with the EU standards of judicial protection could be addressed without raising the question whether Security Council Resolution 1373 (2001) itself conflicted with these standards.

The *Yusuf*[74] and *Kadi*[75] cases represent the third scenario mentioned above. In these instances the CFI (and subsequently the ECJ) was confronted with a request for annulment of EC Regulations which implemented the blacklisting regime of the Al-Qaeda/Taliban Sanctions Committee.[76] The legal question before the CFI was framed in a manner that also touched on the issue of the legality of the Security Council measures. As these regulations transposed almost word for word the relevant Security Council resolutions, any review of the substance of the challenged regulations necessarily amounts to indirect review of the

---

71 *See Segi* decision (note 68), at paras. 52 *et seq*.

72 Common Position 2001/931/CFSP, *supra*, note 70; *see also Segi* decision, *supra* note 68 at paras. 51-52, para. 54.

73 *See* in particular the opinion of Advocate General Mengozzi, delivered on 26 October 2006, Case C-355/04 P, *Segi, Araitz Zubimendi Izaga, Aritza Galarraga v. Council of the European Union* 2007 ECR I-01657, para. 57. He described the listing of *inter alia Segi* as a completely autonomously by the EU. *See also* Bulterman (note 69), at 757.

74 Case T- 306/01, *Yusuf and Al Barakaat International Foundation v. Council and Commission* 2005 ECR II-3353.

75 Case T-315/01, *Kadi v. Council and Commission 2005* ECR II-3649; hereinafter reference will only be made to the relevant paragraphs of the decision.

76 *See* Feinäugle, in this issue.

legality of the relevant Security Council measures.[77] The CFI concluded that it would not have the right to engage in such a review, except where violations of peremptory norms (*jus cogens*) of international law are at stake.[78] It further concluded that obligations under Article 103 of the Charter – which include binding Security Council decisions – took precedence over all other international obligations, with the exception of *jus cogens* obligations.

Elsewhere this author has extensively criticized the CFI's reasoning.[79] Here it would suffice to say that in light of the very small number of *jus cogens* norms currently recognized in international law, the judicial oversight resulting from the CFI's reasoning is of very little meaning to the affected individuals and would thus not significantly contribute to strengthening the cosmopolitan accountability model.[80] This is reflected *inter alia* by the fact that in accordance with the CFI's reasoning, the Security Council had the competence to suspend the right to a fair trial (as guaranteed by EU and international law) of the blacklisted persons for an unlimited period of time. As this right does not (yet) belong to the corpus of peremptory norms recognized by in public international law, it could be overridden by a conflicting Security Council decision.

The CFI's decision has subsequently been overturned on appeal.[81] Even so, the CFI's reasoning in relation to the very limited boundaries to Security Council powers and the equally restricted roles of regional and

---

[77] Christian Tomuschat, *Primacy of United Nations Law – Innovative Features in the Community Legal Order*, 43 COMMON MARKET LAW REVIEW 543 (2006).

[78] *Kadi* decision (note 75), at para. 221, paras. 225-226.

[79] *See* Erika de Wet, *Holding the United Nations Security Council Accountable for Human Rights Violations through Domestic and Regional Courts: A Case of Beware What You Ask For?, in* SANCTIONS, ACCOUNTABILITY AND GOVERNANCE IN A GLOBALISED WORLD (Jeremy Farrall & Kim Rubenstein eds., forthcoming 2009).

[80] For the very restricted list of *jus cogens* norms generally recognized as such, *see* Report of the International Law Commission, 58th Session of the International Law Commission, UN Doc. A/61/10 (2006) 421. For a different opinion, *see* ALEXANDER ORAKHELASHVILI, PEREMPTORY NORMS IN INTERNATIONAL LAW (2006) (defining *jus cogens* in a much broader fashion).

[81] The decision turned on European law and the ECJ did not address the *jus cogens* arguments raised by the CFI. See Cases C-402/05 P and C-415/05 P, *Yassin Abdullah Kadi and Al Barakaat International Foundation v Council and Commission*, 3 September 2008, available at http://curia.europa.eu.

domestic courts in reviewing such boundaries has already had a significant influence on the practice of other courts. More specifically, it has been confirmed by the *Nada* case of the Swiss Federal Supreme Court.[82] In this case, which also concerned the blacklisting of an individual in accordance with Al-Qaeda/Taliban sanctions regime, the Swiss court effectively copied the reasoning of the CFI. The reasoning was further explicitly confirmed by the English Court of Appeal in the *Al-Jedda* decision.[83] This case concerned an entirely different issue, namely whether the detention without trial of a British/Iraqi national by British forces in Iraq in 2004, on the basis of Security Council Resolution 1546 of 8 June 2004, violated Article 5(1) of the European Convention of Human Rights. In addition, the conflict between the respective Security Council decision and the human rights in question was arguably not as extreme as in the *Yusuf* and *Kadi* cases. Even so, the Court of Appeal relied heavily on the reasoning of the *Yusuf* and *Kadi* decisions. As the House of Lords subsequently did not dwell on this part of the Court of Appeal's reasoning, apart from confirming that the Security Council is bound by *jus cogens*,[84] one could interpret its decision as an approval of the Court of Appeal's reasoning on this particular point.

In essence therefore, it seems that regional and/or domestic courts may remain reluctant to provide meaningful judicial oversight to individuals whose international human rights are suspended by directly conflicting decisions of the Security Council.[85] A different conclusion would per-

---

[82] *Youssef Mustapha Nada v. Staatssekretariat für Wirtschaft,* BGE, No. 1A.45/2007, 14 November 2007. The *Nada* decision was rendered by the Federal Supreme Court, available at: http://www.admin.ch/ch/d/sr/sr.html.

[83] *The Queen (on the application of Hilal Abdul-Razzaq Ali- Al-Jedda) v. the Secretary of Defence*, [2005] EWHC 1809 (Admin).

[84] *R (on the application of Al-Jedda) (FC) (Appellant) v. Secretary of State for Defence (Respondent)* [2007] UKHL 58, judgment of 12 December 2007. *See* in particular the opinion of Lord Bingham of Cornhill, para. 35. However, it is also worth noting that the House of Lords was not inclined to accept a complete displacement of Art. 5(1) of the European Convention of Human Rights by S.C. Res. 1546 of 8 June 2004. The qualification of this right was therefore not to be equated with a complete displacement. *See* in particular the opinion of Baroness Hale of Richmond, paras. 126 *et seq*.

[85] *See Agim Behrami and Bekir Behrami v. France* (Application No. 71412/01), Judgment, 31.05.2007; and *Ruzhdi Saramati v. France, Norway and Germany* (Application No. 78166/01), Judgment, 31.05.2007. Both judgments available at: http://echr.coe.int/echr/en/hudoc. The ECtHR did not accept effective (extra-territorial) control by the Member States in question in Kosovo at

haps be possible if regional and domestic courts were willing to interpret the notion of *jus cogens* in a manner that also includes fundamental (human rights) norms of domestic or EU law – as a limitation to Security Council powers.[86] Another possibility would be to give preference to fundamental (human rights) norms on the domestic or regional level, without entering the debate as to whether the concept of *jus cogens* should be expanded in order to include such a domesticized or regionalized interpretation. This was in fact the strategy followed by the ECJ in the *Kadi* decision on appeal, that granted comprehensive judicial review for those blacklisted by the Al-Qaeda/Taliban Sanctions Committee at EU level on the basis of EU law.[87]

Another technique for strengthening the cosmopolitan accountability model would be to depart from the premise that a suspension of indi-

---

the time when the alleged violation of the right to life (Art. 2) and the right to deny the legality of one's detention (Art. 5) of the ECHR occurred in 2000 and therefore declared the case inadmissible. At the time the states in question formed part of the NATO forces in Kosovo, whose presence was authorized under SC. Res. 1244 of 10 June 1999. The ECtHR's rather distorted arguments in finding an absence of effective control on the part of the Member States arguably reflects the pressure exercised by the troop contributing countries not to review binding Security Council resolutions.

[86] In Switzerland there is an ongoing debate as to whether the concept of *jus cogens* – which is explicitly recognized as a limitation to the legislative (constitutional) process in the federal Constitution of 1999 – should be defined to include also domestic fundamental norms. *See e.g.* Daniel Thürer, *Verfassungsrecht und Völkerrecht, in* VERFASSUNGSRECHT DER SCHWEIZ 179-205 (Daniel Thürer *et al.* eds., 2001); Daniel Thürer, *Wer hat Angst vor dem Völkerrecht? Wer vor den Volksrechten? Keine unlösbaren Widersprüche, sondern gegenseitige Stärkung*, NEUE ZÜRCHER ZEITUNG 17.11.2007; Tristan Zimmermann, *Quelles normes impératives du droit international comme limite à l'exercice du droit d'initiative par le peuple?*, 16 AKTUELLE JURISTISCHE PRAXIS 748 *et seq.* (2007).

[87] Cases C-402/05 P and C-415/05 P, *Yassin Abdullah Kadi and Al Barakaat International Foundation v. Council and Commission*, 3 September 2008, available at http://curia.europa.eu. *See also* the well-known *Solange* decisions of the German Federal Constitutional Court: Collection of Decisions of the Federal Constitutional Court (BVerfGE) 37, 271 of 29 May 1974; BVerfGE 73, 339 of 22 October 1986. These decisions are also available at: www.bundesverfassungs gericht.de. Note that this "dualist" solution could trigger the international law of State responsibility. This would be the case where the domestic or regional obligations which are granted preference conflict with (other) international obligations, such as binding Security Council resolutions.

vidual human rights by Security Council decisions such as the Al-Qaeda/Taliban sanctions regime cannot be assumed unless provided for explicitly.[88] This approach would imply that a resolution such as Resolution 1267 (1999) necessarily (implicitly) allows States the necessary discretion to enforce the respective sanctions regime in accordance with human rights standards, even though this may not be self-evident from the resolution at first sight.

In this context the recent *Möllendorf* decision of the ECJ constitutes an interesting example.[89] This reference request to the ECJ resulted from the fact that the Al-Qaeda/Taliban sanctions regime had unforeseen consequences for the property rights of third parties. A contract of sale concerning immovable property was concluded between the *Möllendorfs* (the sellers) and buyers who were subsequently blacklisted under the Al-Qaeda sanctions regime. At the time of the blacklisting, the buyers were already in possession of the immovable property and the sellers had already received (and spent) the sales price. However, ownership had not yet transferred since the transaction was not yet, as required by German law, registered in the Land Register.[90]

Since registration was no longer possible once the buyers were blacklisted, the question arose whether the sales transaction had to be reversed. This would have been the normal procedure under German civil law when a legal impediment arose against the transfer of property.[91] The sellers objected to repaying the sales price that would result from such a reversal of the transaction, arguing that it would disproportionately limit their right to property.[92] The ECJ supported this position to the extent that it ordered the national authorities to apply the national law to the sellers in a manner that gave effect to EU fundamental rights protection as far as possible.[93] It is important to note that the legality of the sanctions regime itself was not at stake in this case. Instead, it con-

---

88 *See also* José E. Alvarez, *The Security Council's War on Terrorism: Problems and Policy Options, in* REVIEW OF THE SECURITY COUNCIL BY MEMBER STATES, 134 (Erika de Wet & André Nollkaemper eds., 2003).

89 Case C-177/06, *Gerda Möllendorf & Christiane Möllendorf-Niehuus* 2007 ECR I-8361, Judgment of 11 October 2007.

90 *Id.* at para. 24.

91 *Id.* at para. 52.

92 This money would then have to remain in a frozen account for as long as the buyers remained blacklisted. *Id.* at para. 70.

93 *Id.* at para. 76, para. 81.

cerned the scope of the EU implementing measures and in particular their impact ("collateral damage") on third parties. Even so, the case potentially provides an interesting example of how elements of proportionality and human rights protection can be interpreted into a sanctions regime. Neither Resolution 1267 (1999) and subsequent resolutions, nor the EU implementing measures explicitly provide for such protection in instances where the sanctions regime affected the rights of non-listed third parties. The ECJ was nonetheless prepared to read it into the sanctions regime.[94]

Whether regional or domestic courts may be willing to engage in more stringent judicial review of normative acts of international institutions other than the Security Council remains to be seen. The special role of the United Nations Security Council in maintaining international peace and security combined with the primacy clause contained in Article 103 of the United Nations Charter, place the obligations flowing from Security Council decisions in a *sui generis* position compared to those stemming from other international institutions. On the one hand, this may imply that regional and domestic courts would be more willing to engage in rigorous judicial review of decisions of other international institutions, if and to the extent that they are incidentally confronted therewith. On the other hand, it is possible that courts may generally be reluctant to exercise extensive judicial review over international norm-setting activities pertaining to issues closely associated with foreign policy.

This is, for example, reflected by decisions of the German Federal Constitutional Court pertaining to the evolving scope of NATO's goals and competencies. In 2001, the Court reviewed the nature of NATO's New Strategic Concept adopted in 1999 in order to determine whether it amounted to an international treaty or an amendment of the North Atlantic Treaty of 1949.[95] Since Article 59(2) of the German Basic Law requires parliamentary consent for the ratification of certain international

---

[94] Some might question whether the situation of third parties who are indirectly affected by the sanctions regime would at all be comparable with that of persons forming the direct object of the sanctions regime. However, this author submits that the *Möllendorf*-case remains an interesting example of how a court can read some human rights protection into a sanctions regime.

[95] Federal Constitutional Court (BVerfG), 2 BvE 6/99 of 22 November 2001, paras. 130-131; Birgit Schlütter, in ILDC 134 (DE 2001) H1. *See also* the earlier AWACS case, *i.e.* BVerfGE 90, 286 *et seq.*, decision of 12 July 1994, which concerned the NATO Strategic Concept of 1991.

treaties, an affirmative answer would have implied that the Government violated the Basic Law when adopting the New Strategic Concept without the consent of Parliament.[96] The Court determined that the New Strategic Concept did not amount to an international treaty and there was thus no violation of Article 59(2) of the Constitution, as the further development of a system of mutual collective security that did not involve the amendment of the treaty and thus did not require the consent of the federal Parliament.[97]

However, the Court did warn that Parliament's right to participate in the exercise of foreign policy would be violated if the Government's involvement in the development of NATO's competencies resulted in a fundamental structural departure from NATO's constitution and its orientation towards the maintenance of peace. This followed from Article 59(2) in combination with Article 24(2) of the Basic Law, which authorizes the Government to enter into collective security systems aimed at the maintenance of peace.[98] However, no such departure took place in this instance. One could not infer from the content of the New Strategic Concept that NATO intended to abandon its commitment to the aims of the United Nations and the compliance with its Charter.[99] The Court subsequently reiterated this position in a decision in 2007.[100] In that instance the Court was not prepared to accept that NATO's involvement outside the Euro-Atlantic region (through its involvement in the International Security Assistances Force in Afghanistan (ISAF)), or its (limited) cooperation with Operation Enduring Freedom in Afghanistan (which is lead by the United States of America), constituted a fundamental departure from the NATO Constitution or goals.[101]

---

96 BVerfG, 2 BvE 6/99 of 22 November 2001, para. 150; Birgit Schlütter, in ILDC 134 (DE 2001) C5.

97 *Id.* at para. 130.

98 *Id.* at paras. 154, 161; ILDC 124 (DE 2001) H10-H11.

99 BVerfG, 2 BvE 6/99 of 22 November 2001, para. 157, para. 161. The New Strategic Concept did not call into question the mandatory prohibition on the threat or use of force contained in Art. 2(4) of the Charter; the accepted Charter prerequisites for the use of military force (which include a Security Council mandate in accordance with Art. 42 and Art. 48 of the Charter or to regional organizations in accordance with Art. 53 of the Charter); collective defense also of third states; intervention by request; and the proportionality of such action.

100 BVerfG, 2 BvE 2/07, decision of 3 July 2007, para. 45, para. 87.

101 BVerfG, 2 BvE 2/07, decision of 3 July 2007, para. 45, para. 87. The violation of international law by an individual NATO operation could be an indica-

In these instances the review was not directed at determining the legality of the manner in which NATO exercised its competencies in accordance with international (human rights) law. It was thus not directed at strengthening the cosmopolitan accountability model. Instead, the constitutional complaints were exclusively based on potential violations of domestic constitutional law and aimed at strengthening democratic control over executive participation in international norm-setting in the area of collective security. The procedure was essentially directed at strengthening the liberal democratic accountability model. This attempt was unsuccessful. The Court interpreted Article 59(2) of the Basic Law narrowly and did not consider any other form of modern international law-making beyond that of the NATO Treaty of 1949 as relevant for its decision.[102] It also gave a broad interpretation to the meaning of collective security systems directed at the maintenance of peace in accordance with Article 24(2) of the Basic Law. From this one can conclude that the Court will remain reluctant in future to extend parliamentary oversight in relation to executive participation in international norm-setting pertaining to collective security, despite the fact that such extension remains possible in theory.

C. Conclusion

The foregoing analysis illustrates that accountability of international institutions in the form of retroactive oversight remains under-developed on various levels. First, the oversight mechanisms are still very much oriented towards Member States in accordance with the sovereign equality of States model. In instances where the oversight mechanisms are representative of the international community (of States) as a whole, they also resemble the internationalist accountability model. In contrast, the presence and impact of the cosmopolitan model and in particular the liberal democratic model of accountability remain limited.

---

tion of such a fundamental structural departure, but does not need to be the case.

[102] Birgit Schlütter, in ILDC 134 (DE 2001) C5. *See also* Andreas L. Paulus, *Quo vadis Democratic Control? The Afghanistan Decision of the Bundestag and the Decision of the Federal Constitutional Court in the New Strategic Concept Case*, 3 GERMAN LAW JOURNAL no. 1 (2002); Heiko Sauer, *Die NATO und das Verfassungsrecht: Neues Konzept – alte Fragen*, 62 ZEITSCHRIFT FÜR AUSLÄNDISCHES ÖFFENTLICHES RECHT UND VÖLKERRECHT 317 (2002).

This is *inter alia* reflected by the fact that individualized oversight mechanisms within international institutions remain the exception to the rule and where they do exist, do not amount to binding judicial proceedings resulting in enforceable decisions.

Second, the oversight mechanisms directed towards Member States are not necessarily forceful either. This is reflected by the different manifestations of vertical and intermediate oversight identified in the case studies. For example, vertical or intermediate oversight by Member States does not always provide for the possibility of overruling a decision of a lower body or the replacement of the persons composing the lower entity that is responsible for the normative decisions. This aggravates the perception that international institutions function in an autonomous environment that insulates them from accountability towards Member States and other constituencies alike.

The analysis has further revealed that the weak general mechanisms of oversight and centralized individual complaints procedures can be complemented by incidental judicial review of international normative acts before regional and domestic courts. This type of oversight could strengthen accountability along the lines of the cosmopolitan model, notably in relation to individuals affected by the international exercise of public power. The (still rather limited) court practice reflects that such review is particularly meaningful where the international normative decision leaves room for interpretation. Such discretion enables regional and domestic courts to strike a balance between the rights and interests of different affected constituencies.

However, practice also reveals the hesitance of regional and domestic courts in exercising judicial review in instances where normative measures stemming from a powerful international institution directly conflict with human rights obligations. This is particularly the case where such a conflict concerns human rights versus collective security obligations. Similarly, regional and domestic courts are unlikely to strengthen the liberal democratic accountability model through judicial review of the national executive, where the latter participates in international norm-setting activities that touch upon sensitive areas of foreign policy.

This reveals that decentralized judicial review cannot in and of itself ensure the sufficient protection of the rights and interests of private individuals and other constituencies affected by the norm-setting activities of international institutions. In other words, it cannot entirely compensate for deficient oversight mechanisms within the international institution itself, but remains a residual mechanism that has to be imbedded in a broader system of oversight consisting of centralized and decentralized components aimed at creating balanced and effective oversight.

International Composite Administration: Conceptualizing Multi-Level and Network Aspects in the Exercise of International Public Authority

*By Armin von Bogdandy & Philipp Dann**

---

* We are grateful to Ute Mager, Christoph Möllers and Eric Pickett, as well as the members of the Max Planck Institute for Comparative Public Law and International Law participating in this project for their critical and helpful comments on an earlier version.

A. von Bogdandy et al. (eds.), *The Exercise of Public Authority by International Institutions*, Beiträge zum ausländischen öffentlichen Recht und Völkerrecht 210, DOI 10.1007/978-3-642-04531-8_31, © Springer-Verlag Berlin Heidelberg 2010

A. Introduction

The administration of the traditional nation-state used to operate as a rather closed system to the outside world. Today, cooperation between the public authorities of different States and between States and international bodies is a common phenomenon. Yet the characteristics and mechanics of such cooperation can hardly be understood using the concepts domestic public law or public international law currently on offer. Conventional concepts, such as federalism, confederalism or State-centered "realism" hardly fathom the complexity of interactions or reflect the changed role of the State, while more recent concepts, such as multi-level systems or networks, seem to encompass only parts of the phenomena at hand. Given this void, we propose to explore the notion of "composite administration" (*Verbundverwaltung*) and argue that it offers a concept which can combine more coherently the seemingly diverging legal elements of cooperation and hierarchy that distinguish administrative action in what often is called a multi-level administrative system.[1] Even though the concept of composite administration was originally designed[2] and further developed[3] with respect to the largely

---

[1] Eberhard Schmidt-Aßmann, *Der Europäische Verwaltungsverbund und die Rolle des Europäischen Verwaltungsrechts*, *in* DER EUROPÄISCHE VERWALTUNGSVERBUND 7 (Eberhard Schmidt-Aßmann & Bettina Schöndorf-Haubold eds., 2005). For a similar approach, *see* GIACINTO DELLA CANANEA, L'UNIONE EUROPEA. UN ORDINAMENTO COMPOSITO 6, 146 (2003).

[2] ARMIN VON BOGDANDY, SUPRANATIONALER FÖDERALISMUS ALS WIRKLICHKEIT UND IDEE EINER NEUEN HERRSCHAFTSFORM 11 (1999); Sabino Cassese, *Der Einfluß des gemeinschaftsrechtlichen Verwaltungsrechts auf die nationalen Verwaltungsrechtssysteme*, 33 DER STAAT 25 (1994).

[3] Gabriele Britz, *Vom Verwaltungsverbund zum Regulierungsverbund?*, 41 EUROPARECHT 47 (2006); Jens-Peter Schneider, *Verwaltungsrechtliche Instrumente des Sozialstaats*, 64 VERÖFFENTLICHUNG DER VEREININGUNG DER DEUTSCHEN STAATSRECHTSLEHRER (VVDSTRL) 262. For a similar treatment but with his own terminology, *see* GERNOT SYDOW, VERWALTUNGSKOOPERATION IN DER EUROPÄISCHEN UNION (2004).

federal European administrative space, we suggest testing the concept in the wider context of international cooperation.[4] We believe that it offers valuable insights and raises critical questions, even though we do not intend to insinuate any proto-federal prospects of the institutions discussed in this paper.[5]

The present article analyzes the multi-level and network aspects of the exercise of public authority and the legal structures providing the basis for cooperation between national and international authorities in light of the composite administration model. It aims to provide a legal phenomenology of international administrative cooperation in order to test whether the concept of composite administration can be fruitfully applied in this arena.[6] The article proceeds in three steps: the first will outline the basic concept of composite administration, its limits and its context (B.). In the second, more extensive part, we will analyze five elements that characterize the interlinked operation of international and domestic institutions as features of international composite administration (C.). To that end, we will focus on the normative basis of cooperation in composite structures, examine more closely informational exchange and expert committees, the various modes of implementation and analyze cross-linkages between institutions and their law. In a third step (D.), we will summarize our arguments on why we think that the notion of composite administration is helpful to conceptualize inter-authority cooperation and point to some important differences between European and international forms of composite administration.

4 On the catalytic role of European concepts for international phenomena, *see* Matthias Ruffert, *Perspektiven des Internationalen Verwaltungsrechts, in* INTERNATIONALES VERWALTUNGSRECHT 412 (Christoph Möllers, Andreas Voßkuhle & Christian Walter eds., 2007); Anne-Marie Slaugther & William Burke-White, *The Future of International Law is Domestic (or, The European Way of Law)*, 47 HARVARD INTERNATIONAL LAW JOURNAL 327 (2006).

5 On the differences between European and international composite administration, *see* Part C. Against proto-federal concepts in the analysis of global governance, *see* von Bogdandy, in this volume.

6 The notion of "administration" is understood here primarily in its operational (not its organizational) meaning, *i.e.* focused on activity. On the terminology, *see* von Bogdandy, Dann & Goldmann, in this volume.

B. The Concept of Composite Administration

I. Basic Idea

The concept of composite administration aims to reconcile "autonomy, mutual considerateness and the ability to undertake common action".[7] Considering the growing demand for understanding international cooperation, a concept combining these features promises to be useful. It should be noted that such a concept is, first of all, a proposal; its power lies in its descriptive (and partly figurative) value, it is not a legal term.[8] It may facilitate understanding the *operations* conducted within and by such multi-layered structures. The concept does not focus on powers, organizational structures or the relation of legal norms as such,[9] but rather on bureaucratic cooperation and the interaction of institutions in the exercise of public authority.[10] At the same time, one should note that the concept does not focus on processes *within* one organization but encompasses the *entirety* of cooperation between international institutions and member States.[11] Some might wonder whether such a concept would be too broad and rather obfuscate the problems. However, this would misread our intention and the concept's purpose: Sabino Cassese recently remarked that "between the global and the domestic sphere there is a gray area of mixed bodies and procedures, joint decisions and parasitical systems".[12] Our aim is to put this "gray area" under a magnifying glass and to analyze what we find there in detail. The concept of composite administration might help to get hold of what we find and in fact focus our research. Its basic idea can be summed up in the following terms:

---

7 Schmidt-Aßmann (note 1), at 7 [translation by the authors].

8 Britz (note 3), at 47.

9 On these issues, *see* International Law Commission, Fragmentation of International Law, 58th session, General Assembly A/CN.4/L.682; DAN SAROOSHI, INTERNATIONAL ORGANIZATIONS AND THEIR EXERCISE OF SOVEREIGN POWERS (2005); CHRISTOPH MÖLLERS, GEWALTENGLIEDERUNG. LEGITIMATION UND DOGMATIK IM NATIONALEN UND INTERNATIONALEN RECHTSVERGLEICH 253 (2005).

10 It is easier to express this very point in German: we focus on *Verbundverwaltung*, not on the *Verwaltungsverbund*.

11 On the different dimensions of cooperation, *see* Part B.II.

12 Sabino Cassese, *Administrative Law without a State?*, 37 NEW YORK UNIVERSITY JOURNAL OF INTERNATIONAL LAW AND POLITICS 684 (2005).

The first hallmark is one of functional and routinized cooperation between bureaucratic institutions which maintain organizational separation.[13] Composite administration takes place when a plurality of legally independent public authorities pursues aims of public concern as a common task. These authorities are, in contrast to those of a federal State, not part of a comprehensive body politic. Whereas in a federal State, all authorities are conceived as being part of one body politic (*Verband*), this is not the case in instances of composite administration which only forms a compound or composite arrangement (*Verbund*).[14] What is missing is the idea of an overarching political and legal unity.[15] The common operation is principally based on the idea of a division of labor.[16] Hence, functional cooperation and organizational separation form structural principles on which a composite administration rests.

The codependence of the participants is also characteristic of composite administration. Standards, be they binding legal acts or soft law requirements, are not only developed, but also implemented in a cooperative way. Especially implementation as composite administration is characterized by manifold forms of interaction with respect to the exchange of information, procedural alliances or even forms of institutional combinations in order to ensure implementation and to avoid the prisoners' dilemma. In effect, while the organizations are legally separate, their exercise of public authority can often not be attributed to one level; rather, is an interconnected effort of functionally interwoven bureaucratic actors. This form of codependence is therefore another structural principle of composite administration. A further characteristic element of composite administration is a difference in the territorial scope of the authorities involved. There is usually one public authority, often con-

---

13 By composite administration we therefore focus on a smaller range of institutions than the overall project.

14 In German, the terms "*Verband*" and "*Verbund*" easily express the difference between these two forms of association. In English such wordplay is not possible. On the notion of *Verband* (organization/association) as a social relationship that is closed or limited in the admission of outsiders and the regulations of which are enforced by specific individuals, *see* MAX WEBER, ECONOMY AND SOCIETY §§ 12, 17 (Gunter Roth & Claus Wittich eds., 1978).

15 DANIEL ELAZAR, FEDERALISM AND POLITICAL INTEGRATION (1979). For a comparative perspective, *see* MICHAEL BOTHE, DIE KOMPETENZSTRUKTUR DES MODERNEN BUNDESSTAATES IN RECHTSVERGLEICHENDER HINSICHT (1977).

16 *See* Venzke, in this volume.

ceived as the "upper level", that operates for the entire territory covered by the regime, and a plurality of further institutions, often seen as the "lower level" which are territorially more limited.[17] Most importantly, the territorially more limited institutions (usually a nation-state) generally carry more legitimacy.[18] As public law gravitates around the issue of legitimacy, this feature deeply informs the structure and operation of composite administration. It also proves how misleading the use of the terms "upper" and "lower" in this context can be.

II. Dimensions of Cooperation – The Problem of Hierarchy

Cooperation between public authorities is often conceived as taking place in different "dimensions". The most common way is to distinguish between a vertical and a horizontal dimension: the vertical dimension is mostly understood in terms of the multi-level metaphor, meaning the cooperation between an "upper" and "lower" level.[19] The levels

---

[17] On the notion and legal contours of level (*Ebene*), *see* MÖLLERS (note 9), at 210-218 (2005); Franz C. Mayer, *The European Constitution and the Courts*, *in* PRINCIPLES OF EUROPEAN CONSTITUTIONAL LAW 320 (Armin von Bogdandy & Jürgen Bast eds., 2006).

[18] Daniel Bodansky, *The Legitimacy of International Governance: A Coming Challenge for International Environmental Law?*, 93 AMERICAN JOURNAL OF INTERNATIONAL LAW 596 (1999); Rainer Wahl, *Der einzelne in der Welt jenseits des Staates, in* VERFASSUNGSSTAAT, EUROPÄISIERUNG, INTERNATIONALISIERUNG 62-66 (Rainer Wahl ed., 2003); Joseph H. H. Weiler, *The Geology of International Law – Governance, Democracy and Legitimacy*, 64 ZEITSCHRIFT FÜR AUSLÄNDISCHES ÖFFENTLICHES RECHT UND VÖLKERRECHT (ZAÖRV) 547 (2004); Wolfrum, in this volume; Michael Zürn, *Global Governance and Legitimacy Problems*, 39 GOVERNMENT AND OPPOSITION 260 (2004).

[19] The concept of multi-level systems made a fast career since the 1990s in political science as well as law. For political scientist's perspective, *see* Beate Kohler-Koch & Markus Jachtenfuchs, *Regieren im dynamischen Mehrebenensysten, in* EUROPÄISCHE INTEGRATION, 15 (Beate Kohler-Koch & Markus Jachtenfuchs eds., 1996); DAS EUROPÄISCHE MEHREBENENSYSTEM (Thomas König, Elmar Rieger & Hermann Schmitt eds., 1996); Gary Marks & Liesbet Hooghe, *Contrasting Visions of Multi-Level Governance*, *in* MULTI-LEVEL GOVERNANCE 15 (Ian Bache & Matthew Flinders eds., 2004). For the perspective of legal scholarship, *see* Thomas Groß, *Verantwortung und Effizienz in der Mehrebenenverwaltung*, 66 VVDSTRL 154-157 (2006); Wahl (note 18); Ingolf Pernice, *The Global Dimension of Multilevel Constitutionalism*, *in* VÖLKER-

are characterized by their territorial scope, quite often complemented by an implicit Kelsenian understanding of a *Stufenbau*, distinguishing an international, supranational, national and regional level.[20] The horizontal dimension is understood as meaning cooperation between organizations on the same level.

However, this terminology is problematic. Although intuitively appealing and helpful for approaching the topic, it might convey an idea of hierarchy which is misleading in comprehending today's reality of the relationships and interactions between the various actors and levels. It implies a traditional meaning of hierarchy, in which the "upper" level dominates the "lower" level and in which hierarchy is organized mostly in formal instruments. This, however, would today be equally wrong as describing all international cooperation as cooperation of equal and sovereign subjects of international law, acting on neatly separated levels. Instead, the concept of composite administration takes into account the multiple forms of interconnectedness which are characteristic of today's global governance system. At the same time, the concept does not disguise the existence of hierarchy in the sense of power imbalances. On the contrary: obviously, power imbalances shape the relations between actors, but such power is rather based on informal and non-legal facts, such as economic, military or cultural advantages.[21] This non-legal power finds its expression in the way processes are created (or blocked), used (or abused) or publicly communicated (or not reported) and not so much by the formal status of actors or their positions on an upper or lower level. It taints the concept of "multi-level systems" that it is not able to avoid such a (mis)conception.[22]

RECHT ALS WERTORDNUNG. FESTSCHRIFT FÜR CHRISTIAN TOMUSCHAT, 973 (Pierre-Marie Dupuy ed., 2006).

20 HANS KELSEN, REINE RECHTSLEHRE 228 (1960). Against a hierarchical understanding of levels, *see* FRANZ C. MAYER, DIE INTERNATIONALISIERUNG DES VERWALTUNGSRECHTS 320-321 (forthcoming).

21 ANDREW HURRELL, ON GLOBAL ORDER. POWER, VALUES AND THE CONSTITUTION OF INTERNATIONAL SOCIETY (2007); JOSEPH NYE, SOFT POWER (2004). On how these aspects play out in the field of development cooperation, *see* Philipp Dann, *Grundfragen eines Entwicklungsverwaltungsrechts, in* INTERNATIONALES VERWALTUNGSRECHT 44 (Christoph Möllers, Andreas Voßkuhle & Christian Walter eds., 2007).

22 Another way of defining different dimensions could focus on the central instrument of action: if this is unilateral (*e.g.* an administrative act, a regulation, a binding resolution, a decision) one assumes that a vertical dimension is at

For similar reasons, the concept of network administration is unconvincing. Moreover, the term *network* is often meant to focus on informal relationships.[23] While such relationships need to be considered for a full understanding of institutional and procedural rules, it appears problematic from a legal perspective to concentrate on a concept that largely does away with the central research object, *i.e.* positive rules.[24] These problems of adequately naming dimensions of interaction show the urgency in developing less metaphorical concepts for such legal phenomena. The notion of composite administration therefore sets aside such terms yet combines their perspectives. In effect, composite administration captures various modes and dimensions of cooperation between the actors involved.

III. Participants and Constellations of Composite Administration

This leads to a second set of questions concerning the notion of composite administration, namely the questions of who takes part in it, what are the regular configurations and what would *not* be considered composite administration. In response to these questions one has to realize that the concept of composite administration alludes to more than

stake, while conventional bilateral or multilateral acts (*e.g.* contracts, treaties) indicate a horizontal dimension. However, the problem of this approach is that the difference between a horizontal instrument and a vertical one does not necessarily reveal the power relationship between the actors involved. This is easily demonstrated by examples from the law of subsidies, where these are agreed in contractual form, but often on terms of the (donating) State or parallel cases of development assistance.

[23] On the notion of networks, *see* ANNE-MARIE SLAUGHTER, THE NEW WORLD ORDER 18-23 (2004); GUNNAR FOLKE SCHUPPERT, VERWALTUNGSWISSENSCHAFT 384 (2000).

[24] For further problems of the concept of networks, *see* Matthias Goldmann, *Der Widerspenstigen Zähmung, oder: Netzwerke dogmatisch gedacht*, *in* NETZWERKE 226 (Sigrid Boysen *et al.* eds., 2007); Eyal Benvenisti, *"Coalitions of the Willing" and the Evolution of Informal International Law*, TEL AVIV UNIVERSITY LAW SCHOOL, FACULTY PAPERS 31/2006; more appreciative of the ambiguities of the notion, Christoph Möllers, *Transnationale Behördenkooperation*, 65 ZAÖRV 380 (2005).

the interaction of an organization and its members. Inter-institutional cooperation as composite administration can occur in three ways:[25]

First, it takes into account the fact that organizations deal with their members not only as members but also as external partners.[26] When UNDP conducts a Good-Governance-project in the Sudan, both the UNDP and the central administration of Sudan act as independent legal entities administering the project. Hence, there is an external relationship between both which can include the exercise of public authority. If this cooperation is continuous and routinized, and not just *ad hoc*, such cooperation would be an example of composite administration.[27] On the other hand, the participation of member States in the bodies of the organization is not an expression of a composite administration.

Second, an international institution can also cooperate with other external partners, namely other international institutions, non-member States or non-governmental organizations. The common and concrete unity of action and the regular exercise of public authority with regard to an agreed purpose marks composite administration.[28] We can therefore observe such administration when the FAO regularly cooperates with the World Health Organization on issues of fisheries, or when CITES cooperates with certain NGOs to assemble and assess data, but we cannot assume a composite administration between FAO and WIPO just because both of them are part of the UN family.[29]

Third, there can also be cooperation among the member States of an organization (or some of them), for example in order to coordinate the implementation of common obligations. This type of transnational cooperation has become especially relevant within the European compos-

---

25 With respect to the European composite administration, Eberhard Schmidt-Aßmann writes of the "triadic structure of roles" (translation of the authors) of Member States – as masters of the treaties, as partners of the Commission and as subjects of control, *see* Schmidt-Aßmann (note 1), at 7; VON BOGDANDY (note 2), at 11-14.

26 HERNY G. SCHERMERS & NIELS BLOKKER, INTERNATIONAL INSTITUTIONAL LAW § 1688 (2003, 4th ed.).

27 On the special question of host States, *see* A. S. MULLER, INTERNATIONAL ORGANIZATIONS AND THEIR HOST STATES (1995).

28 Irrelevant is also whether an organization is part of a "family of international organizations". On these, *see* SCHERMERS & BLOKKER (note 26), at §§ 1691-1701.

29 *See* Paul C. Szasz, *The Complexification of the United Nations System*, 3 MAX PLANCK YEARBOOK OF UNITED NATIONS LAW (UNYB) 1 (1999).

ite administration.[30] Needless to say, not every cooperation between States, which (also) happen to be members of the same organization, constitutes composite administration.

In sum, composite administration includes the cooperation of international institutions with other legal entities (be it member States or other institutions) if the institutions are bureaucratic in nature, the purpose of this cooperation is the exercise of public authority, the exercise of public authority also involves instruments external to the organization and the cooperation is continuous, not just *ad hoc* in nature. The concept thus aims to grasp cooperation outside the regular shell of an organization, and it implies that an organization can take part in different instances of composite administration and with different partners.

C. Elements of International Composite Administration

There is not one fixed form of international composite administration, but rather several typical elements that characterize it and the dynamics in it. In the following section, we want to highlight five elements; others could be added.

I. Normative Basis

A starting point for understanding international composite administration is the question of its respective normative basis. This might be surprising, since the normative basis for any cooperation between the international institution and its member States (or third parties) can be found in the general principles of *pacta sunt servanda* and *good faith*, Articles 26 and 31 VCLT. These doctrines oblige the respective parties to honor the terms of the treaty and to collaborate in its framework.[31] It

---

[30] Jürgen Bast, *Transnationale Verwaltung des europäischen Migrationsraums. Zur horizontalen Öffnung der EU-Mitgliedstaaten*, 46 DER STAAT 8, 27 (2007); Giacinnto della Cananea, *The European Union's Mixed Administrative Proceedings*, 68 LAW AND CONTEMPORARY PROBLEMS 197 (2006); Hans Christian Röhl, *Verantwortung und Effizienz in der Mehrebenenverwaltung*, DEUTSCHE VERWALTUNGSBLÄTTER 1078 (2006).

[31] Jean Salmon, *Article 26, in* LES CONVENTIONS DE VIENNE SUR LE DROIT DE TRAITÉS, 1075 (Olivier Corten ed., 2006); Jean-Marc Sorel, *Article 31, in* LES

is an interesting and telling fact, however, that the treaties usually contain more specific norms. A central aspect of the European composite administration is its legal anchor in Art. 10 EC Treaty. Similar provisions can be found in a number of treaties in the international sphere. For example, Art. 4.1 of the FAO-Code of Conduct for Responsible Fisheries stipulates that: "All members and non-members should collaborate in the fulfillment and implementation of the objectives and principles contained in this Code."[32] Similarly, Art. 6 of the UNESCO World Heritage Convention states that: "Whilst fully respecting the sovereignty of the States on whose territory the cultural and natural heritage [...] is situated, [...] the States Parties [...] recognize that such heritage constitutes a world heritage for whose protections it is the duty of the international community as a whole to co-operate." Art. 2.2 and 2.5 of the UN Charter express an equivalent idea.

It is difficult to construe these provisions as imposing concrete obligations of collaboration in specific cases.[33] But it would also be unconvincing to consider them as simply repeating the basic principles of *pacta sunt servanda* and *good faith*, for this would be redundant and without additional value.[34] Rather, these provisions highlight the fact that member States in a composite administration play more than one role. They are creators of the treaty but also members and partners of the international institution, entrusted with the obligation to contribute to its effectiveness, as well as addressees of binding obligations imposed by such institution.[35] The analysis of the following elements might provide instances for where an obligation to cooperate as a member of the institution can be relevant. This might, for example, include the obligation to provide information, to comply with soft forms of coordination measures or to cooperate in implementation schemes.

CONVENTIONS DE VIENNE SUR LE DROIT DE TRAITÉS, 1289 (Olivier Corten ed., 2006).

32 FAO, The Code of Conduct for Responsible Fisheries, Report of the Conference of FAO, Twenty-eighth Session, 20-31 October 1995, Appendix I, also available at: ftp://ftp.fao.org/docrep/fao/005/v9878e/v9878e00.pdf; *see also* Art. 11 FAO-Constitution, OECD, Art. 3.

33 *See* von Bogdandy (note 5).

34 On this tension, *see* JAN KLABBERS, INTRODUCTION TO INTERNATIONAL INSTITUTIONAL LAW 194 (2002).

35 SCHERMERS & BLOKKER (note 26), at § 156; *see also* Schmidt-Aßmann (note 1), at 8.

II. Informational Exchange

Gathering, analyzing and channeling information are pivotal exercises in international composite administration. Appropriate solutions and rational administration rest on a sound basis of knowledge and analysis. The collection, processing, and distribution of information are important functions of many international institutions, and one basis of their communicative power. Yet international institutions and especially their secretariats seldom have the capacity to make inquiries and do research themselves. By their nature and position, they are detached from a larger administrative system which could furnish them with information internally. They thus depend on input from other sources. In addition, providing common data is the basis for creating a unified understanding of tasks and possible solutions. Establishing common data is hence a necessary step towards the perception of organizational unity and a sense of being connected.[36] Rules on the exchange of information are therefore important in the legal regimes of international organizations. While there are a number of such rules, three distinct typical structures have emerged.

There are, first of all, obligations of member States or parties to provide the central bureaucracy with relevant information. These obligations may arise at different stages of the policy-making process. UNESCO, for example, requires that its State parties provide an extensive dossier about the site that is supposed to be listed as a World Heritage.[37] State parties hence provide the main factual basis of the listing procedure.

Reporting obligations with respect to the implementation of international commitments are another form of bottom-up information channeling.[38] The FAO fisheries regime contains an extensive though voluntary system of reporting on the implementation of the central Code of Conduct and specific Plans of Action.[39] These reports are guided by a

---

[36] Schmidt-Aßmann (note 1), at 16.

[37] Art. 11(1) of the Convention; para. 32 Operational Guidelines 2005. On the UNESCO World Heritage regime in general and on these informational connections in particular, *see* Diana Zacharias, in this volume.

[38] On such reporting duties, *see* Röben, in this volume.

[39] *See* Friedrich, in this volume.

questionnaire that the Secretariat provides. The results from the reports then provide a basis for general annual reports to the member States.[40]

In addition to these bottom-up channels of information, international composite administration is often characterized by cooperation with non-members and expert NGOs which provide or evaluate data. An especially telling example in this respect is CITES.[41] The CITES Secretariat regularly contracts out research and analysis to two global NGO-networks[42] regarding the situation of certain species and trade in them. It can thus tap into a massive pool of expertise. At the same time, it depends, in its information gathering, on annual reports from its member States, which are then compiled and analyzed by another external organization, the World Conservation Monitoring Center (UNEP-WCMC). Moreover, CITES keeps in touch with a wide variety of NGOs which provide information.

Finally, certain variants of international composite administration have evolved in which little happens beyond collecting and sharing information. No further administrative activity occurs here; the main task is the assessment and channeling of information. Perhaps the most important example of this kind occurs in the International Criminal Police Organization (Interpol).[43] Interpol's central task is not to take police actions itself, not even to collect data by itself, but only to channel information that it receives from its members and to ensure the integrity of the in-

---

40 *See* de Wet, *Governance through Promotion and Persuasion: The 1998 ILO Declaration on Fundamental Principles and Rights at Work*, in this volume (on extensive reporting on implementation).

41 *See* Fuchs, in this volume (on CITES).

42 Trade Records Analysis of Fauna and Flora in Commerce (www.traffic.org) and International Union for the Conservation of Nature and Natural Resources (www.iucn.org/). On these links, *see* Rosalind Reeve, *Enhancing the International Regime for Protecting Endangered Species: The Example of CITES*, 63 ZAÖRV 339 (2003).

43 *See* Schöndorf-Haubold, in this volume; MATTHIEU DEFLEM, POLICING WORLD SOCIETY 124 (2002). A similar role is played by different committees of the OECD. They too serve to compile information and provide statistics rather than to administer (OECD-DAC, *see* Schuler, in this volume).

formation.[44] It hence provides a central database and serves as a transmitter of information and searches (so-called notices).[45]

Composite administration by way of information networks does not reach the level of institutionalization as known in the European Union,[46] but the amount of attention and legal regulation that concerns the administration of information in such international systems is becoming ever more obvious. They are therefore an integral part of composite structures.

III. Expert Committees

Another typical element of international composite administration is the role played by expert committees. Often an integral part of policy-making procedures, they are used to provide expertise and knowledge as well as to test concepts stemming from the international or national participants of composite administration. In their somewhat detached institutional position (being neither organs nor unrelated actors) and due to their mandate of objectivity, they are intended to avoid political impasses and provide legitimacy to international institutions and their decisions.[47]

The membership in such committees is based on scientific qualification and not based on member State representation. An example can be seen in the Advisory bodies of the UNESCO World Heritage Convention.[48]

---

44 *See* Art. 10.1(a) of the Rules on the processing of information for the purposes of international police cooperation, adopted as Resolution No. AG-2003-RES-04 by the General Assembly in 2003.

45 Schöndorf-Haubold, in this volume.

46 *See* Armin von Bogdandy, *Links Between National and Supra-national Institutions*, *in* LINKING EU AND NATIONAL GOVERNANCE, 24 (Beate Kohler-Koch ed., 2003); Armin von Bogdandy, *Informationsbeziehungen innerhalb des Europäischen Verwaltungsverbundes*, *in* II GRUNDLAGEN DES VERWALTUNGSRECHTS 347 (Wolfgang Hoffmann-Riem, Eberhard Schmidt-Aßmann & Andreas Voßkuhle eds., 2008).

47 On the role of such experts in international institutions, *see* von Bernstorff, in this volume; Venzke, in this volume. Expert committees also play a major role in the European governance system, *see* EU COMMITTEES (Christian Joerges ed., 1999).

48 Art. 13(7) and Art. 14(2) Convention, (*see* Zacharias, in this volume).

These are composed of two independent non-governmental organizations[49] and a separate intergovernmental organization[50] which evaluate properties named for the listing as World Heritage, monitor the state of conservation of properties and basically advise the UNESCO committee. A similar example is provided by the expert bodies to the Codex Alimentarius Commission.[51] Its Joint FAO/WHO expert bodies[52] are consulted at the beginning of the procedure of establishing food standards. As in the case of UNESCO, they are composed of independent experts.

It is especially important to examine the role of these committees in relation to the political bodies. Their relationship is supposed to be characterized by a functional separation between scientific assessment and political judgment, for example in the case of food standards and the work of the Codex Alimentarius Commission. Here, risk *assessment* is primarily assigned to the Joint FAO/WHO expert bodies and their consultation in the standard setting procedure, whereas risk *management* is supposed to lie with the Commission and its subsidiary bodies.[53] These in turn are not composed of scientific experts, but of government representatives from the domestic level.[54] However, the idea that the tasks of scientific consultation and political decision-making can therefore be neatly separated with a mutual gain of legitimacy in both parts of the process (the expert committee not being tainted by having to make final decisions, the political body expected to take into account scientific advice and common welfare considerations) might be premature. One can doubt whether scientific consultation can ever be free of subjective interests and specific agendas. Also, one has to wonder to what extend political decision-makers can understand the specific

---

49 International Council on Monuments and Sites (ICOMOS) and International Union for Conservation of Nature and Natural Resources (IUCN), now called World Conservation Union.

50 International Centre for the Study of the Preservation and Restoration of Cultural Property in Rome (ICCROM).

51 On the structure in detail, *see* Pereira, in this volume.

52 Joint FAO/WHO Expert Committee on Food Additives (JECFCA); Joint FAO/WHO Meeting on Pesticides Residues (JMPR); Joint FAO/WHO Expert Meetings on Microbiological Risk Assessment (JEMRA).

53 CAC, Working Principles for Risk Analysis for Application in the Framework of the Codex Alimentarius (ALINORM 03/41, para. 146 and Appendix IV).

54 Pereira, in this volume.

advice and still make a sound and independent judgment.[55] In sum, one has to ask to what extent such experts really help to de-politicize decision-making or rather disguise certain interests and power imbalances. Often, the question will be how such experts are selected, where they come from and whose interest they are closest to. Informal pressure and power might tilt the expertocratic balance.

IV. Various Modes of Implementation

The implementation of international legal obligations is a critical aspect of global governance, and it has taken on a new complexity, as various new modes are being developed that complement the conventional State-centered model.[56] Traditionally, the implementation of international obligations was part of a two-step procedure. International obligations were first agreed upon among contracting parties, and then, in a second step, implemented by the State parties.[57] Implementation in this model was principally *legislative* implementation, *i.e.* by means of general rules. In the current system of global governance, this concept has not been replaced, but it is complemented by a wide variety of other models and techniques to make obligations operative in domestic law.[58]

We shall analyze these techniques by, first, distinguishing different models of implementation (1.), then taking a closer look at the instruments of central bureaucracies to coordinate the implementation in the member States (2.) and finally focusing on technical and financial assistance as specific instruments of international institutions to ensure the correct implementation of their rules (3.).

---

55 On such doubts, *see id.*

56 Implementation is understood here as encompassing all measures parties take to make international agreements operative in their domestic law. *See* Catherine Redgwell, *National Implementation*, *in* OXFORD HANDBOOK OF INTERNATIONAL ENVIRONMENTAL LAW 925 (Daniel Bodansky, Jutta Brunnée & Ellen Hey eds., 2007).

57 At least according to a dualist approach, *see* IAN BROWNLIE, PRINCIPLES OF PUBLIC INTERNATIONAL LAW 31 (2003, 6th ed.).

58 MAYER (note 20), at 235. On the limited use of traditional models with respect to the hierarchy between national and international norms, *see* Ruffert (note 4), at 413.

1. Different Models

Different models of implementation can be distinguished according to the relevant actor or the primary instrument.[59] We will use both yardsticks here and look at five types of implementation. All these models demonstrate to what extent authorities are codependent in their exercise of public authority and point to further instances where the normative bases, as named above, and/or the perception as composite administration entail a heightened normative expectation to act cooperatively to achieve the commonly agreed purpose.

(a) The conventional (and still most common) model of implementation is that of legislative implementation. International rules set by an agreement between States are implemented by the public authorities of the member States through general norms. Although the final act might be enacted by parliament, it is usually drafted by the ministerial bureaucracy; that is why the implementation procedure can count as composite administration. A typical example of an organization that primarily relies on this kind of mechanism is the International Labor Organization (ILO). The ILO promulgates Conventions, which lay down labor standards. These Conventions are international treaties and thus open to ratification by member States.[60] Multi-level cooperation hence takes on the form of legislative cooperation and international standards are made operative by national (or regional) norms.[61]

(b) Implementation can, secondly, take place through administrative action by the relevant domestic authorities. Such administrative implementation hence concerns cases in which individual decisions are taken

---

[59] *See* Benedict Kingsbury, *Global Environmental Governance as Administration, in* OXFORD HANDBOOK OF INTERNATIONAL ENVIRONMENTAL LAW 72-83 (Daniel Bodansky, Jutta Brunnée & Ellen Hey eds., 2007); Redgwell (note 56), at 929.

[60] de Wet (note 40). It should be added that even though the ILO Declaration of 1998 is itself a non-binding declaration, its aim is to promote the legislative implementation of the core ILO Conventions.

[61] Two special aspects of such legislative implementation should be pointed out, as they demonstrate the variety of today's implementation regimes. First, in areas of regional integration the implementation can be done by regional (and not national) legislatures, esp. in the EU (*see* Friedrich, in this volume). And secondly, the international norms do not have to be binding. To an ever growing extent, non-binding norms are agreed on the international level yet domestic authorities deem it expedient to implement them. Many OECD Guidelines can serve as examples (*see* Schuler, in this volume).

domestically on the basis of international agreements. A prominent example in this respect are the export or import permits issued in accordance with and on the basis of CITES appendices. These appendices contain lists of species which require special protection; the import and export of them is therefore regulated. National Management Authorities are designated to grant individual permits if animals or plants on one of the CITES Appendices are concerned.[62] CITES rules are hence executed directly by domestic authorities.

(c) While *national* authorities are responsible for the implementation in these first two models, *international* authorities are decisive in the following three. The first of these three can be called "international direct implementation". Here, an international authority is itself responsible for executing an international agreement vis-à-vis a private individual or a State. The most prominent of this revolutionary, although still extremely rare form of implementation can be found in the UNHCR's system of refugee status determination.[63] Here, the UNHCR staff makes a decision as to whether an asylum seeker falls within the criteria for international refugee protection. This determination can[64] have the effect that a national authority has no further discretion with respect to accepting a person's status. The decision of an international institution is hence directly operative in domestic law.[65]

(d) A second type of international implementation might be termed "integrated implementation". Here, the final decision vis-à-vis an individual actor is also taken by an international authority, but it has been prepared by a national authority which was given authority to make a preliminary decision. Implementation here is therefore an integrated procedure involving national and international authorities. A prominent example of this type is the Clean Development Mechanism (CDM) under the Kyoto protocol.[66] In this case, the CDM member States set up

---

62 In more detail, *see* Fuchs, in this volume.

63 *See* Smrkolj, in this volume.

64 The effect depends on the concrete legal relation between UNHCR and the host country in question. In more detail, *id.*

65 Another example of such direct international implementation can be found in the WIPO's Madrid System of registering trademarks. There, a legal effect of the (international) registration sets in automatically, unless a country raises an objection. *See* Kaiser, in this volume.

66 Mindy G. Nigoff, *The Clean Development Mechanism: Does the Current Structure Facilitate Kyoto Protocol Compliance?*, 18 GEORGETOWN INTERNATIONAL ENVIRONMENTAL LAW REVIEW 249 (2006).

national contact points, so-called designated operational entities (DOE). If a company now wants to propose a CDM project, it will first have to turn to the (national) DOE. This examines the project and verifies its emissions reduction. The certification by the DOE will automatically result in the issuance of the specified number of certified emission reductions by the CDM registry administrator, *unless* the CDM Executive Board exercises its powers of review and, for example, detects fraud. Hence, legal effect comes from the international certificate, but the *de facto* implementing decision is made by a "loaned" national contact point.[67]

(e) Finally, the fifth type of international administration is in essence a model of shared implementation. Here, an international decision is taken and valid as such. However, national authorities are required to complement the international decision to make it effective. Such a model can be found in the listing of a site as a World Heritage site by the UNESCO. The listing decision is taken autonomously by the international committee. This listing decision then triggers a whole variety of obligations for the respective municipality to protect and preserve the listed sight.[68]

These five modes of implementation can be used simultaneously by one organization for its different tasks. CITES is an example for this.[69] However, they underline how the interaction between the international and the domestic level has moved away from State-centered ratification and become a more cooperative and varied common effort. They also highlight the codependence of authorities in composite administration. And, last but not least, they indicate to what degree the idea of international cooperation as always free and equal cooperation has been eroded and become inadequate to describe the reality of the situation. The modes of international direct and integrated implementation (c and d above) contain elements (even though in small doses) of hierarchy in favor of the international authority. If these two modes of cooperation

[67] The registration of domain names for the internet follows a similar, though slightly different procedure. ICANN, the global internet administration, does not have the competence to register domain names itself but has contracts with national registries. These can be public authorities or private companies but they are accredited with ICANN.

[68] On the legal effect of listing in detail, *see* Zacharias, in this volume.

[69] CITES obligations are implemented through legislative and administrative instruments and by national and international actors (*see* Reeve (note 42), at 338).

are admittedly rare cases, the next two sections provide examples for further soft and not so soft instruments of power.

2. Instruments of Coordinated and Consistent Implementation

Even if responsibilities for the implementation of international rules are laid down, questions on how exactly to implement them can remain, especially where the implementation is done in a decentralized way. The question therefore remains as to how the implementation of rules can be ensured to be correct and consistent.[70] To counter this problem, manuals or guidelines instructing those actually implementing the rules on how to understand and apply them have become a central instrument of coordination. Such manuals are often formulated in general terms and hence resemble norms themselves; they are promulgated by the international bureaucracies.

Several examples demonstrate the growing insistence on such coordination: the OECD provides official commentaries on its draft agreements on double taxation to orchestrate the unified application of these.[71] FAO hands out so-called Circular Letters that give guidance on questions of implementation.[72] CITES is slightly stricter as it promulgates binding interpretations for the central provisions of its Convention as well as resolutions that concretize it.[73] The UNESCO uses a "reactive monitoring" system in which a "Policy Guidance Tool" directs the handling of listed places.[74]

All in all, there is thus a broad variety of such instruments of coordination. In most cases, these instruments are soft instruments, proposing interpretations, nudging parties to keep in line with obligations or the like. Although being soft, these instruments can also be read together with the norms on the duty to mutual cooperation[75] and thereby be normatively "hardened". Obviously, there is no court to enforce such

---

[70] SCHERMERS & BLOKKER (note 26), at § 1739.

[71] Ekkehart Reimer, *Transnationales Steuerrecht*, *in* INTERNATIONALES VERWALTUNGSRECHT 187 (Christoph Möllers, Andreas Voßkuhle & Christian Walter eds., 2007).

[72] Friedrich, in this volume.

[73] Fuchs, in this volume.

[74] Operational Guidelines, para. 169; Zacharias, in this volume.

[75] Zacharias, in this volume.

duties, but central bureaucracies can nevertheless make an argument from general provisions of mutual and loyal cooperation and remind lax members of their respective commitment. And often enough, central bureaucracies have further resources to back up their demands, as – for example – the next section demonstrates.

3. Supported Implementation: Technical and Financial Assistance

Providing technical and financial assistance is another instrument that has become central to the effective and consistent implementation of international agreements or decisions.[76] In the process of composite administration such assistance is often available to developing countries that need additional means or expertise to fulfill their obligations.[77] Providing such assistance is hence often a necessary pre-condition or complement for implementation to take place at all or in the envisioned form. The allocation is organized and controlled by the institution that is also responsible for setting the international obligation.[78]

The UNESCO World Heritage Convention provides a fine example. Art. 15 of the World Heritage Convention establishes a World Heritage Fund, while art. 13 sets out a procedure according to which the central decision-making body, the World Heritage Committee, has to decide on requests for funding.[79] Such assistance may be requested for emergency assistance for sites that have suffered due to natural or man-made incidents, preparatory assistance for the preparation of nominations for the World Heritage List, technical cooperation covering the provision of experts and/or equipment for the conservation or management of

---

[76] Laurence Boisson de Chauzournes, *Technical and Financial Assistance*, *in* OXFORD HANDBOOK OF INTERNATIONAL ENVIRONMENTAL LAW 948 (Daniel Bodansky, Jutta Brunnée & Ellen Hey eds., 2007); Nele Matz, *Environmental Financing: Function and Coherence of Financial Mechanisms in International Environmental Agreements*, 6 UNYB 473 (2003); Lothar Gündling, *Compliance Assistance in International Environmental Law*, 56 ZAÖRV 796 (1996).

[77] Such programs are not exclusive to the international sphere. The EU also used a wide number of such programs to help countries to prepare for accession (*see* Armin von Bogdandy, *The European Union as Situation, Executive, and Promoter of the International Law of Cultural Diversity*, 19 EJIL 241 (2008)).

[78] *See* Philipp Dann, *Accountability in Development Aid Law: The World Bank, UNDP and Emerging Structures of Transnational Oversight*, 44 ARCHIV FÜR VÖLKERRECHT 394 (2006).

[79] *See* Zacharias, in this volume.

world heritage sites, or assistance for the training of specialized staff or for education, information and awareness-raising.[80] Between 1998 and 2005 there were 787 grants with a total amount of nearly US$ 20 million approved. And obviously, such grants are not ineffective instruments. Any poorer country with an important tourism industry depends on retaining the status of its sites. Granting or refusing such money is therefore a powerful tool to ensure that proper "cooperation" takes place.

V. Cross-Linkages

Another characteristic element of international composite administration should be highlighted: the importance of cross-linkages, *i.e.* cooperation across one level. Such ("horizontal") cooperation takes place between domestic authorities, between international bureaucracies or between bureaucracies and non-State actors and contributes greatly not just to broadening the viewpoint but also to the effects of international administration.[81] The horizontal dimension of composite administration is thus central in order to grasp the nature of today's global governance system. Two media of such cross-linkages shall be distinguished here: institutional and instrumental linkages.

1. Institutional Cross-Linkages

Cross-linkages can, first of all, mean the *institutional* cooperation between different organizations. The regular participation of representatives of other organizations as observers in meetings and decision-making procedures of an organization is one example. Such observers do not have a right to vote, but often enough they have a right to speak. They can attend the meetings of different bodies. FAO, for example, permits observers in its Conference and also its topical committees (esp. in the COFI).[82] The identity of such observers can vary; they can be

---

80 *See* Arts. 22 and 23 of the World Heritage Convention; paras. 235 and 241 of the Operational Guidelines 2005. Available at: http://whc.unesco.org/archive/opguide05-en.pdf.

81 Cassese (note 12), at 675.

82 Art. III(5) and Art. V of FAO General Rules of Organization; Art. XXX General Rules of the Organization (FAO) and Rule III of RoP COFI.

other international organizations but also private, non-State actors. FAO, to stick to this example, allows other international organizations, non-member States and non-State actors to attend.[83] Decisions about their admission rest with the Director General. In the case of the OECD's Export Credit Arrangement, it is generally the respective member State's Export Credit Agency that is invited to the sessions (Para. 3 ECA). The WTO also takes part here.

A different form of institutional cross-linkage is found where an organization is not part of an agreement but provides the forum and the organizational structure to a meeting of parties. A special example of such forum-function can be found in the Development Aid Committee (DAC) of the OECD. This, together with staff members of the World Bank, organizes a continuous exchange between donors and between donors and recipients.[84] The DAC obviously has no hierarchical means at hand to order participation, but it serves as host and provides the logistical (and financial) support for the process.

Both occurrences of horizontal institutional cross-linkages demonstrate the permeability and perhaps even openness of some international institutions and the flexibility of processes, at least in certain circumstances. Instead of being closed and complete systems, organizations seek an exchange with other organizations. The reasons for such permeability will be addressed below.

2. *Instrumental Cross-Linkages*

Another type of cross-linkage is of a rather instrumental character. It is the mutual use of norms by means of reference.[85] An organization can incorporate provisions of other organizations by reference in its legal framework. This can take place in explicit or implicit form. For example, the UN Convention on the Law of the Sea (UNCLOS) and the UN Fish Stocks Agreement refer implicitly to the FAO Code of Conduct for Responsible Fisheries when they demand respect for "gener-

---

[83] FAO, Conference Resolution 39/57 and 44/57.

[84] Dann (note 21), at 17.

[85] MAYER (note 20), at 281. On the problems of such references from the perspective of rule of law and democratic legitimacy, *see* CHRISTIAN TIETJE, INTERNATIONALISIERTES VERWALTUNGSHANDELN 599 (2002).

ally recommended international minimum standards".[86] The Lake Tanganyika Convention, on the other hand, refers explicitly to the FAO Code of Conduct in order to establish the relevant standards that are to be applied pursuant to the Lake Tanganyika Convention.[87] Other examples can be added: the OECD Export Credit Arrangement incorporates norms which the Bern Union has promulgated and which are laid down in the Bern Union General Understanding. The WTO has incorporated norms of this agreement in its Agreement on Subsidies and Countervailing Measures.[88] All of these examples underline the interconnectedness of legal regimes on the international plane and even a surprising degree of normative collaboration.[89]

D. Comparative Summary

The previous parts have examined a wide range of international institutions in their interaction with national authorities, other international institutions and non-State actors. It was asked what recurrent forms of interaction occur and how they can be explained. The central idea put forward was to conceptualize these interactions as composite administration, hence with a model that offers a wider horizon of such interaction and emphasizes the specific interplay of cooperation and power, autonomy and interdependence in it.

The following section sums up these analyses from a comparative angle. It is guided by two questions: first, we ask to what extent the concept of international composite administration might provide a convincing framework which captures the characteristics of international cooperation between public authorities (I.). In a second step we inquire into the

---

86 Art. 5(b), 10(c) Fish Stocks Agreement; Art. 61(3), Art. 119(1)(a) UNCLOS. *See* Friedrich, in this volume.

87 Art. 7(2)(b) Convention on the Sustainable Management of the Lake Tanganyika.

88 WTO Agreement on Subsidies and Counterveiling Measures, Annex I, lit. (k), para. 2. *See* Janet K. Levit, *The Dynamics of International Trade Finance Regulation*, 45 HARVARD INTERNATIONAL LAW JOURNAL 65, 120-121 (2004).

89 A perhaps rather troubling instance from a rule of law perspective concerns CITES. Its Art. VIII(1)(a) obliges the member States to penalize trade in protected species, which has been implemented, for example by Germany, with a dynamic reference in its penal code to the CITES appendices. *See* Fuchs, in this volume.

differences between the *international* type of a composite administration vis-à-vis the *regional* (European) type (II.). Even though these two types share common basic features, it is necessary to point to some fundamental differences.

I. International Composite Administration: Why Propose a New Term?

Different reasons can be put forward to argue that the new term and concept helps to better grasp the nature of cooperation between public authorities than other concepts.

For one, the concept should work as a magnifying glass and as a tool to frame and focus scholarly attention on this increasingly important aspect of global governance. The concept of composite administration, as outlined here, is more specific than concepts of multi-level-structures or networks, which can include various aspects such as competences, organizational structure or procedures alike. Our concept of composite administration, instead, concentrates on the exercise of public authority, hence on the operational side. It focuses on the routine forms of cooperation that are bureaucratic in nature. It therefore concentrates on only one aspect of what other concepts take into consideration.

At the same time, composite administration as a concept might help to avoid the terminological ambiguities of multi-level and network analysis, which are grounded in a misleading understanding of hierarchy. It does not insinuate top-down hierarchy (multi-level) or the absence of hierarchy (networks). Instead, it stresses the interwoven structure of authorities and the end of clear-cut levels. Yet by acknowledging this "marble cake situation", it can move on and uncover disguised power imbalances and thus informal hierarchies.

Moreover, even though it is not a legal term, the concept of composite administration can be connected to normative bases and impart certain normative meaning. In connection with a concrete legal basis (see B.I.), it can provide an argument for heightened obligations to cooperate, for example to provide information or to implement a program faithfully. In this respect, the term can help to accentuate normative consequences.

Finally, the term connects to an existing body of scholarship, which has been dealing intensely with similar phenomena in the European

Union.[90] While the European sphere is certainly different in many respects, as we shall see in the next section, the basic phenomena and issues are the same. The term "composite administration" therefore helps to strengthen the intra-disciplinary exchange.

However, the concept of composite administration also has flaws – and it is important to name them. First of all, it is still very broad. It does not focus on one issue area, a specific regime or a special mechanism of interaction, but tries to grasp the whole area of inter-institutional interaction. More important perhaps is another limitation: the concept of composite administration does not indicate how to resolve the central problem of the "gray area" where the lines of responsibility are blurred. It might help to better indicate where power imbalances and informal hierarchies exist, but it provides no recipe of how to deal with them. Like many current notions, it rather highlights the cooperative and efficiency enhancing aspects but does not indicate standards or critical expectations. However, the term is meant as a tool for further research. Using it as a magnifying glass and with these limitations in mind should help to address such issues.

II. International and European Composite Administration: Where Are the Differences?

While the concept of composite administration has so far not been used for the international sphere, it has played a remarkable role in the analysis of European administrative cooperation.[91] We should therefore inquire as to the differences between the European and international examples, for even though composite administration in different settings shares defining features, important distinctions have to be made.

1. Controlling Applicability and Impact

A first and fundamental distinction can be drawn with respect to the surrounding legal order. Here, the question arises of which legal order is determining the impact and applicability of common or "higher" level law on the particular or "lower" level. In the European example, the instruments of primacy and direct applicability assign this compe-

[90] *See* notes 1-3.

[91] *See* notes 1-3 (including literature cited).

tence to the "higher" level.[92] In the international sphere, this is not the case. Here, the constitutional mechanisms of member States or parties act as "gatekeepers" concerning the applicability and implementation of decisions taken by the international level.[93] This "reversed order" and the dominant role of nation-states has manifold repercussion when it comes to the mechanics of administrative cooperation, be it in the instruments used, the need for coordination or the supervision of implementation and compliance control.

2. *Topos and Telos: "Sectorality" vs. Universality*

Another difference between European and international forms of composite administration lies in their *topos*, and ultimately their *telos*. Composite administration in the *supranational* European Union is a process within one polity, whose organs act within a (mostly) unified institutional framework and which offers thematic universality, *i.e.* acts on a broad variety of fields. *International* composite administration, on the other hand, does not contain a proto-federal *telos*, but follows the logic of functional differentiation. The exercise of public authority here is principally focused on one theme, one sector, hence its regulatory perspective is in principle functionally limited. Moreover, it is not bent on political integration but technocratic perfection. This has profound consequences.

For one, an exchange of legal concepts between different sectors is much more difficult in the international context. A mechanism of "traveling concepts" that profoundly shaped today's coherence of European administrative law (*e.g.* the emphasis on procedural safeguards or the relevance of proportionality considerations) is lacking.[94] With respect to

---

92 KOEN LENAERTS & PIET VAN NUFFEL, CONSTITUTIONAL LAW OF THE EUROPEAN UNION 665 (2005, 2nd ed.); Franz C. Mayer, *Supremacy – Lost?*, *in* THE UNITY OF THE EUROPEAN CONSTITUTION 87 (Philipp Dann & Michal Rynkowski eds., 2006).

93 For a recent defense of this mechanism, *see* Advisory Opinion of Advocate General Maduro in the ECJ-Case C-402/05 (*Kadi vs. Council*).

94 For the principle of proportionality, *see* PAUL CRAIG, EU ADMINISTRATIVE LAW 658-666 (2006); for the exchange of concepts between EU and member states, *see* ECJ, Case C-28/05, *Dokter*, 2006 E.C.R. I-5431, paras. 71-75; Armin von Bogdandy, *Pluralism, Direct Effect, and the Ultimate Say*, 6 INTERNATIONAL JOURNAL OF CONSTITUTIONAL LAW 397 (2008).

its *telos* (integration or expertise) and its *topoi* (activities across the range of issues or functional specialization) composite administration can thus take place in profoundly different environments.

The sectoral specialization goes along with organizational and legal fragmentation.[95] While there is only one institutional and legal system for European composite administration, the various international regimes produce distinct systems in which public authority can be exercised as composite administration. This multitude heightens the problem of coordination. Especially with respect to actors on one level and overlapping jurisdictions, coordination becomes a major task.[96] It is from this perspective, that the cross-linkages gain special importance.

3. Permeability: The Boundaries of Composite Administration

International and European composite administration are also distinct with respect to the permeability of their boundaries. It is typical that the organs of international institutions involved in composite administration are open to representatives from other organizations which often take part in their deliberations. Their institutional boundaries are hence less hermetic than those of domestic authorities.

The reasons for this permeability can be found, first, in the functional need for cooperation and external advice. In European instances of composite administration, the exchange between the "branches of government" is a natural aspect of European governance and politics,[97] but not so in the international sphere. Another reason could lie in the fact that international bodies do not form polities. Their organs therefore have more of a functional than a representational role. This would also mean that the question of who is present and can voice his concerns is seen as less strict.

---

95 PROLIFERATION OF INTERNATIONAL ORGANIZATIONS (Niels Blokker ed., 2001); International Law Commission, Fragmentation of International Law (note 9).

96 SCHERMERS & BLOKKER (note 26), at §§ 1706-1739.

97 *See* FLORIAN WETTNER, DIE AMTSHILFE IM EUROPÄISCHEN VERWALTUNGSRECHT (2005); CRAIG (note 94), at 57.

4. Density of Cross- or Horizontal Cooperation

Another difference becomes apparent when we compare typical elements of international and European composite administration, namely the central role of horizontal interaction. In the European setting, composite administration often takes place as cross-linkages and cooperation between member States.[98] In other words, in the European setting composite administration also frequently takes place as cooperation at the purely national level between the various national agencies and authorities. However, this cooperation between the member States (cross-linkage at the national level) can hardly be observed in the international examples of composite administration. Member State cross-linkage, let us say, in CITES or the World Bank, is rather limited. On the other hand, cooperation between international institutions is frequent in international composite administration.[99] This lack of member State to member State cooperation in international composites may be explained by the fact that there is less trust between the national bureaucracies, much less an understanding of organizational unity and thus less willingness to cooperate.

5. Collusion of Powers – or the Lack of Institutional Counter-Bearings

A characteristic feature in the exercise of international public authority by composite administration lies in the significance of separation of powers mechanisms for them – or rather, the lack thereof. This is to some extent similar to the EU. In both cases, legislative, executive and judicial functions are exercised by several organs.[100] Legislative and executive functions are mostly exercised by identical actors, rendering this distinction almost meaningless on the supra- and international plane. However, the lack of judicial organs that can serve as institutional counter-balances to the norm-setting organs is more problematic, and in sharp contrast to the European composite administration. It would be the task of judicial organs, especially on the central level and thus with effect for all members, to establish and shape guiding principles and to lay down the normative standards for the composite exercise of

---

98 Bast (note 30).

99 *See* Part C.V.1.

100 Koen Lenaerts, *Some Reflections on the Separation of Powers in the European Community*, 28 COMMON MARKET LAW REVIEW 15 (1991); MÖLLERS (note 9), at 253.

public authority. Yet, while in the European context the ECJ and the ECHR play this role, judicial organs are rare on the international level and it seems more likely that decentralized courts, *i.e.* national or regional courts, will take on the task of judicial oversight.[101] This, however, could have problematic consequences, *e.g.* for the coherence of their rules or the protection of common concerns.

E. Conclusion

The concept of composite administration has been presented here as a conceptual tool for a better legal understanding of the various and heterogeneous norms concerning the exercise of public authority through the interplay between international institutions and national administrations, between various member State administrations as well as between various international institutions. In doing so, the concept should demonstrate its usefulness for the legal analysis of such forms of administrative collaboration, and its difference to the concepts of multi-level systems and networks. The aim of the concept is therefore not one of critique. The legitimacy of composite administration has not been the central focus. The concept's aim is rather to provide an analytical concept to mark typical elements, name recurrent problems and indicate further areas of research.

However, even though the main purpose of the concept is heuristic, it carries a normative component as it is embedded in a normative vision of peaceful cooperation between polities organized by international institutions which live up to their publicness.[102] International administration does not always conform to this vision: distrust, neglect, or hegemonic aspirations are not unfamiliar phenomena. Yet we believe that the vision which underlies the concept of composite administration has a sufficient legal basis in order to inform the construction of positive law and provide a meaningful general idea.

---

[101] On the role of decentralized courts, *see* de Wet (note 40); on the potential role of the ICJ, *see* Eyal Benvenisti, *The Interplay Between Actors as Determinant of the Evolution of Administrative Law in International Institutions*, 68 LAW AND CONTEMPORARY PROBLEMS 336 (2005).

[102] On this notion, *see* von Bogdandy, Dann & Goldmann, in this volume.

International Composite Administration

*Comment by Ute Mager**

Armin von Bogdandy's and Philipp Dann's contribution takes the heuristic model of composite administration as its basis. Compared with the alternative models of multi-layered administration and networks, this model has the advantages mentioned in the text. In fact, while the notion of multi-layered administration evokes the idea of hierarchy where no such hierarchy exists, the notion networking, though negating the concept of hierarchy, eliminates the fact of legal relations itself and therefore is unable to encompass most of the interesting phenomena, as the authors point out. The term "international composite administration" is a valuable contribution to legal scholarship because it includes terms and concepts known in the legal sphere – international and administration – whereas the adjective composite indicates the direction for further research.

I do not agree with the argument that the concept of international composite administration "does not disguise the existence of hierarchy in the sense of power imbalances". The notion of hierarchy is not sufficiently defined by the concept of "power imbalances". Hierarchy is a very special term which possesses a normative content: there is hierarchy between different agents of public authority in the case that the power of one agent derives from the power of the other agent. In a very strict sense of hierarchy, the power of both agents should have the same source of legitimacy. In contrast, the criterion of power imbalances is not sufficiently defined. This lack of precision means that the concept of power imbalances is not very helpful for legal analyses.

---

* I would like to thank Eric Pickett for his very helpful comments on a previous draft of this article.

A. von Bogdandy et al. (eds.), *The Exercise of Public Authority by International Institutions*, Beiträge zum ausländischen öffentlichen Recht und Völkerrecht 210,
DOI 10.1007/978-3-642-04531-8_32,

The authors present an overview of legal relations which they subsume under the notion of international composite administration: relations between an international organization and a member State, relations between different international organizations and relations between member states of a special international organization. The precondition is that the international organization in question is established to fulfil functions of international public authority. The concept of public authority in the sphere of international law is not as clear as it may seem at first glance. Nevertheless, the problems created by the lack of crisp boarders defining the notion of international public authority should not be overestimated. Where international organizations founded by states exercise authority or states fulfil public functions on the basis of rules or decisions taken by international organizations (whoever founded them), there is little doubt that the notion public authority fits well. Thus, while the term serves well in clear cases, it must also be pointed out that further legal research is required to develop a more specific definition.

The authors' comparison of the elements and structures of international composite administration with the elements and structures of European composite administration (*Europäischer Verwaltungsverbund*) is particularly useful. This comparison provides a deeper understanding of international composite administration, which the authors define as "a functional and routinized cooperation between bureaucratic institutions which maintain organisational separation". The deeper understanding is not obtained because international and European administrations are so very similar but because the differences are so enlightening. I would like to add to this comparison the perspective of a national composite administration in a federal state like Germany.

Looking first at the normative basis of administration one can see that in a state like Germany there is a complete hierarchy of norms. In the European Union we find the supremacy of European law, the effect of which is very similar to the establishment of a hierarchy of norms. In contrast, the status of an international norm in relation to national regulation depends in most cases on the decision of the state concerned. These differences correlate with the fact that a state is regarded as an entity which has one source of legitimacy, encompasses competences in all political fields and has a completely integrated administration as well as comprehensive jurisdiction. On the other hand, international cooperation is limited to a special issue with administrative cooperation strictly focused on this issue and determined by the function it has to fulfil. Mostly there is no other legal control than by national courts. The legitimacy of an international organization's actions is rooted in the agreed function it has to fulfil. In between the national model and the international model (but not in the middle) there is the European Union, which encompasses shared values and political goals. The European Union enjoys broad, though nonetheless limited, powers in a wide variety of political fields. The repercussions of these limitations can be seen in the sort of patchwork administration characteristic of the European Union and the fact that the European Court of Justice is not a European Supreme Court.

To summarize, it can be said that, whereas in national composite administration there is hierarchy in the normative basis and in the decision-making processes, in European composite administration the normative basis is the supremacy of European law, which results in some elements of hierarchy in the decision-making processes being reproduced, and in international composite administration there is fragmentary functional cooperation and often no international jurisdiction at all.

The great advantage of the international composite administration model is that it allows a comparison of phenomena on the international level with similar phenomena on the European and even national level. The differences which become visible from this broad comparative perspective are enlightening. They open the field for further questions, for example if there are good reasons for these differences or whether developments on the international level have to be advanced. The concept is forward-looking because it transcends the state-focused perspective by using a more functional but still legal perspective.

Legitimacy of International Law and the Exercise of Administrative Functions: The Example of the International Seabed Authority, the International Maritime Organization (IMO) and International Fisheries Organizations

By Rüdiger Wolfrum

A. Introduction

It is possible to speak of international administration only if an international entity is truly exercising functions equivalent to those of States. While such cases are rare, as *Joseph Weiler*[1] emphasized in a different context, they do exist. One such case is the International Seabed Authority, which exercises legislative as well as executive functions in respect of the international seabed (the "Area") and its resources. Fur-

[1] J.H.H. Weiler, *The Geology of International Law – Governance, Democracy and Legitimacy*, 64 ZEITSCHRIFT FÜR AUSLÄNDISCHES ÖFFENTLICHES RECHT UND VÖLKERRECHT 547 *et seq*. (2004).

A. von Bogdandy et al. (eds.), *The Exercise of Public Authority by International Institutions*, Beiträge zum ausländischen öffentlichen Recht und Völkerrecht 210,
DOI 10.1007/978-3-642-04531-8_33,

thermore, the legal regime relating to the international seabed comprises a fully elaborated system for the settlement of disputes that is available to public and private actors involved in the exploration and exploitation of mineral resources in the Area. The functions assigned to the International Maritime Organization (IMO) and some fisheries organizations have not quite reached this level. Nevertheless, one can observe that these organizations, too, prescribe binding rules, at least *de facto*. However, they lack the jurisdiction to enforce such rules directly; in that respect they are relying on States acting in different capacities – such as flag States or port States – to enforce such rules. One may consider these legal regimes as belonging to a multilevel system (Mehrebenensystem), where the prescriptive and executive functions are vested in different levels.

The following contribution will examine why legitimacy is crucial for entities engaged in the exercise of functions which may be qualified as international administrative law (B.) and whether the International Seabed Authority (C.), the IMO (D.) and the Northwest Atlantic Fisheries Organization (E.) are particularly developed in this respect, and whether they possess such legitimacy.

B. Legitimacy in International Law

In recent years, the issue of the legitimacy of international law has been discussed quite intensively.[2] Different authors mean different things by the term legitimacy, although it mainly refers to the justification of authority, this notion being understood as the equivalent of having the

---

[2] T.M. FRANCK, THE POWER OF LEGITIMACY AMONG NATIONS (1990); M. Kumm, *The Legitimacy of International Law: A Constitutionalist Framework of Analysis*, 15 EUROPEAN JOURNAL OF INTERNATIONAL LAW 907 (2004); THE LEGITIMACY OF INTERNATIONAL ORGANIZATIONS (J.-M. Coicaud & V. Heiskanen eds., 2001); J.L. GOLDSMITH & E.A. POSNER, THE LIMITS OF INTERNATIONAL LAW (2005); A. BUCHANAN, JUSTICE LEGITIMACY, AND SELF-DETERMINATION: MORAL FOUNDATIONS FOR INTERNATIONAL LAW (2004); H.L. HART, THE CONCEPT OF LAW (1961); T.M. Franck, *The Power of Legitimacy and the Legitimacy of Power: International Law in an Age of Power Disequilibrium*, 100 AMERICAN JOURNAL OF INTERNATIONAL LAW (AJIL) 88 (2006); R. Wolfrum, *Legitimacy in International Law, in* THE LAW OF INTERNATIONAL RELATIONS, LIBER AMICORUM HANSPETER NEUHOLD, 470 *et seq.* (A. Reinisch & U. Kriebaum eds., 2007).

power to take binding decisions, be they prescriptive or executive. Such decisions may be general or specific in nature, a distinction which may be of relevance to their legitimacy. Scholars have suggested a variety of approaches concerning the elements which may give legitimacy to a particular authority. Theoretically they may be source-, procedure- or result-oriented, or a combination thereof.

First, authority can be legitimated through its original source of power. One example is State consent to international treaties. International law proceeds from the assumption that States have the authority to negotiate and to adhere to international agreements and the duty to comply with such agreements. States which become parties to such agreements accept obligations *vis-à-vis* the other partners to that agreement and, *de facto*, towards a larger community.

Second, authority can also be legitimate because it involves procedures considered to be adequate or fair.[3] Rules concerning the composition or establishment of an institution and its rules pertaining to the taking of decisions are to be seen from this point of view (procedural legitimacy). Procedure, or rather adhering to a pre-agreed procedure which is considered to be adequate and fair, thus has a legitimizing effect in international law, just as it has in national law.[4]

Finally, authority can be legitimated or delegitimized by the outcome of its decisions (substantive legitimacy). This is a crucial issue and one which deserves careful consideration. If a particular body, such as the Security Council or an international court or tribunal, although established according to the applicable rules and taking decisions pursuant to the established procedure, does not achieve results that the community to which these decisions are addressed considers to be adequate or fair, this may, in the long run, lead to an erosion of its legitimacy. In other words, an international organization's legitimacy is based on its procedural as well as its substantive legitimacy. The fate of the Commission on Human Rights provides a useful example. The dissatisfaction of the international community with the performance of the Commission has led to the establishment of the Human Rights Council, whose composition differs from the former Commission on Human Rights. In this re-

---

3 FRANCK (note 2), at 91 *et seq.* (emphasizing the "right process"); D.A. Wirth, *Reexamining Decision-Making Processes in International Environmental Law,* 79 IOWA LAW REVIEW 798 (1994) (pointing out that procedural integrity in itself is an important source of legitimacy for international law).

4 N. LUHMANN, LEGITIMATION DURCH VERFAHREN (2nd ed., 1989).

gard, it is of particular relevance that a member of the Human Rights Council may be expelled if it significantly and systematically violates internationally protected human rights. However, having said that, it cannot and does not mean that the legitimacy of an international body should be judged merely on whether its decisions are considered as being satisfactory by a State, a group of States or a community to which they are addressed. A further element of substantive legitimacy may be efficiency. However, this element should not be overrated. Frequently, the rules on decision-making of organs provide for the protection of particular States or groups of States, as provided for, for example, in Article 27 UN Charter. The inability to overcome this threshold has often, but wrongly, been considered to be inefficiency.

A discussion on the legitimacy of international law should begin with international treaties, as the primary source of international law. International treaty law is developed on a consensual basis. States' representatives negotiate international rules, which are subsequently adopted by the national institutions in a procedure designed by national law. Depending on the national system, this may include parliamentary approval. Thus, it is for the national law to ensure that there is a "legitimacy chain" that justifies the implementation of treaty-based international obligations through national institutions. As a matter of principle, one may say that – as far as consent-based international law is concerned – the legitimacy of the obligations deriving from the original consent is also to be established at the national level through nationally established mechanisms.

In practical terms, consent by States can have two different meanings; namely a specific one in which a State accepts a particular obligation, and a more general one in which a State accepts the establishment of a regime or a system of governance combining prescriptive and executive functions, which – after having been set up by consent – develops a legal life of its own.[5] These two options are not as distinct as one may assume; rather, in practice, they tend to blur into one another.

The consent of a State will undoubtedly suffice if the obligation is a specific one and can be implemented by an isolated act or omission. The same is true even if the obligation is of a continuing nature and requires continuous activities or omissions. However, there remains the risk that the legitimizing effect of the original consent may be eroded over time. This would be particularly true if, due to changing circumstances, the

---

5 D. Bodansky, *The Legitimacy of International Governance*, 93 AJIL 604 (1999).

burden of implementing this obligation increased significantly. Nevertheless, international law proceeds from the assumption that the originally valid consent provides legitimacy for continuous obligations. The mechanism to re-establish legitimacy if such an obligation has, over time, become factually illegitimate, is either through the mechanism of renunciation of the respective obligation, or recourse to the *clausula rebus sic stantibus*. In particular, the latter is intended, within limits, to adjust continuing legal obligations to the equilibrium originally envisaged by the parties.[6]

As will be seen below, the matter may become more problematic if States have agreed to establish a regime or system that exercises prescriptive and executive, and possibly also adjudicative, competences. Although the establishment of such a system or regime may be considered as being similar to having continuing obligations, they constitute a particular challenge to the legitimizing effects of the original consent through which the regime or system has been established.[7]

It is widely accepted that international law has changed in the last decades in terms of its scope, impact on national law, addressees, and the procedures through which international norms are created, as well as the value system upon which public international law is based.[8] Of particular relevance is the fact that international law increasingly addresses individuals, as well as corporations, directly.[9] Furthermore, international law is now increasingly being developed not only through international agreements but also by other, more flexible, means, specifically through the prescriptive and executive functions of international decision-making bodies.[10] International environmental law, in particular, has made use of the mechanism of further developing international law

---

6 *See* G. DAHM, J. DELBRÜCK & R. WOLFRUM, I/3 VÖLKERRECHT 743 (2nd ed., 2002).

7 Weiler (note 1), at 557 *et seq*.

8 *See* C. Tomuschat, *International Law: Ensuring the Survival of Mankind on the Eve of a New Century*, 281 RECUEIL DES COURS 63 et seq. (1999); B. Fassbender, *Der Schutz der Menschenrechte als zentraler Inhalt des völkerrechtlichen Gemeinwohls*, 30 EUROPÄISCHE GRUNDRECHTE-ZEITSCHRIFT 2 et seq. (2003).

9 *See* A. Seibert-Fohr & R. Wolfrum, *Die einzelstaatliche Durchsetzung von Mindeststandards gegenüber transnationalen Unternehmen*, 43 ARCHIV DES VÖLKERRECHTS 153 (2005).

10 DEVELOPMENTS OF INTERNATIONAL LAW IN TREATY MAKING (R. Wolfrum & V. Röben eds., 2005).

by means of decisions taken by meetings of States Parties. The norms resulting therefrom are not merely of a technical nature but often constitute either additional obligations for States Parties, guidelines for individuals and corporations, or recommendations on national measures to be taken to accelerate the implementation of obligations already stipulated in the original treaty. Although the decisions are based upon an international treaty, they are not necessarily treaties, as such, themselves.

The UN Security Council, to take another example, has not only interpreted its mandate broadly but has also assumed new functions. Making use of its power under Chapter VII of the UN Charter, it has acted in at least two areas as an international legislator: in the fight against terrorism and in the prevention of the proliferation of weapons of mass destruction. Here, the decisions of the Security Council require States to take action not only to deal with a particular incident but also to enact national legislation to tackle general problems concerning terrorism and the proliferation of weapons of mass destruction.[11]

These examples are indicative of a trend as far as the functioning of international decision-making bodies/mechanisms is concerned, and one which has resulted in strengthening their functions *vis-à-vis* States. Certainly, they remain institutions created by the will of national governments and act under their control. Whether this control is exercised effectively is a different matter.[12] In any case, none of them has yet reached the level of independence of the European Union, with its broad mandate. Such control of international institutions rests, though, with the national governments, whereas national democratic legitimacy is based, at least in principle, upon the people's consent. Even if the democratic character of many Member States is taken into account, as well as the democratic values upon which such international organizations may be built, the connection between individuals and international institutions remains a mediated and remote one. The broadening of the mandate of international institutions, combined with a more effective decision-making process and, in particular, the strengthening of their secretariats (international bureaucracies), results in increased independ-

---

[11] *See* S/RES/1373 (2001) of 28 September 2001 and S/RES/1540 (2004) of 28 April 2004.

[12] The Meeting of States Parties has, on some occasions, developed into such a control mechanism, which not only covers budgetary matters but also matters such as the exercise of functions and the recruitment of staff. This is ignored by those complaining about the increasing power of international bureaucracies.

ence and correspondingly weakens the possibility for governments to control them, although their collective control is not put into question.[13]

Finally, the establishment of new institutions – or the revival of existing ones – for the settlement of international disputes and the creation of new mechanisms to monitor the implementation of international obligations, should be mentioned. Such international courts, tribunals or compliance committees not only apply the respective law *stricto sensu*, but also add, either explicitly or implicitly, to the understanding of the law in question. Taking into consideration that international law, treaty law, as well as customary international law, are – by their very nature – less concrete, the contribution of these institutions to the corpus of international law should not be underestimated.

To summarize, three trends may be identified in the current development of international law. As far as the creation of norms is concerned, a shift of competences from the national to the international level is occurring. This shift may be characterized by the trends towards denationalization in favor of internationalization and "deparliamentarization" in favor of strengthening the role of the executive. Another visible trend is that individuals, including corporations, have increasingly become addressees of international law. Finally, the role of the judicial settlement of legal disputes has been strengthened. A factor which is common to all these new trends is that the direct influence of national governments – and most notably of the national legislature – on the shaping of international law decisions or international law in general, has been reduced; the chain of legitimacy connecting people to the international organization has been further mediated.

It is evident that such a development increases the dilemma over legitimacy. Exercising authority over individuals or corporations requires legitimacy which, in the absence of the traditional sources of international law, cannot be based entirely on State consent.

What possible means can be found to overcome the legitimacy dilemma? One should seek to rely on legal legitimacy, through which the continuing authority of the system or regime is connected to its original

---

13 Weiler (note 1), at 550 (referring to further examples): "The regulatory regime is often associated with an international bureaucratic apparatus, with international civil servants, and, critically, with mid-level State officials as interlocutors. Regulatory regimes have a far greater "direct" and "indirect" effect on individuals, markets and more directly if not always visible as human rights, come into conflict with national social values."

basis, namely State consent. The main element of legal legitimacy is that the respective institution keeps strictly within the limits of its mandate and follows the procedures set out for decision-making. A further means of providing legal legitimacy is strengthening the possibility of judicial review. This is a logical consequence in light of the functions being assumed by international administration: if international institutions are taking over governmental tasks equivalent to those of national institutions and – one should add – to the detriment of the latter, they should come under the same restrictions as States in adhering to the principle of the rule of law. If, for example, an institution such as the International Seabed Authority assumes legislative competences, or competences that directly affect the rights of individuals, such an increase in power calls for a counter-balance through judicial review.

Since the primary issue regarding the gap in the legitimacy chain was identified as being the linkage between the international organization and the national level, efforts should be undertaken to reinforce this linkage or – in other words – to make such linkage commensurate with the governmental authority exercised at the international level. Such a need arises in all cases where prescriptive measures or individual acts are undertaken at the international level, which replace equivalent legislative measures or decisions at the national level. The consent – including subsequent approval – of the competent national institutions, as the major source of legitimacy, is to be construed in such a way that it covers the consequences of the international commitment in the short term as well as the long term.

A further option, less rooted in the traditional approach, which seeks legitimacy through the consent of States, may be to consider alternative mechanisms of legitimizing international governance that are not modeled on the blueprint of national democratic governance. A body of experts, who are entrusted with making decisions, as opposed to a representative body of States, may be considered as one such mechanism. This mechanism is the one used by the Legal and Technical Commission of the International Seabed Authority. Although, formally speaking, this Commission merely has consultative power as far as the review of formal written plans is concerned, such recommendations may only be overturned by the Council by a qualified majority.

C. The International Seabed Authority: Objective and Functions

I. Introduction

The International Seabed Authority ("the Authority") is the principal component of the deep seabed regime established by the United Nations Convention on the Law of the Sea ("the Convention"). It was established pursuant to Part XI, Annexes III and IV of the Convention,[14] in conjunction with the Agreement Relating to the Implementation of Part XI of the United Nations Convention on the Law of the Sea, 1994 ("Implementation Agreement").[15] According to the Implementation Agreement, the establishment and function of the organs and the subsidiary bodies of the Authority are based on an evolutionary approach, which has not yet been fully completed. The organization of the Authority and its functions will therefore grow in accordance with the development of deep seabed activities.

1. Objective, Functions, Institutional Set-Up

The Authority is an international organization with legal personality at the international as well as at the national level. It enjoys privileges and immunities; its property, wherever it is located and by whomsoever held, is immune from search, expropriation, and all forms of seizure and writs of execution, by way of administration or legislation.

Article 157 (1) of the Convention defines the Authority's objective as follows:

> The Authority is the Organization through which States Parties shall, in accordance with this Part [Part XI], organize and control activities in the Area, particularly with a view to administering the resources of the Area.[16]

---

14 United Nations Convention on the Law of the Sea (concluded 10 December 1982, entered into force 16 November 1994), 1833 UNTS 3.

15 Agreement Relating to the Implementation of Part XI of the United Nations Convention on the Law of the Sea of 10 December 1982 (adopted 28 July 1994, entered into force provisionally 16 November 1994 and definitively 28 July 1996), UNGA RES. 48/263 of 28 July 1994, 1836 UNTS 3.

16 The "Area" is the deep seabed and ocean floor and subsoil thereof beyond the limits of national jurisdiction.

At first glance, Article 157 (1) of the Convention seems to be in conflict with Article 137 of the Convention, which states that the Authority acts in the name of mankind as a whole. This may even be seen as a conflict of legitimacy. How can it be that a group of States acts on behalf of mankind as a whole? This conflict is exacerbated by the statement in Article 157 (3) of the Convention that the Authority is based on the principle of the sovereign equality of all its members.

The apparent conflict between the two articles in question exists, however, only in theory. Article 137 of the Convention contains a specific objective and refers to the mandate of the Authority – administration of the deep seabed in the general interest of mankind – thus including the interests of that part of mankind not represented by the Authority's Member States. Article 157 of the Convention, on the other hand, is aimed at establishing the Authority, and thus structures the decision-making process. The Convention and, accordingly, the International Seabed Authority, has a broad membership and encompasses entities other than States. This very much reflects the idea that the Authority is meant to administer the Area and its resources for the benefit of mankind as whole, acknowledging that mankind may exist beyond the realm of States Parties.[17]

There is, nevertheless, no doubt that States are the main actors in this respect. Article 137 of the Convention is one of the cornerstones of the legal regime that structures the administration of the deep seabed. It reconfirms the system of common values on which this legal regime is based, namely that the deep seabed and its resources are the common heritage of all mankind – compared to the particular interests of individual States – and that this principle is to provide guidance for the policies to be pursued by the International Seabed Authority in the exercise of its competences.

According to Article 158 of the Convention, the Authority has three principal organs: the Assembly, the Council and the Secretariat. Its basic structure is thus no different from that of other international organizations. In addition, the Authority can also establish subsidiary organs. Some of the Council's subsidiary organs were already explicitly referred to in the Convention and the Implementation Agreement. These include the Economic Planning Commission (Article 163 (1) (a)), the Legal and Technical Commission (Article 163 (1) (b)), and the Finance Committee (Implementation Agreement, Annex Sec. 9). The Economic

---

17 *See* Art. 305 of the Convention.

Planning Commission will only be established at a later stage. Article 158 (2) of the Convention names the "Enterprise" as a further organ of the organization. It has special status, its own legal personality and will be in charge of its own organization (Article 170 of the Convention). Until the Enterprise begins to function independently, the Secretariat performs the functions of the Enterprise (Implementation Agreement, Annex, Sec. 2).

The Assembly is the plenary body and, as such, the supreme organ of the Authority (Article 160 (1) of the Convention). Each member has one representative in the Assembly. It meets in regular annual sessions and in such special sessions as may be decided by the Assembly, or convened by the Secretary-General at the request of the Council or a majority of the members of the Authority. Every State has one vote in the Assembly. Decisions on questions of substance are taken by a two-thirds majority of the members present and voting, provided that such majority includes a majority of the members participating in the session.

The Council is an organ with a limited membership. It consists of 36 members of the Authority (Article 161 (1) of the Convention) elected by the Assembly. The members must be taken from five different groups, four of which can be described as interest groups. The Implementation Agreement substantially modifies Article 161 of the Convention. These modifications have resulted in the establishment of a chamber system – a term expressly used in Sec. 3 (9) (a) of the Annex to the Implementation Agreement. Four members represent those States which are the main consumers or importers of minerals produced from the categories of minerals derived from the Area. One of these four must be a State from the Eastern European region, with the largest economy in that region in terms of gross domestic product, and another must be the State having the largest economy in terms of gross national product on the date of the entry into force of the Convention (Article 161 (1) (a) of the Convention, in connection with paragraph 15 (a) Implementation Agreement). Four other Council members are to be selected from the eight States which have made the largest investments in preparation for and in the conduct of activities in the Area, either directly or through their nationals (paragraph 15 (b) Implementation Agreement). Four further Council members must belong to the group of States which, based on their production figures, are major net exporters of the categories of minerals to be derived from the Area (paragraph 15 (c) Implementation Agreement). At least two of these States must be developing countries with economies that are considerably influenced by the export of such minerals. Another six members are to be taken from the group of developing countries, provided that these represent special interests. The special interests to be represented shall include those of States with large populations, States which are land-locked or geographically disadvantaged, island States which are major importers of the categories of minerals to be derived from the Area, States which are potential producers of such minerals, and least developed States (Article 161 (1) (d)). The discretionary power of the Assembly in electing the Council members from these categories is subject to certain restrictions. Before electing the members of the Council, the Assembly shall establish a list of countries fulfilling the criteria for membership of each category. Each group of such States shall be represented in the Council by those members nominated by that group (Implementation Agreement, Annex, Sec. 3). The final 18 members are to be chosen according to an equitable geographical distribution. The exceptional feature here is not that these 18 seats should be evenly distributed geographically, but that the Council as a whole should display an equitable geographical distribution. Every regional group shall have at least one seat in this category.

The Implementation Agreement significantly modifies the decision-making process. As a general rule, which applies to all organs of the Authority, decisions should be reached by consensus. Only once all efforts to reach a decision by consensus have been exhausted, can the decision be put to the vote. The Council has four different voting procedures for making decisions.[18]

Decisions on questions of procedure shall be taken by a majority of members present and voting. Decisions on questions of substance shall be taken by a two-thirds majority of members present and voting, provided that such decisions are not opposed by a majority in any one of the Chambers. These clauses may mitigate the influence of the group of developing countries, which is likely to have a two-thirds majority in the Council. However, given their different economic interests, one should not expect the developing countries to vote as a homogeneous bloc.

---

[18] The four different voting procedures include a vote by show of hands or a roll-call in the absence of voting by mechanical means, and a non-recorded vote or a recorded vote in the case of voting by mechanical means. *See* Rule 60 in Part X of the Rules of Procedure of the Council of the International Seabed Authority.

Additionally, there are several categories of policy questions which can only be decided by way of consensus. These include decisions concerning production policy leading to the reduction of deep seabed mining; recommendations to the Assembly regarding rules, regulations and procedures on the equitable sharing of financial and other economic benefits, as well as the adoption and provisional application of rules, regulations and procedures; and, finally, adoption of amendments to Part XI. In addition, decisions which do not fall under any other category but which the Council is authorized to take, must also be adopted by consensus. The majority requirement can also only be reduced by way of consensus. Finally, the approval of plans of work (for mining activity) is subject to a special procedure; here, the majority required depends upon the decision taken by the Legal and Technical Commission. If that Commission recommends the approval of a plan of work, the Council is deemed to have approved it if a two-thirds majority of the members of the Council present and voting, including a majority in each of the chambers of the Council, do not disapprove the plan. If the Commission, on the other hand, recommends the disapproval of a plan of work or does not take a decision, the Council may nevertheless approve it in accordance with the rules for decisions on questions of substance.

The division of the Authority's functions between the Assembly and the Council is highly complicated. The Implementation Agreement has resulted in the strengthening of the Council's powers. Basically, the Assembly is a legislative organ, which rules on the budget and determines the Authority's general policy (Article 160 of the Convention), whereas the Council is described as the executive organ (Article 162 of the Convention). One cannot say, however, that the Assembly actually has precedence over the Council. In many areas, the Council and the Assembly have to co-operate. Decisions of the Assembly on any matter for which the Council also has competence, or on any administrative, budgetary or financial matter, shall be based on the recommendation of the Council. If the Assembly disagrees with the Council, the matter shall be returned to the latter and reconsidered.[19] This occurs mainly in the field of law-making, as the respective rules and regulations are drawn up by the Council and the Legal and Technical Commission (the first – and in practice definitive – draft will come from the Preparatory Commission) and provisionally applied by the Council. The rules, regulations and procedures finally come into force after having been

---

19 Implementation Agreement, Annex, Sec. 3.

approved by the Assembly. The Council's main area of competence lies in authorizing the plans of work, which strictly regulate the deep seabed mining activities. These plans of work formally summarize all applicable requirements for a given mining activity. They must also be consistent with the framework of the Convention, the Implementation Agreement and the rules and regulations issued by the Authority.

The Secretariat of the Authority (Article 166 of the Convention) and the status of the Secretary-General are no different from the basic model developed for other organizations. The Secretary–General is the chief administrator of the Authority. His or her main task is the preparation of the meetings of the various organs. Although this is intended to be a service function, he or she may exercise considerable influence on the conduct of activities of the Authority.

The Enterprise is the organ of the Authority through which it takes part in deep seabed activities. The term "organ", as it is used in Article 158 (2) of the Convention, imprecisely defines its position in the Authority and the functions assigned to it. Its relationship with the Authority is comparable with that between the Euratom Supply Agency and Euratom itself. The duties carried out by the Enterprise correspond to those of a privately-run enterprise. Basically, co-operation among States concerning deep seabed activities has been institutionalized in the Enterprise. The latter has a Governing Board, a Director-General and a Secretariat. The Governing Board is to be composed of 15 members, who are elected by the Assembly at the Council's recommendation for a period of four years, according to the principle of equitable geographical distribution, and who shall direct the Enterprise's operations. The Director-General's duties are purely administrative and are subject to review by the Governing Board. All in all, the Enterprise's organizational structure does not display any exceptional features and corresponds to the model of other international economic organizations.

2. *Mandate of the Authority*

Under the heading "Nature and fundamental principles of the Authority", Article 157 of the Convention describes the mandate of the Authority. According to this article, it is for the Authority to "*organize and control* activities in the Area, particularly with a view *to administering* the resources of the Area."[20] When referring to the organization of

---

[20] Art. 157 of the Convention, emphasis added.

activities, the Convention in fact refers to the prescriptive functions of the Authority. It's prescriptive jurisdiction includes the adoption of rules, regulations and procedures for, *inter alia*, the appropriate conduct of activities in the Area,[21] the protection of the marine environment,[22] the protection and conservation of natural resources of the Area,[23] and the protection of human life with respect to the activities in the Area.[24] The most essential regulatory function is the development of regulations governing activities in the Area. The Convention specifies some objective criteria concerning the operational face of the activities, such as determination of the size of the Area, duration of operations, performance requirements and specification of categories of resources, etc. The Authority – in fulfilling these functions – does not confine itself to establishing regulations for harmonizing the activities concerning the deep seabed. In fact, the regulations envisage practical measures which have far-reaching implications for the operator.

These regulations are fully enforced by the Authority itself.

Pursuant to Article 162 (2) of the Convention, in July 2000, the Council of the Authority adopted by consensus and provisionally applied the Regulations on Prospecting and Exploration of Polymetallic Nodules in the Area. These regulations contain provisions on issues such as the conduct of prospecting activities, notification of prospecting activities to the Authority, the application for a plan of work for exploration activities, the conduct of exploration activities, the term of the contract, the rights of the contractor, the size of the exploration area, relinquishment of the area, responsibility and liability, training obligations, and obligations concerning protection of the marine environment. The Assembly approved these regulations without amendment[25] and they en-

---

21 Art. 17 of Annex III to the Convention.

22 Art. 145 (a) of the Convention.

23 Art. 145 (b) of the Convention.

24 Art. 146 of the Convention.

25 ISPA/6/A/18, Annex: Selected decisions 6, 31; Basic texts 226-270. These regulations are sometimes referred to as the Mining Code, although they form only part of that Code because they deal only with one of the mineral resources of the deep seabed and do not deal with exploitation. For an evaluation of these regulations, *see* M.W. Lodge, *The International Seabed Authority's Regulations on Prospecting and Exploration for Polymetallic Nodules in the Area*, 20 JOURNAL OF ENERGY AND NATURAL RESOURCES LAW 270 *et seq*. (2002); R. Wolfrum, *Rechtsstatus und Nutzung des Tiefseebodens des Gebiets, in* HANDBUCH DES SEERECHTS, 333 (W. Graf Vitzthum ed., 2006); *See also* M.C. Wood,

tered into force without having to be ratified by the States Parties. The regulations are directly binding for States Parties and private operators engaged in deep seabed activities and they are implemented through the work contracts that operators have to negotiate and accept before engaging in deep seabed activities.

However, the Authority's power to draft regulations is subject to certain restrictions. The Convention contains several restrictions, compliance with which is monitored by the International Tribunal for the Law of the Sea.

These regulations are binding on the Authority itself. This is of particular relevance for the negotiation and conclusion of work contracts. There is thus a hierarchy of norms which is similar to that found in national public law: namely the Convention (the "constitutional level"), the regulations issued by the Authority (the "statutory level") and work contracts concluded between the Authority and potential operators (the "work contract level"). The Seabed Disputes Chamber of the International Tribunal for the Law of the Sea ensures that this hierarchy of norms is fully respected and implemented.

The Authority also exercises executive functions. It has the competence – and actually the obligation – to ensure that deep seabed mining activities are undertaken according to the rules as set out above. These supervisory functions, however, are shared between the States Parties and the Authority, with the States Parties bearing the primary responsibility.

Article 139 (1) of the Convention stipulates that:

> States Parties shall have the responsibility to ensure that activities in the Area, whether carried out by States Parties, or state enterprises or natural or juridical persons which possess the nationality of States Parties or are effectively controlled by them or their nationals, shall be carried out in conformity with this Part [Part XI].

In order to ensure that the States Parties comply with this obligation, Article 153 (4) of the Convention grants the Authority the right to "exercise such control over activities in the Area as is necessary for the purpose of securing compliance with the relevant provisions of the Convention." This control function on the part of the Authority is independent from the affirmative consent of the States Parties or the companies engaged in the deep seabed mining activities. The Authority

---

The International Seabed Authority: Fifth to Twelfth Session (1999-2006), 11 MAX PLANCK UNYB (MAX PLANCK YEARBOOK OF UNITED NATIONS LAW) 47 *et seq.*, 85 *et seq.* (2007).

has a right to take any measure within the framework of the Convention's provisions, including inspection of installations in the Area, which is necessary to ensure compliance. Furthermore, the Convention envisages the inclusion of provisions concerning the Authority's supervisory authority and criteria governing the particular contract between the Authority and the applicant. This supervisory role may be further refined through regulations to be adopted by the Authority. In the event that the States Parties concerned are in breach of their obligations, they are internationally liable or, if they are directly involved in deep seabed mining, they may lose their right to continue conducting deep seabed mining activities.

The same is true for natural or juridical persons. In case of a breach of either the Convention or the terms of the contract, the licence to undertake deep seabed mining may be suspended or terminated.[26] This sanction would have significant economic consequences. In lieu of termination of the contract, the Authority may fine operators for willfully and persistently violating the fundamental terms of the contract or the applicable legal provisions. Such sanctions enacted *vis-à-vis* States Parties or natural or juridical persons may be reviewed by the Seabed Disputes Chamber of the International Tribunal for the Law of the Sea.[27]

Finally, the Authority enjoys the right to carry out deep seabed mining through its own company (Enterprise). This competence is unparalleled, even though it is limited by the Implementation Agreement. Generally speaking, deep seabed mining activities may, in accordance with the Convention, be undertaken by the Authority (through Enterprise), as well as by States and private and State-owned entities. According to the Implementation Agreement, Enterprise shall conduct its initial deep seabed mining operations through joint ventures. The reference to "initial deep seabed mining operations" indicates that, after a certain stage of development has been reached, Enterprise may undertake mining activities in its own right, as had originally been contemplated at the Third UN Conference on the Law of the Sea. Initiatives for the establishment of joint ventures may come from Enterprise or a contractor, in

---

[26] Art. 18 Annex III, Convention on the Law of the Sea.

[27] Art. 18 (3), Annex III, Convention on the Law of the Sea stipulates that sanctions may, as a matter of principle, be executed only after the operator in question has had the opportunity to exhaust the legal remedies available.

particular one which has contributed a particular area to the Authority as a reserved area (banking system).[28]

3. Conclusions on the International Seabed Authority

The Authority is, without question, a prime example of what may be referred to as an international administration. It exercises prescriptive as well as executive functions directly *vis-à-vis* States and natural and juridical persons. The Authority's legitimacy is based upon the original consent given by the States Parties when ratifying the Convention. The structure and the voting procedure of the Authority also provide legitimacy, particularly since the Authority has a plenary organ which is involved in legislating binding secondary rules. Equally, the Meeting of States Parties to the Convention on the Law of the Sea, which meets once a year and exercises supervisory functions, further contributes to the Authority's legitimacy. Finally, the elaborate dispute settlement procedure, which is open to States as well as natural and juridical persons, upholds the rule of law as far as the management of the deep seabed and its resources is concerned. It thereby contributes significantly to the legitimacy of this regime. The international administration of the deep seabed does not, therefore, have just one basis for legitimacy but several, which complement and reinforce each other.

D. International Maritime Organization

The International Maritime Organization (IMO) was established in 1948 (until 1982 it was named the Inter-Governmental Maritime Consultative Organization). According to Article 1 of the IMO Convention, the main purpose of the organization is to provide machinery for co-operation among Governments in the field of governmental regulation and practices relating to technical matters of all kinds affecting shipping engaged in international trade, and to encourage the general adoption of the highest possible standards in matters concerning maritime safety (efficiency of navigation and prevention and control of marine pollution from ships).

Over the years, the IMO has promoted the adoption of many conventions, protocols and mandatory and non-mandatory codes and guide-

---

[28] For details, *see* Section 2 of the Annex to the Implementation Agreement.

lines, the most important of which are the International Convention for the Safety of Life at Sea (SOLAS), the Convention on the Prevention of Marine Pollution by Dumping of Wastes and Other Matter, and the International Convention for the Prevention of Pollution from Ships (MARPOL). The main bodies of the IMO are the Assembly, the Council and several Committees, in particular the Maritime Safety Committee and the Legal Committee.

The IMO has neither direct prescriptive nor executive functions that go beyond State consent. Nevertheless, it exercises significant authority by promulgating international rules and standards concerning the safety of navigation, the safety of ships and the prevention of marine pollution from ships. Its role has been enhanced by the Convention, in particular.[29] For example, according to Article 211 of the Convention, States acting through the competent international organization (i.e. the IMO) shall establish "international rules and standards to prevent, reduce and control pollution of the marine environment from vessels and promote the adoption, in the same manner, wherever appropriate, of routing systems designed to minimize the threat of accidents which might cause pollution of the marine environment." States are, at the same time, obliged to adopt national laws and regulations concerning ships flying under their flag to prevent, reduce and control marine pollution from ships (Article 211 (2) of the Convention). Coastal States may take action against any violation of their national laws and regulations adopted in accordance with the Convention or applicable international rules and standards for the prevention, reduction and control of pollution (Article 220 (1) of the Convention). Equally, port States may enforce "applicable international rules and standards established through the competent international organization" (Article 218 (1) of the Convention).

The above-mentioned international conventions concerning the safety of ships and the protection of the marine environment developed under the auspices of IMO have become applicable "international rules and standards" as referred to in Articles 218 and 220 of the Convention, after having been accepted by a significant number of States. The acceptance was not universal, however, and was not necessarily given by the flag States of those ships against which the rules and standards may be enforced – the enforcement mechanism resting within the competence of the coastal States or the port States, as the case may be.

---

29 *See* Implications of the United Nations Convention on the Law of the Sea for the International Maritime Organization, IMO Doc. LEG/MISC/3/Rev.1 (6 January 2003).

Although one cannot qualify the activities of the IMO as being purely legislative in nature, the IMO significantly determines the substance of the corresponding national laws, which implement the rules developed under the IMO.

In addition, the dispute settlement mechanism of the Convention operates as a safeguard, so that national law does not go beyond such international rules and standards. The flag States of ships arrested or sanctioned by port States or coastal States may initiate proceedings under the Convention against national measures that seek to enforce higher standards.[30] In such a case, the dispute settlement body will assess whether the national law provides a basis for the national measure taken and whether the national law, as well as the measures taken, conform to the applicable international rules and standards and are proportionate to the alleged offence. The Convention thus establishes a coherent system of norm-setting through the interplay between prescriptive acts – based on both international sources such as the Convention and the international rules and standards established by the IMO, and on national law enforced by national organs – and an international judiciary.

The IMO has developed one further mechanism that can be considered to be of a prescriptive nature. The IMO may, upon the request of a coastal State, designate an area as a "particularly sensitive sea area" (PSSA). This power has been granted to the IMO pursuant to Annex II to IMO Resolution A.927 (22). PSSAs are areas which need special protection because of their significance for recognized ecological, socio-economic or scientific reasons and their vulnerability to damage caused by international shipping activities. The legal basis for the IMO's having such power may be found in Articles 192, 194 and 211 (1) of the Convention, in conjunction with the consent of the coastal State concerned. If approved by the IMO, an area will be designated as a PSSA and the IMO will adopt one or more "associated protective measures" that ships must follow in the PSSA. It is to be noted that the designation of a particularly sensitive sea area has no binding effect whereas the "associated protective measures" are mandatory.[31]

The type of measures that may be adopted is at the IMO's discretion. To date, the IMO has prescribed ship routing measures and ship report-

---

30 The procedures are set forth in Part XV of the Convention on the Law of the Sea.

31 *See* Revised Guidelines for the Identification and Designation of Particularly Sensitive Sea Areas, IMO Assembly Resolution A. 982(24), IMO Assembly 24th Session, adopted on 1 December 2005.

ing systems under SOLAS, special areas under MARPOL and a range of other measures adopted through IMO resolutions. To the extent that such measures have been based on existing international agreements, the resulting restrictions imposed upon navigation can be considered as justified.[32]

So far, the IMO has established at least 10 PSSAs, one of which (the Western European Waters PSSA) covers the territorial sea and at least part of the exclusive economic zone from the southern maritime border of Portugal to the Shetland Islands. In this area, traffic separation schemes and mandatory ship reporting systems are applicable.[33] Other PSSAs include the Great Barrier Reef, the Baltic Sea and the maritime areas around the Canary Islands.

Here again, binding international rules are being issued that have their legal basis in the consent of the coastal State in question, IMO resolutions and a general mandate in the Convention. The fact that PSSAs can only be established with the consent of the coastal State concerned is, in itself, not a sufficient legitimization, since PSSAs also encompass exclusive economic zones. In these areas, the coastal States have only limited competence to prescribe and enforce measures against international navigation. The associated protective measures go beyond those which could be prescribed and enforced unilaterally by coastal States. This is why co-operation with the IMO becomes necessary.

As indicated above, the IMO possesses neither direct prescriptive powers nor executive powers. Nevertheless, the IMO significantly shapes the development of the international rules on shipping and thereby indirectly but materially influences respective national rules. The authority to establish PSSAs is based upon the IMO's internal rules, whereas the issuance of associated protective measures is based upon international agreements. Thus, the powers of the IMO are primarily derived from the Convention and other international agreements, as well as the consent of the States Parties concerned. However, this basis for legitimacy is under strain. Although the IMO has so far interpreted its mandate narrowly, by refraining from acting at its own discretion and by

---

32 *See* J. P. Roberts, T. Workman, B.M. Tsamenyi & L. Johnson, *The Western European PSSA proposal: a "politically sensitive sea area"*, 29 MARINE POLICY 431 (2005).

33 *See* Particularly Sensitive Sea Areas, (IMO ed., 2007 edition).

prescribing broad measures, it is now coming under pressure to act outside the scope foreseen in the Convention.[34]

E. Northwest Atlantic Fisheries Organization

International fisheries organizations have traditionally been established to co-ordinate fishing activities in particular areas or concerning particular species. In the middle of the 20th century, these organizations clearly had neither prescriptive nor executive authority. However, in general terms, their powers have been expanded. This expansion of power has two sources. Firstly, there is the issue of overfishing and the associated sharp decline of certain fish stocks, and secondly, there is the legal source, namely, the Convention and the rules promulgated thereunder. It has become the task of the fisheries organizations to prescribe in detail the management and conservation measures to be undertaken. These secondary rules are based upon the treaty establishing the respective fisheries organization, which describes in detail the organization's prescriptive powers. By comparison, the executive powers of these organizations are limited; as far as enforcement is concerned, they rely on the States Parties.

The Conservation and Enforcement Measures[35] of the Northwest Atlantic Fisheries Organization (NAFO) are particularly advanced in this respect. Amongst other more traditional measures such as inspections at sea, inspections in ports, monitoring on the basis of reports to be submitted, a licensing system, electronic tracking of fishing vessels, etc., NAFO establishes a list of "presumed IUU[36] activities". This list is based upon information received by States Parties and includes vessels from both States Parties and non-States Parties. The States concerned are informed when vessels under their flag have been listed and they are given the reasons for the listing. The consequence of such a listing is that the States Parties to the Convention must deny access to their ports

---

[34] For example, Australia's attempts to induce the IMO to prescribe mandatory pilotage in the Torres Strait, a measure which may not have a basis in the Convention. In detail: R.C. Beckman, *PSSAs and Transit passage – Australia's Pilotage System in the Torres Strait Challenges the IMO and UNCLOS*, 38 OCEAN DEVELOPMENT AND INTERNATIONAL LAW 325 *et seq*. (2007).

[35] Available at: http://www.nafo.int/fisheries/fishery/iuu/list.html.

[36] Illegal, unreported and unregulated fishing.

by fishing vessels and all supporting vessels under this particular flag and also deny access to all services, except in cases of emergency. Furthermore, States Parties must prohibit the landing of fish, the reflagging of the vessel, or the change of crew, etc.[37] This listing procedure is similar to the one under the jurisdiction of the Security Council for the suppression of terrorism,[38] and States whose flag has been listed may be delisted if they can prove that they have effective control over fishing vessels flying their flag.

The listing mechanism works on two levels. Whereas the prescription of the applicable rules rests at the international level, enforcement is vested in the States. Recourse against the listing may be sought before the national courts of the State enforcing the listing.

The legitimacy of this mechanism rests on the consent by the States Parties to the Convention establishing the Northwest Atlantic Fisheries Organization and ultimately on the Convention, which calls for close co-operation by States in the conservation and management of fishing resources. Since the enforcement measures are taken under the authority of the enforcing State, such measures enjoy the legitimacy of the relevant national law.

F. Conclusion

The three examples dealt with in this contribution show that legal regimes have developed which may be qualified as international administrative law, either as a single level system or a multilevel system. These are not the prime examples that are often referred to in the growing literature on this issue, since many authors generally begin from a rather theoretical starting point. But it is unsustainable to assume the exercise of authority in international law without discussing whether such exercise really exists and what it entails. To then make far-reaching demands concerning changes in respect of international law or – even worse – to question the relevance of international law for the conduct of international relations on the basis of such an assumption, is equally unsustainable.

Having said that, it is equally evident that legal regimes which provide for an international administration must be scrutinized from the point

---

37 *See* Art. 53 of the Conservation and Enforcement Measures.

38 *See* Feinäugle, in this volume.

of view of legitimacy. Given their particular functions, it would not be sufficient to merely refer to the consent of States Parties to the constituent instrument, although this consent may (theoretically) cover all the measures taken under these regimes. Hence, the chain of legitimacy needs to be a continuous one. The International Seabed Authority, having been set up for the administration of the Area, provides such a coherent system and therefore does not have a legitimacy deficit. The situation may differ in cases where traditional international organizations or institutions gradually assume international administrative functions, as is the case with the IMO. The legal framework of these organizations and institutions should be reconsidered to strengthen the legitimacy of their measures, whether prescriptive or executive. However, the main task lies with the national legislator. It is for the latter to provide for an efficient and continuous chain of legitimacy in such cases.

Finally, NAFO demonstrates how the legitimacy of measures may be established or strengthened by having recourse to national law or in other words, by making use of the multilevel system where each level has its own chain of legitimacy and the two supplementing each other.

IV. Context

The Internationalization of Administrative Relations as a Challenge for Administrative Law Scholarship

*By Eberhard Schmidt-Aßmann**

A. Introduction

One does not approach a challenge with a backward view. Rather, we take on challenges by looking forward. In scholarship, taking a forward

* This is a translation of *Die Herausforderung der Verwaltungsrechtswissenschaft durch die Internationalisierung der Verwaltungsbeziehungen,* 45 DER STAAT 315 (2006). The original is a supplemented text of a speech given upon the conferral of the status of professor emeritus on 16 February 2006, Alte Aula of the University of Heidelberg. Translation by Joseph Windsor.

A. von Bogdandy et al. (eds.), *The Exercise of Public Authority by International Institutions*, Beiträge zum ausländischen öffentlichen Recht und Völkerrecht 210,
DOI 10.1007/978-3-642-04531-8_34,

view is known as *research*. Law schools define themselves by their research. Scholarly work is what garners prestige from without and solidarity from within. Without a doubt, teaching itself also ranks highly, but excellent teaching begins with proper research. The connection between research and teaching is indispensable. Teaching flourishes where students are gradually introduced to the processes of research, giving them a feeling for the excitement of scholarly work. This forms the nexus between the older and younger generations of academics, continually opening and reopening their perspectives to innovation and the undiscovered. *Semper apertus* reads the seal of the University of Heidelberg from 1386.

Research requires much stamina. The systematic search for new insights and ideas proceeds according to rules different from those governing politics and economy. It succeeds only where researchers forgo actionism. Research with stamina, of course, does not mean longwinded research. Mere reproduction of what is already known and established is not research. One also cannot rationalize research by simple reference to the law's peculiar stabilizing function. Phenomena draw and merit scholarly attention precisely because of their novelty or unusualness. We may find them agreeable, or, owing to the threat they represent to the familiar, traditional framework, they may seem disagreeable. But administrative law scholarship has the task – the responsibility! – to recognize anything and everything that exists within the realm of administrative reality, to scrutinize it systematically, and to locate it within the context of previous knowledge and insight.

One such research topic is the internationalization of administrative relations, which is taking place within the tension between the traditional and the novel: not a standard topic, if also not completely new. Since the mid-19th century, legal issues arising out of international administrative treaties and international administrative unions have been dealt with in a broad, international discourse. Contemporary literature clearly recognized that international law and administrative law were converging and needed to be placed on a new foundation – international law as the law of state cooperation, and administrative law as a body of law reaching above and beyond the traditional notion of sovereignty. Georg Jellinek fittingly captured both the aspect of an increase in legal structuring and the aspect of an alteration of the prior understanding: "That definition of the term *sovereignty*, which characterizes state power as inherently absolutely limitless, cannot be reconciled with the historical reality of states bound by a system of administrative treaties."[1] By 1882, he had already formulated it positively in his treatise on the relationships of states: in the large administrative associations, states show "that, in their reciprocal relations, they are not only powers, that is, not only physically acting forces, but also orders".[2]

Many of these insights were shaken by the Second World War with some forced into the background, while post-1945 German public law – understandably, but exaggeratedly – concentrated on domestic issues.[3] Recently, however, one can observe a resurgence in scholarly interest in the internationalization of administrative law.[4] This provides us with our starting point.

As I understand it, the internationalization of administrative activity means processes of an administrative nature extending beyond national administrative borders, either because they have evolved beyond such borders or because they were, from the outset, conceived without consideration of such borders. Diminished territoriality is their hallmark. If, however, the principle of territoriality can be counted among the "classic" premises of administrative law,[5] then internationalization represents a substantial challenge.

---

1 GEORG JELLINEK, ALLGEMEINE STAATSLEHRE 740 (3rd ed., 1913).

2 GEORG JELLINEK, DIE LEHRE VON DEN STAATENVERBINDUNGEN 111 (1882).

3 Konrad Hesse, *Einleitende Bemerkungen zum Kolloquium*, *in* DIE WELT DES VERFASSUNGSSTAATES 11 (Martin Morlok ed., 2001); Rainer Wahl, *Die zweite Phase des Öffentlichen Rechts in Deutschland: Die Europäisierung des Öffentlichen Rechts,* 38 DER STAAT 495 (1999).

4 CHRISTIAN TIETJE, INTERNATIONALISIERTES VERWALTUNGSHANDELN (2001); CHRISTOPH MÖLLERS, GEWALTENGLIEDERUNG (2005); CHRISTOPH OHLER, DIE KOLLISIONSORDNUNG DES ALLGEMEINEN VERWALTUNGSRECHTS (2005); FRANZ C. MAYER, DIE INTERNATIONALISIERUNG DES VERWALTUNGSRECHTS (forthcoming); Matthias Ruffert, *Rechtsquellen und Rechtsschichten des Verwaltungsrechts, in* 1 GRUNDLAGEN DES VERWALTUNGSRECHTS 149 *et seq.* (Wolfgang Hoffmann-Riem, Eberhard Schmidt-Aßmann & Andreas Voßkuhle eds., 2006). For earlier works, *see* Hans-Heinrich Trute, *Die Wissenschaft vom Verwaltungsrecht,* DIE VERWALTUNG, Beiheft 2, 9, 21 *et seq.* (1999); Jan Ziekow, *Die Funktion des Allgemeinen Verwaltungsrechts bei der Modernisierung und Internationalisierung des Staates, in* INTERNATIONALISIERUNG VON STAAT UND VERFASSUNG IM SPIEGEL DES DEUTSCHEN UND JAPANISCHEN STAATS- UND VERWALTUNGSRECHTS 187 (Rainer Pitschas & Shigeo Kisa eds., 2002).

5 OTTO MAYER, II DEUTSCHES VEWALTUNGSRECHT 454 (1st ed., 1896).

My thoughts here are developed in three steps. Part II describes internationalized administrative relations. In light of this survey, part III addresses the specific challenges confronting administrative law scholarship. Part IV undertakes, in the form of a research agenda, to draft a blueprint for a law on international administrative relations. Part V concludes the discussion with a plea for a redefinition of international administrative law. Before proceeding with examples, two limitations on the scope of the present discussion should be kept in mind:

The *Europeanization* of administration and administrative law[6] is not dealt with, although it can certainly be viewed as a particular form of internationalization. It is set aside nonetheless because of the particular circumstances of supranational lawmaking (most prominently, those of EC law) have allowed it to develop its own independent legal configuration and because it is, therefore, significantly distinct from what one might call "normal" internationalization.

I also avoid an association with the concept of *global administrative law*, although it is currently the subject of a rich, scholarly discussion, especially in the USA[7] and Italy,[8] but also elsewhere.[9] A portion of the phenomena handled in those debates will indeed be addressed here. However, the (over)extension into the global sphere shifts the focus too quickly away from the (relatively speaking) more readily comprehensible factual constellations; therewith, certain experiences and potential solutions remain unutilized, although they are certainly already available in the practice-related material of comprehensible, relatively small-scale situations of administrative cooperation, both bilaterally and between adjacent countries.

---

[6] STEFAN KADELBACH, ALLGEMEINES VERWALTUNGSRECHT UNTER EUROPÄISCHEM EINFLUß (1999); DER EUROPÄISCHE VERWALTUNGSVERBUND (Eberhard Schmidt-Aßmann & Bettina Schöndorf-Haubold eds., 2005); JÜRGEN SCHWARZE, EUROPÄISCHES VERWALTUNGSRECHT CXII (2nd ed., 2005).

[7] Benedict Kingsbury, Nico Krisch & Richard B. Stewart, *The Emergence of Global Administrative Law*, 68 LAW & CONTEMPORARY PROBLEMS 15 (2005).

[8] Conferences on Global Administrative Law in Viterbo, 10-11 June 2005 and 9-10 June 2006.

[9] JEAN-BERNARD AUBY, LA GLOBALISATION, LE DROIT ET L'ÉTAT (2003); MATTHIAS RUFFERT, DIE GLOBALISIERUNG ALS HERAUSFORDERUNG AN DAS ÖFFENTLICHE RECHT (2004).

B. The Functions of Administrative Law

A law on international administrative relations should thus also be framed in terms of the same dual function which shapes domestic administrative law:[10] it must protect the individual's rights against the administration, and it must make legal procedures and instruments available to the administration, so that it can effectively carry out its tasks. Administrative law scholarship has the peculiar responsibility to defend this dual function against fluctuations in lawmaking and in adjudication, for only academia maintains the distance necessary to an overview of developments in the longer term.

Today, such fluctuation also includes the fact that the discourses on administrative law begun on the national level grow far beyond these borders. Fortunately, more has occurred on this point in the last two decades than is generally recognized – initially in comparative administrative law but, more recently, increasingly in collaboration on substantially similar problems.[11]

I. The Law's Formative Force

An inquiry into the functions of administrative law scholarship is simultaneously an inquiry into the effectiveness of the law:

Because many occurrences take place in much greater dimensions and with much stronger developmental dynamics than the law, do they not thus fall outside the law's sphere of influence? The prototypical example is electronic communications technology, which can hardly be approached with a single state's regulatory scheme.

Have not many actors, already for quite a long time, preferred softer means of settlement and compromise instead of waiting for hard legal solutions? Examples include various systems of negotiation, settlement, and plea bargaining, each with its own, situational codes of conduct.

---

10 EBERHARD SCHMIDT-AßMANN, DAS ALLGEMEINE VERWALTUNGSRECHT ALS ORDNUNGSIDEE 16 *et seq.* (2nd ed., 2004); Ziekow (note 4), at 201 *et seq.*

11 For example, in the European Group of Public Law, its annual conferences, and the European Review of Public Law that it publishes, available at: http://www.eplc.gr.

Is not law itself generally on the retreat, being pressed back to the fringes by stronger policy goals? Objections such as this are untenable.

Of course, most of these objections are not specifically caused by internationalization. They can equally be directed against national administrative law and have been dealt with at length, particularly in the discussion of administrative legal reform.[12] At no time was it seriously in doubt, whether the law could, or would, continue to have effective influence in its pivotal role as a central standard for the social order. The law is not simply swept helplessly along in an uncontrollable current of "de-formalization". Doomsday scenarios are hardly helpful. Societal processes are, and always have been, a mixture of formal and informal elements. There never was a golden age of immaculately legal administration. Formal elements provide the requisite stability; informal practices maintain the necessary reserves of flexibility. Striking the proper balance between the two is the actual task. And it is a continuous task.[13]

This task demands, however, that administrative law scholarship abandon a restrictive definition of the term *law*, that is, abandon a definition that encompasses only the *traditional* legal instruments and only the *substantive* statutory law that determines, or programs, administrative activity. In reality, the influence of law flows also from procedural law and from the law on institutional structures.[14] The law's governance function does not break down at the border between public and private law; rather, the law's potential to govern embraces both the mode of reasoning based on legal principles and a cautious extension to include those standard works which do not (yet) count among the canonized sources of law.

Admittedly, there are greater challenges to the law within the system of internationalized administrative action than within the national sphere.

---

[12] *See* I-X SCHRIFTEN ZUR REFORM DES VERWALTUNGSRECHTS (Wolfgang Hoffmann-Riem & Eberhard Schmidt-Aßmann eds., 1993-2004); Andreas Voßkuhle, *Die Reform des Verwaltungsrechts als Projekt der Wissenschaft*, 32 DIE VERWALTUNG 545 (1999).

[13] Friedrich Schoch, *Entformalisierung staatlichen Handelns, in* III HANDBUCH DES STAATSRECHTS DER BUNDESREPUBLIK DEUTSCHLAND 131 *et seq.* (Josef Isensee & Paul Kirchhof eds., 2005).

[14] For more detail, *see* GUNNAR FOLKE SCHUPPERT, VERWALTUNGSWISSENSCHAFT 461 *et seq.* (2000); Claudio Franzius, *Modalitäten und Wirkungsfaktoren der Steuerung durch Recht, in* GRUNDLAGEN DES VERWALTUNGSRECHTS 42 *et seq.* (Wolfgang Hoffmann-Riem, Eberhard Schmidt-Aßmann & Andreas Voßkuhle eds., 2006).

Often, even a basic, common legal framework is lacking. Individual, national parliaments have, at best, only limited influence.[15] And the confusing structure of administrative cooperation also does its part to hamper the determination of accountability.

On the other hand, it is precisely international law that is experienced with legal instruments of widely varying degrees of "hardness" and intensity. International law also exhibits greater openness in questions of sources of law – as is evident from article 38 of the ICJ Statute.[16] Law in international relations is by no means necessarily in decline, as is very apparent from recent developments. Dispute settlement in the WTO is seen as a manifestation of increasing juridification.[17] The self-imposed practice among expert panels of setting strict procedural rules shows that the law's legitimizing function is not disposable. Admittedly, the administrative cooperation underlying internationalization was itself only able to develop in a political climate with due respect for the rule of law; nonetheless, the assertion that internationalized administrative relations are indeed amenable to legal systematization remains a very tenable scholarly position.

II. The Meaning of "Open Statehood"

But inquiry into the functions of administrative law scholarship is also inquiry into the state's role in the systematization of internationalized administrative relations. Administrative law owes its traditional form to its close relationship to the nation-state and the associated institutions of constitutional law (separation of powers, legality, judicial review).[18]

---

15 Kingsbury, Krisch & Stewart (note 7), at 34 *et seq.*; RUFFERT (note 9), at 61-62.

16 *See* Christian Tietje, *Recht ohne Rechtsquellen?*, 24 ZEITSCHRIFT FÜR RECHTSSOZIOLOGIE 27, 30 *et seq.* (2003); TIETJE (note 4), at 255 *et seq.*

17 GÖTZ J. GÖTTSCHE, DIE ANWENDUNG VON RECHTSPRINZIPIEN IN DER SPRUCHPRAXIS DER WTO-RECHTSMITTELINSTANZ 88 *et seq.* (2005); Meinhard Hilf, *Das Streitbeilegungssystem der WTO, in* WTO-RECHT 507 *et seq.* (Meinhard Hilf & Stefan Oeter eds., 2005); John Jackson, *Effektivität und Wirksamkeit des Streitbeilegungsverfahrens der WTO, in* VERRECHTLICHUNG – BAUSTEIN FÜR GLOBAL GOVERNANCE? 99 *et seq.* (Bernhard Zangl & Michael Zürn eds., 2004).

18 SABINO CASSESE, GLOBAL ADMINISTRATIVE LAW: AN INTRODUCTION 36 *et seq.* (2005), available at: http://globusetlocus.org/it_data/fil/s_cassese__

With this internationalization, can we now anticipate *Amministrazioni senza Stato* – as the title of a thoughtful Italian study speculates?[19]

Viewed from a purely global perspective, such a prognosis is not unfounded: other actors (international organizations such as the World Bank, mixed expert bodies such as the Codex Alimentarius Commission, and NGOs) play important roles in the processes of administrative decision-making.[20] For instance, the so-called secondary lawmaking of international organizations, an intermediate form of law that is important particularly for administrative execution, does indeed diminish the influence of the individual state.[21]

However, taking the myriad manifestations of internationalized administrative action into an overall view, the scene looks far less dramatic: in police law, tax law, and social welfare law, states and state institutions still determine the situation – international entanglements notwithstanding – and oversee the influence from processes of internationalization. Good examples of this include the detailed regulation of the 1990 Schengen Convention or treaties on double taxation.

In worldwide international intercourse, as well, states ultimately continue to be the most important formative forces.[22] Here, one must be careful not to be dazzled by the spectacular activities of international NGOs or multinational corporations. It is state governments that conclude treaties.[23] It is primarily states' courts that develop customary international law. It is states' executive instruments that are called on to implement treaties. "Whichever way one looks at it, the legitimacy of

---

global_administrative_law.pdf; Giacinto della Cananea, *Beyond the State: The Europeanization and Globalization of Procedural Administrative Law*, 9 EUROPEAN PUBLIC LAW 563, 565-566 (2003).

19 STEFANO BATTINI, AMMINISTRAZIONI SENZA STATO: PROFILI DI DIRITTO AMMINISTRATIVO INTERNAZIONALE (2003).

20 GUNNAR FOLKE SCHUPPERT, STAATSWISSENSCHAFT 869 *et seq.* (2003).

21 JURIJ D. ASTON, SEKUNDÄRGESETZGEBUNG INTERNATIONALER ORGANISATIONEN ZWISCHEN MITGLIEDSTAATLICHER SOUVERÄNITÄT UND GEMEINSCHAFTSDISZIPLIN 195 (2005).

22 VOLKER RÖBEN, AUßENVERFASSUNGSRECHT (Habilitationsschrift) 33-38 (2005); TRANSFORMATION DES STAATES (Stephan Leibfried & Michael Zürn eds., 2006).

23 Anthony Aust, *Domestic Consequences of Non-Treaty Law-Making*, *in* DEVELOPMENTS OF INTERNATIONAL LAW IN TREATY MAKING, 487, 495 (Rüdiger Wolfrum & Volker Röben eds., 2005).

political activity and legal standardization on the international level still relies on the legitimizing structures and processes of nation-states."[24]

In the present context, reconnecting to national constitutional orders is similarly necessary. It is in line with the insight that, internally, the state is the only reliable point of crystallization for civic identity and the only bearer of comprehensive responsibility with respect to the citizenry.[25] States alone are therefore able to counterbalance the strong segmentation of politics on the international level.[26]

Here, too, of course, modern challenges will not be overcome by a concept of statehood, which seeks to maximize insulation from the outside and which, in any case, interprets internationalization above all as a threat. Instead, it will be necessary to take a *concept of open statehood* seriously, as the German Basic Law has done, in articles 23-25 and 59, from its inception by elevating the concept as a normative ideal.[27] The Federal Constitutional Court today fittingly emphasizes that international law "endeavours to form the foundation of legitimacy for every state order".[28]

In light of this sort of constitutional decision, the internationalization of legal and administrative relations is not a distressing side-effect that must be limited with as many "reservations" as possible. Rather, such internationalization should be considered normality for a constitutional state – of course, not without risks and difficulties, which at any rate complicate governmental action in the domestic sphere as well – and should not be viewed as a radical development intruding into and usurping the state's domain.

---

24 Fritz Scharpf, *Legitimationskonzepte jenseits des Nationalstaats, in* EUROPAWISSENSCHAFT 705, 736 (Gunnar Folke Schuppert, Ingolf Pernice & Ulrich Haltern eds., 2005).

25 Rainer Wahl, *Internationalisierung des Staates, in* FESTSCHRIFT FÜR ALEXANDER HOLLERBACH 193, 220-221 (Joachim Bohnert, Christof Gramm, Urs Kindhäuser, Joachim Lege, Alfred Rinken & Gerhard Robbers eds., 2001).

26 *See* Armin von Bogdandy, *Demokratie, Globalisierung, Zukunft des Völkerrechts – eine Bestandsaufnahme*, 63 ZEITSCHRIFT FÜR AUSLÄNDISCHES ÖFFENTLICHES RECHT UND VÖLKERRECHT (ZAÖRV) 853 (2003).

27 RÖBEN (note 22), at 528-530.

28 Bundesverfassungsgericht (BVerfG – Federal Constitutional Court), 2 BvR 955/00, 1038/01 (2004) (original quotation: "... Grundlage der Legitimität jeder staatlichen Ordnung sein will"). *See also* 2 BvR 2259/04 (2005) (discussing the consequences and attention to the structures, content, and legal viewpoints of other states, for example, in legal assistance).

Understood as normality, internationalization would involve our incorporating its various forms of cooperation into that part of administrative law which we consider worth preserving. Doing so would facilitate a better legal comprehension of especially the interface of horizontal and vertical modes of administrative cooperation.

III. Basic Elements: Treaty and Statute

If states are indeed still the most important forces in international politics, then there are good reasons to continue entrusting much to the two main forms of legal structuring: the international treaty and the parliamentary statute. And there are also good reasons to take these two forms as the core building materials for a law on international administrative relations.

1. Treaties

The international treaty constitutes both the foundation and the framework for international administrative relations: treaties concretize obligations to cooperate, install regimes for secondary lawmaking and legal review, and create international organizations as new actors. Treaties are also the means required to raise protective standards above a minimum level of protection under customary international law. Where intensive forms of cooperation have developed without a treaty as basis but with effects reaching into the national sphere, states have the task to "re-file" these forms under treaty law.

The theoretical tenets of the international treaty have found a sufficiently clear doctrinal form in the Vienna Convention on the Law of Treaties.[29] At the same time, they are flexible enough to process the demands of novel developments. The possibility of simplified, continued development and concretization of treaties exists, not least in the potentialities of secondary lawmaking.[30] For its part, states' task here is to act as a decelerator, whenever they have the impression that such administrative activity threatens to run off the rails of individual state authority. And,

---

[29] GEORG DAHM, JOST DELBRÜCK & RÜDIGER WOLFRUM, I.3 VÖLKERRECHT 511-763 (2nd ed., 2002).

[30] *See* the contributions to Wolfrum & Röben (note 23).

for its part, academia's task is to craft an *ultra vires* standard to gauge this connection between states and international administration.

Specifically characteristic of international administrative relations are "regulatory cascades": treaties set up only the framework. Development of the specific content is reserved for further forms of negotiation and decision-making. The primary form comprises administrative agreements which can be concluded as governmental or ministerial agreements or, with the proper authorization, even as implementation agreements by subordinate governmental departments.[31] Considering this canon of modes, recourse to memoranda of understanding should be limited to truly open situations in which the parties concerned reasonably wish to avoid binding themselves legally. For execution of administrative acts, such situations would presumably remain exceptional. Additionally, the practice of publishing agreements still has much room for improvement.

2. *Statutes*

Legislation is the second structuring factor. First of all, however, in parliamentary practice, more attention must be paid to international administrative action. Pains must be taken to make the international dimension present in individual sectoral laws, and a requirement of parliamentary ratification of international treaties fails to achieve this sufficiently. It is necessary not only to create legal bases for the arsenal of international administrative acts, but also to connect them to those existent legal bases that regularly implicate internal administrative action. There are already examples of this: the tax code and the social security code contain a significant number of provisions on the transfer of data to foreign institutions. Police law governs the deployment of German police officers abroad as well as the authority of foreign officers in German territory. These, however, are relatively rare provisions. The law of administrative procedure, in some ways the most important representative of general administrative law in Germany, has completely factored out the international dimension, even though its inclusion, for instance, in official administrative assistance, would have seemed only logical.

---

31 *See* Art. 19 of the Abkommen zwischen der Bundesrepublik Deutschland und Japan, Bundesgesetzblatt (BGBl.) II 876 (1999); Art. 5 of the Vereinbarung zur Durchführung des Abkommens, BGBl. II 896 (1999).

Yet the legislature has recently recognized the meaningfulness of the issue. The new Telecommunications Act, for example, explicitly emphasizes the responsibilities of regulatory agencies with respect to international telecommunications policy, especially their cooperation with international organizations, and specifies that the agencies act in this respect on behalf of the Federal Ministry of Economics (§140). Thus, it goes well beyond the old regulation of cooperative execution (§83 of the Telecommunications Act of 1996); indeed, it has implications for the gubernative powers that have previously been exercised only informally in transnational networks of agencies. At any rate, this is a clear attribution of domestic accountability. The legislature draws on the governance capabilities inherent in its power to adjust the state's structure; thereby, it connects the international administrative network back to the national constitutional order.

IV. "Giving Teeth" to the Legal Order

Treaty and statute "give teeth" to the international legal order and to national legal orders.[32] A statute domestically mandates an application of the law, which then underlies those legal standards by which administrative agencies are bound under article 20(3) of the German Basic Law. Conversely, a treaty opens up the possibility of bringing cross-border administrative cooperation into the statutory systematics, thereby permitting the resolution of incidental issues, such as questions of choice of law or of liability.

From *both* approaches, starting from the treaty or the statute, the international and national legal orders are converging,[33] without, however, consolidating into a homogenous unit. Differences (for instance, in the interpretive methods) and tensions persist. The law on international administrative relations knows no hierarchy of sources of law. This would presume a unified political system, which is more doubtful at the international level than the European level.

---

[32] For a fundamentally similar approach, *see* TIETJE (note 4), at 488, 640 (internationalized administrative activity within the system of national and international law as a functionally coherent unit).

[33] For a clear representation of this point, *see* DANIEL THÜRER, I KOSMOPOLITISCHES STAATSRECHT 75 (2005) (organizational systems engaging with each other).

Tensions between the legal orders can be mitigated by interpretation in accordance with international law and other rules of deference. But the tensions cannot be completely alleviated. The points of tension are well-known from the Federal Constitutional Court's handling of EC law and the ECHR.[34] The tension is, however, no German *Sonderweg* but has parallels with other legal orders. Even the abovementioned judgment of the Court of First Instance on "terrorist monies" is a reaction to the tensions between legal levels, that is, between the international and the European protection of fundamental rights.

Tensions will continue to increase as the administrative activities of international bodies intensify and begin to lead to types and degrees of legal intervention that the international legal order is not yet equipped to deal with. The literature on international environmental law provides a case in point. Scholars rightfully point out that the level of compliance monitoring already achieved should have been flanked by a canon of indispensable procedural principles.[35] The above-cited judgment of the Court of First Instance points in the same direction. It also identifies the two approaches to releasing the tensions:

> The first approach is "bottom-up" and inquires whether strict adherence to international law is not precluded by the legal reservation of an *ordre public* that compels both a more definite disconnection from UN law and scrutiny using a European fundamental rights standard – an *ordre public* that derives from *within* the European legal tradition or that of the Member States. This has heretofore been the usual *decoupling* approach; it takes only the internal act of execution into account, asserting its entitlement to exceptional regulation and refraining from making any statement regarding the law of the higher level.
>
> The Court, however, chose to follow another approach. It inquires whether the UN Security Council's resolutions meet the requirements of UN law and then proceeds to construe the reservation of an *ordre public* in international law, derived from the *jus cogens* of international law. This can be described as the *extending* approach; it is particularly interesting in that it does not limit itself to the internal legal order's demands on the internal act of execution, instead seeking to recognize fundamental protective standards that have already

---

34 *See* Stefan Mückel, *Kooperation oder Konfrontation?: Das Verhältnis zwischen BVerfG und EGMR*, 44 DER STAAT 403 (2005).

35 ULRICH BEYERLIN, UMWELTVÖLKERRECHT 496 (2000).

developed on the higher prescriptive level. It is an approach similar to the one advocated in one of the dissenting opinions in the judgment on the European arrest warrant.[36] Here, much admittedly remains unresolved, including especially the question of jurisdiction.[37]

Nonetheless, everything speaks for the use of both approaches in combination: fundamental standards based on the rule of law (fair trial rights, judicial protection) can today already be developed for activities on the international levels, as well. International organizations cannot demand anything of their members that they are not themselves willing to respect. The necessary *democratic* elements of decision-making are still to be secured primarily by way of a sufficient connection from the national executive actors in the international contexts back to the legitimating sources of their respective constitutions.[38]

C. A Blueprint for the Law on Internationalized Administrative Relations

The above statements have already raised a few specific points that will be addressed in the following discussion, which undertakes a listing of topics that need to be addressed in a systematic representation of a law on international administrative relations. As stated above, only the con-

---

[36] 2 BvR 2236/04 (2005) dissenting opinion of Judge Michael Gerhardt, at 339 *et seq*. For a similar approach to a judgment of the Court of First Instance, *see* Lothar Harings, *Die EG als Rechtsgemeinschaft (?) – EuG versagt Individualrechtsschutz,* 16 EUROPÄISCHE ZEITSCHRIFT FÜR WIRTSCHAFTSRECHT 705 (2005).

[37] Christoph Möllers, Frankfurter Allgemeine Zeitung, 14 February 2006, at 39; regarding this question, *see also* Mehrdad Payandeh, *Rechtskontrolle des UN-Sicherheitsrates durch staatliche und überstaatliche Gerichte,* 66 ZAÖRV 41, 57 *et seq*. (2006).

[38] MÖLLERS (note 4), at 358 *et seq*.; Thomas Puhl, *Entparlamentarisierung und Auslagerung staatlicher Entscheidungsverantwortung, in* III HANDBUCH DES STAATSRECHTS DER BUNDESREPUBLIK DEUTSCHLAND 3 *et seq.* (Josef Isensee & Paul Kirchhof eds., 2005). For a discussion in the context of the European Union, *see* the dissenting opinion of Judge Gertrude Lübbe-Wolff, 2 BvR 2236/04, (2005).

tours of the necessary crafting of the legal doctrine will be sketched here, in the form of a research program.[39]

The opportunity to draw up such programs and to implement them with other, especially younger scholars is perhaps one of the greatest advantages offered by a career as an academic researcher and instructor. In order to take full advantage of this opportunity, however, a certain research climate is required: a high degree of international exchange and a faculty that combines friendly collegiality and prudent distance. Much has already been self-evident for decades and need not now be fought for, requested, or otherwise attained.

As far as the system-building of a law on international relations is concerned, there is something to be said for an orientation along three doctrinal categories: form, procedure, and principle.[40] By centering the legal questions of internationalized administrative relations on forms, procedures, and principles, one proceeds from what is already well-settled; inquires into the larger context, into functional equivalents, gaps in protection, and necessary expansions into related areas; and enables comparison.

I. Administrative Law on Information

One issue, however, must be dealt with preliminarily: the issue of information and the trafficking of information in international administrative intercourse. It cuts across all three doctrinal categories, so to speak. Administrative cooperation in the international sphere is, above all else, the exchange of information. Here, even more than in national administrative law, it holds true: administrative law is first and foremost law on the administration of information! Its regulatory objects can be identified by asking four questions:

1. What information may be collected and exchanged at all?
2. Who has access to the information held by an administrative entity, and who is authorized to make a record of the information?

---

[39] *See* WOLFGANG SCHLUCHTER, HANDLUNG, ORDNUNG UND KULTUR 9-10 (2005) (discussing generally the requirements of a research program).

[40] On their significance in national administrative law, *see* SCHMIDT-AßMANN (note 10), at 297 *et seq.*

3. To what degree is the information open to the public, and how is the necessary confidentiality secured?

4. Who safeguards the quality of information, and who can be held liable for inaccuracy?

Nowadays, the protection of *personal* data is already relatively well secured. At any rate, guidelines for uniform rules are recognizable in social security agreements and double taxation treaties, and such guidelines provide points of reference for the negotiation of administrative agreements or for the development of cooperative practice. In contrast, the protection of business and trade secrets remains uncertain. Here, too, however, international standards need to be developed. This is true, for example, in the case of the transfer of corporate data for purposes of review by environmental law systems – especially when NGOs are involved in such systems.

One problem, the significance of which has hardly been recognized, is the handling of information that has *already* been collected. As a general rule, an agency is not *required* to evaluate information received. But is it *permitted* to do so in all cases? Every utilization of information can make its own unnoticed contribution to the establishment of practices that the given entity is neither authorized to practice itself nor even permitted to tolerate. In the processing of information, thus, scandalous investigative practices in another country, such as torture, cannot be ignored, and *a fortiori* an administrative institution may not, whether directly or indirectly, contribute to such practices itself. On the other hand, administrative law knows no absolute prohibition on the processing of information. In defense against serious threats, especially threats to life and health, information may be extracted from the international administrative intercourse and utilized, even when its collection would be impermissible under domestic law.

II. Procedures and Principles

Forms, procedures, and principles provide the fundamental structure not exclusively for German administrative law, well-known for its systematic approach; rather, they are also evident in other administrative legal orders, including the European order.[41]

---

[41] *See* JÜRGEN SCHWARZE, EUROPÄISCHES VERWALTUNGSRECHT (2nd ed., 2005).

The legal procedure of international administrative relations is, today, still defined largely by the institutions of reciprocal administrative assistance[42] and mutual recognition.[43] The current view holds that both have to be based on an international treaty and that, as yet, there are no unwritten duties of administrative assistance or recognition. By now, though, there is a recognized duty to inform regarding dangers in bordering areas, based on the principle of good neighborliness. It also seems that one cannot rule out the existence of a duty when the situation involves the enforcement of *jus cogens* in international law. Within each treaty-framework, the relations of administrative assistance have been intensifying. Still dominant, of course, is the division of spheres of responsibility that follows from the principle of sovereignty. However, clauses earmarking data for specific purposes are common in data protection law and leave no doubt that external effects must now be taken into consideration.

At this point, it becomes clear that a law on internationalized administrative relations will first have to orient itself toward *principles*, before individual regulations can be developed. Such principles can be derived inductively from national law and international treaties and deductively especially from human rights protections under international law. European administrative law has developed with a similar orientation toward principles.[44] Recently, the rulings of the WTO dispute settlement bodies have proven to be a source of principles as law, which not only has effects on domestic administrative law, but even seeks to bind international authorities: principles such as good faith, due process of law, equal treatment, proportionality, and the protection of legitimate expectations of privacy have been increasingly recognized as spanning multiple levels.[45]

Included among these principles is the notion that interests implicated and those whose interests they are have a chance to be heard. This,

---

[42] *See* Rudolf Geiger, *Legal Assistance Between States in Administrative Matters, in* III ENCYCLOPEDIA OF PUBLIC INTERNATIONAL LAW 186 (Rudolf Bernhardt ed., 1997).

[43] *See* SASCHA MICHAELS, ANERKENNUNGSPFLICHTEN IM WIRTSCHAFTSVERWALTUNGSRECHT DER EUROPÄISCHEN GEMEINSCHAFT UND DER BUNDESREPUBLIK DEUTSCHLAND 52 *et seq.* (2004).

[44] *See generally* Armin von Bogdandy, *Europäische Prinzipienlehre, in* EUROPÄISCHES VERFASSUNGSRECHT 149 (Armin von Bogdandy ed., 2003).

[45] della Cananea (note 18), at 573 *et seq.*; GÖTTSCHE (note 17), at 195 *et seq.*; Kingsbury, Krisch & Stewart (note 7), at 24.

though, raises complicated questions of *representation*. Some of the literature, here, assigns an important role to NGOs and promises that they will deliver a strengthening of democratic values.[46] One should, however, be cautious with overdrawn expectations. When viewed with proper caution for the decisional interdependence on the international levels, insights into the ordering of powers tend rather to speak against expectations of greater legitimacy flowing from a multiplicity of participatory possibilities.[47] It can conversely even confuse a clear view of responsibility, which is a basic prerequisite of democracy. Rather, recourse to national administrations often seems to be a more effective means of securing a basic level of accountability. Thus, what is actually needed is a conceptualization of delegation and review in the national constitutions – a conceptualization that is specifically tailored to international administrative relations.[48]

D. A Plea for a New International Administrative Law

A research area gains in consistency when it can be put succinctly, put in a nutshell, as it were. The law on internationalized administrative relations will yet need to be newly conceptualized, but it should henceforth be understood as the core of *international administrative law*!

However, this term has already been taken,[49] the prevalent usage of *international administrative law* refers to the public law on conflict of laws, developed in linguistic parallel to private international law, which is to say, it refers to national laws on the applications of laws in fact constellations with a foreign link.[50] This parallelization was askew from

---

46 Kingsbury, Krisch & Stewart (note 7), at 22; STEFANO BATTINI, INTERNATIONAL ORGANIZATIONS AND PRIVATE SUBJECTS: A MOVE TOWARD A GLOBAL ADMINISTRATIVE LAW?, Institute for International Law and Justice, NYU School of Law, Working Paper 2005/3, available at: http://www.iilj.org/publications/documents/2005.3Battini.pdf, 22; Zoe Pearson, *Non-Governmental Organisations and International Law: Mapping New Mechanisms for Governance*, 23 AUSTRALIAN YEARBOOK OF INTERNATIONAL LAW 73 (2004).

47 OHLER (note 4), at 329 *et seq.*

48 *See also* TIETJE (note 4), at 585 *et seq.*

49 *See* OHLER (note 4), at 2 *et seq.*

50 For references, *see* CHRISTIAN VON BAR & PETER MANKOWSKI, I INTERNATIONALES PRIVATRECHT 235, 236 (2nd ed., 2003); Ernst Steindorff, *Verwal-*

the outset. What is more, it has been the cause of some contention.[51] The two fields pursue very different goals. Most notably, international administrative law, thus understood, does not deal with choice of law among various legal orders.

Administrative law scholarship should abandon the inaccurate parallel and radically reorder the formation of terminology. International administrative law is to be understood as the administrative law originating under *international law*. It involves processes of reshaping national law and reconstructing international law; these processes resemble Europeanization in their structures (but not in their mechanisms).

As a matter of clarification, it is worth noting that none of this changes the fact that *national* administrative law remains the main point of orientation for the practical administrative activity of most agencies. The laws on the applications of laws, or laws on conflict of laws, are to be systematized within the framework of *national* administrative law for administrative procedures with foreign implications; this is national law which is to be determined by, above all else, the national constitution.[52]

For the newly defined international administrative law, I would propose – in continuance of research on European administrative law[53] – three main functional circles: it is a body of law governing international administrative institutions, a body of law *determinative* of national administrative legal orders, and a body of law on *cooperative* handling of specific associative problems.

I. Law of International Administrative Institutions

As a body of law governing international administrative institutions, international administrative law takes account of the current development that international organizations increasingly carry out administrative activities with external effects.[54] The above discussion has already shown

---

tungsrecht, Internationales, in III WÖRTERBUCH DES VÖLKERRECHTS 581 (Karl Strupp & Hans-Jürgen Schlochauer eds., 1962).

51 Ludwig von Bar, *Internationales Verwaltungsrecht, in* II ENZYKLOPÄDIE DER RECHTSWISSENSCHAFT 278 *et seq*. (Josef Kohler ed., 1914). For an early critique, *see* MAYER (note 5), at 454.

52 For a recent, groundbreaking work, *see* OHLER (note 4), at 112 *et seq*.

53 SCHMIDT-AßMANN (note 10), at 384 *et seq*.

54 *See* Kingsbury, Krisch & Stewart (note 7), at 20 *et seq*.

that international organizations cannot do so without respecting fundamental principles of law, especially those protecting international human rights.

Beyond this, a higher degree of binding legal force must be ascribed to an array of practical rules of procedure, which international institutions have heretofore practiced only as internally binding standards. Gradually, such *practical* rules must be developed into legal rules.

II. Law Determinative of National Administrative Legal Orders

In its second function as a body of law determinative of national administrative legal orders, international administrative law rearranges those national orders by calling for alterations and expansions. One recent example is the Aarhus Convention, concluded under the auspices of ECOSOC. Without establishing particular cooperative relations among national executive branches, the Convention prescribes a reconstruction of national protections in environmental matters, thereby resulting in expansions of both internal administrative procedure and judicial administrative procedure.[55] A separate topic involves the effects that international law has on national laws on application of laws in cases with a foreign link.[56]

III. Law on Cooperative Handling of Multilevel Issues

Merging the two mentioned functions, international administrative law is thirdly a law on horizontal and vertical administrative cooperation and the specific multilevel issues related to such cooperation. It is not enough to perform the central regulatory tasks of administrative law, to protect individual rights, and to ensure administrative accountability, where this all is done separately at each distinct level. Association, in and of itself, creates its own legal problems when accountability becomes unclear and when individual decisions become dependent on specialized voting mechanisms.

---

[55] Christian Walter, *Internationalisierung des Deutschen und Europäischen Verwaltungsverfahrens- und Verwaltungsprozessrechts – am Beispiel der Aarhus-Konvention,* 40 EUROPARECHT 304 (2005).

[56] OHLER (note 4), at 129-130.

International administrative law must find answers to these specifically multilevel challenges. There are certainly models in various fields, among them the interpretive understandings in treaties on double taxation and the comprehensive standards on data transfer found in social legislation as well as agent liability for errors in police information systems and the notion of an *ordre public* in international law. Legal scholars will have the task of taking these components of positive-law material and constructing a systematized law on international administrative relations. A wide-open field of work in comparative law and legal doctrine lies ahead of us. Research takes a forward view: *semper apertus*!

Procedural Due Process of Law Beyond the State

*By Giacinto della Cananea**

1. Two Questions and Their Relationship: A Conjecture

The research carried out by the Max Planck Institute does not only enrich our empirical knowledge about the new trends regarding the exercise of authority. It also raises some challenging theoretical questions. One such question, which has been raised by several observers in the last years and lies at the heart of the ambitious project advanced by the introductory paper,[1] is whether the traditional dichotomy between pub-

---

* This is an enlarged version of the presentation I made at the Heidelberg seminar, which is part of a broader essay. I wish to express my gratitude to Armin von Bogdandy for inviting me to the seminar and for his advice; to Sabino Cassese, Giulia Maria Labriola, Gianluigi Palombella and Giorgio Rebuffa, for reading an earlier version; to Matthias Goldmann for reviewing the text. All errors and omissions, of course, are mine.

A. von Bogdandy et al. (eds.), *The Exercise of Public Authority by International Institutions*, Beiträge zum ausländischen öffentlichen Recht und Völkerrecht 210, DOI 10.1007/978-3-642-04531-8_35, © Springer-Verlag Berlin Heidelberg 2010

lic law within and outside states still makes sense. Another question is whether, in the brave new world in which we live, there are at least some common principles of procedure shared by most (if not all) legal orders.

Since several chapters of this book show how often and the extent to which the separation between the two great provinces of public law fades, a revision of some *idées réçues* is inevitable. But the question raised by the introductory paper is a different one. The question is whether the new world order requires much more than a revision of some theoretical categories. It regards the validity of a paradigm. While other observers argue that the traditional paradigm no longer accurately reflects the reality of our time, their argument is that such a paradigm must be adjusted, not abandoned.

The other question regards the scope of the new procedural principles which govern the exercise of authority. Such principles often derive from bilateral and multilateral treaties. But the research also gives evidence of other ways by which principles of procedural due process of law emerge.[2] In an increasing number of cases they are affirmed by arbitral and judicial bodies. Sometimes, more simply, they grow in the interstices of procedures, for example in internal documents of international bodies.[3] Beyond states, therefore, there are not only the princi-

---

1 *See* A. von Bogdandy, P. Dann & M. Goldmann, *Developing the Publicness of Public International Law: Towards A Legal Framework for Global Governance Activities,* in this volume and A. von Bogdandy, *General Principles of International Public Authority: Sketching a Research Field*, in this volume.

2 I am aware that my distinction between process and substance is conventional and problematic, as argued by J. MASHAW, DUE PROCESS IN THE ADMINISTRATIVE STATE 5 (1986). However, the science of public law has shown that processes matter whatever their results, *see* J. Lever, *Why Procedure is More Important than Substantive Law*, 48 INTERNATIONAL AND COMPARATIVE LAW QUARTERLY 285 (1999) and R.S. Summers, *Evaluating and Improving Legal Processes – A Plea for "Process Values"*, 60 CORNELL LAW REVIEW 1 (1974). Moreover, in modern philosophy the most important work on justice focuses on procedures, J. RAWLS, A THEORY OF JUSTICE (1971).

3 *See* especially C.A. Feinäugle, *The UN Security Council Al-Qaida and Taliban Sanctions Committee: Emerging Principles of International Institutional Law for the Protection of Individuals?*, in this volume; M. Smrkolj, *International Institutions and Individualized Decision-Making: An Example of UNCHR's Refugee Status Determination* (pointing out the importance of UN manuals of procedure), in this volume; J. von Bernstorff, *Procedures of Deci-*

ples of conventional and customary international law. A larger body of principles governing the conduct of both national and international institutions is emerging, though opponents of globalization argue that such principles are not universal.

Whatever the soundness of this opposition, the underlying question may look less relevant, theoretically, than the other one. However, it is not necessarily so. At least, my conjecture is that, *if* we can identify some general principles of law which are not limited to a single class of legal orders, but have a wider scope of application, including international and supranational orders, *then* we should also consider in a different way the traditional divide between the two great provinces of public law. Of course, it would not necessarily follow from this that any distinction between the two fields of public law ought to be abandoned. But we should discuss about distinctions, rather than a divide.

2. The Great Divide Between Internal and External Public Law: Issues of Methodology

Let us consider, initially and briefly, the first question. Its importance is indisputable. Public law was and to a large extent still is conceived as being divided into two parts, within and outside the state. This great divide rests on historic, philosophical and pragmatic considerations.[4] Following

---

sion-Making and the Role of Law in International Organizations, in this volume.

[4] Limits of space preclude a deeper analysis. Suffice it to mention that, beyond the Enlightenment, the principles governing the conduct of nations were conceived as *jus gentium*. During the 19th century, that paradigm was replaced by another, focusing on the network of relationships between states or *international law*, as it was named by Jeremy Bentham. This was, as Carl Schmitt argued, an interstate law, C. SCHMITT, DER NOMOS DER ERDE IM VÖLKERRECHT DES JUS PUBLICUM EUROPAEUM (1950), THE NOMOS OF THE EARTH IN THE INTERNATIONAL LAW OF THE JUS PUBLICUM EUROPAEUM, translated and annotated by G.L. Ulmen (2005). Philosophically, the fact that there was a completely different law within and outside the state was already obvious, almost axiomatic, for Hegel. He argued that the reality of internal public law changes when the relationship between the states are concerned, that is to sat in their external law, *see* G.F.W. HEGEL, GRUNDLINIEN DER PHILOSOPHIE DES RECHTS (1821), translated and annotated by T.M. KNOX, HEGEL'S PHILOSOPHY OF

lowing this line of reasoning, it may be asked whether it is reasonable to assume that the principles developed within national legal orders may be applied to other types of legal orders. It may be contradictory, moreover, to set up new institutions, outside the boundaries of states, while measuring their performance on the basis of the standards which have been elaborated in national contexts. Last but not least, a serious problem arises on more pragmatic grounds. Arguably, international institutions cannot be subject to the same principles which govern national authorities. A generalized, indiscriminate "transplant" of legal principles and tools would entail the risk of jeopardizing the contribution which international institutions are expected to provide precisely because they differ from states.

All these remarks require serious consideration, not only because, especially in a changing legal environment, differences of analysis are to be expected and may be very useful. In my opinion, there are serious flaws in all theories which simply assume that some principles, particularly democracy and in some respects even transparency, may be extended to all public organizations. The underlying assumption is that such principles and rules are valid for every system of government, regardless of its nature. But it is trite wisdom that there are a variety of human societies, which are governed by different rules, as Montesquieu demonstrated admirably.[5] Moreover, all societies adjust their principles. Bringing this argument further, it may be observed that the state itself is an evolving product of history. Accordingly, it cannot be conceived as an archetype.[6]

In addition to agreeing to the *caveat* just mentioned, I also believe that the other two arguments in defense of the traditional paradigm are quite reasonable. A major flaw of most recent works regarding the European Union and even the World Trade Organization is, in fact, the unaware-

---

RIGHT § 259 (1942). H. KELSEN, REINE RECHTSLEHRE (1934), translated and annotated by M. KNIGHT, PURE THEORY OF LAW (1978) was of the same opinion. More recently, John Rawls observed that the international arena may require not only principles established in a different way, but also principles having a different content, RAWLS (note 2), § I.2. For further discussion, *see* M. LOUGHLIN, PUBLIC LAW AND POLITICAL THEORY (1992).

5 MONTESQUIEU, DE L'ESPRIT DES LOIS (1758) (since the *Préface*, he points out the "*infinie diversité de lois et de mœurs*").

6 *See* M.S. GIANNINI, IL PUBBLICO POTERE. STATI E AMMINISTRAZIONI PUBBLICHE 21 (1986).

ness that such institutions differ from those to which we are more accustomed because their role is largely different.[7] The pragmatic argument, too, is reasonable. Legal science, which is a practical science, ought to take it into due consideration.

However, a pragmatic approach need not be synonymous with an intellectually weak one. One thing is to say, in normative terms, that distinct spheres of human conduct require distinct legal principles. Another thing is to verify whether such a distinction may be conceptualized as a separation or, alternatively, it is less evident than it used to be. In the last years, this point has been emphasized by several observers, on both side of the Atlantic. Their starting point is that procedural safeguards have not grown only within national legal orders, in order to protect individuals from the arbitrariness of both governors and administrators.[8] Indeed, such procedural safeguards are no longer an exclusive feature of national legal orders. Regional and global regulatory regimes increasingly impose procedural duties on contracting parties. The European Union, with its quasi-state institutional framework is the clearest example of this. But it is not the only one. The recent experience of UN actions against terrorism confirms it.[9] Only recently did the growing pressure exerted on the Security Council determine a gradual change of its rules. Both a partial duty to give reasons and the possibility to seek to obtain the reformation of the decision has been provided to individuals by Resolution 1830 (2006). All this strengthens the argument that an increasing part of global law may or should be conceptualized as

---

7 For this argument, *see* S. CASSESE, *Administrative Law Without the State? The Challenge of Global Regulation*, 37 NEW YORK UNIVERSITY JOURNAL OF INTERNATIONAL LAW & POLITICS 663, 671 (2005).

8 *See* B. Kingsbury, N. Krisch & R.B. Stewart, *The Emergence of Global Administrative Law*, 68 LAW & CONTEMPORARY PROBLEMS 15 (2005) (for the thesis that such developments cannot be properly understood in terms of classical international law); S. Cassese, *Global Standards for National Administrative Procedure*, 68 LAW & CONTEMPORARY PROBLEMS 109 (2005) (observing that global standards have different sources and goals); N. Krisch & B. Kingsbury, *Introduction: Global Governance and Global Administrative Law in the International Legal Order*, 17 EUROPEAN JOURNAL OF INTERNATIONAL LAW (EJIL) 1 (2006) (pointing out that globalization and global governance are transforming the structure of international law).

9 *See* J. Reich, *Due Process and Sanctions Targeted Against Individuals Pursuant to U.N. Resolution 1267* (1999), 33 YALE JOURNAL OF INTERNATIONAL LAW 491 (2007).

administrative law. Regardless of the theoretical foundation (international institutional law, global administrative law or else), there is widespread awareness that the exercise of such powers requires proper procedural safeguards in coherence with the ideals of rule of law while raising the question of democratic control of the executives. It would be awkward, to say the least, to give up all or many of the safeguards obtained throughout centuries within national constitutional frameworks, only because some decisions require an enhanced cooperation at the global level.

All this shows that we are confronted with two different paradigms, each justified by several arguments. Rather than seeking to verify the validity of either paradigm, I believe that a twofold methodological remark may be useful. First, every researcher has a twofold obligation: being aware of referring to one paradigm or the other and making the choice as clear as possible. In other words, what must be absolutely avoided is the risk of opacity or, even worse, of presenting a research as if it were epistemologically neutral. Quite the contrary. Not only must the starting point be clarified, but also the results must be evaluated on the basis of such a starting point. My second methodological claim is that the existence of the traditional divide between internal and external public law should not be regarded as an axiom. It must be confronted with the data provided by empirical analysis. Therefore, even for those who are convinced that the great divide still makes sense, it should not be excluded that the two cultures of public law may be closer, even more integrated, with reciprocal benefit. With this *caveat*, we may now turn to the other question initially mentioned which concerns *procedural due process of law* principles.

3. Universal or Relative Principles?

Whether there are at least some procedural principles of universal validity, is a fascinating perspective. It echoes the Kantian thesis of the need for universal public law in view of an eternal peace.[10] It supports the

[10] *See* I. KANT, ZUM EWIGEN FRIEDEN (1795), translated and annotated by C.J. FRIEDRICH, INEVITABLE PEACE (1948).

idea that justice, not only the market, is increasingly globalized.[11] However, the problems that such a perspective raises are neither few nor irrelevant. Such problems emerge from an overview of the three main doctrinal positions.

A first position roughly corresponds to the two paradigms examined in the previous paragraph, namely international institutional law and global administrative law. Although their cultural premises differ in some respects, both those paradigms observe that the new regulatory regimes and legal orders raise questions concerning the exercise of authority. At least some of those questions are faced by way of general principles of law. Some of them grew on the basis of broader principles, such as those prohibiting any discrimination on grounds of nationality. Other procedural constraints on governments, instead, were largely influenced by the principles elaborated within national legal orders during the last centuries. In sum, through a process which is not uniform, but clear enough in its effects, public law has changed and is increasingly changing. This obliges scholars to verify if the theoretical tools elaborated in the past may still be used, if necessary at the cost of some adaptations, or need to be replaced.[12]

A second position recognizes the importance of the principles influenced by national legal traditions. However, it puts much less emphasis on the fact, albeit historically relevant, of the acceptance of such principles. It emphasizes, rather, the importance of the general principles of law which must be respected by any legal order as such. An attentive reader may have noted that in the preceding sentence the language of "recognition" was shifted in the language of "duty". The shift was non-accidental. What characterizes the second position is precisely the idea of the intrinsic value of at least some general principles of law, such as the right to be heard. Without those principles, it is argued, there is not a legal order.[13] This line of reasoning clearly reveals the influence of an

---

11 M. DELMAS-MARTY, TROIS DÉFIS POUR UN DROIT MONDIAL (1998), translated and annotated by N. NORBERG, GLOBAL LAW: A TRIPLE CHALLENGE (2003).

12 *See* Kingsbury, Krisch & Stewart (note 8), at 15; Cassese (note 8), at 109.

13 M. Koskenniemi, *General Principles: Reflexions on Constructivist Thinking in International Law* (1985), *in* SOURCES OF INTERNATIONAL LAW, 359 (M. Koskenniemi ed., 2000), (for the thesis that the maxim *audi alteram partem* identifies one of such principles); *id.*, *Constitutionalism as Mindset: Reflections on Kantian Themes About International Law and Globalization*, 8 THEORETI-

old tradition, that of natural law. The idea of a universal legal patrimony has, moreover, gained a renewed importance when lawyers became aware of the excess of positivism and nationalism.[14]

Not only the usefulness, but even the possibility to identify such a universal legal patrimony is criticized, if not refuted, by other scholars. Their positions, however, are diversified. Some of them demonstrate empirically that established principles of Western legal culture, such as transparency and judicial review, do not fit with some specific cultures, for example that of the Malaysian indigenous population of *Buimiputera*.[15] Other observers bring this argument one step further. They argue that procedural safeguards are not at all neutral, but reveal strong connections with value judgments. Such value judgments are shared within national communities and, more rarely, within "regional" organizations, such as the European Union. They are, however, but "western constructs", inapplicable elsewhere.[16] Otherwise, there is the risk of a new type of imperialism, due especially to the dominance of the American legal culture.

The distinctive features just outlined determine different outcomes, which may be considered with regard to a specific question. The question is whether a public authority has to provide individuals and groups with a reasonable opportunity to be heard before it takes a decision adversely affecting their interests. National legal orders, in this respect, are not at all governed by the same set of rules. Even a quick glance to Western countries shows that procedural rules and practices differ. Dif-

---

CAL INQUIRIES IN LAW 29 (2007); O. SCHACHTER, INTERNATIONAL LAW IN THEORY AND PRACTICE (1991) (who identifies three categories of principles different from those recognized by civilized nations: those "*intrinsic to the idea of law and basic to all legal systems*", those "*valid through all kinds of societies*" and, finally, those founded on the "*very nature of man as a rational and social being*").

14 N. BOBBIO, PRINCIPI GENERALI DEL DIRITTO, NUOVISSIMO DIGESTO ITALIANO 889 (1968).

15 *See* C. McCrudden & S.G. Gross, *WTO Government Procurement Rules and the Local Dynamics of Procurement Policies: A Malaysian Case Study*, 17 EJIL 151 (2006).

16 For further remarks, *see* C. Harlow, *Global Administrative Law: The Quest for Principles and Values*, 17 EJIL 168 (2006) and U. Mattei, *A Theory of Imperial Law: A Study on U.S. Hegemony and the Latin Resistance*, 10 INDIANA JOURNAL OF GLOBAL LEGAL STUDIES 383 (2002).

ferences become more evident the more we move from adjudication (such as disciplinary procedures or those giving rise to sanctions) to rule-making and planning procedures.[17] However, when the Appellate Body (AB) of the WTO adjudicated the dispute concerning the import of shrimp and shrimp-related products, it did not only rely on due process principles. It also assumed that such principles are necessary in any country member of the WTO, in order to prevent arbitrary and capricious limits to free trade. Some Asian countries had argued that, though US limits explicitly intended to protect environmental resources (sea turtles), the intent or the effect was to discriminate against their products. While the AB dissented from the panel on the grounds that environmental protection might justify limits to free trade, it found that such limits were flawed. Indeed, basic procedural due process of law requirements had been disregarded. First, no notice and comment requirements had been observed. In the words of the AB, "there was no formal opportunity for an applicant country to be heard or to respond to any arguments that may be made against it".[18] A second and related flaw was that national authorities failed to provide adequate reasoning. Indeed, "no formal written, reasoned decision" was issued in relation to applications. For all these reasons, the AB came to the conclusion that "exporting members applying for certification [...] are denied *basic fairness and due process* and are discriminated".[19] It is an irony that the

---

17 *Cf.* G. della Cananea, *Equivalent Standards under Domestic Administrative Law: A Comparative Perspective*, *in* INVESTMENT TREATY LAW – CURRENT ISSUES, volume II (L. Liberti, F. Ortino, A. Sheppard & H. Warner eds., 2007).

18 Report of the Appellate Body, WT/DS58/AB/R 12 October 1998, § 180. For a comparison between the US and European conceptions of the right to state reasons, *see* M. Shapiro, *The Giving Reasons Requirement*, UNIVERSITY OF CHICAGO LEGAL FORUM 178 (1992); J. Mashaw, *Reasoned Administration: The European Union, the United States, and the Project of Democratic Governance*, 76 GEORGE WASHINGTON LAW REVIEW 101 (2007).

19 Report of the Appellate Body, § 181, italics added. For a similar claim made by India in another dispute, *see* R. Howse, *Back to Court After Shrimp/Turtle: India's Challenge to Labour and Environmental Linkages in the EC Generalized System of Preferences*, *in* WTO LAW AND PROCESS, 251 (M. Andenas & F. Ortino eds., 2005). *See also* A. von Bogdandy, *Law and Politics in the WTO*, MAX PLANCK YEARBOOK OF INTERNATIONAL LAW 613 (2000), (for the thesis that the AB creates law, thus protecting the rights of non-citizens) and R. Howse, *The Appellate Body Rulings in the Shrimp/Turtle Case: A New Legal Baseline for the Trade and Environment Debate*, 27 COLUMBIA JOURNAL

conduct of US authorities has been deemed arbitrary for failure to observe principles which are rooted in American public law. But the effects of this case are far-reaching.

For those who share the first theoretical position, this report is particularly important to the extent to which it confirms the transplant of legal principles, tools and techniques from national contexts to the new regional and global regulatory regimes. They stress, however, the importance of some distinctive features. It is evident, particularly, that procedural due process requirements are neither invoked directly by economic actors nor to be used by them. Rather, the AB held that their states should avail themselves of such safeguards.

From the point of view of theories which emphasize the importance of natural law, the report of the AB is neither surprising nor dangerous. It simply acknowledges the existence of a general principle of law common to all legal orders because it is a necessary requirement. The question is not, therefore, whether such a general principle of law exists. Nor is there any need for an enabling clause. It remains to be seen, rather, how existing variables may be explained. One possible solution is to affirm that while a procedural safeguard has a clear "essence", it may be declined and applied differently by the various legal orders.[20] Of course, the underlying assumption, notably that all legal orders share a minimum content, may be viewed in very different terms by both positivists and advocates of national cultures. However, the distinction between what may be defined as a sort of essential content of a procedural principle and its concrete manifestations is quite important for our purposes, as it will be argued in section 6.

That said, a sharper difference emerges between the two positions just considered, especially the latter, and the last one. Such a difference does not only emerge with regard to the way of considering the impact of regional and global regulatory regimes. There is a deeper and more important distinctive element. Such an element is philosophical, rather

---

OF INTERNATIONAL LAW 514 (2003) (criticizing the "illegitimate judicial activism") and T.U. Shivasan, *Development, Domestic Constraints and External Opportunities from Globalization*, 26 MICHIGAN JOURNAL OF INTERNATIONAL LAW 63, 82 (2004-5) (same critique).

[20] A similar position, concerning the *rule of law*, is expressed by D. Dyzenhaus, *The Rule of (Administrative) Law in International Law*, 68 LAW & CONTEMPORARY PROBLEMS 127 (2004).

than empirical, since the third position has a radically different intellectual premise. It denies the existence of principles shared by all national legal orders, because the underlying values differ. For this reason, while pointing out a variety of concrete problems, including the risk of regulatory capture, the third position basically puts such problems into a secondary rank. The real problem, it argues, lies at the ethical and political roots of such procedural principles. Since such roots largely diverge, it is not at all possible to take for granted that common procedural values governing the conduct of public authorities exist. More clearly, there is no such thing as general principles of procedure. Moreover, insisting on such principles is misleading. It obscures the real problem, that is to say substantive justice, such as peace and prosperity for all.[21]

4. Normative and Empirical Arguments: An Overview

In my opinion, the critical remarks just mentioned cannot be simply dismissed as isolated or eccentric. Indeed, the questions they pose are, again, both questions of value and questions of technique. Moreover, questions of value are not only raised by some academics and other observers. Such questions are increasingly raised by policymakers, either tactically or for a true belief. For all these reasons, they must be taken seriously. But this does not necessarily mean that such critical remarks ought to be accepted. Indeed, they suffer from two methodological flaws.

Their first flaw regards the critique of the cultural hegemony exercised by Western culture. In this critique there is a frequent confusion between two distinct levels of analysis. One thing is whether, in the real world, there are symptoms of a convergence between the procedural safeguards traditionally provided by some national legal orders and those introduced by regional or global regulatory regimes. Another thing is, provided that such a convergence emerges, whether it is inevitably in contrast with the founding values of other cultures of the

---

21 This is, of course, an oversimplification, since the ideas expressed by critics are much more articulated, *see*, *e.g.*, Mattei (note 16), at 386 and B. Chimni, *International Institutions Today: An Imperial Global State in the Making*, 15 EJIL 1 (2004).

world. Of course, it may not be excluded that such a contrast exists. Nor may it be excluded, however, that such a contrast either does not exist or is less serious than it was thought earlier. All this implies that we must not limit our analysis to value judgments. Empirical judgments must be considered, too. And empirical analysis may reveal, as Amartya Sen has consistently argued, that sometimes national or "regional" values are more similar than it was expected.

Another methodological flaw regards the way of conceiving variables. Less recent theories of public law have been convincingly criticized for their abstractness. We need not repeat here that criticism, especially against the methodology used to build the German *Allgemeine Staatslehre*. Its main weakness was not the insufficient attention paid to the innumerable variables emerging from the concrete reality. It was, rather, an adequate awareness of the historical nature of legal institutions. Since legal institutions are products of history, they are inevitably subject to change. Even the state, far from being an absolute (to use again a Hegelian terminology) and immutable form of legal organization, is a historic achievement, with its parable.[22] Precisely because states change, as a response to new needs, they create the new international regimes and legal orders. The latter, however, increasingly bind states' powers. As a result, the old theories of the state may hardly explain the new phenomena. Similar concerns regard modern theories, such as those of *law and economics*. It may be argued that there is not a single economic orthodoxy. Nor, as a result, is there a single set of legal principles and rules capable of achieving an optimum legal discipline. To bring the argument to its logical conclusion, serious doubts must be cast on any attempt to elaborate a normative theory of procedural due process of law valid for all countries, contexts and seasons.

While all this confirms that identifying common procedural principles is not an easy task, it shows that normative arguments, based on value judgments, are not sufficient. Such arguments should be combined, and confronted with empirical judgments. In the search of reasons for using procedural safeguards, it is not irrelevant whether public authorities operating in different institutional frameworks face more or less the same problems and try to use similar solutions. The question whether

---

[22] GIANNINI (note 6), at 19 *et seq.* (holding that this parable is today on the decline), and 25 (on the limits of the theories elaborated by 19th century German legal scholarship).

there are at least some universal procedural principles can thus be properly answered only by addressing it from different points of view.

On this basis, I will try to expose some arguments, both normative and empirical, which should show the persuasiveness of a positive answer to the question whether some universal principles of procedural justice do exist. The first of such arguments emphasizes the intrinsic value of procedural due process of law. As a matter of fact, procedural safeguards are essential for the adequacy of any legal order. On the one hand, if the history of constitutionalism is of some guide we need some procedural safeguards to limit the exercise of authority.[23] This is still more evident when considering the greater impact of authority on individual and collective interests. On the other hand, the more recent history shows that we need adequate procedures that can fulfill further functions. Such functions include mediating conflicts between competing interests, shaping public action and strengthening its legitimacy.[24]

Such procedural safeguards, it may be argued, are all the more indispensable if there are a variety of interests, opinions and value judgments. Obviously, a situation of this kind characterizes all political regimes where power lacks a single foundation, be it religious or political. However, such a situation or some sort of approximation is not necessarily unknown in other types of political regimes, such as those which Rawls defined as well-ordered hierarchical regimes.[25] Even in such regimes, the exercise of power may and often does affect the interests of foreign citizens and those of other states. An authoritarian state, for example, may be bound by a bilateral treaty laying down the principle that fair and equitable treatment must be given to the investors of the other state. All this makes a *prima facie* case for arguing that, in an increas-

---

23 *See* K.C. DAVIS, DISCRETIONARY JUSTICE. A PRELIMINARY INQUIRY (1969), holding that discretionary powers must be limited, structured and checked, in order to make them accountable to the people, and MASHAW (note 2), for the thesis that in modern US law due process has a plurality of rationales, including appropriateness, competence and dignity of the human being. My argument differs from that of F.A. VON HAYEK, LAW, LEGISLATION, AND LIBERTY (1986), who identifies the history of constitutionalism with the fight against legal positivism and the omnipotent state. The problem, in my opinion, lies in authority as such, in this sense *see* the classical portrait of constitutionalism by C.H. MCILWAIN, CONSTITUTIONALISM: ANCIENT AND MODERN (1947).

24 *See* N. LUHMANN, LEGITIMATION DURCH VERFAHREN (1977).

25 *See* J. RAWLS, THE LAW OF PEOPLES (1996).

ingly globalized world, we need some procedural principles which are capable of ensuring some kind of protection for such interests.

Of course, the discontents of procedural values may argue that this way of reasoning simply overlooks some fundamental problems. It ignores the basic tension between the values which characterize national cultures. Moreover, it neglects the procedural safeguards which are required by Western governments for protecting the interests of their firms. Once again, there is some truth in these objections. However, reality is more complex. From the first point of view, as it was suggested earlier, the relevant dimension is that of general principles of public law and this is quite important. Its importance lies in the fact that, unlike rules, general principles convey broad values. Their logic, moreover, is not an "all-or-nothing" one, but, rather, that of balancing. Precisely for these reasons, it has always been relatively easier to find common principles in different jurisdictions, than to identify common rules.

That newcomers are substantially obliged to accept a variety of conditions if they want to join regional and global regulatory regimes, is another question. It does not necessarily imply, however, that procedural safeguards protect Western countries. Consider again the dispute between Asian exporting countries and the US government. What was at stake was not the enforcement of global procedures within the legal orders of the former. It was, rather, the procedural duties of the latter. Hence the importance of the AB's ruling. Critics of globalization may argue that cases such as that just mentioned are but Trojan horses to introduce procedural values in other legal orders, undermining their cultures. Such a risk is not simply hypothetical. Yet, the underlying assumption, namely that emphasizing the importance of procedures is only a Western obsession, is far from convincing. Normative and empirical arguments, in sum, are intertwined, though in the next pages they are separately taken into account.

5. The Intrinsic Value of Procedural Safeguards

When addressing the intrinsic value of procedural due process requirements, whatever their effectiveness,[26] a question of methodology soon

---

26 Although procedural requirements, in the context of this paper, do not correspond to human rights, also because they may be invoked by other sub-

arises. Once again, the Kantian strand of liberal tradition is appealing.[27] It also looks relatively easy to use. Once a basic value is established *a priori*, namely equality, it determines a series of consequences. Focusing on equality has another advantage. It makes sense of procedural principles with regard to both private parties, within a national or supranational legal order, and to states in the global arena. Yet, a Kantian perspective of this kind is troublesome in a twofold respect. On the one hand, it assumes a common conception of the good, which is challenged not only by positivists, but also by advocates of relativism. On the other hand, it does not provide us with an adequate explanation of all the cases in which written rules and case-law follow an instrumentalist perspective, explicitly excluded by Kant. Consider, for example, the principle expressed by the maxim *ne bis in idem*. Also claims of accuracy are important in the global arena, especially with regard to controversial issues such as the use of genetically modified organisms (GMO), mentioned later. Notwithstanding its appeal, a deductive approach may thus raise more problems than it may solve.[28] Rather than deducting procedural principles from, say, natural justice, my intent is to try to verify whether their necessity may be demonstrated inductively. Such a position is ideally closer to that of Edmund Burke than to that of his French antagonists.[29]

From this point of view, it is useful to look briefly at two cases decided in the last years by the European Court of Human Rights, *Taskin v.*

---

jects as well, an important lesson may be drawn from the rich literature concerning human rights. It is certainly correct to point out that what matters today is not their recognition, but their protection, *see* N. BOBBIO, L'ETÀ DEI DIRITTI (1992), translated by A. CAMERON, THE AGE OF RIGHTS (1996). This shows the importance of empirical research about the effectiveness of treaties recognizing human rights, *see* O.A. Hathaway, *Do Human Rights Treaties Make a Difference?*, 111 YALE LAW JOURNAL 1935 (2001-2002). However, as A. CASSESE, HUMAN RIGHTS IN A CHANGING WORLD (1990), convincingly argued, the infringements of human rights do not impinge on their normative value, which is confirmed by the use of such a category to qualify them.

27 MASHAW (note 2), at 191.

28 For a defence of the inductive and comparative method, *see* G. SCHWARZENBERGER, THE INDUCTIVE APPROACH TO INTERNATIONAL LAW (1965).

29 I refer to BURKE'S REFLECTIONS ON THE REVOLUTION IN FRANCE (1790).

Turkeye and *Tysiac v. Poland*.[30] In the former case, dozens of Turkish citizens were tragically affected by the effects deriving from the use of cyanide in a gold mine. There is no doubt that their substantive rights to health and to the integrity of family life had been infringed. However, when looking at the way in which the Strasbourg Court dealt with the dispute, it soon becomes evident that it did its best not only to respect the margin of appreciation which the Convention leaves to each Member State, but also to show that it was paying due respect to it. Precisely for this reason, the Court did not weigh the interests at stake. Rather, it easily demonstrated that such interests had not been duly balanced. Indeed, before the mining license was released, no analyses of its impact on the environment had been carried out. Accordingly, the national administrative judge annulled such license. And the government's refusal to comply with the judgment of the national judge was but a further procedural ground for holding that the Convention had been violated, this time on the basis of article 6.

The other case was even more delicate, since it dealt with abortion, itself a highly sensitive issue and one that is perceived very differently by European people. Hence the lack and even the impossibility of a common European legal framework in this respect.[31] Understandably, the Strasbourg Court clarified that it did not intend to reconsider the balance struck by the Polish Parliament between women's self-determination and the protection of the unborn. Whatever the soundness of such a balance, the Court held, when a national procedure has been established, such a procedure must be taken seriously by the administration. No officer, therefore, is allowed to disregard the evidence produced by the woman, regardless of the antagonism between her personal interest and the will of the majority. Nor may she be refused a reasonable chance to express her point of view or be heard by an absentminded public officer in a formalistic way taking only a few minutes.

In both cases, the fundamental question was not whether public officials exercised their powers correctly. Of course, the dimension of accu-

---

30 *Taskhin v. Turkey*, application no. 46117/99, 2004; *Tysiac v. Poland*, application no. 5410/03, 2007.

31 For a similar line of reasoning, *see* J.H.H. Weiler, *Fundamental Rights and Fundamental Boundaries: On the conflict of standards and values in the European legal space*, *in* THE CONSTITUTION OF EUROPE, 102 (J.H.H. Weiler ed., 1999). *See also* F. Sudre, *Existe-t-il un ordre public européen?*, *in* QUELLE EUROPE POUR LE DROITS DE L'HOMME?, 39 (P. Tavernier ed., 1996).

racy and appropriateness did matter. However, at the heart of both cases there was not simply a demand for sound administration. Procedural dysfunctions do not simply lead to unacceptable outcomes of both individuals and groups. They may affect human dignity. "Dignity", in this sense, must not be seen in substantive terms, as it happens for example when dignity is conceived as a shield against inhuman treatments or torture. What is at stake is not the outcome, but the process. Of course, we must take into account the fact that people tend to gauge the fairness of decision-making process by the quality of their participation. However, the process itself matters. It may be detrimental to one's sense of dignity, by denying a minimum standard of procedural fairness. If a human being is not taken seriously as a person, not only his individuality, but the elementary sense of justice is violated.[32]

Procedural safeguards are not less important when they are invoked by other entities, notably legal persons or foreigners. Thus, to take the GMO dispute before the AB as an example, issues of appropriateness and scientific competence had more weight than the issues of natural justice.[33] However, what matters is the broader meaning of the dispute. It concerned the EU ban on GMO. For all multinationals, a vast majority of the regulations which they are obliged to respect are by definition *foreign* regulations. The question thus arises if and how it is possible to ensure that such regulations and the corresponding checks are not vitiated by partiality and capriciousness. Both the AB and the Italian administrative court did all they could in order not to engage in complex policy issues (in particular, whether GMO should be introduced). Rather, their approach has been that, if the body which has the responsibility to carry out a scientific assessment has not identified risks for human health and the environment, then the political authority may not

---

32 I am indebted with professor Mashaw for his thoughtful comments on this point. *See* his DUE PROCESS IN THE ADMINISTRATIVE STATE (note 2), at 162; *id.*, *Administrative Due Process: The Quest for a Dignitary Theory*, 61 BOSTON UNIVERSITY LAW REVIEW (1981).

33 *See* the report of the AB, WT/DS291/R, WT/DS202/R, WT/DS203/R, *European Communities – Measures Affecting the Approval and Marketing of Biotech Products,* 2006 and the judgment of the Italian administrative court for Regione Lazio: section I, n. 14477 /2004. For a comparison, *see* S. Battini, *Le due anime del diritto amministrativo globale*, *in* IL DIRITTO AMMINISTRATIVO OLTRE I CONFINI. OMAGGIO DEGLI ALLIEVI A SABINO CASSESE, 6 (C. Franchini et al. eds., 2008).

ban GMO. Clearly, this means considering complex political issues in a way which is no more than a search of competence and appropriateness. Whether this approach to due process requirements is satisfying remains to be seen. What is more relevant for our purposes, anyway, is the fact that both the AB and the national judge framed the problem in procedural terms. Of course, none of them implied that there is a single way to deal with such a problem. Rather, they assumed that some minimum standards of procedural justice must be respected. All this applies to other cases, such as those concerning foreign investment. National authorities may take decisions adversely affecting investors only if and to the extent to which either a hearing has been provided or (adequate) reasons have been stated. Disregard of such procedural safeguards should be regarded as a proof of the denial of justice, which is mainly (if not only) a procedural concept.[34]

A full procedural due process of law is required, too, for a non-citizen, such as Kadi. A Saudi Arabian citizen living in the UK, Kadi was included in the list of persons and other entities subject to the freezing of funds aiming at weakening support to international terrorism. Not being a UK citizen, he could not avail himself of political safeguards. Nor, as a suspect supporter of terrorism, could he exercise his right to be heard before a decision was taken affecting his interests. He could only invoke ex-post remedies. But even the courts were reluctant to ensure full protection of his procedural rights. A UK court was unable to do so. Nor did the Court of First Instance of the EU apply the usual standards of review. It deferred to UN law. It underlined the need to give the precedence to collective security. Whatever the effectiveness of measures aiming at maximizing this collective interest, there is however a limit to such measures. That limit derives from the risk that unlimited discretionary powers degrade into arbitrariness, against which every social structure seeks a defense.[35] Precisely to prevent such a risk, when

---

34 J. Paulsson, Denial of Justice in International Law 98 (2003). Two examples of this are the ELSI judgment of the International Court of Justice, *Elettronica Sicula S.p.a.* (United States of America v. Italy), ICJ Reports 1989, 13; and the ICSID tribunal award on *Loewen v. United States of America,* Case no. ARB(AF)/98/3 (2003).

35 *See* R. Dworkin, *What the Court Really Said*, 51 New York Review of Books 1 (2004); J. Bacchus, *Turning to Tacitus (Lessons from Tacitus Regarding the Rule of Law and Freedom when Confronted by Terror),* 16 Vanderbilt Journal of Transnational Law 631 (2004), for the thesis that abandoning

considering Kadi's appeal, the ECJ recognized that some minimum procedural rights, consisting either in some kind of hearing or in an *ex-post* review,[36] had to be granted. What was at stake, therefore, was not the weight of the interests involved by the freezing of the funds, but a minimum of procedural fairness.[37] This case also reveals the connections between regulatory regimes. A very clear connection emerged between the EU and the ECHR. Not only did the ECJ mention the Convention, but it also repeatedly quoted the case-law of the other court. In addition to this horizontal relationship, another relationship, of vertical nature, emerged. It is possible to consider the decision of the ECJ in *Kadi* as a reaction to UN Security Council's disregard for basic procedural protections. But, if we look more closely at the judgment, we understand that the Court noted the progresses occurred at UN level.

Procedural protections are not at all less important when the interests of states are at stake within supranational or international organizations. Consider, for example, the dispute between the Commission and the Ecofin as far as the deficits of France and Germany were concerned. The need to ensure a fair and accurate decision was channeled through a set of procedural safeguards. Such safeguards included the *audi alteram*

---

the *rule of law* in order to maximize security would not only morally controversial, but also ineffective. *See* CFI, Cases T-315/01, *Abdullah Kadi v. Council and Commission* and C-306/01, *Yusuf and Al Barakaat v. Council*. For a critical assessment, *see* C. Tomuschat, *Comment to Case T-315/01, Abdullah Kadi v. Council and Commission*, 43 COMMON MARKET LAW REVIEW 549 (2006); P. Eeckhout, *Community Terrorism Listings, Fundamental Rights and UN Security Council Resolutions. In Search of the Right Fit*, 3 EUROPEAN CONSTITUTIONAL LAW REVIEW 183 (2007).

36 *See* H.J. Friendly, *Some Kind of Hearing*, 123 UNIVERSITY OF PENNSYLVANIA LAW REVIEW 1267, 1316 (1975) (holding, however, that the Supreme Court had gone too far in affirming "that the adversary system is the only appropriate model").

37 Joined Cases C-402/05 P and C-415/05 P, *Yassin Abdullah Kadi Al Barakaat International Foundation v. Council*. For further comments, *see* T. Tridimas, *Terrorism and the ECJ: Empowerment and Democracy in the EC Legal Order*, 34 EUROPEAN LAW REVIEW 103 (2009) (arguing that "this is the most important judgment ever delivered by the" ECJ with regard to the relationship between EC law and international law), and A. Gattini, *Comment*, 46 COMMON MARKET LAW REVIEW 213 (2009) (arguing that the ECJ jeopardized "the coherence between the international legal system and the promotion of an effective dialogue between international courts and international organizations").

partem principle. This allowed both national governments to present evidence and arguments. But each of them was not allowed to vote in their own procedure, coherently within the principle of impartiality. A blocking minority was equally reached, preventing the adoption of sanctions. That the Council may do so was not disputed by the ECJ. Nor did the ECJ contest the Council's wide discretionary powers in the choice of the appropriate means to seek the observance of deficit targets. However, the Court annulled the final outcome, because of the improper use of the powers which the Treaty confers on the Council of Ministers. The latter has, in fact, chosen a new procedure. In other words, the Court articulated and defended a process-oriented conception of due process aiming at preserving checks and balances within the EU and, with it, the confidence of the public in European fiscal rules.[38]

A process-oriented conception emerges from the case-law of the AB and of the WTO, too. Even a first glance reveals that the due process premises of its rules of procedure were kept. On several occasions the AB specified those rules. In particular, it emphasized that all contracting parties had a *full opportunity of defense of interests*.[39] It may be argued that this is the underlying assumption of the AB's decision to admit *amicus curiae* briefs presented by another party. Quite the contrary. The admission of the briefs presented by environmental associations was a response to the growing demand for a new approach that sought to involve in the process of decision-making all the groups affected by any action of the WTO.[40]

At this point, we must beware of overemphasizing the relevance of both the EU and the WTO in a discourse which regards the global arena.[41] Indeed, this is characterized by many other regulatory regimes.

---

[38] *See* ECJ Case C-27/04, 2004, *Commission v. Council.*

[39] *See Report of the Appellate Body*, 22 July 2003, WT/DS219/AB/R, *European Communities – Anti-Dumping Duties*, § 149.

[40] This was contested, *see* R. Howse, *Membership and its Privileges: The WTO, Civil Society and the Amicus Brief Controversy*, 9 EUROPEAN LAW JOURNAL 499 (2003).

[41] For this remark, Harlow (note 16), 175, and for the thesis that such regimes were created by the same club of nations and had largely similar purposes, that is to say to ensure a certain degree of free trade, J.H.H. Weiler, *Cain and Abel – Convergence and Divergence in International Trade Law*, *in* THE EU, THE WTO, AND THE NAFTA. TOWARDS A COMMON LAW OF INTERNATIONAL TRADE, 4 (J.H.H. Weiler ed., 2003).

And the latter differs from the former, sometimes remarkably. As a result, it cannot be asserted that the same principles govern other regimes. But there is some evidence that procedural principles gradually emerge in other regimes as well. This applies both to multilateral institutions, as the adjustment of UN rules on listing shows, and to bilateral agreements. The same applies to the denial of the authorization to build a plant, requested by a foreign investor, as it happened in the *Metalclad* case.[42] Metalclad Corporation, a US waste disposal company, challenged the denial of the permit to build which was based on preoccupations for externalities, particularly for the environment. It instituted arbitration proceedings against Mexico under the ICSID rules and the arbitral tribunal reached the conclusion that the denial of the permit was unlawful. It found that the Municipality's denial of the permit did not make any reference to any aspect of the facility which the investor aimed at building. As a consequence of this, the decision lacked proper reasons, with the further consequence that Mexican authorities had failed to ensure a fair treatment.

6. Conflicting Interests and Values: Implications for Due Process Protections

There is another reason which suggests that the diversity between the values[43] shared within a specific country and, to a larger extent, between the various countries of the world does not diminish the importance of procedural due process of law. Quite the contrary, such diversity accentuates the need for some procedural protections.

---

42 *Metalclad v. Mexico* (2000). *See* Battini (note 33), 11; V. Been & J.C. Beauvais, *The Global Fifth Amendment: NAFTA's Investment Protections and the Misguided Quest for International "Regulatory Takings" Doctrine*, 78 NEW YORK UNIVERSITY LAW REVIEW 83 (2003).

43 The term "values" is increasingly often used, though it is less precise than principles. It also generates the inconveniences pointed out by C. SCHMITT, DIE TYRANNEI DER WERTE (1967).

The bases of this line of reasoning are still those pointed out by Adam Smith in his theory of moral sentiments.[44] According to such a theory, market economy is vital only if ethics and law, imposing the respect of other interests, limit individual selfishness, though the latter is the engine of the economy. The role of ethics is potentially more relevant if the community is more cohesive, although this does not prevent contrasts and even conflicts. Such a role becomes weakened, instead, when the community widens, becomes more diversified and is influenced by new instances and ideas. When this happens, ethics, customs and traditional practices gradually become insufficient. The legal order must fill the gap. It must provide some guidance to individuals and ensure legal certainty or make the results of their conducts reasonably foreseeable. Such a need emerged very clearly in the *Metalclad* decision, just mentioned. The tribunal noted, the preamble of NAFTA sets the goal of ensuring a "predictable commercial framework for business planning and investment". The underlying idea is not simply that the rule of law must be respected, as more or less solely legal systems impose. It is, rather, echoing Lon Fuller's assumption that there are requisites of any legal system,[45] that the rule of law as such is violated if: a) there are not adequate legal rules, preventing those wielding authority to decide on a case-to-case basis; b) their decisions are not clearly grounded on such rules.

This does not only apply to commercial litigation. Consider, again, the *Kadi* case. Let us imagine that Kadi was actively involved in an intense anti-Western or even in favor of a radical Islamic group's propaganda, for which he collected funds. This may explain the reaction of the host country's government, its effort to prevent such activities. Prevention was justified, more precisely, by the risks to which collective security is exposed. However, the enforcement of such measures raises a twofold problem. On the one hand, while there is a strong case for a high level of accuracy, there is no evidence that such a level was achieved. On the other hand, the question arises whether some degree of fundamental fairness must be ensured to Kadi and all other legal entities. Under UN resolutions, no judge intervenes before such measures produce their effects. Nor are any of the affected parties informed that a decision ad-

---

[44] *See* A. SMITH, THE THEORY OF MORAL SENTIMENTS (1790), in particular § VII.4.36. For a reading of Smith which accentuates the connection between ethics and economy, A. SEN, ON ETHICS AND ECONOMICS (1988).

[45] L. FULLER, THE MORALITY OF LAW (1967).

versely affecting them has been taken. This lack of safeguards against the exercise of administrative powers becomes all the more serious due to the lack of other protections. In fact, no diplomatic protection came to Kadi from his country. Even in the case in which his country had somehow decided to act, it could do so ambiguously or even capriciously. Hence the partnership of fundamental fairness and appropriateness, as rationales of procedural due process of law.

This is not merely a pragmatic approach. From the recent philosophical literature concerning questions of justice a similar preoccupation emerges, that is to say to find minimum standards of procedural justice. A similar approach lies at the heart of Rawls's *A Theory of Justice*, possibly the most influential work in this field.[46] His basic premise is that the primary task of every political regime is to ensure conditions acceptable for everybody under the veil of ignorance. As a result, we may consider the principles of procedure as safeguards that everybody would be inclined to accept. As to the extent to which we ignore whether our values coincide with those of the majority or at least are compatible with them, we are interested in fair procedures being available for all. We do not need, instead, to share the belief that liberal and democratic polities must be preferred to others.[47] Precisely because different interests and values emerge, we need processes. Such processes do not inevitably lead to bargaining and compromises, at least on some issues. But due process principles are even more necessary.[48] This does not imply that such principles are absolute and immutable truths. However, they are particularly important because, and to the extent to which, they are valid for all.

However, the question thus arises how we may identify such principles. There are, of course, many ways to do so. Montesquieu used an inductive method, when he affirmed that only barbarian peoples used to condemn somebody without providing any opportunity to be heard. Lon Fuller used, instead, a deductive method. He deduced a series of

---

46 RAWLS (note 2).

47 *See* J. RAWLS, POLITICAL LIBERALISM (1996) (where the idea of an *overlapping consensus* is introduced, that is to say an agreement on *justice as fairness* between citizens who hold different religious and philosophical views or conceptions of the good). For critical remarks, *see* J. GRAY, THE TWO FACES OF LIBERALISM (2000).

48 *See* S. HAMPSHIRE, JUSTICE IS CONFLICT 37 (2000).

corollaries not from an abstract idea of justice, but from the concept of legal order. One of such corollaries is the principle expressed by the old maxim *nulla poena sine lege*. Interestingly, Fuller included this between the principles that all civilized nations must respect.[49]

Of course, we may wonder whether this approach is acceptable within different polities, for example in single-party regimes or in those dominated by religious authorities which pursue a single idea of the good. In the liberal and democratic tradition, these are less than well-ordered states.[50] Yet, if we look at the world as it is, it soon becomes evident that there are plenty of such states. But, with the exception of some isolated totalitarian regimes, even less than well-ordered states would look for some kind of procedural justice outside their borders. The more regional and global regulatory regimes deal with the essential interests of national communities, the more acute their governments call for reasonably accurate processes of decision making. That they do so instrumentally, in order to protect their own interests, is no surprise. What matters is the widespread demand of fair procedures.

This demand characterizes two basic legal structures: intergovernmental negotiations and the judicial process. As far as the former are concerned, of course, nothing may replace the political will to stipulate an agreement. No obligation *de contrahendo* would be enforceable. However, it may introduce some obligations *de negotiando*, incentives and disincentives. Consider, again, the dispute between the US and some Asian importers of shrimps and shrimps-related products. The AB refused to exclude that the US ban on those products could be justified by the need to protect sea turtles. However, such a ban had to meet a severe test of non-arbitrariness. It failed to meet the test for two reasons. First, the US government had only negotiated with some American partners, ex-

---

49 FULLER (note 45), 59; J. Boyle, *Legal Realism and the Social Contract: Fuller's Public Jurisprudence of Form, Private Jurisprudence of Substance*, 78 CORNELL LAW REVIEW 377 (1992-93) (holding that Fuller intended to expose universal principles, rather than a normative theory limited to the US); R.J. Blackman, *There is There There: Defending the Defenseless with Procedural Natural Law*, 37 ARIZONA LAW REVIEW 285 (1995) (for a confutation of positivist objections to "procedural natural law"). *See also* International Criminal Tribunal for the Former Yugoslavia, *The Prosecutor v. Tadic*, Appeals Chamber, Judgment in Sentencing Appeals, 26 January 2000, and the dissenting opinion of Antonio Cassese.

50 RAWLS (note 2).

cluding Asian ones. Second, the latter had not been provided with a fair opportunity to be heard within national administrative procedures. In positive terms, this confirms the need of fair procedures. The fairness of a procedure is an essential requisite for the acceptability of the final outcomes. For this reason, established organizational principles governing the judicial process, such as that expressed by the maxim *nemo judex in causa propria*, do not suffice to ensure a proper standard of justice. This requires, at least the respect of the other maxim, *audi alteram partem*.

That the observance of such a maxim is increasingly required in administrative procedures, is very important for a practical reason. It regards the risk of capture of the regulators. Such a risk emerged in Western countries for many decades. Of course, it may not be excluded that such a risk occurs when regulatory or global regulatory regimes provide participatory procedures. Nor may it be excluded that such procedures, more simply, favor stronger economic actors, in particular multinationals. However, empirical research offers evidence that at least in some cases open procedures produce the opposite outcomes.

One such case concerned the construction of a highway in Mumbai. The project would have sensibly improved transfers by buses and rails services. However, it would have required the relocation of business and the involuntary resettlements of both inhabitants and shopkeepers. Many of them protested against resettlement. Some non-governmental organizations backed their protests. A request for inspection was sent to the Inspection Panel of the World Bank. Further requests followed. Eventually, an inspection was carried out. The Panel found that shopkeepers had not been consulted regarding alternatives to resettlement of the sites for their shops. Moreover, the necessary documentation to ensure that all environmental consequences had been considered was unavailable. This led the Bank to suspend some lines of payment. The Management's response recognized these shortcomings. It took the commitment to place increased emphasis on consultation, which should be supplemented by "effective and timely dissemination ... of information".[51] Interestingly, assuring due process did not demand particular

---

[51] *See* the Inspection Panel, *India-Mumbai Urban Transport Project*, Report no. 34725 of 21 December 2005; Management, *Response and Reconsideration in Response to the Inspection Panel Report*, 27 February 2006. For an assessment of this mechanism, *see* I. SHIHATA, THE WORLD BANK INSPECTION PANEL 85 (2002); E. Suzuko & S. Nannani, *Responsibility of International Organizations:*

forms or expenses, but rather an accurate investigation. Nor was due process detrimental to collective interests. Quite the contrary, it gave voice to the less protected individuals and groups. Information and consultation, initially excluded, were provided.

7. Values, Principles and Rules

The Mumbai traders' case does not only provide us with an interesting refutation to the empirical critique raised by relativists, that is to say that due process inevitably favors the wealthier ones. It also holds out the prospect of confining due process values within the family of individualistic concerns which are so often criticized by the advocates of Asian values. However, some relativists may contest the use of procedural safeguards made by international authorities, arguing that this is another technique to impose the Western cultural model.

I do not raise this problem merely to dismiss it. As it was observed earlier, not only is this problem raised by many, but it is also a real one, which should not be overlooked. While one of the basic international documents, the Statute of the International Court of Justice, still includes between its legal sources the "general principles of law recognized by civilized countries", its meaning has changed. As to the extent to which the international community is much more differentiated, even the possibility of drawing a line distinguishing civilized from non-civilized countries is, at least, controversial. Moreover, the development of conventional sources suggests that, while that provision is unchanged, its legitimating function has become weaker. Or, more correctly, it is important to be aware of its limited role. However, too often judicial and arbitral bodies neglect this. They simply confront civil law and common law countries. This is all the more questionable when one considers the extent to which comparative analysis is used to introduce new norms in a legal order.[52]

The Accountability Mechanisms of Multilateral Development Banks, 27 MICHIGAN JOURNAL OF INTERNATIONAL LAW 177 (2005).

52 M. DELMAS-MARTY, LE RELATIF ET L'UNIVERSEL 15 (1999). *See also* E. Jouannet, *Universalism and Imperialism: The True-False Paradox of International Law?*, 18 EJIL 379 (2007). Limits of space do not permit to devote sufficient analysis to the importance of article 38 of the Statute of the ICJ. The rele-

A better awareness of the historic and conventional nature of so many important legal principles and rules is, therefore, necessary. It can provide a better theoretical grounding for comparative analysis, in the sense that every legal order must be considered for its own morphological features and cannot be considered as an archetype.[53] It can provide a more satisfying basis for analyzing the concrete problems which emerge in a more globalized world. It may promote judicial restraint, or simply accuracy, while sometimes expanding judicial action.

That said, the relativist critique, as I portray it, remains troublesome from a twofold perspective. First, its underlying assumption, notably that procedural values are but Western constructs, is at least questionable. It is flawed from an epistemic point of view, as the recent studies carried out by Amartya Sen show. Moreover, the history of political and administrative institutions is replete with exchanges and transplants. Historic and comparative analysis may thus show that, while we may not assume that some principles are accepted everywhere, it cannot be excluded that they are shared by very different cultures. My second argument, in the next paragraph, takes a quite different form. It focuses on the importance of regional and global regulatory regimes and institutions. It attempts to provide a direct linkage between the choice either to set up such regimes and institutions or to apply for membership and the evolving values which all communities, including less than well-ordered communities protect and enhance. Its main thrust is to reinterpret the perspective of values in a dynamic way, which takes into account the increasing web of bilateral and multilateral relations.

After emphasizing the risk of giving too much weight to the principles shared by Western polities, it ought to be observed that this is not the only risk which must be avoided. Another, and symmetrical one, consists in leaving unchallenged the currently widespread relativist ap-

---

vant literature is examined in my chapter *Dai vecchi ai nuovi principi generali del diritto: il due process of law*, *in* I PRINCIPI DELL'AZIONE AMMINISTRATIVA NELLO SPAZIO GIURIDICO GLOBALE, 11 (G. della Cananea ed., 2007). *See also* J. von Bernstorff, *The Changing Fortunes of the Universal Declaration of Human Rights: Genesis and Symbolic Dimensions of the Turn to Rights in International Law*, 19 EJIL 903 (2008). On the question of standards, *see* J. GONG, THE STANDARDS OF CIVILIZATION (1984) (holding that such standards inevitably changed when the international community widened).

[53] M.S. Giannini, *Le relazioni tra gli elementi degli ordinamenti giuridici*, 40 RIVISTA TRIMESTRALE DI DIRITTO PUBBLICO 1014 (1991).

proach. That there are no similar principles and tools in different legal orders is certainly possible. But it cannot be viewed as an axiom. As Amartya Sen has convincingly argued, such an approach is vitiated by a half-hidden form of racism. The latter becomes more visible when it is affirmed, as if it were evident, that some values, such as democracy, are an exclusive patrimony of some nations or parts of the world. The least that can be said is that, epistemologically, this way of looking at modern cultures rests on a selection of non-Western cultures, which is debatable.[54] It may be added that cultures, including legal cultures, generally do not develop in full isolation, but interact. Whether they do it peacefully or not, on the basis of symmetry or not, is another question. What matters for our purposes is that while all these forms of interaction generate risks, which cannot be neglected, they also provide opportunities for change and correction of old imbalances.

A related point is that the historic origins of a specific principle or of a set of principles must not be confounded with their validity in the present reality. The merit system offers a very good example of this. It was elaborated in a non-Western, authoritarian institutional framework, such as the Chinese Empire. Though it was functional to the preservation and exercise of authority, it also had an important function in terms of openness to talents, wherever they came from socially. Both rationales, effectiveness of public action and openness, justified its gradual introduction by Western countries. It was simply much better than the purchase of public offices and political patronage. The same applies to the introduction of administrative justice within the Ottoman Empire. In the middle of the 19th century its decadence was quite evident. Its governors thought that such a decline did not only depend on technology and military power, but also on legal and administrative factors. They decided to introduce changes in the administration of justice. However, conferring powers on independent courts looked irreconcilable with the authority of the sovereign. As a result, since the 1860's, they chose to set up judicial institutions based on the French model. Such institutions were closely connected with the executive power. But this does not imply that Turkish administrative courts should be less concerned with protecting individual and collective rights. As the discussion of *Taskhin* illustrates, the Supreme administrative court has shown its allegiance to due process rights and with the underlying value of the rule of law. The same value lies at the basis of the constitutional

---

[54] A. SEN, DEMOCRACY AS A UNIVERSAL VALUE (1999).

provisions which impose due process requirements not only within the criminal proceedings, but also within some administrative procedures, such as those having disciplinary nature.[55] Last but not least, the Turkish case clearly holds out the possibility of explaining exchanges and transplants in terms of coercion.

The Korean case is equally instructive. In Korea, too, since the end of the 19th century there has been a growing awareness of the need to know the basic concept of international law, as it was elaborated by Western countries. At least one element is worth mentioning. The Constitution adopted in 1899 established that the promulgation and implementation of statutes was based on national public law. However, it also provided that in both cases the codes "common to all nations" had to be taken into account. After 1945, (South) Korea did not only adopt a framework of economic law of the Western variety. It also introduced procedural safeguards, including a due process clause. Of course, more than one century of influence did not suffice to alter the traditional structures of the two legal systems. However, there is evidence that values and structures are not immutable, but evolve.[56] Of course, they are influenced by changing social demands as well as by bilateral and multilateral relations with other nations. The relationship between autono-

---

[55] I am indebted to Professor Il Han Ozay, of the Balcehir University of Istanbul, for drawing my attention to Turkish public law and to the essay of the late Professor S. Sami Omar, *Des rapports et des resemblances existant entre les Conseils d'Etat turc et français*, *in* CONSEIL D'ETAT, LIVRE JUBILAIRE POUR LE CENT CINQUANTIEME ANNIVERSAIRE 555 (1952). The influence of French culture on the Ottoman Empire is pointed out by recent historic analysis, *see* the last chapter of the *Histoire de l'Empire ottoman*, sous la direction de R. Mantran (1989); E. Stein, *Use, Non-Use and Abuse of Comparative Law*, 72 NORTHWESTERN UNIVERSITY LAW REVIEW 198 (1977). As regards constitutional reform, *see* Ozay's *Sintesi storica dell'evoluzione costituzionale della Turchia*, part I, 42 ANNALES DE LA FACULTÉ DE DROIT D'INSTANBUL 577 (1979); part II vol. 43, 449 (1980); part III vol. 44, 511 (1981); part IV vol. 44, 79 (1982).

[56] I owe this information to Professor Chongko Choi, of the Law School of the University of Seoul and to his *Law and Justice in Korea. South and North* (2005). A particularly relevant provision of the Korean Constitution is article 12, which refers to due process with regard to criminal proceedings. Article 31 of the Japanese Constitution has a similar content, with an even stronger influence of US law.

mous adjustments and external influences is so close that they may not be easily separated. Even a distinction is analytically difficult.[57]

Rather, it is useful to focus on another distinction, that between principles and rules. Empirical analysis confirms the distinction elaborated by the philosophy of law.[58] While principles have a broad, undetermined scope, rules aim at regulating specific categories either of subjects or of conducts. While principles have a broad meaning, and may be interpreted in different ways, rules impose, admit or prohibit specific conducts. Accordingly, while contrary rules may not be applied simultaneously, general principles may be, and usually are, balanced. All this explains why it is more difficult to find affinities at the level of rules, even beyond countries which share the same legal culture. For this reason, while the social and economic forces which act in favor of localism and universalism may alternatively prevail, the latter prevail more easily at the level of general principles.

8. Sovereignty, Membership of Regulatory Regimes and the Calculation of Conveniences

A concurrent explanation – and my last argument – is that procedural values are more intensely asserted as fundamental by international and supranational institutions. Whether this has produced, or may produce, a consensus set of values, it remains to be seen. Further empirical analysis is needed, not only at the level of norms, but, more broadly, for their

---

[57] *See* P. CRAIG, ADMINISTRATIVE LAW 209 (2007), emphasizing the "spill-over effect"; J.P. Costa, *Some Aspects of the Influence of the European Convention on Human Rights on Domestic Law*, *in* COMPARATIVE LAW BEFORE THE COURTS, 85 (G. Canivet, M. Andenas & D. Faigrieve eds., 2004), distinguishing the similarities existing prior to the accession to the ECHR and its implications; S. Cassese, *Mercatizzazione dello Stato o arena pubblica*, *in* LA CONCORRENZA TRA ORDINAMENTI GIURIDICI, 214 (A. Zoppini ed., 2004), holding that arbitrages do not determine a competition among legal orders, but, rather, a competition in adjusting such legal orders to the new reality.

[58] Mention must be made, at least, of the debate between Hart and Dworkin (*see* TAKING RIGHTS SERIOUSLY, 1977) in the second half of the twentieth century, after which Hart recognized, in the second edition of THE CONCEPT OF LAW (19) that he should have recognized the greater importance played by principles.

application to cases such as those that have punctuated the discussion of the intrinsic value of procedural safeguards. Those cases, nevertheless, shed some light on the debate raised by another strand of criticism against universal principles of law, which is based on traditional ideas of sovereignty.

The concept of sovereignty, however, may be misleading if intended on the basis of the paradigm of international law elaborated by Grotius. That paradigm conceived states as the public authorities by excellence, if not by anonymity. They were the exclusive holders of sovereign powers and exercised them with regard to trade and war. In this context, there was some room for cooperation, by way of treaties, of amity and peace, of trade and alliance. However, such cooperation was merely potential. Its importance was more accentuated in the other paradigm which was elaborated by Kant. However, even the latter did not contest the unilateral powers of states, of any state.[59]

Probably it was not fortuitous, therefore, that Adam Smith's theory about the role of the "invisible hand" was based on the premise that states decided and behaved unilaterally. He intended, surely, to demonstrate that protectionism was wrong, that the removal of all barriers to trade would increase the wealth of all nations. He relied on Montesqieu's argument that mutual dependency discourages war, although the contribution of Montesquieu, as an economist, to economic analysis has not been regarded as particularly relevant by more recent theorists.[60] Probably it was not fortuitous that David Ricardo elaborated a theory of the comparative advantages which freedom of trade was likely to produce. A discontinuity in the ways of achieving the wealth of nations would produce, he argued, evident advantages. Historically, such wealth was achieved at the expenses of others. It depended either on wars or unequal treaties. If we use the order of concepts introduced recently by game theory, those were games with a null outcome.

Of course, a mathematical comparison of advantages and disadvantages is quite difficult both *a priori* and empirically. Perceptions of utility

---

[59] *See* GROTIUS, DE JURE BELLI AC PACIS § XVII (1625); translated into French by P. PRADIER-FODÉRÉ, LE DROIT DE LA GUERRE ET DE LA PAIX (1999).

[60] This is an important point, which cannot be fully developed in this context, for further comments, *see* R. Howse, *Montesquieu on Commerce, Conquest, War and Peace*, 31 BROOKLYN JOURNAL OF INTERNATIONAL LAW 693, 708 (2006).

may vary between the parties and even diverge sensibly. The outcomes, moreover, may differ from expectations and disproportionally favor one party. However, all this raises the question of equality in the enjoyment of the benefits of cooperation, but does not cast any doubt on the new perspectives of cooperation in our epoch.[61] The 19th and especially the 20th centuries were characterized by games with a positive sum, made possible by consistent increases in the exchanges of goods and services.[62] While the economy has been the driving force, it has not been the only one. The fact that the environment has undergone unprecedented changes, with serious implications for human health, has made international cooperation inevitable.

All this shows a change which is not simply of degree, but of nature. While Bismarck's period was characterized by a few, great interstate conferences, in the second half of the 20th century there have been hundreds of them.[63] And they have produced remarkable outcomes, such as thousands of treaties, many of which set up new regulatory regimes. In the contemporary international system, characterized by growing interdependence, sovereignty is no longer unilaterally exercised. Rather, it is exercised by joining regional and global regulatory regimes.[64] This does not exclude that, coherently within the traditional realist paradigm of international relations, the power to negotiate a treaty and join a specific regulatory regime or organization still includes the exit option. However, such an exit option is more theoretical than concrete, because the best way to protect and promote national inter-

---

61 The classical point of view is stated by H. BULL, THE ANARCHICAL SOCIETY. A STUDY OF ORDER IN WORLD POLITICS (2002). More recent changes are pointed out by R.O. Keohane, *The Concept of Accountability in World Politics and the Use of Force*, 24 MICHIGAN JOURNAL OF INTERNATIONAL LAW 1121 (2003); A.M. SLAUGHTER, A NEW WORLD ORDER (2005).

62 During the nineteenth century such exchanges passed from 1 to 7 % of gross national product, *see* P. CIOCCA, DOPPIARE IL SECOLO (1997), ora in IL TEMPO DELL'ECONOMIA. STRUTTURE, FATTI, INTERPRETI DEL NOVECENTO 105 (2002).

63 *See* J.C. Yoo, *Globalism and the Constitution: Treaties, Non-Self-Execution, and the Original Understanding*, 99 COLUMBIA LAW REVIEW 1955 (1999) ("we live in a world of treaties").

64 *See* A. CHAYES & A. HANDLER CHAYES, THE NEW SOVEREIGNTY. COMPLIANCE WITH INTERNATIONAL REGULATORY AGREEMENTS 27 (1986).

ests is to take part in negotiations within multilateral fora.[65] For our purposes, there is no need to focus on a possible objection, concerning the use of force. There are plenty of contrary examples of this kind. However, such examples show that there is a different category of phenomena, which should be considered per se. They do not contradict the relevance of all the other situations regarding market regulation or environmental protection. Their relevance is caught by that part of science of international law which redefines sovereignty in terms of interdependence and cooperation.[66]

9. Conjectures and Implications

Thus, in the end, my argument comes to these two points. The first regards my initial conjecture. There are probably several convincing arguments, both theoretical and pragmatic, for distinctively considering the two great provinces of public law, within and beyond the state. However, it should not be forgotten that such a traditional divide was an intellectual representation of reality (not without normative intents) and reality has changed. It is true that beyond the state there are non-elected parliaments which, and magistrates who, have the monopoly over the legitimate use of the force. Yet, this does not undermine the relevance and meaning of both transnational processes and intergovernmental negotiations. Such processes and negotiations determine a growing need for legal regimes and these give rise to litigation. Whatever the risks of such an increasing juridification, there is evidence that

---

65 M.R. Ferrarese, *Hormones and Democracy. Inclusion, no "Exit-Option" and Some "Voice": "Democratic" Signals in International Law?*, 6 GLOBAL JURIST TOPICS issue 2, Article 2 (2006). E. Benvenisti, *Exit and Voice in an Age of Globalization*, 98 MICHIGAN LAW REVIEW 167, 178 (1999) (holding that global regimes *de facto* favor more powerful states, by making exit options more expansive).

66 *See* CHAYES & HANDLER CHAYES (note 64) and SLAUGHTER (note 61). *See also* J. Ziller, *Sovereignty in France: Getting Rid of the Mal de Bodin*, *in* SOVEREIGNTY IN TRANSITION, 261 (N. Walker ed., 2002). The argument according to which, when considering principles, the emphasis should placed on the *id quod plerumque accidit*, rather on exceptions, has been used by R. ALEXY, THE ARGUMENT FROM INJUSTICE. A REPLY TO LEGAL POSITIVISM, translated by B.L. Paulson and S.L. Paulson (2003).

a growing body of legal principles, both written and unwritten, is emerging. And this body of legal principles is largely common – precisely because these principles are general – to different realities. At least some principles of procedural due process of law do not only apply to liberal and democratic polities. Such principles apply, too, within less than well-ordered ones, to borrow again Rawls' words. Whether this depends on the common reactions to problems which are basically the same everywhere or to the influence of regional and global regulatory regimes, is another question, and not a fundamental one for my argument. What matters is, rather, as suggested by Montesquieu, that the particularities of domestic legal orders do not depend only on fundamental beliefs and values, but also on other factors. This may provide us with an answer as to why a certain kind of universalism is not necessarily in contrast with different legal traditions.[67]

It is in the light of this moderate universalism, that some procedural safeguards, including the right to be heard and the duty to give reasons, have an increasing importance. Such constraints on government are no longer distinctive and exclusive features of national legal orders. Quite the contrary, they apply equally to national authorities and to the institutions which they set up to deal with common problems. Precisely because such principles of law are general, the usual *caveat* applies: their operating mode is not the same for rules. This leaves wide room for distinctions and adjustments to specific contexts. But it must be clear that between the two great provinces of public law there is a series of distinctions, though sometimes quite important, rather than the divide which Hegel asserted as a postulate. Any attempt to restore or restate such a divide, especially if based on unawareness of its philosophical underpinnings, simply does not fit with the new world order. This world, whether we like it or not, is characterized by the growth of a new public law, which is neither simply international nor national, but to an increasing extent transnational. As Alexis de Tocqueville convincingly argued while describing the democracy that he witnessed in the US, a new world requires new paradigms.[68]

---

67 *See* Howse (note 60) and S. Cassese, *The Globalization of Law*, 37 NEW YORK UNIVERSITY JOURNAL OF INTERNATIONAL LAW & POLITICS 973, 991 (2005).

68 A. DE TOCQUEVILLE, DE LA DÉMOCRATIE EN AMERIQUE 62 (1835) (ed. 1981), ("il faut une science politique nouvelle à un monde tout nouveau").

My other conjecture was that it was possible to avoid the flaws of legal positivism and at the same time to identify some principles of procedural due process of law without trying to deduct them from other principles established *a priori* and in a categorical way. Such a conjecture does not prevent the possibility of giving a precise meaning to the broad provisions which include the general principles of law among the norms of which the ICJ and the ECJ, respectively, must ensure the observance. But the scope, meaning, and effectiveness of such general principles depend on a series of variables. Only an inductive analysis, whilst providing evidence of the formation of some principles more specific than those of natural justice and fair and equitable treatment, catches the evolution of public law. The fact that it is an evolution, rather than a revolution, assumes a precise meaning in two respects. On the one hand, change coexists with stability, or, as Schmidt-Aßmann has observed, legal orders need a certain degree of stability in order to accommodate change.[69] Moreover, in spite of its growth, the new public law is still more similar to the rudimentary stage of administrative justice in France before 1872 than to the developed legal systems of our epoch.[70] Especially as far as the relationship between public authorities is concerned, this public law is more influenced by the *raison d'État*. All this justifies the caution invoked by some observers against a certain enthusiasm for the new principles. On the other hand, since an evolution emerges, it implies that administrators, judges and arbitrators should take it into account when adjudicating. A theoretical perspective that emphasizes the autonomy of existing legal orders, whilst recognizing the importance of some common principles, implies a *prima facie* argument. This argument suggests that, among the various possible interpretations of existing rules, some are to be preferred. A preference must be given to those interpretations which are coherent with such common principles of due process of law and are likely to promote a more adequate perception of transnational processes.[71]

---

[69] E. Schmidt-Aßmann, *La contribution de l'autorégulation à la systematization du droit administratif*, 18 EUROPEAN REVIEW OF PUBLIC LAW 1255 (2006).

[70] S. CASSESE, OLTRE LO STATO 47 (2007).

[71] For a similar line of reasoning, *see* J. Martinez, *Towards an International Judicial System*, 56 STANFORD LAW REVIEW 529 (2003), arguing that the courts should apply a sort of "antiparochialism" canon.

List of Contributors

Ravi Afonso Pereira

Doctoral Candidate, Universidade Nova de Lisboa School of Law. Email: rafonsopereira@fd.unl.pt.

Jochen von Bernstorff

Dr. iur., LL.M. (EUI), Senior Research Fellow at the Max Planck Institute for Comparative Public Law and International Law, Heidelberg. Email: jvbernst@mpil.de.

Armin von Bogdandy

Dr. iur., Director at the Max Planck Institute for Comparative Public Law and International Law, Heidelberg; Professor of Law, University of Frankfurt. Email: bogdandy@mpil.de.

Sabino Cassese

Professor of Law, University of Rome and Scuola Normale Superiore of Pisa; Justice, Italian Constitutional Court. Email: sabino@sabinocassese.eu.

Philipp Dann

Dr. iur., LL.M. (Harvard); Senior Research Fellow at the Max Planck Institute for Comparative Public Law and International Law, Heidelberg. Email: pdann@mpil.de.

Giacinto della Cananea

Ph.D. (EUI Florence); Full Professor of Administrative Law and EU Administrative Law, University of Naples "Federico II". Email: giacinto.dellacananea@fastwebnet.it.

Erika de Wet

Dr. iur., LL.M. (Harvard); Professor of International Constitutional Law, Universiteit van Amsterdam; Extraordinary Professor, North-West University (Potchefstroom campus South Africa) and University of Pretoria. Email: e.dewet@uva.nl.

Anuscheh Farahat

Maîtrise en droit (Paris X); Research Fellow at the Max Planck Institute for Comparative Public Law and International Law, Heidelberg. Email: afarahat@mpil.de.

Isabel Feichtner

LL.M. (Cardozo), Senior Research Fellow at the Max Planck Institute for Comparative Public Law and International Law, Heidelberg. Email: ifeichtn@mpil.de.

Clemens A. Feinäugle

Senior Research Fellow, Max Planck Institute for Comparative Public Law and International Law, Heidelberg. Email: cfeinaeu@mpil.de.

Jürgen Friedrich

LL.M. (McGill), former Research Fellow at the Max Planck Institute for Comparative Public Law and International Law, Heidelberg. Email: juergen.friedrich@live.de.

Christine Fuchs

Research Fellow at the Max Planck Institute for Comparative Public Law and International Law, Heidelberg. Email: cfuchs@mpil.de.

Matthias Goldmann

Research Fellow at the Max Planck Institute for Comparative Public Law and International Law, Heidelberg. Email: mgoldman@mpil.de.

Dirk Hanschel

Dr. iur., M.C.L., Postdoctoral Research Fellow at the Faculty of Law and Economics, University of Mannheim. Email: hanschel@uni-mannheim.de.

Matthias Hartwig

Dr. iur., Senior Research Fellow at the Max Planck Institute for Comparative Public Law and International Law, Heidelberg. Email: mhartwig@mpil.de.

Stefan Kadelbach

Dr. iur., Professor of Law, University of Frankfurt am Main. Email: S.Kadelbach@jur.uni-frankfurt.de.

Karen Kaiser

Dr. iur., Research Fellow, Federal Constitutional Court, Karlsruhe. Email: karenkaiser@web.de.

Jan Klabbers

Dr. iur., Professor of International Organizations Law, University of Helsinki; Director, Academy of Finland Centre of Excellence in Global Governance Research. Email: Jan.Klabbers@helsinki.fi.

Petra Lea Láncos

Assigned Lecturer at the Pázmány Péter Catholic University of Budapest, Faculty of Law and Political Sciences. Email: petra_lancos@hotmail.com.

Stephan Leibfried

Dr. rer. pol., Professor of Public and Social Policy at the University of Bremen; Director of the German National Science Foundation Research Center Transformations of the State (TranState). Email: stephan.leibfried@sfb597.uni-bremen.de.

Steven Less

Dr. iur., J.D. (Seton Hall), Esq.; Senior Research Fellow at the Max Planck Institute for Comparative Public Law and International Law, Heidelberg. Email: sless@mpil.de.

Ute Mager

Dr. iur., Professor of Public Law, University of Heidelberg. Email: ute.mager@jurs.uni-heidelberg.de.

Volker Röben

Dr. iur., LL.M. (Boalt), LL.M.Eur. (Bruges), Professor of Law, Swansea University Law School. Email: v.roeben@swansea.ac.uk.

Eberhard Schmidt-Aßmann

Dr. iur. Dr. h.c., Emeritus Professor of Law, University of Heidelberg. Email: ivr@uni-hd.de.

Bettina Schöndorf-Haubold

Dr. iur., Postdoctoral Research Fellow at the Institute for German and European Administrative Law, University of Heidelberg. Email: bsh@uni-hd.de.

Gefion Schuler

Doctoral Candidate at the Law Faculty of the University of Heidelberg. Email: gefion.schuler@yahoo.de.

Maja Smrkolj

LL.M. (Heidelberg), Research Fellow, Max Planck Institute for Comparative Public Law and International Law, Heidelberg. Email: msmrkolj@mpil.de.

Christian Tietje

Dr. iur., LL.M. (Michigan), Professor at the Law School of the University Halle-Wittenberg, Chair for Public Law, European Law, and International Economic Law, Director of the Institute for Economic Law and the Transnational Economic Law Research Center (TELC). Email: christian.tietje@jura.uni-halle.de.

Ingo Venzke

LL.M. (London), Research Fellow at the Max Planck Institute for Comparative Public Law and International Law, Heidelberg. Email: ivenzke@mpil.de.

Joseph Windsor

J.D., LL.M. (Heidelberg), Attorney Editor for The Government Contractor at Thomson Reuters/West, Washington, D.C. Email: joseph.windsor@thomsonreuters.com.

Rüdiger Wolfrum

Dr. iur. Dr. h.c. mult., Judge at the International Tribunal for the Law of the Sea; Director at the Max Planck Institute for Comparative Public Law and International Law; Professor of Law, University of Heidelberg. Email: sekrewol@mpil.de.

Diana Zacharias

Dr. iur., LL.M. (Sydney), Senior Research Fellow at the Max Planck Institute for Comparative Public Law and International Law, Heidelberg. Email: dzachari@mpil.de.

Max-Planck-Institut für ausländisches öffentliches Recht und Völkerrecht

Beiträge zum ausländischen öffentlichen Recht und Völkerrecht

Hrsg.: A. von Bogdandy, R. Wolfrum

Bde. 27–59 erschienen im Carl Heymanns Verlag KG Köln, Berlin (Bestellung an: Max-Planck-Institut für Völkerrecht, Im Neuenheimer Feld 535, 69120 Heidelberg); ab Band 60 im Springer-Verlag Berlin, Heidelberg, New York, London, Paris, Tokyo, Hong Kong, Barcelona

---

211 Georg *Nolte* (ed.): **Peace through International Law. The Role of the International Law Commission.** 2009. IX, 195 Seiten. Geb. € 64,95 zzgl. landesüblicher MwSt.

210 Armin *von Bogdandy*, Rüdiger *Wolfrum*, Jochen *von Bernstorff*, Philipp *Dann*, Matthias *Goldmann* (eds.): **The Exercise of Public Authority by International Institutions.** 2010. XIII, 1005 Seiten. Geb. € 149,95 zzgl. landesüblicher MwSt.

209 Norman *Weiß*: **Kompetenzlehre internationaler Organisationen.** 2009. XVIII, 540 Seiten. Geb. € 99,95

208 Michael *Rötting*: **Das verfassungsrechtliche Beitrittsverfahren zur Europäischen Union.** 2009. XIV, 317 Seiten. Geb. € 79,95

207 Björn *Ahl*: **Die Anwendung völkerrechtlicher Verträge in China.** 2009. XIX, 419 Seiten. Geb. € 89,95

206 Mahulena *Hofmann*: **Von der Transformation zur Kooperationsoffenheit?** 2009. XIX, 585 Seiten. Geb. € 99,95

205 Rüdiger *Wolfrum*, Ulrike *Deutsch* (eds.): **The European Court of Human Rights Overwhelmed by Applications: Problems and Possible Solutions.** 2009. VIII, 128 Seiten. Geb. € 59,95 zzgl. landesüblicher MwSt.

204 Niels *Petersen*: **Demokratie als teleologisches Prinzip.** 2009. XXVII, 280 Seiten. Geb. € 79,95

203 Christiane *Kamardi*: **Die Ausformung einer Prozessordnung sui generis durch das ICTY unter Berücksichtigung des Fair-Trial-Prinzips.** 2009. XVI, 424 Seiten. Geb. € 89,95

202 Leonie F. *Guder*: **The Administration of Debt Relief by the International Financial Institutions.** 2009. XVIII, 355 Seiten. Geb. € 84,95 zzgl. landesüblicher MwSt.

201 Silja *Vöneky*, Cornelia *Hagedorn*, Miriam *Clados*, Jelena *von Achenbach*: **Legitimation ethischer Entscheidungen im Recht.** 2009. VIII, 351 Seiten. Geb. € 84,95

200 Anja Katarina *Weilert*: **Grundlagen und Grenzen des Folterverbotes in verschiedenen Rechtskreisen.** 2009. XXX, 474 Seiten. Geb. € 94,95

199 Suzette V. *Suarez*: **The Outer Limits of the Continental Shelf.** 2008. XVIII, 276 Seiten. Geb. € 79,95 zzgl. landesüblicher MwSt.

198 Felix *Hanschmann*: **Der Begriff der Homogenität in der Verfassungslehre und Europarechtswissenschaft.** 2008. XIII, 370 Seiten. Geb. € 84,95

197 Angela *Paul*: **Kritische Analyse und Reformvorschlag zu Art. II Genozidkonvention.** 2008. XVI, 379 Seiten. Geb. € 84,95

196 Hans Fabian *Kiderlen*: **Von Triest nach Osttimor.** 2008. XXVI, 526 Seiten. Geb. € 94,95

195 Heiko *Sauer*: **Jurisdiktionskonflikte in Mehrebenensystemen.** 2008. XXXVIII, 605 Seiten. Geb. € 99,95

194 Rüdiger *Wolfrum*, Volker *Röben* (eds.): **Legitimacy in International Law.** 2008. VI, 420 Seiten. Geb. € 84,95 zzgl. landesüblicher MwSt.

193 Doris *König*, Peter-Tobias *Stoll*, Volker *Röben*, Nele *Matz-Lück* (eds.): **International Law Today: New Challenges and the Need for Reform?** 2008. VIII, 260 Seiten. Geb. € 69,95 zzgl. landesüblicher MwSt.

192 Ingo *Niemann*: **Geistiges Eigentum in konkurrierenden völkerrechtlichen Vertragsordnungen.** 2008. XXV, 463 Seiten. Geb. € 94,95

191 Nicola *Wenzel*: **Das Spannungsverhältnis zwischen Gruppenschutz und Individualschutz im Völkerrecht.** 2008. XXXI, 646 Seiten. Geb. € 99,95

190 Winfried *Brugger*, Michael *Karayanni* (eds.): **Religion in the Public Sphere: A Comparative Analysis of German, Israeli, American and International Law.** 2007. XVI, 467 Seiten. Geb. € 89,95 zzgl. landesüblicher MwSt.

189 Eyal *Benvenisti*, Chaim *Gans*, Sari *Hanafi* (eds.): **Israel and the Palestinian Refugees.** 2007. VIII, 502 Seiten. Geb. € 94,95 zzgl. landesüblicher MwSt.

188 Eibe *Riedel*, Rüdiger *Wolfrum* (eds.): **Recent Trends in German and European Constitutional Law.** 2006. VII, 289 Seiten. Geb. € 74,95 zzgl. landesüblicher MwSt.

187 Marcel *Kau*: **United States Supreme Court und Bundesverfassungsgericht.** 2007. XXV, 538 Seiten. Geb. € 99,95 zzgl. landesüblicher MwSt.

186 Philipp *Dann*, Michał *Rynkowski* (eds.): **The Unity of the European Constitution.** 2006. IX, 394 Seiten. Geb. € 79,95 zzgl. landesüblicher MwSt.

185 Pál *Sonnevend*: **Eigentumsschutz und Sozialversicherung.** 2008. XVIII, 278 Seiten. Geb. € 74,95

184 Jürgen *Bast*: **Grundbegriffe der Handlungsformen der EU.** 2006. XXI, 485 Seiten. Geb. € 94,95

183 Uwe *Säuberlich*: **Die außervertragliche Haftung im Gemeinschaftsrecht.** 2005. XV, 314 Seiten. Geb. € 74,95

182 Florian *von Alemann*: **Die Handlungsform der interinstitutionellen Vereinbarung.** 2006. XVI, 518 Seiten. Geb. € 94,95

181 Susanne *Förster*: **Internationale Haftungsregeln für schädliche Folgewirkungen gentechnisch veränderter Organismen.** 2007. XXXVI, 421 Seiten. Geb. € 84,95

180 Jeanine *Bucherer*: **Die Vereinbarkeit von Militärgerichten mit dem Recht auf ein faires Verfahren gemäß Art. 6 Abs. 1 EMRK, Art. 8 Abs. 1 AMRK und Art. 14 Abs. 1 des UN Paktes über bürgerliche und politische Rechte.** 2005. XVIII, 307 Seiten. Geb. € 74,95

179 Annette *Simon*: **UN-Schutzzonen – Ein Schutzinstrument für verfolgte Personen?** 2005. XXI, 322 Seiten. Geb. € 74,95

178 Petra *Minnerop*: **Paria-Staaten im Völkerrecht?** 2004. XXIII, 579 Seiten. Geb. € 99,95

177 Rüdiger *Wolfrum*, Volker *Röben* (eds.): **Developments of International Law in Treaty Making.** 2005. VIII, 632 Seiten. Geb. € 99,95 zzgl. landesüblicher MwSt.

176 Christiane *Höhn*: **Zwischen Menschenrechten und Konfliktprävention. Der Minderheitenschutz im Rahmen der Organisation für Sicherheit und Zusammenarbeit in Europa (OSZE).** 2005. XX, 418 Seiten. Geb. € 84,95

175 Nele *Matz*: **Wege zur Koordinierung völkerrechtlicher Verträge. Völkervertragsrechtliche und institutionelle Ansätze.** 2005. XXIV, 423 Seiten. Geb. € 84,95

174 Jochen Abr. *Frowein*: **Völkerrecht – Menschenrechte – Verfassungsfragen Deutschlands und Europas. Ausgewählte Schriften.** Hrsg. von Matthias *Hartwig*, Georg *Nolte*, Stefan *Oeter*, Christian *Walter*. 2004. VIII, 732 Seiten. Geb. € 119,95

173 Oliver *Dörr* (Hrsg.): **Ein Rechtslehrer in Berlin. Symposium für Albrecht Randelzhofer.** 2004. VII, 117 Seiten. Geb. € 54,95

172 Lars-Jörgen *Geburtig*: **Konkurrentenrechtsschutz aus Art. 88 Abs. 3 Satz 3 EGV. Am Beispiel von Steuervergünstigungen.** 2004. XVII, 412 Seiten (4 Seiten English Summary). Geb. € 84,95

171 Markus *Böckenförde*: **Grüne Gentechnik und Welthandel. Das Biosafety-Protokoll und seine Auswirkungen auf das Regime der WTO.** 2004. XXIX, 620 Seiten. Geb. € 99,95

170 Anja *v. Hahn*: **Traditionelles Wissen indigener und lokaler Gemeinschaften zwischen geistigen Eigentumsrechten und der public domain.** 2004. XXV, 415 Seiten. Geb. 84,95

169 Christian *Walter*, Silja *Vöneky*, Volker *Röben*, Frank *Schorkopf* (eds.): **Terrorism as a Challenge for National and International Law: Security versus Liberty?** 2004. XI, 1484 Seiten. Geb. € 169,95 zzgl. landesüblicher MwSt.

168 Kathrin *Osteneck*: **Die Umsetzung von UN-Wirtschaftssanktionen durch die Europäische Gemeinschaft.** 2004. XXXIX, 579 Seiten. Geb. € 99,95

167 Stephan *Sina*: **Der völkerrechtliche Status des Westjordanlandes und des Gaza-Streifens nach den Osloer Verträgen.** 2004. XXI, 410 Seiten. Geb. € 84,95

166 Philipp *Dann*: **Parlamente im Exekutivföderalismus.** 2004. XXIII, 474 Seiten. Geb. € 89,95

165 Rüdiger *Wolfrum* (Hrsg.): **Gleichheit und Nichtdiskriminierung im nationalen und internationalen Menschenrechtsschutz.** 2003. VIII, 299 Seiten. Geb. € 74,95

164 Rüdiger *Wolfrum*, Nele *Matz*: **Conflicts in International Environmental Law.** 2003. XI, 213 Seiten. Geb. € 64,95 zzgl. landesüblicher MwSt.

SPRINGER NATURE

GPSR Compliance

The European Union's (EU) General Product Safety Regulation (GPSR) is a set of rules that requires consumer products to be safe and our obligations to ensure this.

If you have any concerns about our products, you can contact us on ProductSafety@springernature.com

In case Publisher is established outside the EU, the EU authorized representative is:

Springer Nature Customer Service Center GmbH
Europaplatz 3
69115 Heidelberg, Germany